LITTLE, BROWN AND COMPANY

Law School Casebook Series

The Employment Relation and the Law. Edited by BENJAMIN AARON, Professor of Law and Director, Institute of Industrial Relations, University of California at Los Angeles

Federal Income Taxation: Cases, Problems, Notes. WILLIAM D. ANDREWS, Professor of law, Harvard University

Antitrust Analysis: Problems, Text, Cases. PHILLIP AREEDA, Professor of Law, Harvard University

Land Transfer and Finance. ALLAN AXELROD, Professor of Law, Rutgers University, CURTIS J. BERGER, Professor of Law, Columbia University, and QUINTIN JOHNSTONE, Justus S. Hotchkiss Professor of Law, Yale University

Land Ownership and Use: Cases, Statutes, and Other Materials. CURTIS J. BERGER, Professor of Law, Columbia University

International Law: Cases and Materials. Third Edition. WILLIAM W. BISHOP, JR., Edwin M. Dickinson Professor of Law, University of Michigan

Federal Income, Estate and Gift Taxation. Fourth Edition. BORIS I. BITTKER, Southmayd Professor of Law, Yale University, and LAWRENCE M. STONE, Professor of Law, University of California at Berkeley

Materials on Reorganization, Recapitalization and Insolvency. WALTER J. BLUM, Professor of Law, University of Chicago, and STANLEY A. KAPLAN, Professor of Law, University of Chicago

Civil Procedure: Cases and Comments on the Process of Adjudication. PAUL D. CARRINGTON, Professor of Law, University of Michigan

Estate Planning. Third Edition. A. JAMES CASNER, Weld Professor of Law, Harvard University

Cases and Text on Property. Second Edition. A. JAMES CASNER, Weld Professor of Law, Harvard University, and W. BARTON LEACH, Story Professor of Law, Emeritus, Harvard University

International Legal Process. ABRAM CHAYES, Professor of Law, Harvard University, THOMAS EHRLICH, Professor of Law, Stanford University, and ANDREAS F. LOWENFELD, Professor of Law, New York University

Cases and Materials on Debtor and Creditor. VERN COUNTRYMAN, Professor of Law, Harvard University

The Lawyer in Modern Society. VERN COUNTRYMAN, Professor of Law, Harvard University, and TED FINMAN, Professor of Law, University of Wisconsin

Commercial Law: Cases and Materials. VERN COUNTRYMAN, Professor of Law, Harvard University, and ANDREW L. KAUFMAN, Professor of Law, Harvard University

Law, Medicine and Forensic Science. WILLIAM J. CURRAN, Frances Glessner Lee Professor of Legal Medicine, Harvard Medical School, Harvard School of Public Health, and E. DONALD SHAPIRO, Adjunct Professor of Law, New York University

Family Wealth Transactions. JESSE DUKEMINIER, Professor of Law, University of California at Los Angeles, and STANLEY M. JOHANSON, Professor of Law, University of Texas

Political and Civil Rights in the United States. Third Edition. THOMAS I. EMERSON, Lines Professor of Law, Yale University, DAVID HABER, Professor of Law, Rutgers University, and NORMAN DORSEN, Professor of Law and Director, Arthur Garfield Hays Civil Liberties Program, New York University

Cases and Materials on Family Law. CALEB FOOTE, Professor of Law and Criminology, University of California at Berkeley, ROBERT J. LEVY, Professor of Law, University of Minnesota, and FRANK E. A. SANDER, Professor of Law, Harvard University

Constitutional Law: Cases and Other Problems. Third Edition. PAUL A. FREUND, Carl M. Loeb University Professor, Harvard University, ARTHUR E. SUTHERLAND, Bussey Professor of Law, Emeritus, Harvard University, MARK DE WOLFE HOWE, late Charles Warren Professor of American Legal History, Harvard University, and ERNEST J. BROWN, Langdell Professor of Law, Harvard University

Cases and Materials on Corporations. ALEXANDER H. FREY, Algernon Sidney Biddle Professor of Law, Emeritus, University of Pennsylvania, C. ROBERT MORRIS, JR., Professor of Law, University of Minnesota, and JESSE CHOPER, Professor of Law, University of California at Berkeley

Cases and Materials on Torts. Second Edition. CHARLES O. GREGORY, John B. Minor Professor of Law, Emeritus, University of Virginia, and HARRY KALVEN, JR., Professor of Law, University of Chicago

Land-Use Planning: A Casebook on the Use, Misuse, and Re-use of Urban Land. Second Edition. CHARLES M. HAAR, Professor of Law, Harvard University

Administrative Law: Cases and Materials. Third Edition. LOUIS L. JAFFE, Byrne Professor of Administrative Law, Harvard University, and NATHANIEL L. NATHANSON, Frederic P. Vose Professor of Law, Northwestern University

Criminal Law and Its Processes: Cases and Materials. Second Edition. SANFORD H. KADISH, Professor of Law, University of California at Berkeley, and MONRAD G. PAULSEN, Dean and John B. Minor Professor of Law, University of Virginia

Constitutional Law: Cases and Materials. Fourth Edition. PAUL G. KAUPER, Henry M. Butzel Professor of Law, University of Michigan

Contracts: Cases and Materials. Second Edition. FRIEDRICH KESSLER, Professor of Law, University of California at Berkeley, and GRANT GILMORE, Harry A. Bigelow Professor of Law, University of Chicago

Basic Business Associations: Cases, Text and Problems. ELVIN R. LATTY, Dean Emeritus and William R. Perkins Professor of Law, Duke University, and GEORGE T. FRAMPTON, Professor of Law and Vice-Chancellor for Campus Affairs, University of Illinois

Cases and Text on the Law of Wills. Second Edition, 1960 Revision. W. BARTON LEACH, Story Professor of Law, Emeritus, Harvard University

Labor Law: Cases, Materials, and Problems. BERNARD D. MELTZER, Professor of Law, University of Chicago

Commercial Transactions: Cases and Materials. SOIA MENTSCHIKOFF, Professor of Law, University of Chicago

Legislation: Cases and Materials. FRANK C. NEWMAN, Professor of Law, University of California at Berkeley, and STANLEY S. SURREY, Jeremiah Smith, Jr., Professor of Law, Harvard University

Family Law: Cases and Materials. Second Edition. MORRIS PLOSCOWE, Adjunct Professor of Law, New York University, and HENRY H. FOSTER, JR., Professor of Law, New York University and DORIS JONAS FREED, of the New York and Maryland Bars

State and Local Government Law. SHO SATO, Professor of Law, University of California at Berkeley, and ARVO VAN ALSTYNE, Professor of Law, University of Utah

Problems and Materials on Decedents' Estates and Trusts. EUGENE F. SCOLES, Dean and Professor of Law, University of Oregon, and EDWARD C. HALBACH, JR., Dean and Professor of Law, University of California at Berkeley

Cases and Other Materials on Civil Procedure. AUSTIN WAKEMAN SCOTT, Dane Professor of Law, Emeritus, Harvard University, and ROBERT B. KENT, Professor of Law, Boston University

Select Cases and Other Authorities on the Law of Trusts. AUSTIN WAKEMAN SCOTT, Dane Professor of Law, Emeritus, Harvard University, and AUSTIN WAKEMAN SCOTT, JR., late Professor of Law, University of Colorado

The Civil Law System: Cases and Materials for the Comparative Study of Law. ARTHUR TAYLOR VON MEHREN, Professor of Law, Harvard University

The Law of Multistate Problems: Cases and Materials on Conflict of Laws. ARTHUR TAYLOR VON MEHREN, Professor of Law, Harvard University, and DONALD THEODORE TRAUTMAN, Professor of Law, Harvard University

Labor Relations and the Law. Third Edition. THE LABOR LAW GROUP TRUST Under the Editorship of JERRE WILLIAMS, Rex G. and Edna Heflin Baker Professor of Constitutional Law, University of Texas, and Others

Federal Income Taxation of Business Enterprise. BERNARD WOLFMAN, Dean and Professor of Law, University of Pennsylvania

Law School Textbook Series

Public Law Perspectives on a Private Law Problem: Auto Compensation Plans. WALTER J. BLUM, Professor of Law, University of Chicago, and HARRY KALVEN, JR., Professor of Law, University of Chicago

American Civil Procedure. WILLIAM WIRT BLUME, Professor of Law, University of California, Hastings College of Law

Readings in Jurisprudence and Legal Philosophy. MORRIS R. COHEN, late Professor of Law, City College of New York, and FELIX S. COHEN, late Visiting Professor of Law, City College of New York, and Visiting Lecturer, Yale University

Handbook of Modern Equity. Second Edition. WILLIAM Q. DE FUNIAK, Visiting Professor of Law, McGeorge School of Law, University of the Pacific

The Fundamentals of Legal Drafting. F. REED DICKERSON, Professor of Law, University of Indiana (Bloomington)

The Growth of American Law: The Law Makers. JAMES WILLARD HURST, Vilas Professor of Law, University of Wisconsin

Judicial Control of Administrative Action. Abridged Student Edition. LOUIS L. JAFFE, Byrne Professor of Administrative Law, Harvard University

Civil Procedure. FLEMING JAMES, JR., Sterling Professor of Law, Yale University

Trial Tactics and Methods. ROBERT E. KEETON, Professor of Law, Harvard University

Securities Regulation. Student Edition. LOUIS LOSS, William Nelson Cromwell Professor of Law, Harvard University

A Concise History of the Common Law. Fifth Edition. THEODORE F. T. PLUCKNETT, Late Professor of Legal History in the University of London

Effective Legal Research. Third Edition. MILES O. PRICE, late Professor of Law and Law Librarian, Columbia University, and HARRY BITNER, Professor of Law and Law Librarian, Cornell University

Scott's Abridgment of The Law of Trusts. AUSTIN WAKEMAN SCOTT, Dane Professor of Law, Emeritus, Harvard University

Handbook of Law Study. FERDINAND FAIRFAX STONE, W. R. Irby Professor of Law and Director of Institute of Comparative Law, Tulane University

Cases and Materials on
Family Law

Cases and Materials on

Family Law

Caleb Foote

PROFESSOR OF LAW, UNIVERSITY OF CALIFORNIA, BERKELEY

Robert J. Levy

PROFESSOR OF LAW, UNIVERSITY OF MINNESOTA

Frank E. A. Sander

PROFESSOR OF LAW, HARVARD UNIVERSITY

LITTLE, BROWN AND COMPANY

BOSTON AND TORONTO   1966

*Published simultaneously in Canada
by Little, Brown & Company (Canada) Limited*

PRINTED IN THE UNITED STATES OF AMERICA

PREFACE

As in the case of the widow during the reign of Henry VI who, it is reported, "might give birth to a child *seven years* after her husband's death without injury to her reputation," see page 43 note 29 infra, the gestation period of this book has been of long duration. It began in 1956 at the University of Pennsylvania Law School as part of a project, supported by a grant from the National Institute of Mental Health, whose purpose was to develop methods and materials for training law students in behavioral science. Others associated with that project, notably Drs. Julius Wishner, Jefferson Bitterman, Andrew S. Watson, and Richard G. Lonsdorf, have made invaluable contributions to our conception of the relationship of legal and scientific materials in the analysis of the family.

Since much of our conception of this book is set forth in the Prologue (see pages 3-10 infra), we have felt it unnecessary to reiterate these matters here. By the nature of the task we set for ourselves, the casebook is an unfinished product. Subsequent editions will certainly include examination of the problems presented by aged and mentally incompetent family members, a project of such scope and complexity that we felt warranted in putting it off so as not further to delay this volume. We also recognize that the body of behavioral and social science data relevant to legal doctrine and practice is constantly growing, so that some of our selections will be dated almost by the time of publication. We expect that with further experience this "nonlegal" aspect of the book can be substantially improved. In the meantime, perhaps its publication now will add some impetus to what we hope we can call a trend of increasing recognition of the importance to law of such nonlegal data.

In addition to the individual case presentations which are included in the book (see pages 417 and 866) we have collected other material of this type which we think may be useful as either supplementary reading or for more exhaustive examination in a seminar setting. As the book is already long for what has been the standard family law course, these additional materials have been incorporated in a separately available supplement, to which reference is made in these pages from time to time. We acknowledge the assistance of the National Council on Legal Clinics in the preparation of the individual case materials.

In editing selections we have freely omitted footnotes and renumbered those which have been retained. Unless otherwise indicated, any material in a selection which is enclosed in brackets represents our editorial insertion. Because our method of organizing the materials is substantially different from that usually employed, we have sought to facilitate reference to particular subject matter by the provision of a detailed table of contents, a comprehensive index and table of cases at the back of the volume, and frequent cross-references in the text. We have also used the following short forms of citation for these frequently cited references:

Association of American Law Schools, Selected Essays on Family Law (1950), cited as Selected Essays on Family Law

Justice for the Child (Rosenheim ed. 1962), cited as Justice for the Child

Pollock and Maitland, The History of English Law (2d ed. 1898), cited as Pollock and Maitland

Vernier, American Family Laws (1931-1938), cited as Vernier

We gratefully acknowledge our indebtedness to countless colleagues, research assistants, students, and secretaries who in various ways have contributed so much to the final product. We owe a special debt to Sheila Mulvihill, who performed so ably and cheerfully the thankless task of preparing the manuscript for publication.

CALEB FOOTE
ROBERT J. LEVY
FRANK E. A. SANDER

ACKNOWLEDGMENTS

We gratefully acknowledge the permission extended by the following authors, publishers, and organizations to reprint excerpts from the works indicated: Ellzey, Marriage or Divorce?, 22 University of Kansas City Law Review; Haskins, Law and Authority in Early Massachusetts; Cook, Eugenics or Euthenics, 37 Illinois Law Review; Gebhard et al., Sexual Behavior in the Human Female, and Pregnancy, Birth and Abortion; Lindman and McIntyre, The Mentally Disabled and the Law (American Bar Foundation); Younghusband, The Dilemma of the Juvenile Court, 33 Social Service Review; Abbott, The Child and the State (U. Chicago Press); Davis, Illegitimacy and the Social Structure, 45 American Journal of Sociology; Keith-Lucas, Child Welfare Services Today: An Overview and Some Questions, 355 Annals; Schulze, Man's Contracting World in an Expanding Universe (Brown Univ. Press); Hart, Law, Liberty and Morality; Vernier, American Family Laws; Prosser, Handbook of the Law of Torts (West Publishing Co.); McCormick, Handbook of the Law of Evidence (West Publishing Co.); Storke, Annulment in the Conflict of Laws, 43 Minnesota Law Review; Wels, New York: The Poor Man's Reno, 35 Cornell Law Quarterly; Comment, Rights of the Putative and Meretricious Spouse in California, 50 California Law Review; Boulas, Moore and Preucel, Therapeutic Abortion, 19 Obstetrics and Gynecology; Schwartz, Book Review, 96 University of Pennsylvania Law Review; Waelder, Psychiatry and the Problem of Criminal Responsibility, 101 University of Pennsylvania Law Review; Note, The Administration of Divorce: A Philadelphia Story, 101 University of Pennsylvania Law Review; Freeman, A Remonstrance for Conscience, 106 University of Pennsylvania Law Review; Champlin and Winslow, Effective Sterilization, 106 University of Pennsylvania Law Review; Guides for Juvenile Court Judges (National Council on Crime and Delinquency); Goldman, Differential Selection of Juvenile Offenders for Court Appearance (N.C.C.D.); Polier, A View from the Bench (N.C.C.D.); McCrea, Juvenile Courts and Juvenile Probation, 3 National Probation and Parole Association Journal (N.C.C.D.); Shaw, Juvenile Institutions and Juvenile Parole, 3 National Probation and Parole Association Journal (N.C.C.D.); Berg, Utilizing the Strengths of Unwed Mothers in the AFDC Program, 43 Child Welfare; Alexander, The Follies of Divorce — A Therapeutic Approach to the Problem, 1949 University of Illinois Law Forum; Woodside, Sterilization in North Carolina; Broeder and Barrett, Impact of Religious Factors in Nebraska Adoptions, 38 Nebraska Law Review; Kingsley, The Law of Infants' Marriages, 9

Vanderbilt Law Review; Rheinstein, The Law of Divorce and the Problem of Marriage Stability, 9 Vanderbilt Law Review; Selznick, Legal Institutions and Social Controls, 17 Vanderbilt Law Review; Ulman, A Judge Takes the Stand; Williams, The Sanctity of Life and the Criminal Law; Williams, The Legalization of Medical Abortion, 56 Eugenics Review; Puxon, Collusion — II, 103 Solicitors' Journal; Chafee, Some Problems of Equity; Packer and Gampbell, Therapeutic Abortion: A Problem in Law and Medicine, 11 Stanford Law Review; Harmsworth and Minnis, Nonstatutory Causes of Divorce: The Lawyer's Point of View, 17 Marriage and Family Living; Burchinal, Characteristics of Adolescents from Unbroken, Broken, and Reconstructed Families, 26 The Journal of Marriage and the Family; Weyrauch, Informal and Formal Marriage — An Appraisal of Trends in Family Organization, 28 University of Chicago Law Review; Comment, 28 University of Chicago Law Review; Fonzi, Divorce Philadelphia Style, Greater Philadelphia Magazine, February, 1964; Chattanooga Divorce Report, 19 Tennessee Law Review; Connolly, Divorce Proctors, 34 Boston University Law Review; Note, Annulments for Fraud — New York's Answer to Reno?, 48 Columbia Law Review; Drinker, Problems of Professional Ethics in Matrimonial Litigation, 66 Harvard Law Review; 1 Proceedings, Institute of Church and State, Villanova University; Young, Wednesday's Children; Kempe, The Battered-Child Syndrome, 181 American Medical Association Journal; 193 The Economist; Davis, The Theory of Change and Response in Modern Demographic History, 29 Population Index; Bogue, The Demographic Breakthrough: From Projection to Control, 30 Population Index; Pound, Foreword, A Symposium in the Law of Divorce, 28 Iowa Law Review; Current Topics, 35 Australian Law Journal; Kolb and Noyes, Modern Clinical Psychiatry; Arther and Reid, Utilizing the Lie Detector Technique to Determine the Truth in Disputed Paternity Cases, 45 Journal of Criminal Law, Criminology and Police Science; Goode, After Divorce; Anderson, Islamic Law in the Modern World; Allen, The Borderland of Criminal Justice; Bell, Aid to Dependent Children; Schatkin, Should Paternity Cases Be Tried in a Civil or Criminal Court?, 1 Criminal Law Review; Schatkin, Paternity Proceedings — A Changing Concept, 42 Journal of Criminal Law, Criminology and Police Science; Brinton, French Revolutionary Legislation on Illegitimacy 1789-1804; Witmer, Herzog, Weinstein and Sullivan, Independent Adoptions (Russell Sage Foundation); Gellhorn, Children and Families in the Courts of New York City; Virtue, Family Cases in Court; Garrett, Interviewing: Its Principles and Methods (Family Service Association of America); The Lawyer and the Social Worker (Family Service Association of America); Pound, The Spirit of the Common Law; Hill, Stycos and Back, The Family and Population Control; Weaver, Social Problems; Monahan, Does Age at Marriage Matter in Divorce?, 32 Social Forces; Moore, The Paternity Scandal, 121 The Nineteenth Century and After; Clark, Estoppel Against Jurisdictional Attack on Decrees of Divorce, 70 Yale Law Journal; Restatement Second, Conflict of Laws (Tent. Draft No. 4); Model Penal Code (Tent. Draft No. 9); O'Gorman, Lawyers and Matrimonial Cases; Cheney, A Suggested Statute and Policy for Child Welfare Protective Services in Connecticut: A Report for the Legislature; Young, Out of Wedlock; Sussman, 1 Journal of Forensic Sciences; Power, Letter, 41 Child Welfare; Maas, The Young Adult Adjustment of Twenty Wartime Nursery Children, 42 Child Welfare; Murphy, Shirley and Witmer, Incidence of Hidden Delinquency, 16 American Journal of Orthopsychiatry; Eisenberg, The Sins of the Fathers: Urban Decay and Social Pathology, 32 American Journal of Orthopsychiatry; Watson, The Conjoint Psychotherapy of Marriage Partners, 33 American Journal of Orthopsychiatry; Simms, Abortion — A Note on Some Recent Developments in Britain, 4 British Journal of Criminology; Christensen, Cultural Relativism and Premarital Sex Norms, 25 American Sociological Review; Spellman, Successful Management of Matrimonial Cases; Matza, Delinquency and Drift; Vincent, Unmarried Mothers; Vincent, Illegitimacy in the Next Decade, 43 Child Welfare; Orlansky, Infant Care and Personality, 46 Psychological Bulletin; Wootton, Social Science and Social Pathology; Rheinstein, Divorce and the Law in Germany: A Review, 65 American Journal of Sociology; excerpts from the following essays in Rosenheim, Justice for the Child: Rosenheim, Perennial Problems in the Juvenile Court, Alexander, Constitutional Rights in the Juvenile Court, Fradkin, Disposition Dilemmas of American Juvenile Courts, and Shireman, Foreword; Brieland, An Experimental Study of the Selection of Adoptive Parents at Intake (Child Welfare League of America); Fanshel, Approaches to Measuring Adjustment in Adoptive Parents, in Quantitative Approaches to Parent Selection (Child Welfare League of America); Schapiro, A Study of Adoption Practice (Child Welfare League of America); Wolins and Piliavin, Institution or Foster Family, A Century of Debate (Child Welfare League of America); excerpts from the following essays in Witmer, Maternal Deprivation (Child Welfare League of America): Witmer, Introduction, Yarrow, Toward an Empirical and Conceptual Re-evaluation, and Ainsworth, Reversible and Irreversible Effects of Maternal Deprivation on Intellectual Development; Standards for Adoption Service, and Standards for Child Protective Service (Child Welfare League of America).

SUMMARY OF CONTENTS

Part III. DISSOLUTION OF THE FAMILY

T A B L E   O F   C O N T E N T S

CHAPTER 2

MARRIAGE   170

Part II. THE GOING FAMILY

CHAPTER 3

LEGAL RELATIONS OF THE FAMILY

CHAPTER 5

AUGMENTATION OF CHILDREN 472

CHAPTER 8

THE ROLE OF THE LAWYER IN COUNSELING DIVORCE CLIENTS

CHAPTER 11

FAMILY DISSOLUTION PLANNING — THE SEPARATION
AGREEMENT   942

Cases and Materials on
Family Law

PART I

The Formation of the Family

CHAPTER 1

The Problem of Illegitimacy

A. PROLOGUE

1. *Introductory Note*

The first part of this book deals with the various ways in which a family comes into existence and examines the legal consequences of different kinds of family formation. In a social sense one can say that a family is created, at least at a rudimentary level, whenever a man and woman share a common household or where one or both parents are sharing such a household with their minor children. The family in its legal sense, however, is a much more restricted concept. Formal ceremonial marriage is the usual prerequisite of the legal family, and the law both restricts freedom of entry into marriage and even more sharply inhibits the right to terminate that legal status.

Any family, whether or not legally sanctioned, may serve important human needs. It can provide the outlet for satisfactory sexual expression, create the protective environment demanded by the prolonged helplessness and dependence of the human child, provide an economic framework for the woman who is herself incapacitated from other productive labor because of the demands of bearing and rearing children, and serve basic psychological needs by providing the satisfactions which result from bonds of affection created by family living and sharing. The legal status of marriage is designed to serve and strengthen these essential family functions. It gives formal moral approval to the sexual relationship and seeks to ensure its exclusiveness, and it greatly improves the social and economic position of the wife and children. This system of advantages and concomitant penalties offers powerful incentives to conformity with the legal norm and serves as a deterrent against the creation of informal, extralegal relationships.

Unfortunate corollaries of legal restriction and protection of family status, however, arise from the obvious fact that sexual relations and living together can and do take place outside of the legally sanctioned marriage relationship. By-products of the relatively strict legal regulation of family status are such institutions as prostitution or concubinage, the birth of children outside of wedlock, and the existence of de facto families where the consummation of a legally approved marriage is neglected due to different cultural traditions or is legally impossible because of consanguinity, age, race, or, most commonly, because one or both partners have a prior undissolved marriage. To a greater or lesser degree the law and the culture it reflects penalize and stigmatize the participants in such arrangements, both the parents who created the situation more or less knowingly and the children whose legally unfortunate choice of parents was beyond their control.

Both illegitimacy and the nonlegal, de facto family have been serious problems in most cultures, and the difficulties they pose have been aggravated in modern times because of the profound changes in family structure which have been wrought by the industrial revolution and the cultural and social concomitants of that revolution. We have been speaking of family in its narrow sense of parents and minor children, but until relatively recent times the concept more often implied a broader base which included many or most of those who shared a common descent. Such a broader family typically embraced more than just two generations and retained at least some siblings in the home even after they had reached adulthood. Such a unit might achieve a degree of economic self-sufficiency with productive work for its own immediate needs often centered in the home. It was self-sustaining in recreation and sometimes in education, and the size of the institution permitted it to assume responsibility for its weaker members — the aged, the mentally defective, the injured, the unemployable. Although we have no historical statistics, it would be reasonable to assume that the many-sided importance of such a broad family unit and the utter dependence of many family members upon the group served to stabilize and preserve it. It does not follow, needless to say, that greater stability necessarily meant greater happiness or better performance of child-rearing functions.

Profound social changes, however, have substantially depreciated most of these economic functions of the family. Even in rural areas, where the change has come about more slowly, families produce less and less for their own consumption and more and more for the market, with a resulting decline in the economic dependence of family members upon the family group. Production for the market, moreover, has taken adults away from the home; artisans have become wage earners, and doctors' offices have moved from home to office building. Modern food processing and new work-saving devices, the TV dinner and the laundromat, have given women a substantial measure of freedom from kitchen and laundry. The social and cultural products of this economic revolution have further enhanced the relative importance of individualism at the expense of family unity. Feminism and changed attitudes towards the "rights" of children, as well as the emergence of the automobile as a staple of American life, have afforded members of the family an independence and mobility which would have been unthinkable fifty years ago. When the minor child is still in the home, community institutions have replaced the home in supplying most of his educational and recreational needs, and upon reaching adulthood, he typically moves away. Welfare functions formerly assumed in the family have substantially disintegrated and been transferred, first to private charity and now increasingly to the state.

This decline in family functions, in particular the economic devaluation of the family, probably accounts for many of the new patterns which are emerging in family formation and dissolution. The incidence of premarital and extramarital sexual relationships rose sharply early in this century and has continued at high levels. The divorce rate has climbed even more sharply, although leveling off in the nineteen-fifties. The incidence of illegitimacy apparently continues to climb. The median age of marriage has slowly but steadily declined in recent decades, until today more than half of all brides at first marriage are teenagers. An increasing proportion of law students get married before rather than after completing legal education, the economic role of their wives being transformed from that of liability to asset.

However, there is little indication that these changes, profound as they are, herald a total disintegration of the family.[1] The psychological satisfactions of marriage and child-rearing offer as much attraction as ever, and the peculiar fitness of the monogamous marriage for the nurture of children would appear to make the basic family unit almost immune to destruction. Basic facts of psychological and physical life protect the family institution against the most persistent disintegrating forces. The helplessness of the human infant for a prolonged period following birth, the child's need for protection and affection during a protracted period of immaturity, the needs of the mother during pregnancy, childbirth, and child-rearing, and the emotional bonds which this process forges among parents and children all tend to ensure family survival.

In some cultures today the significance of the parental role in raising children has been reduced in favor of increased state or other collective control over childrearing. To some extent this has been true of the Israeli kibbutz, where much of the care of children has been shifted to community institutions, but with close parental relationships also being retained.[2] At certain periods in both German and Soviet history, and currently in Communist China, it has been deliberate state policy to weaken the family by weaning the infant from its parents as rapidly as possible. By and large, however, our times are characterized by an increasing concern for strong parent-child relationships. The relative decline of economic activities within the family invites increasing attention to more basic questions of the welfare of the child and improvements in family stability. The past has concentrated almost exclusively upon the economic welfare of de-

[1] For a more pessimistic view of the future of the family, see Moore, Political Power and Social Theory 161-162 (1958).
[2] See Spiro, Children of the Kibbutz (1958).

pendent family members; the present and future are far more concerned with psychological adjustment and an exploration of the interrelationship between family happiness and such basic human problems as mental health, aggression, and crime. A strong case could be made for the proposition that the family, far from disintegrating, is only now beginning to recognize its full potentialities for human satisfaction. Social revolutions, however, pose tremendous difficulties for those who must live through them. To a considerable extent morals follow economics, but as economic patterns change, a nostalgia for the old order perpetuates moral attitudes long after they have become an impediment to achieving a satisfactory adjustment to changed conditions. It is this tendency to evaluate the new order by criteria evolved long ago under entirely different conditions which accounts for many of the cries of alarm about family disintegration so characteristic of our times.

Among human institutions law is often the most conservative and the last to adjust to changes in economic and social conditions. Dean Pound reports a delightful example of this conservatism from England before the establishment of divorce as a statutory remedy. A judge was called upon to sentence a workingman convicted of bigamy.

On being asked what he had to say why sentence should not be pronounced, the accused told a moving story of how his wife had run away with another man and left him with a number of small children to look after while barely earning a living by hard labor. After waiting several years he remarried in order to provide a proper home for the children. Mr. Justice Maule shook his head. "My good man," said he, "the law did not in any wise leave you without a sufficient remedy. You should first have brought an action in Her Majesty's Court of Common Pleas against this man with whom, as you say, your wife went away. In that action, after two or three years and the expenditure of two or three hundred pounds you would have obtained a judgment against him which very likely would have been uncollectible. You should then have brought a suit against your wife in the ecclesiastical court for a divorce from bed and board, which you might have obtained in two or three years after expenditure of two or three hundred pounds. You would then have been able to apply to Parliament for an absolute divorce, which you might have obtained in four or five years more after spending four or five hundred pounds. And," he continued, for he saw the accused impatiently seeking to interpose and to say something, "if you tell me that you never had and never in your life expect to have so many pennies at one time, my answer must be that it hath ever been the glory of England not to have one law for the rich and another for the poor." . . .[3]

One of the fascinations of family law in this period of transition of family function is to observe the stresses which accompany change and the resulting tensions for members of the legal profession. As more is ex-

[3]Pound, The Spirit of the Common Law 211-212 (1921).

pected of the family than simple economic justice, so more is demanded of the practitioner of family law than drafting separation papers or filing a paternity action. To be a counselor in family problems requires wisdom as well as technical skill.

The problem of illegitimacy to which we turn first may not represent the most typical instance of family formation, but it is a particularly illuminating vehicle for an examination of the interaction of history, law, cultural forces, and psychological knowledge. Pedagogically, it places before us at the outset the most elemental family functions: the mother-child relationship and the physical and psychological needs of infants. By permitting us to examine the standards for evaluating the competing claims in cases involving illegitimate children, it gives us a useful background for the resolution of other family controversies. It brings us face to face with such a typical family law problem as whether support money should be extracted from the father who is often estranged from the mother and child and who commonly either has no resources or has strong competing demands for his limited resources. If so, how is the question of paternity to be established in cases of doubt, when, by the nature of things, the only testimony normally available is the sharply conflicting and self-serving evidence of the mother and putative father? Or should some form of social insurance be developed instead to deal with this problem? Indeed, the plight of the illegitimate child and his relationship to his mother and father presents in microcosm most of the social and legal problems with which this book will deal.

First, the law in this area is struggling to free itself from the shackles of the past. The materials in this chapter provide dramatic illustrations of the revolutionary social changes which have occurred in the treatment of illegitimates and unwed mothers. Typically, as we have already indicated, legal change lags far behind social change, so that laws dealing with illegitimacy often continue to illustrate historical determinants which clash with current knowledge and outlook.

A *second* way in which the law of illegitimacy typifies the whole subject of family law is in its reflection of a complicated interaction between strong moral feelings and pragmatic concern for the welfare of particular individuals. The moral condemnation which was a major causative factor in old laws continues as a muted but still potent force in modern society. In dealing with the family we examine many situations in which our moral and religious principles are deeply involved. To a somewhat lessening extent society still proceeds from the premise that the unwed mother is a sinner with a stigma that also attaches to her offspring.

These moral overtones raise important problems of practice, reform, and policy. Of immediate significance for the family lawyer is the fact that his own strong convictions about the immorality of conduct in whose legal consequences he is involved may incapacitate his ability to function as a wise and dispassionate counselor or as a loyal advocate. Moreover, in light of these deep-seated moral feelings, the written law is often far stricter than the law which we tolerate in practice or are willing to enforce, as, for example, is the case with respect to our criminal sanctions against adultery and fornication, or our theoretically very rigid restrictions upon divorce. The resulting disparity between theory and practice poses a particularly difficult ethical dilemma for the practicing lawyer who is asked to ameliorate the harshness of the written law through the use of more or less accepted evasionary tactics.[4]

For the lawyer in the legislature or bar association who is carrying on the bar's historic role of law reform, the moral climate in which the family functions also poses something of a paradox. We use our written law to state our ideals of right conduct and to support community censure with legal sanction. As society's moral outlook changes, however, the statement of the ideal in legislation may be unresponsive to this change and reflect only the ideal adhered to by a minority.[5] Yet attempts to bring the law into greater conformity with current practice or revised community standards often invite the reply that such reform will weaken the moral norm and encourage immoral conduct.

These arguments, of course, raise basic policy questions as to the role of law in its relation to the family. To what extent is society justified in regulating essentially private consensual conduct? What role is to be given to law in fashioning people's family conduct? If the law is to have a deterrent function with respect to the control of such social conditions as illegitimacy or family disintegration, how is society to resolve the inevitable conflict between carrying out that policy and the desirability of not stigmatizing families, particularly innocent children?

Third, the lawyer's place in dealing with mothers of illegitimate children or with potential adoptive parents illustrates the delicate counseling role which the legal practitioner must assume in family law cases. People in trouble may turn to a religious counselor or to a psychiatrist or to a social agency or to a lawyer, and in many instances the selection of a particular profession in the search for help turns more on cultural and personal factors than on an objective assessment of the kind of help which is needed. Like clergymen or doctors, lawyers are members of a profession. "The professional man," Talcott Parsons has said, "is not thought of as engaged in the pursuit of his personal profit, but in performing services to his patients or clients, or to impersonal values like the advancement of science." [6] Thus in an acquisitive society dominated by the pursuit of personal economic gain, professional men "have been thought of as standing above these sordid considerations, devoting their lives to the 'service'

[4] Mr. Henry Drinker, in his article Problems of Professional Ethics in Matrimonial Litigation, 66 Harv. L. Rev. 443, 444 (1953), refers to these devices as "fictions or quasi fictions — the 'growing pains of the law.' "

[5] See particularly Cohen, Robson & Bates, Parental Authority: The Community and the Law (1958), which relates existing legal norms in Nebraska to the values of the Nebraska community as determined by a poll designed to ascertain that community's moral sense on selected family law issues pertaining to parental control over children. Summarizing their findings, the authors state that "There are at least twice as many issues concerning which the community views are in disagreement with the law as there are [issues] on which the community views and the law are in harmony." Id. at 193.

[6] Parsons, The Professions and Social Structure, in Essays in Sociological Theory 35 (rev. ed. 1954).

of their fellow men." [7] Lawyers are not tradesmen selling prescriptions on demand, and clients typically expect more of a lawyer than the mere purchase of predetermined legal services. Justice Brandeis long ago made this same point in stressing the view of a lawyer as a "counsellor." [8]

The proper discharge of this counseling role requires considerable insight:

> When the client comes to the lawyer, he may be affected by fear, anxiety, and helplessness. The lawyer cannot successfully handle such a person on a wholly impersonal basis. To do an effective job, the lawyer must be aware of the client's personal situation; he must seek to understand and evaluate the client. . . .[9]

Moreover, the only problems of many family law clients may be nonlegal; thus the unmarried pregnant woman who comes to a lawyer is likely to be charged with suppressed emotional turmoil, and in many cases her purported legal problem is a mask through which she actually seeks wisdom and guidance. No lawyer can escape these situations, and he must resolve them, even if the resolution is the unprofessional and unsatisfactory one of ignoring the existence of the nonlegal problem. Furthermore, from the client's viewpoint the interview with the lawyer is a significant step, often being the culmination of long uncertainty and hesitation about seeking help. Even if the lawyer does not take the case and terminates the relationship after a single interview, the client will be helped or harmed in the process, depending upon the sensitivity and skill of the lawyer.

Fourth, this broader counseling role points up the necessity for some familiarity with the nonlegal professions and their contributions to the solution of family problems. Any lawyer with a substantial family practice inevitably must deal with social workers and psychiatrists. To profit from such interdisciplinary relationships, he must have some understanding of where these persons usefully fit into the total scheme of things. Not infrequently they will take a dim view of what they regard as the lawyer's narrow and legalistic attitude towards the client's problem, and some prior awareness of this on the lawyer's part cannot but help to facilitate his dealings with them. Moreover, to be able to understand the total situation of a client such as an unwed mother, the lawyer needs to be equipped with some knowledge of what the social and behavioral sciences have found out about such persons. This does not imply that the family lawyer must have technical training in psychiatry, social work, or sociology. It does mean, however, that the lawyer must have sufficient familiarity with relevant disciplines beyond the limits of his own profession so that he can detect nonlegal aspects of the client's problem, recognize the

---

[7] Id. at 43.

[8] See Harvard Law School, Occasional Pamphlet No. 3, Proceedings in Honor of Mr. Justice Frankfurter and Distinguished Alumni 5 (1960). For a recent analysis of the lawyers' neglect of their important counseling function, see Pilpel, The Job the Lawyers Shirk, Harper's, Jan. 1960, p. 67.

[9] Griswold, Law Schools and Human Relations, 1955 Wash. U.L.Q. 217, 223.

nonlegal implications of alternative courses of legal action, and distinguish those cases in which consultation with or reference to nonlegal experts is advisable. Of course, just as there is a danger in lawyers not knowing anything about these areas, there is an equally great danger that they will think they know enough to attempt to handle "by common sense" complex emotional problems requiring expert professional help.

In divorce practice, for example, the competent lawyer, in addition to possessing the necessary legal skill, must (1) be sensitive to the critical psychological aspects of his counseling role in dealing with emotionally disturbed clients; (2) be sufficiently aware of the nature of marital discord to be able to diagnose cases where reconciliation is a possibility or where the client is in need of psychiatric therapy or other skilled nonlegal counseling; (3) have informed himself of the existence and methods of operation of the psychiatric, counseling, and child welfare facilities in his community to which he can refer appropriate cases and have acquired skill in the delicate task of accomplishing such a referral; and (4) be able to advise clients of the economic, social, and psychological problems incident to family dissolution. In the problem with which we are immediately concerned — the illegitimate child and his parents — the lawyer's craftsmanship will have profound effects upon a helpless infant as well as upon the mother or father who is the formal client. In some European countries there is legal provision for the appointment at or even before birth of a guardian to protect the interests of an illegitimate child. Any conscientious lawyer involved in a paternity situation will, at least to some degree, assume this guardianship role. In recent decades the behavioral sciences have amassed impressive evidence attesting to the critical importance of the early months and years of a child's life. There is now substantial empirical and other evidence cutting across many scientific disciplines that supports the general agreement that very early childhood experiences will profoundly affect subsequent susceptibility to mental illness, delinquency, or chronic immaturity. Some acquaintance with this knowledge is an important tool for the lawyer who counsels the unwed father or mother, for legal counseling and action should be geared to the promptest possible assimilation of the child into a family environment which offers reasonable prospects for permanence and emotional nurture. Similarly, a sensitive handling of the unwed mother demands some awareness of the psychological and social factors which are operative in this area. As is to be expected, the development of appropriate legal remedies for this situation often lags far behind our developing knowledge of the need for regulation and guidance, and an able lawyer who is aware of the complexity and importance of the social problem can do much to bridge the gap between scientific knowledge and the frequent inadequacy of the legal response to that knowledge.

2. *A Brief Historical Note*

1 BLACKSTONE, COMMENTARIES
*454-459

1. Who are bastards. A bastard, by our English laws, is one that is not only begotten, but born, out of lawful matrimony. The civil and canon laws do not allow a child to remain a bastard, if the parents afterwards intermarry: and herein they differ most materially from our law; which, though not so strict as to require that the child shall be *begotten,* yet makes it an indispensable condition that it shall be *born,* after lawful wedlock. And the reason of our English law is surely much superior to that of the Roman, if we consider the principal end and design of establishing the contract of marriage, taken in a civil light; abstractedly from any religious view, which has nothing to do with the legitimacy or illegitimacy of the children. The main end and design of marriage therefore being to ascertain and fix upon some certain person, to whom the care, the protection, the maintenance, and the education of the children should belong; this end is undoubtedly better answered by legitimating all issue born after wedlock, than by legitimating all issue of the same parties, even born before wedlock, so as wedlock afterwards ensues: 1. Because of the very great uncertainty there will generally be, in the proof that the issue was really begotten by the same man; whereas, by confining the proof to the birth, and not to the begetting, our law has rendered it perfectly certain, what child is legitimate, and who is to take care of the child. 2. Because by the Roman laws a child may be continued a bastard, or made legitimate, at the option of the father and mother, by a marriage ex post facto; thereby opening a door to many frauds and partialities, which by our law are prevented. 3. Because by those laws a man may remain a bastard till forty years of age, and then become legitimate, by the subsequent marriage of his parents; whereby the main end of marriage, the protection of infants, is totally frustrated. 4. Because this rule of the Roman laws admits of no limitations as to the time, or number, of bastards so to be legitimated; but a dozen of them may, twenty years after their birth, by the subsequent marriage of their parents, be admitted to all the privileges of legitimate children. This is plainly a great discouragement to the matrimonial state; to which one main inducement is usually not only the desire of having *children,* but also the desire of procreating lawful *heirs.* Whereas our constitutions guard against this indecency, and at the same time give sufficient allowance to the frailties of human nature. For, if a child be begotten while the parents are single, and they will endeavour to make an early reparation for the offence, by marrying within a few months after, our law is so indulgent as not to bastardize the child, if it be born, though not begotten, in lawful wedlock: for this is an incident that can happen but once; since all future children will be begotten, as well as born, within the rules of honour and civil society. Upon reasons like

these we may suppose the peers to have acted at the parliament of Merton, when they refused to enact that children born before marriage should be esteemed legitimate.

From what has been said it appears, that all children born before matrimony are bastards by our law; and so it is of all children born so long after the death of the husband, that, by the usual course of gestation, they could not be begotten by him. . . .

2. Let us next see the duty of parents to their bastard children, by our law; which is principally that of maintenance. For, though bastards are not looked upon as children to any civil purposes, yet the ties of nature, of which maintenance is one, are not so easily dissolved: and they hold indeed as to many other intentions; as, particularly, that a man shall not marry his bastard sister or daughter. The civil law therefore, when it denied maintenance to bastards begotten under certain atrocious circumstances, was neither consonant to nature, nor reason, however profligate and wicked the parents might justly be esteemed.

[Blackstone then discusses affiliation proceedings.]

3. I proceed next to the rights and incapacities which appertain to a bastard. The rights are very few, being only such as he can *acquire;* for he can *inherit* nothing, being looked upon as the son of nobody, and sometimes called filius nullius, sometimes filius populi. Yet he may gain a sirname by reputation, though he has none by inheritance. All other children have a settlement in their father's parish; but a bastard in the parish where born, for he hath no father. However, in case of fraud, as if a woman be sent either by order of justices, or comes to beg as a vagrant, to a parish which she does not belong to, and drops her bastard there; the bastard shall, in the first case, be settled in the parish from whence she was illegally removed; or, in the latter case, in the mother's own parish, if the mother be apprehended for her vagrancy. The incapacity of a bastard consists principally in this, that he cannot be heir to any one, neither can he have heirs, but of his own body; for, being nullius filius, he is therefore of kin to nobody, and has no ancestor from whom any inheritable blood can be derived. A bastard was also, in strictness, incapable of holy orders; and, though that were dispensed with, yet he was utterly disqualified from holding any dignity in the church: but this doctrine seems now obsolete; and in all other respects, there is no distinction between a bastard and another man. And really any other distinction, but that of not inheriting, which civil policy renders necessary, would, with regard to the innocent offspring of his parents' crimes, be odious, unjust, and cruel to the last degree: and yet the civil law, so boasted of for [its] equitable decisions, made bastards in some cases incapable even of a gift from their parents. A bastard may, lastly, be made legitimate, and capable of inheriting, by the transcendent power of an act of parliament, and not otherwise: as was done in the case of John of Gant's bastard children, by a statute of Richard the second.

NOTE

1. The logic of the doctrine of filius nullius created other difficulties in addition to the incest problem to which Blackstone made reference. In the Middle Ages whether or not a man was born free or serf depended upon the condition of his father, and by the reign of Edward II the courts "pressed this rule to the absurd, if humane, conclusion that a bastard is always born free since he has no father." 1 Pollock & Maitland 423.

2. Community disapproval of illegitimacy, however expressed, does not necessarily prevent the birth of children out of wedlock, but it may intensify the unmarried mother's desire to avoid detection. How strong community pressures must once have been is poignantly illustrated by an entry in Winthrop's Journal for 1647:

> There fell out at this time a very sad occasion. A merchant of Plymouth in England, (whose father had been mayor there,) called . . . Martin, being fallen into decay, came to Casco Bay, and after some time, having occasion to return into England, he left behind him two daughters, (very proper maidens and of modest behavior,) but took not that course for their safe bestowing in his absence, as the care and wisdom of a father should have done, so as the eldest of them, called Mary, twenty-two years of age, being in [the] house with one Mr. Mitton, a married man of Casco, within one quarter of a year, he was taken with her, and soliciting her chastity, obtained his desire, and having divers times committed sin with her, in the space of three months, she then removed to Boston, and put herself in service to Mrs. Bourne; and finding herself to be with child, and not able to bear the shame of it, she concealed it, and though divers did suspect it, and some told her mistress their fears, yet her behavior was so modest, and so faithful she was in her service, as her mistress would not give ear to any such report, but blamed such as told her of it. But, her time being come, she was delivered of a woman child in a back room by herself upon the [thirteenth of December] in the night, and the child was born alive, but she kneeled upon the head of it, till she thought it had been dead, and having laid it by, the child, being strong, recovered, and cried again. Then she took it again, and used violence to it till it was quite dead. Then she put it into her chest, and having cleansed the room, she went to bed, and arose again the next day about noon, and went about her business, and so continued till the nineteenth day, that her master and mistress went on shipboard to go for England. They being gone, and she removed to another house, a midwife in the town, having formerly suspected her, and now coming to her again, found she had been delivered of a child, which, upon examination, she confessed, but said it was still-born, and so she put it into the fire. But, search being made, it was found in her chest, and when she was brought before the jury, they caused her to touch the face of it, whereupon the blood came fresh

into it. Whereupon she confessed the whole truth, and a surgeon, being called to search the body of the child, found a fracture in the skull. Before she was condemned, she confessed, that she had prostituted her body to another also, one Sears. She behaved herself very penitently while she was in prison, and at her death, [on the eighteenth of March] complaining much of the hardness of her heart. She confessed, that the first and second time she committed fornication, she prayed for pardon, and promised to commit it no more; and the third time she prayed God, that if she did fall into it again, he would make her an example, and therein she justified God, as she did in the rest. Yet all the comfort God would afford her, was only trust (as she said) in his mercy through Christ. After she was turned off and had hung a space, she spake, and asked what they did mean to do. Then some stepped up, and turned the knot of the rope backward, and then she soon died.[10]

The high rate of stillbirths for illegitimate children and the ease with which this defense could be invoked by a mother suspected of infanticide led to legislation to ease the prosecution's burden of proof. Thus a Massachusetts statute enacted in 1696 provided:

Whereas many lewd women that have been delivered of bastard children, to avoid their shame, and to escape punishment, do secretly bury or conceal the death of their children, and after, if the child be found dead, the said women do allege that the said child was born dead, whereas it falleth out sometimes (although hardly it is to be proved) that the said child or children were murdered by the said women their lewd mothers, or by their assent or procurement,

Be it therefore enacted by the lieutenant governor, council and representatives, convened in general assembly, and it is hereby enacted by the authority of the same, that if any woman be delivered of any issue of her body, male or female, which, if it were born alive, should by law be a bastard, and that she endeavour privately, either by drowning, or secret burying thereof, or any other way, either by herself, or the procuring of others, so to conceal the death thereof, that it may not come to light, whether it were born alive or not, but be concealed, in every such case the mother so offending shall suffer death, as in case of murder, except such mother can make proof by one witness at the least, that the child whose death was by her so intended to be concealed was born dead.[11]

3. Although harsh sanctions were imposed against the unwed mother, there was concern for the life and health of the child, and this concern inevitably produced opportunities for "lewd women . . . to avoid their shame, and to escape punishment" in return for the life of the infant.

[10] 2 Winthrop's Journal, "History of New England" 1630-1649, pp. 317-318 (Hosmer ed. 1908). (The first bracketed word is bracketed in original.)
[11] The Charters and General Laws of the Colony and Province of Massachusetts Bay 293 (Dane, Prescott & Story eds. 1814).

Thus, Frederick the Great, complaining to Voltaire in 1777 about the large number of executions in Germany of mothers convicted of infanticide, described his own efforts to relieve the pressures on unwed mothers:

Among the delinquents the majority are women who have destroyed their children; there are few murders committed, and still less highway robberies. But, of the wretches who have so cruelly treated their offspring, none but those against whom the murder has been well proved are put to death. I have done everything in my power to prevent them from thus ridding themselves of the fruit of their womb. Masters are obliged to send information, when their maids are with child. Formerly, such poor girls were obliged to do public penance in the churches; from which I have relieved them. There are houses appointed, in each province in which they may lie in, and where their children are educated.

Notwithstanding all these conveniences, I have not yet been able to root the unnatural prejudice from their minds which induces them to destroy their children.[12]

The church's concern for illegitimate children goes back at least to the fourteenth century, when what was apparently the first institution to shelter unwed mothers and foundlings was established in Florence. In convents all over Europe a device called the *tour* (turnbox) came into existence by the late Middle Ages.[13] The *tour* was placed at the door or in the wall of a convent, monastery, or foundling home. It was an enclosed round box, which pivoted on an axis so it could be rotated, with an opening on one side. An object was placed in the opening from the outside which, when the box was rotated, could be removed by someone inside the building.[14] Thus nuns could receive deliveries from the outside world without either seeing or being seen by the visitor. Whether or not the *tour* was explicitly developed to provide for the delivery of unwanted infants, it was admirably suited to this purpose and enabled the mother to dispose of her child humanely yet without the need to identify herself.

Abandonment and infanticide became so common in France[15] that in 1811 Napoleon issued a decree requiring that all foundling homes be equipped with a *tour*.[16] Some years later, however, it was alleged that the *tour* encouraged parents to abandon their responsibilities to the church; it was suppressed by a circular of July 27, 1838, and finally totally forbidden in 1860.[17]

[12] 8 Posthumous Works of Frederic II King of Prussia 536-537 (Holcroft transl. 1789).

[13] 31 La Grande Encyclopedie 224 (1886-1902).

[14] For an illustration and further discussion, see 7 Nouveau Larouse Illustré 1069 (Ange ed. 1898-1909).

[15] In Paris in 1772 the number of foundlings was equal to about 40 per cent of the baptisms, and the death rate for foundlings often surpassed 500 per 1000. Krause, Some Implications of Recent Work in Historical Demography, in 1 Comparative Studies in Society and History 164, 177 (1959).

[16] Law of January 19, 1811, [1811] Bulletin des Lois (4th ser.), pt. 1, p. 82.

[17] 7 Nouveau Larouse Illustré 1069 (Ange ed. 1898-1909).

B. STATUS OF CHILDREN BORN OUT OF WEDLOCK

1. *Disabilities of Illegitimates*

WILSON v. INGRAM

61 S.E.2d 126 (Ga. 1950)[18]

J. W. Buttrum died on September 23, 1948, leaving a will which provided, in so far as is material here, as follows: "The remainder of the aforesaid life estate and all of the remainder of my property shall be divided between my children, share and share alike. . . ." [Quotation abbreviated by Eds.] . . .

The petitioner, Mary Elizabeth Wilson, . . . filed her petition in the Bartow Superior Court, seeking to recover a child's share in the estate of J. W. Buttrum, in which she alleged: that she was the daughter of J. W. Buttrum; that she was born in Bartow County on April 19, 1905, and that her mother was Georgia Ida Brownlow; . . . that, shortly after her birth, J. W. Buttrum, her father, took her into his home under an agreement with her mother to adopt her as his own child; that the testator reared the petitioner as his legitimate child, and treated her in the same manner and on the same basis as his other children; that the petitioner did not know until she was almost an adult that she was not the legitimate child of J. W. Buttrum; that J. W. Buttrum referred to her as his daughter and legitimate child on numerous occasions; that J. W. Buttrum executed an affidavit in which he stated that he had always accepted her as his legitimate child and on the same footing as the other children born to him. . . .

WYATT, J. 1. Counsel in the instant case devote much of their argument to the question of whether or not the allegations of the petition are sufficient to authorize a court of equity to decree that there had been a virtual adoption of the petitioner by the testator. In the view we take of this case, it is not necessary to pass upon that question here. . . .

3. Granting, but not deciding, that the allegations of the petition are sufficient to show a virtual adoption, can the petitioner recover as a child under a will devising property "to my children, share and share alike"? This court in Comer v. Comer, 195 Ga. 79, 87, 23 S.E.2d 420, 425, said: "Generally, the terms 'issue,' 'children,' 'heir,' and words of similar import, in a will, are intended to refer to natural or blood relationships, and would not include an adopted child in the absence of circumstances clearly showing that the testator so intended. The artificial relation created by adoption is an unusual and exceptional one, and hence would not fall within the ordinary signification of such terms." . . .

4. The next question is: Does the term "children" include the petitioner, who is an illegitimate child of the testator? It has been held many

[18] A summary of the case, but not the opinion of Wyatt, J., also appears in 207 Ga. 271.

times by this court that the term "children" does not include an illegitimate child. [Citations omitted.]

5. It is contended that a certain affidavit executed by the testator some six years prior to his death, stating in effect that the petitioner was his child, together with the fact that the petitioner lived in the testator's home, and that the testator referred to the petitioner as his child, is sufficient to show that the testator in the instant case intended to include the petitioner in the term "children" as used in his will. The intention to include persons other than natural, legitimate children within the term "children" in a will must be found in the will itself, extraneous evidence being inadmissible to give it a more inclusive meaning. [Citations omitted.] The will in the instant case uses the word "children" without any qualification whatever. . . . We therefore hold, under the rulings above made, that the term "children" as used in the will in the instant case does not include the petitioner, either as an adopted child or as an illegitimate child of the testator. Accordingly, it was not error to sustain the general demurrer to the petition.

Judgment affirmed.

NOTE

Compare Old Colony Trust Co. v. Attorney General, 326 Mass. 532, 95 N.E.2d 649 (1950) (where testator knew that mother had only two children, one of whom was illegitimate, and knew that mother was dead, use of plural form "children" sufficiently indicates his intention to allow illegitimate child to take despite rule that "children" normally excludes illegitimate children), with Eaton v. Eaton, 88 Conn. 269, 278, 91 Atl. 191, 194 (1914) (the "harsh and inhumane doctrine of the English common law" has never been applied in Connecticut; presumptively the word "child" or "children" in a will includes all of a mother's children, legitimate and illegitimate, unless a different intention is to be gathered from the will).

Matter of CADY
257 App. Div. 129, 12 N.Y.S.2d 750, aff'd mem.,
281 N.Y. 688, 23 N.E.2d 18 (1939)

Hill, P.J. Appeal from a decree of the Cortland County Surrogate's Court which revoked letters of administration earlier issued to an illegitimate son of a deceased sister of the intestate upon the ground that he was not entitled to take or share in the personal property left by intestate and, therefore, was not qualified to act as administrator. (Surr. Ct. Act, §118.)

It is argued on behalf of appellant that under the new Statute of Distribution (Dec. Est. Law, art. 3, Laws of 1929, chap. 229, and later amendments) he is entitled to share in the estate of a deceased brother of his mother, irrespective of his own illegitimacy. The steps by which his counsel reaches this conclusion follow: (1) That as "all existing modes, rules and canons of descent are . . . abolished" (§81, supra) by the new statute, all the former common law and statutory disability as to inheritance by illegitimates was terminated.   (2) That the inhibition against inheritance by illegitimates, except from the mother, contained in former section 89 of the Decedent Estate Law, because of the final sentence, "In any other case illegitimate children or relatives shall not inherit," is omitted in the comparable provision in the new act (§83, subd. 13), which reads: "If a woman die, leaving illegitimate children, or the legitimate descendants of deceased illegitimate children and no lawful issue, such children or descendants inherit her real and personal property as if such children were legitimate."   (3) That appellant is entitled to take this estate under subdivision 6 of section 83, as he is the sole descendant of his mother, who was the only sister of intestate.   This paragraph provides for per stirpes inheritance by brothers and sisters and their descendants; the estate is to "be distributed to such descendants in whatever degree, collectively."

We are unable to agree with the foregoing argument, as the repeal of former "modes, rules and canons of descent" (§81) did not change the common-law rule that an illegitimate was nobody's son (nullius filius). The common-law rule was not a Statute of Distribution; rather it established that the illegitimate was not to be regarded the child or descendant of any one. [Citations omitted.]   Under appellant's argument an illegitimate would be more favored in the distribution of the estates of his collateral relatives than in the distribution of the estate of his mother, for he may only inherit from her in the event there is "no lawful issue" (§83, subd. 13), while he would compete, in the event of his mother's death, with lawful issue in the distribution of the estates of his mother's brothers and sisters, as he would be included under the general term "descendant." So paradoxical a result could not have been intended by the Legislature. It is a general rule of construction that when the words "child," "children" or "descendants" are used in a statute the meaning is legitimate or lawful children or descendants. [Citations omitted.]

None may gainsay the harshness and seeming unfairness of the discrimination against those unfortunate enough to have been born out of wedlock, but, as the inheritance of property is governed by statute the remedy must be obtained from the Legislature.   The appellant adverts to the fact that had he died after the death of his mother and had her deceased brother survived the latter would have inherited from appellant.   This is only another example of the unfairness of the statute, but courts have no remedy.

The decree should be affirmed.

[Dissenting opinion of Bliss, J., omitted.]

HARGROVE v. LLOYDS CASUALTY CO.
66 S.W.2d 466 (Tex. Civ. Ct. App. 1933)

GRAVES, J. [Deceased worker at the time of his death and for eighteen months prior thereto was living and cohabiting with a woman who was married to another, and after the worker's death a child of this union was born. The lower court denied workmen's compensation benefits.]

No extended discussion of the matter is deemed necessary; the directly applicable portions of our statutes, R.S. art. 8306, §8a, and article 8309, are these: "The compensation provided for in the foregoing section of this law shall be for the sole and exclusive benefit of the surviving husband who has not for good cause and for a period of three years prior thereto, abandoned his wife at the time of the injury, and of the wife who has not at the time of the injury without good cause and for a period of three years prior thereto, abandoned her husband, and of the minor children, parents and stepmother, without regard to the question of dependency, dependent grandparents, dependent children and dependent brothers and sisters of the deceased employee. . . . The words 'legal beneficiaries' as used in this law shall mean the relatives named in section 8a, part 1, of this law."

Without much ado, our own courts have held . . . that the words "children" and "dependent children" as used in these acts mean legitimate children, wherefore illegitimate ones are not capable of taking the benefits therein provided.

Most if not all the authorities cited and relied upon in the able brief of the appellant for a contrary conclusion are interpretations of statutes in other states which provide for compensation to the members of deceased's "family or household"; notable among these is the Massachusetts act, upon which, in some respects at least, our own was based, the provision there being this: " 'Dependents' shall mean members of the employee's family or next of kin who were wholly or partly dependent upon the . . . employee for support at the time of the injury." Part 5, §2, Massachusetts Workmen's Compensation Act (St. 1911, c. 751, pt. 5, §2). See, also, Gritta's Case, 236 Mass. 204, 127 N.E. 889.

From and upon such statutes the courts seem to have built what may perhaps not inappropriately be denominated the "family doctrine" in holding that illegitimate children are capable of taking the benefits thereunder; but there is a distinct line of cleavage between statutes and decisions of that sort and our own, where no such statutory intendment exists, as is pointed out by the Supreme Court of Michigan in Bassier v. J. Connelly Construction Company, 227 Mich. 251, 198 N.W. 989; see, also, Scott v. Independent Ice Co., 135 Md. 343, 109 A. 117.

It is true that our act, along with such laws generally, is entitled to be liberally construed with a view toward effectuating the purposes of its enactment, but it would seem to be carrying that rule over the brink to assume one of those objectives to have been the encouragement of men and women to lie up ad libitum in illicit relationships and produce illegitimate offspring — as these negroes did in this instance — with the expectation of their being accorded the same rights under this expressed policy of the state as children born in lawful wedlock; at any rate, this court cannot, with the lights before it, so hold.

The judgment of the learned trial court will therefore be affirmed.

NOTE

1. The intestate inheritance rights of illegitimate children are governed by explicit statutory provision in most states. New York has recently amended its statute by repealing §83, subd. 13 of the Decedent Estate Law that was cited in the Cady case and substituting, inter alia, the following:

  a. An illegitimate child is the legitimate child of his mother so that he and his issue inherit from his mother and from his maternal kindred.

  b. An illegitimate child is the legitimate child of his father so that he and his issue inherit from his father if a court of competent jurisdiction shall have found the decedent to be the father of such child and shall have made an order of filiation declaring paternity in a proceeding instituted during the pregnancy of the mother or within two years from the birth of the child.

  c. The approval of any agreement or compromise without the making of an order of filiation declaring paternity shall not enable the child to inherit from the respondent in any such proceeding.[19]

How would this affect the Cady result? Compare Cal. Prob. Code §255, page 32 infra. As is evident from these two samples, the subject of intestate inheritance is immensely complicated by different requirements in the various statutes, depending upon whether the illegitimate child is attempting to inherit from his mother, his father, or the kindred of either, or whether any of these are trying to inherit from or through him. For a compendious chart detailing all these situations, see Note, 26 Brooklyn L. Rev. 45, 76-79 (1959).

As to the problem involved in Hargrove, see Staker v. Industrial Commission, 127 Ohio St. 13, 17, 186 N.E. 616, 617 (1933) ("we think it is obvious that in [the workmen's compensation statute] the Legislature intended to use the word 'child' *in its usual and ordinary sense* [excluding illegitimates]") (emphasis supplied). See also Annot., 72 A.L.R.2d 1235 (1960), concerning the rights of illegitimate children under wrongful death statutes, and Annot., 13 A.L.R. 686 (1921), as supplemented, concerning the rights of such children under workmen's compensation acts.

Miscellaneous situations in which illegitimate children have recovered include: under state veterans' compensation as a "minor child";[20] under the New York City Employees' Retirement System, where the statute mentioned "dependents" as well as "child";[21] under an insurance policy naming "children" as beneficiaries;[22] and as "children" under Federal

---

[19] Decedent Estate Law §83-a, as added by N.Y. Sess. Laws 1965, c. 958, §1.

[20] Miller v. Miller, 116 Kan. 726, 229 Pac. 361 (1924).

[21] Ciarlo v. New York City Employees' Retirement System, 270 App. Div. 594, 61 N.Y.S.2d 751 (1946), aff'd mem., 296 N.Y. 962, 73 N.E.2d 269 (1947).

[22] Turner v. Metropolitan Life Ins. Co., 56 Cal. App. 2d 862, 133 P.2d 859 (1943).

Employees Group Life Insurance.[23] In the last case, the child was assisted by Md. Ann. Code art. 1, §16 (1957): "The word child or its equivalent shall be construed to include any illegitimate child, except in matters of inheritance, descent or distribution of real and personal property, unless such a construction would be unreasonable."

2. A great many federal statutes raise similar interpretative problems when the claimant is an illegitimate child. Some of these statutes expressly incorporate state law. See, e.g., the Social Security Act, which provides that for the purpose of "determining whether an applicant is the child . . . , the Secretary shall apply such law as would be applied in determining the devolution of intestate personal property by the courts of the State in which such insured individual is domiciled." 42 U.S.C.A. §416(h)(2)(A) (1964). See also the Federal Tort Claims Act, which, generally speaking, imposes liability on the United States if a private person engaging in the conduct in question "would be liable to the claimant in accordance with the law of the place where the act or omission occurred." 28 U.S.C.A. §1346(b) (1962). Other federal statutes are more specific as to who are the intended beneficiaries of the statutory benefits, but by using such undefined terms as "child" or "children," have left it to the courts to determine whether federal or state law should be utilized in interpreting such terms, and whether, if the latter, what part of the state's law should be looked to. In De Sylva v. Ballentine, 351 U.S. 570, 580-581 (1956), the Court held that the word "children" in §24 of the Copyright Act, which regulates the descent of an author's renewal rights, should be interpreted according to state law:

> We think it proper, therefore, to draw on the ready-made body of state law to define the word "children" in §24. This does not mean that a State would be entitled to use the word "children" in a way entirely strange to those familiar with its ordinary usage, but at least to the extent that there are permissible variations in the ordinary concept of "children" we deem state law controlling. [Citation omitted.]

The Court then concluded that although the claimant had not met the requirements of the California legitimation statute, see page 27 infra, he could nevertheless claim his deceased father's copyright renewal rights since he had been acknowledged in writing by his father as provided in the intestate succession statute, see page 32 infra. See also Bowen v. New York Cent. R.R., 179 F. Supp. 225 (D. Mass. 1959), holding that the word "children" in the Federal Employer's Liability Act must be interpreted by state law; since in Massachusetts the term "children" in a will or trust does not normally include illegitimate children, the latter could not intervene in an FELA action. But cf. Hammond v. Pennsylvania R.R., 31 N.J. 244, 156 A.2d 689 (1959). And see Middleton v. Luckenback S.S. Co., 70 F.2d 326 (2d Cir. 1934), interpreting the phrase "parent, child, or dependent relative" in the Federal Death on the High Seas Act, 46 U.S.C.A. §761 (1958), by federal rather than state standards, and allowing recovery

[23] Johnson v. Brooks, 28 U.S.L. Week 2204 (Md. Cir. Ct., Oct. 29, 1959).

to an illegitimate child even though such child would not be allowed to inherit his father's property.

Finally there are federal statutes which expressly define the class of intended beneficiaries. See, e.g., 38 U.S.C.A. §101(4) (Supp. 1964) (veterans' benefits):

> The term "child" means . . . a person . . . who is a legitimate child, a legally adopted child, a stepchild who is a member of a veteran's household or was a member at the time of the veteran's death, or an illegitimate child but, as to the alleged father, only if acknowledged in writing signed by him, or if he has been judicially ordered to contribute to the child's support or has been, before his death, judicially decreed to be the father of such child, or if he is otherwise shown by evidence satisfactory to the Administrator to be the father of such child. . . .

In general, see Note, 76 Harv. L. Rev. 337 (1962).

PROBLEMS

1. Wilson, a twenty-three-year-old bachelor, was employed by the Kingswood Trucking Company at a wage of $90 a week. He lived at home with his parents, contributing $10 a week for board and room. On September 10, 1958, he pleaded guilty to a charge of fornication. Sentence was suspended when he signed an agreement to pay the pregnant girl involved, Mary Jane, $300 for her confinement expenses and loss of wages and to pay $10 weekly for the support of the child-to-be until the child was fourteen years of age. On November 29, Wilson was killed in an accident while at work, and on December 2, Mary Jane gave birth to Susan. Both Wilson's parents and Mary Jane (in behalf of Susan) have filed claims for workmen's compensation benefits. The Kingswood Trucking Company, admitting liability, asks you which claimant it should pay. The relevant statute provides as follows:

> §561. In the case of death, compensation shall be computed on the following basis, and distributed to the following persons:
>
> 1. If there be no widow nor widower entitled to compensation, compensation shall be paid to the guardian of the child or children. . . .
>
> 5. If there be neither widow, widower, nor children entitled to compensation, then to the father or mother, if dependent to any extent upon the employee at the time of the accident, twenty-five per centum of wages, but not in excess of nine dollars per week: Provided, however, that in the case of a minor child who has been contributing to his parents, the dependency of said parents shall be presumed . . .
>
> §562. Compensation shall be payable under this section to or on account of any child, brother, or sister, only if and while such child,

brother, or sister is under the age of sixteen. No compensation shall be payable under this section to a widow, unless she was living with her deceased husband at the time of his death, or was then actually dependent upon him and receiving from him a substantial portion of her support. No compensation shall be payable under this section to a widower, unless he be incapable of self-support at the time of his wife's death and be at such time dependent upon her for support. If members of decedent's household at the time of his death, the terms "child" and "children" shall include stepchildren, adopted children, and children to whom he stood in loco parentis, and shall include posthumous children.

2. Assume that Congress is about to pass new legislation providing free medical care for certain indigent persons and their dependents. The question has arisen whether illegitimate children are to be entitled to benefits under this act, and if so, under what circumstances. As among the three possible alternatives for denominating the beneficiaries entitled to aid under the act — express incorporation of state law, use of incompletely defined federal terms such as "child," and express definition in the federal act — which should Congress choose? What are some of the considerations pro and con? If state law is to be looked to, what particular part of the state's law should be referred to? Would your answer to this question be the same for any other proposed federal compensatory legislation, or would it depend upon the precise subject matter of the act in question? Suppose that Congress has chosen the second alternative and the case comes before a court for determination whether the term "child" in the act extends to illegitimate children. How should the court decide this question (i.e., by reference to what law)?

2. *Legitimation*

Estate of LUND
26 Cal. 2d 472, 159 P.2d 643 (1945)

SCHAUER, J. Bert A. Lund, petitioner herein, appeals on a settled statement from an order denying his petition to determine heirship. Petitioner was born the illegitimate (it is assumed) son of Andrew Lund, now deceased, from whom he seeks to inherit. He was received into his father's family, with the consent of the father and his wife (not petitioner's mother), while they were domiciled in another state, and thenceforth was publicly acknowledged and in every respect treated by his father as a legitimate son. The father died a resident of California, leaving estate herein. The family status and relationship do not appear ever to have been disavowed. We have concluded that by virtue of the provisions of section 230 of the Civil Code, upon the facts shown, petitioner is entitled to share in the estate of decedent pursuant to the statutes of descent of California.

Petitioner was born in Norway in 1883. His father (decedent) and mother are not shown to have ever married and for the purposes of this opinion we assume that the evidence establishes that they did not marry. Decedent came to Minnesota and married another. There were two children of the marriage, Lillian Blanche and Frank. In 1904 petitioner, at the request of decedent and his wife, came from Norway to Minnesota and was received into the family with the consent of the wife and publicly recognized and acknowledged by decedent as a son. In 1906 decedent moved to New Mexico; he took petitioner with him and the rest of the family soon joined them; petitioner continued to live as a member of the family and was publicly recognized and acknowledged by decedent as a son. It does not appear that this publicly established family status (whatever its legal effect) was ever broken up or disavowed prior to decedent's death. Petitioner was known by the name "Lund" in Norway. Although his mother's name was Anderson he came to this country under the name "Lund," and has continued to use it.

In 1941 Andrew Lund, the father, then a resident of California, died, leaving estate herein. It does not appear exactly when decedent became a resident of this state or, expressly, that petitioner did or did not join his father in becoming domiciled in California. Petitioner, it appears, was of adult age before the family moved to California — in fact, before they moved to New Mexico — but there is no showing that he ever married or established a separate domicile. It does appear that his half-brother and half-sister are residents of this state and he is now appearing in the courts of this state, invoking their jurisdiction.

Decedent left a will which devised all his estate to his son Frank Lund and his daughter Lillian Blanche Imel. Such will was admitted to probate. Petitioner, who was not mentioned or provided for in the will, claims that he, as pretermitted heir, is entitled to share in the distribution of the estate.

Statutes under which a child born illegitimate can, by virtue of subsequent conduct of his father (or of both parents) become capable of inheriting from the father, are usually classified as either statutes of legitimation (under which the child can, in some jurisdictions, attain the full status of legitimacy) or statutes of succession (under which the child, although remaining illegitimate in social status, can, at least to a limited extent, inherit as if he were legitimate, or, as is sometimes said, under which he is legitimated for the purpose of inheritance only). [Citations omitted.] Whether a child shall succeed to the estate of his father is determined in the case of land by the law of the situs of the land [citations omitted] and in the case of movables by the law of the domicile of the father at the time of his death unless the law of the situs of the property provides that the law of the decedent's domicile shall not govern [citations omitted]. As to what law governs (as precluding, permitting, or creating) the attainment of the full status of legitimacy, the reports of decisions and the texts of academic writers disclose a wide and heterogeneous conflict of authority and uncertainty of theory. As appears later herein it is upon the particular theory and policy adopted in California that the determination of this case depends.

At the time the family of Andrew Lund resided in Minnesota there was in that state no statute whereby petitioner could, by virtue of the father's receiving him into the family, etc., attain the status of legitimacy or otherwise become capable of inheriting from the father. And at the time the family moved to New Mexico the only statute there pertinent (N.M. Comp. Laws, 1897, §2038) declared that illegimate children shall, *when there are no legitimate children,* inherit from the father whenever they have been recognized by him as his children, provided that such recognition must have been general and notorious, or else in writing. The exception when the father left legitimate children was eliminated by amendment in 1915 (N.M. Laws, 1915, ch. 69, §1). Whether at that date Andrew Lund and his family were still residing in New Mexico or had moved to California does not appear from the record before us. In any event the New Mexico statute probably is not applicable here and is not relied upon by us because although the Supreme Court of New Mexico, so far as our research discloses, has not had occasion to decide whether the statute above referred to (later N.M. Comp. Stats. 1929, §38-114, now N.M. Comp. Stats. 1941, §31-118) is a statute of succession as opposed to a statute regulating status, it has consistently referred to the section as a statute of descent [citations omitted] and we should probably feel constrained to regard such references as at least tending to show an interpretation of the statute placed on it by the courts of the state in which it is enacted, which interpretation we should therefore respect (Osborne v. Home Life Ins. Co. (1899), 123 Cal. 610, 612 [56 P. 616]). As a statute of descent it would be immaterial to a determination of the legitimacy status of petitioner in California.

We regard the record here as disclosing no facts which would bring the petitioner within any operative statute of succession otherwise than through legitimation. It thus becomes obvious, from the principles and facts above stated, that the right, if any, of petitioner to inherit from his father depends exclusively on the law of California and that such right, if existent, derives necessarily from our statute of legitimation. In other words, the ultimate question is: Under the laws of California is petitioner legitimated in relation to his father? The reasons which impel our affirmative answer to this question appear in the discussion which follows.

As previously stated there is a wide and heterogeneous conflict in authority and theory as to what law governs the attainment of the status of legitimacy. Support may be found for at least five different theories: (1) the law of the domicile of the father at the time of the birth of the child; (2) the law of the domicile of the father at the time of his legitimating acts; (3) the law of the place where the legitimating acts occurred; (4) the law of the domicile of the child (of its mother) at birth; (5) the law of the situs of property, succession to which depends on the status of legitimacy in that jurisdiction. [Citations omitted.]

It is contended here that California has no jurisdiction over the status of the relationship of Andrew Lund and the petitioner in that, it is asserted, neither father nor child was domiciled here at the time of the child's birth or at the time the cognizable legitimating acts took place, and that such acts were not performed in California. It is also contended that the legitimation of a child must be effected during his minority or not at all. Upon the record before us we are satisfied that neither of respondent's contentions should be sustained.

The divergence in authorities pointed out above reflects not only the personal attitudes of the justices of the various courts as being conservative or liberal in their interpretation and application of the statutes of the particular states they serve but also is grounded in the respective fundamental policies of those states on the subject of bastardy. On this subject the controversy is as old and deep-rooted as is the conflict between common law and civil law.

The common law was antagonistic to both adoption and legitimation of children and its effect appears in many jurisdictions. . . . The only method of legitimation under the common law in England was by special act of Parliament. [Citation omitted.] The Roman law, however, adopted a more tolerant and liberal view. It provided various modes for legitimation of bastards: "(1) By subsequent marriage of the father and mother; (2) per oblationem curiae, whereby the parent consecrated his child to the use of the state; (3) under the Emperor Anastasius, by adoption merely. This law was, however, abolished by Justin and Justinian. (4) By the last will of the father, confirmed by the emperor. (5) By a special dispensation from the emperor, granted upon the father's petition. (6) By recognition on the part of the father." (7 C.J. §17, p. 947, note 97[c].)

In jurisdictions espousing the strict common-law philosophy it is argued that it is meet to visit the sins of the fathers upon the children and that it tends to discourage bastardy if illegitimate children are denied any right of inheritance or support or recognition from the father. Few jurisdictions adhere absolutely to this rigorous rule. . . .

Many states now have laws subjecting the father of an illegitimate child to liability for its support (see, e.g., Cal. Civ. Code, §196a; Iowa Code, 1939, §12667.01); many have provisions by which the illegitimate may upon various conditions inherit from the father (see, e.g., Cal. Prob. Code, §255; Colo. Ann. Stats., 1935, ch. 176, §8; Ind. Ann. St., 1933, §6-2309; Maine Rev. Stats., 1930, ch. 89, §3); many have enacted statutes by which the illegitimate may attain the full status of legitimacy upon varying conditions (such as subsequent marriage of the parents, in some states dependent upon accompanying express acknowledgment of paternity [see, e.g., Ala. Code, 1940, tit. 27, §10; Ind. Ann. Stats., 1933, §6-2310] and in some jurisdictions regardless of such acknowledgment [see e.g., Cal. Civ. Code, §215; Iowa Code, 1939, §10444; Mont. Rev. Code, 1921, §5852]; public acknowledgment by a father, without marriage of the mother, but accompanied by receipt of the child into his family and treatment as a legitimate child); some states by fiat decree the legitimacy of children born of a marriage void at law (see, e.g., Cal. Civ. Code, §85:

Kan. Gen. Stats., 1935, §23-124); and some states have adopted substantially universal legitimation laws.[24]

It cannot be seriously disputed that the public policy of California disavows the common-law tenets and favors legitimation. A marriage annulled is held to be void ab initio; a decree of nullity is a determination that the marriage never existed as a valid marriage. [Citations omitted.] But "A judgment of nullity of marriage does not affect the legitimacy of children conceived or born before the judgment . . ." (Civ. Code, §84) and "The issue of a marriage which is void or annulled . . . is legitimate" (Civ. Code, §85). "All children born in wedlock are presumed to be legitimate" (Civ. Code, §193); "All children of a woman who has been married, born within ten months after the dissolution of the marriage, are presumed to be legitimate children of that marriage" (Civ. Code, §194); "The father as well as the mother, of an illegitimate child must give him support and education suitable to his circumstances" (Civ. Code, §196a); "If a parent chargeable with the support of a child dies, leaving it chargeable to the county, and leaving an estate sufficient for its support, the supervisors of the county may claim provision for its support from the parent's estate by civil action" (Civ. Code, §205); "A child born before wedlock becomes legitimate by the subsequent marriage of its parents" (Civ. Code, §215); and "The father of an illegitimate child, by publicly acknowledging it as his own, receiving it as such, with the consent of his wife, if he is married, into his family, and otherwise treating it as if it were a legitimate child, thereby adopts it as such; and such child is thereupon deemed *for all purposes legitimate* from the time of its birth. The foregoing provisions of this chapter [entitled "Children by Adoption"] do not apply to such an adoption" (Civ. Code, §230). (Italics added.)

The last quoted statute is that upon which petitioner relies. It is, on its face, primarily a law governing legitimation or status but if under it

---

[24] See Ariz. Ann. Code, 1939, §27-401, which provides that "Every child is the legitimate child of its natural parents and is entitled to support and education as if born in lawful wedlock, except the right to dwelling or a residence with the family of its father, if such father be married. It shall inherit from its natural parents and from their kindred heir, lineal and collateral, in the same manner as children born in lawful wedlock. This section shall apply to cases where the natural father of any such child is married to one other than the mother of said child, as well as where he is single." Section 27-402 provides "that the mother of said child shall not be a competent witness [to establish parentage] if the alleged natural father of said child is dead at the time of the trial."

See also Ore. Stats., ch. 269, Gen. Laws of 1925, which provides that "In case a man and woman, not otherwise married heretofore, shall have cohabited in the state of Oregon as husband and wife, for over one year, and children shall be living as a result of said relation, said cohabitation, if children are living, is hereby declared to constitute a valid marriage and the children born after the beginning of said cohabitation are hereby declared to be the legitimate offspring of said marriage." . . . [This statute was repealed in 1929, Ore. Gen. Laws 1929, c. 149, and the following statute is now in force: "The legal status and legal relationships and the rights and obligations between a person and his descendants, and between a person and his parents, their descendants and kindred, are the same for all persons, whether or not the parents have been married." Ore. Rev. Stat. §109.060 (Supp. 1963)].

the petitioner has attained the status of legitimacy "for all purposes" in California then he is entitled to the benefit of the general succession statutes. In some of the cases and texts there appears considerable confusion in the differentiation and respective applications of statutes of succession and statutes of legitimacy. It seems to be the concept of some authors that a statute of succession may be given application in situations where a statute of legitimacy would be wholly inoperative. Yet in truth the statute of legitimacy is the broader law. While a statute of succession is just a law of devolution of property, and no more, a statute of legitimacy is, in effect, all of that and more. The attainment of the full and unqualified status of legitimacy carries with it as an incident thereof the right to inherit. Certainly, then, a sovereign state should be no less zealous or unfettered in the application of its legitimation statutes than of its pure descent statutes.

In respondent's argument that the rights of petitioner as to status, and consequentially his right to inherit from his father, are not to be determined by California law, stress is laid on . . . [an] assertedly general rule . . . stated in the Restatement, Conflict of Laws, page 207, section 140, as follows: "An act done after the birth of an illegitimate child will legitimize the child as to a parent from the time of the act if the law of the state of domicil of that parent at that time so provides. . . . The law must be that of the state in which the parent is domiciled at the time of the act; it is not enough that he later becomes domiciled in a state whose law provides for the legitimizing upon the doing of the act." . . .

It is obvious that the question with which we are dealing is one of comity, and is not controlled by the constitutional provision as to "full faith and credit." Thus, in Olmsted v. Olmsted (1910), 216 U.S. 386, 395, the United States Supreme Court held that (as well epitomized in the annotation at p. 942 of 73 A.L.R.) "the courts of one state are not required by the full faith and credit clause of the federal Constitution to give effect to the statute of another state legitimizing children born prior to the marriage of their parents, so as to control the devolution under a will of the title to lands in the state, particularly where to give effect to such statute would disturb interests already vested when the statute was enacted." Of course it is obvious that if a state is not bound to recognize a status of legitimacy created in another state it is not obligated to leave unchanged a status of illegitimacy existing in such other state.

We deem it uncontestable that each state may formulate its own public policy in respect to legitimation and can enact laws to carry out its policy. There is no federal constitutional proscription against a state's adopting legislation which makes legitimate within the operation of its laws children who are illegitimate in other jurisdictions nor is there any constitutional requirement that such laws be limited in their applicability to children who were born in the state or whose parents (either or both) were domiciled in the state at the time of their birth or that such laws be dependent for operation on acts occurring within the state. . . .

It will be noted that in none of the legitimation provisions of the California law hereinabove quoted is there any express or apparent requirement that the precedent marriage, void or otherwise, has been solemnized in California; or that the child of the marriage, void or otherwise, has been born in California; or that the parents, or either of them, or the child, at any time have been domiciled in California; or that the subsequent marriage of the parents of an illegitimate child be contracted in California; or that the legitimating acts specified in section 230, occur in California. . . .

It is thus apparent that the failure of the proof to expressly establish that petitioner himself became domiciled in California during his father's lifetime (assuming that because he was of adult years his domicile did not follow that established by his father) does not defeat his claim. We are also satisfied that the broad and sweeping language of section 230, considered in the light of the public policy evidenced thereby, does not contemplate that the operation of that section shall be limited by judicial construction to the legitimation of those children only whose respective fathers were domiciled in California at the time of their birth. No sound basis for any such classification among illegitimates appears and to indulge it would not only write into the statute a limitation not placed there by the Legislature but would defeat in many cases the policy which dictated the legislation.

We likewise are satisfied that it would be contrary to the purpose of the statute and the public policy of this state, and an unwarranted restriction upon the language used, to interpret it as applying only to *minor* children. Certainly an adult is as interested as is a minor in transmutation of status from illegitimacy to legitimacy and we perceive no compelling reason why the policy of the state favoring legitimation of children should be cut off upon their attaining majority. . . . We think it reasonable, therefore, and more consonant with our view of the state's policy, to construe the statute as it stands enacted, neither adding to nor subtracting from its words, and to hold that its benefits are available to all so-called illegitimate children (who in truth could be more accurately referred to as the natural children of illegitimate parents) whether they be minors or adults and whether the acts essential to effectuate their legitimation occur during their minority or later. "When a statute . . . is equally susceptible of two interpretations, one in favor of natural right, and the other against it, the former is to be adopted." (Code Civ. Proc., §1866.) . . .

We are satisfied that the public, unconditional, and long continued acknowledgment of a child by his father, with full knowledge of the facts, accompanied by reception of the child into the family and treatment as a legitimate child, constitutes a continuing representation to the whole world of a permanent de facto family status which is the very essence of the requirements of section 230 of our Civil Code; that such representation is of a fact which by its nature is inherently permanent and continuing and goes with the father wherever he goes. The factual significance of the father's acts, proclaimed to the whole world, was the same in California as in Minnesota or New Mexico. The fact that the legal effect of those acts may have been inconsequential in Minnesota and New Mexico is immaterial in California. When Andrew Lund came here and established his domicile he did so in the light of the factual significance of his previous acts. His conduct in California in remaining silent in respect to the facts surrounding the birth of petitioner is consistent with his prior acts and amounts to a continuing representation of the facts and de facto status which he had publicly proclaimed. His acts were, it is repeated, inherently of a permanent and continuing character. The biological relationship of father and son, and the de facto family relationship which the father had established, are not transient or volatile things which may exist one moment and be nonexistent the next, or which depend for their continuance upon repetitions of the original words or acts. Once proclaimed and established they exist as facts for all time and in all places. And when the living proclaimer of those facts comes to California and establishes his domicile herein and leaves estate to be distributed according to our laws of succession, the courts of California need not ignore those facts and are not powerless to apply them. Their legal effect within this state will be admeasured by the laws of this state.

For the reasons hereinabove stated the order appealed from is reversed and the cause is remanded to the trial (probate) court with directions to enter its decree establishing the right of petitioner to share in the estate of his father as a legitimate son.

EDMONDS, J. I cannot concur in the conclusions upon which this case is decided and am of the opinion that the judgment of the probate court should be affirmed. . . .

Section 230 of the Civil Code provides that a child is legitimated for all purposes when the father publicly acknowledges his parentage, receives the child into his family with the consent of his wife, if married, and otherwise treats the child as if it were legitimate. This section, Mr. Justice Schauer states in effect, should be construed as providing that, for the purpose of status in California, any child born out of wedlock may be legitimated by the declaration of the father without regard to the domicile of the parent at the time he acknowledges the relationship. Yet the statute includes no language which, by the broadest construction allowable under fundamental legal principles, properly may be held to give it unlimited extraterritorial effect in contravention of the established rules concerning conflict of laws.

Certainly, the enactment expresses no intention that its operation shall violate the doctrine by which, in general, status is determinable according to domiciliary law (Beale, Conflict of Laws (1935), vol. 1, §1.8, p. 7; §9.3, p. 91; Goodrich, Conflict of Laws (2d ed. 1938), pp. 25, 26; Stumberg, Conflict of Laws (1937), p. 254). . . .

To supply the obvious deficiency of legal authority to support his conclusions, Mr. Justice Schauer relies upon theories having no support in law. For example, as a final ground of decision, he attempts to ignore the fact that the father of Lund made no legitimating declaration while domiciled in this state by holding that the acts done in Minnesota and New Mexico, as a matter of law, were repeated wherever the father went and must be presumed to have continued at all times unless expressly revoked. The authorities clearly refute any such artificial and unwarranted presumption; they squarely hold that it is not sufficient that the father later acquires a domicile in a state recognizing the acts as conferring legitimacy.

As justifying the departure from established legal principles, Mr. Justice Schauer also mentions the present day change of attitude toward those born outside of the marriage relation, and concludes that any divergence of opinion, as evidenced by the present controversy, reflects "the personal attitudes of the justices of the various courts as being conservative or liberal in the interpretation and application" of legitimation statutes. But neither sentiment nor the desire to reach a particular result is a sound basis for evading or overturning long accepted rules of decision and only by judicial legislation may it be said that the law of California affords any relief upon the facts shown by the record in the present case. . . .

For these reasons, in my opinion, the judgment should be affirmed.

SHENK, J., and TRAYNOR, J., concurred [in the views of Edmonds, J.].

NOTE

1. Goodrich, Conflict of Laws 436 n.8 (3d ed. 1949), found this case "difficult to explain," but a more recent edition of the same treatise indicated that "[m]any other courts have been moved to analogous results." Goodrich, Conflict of Laws 284 (4th ed. Scoles 1964). Under the court's view, when, precisely, did the legitimation occur? Suppose the decedent had returned to and re-established his domicile in New Mexico or Minnesota shortly before his death. The statutes pertaining to inheritance by illegitimate children in those states, like that of California, require a recognition in writing. Minn. Stat. Ann. §525.172 (1947); N.M. Stat. Ann. §29-1-18 (1954). Do you think those states would have allowed the petitioner to share in his father's estate?

2. Although Mr. Justice Schauer purports to distinguish between legitimation and succession statutes, and although he asserts that the statute here involved is of the former type, does his decision really hold anything more than that for purposes of the devolution of this California property, Bert Lund is entitled to share along with the decedent's two other children? Suppose that after this decision Bert Lund had claimed a share of some of his father's property located in New Mexico or Minnesota. Must those states recognize Mr. Lund's claim? If not, on what theory can they fail to give full faith and credit to the California decree of legitimation? And if the California decision has no extraterritorial effect, what is the difference between a legitimation and a succession determination by the California court?

3. In order to understand properly the setting in which the Lund case arose, the full complex of the relevant California statutes must be considered. The legitimation statute on which the case was based is California Civil Code §230, quoted at page 27 supra. The pretermission statute, which was also involved in the case, reads:

When a testator omits to provide in his will for any of his children . . . whether born before or after the making of the will . . . and such child or issue are unprovided for by any settlement, and have not had an equal proportion of the testator's property bestowed on them by way of advancement, unless it appears from the will that such omission was intentional, such child or such issue succeeds to the same share in the estate of the testator as if he had died intestate.[25]

Finally there is the succession statute which at that time read:

Every illegitimate child is an heir of his mother, and also of the person who, in writing . . . , acknowledges himself to be the father, and inherits his or her estate . . . in the same manner as if he had been born in lawful wedlock; but he does not represent his father by inheriting any part of the estate of the father's kindred, either lineal or collateral, unless, before his death, his parents shall have intermarried, and his father, after such marriage, acknowledges him as his child, or adopts him into his family; in which case such child is deemed legitimate for all purposes of succession. . . .[26]

The interrelationship of these three provisions raises some interesting problems of statutory construction. Since the decedent in the Lund case left a will which did not provide for the petitioner, this initially brought the pretermission statute into play. Did the court have to go any further than this statute? In a previous case, Estate of Wardwell, 57 Cal. 484 (1881), an illegitimate child, who had never been legitimated, claimed a share of her mother's estate as a pretermitted heir. The court held that the petitioner was entitled to a distributive share of the estate. In effect it construed the word "children" in the pretermission statute to include illegitimate as well as legitimate children. Could the court in the Lund case more easily have reached the same result merely by following Wardwell?

Apparently the court assumed that the pretermission statute could be applied only in conjunction with either the succession or the legitimation statute. And since there was no writing by the father acknowledging the petitioner as his son, the succession statute could not be applied. The court seemed to regard the succession statute and the legitimation statute as independent, so that the result which could not be reached by the former could be reached by the latter. Was this sound as a matter of statutory construction? Why should the statute regulating inheritance by an illegitimate child be wholly unrelated to, and provide different requirements from, the general statute on legitimation of such children?

The court faced a more difficult problem of reconciling these two statutes four years later in a case where the petitioner was also an illegitimate child who had been legitimated by his father under §230. His mother and his father had not married, however. Petitioner sought recovery of his share as heir in the distribution of the estate of his father's sister.

25 Cal. Prob. Code §90.
26 Id. §255.

What result? See Estate of Garcia, 34 Cal. 2d 419, 210 P.2d 841 (1949).

4. As indicated in Justice Schauer's opinion, we have come a long way since the ancient days of filius nullius. There are now two major ways in which an illegitimate child may be legitimated (quite apart from special provisions such as Cal. Prob. Code §255, which remove particular common law disabilities such as the inability to inherit). Perhaps the most common method of legitimation is through intermarriage of the parents.[27] See Cal. Civ. Code §215 and other statutory provisions cited in the opinion; see also N.Y. Dom. Rel. Law §24 and §1 of the English Legitimacy Act, 1959, 7 & 8 Eliz. 2, c. 73, applying this doctrine even to a child born of an adulterous relationship. The other type of legitimation statute is the kind involved in the Lund case, requiring some form of recognition or acknowledgment by the putative father. The statutes vary widely, some requiring a writing, others, like the California statute, requiring some more or less informal conduct (such as a "public acknowledgment" or a "receiving of the child into one's home") designed to show the recognition of the child as one's own. Several statutes (including that of California) use the confusing word "adopts" or "adoption" to refer to this type of legitimation. See generally Annot., 33 A.L.R.2d 705 (1954). See also Note, The Status of Illegitimates in New England, 38 B.U.L. Rev. 299 (1958); Lasok, Legitimation, Recognition and Affiliation Proceedings, 10 Int. & Comp. L.Q. 123 (1961); Ester, Illegitimate Children and Conflict of Laws, 36 Ind. L.J. 163 (1961); Annot., 87 A.L.R.2d 1274 (1963).

So far our emphasis has been on children born out of wedlock. Brief reference should be made, however, to two situations involving children born in wedlock which raise conceptually related problems. The first relates to children born during a marriage which is subsequently annulled. Under generally prevailing doctrine, most such annulments render the marriage void ab initio, and hence would illegitimize any children born during the marriage. See pages 172-177 infra. However, here again modern statutes tend to protect the status of the children in varying degrees, depending upon such factors as the ground of the annulment and the good faith of the parties. See, e.g., N.Y. Dom. Rel. Law §145. Compare §2 of the English Legitimacy Act, 1959, 7 & 8 Eliz. 2, c. 73, legitimating any child of a void marriage if at the time of the intercourse resulting in the birth "both or either of the parties reasonably believed that the marriage was valid." This latter provision is discussed in 9 Int. & Comp. L.Q. 319 (1960).

The second situation relates to a child born during the marriage but where there is some question whether the husband or another is the father. The Royal Commission on Marriage and Divorce disapproved a suggestion that an illegitimate child of a married woman be considered

[27] Apparently it is not only the courts which are occasionally willing to go to considerable lengths to spare children the disabilities of illegitimacy. According to a dispatch in The New York Times, Aug. 28, 1960, p. 42, col. 4, the French National Assembly, with the approval of President de Gaulle, passed a special law permitting the unwed mother of a one-month-old child to marry (apparently with retroactive effect) a man who had died eight months previously in a catastrophic flood.

the child of her marriage to her husband if the child is accepted as one of the family by her husband. The Commission majority argued:

> Legitimacy is the status held by a lawful child of the marriage. Any departure from that conception can only be made by ignoring the essential moral principle that a man cannot, during the subsistence of his marriage, beget lawful children by another woman. It is unthinkable that the State should lend its sanction to such a step, for it could not fail to result in a blurring of moral values in the public mind. . . .
>
> The fact that an illegitimate child may be adopted and can thus acquire property rights shows that such a child need not at present be at any serious material disadvantage. It is right that it should be possible to mitigate the material consequences for the child. It is quite another thing to suggest that no distinction should be made between the lawful children of the marriage and children who were born of an adulterous union.[28]

This problem also brings into play the so-called presumption of legitimacy, which is explored in the case that follows.

KUSIOR v. SILVER
54 Cal. 2d 603, 354 P.2d 657 (1960)

Dooling, J. Plaintiff appeals from a judgment for defendant [Dr. Silver] in an action to establish the paternity and to provide for the support of her child. Plaintiff's child was born July 29, 1954, nine days after the entry of a final decree of divorce dissolving her marriage to Thaddeus Kusior.

It appears from the settled statement that plaintiff and her husband separated in February, 1953, and that an interlocutory decree of divorce was secured in July, 1953. The child was probably conceived in October or November, 1953.

Both plaintiff and her husband testified that sexual relations between them ceased at the time of separation. However, Mr. Kusior exercised his right to visit their 8-year-old daughter at regular intervals. On these occasions, he would perform maintenance work on the property, and he took plaintiff and their daughter out to dinner on at least one occasion. Several times he remained in plaintiff's home until the early hours of the morning. Plaintiff testified: "I had to have someone to talk to. Yes, we sat and talked until 3 or 4 in the morning." Mr. Kusior continued these visits even after their daughter was sent east on a visit in May, 1954, but plaintiff had long since been pregnant at that time.

Two neighbors testified that Mr. Kusior was seen by them, sometimes in the evenings, during the period of possible conception. They were unable to say whether he stayed all night but did state that plaintiff and her husband did "not live together" after the separation.

[28] Report 1951-1955, Cmd. No. 9678, pars. 1180-1181 (1956).

Mrs. Nelson lived in the house as a roomer until some time in October. She testified that plaintiff did not live together with any man during that period, although she did see one man, not Mr. Kusior, both in the evening and the following morning. There were, however, as many as 10 men who visited plaintiff; they would sit with her in the den and sometimes bring groceries. Mrs. Nelson also saw one man leave amidst a commotion at 4 o'clock one morning.

Plaintiff testified that she first had intercourse with defendant early in June, 1953, and subsequently about four more times until she underwent an operation in September of that year. She testified that she had intercourse with defendant several times thereafter. He slept in the den the first time he came to her house, about the middle of October, 1953, shortly after Mrs. Nelson moved out of the house. Mrs. Nelson testified that she never saw defendant until her appearance in court.

Plaintiff also testified that she went out with other men during the period of possible conception, and also frequented a certain cocktail bar. She stated, however, that defendant was the only man with whom she had intercourse.

Blood tests were taken of the parties pursuant to section 1980.3 of the Code of Civil Procedure. These tests established that plaintiff's husband could not have been the father of the child but that defendant was within the class of persons who could have been.

The sufficiency of the evidence to support a judgment for defendant is not disputed, but plaintiff contends that certain instructions involving the effect of the blood tests and the presumptions of legitimacy were in error, and could have caused the jury to dispose of the proceedings by improperly determining that Mr. Kusior must be considered to be the child's father.

The trial court gave instructions based on the following sections of our code, which set forth conclusive and rebuttable presumptions of legitimacy. Code of Civil Procedure, section 1962, subdivision 5, provides: "Notwithstanding any other provision of law, the issue of a wife cohabiting with her husband, who is not impotent, is indisputably presumed to be legitimate." Section 1963, subdivision 31, sets forth as a disputable presumption: "That a child born in lawful wedlock, there being no divorce from bed and board, is legitimate." Civil Code, section 193, provides: "All children born in wedlock are presumed to be legitimate." Section 194 makes that presumption applicable to all children born within 10 months of the "dissolution of the marriage." Section 195 provides that the only persons who can dispute that presumption are the state in an action for support under section 270 of the Penal Code, or the "husband or wife, or the descendant of one or both of them."

The instructions given to the jury based on these sections were to the effect that a conclusive presumption, which none of the other evidence in the case can contradict, would apply if there was a failure to show that there was not "a reasonable possibility of access." The jury was also instructed that if they found that the conclusive presumption did not apply, then only the rebuttable presumption applies, and any evidence, including the blood tests, might be considered to rebut it. . . .

Appellant contends that the instructions defining the scope of the conclusive presumption were too broad in that "cohabiting," as used in subdivision 5 of section 1962 of the Code of Civil Procedure, should properly be construed as "the living together of a man and woman ostensibly as husband and wife" (Estate of Mills, 137 Cal. 298, 301 [70 P. 91]) and that certain comparatively recent cases in the District Courts of Appeal which have, or appear to have, broadened the definition of "cohabiting," as used in this section, to include "a reasonable possibility of access" constitute an unwarranted extension of the meaning of that section. We have concluded from an examination of the decisions of this court dealing with the proper construction of section 1962, subdivision 5, that the definition contended for by appellant is clearly the one originally adopted by this court, and that the cases in the District Courts of Appeal which have, or appear to have, broadened this definition find no support in any decision of our court. . . .

. . . [A]ll doubt on this score was resolved by this court in its consideration of Estate of Walker on two successive appeals, 176 Cal. 402 [168 P. 689] and 180 Cal. 478 [181 P. 792]. In Walker the spouses were not living together but the opportunity for intercourse existed. The court did not consider section 1962, subdivision 5, applicable but held on both appeals that the case was governed by the disputable presumption of section 194 of the Civil Code. That this was no mere oversight is apparent from the following quotation from the second Walker opinion: "The English rule would seem to go so far as to permit evidence of nonintercourse even where the parties are cohabiting, i.e., *living together in the same house or apartments.* Such is not the rule in this state. (Code Civ. Proc., §1962, subd. 5; Estate of Mills, 137 Cal. 298 [70 P. 91.]) But with this statutory exception the true rule in America, as well as England, is, we believe, that if it is possible by the laws of nature for the husband to be the father (that is, if there was coition and no impotency), no inquiry will be permitted into the probabilities of the case one way or the other, but the presumption of legitimacy is conclusive; and, on the other hand, it is always permitted to show that it was not possible by the laws of nature for the husband to be the father, as by showing impotency on his part, *want of intercourse during the possible period of conception,* or that the child is of a race or color such that it could not have been conceived by the husband." (Emphasis added; 180 Cal. 491.)

Taken together, the Mills and Walker cases clearly limited the application of the conclusive presumption of section 1962, subdivision 5, to cases where the parties were "living together . . . ostensibly as husband and wife" (Mills) or "living together in the same house or apartments" (Walker) and in all other cases applied only the rebuttable presumptions. . . .

Although a variety of meanings have been ascribed by various courts to the words "cohabit" and "cohabitation" (see e.g., 14 C.J.S. 1311-1312), their primary etymological meaning is living *with* or *together,* from the

Latin "co-" ("co- signifies in general *with, together, in conjunction, jointly. . . ."* Webster's New International Dictionary, 2d ed., unabr., p. 510) . . . .

Our courts so defined the words in determining the statutory requirement of a "common-law (i.e., nonceremonial) marriage" under the former section 55 of the Civil Code, which required "a mutual assumption of marital rights, duties, or obligations." In Kilburn v. Kilburn, 89 Cal. 46, 50 [26 P. 636], this court said: ". . . there is no assumption of marital rights, duties, or obligations, within the meaning of section 55 of the Civil Code, until the commencement of cohabitation by the parties to the agreement. And by cohabitation is not meant simply the gratification of the sexual passion, but 'to live or dwell together, to have the same habitation, so that where one lives and dwells there does the other live and dwell also.'" . . . [T]his court in Estate of Mills, supra, 137 Cal. at page 301, . . . gave to the word "cohabiting" in section 1962, subdivision 5, the same peculiar and appropriate meaning. . . .

. . . We conclude that "cohabiting" in section 1962, subdivision 5, should be construed to mean "living together as husband and wife," and any language giving or suggesting a broader meaning in any of the cases in the District Courts of Appeal [citations omitted] is to that extent disapproved.

We conclude that the trial court committed error in instructing that the conclusive presumption applies if the husband had "access" or "reasonable possibility of access" to his wife during the period of conception.

Appellant also contends that the instructions with regard to the conclusive presumption should not have been given at all in view of the fact that the blood tests showed that her husband could not have been the father. She argues that the conclusive presumption is subject to well-recognized exceptions, and that blood tests should be added to the exceptions. She relies principally on the explanation for the exceptions set forth in Estate of McNamara . . . , 181 Cal. 82, 96: "The reason why the conclusive presumption is not applied in such instances is that the element of indeterminability which is the reason for the presumption in the ordinary case is absent. . . . The actual fact, in other words, is capable of definite determination, and for this reason the conclusive presumption which is a substitute for such determination is not properly applicable."

Appellant cites the scientific reliability of blood-grouping tests (see concurring opinion of McComb, J., in Berry v. Chaplin, 74 Cal. App. 2d 652, 667-668 [169 P.2d 442]), which was accorded recognition by the adoption of the Uniform Act on Blood Tests to Determine Paternity (Code Civ. Proc., §§1980.1-1980.7), and argues that the "actual fact" is here capable of definite determination, and thus under the reasoning in Estate of McNamara, supra, "the conclusive presumption is not applicable." However, the actions of the Legislature have clearly established the effect of the blood-grouping tests in relation to the application of the conclusive presumption to be otherwise.

. . . [T]he Legislature in 1953 enacted our version of the Uniform Act on Blood Tests to Determine Paternity, providing: "In a civil action, in which paternity is a relevant fact, the court . . . may . . . order the mother, child and alleged father to submit to blood tests." (Code Civ. Proc., §1980.3.) "If the court finds that the conclusions of all the experts . . . are that the alleged father is not the father of the child, the question of paternity shall be resolved accordingly." (Code Civ. Proc., §1980.6.) However, the Legislature significantly refrained from adopting section 5 of the Uniform Act, which provides: "The presumption of legitimacy of a child born during wedlock is overcome if the court finds that the conclusions of all the experts, as disclosed by the evidence based upon the tests, show that the husband is not the father of the child." Our law emerged without this section or any reference to the subject matter contained therein.

Statutes are to be interpreted by assuming that the Legislature was aware of the existing judicial decisions [which in this instance had excluded blood test evidence to dispute the conclusive presumption of legitimacy]. [Citation omitted.] Moreover, failure to make changes in a given statute in a particular respect when the subject is before the Legislature, and changes are made in other respects, is indicative of an intention to leave the law unchanged in that respect. . . . [T]he failure of the Legislature to enact that part of the act which would specifically have enabled the result of a blood test to overcome the conclusive presumption declared in section 1962, subdivision 5, must be deemed an intention not to change the [pre-existing rule]. . . .

Appellant contends that such a construction is not consistent with constitutional principles in that there is no reasonable relationship between the presumption and the fact sought to be presumed in a case in which there is scientific evidence to the contrary. [Citation omitted.] However, appellant does not suggest that the Legislature has no interest in or power to determine, as a matter of overriding social policy, that given a certain relationship between the husband and wife, the husband is to be held responsible for the child. There are significant reasons why the integrity of the family when husband and wife are living together as such should not be impugned. A conclusive presumption is in actuality a substantive rule of law and cannot be said to be unconstitutional unless it transcends such a power of the Legislature. (Morgan, Federal Constitutional Limitations Upon Presumptions Created by State Legislation, Harvard Legal Essays (1934) 323, 328.)

Appellant's final contention is that the trial court was in error in instructing the jury that the blood tests were not conclusive as against the rebuttable presumption but were only evidence to be weighed with all the other evidence. A similar argument was rejected in McKee v. McKee, 156 Cal. App. 2d 764 [320 P.2d 510], a case in which the conclusive presumption was inapplicable, but the judgment was affirmed on the basis of the rebuttable presumption despite a blood test which negatived paternity. . . . Although a rebuttable presumption is treated by our court as evidence which may outweigh positive evidence against it, there has been a legislative determination here that blood test evidence is conclusive. (Code Civ. Proc., §1980.6.) Unless there can be found a manifested intent that this section specifically dealing with the effect of blood tests does not define the effect of such blood tests in every case in which they are admissible into evidence, then it seems clear that since they have always been admissible for whatever their worth as evidence capable of overcoming a rebuttable presumption (McKee v. McKee, supra, even assumes that they are), they ought, in view of the overall recognition by the statute of their accuracy, to be conclusive against a merely rebuttable presumption. . . . The fact that section 5 of the Uniform Act was omitted can be explained by assuming that the Legislature did not intend to affect the conclusive presumption, but that the statute as enacted was to have whatever effect on the rebuttable presumption a reasonable interpretation thereof would give it. If we did not have the dual system of presumptions, then we might be forced to give a greater weight to the omission, but in the face of the dual system, we need not do so.

We conclude that the result of blood tests taken under the Uniform Act [citation omitted] may not be used to controvert the conclusive presumption . . . but that . . . where the tests so taken establish that the mother's husband could not be the father of the child the rebuttable presumptions of paternity are conclusively rebutted. The dictum in McKee v. McKee, supra, 156 Cal. App. 2d 764, inconsistent with this conclusion, is disapproved. . . .

The judgment is reversed.

NOTE

1. If you were the trial judge to whom this case was remanded, would you enter judgment for plaintiff or order a new trial? If the latter, what instructions would you give to the jury?

2. This case illustrates the strong force of the presumption of legitimacy, which is applicable throughout the United States. See 9 Wigmore, Evidence §2527 (3d ed. 1940), and Comment, 23 So. Cal. L. Rev. 538 (1950). What is the purpose of the presumption? Does it have any place in a situation such as Kusior, where a child was born after the final divorce of its mother?

Also relevant in this connection is Lord Mansfield's rule, which bars a husband or wife from testifying as to the other spouse's nonaccess if the effect thereof would be to illegitimize the child. The rule has been generally accepted in this country. See 7 Wigmore, Evidence §2063 n.13 (3d ed. 1940). However, it has been modified in some states, see, e.g., N.Y. Family Ct. Act §531 (testimony permitted only in paternity proceedings), and was abolished altogether in England in 1949. Law Reform (Miscellaneous Provisions) Act, 12, 13 & 14 Geo. 6, c. 100, §7. Although California is one of the handful of states that has rejected the Mansfield rule and hence allows a spouse's testimony as to nonaccess, Cal. Civ. Code §195, it does not permit evidence as to nonintercourse while the spouses are cohabiting, on the ground that the conclusive presumption renders such evidence immaterial, Estate of Mills, 137 Cal. 298, 70 Pac. 91 (1902).

Lord Mansfield's rule may be seen as an evidentiary ally of the presumption of legitimacy. But, as one recent commentator has noted, the perfection of blood testing has made it possible to rebut the presumption without proof of nonaccess, and thus has underscored the desirability of abolishing the evidentiary rule as part of a general re-examination of the presumption itself. According to this writer, the issue posed by the presumption is essentially one of standing. The child (or the mother on its behalf) should be permitted to waive the benefit conferred by the presumption if support is viewed as more significant than status. The putative father, although having an interest adverse to that of the child, has a legitimate stake in avoiding responsibility for the support of a child which he can show to be not his own. Accordingly, he, too, should be permitted to rebut the presumption by any probative evidence, provided that he acts reasonably promptly after the child's birth. Subject to these (and one or two other minor) exceptions, the presumption should be regarded as conclusive. See Note, 112 U. Pa. L. Rev. 613 (1964).

3. The study of the Kinsey Institute suggests that the incidence of the problem raised by Kusior v. Silver is probably not very significant. See Gebhard, Pomeroy, Martin & Christenson, Pregnancy, Birth and Abortion 83-84, 92, 99 (1958):

> Of our 2221 ever-married women, 26 reported a total of 32 pregnancies known or believed to have been the result of extra-marital coitus. Of course there must be an additional number of extra-marital conceptions not recognized as such even by the women involved; these conceptions make a study of the frequency of extra-marital conception correspondingly unreliable. . . .
>
> . . . The 26 women of our sample who reported that they conceived, while married, by males other than their husbands are unlike our total sample of married women in one other respect: they are, as a group, irreligious. Twenty of them reported that they never attended church or synagogue, five did so very rarely, and only one attended regularly. By our definition, therefore, 25 of the 26 fall in the category of religiously inactive, and one in the devout category. . . .
>
> . . . All the 32 conceptions resulting from extra-marital coitus ended within the marriage during which they occurred. How they ended is rather interesting: 22 in induced abortions (one being therapeutic), 5 in spontaneous abortions, and 5 in the birth of children who were reared in the home. . . . In 2 of the 5 cases the husband was aware that he had not fathered the child.

C. SUPPORT FOR ILLEGITIMATE CHILDREN

1. *Private Paternity Actions*

COMMONWEALTH v. WATTS
179 Pa. Super. 398, 116 A.2d 844 (1955)

GUNTHER, J. The defendant was tried on an indictment charging fornication and bastardy. The prosecutrix testified that she had intercourse with defendant three times, the last time being sometime in September, 1953. The child was born August 6, 1954. Defendant was found guilty, an order of support was entered, and defendant has appealed.

Appellant's primary contention is that the medical testimony was insufficient to sustain the conviction. The medical testimony was given by the doctor who delivered the child. She testified that the normal gestation period is nine months or 282 days, give or take two weeks either way. The defendant admitted having intercourse and asserted that the last time occurred on September 21, 1953. If the latter date is correct, the gestation period would have been almost 320 days. The prosecutrix testified that she did not have intercourse with any other man during the possible gestation period. Defendant now complains that even assuming conception on the last day of September, as from the testimony of the prosecutrix, the gestation period would be 310 days, which is longer than any outside limit given by the medical witness.

The court charged the jury that the field of medicine has found that gestation can vary from 220 to 330 days, the average being 270 days. This charge is alleged to be error and defendant cites several cases to sustain his contention that the possible gestation period must be related to the testimony given. In Com. v. Jodlowsky, 163 Pa. Superior Ct. 284, 60 A.2d 836, a conviction of bastardy was reversed where the gestation period was allegedly 252 days and the only medical testimony gave a leeway of from 260 to 340 days. . . . [T]he medical witness in this case was never specifically asked for the medically accepted time span for the duration of pregnancies. Her remark that there could be a two weeks leeway in either direction was obviously a quick generalization. The pregnancy here occurred within the medically accepted time possibilities and the jury was properly charged. . . .

Judgment of sentence and order of support affirmed.

WOODSIDE, J. [dissenting]. I do not agree with the majority in this case.

The defendant was charged with bastardy. He should not have been convicted unless the evidence established his guilt beyond a reasonable doubt. It is my opinion that incontrovertible facts raise a reasonable doubt as to his guilt, — and that the true significance of these facts was not only withheld from the jury, but so presented as to mislead it.

The prosecutrix testified that she had sexual intercourse with the defendant three times during the month of September 1953, and not there-after. A letter introduced by the Commonwealth indicates the defendant was in North Carolina and the prosecutrix in Pennsylvania during the last two days of September. The child was born August 6, 1954. That was 312 days after the 28th of the previous September. At the hospital she gave her last menstrual period as October 27, 1953. That was 283 days before the birth. She testified that she had sexual relations with no other men during September, October and November of 1953. She was not asked about December, the first day of which was 248 days before the birth.

There was no evidence concerning the length, weight or condition of the child at birth, and no evidence concerning the prosecutrix's preg-nancy except that relating to her last menstrual period.

I should like to make it clear at the outset that *I do not* think it is *impossible* for this child to be the child of the defendant. I do think that the probability of its being his is so extremely *remote* that it raises a doubt which should permit a conviction only after the jury is fully ad-vised of the improbability of such a protracted period of gestation.

The purpose of the trial in this case was to determine whether the de-fendant *was* the father of the child born to the prosecutrix, not whether he *could have been*. We are thus dealing with probabilities and not possibilities. . . .

Although admittedly it cannot be known with mathematical certainty, an examination of the authorities and an analysis of the recorded cases of prolonged pregnancies indicate that a pregnancy of the length here sup-posed is not likely to happen one time in some millions of births.

Before considering any of the authorities on the duration of pregnancy we should note that time is computed from the date of three different occurrences in the life of the mother; one is the first day of the last men-strual period, one is the time of intercourse, and one is the time of fertili-zation of the ovum. As the three occurrences usually take place on differ-ent dates, care should be taken not to confuse the number of days figured from the different occurrences. Both medical authorities and courts have been careless in their comparisons.

Computing from the last menstrual period is an inaccurate test of the actual time of conception, but it is the most practical way to predict the date of birth in most cases, and is the time recorded in most records and studies of the duration of pregnancies. . . .

What we are concerned with here is the time between intercourse and birth.

H. L. Stewart, M.D., of Detroit recently made a study of the duration of pregnancy . . . [in which] he concluded . . . that "Decisions establish-ing paternity within a period of 300 days from the last coitus are reason-able, but longer periods seem most questionable, and are conspicuous by the complete absence of any supporting data from this study." Journal of American Medical Association (March 29, 1952). . . .

Nicholson J. Eastman, M.D., a professor of Johns Hopkins University, [refers] in the 10th edition of Williams Obstetrics (1950) . . . to a record of 144,079 cases in which only 42 had pregnancy extending more than 31 days after the expected date. This would mean that only 3 cases out of a thousand had pregnancies extending more than 298 days computed from conception to birth. . . .

. . . Wharton & Stille's, Medical Jurisprudence Vol. III (1905) also collected and reviewed cases of prolonged pregnancy known to medical literature. Among these cases can be found some, considered authentic by medical authorities, in which birth was more than 312 days after intercourse. The number of such cases, however, in all of modern medical history has not exceeded approximately a dozen. The cases collected by these authorities are from prior to 1867 to the present time and from all over the western world. During that time there were hundreds of millions of births attended by physicians who in most cases would have been quick to report such an unusual medical phenomenon. . . .[29]

A study of these and other authorities substantiates the conclusion that the chance of a birth being caused by intercourse 312 days earlier is less than one in a million.

There is a *possibility* that the mother is telling the truth when she says the child was conceived in September, but with the improbabilities of such a protracted pregnancy, is not there a *reasonable doubt of the defendant's guilt?* Is not the probability of the mother withholding information concerning a subsequent intercourse with another man so much greater than the probability of her pregnancy lasting 312 days that by the mere comparison of probabilities, a reasonable doubt of the defendant's guilt is created?

There is, of course, a presumption that the witness is telling the truth, particularly in light of the jury's findings. Nevertheless, it must be remembered that the outcome is extremely important to her. Assuming the order continues at its present rate until the child is 18, it will involve over $7500. Furthermore, whether she ever had intercourse with another man about the time of conception is a fact which she could hide from the court and the defendant with ease, and with little fear of ever being caught. . . .

RHODES, P.J. [concurring]. The majority opinion properly sustains the conviction of the defendant.

The dissenting opinion ignores the fact that the guilt or innocence of

---

[29] It is interesting, if not relevant, to find the statement that Scotland, France and Italy define 300 days as the maximum time for legitimacy in contested paternity cases and that in Austria the law recognizes the legitimacy of a child born 307 days, in Germany 302 days, and in Switzerland 300 days after the death of the husband. England has no such limits. Its law, unchained to science or reality, was let free to hold during the time of Edward II that the child of the Countess of Gloucester born *one year and seven months* after the death of the Duke was legitimate. That the absurdities knew no bounds in the land and age of chivalry is shown by the opinion of Baron Rolfe expressed, it is said, with apparent gravity during the reign of Henry VI that a widow might give birth to a child *seven years* after her husband's death without injury to her reputation. 7 A.L.R. 330. [The preceding paragraph is taken from another part of Judge Woodside's opinion, 179 Pa. Super. at 407-408, 116 A.2d at 849.]

the defendant in this case turned on the credibility of the prosecutrix which was solely a matter for the jury. . . .

BERRY v. CHAPLIN
74 Cal. App. 2d 652, 169 P.2d 442 (1946)

WILSON, J. This is a filiation proceeding commenced under sections 196a and 231 of the Civil Code by the grandmother of plaintiff as guardian ad litem prior to plaintiff's birth in which a judgment was prayed that defendant be declared to be the father of plaintiff, and that he be required to pay for medical care during pregnancy and birth for the mother of plaintiff, and for the support of plaintiff after birth, together with attorneys' fees and costs.

Following the commencement of the action a stipulation was signed by the guardian ad litem and the attorneys then representing her and plaintiff, and by defendant and his attorneys, which recites the claim of Joan Berry, the mother of the prospective child, that she was then with child begotten by defendant on or about December 20, 1942, and the denial of defendant that he was the father of said child. The stipulation, the details of which will be stated hereinafter, provides for the making of tests of the blood of the child, of Joan Berry, and of defendant. Said stipulation was approved by the Honorable William S. Baird, a judge of the superior court. After the birth of the child blood tests were made by physicians, chosen as provided in the stipulation. They unanimously reported their conclusion from the tests that defendant was not the father of the child. Counsel who at that time represented plaintiff did not, as provided in the stipulation, file a dismissal of the action upon the receipt of said report. Thereupon defendant made a motion for dismissal based upon the terms of the stipulation and the physicians' report. Counsel who now represent plaintiff were substituted for the attorneys who commenced the action and who entered into said stipulation, and the present guardian ad litem was substituted for the grandmother. . . .

. . . The stipulation to which reference has been made contains the following, among other provisions: That subsequent to the making of said claim by Joan Berry defendant voluntarily agreed to pay to her the sums of money set forth in the stipulation for medical care and for her support and for all hospital and medical expenses necessary for her proper care during the period of her pregnancy and confinement and attendant upon the birth of the child, upon condition that she would voluntarily submit said child after its birth to medical tests for the purpose of determining its paternity and that she would make herself and said child available at all times so that said tests could be made by competent medical experts; that an order be made by the superior court whereby defendant shall be required to pay to the guardian ad litem the amounts set forth in the stipulation for said purposes, and that attorneys' fees in the sum of $5000 shall be paid directly to the attorneys for plaintiff; that if the action shall be tried defendant shall pay an additional sum of $5000 as attorneys' fees; that the action shall not be brought to trial until at least four months after the birth of the child and not until appropriate tests shall have been conducted as provided in the stipulation; that after said child shall have lived for a period of not less than four months it shall be made available for the purpose of having such tests made; that one physician shall be named by defendant, one by the guardian ad litem, and the two physicians so chosen shall select a third "who shall be especially skilled in such matters, who shall make a blood test or other tests accepted by medical science for the purpose of proving and establishing paternity, and who shall report their findings and conclusions with respect to the paternity of said child to the said guardian ad litem and to the defendant"; that said Joan Berry shall be bound by said stipulation as if she were the plaintiff and real party in interest; that defendant, by entering into the stipulation, shall in no way be deemed or construed as thereby admitting any allegation in the complaint, but on the contrary denies that he is or could be the father of the child. . . .

The guardian ad litem and her attorneys were without power to enter into and the court was without power to approve the stipulation. . . .

Neither the guardian ad litem nor the attorneys for the minor, nor both, had power to consent to a judgment depriving the minor of its right to claim support from defendant without the opportunity of a trial at which all available evidence could be introduced for consideration by the jury, not merely such evidence as the parties considered proper for the determination of the issue involved. . . .

. . . *Did plaintiff make out a prima facie case against defendant?* "Prima facie evidence is that which suffices for the proof of a particular fact, until contradicted and overcome by other evidence." . . . She testified that she and defendant had four acts of sexual intercourse at or about the date when, in the ordinary course of nature, the child must have been begotten. These acts occurred on the 10th, 23d, 24th and 30th days of December, 1942. This evidence alone was sufficient not only to constitute a prima facie case but to sustain the verdict although denied by defendant. [Citation omitted.] Her testimony was corroborated by defendant's butler as to the fact that she arrived at defendant's home on the evening of December 23d and remained there until some time in the afternoon of December 24th, occupying either defendant's room or a room connected therewith by a bathroom, and that defendant was present in the room during at least a portion of the night of the 23d and in the morning of the 24th. . . .

The burden of proof did not rest on defendant to prove that he was not the father of the child. Nevertheless, in his attempt to show that Miss Berry had had illicit relations with other men it was incumbent upon him to show that such relations were had at or about the time when, in the ordinary course of nature, the child must have been conceived. . . .

When a verdict is attacked as being unsupported by the evidence the power of the appellate court is limited to a determination whether there is any *substantial* evidence, contradicted or uncontradicted, that will support the conclusion of the jury. [Citations omitted.]

[The court held that although the blood tests indisputably established

that Charles Chaplin "cannot be the father of the child," it was nevertheless proper for the trial court to treat them simply as part of the evidence
to be weighed by the jury. This result was said to be required by a
governing decision of the California Supreme Court that was subsequently changed by statute. See Kusior v. Silver, page 34 supra.]

*. . . Did the court err in requiring defendant to stand in front of the jury
with Miss Berry and plaintiff?* Defendant complains of the order of the
court directing him to stand in front of the jury in close proximity to the
mother holding her child in her arms in order that the jurors might study
and compare the physical features of the infant plaintiff with those of
defendant. We see no reason why they should not have been given the
benefit of personal observation of the parties and we have not been referred to any authority to the effect that such an order of the court is
improper or prejudicial. . . . The jurors were entitled to the ocular
demonstration ordered by the court, and it will be assumed that they
exercised their powers of observation rather than of imagination.

We are not impressed with the thought advanced by counsel for defendant that the sympathy of the jurors could have been aroused by the
juxtaposition of the three parties in interest. The apprehension expressed by counsel that plaintiff in the arms of her mother caused compas-
sionate visualization of the ancient masterpieces of "Madonna and Child"
is dispelled by the character of the evidence in the case which kept the
minds of the jurors fixed on the unspiritual and terrestrial affairs of the
mother and defendant. . . .

McComb, J. I concur in the judgment because of the fact that this
court is bound by the decision of the Supreme Court in Arais v. Kalensni-
koff, 10 Cal. 2d 428 [74 P.2d 1043, 115 A.L.R. 163]. I believe, however,
that that court was in error in its determination of the case. . . .

In the case at bar a widely accepted scientific method of determining
parentage was applied. Its results were definite. To reject the new and
certain for the old and uncertain does not tend to promote improvement
in the administration of justice.

UNIFORM ACT ON PATERNITY (1960)[30]

PREFATORY NOTE

This act . . . . was originally drafted as a revision of the Uniform Illegitimacy Act, but experience with it at two annual conferences demonstrated that on some of the collateral matters included there were apparently irreconcilable points of view. Therefore the drafting committee
discarded the pattern. As a result there is presented here a comparatively
brief act confined to setting up the suggested civil action, wherever pos-

---

[30] 1960 Handbook of the National Conference of Commissioners on Uniform
State Laws 179. See also 9B U.L.A. 155 (Supp. 1964). Most of the drafters' comments have been omitted, as have §§14-18 (dealing with, inter alia, venue, interpretation, and effective date); all bracketed material in this Act is bracketed in
original.

sible utilizing existing law. Excursions into collateral problems such as legitimation, effect of adoption, and rights of inheritance, have been left to other legislation. It is hoped that this act will furnish an acceptable modernized procedure for handling this troublesome social problem, and that it will prove a valuable adjunct to the Uniform Reciprocal Enforcement of Support Act.

SECTION 1. [*Obligations of the Father.*] The father of a child which is or may be born out of wedlock is liable to the same extent as the father of a child born in wedlock, whether or not the child is born alive, for the reasonable expense of the mother's pregnancy and confinement and for the education, necessary support and funeral expenses of the child. A child born out of wedlock includes a child born to a married woman by a man other than her husband.

SECTION 2. [*Enforcement.*] Paternity may be determined upon the [petition] [complaint] of the mother, child, or the public authority chargeable by law with the support of the child. If paternity has been determined [or has been acknowledged according to the laws of this state], the liabilities of the father may be enforced in the same or other proceedings (1) by the mother, child, or the public authority which has furnished or may furnish the reasonable expenses of pregnancy, confinement, education, necessary support, or funeral expenses, and (2) by other persons including private agencies to the extent that they have furnished the reasonable expenses of pregnancy, confinement, education, necessary support, or funeral expenses.

SECTION 3. [*Limitation on Recovery from the Father.*] The father's liabilities for past education and necessary support are limited to a period of [four] years next preceding the commencement of [an action] [a proceeding].

SECTION 4. [*Limitations on Recovery from Father's Estate.*] The obligation of the estate of the father for liabilities under this Act is limited to amounts accrued prior to his death [and such sums as may be payable for dependency under other laws].

COMMENT

This section is intended to prevent judgments under the act from being enforced in such a way that the illegitimate child might be preferred over the legitimate child, who may be partly or wholly disinherited by will. The bracketed language at the end is intended to suggest adjustment to other laws regarding "family allowances" or similar provision for temporary support of dependents.

SECTION 5. [*Remedies.*] The [   ] court has jurisdiction of [an action] [a proceeding] under this Act and all remedies for the enforcement of judgments for expenses of pregnancy and confinement for a wife or for education, necessary support, or funeral expenses for legitimate children apply. The court has continuing jurisdiction to modify or revoke a judgment for future education and necessary support. [All remedies under the Uniform Reciprocal Enforcement of Support Act are available for enforcement of duties of support under this Act.]

SECTION 6. [*Time of Trial.*] If the issue of paternity is raised in [an action] [a proceeding] commenced during the pregnancy of the mother, the trial shall not, without the consent of the alleged father, be held until after the birth or miscarriage [but during such delay testimony may be perpetuated according to the laws of this state].

[SECTION 7. [*Authority for Blood Tests.*] The court, upon its own initiative or upon suggestion made by or on behalf of any person whose blood is involved may, or upon motion of any party to the [action] [proceeding] made at a time so as not to delay the proceedings unduly, shall order the mother, child and alleged father to submit to blood tests. If any party refuses to submit to such tests, the court may resolve the question of paternity against such party or enforce its order if the rights of others and the interests of justice so require.]

COMMENT

This section and sections 8, 9 and 10 are taken, with the minimum necessary adjustments, from the Uniform Act on Blood Tests to Determine Paternity. In states that have adopted this act these sections should be eliminated as unnecessary.

[SECTION 8. [*Selection of Experts.*] The tests shall be made by experts qualified as examiners of blood types who shall be appointed by the court. The experts shall be called by the court as witnesses to testify to their findings and shall be subject to cross-examination by the parties. Any party or person at whose suggestion the tests have been ordered may demand that other experts, qualified as examiners of blood types, perform independent tests under order of court, the results of which may be offered in evidence. The number and qualifications of such experts shall be determined by the court.]

[SECTION 9. [*Compensation of Expert Witnesses.*] The compensation of each expert witness appointed by the court shall be fixed at a reasonable amount. It shall be paid as the court shall order. The court may order that it be paid by the parties in such proportions and at such times as it shall prescribe, or that the proportion of any party be paid by [insert name of the proper public authority], and that, after payment by the parties or [insert name of the public authority] or both, all or part or none of it be taxed as costs in the action. The fee of an expert witness called by a party but not appointed by the court shall be paid by the party calling him but shall not be taxed as costs in the action.]

[SECTION 10. [*Effect of Test Results.*] If the court finds that the conclusions of all the experts, as disclosed by the evidence based upon the tests, are that the alleged father is not the father of the child, the question of paternity shall be resolved accordingly. If the experts disagree in their findings or conclusions, the question shall be submitted upon all the evidence. If the experts conclude that the blood tests show the possibility of the alleged father's paternity, admission of this evidence is within the discretion of the court, depending upon the infrequency of the blood type.]

SECTION 11. [*Judgment.*] Judgments under this Act may be for periodic payments which may vary in amount. The court may order payments to be made to the mother or to some person, corporation, or agency designated to administer them under the supervision of the court.

SECTION 12. [*Security.*] The court may require the alleged father to give bond or other security for the payment of the judgment.

SECTION 13. [*Settlement Agreements.*] An agreement of settlement with the alleged father is binding only when approved by the court.

NOTE

1. The Uniform Act restates the generally prevailing rule that if the defendant's paternity can be established according to the requisite standard of proof, the father will be liable for the child's support. But compare Va. Code Ann. §20-61.1 (1960), which provides that the father is liable only if he admits paternity in open court or has signed in writing under oath a voluntary admission of paternity. In Distefano v. Commonwealth, 201 Va. 23, 109 S.E.2d 497 (1959), a man who lived with a woman for several years, fathering two children whom he promised in writing to support, was held not liable when the woman sued to enforce this agreement since the requisite admission of paternity was not under oath. In addition to the other indicia of paternity, the father had for some years claimed the children as dependents on his federal and state income tax returns.

2. The scope and duration of the father's duty to support vary considerably. Some statutes prescribe specific dollar amounts, depending on the age of the child. See, e.g., Fla. Stat. Ann. §742.041 (1964). Others stipulate simply "a fair and reasonable sum for the support and education of the child until the child is twenty-one" (N.Y. Family Ct. Act §545), thus leaving the precise amount to the discretion of the court, depending upon such factors as the needs of the child and the ability of the parents. Compare §1 of the Uniform Act, page 47 supra. The statutes not uncommonly impose liability also for the mother's expenses of pregnancy and confinement. See, e.g., N.Y. Family Ct. Act §514.

Matter of "Wood" v. "Howe," 15 Misc. 2d 1048, 182 N.Y.S.2d 992 (Child. Ct. 1959), concerned the effect of an illegitimate child's adoption on the mother's right to claim her pregnancy and confinement expenses from the child's father. The father denied paternity and claimed that the adoption which occurred more than a year prior to the paternity action constituted a complete severance of the bonds between the child and its natural parents. Accordingly he claimed that he was no longer liable for the child's support or any expenses related thereto. What should be the result?

3. Establishing the defendant's paternity — the sine qua non of liabil-

ity under American law[31] — has been considerably facilitated by the development of blood testing. It should be noted, however, that the blood tests presently utilized rarely prove the paternity of the defendant; they are characteristically introduced by the defendant to show that he could not have been the father. Although very few jurisdictions have adopted the Uniform Act as such, most states now permit the admission and/or compulsion of blood tests in paternity proceedings. See, e.g., Maine Rev. Stat. Ann. c. 19, §262 (1964); Mich. Stat. Ann. §25.496 (1957); N.J. Stat. Ann. §2A:83-3 (1952). Whether blood tests can be used in other types of actions that may involve questions of paternity — such as a claim for child support in a divorce action — is not wholly clear. See Commonwealth ex rel. Goldman v. Goldman, 199 Pa. Super. 274, 184 A.2d 351 (1962) (Uniform Act applicable in action by wife to compel support of child conceived and born during wedlock as well as child conceived and born following parties' separation). But cf. Commonwealth ex rel. Weston v. Weston, 201 Pa. Super. 554, 193 A.2d 782 (1963) (husband estopped to question paternity of child two and one-half years after its birth).

As the Berry case demonstrated, the admissibility of blood tests does not necessarily determine the weight to be given to such evidence. In California, the Berry result has been changed through adoption of a provision comparable to the first sentence of §10 of the Uniform Act. See Kusior v. Silver, page 34 supra. See also, e.g., Pa. Stat. Ann. tit. 28, §307.4 (Supp. 1964). Some states have reached the same result by judicial decision. See, e.g., Commonwealth v. D'Avella, 339 Mass. 642, 162 N.E.2d 19 (1959). Others apparently still leave the issue to the jury.

Note that §10 of the Uniform Act, unlike most state statutes, deals not only with the case where the blood tests clearly exclude the defendant's paternity, but also covers two other situations. Why is the court given discretion to exclude the blood test evidence where it shows the possibility of the defendant's paternity? There is still a fourth situation that is not explicitly provided for in the Act. What if the best presently available medical testimony indicates an extremely high probability, albeit not certainty, of exclusion? Compare Miller v. Domanski, 26 N.J. Super. 316, 97 A.2d 641 (1953) (testimony summarily excluded since doctor could not assert definite exclusion), with Groulx v. Groulx, 98 N.H. 481, 103 A.2d 188 (1954) (although tests do not absolutely exclude paternity, they are entitled to evidentiary weight like all other expert opinion).

For a compilation of court decisions on the use of blood tests, see Annots., 163 A.L.R. 939 (1946) and 46 A.L.R.2d 1000 (1956). See also Harris, Some Observations on the Un-Uniform Act on Blood Tests to Determine Paternity, 9 Vill. L. Rev. 59 (1963). Concerning the reliability of blood tests, see page 55 infra.

4. Jordan v. Mace, 144 Me. 351, 69 A.2d 670 (1949), concerned twins, and the blood tests excluded defendant's paternity only as to one of them.

---

[31] Compare the statutes described at page 59 infra which impose joint and several liability on any persons who had intercourse with the plaintiff around the probable time of conception.

The court assumed that the father of twins must be one and the same man.   The same situation arose in State v. Pernell, 29 U.S.L. Week 2093 (Md., Balt. Crim. Ct., Aug. 5, 1960), where the court considered the possibility that the twins might have different fathers by fertilization of two ova in different acts of coitus within a short time (superfecundation) or with the intervention of several weeks (superfetation).   The court ruled for the defendant, finding that such an occurrence "has not been sufficiently established in medical literature, particularly with regard to its frequency, to form the basis for a legal conclusion."   See Casenote, 22 Md. L. Rev. 333 (1962).   Compare a press dispatch from Horsens, Denmark, Sept. 30, 1960, quoted in 2 Fam. Law., Oct. 1960, p. 3 (A.B.A. Sect. of Fam. L.), where the evidence apparently showed that the mother of twins had had intercourse on the same day with her husband and with another man now dead.   Blood tests excluded the husband's paternity of one child. Ironically, the now-divorced husband was asserting paternity of both twins in order to obtain custody of them.   The court apparently recognized the possibility of diverse paternity of the twins.

5. Suppose that in the Chaplin case, Miss Berry, the plaintiff, had admitted under cross-examination that she had had intercourse with other men during the time of possible conception, or that the jury had so found. Such evidence, known as the exceptio plurium in the civil law, generally constitutes a complete defense.   See Commonwealth v. Rex, 147 Pa. Super. 121, 24 A.2d 98 (1942); People v. Rasmusson, 286 App. Div. 860, 141 N.Y.S.2d 599 (1955).   Why should this be so?   What if the plaintiff had intercourse with the defendant ten times and with any other man only once during the relevant period?   Could the plaintiff in such a case introduce the blood tests of the alleged "corespondent" in an attempt to show that he could *not* have been the father and that therefore the exceptio plurium element should disappear from the case?   Would the Uniform Act permit such evidence?   See Kusior v. Silver, page 34 supra, where the plaintiff sought to introduce the blood tests to show that her husband could not have been the father of the child.   And note that those jurisdictions which impose joint and several liability on any persons who had intercourse with the plaintiff about the time of probable conception generally permit the introduction of blood tests to exclude one or more of the defendants.   See pages 59-61 infra.   Compare also La. Civ. Code Ann. art. 210 (1952):

> The oath of the mother, supported by proof of the cohabitation of the reputed father with her, out of his house, is not sufficient to establish natural paternal descent, if the mother be known as a woman of dissolute manners, or as having had an unlawful connection with one or more men (other than the man whom she declares to be the father of the child) either before or since the birth of the child.

Of course, if the defendant merely introduces evidence that the plaintiff had intercourse with other men about the time of probable conception, and, as is customary, this evidence is denied by plaintiff, then there is simply a further question of credibility presented for the jury.

6. On what basis did the Berry case reject the agreement entered into between the parties? Compare Wis. Stat. Ann. §52.28 (Supp. 1965):

> A woman who has borne a child out of wedlock or who is pregnant with a child which is likely to be born, out of wedlock, may enter into an agreement with the person claimed by her to be the father of the child. Such agreement may be entered into at any time prior to final judgment, either before or after issuance of process, or at any time while said judgment is still in effect. No agreement shall be entered into before the birth of the child unless the court finds that there are special circumstances making it advisable to do so. . . . All agreements referred to in [certain specified sections of this statute] shall be drawn by the district attorney. No other agreement or settlement of any paternity proceeding shall be valid.

See also N.Y. Family Ct. Act §516 (agreement binding only if court approves and determines that it makes "adequate provision" for the child and is fully secured); Annot., 84 A.L.R.2d 524 (1962). In Haag v. Barnes, 9 N.Y.2d 554, 175 N.E.2d 441 (1961), a New York resident had become pregnant as a result of intercourse in New York with an Illinois resident. The child was born in Illinois, and there the parties signed an agreement under which the father was to pay $275 per month for the child's support until it reached the age of sixteen. The agreement contained a release of all actions for support of the child, and provided that it was to be governed by Illinois law. Although the father made all the payments required under the agreement, the mother sued in New York for additional support, citing the predecessor to §516. The defendant, in support of a motion to dismiss, relied on the provision of the Illinois statute which made any such agreement for a sum not less than $800 a bar to any further action for support. The Court of Appeals affirmed dismissal of the complaint, pointing out that Illinois had the most significant contacts with this transaction, and that New York's enforcement of the Illinois agreement was not so offensive to New York public policy as to warrant its application of its own law. See Ehrenzweig, The "Bastard" in the Conflict of Laws — A National Disgrace, 29 U. Chi. L. Rev. 498 (1962); Annot., 87 A.L.R.2d 1306 (1963).

If the mother and father enter a valid settlement agreement, would the child (or the welfare department in case the child becomes a public charge) be bound? Cf. Commonwealth v. Pewatts, 200 Pa. Super. 22, 186 A.2d 408 (1962) (although judgment in fornication and bastardy proceeding required father to pay support only until the child's fourteenth birthday, father could be compelled under criminal nonsupport statute to support the child after it had reached that age); State ex rel. Acorman v. Pitner, 80 N.J. Super. 91, 193 A.2d 143 (1963) (judgment of "not guilty" entered in Pennsylvania fornication and bastardy prosecution pursuant to financial settlement between mother and putative father was not binding upon child in subsequent suit against putative father for support). Compare page 922 infra concerning the continuing modifiability of a child support decree upon divorce. See also N.Y. Family Ct. Act §516 (complete performance of a court-approved agreement, following due notice to appropriate welfare official, "bars other remedies of the mother or child for the support and education of the child").

7. What, if any, effect should be given to an adjudication of paternity after the father's death? Compare §4 of the Uniform Act with §513 of the N.Y. Family Ct. Act:

If a parent dies, an order of support or a judicially approved settlement made prior to that parent's death shall be enforceable as a claim against the deceased parent's estate in an amount to be determined by the surrogate's court not greater than is provided in said order or settlement, having regard to the age of the child, the ability of the surviving parent to support and educate it, the amount of property left by the deceased parent and the number, age and financial condition of those other persons legally entitled to support by the deceased parent during his or her lifetime.

See also page 20 supra respecting the child's intestate succession rights.

8. Where the father or mother of the child cannot be located or are incapable of supporting the child, the question sometimes arises whether other relatives are responsible for the illegitimate child's support. In State Board of Child Welfare v. P.G.F., 57 N.J. Super. 370, 154 A.2d 746 (Juv. & Dom. Rel. Ct. 1959), it was held that although New Jersey law makes a grandfather, among others, responsible for a child's support, this provision does not compel a man to support the illegitimate child of his illegitimate daughter.

PROBLEM

A client comes to you in July and hands you a complaint which has just been served upon him, alleging in substance as follows: (1) that plaintiff is and always has been unmarried; (2) that eighteen months previously about midnight on January 31, defendant, after taking her to a movie theater and then to a restaurant, had sexual intercourse with her in his automobile, and as a result thereof she became pregnant, and defendant acknowledged that he was responsible for her pregnancy; (3) that on the following September 29, she gave birth to a female child; (4) that defendant is the father of the child and that he acknowledged on many occasions that he is its father; (5) that before the child was born, defendant agreed to pay all her medical and miscellaneous expenses and to compensate her for the loss of her salary caused by the child's birth, and also to pay her ten dollars per week for its support until it reached the age of twenty-one, upon condition that she would not institute bastardy proceedings against him as long as he made the payments in accordance with the agreement; (6) that she claimed the following sums: Union Memorial Hospital, $170; Dr. George Merrill, her physician, $95; miscellaneous expenses, $90.80; loss of earnings for twenty-six weeks, $1105; support of the child to date,

$380; total, $1840.80; and (7) that defendant paid her only $550.80, and she demanded that he pay her the further sum of $1290, the balance due under the agreement, but he failed and refused to pay the same.

Your client tells you (a) that he took the plaintiff out on the night in question but that he did not have intercourse with her then or on any other occasion; (b) that he has never admitted paternity; (c) that he never made any oral agreement with her to pay her any money for any purpose; (d) that he did pay her medical expenses and some additional money at intervals for five months after the child's birth, these payments totaling $550.80 as alleged in par. 7 of the complaint, but only because she threatened him with a bastardy prosecution and his father urged him to pay because his mother had a heart condition and he wished to keep the matter away from his mother, the public, and the courts; (e) that about four months ago he went to plaintiff's physician to make inquiry about blood tests, that blood tests were made, and that said blood tests excluded the possibility of his paternity; (f) that since receiving the blood test reports he has refused to make any payments; (g) that his friend, Tom, recently admitted to him "privately and confidentially" that he had intercourse with the plaintiff on at least four occasions during the first ten days of the January preceding the birth of plaintiff's baby; and (h) that in any event the whole problem could be solved if plaintiff would only give the baby up for adoption, which would be better for the baby anyway, as plaintiff is unfit to be a mother.

1. Advise the client and plan his defense.

2. If the client had come to you before the child was born and before he had made any payments in response to the woman's demands, how would you have handled the case?

RELIABILITY OF EVIDENCE IN PATERNITY CASES

"The woman always pays!" Indeed, she does not. She stands to win every time in an "affiliation" case. It is the man who pays, almost automatically, for our English magistracy is apt to assume he is guilty unless he can prove his innocence — which is practically impossible. . . .[32]

Proof problems in paternity actions have long been a matter of concern. Seventeenth century Massachusetts statutes put great weight upon the testimony of the woman while in the throes of labor. Even if the evidence was insufficient to sustain a criminal conviction of an accused father,

then the man charged by the woman to be the father, she holding constant in it, (especially being put upon the real discovery of the truth of it in the time of her travail) shall be the reputed father, and accordingly be liable to the charge of maintenance as aforesaid . . . unless the circumstances of the case and pleas be such . . . that the

[32] Moore, The Paternity Scandal, 121 The Nineteenth Century and After 394 (1937).

court that hath the cognizance thereof shall see reason to acquit him. . . .[33]

This evidentiary concept that a charge made by a woman while in labor is entitled to special weight is still retained in our law notwithstanding the humanization of obstetrical practice; see Pa. Stat. Ann. tit. 18, §4506 (1963). While we have no empirical evidence to support the premise that the experience in the delivery room is a deterrent against falsehood, there is now ample evidence that the veracity of unwed mothers when not in labor leaves a good deal to be desired. Schatkin, a leading authority in the field, makes the following claims:

> Science — not social service activity — has come to the aid of the [putative father]. Blood tests, in effect in New York since 1935, have shown that approximately 30 per cent of the accused men in New York City, who deny paternity and demand a blood test, are not the fathers of the disputed children. False claims of paternity are no novelty. The late Dr. Fritz Schiff, who by May 1, 1931 had carried out 5512 blood tests ordered by the German Courts, declared that, "In those lawsuits in which the blood test has been applied, roughly every second man has been denounced unjustly."
>
> Paternity offers a fertile field for blackmail, extortion and "shakedown" on the part of an unscrupulous woman. The average normal woman, of course, is not unscrupulous, nor will she be guilty of extortion. Nevertheless, a normal single woman who becomes pregnant is trapped — desperate, virtually compelled to designate a father for her expected child.
>
> Now, however, the complete blood test (A-B-O, M-N, and Rh-Hr) will detect 55 out of 100 false accusations of paternity. In actual practice, out of 100 blood tests ordered by the court, 18 exclusions result. The ratio of 18 to 55 being $33\frac{1}{3}$ per cent, it follows that one-third of the paternity cases brought to the Court of Special Sessions in New York City are false charges.[34]

If Schatkin's concept of a "false accusation" and his mathematical computations are accepted, he probably understates the proportion of false charges. Gellhorn reports that blood tests are not given in all cases in New York. "Because many of the defendants in these matters are too impecunious to pay out $50 for laboratory tests that have only a dimly perceived significance, the tests are not administered in every case where their results might be revealingly helpful." [35]

Dr. Leon N. Sussman, in Blood Grouping Tests in Disputed Paternity

[33] The Charters and General Laws of the Colony and Province of Massachusetts Bay 116 (Dane, Prescott & Story eds. 1814).

[34] These three paragraphs are adapted from two of Schatkin's articles: Should Paternity Cases Be Tried in a Civil or Criminal Court?, 1 Crim. L. Rev. (N.Y.) 18, 23 (Spring 1954), and Paternity Proceedings — A Changing Concept, 42 J. Crim. L., C. & P.S. 821, 823 (1952). Schatkin is also the author of the standard text in the field, Disputed Paternity Proceedings (3d ed. 1953).

[35] Gellhorn, Children and Families in the Courts of New York City 207 (1954).

Proceedings and Filial Relationship, J. Forensic Sciences, July 1956, pp. 25, 26-27, states that "positive identification of a person by means of blood testing is a goal for the future," but that ultimately this may be possible "as it is believed that the complete blood group of a person is more individual than even his fingerprint." While testing today is limited to three systems, "[a]ctually 13 well-recognized systems are known but the unavailability of testing serums, the difficulties with the technics, and insufficient statistical experience limit their usefulness in all but research laboratories. . . . [U]sing the 3 available acceptable systems, there are 216 varieties of blood demonstrable." But when the additional systems become available, "approximately 100,000 serologically different individuals can be identified by their blood groupings."

Errors in making the tests are possible. See United States ex rel. Lee Kum Hoy v. Murff, 355 U.S. 169, 170 (1957) (judgment of lower court vacated because it appeared that "the blood grouping tests made herein were in some respects inaccurate and the reports thereof partly erroneous and conflicting"). See also Committee on Medicolegal Problems, Medicolegal Application of Blood Grouping Tests, 149 A.M.A.J. 699, 703 (1952). ("It is the duty of the court to examine the evidence in order to convince itself that the tests have been properly carried out by qualified experts"; retesting by independent expert suggested). And compare the Uniform Act's reference to "experts" (page 48 supra), which has been interpreted to make testimony by only one expert nonconclusive. See State v. Sargent, 100 N.H. 29, 118 A.2d 596 (1955). In general, see Ross, The Value of Blood Tests as Evidence in Paternity Cases, 71 Harv. L. Rev. 466 (1958).

ARTHER and REID, UTILIZING THE LIE DETECTOR TECHNIQUE TO DETERMINE THE TRUTH IN DISPUTED PATERNITY CASES

45 Journal of Criminal Law, Criminology and Police Science 213 (1954)

When testifying in court on his own behalf, the defendant usually invokes one of two defenses. First, he may deny any sexual intercourse with the complainant during the possible period of the child's conception. Second, he may admit intercourse during the conception period but claim that the complainant also had intercourse with other men during this same period, and that he should not be held responsible since one of the others could be the father.

In almost every case, of course, the complainant will claim that during the conception period the defendant is the only one with whom she had sexual intercourse. In paternity cases, therefore, one of the two parties probably will be lying . . . .

For 16 years a number of judges of the Chicago Municipal Court have consistently availed themselves of the lie-detector technique to assist them in their decisions. Upon such occasions both the accused and the mother are requested by the judge to take a lie-detector test. This request is ordinarily made at the conclusion of the testimony given by both the complainant and the accused.

On the basis of a six-year study of the 312 disputed paternity cases handled at the Chicago laboratory of John E. Reid and Associates, it was determined that 93 per cent of the tested parties lied in some respect when they testified in court as to their sexual relationship! The lying ranged from the defendant's complete denial of any intercourse with the complainant, when he actually did have it with her during the conception period, to the complainant simply exaggerating the number of times intercourse did take place with the defendant during the conception period.

Even when a witness testifies in a paternity case, usually for the defendant, the judge or jury can not assume that he is telling the truth. Such a witness will swear in court that he had sexual intercourse with the complainant during the baby's conception period. This is supposed to prove false the mother's claim that during the conception period the defendant was the only one with whom she had intercourse. Yet when the witnesses were given lie-detector tests, 57 per cent of them confessed to the lie-detector examiner that they had not had sexual intercourse with the mother during the conception period. In fact, many of them confessed that they never did have sexual intercourse with the mother.

Following their lie-detector tests, approximately 82 per cent of the paternity complainants, alleged fathers, and witnesses confessed to the lie-detector examiner that they committed perjury when testifying in court! The fact that over 40 per cent of the tested mothers confessed to having had sexual intercourse with others during the conception period is enough to warrant a more extensive use of the lie-detector in paternity proceedings. . . .

The first contention, that the accused never had sexual intercourse with the mother, was found to be true in only 1 of the 312 cases studied.[36] The second contention, that he had intercourse with the mother but not during the period of conception, is the most prevalent defense. It was found to be true in only 26 of the other 311 cases. The third defense position, the admission of one or more acts of intercourse during the conception period, is used by the man who has had intercourse with the mother during the period and is trying to be as truthful as possible. However, this man desires the lie-detector tests because he believes that another man or men have had intercourse with her during the same period. If his belief is right, that is, that she did have intercourse with others during the conception period, he is usually declared innocent and acquitted.

Regardless of the defense used by the accused men, 88 per cent of them confessed to the lie-detector examiner that they lied in court regarding the number of times they had intercourse with the mother. Seventy-one of those who previously denied any intercourse with the mother during the conception period confessed to having had intercourse with her during that time. Even those men who admit intercourse during the conception period, but contend that other men were also involved, often confess

[36] Unfortunately the authors do not state how many of the 312 men made this contention. — Ed.

that they lied in court, in that they withheld the number of times they actually did have intercourse with the mother during the period. . . .

. . . Only once, however, was a complainant found to be lying altogether regarding her accusation that she had had intercourse with the defendant. In 26 of the other 311 cases she was lying when she claimed to have had intercourse with him during the conception period. In 149 of the total number of cases, or 47.75 per cent, she was reported lying when she denied having intercourse with any one else but the defendant during the conception period.

In the great majority of cases the lying mother confessed to the lie-detector examiner that she had lied in court. Many times damaging admissions are given even before the running of the first test. Of the 149 complainants reported lying when they denied intercourse with anyone else but the defendant during the conception period, 128 of them confessed that fact to the examiner! If just blood tests were used on these 149 women, only 82 of them, instead of 128, would have been definitely shown to have filed a false paternity suit. . . .

STATISTICS OF LIE-DETECTOR TESTS IN PATERNITY CASES
(January 1948 to September 1953)

1. Total number of cases 312
2. Total number of subjects 589
3. Number of cases where the defendant was reported to have been the only one to have intercourse with the mother during the conception period 158
4. Number of cases where the mother had intercourse with others during the period as well as with the defendant 122
5. Number of cases where the mother had intercourse with others during the period but not with the defendant 27
6. Total number of mothers' confessions to intercourse with other men during the period 128
7. Total number of defendants who in court denied any intercourse with the mother during the period, then admitted it to the lie-detector examiner 71
8. Number of cases where no definite report could be given to the court .... 5 [37]

NOTE

1. Evidence of lie detector test results is usually inadmissible unless both parties have stipulated before any tests that the results are to be admitted regardless of their outcome. The authors give a suggested form for such a stipulation at 219-220.

2. The authors state that "The latest estimation accords to the lie-detector technique, when properly used, an accuracy of 95%, with a 4%

[37] In each of these 5 cases only one party was tested instead of both. Two of these five "indefinite" subjects had been previously confined to a mental institution, two of them were of extremely low intelligence, and the fifth was unresponsive to the technique.

margin of indefinite (inconclusive) determinations and a 1% margin of maximum possible error." Id. at 216 n.5. The apparent source of this assertion is Inbau & Reid, Lie Detection and Criminal Interrogation 111 (3d rev. ed. 1953), where it is stated that "The percentage of *known error* was .0007 per cent — in other words 3 known errors out of 4093 subjects" (emphasis supplied). But the authors concede: "There is no assurance, of course, that all errors were discovered. It does appear, however, that the one per cent estimate will cover whatever errors may be present." If the authors have figures to support this assertion, they do not give them. According to their figures, of the total 4280 cases studied, the results in 187 cases were indefinite. Of the balance of 4093, the test reported 2759 as innocent and 1334 as guilty. The only "verification" of these results is that 486 of those who tested guilty made a confession and in 323 of the "innocent" cases the finding of innocence was "verified" by another's confession. Accepting these as verifications, there remain 3284 or 80 per cent of the 4093 cases where the validity of the test is unknown. For a collection of materials on the reliability of lie detector tests, see Levin, Evidence and the Behavioral Sciences, p. III-B-235 (mimeo., Univ. Pa. Law School 1956). For opposing analyses of reliability, compare Trovillo, Scientific Proof of Credibility, 22 Tenn. L. Rev. 743 (1953), with Levitt, Scientific Evaluation of the "Lie Detector," 40 Iowa L. Rev. 440 (1955). See also Skolnick, Scientific Theory and Scientific Evidence: An Analysis of Lie-Detection, 70 Yale L.J. 694 (1961).

3. The lie detection data suggest that many, perhaps most, of those whom Schatkin assumed to be "denounced unjustly" on the basis of blood test exclusion may in fact have had intercourse with the mother during the time of possible conception. The problem of providing support for the child where the evidence shows that two or more men may be the possible father has been the subject of legislation in several countries. Nova Scotia Rev. Stat. c. 31, §5 (1954), provides that "Where any one of a number of persons may be the possible father," then all can be joined as defendants and an order for support may be directed "against any number or all of such persons." Indeed, if a putative father produces a defense witness whose testimony "indicates that it is possible that the mother was pregnant by the witness," then the witness can be joined as an additional defendant. A 1961 amendment, however, permits the use of blood tests to exclude any of the putative fathers. Laws 1963, c. 16.

In Norway, 1915 legislation provided for a finding of paternity which entitled the child not only to support from the natural father but also to the father's name, to equal standing before the law with the father's legitimate children, and to equality of inheritance from the father. The act then set up a second category of persons who, although not adjudged the natural father, were nonetheless liable for support if it was "proved that he has had intercourse with the mother within such a time that in the ordinary course of nature he might be the father of the child." If more than one person was in this category, each could be ordered to contribute to maintenance and each was "severally responsible for the entire amount of the prescribed contribution." [38]   Arnholm reports the subsequent history of this radical legislation:

> Thus at this time there were three categories of illegitimate children: those who entered into a regular family relation with one father, those who enjoyed support without paternity and those children as to whom it was not even possible to establish a duty of support.   And within the group enjoying support only, there was a division between cases where one person only was liable to support and cases where several men were so liable. . . .
>
> The part of the Act which caused most criticism as time went by was that containing the rules providing for the establishment of a duty of support unconnected with paternity. . . .   [B]y taking up the fundamental position that illegitimate children were entitled to a regular family status with regard to the father, the 1915 Act — much against the intention of the legislature — came to depress the social position of those children whose right of support was granted without the establishment of paternity.   Such a decision involved an assumption of the sexual promiscuity of the mother during the period of conception, and the scheme of support served to remind the child of this very fact during the whole of its adolescence.   This means placing a severe psychological strain on the child.   Experienced social workers affirm that children settle down more easily where no duty of support is imposed at all.   The child can then find refuge in the thought that the mother has only had sexual relations with one man, who has deserted her and who cannot be found. . . .
>
> . . . By the 1956 Act the intermediate solution of imposing a duty of support without conferring family status was abolished.   The choice is now between full paternity with family status and nothing at all.
>
> . . . The requirements under the previous law for the establishment of paternity have now been reduced.   Some of those children who would have been in the intermediate category under the 1915 Act will qualify for the establishment of regular paternity under the new law.   [Other children who cannot qualify under the new requirements may now be eligible for public assistance.]
>
> Under the 1956 Act the requirements for establishing paternity are partly of a positive character — proof that the man indicated has had sexual intercourse with the mother at a time when the child may have been begotten; and partly of a negative character — that no circumstances are established making it "unlikely" that he is the true father.   Perhaps this term is not very precise, but the intention is to require a high degree of probability in favour of paternity. . . .
>
> The practical importance of the fact that the Act no longer unconditionally permits exceptio plurium concumbentium cannot be

---

[38] U.S. Children's Bureau Pub. No. 31, Norwegian Laws Concerning Illegitimate Children 14-21 (Magnusson trans. 1918).   Denmark and Iceland had similar legislation.   Arnholm, The New Norwegian Legislation Relating to Parents and Children, in 3 Scandinavian Studies in Law 9, 11 (Schmidt ed. 1959).

measured with any certainty until the Act has been in force for some years. But some extreme cases are already clear. If it is established in court that both A and B have had sexual relations with the mother in circumstances permitting the inference that either of them could be the father, and if the court does not believe that there is anybody else involved, paternity is to be imposed on A if the blood-groups exclude B but not A. And the law does not require even so high a degree of certainty as this. One may assume, for instance, that the mother has had intercourse on various occasions with her fiancé A, but she has also had intercourse on a single occasion with B somewhere near the limits of the possible conceptive period. In this case, unless there are established special circumstances which exclude A, the law requires that he be held to be the father.[39]

PROCEDURE IN PATERNITY ACTIONS

There are wide differences in procedure among the various states. Some, like Massachusetts and Pennsylvania, provide that bastardy is a crime and may combine it with a prosecution for fornication. Other states provide explicitly that the action is civil. New York, prior to the recent establishment of a state-wide family court, provided for trial in criminal courts in New York City and in civil courts in the rest of the state. For some of the implications of the label attached, see pages 64-65 infra.

The excerpt which follows conveys something of the flavor of these unedifying proceedings.

GELLHORN, CHILDREN AND FAMILIES IN THE COURTS OF NEW YORK CITY
192, 198, 204-205, 208-209 (1954)

The Court of Special Sessions, by law an "inferior court of criminal jurisdiction," is the sole tribunal of the City of New York empowered to entertain "proceedings to establish paternity and to provide for the support of natural children and their mothers . . ." Despite the explicit language of the statute, occasional efforts have been made by strong-willed judges of other courts to trench upon the exclusive power of Special Sessions. Beyond any real doubt, however, the filiation and support problems of children born out-of-wedlock fall within the province of the Court of Special Sessions and no other. . . .

[In 1951 the Court of Special Sessions disposed of 1079 complaints, of which 162 were dismissed; in 837 filiation was ordered on the defendant's admission (before a single judge), and 80 went to trial (before a court of three judges); of those tried, filiation was ordered in 36 and denied in 44 cases. See Table 22 at 198.]

The preceding table exhibits only a part of the Court's judicial labors in these matters. When a support order has been entered, Special Ses-

[39] Id. at 15-20.

sions automatically places the defendant on nominal probation. In point of fact, the terms of the probation are as a rule essentially the same as the terms of the support order. The "probationer" is under command to maintain the payments he has been ordered to make. Rarely is there any pretense that the purposes of the probation are rehabilitative or advisory. In short, the routine invocation of the probation terminology is a psychological weapon, rather than the prelude to active casework with the maladjusted men, women, and children whose personal unhappinesses are laid bare by paternity proceedings. When defendants fall into arrears in their prescribed payments, they are brought once more before a justice of the Court, presiding over a probation session of the Paternity Part. . . . The Court's reports do not show the volume of these supplementary proceedings. In 1947 the then Chief Justice estimated that "at least 2500 cases are reviewed yearly in this manner by the Court." . . .

An initial issue in a contested case is whether the defendant had sexual intercourse with the complainant mother at about the time of conception. The defense, if unable to dispute the allegation that intercourse did occur, may seek to show that other men also enjoyed the complainant's favors. In order that the judges on their high bench may hear the testimony above the distracting noises of a bustling courtroom, each witness is constantly admonished to speak loudly and clearly. Counsel have been advised to "ask questions in a voice that carries" and to stand in as remote a spot as possible in order to draw audible answers from "the unwed mother on the witness stand [who] is usually a timid and reticent witness." Then, with counsel and witness vying with one another to be heard in the far corners of a mammoth chamber packed with onlookers, answers are sought to questions of which the following sequence is aptly illustrative:

> "When did you start having acts of sexual intercourse with the defendant?"
> "How often per week from that time on did you have sexual intercourse with the defendant?"
> "When was the last act of intercourse you had with the defendant before the baby was born?"

A 27-year old complainant, attended in court by her 4-year old child, is asked: "How old were you when you first had intercourse with the defendant?" She lowers her head and mumbles a response. A judge complains that he cannot understand her answer. "It was when I was thirteen," she then bellows, mindful of the necessity of "speaking so the judges can hear you."

And so it goes.

The wretched chronicles that unfold before the Court are likely to thrill none but the depraved. They rarely bring joy in the telling either to the complainant or to the defendant. The circumstances of the telling, however, may well be an invitation to abuse of the Court's processes by private complainants. As already noted, the bulk of paternity proceedings are forced to trial by the Welfare Department; in those cases the mother is a reluctant participant, and in any event cases are not brought on for trial until the evidence has been responsibly reviewed by a highly competent law officer of the City of New York. In "private" litigation, on the contrary, the defendant may be the victim of a scheming woman who, by threatening to shout her accusations in a public forum, may exact a substantial settlement regardless of the merits. The occasional exposure of unsuccessful efforts to use paternity proceedings for extortion, leads one to suspect that other efforts have escaped detection. . . .

. . . The Court of Special Sessions deserves to be applauded for attempting honorably to discharge its duties toward children born out-of-wedlock. Nevertheless, the entire jurisdiction over paternity proceedings is misplaced. It should now be transferred from Special Sessions to the Domestic Relations Court. . . .

. . . Special Sessions is primarily a criminal court, with the attitudes and atmospheres that typify the enforcement of penal statutes. Filiation proceedings do not fit easily within that framework. Their just purpose is not to punish the father or the mother of a child born out-of-wedlock. It is, rather, to fix the responsibilities of adults in order to protect the well-being of an infant. The methods of social investigation do not come easily to a tribunal that is daily absorbed in a very different type of adjudication with its own traditional techniques. . . .

Hearings in Family Court seem on the whole to be conducted in a more helpful spirit than are their counterparts in Special Sessions. Cases are reached for trial with few delays. The holding of hearings in small courtrooms without the crowds that fill the seats of Special Sessions, conduces to a natural, relaxed, and unsensational presentation of the facts.[40]

NOTE

1. Another court observer has reached conclusions similar to Gellhorn's. Virtue, Family Cases in Court 36-37, 43-44 (1956), describes paternity proceedings in San Francisco courts as exhibiting the

war of the sexes at its most implacable. So bitter are these conflicts, and so punishing for all the parties, that some scholars in the social work field have wondered whether society is wise in attempting to identify the father of an illegitimate child and exacting financial payments from him. The courtroom presentation of a bastardy case is at best a sordid spectacle. . . .

Virtue describes one case observed in San Francisco in which the complaining witness, seven months pregnant, was subjected to prolonged and gruelling cross-examination. Virtue speculated that perhaps

[40] Judges of Special Sessions defend their public proceedings as tending to discourage the filing of fraudulent claims of paternity, because the plaintiff must expose herself to a trial in an open courtroom. It is at least arguable, however, that the open courtroom may hold more terror for a defendant (if he is a man of substance and standing) than for the plaintiff. It may well be that the threat of exposure to a public airing of the paternity charges may be a means of furthering fraudulent claims, rather than discouraging them.

the attorney for the defendant was not only reflecting his client's emotional position towards the girl, but was actively enjoying the opportunity to act out his own sex hostility. . . .

. . . There seems little question that the facts which were actually gleaned from this hearing could have been obtained in a fraction of the time by a trained court investigator, and that such questioning by an objective worker of this kind would have done violence to the legal position of neither party. In addition, it would have eliminated the factor of hostility, which appears to have been a detriment rather than an aid to accomplishing the purpose for which the judicial process was invoked here.

For opposition to Gellhorn's view that paternity cases should be tried in a family court, see Schatkin, Should Paternity Cases Be Tried in a Civil or Criminal Court?, 1 Crim. L. Rev. (N.Y.) 18, 23-24 (Spring 1954):

We all sympathize with the innocent child, but we cannot completely lose sight of the question of the protection of the defendant's rights.

The Court of Special Sessions — a criminal court — is well suited to protect the rights of a defendant in a paternity case. Every legal safeguard of the Constitution, the statutes and the rules of evidence of a criminal court are thrown protectively around the defendant. The complainant is made to prove her case by entirely satisfactory evidence. The Court of Special Sessions recognizes the inherent potentialities for fraud in these cases.

The Family Court does not seem to realize there is more to the problem than meets the casual eye, that approximately 30% of the men charged are simply not the fathers. The Family Court seems to be interested chiefly in a private hearing for the mother, the sparing to her of humiliation, etc. If the percentage of false claims of paternity were only minimal, then by all means let the cases go to the Domestic Relations Court. But in this field we have the widest area of legal "shakedown" that is known to exist.

Does it necessarily follow, however, that paternity actions must be labeled "civil" or "criminal" in order that we may determine what procedure is to be applied, or that the extent of the defendant's procedural protections should turn on whether the case is assigned to a criminal court or to a civil court? Such an analysis inevitably leads one into a morass, for paternity actions cannot be readily classified by such dichotomous reasoning. They are civil in the sense that the judgment is typically not for the primary purpose of punishing the defendant but to provide support for the child. The judgment, however, imports the stigma which attaches to a finding that the defendant has been criminally immoral, while the imprisonment which looms in the background as a means of enforcing the support order and the initiation of the proceedings by the defendant's arrest and imprisonment or release on bond show that this is no ordinary civil proceeding. For a collection of cases showing the attempt of the courts to resolve procedural questions by a labeling process, see Wysong,

The Jurisprudence of Labels — Bastardy as a Case in Point, 39 Neb. L. Rev. 648 (1960). Wysong analogizes to the examination of a porpoise, which swims like a fish, looks like a fish, and inhabits the ocean like other fish. On the other hand, the porpoise suckles its young, takes its oxygen from the air, and is warm-blooded. Depending upon which attributes are summed, the classification can go either way. "Absent is the penetrating inquiry requiring answers to questions concerning purpose, function, significant behavior and prime consequences." Id. at 658. The following are some of the questions which Wysong discusses and whose answers typically turn on the label applied:

a. Must probable cause be shown before a defendant can be held for trial?

b. Should the case of a juvenile defendant be transferred to the juvenile court?

c. Will the court have jurisdiction if the child is begotten in another state?

d. Will the frequently shorter statute of limitations applicable to criminal cases apply?

e. Is a contract by a putative father to support the child upon condition that bastardy proceedings not be instituted a contract to compound a criminal prosecution, and hence against public policy?

f. Upon trial is the defendant protected by such typically criminal evidentiary concepts as the requirements of proof beyond a reasonable doubt, corroboration, prohibition of prosecution comment upon the defendant's failure to testify, and admissibility of character evidence? Must a defendant, as in criminal cases, give prior notice of intention to rely upon an alibi defense?

g. Can the complainant appeal from a judgment for the defendant?

In many situations it is apparent that neither the civil nor criminal procedure will provide the most satisfactory result. If blackmail using the threat of public exposure is a serious problem, the public criminal preliminary hearing and its requirement of probable cause as a protection against unfounded prosecutions comes too late. Cf. D.C. Code Ann. §11-953 (1961): before prosecution can be started, "[t]he Complainant shall be examined under oath by an Assistant Corporation Counsel to determine the validity of the accusation." Paternity likewise presents a special statute of limitations problem, for nature inexorably brings the cause of action to a climax in a matter of months, and the only apparent result of any other than a very short limitations period would appear to be to facilitate blackmail.

PROBLEM

In the light of the preceding materials, does the Uniform Paternity Act (page 46 supra) satisfactorily solve the problems raised by paternity actions? Would you recommend any additional provisions?

2. Public Support for Dependent Children

If the primary purpose served by a paternity action is to provide support for the children, the device can hardly be labeled a great success. Gellhorn has reported:

> By and large the defendants in these matters are men and boys whose earnings are low, whose prospects are dim, and whose irresponsibility is manifested by the very fact of their being before the court. The order finally entered by the court is as a rule for a picayune amount, wholly insufficient to sustain the child whose father has just been judicially certified.
>
> It is only when the payments are aggregated in a common fund that they become impressive. During the years 1947-1951, inclusive, the average of annual collections by the Welfare Department's "Filiation Accounts Section" (which is located in the court building and serves as the court's support bureau) came to $579,773.16. . . .
>
> We must note, however, that the court has claimed credit not only for payments made pursuant to its orders, but also for all the payments that were made voluntarily in accordance with agreements between the Welfare Department and the putative fathers.
>
> There are those, in any event, who question whether the financial justification suffices. The proceedings are in themselves shattering experiences for all who participate. These include not only the mother and father, but also the father's other dependents and, often enough, the affected children themselves, who can be seen in the courtroom while the haggling is in process. In many instances the consequences are almost certainly reflected in later social expenses — for institutionalization of the parties, for lawlessness by men whose latent grudges against society are aroused, and for the economic and emotional wounds that may be suffered by the defendant's "other family." In short, there are hidden as well as direct costs in collecting these moneys.[41]

At least one country, apparently troubled by the proof and collection problems that are implicit in private paternity actions, has taken up Gellhorn's implied suggestion and abolished altogether the father's responsibility for support of his illegitimate child. The mother is granted an allowance directly from the state. See Berman, Soviet Family Law in the Light of Russian History and Marxist Theory, 56 Yale L.J. 26, 50-52 (1946). But see N.Y. Times, Feb. 17, 1964, p. 1, col. 8, reporting a proposal for restoration of the private paternity action.

In the United States over 300,000 illegitimate children are presently being supported largely by federal and state financial aid rather than their fathers. Indeed, since passage of Title IV of the Social Security Act in 1935,[42] both the federal and state governments have been deeply in-

[41] Gellhorn, Children and Families in the Courts of New York City 195-196 (1954).

[42] 99 Stat. 620 (1935), as amended, 42 U.S.C.A. §§301-1394 (1964).

volved in providing financial support to needy children in their own homes. The Aid to Dependent Children program authorizes federal grants to the states of 50 per cent of the cost of state aid to dependent children.[43]

A dependent child was defined in the original Act as a child under sixteen years of age "who has been deprived of parental support or care by reason of the death, continued absence from the home, or physical or mental incapacity of a parent," if the child was living in the home of any of a specified list of relatives including the other parent.[44] Although a state plan for aid must comply with standards established in the Social Security Act to qualify for federal contributions, a national standard of need was not provided

> partially because the heterogeneity of the country was felt to make a single standard unrealistic and possibly disruptive to the economic and social structure. Nor were states obliged to provide sufficient assistance to meet minimum standards of health and decency. The level of public support to be provided . . . was entirely within the discretion of the state. Also, all matters relating to the selection, qualifications, tenure, and compensation of personnel were initially reserved to states.[45]

In 1957, the Pennsylvania requirements for assistance were:

> 1. The recipient must be in need. This means that a person's own income and other means of support must be less than the amount the DPA [Department of Public Assistance] is authorized to grant to maintain certain minimum necessities for living.
>
> 2. One year's residence in Pennsylvania (all but ten states have residence requirements of at least one year).

---

[43] Under the 1962 amendments, the federal government will pay up to 75 per cent of the cost if the state program complies with more rigorous federal requirements relating to child welfare services. See generally pages 416-417 infra; Bell, Aid to Dependent Children (1965). There are four other financial aid programs partially financed with federal funds: Old Age Assistance; Medical Aid to the Aged; Aid to the Permanently and Totally Disabled; Aid to the Blind. An illegitimate child may also receive funds through a general assistance program (often designated "relief") financed wholly by state or local funds or a combination of both. "Recipients of general assistance usually are persons not eligible for Federal-State public assistance because of age or residence. The Bureau estimates from reports by most of the States that there were in the Nation about 775,000 recipients of general assistance in June 1963. During the fiscal year, an estimated $282 million was paid to recipients." Dept. H.E.&W., Ann. Rep. 75 (1963). Of course, not all of these sums are used for the support of illegitimate children, nor even for children whose families are broken.

[44] 49 Stat. 629 (1935), as amended, 42 U.S.C.A. §606 (1964). Under the provisions of the 1962 amendments, ADC aid may be provided even if both parents are in the home if one of the parents is unemployed or incapacitated. Also the age limit has been raised to eighteen.

[45] Bell, Aid to Dependent Children 21 (1965). Space does not permit complete treatment of the history or current operations of the program. Some of the problems of federal-state relationships which it has posed are mentioned at page 121 infra.

3. Children may qualify for ADC if:

    a. They are deprived of normal parental support, care, or guidance, because of the death, continued absence from home, or physical or mental incapacity of either or both parents (other [states'] definition of "continued absence" varies from one month to one year).

    b. They are under sixteen years of age, or eighteen if attending school.

    c. They are living with a parent or specified relative (in twenty-three states the child must live in a "suitable home").[46]

In fiscal 1963, 3.9 million children received ADC grants (including those eligible under the 1962 amendments) at a total cost for that year of over $1.4 billion. The federal government supplied approximately 60 per cent of the funds. (The precise proportion varies from state to state.) The average payment per month per recipient varied from $8.91 in Mississippi to $47.40 in Minnesota; average payments per family receiving aid per month (including medical care) ranged from $36.02 in Mississippi to $198.89 in Illinois.[47] Although the ADC program supports largely legitimate children in broken homes, illegitimate children living with their mothers or other relatives are also eligible for payments. The number of unwed mothers receiving ADC rose sharply (91 per cent) from 1948 to 1955. This increase reflected in part a general increase in ADC recipients, but the ratio which unwed mothers bore to all families receiving aid also increased from 14.8 per cent in 1948 to 22.7 per cent in 1955, with more recent figures tending to show a leveling off of this percentage at approximately 20 per cent.[48]

Berg, Utilizing the Strengths of Unwed Mothers in the AFDC Program, 43 Child Welfare 333, 334 (1964), provides some additional data:

Of approximately 2,659,000 children receiving ADC at the end of 1961, 53 percent were white and 47 percent were nonwhite. Of the white children, 6.5 percent were illegitimate; of the nonwhite, 17.5 percent were illegitimate. In the three states of New York, New Jersey, and Pennsylvania, however, 58 percent of the children on ADC were nonwhite, and 24 percent of them were illegitimate. [Illinois] figures, heavily weighted by those for Chicago, show 76 per-

---

[46] Foster, Dependent Children and the Law, 18 U. Pitt. L. Rev. 579, 589-590 (1957).

[47] All but the last set of figures have been taken from tables in Dept. H.E.&W., Ann. Rep. 114-120 (1963). The family payment figures relate to 1961 and are taken from id. at 77.

[48] Kaplan, Support from Absent Fathers of Children Receiving ADC 1955, p. 27 (U.S. Bureau of Public Assistance Rep. No. 41, 1960). See also U.S. Bureau of Public Assistance, Illegitimacy and its Impact on the Aid to Dependent Children Program 35 (1960): "The great majority of all children born out of wedlock — about 87 percent — are being supported by parents, relatives, or through sources other than aid to dependent children." This figure is calculated against a base which includes all illegitimate children, whether or not adopted. See id. at 35-36.

cent of the children as nonwhite, 33 percent of them illegitimate. Missouri, the District of Columbia, and the states of the South also have a high percentage of nonwhite child recipients and a high percentage of illegitimacy among them.[49]

It has been estimated that, prior to the 1962 amendments, approximately one third of ADC funds were used for the support of illegitimate children.[50]

It is not surprising that illegitimate children and their mothers create a heavy financial burden for the community. In 1954 the median income of all families headed by a woman was only about half that of families headed by a male, and the discrepancy is probably growing larger because the income of such families is increasing at a much slower rate than that of male-headed families. Moreover, there is reason to believe that the income of families whose head is an unwed mother is probably less than that of other families headed by a woman, since an increasing proportion of illegitimate children are nonwhite and from low economic strata.[51]

Public opinion and legislative policy, however, are united in insisting that through vigorous prosecution of private paternity actions the fathers of illegitimate children should be made to share as much of the financial cost as possible. In New York City, for example, "99 per cent of all [paternity] cases that progressed to a decision within the past five years, it has been responsibly estimated, were initiated by the Commissioner of Welfare."[52] To obtain relief the unwed mother must disclose the name of the father and request the initiation of proceedings. "The mother practically admits that she would not now be taking him to court, except for her desire to obtain home relief from the City."[53]

In 1952 the Social Security Act was amended to require that state plans for aid to dependent children provide for prompt notice to appropriate law enforcement officials of the furnishing of aid to families with dependent children in respect of a child who has been deserted or abandoned by a parent. 42 U.S.C.A. §602(a)(10)(1964).

It was thought that the law-enforcement officials could use these notices to identify situations in which prosecution under a State law concerning desertion and abandonment might be warranted. It was also hoped that both public assistance agencies and law-enforcement officials would increase their efforts to obtain greater support from absent fathers.[54]

On a national basis, however, Kaplan's study for the Bureau of Public Assistance suggests that private support actions are not likely to produce

[49] For a more complete statistical picture of illegitimacy, see pages 77-89 infra.
[50] 196 Economist 989 (1960).
[51] Kaplan, Support from Absent Fathers of Children Receiving ADC 1955, pp. 1, 29 (U.S. Bureau of Public Assistance Rep. No. 41, 1960).
[52] Gellhorn, Children and Families in the Courts of New York City 194 (1954).
[53] Schatkin, Disputed Paternity Proceedings 564 (3d ed. 1953).
[54] Kaplan, Support from Absent Fathers of Children Receiving ADC 1955, p. xi (U.S. Bureau of Public Assistance Rep. No. 41, 1960).

significant savings in relief costs.[55]   Of 125,220 families with illegitimate
children receiving ADC assistance, in only 10.2 per cent of the cases were
the families receiving contributions from the fathers,[56] and almost all the
contributions were less than $50 a month.   One reason for this low rate of
return was that in 61.2 per cent of the cases the whereabouts of the father
was unknown.   Of all cases studied, the notice required by the Social
Security Act had been given in 46.6 per cent.   Court orders requiring
support were outstanding in 10.4 per cent of the cases, and in an additional 7.3 per cent the father had entered into an agreement to provide
support.

"It is estimated that, on an annual basis, aggregate contributions
amounted to about $4.6 million in 51 States in 1955." [57]   This does not
represent a net saving in relief costs, however, both because some part of
the contribution may be used to meet family needs that cannot be met
within the maximum ADC payment[58] and because there is substantial
administrative cost in collecting these contributions.   Foster reports that
in Pennsylvania "locating the father becomes a major task for DPA employees," [59] manpower which is presumably drained away from casework
with the mothers and the children.   In any event, considering the amount
of public funds involved in the whole program, it would appear that even
if more vigorous enforcement could produce a 50 per cent increase in the
fathers' contribution rate (an unlikely prospect), the taxpayer's burden
for illegitimate children would be affected by not more than one per cent.

To these considerations we must add the possible "later social expenses" of collecting the money that were mentioned by Gellhorn, and
the impact of a paternity action on casework with the mother.   One social
worker in private agency practice observed that "from a purely casework
point of view, we have long since moved from establishing paternity as an
end in itself, knowing that as such little is to be gained. . . .   In our
agency [in Cleveland] very few cases are brought to court action."   Hay-
nam, Casework Treatment of the Unmarried Mother 7-8 (paper prepared
for Committee on Unmarried Parents (now National Council on Illegitimacy), National Conference of Social Work, 1947; reproduced by U.S.
Children's Bureau in 1947 and 1949).   Another caseworker commented:

Rigorous requirements for paternity hearings should not be insisted upon, since it is frequently desirable for the girl and for the

[55] Id. at 5-6. The data are based on a study made during a summer month of
1955. At that time it was estimated that ADC aid was being given to 138,100
families with 308,800 children where the father was never married to the mother
of the children. The study covers 125,220 of these families in all states except
California and Nevada.

[56] In 43.5 per cent of the families more than one father was involved for the
children in a single family. Id. at 5. The data from which the statements in the
text in this paragraph are taken are to be found in id. at 1, 5-6, 38-39.

[57] Id. at 39.

[58] On the basis of figures for nineteen states, it would appear that about 83
cents of every dollar contributed by fathers goes to the reduction of ADC payments. Ibid.

[59] Foster, Dependent Children and the Law, 18 U. Pitt. L. Rev. 579, 603 (1957).

future welfare of the baby that all ties with the father be broken. Unless the future welfare of the child seems seriously jeopardized, it is important that the mother be given the right to determine whether or not she wishes to institute such hearings. This is particularly important of course in situations where adoption is considered, since a clean break with previous ties is clearly indicated here.[60]

These observations suggest that other values besides purely practical financial considerations may be at issue. But even if the financial returns are not important and if rigid paternity action enforcement often conflicts with sound casework principles, it could be argued that abolition of legal liability for paternity would imply a lessening of moral standards. It is to these broader social policy considerations that we now turn.

D. An Evaluation of Legal Policies Aimed at Illegitimacy

PROBLEM

Ten years ago Mary married George, and they had a child, Lucy, now seven years old. George died five years ago and Mary never remarried. Three years ago Mary gave birth to a daughter, Joy. In a subsequent paternity proceeding the court found that Henry was the father and ordered him to pay $20 a week for Joy's support. At that time Henry was married to Anita, by whom he had had a son, Sammy, now five years old. Recently Mary died following a short illness, and Henry and Anita were killed in an airplane crash. Neither Mary nor Henry left a will, but both left considerable estates.

Statutes of the jurisdiction contain the following provisions:

Sec. 1. If a woman dies, leaving illegitimate children, or the legitimate descendants of deceased illegitimate children and no lawful issue, such children or descendants inherit her estate as if such children were legitimate.

Sec. 2. If the deceased was illegitimate, and leaves a mother, and no child, or descendant, or surviving spouse, such mother shall take the whole estate . . . If the mother of such deceased be dead, the relatives of the deceased on the side of the mother shall take in the same manner as if the deceased had been legitimate . . .

Sec. 3. The estate of a decedent not disposed of by will or otherwise shall descend as hereinafter provided . . .

Sec. 3.2. The share of the estate, if any, to which the surviving spouse is not entitled, and the entire estate if there is no surviving spouse, shall descend in the following order: (a) to the issue of the decedent in equal shares . . .

Sec. 4. The word child or its equivalent shall be construed to include any illegitimate child, except in matters of inheritance, de-

---

[60] Brower, What Shall I Do with My Baby?, 12 The Child 166, 169 (1948).

scent, or distribution of real and personal property, unless such a construction would be unreasonable.

In litigation involving settlement of Mary's estate, counsel appointed for Mary's illegitimate child, Joy, claims half the estate for Joy. Among the arguments advanced by Joy's counsel is that the foregoing statutes are unconstitutional. In a preliminary oral skirmish counsel says:

The statutory pattern imposing such gross disabilities upon inno- cent children is patently irrational and discriminatory. It is well settled that a legislative classification must be reasonably related to the purposes of a statute. Cf. Skinner v. Oklahoma ex rel. William- son, 316 U.S. 535 (1942). Even with respect to Goessart v. Cleary, 335 U.S. 464 (1948), where a divided Court upheld a statute provid- ing that no female could be licensed as a bartender unless she was the wife or daughter of the male owner of a licensed liquor establish- ment, an argument could be made that the alleged discrimination was to protect the morals and safety of the particular class involved. Here, however, in no conceivable way can the statutes be construed as advancing the welfare of illegitimate children.

Rather, the policy of these statutes is capriciously to select Joy and penalize her in order to carry out the state's policy of discouraging illegitimacy, even though Joy herself had no responsibility for her own illegitimacy. In the Kirchner case, the California Supreme Court struck down a statute which made a daughter liable for the support of her involuntarily committed mother in a state mental hos- pital. The court found that civil commitment of the mentally ill served the state function of protecting society, as well as protecting and possibly reclaiming the confined person, and that the cost of such a state function "cannot be arbitrarily charged to one class in the society." [61]

It is also well settled that a classification can be invalid because it is repugnant to our basic notions of equality. See Edwards v. Cali- fornia, 314 U.S. 160 (1941), holding invalid a statute which discrimi- nated against indigents attempting to enter California. While the majority in that case went no further than to reach this result on the commerce clause, there is undoubtedly general agreement today with Mr. Justice Jackson's concurring opinion finding a violation of the equal protection clause and stating: "The mere state of being with- out funds is a neutral fact — constitutionally an irrelevance, like race, creed, or color." [62] See particularly the line of equal protection

---

[61] Dept. of Mental Hygiene v. Kirchner, 60 Cal. 2d 716, 720, 388 P.2d 720, 722 (1964), vacated, 380 U.S. 194 (1965) (remand by Supreme Court because of uncer- tainty whether state judgment rested solely on equal protection clause of the four- teenth amendment or also on equivalent provisions of California constitution), former state judgment reiterated, 62 Cal. 2d 586, 400 P.2d 321 (1965) (judgment rests on state law, but court also reiterates view that same result compelled by fourteenth amendment).

[62] Edwards v. California, 314 U.S. 160, 181, 184-185 (1941) (concurring opinion).

cases that have followed Griffin v. Illinois, 351 U.S. 12 (1956), particularly Draper v. Washington, 372 U.S. 487 (1963). These decisions have stressed the fact that in criminal appeal practice even the laudable objective of restricting frivolous appeals to save unnecessary expenditures of a state's money and judicial resources cannot be accomplished by methods which draw invidious discriminations against indigent defendants. In these cases the courts protected persons already convicted of a crime. Will they do less for Joy, whose only wrong was the manner in which she was conceived? Surely in this day and age the bar sinister is as much an irrelevance constitutionally as is poverty.

The blatant discrimination of the statute is also apparent from a comparison of §2 with §1. How can the discrepancy between these sections be justified on any rational grounds?

I concede that Mary could have left a will discriminating against one or both of her daughters. But she did not do so, and for the state to step in and exclude Joy, who is every bit as much the fruit of her mother's body as Lucy, is an arbitrary act which violates Joy's rights under the equal protection clause of the fourteenth amendment.

1. You represent the child Lucy; prepare to argue that she should take Mary's entire estate.

2. Would your analysis be different if you represented Henry's legitimate son, Sammy, and Joy's counsel used the same reasoning to advance Joy's claim to half of Henry's estate?

3. What sort of data would you expect counsel on both sides to utilize to document or refute the claim of Joy's lawyer that the statutory policy is "patently irrational and discriminatory"? How much of the data reproduced below would be useful? What other kinds of data would help?

This problem, like several others appearing later in this book, is designed to test your skill in applying a large body of material to resolve a specific controversy. To integrate legal and nonlegal data in a concise, well-reasoned legal argument, you will need to have studied the materials through page 128 infra and to incorporate relevant doctrine from the earlier sections of this chapter.

1. *Legal Policy and Scientific Data*

Intelligent discussion of the preceding Problem requires precision in (1) defining the social problem at issue, (2) identifying the factual assumptions upon which value judgments about the social problem are likely to be based, (3) determining the policy goals of the stipulated legislation, and (4) ascertaining whether the means adopted in the statute are reasonably related to the goals. Thus, although it is obvious that the statute in question is concerned with "the problem" of illegitimacy, it is nonetheless far from clear what acts by what persons the statute is ultimately designed to affect. At least three people are involved in every illegitimate birth transaction: child, mother, and one or more men who had intercourse with the mother during the period of possible conception. Moreover, "the problem" may not include all illegitimate births. One class of illegitimate children are those adopted shortly after birth; such babies fill the presumably useful (and socially approved) role of allowing childless couples to complete their families. Another class of illegitimate children, not always identified as part of "the problem" of illegitimacy, includes those who are raised by their mothers or other relatives without public involvement. At least if press comment and legislative activities on other fronts (see pages 117-122 infra) are taken as an index, "the problem" of illegitimacy centers upon the unwed mothers and illegitimate children who wind up on public relief. But this end product is produced only with the concurrence of all the following variables: mother and father have intercourse out of wedlock; they fail to utilize effective contraceptive devices; the mother becomes pregnant; she does not have a spontaneous abortion (miscarriage); she fails to obtain an induced abortion; the mother and father fail to get married during the nine months between conception and birth; the mother decides not to release the child for adoption, or the child is unadoptable because it fails to meet health, racial, or other criteria demanded by adopting parents or by law; and the mother, due to her poverty and the financial irresponsibility of the father, is unable to support the child without help from the taxpayers. Judgments about the statute cannot be made without first determining which of these causative variables society is trying to affect.

It is possible, however, that the statute does not respond to any clearly segregable social problem. It may simply reflect a hostile public reaction to "illegitimacy" — and constitute an indirect effort, sanctioned by history and morals, to punish illegitimate children. It is obviously very difficult to untangle such a legislative motive from others which are more appropriate, to determine why the birth of illegitimate children may arouse an urge to punish, or to estimate the strength of that urge and its precise manifestations in present society. Yet if the constitutional decision includes a judgment as to the rationality of the legislative classification, an effort must be made to answer such questions. Vincent, Unmarried Mothers 23 (1961), noted that in the early nineteen fifties in both Japan and the United States there was substantial critical "press publicity given the illegitimate children sired by U.S. troops in Japan" which grossly exaggerated the number of such children. He observed (id. at 23-24):

   The highly exaggerated estimates and severe criticisms in the U.S. and Japanese presses reflected attitudes which ostensibly were extremely censorious of illegitimacy in general and of unmarried fathers in particular. However, we interpret them as having been primarily a means enabling the Japanese people covertly to express their growing resentment of American occupation troops and policies; and a means enabling the American people covertly to express their solicitous concern, if not guilt, about the use and consequences of the Atomic bomb. . . . [This] press publicity . . . was far more critical of the 3490 illegitimate children sired by U.S. servicemen in

Japan *over a period of several years* than of the approximately 20,000 indigenous illicit births and one million abortions in Japan *each year* during the middle 1950's.

If a court were persuaded that the disability statute in question exemplified such a "displacement phenomenon," what, if any, bearing would this have on the constitutional issue?

Even if a court were to decide that the expression of public hostility to illegitimacy constituted an appropriate legislative goal, public opinion might in fact be neutral or perhaps even opposed to imposing disabilities on illegitimates, in which case the statute may be no more than a monument to the lag between changes in public mores and law reform. But recourse to public opinion data entails very difficult technical and scientific problems.[63] How should the public attitude be measured? Should the public attitude toward premarital intercourse be determined from what people say they believe when queried by a pollster or from what they have actually done in their own lives as determined by a researcher like Kinsey? Whichever criterion is selected, such a determination involves the familiar problem of ensuring that the sample studied is representative of the population whose opinion is our concern. Determining what constitutes an adequate sample, the methods of obtaining representative data from the sample selected, and the extent to which findings can be generalized to a broader population are all technical questions for experts. The attempt by Cohen, Robson, and Bates to apply polling techniques to a random sample of a state population in order to ascertain the community's verbal opinion on some relatively simple and emotionally uncharged family law issues indicates how difficult such an enterprise can be.[64] Yet even if the technical problems can be resolved, a basic policy issue remains: is it necessary or desirable that there be a concurrence of legislative policy and public opinion? A criticism of the polling research of Cohen, Robson, and Bates questioned whether the role of law making should be "an effort to 'narrow the distance between lawmakers and their subjects'; i.e., to make 'popular' law." Rather, it was suggested that we should be "engaged in making rational, useful law which we hope can be popularized by education." "[A]s respects law reform, precise knowledge of prevailing public attitudes can hardly do more than indicate the limit of mass tolerance for immediate changes."[65]

[63] See, e.g., Blum & Kalven, The Art of Opinion Research: A Lawyer's Appraisal of an Emerging Science, 24 U. Chi. L. Rev. 1 (1956).

[64] Cohen, Robson & Bates, Parental Authority and the Law (1958).

[65] Schwartz, Comment, 8 J. Legal Ed. 319, 320 (1955). For the original statement of Cohen, Robson, and Bates which led to this exchange, see Ascertaining the Moral Sense of the Community, id. at 137, 141: "If the ascertainment of the moral sense of the community is relevant to the lawmaking process, either as a norm for the lawmaker to consider or as a norm to follow, it is our view that it need not be left to conjecture, to hunch, or to intuition, and that modern social science techniques could more reliably be utilized for the task." See also id. at 469 for the social scientists' reply to Professor Schwartz's comment.

Compare the account of Professor Adam Podgórecki of the University of Warsaw of the method followed in Poland in the preparation of the Family and

Even if it is clear that the legislation seeks appropriate goals — e.g., reinforcing family stability by deterring illegitimate births — the statutory means must be reasonably related to those goals. Resolution of the underlying issues might, but does not always, involve a number of factual investigations. For example, the assumed magnitude of "the illegitimacy problem" may have an important bearing on one's judgment about the reasonableness of the methods chosen by the legislature to deal with the problem. Is the purported rise in illegitimacy substantial and an alarming new crisis, is the increase substantial but nothing new, or is the rise slight or illusory? Moreover, the statutory means themselves merit careful investigation. If the disability legislation makes assumptions as to the personality or economic characteristics of women who give birth to illegitimate children, are those assumptions warranted? Does the legislation affect the incidence of illegitimacy or the stability of the family? Would abolition of the disabilities cause a rise in the illegitimate birth rate, or, conversely, if the sanctions against unwed motherhood and the disabilities were made more drastic and were more vigorously enforced, would the illegitimate birth rate decline? Investigation of other social phenomena closely related to illegitimacy is also warranted; tinkering with a complex social problem is likely to have not one but many results. Thus changes in legal sanctions against illegitimacy might affect not only the illegitimate birth rate, but also the incidence of induced abortions, forced marriages, falsification of birth records, or sale of babies on the adoption black market.

Although it is important to amass and analyze all relevant factual data, we must recognize that legislatures and courts often have to act on insufficient or inconclusive data. Assumptions thus cannot be avoided, but if the process is conscious, it may be possible to identify the assumptions and to estimate their reliability.

The materials that follow include a small sample of the data which may be relevant to the constitutional issue posed in the Problem. In light of the preceding comments, the data will appear to emphasize primarily how

Guardianship Code of 1965: "The characteristic and common trait of all the laws enacted by the Seym [legislature] is the method used in drafting them. Prior to this the chief basis for legislative proposals was the individual experience of experts on the theory of law and of celebrated practitioners (primarily professors of law and judges of the Supreme Court). Now, however, other persons have been included. In the method now adopted collective experience is drawn upon, hence a sort of nation-wide poll is addressed to the entire population of the country. In this manner various categories of persons and institutions are called upon to give their opinion on a given draft measure. Among these are: professors of law, judges, lawyers, prosecutors, legal counsellors, civic guardians, educators, women's and youth organizations, physicians." Podgórecki, Family Law, Poland [Illustrated Magazine], Sept. 1965, p. 28a. Among the examples cited is the Code provision raising the minimum age of marriage for men from eighteen to twenty-one, adopted after determining that 98.7 per cent of "the test sample of [the] adult population" opposed a minimum as low as eighteen years. Ibid. Podgórecki also states that the new Code embodies the "elimination of the concept of illegitimate children," but does not state how this was done or whether this issue was submitted to the public. Ibid.

little we still know about the subject of illegitimacy. Yet our ignorance is itself relevant: to what extent should our insufficient knowledge be taken into account in formulating statutory policy or in ruling on constitutional questions?

a. STATISTICS — NUMBERS, RATES, AND SOME FACTORS ASSOCIATED WITH RATES

TABLE 1. ESTIMATED NUMBER OF ILLEGITIMATE LIVE BIRTHS BY COLOR, AND ILLEGITIMACY RATES AND RATIOS: UNITED STATES, 1940-1962

Year	Number			Rate	Ratio		
	Total	White	Nonwhite	Total	Total	White	Nonwhite
1962	245,100	93,500	147,500	21.5	58.8	27.5	229.9
1960	224,300	82,500	141,800	21.8	52.7	22.9	215.8
1958	208,700	74,600	134,100	21.0	49.6	20.9	212.3
1956	193,500	67,500	126,000	20.2	46.5	19.0	204.0
1954	176,600	62,700	113,900	18.3	44.0	18.2	198.5
1952	150,300	54,100	96,200	15.6	39.1	16.3	183.4
1950	141,600	53,500	88,100	14.1	39.8	17.5	179.6
1948	129,700	54,800	74,900	12.5	36.7	17.8	164.7
1946	125,200	61,400	63,800	10.9	38.1	21.1	170.1
1944	105,200	49,600	55,600	9.0	37.6	20.2	163.4
1942	96,500	42,000	54,500	8.0	34.3	16.9	169.2
1940	89,500	40,300	49,200	7.1	37.9	19.5	168.3

Source: Selected years from 1 Vital Statistics of the United States 1962, p. 1-18, Table 1-21; 1 Vital Statistics of the United States 1958, p. 3-27, Table 3-W.

The figures are based on information from birth records in the thirty-five states which record illegitimacy, adjusted to include an estimate from the states not reporting this item. Estimates are rounded to the nearest hundred without being adjusted to group totals which are independently rounded. No adjustment is made for misstatements concerning legitimacy on birth certificates or for illegitimate births which are not registered.

The *rate* is per 1000 unmarried female population aged fifteen to forty-four years.

The *ratio* is per 1000 total live births in specified groups.

NOTE

Any remotely useful measure of illegitimacy must start by counting illegitimate births. While the raw totals which are thus cumulated may be of value for some purposes, e.g., to guide social agencies in program planning, for most purposes we are more interested in trends, and we seek to neutralize the influence of factors which a priori we decide are irrelevant to the phenomenon of illegitimacy. Thus within a given city over a twenty-year period the number of illegitimate births may double. Social agencies might then be required to employ more social workers to handle the increased caseload, but if concurrently the city's population has tripled, our analysis of the "illegitimacy problem" is likely to be different than if the increased gross illegitimacy occurred against a background of a declining total population. The second problem, therefore, is to determine what base to use in constructing an index which will give us the best indication of changes and trends in illegitimacy. Choice of a base line against which to measure the change may have a critical effect on the resulting index; compare, for example, the percentage change between 1940 and 1962 according to each of the two indexes in Table 1.

TABLE 2. NUMBER, PERCENT, AND RATE OF ILLEGITIMATE
BIRTHS IN 1938, 1957, AND 1962, BY AGE OF MOTHER

			Age of Unmarried Mother				
Year	Under 15	15-19	20-24	25-29	30-34	35-39	40 and Over
			Number of Illegitimate Births				
1938	2,000	40,400	26,400	10,000	5,000	3,100	1,000
1957	4,600	76,400	60,500	29,800	18,000	9,400	2,800
1962	5,100	94,400	77,300	34,000	19,800	11,100	3,200
Change from 1938 to 1957	+130%	+89%	+129%	+198%	+260%	+204%	+180%
Change from 1957 to 1962	+12%	+24%	+28%	+14%	+11%	+18%	+14%
			Per cent of All Illegitimate Births				
1938	2.3	45.9	30.0	11.4	5.6	3.5	1.2
1957	2.3	37.9	30.0	14.8	9.0	4.7	1.4
1962	2.1	38.5	31.5	13.9	7.7	4.5	1.3
Change from 1938 to 1957	0	−18%	0	+30%	+61%	+35%	+20%
Change from 1957 to 1962	−7%	+2%	+5%	−6%	−14%	−4%	−4%
			Rate of Illegitimacy (per [1000] unmarried females)				
1938	0.3	7.5	9.2	6.8	4.8	3.4	1.1
1957	0.6	15.6	36.5	37.6	26.1	12.7	3.3
1962	0.6	14.9	41.8	46.4	27.0	15.1	3.8
Change from 1938 to 1957	+100%	+108%	+297%	+453%	+444%	+274%	+200%
Change from 1957 to 1962	0	−4%	+14%	+23%	+3%	+19%	+16%

Source: Vincent, Illegitimacy in the Next Decade: Trends and Implications, 43 Child Welfare 513, 514 (1964).

An index which reports only an ultimate or global measurement of a phenomenon will probably be crude and can be seriously misleading.[66]

[66] For a helpful and not forbiddingly technical discussion illustrated with research which attempted to separate the relationships of such factors as wetness, Catholicism, and urbanization to Al Smith's vote in the 1928 presidential election in counties, see Stouffer, Problems in the Application of Correlation to Sociology, 29 J. Am. Statistical Assn. 29, Supp. 52-58 (1934), reprinted in Stouffer, Social Research to Test Ideas 264 (1962). Stouffer notes (ibid.): "Sociologists are gradually discovering that there is rather little place for simple correlation between two variables in their field. As Frank A. Ross said, . . . a sociological problem seldom involves a simple relationship between A and B, but usually involves a relationship between A, B, C, D, and other factors."

Thus a third problem in the measurement of trends or changes concerns the refinement of precisely what is to be measured. Consider, for example, a governor's commission stimulated by the publicity given teen-age illegitimacy having only the total numbers and rates reported in Table 1 before it; on the basis of this data it urges a crash preventive program to combat the rising tide of illegitimacy. Because it assumes that the rising rate reflects at least in part an accelerating breakdown of youth morality, it recommends concentrating the state's limited resources on work with teen-age girls. When, however, the variable of mother's age is controlled, as reported in Table 2, a much more complex picture emerges. Even if one accepts for this purpose the commission's assumption of a correlation between a rise in illegitimacy rates and immorality, it is hardly self-evident that it is the teenagers who stand in direst need of moral rehabilitation.

Mother's age is only one of an indefinite number of criteria or variables which might be isolated in an attempt to evaluate the meaning of our overall illegitimacy statistics. The availability of statistics on this factor is probably an accident — custom has dictated that age of the mother, like her race (see Table 1), be included in birth records, and the data are therefore relatively accessible. Deliberate selection of criteria by which to judge possible causal factors of illegitimacy and the testing of these criteria or hypotheses by research remains largely a task for the future.

Problems are posed at all three levels of this measurement process — counting, base determination, and selection of differentiating criteria to study separate elements of the overall phenomenon.

1. In examining the total number of illegitimate births, consider the following counting problems.

a. As the title of Table 1 indicates, the national totals are only estimated figures, and among the quarter of our jurisdictions which do not record and tabulate illegitimate births (ostensibly to benefit the illegitimate by keeping any indication of his status off his birth record) are such key states as New York, California, and Massachusetts. The estimates are derived by dividing the country into nine geographic divisions. To compute the number of illegitimate births in each division, the illegitimacy ratio of the reporting states is applied to the total number of live births in that division. See Illegitimate Births: United States, 1938-57, 47 Vital Statistics — Special Reports 225, 248 (No. 8, 1960) (hereinafter Special Reports). Thus for New England, one of the geographic divisions, the ratio in Maine and Rhode Island, which report illegitimate births, is used as the basis for estimating the number of illegitimate births in the nonreporting states of Connecticut, Massachusetts, New Hampshire, and Vermont. Id. at 247. One noteworthy aspect of this procedure is that although the illegitimacy rate is generally preferred to the illegitimacy ratio as a more meaningful index, the national rate is computed in part by extrapolating from the ratio in reporting states to make up for the lack of data in the nonreporting states.

Although these deficiencies are not the fault of the National Office of Vital Statistics, they do illustrate the difficulties of research in social science, where critical data are simply not available and can be obtained only at great expense. A national statistician can do nothing about states which as a matter of policy refuse to tabulate illegitimate births, and since population estimates for unmarried women are available only on a national basis, it is impossible to compute state illegitimacy rates. Id. at 243. The problem, therefore, is one of sampling: are illegitimacy patterns in Maine and Rhode Island sufficiently representative of all of New England to warrant generalizing from those two states to the whole region? The lawyer is not expected to answer that question;

> for any substantial statistical problem in sampling, a technician must be consulted. The great difficulty, however, is not in the statistical problems of sampling, but in determining and dealing with the characteristics which must be accounted for if the findings of a study are to be generalized beyond the population actually sampled . . . .[67]

As will be noted below in connection with our examination of Vincent, Unmarried Mothers (1961), a plausible hypothesis is that some (but not all) classes of unwed mothers migrate to a large city in another state to have their babies, in order that birth and subsequent surrender of the baby for adoption can be as anonymous as possible. It may also be that some of these mothers deliberately select a state that does not record the fact of illegitimacy. To the extent that Maine mothers go to Boston to achieve such anonymity, the incidence of illegitimacy is artificially reduced in Maine and inflated in Massachusetts; yet the Massachusetts incidence is statistically derived from the Maine ratio. Beyond this kind of doubt, we know that for the thirty-five reporting states whose data were collected in the Special Reports, the ratios varied markedly from state to state; the white ratio decreased from 58.8 (D.C.) to 11.3 (Utah); the non-white from 324.0 (Del.) to 88.6 (Wash.) and 41.8 (Utah). Special Reports 249-250. Even within a single state there are striking and largely unexplained differences; among the eight largest cities in Ohio, for example, the range of the white ratio is 17.0 to 44.5, of the nonwhite 140.3 to 275.8. Id. at 245.

b. "Probably the most important deficiency in these data arises from misstatements on the record concerning the legitimacy of birth." Id. at 246. Whether a given child is recorded as legitimate or illegitimate depends upon the information supplied by the mother and the thorough-

---

[67] Herzog, Some Guide Lines for Evaluative Research 58 (U.S. Children's Bureau Pub. No. 375, 1959). This 100-odd-page booklet, which includes an extensive bibliography, was written "chiefly for the use of administrators and others who are considering setting up evaluative research in their agencies or are wanting to know how much reliance to put on the reported findings of such studies." (From the Foreword, unpaginated, by Children's Bureau Chief Oettinger.) The particular problem dealt with concerns research which seeks to determine "the effectiveness of efforts to bring about social or emotional change in individuals," ibid., e.g., psychiatric therapy or social work counseling. Herzog's discussion of the formidable difficulties of such research and her explanation of the technical problems would be helpful to many lawyers.

ness of the recording official (doctor, hospital nurse, local clerk). The latter may simply assume that the mother is married, he may ask a casual question, or he may conduct a close cross-examination. Herzog states:

> Before depending on any measurement or rating, it is necessary to assess its *reliability*. That is, it is necessary to determine to what extent the differences it reveals arise from inconsistencies in the measuring or rating rather than from differences in what is measured or rated. . . .[68]

We have no estimate of the amount of error which is introduced when legitimacy is determined from rigorous questioning of the mother, i.e., what proportion of mothers are persistent and successful liars. More important, we can only speculate as to the extent to which differences in rates between older and younger women, or between white and nonwhite women, or between middle-class women and women on relief, reflect not differences in the actual incidence of illegitimacy in these categories but inconsistency in the way the information is obtained. It is at least plausible that a higher proportion of actual illegitimacy is discovered and recorded if the mother is young or nonwhite or poor and that the data are therefore somewhat unreliable.

c. In 1940 the estimated completeness of birth registration was 94.0 per cent for the white population and 81.3 per cent for the nonwhite; in 1958 the respective figures were 99.3 per cent and 96.1 per cent. 1 Vital Statistics of the United States 1958, p. 3-16. What weight should be given to this fact in analyzing the data?

d. The data record births, i.e., numbers of children, but from the standpoints of social welfare planning, legal policy, or the significance of apparent racial differences, it is the number of unwed mothers that is significant, for only the mothers can be deterred or aided. Particularly when comparing the white with the nonwhite population, significant error may creep in by making assumptions about the number of mothers that are derived from data about the children. See, e.g., Vincent, Unmarried Mothers 58 (1961), who reports on 467 unwed mothers in Alameda County, California, in 1952-1954. The 246 white mothers stated that they had had 262 illicit births; the 221 Negro mothers, 403 illicit births.

e. The statistics do not include some categories of children who may be regarded as illegitimate in the eyes of the law, e.g., children of void or de facto marriages which are legally ineffective, but who are treated as legitimate for the purpose of hospital records.

The combined weight of these possible counting errors may underlie the Kinsey observation that "The actual facts might multiply the official figures several times." [69]

---

[68] Id. at 37 (emphasis supplied).
[69] Kinsey, Pomeroy, Martin & Gebhard, Sexual Behavior in the Human Female 326 (1953).

2. The base from which the rate is computed is the number of women who are at risk, i.e., the unmarried females of specified age. The size of this base has declined in recent decades. Thus for the 25-29 age group, where the illegitimacy rate has shown its largest increase (see Table 2), the number of unmarried women declined 46.3 per cent between 1938 and 1957.[70] The base for the ratio is the number of all live births; the ratio is thus affected not only by the age and marital composition of the female population but by the fertility rate of married women, and "its value as an analytical tool is limited."[71] From 1945 to 1959 the overall fertility rate increased from 86 to 120 births per 10,000 women aged fifteen to forty-four years.[72]

In 1958 out-of-wedlock births represent about one percentage point more than in 1938, as a proportion of all live births. . . . [G]radually, over a considerable period, births out of wedlock have shown the same tendency to increase that characterizes all births. . . . Why should the things that make total births go up also affect illegitimate births?[73]

3. An examination of Table 1 shows startling apparent differences between the total illegitimacy rate, the white ratio, and the nonwhite ratio. This has provoked an attempt to find cultural explanations to account for the difference. One is what Herzog calls "the slavery-specific culture thesis: that is, the proposition that illegitimacy rates among low-income Negroes derive primarily from a 'Negro culture' produced by the situation under slavery."[74] Herzog questions this proposition, both because "slavery is a hundred years behind us" and because "some characteristics lumped under the slavery-legacy label are characteristically found also among low-income whites."[75] Certainly to some extent this is true; the social pressures that tend to produce conformity to prevailing mores among the middle and upper classes will be much less significant among those who live in poverty, whether they are white or Negro. But the prejudice and segregation which has depressed the Negro culture economically and effectively isolated low-income Negroes from the dominant white culture is a process which is to considerable degree unique to the Negro, and its antecedents are certainly an exclusively Negro heritage.[76]

---

[70] Illegitimate Births: United States, 1938-57, 47 Vital Statistics — Special Reports 225, 232 (No. 8, 1960).

[71] Id. at 229.

[72] Adams & Gallagher, Some Facts and Observations about Illegitimacy, 10 Children 43 (1963).

[73] Herzog, Unmarried Mothers: Some Questions to Be Answered and Some Answers to Be Questioned, 41 Child Welfare 339, 341 (1962).

[74] Id. at 347.

[75] Id. at 347-348.

[76] Compare the discussion of the very high Negro illegitimacy rates in Caribbean countries. E.g., Goode, Norm Commitment and Conformity to Role-Status Obligations, 66 Am. J. Soc. 246, 255 n.34 (1960): "An apparently widespread structural characteristic of the lower-class family [in the Caribbean] is its social isola-

Prior to the Civil War all slaves were by law illegitimate, and the case law of the time rings with phrases reminiscent of the English common law on bastardy, e.g., "the father of a slave is unknown to our law." [77] Not only did Southern law refuse any recognition to slave marriages,[78] but it was unable to devise any method to protect the de facto families which existed.[79] No segment of our white population was subjected to any comparable cultural force.

However plausible such a theory may be, there remains considerable question about its significance. The slavery hypothesis assumes that the nonwhite population (which is more than 90 per cent Negro) has a higher illegitimacy rate, and by seeking an explanation in Negro history and culture, seeks to suggest a causal relationship. Our discussion of reliability has indicated that inconsistency in the way illegitimacy data are collected casts doubt on at least the size of the apparent discrepancy between white and nonwhite rates. Even if the data are technically reliable in the sense that white and nonwhite data are collected consistently, it does not follow that the resulting differences have validity. The distinction between reliability and validity is worth emphasis: "By reliability is meant: Does the index measure something consistently? By validity is meant: Granted that the index measures something consistently, is it really describing what we think it is describing?" [80] It is self-evident that if data lack reliability, there can be no validity; thus in our problem if the figures do not accurately reflect the relative rates of white and nonwhite illegitimacy, they tell nothing about a possible real correlation between race and illegitimacy. Even if the data are reliable, however, validity does not necessarily follow. An essential aspect of research is controlled observation, so that a limited number of things are observed, while other variables are being controlled or randomized. Absent such control, if a number of different and possibly causal elements contribute to a research result, it is impossible to determine the extent to which each contributes, if at all, to the final product.

Tables 3 and 4 and the Notes which follow illustrate some of the factors besides race which have not been adequately controlled in research on illegitimacy and which raise questions about the validity of the apparent correlation between race and illegitimacy.

---

tion and, correspondingly, the social isolation of the adolescent girl" from wider community pressures to induce what that wider community regards as socially appropriate behavior. See also Dept. of Labor, The Negro Family (1965) (the so-called Moynihan report).

[77] Frazier v. Spear, 2 Bibb 385 (Ky. 1811). Many fascinating cases on family law under American slavery are included in Catterall, Judicial Cases Concerning American Slavery and the Negro (1932).

[78] Cobb, Law of Negro Slavery 242-243 (1858).

[79] See, for example, id. at 246, where Cobb expressed his concern because of the law's impotence against separation by sale of slave families, but was unable to suggest any remedy save an appeal to "Christian philanthropy" because the law could not "fasten upon the master of a female slave, a vicious corrupting Negro."

[80] Stouffer, Social Research to Test Ideas 265 (1962).

TABLE 3. FAMILY INCOME, UNITED STATES, 1961

				Cumulative per cent, stated amount or less		
Total money income	*Total*	*White*	*Nonwhite*	*Total*	*White*	*Nonwhite*
Number (thousands)	46,341	41,888	4,453	46,341	41,888	4,453
Per cent	100.0	100.0	100.0	100.0	100.0	100.0
Under $1,000	5.0	4.2	12.7	5.0	4.2	12.7
$1,000 to $1,499	3.6	3.1	9.0	8.6	7.3	21.7
$1,500 to $1,999	4.1	3.5	9.0	12.7	10.8	30.7
$2,000 to $2,999	8.7	7.8	16.8	21.4	18.6	47.5
$3,000 to $3,999	9.4	9.1	12.7	30.8	27.7	60.2
$4,000 to $4,999	10.5	10.3	11.7	41.3	38.0	71.9
$5,000 to $7,999	31.0	32.4	18.1	72.3	70.4	90.0
$8,000 and over	27.6	29.4	10.3	—	—	—
Median income	$5,737	$5,981	$3,191	—	—	—

Source: Adapted from Income of Families and Persons in the United States: 1961, Current Population Reports, Series P.-60, No. 39, March 14, 1963, Table 18, p. 26.

To abridge this table some income categories have been consolidated and percentages added; hence totals do not round off to exactly 100.0 per cent.

Family income is the total income of two or more related persons living together; for the income of unrelated individuals by race, see the second part of the same table, omitted here. The pattern for unrelated individuals is similar but the median income is markedly lower.

EXCERPTS FROM THE KINSEY STUDIES

[The text on the incidence of premarital coitus which follows is excerpted from Kinsey, Pomeroy, Martin & Gebhard, Sexual Behavior in the Human Female 287-304 (1953) (hereinafter Female Behavior); Table 4, dealing with outcomes of premarital conceptions, is adapted from three tables in Gebhard, Pomeroy, Martin & Christenson, Pregnancy, Birth and Abortion 78, 161, 178 (1958) (hereinafter Pregnancy).

[Data reported in both volumes are derived from the thousands of case histories obtained by the Institute for Sex Research at Indiana University, founded by Kinsey. Substantially the same case histories are used in both reports, although of the sample used in Pregnancy, about six per cent of the case histories were collected after data gathering for Female Behavior was closed, while some cases used in Female Behavior were excluded from Pregnancy. See Female Behavior at 43, Pregnancy at 11 n.1, 15.

[The principal sample in both studies consisted of white nonprison females; 5940 case histories were used in Female Behavior (at 22), and 5293 in Pregnancy (at 11). The composition of the sample, method of obtaining the data, and problems of sampling and reliability are discussed in detail in Female Behavior at 22-57 (sampling) and 58-97 (the data and its sources). As described in Pregnancy at 15-17, the sample was almost entirely urban and heavily concentrated in the Northeast and North Central regions. About four fifths of the sample were women aged 16-30 at the time their histories were taken. By years of education, 2.3 per cent had 0-8 years; 15.3 per cent, 9-12 years; 60.8 per cent, 13-16 years; 21.6 per cent, 17 or more years. The authors state (Pregnancy at 17):

While the sample, taken as a whole, can be used as a basis for inferences only for the educationally upper 20 per cent of the U.S. population, it should be said that as the sample is subdivided, some of its categories (e.g., the high school educated) provide findings applicable to larger segments of the urban white population. . . .

[The separate and much smaller samples of Negro nonprison, Negro prison, and white prison women which are reported in part of Table 4 are briefly described in the Notes following Table 4.]

Very nearly 50 per cent of the females who were married by age twenty had had pre-marital coitus. Similarly those who were married between ages twenty-one and twenty-five had had pre-marital coitus in nearly 50 per cent of the cases. Those who were married between the ages of twenty-six and thirty had had pre-marital coitus in something between 40 and 66 per cent of the cases. . . . [Page 287.]

. . . Restricting our data [about those who had premarital coitus] to the married females in the sample, because they had completed their premarital histories, the record shows that 53 per cent had had coitus with only a single partner prior to marriage. A third (34 per cent) had had coitus with two to five partners, and 13 per cent had had coitus with six or more . . . However, it should be pointed out again that the sample does not adequately represent the lower educational levels, and we do not have sufficient information to predict whether the data from those groups would show a greater or lesser promiscuity. Neither does the sample include histories of females who had done time in penal institutions, and our calculations show that that group is much more promiscuous in its pre-marital activity. Consequently, the present record is based on only middle class and upper social level females. While the promiscuity in these groups may surprise some persons, it does not approach the promiscuity of the male.

Among the married females in the sample who had had pre-marital coitus, 87 per cent had had at least a portion of it with the men whom they subsequently married . . . Some 46 per cent had confined their coitus to the fiancé. This means that 41 per cent of all the females who had had any such coitus had had it with both the fiancé and with other males. Some 13 per cent had had it with other males but not with the fiancé. In this respect, females of the older and younger generations represented in the sample had not been particularly different. Among the females who had married at an earlier age, a somewhat higher percentage (54 per cent) had had pre-marital coitus with the fiancé only, while among those who did not marry until they were past thirty, only 28 per cent had confined their coitus to the fiancé. . . .

. . . If calculations of the accumulative incidences of pre-marital coitus are based upon the total sample, irrespective of the age of marriage, there appears to have been a marked correlation between the educational levels which the females had ultimately attained, the ages at which they began their pre-marital coitus, and the percentages which were ultimately involved . . . The females in the grade school sample had started coitus five or six years before the females in the graduate sample. Ultimately only 30 per cent of the grade school group had had pre-marital coitus, in contrast to 47 per cent of the high school group and more than 60 per cent of the girls who had gone on into college. Strangely enough, these findings appear to be diametrically contrary to the record which we secured . . . from the pre-marital coital histories of the males in our sample. For instance, about 67 per cent of the males who had gone on to college, but 98 per cent of certain of the male groups which had never gone beyond grade school, had had coitus before marriage.

Further analyses indicate, however, that these correlations between the female's pre-marital coital history and her educational background are wholly dependent upon the fact that marriage occurs, on an average, at quite different ages in these several educational levels . . .

Among the females who had married at a given age, approximately the same percentages had had pre-marital coitus, irrespective of whether they belonged to high school, college, or graduate groups . . . This was true for the females who had married between the ages of sixteen and twenty, for the females who had married between the ages of twenty-one and twenty-five, and for those who had married between the ages of twenty-six and thirty. The close conformance of the incidence figures within any one of these groups is very striking. It emphasizes the fact that most social factors had had a minimum effect upon the pattern of sexual be-havior among the females in the sample, but whether they had or had not had pre-marital coitus had been definitely correlated with the age at which they had married. . . . We reported . . . that social factors do affect the male's pattern of sexual behavior, and a recalculation of our data on the basis of the ages at which the males had married indicates that the correlations with the educational backgrounds of the male are still real and are not eliminated by any corrections for their ages at marriage. [Pages 292-295.]

. . . Among the females in the sample who were born before 1900, less than half as many had had pre-marital coitus as among the females born in any subsequent decade . . . For instance, among those who were still unmarried by age twenty-five, 14 per cent of the older generation had had coitus, and 36 per cent of those born in the next decade. This increase in the incidence of pre-marital coitus, and the similar increase in the inci-dence of pre-marital petting, constitute the greatest changes which we have found between the patterns of sexual behavior in the older and younger generations of American females.

As in the case of pre-marital petting . . . , practically all of this in-crease had occurred in the generation that was born in the first decade of the present century and, therefore, in the generation which had had most of its pre-marital experience in the late teens and in the 1920's following the first World War. The later generations appear to have accepted the new pattern and maintained or extended it.

An examination of the possible correlations indicates that changes in the age of marriage of the females in the sample were not responsible for these decade effects. . . . [Pages 298-299.]

. . . The accumulative and active incidences of pre-marital coitus had been distinctly higher among those females in the sample who were less actively connected with religious groups, and lower among those who were most devout . . . This, in general, was true for the Protestant, Catholic, and Jewish groups. In many instances the differences between devout and inactive members of particular groups were very marked. The differences between Protestant, Catholic, and Jewish females of the same degree of devoutness were usually less than the differences between the various levels within any one religion. There appear to be no other factors which affect the female's pattern of pre-marital behavior as markedly as the decade in which she was born and her religious background.

The accumulative incidence curves for the females in the sample who had not yet married had risen at thirty-five years of age to about 63 per cent among the religiously inactive Protestants, to nearly the same point among the non-devout Jewish females, and to perhaps 55 per cent among the inactive Catholic females . . . In contrast, hardly more than 30 per cent of the devout Protestants and 24 per cent of the devout Catholics had become involved. The females who were intermediate in their religious devotion stood midway between the devout and the less devout groups. [Page 304.]

TABLE 4. OUTCOMES OF PREMARITAL CONCEPTIONS BY RACE, EDUCATION, AND PRISON STATUS

	White nonprison sample			White prison females (see Note B)		Negro nonprison sample (see Note A)			Negro prison females (see Note B)
	Years of education					Years of education			
	9-12	13-16	17 up	A	B	0-8	9-12	13 up	—
Outcome:									
Illegitimate birth	10.1	2.4	1.6	38.7	42.2	25.9	40.8	7.5	51.7
Spontaneous abortion	3.7	4.3	6.2	14.1	17.8	27.6	8.6	3.8	20.0
Induced abortion	63.3	81.7	82.9	9.9	23.3	18.9	24.7	81.2	5.5
Live birth in marriage	22.9	11.6	9.3	37.3	16.7	27.6	25.9	7.5	22.3
Total number of conceptions	109	164	129	142	90	58	81	53	145

Source: See page 84 supra.

NOTES TO TABLE 4

Note A. The Negro nonprison sample is of 572 individuals, 91 per cent urban as adults; 53 per cent aged 25 or younger; 23 per cent had had grade school, 36 per cent, high school, and 40 per cent had entered college. While characterized as Northern Negroes, 48 per cent had lived one or more years in the South. Pregnancy at 153.

Note B. Interviews with 1250 prison women (900 white, 309 Negro) were taken at three institutions. Prison A was an "institution in a midwestern state . . . populated chiefly by women convicted of misdemeanors" (id. at 169), from which 698 white and 188 Negro histories were obtained. The white population was largely small town or rural in background. Prison B derived its population from a large, eastern, almost wholly urban metropolis; 202 whites and 71 Negroes were interviewed. Prison C was a small eastern training school for Negroes and contributed 50 Negro histories. In the table, Negro prison females from all three institutions are treated together, but the whites are tabulated separately for institutions A and B. The authors state, discussing the white prison sample (id. at 180-182):

> At the lower end of the scale of the grade school educated are the impoverished, the underprivileged, the untrained, and the rejects of society. These are the women who constitute a large part of our prison sample. . . .
>
> [Among these women we find, "based upon our case histories and upon our personal impressions during interviews," that coitus] is looked upon as natural and inevitable, and as one of the chief pleasures available. Virginity is encouraged verbally but not expected. Pre-marital coitus, especially between persons contemplating marriage, is common and pre-marital pregnancy is also a frequent precursor of marriage. If the marriage does not occur, this is considered a misfortune, but the unwed mother is not stigmatized; disapproval is apt to be directed at the male who escaped the marriage. Since there is relatively little social disapproval of illegitimacy, the women do not have such a strong reason to seek an abortion. Also, for these people the cost of an abortion is often prohibitive, and many of them have a general distrust and fear of physicians. . . .
>
> . . . All these factors combine to produce a high pre-marital live birth rate and to minimize induced abortion. With induced abortion low, and in an economically depressed group, it is no surprise to find spontaneous abortion common. . . .

NOTE

1. Consider Vincent, Illegitimacy in the Next Decade: Trends and Implications, 43 Child Welfare 513, 517 (1964):

> About 70,200 illegitimate children were adopted in the United States in 1962, or 29.2 percent of the number of illegitimate children born in 1961. About 66,100 illegitimate children were adopted in 1961, or 29.4 percent of the total illegitimate children born in 1960. There does not appear to have been any great fluctuations (the range has been from about 29 percent to 31 percent) in the proportion of illegitimate children adopted during the past 20 years. Of the estimated 3 million illegitimate children under 18 years of age in the United States in December of 1961, 31 percent had been adopted. The proportions are strikingly different by race, however; 70 percent of the white and only 5 percent of the nonwhite illegitimate children under 18 years of age were adopted.

2. U.S. Bureau of Public Assistance, Illegitimacy and its Impact on the Aid to Dependent Children Program 35-36 (1960):

> Of an estimated 2.5 million surviving children registered as illegitimate at birth from 1940 through 1957, 1 million were white and 1.5 million, nonwhite. In late 1958, fewer than 10 percent of the white, and fewer than 16 percent of nonwhite, children in this group were living in aid to dependent children families in which the father had not married the mother.
>
> . . . Possibly as many as 70 percent of all white illegitimate children are given for adoption, but only between 3 and 5 percent of the nonwhite illegitimate children are adopted. . . .
>
> Of the children who are not adopted, about 30 percent of the white children and about 16 percent of the nonwhite children are receiving aid to dependent children. . . .

Even in a city like Philadelphia, with a high Negro population, a recent sample study of 777 children on ADC reported 61.6 per cent legitimate and 38.3 per cent illegitimate. Kronick, Norton & Sabesta, The Legitimacy Status of Children Receiving AFDC, 42 Child Welfare 339, 341 (1963). See also pages 68-69 supra.

b.   CHARACTERISTICS OF THE UNWED MOTHER

From a voluminous literature about unwed mothers, two illustrative examples are excerpted here. The most striking contrast between them is in methodology; as you read them, consider the following assertions:

1. Herzog, Who Are the Unmarried Mothers?, 9 Children 157, 157-158 (1962):

> The prevalent answer to the recurrent question has varied from year to year, although there are always dissenting minorities. . . .
>
> Clark Vincent presents the answers typical of different decades in brief sketches, further condensed (and oversimplified) here:

The period	*Emphasis on* —
Before 1930	"Inborn" immorality, bad companions, mental deficiency
During the 1930's	Environmental sources of behavior (poverty, broken homes)
Late 30's-early 40's	Culture, life ways
The 40's-early 50's	Psychological and psychiatric explanations
Mid- and late 50's	The sick society

> Vincent's summary (as he gives it) brings out, not only the changing emphasis, but also the fact that each successive theory was documented by reports of the particular kind of unmarried mothers that would confirm it. . . .
>
> Therefore, as Vincent comments, "much — if not most — of the existing data about unwed mothers may tell us less about factors con-

tributing to illegitimacy than about the clientele of given charity institutions, social agencies, outpatient clinics, and physicians in private practice." [81]

2. Alexander, Book Review, 41 J. Crim. L. & Criminology 751, 752-753 (1951):

A few representative cases of criminal individuals studied intensively by the psychoanalytic method reveal more about the causes of delinquency than the study of a thousand cases by more or less superficial methods. . . . Personality cannot be split up into artificial units but must be studied in its totality, in the specific configuration of its constituent parts. The study of separate trends with pseudo-quantitive measurements may produce material which is suited for statistical treatment; however, it is more or less lifeless and artificial material. . . .

YOUNG, OUT OF WEDLOCK
16-80 (1954)

A cross section of unmarried mothers reaching social agencies indicates a rather general scattering of social and economic backgrounds, with the exception of the top economic group. Girls from this group would have considerable money, and it is reasonable to assume that they or their families would handle the situation without any recourse to outside assistance and with a maximum of secrecy. . . .

Educationally they also cover a wide variation. In the absence of statistics exact distribution cannot be known. However, observation of a considerable number of unmarried mothers shows that most of them have at least completed grammar school, and many of them are high-school graduates. A much smaller percentage are college graduates, and a very few have had some type of professional training. In intelligence they seem to be pretty much representative of the population as a whole. . . .

Since only unmarried mothers who come to some type of social agency can be studied, definitive conclusions in this area are impossible. . . . [Pages 16-18.]

Why does a girl become an unmarried mother? In the past the answer was obscured by specious and erroneous preconceptions of her behavior. Whether these explanations were punitive or kindly, they lacked any solid foundation in fact. Not until the discoveries of Freud proved that human behavior is purposive, not haphazard, and demonstrated how personality is developed could the question even be raised with any hope of an accurate answer. Not until we were free to observe and record the case histories of many unmarried mothers, to consider them from a scientific rather than a moral point of view, to note similarities and contradictions, and to follow the fine thread of continuity between cause and effect could we begin to learn some of the answers to this difficult and troubling

[81] Vincent, Unmarried Mothers 21 (1961). — Ed.

problem. When certain facts appeared over and over in hundreds of cases, there was justification for assuming that they possessed real significance in the psychology of the unmarried mother. And when these facts were consistently at odds with normal behavior, they obviously required an explanation and indicated that the individual was having more than average difficulty in adjusting herself to society.

One of the first myths to disappear under the light of these facts was the idea that having an out-of-wedlock child is something that just happens. On the contrary, everything points to the purposeful nature of the act. Although a girl would obviously not plan consciously and deliberately to bear an out-of-wedlock child, she does act in such a way that this becomes the almost inevitable result. At the same time she conceals the portent of her actions from herself by various superficial explanations that rarely stand the test of objective scrutiny. . . .

An astonishing number of unmarried mothers meet the fathers of their babies in casual, unconventional fashion. They "pick up" a man in trains, in hotels, at dances and large parties, or they meet him on "blind dates" with casual acquaintances. Sometimes they have a steady "boy friend" at the same time they do this, but they show little feeling for this boy, even when he continues to stick by them, and do not have the baby by him. This sexual experience frequently occurs at a time of stress in the girl's life. It may be precipitated by her first attempt to leave home and stand on her own feet, or by strain and changes within the family, or occasionally by the legitimate pregnancy of a sister with whom she has been competitive.

Dolores, a young girl in her late teens, was a striking example of this competition. She walked into the office of an agency for unmarried mothers, seeking shelter and help. She was accompanied by her two older sisters, both married and both pregnant, who cruelly emphasized the virtue of their status by promptly producing their marriage certificates, leaving her the forlorn outcast. She had become pregnant following the knowledge of their pregnancies. Her explanation of what had happened was simply that for the first time in her life she had made alone a short journey to a neighboring city, had lost her way, and had asked directions of a man in the street. He had struck up an acquaintance with her, had accompanied her to her home town, although not to her home, and had met her by arrangement once afterward. She knew nothing further about him and had no further interest in him. She ignored the obvious fact that she must have encouraged his interest and permitted him to accompany her. That it was herself and not the case worker whom she was interested in deceiving was apparent from the absurdity of her story, which sought to fix the explanation for her actions upon the contrived and irrelevant detail of getting lost and asking directions of a man. Had she wanted to deceive others and protect herself, she would have invented a more plausible tale. She was not a stupid person. Instead she stated the literal facts and ignored totally her own part in initiating and encouraging this brief sexual contact which resulted in pregnancy. She made no conscious connection between her abrupt departure from her prior pattern of behavior and her knowledge that her two older sisters were having babies within the approved shelter of wedlock.

To observe this is clearly not to explain why this girl did what she did, but it is apparent that this was not something which just happened without interest and responsibility on her part. Up to this point, Dolores had shown a conspicuous lack of interest in boys, had been carefully sheltered in a strict, moral home by parents who sought to protect her from any such possible danger, and she had seemingly been content to remain within this protection. This was almost certainly her first sexual experience, and following the birth of her child she returned to the protection of her home.

If this were a rare or isolated case, one might consider it of little validity. But the same contradictions, discrepancies, and absurdities appear to some degree in almost every situation (with the exception of those girls coming from a cultural pattern which accepts as normal an out-of-wedlock pregnancy). Not always as obvious or as naïve as the situation described, each nevertheless shows the same basic outline. . . .

The purposive nature of her behavior appears clearly in another area. . . . Questioning of a large number of girls as to whether they had considered the use of contraceptives brought always the same response, an expression of flat astonishment and bewilderment and the answer "no." When asked whether she knew in advance that sexual intercourse might well result in pregnancy for her, every girl admitted readily and without hesitation that she had known this. The further and obvious query of why she had not then considered contraception brought only deepening confusion and the answer "I don't know; I just never thought about it." A few girls were able to take the logical next step and say, "I don't know why I did such a thing," although usually they referred to the sexual action rather than the failure to protect themselves. . . . [Pages 21-25.]

Why should a girl so blind herself? What does she want so badly that she is willing to pay so high a price for it? Only a very strong desire could motivate such extreme behavior, and only a very strong prohibition could result in such exhaustive efforts to conceal its existence from the girl herself.

Obviously, she wants a baby — but, specifically, an out-of-wedlock baby — without a husband. [Page 28.]

It is interesting to note that there is no discernible conflict in this unconscious urge. The same girl who consciously may be unable to make the simplest decision and wavers helplessly between two alternatives moves directly and decisively, however blindly, toward realizing this wish and counts no cost too great to achieve it. Whatever her relationship to the man, even if, as occasionally happens, she later marries him, the fact remains that she has a child unshared with him and belonging only to her. In a large number of cases she excludes him altogether and shows little if any continuing interest in him. . . . [Page 30.]

There can be no doubt that the drive which propels an unmarried mother results in compulsive action. To say that her behavior is the result of immorality or of free choice is to ignore all the evidence. . . . What these girls seem to be saying is that they had a compulsive necessity to act out an infantile fantasy before they could be free to be themselves as adults and do what they as adults consciously wanted to do. Interestingly, a number of these girls, who had a considerable degree of emotional health, acted in exactly this fashion. Almost without exception they placed their babies for adoption and then, as if they had really completed a necessary phase of their lives, went ahead to do new and different things which they had not felt free to tackle before. Some of them went into new fields of work, secured additional training, made new and happier living arrangements. A number of them married. One can only conclude that, having acted out this necessary fantasy successfully, they were able to let it go, put it behind them, and had sufficiently healthy personalities to move ahead and make a happier, more satisfying life for themselves on an adult level. [Page 36.]

Why does a girl have to bear a baby at such a cost to herself? The answer can only be sought in her past life, her home and her childhood. Like every human being she responds dynamically to her particular life situation. The question is what particular combination of factors and circumstances produces that psychological development which finds its expression in an out-of-wedlock child.

If one factor can be considered fundamental in the family background of unmarried mothers, it is the consistent pattern of domination of the home by one parent. With monotonous regularity one hears from girl after girl, as she describes her early life, of a family which has been shadowed by the possessiveness and unhealthy tyranny of one of the parents. . . .

The great majority of unmarried mothers come from homes dominated by the mother. The basic pattern is consistent in all of them although it varies in degree. The mother is basically a woman who has never accepted her own femininity and whose life adjustment is a constant struggle with that fact. To a greater or lesser degree she both envies and despises her husband, and she generally marries a passive man who cannot or will not oppose her domination of the family. Possessive of the children in most cases, she has been both seducing and rejecting in her attitude toward them. While much has been written about the damage done by this kind of mother to her son, she can be equally damaging to a daughter.

Anyone who has interviewed any considerable number of the mothers of unmarried mothers is familiar with the startling uniformity of their attitudes and even their way of expressing these attitudes. Over and over again one hears a mother say, "I don't see how this could have happened to my daughter. She's always been such a good girl and has never given me a moment's worry or trouble until now." . . . [Pages 39-41.]

. . . The mothers of these girls are not all equally rejecting or equally dominating, and there can be love and concern as well as possessiveness and hostility. Correspondingly the fathers are not all equally passive or equally withdrawn from relationships with their children. Nevertheless to some extent the mother consumes part of the vital area of the girl's personality and to that degree leaves her emotionally crippled. The girl loses part or sometimes all of her confidence in and ability to express her own femininity and in some cases becomes a pale shadow of her mother as well as a relatively impotent victim. Girls with this kind of family background almost invariably describe their fathers as quiet, gentle men who are "strangers" to them. They cannot discuss them as people; one gets an impression of a kind of amorphous ghost who flits about the edges of their lives. While these fathers are unquestionably passive men, they cannot possibly be as vague as their daughters describe them. It is clear that the girl has had to repress most of her knowledge of and feelings for her father. Her hazy description and her pale sympathy are all that are consciously left. She has had to make her father a stranger. Her mother has forbidden the tie between them and made anything else impossible.

Toward their mothers these girls express one of two attitudes. Most commonly they affirm their love and devotion and permit themselves no critical observations. Dependent to an infantile degree upon their mothers, they can scarcely afford the luxury of criticism or overt resentment. They often express guilt and sorrow that they have so hurt and disgraced their mothers by what they have done. A frequent remark from them is "I want to do what I can now to make up to my mother for what I've done to her. I'll do whatever she says." They describe their mothers as someone who has always taken care of them and protected them, although occasionally a girl adds that her mother was "strict." They are quite unaware that they speak like small children and with considerably less spirit and independence than the average small child. They are also unaware that their words say they "did" this to their mothers and thus indicate something of the motivation. Viewed objectively, this is something they "did" to themselves and to their babies, but for them this is largely irrelevant. The focus is on Mother.

A smaller number of them, on the other hand, express intense hate and resentment toward their mothers. Like its seeming opposite, the slavish devotion, it is a blanket emotion that permits no deviation. These girls blame their mothers for everything, deny that they ever received anything positive from them, and will go to any lengths to oppose them. While superficially their open rebellion seems healthier than the submission of their sisters, they are actually just as bound to the mother and just as exclusively focused on what she thinks and wants. What the girl herself feels and wishes and the needs of her baby are unimportant to her. What matters is to know what Mother wants and then do the opposite. The girl is unaware of the fact that she is still completely bound to her mother by her own spite and hate and that her actions but affirm and reinforce that tie. . . .

[Young then discusses the fact that "girls from this type of family background" hardly know or cannot remember the father of the child, and uses as an illustration of this class of unmarried mothers a "borderline psychotic."] A professional woman in her early thirties, she had always lived with her mother. She went out one evening on a "blind date" with another couple. At the end of the evening the two couples separated, and the man brought her home. He "raped" her in her own house with her mother asleep upstairs. When asked why she did not struggle and call out, she said that any commotion would have roused the neighbors and created a scandal. This would have embarrassed her mother as well as herself. She insisted, however, that the man had not penetrated inside of her, and hence she had refused to believe for months that she could be pregnant. Interestingly, this same woman said a few moments later that she wished to place the baby for adoption because she could not keep a child "conceived in revenge." She was unaware of the contradiction in her story but when asked, "Revenge against whom?" refused to answer. It is hard to see how that person could be anyone but her mother. . . .

All the evidence points to the fact that most of the girls in this group are truly disinterested in the actual fathers of the babies. Whether they know them or not, that basic fact remains unaltered. They do not have a poor relationship with men; they have no relationship at all. For such a girl, the man is apparently a necessary biological accessory who serves only one purpose — to make her pregnant — and then is of no further interest or concern. She is not hurt or worried when he abandons her because in a sense that is what she wanted him to do. One intelligent young woman with an unusual degree of insight remarked of the father of her baby, "I never really cared anything about him, but I felt as if I were grabbing something from him." [Pages 44-50.]

The unmarried mothers whose fathers have dominated the family are fewer in number than the girls coming from mother-dominated homes, but they too represent a distinct group, with common factors in background and personality patterns. [Page 60.] [Young then discusses this group at length at pp. 60-79, concluding that the father's rejection has convinced the girl that femininity is of little worth; such girls] not only have accepted this verdict as fact but have adopted it as their own. They act this out very clearly whether they submit to it hopelessly and gain their only satisfaction by becoming the abused victim of a man or whether they rebel impotently against it by seeking to punish and destroy the man. In neither case do they ever question the essential veracity of their conviction. They demonstrate over and over again that as women they have no value in their own eyes, no right to spontaneous and freely given admiration, love, and protection from men, no hope of ever attaining the freedom and power which they attribute only to men. With such a philosophy, the violent hate and jealousy they exhibit toward their own fathers and toward the fathers of their babies is very understandable. Their rage is insatiable because nothing they do can remove the brand of their inferiority. Nor is it surprising under these circumstances that they have little love for the babies. To a normal woman a baby is a source of joy and fulfillment; to these girls a baby is a source of power who can hopefully balance the unfair odds in their battle to compete with men. . . .

With its endless diversity and variety, human personality defies airtight classifications always. Unmarried mothers are no exception, despite the striking consistency of their patterns. There is a small group of girls who do not seem to conform to either of the psychological and family patterns previously discussed. There is no overt indication that the home has been dominated by either of the parents, nor do the girls themselves seem to follow any similar, clearly defined psychological pattern. [Pages 79-80.]

[The balance of the discussion of this "small group" is omitted, as are the chapters of the study which deal with adolescents, the effects of the social setting on the girl's unconscious motivation, the unmarried father, the illegitimate child, and a lengthy section on "Dealing with the Problem."]

VINCENT, UNMARRIED MOTHERS
55-119 (1961)

[This study reports data collected during a pilot investigation in 1952 and a full study in 1954. From the mass of data collected three kinds have been excerpted here: the social and economic characteristics of the mothers, their relationships with their sexual partners, and some data on family and personality.]

[1. THE MOTHERS' SOCIAL AND ECONOMIC BACKGROUNDS]

In January, 1953, 576 physicians representing all general practitioners, gynecologists, obstetricians, osteopaths, and surgeons in Alameda County, California, were asked to complete a questionnaire for each unwed mother they had attended in private practice within Alameda County during 1952. Four hundred and nine (71 per cent) physicians returned the questionnaire. One hundred and thirty (32 per cent) had attended at least one unwed mother; the total of unwed mothers thus attended was 252 that year.

One hundred and fifteen of these unwed mothers were divorced, separated, or married to someone other than the father of the baby. They were excluded from the study. The remaining 137 were single and had never been married, and are reported as a separate subgroup in this chapter. . . . However, the fact that they were all physicians' private patients during pregnancy undoubtedly introduced a socio-economic bias. . . . Thus we designed a survey study that would include, hopefully, *all* unwed mothers attended in Alameda County during 1954. . . .

Illegitimacy is not indicated on California birth records. Therefore, arrangements for collecting data were made with the physicians and authorities in the three situations in which unwed mothers were attended during 1954 in Alameda County, a metropolitan area with an estimated population of 838,900 in 1954.

PRIVATE PRACTICE

At the beginning of 1954, the 546 general practitioners, gynecologists, obstetricians, osteopaths, and surgeons in Alameda County were asked to keep current records . . . throughout the year on each unwed mother attended in private practice, though not those attended in the county and the maternity-home hospitals. Four hundred and eighty-four (89 per cent) returned the requested information at the end of the year. Ninety-four (30 per cent) had attended at least one unwed mother apiece; the ninety-four had attended, in total, 175 cases.

BOOTH MEMORIAL HOSPITAL

Social caseworkers administered questionnaires . . . and the California Psychological Inventory to obtain data about 189 unwed mothers attended during 1954 at the Booth Memorial Hospital (Salvation Army Maternity Home and Hospital) in Alameda County.

ALAMEDA COUNTY HOSPITAL

A questionnaire . . . and caseworkers' records provided data for the 373 unwed mothers attended during 1954 at Highland Hospital (the Alameda County Hospital).

The 736 unwed mothers in these three situations accounted for 3.2 per cent of the total 23,384 live births occurring in Alameda County during 1954.

*Table 1 — Distribution of 736 Unwed Mothers Attended
in Alameda County During 1954 (by Marital Status
and by Situation in Which Attended)*

| | Situation in Which Attended | | | |
Marital Status	Private Practice	Booth Hospital	County Hospital	Totals
Single-never-married	106	153	280	539
Divorced/Separated more than 9 months	47	21	69	137
Married, but not to baby's father	18	8	2	28
Marital status not reported	4	7	21	32
Totals	175	189	372	736

The 539 "single-never-married" mothers form the primary subjects of the data reported . . . Mothers in other marital-status categories have been excluded, since we thought that their illicit pregnancies represented phenomena quite different from those represented by the illicit pregnancies of single-never-married females. The 137 private-practice cases from the 1952 study have been reported separately [at some points for purposes of comparison but are not included in totals]. . . .

[The following two tables summarize other pertinent data about the unwed mothers.]

Table 2 — Distribution of Unwed Mothers, by Race and by Situation in Which Attended [and of all Live Births by Race] in Alameda County

Race	Situation in Which Attended				Totals (1954 only) (N=539)	All Live Births in County (1954) (N=23,284)[82]
	Private Practice 1952 (N=137)	1954 (N=106)	Booth Hospital (N=153)	County Hospital (N=280)		
	(Per cent)					
White	84	82	87	13	47	84
Negro	13	15	10	79	47	13
Other[83]	2	3	3	4	4	3
No data	1	—	—	4	2	—
	100	100	100	100	100	100

Table [3] — Distribution of Unwed Mothers, by Age and by Situation in Which Attended

Ages	Situation in Which Attended				Totals (1954 only) (N=539)
	Private Practice 1952 (N=137)	1954 (N=106)	Booth Hospital (N=153)	County Hospital (N=280)	
	(Per cent)				
17 and younger	15	18	42	29	31
18-19	21	28	22	18	21
20-21	13	17	18	17	17
22-25	33	27	13	19	18
26 and older	18	10	5	17	13
	100	100	100	100	100

Education data . . . are misleading and easily misinterpreted when age is not held constant. . . . Table [4] reports data for only those unwed mothers who were eighteen and older . . . . [It] indicates that, *when age differences are partially controlled, the educational attainment of the unwed mothers approximates that of all females in Alameda County.* This statement, based on comparisons of data in the last two columns, is qualified by several unknowns. Since information about education of females in Alameda County has been available only for women who were twenty-five and older, unwed mothers have been at a comparative disadvantage. Most of them are younger than twenty-five; some of them, presumably, will continue their educations after their pregnancies have been completed. On the other hand, including all females twenty-five and older in the comparative group would mean including older women in whose generation higher education was not emphasized as it is today. These two disadvantages may or may not cancel each other; the comparatively high educational attainment of the 285 unwed mothers who provided educational data is noteworthy, especially since 34 per cent of them were Negroes, 83 per cent of whom were attended at the county

[82] This column not included in Table 2, but taken from unnumbered table on p. 57. — Ed.
[83] Includes 13 Mexican, 1 Oriental, 2 Filipino, 2 Indian, and 2 Mexican-Indian.

hospital — less than 15 per cent of the comparative group of all Alameda County females were Negro. The educational distribution of the unwed mothers was affected by this component proportion of Negroes attended at the county hospital, as may be observed in the comparative distributions of the "whites only" and "Negroes only" columns.

Table [4] — Distribution[84] of Alameda County Unwed Mothers, Aged Eighteen and Older, in 1954, by Education, by Situation in Which Attended, and by Race: Distribution of All Alameda County Females Aged Twenty-five and Older, in 1950, by Education

	Unwed Mothers Aged Eighteen and Older						*Alameda County Females Twenty-five*
	Situation in Which Attended in 1954			*Alameda Co. Totals*			*five*
	Private Practice	*Booth Hospital*	*County Hospital*	*Whites Only*	*Negroes Only*	*All Races*	*and older in 1950* [85]
EDUCATION:				(*Per cent*)			
Completed college	29	3	—	13	3	9	9
Attended college	25	34	7	24	15	20	12
Completed high school	26	35	19	30	20	26	33
Attended high school	18	28	66	32	54	41	18
Eight years or less	2	—	8	1	8	4	28
	100	100	100	100	100	100	100
("No-Data" Cases)[86]	(3)	(—)	(84)	(13)	(74)	(87)	(—)
(Cases with Data)[84]	(84)	(89)	(112)	(175)	(96)	(285)[87]	(242,495)

[Among the facts that led to the author's conclusion that the unwed mothers "were not predominantly of low socio-economic status, nor even predominantly of any one particular socio-economic stratum" (p. 64) were data about the unwed mothers' occupations and their parents' education. Only the first category of data is reproduced here, in Table [5], which also includes the occupational distribution of the total female labor force in Alameda County.] The total female labor force in Alameda County had higher occupational attainments than the combined groups of unwed mothers, in part, because of the older ages contained in the former category. The youth of the unwed mothers undoubtedly limited their proportionate representation in the professional and managerial positions usually filled by older women.

[84] Percentages are based only on cases reporting data.

[85] Adapted from United States Census of Population: 1950 (Vol. 11, Characteristics of the Population, Part 5, California; Chap. C [Washington, 1952]), Table 42, pp. P5-162.

[86] Percentages are based only on cases reporting data. [In a footnote to an omitted table (p. 63) Vincent states that data were incomplete for many of the county hospital cases because "these unwed mothers seldom gave any advance notice to the hospital, but came as emergency cases when in labor and left within two or three days." It was usually impossible to interview them, and the social workers' records apparently were often incomplete.]

[87] Includes fourteen cases other than Negro or white.

Table [5] — Distribution[88] in Alameda County of Unwed
Mothers, by Occupational Grouping, and by Situation
in Which Attended; and of Total Female Civilian
Labor Force, by Occupational Grouping

	UNWED MOTHERS					Female
	Situation in Which Attended in					Labor Force
	Alameda County				Totals	Alameda
	Private Practice		Booth	County	1954	County
	1952	1954	Hospital	Hospital	Only	in 1950 [89]
OCCUPATION:			(Per cent)			
Professional & managerial	24	22	8	—	8	19
Clerical & sales	49	42	52	10	30	42
Craftsmen & operatives	9	11	20	22	20	16
Private household & service workers	8	5	13	19	15	18
Not working	10	20	7	39	27	9
	100	100	100	100	100	100
("No-Data" Cases)[88]	(13)	(10)	(3)	(131)	(144)	(—)
(Cases with Data)[88]	(88)	(63)	(60)	(110)	(233)[90]	(98,019)

[Omitted are data which show, inter alia, that most college educated white unwed mothers came from a state other than California, that a majority of high school white mothers and of college educated Negro mothers came from a California county other than Alameda, and that only for Negro mothers of high school or less education did the overwhelming majority come from Alameda County.]   [Pages 55-69.]

[2. UNWED MOTHERS AND THEIR PARTNERS]

. . . [W]e present pair data for illicit sex partners [in part to] posit several theoretical and research implications of the association found between the unwed mother's degree of ego-involvement in sexual relations and her socio-economic status. . . .

The increasing interest in data concerning unwed mothers coming from a variety of socio-economic levels raises the problem of a theoretical framework within which such data may be interpreted. This issue is explored here by means of data which are interpreted as showing that an unwed mother's degree of ego-involvement in sexual relations is closely associated with her socio-economic status, and that a high degree of ego-involvement demands a "primary" relationship as a prerequisite to illicit sexual intercourse. . . .

The 850 unwed mothers [including some from San Francisco not reported in the primary study] for whom data are reported and discussed include all who chose one of the first three of the following responses to the question, "What was the relationship between you and the father of your baby?"

88 Percentages are based only on cases reporting data.
89 U.S. Bureau of the Census, op. cit. [note 85], Table 43, pp. P5-167.
90 Excludes 162 students from the initial total of 539.

	Number	Per cent
(1) "A love relationship of some duration"	(344)	32
(2) "A close friendship relationship"	(248)	23
(3) "A casual relationship"	(258)	25
	(850)	
(4) "Don't know" or "No answer" [91]	(182)	17
(5) "Rape, force, or incest"	(30)	3
	(1,062)	100

We assumed that a reported "love relationship" reflected the most, and that a reported "casual relationship" the least, ego-involvement of the respondents. Our hypotheses were that, on a *group basis*, (*a*) white mothers of middle and upper-middle socio-economic status would report a "love relationship"; (*b*) white mothers of low socio-economic status would report a "casual relationship"; and (*c*) Negro mothers would report a "casual relationship," regardless of socio-economic status.

The assumption and working hypotheses were derived from the following rather general notions, found in case histories and in textbooks concerning socio-economic differences in female orientation to sexual relations. In very general terms, females of middle and upper-middle socio-economic status are believed to be more likely to personalize sex, to require considerable courting and preliminary love-making, and to need a more total acceptance, if not love, from the male. Women of low socio-economic status are considered to be more likely to perceive "sex as sex," to participate fairly directly after minimum preliminary sex play, and to acknowledge that the sexual union contains its own enjoyment and justification. The attitudes concerning sexual relations held by Negro females are generally regarded as similar to those held by white females of low socio-economic status. . . .

The data for marital status and age subgroups show that the Negroes and whites have a *similar direction but different degree of* increased ego-involvement as we move from the "single" to the "married" [citing an omitted table], and from younger to older [citing another omitted table] (the Negroes change from "casual" to "friendship"; the whites, from "friendship" to "love"). [Other data show that these differences by age and marital status] are primarily a function of socio-economic status. . . .

The data in [Table [6], below, and an omitted table] provide very clear evidence that, on a *group basis,* the degree of ego-involvement in illicit sexual relations by the unwed mothers in this substudy is (*a*) closely associated with their socio-economic status, and (*b*) associated more closely with their socio-economic status than with their race. (However, at any given socio-economic status level, proportionately more whites than Negroes report a love relationship, and proportionately more Negroes than whites report a casual relationship.)

[91] This includes forty-one who were not Negro or white, but too few for separate treatment.

We have accepted these data at face value as reported anonymously by the unwed mothers; but we recognize the possibility that more high than low socio-economic status respondents might report a "love relationship" when one did not exist. However, we infer that this inclination in itself reflects ego-involvement in sexual relationships. . . .

Table [6] — Relationship between Illicit Sex Partners, by Race, Education, Occupation, and Income of the Unwed Mother (as Reported by the Unwed Mothers)[92]

	White			Negro		
	EDUCATION OF UNWED MOTHER					
Reported Relationship:	*Attended or completed college* (N=146)	*High-school graduate* (N=143)	*Less than 12 years* (N=194)	*Attended or completed college* (N=22)	*High-school graduate* (N=34)	*Less than 12 years* (N=142)
	(Per cent)					
"Love"	81	56	42	50	47	6
"Friendship"	14	38	40	36	35	26
"Casual"	5	6	18	14	18	68
	(X^2 59.2, df=4; P < .001)			(X^2 60.2, df=4; P < .001)		
	OCCUPATION OF UNWED MOTHER					
	Professional, secretarial, & stenographic (N=108)	*Clerical: sales & office* (N=133)	*Skilled, semi-, & unskilled* (N=98)	*Professional, secretarial, & stenographic* (N=20)	*Clerical: sales & office* (N=37)	*Skilled, semi-, & unskilled* (N=79)
	(Per cent)					
"Love"	80	14	9	45	8	4
"Friendship"	13	62	42	45	65	25
"Casual"	7	24	49	10	27	71
	(X^2 178.3, df=4; P < .001)			(X^2 46.9, df=4; P < .001)		
	MONTHLY INCOME OF UNWED MOTHER					
	$250. or more (N=91)	*$249. to $150.* (N=67)	*$149. or less, or county aid* (N=97)	*$250. or more* (N=26)	*$249. to $150.* (N=36)	*$149. or less, or county aid* (N=143)
	(Per cent)					
"Love"	77	39	19	58	25	5
"Friendship"	19	46	33	35	53	20
"Casual"	4	15	48	7	22	75
	(X^2 87.1, df=4; P < .001)			(X^2 81.9, df=4; P < .001)		

[92] The notations at the bottom of each of the six groups of data in this table require explanation. The first such notation reads: X^2 59.2, df = 4; P < .001. "P" is the probability that the indicated disparities are statistically significant and not merely the result of chance. Significance is not an all-or-nothing matter, but one of degree. A result which may be expected by chance once in every twenty repetitions of an experiment is said to be statistically significant at the 5 per cent level (P equals 5 per cent, or .05), while a result to be expected by chance once in every 100 repetitions is significant at the 1 per cent level (P equals .01). The lower the P, the less the likelihood that the result might have occurred by chance and the greater our confidence in what the figures seem to tell us about a problem. Little confidence is placed in findings which do not reach the .05 level of signicance; we begin to be quite confident about results which reach the .01 level.

[A very long omitted table paired each unwed mother by occupation and type of relationship with the occupation of her sex partner. The data revealed] three patterns which are *most evident* for the unwed mothers in professional positions, and *least evident* for those in semi- and unskilled jobs. (1) Unwed mothers reporting a "love relationship" had partners whose occupations were closely related to, but at higher levels than theirs. (2) Those reporting "friendship" had partners whose occupations were less closely related, but more equal, to theirs. (3) Those reporting a "casual" relationship had partners whose occupations were at lower levels and not directly related to theirs. . . .

The occupational associations between the unwed mothers and their sex partners illustrate the inadequacy of the evil-causes-evil theory, inasmuch as they reflect social practices and personal ideology designed to be means to "good" goals. The loss of motivation for, and the diminution of creative rewards from, work tend, in C. Wright Mills's terms, to lead individuals to "sell little pieces of themselves in order to try to buy them back each night and week-end with the coin of 'fun,' . . . love . . . [and] vicarious intimacy." Dissatisfaction with work is countered by personnel ideology's emphasis on ways to make work and working conditions enjoyable; and feeling that one's shop or office co-workers constitute "one big happy family" is regarded as promoting high productivity. For these reasons, one's companions in the "fun, love, and vicarious intimacy" are frequently selected from shop, office, or factory.

This does not mean that such attitudes are causes of illegitimacy. They are only facets of a very complex configuration of social practices and values affecting opportunities for intimacy; within Sutherland's concept of "differential association," they have the effect of encouraging permissive sexual attitudes. So do the current philosophy of fun morality, which justifies enjoying one's self, and doing so elsewhere when home life is unhappy and work unrewarding; the themes in novels, plays, and movies that "sex is fun," and the minimization of the adultery stigma by

---

While it is unnecessary for the lawyer to understand the statistical methods by which P is determined, it being sufficient if he simply grasps the meaning of the concept of significance, a brief description of the method used here will explain the remaining notations. That part of the table under discussion (education of white mothers) is a 3×3 table containing nine cells or figures. "X^2" is a chi square, a common index of significance. The first step in computing X^2 is to determine the values to be expected in each cell on the hypothesis that there is no true relation between the factors across the top and down the side of the table; this is the so-called null hypothesis. The difference for each cell between the result to be expected by chance and the value actually obtained is then squared and divided by the expected value, and X^2 is the sum of the quantities so obtained for each cell — in this instance, 59.2. To determine P from the X^2, special statistical tables are used; these tables in turn require determination of the degrees of freedom (df). In general, the number of degrees of freedom is equal to one less than the number of rows multiplied by one less than the number of columns; here, with three rows and three columns, we reach the result stated: $df = 4$. A X^2 table shows that where there are four degrees of freedom, a X^2 of 9.48 has a significance level of .05, and a .01 level is reached at a X^2 of 13.27; 59.2 far exceeds this level, and the null hypothesis may be said to be false. — Ed.

replacing the *Scarlet Letter* "A" of former years with the current, more therapy-oriented rationale expressed in *Tea and Sympathy;* the widespread exploitation of sex in selling and advertising; and, finally, the acceptance of "escort service bureaus" as a means of attracting business conventions.

Such practices are particularly germane for an understanding of illegitimacy among females of middle and upper-middle socio-economic status, whose high degree of ego-involvement assumes sex is a *means* of self-enhancement. Self-enhancement, whether as ego-gratification, status recognition, marriage, or material gain, is in evidence when the women have sexual relations with males of higher socio-economic status than their own. It is also present when they require a primary relationship as a preliminary, to assure themselves that they, and not just sex, are of value. *This concept of sex as a means is supported by the exploitation of sex to achieve higher productivity, increased sales, and more visiting conventions. . . .*

[Vincent notes that the sixty high school mothers were an exception to the general rule, reporting "friendship" regardless of socio-economic status. He also discusses the doubt his figures cast on "the 'subculture ethos' as an explanation of Negro illegitimacy" and points to the need of more research in both these areas.] [Pages 73-94.]

[3. FAMILY AND PERSONALITY]

[Another substudy reported by Vincent obtained family and psychological data for a group of unwed mothers and compared them with the same data for a control sample of "single-never-pregnant (SNP)" females. For practical reasons imposed by the limited resources of the investigation, the only unwed mothers for whom the psychological data were obtained were the maternity home cases. The relative youth of these mothers necessitated using a high school senior sample for the comparative sample of SNP females. A family questionnaire and a standard test, the California Psychological Inventory (CPI), were administered to 212 maternity home unwed mothers and to 257 high school seniors, the latter representing 97 per cent of the girls in a senior class in one high school. Various matchings of the two groups were employed to control such variables as age, education, broken home, and socioeconomic status of parents. The major group matchings paired 50 SNP and 50 unwed mothers from broken homes and 50 SNP and 50 unwed mothers from unbroken homes. Only a few of the results are reported here.] [Pages 101-102.]

The absence of any statistically significant familial differences, in our results, between the comparable groups of unwed mothers and SNP females, was surprising, because so many previous studies of unwed mothers have emphasized disturbed parent-child relationships. However, our failure to find significant differences does not mean that the familial relationships of the unwed mothers studied here were unrelated to their illicit pregnancies. It simply illustrates the limitations and oversimplifications involved when group data on selected samples of unwed mothers form the basis for generalizations about the causes of illegitimacy. For example, the fact that 35 per cent of the 212 maternity-home mothers came from broken homes might easily be taken as evidence that broken homes are closely correlated with unwed motherhood. Such an interpretation is obviously quite misleading, however — 31 per cent of the 257 SNP females came from broken homes (based on figures before groups were matched); and 65 per cent of the 212 unwed mothers came from homes that were not broken.

If we had not obtained comparative data on the familial relationships of the SNP females, we might well have given undue significance to some of the data for the unwed mothers. For example, Leontine Young, in her very insightful study of unwed mothers, states: "If one factor can be considered fundamental in the family background of unwed mothers, it is the consistent pattern of domination of the home by one parent . . . The great majority of unmarried mothers come from homes dominated by the mother." [93] The limitation of this generalization concerning unwed mothers is indicated by the probability that the majority of females in the United States come from homes dominated by one parent — usually the mother. In the present study, the unwed mothers appear to corroborate Young's observation, in their responses to the following questionnaire items: Which parent made the important decisions and was definitely dominant in husband-wife discussions? What per cent of the respondent's discipline, rewards, and love came from each parent, both before and after the age of thirteen? Which parent influenced the respondent most, both before and after the age of thirteen? and, How close was the respondent to each parent, both before and after the age of thirteen? In reply, 54 per cent of the unwed mothers from unbroken homes, and 62 per cent of the unwed mothers from broken homes, described their mothers as being consistently dominant and predominant in all areas designated by these items.

The ostensible confirmation disappears, however, when we consider the responses of the SNP females to these items: 58 per cent of those from unbroken homes, and 66 per cent of those from broken homes, reported their mothers as consistently predominant and dominant in all the designated areas.

We hasten to add that Young's observation was based on intensive interviewing and therapy sessions with individual unwed mothers over a period of time. She could thus obtain a more accurate picture of their home situations than a questionnaire could. But this raises the issues noted in earlier chapters. How representative of unwed mothers in general are those who seek and/or receive therapeutic help? and would data from comparable groups of SNP females who seek and/or receive such help reveal their parent-child relationships and personality disturbances to be similar to those of the unwed mothers?

We accept as given the limitations of questionnaire-type research in this area, and the absence of either representative samples or control groups in most of the intensive investigations that have emphasized the neurotic components and disturbed familial relationships in unwed motherhood.

[93] Leontine Young, [Out of Wedlock (1954)], pp. 40-41. See also Rose Bernstein, "Are We Still Stereotyping the Unmarried Mother?" Social Work, V (July, 1960), pp. 22-28.

The focal point of our criticism is that descriptive data for selected groups of unwed mothers are too frequently interpreted as causal explanations of illegitimacy.

In this connection, the CPI data consistently indicated less positive personality profiles for the unwed mothers than for the SNP females, whether the comparisons were between matched or unmatched groups. But the differences were smaller than anticipated. Also, except in four of the eighteen scales (*Re, So, To,* and *Fe*), the *direction* and *pattern* of the group profiles were similar in all comparisons made between the unwed mothers and the SNP females. Moreover, the fifty SNP females from broken homes had a group CPI profile very similar to that of the fifty unwed mothers from unbroken homes. [Pages 117-119.]

C. CULTURAL VARIABLES AFFECTING CONDUCT

CHRISTENSEN, CULTURAL RELATIVISM AND PREMARITAL SEX NORMS
25 American Sociological Review 31 (1960)

In noting that behavioral standards vary over time and from society to society, William Graham Sumner made the now classic statement: "The mores can make anything right." By this he meant that moral problems are interpreted differently by different societies — that questions of right and wrong are relative to the particular culture in which the behavior occurs. This theory has been labeled *cultural relativism*. It challenges the notion of absolute standards of judgment to be applied uniformly regardless of time or place. . . .

This paper is an attempt to illuminate further the notion of cultural relativism by applying it to differing sets of premarital sex norms. . . .

Specifically, it is hypothesized that the more permissive the culture regarding sexual matters, the greater will be the incidence of premarital pregnancy, *but the lesser will be the effects of such pregnancy as pressure either for hasty marriage or for subsequent divorce.* . . .

In order to treat culture as a variable, we have made identical observations in three widely divergent areas. The first is the state of Utah, where the Mormon Church is dominant and premarital sex norms tend to be extremely conservative, almost to the point of being puritanical. Here, religion is a motivating force in the lives of most people, and the religious interpretation of premarital sexual intercourse is that it is an extremely grievous sin. Waiting until marriage for sexual intercourse — "keeping the law of chastity" — is regarded as one of the highest of virtues.[94]

The second is the state of Indiana, which in many ways is typical of the

---

[94] In this connection, it is interesting to recall Kinsey's finding to the effect that religiously devout men and women participate less in all socially disapproved forms of sexual behavior. He regarded religion as being the "most important factor in restricting premarital activity in the United States." See Alfred C. Kinsey et al., Sexual Behavior in the Human Female, Philadelphia: Saunders, 1953, pp. 324, 686-687, and passim.

United States as a whole. It is centrally located and heterogeneous in culture. It is approximately an average state in size, in rural-urban distribution, in population numbers and composition, and in various social indices such as median income, school attendance, and marriage, birth, and divorce rates. The "chastity norm" is a part of the prevailing culture in Indiana as in most of the United States — in prescription even if less so in practice. And there are religious incentives, promoted by a variety of denominations, which give support to the sexual mores.

The third location is Denmark, which, like all of Scandinavia, has a long tradition of sexual intercourse during the engagement. This goes back three or four centuries at least, in spite of efforts by the State Lutheran Church to establish a chastity code. In this connection, it is important to point out that, although most Danes have their names on the church records, they seldom attend church services. Except for a few, religion in Denmark is not a strong motivating force in the lives of the people. Croog notes the importance of understanding the *ring engagement* — which has almost the status of a formal marriage, including rights to sexual intercourse, and obligations to marry if pregnancy results — as background for interpreting sexual behavior in Denmark. He also explains how this pattern of sexual freedom is spreading to include the more informal "going steady" relationships; and how these practices are encouraged by a liberal clergy, by welfare laws which make abortion and unmarried motherhood relatively easy, and by the facility with which premarital sexual behavior can be rationalized since "everyone is doing it." [95] Svalastoga cites five recent empirical studies to support his claim that: "Coitus before marriage may now safely be considered the rule and chastity the exception in Scandinavia." [96] . . .

For any accurate measure of premarital conception, one needs to know three quantities: abortion among the unmarried, both spontaneous and induced; illegitimacy, that is, birth outside of marriage; and the number of weddings that are preceded by pregnancy.[97]

Unfortunately, there are no available statistics to enable us to make comparisons on the relative numbers of abortions.

With regard to illegitimacy, official statistics for 1955, which are typical of recent years, show the per cent of all births occurring outside of wedlock to be .9 for Utah, 2.9 for Indiana, and 6.6 for Denmark. . . . Thus, in these societies, illegitimacy increases with each advance in the sexual permissiveness of the culture.

---

[95] Sydney H. Croog, "Aspects of the Cultural Background of Premarital Pregnancy in Denmark," Social Forces, 30 (December, 1951), pp. 215-219.

[96] Kaare Svalastoga, "The Family in Scandinavia," Marriage and Family Living, 16 (November, 1954), pp. 374-380; quotation from p. [377].

[97] [Strictly] speaking, early birth within marriage provides the only available accurate measure of premarital conception. Some unmarried women have abortions and illegitimate births; the term "premarital" hardly describes them. Yet, since it is likely that the majority of such women later get married, no great violence is done in using the concepts in this way. In Denmark, for example, one study has shown that by age six well over half of all children born out of wedlock are then living with their mother who has since been married — in most cases to the child's father. [Citation omitted.]

Although illegitimacy rates can be obtained from published statistics for whole populations, it has been necessary to conduct sample studies for measures of the premarital conceptions which end in postmarital births.[98] As a consequence, the following analysis relies heavily upon the writer's earlier record linkage studies of Utah County, Utah, and Tippecanoe County, Indiana, and his more recent parallel investigation of Copenhagen, Denmark. The Utah County data were derived by comparing marriages occurring during the years 1905-7, 1913-15, 1921-23, and 1929-31 with birth records for four years following each wedding, in order to find the date of the first birth. This process yielded 1670 cases. The Tippecanoe County data were derived by taking marriages which occurred during the years 1919-21, 1929-31, and 1939-41, matching them with the birth records searched for five years following the wedding, and finally checking against the divorce records to discover which marriages ended in failure. The result consisted of 1531 cases involving a first child, with 137 of these cases terminating in divorce. The Copenhagen data were derived by taking every third marriage which occurred during a single year, 1938, eliminating cases involving remarriage and those in which the wife was thirty or more years of age, and then checking both birth and divorce recordings for sixteen years following the wedding. These steps provided a sample of 1029 cases involving a first child, with 215 ending in divorce.

These samples from three cultures are not, of course strictly comparable. They were drawn in slightly different ways and have somewhat different compositions. Nevertheless, the contrasts reported below are of sufficient magnitude to suggest at least tentative answers to the problem posed.

From [an omitted table], it may be observed that the same general pattern holds for this phenomenon as was previously noted for illegitimacy. The six months index, which is a sure minimum measure of premarital conception, makes the clearest comparison. It shows the lowest incidence of premarital pregnancy in Utah [9.0 per cent of all marital first births occurring within six months], a somewhat higher incidence in Indiana [9.7], but a considerably higher incidence in Denmark [24.2 in Copenhagen, 32.9 in whole country]. The nine months index is less valuable since it includes unknown numbers of postmarital conceptions. The higher rate for Utah [30.9] than for Indiana [23.9] may simply reflect the tendency to earlier postmarital conceptions in Utah. . . .

Not only does the incidence of premarital pregnancy differ from culture to culture, as demonstrated above, but it varies among certain subgroups within each culture. . . . [T]here are strong and consistent tendencies for premarital conception to be higher with young age at marriage in contrast to the older ages, with a civil wedding in contrast to the religious ceremony, and with a laboring occupation in contrast to the more skilled and professional ways of earning a living. Each of these differences was found to be in the same direction and to be statistically significant for each of the three cultures studied, which is evidence of certain cross-cultural regularities.

[98] Denmark has published nation-wide statistics on this phenomenon, but the United States has not.

[An omitted table to document this statement shows, e.g., the per cent of first births premaritally conceived for husband's occupation:

Factors	Utah	Indiana	Denmark
Laborer	17.9	16.0	30.0
All Other	8.6	7.2	18.2]

. . . [T]here is the strong suggestion here that broad cultural norms may be to some extent overruled by the operation of other factors. . . .

. . . Figure 1 . . . has been constructed from estimated dates of conception calculated by counting back 266 days from each date of birth. It may be noted that, whereas in the Utah and Indiana samples the modal time of conception is one lunar month after marriage, in the Danish sample it is five lunar months *before* the marriage. As a matter of fact the Danish data show many more couples conceiving about five months before the marriage than at any other time; in that culture, therefore, premarital conception coupled with subsequent delayed marriage must be considered as the norm. The Indiana curve is bimodal, with the peak for premarital conceptions at two lunar months prior to marriage — suggesting a tendency to get married as soon as possible after the second menstrual period has been missed and the doctor's positive diagnosis has been given. The Utah curve starts low and moves up regularly until the time of marriage and immediately thereafter, when it is the highest of all three. . . .

FIGURE 1. PREGNANCY INCEPTION AS RELATED TO TIME
OF MARRIAGE: A CROSS-CULTURAL COMPARISON

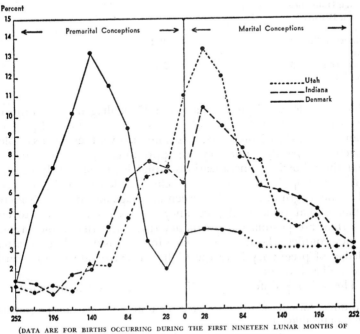

(DATA ARE FOR BIRTHS OCCURRING DURING THE FIRST NINETEEN LUNAR MONTHS OF
MARRIAGE AND ARE EXPRESSED AS PERCENTAGES.)

Apparently, in Denmark there is little pressure to hurry marriage merely because of pregnancy. In Indiana the tendency is to marry immediately after the pregnancy is definitely known so as to hide the fact from the public. Couples who have premarital sexual intercourse in Utah, on the other hand, seem to hurry marriage because of that fact alone, without waiting for pregnancy to force them into it (religious guilt is a sufficient sanction once the "law of chastity" has been broken). . . .

TABLE 3. DIVORCE RATE COMPARISONS BY INTERVAL TO FIRST BIRTH
(For Births Occurring Within 5 Years of the Wedding)

Classification	Copenhagen, Denmark			Tippecanoe County, Indiana		
	Number of Cases	Number Divorced	Per Cent Divorced	Number of Cases	Number Divorced	Per Cent Divorced
Interval Between Marriage and First Birth						
(1) 0-139 days (premarital pregnancy, marriage delayed)	176	60	34.1	71	14	19.7
(2) 140-265 days (premarital pregnancy, marriage hurried)	129	31	24.0	276	39	14.1
(3) 266 days-4.99 years (postmarital pregnancy)	572	111	19.4	1184	84	7.1
Percentage Difference Between Divorce Rates						
(4) Between lines 2 and 1			42.1			39.7
(5) Between lines 3 and 2			23.7 [99]			98.6 [99]

Table 3 is designed to compare the Copenhagen and Tippecanoe County samples concerning possible effects of premarital and postmarital pregnancy upon the divorce rate. As noted above, these two samples are not strictly comparable, but they are approximately so. It seems probable that the following generalizations are at least tentatively justified:

(1) In both populations there is the clear tendency for the divorce rate to fall as the length of interval between marriage and first birth increases. This means that premarital pregnancy cases are more likely to end in divorce than are postmarital pregnancy cases, and that those premarital pregnancy couples who delay marriage for a considerable time after the knowledge of pregnancy have the highest divorce rate of all — in Denmark as well as Indiana.

(2) The *relative* difference in divorce rate between premarital preg-

[99] No direct formula has been located for testing the statistical signifiance of this intersample difference . . . .

nancy couples who hurried marriage and those who delayed it is essentially the same for both populations. Thus, Copenhagen figures show a 42.1 per cent difference between these two rates as compared with a difference of 39.7 per cent in Tippecanoe County, an intersample difference that is not significant.

The facts that both samples show substantially higher divorce rates for couples who delay marriage after knowledge of pregnancy and that the differentials in this respect are about the same in the two cultures suggest universal tendencies for certain pregnant couples to marry under the pressure of social responsibility (for example, sympathy for the lover, consideration for the future child, or parental influence). The data also suggest that, statistically speaking, such "shot gun" marriages do not turn out well.

(3) The *relative* difference in divorce rate between postmarital pregnancy couples and the premarital couples who married soon after the discovery of pregnancy is four times greater in the Indiana sample (98.6 per cent compared with 23.7 per cent), an intersample difference that by some tests is statistically significant. . . .

The fact that the postmarital pregnancy divorce rate is lower in both cultures is evidence that premarital pregnancy — even when associated with an early wedding — tends generally to make marriage's survival chances less than even. This may be because some marriages take place under pressure from others and are therefore accompanied by resentment, or because in their haste to escape public scorn the couple marries without adequate preparation, or in the absence of love, or in the face of ill-matched personalities. But the fact that the postmarital-premarital pregnancy divorce rate differential is substantially less in Denmark, gives strong support to [the hypothesis stated earlier that the more liberal the culture the *less* likely is premarital pregnancy to be followed by divorce]. It seems probable that in Denmark, where sexual relations outside of marriage are more or less accepted, premarital pregnancy will have less negative effect upon marriage than in Indiana, where it is expected that sexual intercourse and pregnancy be confined to marriage. . . .[100]

In some respects our data give support to the idea of cultural relativism. . . .

But there are also *regularities* among the cultures studied. . . .

---

[100] As noted above, divorce rate comparison does not include the Utah sample since data were not available. It is believed, however, that the Utah divorce rate differential (between premarital and postmarital pregnancy cases) probably is the greatest of the three areas — because premarital sexual intimacy is most strongly condemned there.

This unestablished assumption can be argued by an analogy. The drinking of alcoholic beverages is also strongly condemned in Utah (and in the rest of Mormon culture). Research shows that Mormon college students have the lowest incidence of drinking among religious groups, but that, of the drinkers, Mormon students have a very high rate of alcoholism. This suggests that cultural restrictions can lower the incidence of the condemned practice, but that for those who indulge, the negative effects are apt to be extreme. Cf. Robert Strauss and Selden D. Bacon, Drinking in College, New Haven: Yale University Press, 1953, passim.

[T]his suggests the existence of certain universals which are to some extent independent of the cultural variable. . . .

2. Controls on Illegitimacy — Morality and Ambivalence

Many legal rules and policies whose objectives have at most a tangential relevance to the control of illegitimacy nonetheless may have some influence on its incidence. The most obvious examples are marriage and divorce legislation, legal restrictions on the dissemination of contraceptive devices, and the typical prohibition of induced abortions except under very limited conditions.[101]

There has been a slow but steady trend in this century to tighten up restrictions upon marriage. Bradway, for example, analogizes marital screening processes to admission to the bar, and suggests that the applicant should be required to show requisite qualifications and moral character to obtain permission to marry.[102] It is apparent that such a policy would increase the proportion of children who are illegitimate. For a variety of complicated reasons many persons form families without marital formalities or break up their existing families in order to form new relationships. Withholding legal recognition from these de facto families may deter some persons from forming such relationships, but for those who are not deterred, the immediate effect is to bastardize any children of the de facto family.[103]

Similarly, the paradoxical result of restricting the availability of contraceptive devices and induced abortion is to increase the likelihood of conception in nonmarital intercourse and, once conception has taken place, to assure that the birth of an illegitimate child will follow unless interrupted by natural causes or legitimated by marriage. But the Kinsey Institute studies (page 84 supra) suggest that most nonmarital intercourse does not result in conception and that where it does, the pregnancy is terminated by induced abortion in up to 90 per cent of the cases. This might suggest that strict abortion laws cannot be rigorously enforced as a practical matter and that a relaxation of abortion laws would have little effect on the incidence of illegitimacy, as most of those who would consider using abortion are already employing it illegally.

An Ohio court has suggested that an objective of abortion legislation is "to discourage . . . immorality between the sexes," [104] but this is doubtless an insignificant consideration compared with the dominant concern about the sanctity of human life. Furthermore, statistical studies report

---

[101] All of these subjects will be treated fully later in this book, but some note should be taken of their all too frequently ignored implications for the problem of illegitimacy.

[102] Bradway, Divorce Litigation and the Welfare of the Family, 9 Vand. L. Rev. 665, 678-679 (1956). For treatment of a range of restrictions, see Chapter 2.

[103] A legitimation statute may, under some circumstances, avoid this result. See page 33 supra.

[104] State v. Tippie, 89 Ohio St. 35, 40, 105 N.E. 75, 77 (1913).

that up to 90 per cent of all abortions are committed on married women.[105]

In addition to these policies, there are a number of societal sanctions which seem to be designed to control illegitimacy, whether directly or indirectly.

First, there are criminal sanctions against nonmarital intercourse which operate directly as deterrents upon the parents but which are only indirectly related to illegitimacy. No doubt the primary objective of fornication, adultery, and seduction statutes is to discourage immoral conduct rather than explicitly to reduce the incidence of illegitimacy. But one reason we regard nonmarital intercourse as socially undesirable is the risk it creates of begetting children outside of the protective institution of legal marriage. Furthermore, at least in abstract theory, sanctions against nonmarital intercourse could affect the illegitimacy rate, for to the extent that these sanctions against the basic conduct which creates the possible risk of illegitimacy were effective, the number of illegitimate children would be held down.

Second, there are sanctions which operate directly on the unwed mother and father because they have had an illegitimate child.

Third, there are sanctions which may tend indirectly to influence the parents because of disabilities imposed on their illegitimate children. Apart from the issues of fairness and effectiveness which are raised by such indirect sanctions, they squarely put in issue the usual principle that the welfare of the child is the paramount consideration in formulating or interpreting laws affecting children.

a. CRIMINAL SANCTIONS ON NONMARITAL INTERCOURSE

The American tendency to regard consensual intercourse between adults outside of marriage as a crime is something of an anomaly in the modern world. H. L. A. Hart, in Law, Liberty and Morality 26 (1963), has noted:[106]

> In America a glance at the penal statutes of the various states of the Union reveals something quite astonishing to English eyes. For in addition to such offences as are punishable under English law, there seems to be no sexual practice, except "normal" relations be-

---

[105] Full discussion of abortion will be found in Chapter 6.

[106] Compare also the position of another distinguished Englishman, Earl Jowitt, who stated in the House of Lords, 187 H.L. Deb. (5th ser.) 745-746 (1954): "Never let us make the mistake of thinking that we should attempt to make the area covered by our criminal law coextensive with the area covered by the moral law. . . . For instance, take the case of adultery, which I certainly think is a great evil in this country to-day. No one would suggest that we should once more make adultery a criminal offence. It is not that we desire to condone or support adultery or anything of that sort; it is just that we realise that the criminal law and the moral law are two wholly different concepts . . ." Hart's book is an illuminating discussion of the problems involved in using the criminal law to enforce morality; somewhat similar questions are posed by the use of civil sanctions. See also Devlin, The Enforcement of Morals (1965).

tween husband and wife and solitary acts of masturbation, which is not forbidden by the law of some state. In a very large number of states adultery, which has not been criminally punishable in England since Cromwell's time, is a crime, though, in a minority of states, this is so only if it is open, notorious, or continuous. Fornication is not a criminal offence in England or in most countries of the civilized world, but only a minority of American states do not have statutes making fornication under certain conditions punishable, and some states make even a single act punishable.[107] Besides these statutory provisions there is an unknown quantity of local or municipal enactments which, in some cases, are more restrictive than the state laws, and though these are for that reason of doubtful validity, they have been enforced. . . .

Most American states also make seduction under some circumstances a criminal offense. What is probably the most severe statute provides:

> Any person who shall, by persuasion and promises of marriage or other false and fraudulent means, seduce a virtuous unmarried female and induce her to yield to his lustful embraces and allow him to have carnal knowledge of her, shall be punished by imprisonment and labor in the penitentiary for not less than two nor more than 20 years.[108]

A curious feature of many seduction statutes is that marriage is made a bar to prosecution, although the bliss of the honeymoon may be somewhat clouded by the requirement in one state that the husband post a bond to cover his wife's support for five years,[109] or in another that the suspended prosecution will be resumed if the wife is deserted or given grounds for divorce within three years.[110] Is this defense by marriage intended to aid the defendant, save the girl, or provide an added in terrorem deterrent?

In some instances conduct violative of these state statutes may also be a federal offense; see, e.g., Note, Interstate Immorality: The Mann Act and the Supreme Court, 56 Yale L.J. 718 (1947).

Regarding the enforcement of such legislation, Hart says:

> No doubt much, and perhaps most, of this American legislation against sexual immorality is as dead a letter as it is commonly said to be. But the facts as to law enforcement are at present very hard to establish. In many states, California among them, the annual criminal statistics do not usually break down figures for sex crimes further than the two heads of "Rape" and "Other sexual offences." But in Boston as late as 1954 the sex laws were reported to receive "normal" enforcement, and in 1948 there were 248 arrests for adultery in that

---

[107] See, for a short summary, the American Law Institute, Model Penal Code, Tentative Draft No. 4, pp. 204-10.
[108] Ga. Code Ann. tit. 26, §6001 (1953).
[109] Id. §6002.
[110] Ky. Rev. Stat. Ann. §436.010 (1963).

city.[111] No one, I think, should contemplate this situation with complacency, for in combination with inadequate published statistics the existence of criminal laws which are generally not enforced places formidable discriminatory powers in the hands of the police and prosecuting authorities.[112]

The striking discrepancy between the alleged frequency of the proscribed conduct and the alleged nonenforcement of the criminal law has been emphasized in the first Kinsey study:

> It will be recalled that 85 per cent of the total male population has pre-marital intercourse . . . , 59 per cent has some experience in mouth-genital contacts . . . , nearly 70 per cent has relations with prostitutes . . . , something between 30 and 45 per cent has extra-marital intercourse . . . , 37 per cent has some homosexual experience . . . , 17 per cent of the farm boys have animal intercourse . . . All of these, and still other types of sexual behavior . . . , are illicit activities, each performance of which is punishable as a crime under the law. The persons involved in these activities, taken as a whole, constitute more than 95 per cent of the total male population. . . . [The demand for enforcement of sex laws is], in fine, a proposal that 5 per cent of the population should support the other 95 per cent in penal institutions. . . .[113]

If the Kinsey incidence figures are accepted as a proper criterion for evaluation of these laws, does the report's conclusion follow from the authors' own statistics? As to whether accumulative incidence is a proper criterion, compare Goode, Norm Commitment and Conformity to Role-Status Obligations, 66 Am. J. Soc. 246, 254 n.32 (1960):

> When we question the stability of the modern social structure, however, with its apparent lack of consensus and weak norm commitment, we must measure conformity not by the proportion of people who ever violate a given norm but by a rate of violation, the proportion of violators in a given time. Thus, though perhaps everyone in our society steals at some time in his life, the proportion of adults who steal in a given year is probably not high.

For a view opposed to that implied by the Kinsey report, see Schwartz, Book Review, 96 U. Pa. L. Rev. 914, 915-916 (1948):

> If the conduct proscribed by these laws is undesirable, evidence of promiscuous violation would, with greater logic, support an increase in penalties and more rigorous enforcement. The test of a criminal law is not its correlation with actual behavior, but its correspondence to behavior ideals and its efficiency in promoting those ideals. The report itself demonstrates that people who engage in forbidden prac-

[111] American Law Institute, Model Penal Code, Tentative Draft No. 4, p. 205, n.16.
[112] H. L. A. Hart, Law, Liberty and Morality 27 (1963).
[113] Kinsey, Pomeroy & Martin, Sexual Behavior in the Human Male 392 (1948).

tices nevertheless subscribe to the law and morality which condemn their conduct. This is not hypocrisy, although hypocritical people may take such positions. This is only a recognition that there may be a better way of life than one is personally able to follow in every situation. . . .

Now that Kinsey has let the cat out of the bag, shall we see major modifications of the sex laws comparable to the repeal of prohibition? I think not.[114] Prohibition went out not merely because violation was frequent, but because of increasing doubts that the forbidden conduct was undesirable and much evidence that the cost and consequences of enforcement were intolerable. The situation of the sex laws is much more comparable to the perjury problem. If cumulative incidence figures were compiled on conscious sworn fabrications in court proceedings, tax returns, etc., they would no doubt lend apparent support to the proposition that the perjury laws were "unrealistic" and "barbarous" contradictions of "normal" human behavior. But not a voice would be raised for repeal, because we would all go on believing that perjury was an evil and the threat of punishment plus the subtle influence of penal sanctions on the general moral climate of the community do tend to restrain it to some extent. Accordingly, Kinsey has not disproved the basic postulates of the sex laws: that the forbidden conduct is undesirable, that it can be deterred, and that the social cost of the deterrence program is not excessive.

b.   DIRECT SANCTIONS ON PARENTS OF ILLEGITIMATE CHILDREN

We have already noted the father's support liability, which in some states arises as a consequence of a criminal conviction for fornication and bastardy. While this is primarily oriented to the child's welfare and the taxpayer's purse, does it serve a significant deterrent function as well? Even a relatively small sum can become a severe cumulative sanction; $25 a month continued over eighteen years amounts to more than $5000.

A possibly more sweeping tort liability which would hold the father

[114] Compare the report of Professor Fowler Harper of Yale, Book Review, 63 Yale L.J. 895, 898 (1954), on the attitudes of the legislature of "a typical New England state." He canvassed a random sample of the lower house and all of the upper house, presenting the legislators with data from both the male and female Kinsey studies (id. at 899): "None thought that the criminal law relating to adultery (punishable by up to five years' confinement) should be made stricter, but only 40% thought the penalty should be reduced. As to fornication (punishable by a maximum penalty of six months), 20% thought the law should be strictly enforced, 37.5% thought it should remain the same but not strictly enforced, and 20% wanted the statute repealed. As to homosexuality and other forms of sodomy (punishable by imprisonment up to thirty years), 57.5% wanted no change in the law while only 32.5% thought it should be made less strict.

"Asked whether or not they thought studies such as Kinsey's were of value to them as legislators, 45% thought so, 50% thought not, and 5% did not think." — Ed.

responsible directly to the child for damages resulting from illegitimacy was at issue in Zepeda v. Zepeda, 41 Ill. App. 2d 240, 190 N.E.2d 849 (1963), cert. denied, 379 U.S. 945 (1964). The court found that by causing conception out of wedlock the father had committed a tortious act against the child, that as a result the child had suffered injury (whose nature and extent were left rather vague), but that judicial recognition for what the court christened "a cause of action for wrongful life" was precluded because it might have such sweeping and far-reaching consequences. The court said (41 Ill. App. 2d at 260, 190 N.E.2d at 858):

> What does disturb us is the nature of the new action and the related suits which would be encouraged. Encouragement would extend to all others born into the world under conditions they might regard as adverse. One might seek damages for being born of a certain color . . . , another for inheriting unfortunate family characteristics . . . .

But see Williams v. State, 46 Misc. 2d 824, 260 N.Y.S.2d 953 (Ct. Cl. 1965), refusing to dismiss an illegitimate infant's action against the State of New York for damages arising out of illegitimacy. The infant alleged that she was conceived because of the state's negligence in failing to protect her mother, a patient in a state mental hospital, from being sexually assaulted. The court was not impressed by the "asserted ingenious analogies" advanced in Zepeda; "[t]angential reasoning should not be utilized as a sledge hammer or chisel to destroy a fundamental right which cries out for justice." Id. at 959.

Denial of relief payments to illegitimate children under the Aid to Dependent Children program or some comparable state programs is in some respects a direct sanction upon the parents. As the children concerned are very young, the money is paid to the parent and in fact forms all or a considerable part of the economic livelihood of many families. As it is presumably not proposed that infants and children should starve, denial of a family's livelihood is thus in effect an implied threat that the children will be removed from their parents and placed in foster homes.[115]

Perhaps more important in this context, at least some states have passed legislation which is frankly aimed at punishing the parents. The Louisiana legislature created a new crime, punishable by a fine of up to $1000 or imprisonment up to one year: "Conceiving and giving birth to two or more illegitimate children is hereby declared to be a crime. Both the father and mother of such children shall be equally guilty of the commission of this crime. Each such birth shall be a separate violation hereof."[116]

---

[115] The ADC problem is discussed at page 121 infra.

[116] La. Rev. Stat. Ann. §14:79.2 (Supp. 1964). The statute also provides that the birth certificate is prima facie evidence of an illegitimate birth. Quere how the father can violate this statute if it requires "giving birth"? What if the defendant's first child out of wedlock is by a woman who has already given birth to one illegitimate child; has he violated the statute? Suppose he subsequently fathers an out of wedlock child by another woman who has never given birth before? And what if twins are born the first time?

Although there is reason to believe that racial tensions in the South may be primarily responsible for this legislation, and that the concern with illegitimacy is collateral to that broader issue,[117] such a deterrent approach is not limited to the deep South. For example, a California trial court conditioned the grant of probation to a mother of illegitimate children who was convicted of relief fraud upon her agreement not to establish any other extramarital relationships, and the probation was re- voked when she gave birth to another illegitimate child.[118] A bill in the 1960 session of the Maryland General Assembly would have made it a misdemeanor punishable by imprisonment up to three years "for any fe- male person to give birth within this State to more than two illegitimate children," and upon conviction the statute provided that the woman should be sterilized "forthwith," permanently barred from any future welfare payments, and "any of her existing children and . . . any child of hers en ventre sa mere . . . shall be removed permanently from the care, custody and control of the mother." [119] As modified by striking the sterilization clause and making conviction only prima facie evidence of unfitness for custody, the bill passed the Senate but died in a House com- mittee.

It bears emphasis that community disapproval and penal sanctions against the mother may intensify the mother's desire to protect her ano- nymity and rid herself of the infant. Although the incidence of infanti- cide and abandonment are not as great as they were in Puritan days (see page 15 supra),[120] the pressure on the modern unmarried mother may result in either illegal induced abortion or anonymous release of the child for adoption. One of the common reasons for "gray market" adoptions (those which are privately arranged through an obstetrician or lawyer intermediary) is the mother's effort to prevent disclosure of her pregnancy to her family and to the community. It seems fairly well established that the secrecy which often attends an illegitimate pregnancy poses dispropor- tionate health risks for both mother and child. Unwed mothers receive less adequate prenatal medical care than married mothers, and there

---

[117] The bills were part of a much larger anti-integration package passed at an emergency session of the legislature, and the impact of the antirelief measures was estimated to fall 95 per cent on Negroes. N.Y. Times, Aug. 28, 1960, p. 62, col. 4.

[118] See In re Turrieta, 54 Cal. 2d 816, 356 P.2d 681 (1960), where the California Supreme Court reversed this disposition for denial of right to counsel at the revo- cation hearing.

[119] S. 91, General Assembly of Maryland, 1960 Session. The author of a recent letter to The New York Times, in commenting upon the Newburgh Welfare Code discussed at page 122 infra, explicitly suggested legislation under which "any mother who has more than one illegitimate child would lose all her children," to which the publicist Harry Golden replied: "A more practical solution to this problem would be to enlarge the Federal Mann Act and arrest every young man who has expressed interest or desire in a sexual union with an unwed girl." N.Y. Times, Aug. 14, 1961, p. 24, col. 6, and Aug. 21, 1961, p. 22, col. 6.

[120] England, which still keeps separate statistics for the murder of infants under one year of age, reported an annual average of ten such murders for the years 1952-1957 and not all of these were infanticides of newly born infants. Criminal Statistics: England and Wales 1957, Cmd. No. 529, p. xxxv (1958).

seems to be a direct causal relationship between this fact and unmarried status.[121]   Particularly among white mothers, a substantially higher proportion of illegitimate babies are "immature" at birth,[122] and the fetal death ratio for illegitimate births in 1957 (27.0 per 1000 live births) was more than 70 per cent higher than for legitimate births.[123]   It is not surprising that private adoption agencies, and to an increasing extent public agencies as well, have sought to protect the health of illegitimate children and to eliminate the evils of privately arranged adoptions by offering anonymity to unwed mothers.[124]

Under modern social conditions, therefore, the ambivalence exemplified by the history of the *tour* in France, see page 15 supra, is repeated in the unresolved policy clash between the application of deterrent pressures on unwed mothers and their protection from public exposure for their children's sake.

C.   SANCTIONS ON ILLEGITIMATE CHILDREN

The first big reform in behalf of illegitimate children in relatively modern times occurred during the French Revolution, and the revealing history is delightfully told in Crane Brinton's French Revolutionary Legislation on Illegitimacy 1789-1804 (1936).   The principles of the French Revolution were felt to include equality among all children, legitimate or illegitimate.   Under the triumphant slogan, "Il n'y a plus de batards en France," the Revolution in 1794 "abolished" illegitimacy, and if the legislation left the "details" to be worked out in subsequent enactments and still discriminated against adulterine bastards in the interests of marital stability, it was forthright in declaring that all children were legitimate. Bastards became "orphans" or "children of love" [125] or "natural chil-

---

[121] Adams, Two Studies of Unmarried Mothers in New York City, 8 Children 184 (1961); Protecting Children in Adoption 9 (U.S. Children's Bureau Pub. No. 354, 1955).

[122] Illegitimate Births: United States, 1938-1957, 47 Vital Statistics — Special Reports 241 (No. 8, 1960).

[123] Id. at 243.

[124] Recent New York legislation authorized public welfare officials to give maternity care away from the unwed mother's home and to waive the requirement that her legally responsible relatives be investigated and required to contribute to the cost of such care.   N.Y. Soc. Welfare Law §398(5)(a).   In his statement on the bill the Governor quoted from a memorandum by the State Charities Assn.: "Agencies working with unwed mothers have long recognized that in some cases the unwed mother's fear of her parents' reaction, should they learn of her pregnancy, leads some of these girls to proceed secretly and place their babies through gray or black market channels rather than seek aid through authorized agencies. . . . A number of leaders in the field of adoption have pointed out that this measure would . . . result in improvement of protections and benefits involving both mothers and children."   Governor's Memorandum on c. 525, 1959 N.Y. State Legis. Ann. 423.

[125] Brinton notes the romantic-genetic assumption that "the child of passion will be a better biological achievement than the child of routine marriage" and cites Shakespeare, King Lear, Act I, Scene 2:

dren" or simply "children born out of wedlock." Thus, says Brinton (id. at 33), "by the simple expedient of abolishing a word, the Convention had all the satisfactions of abolishing a condition, and not nearly so many of the inconveniences." But the pendulum swung, and rapidly. It was alleged that such a revolutionary doctrine would destroy marriage, that women required the protection of marriage, and that the best form of protection was to prevent the fathers and husbands of France from being harassed by paternity actions. Brinton comments (id. at 62):

> Now that they know they cannot foist their children on some rich and respected gentleman by the vicious procedure of *la recherche de la paternité,* women will be more careful of their virtue. Presumably now that they have to answer to their conscience instead of merely to the law for their bastards, men will also think twice before they procreate them. At any rate, morality, which a few years ago was all with Nature in favor of equal treatment of all children, has now decided with equal vigor against such equality of treatment.

Napoleon's declaration that "society has no interest in the recognition of bastards" (quoted id. at 66) hastened the result, and what began as an outpouring of egalitarian idealism ended ten years later in the most repressive legislation of modern times. The Napoleonic Civil Code abolished the paternity action[126] and left the illegitimate child and unwed mother worse off than they were before the Revolution. Like other societies before and since, France had not been able to resolve the apparent dilemma between helping the out-of-wedlock mother and child and rocking the boat of matrimonial security. Brinton says of the legislators (id. at 82-83):

> Along one pleasant track their minds passed easily to the full rehabilitation of these children of nature, once called bastards; on an equally pleasant track their minds arrived at a France filled with virtuous, happy married couples. Now bastardy and marriage in this world are quite complementary — you cannot have one without the other. In another world, you may indeed separate the two institu-

---

> Why brand they us
> With base? with baseness? bastardy? base, base?
> Who in the lusty stealth of nature, take
> More composition and fierce quality
> Than doth, within a dull, stale, tired bed,
> Go to the creating a whole tribe of fops,
> Got 'tween asleep and wake?

Brinton, French Revolutionary Legislation on Illegitimacy 1789-1804, pp. 14-15 (1936).

[126] "La recherche de la paternité est interdite." French Civil Code of 1803, art. 340. The Code also prohibited the fruits of an incestuous or adulterous intercourse from establishing even maternity or from being legitimated or recognized in any way (arts. 331, 335, 342) and provided that even children acknowledged by the father cannot have the rights of a legitimate child (art. 338). These provisions were slowly modified in succeeding generations until in 1912 Article 340 was in effect repealed.

tions and eliminate one of them, either by having marriage so perfect — in various senses — that no one will ever commit fornication or adultery, or by having fornication so perfect that no one will ever commit marriage.   But these are definitely other worlds. . . .

The perpetuation of discriminations against children born out of wedlock poses in its baldest form the dichotomy between the welfare of the child and the desire to deter illegitimacy.   Although the extreme sanction imposed in the Napoleonic Code — abolition of private paternity actions — has not been suggested,[127] many of the recent proposals to cut off public relief in cases of multiple production of illegitimate children can hardly be considered mild.   A 1960 Louisiana act amending that state's ADC plan provided:

> [No] assistance shall be granted to a child living with its mother, if the mother has had an illegitimate child after receiving assistance from the department of public welfare, unless and until proof satisfactory to the parish board of public welfare has been presented showing that the mother has ceased illicit relationships and is maintaining a suitable home for the children.[128]

The Department of Health, Education, and Welfare ruled that the Louisiana plan was inconsistent with the Social Security Act:

> A State plan for aid to dependent children may not impose an eligibility condition that would deny assistance with respect to a needy child on the basis that the home conditions in which the child lives are unsuitable, while the child continues to reside in the home.   Assistance will therefore be continued during the time efforts are being made either to improve the home conditions or to make arrangements for the child elsewhere.[129]

A 1951 Georgia statute also provided that public welfare funds could not be paid under the ADC program to more than one illegitimate child in any family,[130] but the state's Attorney General ruled the provision unconstitutional as "an unreasonable and arbitrary division of a classification without any recognizable or reasonable basis for difference be-

[127] Except, of course, in the rather different context of substituting a program of public support, see page 66 supra.

[128] La. Acts 1960, No. 306, §1.   This was replaced by La. Acts 1962, No. 28, see La. Stat. Ann. §233(D) (Supp. 1964), which listed factors to be considered in determinations of home suitability, including the existence of an illicit union or having an illegitimate child "after having received a public assistance check."

[129] State Letter No. 452 (U.S. Bureau of Public Assistance, Jan. 17, 1961).   For a full review of the controversy, including the texts of the government rulings, see 35 Soc. Serv. Rev. 203 (1961).   See also Note, 70 Yale L.J. 1192 (1961).   By Pub. Law 87-31, 75 Stat. 75 (1961), Congress approved this interpretation of the Social Security Act but postponed its effective date to Sept. 1, 1962, to give states with "suitable home" requirements additional time to conform their legislation to the new policy.

[130] Ga. Laws of 1951, No. 445.

tween the two of illegitimate children within the same classification." [131] The controversial Welfare Code enacted in 1961 by the town of Newburgh, New York, included the provision that "All mothers of illegitimate children are to be advised that should they have any more children out of wedlock, they shall be denied relief." [132] See generally Bell, Aid to Dependent Children (1965).

The same ambivalence which swings between protection of the child from stigma and disability and use of the child's status as a deterrent sanction is apparent in the policy adopted towards birth certificates. Problems of record-keeping can arise in a number of different contexts which need to be distinguished: (1) where an adulterine bastard is accepted by the mother's husband into a family which includes other legitimate children and the husband and wife wish to conceal the irregularity and have the illegitimate child treated in all respects as the equal of the legitimate children; (2) where an illegitimate child is adopted by unrelated persons and the adoptive parents, particularly if they have natural children as well, wish to conceal the fact of adoption with its implication of probable illegitimate birth; (3) where the natural mother keeps the child and subsequently marries a man who is not the child's father but who accepts the child and wishes it treated as the equal of subsequent legitimate children; and (4) where the child remains illegitimate and does not fall into any of the above family situations, as where the mother keeps the child and remains unmarried.

The birth record typically includes not only the name and sex of the child and date and place of birth but also the names of the father and mother. Any discrepancy in the indication of parentage (different surnames or omission of the father's name) makes illegitimacy apparent even if the original certificate does not affirmatively proclaim that status, as by stamping the face thereof with the letters "OW" (out of wedlock).[133] The evolution of legal reform, noteworthy for its slow pace, has provided a partial solution to this problem through the use of a short-form certificate which omits the telltale indicia of parentage on the original record. See, e.g., the confidentiality provided for by the Uniform Vital Statistics Act §23(2), 9C U.L.A. 364 (1957), which is in force in a number of states:

> Disclosure of illegitimacy of birth or of information from which it can be ascertained, may be made only upon order of a court in a case where such information is necessary for the determination of personal or property rights and then only for such purpose.

[131] This opinion is apparently unpublished; it is quoted in Illegitimacy and its Impact on the Aid to Dependent Children Program 54 (U.S. Bureau of Public Assistance 1960).

[132] N.Y. Times, June 29, 1961, p. 32, col. 2. Enforcement of the Code was enjoined on the ground that it violated both state and federal law. State Bd. of Social Welfare v. Newburgh, 28 Misc. 2d 539, 220 N.Y.S.2d 54 (Sup. Ct. 1961).

[133] The example is from New York before 1936; the slow but progressive movement towards reform of birth certification practice in New York is traced in Note, Illegitimacy under New York Law, 23 Brooklyn L. Rev. 80, 83-84 (1957).

This does not, however, resolve the problem in any of the first three situations noted above in which there is objection to disclosure of the fact of illegitimacy or adoption for any purpose whatsoever. This problem is interesting not only for its legal difficulty but as an indication of the emotional undercurrents with which the subject of illegitimacy is still charged. During a House of Commons debate in 1959 on a bill to change the law relating to illegitimate children, for example, the following amendment was proposed by Mr. Parker:

> Any child born to a married woman, and accepted as one of the family by her husband, shall be deemed to be the child of her marriage to her husband, provided she was married at the time of the child's birth, and upon acceptance by the husband, the birth certificate shall be amended to provide that the said child is the legitimate child of the marriage.[134]

This amendment was withdrawn after it was subjected to a storm of criticism as permitting "legalised forgery"[135] of the birth register and as encouraging a "serious weakening in respect for marriage":[136]

> Steps such as this — and we see the same thing in regard to such evils as prostitution — are but palliatives. They have nothing to do with the main problem. . . .
> . . . The real answer is not to remove every restraint there should be upon a mother or upon a father by saying, "Even if you have an illegitimate child nothing will happen to the child. It can be put into a position equivalent to that of your lawful children." There is still, and there should be, some restraint on people giving way to their passions, and one restraint is the consequences on other people.
> . . . [I]n my view it would be unwise, in our present situation, to take from husbands or wives — on whatever specious and well-intended grounds — their sense of responsibility to their children.
> Parents must not confuse their progeny, and I believe that confusion of progeny — disputes about legitimacy and illegitimacy — would be a bad thing for family life. It is true, as the hon. Gentleman said, that it would be — or could be — very nasty in family life to have some legitimate and some illegitimate children. The answer is for husbands and wives to remember that before they indulge their passions.
> To change the name from illegitimacy to legitimacy is not the answer — it is only changing the name. The wife or husband remains dishonoured. It is no good their saying that the child is legitimate — in the circumstances foreseen someone has been dishonourable, and no change in name can change what was an act of dishonour into an act of honour.

---

134 605 H.C. Deb. (5th ser.) 760 (1959).
135 Id. at 767.
136 Quoted id. at 774.

. . . [I]n nature, there remains a difference between someone born of a loyal and honourable union and the unhappy person who is not. We should face that fact. [Mr. Bell] [137]

The same arguments were adopted by the majority of the Royal Commission on Marriage and Divorce:

A powerful deterrent to illicit relationships would be removed [if such a statute were adopted], with disastrous results for the status of marriage as at present understood. The issue is fundamental but perfectly plain. If children born in adultery may subsequently acquire the status of legitimate children, an essential distinction between lawful marriages and illicit unions disappears.[138]

Similar considerations have been advanced in this country; thus Eldredge has objected to the practice of changing the birth records of an adopted child to show him as the natural child of the adoptive parents:

Regardless of what the majority of adopting parents and adopted children may or may not want to have known, this does not justify a conspiracy between the adoptive parents and a State agency to have the latter issue an official document which contains factual information which is untrue and is known to be untrue. The certified copy of the birth certificate . . . will be used to induce some kind of action to be taken by a person who has no knowledge of the facts, and who is induced to act in reliance upon the accuracy of the facts as stated in an official document carrying the seal of the governmental bureau. . . .

. . . [The] argument of the social workers, that we must lie to illegitimate adopted children about their ancestry "for their own good," leaves me cold. But I become hot with anger when I realize that they have carried this to the point where you responsible officials, who are charged with the important public duty of issuing accurate certifications of vital statistics, are compelled to issue false and fraudulent certificates. . . .[139]

In evaluating this controversy and in considering why Eldredge becomes "hot with anger," it may be helpful to distinguish the purposes for which birth records are used. Almost everyone has some occasion to produce a birth certificate: e.g., to establish citizenship as when re-entering the country or applying for a passport; to prove age upon first school admission, registration for voting, obtaining a driver's license, or showing eligibility for an old-age pension. The short-form birth certificate without indication of parentage is sufficient for most of these secondary pur-

[137] Id. at 770-771.

[138] Royal Commission on Marriage and Divorce, Report 1951-1955, Cmd. No. 9678, par. 1180 (1956).

[139] Eldredge, How Reliable Are Official Certifications by Bureaus of Vital Statistics? (Address to Am. Assn. for Vital Records & Public Health Statistics, June 17, 1960).

poses. The issue turns, therefore, on the limited situations remaining where the child's status determines some legal right: eligibility for Social Security benefits, intestate succession, or instances noted by Eldredge such as inheritance as a lineal blood descendant or eligibility for admission to an hereditary society. Aside from the weight given to the abstract proposition that public records should never lie, one can try to balance the risk of deception and the interest of the person who might be deceived against the values which misrepresentation of the records can achieve for the child and his family.[140] The position of Bell in the House of Commons and of the Royal Commission is of particular interest because the Parker amendment would have changed the record only to have it accord with a factual situation which the husband of the adulteress had already accepted; there was therefore no issue of deception of the husband. Presumably the likely victims of deception would be the illegitimate's purported siblings who might be able to exclude him as heir if they knew he was illegitimate and the father died intestate. As the husband would have already determined by changing the record that he wished the children treated equally, what social policy is being advanced by permitting the legitimate children to thwart his wishes if he neglects to make a will?

The magnitude of the risk of deception is also contingent upon the extent of the substantive disabilities and the force of the traditional view which has insisted that the blood line is a critical factor that must be given formal recognition even if the immediate family wishes to obliterate blood differences. In either of the stepparent situations noted above the illegitimate child can be accorded most of the legal consequences of legitimacy if he is adopted by the stepparent.[141] But the adoption proceeding and the record of it on an amended birth certificate only emphasize the distinction which the parents wish to conceal.

Consider again, also, the opposition to changes in the law of legitimation which we have already noted. When the 1960 Uniform Act on Paternity, page 46 supra, was being prepared, the first tentative draft included the following as optional sections, but they were omitted from the final version because, as the Commissioners noted in their Prefatory Note, "there were apparently irreconcilable points of view":

[SECTION 32. [*Inheritance from Mother.*] Children born out of wedlock inherit from their mother, and she from them.]

[SECTION 33. [*Inheritance from Father.*] They shall inherit from the father when the paternity is proven during his life, or they have been recognized by him as his children; but such recognition must have been general and notorious, or in writing. Under such circum-

---

140 Compare Professor Ernst Freund's comment that "surely, the interest of the child should be paramount, and the abstract desirability of complete data for registration or statistical purposes should take a second place." Freund, The Present Law Concerning Children Born Out of Wedlock, and Possible Changes in Legislation, in Standards of Legal Protection for Children Born Out of Wedlock 26, 33 (U.S. Children's Bureau Pub. No. 77, 1921).

141 But see pages 565-574 infra for situations in which the legal status of an adopted child is not equivalent to that of a legitimate natural child.

stances, if the recognition has been mutual, the father may inherit from his child born out of wedlock.][142]

In 1921, Professor Freund, apparently accepting as an ideal the Norwegian law under which the father of every illegitimate child was compelled by the state to assume the full obligation that is owing to a legitimate child, see page 59 supra, was troubled by the fact that "the practical difficulties in the way of indisputably establishing paternity in many cases are undeniable." [143]   But the proof problem is not a complete explanation of the law's policy, for the illegitimate child's connection with his mother is not difficult to establish; yet the law occasionally continues to restrict the child's right to take from or through his mother, and at least in many cases proof of paternity can be established beyond dispute. Freund also noted that "it is clear that intense prejudices prevail upon the subject," [144] and it becomes a matter of no small importance to the would-be reformer to try to determine why Bell, Eldredge, the members of the Royal Commission, and many other people feel so strongly on this matter.

If the theoretical desirability of equality in inheritance and other rights between legitimate and illegitimate children is assumed, can such a change be effectuated legislatively, and if so how? [145]   In this connection consider the following comments:

1. Freund, The Present Law Concerning Children Born Out of Wedlock, and Possible Changes in Legislation, in Standards of Legal Protection for Children Born Out of Wedlock 26, 34-35 (U.S. Children's Bureau Pub. No. 77, 1921):

> Waiving the difficulties encountered in an adverse public opinion, it is necessary to realize that the policy of general compulsory legitimation involves a revision of the law of testamentary liberty.   In Europe a child has an absolute right of inheritance; in America it has not.   [Here t]he lawful child can count on the normal paternal instinct for a share in the inheritance, but a child forced on a man against his will is likely to find himself disinherited upon the father's death unless the law provides against this.   Compulsory legitimation logically involves compulsory inheritance, and without this it is a precarious gift.   The change of the law is theoretically possible.   But is it likely that the child born out of wedlock would be accorded a right which the child born in wedlock has not?   Even a legislature favorably disposed toward children born out of wedlock may object to a discrimination making their rights superior to those of the law-

---

[142] 1958 Handbook of the National Conference of Commissioners on Uniform State Laws 275, 280-281.   All bracketed material is bracketed in the original.

[143] Freund, note 140 supra, at 27.

[144] Ibid.

[145] Compare Article 6(5) of the German Constitution (Federal Republic): "Illegitimate children shall be provided by legislation with the same opportunities for their physical and spiritual development and their position in society as are enjoyed by legitimate children."

ful child.[146] A compulsory legitimation measure must deal with the problem of the married father and his wife; with the question of the right of custody and education; and with the question of the name of the child. . . . It would be interesting to see a compulsory-legitimation law formulated, if merely as a basis of detailed consideration and discussion; but the most sanguine advocates of such legislation will hardly venture to predict its speedy adoption in many States.

2. Davis, Illegitimacy and the Social Structure, 45 Am. J. Soc. 215, 228, 231-233 (1939):

> Given our institutional patterns and the sentiments supporting them, the position of the illegitimate child seems inevitable. . . . A child whose physical parents are not his full sociological parents because not married to each other, or who is living with adoptive parents, must necessarily feel different from other children, even though he is never directly insulted. He is supposed, for example, to cherish his mother and to view as an outrage any reflection upon her virtue; but illegitimate pregnancy is in itself a great blotch upon a woman's virtue. Hence, in so far as the child identifies himself with his physical mother — as he is bound to do in our culture — he will profoundly be affected by the knowledge of his illegitimacy. . . . [This] emphasizes the inescapable emotional conflict that must result for the person whose "real" parents are not what they should be.[147]
>
> [Davis then discusses what he regards as the only methods of "abolishing" illegitimacy, first,] by eliminating marriage and the family [or second, by an hypothetical program which would provide free contraceptives and compulsory education in their use combined with a program of abortion] to be performed freely and scientifically, and perhaps compulsorily, upon all pregnant women not mar-

[146] This is precisely what has happened in New York, where a father can legally disinherit his legitimate children but a paternity support order against him may be enforceable against his estate. See page 53 supra. Compare §4 of the 1960 Uniform Act on Paternity ("The obligation of the estate of the father for liabilities under this Act is limited to amounts accrued prior to his death") with §6 of the first tentative draft of this act ("The obligation of the father, where his paternity has been judicially established in his life time, or has been acknowledged by him in writing, is enforceable against his estate in such an amount as the court may determine, having regard to the age of the child, its inheritance from the father, the ability of the mother to support it, the amount of property left by the father, the number, age, and financial condition of the lawful issue, if any, and the rights if the widow, if any." Provision is made for periodic or lump sum payments). The text of the draft appears in 1958 Handbook of the National Conference of Commissioners on Uniform State Laws 275.

On the general question whether legitimate children, like wives, should have compulsory inheritance rights, see page 311 infra. — Ed.

[147] . . . William Healy, in Mental Conflicts and Misconduct (Boston, 1917), pp. 47, 73, 213-17, discusses the connection between misconduct and worry over parentage. The strength of such feelings is attested by an apparently frequent child complex, the compulsive doubt as to whether one's parents are one's real parents.

ried to the partner in conception [and a severe penalty for procreating an illegitimate child.] . . .

In the last analysis our hypothetical scheme is not far removed from the radical proposal to abolish marriage. If we were so emancipated from the mores as to sanction contraception and abortion, why should we worry about illegitimacy? . . . If we look at social matters so objectively that we could eliminate illegitimacy by deliberate planning, we would cease to abhor illegitimacy itself and would feel no necessity of putting our plan into effect. Illegitimacy and marriage would both have disappeared. We may conclude, therefore, that such a bizarre plan will not be adopted, and that the future changes in our reproductive institutions, whatever they may be, will not embrace among their fruits the abolition of illegitimacy, but merely alterations in the amount, kind, and circumstances of it.

PROBLEM

The following statute, patterned after one in effect in North Dakota from 1917 to 1945, has been proposed for adoption in your state. What objectives does it seek to attain? How well is it conceived to achieve its objectives? Would you recommend its adoption? What amendments would you propose?

Every child is hereby declared to be the legitimate child of its natural parents and as such is entitled to support and education, to the same extent as if it had been born in lawful wedlock. It shall inherit from its natural parents and from their kindred heir lineal and collateral.

This section shall apply to cases where the natural father of any such child is married to one other than the mother of said child, as well as where he is single. Provided, however, this law shall not be so construed as to give to said child a right to dwelling or a residence with the family of its father, if such father be married.

E. Disposition of Illegitimate Children

PROBLEM

Your secretary informs you that a Miss Angela Stevens is on the phone and wishes to see you "as soon as possible." In view of her insistence, an appointment is made for this afternoon. Shortly thereafter the morning mail brings you a letter from a college classmate, Jim Larsen:

Recently I saw my cousin, Angela Stevens, and have urged her to see you without delay. She's in a mess, has been having an affair with a married man, Nicholas Johnson, and now she's some months pregnant. Angela thinks she is very much in love with Johnson, but he has two young children and won't, I think, divorce his wife for religious reasons. The wife apparently knows nothing about this.

Angela wants to keep the baby, but I am not at all sure she will be able to support it. Johnson has a fairly good job as a buyer in a large department store, and Angela thinks he earns about $140 a week. The reason for needing your help is that he's not being very reasonable — first tried to get her to have an abortion, and now he's pressuring her to put the baby out for adoption, which she very much opposes, because she wants to give it a good home with a mother's love.

If she sees you, Angela will give you the rest of the story. I might add that she's 22, and the second of five children; her father (who was a druggist) and her mother are now dead, and after one year of college she had to withdraw because of financial difficulties. After she left college and mastered a certain amount of shorthand and other office skills, she took a job as secretary to an executive in a small corporation, where she makes $80 a week.

Prepare to interview the client. What additional facts will you seek? On the basis of the above facts, what is the best course of action to pursue?

(To deal adequately with this problem, you will need to review the earlier parts of this chapter, as well as study the materials through page 169 infra.)

1. *Note on Counseling Problems*[148]

Many of the problems in these materials place the student in the role of the lawyer at his point of initial contact with a client. These situations are of immediate practical importance, and many of them (such as the problem above) are drawn from an actual case. Like any legal problems, the ones in these materials require sound diagnostic judgment, the ability to isolate the particular narrow legal issues involved without which appropriate research and action are impossible. Usually, however, more than narrow technical legal skill is required. Most clients who seek consultation about a family law problem are people in trouble seeking help, and the real or fancied legal issue which has brought them to a lawyer is often only one facet of a complex and highly charged situation.

This difficulty is not unique to family law. No competent lawyer will draw a will or draft a contract without first informing himself of and assessing all the relevant facts, nonlegal as well as legal. He knows that a legal solution which is usually applicable to the type of problem before

---

[148] In general, see Freeman, Legal Interviewing and Counseling (1964), a series of problem cases presented by the lawyers who handled them, followed by critical comments from members of various professions. See also Watson, The Lawyer As Counselor, 5 J. Fam. L. 7 (1965). For further background and additional bibliography, see Heller, Polen & Polsky, An Introduction to Legal Interviewing (1960), which can be purchased from the National Legal Aid and Defender Assn., 1155 E. 60th St., Chicago 37, Ill. ($1.00). For some useful examples of transcribed interviews with analytical comments, see Gill, Newman & Redlich, The Initial Interview in Psychiatric Practice (1954); Pittenger, Hackett & Danehy, The First Five Minutes (1960).

him may be inappropriate because of legally irrelevant but psychologically critical circumstances of the individual case. Moreover, he must
anticipate eventualities which the client may have overlooked, and in
many situations this may involve helping the client face up to unpleasant
realities which he has consciously or unconsciously tried to avoid. In
addition, the legal problem is usually enmeshed in a broader factual
framework; counsel for a seller drafting a disclaimer clause for inclusion
in a sales contract, for example, cannot ignore the market (a nonlegal
fact) lest he end up with a contract which protects his client so well that
no one wishes to buy his goods.

Moreover, the client's best interests are not the only concern of the
lawyer. While he is obligated "to represent the client with undivided
fidelity," he is also "an officer of the law charged . . . with the duty of
aiding in the administration of justice." [149] An even more serious problem in family law cases is the interest of other and often unrepresented
parties whose affairs are inextricably interwoven with those of the client.
In the instant problem the welfare of the unborn baby must certainly
weigh heavily upon the lawyer's conscience. If he does not also "represent" the baby, no one else is likely to fill the void. The same difficulty
arises in divorce cases where children are involved.

Any law office initial interview is difficult, and the ability to handle it
requires experience. Typically it consists of a disorderly presentation of
bits of legally relevant and irrelevant fact and opinion as they are filtered
through a biased informant. In most family law situations, moreover, the
client is not only biased, but his perception is further distorted because of
his emotional turmoil. The very situations which bring him to a lawyer
are charged with feeling which, although perhaps disguised at first, boils
to the surface on slight provocation: the shame and anger of an unmarried pregnancy, the desperation over an apparently hopeless marital situation, the bitterness of a custody fight. In these instances the emotional
overtones are obvious, but even where less apparent they may be just as
important. The situation is aggravated by the fact that the lawyer will
often have to probe some of the most intimate aspects of the client's life,
e.g., his religious scruples or his sexual experiences.

Ideally this aspect of legal education should come from clinical training
comparable to that given in medical schools. As this is usually impracticable,[150] some of the problems in these materials offer an opportunity to
consider the interview situation, and a few introductory remarks about
handling these problems may be helpful. In each of these situations you
must put yourself in the role of the lawyer and use your imaginative powers to visualize the client:

— How will I begin the interview?
— What will I look for, and how?
— What will I do if the client breaks down and sobs?

[149] A.B.A., Canons of Professional Ethics, Canons 6, 22.
[150] But see National Council on Legal Clinics, Education for Professional Responsibility — Preliminary Reports on Seven Experimental Projects (1962).

— How will I raise the problem of setting a fee?

The client has sought your professional skill because he is looking for help, and his expectations are comparable to those he would have if physical distress took him to a doctor. If you accept his case, the first interview is the critically important base upon which a continuing relationship will be built. If you decide not to take the case, how can the interview nonetheless serve a constructive purpose rather than leaving the client further harassed or embittered?

Applying these considerations to our problem will illustrate their complexity. Ultimately an unmarried pregnant woman must seek assistance from someone; few today would be as hardy or unwise as the poor girl, described at page 13 supra, who kept her secret and delivered herself in a back room. She will seek help — from relatives, from her pastor or priest, from a psychiatrist, from an obstetrician, from a public health nurse, from a social agency — or from a lawyer. What motivates a particular client first to seek legal counseling instead of spiritual, medical, or social work counseling? We know very little about this decision-making; in many instances the motivation stems from the culture or experience of the client. Depending upon her choice of a helping profession, she may select one particular facet of her problem for initial presentation. When she decides upon a lawyer, we can reasonably assume that her selection process is not exclusively rational and that the legal excuse for the interview is, like the visible part of an iceberg, only a symptom of something much vaster and more complicated. It is also probable that the client herself lacks understanding of her problem or her own actions. The lawyer, therefore, must be prepared to recognize unconscious behavior. The following paragraphs may be helpful in the lawyer's attempt to understand Angela Stevens:

> The reasons underlying some forms of human behavior are obvious both to the actor and to outside observers. Sometimes they are concealed from outsiders but are recognized more or less clearly by the actor. Sometimes they are unknown even to him. For example, a man applying for a job insults his prospective employer. How can such behavior be understood? Did he not know he was being insulting? Or didn't he know that an insult would prevent his being hired? Or didn't he really want the job? Or what? In seeking to explain his failure to get the job, he might say, "The foreman was unreasonable." But very likely he would himself be aware of the unsatisfactoriness of such an explanation. Often people who behave in some such irrational way as this are as much puzzled by their behavior as is anyone else.

> We can sympathize more readily with such a person's bewilderment if we realize that there is much of our own behavior we find hard to explain. Our glib rationalizations do not satisfy even ourselves. Why do we sometimes fly into a rage if we are kept waiting for a minute when at other times we'll wait in line fairly patiently for

half an hour? Why do we sometimes punish a child severely for a slight fault and at other times let more severe misbehavior go unremarked? Why do some people in particular "get our goats"?

If we knew all, we would doubtless understand all. Bizarre behavior, like more usual behavior, has its causes, but sometimes they are deeply hidden. In dealing with others it is seldom possible or essential to understand fully the causes of their actions. It is essential, however, to realize that their behavior is motivated. Its source may lie hidden in the depths of their personalities where neither they nor we can readily discover it. In a complex personality with its many interconnected causal chains, the factors underlying a given bit of behavior are usually many and varied. A single cause cannot be isolated, and to attempt to force the individual to name one is to demand the impossible. He will be forced to resort to an inadequate rationalization.

The recognition that much human motivation is unconscious will enable the interviewer to be more tolerant, less condemnatory, and thus better able to help his client effectively. Instead of becoming impatient with rationalizations, he will realize that motives that the client disguises even to himself are probably sources of deep and painful anxiety to him.

Unconscious motivation is much more common than we ordinarily recognize in our attempt to understand people. We seek too often for intellectual *grounds* for behavior rather than for psychological *causes* rooted in feelings and emotions. "Drives" are emotional affairs, and actions controlled by them have their source in feeling rather than in intellect. A person who apparently likes, but really dislikes, another "forgets" a luncheon engagement with him, and in extenuation pleads a busy day. A man fired from a job because of incompetence "explains" that the work was too heavy for him. Why a client says certain things and leaves others unsaid, why a child with a high I.Q. flunks in school, why a wife who effusively protests her love for her husband continually belittles him, are questions whose answers are to be sought not in intellectual but emotional terms. Explanations such as, "He's deceitful," "He's lazy," "She's just being modest about him," are obviously inadequate. Yet for many people such remarks conclude the discussion and block any real understanding.[151]

It goes without saying, therefore, that the lawyer should watch for the irrational, for emotions, silences, and other nonverbal communication which are significant expressions of unconscious determinants.

Getting from an interview all the facts necessary to make professional judgments is exceedingly difficult. The lawyer should be a sympathetic, interested listener; the client has probably undergone ample punishment, self-inflicted or otherwise, and what he most needs is understanding. In-

---

[151] Garrett, Interviewing: Its Principles and Methods 12-13 (Family Service Assn. of America 1942).

deed, often that is all the client wants. It has been suggested that for some clients the primary need is to obtain

> an attentive captive audience. With the aid of a respectful ear he can ventilate his resentment, apprehension, hope, guilt or other emotionally charged ideas; whereupon he feels greatly relieved and drops the case. Divorce lawyers recognize this familiar chain of events; and it is commonplace in psychiatric practice. Its constructive value in averting or postponing damaging action should not be scoffed at.[152]

Such a natural, friendly approach must maintain a delicate balance between being constructive and confident without making promises that cannot be fulfilled or communicating opinions resulting from conclusions based on fragmentary evidence. Nothing will contribute more to the desired atmosphere than the lawyer's willingness to adopt a passive role, giving the client his entire unhurried attention while allowing the client to tell his story in his own meandering fashion. It will probably help if the lawyer conducts the interview in relaxed surroundings with as few interruptions as possible, if he takes as few notes as possible (writing up the interview later), and if at least initially he asks only such indirect questions as are necessary to keep the client talking. At the same time, one must not lose sight of the fact that the lawyer, unlike the long-range therapist, usually has an immediate problem to contend with. In our Problem, for example, what, if any, action should Angela take against Nick? What plans should she be making for the baby? Sound resolution of such questions means that the lawyer must elicit the relevant information and be prepared at least to outline alternative courses of action for the client.

Whether or not the interview develops that rapport which opens the door to the fullest communication from the client often turns on unconscious factors. Although written for social workers, Garrett's explanation of this process and of the desirable mean which the interviewer should seek is equally pertinent for lawyers:

> For many a client it is a unique experience to talk with someone who, instead of criticizing or admonishing, listens with non-judgmental understanding. This relationship with a person who does not ask anything for himself personally but focuses his interest entirely on the client and yet refrains from imposing advice or control is a very satisfying one. The discovery of these characteristics in the interviewer, accompanied as it is by the absence of closer knowledge of the interviewer's personality with its inevitable personal whims and foibles, leads the client to idealize him. The client's feelings are unchecked by personal knowledge of the interviewer which might dilute them. He thus endows the worker with the ideal characteristics one is always searching for, quite independently of whether or not the worker actually is such an ideal person. . . .

---

[152] Modlin, The Client and You — What You Are, 16 Bar Bull. 151 (N.Y. County Lawyers Assn. 1959).

The opposite sort of situation also arises in interviewing. Again quite independently of the interviewer's actual character, the client, because of his own anxieties, insecurity, and deprivations, may endow him with negative characteristics and build up antagonism toward him. Much depends on the client's previous experiences with his parents or with others in authority. . . .

The development of excessive negative or positive feelings by the client is often alarming to the interviewer who may be unaware of having done anything to arouse such feelings. An interviewer tends to want his clients to like him, but sometimes in his eagerness to achieve this end he unwittingly encourages more dependency than he had realized was potentially present. A worker should realize that the development of an emotional rapport, positive or negative, between the client and himself is not abnormal but inevitable, and that he should direct his attention not to eliminating this relationship but to controlling its nature and intensity. He must guard against misleading the client into an overly dependent relationship through appearing too personally friendly or appearing to promise too much, but on the other hand he must not lean over backward in avoiding this danger and make the client feel that he is an unresponsive and unsympathetic listener. It is easy, when one is treated like God, to assume the characteristics of that role, and it is easy to over-correct this tendency.

If an interviewer notices that the relationship with his client seems to be developing negatively, he should not become overly alarmed because this may be due not at all to him but to factors deeply hidden in his client's personality. He should review his own activity in the case and make sure that he has given no objective grounds for the antagonism the client seems to feel for him. He may have given inadequate help, broken an appointment, or himself have developed negative feelings toward the client of which he was not fully aware. If there are no such objective sources for his client's negativism, he can assure the client by a continued attempt to understand the reasons for his difficulties that he is not retaliating with disapproval of his own.

The development of an inter-relationship of this general sort, positive or negative, between interviewer and interviewee is not at all a unique phenomenon but a universal one. It is a commonplace that people tend to become dependent upon their doctors, lawyers, and ministers. Toward the end of her pregnancy a woman often relies more on her physician than on her husband. A patient under psychoanalysis develops a strong emotional attachment to the analyst. The analyst has developed methods of making therapeutic use of such a relationship. He calls it technically "transference." . . .[153]

Many family questions brought to lawyers turn out not to be legal problems at all, or the legal issue is found to be subsidiary to pressing

[153] Garrett, note 151 supra, at 19-20.

nonlegal problems. How can the lawyer handle such situations? For example, a middle-aged woman comes to her lawyer because "I need some legal advice — I will only take a moment of your time." She continues: "I plan to visit my sister in California for six months. I want to know if that will give my husband grounds to divorce me for desertion." Although she speaks calmly, she is full of tension, and to a sensitive observer she is saying, very simply, "help me." Her question, however, is superficially easy, and the lawyer may well be tempted to reassure her with a negative response and quickly usher her from his office before he gets involved. Does he have a responsibility to do more? He might, for example, say: "I'd have to know more about the whole situation before I could advise you. Suppose you go ahead and tell me all about your problem." During the next hour (or more) the following story emerges, punctuated by long silences and accompanied by substantial consumption of Kleenex. She has been married for twenty years, her husband is a professional man, they have no children, and she is a writer. Although for the last year or two her husband had seemed to be required to work many evenings and sometimes to stay away overnight, she was busy with her writing and had no idea that anything was wrong. Then a month ago at breakfast he suddenly announced that he wanted a divorce, that for a year he had been hopelessly in love with a much younger woman who was associated with him in his work, that he was going to marry her as soon as she had divorced her present husband. He had not, however, moved out of their house, which they continued to share in a state of uneasy truce. Now more legal problems emerged: Can she block his attempt to get a divorce and so prevent him from marrying the other woman? What shall she do if he suddenly takes off for Reno, the haven to which his lover has recently gone? She has to get away from him; yet she wants to make sure that he does not divorce her. She seethes with anger, frustration, and humiliation ("everyone's known about this except me; they've all been laughing behind my back; I even entertained that woman in my house a few months ago"). Yet her emotional ambivalence comes out clearly in her hope that her husband will come to his senses, her prediction that the other woman is just playing him for a fool and will never marry him, her repeated question: "What did I do that was wrong?"

At this point it has become apparent that the legal problems which are implicit in this case have not yet ripened and that the immediate need is for marital counseling. The lawyer can help the client realize this need and direct her to avenues of possible help by asking questions that will emphasize the extent of her emotional ambivalence, so that she will become aware that she herself does not know what she wants to do. He can ask her why she waited a month before talking to anyone, why she then came to a lawyer instead of a member of some other profession, whether she has a pastor with whom she would feel it appropriate to talk, whether she is aware of the work of marriage counselors and agencies like family service associations. Hopefully he could terminate the interview by making her aware of and desirous for such help, in which case the best procedure is to use the telephone forthwith to make an appointment for her with whatever counselor she selects. Questions such as the following are bound to arise in practice, and the lawyer will need to prepare himself to answer them.

1. What kind of expert help does the client require? Some knowledge of the different kinds of services rendered by social workers, marriage counselors, clinical psychologists, and psychiatrists will help in making decisions about an appropriate referral. The nonlegal materials in this book illustrate some of the different skills of such specialists.

2. What services are available in the lawyer's community? In a big city knowing the resources (the extent of free services and the cost of private treatment) means finding out about the various services and making contacts with at least some practitioners and agencies in order to be prepared when the need for referral arises. In smaller communities many services may be inadequate or nonexistent, for there is an acute shortage of competent, trained personnel in all these allied professions. It is important to ascertain the exact situation in a community, for there is little value in persuading a client to accept a service which then proves to be unavailable or inadequate. Even if there are some psychiatrists and social agencies available, the lawyer should find out if they are overtaxed. "One of the real barriers to effective co-operation with the legal profession in our community," a social worker has reported, "is the waiting list. In general, when attorneys wish to make a referral for social work help the situation is urgent and waiting for counseling is destructive." [154]

Even if facilities are available, referral to a nonlegal profession may be inexpedient because of the client's resistance to the idea. This may happen where the client fears a breach of anonymity and confidentiality, or where she has an antagonism toward or fear of the other profession (which may be why she selected a lawyer to come to in the first place). The client may have no confidence in the professional ability of social workers or psychiatrists, or a middle-class client may think social work is just for poor people, or that proposed referral to a psychiatrist (always a delicate task at best) implies that the lawyer thinks the client is crazy. In these situations the lawyer will have to terminate the relationship as constructively as possible, or decide to counsel himself, or undertake limited counseling in the hope that after a few hours he will be able to complete a referral. For the moment, we merely note the existence of this problem. In Chapter 8 we present some materials and suggest readings designed to aid those who decide to do some counseling.

2. *Alternative Dispositions*

Whenever the lawyer deals with an unwed mother, he must consider the range of possible solutions of the problem:

a. Should the mother be encouraged to marry the baby's father? There is a wide difference of opinion on this matter among those engaged in

[154] Report of Committee on Lawyer-Family Agency Cooperation 11 (Family Service Assn. of America 1960).

counseling unwed mothers. In a questionnaire study comparing the counseling practices of members of five professions (not including lawyers) who deal with unmarried mothers, 80 per cent of 68 responding pastors but only 42 per cent of 169 doctors and 14 per cent each of 44 social workers and 37 public health nurses favored marriage as the recommended solution to the unmarried mother problem.[155] To some extent these differences may reflect the different socioeconomic status of the mothers who typically approach a pastor on the one extreme and a public health nurse on the other. A cross-cultural study of 1062 unwed mothers has reported that for 90 per cent of white mothers and 79 per cent of Negro mothers in upper socioeconomic levels, the pregnancy out of wedlock resulted from "a love relationship of some duration," whereas for the overwhelming majority of both whites and Negroes in the lowest socioeconomic grouping, intercourse resulting in pregnancy was part of "a casual relationship" with the father.[156] If those of upper socioeconomic status typically go to pastors and those of low status to agencies or public health nurses, this would go far to explain the different images of these professions. Some of the problems and implications of forced marriages are discussed below in connection with other marriage problems. As to the outcomes of marriages where conception precedes marriage, see Christensen, page 106 supra. In any event, in many situations (as in our current Problem, where the father already has a wife and children) marriage is legally or practically impossible.

b. A remotely possible outcome is custody to (and possible legitimation or adoption by) the father without marriage to the mother. In most cases, however, the father will not be interested in the child.[157]

c. Should the mother be urged to give up all her rights in the baby and sign a release which will permit the baby's adoption by strangers? In some states this course of action will require the intervention of a licensed social welfare agency. In most states an adoption privately arranged by a lawyer or obstetrician is legal but poses serious problems.

d. Should the mother keep the baby herself? Where this course of action is proposed or considered, serious counseling and practical problems almost always arise. First, there must be consideration of the mother's motives for wanting to keep the child. Second, the effect upon the baby will turn in part upon the mother's economic status, the likelihood that

---

[155] Strand & Larson, Five Professions View the Unmarried Parent, 6 Int. J. Social Psychiatry 269, 271 (1960).

[156] Vincent, Ego Involvement in Sexual Relations: Implications for Research on Illegitimacy, 65 Am. J. Soc. 287, 288 (1959). For a more complete report of the study, and some suggestions as to its limitations, see page 96 supra.

[157] Compare Commonwealth v. Rozanski, 206 Pa. Super. 397, 213 A.2d 155 (1965) (3-2 decision) (father of illegitimate child granted visitation rights), with Wallace v. Wallace, 60 Ill. App. 2d 300, 210 N.E.2d 4 (1965) (claim by illegitimate child to society and companionship of father denied). See also English Legitimacy Act, 1959, 7 & 8 Eliz. 2, c. 73, §3, which appeared to grant the father of an illegitimate child expanded rights; but see Adoption Application 41/61, [1963] 1 Ch. 315. See also pages 372 and 491-493 infra.

she will marry and thus regularize the child's position, and the mother's cultural environment which will determine the extent to which an unmarried mother and child will be accepted.

To the extent that unwed motherhood is symbolic of deeper psychological problems, the difficulties of keeping the child would seem likely to aggravate the situation. Unless she has independent means, the mother will be forced to depend upon (1) assistance from the father (which is statistically improbable in any adequate amount), (2) her own earnings (which will have to be large enough to provide for day care for the child while the mother works, an unlikely prospect for those in lower socioeconomic levels), (3) support from her relatives, which may intensify family-oriented psychological problems, or (4) public relief, which is probably the likeliest result. A major phase in counseling unwed mothers will be the need to achieve a realistic appraisal of the usually grim economic prospects of the mother who thinks she wishes to keep her child. For the lawyer or counselor a proposal that the mother keep the child needs to be viewed in light of the unlikelihood that the mother in fact will keep the child permanently. An outcome which postpones a decision about adoption until the child is older or which results in institutional or transitory foster home care for the child may well be unfortunate for the child — and probably for the mother as well.

a.   THE ROLE OF SOCIAL AGENCIES

In many cases involving unwed motherhood it is apparent that both lawyer and client will benefit from the advice and counseling services of social agencies. The agency can quiet the client's fears of publicity, danger, and disgrace. It will arrange for proper medical care and for admission to a responsible maternity home if that is the best plan.

The first excerpt below describes the training and function of the social worker; the second illustrates the application of social casework principles to the problem of unwed motherhood.

THE LAWYER AND THE SOCIAL WORKER 13-16
(Family Service Assn. of America 1959)

THE SOCIAL CASEWORKER AND HIS FUNCTION

The profession of social work is devoted to helping people deal with the pressures of life — pressures that originate either in society or in the individual. The branch of social work that is most concerned with helping individuals, as contrasted with helping groups or communities, is social casework. The social caseworker's task is to help individuals and families mobilize the resources within themselves and society to cope with many problems in everyday life.

The trained social caseworker, like the lawyer, is the product of a long and intensive educational process. Owing to the severe shortage of trained workers, social agencies may be forced to employ untrained persons. However, high standards of professional education for social work have been established, and the number of trained workers is increasing. The professionally trained social caseworker has completed two years of education in a graduate school of social work, following four years of college, and holds a Master's degree. Many schools of social work offer a doctorate in social welfare, and agencies provide various forms of in-service training to raise the standards of social work practice. As part of his graduate studies, the caseworker has had closely supervised practical experience in one or more social agencies.

During his early years of employment in a social agency, the caseworker continues to receive close supervision of his practice. Twenty-two thousand social workers are members of the National Association of Social Workers, a professional organization which represents to social workers what the American Bar Association represents to practicing lawyers. Like lawyers, social workers, too, have developed a code of professional ethics.

Most caseworkers are employees of social agencies, both public and voluntary, although some caseworkers are engaged in the private practice of social work. The voluntary social agency's policies and programs are established by a board of directors. Such a board almost always includes one or more lawyers in its membership. The agency is responsible to the community for the quality of its casework service. The caseworker is responsible to the agency for giving professional counseling help of the highest caliber to persons with problems in social adjustment.

The caseworker is to be found in a variety of settings — family service agencies, child placement and adoption agencies, public welfare departments, schools, probation and parole departments, clinics, hospitals, the armed services, industry, and so forth. Regardless of the setting in which he works, he uses his professional knowledge and his skill in dealing with people to help his clients work out a better social adjustment. The practice of casework, like the practice of law, is an art in which a special body of knowledge is put to use in behalf of the client.

Suggestive of the range of persons with problems who can benefit from the services of a caseworker are the following:

Married couples, torn by discord or temporarily in conflict with each other;
Parents baffled by their child's behavior or distressed over their relationship with him;
Childless couples who want to complete their family through adoption;
Unmarried mothers who need help in planning for their own and their child's future;
Persons of all ages who, owing to unemployment, chronic illness, or desertion, require public assistance funds in order to maintain a normal life;
Industrial workers beset by difficulties that are endangering their capacity to hold a job;

Persons whose lives have been disrupted by long or severe illness or incapacity and who need help in regaining their place in society;

Adolescents who need guidance in choice of a vocation or in making healthy social relationships and whose ties with their parents are strained;

Aging persons who need to readjust their lives following retirement or who are incapacitated by illness.

The above listing is by no means all-inclusive. The lawyer will recognize in this list, however, situations and problems that complicate the lives of some of his own clients. He will be aware, too, that all of these situations involve more than one person — they represent problems of *families,* not merely of individuals. They cannot be solved unless the needs and the capacities of the various members of the family group are taken into account.

Social casework counseling is predominantly family-oriented. The caseworker, in seeking to help a person who is a member of a family group, must, perforce, understand the interrelationships within the family and how each person is affecting the well-being of the others. He makes a family diagnosis, on which he bases a casework treatment plan. Although he may work primarily with one member of the family, he never loses sight of the effects of his counseling service on all members of the family unit.

This family orientation on the part of the caseworker is obviously different from the orientation of the lawyer. The lawyer must keep the individual client uppermost in his concern and must keep his case within the confines of definable legal issues that involve his client. The caseworker's field of concern, on the other hand, must include a wide range of psychological and social issues since these are central to the social problems with which the client has come to him for help. He must be concerned with the relations between husband and wife, between parent and child, between worker and employer, and so on. The issue, for the caseworker, is adjustment in life situations, and nothing is irrelevant that has impact or influence upon the quality of the interpersonal relationships that are involved.

In offering his counseling service, the caseworker does not limit himself to contacts with the client and the members of his immediate family. He reaches out to whatever resources the client may need — child care centers, mental health clinics, employment agencies, public housing, and so on. He also enlists the help of other professional persons — physicians, psychiatrists, ministers, and lawyers — to ensure that the client receives the help he needs. When the client's social situation is entangled in legal difficulties, the lawyer becomes the logical source of help on whom the caseworker must call.

BROWER, WHAT SHALL I DO WITH MY BABY?
12 The Child 166 (1948)

We, as social workers, have long felt that one of the most complex problems facing us is the task of helping the unmarried mother reach a decision about plans for the future care of her child.

Our close contact with the unmarried mother makes us quickly aware of the conflicts and anxiety that she feels when faced with the necessity of making a decision about her child; and her vital emotional stake in the problem is clearly evident to us.

At the same time, the worker is equally aware of what society as a whole feels about the problem, and the stake that society has in the future planning and well-being of the child, as well as society's concern with the problem of the unmarried mother herself, a concern which has been sometimes punitive and other times reformist. . . .

We in Chicago have been giving a good deal of thought to the problem of helping the unmarried mother in her decision about the baby. An institute was recently held here . . . dealing with the problems . . . .

The major point of discussion seemed to be whether our primary emphasis lay with the interest of the mother or the child. Which of the two was the major responsibility of the agency? And upon which was the primary emphasis of our work to be placed?

. . . [W]e emerged with the definite feeling that not only was there no single plan of action that was preferable in all situations, but also, except for rare instances, there was no basic conflict between the best interests of child and mother.

We realized also that our best possibility for working out a sound plan for the future welfare of the child lay in helping the mother to work out her own problems, since it was only in this way that she could be free to make a sound plan for her child.

We have long recognized the complexity of emotions and behavior, and we know that for this reason the decision regarding the child could not be an isolated factor in the life of the unmarried mother.

We know that this decision would be influenced by the same emotional factors that had entered into the pregnancy and the total behavior pattern of the unmarried mother, and that it was through an understanding of these factors that we and she could best ascertain the meaning of the child to her.

We have seen this in many situations where a thorough exploration of the present situation has clearly indicated the inadvisability and even the impossibility of the mother's keeping her baby.

The mother herself has participated and is in agreement with this conclusion. Nevertheless, she finds herself completely unable to carry out the decision that she herself expresses as being best for herself and for her child. . . .

It then becomes the function of the case worker to help the girl understand the psychological pressures and to relate them to the realities of the present situation. . . .

Let us briefly consider some of the plans that these girls bring to us.

Many of the girls who come to us state with fixed determination that they plan to keep their babies. Some of them have the backing of their families in this decision, and the circumstances of their lives indicate that despite many hazards the baby may have some degree of security in living with its mother.

Many more, however, have little mature warmth or security to offer the child, and the plan seems to offer serious disadvantages both to the girl and her baby. What, then, impels these girls to cling to their babies?

Dr. Margaret Gerard of the Institute for Psychoanalysis in Chicago recently pointed out that many of the unmarried mothers coming to us for help are impulsive and infantile individuals, whose own dependency needs may lead them to hold tenaciously to their babies. Sometimes this is because the girl feels that her family, or perhaps the worker, expects it of her. Or she may cling to the child through inability to relinquish any possession for fear that she may regret its loss at some time in the future. One factor that Dr. Gerard pointed out is of particular importance for us who must help the mother in making a decision.

Repeated experience has shown that the more dependent, immature women whom we know to be inadequate mothers practically always choose to keep their babies once they have seen and handled them. This choice grows, not out of an ability to care for the child, but out of the wish for pleasure for herself. We have all known mothers who, long after taking the baby, have found the difficulties which faced her overwhelming, and have come to us, saying, "If I only hadn't seen my baby I could have given him up." They have blamed the worker for not having helped them to make a plan that would have made this possible. . . .

Many other unmarried mothers need to cling to the child because of their attachment to his father, and the hope that through the baby they can still maintain a tie with him. Others who have been led into pregnancy as a result of their own disturbed family relationships, need to keep their babies as a help in working out these relationships. Some need to reinforce their dependence upon their families; others, to bring about their emancipation from an overly dominating family. . . .

The next large group we meet is made up of girls who plan to have their babies adopted. Social workers always feel some security in dealing with this group since they know that if a placement is made through an authorized agency the baby at least will have some security for the future.

Sometimes, however, because of our reassurance about the baby we tend to neglect the emotional needs of this group of mothers. This is understandable in many ways since the pressure of work frequently forces us to use our time and effort on situations where the mother is undecided about plans and the future of the baby is in jeopardy. However, we are frequently surprised when all the plans are made, and the mother then changes her mind or is thrown into a panic of indecision. Sometimes this happens because we have not been sufficiently sensitive to her conflict about adoption, and have not helped her deal with her feeling of guilt. Sometimes, even when this kind of mother goes ahead with the adoption plan, her feeling of guilt may lead her into another pregnancy. . . .

The group that concerns us most is composed of girls who ask for long-time foster-home placement for their babies. These girls neither want to keep the children nor are they willing to give them up, but hold on to them through the nebulous tie of keeping them in foster homes. We are all aware of the unhappy situation of such children, children who grow up in a foster home, knowing their own mothers. These children are prevented from forming close ties with the foster parents, but at the same time do not get the affection and security that they crave from their own mothers. Frequently the child feels divided allegiance, and a rivalry is created between his own mother and the foster mother. As this goes on, the child may be impelled to repeat the neurotic pattern of the mother which had been the cause of the original situation.

As for the mother, this kind of solution has frequently enabled her to put off facing any of her own problems, because she is able to escape into this indefinite plan for long-time placement of the baby. . . . It is true, of course, that long-time foster-home care is sometimes necessary, but this is usually a last resort. . . .[158]

In considering the role of the social worker it is important that she be prepared to accept her own responsibility for helping the unmarried mother reach her decision about the disposition of the child. . . .

In our eagerness to permit our client the right to self-determination, we have frequently avoided our own responsibility in helping her to face one of the most vital problems that a girl can be called upon to meet. In many records we read such examples as the case worker who insists upon discussing alternate plans with the girl who has already resolved upon adoption for her baby, thereby confusing the girl and making her feel that the case worker, and therefore society, looks upon her as a bad mother for wishing to give up her child. We have all also read records where the mother specifically asks the case worker for advice and counsel, only to be turned aside by the worker who states, "It's all up to you."

We have all learned that one of the most important tools of case work comes through the relationship that is developed between the client and the worker. If we accept this premise, how then can we remain aloof and apart from so vital a decision? It is important to realize that any decision which the girl makes will have some painful aspects, and that it will be necessary to help her work through the feelings that may arise before and

[158] For a more recent and sobering study of children in foster care, see Maas & Engler, Children in Need of Parents (1959). After examining foster care in nine different kinds of communities, the authors found that more than half the children face the dismal prospect of having to continue to live in foster care for most of their childhood, typically moving through a series of families without continuing close ties to any adult; it is hardly surprising that the effects on the children were deleterious. For a discussion of the problems of foster care, see pages 460-464 infra. — Ed.

after her decision.   It is also important that we fully convey to her the fact that even if she does not make the decision that we feel is best, we are still interested in her, and she can still turn to us for help. . . .

NOTE

Both the counseling problem of how strongly to urge unwed mothers to keep or to give up their children and the legal policy problem of the extent to which release of illegitimate infants for adoption should be impeded, facilitated, or compelled by law pose extremely difficult questions affecting the basic rights of mother and child.   Solution of such problems would be eased by comparative studies of the outcomes of samples of illegitimate children who are kept by their mothers, placed in institutions, placed in foster care, or adopted; presumably these studies would have to control such variables as race and socioeconomic class.   This knowledge is not presently available, and in its absence both the counseling practices of lawyers in their offices and legislative and judicial decisions will have to rest on what appear to be the most plausible hypotheses derived from limited and inadequate data.   The three examples below are representative of what little is known about the capacity of unwed mothers.

1. Vincent, Unmarried Mothers 185-200 (1961), compared 71 white unwed mothers who gave up their children for adoption with 34 white unwed mothers who kept their children, the sample being derived from the same study reported in more detail at pages 96-106 supra.   Nonwhite mothers were excluded because they "had few adoption outlets for their children."   Id. at 186.   For each mother a psychological test (the California Psychological Inventory, or CPI) was administered and home and family data elicited by questionnaire.   It was found that the mothers who kept their children, as a group, showed significantly less favorable personality patterns on the psychological test than the mothers who released their children for adoption, e.g., their group mean scores were lower for such factors as poise, self-assurance, responsibility, maturity, and intellectual efficiency.   Similarly the study of home and family data provided parallel findings: the mothers who kept their children were significantly more likely to come from lower socioeconomic, broken, unhappy, loveless homes and to have more negative attitudes towards sex.   Vincent comments (id. at 191):

> The above CPI and family questionnaire data tend to corroborate the opinion expressed by many individuals who provide counseling, casework, and therapeutic services for unwed mothers: namely, that (although there are individual exceptions) many of the unwed mothers who are the most insistent on keeping their children appear the least likely, because of personality and family-life experiences, to become adequate mothers.

2. A study of 92 illegitimate children who have remained in their mother's custody under casework supervision of the Child Welfare Council of Toronto compared the school progress, health conditions, behavior

problems, and home adjustments of the children who were living with mother and stepfather (37), living with mother and her relatives (26), living with mother alone (17), and boarded by the mother in an institution (12). Owen, Children Born Out of Wedlock (Child Welfare Council of Toronto 1943). The samples are small, other variables are of unknown magnitude, and reliability of judgments about the criteria are not given — research defects which are unfortunately typical of such investigations. For what they are worth, the most important results were:

a. Of the 19 mothers for whom there were mental test results, 14 were subnormal and one psychotic; of 66 other mothers about whom social workers recorded an opinion of mental status, 34 were said to be normal and 32 subnormal.

b. Financial difficulties were "the most ominous part" of the mother's struggle, a result probably to be expected in agency cases. Economic resources were usually grossly inadequate.

c. The study's conclusions were that where the mother was living alone with the child, "the general social conditions surrounding the child, taking into account the mother's loneliness and dependence on him, are not desirable." Where the child was with mother and relatives, there was the greatest strain and least satisfactory adjustment. The best arrangement was where a stepfather was present, which approximated the ordinary conditions of a normal home. The most disadvantaged children were those put into a boarding home or institution by the mother at her own expense. The statistical support for these conclusions was sketchy.

3. Berg, Utilizing the Strengths of Unwed Mothers in the AFDC Program, 43 Child Welfare 333, 334-339 (1964), reports on an interview study with 30 Aid to Dependent Children recipients in Philadelphia in the summer of 1961. The sample was drawn from a group of women who had two or more illegitimate children, and 28 of the 30 were Negroes. The mothers were found to place great value on motherhood, had high aspirations for their children's educational and occupational advancement, spent their limited money well in managing their homes on inadequate incomes, maintained adequate control over their children, and expressed strong feelings in favor of an unwed mother bringing up her children herself.

Vincent (supra, at 199) makes "a highly qualified prediction of an emerging pattern or trend":

> We predict that — *if* the demand for adoptable infants continues to exceed the supply; *if* more definitive research, using additional sample sources, substantiates our hypothesis that the majority of the unwed mothers who keep their children lack the potential for "good motherhood"; and *if* the laws and courts continue to emphasize that the "rights of the child" supersede the "rights of the parents" [159] — then it is quite possible that, in the near future, unwed mothers will

[159] As you study proceedings to terminate parental rights (pages 159-169 infra and Chapter 4), adoption (Chapter 5), and custody (Chapter 9), consider whether Vincent's assumption about "laws and courts" is correct. — Ed.

be "punished" by having their children taken from them right after birth. A policy like this would not be executed — nor labeled explicitly — as "punishment." Rather, it would be implemented through such pressures and labels as "scientific findings," "the best interests of the child," "rehabilitation of the unwed mother," and "the stability of the family and society." . . .

Vincent stresses, however, the difficult value judgments which arise in the application of group statistical probability data to individual decision-making and legislative policy formulations. He states (id. at 199-200):

We consider that the probability that such policy and practice will emerge necessitates precautions to prevent the misapplication of group data to individuals. It would be most unfortunate if such group data were interpreted or misused to claim that any individual unwed mother desiring to keep her child is ipso facto an inadequate mother and a disturbed person. Such misapplication or misuse of data would do grave injustice to those individual unwed mothers having the desire and the ability (latent or manifest) to be very good mothers to their children, and who may subsequently establish homes with fathers for these children.

Should the lawyer approach an interview with an unwed mother-to-be client with an initial presumption that he should try to steer the case towards release of the child for adoption? What kinds of evidence would be sufficient in his mind to rebut the presumption in an individual case? What are the implications of such group statistical probabilities for a legislator formulating standards for a statute governing the termination of parental rights of an unwed mother in order to permit adoption against the mother's will? See pages 167-169 infra.

b. THE NEEDS OF INFANTS

The two major issues in the care of infants which are relevant to law are the continuity and quality of maternal care. When quality falls below an acceptable level, the law can step in and compel removal of the child from his parents to an environment deemed more suitable to his needs. The ability of the law to influence the factor of continuity is more indirect but nonetheless substantial, for legal standards can be deliberately designed to reduce the risk of discontinuity. The two factors are obviously related; removal of a child because of poor care necessarily entails a change in the child's environment, and this discontinuity in turn may affect quality. A decision to remove, therefore, presumably should require a finding that the risk of continued poor quality care is so substantial that it outweighs the risks that discontinuity entails. This reciprocal relationship of poor quality care and discontinuity as potential adverse personality determinants for the child also plagues scientific research on the relative influence of the two factors; determination of the causative force of either requires research control of the other, and in practice such control is at best extraordinarily difficult.

In the last section we examined data which suggest that white unwed mothers who want to keep their children are likely to have personality structures such that most of these mothers either may later have to give up their children or else will be able to provide the children only with very low quality care. In the frequent cases where one of these outcomes occurs, the state may have to step in to free the child for adoption so that he can be placed in a more favorable and stable environment, even at the expense of discontinuity in his maternal care. In the next section we examine judicial proceedings to terminate the unwed mother's parental rights. We will also be concerned with the very difficult evaluations of quality and discontinuity in later chapters where we deal with (1) other aspects of the state's power to deprive parents permanently of their children (Chapter 4); (2) the screening of adoptive parents, competing claims of natural and adoptive parents, and the relative success of various kinds of adoption (Chapter 5);[160] and (3) the resolution of disputed custody cases following divorce (Chapter 9). These various legal topics are necessarily fragmented in the structure of this book, but the material on maternal care that follows is relevant to all of them.

Any child may find itself in a situation which involves discontinuity of maternal care, e.g., if his mother dies or is afflicted with disabling illness. There is ample evidence, however, that the illegitimate child is subject to a disproportionate risk in this regard. Many illegitimate children are released for adoption immediately after birth, the natural mother frequently never seeing her infant. Even if the infant is immediately placed with permanent adoptive parents, maternal care following birth is provided by a different person from the one with whom the child had a symbiotic relationship for the preceding nine months. The effect of this discontinuity on future development is apparently unknown, and the hypothesis that, all other factors being equal, a substitute mother is not likely to provide as good maternal care as the natural mother is neither proven nor disproven. The discouragement of adoption in some countries like Denmark as well as some judicial decisions in this country favor-

160 The rise of unrelated adoptions which permit the illegitimate child to be completely cut off from his natural parents and integrated into a new family is one of the most striking phenomena of modern social history. The availability of this outlet for white, unwed, illegitimate children has drastically reduced the incidence of less desirable alternatives such as infanticide, abandonment, and large-scale institutional care.

To some extent we will deal with freeing the illegitimate child for adoption in this chapter, but our consideration will be limited to the threshold problems of counseling the unwed mother and terminating her parental rights. We reserve for treatment in Chapter 5 the legal and social problems of the adoption process, which involve not only the natural mother and child but also the interests of the adopting parents and the complexities of social work regulatory practice. To some extent this division is artificial, for we will have to return at that time to some of the problems of the unwed mother, e.g., the voluntariness of her consent to adoption, the scope of her right to revoke her consent and reclaim the child from the adoptive parents, and the extent to which her behavior may constitute an "abandonment" of the child. But the intricacies of adoption law and practice involve a complex of social policies and values which can best be considered as an integral unit.

ing natural over adoptive parents are apparently based in part on the assumption that this hypothesis is true.

However this may be, many illegitimate children released for adoption are for one reason or another not placed in a permanent adoptive home for months or years following birth and hence will have at least one change of mother figure during infancy. Where the mother is ambivalent and postpones her decision to consent to the child's adoption, the infant may have to adjust to progressive changes from natural mother to intermediate foster or institutional care to an adoptive family. During her period of ambivalence, moreover, the natural mother may subject the infant to frequent discontinuity, alternating between self-care and foster care, confusing him as to the identity of his "real" mother or causing anxiety because of her frequent "desertions." We have already noted the danger that an ambivalent natural mother may keep her child in limbo for years and that, when she finally gives him up, it may be too late to consummate an adoption, resulting in prolonged foster or institutional care with changing mother substitutes.[161]

Both substantive law and legal practice can and do affect the incidence of such discontinuities. A child may be severed from his natural mother by her voluntary consent to his adoption, by a waiver of her parental rights tantamount to an abandonment, or by the judicial termination of her parental rights against her will. Any of these three methods will give a court jurisdiction to complete an adoption. If the law of a jurisdiction makes void any consent for adoption executed before the child is six weeks old, 7 & 8 Eliz. 2, c. 5, §5, because "a mother needs about six weeks to recover physically and psychologically from the effects of confinement," [162] one effect of such solicitude is to postpone the possibility of adoption and to increase the relative incidence of discontinuity after age six weeks. Strict construction of the requisites of an abandonment or a rule permitting a mother to revoke a consent months after its execution will have similar results. In such jurisdictions both the incidence of discontinuity and the ages at which it will most frequently occur can be altered by making consent irrevocable,[163] or by permitting a court to decree an adoption notwithstanding the absence of consent,[164] or by a relaxation of the standards of proof required to show an abandonment.[165]

These statutory policy problems will recur in our discussion of adoption in Chapter 5. For present purposes it is sufficient to note that assessment of the magnitude of the risk which results from discontinuity of maternal care is an important factor in legal policy and practice concerning illegitimate children. If it were established that changes in the infant's mother figure among natural, adoptive, foster, or institutional parent during a certain period, such as between ages six months and two years, exposed the child to a serious risk of permanent damage to his

---

[161] See page 143 supra; see also pages 149 and 168 infra.

[162] Departmental Committee on the Adoption of Children, Report, Cmd. No. 9248, par. 56 (1954).

[163] Cf. Cal. Civ. Code §§226, 226a.

[164] E.g., Md. Ann. Code art. 16, §74 (1957).

[165] Cf. N.Y. Dom. Rel. Law §111.

personality structure or intellectual functioning, such knowledge should cause a major reappraisal of the legal structure. It will be recalled that one of the most significant chapters in the history of law over the past century has been the extension of legal protection against the hazards implicit in immaturity, and if discontinuity is such a hazard, the law should respond.

The psychiatric and social work theory of maternal deprivation has advanced just such an assertion of the probability of lasting damage to the child as a result of at least some kinds of interference with the normal one-mother mothering process. The theory came into full prominence in 1952 with the publication of Bowlby's Maternal Care and Mental Health. This volume promptly became "something of a bible for social workers" [166] and had a profound influence on child welfare theory and practice. It was also subjected to searching criticism, and Bowlby's major conclusions were alleged to be nothing more than "quite unproven hypotheses." [167] Accordingly, the brief excerpts from Bowlby below are followed by a small sampling of this criticism, of later research, and of the qualifications of his findings which are coming to be widely accepted.

When you have finished this material, consider what conclusions for legal policy and practice are to be drawn from it. We would wish, of course, that the evidence were less equivocal and that it were more precisely focused on the particular kinds of deprivation which are involved in the discontinuities with which the law is concerned. Still, as lawyers we are in a different position from a scientist. It is not enough for us to say "unproven" and await further developments. We have to act today — as in making decisions in the case of Angela Stevens — and the necessity for that action includes the responsibility of making the most reasonable assumptions of fact as to the magnitude of the risks of discontinuity of maternal care to which an unborn child will be subject. Consider, for example, the following study by Rome that is discussed by Bowlby:

> [She] studied 30 mothers who had committed their illegitimate babies to an institution pending a final decision . . . Of the 30, only 8 were finally taken home by their mothers, 4 were adopted and, after a lapse of three years, 15 remained in the institution or in foster-homes. But not only does she demonstrate that, after three years, half these mothers were still unable to come to a long-term decision, but she points to the fact that the outcome could with a high degree of certainty have been predicted from the time of the baby's birth. Only if at least four of the following conditions are present is the mother likely to take the baby home: that she is of stable personality, takes a realistic attitude towards her problem, is loving and accepting of the child, had a positive relation to the putative father, and has a family which does not insist on the child being disposed of. . . .[168]

[166] Witmer, Introduction, Maternal Deprivation 1 (Child Welfare League of America, Inc. 1962).

[167] Wootton, Social Science and Social Pathology 156 (1959).

[168] Bowlby, Maternal Care and Mental Health 98-99 (World Health Organization Monograph Series No. 2, 1952).

If an unwed mother client proposes a course of action which seems to create a high risk of later discontinuity of care for the child, can either lawyer or social worker disavow a responsibility for assessing the risk to the unrepresented child? In this context, what is the meaning of "[t]he obligation to represent the client with undivided fidelity"?[169]

BOWLBY, MATERNAL CARE AND MENTAL HEALTH

15-103 (World Health Organization Monograph Series No. 2, 1952)

Evidence that the deprivation of mother-love in early childhood can have a far-reaching effect on the mental health and personality development of human beings comes from many sources. It falls into three main classes:

(*a*) Studies, by direct observation, of the mental health and development of children in institutions, hospitals, and foster-homes — direct studies.

(*b*) Studies which investigate the early histories of adolescents or adults who have developed psychological illnesses — retrospective studies.

(*c*) Studies which follow up groups of children who have suffered deprivation in their early years with a view to determining their state of mental health — follow-up studies.

The extent to which these studies, undertaken by people of many nations, varied training and, as often as not, ignorant of each others' conclusions, confirm and support each other is impressive. What each individual piece of work lacks in thoroughness, scientific reliability, or precision is largely made good by the concordance of the whole. Nothing in scientific method carries more weight than this. Divergent voices are few. Indeed, only three have come to light, all follow-up studies, but of a quality which bears no comparison with that of the research the conclusions of which they challenge. [Page 15.]

[The discussion of only one of the studies upon which Bowlby relies is included here.]

The outstanding quality of Goldfarb's work derives from its having been scientifically planned from the beginning to test the hypothesis that the experience of living in the highly impersonal surroundings of an institution nursery in the first two or three years of life has an adverse effect on personality development. With this end in view he selected his samples so that, so far as is possible, they were similar in heredity, and thereby controlled a variable which has been the bugbear of most other investigations. Altogether he has done three main studies. In each he has compared the mental development of children, brought up until the age of about three in an institution and then placed in foster-homes, with others who had gone straight from their mothers to foster-homes in which they had remained. In both samples the children had been handed over by their mothers in infancy, usually within the first nine

[169] A.B.A., Canons of Professional Ethics, Canon 6.

months of life. The sample most thoroughly studied consisted of 15 pairs of children who, at the time of the examination, ranged in age from 10 to 14 years. One set of 15 was in the institution from about 6 months of age to $3\frac{1}{2}$ years, the other set had not had this experience. Conditions in the institution conformed to the highest standards of physical hygiene but lacked the elementary essentials of mental hygiene:

"Babies below the age of nine months were each kept in their own little cubicles to prevent the spread of epidemic infection. Their only contacts with adults occurred during these few hurried moments when they were dressed, changed or fed by nurses."

Later they were members of a group of 15 or 20 under the supervision of one nurse, who had neither the training nor the time to offer them love or attention. As a result they lived in "almost complete social isolation during that first year of life" and their experience in the succeeding two years was only slightly richer. Goldfarb has gone to great pains to ensure that the foster-homes of the two groups are similar in respect of all observable criteria and demonstrates further that, in respect of the mother's occupational, educational, and mental status, the institution group was slightly superior to the controls. Any differences in the mental states of the two groups of children are, therefore, virtually certain to be the result of their differing experiences in infancy. . . .

TABLE VI. DIFFERENCES BETWEEN CHILDREN WHO HAD SPENT
THEIR FIRST THREE YEARS IN AN INSTITUTION AND CONTROLS
WHO HAD NOT (GOLDFARB)

Function tested or rated	Test or rating method	Result expressed as	Results Institution group	Control group
Intelligence	Wechsler	mean IQ	72.4	95.4
Ability to conceptualize	Weigl	mean score	2.4	6.8
	Vigotsky	mean score	0.5	4.7
Reading	standard tests	mean score	5.1	6.8
Arithmetic	standard tests	mean score	4.7	6.7
Social maturity	Vineland Scale completed by case-workers	mean social quotient	79.0	98.8
Ability to keep rules ..	frustration experiment	number of children	3	12
Guilt on breaking rules		number of children	2	11
Capacity for relationships	case-worker's assessment	number of children able to make normal relationships	2	15
Speech		number of children up to average	3	14
Number of children (total)			15	15

Note: In the case of all differences shown, P is less than .01.

The number and consistency of these differences is truly remarkable. . . . [Pages 36-37.]

. . . One shortcoming in his discussion should, however, be noted — namely, his tendency to imply that all institutions and their products are the same. [Page 39.]

[After his review of many studies, including some of his own research, Bowlby states several conclusions.]

. . . It is submitted that the evidence is now such that it leaves no room for doubt regarding the general proposition — that the prolonged deprivation of the young child of maternal care may have grave and far-reaching effects on his character and so on the whole of his future life.

. . . It is, of course, true that there are still far too few systematic studies and statistical comparisons in which proper control groups have been used. Relatively few studies taken by themselves are more than suggestive. But when all the evidence is fitted together it is seen to be remarkably consistent . . . .

. . . [But] although the main proposition may be regarded as established, knowledge of details remains deplorably small. . . .

. . . The fact that some children seem to escape is of no consequence. The same is true of the consumption of tubercular-infected milk or exposure to the virus of infantile paralysis. In both these cases a sufficient proportion of children is so severely damaged that no one would dream of intentionally exposing a child to such hazards. Deprivation of maternal care in early childhood falls into the same category of dangers. [Pages 46-47.]

[Bowlby's other conclusion relates to the conflicting findings on the possibility of later correcting deficiencies which result from deprivation. He discusses some experiments in treatment in Sweden and the United States which may be promising, but notes that it] will be many years before the success of these methods can be judged.

The evidence available suggests that nothing but prolonged residence with an adult, with insight into the problem, skill in handling it, and unlimited time to devote to her charge, is likely to be of much avail. This is not only very expensive but could never be made available to more than a tiny fraction of cases. Far more practicable, and in the long run far cheaper, is to arrange methods of care for infants and toddlers which will prevent these conditions developing. [Page 51.]

[Of immediate interest are Bowlby's conclusions about the implications of his findings for illegitimate children and adoption.] It is urgently necessary in many countries to make studies of what in fact happens to the illegitimate children of today — how many achieve a satisfactory home life with their mothers or immediate relatives, how many eke out their existence in foster-homes or institutions, and how many are adopted and what is the outcome. . . . It may perhaps be that, in some cases, encouraging her [the natural mother] to take the responsibility for her baby will help her become a more responsible citizen, but to act on the assumption that this is always the case is not only to be unrealistic but to be socially irresponsible ourselves. For it is a very serious thing to condemn a child to be parked in an endless succession of foster-homes or to be brought up in an institution when there are long waiting lists of suitable parents wishing to adopt children. . . .

The evidence given in . . . this report points unmistakably to its being in the interests of the adopted baby's mental health for him to be adopted soon after birth. No other arrangement permits continuity of mothering and most other arrangements fail even to ensure its adequacy. If the baby remains with his mother, it is not unlikely that she will neglect and reject him. The work of Rheingold and Levy has shown that if he is parked temporarily in a nursery or group foster-home his development will often suffer in some degree. . . . Nothing is more tragic than good adoptive parents who accept for adoption a child whose early experiences have led to disturbed personality development which nothing they can now do will rectify. Very early adoption is thus clearly in the interests also of the adoptive parents. . . .

. . . On psychiatric and social grounds adoption in the first two months should become the rule, though some flexibility will always be necessary to permit mothers to work their way to a satisfactory decision. . . . [Pages 100-103.]

NOTE

1. For a hard-hitting criticism of Bowlby which summarizes much of the scientific skepticism about his data and its interpretation, see Wootton, Social Science and Social Pathology 136-156 (1959). She cites other studies which do not support Bowlby's conclusions and challenges his reliance on the cumulative impact of imperfect studies as coming "near to an assertion that it does not greatly matter if all the work is slipshod, so long as all the answers are much the same" (id. at 154). She also emphasizes (id. at 151-152) that his data are not controlled by comparative studies to determine

the incidence in the population at large of comparable infantile experiences. . . .

. . . No matter how intensively we may study the experience of those among the separated who are known to suffer from such symptoms, we can never assess the pathogenic nature of that experience so long as we have no idea how often others with similar histories manage to make out at least as well as the rest of us. To attempt such an assessment in the absence of this vital information is on a par with trying to calculate the insurance premiums to be charged for fire risks by reference only to those houses which have actually caught fire.

Finally she notes (id. at 146):

Advocates of the maternal deprivation hypothesis are criticized also for the degree to which they have relied upon the experience of children in institutions, and in arbitrarily selected institutions at that, and for their disregard of the many variables introduced by this procedure. . . . An institution is not a standard unit; and there can be good institutions as well as bad ones. . . . Nor has sufficient weight generally been given to the possibility that communal homes for children may differ from families in other respects beside the opportunity which they offer for intimate affectionate relationships. How, one would like to know, were the institutionalized children fed? Could their backwardness have been due, in any degree, to dietary deficiencies? Little seems to have been done to control such important variables as these. . . .

Nor has adequate information been produced about the reasons which led to the children studied being uprooted from their homes; or about the conditions in which they had lived before this happened.

2. Also subsequent to Bowlby are two notable collections of papers, Deprivation of Maternal Care: A Reassessment of Its Effects (World Health Organization Public Health Paper No. 14, 1962) and Maternal Deprivation (Child Welfare League of America, Inc. 1962). Contributors to both volumes place emphasis on Bowlby's controversial assertion that damage may be "grave and far-reaching . . . on the whole of [the child's] future life." Bowlby, supra, at 46. Ainsworth notes three possible theories about the nature of development which may be relevant to the question of whether damage from deprivation is "reversible":

i. Learning theory, influenced originally by Watsonian behaviorism, implies that development is entirely or almost entirely a matter of environmental stimulation. When the appropriate environmental conditions are provided, learning will take place, and what has not been learned earlier can be learned later when the appropriate conditions are provided. According to this position, the child, initially retarded because of deprivation of environmental stimulation, can eventually catch up, provided that deprivation is relieved and given enough time.

ii. The psychoanalytic position would imply that an early experience can set up certain dynamic processes that become consolidated and ingrained and that tend to continue despite the subsequent alteration of the environmental situation. One variant of this position would view the retardation attributable to deprivation of maternal care as a result of defensive operations, which perhaps serve to insulate the child against the painful frustration of seeking an interaction with an environment that is unstimulating or unresponsive. Once consolidated, this defensive operation tends to maintain itself, insulating the child against interaction with an environment that could prove supportive, responsive, and helpful if he would, or could, only be receptive. According to this position, reversibility would be a question of how consolidated the defensive operations are and how effective the efforts are in breaking them down. Some of Bowlby's publications imply this position . . .

iii. The "sensitive phase" position, which in psychology has been much influenced by the sister science of ethology, suggests that it is possible that in the course of human development there are certain periods during which certain kinds of development proceed normally if adequate environmental conditions are present, but that if these conditions are inadequate during the sensitive phase for the function in question, development not only will be arrested with respect to the function, but it will either be impossible or very difficult for subsequent stimulation to rectify matters. . . .

The ethologists are concerned with species-specific patterns of behavior, genetically determined, that may be evoked by a specific pattern of environmental stimuli or a "releaser," but, in many instances if the behavior is not released during a sensitive phase of development in the young organism, it cannot subsequently be released. It is dangerous to extrapolate from animals to humans, especially with respect to responses that have been demonstrated to be species-specific, but it behooves us to ask whether there are such species-specific patterns of behavior in humans, what the effective "releasers" are, and what the pertinent critical periods are. This seems to me to be one of the more productive avenues along which research in child development can presently proceed . . .

I believe that there is some truth in all three positions — the learning theory position, the psychoanalytic position, and the "sensitive phase" position. With respect to some functions learning is the important thing, and some things that were not learned during a period of deprivation can be caught up later. Dynamic processes, however, may sometimes become so consolidated as to interfere with subsequent environmental influences unless these processes themselves are reversed through special intervention. With respect to some processes there may well be sensitive phases during which modifications may most readily take place, and if appropriate stimulating conditions are lacking at the time, the modifications may be very difficult and perhaps even impossible to evoke at a later time. Indeed it seems likely that the psychoanalytic and "sensitive phase" positions are essentially the same, and that what blocks subsequent modifications are incompatible processes that have become established in the meantime.[170]

Distinguishing between effects on intellectual functioning and personality development, Ainsworth says:

In conclusion, it must be confessed that there is but scanty evidence for a sensitive phase for intellectual development, with relative irreversibility if deprivation of the adequate environmental stimulation is withheld beyond the upper limits of the period. We have presented a hypothesis rather than established fact. If further research proves the hypothesis to be ill-founded, we must then fall back upon some other concept of defensive interference with learning to explain the incontrovertible facts that some children who have

[170] Ainsworth, Reversible and Irreversible Effects of Maternal Deprivation on Intellectual Development, in Maternal Deprivation 42, 46-47 (Child Welfare League of America, Inc. 1962).

suffered extreme and prolonged deprivation of maternal care beginning early in life are highly resistant to reversing their intellectual
retardation in response to environmental stimulation, while for some
children less severely deprived, or whose deprivation was for a shorter
time or began later in life or was perhaps less reinforced by subsequent events, environmental stimulation serves to facilitate development so that, over the years, such children eventually catch up to
average children, at least in regard to global measures of intellectual
development.

. . . The evidence on reversibility or irreversibility of personality
functions is even more difficult to evaluate, perhaps because we lack
global, quantitative measures like the IQ to assist us. I, personally,
am inclined to believe, after having reviewed the literature extensively and having been involved intimately in research in this area,
that the effects on personality development of deprivation of maternal care in early life, though not completely irreversible, are more
resistant to complete reversibility in more cases than are the intellectual functions . . .[171]

Yarrow is even more cautious: "Conclusions about the long-term effects
of separation are very tenuous. They are based on a few studies in which
the information about the early history is not well-documented." [172]

3. Yarrow notes another limitation of the maternal deprivation data
which points up a particular difficulty in the interpretation of the data
for the purpose of obtaining guidance concerning the disposition of illegitimate children:

On the whole, no distinction has been made among several different
separation experiences: a single instance of separation with reunion,
a single separation without reunion, repeated small doses of separation with consistent reunion with the same mother, and cumulative
separations with repeated changes in mothers. It can be assumed
that each of these experiences provides different learning conditions
for the development of meaningful relationships. The most extreme
outcome, the "affectionless character," may be the result of the most
extreme conditions, i.e., repeated traumatic separations.[173]

4. Some of the underlying Freudian assumptions that are implicit in at
least some formulations of the maternal deprivation hypothesis have been
sharply questioned. See, e.g., Sewell, Infant Training and the Personality of the Child, 58 Am. J. Soc. 150 (1952) (in sample of 162 farm children, none of differences in infant training regarded as crucial in Freudian theory was significantly related to childhood personality adjustment

[171] Id. at 59.
[172] Yarrow, Maternal Deprivation: Toward an Empirical and Conceptual Re-
evaluation, in Maternal Deprivation 3, 21 (Child Welfare League of America,
Inc. 1962). Yarrow's article also appears in 58 Psychological Bull. 459 (1961).
[173] Id. at 32.

as measured by author); Orlansky, Infant Care and Personality, 46 Psychological Bull. 1 (1949). Orlansky says: "The importance of childhood experience to the formation of personality was one of the great findings of psychoanalysis. No social scientist will dispute that general finding." Ibid. But in an extensive review of the literature he found little empirical support for such concrete theses as that the mechanics of, e.g., nursing or sphincter training, or the fact that the infant has one as distinguished from multiple mother figures, has a specific invariant psychological impact. He states (id. at 38):

> We conclude that the rigidity of character structuring during the first year or two of life has been exaggerated by many authorities, and that the events of childhood and later years are of great importance in reinforcing or changing the character structure tentatively formed during infancy. Or one may substitute Horney's formulation: ". . . the sum total of childhood experiences brings about a certain character structure, or rather starts its development. With some persons this development essentially stops at the age of five. With some it stops in adolescence, with others around thirty, with a few it goes on until old age" [citation omitted].

5. An example of the difficulty of proving or disproving Bowlby's major claims and of the unknowns that still surround the whole question of maternal deprivation is provided by Maas's study, The Young Adult Adjustment of Twenty Wartime Residential Nursery Children, 42 Child Welfare 57 (1963). Maas was able to track down twenty young adults who during World War II had been separated from their parents and evacuated from London to one of several residential nurseries. Aged nineteen or more at the time they were interviewed, they ranged in age from two months to sixty-one months at the time of separation and were selected to include five each who were one, two, three, and four years old. The three nurseries in which these children had been institutionalized differed from one another in such factors as ratio of staff to children, degree of permissiveness, and sternness of discipline. The duration of separation before they were returned to their families ranged from twelve to fifty months.

Maas evaluated their young adult adjustment by psychological tests and interviews, examining the five areas where previous maternal deprivation literature had predicted lasting damage as a result of separation: "feeling life" (e.g., apathy), inner controls (extent of extremes of impulsiveness or overcontrol), relationships with other people (e.g., extent of subject's social isolation), performance in key roles (e.g., as spouse or employee), and intellectual functioning. Each of the twenty adults was rated on a five-point scale for each of twenty-four items dealing with the five major variables. One method of analysis was to compare the obtained ratings with assumed frequencies of the same ratings in a metropolitan population. Maas provides the following summary of some of his findings (id. at 66-67):

1. Although these 20 young adults may have been seriously damaged by their early childhood separation and residential nursery experiences, most of them give no evidence in young adulthood of any extreme aberrant reactions. There are no ratings at the extremes for 12 of the 20, and 15 have fewer than 10 percent of their total ratings at the extremes. To this extent, the data support assumptions about the resiliency, plasticity, and modifiability of the human organism rather than those about the irreversibility of the effects of early experience.

2. Where there is evidence in individual cases of aberrancy in the adjustment of these young adults, in almost every case the data on their families seem sufficient to explain it. Although our design called for the inclusion only of persons from intact families without gross pathology, as the families became better known, so did their disabilities. . . . [F]ar from permitting the reversibility of early damage, growing up in some of these families might well have given reinforcement to it; and that, seen against their family and neighborhood backgrounds, a few of these young adults give vivid testimony to the strengths that are either inherent in them or were initially developed during years that included their nursery experiences.

3. The data do support the prediction that children placed in residential group care during the first year of life will show evidence of damage in their young adult years. Every test shows that this age group fared the worst of the four groups. . . . The family data, however, indicate parenting problems in this group that cannot be ignored in explanations of these young adults' adjustment.

4. None of the evidence from the Four-plus [age at separation] group supports the prediction that separation and group care starting at this period are followed by enduring damage that is evident in young adulthood.

5. The Twos fared quite well, better than the Threes, differing from our metropolitan population on only one of the five psychosocial variables. . . . In other words, these findings do not support the assumption that the earlier the child is separated, the more permanent is the damage to the child.

Maas also notes (id. at 67):

When interviewed, 17 of the 20 were gainfully employed in the London labor market, two were married women and mothers who had good employment histories, and the twentieth was a university student in her last year of training as a teacher. In four or five cases, at most, could job histories be characterized as unstable.

But compare Ainsworth, The Effects of Maternal Deprivation: A Review of Findings and Controversy in the Context of Research Strategy, in Deprivation of Maternal Care: A Reassessment of Its Effects 97, 151, 154-155 (World Health Organization Public Health Paper No. 14, 1962), who points out that "the methods of personality appraisal now available are relatively clumsy and imprecise" (id. at 154) and that there may be hidden impairments (id. at 151):

> The findings both that children who have apparently recovered from a separation experience are particularly vulnerable to subsequent threats of separation, and that there is an empirical association between childhood bereavement and adult depressive illness suggest that early experiences may set up processes which may remain covert for a long time but, when subsequently reactivated by some stressful experience (which might well be minor and relatively undisturbing to other people), cause a pathological reaction. . . .

C.   TERMINATION OF THE NATURAL MOTHER'S PARENTAL RIGHTS

In re BABY GIRL LARSON
252 Minn. 490, 91 N.W.2d 448 (1958)

GALLAGHER, J.   This is an appeal from an order of the District Court of Hennepin County, made August 3, 1957, which denied the petition of Margaret M. Larson (1) to vacate a prior order of the court dated *November 30, 1956,* wherein it committed Victoria Larson, the child of petitioner born *September 11, 1956,* to the general guardianship of Lutheran Welfare Society of Minneapolis on the ground that she was dependent and neglected;[174] (2) to vacate a subsequent order dated April 26, 1957, amending the prior order to the extent that the commitment to guardianship order therein was found to be based upon petitioner's written consent thereto dated April 26, 1957, and to adjudge such consent null and void; and (3) to vacate the commitment to general guardianship and restore the child to petitioner.

In a memorandum attached to the order from which this appeal is taken, the trial court stated:

"On all of the evidence . . . it was the feeling of the Court that the child . . . was a dependent and neglected child who needed more realistic and permanent plans made for her under Chapter 260 . . . .

[174] Under the then applicable Minnesota statute, commitment to "general guardianship" was equivalent to termination of the mother's parental rights. Minn. Stat. Ann. §260.12 (1959) (now covered by §260.241 (Supp. 1964)). A "dependent child" was defined as "a child who is illegitimate; or whose parents, for good cause, desire to be relieved of his care and custody; or who is without a parent . . . able to adequately provide for his support, training, and education, and is unable to maintain himself by lawful employment." A "neglected child" was defined as "a child who is abandoned by both parents . . . ; or who is found living with vicious or disreputable persons, or whose home, by reason of improvidence, neglect, cruelty, or depravity on the part of the parents . . . is an unfit place for such child." Minn. Stat. Ann. §260.01 (1959) (comparable provisions now in §260.015 (Supp. 1964)).

State ex rel. Mattes v. Juvenile Court, 147 Minn. 222, 179 N.W. 1006 (1920), held that an illegitimate child can be considered "dependent" only if the child's parent is not able to provide for its proper support. — Ed.

"The petitioner's various plans for the child . . . have centered around unrealistic and unfortunate basis. She claims . . . a promise of marriage by the child's acknowledged father [who, without petitioner's knowledge, had married subsequently] . . . . [And] . . . it was her persistent plan . . . to promote a divorce between this man and his wife so she could marry him . . . .

". . . There seems to be little if any basis for the claim now made by the petitioner that her consent to such commitment that resulted in the order of April 26, 1957, was not voluntary and that it was made under duress."

Shortly after the child was born on September 11, 1956, petitioner, in conjunction with the Hennepin County Welfare Board, made arrangements to have her cared for in a boarding home selected by the board. All expenses therefor were paid for by petitioner with the exception of $44.55 paid by the board for the first month's care. A few weeks thereafter the board, without petitioner's knowledge, filed a petition in the juvenile court of Hennepin County, setting forth that the child was "illegitimate" and "without a parent or lawful guardian able to adequately provide for her support, training and education and that the mother of said child neglects and fails to provide a suitable home for said child"; and praying that the child be brought before the court and her alleged dependency and neglected condition be inquired into and that she be further dealt with in accordance with law.

At the hearing petitioner was not represented by counsel nor advised that she was entitled thereto until subsequent to the submission of all the evidence. The evidence presented fails to indicate anything to support the claims that petitioner had neglected the child or had failed to provide her with a suitable home. Some testimony was presented to create the impression that her only permanent plan for the child was based upon her reliance on the statements of the acknowledged father made without her urging after she discovered that he had married in Illinois that he contemplated obtaining a divorce and thereafter marrying petitioner so that he could care for her and the child. With reference to such plans, petitioner, without the aid of counsel, testified as follows:

"I want to keep the baby very definitely. I have been trying to find a good place to keep her with me but it took time. I didn't want her in a home that wasn't clean or with somebody that maybe couldn't give her enough of the proper attention. . . . I have been interviewing numerous women who are willing to give child care and I have inspected their homes to determine whether or not it would be a satisfactory arrangement. Up until Sunday I was unable to find anything that I felt was suitable. . . . if we [referring to the child's father] were married soon my family and the children [her three sons by a former marriage] would not realize that we had not been married a year ago and they would accept it as a legitimate birth, but I feel at this time that the important thing is to have the baby with me so she recognizes me . . . .

". . . I have found this home where I can keep the baby in town. I cannot have the [two] older boys regardless because Jeffery is to stay with his Big Brother through the school term [and] . . . Rex has been with me only nine months in the last three and a half years . . . . I feel it is kindness to leave Rex where he is [with his father]. . . .

"The Court: What are your ideas about possible marriage in that direction now [to the father]?

"Mrs. Larson: I don't think that is as important as taking care of the baby. I feel that if in the future he is still interested in marriage we could be married . . . . [But] . . . .

". . . I don't want him to make arrangements to get married to me if it's going to hurt them [his present wife and family] but you see I didn't know he was married until just this past April and he had been . . . discussing plans for marriage during — well, two years, so I was not aware of the fact that there was a wife so if it would be any hardship on them I would not encourage him. . . . I don't think we will discuss it any farther but I still feel that I can take care of the baby as well by myself as anyone else and I feel she would add to our family because it would give Tom [her youngest son] companionship and he is the only one I will have with me now."

The order of November 30, 1956, in which the court found the child neglected and dependent and committed her to general guardianship, was made upon the evidence outlined. On December 7, 1956, petitioner was notified that the child had been committed to the general guardianship of the Lutheran Welfare Society and that she would not be notified of any subsequent adoption proceedings. She immediately called upon representatives of the Hennepin County Welfare Board and asked the meaning of the order. She was told to confer with the judge of the juvenile court and thereafter, on December 18, 1956, was advised by the latter that his decision had been made for the best interests of the child. In January 1957 the child's father called upon the court and advised it that, in his opinion, petitioner would be a good mother to the child and wanted its custody. On January 11, 1957, in the midst of these conferences and proceedings, and without petitioner's knowledge or consent, the Lutheran Welfare Society placed the child in an adoptive home.

On April 2, 1957, petitioner moved for an order vacating and setting aside the order of November 30, 1956, and for a further order directing that the child be returned to her. During the pendency of these proceedings, petitioner changed counsel. Counsel selected by her testified that petitioner had called upon him in March 1957 and instructed him to undertake proceedings *to regain custody of the child for her;* that at that time she had paid him the sum of $200 to cover his fees; that he then advised her that the case "had not too much merit"; but thereafter he discussed the case with her several times; that the day before the hearing "the father [of the child] and I . . . talked the case over . . . and finally concluded that for the best interests of the baby, and for Margaret's interests . . . it would be better to have the record show that she consented . . . to the adoption . . . so the record wouldn't indicate the child was taken away." It was not disclosed on what basis counsel had arrived at this conclusion or why he had recommended that the consent to the commitment be made by his client.

In an affidavit with reference thereto, petitioner affirmed that during the last part of April 1957 her counsel told her "it would be best not to try to regain the custody of the baby, and told her to sign a release of the baby and in that way the file would be sealed and that nobody could see it"; that "unless she signed the release, the file would be open to her boys to look at, and for her former husband to look at, and told her that this was the best"; and that she signed the release, protesting that it was not voluntary and not without duress and persuasion as stated in the form submitted therefor.

Thereafter, petitioner, at her own expense, employed other counsel and instructed him to again move to vacate the previous orders and to seek an order discharging the child from guardianship and restoring her to petitioner. At the hearing held thereon on June 12, 1957, evidence was submitted substantially in accordance with that taken at the first hearing.

1. A diligent examination of all the evidence fails to disclose anything to support a finding that petitioner's child had been dependent and neglected prior to either the time the order of November 30, 1956, was made, or to the time it was amended on April 26, 1957. It does reveal that petitioner is qualified financially, physically, and morally to care for the child. She is in sound physical and mental condition. She is employed in a responsible position by an insurance company and is earning in excess of $270 per month, plus a sum withheld monthly under a company pension plan. She is the owner of a large residence in the Kenwood district in Minneapolis, where she can reside with her family or which she may rent if she desires to seek another home where she might live as part of a family so that she could devote more of her time to the child. Her employer testified that she had given them long and faithful service in responsible positions. Her neighbors testified that they had observed her in her home and had observed her family relationships and that she was of good moral character; that her children were well governed; and that her family home was neat and well kept. Her brothers and sisters-in-law testified as to her good character and ability and indicated their willingness to cooperate with her in every way to make a good home for her family.

2. That at one time petitioner contemplated a plan of marriage with the child's father, first formulated when she was not aware that he had married in Illinois, and subsequently adhered to because of her reliance on other false statements he had made to her, would not establish her neglect of the child or that other definite and practical plans submitted by her and not challenged by respondents were not adequate. No doubt similar plans are being followed in numerous cases where mothers in similar situations are required to work outside the home to support their children.

3. With respect to the consent signed by petitioner, we do not feel that it should be given any weight in these proceedings. It was not made until

subsequent to the order of commitment to general guardianship and hence could form no basis for the support thereof. Prior to signing it, petitioner had paid her counsel the sum of $200 *to regain custody of her child,* and not merely to be advised that if she signed a consent to the commitment order she would be left in a more secure position as far as her reputation is concerned. That she was induced to sign the commitment against her own better judgment at a time when she was under the stress and worry involved in the proceedings seems clear, both from the surrounding circumstances and from statements made in her affidavits, which, for the most part, are corroborated by other evidence and are uncontradicted. We cannot escape the conclusion that, under the circumstances, it should be regarded as entirely ineffective in these proceedings. State ex rel. Nelson v. Whaley, 246 Minn. 535, 75 N.W. (2d) 786; In re Adoption of Anderson, 189 Minn. 85, 248 N.W. 657.

4. It is too well settled to require citations that the right of a parent to the custody of a child is paramount or superior to that of any other person; that a mother is presumed to be a fit and suitable person to be entrusted with the care of her child; and that the burden of disproving this presumption rests upon the person challenging it. Further, by statute it is provided (M.S.A. 260.11) that "In no case shall a dependent child be taken from its parents without their consent unless, after diligent effort has been made to avoid such separation, the same shall be found needful in order to prevent serious detriment to the welfare of such child." Under these well-established principles, and in accordance with the provisions of §260.11, we cannot escape the conclusion that, under the evidence submitted as outlined above, the orders of general guardianship are entirely without support and accordingly that the order appealed from should be reversed.

Reversed with directions to vacate the orders of November 30, 1956, and April 26, 1957, and to restore the person and custody of the child, Victoria Larson, to her mother, petitioner herein.

In re LEM

164 A.2d 345 (D.C. Mun. Ct. App. 1960)

Rover, C.J. The mother of Cecelia Lem, a child born out of wedlock, appeals from an order committing her daughter to the legal custody and guardianship of the Department of Public Welfare until her 21st birthday, and permanently depriving her of custody in order that the Welfare Department may consent to the adoption of the child under the provisions of Code 1951, §3-117(3).

The child was born January 11, 1956. Paternity has not been established, but it seems from the mother's own statements that the father was a foreign national student who has since returned to his country. For about four months after the birth of the child a private social welfare agency sought to advise the mother as to the best course for her to follow, but she resisted any definite planning other than foster care for the child. At the expiration of four months, and apprehending that **long-term** planning would be required, the agency referred the case to the Department of Public Welfare. On May 4, 1956, the child came into "emergency care" of the Child Welfare Division of the Welfare Department and was placed in a home for infants.

During the next 14 months the Division sought either to work out a plan whereby the mother would actively assume custody and responsibility for her child, or to persuade her to surrender it for adoption. She cooperated with the Division so long as she was not forced to make a definite decision. When pressed for some definitive action, however, she would state that her psychiatrist had cautioned her about being "rushed" into making a decision, and would become uncommunicative, withdrawn and unavailable.

On July 3, 1957, the Child Welfare Division, pursuant to the provisions of Code 1951, §11-908, filed a petition in the Juvenile Court charging that the child was without adequate parental care. Code 1951, §11-906(a)(6). In an accompanying report it related the mother's history of vacillation and indecisiveness concerning the rearing of the child and recommended that the latter be committed to the Department of Public Welfare for three months "in order to give the mother this additional time either to make her decision to release Cecelia for permanent planning or to offer a satisfactory plan of care for her independent of Child Welfare Division." On July 10, 1957, a hearing was held with the mother's court-appointed counsel present; the court found the child was without adequate parental care and committed her to the Department of Public Welfare until October 9, 1957. This period appears to have been inadequate to accomplish its purpose, and the court on November 11, 1957, after a hearing with the mother and counsel present, committed the child to the Welfare Department for two years until November 4, 1959. The mother consented to this action.

At the end of the latter commitment period a hearing was again held on November 25, 1959. At that time counsel for the mother indicated it was his intention to ask for more time for his client to formulate her plans. The court replied that it would hear no arguments for further temporary commitment, but would confine the hearing to resolving the issue of permanent custody in the mother or the Welfare Department. Counsel for the mother acquiesced in this ruling and the hearing proceeded on that basis.

The case for the Child Welfare Division was presented by one of its social workers. She testified that during the course of the two-year commitment the child had been placed in a suburban foster home. The mother visited her about once every two months throughout the period. The early visits were made at the foster home, but due to criticism on the part of the mother about the care her daughter was receiving, the foster parents requested that the mother arrange for visits through the Child Welfare Division.

It also appears that during this time the mother was requested to make contributions to the support of the child while under the care of the Division. This she failed to do, her reasons therefor being somewhat obscure, but seemingly based upon a notion that she should not be called upon to support her child if she did not have custody. In addition, according to the witness, the mother still refused to cooperate with the Division in devising a plan for the assumption of responsibility for her child. She refused to allow that agency to contact her relatives regarding the problem, which the agency thought reflected some embarrassment due to the circumstances and it respected her wishes.

The mother herself testified that she loved her daughter very much and had developed a close attachment for her during her visits; she also expressed concern about the child's welfare. She said she never thought about the possibility that the child would be taken from her, but since that was the course this hearing was taking, she was now willing to assume custody and responsibility for the child rather than lose her permanently.

This was the first time she evidenced any decisiveness in the matter, and thus we have pointed up the fundamental issue in this case — whether her decision has come too late. The child was by then almost four years old and so far as the record indicates, never had been under the care of the mother for any length of time. . . .

In response to these inquiries the mother stated that she was 39 years old, a college graduate, and at the time she lived in an efficiency apartment and was employed as a clerk in an insurance company earning a take-home pay of $55 per week. She said that one reason she refused to contribute to the child's welfare was that she had encountered heavy medical bills in recent months, and she also felt the Welfare Department was taking an unrealistic position in requesting aid from her. Further, she related how she had spent some money on night courses to advance her education and thus improve her position to provide a better home for the child when she did get custody. She admitted she had been under the care of several psychiatrists over the past few years, but did not feel that would impair her ability to care for her child. She said she was now willing to take her child and to do whatever was required to provide a suitable home.

The court had before it together with the foregoing facts the opinion of the Division that adoption was in the best interests of the child, and that the child was fast approaching an age when it would be difficult to place. At the conclusion of the hearing the court ruled against the mother, and on December 3, 1959, entered the order appealed from. On December 4, 1959, the court denied a motion for rehearing that had been filed in the interim between the date of the hearing and the date of the order.

On December 14, 1959, the mother's attorney filed another motion for rehearing together with affidavits of her psychiatrist and two of her sisters. The court granted this motion and held a hearing on January 12, 1960, limiting the proceedings strictly to the new matter raised by the mother. The psychiatrist testified that while the mother suffered from a personality disorder, it was his opinion that this would not interfere with her ability to care for her child. Only one of the two sisters who submitted affidavits testified at this hearing. She stated that the mother never requested her assistance before, but now that her sister stood to lose her child she had been approached, and was ready to do anything she was able in order that her sister be allowed to keep her child. The affidavit from the second sister was to the same effect. Both these sisters lived out of town and were unmarried. At the close of the testimony the court reaffirmed its order of December 3, 1959, and the mother brings this appeal. . . .

. . . [T]he primary contentions of the mother on appeal are that the action of the court in permanently depriving her of the custody of her child and awarding it to the Welfare Department was not justified by the evidence, and that the ruling was arbitrary and an abuse of discretion. No attack is made on the court's statutory power to act as it did, and indeed none could be sustained in view of the court's plenary power in this area.

Concerning the weight of the evidence, we feel that the facts summarized indicate beyond doubt that the child was without adequate parental care. No reasonable mind could question the proposition that a child deprived of the care and attention of its natural mother and committed to the care of welfare agencies for the first four years of its life is a neglected child within the meaning of the statute. We think the evidence was completely adequate to sustain the court's finding.

Nor do we think that it was an abuse of discretion on the part of the court to fail to award custody to the mother based on her newly asserted willingness to take the child at the time of the last hearings. It is true that the fitness of a parent at the time of the hearing is the controlling factor in the determination of custody rights, and that past conduct of a parent is but an aid in arriving at the parent's present qualifications. But the court fully satisfied this test by having the mother relate at the time of the hearing her present mode of living and how she intended to care for the child if it were awarded to her. Her answers revealed vague and uncertain generalities behind the declared willingness to accept the child; the court clearly could not have given her the child at that time, and it was entitled to conclude from the mother's past history that further temporary commitment would merely mean further procrastination and delay.

We can well sympathize with the mother in the unfortunate situation in which she finds herself; but in this case she was given expert guidance and counseling by trained social workers. She had every opportunity over a four-year period to formulate plans for the rearing of her child before the court took the action of which she complains. We can appreciate that under the circumstances it was very difficult for her to arrive at a decision in the matter but we feel that once the situation had deteriorated to the point of requiring judicial determination she must have been apprised, having been represented by counsel, of the consequences of the failure to utilize the ample time allowed to decide to make definite plans for taking the child.

We feel the record supports the disposition made by the court. This jurisdiction has long followed the rule that the determination of child custody "is one largely, and it may be said almost exclusively, of judicial discretion, and that discretion is never reviewed by an appellate court, except when such discretion has been manifestly abused." This case does not present such an abuse, and we have no right to substitute our judgment for that of the trial court.

Affirmed.

NOTE

1. Most Juvenile Court Acts authorize termination of parental rights when a child has been "abandoned." See, e.g., Minn. Stat. Ann. §260.221(b)(1) (Supp. 1964). Often the term is left undefined. In addition, many adoption statutes make the mother's consent unnecessary if she has "abandoned" the child.[175] Simply because an appellate court would consider the mother's conduct an abandonment when the interests of adoptive parents have intervened, however, does not mean that identical conduct by the unwed mother would be considered an abandonment in a parental termination proceeding. Compare the Lem case with Matter of Anonymous, 286 App. Div. 161, 143 N.Y.S.2d 90 (1955) (where unwed mother has demanded money from foster parents as a condition for not revoking her consent to the adoption, court should consider her consent irrevocable).

In any event, whether the proceeding involves an adoption petition or an effort to terminate the unwed mother's parental rights, the courts have often appeared to prefer (and have been criticized for preferring) the "rights of the mother" to the welfare of the child. In re Mrs. M, 74 N.J. Super. 178, 181 A.2d 14 (1962), for example, involved a writ of habeas corpus by an unwed mother to reclaim from foster parents the child she had given them fourteen months previously. The New Jersey statute authorized parental termination for "abandonment," which was defined as follows:

> any of the following acts by any one having the custody or control of the child: (a) willfully forsaking a child; (b) failing to care for and keep the control and custody of a child so that the child shall be exposed to physical or moral risk without proper and sufficient protection; (c) failing to care for and keep the control and custody of a child so that the child shall be liable to be supported and maintained at the expense of the public, or by child caring societies or private persons not legally chargeable with its or their care, custody and control.[176]

The Superior Court reversed the trial court's refusal to grant the writ of habeas corpus:

> Although it might have been argued that plaintiff *technically* abandoned her daughter, [particularly in the light of clause (c) above],

---

[175] For discussion of cases on what constitutes abandonment for the purpose of adoption laws, see Annot., 35 A.L.R.2d 662 (1954). In Chapter 5 (pages 472-484 infra) we examine abandonment and the legal issues which arise in connection with the validity of the mother's consent to an adoption.

[176] N.J. Stat. Ann. §9:6-1 (1960).

counsel [for the foster parents], in the course of oral argument, forthrightly conceded that there was no *actual* abandonment under the statute or common law. We are also of the view that actual abandonment was not proved. . . .[177]

A memorandum prepared by the Citizen's Committee for Children of New York City, Inc., 1959 N.Y. State Legis. Ann. 207, 208-209, stated:

Section 384 authorizes the termination of parental rights and the appointment of a social agency as guardian in the case of a child who has been abandoned by the natural parents. However, the Social Welfare Law makes no provision for the vastly greater number of children who, though not "abandoned" in the legal sense, have been abandoned in every other sense and are doomed to live in foster homes or institutions because the natural parents are unwilling to provide them with a family life even though able to do so and even though given every assistance by social agencies. . . . Tragically, [minimal contacts with the parents] while so infrequent or superficial as to be meaningless to the child, are a bar to a judicial finding of "abandonment." Consequently, although many of these children could be adopted if the legal rights of the natural parents were terminated, they are, as a practical matter, unadoptable, and continue in custodial care at the cost of blighted lives and at great public expense.

The New York legislature responded with an amendment to the adoption law which provided that the mother's consent would not be required where there has been "a judicial finding that the child is a permanently neglected child." Dom. Rel. Law §111. The 1962 Family Court Act includes a procedure for the requisite adjudication. A "permanently neglected child" is defined as:

a person under eighteen years of age who has been placed in the care of an authorized agency, either in an institution or in a foster home, and whose parent or custodian has failed for a period of more than one year following the placement or commitment of such child in the care of an authorized agency substantially and continuously or repeatedly to maintain contact with and plan for the future of the child, although physically and financially able to do so, notwithstanding the agency's diligent efforts to encourage and strengthen the parental relationship. In the event that the parent defaults after due notice of a proceeding to determine such neglect, such physical and financial ability of such parent may be presumed by the court.[178]

---

[177] 74 N.J. Super. at 187, 181 A.2d at 18.

[178] N.Y. Family Ct. Act §611. To terminate parental rights, the court must also find that "the moral and temporal interests of the child require" the adjudication. Id. §614. The court can suspend judgment for one year (and for a second year under "exceptional circumstances") and impose terms and conditions which "relate to the acts or omissions of the parent . . . responsible for the care of the child." Id. §633. Cf. In re Lem, supra.

2. Most Juvenile Court Acts contain a variety of other grounds for terminating the parental rights of an unwed mother. See generally pages 464-470 infra. The Minnesota statute provides for termination:

(a) With the written consent of parents who for good cause desire to terminate their parental rights; or

(b) If . . . one or more of the following conditions exists:

   (1) That the parents have abandoned the child; or

   (2) That the parents have substantially and continuously or repeatedly refused to give the child necessary parental care and protection; or

   (3) That, although the parents are financially able, they have substantially and continuously neglected to provide the child with necessary subsistence, education, or other care necessary for his physical or mental health or morals or have neglected to pay for such subsistence, education or other care when legal custody is lodged with others; or

   (4) That the parents are unfit by reason of debauchery, intoxication or habitual use of narcotic drugs, or repeated lewd and lascivious behavior, or other conduct found by the court to be likely to be detrimental to the physical or mental health or morals of the child; or

   (5) That following upon a determination of neglect or dependency, reasonable efforts, under the direction of the court, have failed to correct the conditions leading to the determination.[179]

[179] Minn. Stat. Ann. §260.221(a), (b) (Supp. 1964). See In re Booth, 253 Minn. 395, 91 N.W.2d 921 (1958) (unwed mother's parental rights terminated because she kept company with married men and had had intercourse with at least one of them in her apartment; she had carried on extramarital relations with adjudicated father of the children for a period of ten years).

CHAPTER 2

Marriage

A. INTRODUCTION

All states regulate marriage by a licensing system from which only the now relatively infrequent common law (or informal) marriages are exempt. The designated state official who issues licenses is required to obtain from the parties such facts as are necessary for a determination whether the prospective marriage falls into one of the categories prohibited by state law (e.g., miscegenous, consanguinous, underage, etc.). Many states seek to strengthen this preventive regulatory system by imposing criminal penalties upon the licensing official or the person who subsequently solemnizes the marriage for knowingly permitting an invalid marriage. One might have supposed that, as with other regulatory legislation, the licensing device would itself produce a substantial body of litigation in which the validity of a proposed but questionable marriage would be determined before the marriage took place. In fact, however, such litigation is extraordinarily rare. Only infrequently does one see a case of mandamus to compel a clerk to issue a license.[1] And few, if any, states have followed the enlightened example of Pennsylvania, whose legislature has sought to avoid clerical finality by providing a formal procedure of judicial review of the denial of a license.[2]

A licensing procedure can hardly be an entirely effective enforcement device. The licensing official cannot be expected to verify at the time of

[1] See, e.g., Perez v. Sharp, 32 Cal. 2d 711, 198 P.2d 17 (1948) (clerk ordered to issue license to couple of diverse race since miscegenation statute unconstitutional). It is significant that the "defect" in issue might have been immediately apparent to the licensing official. It is not unlikely that the absence of litigation is indicative that licensing officials seldom exercise their regulatory authority.

[2] See Pa. Stat. Ann. tit. 48, §1-9 (Supp. 1964), which provides that where a license is refused by the clerk: "Upon request of the applicants, the clerk of the orphans' court, immediately after such refusal, shall certify the proceedings to the orphans' court of the county without formality or expense to the applicants.

"Such application for a license to marry shall thereupon, at the earliest possible time, be heard by a judge of said court, without a jury, in court or in chambers, during the term or in vacation, as the case may be. The finding of the court that a license ought to issue or ought not to issue shall be final, and the clerk of the orphans' court shall act in accordance therewith.

"The true intent of this section is to secure for applicants an immediate hearing before the orphans' court without delay or expense on the part of the applicants."

See, e.g., F.A. Marriage License, 4 Pa. D. & C.2d 1 (Orphans' Ct. 1955), reported at page 247 infra.

application the parties' compliance with some of the very complex legislative requirements. For example, a prospective spouse who was previously divorced may in good faith believe that his divorce was valid and that he is therefore free to marry. The clerk is not likely (nor is he in any position) to challenge such a belief — even though it may turn out later that the divorce was not in fact valid. Moreover, the practicing lawyer is not likely to be consulted prior to celebration of the marriage. Clients rarely come to him to ask whether they can legally get married. Whether this is due to general ignorance of statutory restrictions or whether it is simply indicative of the impetuosity of people (particularly those in love) is not clear.[3] In any event, as we shall see, the validity of a marriage is almost invariably litigated after the marriage has been solemnized.

The issue of validity may be relevant in a variety of collateral proceedings. The husband may claim in defense of a criminal prosecution for bigamy that his second marriage was invalid. Or the question may arise with respect to an asserted interspousal tort immunity or evidentiary privilege. Most common of the collateral attacks are those in probate proceedings by third parties who stand to gain from the invalidation of a marriage. The spouses themselves occasionally seek a resolution of questionable validity in a declaratory judgment action.[4] In seeking social security, workmen's compensation, or other benefits, a surviving spouse may have to carry the burden of establishing a valid marriage.

Nonetheless, in most instances, the validity of a marriage is only subjected to judicial scrutiny in a proceeding initiated by one of the spouses who wishes to terminate the relationship. A state can, but very rarely does, challenge directly an allegedly invalid marital status by instituting a criminal prosecution for bigamy or for some other offense which involves the element of unlawful cohabitation. In some situations in some states a third party can bring an action to annul or declare the invalidity of another's marriage, e.g., where parents are given standing to annul a marriage by an underage child, or where a former spouse in a sequential marriage situation seeks to upset her ex-partner's subsequent marriage. These are the exceptions; most frequently marriages are declared invalid directly when one of the parties has found the venture unsuccessful and seeks to terminate it. Given the variety of possible contexts in which the judges are asked to determine the validity of a marriage, it should be no surprise that the decisions cannot be categorized with precision; nor should it be surprising that the doctrines vary according to the issue to be decided.

Some commentators insist that

[3] Of course this is not to say that the lawyer has no role whatever in connection with a client's prospective marriage. For example, under many state statutes, marriage, like divorce, revokes in whole or part a previously executed will. See, e.g., Cal. Prob. Code §70.

[4] A few states permit such actions. See, e.g., Winn v. Wiggins, 47 N.J. Super. 215, 135 A.2d 673 (1957). See also Note, 62 Harv. L. Rev. 787, 844-847 (1949); Note, Use of the Declaratory Judgment in Determining Marital Status, 46 Va. L. Rev. 1439 (1960).

every member of the [legal] profession must realize the radical difference between a decree of nullity, declaring that no valid marriage ever took place and a decree of divorce a vinculo matrimonii, dissolving a marriage proved to have been valid and binding. A divorce means that a valid marriage has turned out a failure, while a decree of nullity means that no marriage ever existed.[5]

Nonetheless, this conceptual niceness would be difficult to understand without some historical perspective. "The Catholic Church taught from the very beginning the indissolubility of marriage, and by the tenth century this doctrine had become embodied in the civil law of every Christian country." [6] In England, of course, the ecclesiastical courts were eventually successful in asserting jurisdiction over the entire province of marriage, and at a very early period "the marriage law of England was the canon law." [7] The Church insisted that marriages be relatively easy to enter (see pages 270-271 infra) but impossible to dissolve. Yet the ecclesiastical court could and would declare that a marriage had never existed (although the marriage had to be "void ab initio" to avoid any implication that it was being dissolved). Thus the apparent indissolubility of marriage was

> softened by the wide discretion exercised by the Church in annulling marriages. There was no valid marriage if the parties were within the forbidden degrees of consanguinity or affinity, these degrees being stretched by the medieval canonists to an astonishing extent . . . . The annulling of marriages between parties within the prohibited degrees became a flourishing business of the Church, and for sufficient payment a flaw could be found in almost every union. . . .[8]

For a great many purposes, however, the civil courts had to determine the validity of marriages. Such questions were customarily referred to the ecclesiastical courts, but the canonical doctrine might not be dispositive:

> from the middle of the twelfth century onwards [the temporal law] had no doctrine of marriage, for it never had to say in so many words whether a valid marriage had been contracted. Adultery was not, bigamy was not, incest was not, a temporal crime. On the other hand, it had often to say whether a woman was entitled to dower, whether a child was entitled to inherit. About these matters it was free to make what rules it pleased. It was in no wise bound to hold that every widow was entitled to dower, or that every child whom the law of the church pronounced legitimate was capable of inheriting. The question, "Was this a marriage or no?" might come before it incidentally. When this happened, that question was sent for decision to an ecclesiastical court, and the answer would be one of the

[5] Scott, Nullity of Marriage in Canon Law and English Law, 2 U. Toronto L.J. 319 (1938), reprinted in Selected Essays on Family Law 230, 231.
[6] 2 U. Toronto L.J. at 320, Selected Essays on Family Law at 231.
[7] 2 Pollock & Maitland 367-368.
[8] Comment, 171 Law Times 462, 463 (1931).

[premises] on which the lay court would found some judgment about dower, inheritance or the like; but only one of the [premises].[9]

This jurisdictional bifurcation, coupled with some popular and royal displeasure with the incidental consequences of the Church's flourishing annulment "business," led to the modern distinction between "void" and "voidable" marriages. A statute of Henry VIII's reign prohibited annulment by the ecclesiastical courts of marriages "without the Leviticall degrees" of consanguinity or affinity.[10] In addition, early in the seventeenth century, the common law courts began to intervene

> by writs of prohibition to prevent ecclesiastical courts from granting decrees of nullity after the death of either of the parties to the marriage "because it is to bastard and disinherit the issues who cannot so well defend the marriage as the parties both living themselves might have done." [11]

The canonical disabilities — physical impotence, consanguinity and affinity, "pre-contract" (i.e., a prior marriage), and force and error — thereafter rendered a marriage "voidable" because the ecclesiastical courts could annul the marriage, but only while both parties to it still lived; civil disabilities — such as "prior marriage, want of age, idiocy, and the like" — rendered a marriage "void" without any decree from any court.[12]

Vestiges, but only vestiges, of this history remain today. Legal actions which signify the dissolution of a family fall into four categories: annulment, absolute divorce ("a vinculo matrimonii"), judicial separation (divorce "a mensa et thoro" — often called limited divorce), and actions to enforce support following desertion (the poor man's rudimentary form of

---

[9] 2 Pollock & Maitland 374. The common law courts consistently stated that "[t]he acts which give rights in land should be public, notorious acts." Id. at 375. This concern accounts for the common law's rejection of legitimation by subsequent marriage; a deathbed wedding "may do well enough for the church and may, one hopes, profit [the sinner's] soul in another world, but it must give no rights in English soil." Ibid. These doctrines led the House of Lords to hold in 1843 that at common law a marriage was invalid unless celebrated in the presence of an ordained clergyman. See Pollock and Maitland's criticism of these decisions at 372-374, and see pages 270-271 infra.

[10] Concerning precontract and degrees of Consanguinite, 32 Hen. 8, c. 38 (1540).

[11] Davies, Matrimonial Relief in English Law, in A Century of Family Law 311, 312 (Graveson & Crane eds. 1957), quoting Coke, 2d Inst. 614. According to Bishop, the common law courts early established their authority to restrain the ecclesiastical courts from exercising powers they did not have. Bishop, Commentaries on the Law of Marriage and Divorce §3 (2d ed. 1856).

[12] Id. §55. Doctrinal development was apparently fairly untidy: "The dividing line between canonical and civil disabilities is variable and by no means always clear: prior marriage as a cause of annulment of a subsequent marriage was originally of ecclesiastical cognisance only but bigamy was made a civil statutory felony in 1603: at the same time pre-contract, a canonical disability, . . . co-existed down to 1753." Jackson, The Law Relating to the Formation and Annulment of Marriage 50 (1951). It is not surprising that, with such confused and nonfunctional roots, current doctrines as to "void" and "voidable" marriages are in similar disarray. See page 175 infra.

limited divorce). In theory there are sharp distinctions between annulment and the other remedies. An annulment is appropriate where there has never been a valid marriage because of defects existing at the time of the ceremony, whereas divorce assumes a valid marriage and is granted for conditions which have developed since marriage. Conceptually, the consequences of each form of dissolution should also vary. A divorce terminates the marriage and permits the parties to remarry, although a residuum of marital obligations may continue, such as the duty to support the former wife and children. A judicial separation is simply a declaration that a marriage has failed and that the parties are now authorized to live apart; it provides for support and child custody but does not give the spouses the right to remarry. After an annulment, however, since the marriage is "void ab initio," the "husband" should have no obligations of any sort toward the person who appeared to be his "wife," and any children born during the marriage should be illegitimate.

But logic has never been preferred when important social policies are at stake. Building on the framework provided by the ancient consequences of dual jurisdiction, state legislatures have often subdivided the remedy of annulment: some purported marriages are void ab initio, others are merely voidable. Important procedural consequences follow the distinction, e.g., if a marriage is merely voidable, the number of potential litigants who have standing to annul it may be sharply restricted and its "voidness" may operate only from the date of the decree. Moreover, the ab initio fiction has been riddled with exceptions by courts and particularly by legislatures. A court may hold that a marriage which the legislature had denominated "void" was merely voidable. Harrison v. State, 22 Md. 468 (1864). "Logic must yield to realities," the Massachusetts Supreme Judicial Court said in a case in which a wife, who was injured in an automobile accident in a car driven by her husband, attempted to sue him in tort after an intervening annulment for fraud.[13] The court refused to permit the interspousal suit, giving at least that much effect to the marriage that never was. In another case a husband, prosecuted under a criminal statute which penalized beating one's "wife," defended on the ground that the victim was not his wife because their purported marriage was absolutely void for bigamy. The court conceded the voidness but held that for the purposes of this statute the woman was entitled "to the protection afforded by the statute." State v. Collins, 29 Del. 260, 262, 99 Atl. 87, 88 (1916).[14]

Nor have the legislatures been satisfied with the theoretical simplicity of the annulment concept, particularly when it comes to grounds or standing to bring an action. Consider the state laws relevant to the status and dissolution of a marriage contracted at a time when one of the parties is

[13] Callow v. Thomas, 322 Mass. 550, 555, 78 N.E.2d 637, 640 (1948). Is it of any significance that the court took pains to note that the marriage here was merely voidable, not void? See also page 339 infra.

[14] At common law, the ecclesiastical courts, and for a time even the civil courts, deemed legitimate children born prior to annulments for some defects. See 2 Pollock & Maitland 376-377.

insane. Under the canon law such a marriage can be annulled because it fails to meet Canon 1081's requirement that there be consent "lawfully expressed between parties capable according to law." [15] From a policy viewpoint, this ground presents as compelling a reason as any for refusing to give the purported marriage effect. The insane spouse has had no effective free choice, and the sane spouse has probably unwittingly taken on a burden that renders normal marriage impossible from the outset. From society's viewpoint such a marriage offers scant prospects of developing into a stable union and poses disproportionate risks for potential children. The statutes reveal a confused tangle of labels, remedies, standing, and policy objectives.[16] The labels attached to the marriage by various state legislatures are "absolutely void," "void," "void from the time of the court action," and "voidable." In two states the remedy is divorce, while in a handful of other states no remedy is needed as the marriage is void and another marriage can be contracted without obtaining court action. Where a judicial declaration is required, the provisions for standing to sue embrace the following variations. An action can be brought by:

either party;

either party unless cohabitation after reason restored;

only by the incapable party;

only by the incapable party and his guardian;

only by the incapable party or his guardian or relatives;

only by the sane party or the incapable party's guardian or relatives;

only by the sane party;

only by the sane party, and then only if without knowledge of the insanity at the time;

only by the "injured party," which in the context of the particular statute, surprisingly, means the sane party.

There is little correlation between these provisions as to remedy and standing to sue and the label attached to the marriage; indeed, in one state where the label is "absolutely void," the only available remedy is by divorce. Finally, as we shall see, the judicial definition of the prerequisite "insanity" may vary with the parties, the issue, or the time at which validity is questioned. In its practical connotations, the termination of a void or voidable marriage by annulment is much more closely akin to divorce than to the conceptual theory of nullity. Certainly this is true of the "avoidance annulments" of voidable marriages.[17] The marriage continues until there is a decision by one or both parties to terminate it. The availability of an avoidance annulment merely provides another possible ground for dissolution in addition to those set forth in the divorce statute.

[15] See Note, The Effect of Insanity at the Time of Marriage, 16 La. L. Rev. 511, 512 (1956).

[16] See the excellent tables in a comprehensive recent report of the American Bar Foundation, The Mentally Disabled and the Law 207-210 (Lindman & McIntyre eds. 1961). The discussion which follows is based on this study.

[17] Storke, Annulment in the Conflict of Laws, 43 Minn. L. Rev. 849, 850 (1959).

The decision for the lawyer becomes primarily one of tactics, weighing the possible grounds for dissolution and the advantages or disadvantages of annulment compared with some other form of dissolution. Storke provides the following hypothetical dialogue:

> MRS. JONES consulted her lawyer about her teen-age daughter. "Sally has only been married a month," she said, "and now she wants a divorce."
>
> "Wouldn't an annulment be better?" the lawyer inquired.
>
> "What's the difference?"
>
> "A divorce terminates a valid marriage," said the lawyer. "An annulment establishes that the parties were never legally married."
>
> "But they were married," said Mrs. Jones. "Married in church, and everybody knows it. Besides, they have been sleeping together. Isn't an annulment something that people get when they have never slept together?"
>
> "Not necessarily. In this state a girl who marries before she is eighteen can have the marriage annulled any time before her nineteenth birthday, regardless of consummation."
>
> "For all I know," Mrs. Jones objected, "Sally may be pregnant. If she is, I don't want people going around saying she has never been married."
>
> "Why not wait until we know?" the lawyer suggested. "If she is pregnant, we will get her a divorce. If not, we will go for an annulment." [18]

There are many other tactical considerations besides the stigma of unwed motherhood that come into operation when, after one month or many, Sally decides that she has had enough. Depending upon the particular jurisdiction's law as applied to the particular facts, there may be many reasons why one or both parties would prefer annulment to divorce, notwithstanding on occasion even possible bastardization of the offspring (if any). Rules relating to jurisdiction, residence requirements, or choice of law may be different from and more favorable in a particular case than those applicable to divorce. For many persons the stigma attached to the status of divorce is reduced if the decree is one of annulment, and this factor may be particularly persuasive for those affiliated with religions which frown on divorce. Related to this is the right after an annulment immediately to resume a maiden name. For the husband an annulment may offer the prospect of avoiding liability for alimony, and there may be other important differences in the resolution of the couple's property interests. Some jurisdictions delay or impede the right to remarriage as a consequence of a divorce decree, and for the impatient litigant this may be enough to outweigh all else and militate towards annulment. Similarly, in a few states remarriage is impossible for a guilty party after a divorce for adultery. Another factor which may be present in a sequential marriage situation concerns a wife's possible rights flowing from the termination of a prior marriage. As we shall see (page 916 infra), a

[18] Id. at 849.

woman entitled to alimony, support, or one of various social insurance benefits as a result of having been divorced or widowed normally forfeits these rights by remarriage; in many jurisdictions, however, if the remarriage is annulled, at least some of the benefits stemming from the prior marriage can be reinstated. Conversely, if one's client is an alien whose entry into the United States was contingent upon a valid marriage to a citizen, a decree of annulment declaring the marriage void ab initio may be tantamount to an order for deportation, whereas a divorce will have no such effect.

These are some of the practical problems which will have to be considered and resolved in appropriate cases, but they have little to do with any rational marriage policy. The fact that such tactical gamesmanship persists at all in the law of marital dissolution is a recognition of the dominance of history over logic.

There is another factor as to which avoidance annulment shows striking similarities to divorce. It has frequently been suggested that the legal grounds for divorce bear little relationship to the actual causative factors in marital disruption. There seems every reason to believe that the statement is equally true of annulment. In many cases in which an avoidance decree is sought, the fraud or incapacity which is alleged is probably no more than the tool by which legal acknowledgment is desired to confirm a marital failure previously induced by incompatibility, immaturity, neurosis, alcoholism, religious conflict, etc.

Such statistics as exist lend considerable support to the hypothesis that the overwhelming majority of annulments are of the avoidance type and that, despite the procedural variations, in their essential nature such annulments are merely variant forms of divorce. There were about 12,000 annulments in the United States in 1958.[19] In most states its incidence compared with that of divorce is statistically insignificant. The proportion of annulment to total divorce and annulment dissolutions was less than $1\frac{1}{2}$ per cent in twenty-three states and in only nine states was this figure 3 per cent or higher. Two of these states accounted for 73 per cent of all reported annulments. California, with 5107 annulments representing 11.7 per cent of all California marital dissolutions, establishes for all divorces an interlocutory period of one year's duration during which neither of the parties may remarry. New York, whose 3407 annulments[20] represented 39.4 per cent of its total dissolutions, is not only the only state which limits the grounds for divorce to adultery, but also provides that the guilty party in divorce may not remarry during the lifetime of the other spouse unless, after three years, the court gives permission. Under these circumstances it is not surprising that there has been pressure to utilize annulment as a substitute for what would be divorce in most other

---

[19] 1 Vital Statistics of the United States 1959, Table 2-AG, reports 11,655, but there were no data for Kentucky or Louisiana and the figures for a few other states are listed as incomplete.

[20] Jacobson, American Marriage and Divorce 113-114 (1959), gives somewhat higher figures, stating that in the 1950's New York annulments averaged 4170 per year.

jurisdictions. The remarkably broad and unique doctrine of what constitutes fraud sufficient to void a marriage that was evolved by the New York courts can perhaps also be seen as a response to these pressures.[21] The hypothesis gains limited support from the fact that after California and New York, in five of the remaining seven states where the proportion of annulment to all dissolution was 3 per cent or higher, there were atypical restrictions on divorce, such as interlocutory periods or prohibitions of remarriage, although for shorter periods than in California.

Finally, there is reason for believing that even many declaratory annulments of absolutely void marriages represent no more than another technique for avoiding a marriage which in fact has been tried and found wanting for reasons unrelated to the legal defect. The fact that a court would hold a marriage absolutely void because it is repugnant to public policy is no assurance that the illegal status which results will be terminated or even questioned. No one can approximate the number of persons who have contracted void marriages, lived, had children, died, and had their estates probated with no one the wiser. Presumably countless marriages are contracted where one of the spouses has obtained a Mexican mail order or some other divorce which is legally ineffective to terminate the prior marriage. In most jurisdictions the marriage is therefore bigamous and absolutely void, but if the relationship proves to be a tolerable one the parties will not litigate, and it seems likely that only a fraction of void marriages are subjected to collateral attack. For every probate case where a marriage has been attacked collaterally and held void, there are X cases in which interested relatives who could have had a marriage declared void were unaware of the defect, plus Y cases in which interested relatives who had knowledge of the facts refused to seek a material gain because of the expense and notoriety of protracted litigation. Like the research scientist, the lawyer needs constant reminders that the cases with which he deals are not necessarily representative of any general population.

The distinction between annulment and divorce has proved to be on the one hand so fragile and on the other so troublesome that Judge (then Professor) Goodrich once suggested: "Why would not the best way be to drop the doctrine of nullity, with its relation back and bastardizing of innocent children and otherwise ignoring the existence of a fact, and include the common causes of annulment under divorce?" Goodrich, Jurisdiction to Annul a Marriage, 32 Harv. L. Rev. 806, 824 (1919). As to at least some causes of annulment there has been a marked legislative trend in this direction. One extreme statute even authorizes a divorce for a bigamous or fraudulently entered marriage,[22] the grounds responsible for the overwhelming majority of annulments in this country. The Ohio

[21] See Note, Annulments for Fraud — New York's Answer to Reno?, 48 Colum. L. Rev. 900 (1948). Compare South Carolina, which made no provision for any divorce from 1878 to 1948, but whose law of annulments for fraud nonetheless underwent no comparable enlargement. South Carolinians apparently utilized the other well-known device for avoiding local divorce law restrictions — migratory divorce.

[22] Pa. Stat. Ann. tit. 23, §10 (1955).

Supreme Court held that divorce was the exclusive remedy to terminate a bigamous marriage; one of the legislative objectives had been to give the second wife a right to alimony.[23] As we shall note (page 908 infra), a number of legislatures have expressly provided for alimony in annulment proceedings.

For all the reasons enumerated above, these materials treat annulment as essentially a device to terminate what is at least de facto a marital status. Accordingly we treat some of its grounds, procedures, and consequences in the last part of the book where we examine the problems of dissolution. Our concern in this chapter is largely with regulatory policy — what are the state's appropriate concerns in regulating the establishment of marriages and how should the state's policies be enforced.

In considering the cases and statutes which follow, the student should keep in mind the following questions:

a. What is the purpose of a particular rule or statute? Both spouses, their parents, their present or potential children, and any prior spouses of either party may have an interest in legal regulation of the marital status. It is also said that the state is a party to every marriage. It is important to try to ascertain what interest of the state is being promoted by any given statute or decision. We have already noted the heavy hand of history in the determination of present public policy.

b. What sanctions are available to enforce marriage law restrictions? Much of marriage law is preventive, e.g., the prohibition of underage marriage seeks to insure that the parties will bring to their marriage at least a certain minimum level of maturity. Where there has been a violation of such a preventive policy which was undetected in time to prevent a purported marriage and the creation of a family, it is usually too late for the prevention to be effective as to that particular family. Invalidating such marriages after the parties have cohabited for years, have had children, even after their deaths, might be described as an indirect deterrent sanction. But such indirection is at best of dubious efficacy and often works great hardship. Why has so little been done to apply direct sanctions (e.g., criminal prosecutions for entering into an unlawful marriage) or to tighten up administrative regulation?

The problem of enforcement is complicated by the wide differences among states both in the formulation of a particular policy and in the importance attached to that policy in actual administration and interpretation. One of the most difficult and pervasive problems results from evasion of restrictions of the domiciliary state through marriage in a sister state with more lenient laws.

c. What underlying factors, seldom articulated in the statutes or even the opinions, are in fact often of critical importance when state regulatory policy is enforced after the marriage at the expense of a de facto family relationship? One should be alert to the stage of the relationship at which a marriage is attacked. Has the marriage ever been consummated? If so, have the parties actually cohabited and held themselves out as husband and wife? Have children been born of the union? Is the attack

[23] Eggleston v. Eggleston, 156 Ohio St. 422, 103 N.E.2d 395 (1952).

launched only after the death of one of the parties? What are the consequences which invalidation would visit on the parties themselves and on other persons — children, parents, or other relatives? It is significant that questions of such obvious practical importance have so often been ignored in legislative draftsmanship. What can account for such oversight?

d. How far does and should the law go to mitigate the hardship of invalidation of marriage? Both statute and common law provide devices which give relief from a particular incident of invalidation, e.g., provisions for the legitimation of children of void or unlawful marriages. In many states curative statutes make a marriage valid from the time of removal of an impediment which made the marriage invalid when solemnized. The slow trend towards abolition of common law marriage in most jurisdictions raises acutely the problem of how far social policy should go in giving legal recognition to a family relationship which has existed in fact.

e. Can marriage law play a significant part in promoting greater family stability in a society which is plagued with high divorce and separation rates? "It is a pity," a judge has noted, that marriage "is so easy to get into and so hard to get out of." [24] One writer has attributed much of the increase in our divorce rate to the lax marriage laws prevalent in most states.[25] Another writer has said:

> Until they are satisfied that no inadequacy of law or defect of judicial machinery is contributing to the vast aggregate of heartache and human misery represented by a half-million broken homes a year, the bench and bar of America, national, state and local, and all others interested in the efficient administration of justice, should not cease to scrutinize their statutes and judicial processes with that end in view. . . .
>
> The inquiry might well begin with marriage laws and procedures, since many divorces are but the severing of ties that never should have been made in the first place. . . .[26]

Outside the law, too, much attention has been devoted to the question of how to assure a successful marriage. Many factors allegedly associated with marital success have been explored, such as religion and social background, length of engagement, and the relative stability of marriages across religious lines. The development of marriage prediction tests has even been attempted.[27]

In the materials which follow, we consider first some basic problems of the intentions of the parties and the public policy of the state (Section B),

---

[24] Bok, J., in Bove v. Pinciotti, 46 Pa. D. & C. 159, 161 (1942). With respect to the correctness of the second part of Judge Bok's statement, compare pages 683-701 infra.

[25] Ploscowe, The Truth about Divorce 6 (1955).

[26] Note, The National Tragedy of Divorce, 30 J. Am. Jud. Soc. 180, 181-182 (1947).

[27] See, e.g., Ellis, The Value of Marriage Prediction Tests, 13 Am. Soc. Rev. 710 (1948), concluding that use of these tests for marriage counseling cannot be scientifically encouraged.

and then the detailed provisions for legislative regulation of marriage (Section C).

B. NATURE OF THE MARRIAGE CONTRACT

PROBLEM

Arnold has informed you that he was the remainderman of a trust fund established in his deceased father's will. The terms of the trust were that Arnold was to receive the income and the corpus of the trust upon attaining the age of thirty or his wedding day, whichever happened first. Two years ago, when Arnold was twenty-four and anxious to receive his legacy, he asked Lucy, a neighborhood friend, to marry him and told her of the terms of his father's will. He told her that they could get married, but would not have to live together, and when he received his inheritance, he would reward her for her trouble. Lucy knew Arnold to be a great joke-ster and thought he was joshing her. Wishing to see how far Arnold would carry his little joke, Lucy went with him to the Marriage License Bureau, where they received a license. A week later, while on their way home from a party, Arnold and Lucy were married by a Justice of the Peace. At the time, Lucy remarked to a friend accompanying them, "Oh, that Arnold, he'll do anything for a laugh." Lucy and Arnold then went their separate ways and never cohabited as husband and wife. Arnold would now like to marry his sweetheart Grace, who is pregnant by him, and he would like to have his marriage to Lucy annulled. Lucy would also like to have an annulment.

1. Advise Arnold.
2. Soon after his marriage Arnold consulted you because the trustees of Arnold's father's estate refused to pay him any money. Could he compel them to do so?

(In dealing with this problem, consider the materials through page 193 infra.)

CROUCH v. WARTENBERG
91 W. Va. 91, 112 S.E. 234 (1922)

[Appeal from denial of bill for annulment.]

LIVELY, J.: Plaintiff who was 19 years of age, had known defendant about three months and marriage had been discussed between them. At a party held at one of the hotels on the evening of the 30th day of January, 1920, it was proposed by some one that the plaintiff and defendant proceed to be married on that occasion, and that a license be then obtained. The proposition was made and acted upon in a spirit of jest, but without any apparent intention of its consummation, and was evidently the caprice of exuberant youthful spirits. It became rumored that the parties were to have been married in good faith at that time and for some unexplained cause it failed of consummation, and the press reporters published a "story" with the modern colorings, for public consumption.

Next day, about 2 o'clock P.M., plaintiff was on her way to an appointment with her dentist, when, upon invitation, she entered the automobile
of a member of the party of the evening before, and later defendant got in
the car, and told plaintiff that so many people had heard that they were
going to be married the night before, and that she had refused to do so at
the last minute, that it would ruin him as he was just starting in business
in the city, and it would cause him loss of business unless something was
done to prevent it.   After consultation among themselves and defendant's
friends, it was concluded that the ceremony would be at once performed
in order to save any further embarrassment, but that the marriage should
be in form only and that they would not live or cohabit together.   She
stated to him she did not love him, and did not want to become his wife,
and he agreed that he would not expect anything from her by virtue of
the ceremony, and that he would procure an annulment as soon as possible.   It appears that there was no intention on the part of either that they
should become man and wife in any sense.   It seemed to be an ill-advised
step to relieve him from what he thought was a situation which would
affect his business and social standing.   She was nervous and excited, and
upon his assurances of a speedy annulment of the ceremony, went with
him for the license, while a friend of his procured a wedding ring, thence
to the minister where the ceremony was performed with all outward show
of a valid marriage.   Immediately upon leaving the parsonage, they separated.   She went to a relative's house where she talked with her mother
over the telephone telling her of her escapade, thence she went home.
She never lived or cohabited with defendant.   On the third day after the
marriage ceremony, they went together to consult counsel and the suit for
annulment was immediately instituted.   Subsequently she resumed her
studies in a University.   Defendant does not defend the suit.   The divorce commissioner filed an answer substantially denying the allegations,
upon information and belief.   Defendant was introduced as witness by
the divorce commissioner, and corroborates the statement of plaintiff in
every material part.   He says he did not marry her in good faith, and told
her that he would have the ceremony annulled, or "got rid of" at the
earliest possible time after the ceremony.   He says he never lived or cohabited with her, and while he was in a position to provide her a home,
was never ready or willing to do so; that he did not deceive or coerce her
into marrying him, that they both understood that they would have the
ceremony performed and then cancelled, that they did not intend to live
together, and that the whole matter originated in a jest the night before.
We think the evidence clearly establishes that the ceremony, although
actually entered into and performed in the manner provided by statute,
was the outcome of a jest, and was entered into by the parties, with no
intention of being man and wife in the legal sense, with the understanding that they would not be bound thereby and have no privileges or obligations incident thereto; and that no subsequent acts or conduct on their
part indicated otherwise.   They were both young, illy advised, and were
attempting to extricate themselves from what they considered an embarrassing situation; and, as is usual with inexperienced and impulsive

youth, acted hurriedly without deliberation or consultation with relatives or those upon whom they should have relied. As usually happens in such cases, the result was more serious embarrassment.

A marriage is regarded as a civil contract at its inception. The minds of the parties must meet in good faith for the purpose of carrying out the contract by cohabitation as husband and wife, and the assumption of the duties and obligations incidental to the marriage relation. Without such intent, words and ceremonies will not make a valid marriage contract. . . .   The parties never intended to enter into the relation, separated immediately after the ceremony, and never recognized it as binding by subsequent word or act. On the other hand, it would be against public policy and justice to destroy the lives and happiness of these young persons by forcing them against their will to live together, or forcing the alternative of living lives of celibacy. No home will be destroyed, for none has been formed. Perhaps severe censure is due them for trifling with the outward and legal forms of the sacred relationship, but we do not think the censure should go to the extent of wrecking their lives, and their future usefulness to the state and society. Perhaps the publicity and humiliation brought about by these proceedings is punishment sufficient for them, and to warn others. There was no intent, express or implied, on the part of either of the parties to enter into a contract of marriage. . . .

The plaintiff is entitled to the relief prayed for in her bill, and a decree will be entered here awarding her annulment of the marriage, and her costs in this and the lower court.

Reversed, and decree annulling marriage entered.

NOTE

1. Compare Lannamann v. Lannamann, 171 Pa. Super. 147, 149-150, 89 A.2d 897-898 (1952). Plaintiff was an eighteen-year-old student at Swarthmore College.

On August 18, 1950, she drove to Salisbury, Maryland, and had a luncheon engagement with the defendant, whom she had known for some time. He suggested that they get a marriage license; that "it wouldn't hurt and would make him feel better" and as though she was really "his girl." She agreed and the license was obtained. The defendant was well pleased. She returned home and went back to college. She frequently met the defendant but also had "dates" with other boys, and the defendant had "dates" with other girls. In December, 1950, the defendant suggested that they drive to Allen, Maryland, and have a marriage ceremony performed by a named minister. She testified: "[He] more or less dared me, so I said OK." Before they got to Allen, Maryland, she wanted to go back, and the defendant said that they were just going to go through the ceremony, and that later if it was regretted, "it probably won't be too hard for your Mother to get it annulled." She stated that he argued with her

and said it didn't really mean anything, that if they didn't go
through the ceremony it would finish everything between them, and
that they had at least from December to June to decide whether they
wanted to "take it seriously"; and that "he rationalized that it would
make me feel more secure if we went through a ceremony." The
marriage was never consummated; and she returned to college and
the defendant went back to work. They saw each other as they did
before. She testified that they concluded that they had been unwise,
that their parents should be told, and that they ought to "[get] it
cleaned up"; and if at any later date they wanted to get married they
would have the ceremony performed in a church, with their families
and friends present. On March 31, 1951, they told the plaintiff's
mother. The defendant was about to enter the Navy and desired
that the marriage ceremony be translated into reality. To this she
would not agree.

This was certainly not a marriage ceremony performed "in jest,"
and it was not void ab initio. Actually the parties were married,
under an agreement that the marriage should not be immediately
consummated, and that they could change their minds thereafter.
In other words, they agreed that it should be a trial marriage, and
that either or both had a six month option to annul it. Since in
getting married both the parties did only what they intended to do,
and since there was no fraud, duress or lack of mental capacity, the
marriage is valid. . . .

2. For a discussion of other "joke marriage" cases, see Annot., 14
A.L.R.2d 624 (1950).

3. On the question of intoxication as it bears on the absence of deliberate consent, see Annot., 57 A.L.R.2d 1250 (1958).

4. For cases dealing with duress upon one or both parties as a ground
for annulment, see Annot., 91 A.L.R. 414 (1934). Cases in which relief is
granted understandably appear to be rare. The most frequent marriage
in which some form of compulsion is alleged is where the threats are of
criminal prosecution or exposure of a criminal sexual offense such as statutory rape or seduction. It is usually held that this is not enough to
constitute duress for the purpose of avoidance. On the problem of duress
exercised by a third party without procurement or connivance of the defendant, see Note, 30 Colum. L. Rev. 714 (1930).

5. The court in Crouch purported to apply contract principles in resolving the validity of the marriage. How valid was this analogy as it was
applied in this case? Would one expect to find comparable cases in orthodox contracts law where the contracts typically concern economic bargains? Do the courts use this analogy because remedies for breach of
contract are useful in resolving marital problems, or for some other reasons?

6. In an Australian case petitioner sued for a declaration of nullity of
an alleged marriage performed more than three years before; the Attorney General insisted that he was entitled only to a divorce for desertion.

The parties had gone to a minister to be married. The ceremony proceeded to the stage where petitioner had said that he took respondent to be his wedded wife till death should part them, and the respondent had made a corresponding declaration. The minister then invited the petitioner to place a ring on respondent's finger, and as he did so, she pulled it off, threw it on the ground, said "I will not marry you," and ran from the premises. The respondent testified that she had been a willing party until that moment. What judgment? See Quick v. Quick otherwise O'Connell, [1953] Vict. L.R. 224, in which a divided court produced three opinions covering twenty-five pages.

LUTWAK v. UNITED STATES
344 U.S. 604 (1953)

MINTON, J. The petitioners, Marcel Max Lutwak, Munio Knoll, and Regina Treitler, together with Leopold Knoll and Grace Klemtner, were indicted on six counts in the Northern District of Illinois, Eastern Division. The first count charged conspiracy to commit substantive offenses set forth in the remaining five counts and conspiracy "to defraud the United States of and concerning its governmental function and right of administering" the immigration laws and the Immigration and Naturalization Service, by obtaining the illegal entry into this country of three aliens as spouses of honorably discharged veterans. . . .

We are concerned here only with the conviction of the petitioners of the alleged conspiracy. Petitioner Regina Treitler is the sister of Munio Knoll and Leopold Knoll, and the petitioner Lutwak is their nephew. Munio Knoll had been married in Poland in 1932 to one Maria Knoll. There is some evidence that Munio and Maria were divorced in 1942, but the existence and validity of this divorce are not determinable from the record. At the time of the inception of the conspiracy, in the summer of 1947, Munio, Maria and Leopold were refugees from Poland, living in Paris, France, while Regina Treitler and Lutwak lived in Chicago, Illinois. Petitioner Treitler desired to get her brothers into the United States.

Alien spouses of honorably discharged veterans of World War II were permitted to enter this country under the provisions of the so-called War Brides Act . . .

The first count of the indictment charged that the petitioners conspired to have three honorably discharged veterans journey to Paris and go through marriage ceremonies with Munio, Leopold and Maria. The brothers and Maria would then accompany their new spouses to the United States and secure entry into this country by representing themselves as alien spouses of World War II veterans. It was further a part of the plan that the marriages were to be in form only, solely for the purpose of enabling Munio, Leopold and Maria to enter the United States. The parties to the marriages were not to live together as husband and wife, and thereafter would take whatever legal steps were necessary to sever the legal ties. It was finally alleged that the petitioners conspired to conceal these acts in order to prevent disclosure of the conspiracy to the immigration authorities. . . .

There is an abundance of evidence in this record of a conspiracy to contract spurious, phony marriages for the purposes of deceiving the immigration authorities and thereby perpetrating a fraud upon the United States, and of a conspiracy to commit other offenses against the United States.

Petitioners present three principal contentions: (1) Their conspiracy was not unlawful because the marriages involved were valid marriages; (2) the trial court erred in permitting the ostensible wives of these marriages to testify against their so-called husbands; and (3) the trial court erred in admitting testimony of various acts and declarations of different petitioners, done and said after the conspiracy had ended, without limiting the evidence to the particular defendant who performed the act or made the statement.

I.

At the trial, it was undisputed that Maria, Munio and Leopold had gone through formal marriage ceremonies with Lutwak, Bess Osborne and Grace Klemtner, respectively. Petitioners contended that, regardless of the intentions of the parties at the time of the ceremonies, the fact that the ceremonies were performed was sufficient to establish the validity of the marriages, at least until the Government proved their invalidity under French law. They relied on the general American rule of conflict of laws that a marriage valid where celebrated is valid everywhere unless it is incestuous, polygamous, or otherwise declared void by statute. See Loughran v. Loughran, 292 U.S. 216, 223; Restatement, Conflict of Laws, §§121, 132-134. Neither side presented any evidence of the French law, and the trial court ruled that in the absence of such evidence, the French law would be presumed to be the same as American law. The court later instructed the jury that "if the subjects agree to a marriage only for the sake of representing it as such to the outside world and with the understanding that they will put an end to it as soon as it has served its purpose to deceive, they have never really agreed to be married at all." The petitioners claim that the trial court erred in presuming that the French law relating to the validity of marriages is the same as American law, and they further contend that even under American law these marriages are valid.

We do not believe that the validity of the marriages is material. No one is being prosecuted for an offense against the marital relation. We consider the marriage ceremonies only as a part of the conspiracy to defraud the United States and to commit offenses against the United States. In the circumstances of this case, the ceremonies were only a step in the fraudulent scheme and actions taken by the parties to the conspiracy. By directing in the War Brides Act that "alien spouses" of citizen war veterans should be admitted into this country, Congress intended to make it possible for veterans who had married aliens to have their families join them in this country without the long delay involved in qualifying under the proper immigration quota. Congress did not intend to provide aliens with an easy means of circumventing the quota system by fake marriages in which neither of the parties ever intended to enter into the marital relationship; that petitioners so believed is evidenced by their care in concealing from the immigration authorities that the ostensible husbands and wives were to separate immediately after their entry into this country and were never to live together as husband and wife. The common understanding of a marriage, which Congress must have had in mind when it made provision for "alien *spouses*" in the War Brides Act, is that the two parties have undertaken to establish a life together and assume certain duties and obligations. Such was not the case here, or so the jury might reasonably have found. Thus, when one of the aliens stated that he was married, and omitted to explain the true nature of his marital relationship, his statement did, and was intended to, carry with it implications of a state of facts which were not in fact true.

Because the validity of the marriages is not material, the cases involving so-called limited-purpose marriages,[28] cited by petitioners to support their contention that the marriages in the instant case are valid, are inapplicable. All of those cases are suits for annulment in which the court was requested to grant relief to one of the parties to a marriage on the basis of his own admission that the marriage had been a sham. Where the annulment was denied, one or more of the following factors influenced the court: (1) A reluctance to permit the parties to use the annulment procedure as a quick and painless substitute for divorce, particularly because this might encourage people to marry hastily and inconsiderately; (2) a belief that the parties should not be permitted to use the courts as the means of carrying out their own secret schemes; and (3) a desire to prevent injury to innocent third parties, particularly children of the marriage. These factors have no application in the circumstances of the instant case. Similarly inapplicable are the cases where a marriage was entered into in order to render the wife incompetent to testify against her husband in a pending trial, because in none of those cases was it proved that the parties to the marriage did not intend to enter into the marital relationship in good faith.[29] Much more closely related is the case of United States v. Rubenstein, 151 F.2d 915, 918-919, in which the court held that where two persons entered into a marriage solely for the purpose of facilitating the woman's entry into this country, and with no intention by either party to enter into the marriage relationship as it is commonly understood, for the purposes of that case they were never married at all. In the instant case, as in the Rubenstein case, there was no good faith — no intention to marry and consummate the marriages even

[28] E.g., Schibi v. Schibi, 136 Conn. 196, 69 A.2d 831; Hanson v. Hanson, 287 Mass. 154, 191 N.E. 673. These and the other cases cited by petitioners are collected and discussed in a note, 14 A.L.R.2d 624 (1950).

[29] E.g., Norman v. State, 127 Tenn. 340, 155 S.W. 135; State v. Frey, 76 Minn. 526, 79 N.W. 518.

for a day. With the legal consequences of such ceremonies under other circumstances, either in the United States or France, we are not concerned.

[The Court then went on to hold that (1) the rationale underlying the husband-wife evidentiary privilege did not make it appropriate to apply that rule here, and (2) although evidence as to acts done by different petitioners after the conspiracy ended was properly admissible against all defendants, evidence of a declaration made under similar circumstances was not, but this was harmless error.]

Finding no reversible error in this record, the judgment is

Affirmed.

MR. JUSTICE JACKSON, whom MR. JUSTICE BLACK and MR. JUSTICE FRANKFURTER join, dissenting.

Whenever a court has a case where behavior that obviously is sordid can be proved to be criminal only with great difficulty, the effort to bridge the gap is apt to produce bad law. We are concerned about the effect of this decision in three respects.

1. We are not convinced that any crime has been proved, even on the assumption that all evidence in the record was admissible. These marriages were formally contracted in France, and there is no contention that they were forbidden or illegal there for any reason. It is admitted that some judicial procedure is necessary if the parties wish to be relieved of their obligations. Whether by reason of the reservations with which the parties entered into the marriages they could be annulled may be a nice question of French law, in view of the fact that no one of them deceived the other. We should expect it to be an even nicer question whether a third party, such as the state in a criminal process, could simply ignore the ceremony and its consequences, as the Government does here.

We start with marriages that either are valid or at least have not been proved to be invalid in their inception. The Court brushes this question aside as immaterial, but we think it goes to the very existence of an offense. If the parties are validly married, even though the marriage is a sordid one, we should suppose that would end the case. On the other hand, if the marriage ceremonies were for some reason utterly void and held for naught, as if they never had happened, the Government could well claim that entry into the United States as married persons was fraud. But between these two extremes is the more likely case — marriages that are not void but perhaps voidable. In one of these cases, the parties (on the trial) expressed their desire to stay married, and they were acquitted; and no one contends that their marriage is void. Certainly if these marriages were merely voidable and had not been adjudged void at the time of the entry into this country, it was not a fraud to represent them as subsisting. We should think that the parties to them might have been prosecuted with as much reason if they had represented themselves to be single. Marriages of convenience are not uncommon and it cannot be that we would hold it a fraud for one who has contracted a marriage not forbidden by law to represent himself as wedded, even if there were grounds for annulment or divorce and proceedings to that end were contemplated.

The effect of any reservations of the parties in contracting the marriages would seem to be governed by the law of France. It does not seem justifiable to assume what we all know is not true — that French law and our law are the same. Such a view ignores some of the most elementary facts of legal history — the French reception of Roman law, the consequences of the Revolution, and the Napoleonic codifications. If the Government contends that these marriages were ineffectual from the beginning, it would seem to require proof of particular rules of the French law of domestic relations. . . .

NOTE

1. To attempt to ascertain the French law, it is necessary to make an assumption that the marriages contracted in Lutwak were between citizens of Poland domiciled in France and citizens of the United States. If an action for nullity were brought in France, the French court would first look to the law of the nationality of the petitioning spouse. Thus, if the annulment action had been initiated by the United States spouse, the initial reference would have been to its law, which, generally speaking, looks to the law of the place where the marriage was contracted. In this case, that would bring the French court back to French internal law. (This type of reference to a foreign system and subsequent reference back to the forum is known as renvoi in the conflict of laws.) A 1958 case of the Cour de Paris held void a marriage contracted on strikingly similar facts. A Polish girl who lived in France was anxious to return to Poland to visit her sick mother. However, because she had escaped from Poland for political reasons, she was afraid to return there without the protective acquisition of a non-Polish passport. Accordingly she persuaded Mr. Rodolosi, an Italian who was living in France, to marry her for the sole purpose of giving her Italian nationality and hence an Italian passport. The marriage was performed in Paris, but before the girl had a chance to go to Poland her mother died. Subsequently, the Italian husband brought suit for an annulment in a French court. The court granted the annulment because of the absence of consent to marriage required by Article 146 of the French Civil Code. It presumably looked first to the applicable national law (Italy), which, like the American law, refers back to the place where the marriage was celebrated (France). Rodolosi v. Rodolosi, Cour d'Appel de Paris, Oct. 16, 1958, [1958] Semaine Juridique II.10897.

Even if an American spouse of a Lutwak marriage could have obtained a French annulment, it seems clear that "[t]he nullity of a null marriage must be declared by judgment. Neither the parties nor strangers are authorized, in default of such judgment, to assume the nullity to be established." Amos & Walton, Introduction to French Law 65 (2d ed. 1963); see also Cohn, The Nullity of Marriage: A Study in Comparative Law and Legal Reform, 64 L.Q. Rev. 324, 337, 338 (1948), who states that this is generally true on the Continent. Only in very rare instances of "non-existent" marriages, whose elements were not present in Lutwak, can a court decree be dispensed with.

If these principles of French law had been before the Court in Lutwak, would it have made any difference in the judgment?

2. Compare Silver (orse. Kraft) v. Silver, [1955] 1 W.L.R. 728 (Prob.). There one Springer, an Englishman, while working in Germany, met and lived with a German woman. After Springer returned to England, he wished to bring the German woman with him, but she could not be permanently admitted except as his wife, and Springer was already married with no hope of divorce. Springer's stepbrother, Silver, went to Germany, went through a ceremony of marriage with the woman, and brought her back to Springer in England. Springer and the woman lived together until Springer's death thirteen years later. During this period the woman saw Silver only once, when six months after her arrival they filed a declaration for immigration purposes. Now, desiring to marry another man, she filed a petition seeking a declaration that the marriage was void, or alternatively, a divorce for adultery (Silver in the meantime having married another woman and raised a family).

The court pointed out that although consent procured by fraud or duress is invalid, a mere mental reservation on the part of one or both parties to a marriage freely entered into does not affect its validity. Accordingly the marriage was held valid, but the court granted a divorce. The case is discussed at 69 Harv. L. Rev. 768 (1956).

BOVE v. PINCIOTTI
46 Pa. D. & C. 159 (C.P. 1942)

Bok, P.J. Petitioner asks for the annulment of a marriage which took place under rather unusual circumstances on September 23, 1939. He was then 16½ years old and respondent was 17.

Two months before the ceremony they had sexual relations either once or twice. Petitioner then left to work in Washington and when he returned respondent asked him to marry her, which he refused to do. She gave him a letter, apparently already prepared, and told him to read it when he reached home. It said, "By the time you read this letter I'll be dead and so will your baby." He went back to her home at once but found her bedroom door locked and after breaking it open saw her lying unconscious on her bed with traces of iodine on her lips and an empty bottle beside her. He gave her first aid treatment and called a doctor, who brought the girl around with emetics in about an hour. When she regained consciousness she told petitioner she was pregnant and asked him what he meant to do. He said he'd marry her, but they agreed that it was only to give the child a name and that they would not live together as man and wife. Two days later they applied for a marriage license, which they got by misrepresenting their ages, and were married by a magistrate.

They never lived together, but separated immediately after the ceremony. Petitioner saw respondent on the street about six months later and said she looked normal, which meant to him at the moment that no child was imminent. He did not ask her about it.

Respondent was called by the master, not to contest the case but to fill in the gaps. Her story contradicted petitioner's in minor points but corroborated it in the main. She said that no child was born as a result of her pre-marital intercourse with petitioner, but that she met a Mr. Sparks in New Jersey shortly after her marriage, had intercourse with him in December 1939, and delivered a child on September 13, 1940. She seems not to know where Mr. Sparks is now, and she registered the child's father as unknown, as she said she did not want it to appear as petitioner's child, since it wasn't. The birth certificate of this child, which was offered in evidence, gives no birth date, but it is required to be filed within 10 days after birth and bears a filing date of September 19, 1940.

The imponderables, aside from the law, favor this child. It hasn't much of a heritage apart from the presumption that it was born in wedlock, and we feel it is entitled to that. There is no proof to the contrary save the word of its parents, and the policy of our law is not to allow them to bastardize issue by their own word alone. [Citations omitted.]

Apart from this angle of the case there arises the broad question of whether an annulment may be granted to a couple who have married in proper form but who assert that it was done on conditions: these being, of course, that the marriage should be valid for the purpose of giving the expected child a name but invalid for all other purposes. We are of opinion that the annulment cannot be granted, not only because we believe the policy of the law is against it but because an annulment renders the marriage void ab initio, bastardizes the issue, and hence destroys the very purpose for which the parties married. To say that the failure of the child to materialize is a failure of consideration and hence avoids the point just made is merely to emphasize the artificiality of comparing the marriage contract to the ordinary civil contract. It is not possible to have a marriage for one purpose and no marriage at all for other purposes, for marriage is not only a contract but a status and a kind of fealty to the State as well. It is a pity, sociologically, that it is so easy to get into and so hard to get out of, and in trying to make our decision palatable to these young people, who would doubtless prefer bad law to their hard case, it need only be observed that it is difficult to make the law intelligent when the laws are not. . . .

There is no flaw alleged in the formalities of the marriage before us. It was performed by a proper officer of the law after the issuance of a valid license, the young people were not insane or intoxicated or jesting, there is no allegation of fraud, coercion, or duress. They did in proper legal form precisely what they had intended and agreed to do, namely, to get married. What their private motives or reservations may have been is not enough to upset a marriage regular on its face, particularly when they intended it to be so for at least one purpose. . . .

It should be remarked in passing that release from marriage would be made easy if it were possible for the parties to assert successfully that they never intended to be really married in the first place. To let them out by annulment on such grounds would, through the bastardization of issue, have pernicious effects. We cannot believe that the legislature intended any such consequence. Indeed, the policy of the common law against allowing parents to bastardize their issue prevents us from holding that a marriage is void, in a case where a child has been born, upon the mere statement of the parties that they never intended really to marry. If we cannot give legal effect to the actual situation with regard to parentage, a fortiori we cannot give effect to what was in the parties' minds with regard to a marriage preceding the child's birth. . . .

. . . To grant this annulment because of the sympathy we feel might do more harm than good, as the validity of this marriage might be called into question again years hence should the parties marry and property or other rights arise, and an intervening appellate decision against an annulment in such a case would play havoc with the situation. Were we to grant petitioner's prayer there would be no appeal. We hope petitioner will appeal our decision in order to settle the question.

The exceptions are dismissed, the report of the master is approved, and the petition is dismissed.

NOTE

1. The hope expressed by Justice Bok in the concluding paragraph was not fulfilled, despite the fact that another Pennsylvania judge had reached a contrary result on very similar facts six years earlier. Osgood v. Moore, 38 Pa. D. & C. 263 (C.P. 1940). The court there said (id. at 266):

> [W]e have yet to be cited a case going so far as to say that where the parties have entered into an agreement that the ceremony shall not constitute a marriage, and have carried out the agreement to the extent of living apart from the moment of the ceremony and of failing to cohabit, the State still holds them to the undertakings of the ritual rather than to their explicit contract. . . .

2. In accord with the Bove case is the leading case of Schibi v. Schibi, 136 Conn. 196, 69 A.2d 831 (1949), where it was held that a marriage solely for the purpose of legitimating a child is not annullable, even in the absence of any cohabitation following the ceremony. But compare Stone v. Stone, 159 Fla. 624, 32 So.2d 278 (1947) (marriage for sole purpose of legitimating child of W and H's younger brother annullable).

3. When Justice Bok in the Bove case stated that "marriage is not only a contract but a status and a kind of fealty to the State as well" (46 Pa. D. & C. at 161), presumably the concept of status was being used very loosely. Giving it its generally accepted meaning, Sir Henry Maine described a status as applying only to personal conditions over whose creation the individual has had no control and which are not the immediate or remote results of a contract, e.g., being a slave or a woman or an untouchable or a Jew. See Maine, Ancient Law 174 (Pollock ed. 1906). There are difficulties even with such a relatively narrow definition, for what functional

value is achieved by lumping within a single concept the disabilities incurred by a slave, a mature woman, or a young child? To expand the concept, as courts frequently do in marriage cases, to embrace the legal consequences of a free bargain is to multiply the analytical problems. Does the apparently self-contradictory assertion that marriage is both a contract and a status serve anything other than an emotive function? Is this merely a way of stating that a marriage bargain entails consequences which the parties cannot control, even by their mutual assent? Yet particularly in a regulatory society many kinds of free legal agreements besides marriage entail consequences which the parties cannot alter, e.g., a contract of employment necessarily involves both parties in complications such as maximum hours, minimum wages, unemployment insurance, or workmen's compensation.

Note also that in many of the foregoing cases the courts, directly or implicitly, seem to attach weight to answers to questions such as the following: Have the parties cohabited? Have they held themselves out publicly as husband and wife? Are children involved? On a theory of marriage as either contract or status, or both, how are these questions relevant? Would the result of the Bove case have been different if respondent had not had a child by Mr. Sparks, or if the jurisdiction had provided that "[c]hildren of void or voidable marriages shall be deemed to be legitimate," see Del. Code Ann. tit. 13, §105 (1953)?

C. STATE REGULATION OF MARRIAGE

1. *Representative Statute*

Although it has never been determined whether there is a constitutional right to marry, there is no serious doubt that the states possess broad powers to regulate matrimony and to restrict the classes of persons who may enter that relationship. This much the Supreme Court has made clear in one of its infrequent discourses on the subject:

> Marriage, as creating the most important relation in life, as having more to do with the morals and civilization of a people than any other institution, has always been subject to the control of the legislature. That body prescribes the age at which parties may contract to marry, the procedure or form essential to constitute marriage, the duties and obligations it creates, its effects upon the property rights of both, present and prospective, and the acts which may constitute grounds for its dissolution.[30]

The Delaware Marriage Law reproduced in part below has been selected because it is typical of statutory patterns throughout the United States and because it treats explicitly most of the specific regulations with which we are concerned. We will examine five problem areas posed by such a legislative pattern: the restrictions on who may marry whom, such as consanguinity, affinity, and miscegenation (subsection 2); the underly-

[30] Maynard v. Hill, 125 U.S. 190, 205 (1888).

ing moral premise of monogamy (subsection 3); protections against immature or hasty marriage embodied in age and waiting period regulations (subsection 4); health regulations, enacted either as eugenic devices or to insure meaningful contractual consent, and designed to protect the ill applicant, the healthy prospective spouse, or the possible children of the marriage (subsection 5); and enforcement of regulatory policies, both within a state and in the broader context of a federal system (subsection 6). Subsequently we will consider devices which involve evasion of parts or all of the regulatory pattern, e.g., common law marriage, "curative" statutes and evidentiary presumptions, and the problems of families which exist in fact but where the formal marriage was defective or there was no marriage ceremony at all.

DELAWARE CODE ANNOTATED TITLE 13
(SUPP. 1964)

§101. Void and voidable marriages

(a) A marriage is prohibited and void between —

(1) A person and his or her ancestor, descendant, brother, sister, uncle, aunt, niece, nephew or first cousin;

(2) A white person and a negro or mulatto.

(b) A marriage is prohibited, and is void from the time its nullity is declared by a court of competent jurisdiction at the instance of the innocent party, if either party thereto is —

(1) A person of any degree of unsoundness of mind;

(2) A patient, or has been, in an insane asylum, unless such person first files, with the Clerk of the Peace to whom he makes application for a marriage license, a certificate signed by the superintendent of the asylum in which such person is or was a patient, stating that such person is fit to marry, and unless such person in other respects may lawfully marry;

(3) Venereally diseased, or is suffering from any other communicable disease, the nature of which is unknown to the other party to the proposed marriage;

(4) An habitual drunkard;

(5) A confirmed user of a narcotic drug;

(6) Divorced, unless a certified copy of the divorce decree (last decree if he has been divorced more than once), or a certificate of such divorce from the clerk of the court granting the divorce is inspected by the Clerk of the Peace to whom he makes application for a marriage license, and unless such person may in other respects lawfully marry; and if such decree or certificate cannot be obtained, the Resident Judge of the county where such license is desired, or the person designated by the Resident Judge to grant such certificates as may be accepted under the provisions of this subdivision, may grant a certificate of the facts as stated by the applicant and the certificate may, for the purposes of this chapter, be accepted in lieu of a certified copy of a divorce decree;

(7) On probation or parole from any court or institution, unless

such person first files, with the Clerk of the Peace to whom he makes application for a marriage license, a written consent to his proposed marriage from the chief officer of such court or institution, or from some one who is appointed by such officer to give such consent, and unless in other respects the applicant may lawfully marry.

(c) A marriage between paupers is prohibited, and is void from the time its nullity is declared by a court of competent jurisdiction at the instance of the innocent party.

§102. Entering into a prohibited marriage; penalty

The guilty party or parties to a marriage prohibited by section 101 of this title shall be fined $100, and in default of the payment of the fine shall be imprisoned not more than 30 days.

§103. Issuing license for, or solemnizing, prohibited marriage; penalty

Whoever, being authorized to issue a marriage license, knowingly or wilfully issues a license for a marriage prohibited by this chapter, or, being authorized to solemnize a marriage, knowingly or wilfully assists in the contracting or solemnizing of a prohibited marriage, shall be fined $100, and in default of the payment of such fine shall be imprisoned not more than 30 days.

§104. Entering into prohibited marriage outside the State; penalty

If a marriage prohibited by this chapter is contracted or solemnized outside of the State, when the legal residence of either party to the marriage is in this State, and the parties thereto shall afterwards live and cohabit as husband and wife within the State, they shall be punished in the same manner as though the marriage had been contracted in this State.

§105. Status of children of prohibited marriages

Children of void or voidable marriages shall be deemed to be legitimate.

§106. Solemnization of marriages; production of license; penalty; registration of persons authorized to solemnize marriages.

(a) Any ordained minister of the gospel and every minister in charge of a recognized church and, within the City of Wilmington, the Mayor of the City of Wilmington, may solemnize marriages between persons who may lawfully enter into the matrimonial relation. Marriages shall be solemnized in the presence of at least two reputable witnesses [who shall sign the marriage certificate. Marriages may also be solemnized according to the usages of any religious society of which either party is a member. The license must be produced, and subsection (b) provides that any unauthorized person who solemnizes a marriage is liable to a $100 fine or 30 days].

§107. Marriage licenses; obtaining and delivery; period allowed for performance of marriage.

(a) Persons intending to be married within this State, if one or both of the parties are residents of this State, shall obtain a marriage license at least 24 hours prior to the time of the ceremony. If both of the parties to be married are non-residents of the State, they must obtain a marriage license at least 96 hours prior to the time of the ceremony.

(b) The license must be delivered to the person who is to officiate, before the marriage can be lawfully performed. . . .

[Fees for issuing marriage licenses are provided for in §108, and §109 requires that licenses be obtained from Clerks of the Peace.]

§110. Limitations on issuance of license

No marriage license shall be issued by a Clerk of the Peace when either of the parties applying for license to marry, at the time of making the application, is under the influence of intoxicating liquor or a narcotic drug, or if papers that are required by this chapter are not delivered, or if the issuing officer believes there is any legal impediment, as defined in this chapter, to the marriage of such parties.

[§111 provides for the examination, filing, and confidentiality of papers (e.g., divorce certificates) submitted as part of the marriage application.]

§112. Violations by Clerk of the Peace; penalties

Any Clerk of the Peace or deputy of such, who knowingly or wilfully acts in violation of the provisions of this chapter, shall be fined $100, and in default of payment of such fine shall be imprisoned not more than 30 days.

[§§113-119 deal with forms and records.]

§120. Marriage license application; appearance of parties; exception

Before any marriage license shall be issued by the issuing officer, the parties desiring to marry shall together appear before him and he shall examine both parties upon oath, or affirmation, in the presence and hearing of each other, according to the form prescribed in section 122 of this title, to which the parties applying for the license shall subscribe their names. The license shall be issued only after it has been made to appear that no legal impediment to the proposed marriage exists. In the case of critical illness of one of the parties desiring to marry, the physician attending such party may appear for him and make an application for a marriage license for him, if such physician first make an affidavit and delivers it to the issuing officer stating that in the opinion of said physician the party for whom he is acting, is at the point of death and that he may lawfully marry. . . .

[§121 provides for identification of resident applicants.]

§122. Form of marriage license application[31]

The pages of the Marriage Record Books of Clerks of the Peace and justices of the peace shall be in the following form which shall be the marriage license application:

MARRIAGE LICENSE APPLICATION

State of Delaware ⎤
.... County ⎰ SS.   No. ....

BE IT REMEMBERED, That on this .... day of ....

---

[31] In 1963 the Delaware legislature amended this section and delegated the authority for promulgating marriage license application forms to the State Board of Health. However, the prior version is reproduced here for teaching purposes. — Ed.

A. D. 19............., personally appeared .... and .... and made application for a marriage license, and each party in the presence and hearing of the other, being first duly sworn, (affirmed), according to law, did depose and say that,

Male	Female
Full name	....
Address	....
Age .... years	.... years
Color	....

Names and Addresses of Mother and Father:

Mother .... | ....
.... | ....

Father .... | ....
.... | ....

Applicants' Occupations:

.... | ....

Previously Married .... | ....

　1.　If previously married give place and date:

.... | ....
　(Place)　　　　　(Date)　　　　　(Place)　　　　　(Date)

　2.　If marriage terminated by death give place and date of death:

.... | ....
　(Place)　　　　　(Date)　　　　　(Place)　　　　　(Date)

　3.　If marriage terminated by divorce, give place and date; if divorced more than once give information on last divorce:

.... | ....
　(Place)　　　　　(Date)　　　　　(Place)　　　　　(Date)

　Past or present patient in an insane asylum:

.... | ....

　On Probation or Parole Under any Court or Institution:

.... | ....

　And each party did further depose and say that, to the best of his knowledge and belief he is not:

　Of a prohibited degree of relationship; an epileptic; of any degree of unsoundness of mind; venereally diseased; suffering from any other communicable disease the nature of which is not known to the other party; an habitual drunkard; a confirmed user of a narcotic drug; and is not a pauper.

SIGNATURES OF APPLICANTS

.... | ....

　I believe neither party is now under the influence of intoxicating liquor nor a narcotic drug. I have demanded and examined such papers as are required by law and I am satisfied that they are properly executed. I know of no legal impediment to the proposed marriage of the above applicants.

Time of Application .... A. D. 19.......... .... o'clock .... M.

Shall not marry before .... A. D. 19.......... .... o'clock .... M.

Sworn and subscribed before me the day and year first above written.

....

Issuing Officer.

(Sign name and title)

Date of Marriage .... day of .... A. D. 19.......... .... o'clock .... M.

Ceremony performed by ....

State of Delaware ⎱ SS.
..................County ⎰

The portion of this sheet beginning here is to be filled in only in cases of applicants who claim to be residents of Delaware, neither of whom is known personally to the issuing officer.

BE IT REMEMBERED, That on this .... day of .... A. D. 19......., personally appeared before me, ..., who, being first duly sworn (affirmed) according to law, did depose and say that he personally knows ...., one of the above named applicants, and that the said applicant is a resident of the State of Delaware.

(Signed) ....

Guarantor

Sworn (Affirmed) and Subscribed before me the day and year first above written.

....

Issuing Officer

(Sign name and title)

§123.   Marriage of minors; consent forms

(a) No male under the age of 18 nor any female under the age of 16 shall marry.

(b) If any male applicant for a license to marry is under the age of 21 years, or if any female applicant for a license to marry is under the age of 18 years, the license shall not be issued unless the applicant's parents or a parent, legal guardians or guardian, or curator shall first certify under their hands and seals their consent to the marriage of the minor.   If the minor applicant has no parent, legal guardian or curator, a license shall not be issued unless one of the following persons shall first certify under his hand and seal his consent to the marriage of the minor: [There follows a listing of certain judges.   The section also specifies that a consent must be signed before two witnesses.]

(f) The age and consent limitations imposed by this section shall not be a bar to marriage between persons under the age disabilities fixed by this section in cases where the parties desiring to marry shall acknowledge under oath before the officer to whom the application for license to marry shall be made that they are the parents or the prospective parents of a child, but every application of such persons for a license to marry shall have endorsed thereon the reason for issuing the license.

[§§124 and 125 relate to oaths and the validity of pre-1913 marriages.]

§126.   Validity of common law or other lawful marriages

Nothing in this chapter shall be construed to render any common law or other marriage, otherwise lawful, invalid, by reason of the failure to take out a license as provided by this chapter.

§127. False statement; penalty

If any person applying for a license under this chapter knowingly makes false answers to any of the inquiries of the person issuing the license, after having been sworn or affirmed to answer truly, he shall be guilty of perjury, and if any person executing papers under the provisions of this chapter executes them falsely, he shall be subject to such penalties as the Court may impose.

§128. Performance of marriage ceremony in violation of chapter; false certificate of marriage; penalties

Any person or religious society having authority to solemnize marriages who performs a marriage ceremony without the presentation of a license issued pursuant to this chapter, or who performs the same prior to the expiration of 96 hours from the time of the issuance of the license when both parties are nonresidents of the State, or prior to the expiration of 24 hours from the time of the issuance of the license when one or both parties are residents of the State, or more than 30 days after the time of the issuance of the license, shall be imprisoned not more than 6 months, or fined not more than $500, or both. Any person or religious society having authority to solemnize marriages who shall make any false certificate of marriage shall be fined $100.

§141. Physician's certificate of pre-marital physical examination and serological test; filing

Before any person issues a marriage license, each applicant for a license shall file with the issuing officer a certificate, made not more than 30 days prior to the issuance of the license, from a duly licensed physician which states that the applicant has been given such physical examination, including a standard serological test, as is necessary for the discovery of syphilis and that, in the opinion of the physician, the person either is not infected with syphilis, or if so infected, is not in a stage of this disease which is or may become communicable to the marital partner.

DELAWARE CODE ANNOTATED TITLE 11 (1953)

§381. Bigamy generally

Whoever, having contracted marriage, marries, in the lifetime of his or her spouse, another person, or being unmarried, marries a person having at the time a spouse living, and such fact is known to the unmarried person, shall be guilty of bigamy, and shall be fined not less than $400 nor more than $2000, and imprisoned not less than 3 months nor more than 6 years.

§384. Exceptions to bigamy

No person shall be convicted of bigamy, if the husband or wife, at the time of the second marriage, has been absent for 5 years, and during that time the accused has received no intelligence of his or her being alive, or if there has been other good ground to believe the former husband or wife dead, or if the former marriage has been legally dissolved.

§591. Incestuous fornication or adultery

(a) Whoever commits incestuous fornication or adultery within the degrees of consanguinity or affinity set forth in subsection (b) of this section, shall be fined not more than $500 and imprisoned not more than 7 years.

(b) For the purposes of subsection (a) of this section, the degrees of consanguinity and affinity are as follows:

DEGREES OF CONSANGUINITY

A man and his mother.
A man and his father's sister.
A man and his mother's sister.
A man and his sister.
A man and his daughter.
A man and his granddaughter.
A woman and her father.
A woman and her father's brother.
A woman and her mother's brother.
A woman and her brother.
A woman and her son.
A woman and her grandson.

DEGREES OF AFFINITY

A man and his father's wife.
A man and his son's wife.
A man and his wife's daughter.
A man and the daughter of his wife's son or daughter.
A woman and her mother's husband.
A woman and her daughter's husband.
A woman and her husband's son.
A woman and the son of her husband's son or daughter.

2. *Consanguinity and Affinity*

CATALANO v. CATALANO
148 Conn. 288, 170 A.2d 726 (1961)

MURPHY, J. The plaintiff appealed to the Superior Court from the action of the Probate Court for the district of Hartford in denying her application for a widow's allowance for support from the estate of Fred Catalano. The parties have stipulated as to the facts, and the Superior Court has reserved the matter for the advice of this court.[32]

The material facts are these: Fred Catalano, a widower and citizen of this state, was married on December 8, 1951, in Italy to the plaintiff, his

---

[32] The question upon which advice is desired is: "Was Maria Catalano the surviving spouse of Fred Catalano under the laws of the State of Connecticut as of the date of his death on October 11, 1958, and as such was she qualified to receive support under Section 45-250 of the General Statutes, Revision of 1958?"

niece, an Italian subject. Such a marriage was prohibited by §87 of the Italian Civil Code, but since the parties obtained a legal dispensation for the marriage from the Italian authorities, it was valid in Italy. Fred returned to this country. The plaintiff remained in Italy until 1956, when she joined Fred and they came to Hartford, where they lived as husband and wife until his death in 1958. A son was born to the couple. The plaintiff claims to be the surviving spouse of the decedent and, as such, entitled to an allowance for support under the provisions of §45-250 of the General Statutes.

The determination of the question propounded depends upon the interrelation and judicial interpretation of three statutes, §§46-1, 46-6 and 53-223.[33] . . .

It is the generally accepted rule that a marriage valid where the ceremony is performed is valid everywhere. Davis v. Davis, 119 Conn. 194, 197, 175 A. 574. There are, however, certain exceptions to that rule, including one which regards as invalid incestuous marriages between persons so closely related that their marriage is contrary to the strong public policy of the domicil though valid where celebrated. Restatement, Conflict of Laws §132(b). That exception may be expressed in the terms of a statute or by necessary implication. Pennegar v. State, 87 Tenn. 244, 247, 10 S.W. 305. Section 46-6 only validates foreign marriages which could have been legally entered into in this state at the time they were contracted. As §46-1 created an impediment to the union of uncle and niece in this state, the plaintiff and her uncle lacked the legal capacity which §46-6 makes a prerequisite to the validity, in this state, of such a marriage as theirs. A state has the authority to declare what marriages of its citizens shall be recognized as valid, regardless of the fact that the marriages may have been entered into in foreign jurisdictions where they were valid. Murphy v. Murphy, 249 Mass. 552, 555, 144 N.E. 394.

To determine whether the marriage in the instant case is contrary to the public policy of this state, it is only necessary to consider that marriages between uncle and niece have been interdicted and declared void continuously since 1702 and that ever since then it has been a crime for such kindred to either marry or carnally know each other. At the time of the plaintiff's marriage in 1951, the penalty for incest was, and it has continued to be, imprisonment in the state prison for not more than ten years. Rev. 1949, §8551; General Statutes §52-223. This relatively high

---

33 "Sec. 46-1. KINDRED WHO SHALL NOT MARRY. No man shall marry his mother, grandmother, daughter, granddaughter, sister, aunt, niece, stepmother or stepdaughter, and no woman shall marry her father, grandfather, son, grandson, brother, uncle, nephew, stepfather or stepson; and, if any man or woman marries within the degrees aforesaid, such marriage shall be void."

"Sec. 46-6. WHEN MARRIAGES IN FOREIGN COUNTRIES ARE VALID. All marriages where one or both parties are citizens of this state, celebrated in a foreign country in conformity with the law of that country, shall be valid, provided each party would have legal capacity to contract such marriage in this state. . . ."

"Sec. 53-223. INCEST. Every man and woman who marry or carnally know each other, being within any of the degrees of kindred specified in section 46-1, shall be imprisoned in the State Prison not more than ten years."

penalty clearly reflects the strong public policy of this state. We cannot completely disregard the import and intent of our statutory law and engage in judicial legislation. The marriage of the plaintiff and Fred Catalano, though valid in Italy under its laws, was not valid in Connecticut because it contravened the public policy of this state. . . .

MELLITZ, J. (dissenting). We are dealing here with the marriage status of a woman who was validly married at the place of her domicil and who, so far as the record discloses, was entirely innocent of any intent to evade the laws of Connecticut. Mrs. Catalano was a resident and domiciliary of Italy when her uncle came from America and married her in Italy. Although he returned to America soon after the marriage, she continued to reside in Italy for almost five years before she came to America and took up her residence in Connecticut, where she gave birth to a son. There is no suggestion anywhere in the record that at the time of the marriage she intended to come to America, that the parties had any intention of coming to live in Connecticut, or that the marriage was entered into in Italy for the purpose of evading the laws of Connecticut. If a marriage status resulting from a valid marriage, such as the one here, is to be destroyed, the issue bastardized, and the relations of the parties branded as illicit, it should follow only from an explicit enactment of the legislature, giving clear expression to a public policy which compels such harsh consequences to ensue from a marriage entered into under the circumstances disclosed here.

The cases cited in the majority opinion which deal with the question we have here are all cases where the parties went to a foreign state to evade the law of the domicil and the marriage celebrated in the foreign state was refused recognition in the place of their domicil when they returned to live there after the marriage. . . .

The provisions of §46-1, prohibiting marriages within specified degrees of consanguinity, apply only to marriages celebrated in Connecticut and are not given extraterritorial operation by the provisions of §46-6. The first sentence of §46-6, quoted in the majority opinion, was originally enacted as §1 of chapter 197 of the Public Acts of 1913. It does not purport to invalidate or declare void in Connecticut foreign marriages celebrated in contravention of the laws of Connecticut. It is a validating statute and declares valid the marriage of a citizen of Connecticut celebrated in a foreign country in conformity with the law of that country, provided each party would have legal capacity to contract the marriage in Connecticut. Capacity, in the sense employed in the statute, is defined in 2 Beale, Conflict of Laws §121.6, as follows: "By capacity to enter into a marriage is meant a quality which legally prevents the person in question marrying anyone; it does not refer to some quality which prevents the particular marriage in question, though the person may marry someone else. A typical example of capacity is nonage, or having a living spouse. A typical example of a quality which prevents the particular marriage, though the person has capacity to marry, is consanguinity." . . .

. . . The following from the opinion in Pierce v. Pierce, 58 Wash. 622, 626, 109 P. 45, aptly expresses what I conceive to be the correct view in the situation here. "We know of no public policy which will warrant a court in annulling a marriage between competent parties if there be any evidence to sustain it, and especially so where it appears that the parties have consummated the marriage, a child has been born, and the offending party has been openly acknowledged as a spouse. It will not be done unless it clearly appears that the parties willfully went beyond the jurisdiction of the courts of this state to avoid and defy our laws. It is not clear that they did so in this case." . . .

RESTATEMENT (SECOND), CONFLICT OF LAWS [34]
(*Tentative Draft No. 4, 1957*)

TOPIC 1. MARRIAGE

Introductory Note: Marriage is perhaps the most important of all human relationships. It is of deepest concern to the public and to the immediate parties and their children. The parties' consent to take each other as man and wife, although essential in all common law countries, is therefore not of itself enough to create a valid marriage. A legal union does not result except by operation of law. When all elements of a marriage are grouped in a single state, that state, of course, furnishes the governing law. Where, on the other hand, these elements are divided among two or more states with different laws, choice must be made between them. The rules covering this latter situation will be made clearer by a discussion of the interests, both public and private, which may be involved.

The State of Celebration.

The interest of the state where the marriage takes place relates primarily to the question whether there has been compliance with the formalities prescribed by its law. Other considerations point to the use of this law generally to determine the validity of a marriage. The validity of a marriage is of utmost concern to the parties and their children; so the choice of the governing law should be simple and easy in application and should point to the law most likely to have been consulted by the parties. Furthermore, there is a strong inclination to uphold a marriage because of the hardship that might otherwise be visited upon the parties and their children. Finally, differences among the marriage laws of various states usually involve only minor matters of debatable policy rather than fundamentals. All of these factors together support the general rule that a marriage which meets the requirements of the state of celebration is valid everywhere.

The State of Paramount Interest.

The state where the marriage takes place is not for this reason alone that of paramount interest. Its interest is clearly not as great as that of a

[34] Except as otherwise indicated, the Reporter's Comments and Notes are omitted.

state where at least one of the parties was domiciled at the time of the marriage and where both intend to make their home thereafter. The law of this second state, if such a one exists in a given case, is therefore accorded the decisive voice in determining the validity of the marriage. A marriage which is valid under the law of this state will be valid everywhere even though the requirements of the state where the marriage takes place have not been complied with (see §122). Conversely, a marriage which is invalid under this law will be invalid everywhere even though all of these requirements have been met (see §§131 and 132). Instances of the latter sort are comparatively rare because the state of paramount interest will normally make the validity of a marriage depend upon its compliance with the requirements of the state where it took place.

A Third State.

Once the marriage relationship has been created, the parties may seek to enjoy certain of the incidents arising therefrom in a third state. To the extent that they do so, the interests of this latter state are affected and its law controls. Thus, parties domiciled in state X and married in state Y may seek to cohabit in state Z or, after the death of the husband, the wife may there claim the share of a surviving spouse in the husband's local assets. In the case put, the validity of the marriage itself would, as stated above, be determined under the law of X and Y. But Z law would decide whether the parties can lawfully cohabit within the borders of that state or whether the wife may succeed to assets of her late husband that are located there. As stated in §134, a third state will only prohibit the parties from exercising such incidents of their marriage as are offensive to its strong public policy. And the fact that one particular incident may be interdicted does not mean that this is necessarily true of the rest. So, again in the case put, even though it is illegal for the parties to cohabit within the borders of state Z, the Z courts may nevertheless recognize the children of the marriage as legitimate and permit the wife to succeed upon her husband's death to such of his assets as are located in that state.

§121. Law Governing Validity of Marriage.

A marriage is valid everywhere if valid under the law of the state where the marriage takes place, except as stated in §§131 and 132.

§122. Requirements of State Where Marriage Takes Place.

A marriage is invalid everywhere if a mandatory requirement of the state where the marriage takes place has not been complied with unless the marriage is nevertheless valid under the law of a state where at least one of the parties was domiciled at the time of the marriage and where both intended to make their home thereafter.

[Excerpt from Comments to §122:]

e. Distinction between "law" and "local law." The validity of a marriage is normally determined by the "local law" of the state where it takes place, namely by that state's body of law exclusive of its Conflict of Laws rules. The question, in other words, is whether the marriage would have been valid in that state if both of the parties had been domiciled there and all other elements connected with the marriage had been grouped within its borders. To this there is, at least, one exception. If, because of its foreign elements, the very marriage in question would be valid in the state where it takes place, although local requirements were not complied with, the marriage under the general rule will likewise be valid in other states (see §121, Comment *b*). Therefore, in the case of the state where the marriage takes place the reference is first to the local law of that state and usually then only to its Conflict of Laws rules if this is necessary to sustain the marriage.

On the other hand, the reference is always to the "law" of the state of paramount interest, by which is meant the totality of that state's law including its Conflict of Laws rules. Here, the only inquiry is whether the very marriage in question is valid or invalid in that state. This depends in part upon that state's Conflict of Laws rules because of the foreign element interjected by the fact that the parties were married elsewhere.

[§131 states that if the divorce forum has a prohibition against remarriage, see page 779 infra, a remarriage in another state in violation of such prohibition will not be invalid unless the divorce was not yet final or the divorcing state is the state of paramount interest.]

§132. Marriage Invalid Under Law of State of Paramount Interest.

A marriage is invalid everywhere, even though the requirements of the state where the marriage took place have been complied with, if it is invalid under the law of a state where at least one of the parties is domiciled at the time of the marriage and where both intend to make their home thereafter.

[Excerpt from Comments to §132:]

By the time of their marriage, the parties will usually have decided upon the state where they intend to make their home and, in most of such instances, their intention in this regard will be ascertainable. The parties' testimony as to what they intended to do will, of course, be relevant. Frequently, they will have talked to third persons on the subject and such statements on their part, if made at or around the time of the marriage, will sometimes be admissible into evidence. The situation in which they found themselves at the time is also significant. The fact, for example, that the husband had a job in state X, would naturally suggest that the parties intended to make their home in that state. If, in addition, the husband had always lived in state X, the inference that he intended to continue to live there with his wife would, in the absence of countervailing evidence, be almost irresistible. Furthermore, the validity of the marriage will rarely be placed in issue until some time after the parties have actually settled down in a place to live. And subsequent conduct provides highly persuasive evidence of previously formed intentions. So if after their marriage the parties immediately go to state X and make their home there, the conclusion would naturally follow that such was their intention at that time. There will, of course, be rare occasions where the parties either have not by the time of their marriage decided upon the state where they intend to make their home or where for some reason their intentions in this regard cannot be ascertained. In such a case, the validity of the marriage is determined solely by the law of the state where it took place.

b. Scope of application. The rule of this Section is invoked only in a few situations. Unless a contrary result is required by an overriding public policy, the state of paramount interest should and will recognize the validity of a marriage that meets the requirements of the state of celebration. And it will do so even though the marriage would have been invalid if celebrated within its borders. The present rule comes into play only when the marriage violates a policy of the state of paramount interest which in the eyes of that state is sufficiently strong to outweigh the general policy in favor of upholding the validity of marriage. Instances of this sort usually involve one of the following situations:

1. polygamous marriages,

2. incestuous marriages between persons so closely related that their marriage is contrary to the strong public policy of the state of paramount interest,

3. marriages between persons of different races if these are contrary to the strong public policy of the state of paramount interest.

This enumeration is not intended to be exclusive. If a marriage is invalid under the law of the state of paramount interest, it is invalid in all other states as well.

§134. Effect of Marriage Offensive to Public Policy.

A state refuses to give a particular effect to a marriage contracted in another state if to do so would be contrary to its strong public policy.

[Excerpt from Comments to §134:]

a. Distinction between recognition of marriage and according it a particular effect. The refusal of a state to give a particular effect to a marriage on the ground stated in this Section does not deny the validity of the marriage, but precludes the enjoyment within the state of some particular right or other interest incident to the marriage. Whenever a particularly strong policy of the state which has the paramount interest in the parties at the time of the marriage is concerned, the validity of the marriage may be involved under the rules stated in §§131 and 132 even though the requirements of the state where the marriage took place have been complied with. Otherwise, the case does not fall under §§131 and 132 but may be within the rule of this Section. . . .

c. A state may refuse to give one effect to a foreign marriage and at the same time allow the marriage another effect. Thus a state may prohibit the parties to a polygamous marriage from cohabiting within its borders. Yet it may recognize the legitimacy of the children and the economic interests of the spouses arising from the marriage. Again a state may deny political effect to a marriage, as by failing to permit acquisition by the wife of the husband's nationality, and yet permit the spouses to cohabit within its borders and also to enjoy normal economic interests in each other's property.

NOTE

1. Compare each of the following two cases with Catalano and with each other.

a. At issue in In re May's Estate, 305 N.Y. 486, 114 N.E.2d 4 (1953), was the right of a surviving husband to letters of administration of the estate of his deceased spouse, who was his niece by the half blood. Both Jews, they contracted their marriage in Rhode Island under a special Rhode Island provision exempting Jewish marriages from the consanguinity-affinity prohibitions of the statute, R.I. Gen. Laws §15-1-4 (1956). Although the marriage would have been "incestuous and void" had it been contracted in New York, and although the spouses were both New York domiciliaries at the time of the marriage, returned to New York two weeks after the ceremony, and resided there continuously for thirty-two years, the New York Court of Appeals upheld the validity of the marriage (one judge dissenting). The court applied the usual conflicts rule of lex loci contractus, pointing out that the marriage was "not offensive to the public sense of morality to a degree regarded generally with abhorrence and thus was not within the inhibitions of natural law." 305 N.Y. at 493, 114 N.E.2d at 7.

b. In 1950, one Bucca went from New Jersey to Italy and there married his niece, Antonina. Apparently the marriage was unplanned; at least the dispensation obtained under the same Italian law as that involved in the Catalano case stated that it was granted ". . . especially in order to avoid scandal and by reason of poverty . . ." Bucca v. State, 43 N.J. Super. 315, 321, 128 A.2d 506, 510 (Ch. 1957). Some time prior to 1957, Bucca returned to New Jersey, wished to bring his wife to New Jersey, and, because he had been threatened with prosecution for incest, sought a declaratory judgment that his Italian marriage was entitled to full recognition in New Jersey. The court applied New Jersey law on this reasoning:

> There is nothing in the moving papers to indicate that plaintiff intended to remain in Italy and establish his domicil there. It may, therefore, be inferred that it was the intention of these parties at the time of the ceremony in Italy to establish their family domicil in New Jersey. . . .
>
> Geneticists agree generally that the only effect upon offspring would be an increased chance of transmitting any disease or weakness which already existed in the blood line. Such incestuous relationship may be treated not as biologically harmful but only as sociologically improper.
>
> In spite of the above medical opinion, the court, nevertheless, concludes . . . that such marriages should not be recognized as valid. . . .
>
> . . . [New Jersey statutes] have gradually and progressively become more severe and unyielding . . . ; the term "incest" has be-

come part of the criminal law of this State; the relationship of uncle and niece is clearly comprehended within the term "incest". . . .

Therefore, the plaintiff's prayer for judgment declaring that his marriage . . . is entitled to full recognition in the State of New Jersey, and that plaintiff's cohabitation in the State of New Jersey with his said wife will not be in violation of [the New Jersey criminal incest law] is denied.[35]

Are the Bucca and May cases distinguishable because the parties in one in effect sought a license for continued incestuous cohabitation, while in the other death had terminated a marriage which had had a de facto existence for nearly four decades? What would be Bucca's status if he next moved to a state which applied what the New Jersey court stated to be "the majority opinion [which] grants recognition to such marriages"? 43 N.J. Super. at 318, 128 A.2d at 508.

What criteria are relevant in reaching a sound social result in these cases? How much weight should be given to, e.g., the relevant interests of the parties, their potential children, family harmony, social attitudes toward uncle-niece incest, religious beliefs and traditions, or other uncles who might be tempted to marry their nieces? What is the "interest of the state" in a consanguinity case? Where more than one state is involved, how is the state interest to be partitioned? Suppose that Mr. and Mrs. Bucca, although planning at the time of their marriage to return to New Jersey, had never done so but instead had established a home in New York. Could the Restatement rules be applied to reach a result which is socially sound in the light of the relevant criteria?

2. About two thirds of the states have enacted statutory provisions to govern out-of-state marriage problems. The statutes may be categorized as follows:

a. The simplest statutory solution is that found in the laws of about one fourth of the states, which follow the rules of Restatement (Second) §121, though usually without the exceptions expressed and implied by that and succeeding sections of the Law Institute's draft codification. Some of these states (notably California) have sustained even those marriages patently designed to evade or circumvent important restrictions of the home state. See, e.g., In re Perez Estate, 98 Cal. App. 2d 121, 219 P.2d 35 (1950). Others have been far less liberal and have seized upon whatever doubts might be raised about the validity of the marriage abroad to strike it down at home. See, e.g., In re Vetas' Estate, 110 Utah 187, 170 P.2d 183 (1946), refusing to recognize a common law marriage apparently validly contracted and perpetuated in a common law jurisdiction by persons domiciled in Utah at the time the marriage was contracted.

b. A few states have statutes which declare the out-of-state marriage neither valid nor invalid, but merely require that residents who contract such a marriage file some formal notice or registration of that fact within a specified time after their return home or within a certain period after the marriage itself. Related to this type of provision is the Rhode Island

---

[35] 43 N.J. Super. at 321-322, 128 A.2d at 510-511.

requirement that residents who have married abroad submit within six months to a Rhode Island health examination and procure the requisite certificate of freedom from venereal diseases. R.I. Gen. Laws §15-2-5 (1956).

c. Some states extend only a limited recognition to out-of-state marriages, under statutes providing that marriages entered by residents elsewhere are valid except where such unions are, e.g., bigamous, consanguineous, or miscegenous. One state, Arkansas, will recognize the foreign marriage if "the parties then actually resided" there, whatever that phrase may mean. Ark. Stat. Ann. §55-110 (1948).

d. The most comprehensive regulation of the out-of-state marriage is the scheme of the Uniform Marriage Evasion Act, which has been adopted in only a few states. It provides, as enacted in Mass. Gen. Laws Ann. c. 207 (1958):

§10. Foreign marriages; validity. If any person residing and intending to continue to reside in this commonwealth is disabled or prohibited from contracting marriage under the laws of this commonwealth and goes into another jurisdiction and there contracts a marriage prohibited and declared void by the laws of this commonwealth, such marriage shall be null and void for all purposes in this commonwealth with the same effect as though such prohibited marriage had been entered into in this commonwealth.

§11. Non-residents; marriages contrary to laws of domiciled state. No marriage shall be contracted in this commonwealth by a party residing and intending to continue to reside in another jurisdiction if such marriage would be void if contracted in such other jurisdiction, and every marriage contracted in this commonwealth in violation hereof shall be null and void.

§12. Legal ability of non-residents to marry; duty of licensing officer to ascertain. Before issuing a license to marry a person who resides and intends to continue to reside in another state, the officer having authority to issue the license shall satisfy himself, by requiring affidavits or otherwise, that such person is not prohibited from intermarrying by the laws of the jurisdiction where he or she resides.

§13. Construction. The three preceding sections shall be so interpreted and construed as to effectuate their general purpose to make uniform the law of those states which enact like legislation.

The Act was promulgated by the Commissioners in 1912, and having been enacted in only five states, it was withdrawn as obsolete in 1943 because it "can be effective only if it has widespread adoption; otherwise, it merely tends to confuse the law." Handbook of the National Conference of Commissioners on Uniform State Laws 147 (1943). Why do you suppose that the Act enlisted so little support?

Marriages have been set aside under §10 when the domiciliary state has the Uniform Act, Davis v. Seller, 329 Mass. 385, 108 N.E.2d 656 (1952), or under §11 when the state in which the marriage was contracted has such a statute, In re Canon's Estate, 221 Wis. 322, 266 N.W. 918 (1936). Some courts, however, have refused to invalidate an apparently evasionary marriage in the absence of clear proof of an intention to continue to reside in the domiciliary state after the ceremony, Sweeney v. Kennard, 331 Mass. 542, 120 N.E.2d 910 (1954), and of proof that the couple went to the other state solely for the purpose of evasion, Kattany v. Kattany, 16 Ill. App. 2d 148, 147 N.E.2d 436 (1957).

PROBLEMS

1. Albert Angelo lives in Antioch, Ohio. Last summer, while on an extended trip East, he stayed with his uncle and aunt in Boston and fell in love with their daughter Janie, who lives in Boston with her parents. At the end of the summer they decided to get married with the full blessings of Janie's parents. Following the marriage ceremony, which took place in Boston, they went back together to Ohio, where they have lived since.

Now Albert comes to ask your advice. The marriage has not worked out, and he is anxious to get out of it so that he can marry his childhood sweetheart. Advise him.

Massachusetts has the following statutes:

a. "No man shall marry his mother, grandmother, daughter, granddaughter, sister, stepmother, grandfather's wife, son's wife, grandson's wife, wife's mother, wife's grandmother, wife's daughter, wife's granddaughter, brother's daughter, sister's daughter, father's sister or mother's sister." Mass. Gen. Laws Ann. c. 207, §1 (1958).

b. "A marriage solemnized within the commonwealth which is prohibited by reason of consanguinity or affinity between the parties . . . shall be void without a decree of divorce or other legal process." Id. §8.

c. Uniform Marriage Evasion Act.

Ohio has the following statute: "Male persons of the age of eighteen years, and female persons of the age of sixteen years, not nearer of kin than second cousins . . . may be joined in marriage." Ohio Rev. Code Ann. §3101.01 (Page 1960).

2. Assume the following couples, all Delaware residents, after having been unable to obtain marriage licenses in Delaware, see page 194 supra, were married in a neighboring state which had enacted the Uniform Act but where their marriages would have been otherwise lawful: (a) a Negro who married a white person; (b) a person who married an epileptic; (c) a pauper who married another pauper. In subsequent actions for annulment, what results?

PROPOSED MARRIAGE AND DIVORCE CODES FOR PENNSYLVANIA

Pennsylvania, General Assembly, Joint State Government Commission 18-21 (1961)

[These excerpts are from comments to a proposed statutory provision setting out degrees of consanguinity.]

1. Degrees of affinity are deleted and omitted from this code. As of 1951, there were but 20 American jurisdictions (including Pennsylvania) which recognized affinity as an impediment to marriage: Alabama, Connecticut, District of Columbia, Georgia, Iowa, Kentucky, Maine, Maryland, Massachusetts, Michigan, Mississippi, New Hampshire, Pennsylvania, Rhode Island, South Carolina, Tennessee, Texas, Vermont, Virginia, and West Virginia. There is wide disagreement and substantial variation among these 20 jurisdictions as to just what degree of affinity shall constitute an impediment, and cases differ as to whether the impediment is removed when the former marriage is dissolved by death or divorce so as to terminate the affinity and permit marriage. Walter's Appeal, 70 Pa. 392 (1872), perhaps the leading Pennsylvania case on affinity, held that the marriage of a man and the widow of his deceased son was voidable. Cases are collected and discussed in L.R.A. 1916C 723. See also 35 Am. Jur. §141 on Marriage, which states: "Modern statutes quite generally discard affinity relationship as an impediment to marriage."

Historically, the concept of affinity is an outgrowth of the religious notion that upon marriage husband and wife become one flesh and blood and hence the relatives of each become the blood relatives of the other and therefore any sexual relationship between such relatives would be incestuous. A similar concept occurs in some primitive cultures due to the policy of requiring marriage outside the immediate family to gain members and strength for the family unit and perhaps to raise a taboo in order to discourage "affairs" within the family unit.

Today, the reasons of genetics and social policy which support continuation of consanguinity as an impediment to marriage do not support affinity as an impediment to marriage, except to such extent as the mystical notion of husband and wife being one flesh still persists. Genetically, there can be no objection to a marriage of in-laws. It may also be noted that the Christian concept of affinity is opposed to Jewish law.

It would seem that under present social values and standards of morality, there would be no objection to a man marrying his deceased wife's sister, or a widow marrying her former brother-in-law, and that in fact there might be many social, economic, and other reasons which affirmatively support such a union. It is felt that any in-law competition for the affections of an existing spouse is too remote to justify the wholesale adoption of the affinity impediment, that other sanctions already exist to deter such attempts, and that if such other deterrents are not successful, an affinity bar is not apt to be efficacious. . . .

3. The prohibition against marriage of first cousins is herein abolished by striking it from the degrees of consanguinity table. The present situation in Pennsylvania regarding the marriage of first cousins is peculiar and anomalous. Although such a marriage is declared consanguineous under the 1953 Act, it is not made incestuous by . . . The Penal Code. Moreover, in addition to this difference between the 1953 Act and The Penal Code, there is a further difference in construction of The Marriage Law in the case of first cousin marriages. Although other marriages within the prohibited degrees of consanguinity have been regarded as void due to

the statute and decisions, first cousin marriages performed in Pennsylvania since the prohibition have been regarded as merely voidable. See Mc-Clain v. McClain, 40 Pa. Superior Ct. 248 (1909) (marriage of first cousins merely voidable, a matter for divorce, requiring a judicial decree). And where the first cousins leave Pennsylvania and get married in a state which permits such marriages, the Pennsylvania courts will treat it as a valid marriage. See Schofield v. Schofield (No. 1), 51 Pa. Superior Ct. 564 (1912). . . .

Regardless of the variances and discrepancies in existing statutes and decisions, retention of first cousins within the degrees of consanguinity table in The Marriage Law should be continued if supported by genetics or reasons of morality. Dr. Herluf H. Strandskof, member of the Zoology Department at the University of Chicago, and world famous scholar in the field of genetics, has stated that practically there is no reason for retaining such a prohibition today; that there is, however, a possibility that where there are unfavorable recessive characteristics in the family a marriage of first cousins may bring out such characteristics in offspring; but that this is offset, from the standpoint of the geneticist, by the consideration that if such recessive characteristics are to be cleaned up, they must be brought to light. In substance, the possibility of bringing forth unfavorable characteristics in offspring is also offset by the possibility of bringing forth favorable characteristics which were recessive. It works both ways. The conclusion to be drawn from modern genetics, therefore, is that in the case of first cousins there is no scientific reason why they should not marry, although there is a slight possibility that recessive characteristics may appear in offspring, and such characteristics may be favorable or unfavorable.[36]

From the standpoint of the sociologist or anthropologist, the reasons for taboo being extended to first cousins in primitive cultures are not present in contemporary society. Today, the American family usually is centered around a husband and wife and their children; occasionally a grandparent or some other relative lives in the household. It would be extremely rare to find first cousins living in the same household, and even more rare to find a love affair between them which disrupted the domestic order. Of course, taboos related to blood feuds have no application.

NOTE

In Great Britain there has been a long legislative battle over the prohibition of marriage to a brother-in-law or sister-in-law, a situation immortalized by Gilbert and Sullivan. Not until 1907 did Parliament adopt the Deceased Wife's Sister's Marriage Act, 7 Edw. 7, c. 47 (permitting a widower to contract such a marriage), and not until 1921 did it adopt the Deceased Brother's Widow's Marriage Act, 11 & 12 Geo. 5, c. 24. The

---

[36] For an early attack on the alleged eugenic basis of the first cousin marriage prohibition, see Weightman, Marriage and Its Prohibitions, 17 Am. L. Rev. 166, 167 (1883); see also Moore, A Defense of First Cousin Marriage, 10 Clev.-Mar. L. Rev. 136 (1961), for references to the scientific evidence. — Ed.

Marriage (Enabling) Act, 8 & 9 Eliz. 2, c. 29 (1960), completes the trend and permits a man to marry the sister, aunt, or niece of his former wife during that wife's lifetime as well as after her death; or to marry the former wife of his own brother, uncle, or nephew during the lifetime as well as after the death of the husband so related to him. See Comment, 23 Mod. L. Rev. 538 (1960). The 1960 legislation was vigorously contested:

> "I regard the whole idea as revolting," the Bishop of Lichfield told the House of Lords. The Archbishop of Canterbury argued that "if it is possible to look forward from the fulfillment of a still hesitant desire to an actual remarriage to a sister-in-law, that desire is more likely to grow unchecked, and even to be subconsciously encouraged." . . .[37]

PROBLEM

Arnold and Betty had two sons, Charles and David.

Charles first married Ellen; after she died, he married Fanny, twenty-five years younger than he was, recently divorced her after a year of marriage, and is now unmarried. By his first wife, Ellen, Charles had three sons: Gregory, Harry, and Ishmael.

David married Joan, they had a natural daughter, Karin, and much later they adopted a daughter, Lillian. Karin married and had a daughter, Mary.

Under Delaware law, page 194 supra, how should the following applications for marriage licenses be decided: (a) Harry to marry Mary; (b) Ishmael to marry Lillian; (c) Gregory to marry Fanny? Would it make any difference in (b) if the jurisdiction had a statute identical to 6 & 7 Eliz. 2, c. 5, §13(3) (1958): "For the purpose of the law relating to marriage, an adopter and the person whom he has been authorised to adopt under an adoption order shall be deemed to be within the prohibited degrees of consanguinity"?

NOTE ON MISCEGENATION

Related to consanguinity and affinity by allegedly similar historical, eugenic, and sociological criteria is the ban on miscegenation. The history of legal prohibitions on interracial marriages in the United States dates from a Maryland statute enacted in 1661. Throughout the succeeding period a substantial number of states have enacted miscegenation statutes.[38] Today approximately twenty states, located mainly in the South, still have such statutes. Initially their impact was directed toward Negro-white marriages, but some were later expanded to include "Malayans, Mongolians, American Indians, Chinese, Japanese, Hindus, mestizos, half-breeds, and the brown race." [39]

[37] Time, Feb. 8, 1960, p. 32.
[38] See Note, 11 W. Res. L. Rev. 93 (1959).
[39] Id. at 93-94.

The most searching examination of the miscegenation problem has resulted in a path-breaking decision of the California Supreme Court, Perez v. Sharp, 32 Cal. 2d 711, 712, 198 P.2d 17, 18 (1948), invalidating the statute of that state which provided: "All marriages of white persons with negroes, Mongolians, members of the Malay race, or mulattoes are illegal and void." [40] The court split 4 to 3 and only three members joined in a majority opinion which was based on equal protection, unreasonable discrimination, and void-for-vagueness (especially the undefined use of "mulatto"). A fourth member of the court, while stating neither agreement nor disagreement with the plurality opinion, based the invalidity of the statute on the following reasoning:

> I agree with the conclusion that marriage is "something more than a civil contract subject to regulation by the state; it is a fundamental right of free men." Moreover, it is grounded in the fundamental principles of Christianity. The right to marry, therefore, is protected by the constitutional guarantee of religious freedom, and I place my concurrence in the judgment upon a broader ground than that the challenged statutes are discriminatory and irrational. . . .
>
> Reasonable classification . . . is not the test to be applied to a statute which interferes with one of the fundamental liberties which are protected by the First Amendment. The question is whether there is any "clear and present danger" justifying such legislation [citations omitted], and the burden of upholding the enactment is upon him who asserts that the acts which are denounced do not infringe the freedom of the individual. . . .
>
> The decisions upholding state statutes prohibiting polygamy come within an entirely different category. . . . [T]hese cases rest upon the principle that the conduct which the legislation was designed to prevent constituted a clear and present danger to the well being of the nation and, for that reason, the statute did not violate constitutional guarantees.[41]

Subsequently lower courts in Arizona and Nevada in unreported opinions have held the statutes of their states unconstitutional. However, since the Perez case the courts of Alabama,[42] Louisiana,[43] and Virginia[44] have rejected its reasoning and upheld the validity of their statutes. The United States Supreme Court has never decided the question of constitu-

---

[40] See Barnett, Interracial Marriage in California, 25 Marr. & Fam. Liv. 424, 425 (1963), indicating that in 1959 there were 1422 interracial marriages (all mixtures) out of a total of 101,314 in that state, a rate of 1.4 per cent, which has been fairly stable since 1955.

[41] Edmonds, J., concurring, 32 Cal. 2d at 740-742, 198 P.2d at 34-35.

[42] Jackson v. State, 37 Ala. App. 519, 72 So.2d 114, cert. denied, 260 Ala. 698, 72 So.2d 116, cert. denied, 348 U.S. 888 (1954).

[43] State v. Brown, 236 La. 562, 108 So.2d 233 (1954).

[44] Naim v. Naim, 197 Va. 80, 87 S.E.2d 749, vacated and remanded to clarify record, 350 U.S. 891 (1955), aff'd on original record, 197 Va. 734, 90 S.E.2d 849, appeal dismissed for want of a properly presented federal question, 350 U.S. 985 (1956). See also Loving v. Commonwealth, 243 F. Supp. 231 (E.D. Va. 1965).

tionality; it denied certiorari in one relatively recent case[45] and dismissed an appeal for lack of a properly presented federal question in another.[46] However, in 1964, the Court took what may turn out to be the first step towards the ultimate invalidation of a miscegenation statute when it struck down a Florida criminal statute that prohibited habitual night-time cohabitation by two unmarried persons, one of whom is white and the other Negro. McLaughlin v. Florida, 379 U.S. 184 (1964). Although the Court again refused to pass on the validity of the Florida miscegenation statute, it cast doubt on the continued validity of its prior decision of Pace v. Alabama, 106 U.S. 583 (1883), a case in which the Court sustained a more stringent criminal penalty for interracial fornication and adultery, and one that has been frequently cited and relied upon by defenders of miscegenation statutes.

Typical of the reasoning of the courts which sustain these statutes is the following statement: "A state statute which prohibits intermarriage or cohabitation between members of different races we think falls squarely within the police power of the state, which has an interest in maintaining the purity of the races and in preventing the propagation of half-breed children." [47] The Louisiana court, although refusing to strike down that state's statute on constitutional grounds, nonetheless reversed a conviction thereunder because the trial court had given a charge permitting a finding of miscegenation without proof of interracial intercourse. State v. Brown, 236 La. 562, 108 So.2d 233 (1959). The Arkansas Supreme Court has similarly held that the jury may not convict a defendant of miscegenous activities without proof of cohabitation over a substantial period of time, Poland v. State, 232 Ark. 669, 339 S.W.2d 421 (1960); Hardin v. State, 232 Ark. 672, 339 S.W.2d 423 (1960). Although neither of these cases involved an interracial marriage, but merely the question of miscegenous intercourse, the attitude which they evinced may be indicative. In the same connection, it is significant that the Mississippi Supreme Court has held that its miscegenation statute will not be given extraterritorial effect so as to deny recognition to an Illinois interracial marriage and thus prevent inheritance by one spouse of the other's Mississippi property. This result was reached on the ground that the purpose of the statute was only to prevent cohabitation within the state between whites and Negroes. Miller v. Lucks, 203 Miss. 824, 36 So.2d 140 (1948). See also in this connection Ehrenzweig, Miscegenation in the Conflict of Laws, 45 Cornell L.Q. 659 (1960).

There has been a vast amount of scholarly attention given to the problem. A sampling of that literature includes: Applebaum, Miscegenation Statutes: A Constitutional and Social Problem, 53 Geo. L.J. 49 (1964); Weinberger, A Reappraisal of the Constitutionality of Miscegenation

[45] Jackson v. State, 37 Ala. App. 519, 72 So.2d 114, cert. denied, 260 Ala. 698, 72 So.2d 116, cert. denied, 348 U.S. 888 (1954).

[46] Naim v. Naim, 197 Va. 80, 87 S.E.2d 749, vacated and remanded to clarify record, 350 U.S. 891 (1955), aff'd on original record, 197 Va. 734, 90 S.E.2d 849, appeal dismissed, 350 U.S. 985 (1956).

[47] State v. Brown, 236 La. 562, 567, 108 So.2d 233, 234 (1959).

Statutes, 42 Cornell L.Q. 208 (1957); Riley, Miscegenation Statutes — A Re-evaluation of Their Constitutionality in Light of Changing Social and Political Conditions, 32 So. Cal. L. Rev. 28 (1958); Casenotes on Perez v. Sharp, 37 Calif. L. Rev. 122 (1949), 37 Geo. L.J. 442 (1949), 62 Harv. L. Rev. 307 (1948), 22 So. Cal. L. Rev. 31 (1948); Casenote on Naim v. Naim, 41 Va. L. Rev. 861 (1955); Comment on McLaughlin v. Florida, 25 Md. L. Rev. 41 (1965).

3. *Monogamy*

REYNOLDS v. UNITED STATES
98 U.S. 145 (1878)

WAITE, C.J. [The defendant was a member of the Mormon Church who had been convicted of bigamy in the District Court for the Territory of Utah and sentenced to two years. At his trial the accused proved that an accepted doctrine of the Mormon Church was that its members had a duty, circumstances permitting, to practice polygamy, and one of the errors he alleged was the court's refusal to instruct the jury that plural marriage in conformity with what the accused believed to be a religious duty would be a defense.]

Polygamy has always been odious among the northern and western nations of Europe, and, until the establishment of the Mormon Church, was almost exclusively a feature of the life of Asiatic and of African people. At common law, the second marriage was always void (2 Kent, Com. 79), and from the earliest history of England polygamy has been treated as an offence against society. . . .

By the statute of 1 James I. (c. 11), the offence, if committed in England or Wales, was made punishable in the civil courts, and the penalty was death. As this statute was limited in its operation to England and Wales, it was at a very early period re-enacted, generally with some modifications, in all the colonies. In connection with the case we are now considering, it is a significant fact that on the 8th of December, 1788, after the passage of the act establishing religious freedom, and after the convention of Virginia had recommended as an amendment to the Constitution of the United States the declaration in a bill of rights that "all men have an equal, natural, and unalienable right to the free exercise of religion, according to the dictates of conscience," the legislature of that State substantially enacted the statute of James I., death penalty included, because, as recited in the preamble, "it hath been doubted whether bigamy or poligamy be punishable by the laws of this Commonwealth." 12 Hening's Stat. 691. From that day to this we think it may safely be said there never has been a time in any State of the Union when polygamy has not been an offence against society, cognizable by the civil courts and punishable with more or less severity. In the face of all this evidence, it is impossible to believe that the constitutional guaranty of religious freedom was intended to prohibit legislation in respect to this most important feature of social life. Marriage, while from its very nature a sacred obligation, is nevertheless, in most civilized nations, a civil contract, and usually regulated by law.   Upon it society may be said to be built, and out of its fruits spring social relations and social obligations and duties, with which government is necessarily required to deal.   In fact, according as monogamous or polygamous marriages are allowed, do we find the principles on which the government of the people, to a greater or less extent, rests. Professor Lieber says, polygamy leads to the patriarchal principle, and which, when applied to large communities, fetters the people in stationary despotism, while that principle cannot long exist in connection with monogamy. . . .

In our opinion, the statute immediately under consideration is within the legislative power of Congress. . . .   This being so, the only question which remains is, whether those who make polygamy a part of their religion are excepted from the operation of the statute.   If they are, then those who do not make polygamy a part of their religious belief may be found guilty and punished, while those who do, must be acquitted and go free.   This would be introducing a new element into criminal law.   Laws are made for the government of actions, and while they cannot interfere with mere religious belief and opinions, they may with practices.   Suppose one believed that human sacrifices were a necessary part of religious worship, would it be seriously contended that the civil government under which he lived could not interfere to prevent a sacrifice?   Or if a wife religiously believed it was her duty to burn herself upon the funeral pile of her dead husband, would it be beyond the power of the civil government to prevent her carrying her belief into practice? . . .

[Affirmed.]

NOTE

1. The aftermath of the Reynolds decision was an all-out campaign for the suppression of the deviant religious-sexual Mormon practice.   With obvious satisfaction, President Cleveland was able to report to Congress in 1888 that since 1885 there had been nearly 600 convictions under the bigamy and related statutes.[48]   There is even a report of "six women, three of whom had babies under six months of age" imprisoned in a cell in the Utah penitentiary for contempt of court in refusing to acknowledge the paternity of their children.[49]   In 1887 Congress enacted legislation to provide for a judicial proceeding to terminate the corporate charter of the Mormon Church and for the escheat of its property, and the resulting forfeitures were sustained by a divided Court, Mormon Church v. United States, 136 U.S. 1 (1890).   To disenfranchise Mormons, Idaho adopted an oath for all prospective voters by which they were required to swear that they were not members of any organization advocating polyg-

---

[48] 8 Messages and Papers of the Presidents 1789-1897, pp. 773, 794 (Richardson ed. 1898).   See also a report of the Attorney General during a debate on legislation for the relief of the "wives" and children of these plural marriages. 19 Cong. Rec. 9231 (1888).

[49] Ibid.

amy and, inter alia, "that I do not, and will not, publicly or privately, or in any manner whatever, teach, advise, counsel, or encourage any person to commit the crime of bigamy or polygamy, or any other crime defined by law, either as a religious duty or otherwise." The oath was held constitutional in Davis v. Beason, 133 U.S. 333 (1890), and Mormon political control of Utah was threatened by the proposal of similar legislation for Utah.[50] At this point the Church gave up; its president, "after praying to the Lord and feeling inspired," [51] issued a proclamation in 1890 terminating plural marriage in the Church, and as a result of this change of position, Utah was ultimately admitted as a state and the escheated property returned to the Church.[52]

2. Is there any other way in which the Mormon problem could have been handled? For a recent statement of a position opposed to that of the Court, see Freeman, A Remonstrance for Conscience, 106 U. Pa. L. Rev. 806, 824-826 (1958). Freeman argues that the "religion" protected by the first amendment includes more than Christianity and that the line should be drawn between protection of "the great systems of religion recognized by civilization" and nonprotection of "the forerunners of religion, often referred to as primitive or barbaric." The Court's error in Reynolds was to regard "polygamy [as such] a return to barbarism." Freeman says:

> In 1878 the Supreme Court's knowledge of great religions which authorize polygamy, or its sympathy for other religions, may have been inadequate to recognize the necessity for protecting these religions. . . . Today we have sizable Moslem, Hindu, and Buddhist populations in the United States. Diplomats, workers at the United Nations, students in our colleges adhere to those religions. But polygamy is fast disappearing even under such religions as sanction it. I believe that America could have afforded to tolerate religious polygamy until the culture gradually dried it up. The damage to religious freedom in the first amendment and the brutal tearing apart of polygamous families has been a very high price to pay for our "morality." . . .[53]

Compare also the dissenting opinion of Mr. Justice Murphy in Cleveland v. United States, 329 U.S. 14, 24 (1946). In that case the Court held that transportation by "fundamentalist" Mormons of a woman across a state line for a plural marriage ceremony and subsequent cohabitation was a violation of the Mann Act, which makes it a crime to transport in interstate commerce "any woman or girl for the purpose of prostitution or debauchery, or for any other immoral purpose . . ." 18 U.S.C.A. §2421 (1951). Mr. Justice Murphy said (329 U.S. at 26):

[50] See 6 Roberts, A Comprehensive History of the Church of Jesus Christ of Latter-day Saints 213 (1930).
[51] Id. at 220.
[52] Id. at 310.
[53] 106 U. Pa. L. Rev. at 825.

We must recognize . . . that polygyny, like other forms of marriage, is basically a cultural institution rooted deeply in the religious beliefs and social mores of those societies in which it appears. It is equally true that the beliefs and mores of the dominant culture of the contemporary world condemn the practice as immoral and substitute monogamy in its place. To those beliefs and mores I subscribe, but that does not alter the fact that polygyny is a form of marriage built upon a set of social and moral principles. It must be recognized and treated as such.

. . . It takes no elaboration here to point out that marriage, even when it occurs in a form of which we disapprove, is not to be compared with prostitution or debauchery or other immoralities of that character.

3. Although outcroppings of Mormon fundamentalist polygamy still persist in the United States,[54] in the modern world the focus of attention is on parts of Africa and Asia. In 1954 the Supreme Court of Israel construed a statute prohibiting polygamy as applicable to Muslim citizens of Israel, rejecting the allegation that the statute interfered with the religious freedom of Muslim citizens.[55] In Moslem countries, despite the explicit authorization of polygamy in the Koran, there is a decided trend to outlaw or at least restrict plural marriage. A recent example is Iraq, where polygamy was restricted to men who could prove their financial ability to support more than one wife. N.Y. Times, Jan. 2, 1960, p. 3, col. 4. The process of scriptural "interpretation" by which this reform is being supported is described in Anderson, Islamic Law in the Modern World 48-50 (1959), and rests on the conditions for polygamy stated in the Koran: an equal distribution of the husband's favors and a competence to meet all his financial obligations. The 1953 Syrian Law of Personal Status provided that "the Court may withhold permission for a man who is already married to marry a second wife where it is established that he is not in a position to support them both" (id. at 49), and 1958 Morocco legislation does not permit polygamy "if any injustice is to be feared between co-wives" (id. at 50).

[Such a provision as Syria's] was mild, however, by comparison with the Tunisian Law of Personal Status, 1957, which tersely enacted that "polygamy is prohibited" — a prohibition which is said to find its juristic justification in the other Koranic provision that a man should confine himself to one wife unless confident that he is capable of treating a plurality of wives with equal justice, and the assertion that both experience and revelation have made it clear that such impartiality is in fact unattainable. It is only fair to add, however, that the older jurists had urged, reasonably enough, that the Koran must

[54] See Andersen, Polygamy in Utah, 5 Utah L. Rev. 381 (1957); State in Interest of Black, 3 Utah 2d 315, 283 P.2d 887 (1955).

[55] Malham v. The Sharia Judge, Acre and District, 8 Piskei-Din 910 (1954), translated in United Nations, Yearbook on Human Rights for 1954, pp. 161-163.

not lightly be regarded as contradicting itself; and that the equal justice demanded by the "Verse of Polygamy" must therefore be interpreted in terms of those favors over which a husband has control, not the instinctive inclinations of his heart.[56]

4. In polygynous cultures where two or more wives share the same household, family life is markedly affected. At least in primitive societies the "more universally prevalent" form is where "each wife has her separate household and the husband visits them in turn." [57] This situation has been compared to "a temporarily interrupted monogamy. In such cases there is a series of individual marriages in which domestic arrangements, economics, parenthood as well as legal and religious elements do not as a rule seriously encroach on each other." [58] Contemporary American society exhibits another form of "interrupted monogamy," in our case the interruption being permanent and the assumption of a second family being sequential to rather than concurrent with life with the first family. Certainly monogamy in the strict sense of being restricted to one spouse during the life of both, as in Catholic doctrine, no longer represents the legal norm in any state. Under the American form of remarriage after divorce, Landis estimates that a far larger proportion of American men and women have more than one spouse during a lifetime than in polygamous societies where usually "not more than one out of ten to twenty achieves the polygamous state." [59] The difference is particularly marked for women, for most polygamous societies reserve the privilege of more than one spouse to men (polygyny), and the situation where one woman has many husbands (polyandry) is quite rare. American women have as much right to remarry as American men.

From a social standpoint the assumption by a man or woman of more than one family at the same time would seem to pose a much more aggravated problem than would the assumption of a second family after the first family has been abandoned or otherwise terminated in fact. There is no way in which a man could legalize having more than one family at the same time, but bigamy which consists merely in assuming a second family after abandonment of the first is not so much a moral affront under our existing social patterns as it is a punitive device to force people to obtain formal recognition of family dissolution by a decree of divorce or annulment. Oddly enough, however, American bigamy statutes draw no distinction between what we might thus term "concurrent" bigamy and "sequential" bigamy. The first is probably extremely rare, and most of our legal problems concern situations where the challenged second marriage is sequential to an earlier family already terminated in fact. Four situations should be distinguished:

a. Parties may get married by concealing from the marriage license clerk the fact that one or both of them have a pre-existing but legally undissolved marriage. Particularly at certain socio-economic levels of so-

[56] Anderson, Islamic Law in the Modern World 49 (1959).
[57] Malinowski, Sex, Culture, and Myth 32 (1962).
[58] Ibid.
[59] Landis, Sequential Marriage, 42 J. Home Econ. 625, 628 (1950).

ciety this occurrence, which has been called "common law divorce" or "poor man's divorce," is certainly far more common than the infrequent prosecutions for bigamy would indicate. See, e.g., Foster, Common Law Divorce, 46 Minn. L. Rev. 43 (1961).

b. Parties may get married on the assumption that an earlier marriage of one of them was "void" without obtaining a judicial decree of nullification. Even if a statute of a state classifies a marriage as void, we have seen that this may not automatically give the right to remarry, and more than one state's law may be applicable. See Restatement (Second), Conflict of Laws §122 (Tent. Draft No. 4, 1957).

c. An earlier marriage may have been "terminated" by the disappearance or presumed death of the spouse. Most states have provided by statute (the so-called "Enoch Arden Laws") that if the abandoned spouse remarries after the passage of a specified period (usually five to seven years), believing in good faith and after diligent search that his or her former spouse is dead, then the second marriage is presumed to be valid, at least unless and until the "dead" spouse subsequently reappears. Some of these statutes are designed solely to immunize such marriages from subsequent bigamy prosecution. See, e.g., Del. Code Ann. tit. 11, §§381, 384 (1953), page 199 supra. Other statutes, though in terms broadly drawn, have been interpreted to protect the remarrying spouse only so long as the absent spouse does not reappear. See Townsend v. Morgan, 192 Md. 168, 63 A.2d 743 (1949). Still a third group of statutes establishes a special procedure for obtaining a judicial declaration of the death of the absent spouse; under these statutes, any marriage subsequently contracted is fully protected. See, e.g., N.Y. Dom. Rel. Law §§220, 221; Pa. Stat. Ann. tit. 48, §1-8 (1965) (presumption of death after seven years; exposure "to specific peril" sufficient ground for declaration of death following absence for lesser period), applied in Pest and Kolesnik Marriage License, 4 Pa. D. & C.2d 12 (Orphans' Ct. 1955). In those jurisdictions where this latter type of broadly protective statute does not exist (or though in existence is not invoked), the second marriage is a nullity, unless it can be saved by one of the curative provisions or common law presumptions which we shall examine later. Generally speaking, the presumptions that the first marriage was dissolved by death and that the second marriage was a valid one will serve to uphold the second marriage until the absent spouse does in fact reappear, but they cease to operate at that point. See Anonymous v. Anonymous, 186 Misc. 772, 62 N.Y.S.2d 130 (Sup. Ct. 1946). Similarly, once the defect in the second marriage is actually removed by the death or divorce of the absent spouse, curative provisions may take over to validate retroactively the second marriage and legitimate any children of the marriage. See, e.g., Mass. Gen. Laws Ann. c. 207, §6 (1958). But significant gaps which may prove disastrous in particular cases remain between these curative devices. In general, see Annot., 144 A.L.R. 747 (1943).

d. The most common and troublesome problems involving a determination of whether or not a prior marriage is still in force for remarriage purposes arise after the granting of a divorce or annulment. The complexities of full faith and credit being what they are, it is not always easy for lawyers, not to speak of laymen, to know whether a valid divorce has been obtained. Moreover, as we shall see in considering dissolution, legislative or judicial restrictions on remarriage complicate the problem.

4. *Checks against Immature and Hasty Marriages*

a. AGE RESTRICTIONS

In re BARBARA HAVEN
86 Pa. D. & C. 141 (Orphans' Ct. 1953)

LAUB, J. Petitioner has invoked the provisions of the Act of March 24, 1927, P.L. 64, 48 PS 19, which provides that in special cases a judge of the orphans' court may authorize the issuance of a marriage license where one or both of the parties are under 16 years of age. The child in this case is a female of the age of 14 years and eight months and desires to marry the son of her father's second wife, a young man 22 years of age. Her father has given his consent and now asks us to do likewise.

The testimony which we took at the hearing discloses that this attractive well-developed girl is physically suited for marriage. She has, however, achieved only the eighth grade in school and, although apparently intelligent, her marks are not of the best. She testified that she has been in love with her stepbrother for two years; has planned marriage almost from the inception of her acquaintance with him, and believes that her love for him is genuine and permanent. He is her first "steady" beau although she did attend school dances with other boys when she was 12 years old.

The young man in the case, Robert Bihler, is a typical, fine American youth. He is industrious and ambitious. There is no observable reason why he should not be married and it is evident that he is suited to become the head of a family.

The social aspects of marriage have become so impressed upon us that law-making bodies everywhere have seen fit to impose safeguards against ill-advised unions. Thus, waiting periods, medical examinations, age restrictions, marriages within certain degrees of consanguinity and affinity, and many other controls have been universally imposed by State legislatures in order to preserve and maintain the utmost purity and integrity of the marriage state. As pointed out in Fulcomer v. Pennsylvania Railroad Company, 141 Pa. Superior Ct. 264, 269, while marriage is a civil contract, the rights under it are under the control of the law-making power. The Supreme Court in Moorehead's Estate, 289 Pa. 542, 552, said:

"The marriage contract once entered upon, becomes a relation rather than a contract and invests each party with a status towards the other and society at large . . . [Court's quotation abbreviated by Eds.] And in this aspect marriage is a social institution, publici juris, being the foundation of the family and the origin of domestic relations of the utmost importance to civilization and social progress; hence the State is deeply concerned in its maintenance in purity and integrity."

At common law a boy under 14 or a girl under 12 could not be married: Blackstone, book 1, chap. 15(2). But our legislature enacted the current law, apparently concluding that one in the sunlight of youth, standing on the threshold of life, should not walk precipitously into the marriage chamber, but first should look with calm deliberation whether the step is both desirable and safe. In this concept there has been ample support in aphorism and precept. Certainly it is based upon common experience and logic.

The statute in question . . . fulfills a two-fold function in protecting marriage as an estate and in placing a restraining hand upon the shoulder of impetuous youth. Our duty directs our attention to the interest of society in marriage, but it also commands us to consider the best interests of the minor as well.

The prime reason advanced in behalf of the present petition is the young lady's protestation of affection for the boy. Love has many emotional counterfeits, each as likely as the other, but time and mature appreciation are the only devices known which detect the real from the spurious. . . .

All of this was within the knowledge and contemplation of the legislature when it enacted the present law. When it conferred jurisdiction upon us to set aside the general rule in favor of special cases it could not have meant that our discretion was to be exercised in commonplace situations such as obtains here.

In only a minority of cases do applicants seek marriage licenses without believing sincerely that they are in love and without a compelling desire to unite. . . . Therefore, that which calls for action by us must truly be within the legislative concept of something "special," not something based upon the usual, ordinary or the mere urgent desire of the parties.

The proof offered here merely places these young people within the general category. Both are physically fit; both are fine, young citizens. But, in holding the marriage age to 16, the legislature must have realized that there is more to marriage than physical and mental development. It requires mature understanding and judgment; mature emotional stability. Above all, there must be a deep and abiding concept of marriage as more spiritual than physical, more an estate than a condition. In its wisdom the law-making body felt that an appreciation of these elements must be absent in a young girl of the age of the present applicant. It certainly felt that in fulfilling its function as protector of children, the law should not, in the absence of the most compelling circumstances, consent to the marriage of one so young.

We are constrained, therefore, to conclude that, no special circumstances having been shown, we are without jurisdiction to make the order prayed for. . . .

NOTE

1. The statutory provision at the time Barbara Haven was decided read: "[N]o licenses to marry shall issue, if either applicant therefor be under the age of sixteen years: Provided, That a judge of the orphans' court shall have discretion to authorize a license to be issued by the clerk of the orphans' court in special cases where one or both persons are under the age of sixteen years." Pa. Stat. Ann. tit. 48, §19 (1930). A 1953 amendment modified the provision to read: "No license to marry shall be issued . . . [i]f either of the applicants for a license is under the age of sixteen years, unless a judge of the orphans' court shall decide that it is to the best interest of such applicant. . . ." Pa. Stat. Ann. tit. 48, §1-5 (Supp. 1964). Would Barbara Haven's application have been denied under the 1953 formulation?

2. Minnesota Stat. Ann. §517.02 (Supp. 1964) provides: "A female person of the full age of 16 years may, with the consent of her parents, guardian, or the court, as provided in Minnesota Statutes, Section 517.08, receive a license to marry, when, after a careful inquiry into the facts and the surrounding circumstances, her application for a license is approved by the judge of the juvenile court of the county in which she resides." In administering the statute, the Juvenile Court of Hennepin County (Minneapolis) requires that the applicant, her prospective spouse, their parents, and their clergyman answer a questionnaire about the parties, their backgrounds, and the chances for success of their marriage. The applicants are given a full physical examination; a probation officer interviews them and their parents and makes a full report to the court. The questionnaire[60] to the applicants includes such items as: "How many school dances and parties attended together during last year"; "Presents exchanged last Christmas, birthday (given and received)"; "When first discuss marriage"; "Give prospective spouse ring." The parents are asked to evaluate their child's prospective spouse (e.g., "Is that person as intelligent as your child?"), to describe the future educational needs of their child and the couple's financial prospects, and to assess their feelings about the applicant's pregnancy (e.g., "Would you consent to the marriage now if the girl were not pregnant?" "Would it be better to place the baby for adoption and have the children wait a year or so to get married?").

Prior to January 1, 1964, the Juvenile Court permission provision applied to all males between the ages of sixteen and eighteen and females between the ages of fifteen and sixteen. The number and disposition of applications for 1962, 1963, and the first six months of 1964 are given in the table on the following page.[61]

The Probation Officer handling these applications believes that most of the couples who do not receive Juvenile Court permission go immediately

---

[60] Questionnaire provided by the Probation Officer in charge of youthful marriages, Hennepin County Juvenile Court, Hennepin County, Minnesota.

[61] These data were furnished by the Probation Officer, Juvenile Court, Hennepin County, Minnesota.

to South Dakota and get married in that state by lying about their ages. See pages 263-265 infra.

| | 1962 | | 1963 | | 1964 | |
	Pregnant	Not Pregnant	Pregnant	Not Pregnant	Pregnant	Not Pregnant
Applications	45	8	28	3	29	26
Not Completed	9	3			3	2
Completed Applications	36	5	28	3	26	24
Granted	28	4	24	2	20	20
Denied	8	1	4	1	6	4

3. The Pennsylvania statute has always required consent of "a parent or guardian" to the marriage of any person under the age of twenty-one. Pa. Stat. Ann. tit. 48, §1-5(c) (Supp. 1964). The provision contemplates that the Orphans' Court judge can appoint a guardian if the minor does not have one. Probate Codes in most states authorize appointment of a guardian of the person for infants. See generally Fraser, Guardianship of the Person, 45 Iowa L. Rev. 239 (1960).

See In re Minor's Application for Marriage License, 65 Pa. D. & C. 337 (Orphans' Ct. 1948). A boy of eighteen and a girl of seventeen, both high school seniors, applied for a marriage license. The girl was pregnant; her parents gave their consent. The mother of the boy refused to consent:

> The mother of the boy has had training and experience in social service. She believes that the proposed marriage would not be to the interest of either party or their unborn child, because he could not continue his education and has not the ability to support wife or child, and their marriage would bring only frustration and bitterness. She believes that it would be better for the child if it were adopted into the home of people who are more mature, rather than be brought up by young parents who are so unprepared to give it either security or affection.[62]

The girl's parents offered the couple lodging and financial help until the boy's graduation from high school. The court stated (id. at 338) that the mother's opinion was not the sole consideration:

> nor can our thought be for the boy alone. The name and welfare of the child are to be considered . . . . To the credit of the boy, he is willing to assume the duties of a husband and father, and the welfare and best interests of all the parties demand that their relations be put on a decent and normal basis. . . .

Although the court could find no statutory exception to the requirement of consent by a parent or guardian, "public policy requires a further exception to the act. Marriage laws are always given a liberal interpretation where the legitimacy of issue is in question." Id. at 340. The court

---

[62] 65 Pa. D. & C. at 338.

approved the appointment of the boy's attorney as guardian, but pointed out that he did not have discretion to refuse consent; the court had passed upon the advisability of the marriage and the appointment "was a mere formality to comply with the letter of the statute." Id. at 341.

Several courts have taken the contrary position. See In re King, 55 Lanc. L. Rev. 275, 277 (Pa. Orphans' Ct. 1957) (nineteen-year-old Amish boy wished to marry, and parents refused consent because boy left the Church and was marrying outside his religion; held that the court should not supplant the rights of parents "under the facts and circumstances"— even if the parents had "constructively deserted" the boy, or their conduct emancipated him); Gilbert's Application, 5 Lyc. Reptr. 115 (Pa. Orphans' Ct. 1955) (pregnant seventeen-year-old refused permission to marry because her mother would not consent, even though mother had suggested that the girl obtain an abortion; a guardian should be appointed only if the parents are deceased or have deserted the child).

The Proposed Marriage Code for Pennsylvania, page 210 supra, continues the requirement of parental consent for marriage by minors, but explicitly authorizes the Orphans' Court to issue a license if "it is to the best interest of such applicant." §207(c). That section also provides:

> At the discretion of the court any marriage of such person under twenty-one years which is not so authorized shall be subject to annulment by such minor or his parent or guardian if petition for such annulment is filed during such minority and within sixty days after such unauthorized marriage, but otherwise the validity of such a marriage may not be questioned.

The Reporter for the Code states that

> The premise is that easy marriage promotes easy divorce and that except in rare cases consent of parent or guardian to a minor's marriage should be essential. . . . Moreover, parents or guardian . . . may [also] seek annulment, thus making more meaningful what otherwise is but a nominal requirement of parental consent. Legitimacy of any issue will be saved under other provisions in the code.[63]

In 1931 Vernier reported that only fourteen states, some by express statutory provision, permit a parent to bring an action in his own name for annulment of an underage marriage entered into without parental consent. 1 Vernier 251; Annot., 150 A.L.R. 609 (1944). See Turner v. Turner, 167 Cal. App. 2d 636, 334 P.2d 1011 (1959) (father obtained annulment because his consent had been obtained fraudulently; son had told him that he was responsible for girl's pregnancy and that they had already been married in Mexico).

4. The assumption that youthful marriages are particularly susceptible to divorce has general support from "public attitude" and "most sociologists and authors," [64] although published studies have differed widely:

---

[63] Proposed Marriage and Divorce Codes for Pennsylvania 16-17 (Pa., General Assembly, Jt. State Govt. Commission, 1961).

[64] Monahan, Does Age at Marriage Matter in Divorce?, 32 Social Forces 81, 82 (1953).

compare the conclusion of sociologists Hart and Shields that "marriages in which either party is 19 or younger are from 10 to 100 times as risky as are marriages at the ideal [24-29] age," [65] with that of statisticians Dublin and Spiegelman that "The chances of divorce do not change much within the normal range of age at marriage — from around 17 to 40 — but beyond these very rough limits the likelihood of divorce appears to be greater." [66]

To what extent do the following statistical data support the view that youthful marriages are particularly hazardous?

a. Over-all American statistics reveal that the median ages of brides and grooms at first marriage slowly declined through the middle fifties and then leveled off; for brides, from 21.5 years in 1940 to 20.2 in 1955 and 20.4 in 1963; for grooms, from 24.3 in 1940 to 22.6 in 1955 and 22.8 in 1963.[67] In 1955, 44.5 per cent of all first-marriage brides and 13.5 per cent of all first-marriage grooms were under age twenty at marriage.[68] There are considerable regional variations; in 1964, when the national median for first-marriage brides was 19.9 years, the range was from 18.6 in Idaho to 21.7 in Connecticut, District of Columbia, New Jersey, and Pennsylvania, and 21.8 in Hawaii.[69] The importance of distinguishing first marriages (about 77 per cent of all marriages) from remarriages of divorced (about 17 per cent, or widowed (about 6 per cent) persons is emphasized by the fact that the median age at remarriage is at least fifteen years higher than at first marriage.[70]

b. Data from twelve states show a relatively short duration of time between the date of marriage and the date of divorce or annulment. The median duration is 6.4 years; in 7.6 per cent of the divorce-annulment cases the duration was under one year, in 19.5 per cent one or two years, and in nearly 48 per cent of the dissolutions the duration was five years or less. Of course the time interval between marriage and separation is shorter; one study shows that in about 35 per cent of all divorces granted in a Philadelphia court during 1937-1950 the parties had separated within two years after marriage.[71] In a 1955 sample of six states, over one third of wives whose first marriages ended in divorce that year were age twenty-three or younger at the time of dissolution.

c. One of the most complete studies is reported in Monahan, Does Age at Marriage Matter in Divorce?, 32 Social Forces 81 (1953), based on data derived from 52,722 marriages and 8040 divorces in Iowa between 1945

[65] Hart & Shields, Happiness in Relation to Age at Marriage, 12 J. Soc. Hygiene 403 (1926) (based on a statistical comparison of 500 marriage and 500 desertion and nonsupport cases in Philadelphia).

[66] Dublin & Spiegelman, The Facts of Life from Birth to Death 70 (1951) (no documentation for the statement is given).

[67] Statistical Abstract of the United States, 1964, p. 72.

[68] Percentage derived from figures in 1 Vital Statistics of the United States 1955, p. 67.

[69] Statistical Abstract of the United States, 1964, p. 71.

[70] These estimates are derived from id. at 65. All statistics in these reports are incomplete; for states which are included or excluded as to particular data, see the volumes in the Vital Statistics series.

[71] Kephart, The Duration of Marriage, 19 Am. Soc. Rev. 287, 290 (1954).

and 1947. The sample consisted of (1) all marriages in the state in which the bride was a resident of Iowa, both parties were married once only, and both were native white, and (2) all divorces in the state where the couple had previously been married in Iowa. The limitations as to Iowa residence were imposed to try to minimize the impact of the uncontrolled variable of migratory marriage and divorce. Two tables from this study are reproduced in part; data for the relatively fewer marriages above age thirty are omitted.

TABLE 1. AGE AT MARRIAGE FOR MARRIAGES AND DIVORCES: IOWA, 1945-1947; WHITE COUPLES, BOTH PARTIES MARRIED ONCE ONLY (52,722 MARRIAGES; 8040 DIVORCES)

Age at Marriage in Years	Percentage Distribution			
	Husbands		Wives	
	Marriages	Divorces	Marriages	Divorces
Total	100.0	100.0	100.0	100.0
Under 15		.1	.1	.5
15		.1	.6	2.2
16	.2	.5	2.3	6.0
17	1.0	1.7	5.6	10.1
18	2.7	4.6	14.5	15.1
19	4.5	8.1	14.2	16.0
20	8.3	11.5	13.5	13.3
21	14.3	13.0	12.0	10.0
22	12.3	12.4	9.3	6.7
23	10.7	10.5	6.8	5.4
24	9.1	8.8	5.1	3.7
25	7.6	6.6	3.7	2.7
26	6.1	5.1	2.8	2.1
27	4.9	3.4	2.1	1.5
28	3.8	2.8	1.6	1.0
29	2.9	2.2	1.1	.8
30	2.4	1.9	.9	.6
Average Age at Marriage				
Median	23.6	22.8	21.0	20.0
Mean	24.8	23.8	21.9	20.8

[Table 1 shows that youthful marriages in Iowa appear to be overrepresented in divorce actions, but Monahan makes the following qualification:]

Because divorces in one year do not come from marriages in that particular year, but from all preceding years (in a constantly diminishing degree), a non-comparability obtains when we set marriage and divorce data in tables covering the same time period. This factor could be adjusted if the necessary information were available for a long period of time, lacking which one can only make analytical interpretations. In Iowa, divorces occur largely in the first and second years of married life, dropping off rapidly thereafter. The noncomparability in order of time is less serious in Iowa, therefore, than in some other states. Nevertheless, if the pattern of age at marriage were changing rapidly, such a comparison could be grossly misleading. It is believed unlikely that age at marriage in Iowa has shown any drastic change in the years immediately preceding 1947, from which the preponderance of divorces derived. Should one accept, however, the belief that age at marriage has been declining generally, allowance for such a change in Iowa would not diminish but accentuate the difference found in the two series, because divorces of recent date would have derived from times when persons were marrying at older ages. Allowance for a decline in age at marriage would give stronger affirmation to the contrast shown. In terms of the average age at marriage, as shown in Table 1, divorced couples had married about one year earlier than all couples getting married for the first time. . . .

[Another table, which is not reproduced, shows that the median duration of marriages ending in divorce, while displaying statistical irregularities, tends to increase as age increases up to about age twenty-four, and that the marriages of teenagers are of noticeably shorter duration than those where marriage occurred at an older age.]

TABLE 3. RATIO OF DIVORCES TO MARRIAGES BY RELATIVE AGE AT MARRIAGE: IOWA, 1945-1947; WHITE COUPLES, BOTH PARTIES MARRIED ONCE ONLY

Age of Husband	Total	16 & Under	17	18	19	20	21	22	23	24	25	26	27	28
							Age of Wife at Marriage							
Total	.15	.45	.28	.16	.17	.15	.13	.11	.12	.11	.11	.11	.11	.10
16 & Under	.45	*.44*												
17	.27	.32	.29	*.23*	*.14*									
18	.26	.43	.21	.21	.25	.19								
19	.27	.50	.32	.21	.24	.28	.22							
20	.21	.45	.30	.18	.19	.18	.14	*.21*	*.32*					
21	.14	.41	.23	.10	.13	.12	.10	.16	.11	*.22*				
22	.15	.35	.27	.14	.16	.14	.12	.12	.12	.17	*.17*			
23	.15	.40	.26	.16	.18	.15	.13	.11	.12	.12	.13	*.05*		
24	.15	*.69*	.35	.16	.17	.15	.14	.10	.10	.14	.11	.11	*.16*	
25	.13	*.69*	.31	.15	.17	.10	.11	.08	.13	.10	.14	.15	*.10*	
26	.13		*.23*	.14	.13	.17	.12	.09	.08	.11	.12	.17	.04	*.12*
27	.11			.17	.13	.11	.07	.09	.13	.06	.07	.09	.16	*.05*
28	.11			*.19*	.18	.11	.15	.08	.08	.07	.08	.07	.08	.10
29	.11			*.19*	*.23*	.18	.09	.07	.09	.07	.10	.10	.08	.10
30	.12			*.18*	*.21*	.22	.12	.10	.11	.08	.07	.04	.13	.06
31	.12				*.15*	*.18*	*.12*	*.09*	*.17*	*.08*	*.13*	*.06*	*.04*	

The ratio of divorces to marriages in each relative age cell of husband and wife for the period 1945-1947 is shown in Table 3. [Ratios in italics are based upon fewer than 100 marriages.] In a way more satisfactory than any of the others, this table puts a new perspective on the entire question of age at marriage and (what is actually the basic datum on age), the joint ages of the couples. Miscellaneous statistical nonconformities appear throughout, yet a basic pattern is clearly discernible.

As previously indicated, the mean age of the marriage sample was around 25 years for the men and 22 years for the women. At the central area of marriage ages (husbands 24 to 26 years with wives aged 22 to 24 years) the ratio of divorces to marriages is about .10. If we regard the ratio in this area as unity, as one moves toward a correspondingly younger age spouse, or a younger set of joint ages, the ratio of divorce rises. In this central area as the husband's age gets much older for a given age of wife, or as the wife's age gets older for a given age of husband, the divorce ratio goes up. But as the joint ages increase, there is a slight tendency for the ratio to fall below .10. The influence of mortality in the older marriage age groups, reducing the number of potential divorcees importantly as the years go by, must be given full consideration. With this in mind the low ratios in the higher age at marriage combinations are understandable, in part. But it should be noted that even here, as the age-difference spreads, the ratio of divorce goes up.

The higher probability of divorce for the very youthful marriages, singly considered and also in age-combinations, is immediately apparent in Table 3. Where both parties were 16 years and under at marriage the divorce ratio was about four times that in the central area. . . .[72]

What other variables besides age might affect the increased likelihood of divorce following a teen-age marriage? Monahan notes in very young marriages a probably higher incidence of forced or shotgun marriages and of such disrupting factors as economic difficulties and parental interference. In connection with divorce we will also note other variables that seem to be associated with marriage failure, such as religious differences and disparities in the spouses' social, economic, or educational levels (particularly if the wife is on the higher level). We will also see that the frequency of divorce increases as one goes from high to low in economic or social class status. See page 793 infra. At least some of these variables interact with age, and the question as to which factors are causal and which spurious is not easy to resolve.

Consider another possibility:

Some experts suspect that a majority of the married teen-agers now chafing under wedlock would have had marriage difficulties at any age.

"The teen-age marriages we have been having have not been among a typical cross-section of our teen-age population," according

[72] Monahan, Does Age at Marriage Matter in Divorce?, 32 Social Forces 81, 84-86 (1953).

to David R. Mace, former director of the American Association of Marriage Counselors.

"They have been the marriages of our less mature, more disturbed, less responsible, more confused teen-agers," he said.[73]

5. For a different attitude on the age problem in another part of the world, see the following excerpt:

We in India have solved this problem [unwed motherhood and Kinsey-revealed immorality] to a greater extent, I believe, than almost any society in the world. We not only encourage children of tender age to marry; we arrange the matter ourselves. Over the centuries this has proved to be the most enduring basis for a life-long marital relationship. To be sure, there are those who contend that young people understand "love" and ought to be permitted to arrange their own marriages; I refer them to the latest divorce statistics. In the United States, divorce is fast approaching the rule rather than the exception. In India, the divorce rate for 1961 was less than 2 per cent. What better test is there?

I know this may come as a shock to those who like to think of themselves as "advanced." I assure you, however, that few countries are more biologically sophisticated than India. We've been through it all and are guided by centuries of experience. Why should the United States and Great Britain go through the multiple ordeals of history before they arrive at where we are today? [74]

WILKINS v. ZELICHOWSKI
26 N.J. 370, 140 A.2d 65 (1958)

JACOBS, J. . . . . The plaintiff and the defendant were domiciled in New Jersey as were their respective parents. They ran away from New Jersey to marry and they chose Indiana because they believed "it was the quickest place." The Indiana statutes provide that "females of the age of sixteen" are capable of marriage although they also provide that where the female is within the age of 18 the required marriage license shall not be issued without the consent of her parents. See Burns, Indiana Statutes Anotated, §§44-101, 44-202. After their marriage in Indiana on April 23, 1954 the plaintiff and defendant returned immediately to New Jersey where they set up their home. On February 22, 1955 the plaintiff bore the defendant's child. On April 22, 1955 the defendant, having been convicted on several independent charges of automobile theft, was sent to Bordentown Reformatory where he was still confined at the time of the hearing in the Chancery Division. On January 4, 1956 the plaintiff filed her annulment complaint under N.J.S. 2A:34-1(e) which provides that a judgment of nullity may be rendered on the wife's application upon a showing that she was under the age of 18 years at the time of her

[73] Minneapolis Star, Oct. 1, 1963, p. 2B, col. 3.
[74] S. Roy, M.D., letter to the editor, Saturday Review, Jan. 19, 1963, p. 23.

marriage and that the marriage has not been "confirmed by her after arriving at such age"; the statute also provides that where a child has been born there shall be no judgment of nullity unless the court is of the opinion that the judgment "will not be against the best interests of the child." Although the defendant was duly served he did not file any answer and he chose not to contest the plaintiff's proceeding.

The plaintiff's evidence adequately established that she was 16 years of age when she was married and that she did not confirm her marriage after she had reached 18 years of age and the Chancery Division expressly found that an annulment would be "for the best interests of the child"; nevertheless it declined to grant the relief sought by the plaintiff on the ground that the marriage was valid in Indiana and should therefore, under principles of the conflict of laws, not be nullified by a New Jersey court because of the plaintiff's nonage. In reaching the same result the Appellate Division recognized that the Chancery Division had ample power to nullify the Indiana marriage of the New Jersey domiciliaries [citations omitted] but expressed the view that comity dictated that it should not take such action unless there was an imperative New Jersey policy (which it did not find) against marriages of 16-year-old females. . . .

The vigor of New Jersey's policy against marriages by persons under the prescribed age is evidenced not only by the breadth of the statutory language but also by the judicial decisions. . . .

It is undisputed that if the marriage between the plaintiff and the defendant had taken place here, the public policy of New Jersey would be applicable and the plaintiff would be entitled to the annulment; and it seems clear to us that if New Jersey's public policy is to remain at all meaningful it must be considered equally applicable though their marriage took place in Indiana. While that State was interested in the formal ceremonial requirements of the marriage it had no interest whatever in the marital status of the parties. Indeed, New Jersey was the only State having any interest in that status, for both parties were domiciled in New Jersey before and after the marriage and their matrimonial domicile was established here. The purpose in having the ceremony take place in Indiana was to evade New Jersey's marriage policy and we see no just or compelling reason for permitting it to succeed. . . .

[The court then discusses some cases from New York and New Hampshire refusing to recognize an evasive underage marriage as well as some from California and Colorado reaching a contrary result.]

. . . We are not here concerned with a collateral attack on an Indiana marriage or with a direct attack on an Indiana marriage between domiciliaries of Indiana or some state other than New Jersey. We are concerned only with a direct and timely proceeding, authorized by the New Jersey statute (N.J.S. 2A:34-1(e)), by an underage wife for annulment of an Indiana marriage between parties who have at all times been domiciled in New Jersey. We are satisfied that at least in this situation the strong public policy of New Jersey (see Restatement, Conflict of Laws §132(b), comment b) requires that the annulment be granted. The annulment will not render the plaintiff's child illegitimate (N.J.S. 2A:34-20) and, as the Chancery Division found, it will be for his best interests. The annulment will also serve the plaintiff's best interests for it will tend to reduce the tragic consequences of her immature conduct and unfortunate marriage. The Legislature has clearly fixed the State's policy in her favor and has granted her the right to apply for a judgment nullifying her marriage; we know of no considerations of equity or justice or overriding principles of the law which would lead us to deprive her of the relief she seeks under the circumstances she presents. See Taintor, [Marriage in the Conflict of Laws,] 9 Vand. L. Rev. [607], at 624.

Reversed.

HEHER, J. [joined by Burling, J.] (dissenting). I am not of the opinion that judgment of nullity under N.J.S. 2A:34-1, "will not be against the best interests of the child"; and so I would affirm the judgment of dismissal of the complaint for annulment of the marriage. Compare Caruso v. Caruso, 104 N.J. Eq. 588 (Ch. 1929).

NOTE

1. Writing before the Wilkins case was decided, Professor Kingsley stated that "[w]ith but occasional dissent" the courts have applied the law of the state where the marriage was celebrated, "saying that, while the policy of the forum preferred the wisdom of greater age before assuming the duties of marriage, still the locality would not be so shocked by the spectacle of married infants as to justify denial of legitimacy to a status validly created elsewhere." [75]

2. State policies respecting youthful marriages are commonly enforced, of course, only by suits for annulment such as the one decided in Wilkins. Annulment as a marriage-terminating device is considered in greater detail in Chapter 7 infra. It goes without saying that distinctions are commonly made between void and voidable, directory and mandatory. For present purposes, consult Professor Kingsley's précis of the doctrines:

> At common law, where either party was under the age of seven years a purported marriage was treated as totally without effect; between seven and fourteen years for males, and between seven and twelve years for females, the parties could contract a relationship of imperfect status . . . .
>
> However, in most states, modern statutes have made two types of modification with reference to these age groups . . . While a few cases have suggested otherwise, the weight of authority is that statutes

[75] Kingsley, The Law of Infants' Marriages, 9 Vand. L. Rev. 593, 604 (1956). Factors which have influenced courts to take the view of the Wilkins case and void the marriage include: doubt about validity in the state of contracting as well, Sirois v. Sirois, 94 N.H. 215, 50 A.2d 88 (1946); fraud in obtaining the marriage license abroad, Duley v. Duley, 151 A.2d 255 (D.C. Mun. Ct. App. 1959); or the absence at the time annulment is sought of any indication that the marriage is a viable one, Holland v. Holland, 212 N.Y.S.2d 805 (Sup. Ct. 1961).

. . . raising the "age of consent" . . . repeal the common-law rules, making a purported marriage open to attack in proper manner if contracted by a person under the statutory age, even though such person was over the common-law age. The attitude toward the second type of statute — requiring parental or judicial consent — has, however, been different; courts have there held that the requirement for such consent was merely directory and that absence of such consent did not invalidate a marriage or make it open to disaffirmance except where the terms of the statute involved expressly made such consent an essential condition precedent to a valid marriage. . . .

. . . [T]he cases admit that a nonage marriage is capable of ratification by affirmative act after the parties reach full marriageable age; and that, once so ratified, the marriage becomes a completely valid and binding marriage. . . .

To this extent, then, an infant's marriage is not void; if it were, there could be no marriage without satisfaction, after age of consent, of all the formalities of a new marriage, and the status would exist only from the time of a new ceremony.

. . . [T]he more difficult problem is whether or not such a ratification is necessary in order to keep the marriage in force after that date. The weight of authority would seem to be that it is not, that, unless there is appropriate disaffirmance, and until such disaffirmance, the infant's marriage is binding on him and on the world. . . .

In connection with ordinary contracts, it is the general rule that an infant is not estopped to rely on his infancy by having fraudulently misrepresented himself to be of age. . . . In the few cases . . . all except one have said that the infant's power to disaffirm was absolute. . . .[76]

3. Despite an ambiguous statute, N.J. Stat. Ann. §2A-34-14 (1952), in New Jersey, a parent apparently cannot bring an action to annul an underage marriage, Niland v. Niland, 96 N.J. Eq. 438, 126 Atl. 530 (1924), unless the minor is also insane, Naylor v. Naylor, 113 N.J. Eq. 126, 165 Atl. 875 (1933). If New Jersey's policy against underage marriages is as strong as the Wilkins opinion claims, why should standing to raise the defect be limited to the parties?

There are other methods of harassing youthful marriages. See, e.g., State in the Interest of I., 68 N.J. Super. 598, 173 A.2d 457 (Juv. & Dom. Rel. Ct. 1961). A seventeen-year-old boy and a sixteen-year-old girl, both New Jersey residents, had an affair which resulted in the girl's pregnancy. They eloped to Maryland, where they were validly married because Maryland waives the requirement of parental consent where the girl is proved to be pregnant. They went to Pennsylvania and rented an apartment. Both were then charged in New Jersey with juvenile delinquency on a complaint filed by the girl's parents, were forcibly returned to New Jersey, and found to be delinquent on the basis of their premarital sexual relations. The court assumed that under Wilkins the marriage could

---

[76] Kingsley, The Law of Infants' Marriages, 9 Vand. L. Rev. 593-600 (1956).

be annulled at the suit of either juvenile. Do you agree with the assumption?

In the last decade secondary school educators have made vigorous efforts to solve the problem of teen-age marriages. Although there are no reliable figures to suggest how common the practice is, a great many schools and school districts try to deter marriage among high school students by placing restrictions on those who marry. The restrictions vary from prohibitions on extracurricular activities to outright expulsion. Landis[77] reports that most high schools do not require married students to attend, that only a small minority encourage or require withdrawal, but that expulsion is the predominant policy for married girls who are also pregnant. A nationwide poll of school directors and principals reported that 78 per cent of those responding stated that they would permit both male and female married students to attend classes, 16 per cent would prohibit both, 5 per cent would permit only husbands to attend classes, and 1.5 per cent would permit only wives.[78]

McLeod v. State, 154 Miss. 468, 122 So. 737 (1929), and Nutt v. Board of Education, 128 Kan. 507, 278 Pac. 1065 (1929), invalidated policies adopted by school boards excluding married students, otherwise qualified, from high school classes. But see State ex rel. Thompson v. Marion County Board of Education, 202 Tenn. 29, 302 S.W.2d 57 (1957) (Board's action in suspending recently married student for one term reasonable because her presence in school for the first few months after her marriage would have a detrimental influence on her fellow students). In Cochrane v. Mesick Consolidated District, 360 Mich. 390, 103 N.W.2d 569 (1960), the plaintiffs were members of the high school football team. After consulting with the Board of Education and being informed that marriage would not result in any restrictions, they both married. The Board later adopted a policy prohibiting married students from engaging in any extracurricular activities. The plaintiffs sought a writ of mandamus compelling the Board to permit them to play on the football team. The trial court denied the writ and the Supreme Court of Michigan affirmed by an equally divided vote. Four members of the court thought the Board's policy was unconstitutional; three Justices thought that the Board had not abused its discretion because the rule was adopted for a consolidated school, located in a small town, which had experienced a high marriage and dropout rate; one Justice voted to affirm because the question was moot — the plaintiffs had already graduated.

b.   WAITING PERIODS

Banns, or public proclamations of intention to marry, have had a long history. See 2 Pollock & Maitland 370. In 1639 a law that is probably the earliest American marriage statute imposed an inflexible waiting period of at least fourteen days, during which the intentions of the parties

---

[77] Landis, Attitudes and Policies Covering Marriage Among High School Students, 18 Marr. & Fam. Liv. 128-136 (1956).

[78] Opinion Poll, 58 Nation's Schools 86, 88 (Nov. 5, 1956).

were to be "3 times published at some time of publike lecture or towne meeting, in both the townes where the parties, or either of them, do ordinarily reside"; or, where there are no lectures, posted "so as it may easily bee read." 1 Records of the Governor and Company of the Massachusetts Bay in New England 275 (Shurtleff ed. 1853).

In view of this background and of what one would suppose would be at least some relationship between successful marriages and a minimum premarital acquaintance and planning, the present state of American law is surprising. Waiting periods required between application for and issuance of a marriage license range from the substantial number of states which require none to the relative handful which require four or five days. These times are for residents; a few states, like Delaware, require a longer waiting period for nonresidents. See page 195 supra. Most of these waiting periods can be waived. Some additional delay may be occasioned by the requirement of a blood test for venereal disease, but this too can be waived in most states.

The Royal Commission on Marriage and Divorce, Report 1951-1955, Cmd. No. 9678 (1956), noted the fact that marriages can be entered into so easily as a factor going "far to explain why so many marriages are predisposed to break down under the first sign of serious strain" (par. 329). It reported that many of the witnesses before the Commission urged "amendment of the marriage laws so as to put a brake upon hasty and ill-considered marriages." The Commission found this question outside its terms of reference, but urged a review of marriage law (par. 330). Two examples of the testimony before the Commission follow.

1. The Catholic Union of Great Britain, in proposing systematic education for marriage, stated (id., Minutes of Evidence 427, 429):

> In Manchester and Liverpool successful experimental classes in marriage training have been held where young engaged couples have had the opportunity of discussing with experts in many fields the things that go to the building-up of a happy married life. But the training requires time, and if young persons can be married within three weeks of the application referred to above, time is not available before marriage. We submit for the consideration of the Commission that in the case of couples either of whom is under twenty-five a minimum period of six weeks should elapse between such application and marriage, whether the marriage is in a church or before a registrar. . . . We recognize, of course, that good reasons may sometimes exist for a hasty marriage but we submit that these reasons should be given and proved . . .

2. A solicitor with twenty years' experience of 300 or more cases annually in a provincial town proposed the following (id. at 308):

> (i) No marriage to take place without a special licence unless there were evidence that there had been a formal engagement registered at least three months beforehand.
>
> (ii) The engagement would be registered with the minister, if a

church marriage is intended, or otherwise the registrar. He would have an interview [before the registration] with both applicants and satisfy himself that the parties had gone into the matter thoroughly and had sufficient knowledge of each other to justify the marriage proceeding. Probably a questionnaire would be filled in by both parties and the interview would follow. The questionnaire would disclose whether they have been introduced to each other's family; the amount of their respective incomes; where they are going to live; and whether they can buy furniture, or if not, how long it will be before they are in a position to have any furniture of their own; the health records, and whether there have been any court convictions; whether either party refuses to have children, and similar matters.

Although the questions may seem an interference with personal liberty, they are of such importance that it is right that some person representing society, and the interests of future children, should have a say in them, and help people to face realities.

The person taking these particulars should ask the parties to consider carefully any points of difficulty, and should have power to postpone the performance of the ceremony if he were not satisfied; against which, however, there should be an appeal to either the magistrates' court or the judge in chambers.

Compare the Wisconsin Family Code, which requires that each applicant for a marriage license be given a printed message to ponder during the five-day waiting period. The message is taken from Wis. Stat. Ann. §245.001 (Supp. 1965), which sets out the Code's intent and which includes the following: "The seriousness of marriage makes adequate premarital counseling and education for family living highly desirable and courses thereon are urged upon all persons contemplating marriage."

Wisconsin also requires that where one of the parties is a resident the license application be made in the "county in which one of the parties has resided for at least 30 days immediately prior to making application therefor." §245.05. Section 245.11 provides for immediate public posting, and makes provision for a legal action in which possible incompetence of the parties or false statements in the application can be raised by a parent, grandparent, child, brother, sister, or guardian of either applicant, or by the district attorney or family court commissioner. Such an objection stays issuance of the license pending court adjudication. §245.11.

Disregard of waiting period requirements and an apparent correlation between hastily entered evasive marriages and a high divorce rate were described by a Chattanooga Bar Association committee in an investigation of divorce practice in that city. See Chattanooga (Tenn.) Times, Nov. 24, 1946, p. 24, col. 1, at col. 3, p. 26, cols. 6, 7. The committee reported:

Out of the 1000 sample [divorce] cases, 698 (69.8 per cent) of the marriages were consummated in the state of Georgia; 129 (12.9 per cent) in Tennessee, and 138 (13.8 per cent) in other states. In the remaining 34 cases the state of marriage did not appear. In other words, more than five times as many marriages were consummated in Georgia as in Tennessee.

Of the Georgia marriages, the average elapsed time between the marriage and the divorce decree was five years. In Tennessee, the average was 13 years, and in other states eight years. . . .

Why do our citizens rush to Georgia to get married? . . .

[The report notes that although Georgia has a five-day waiting period, this can be waived "in the case of an emergency or extraordinary circumstance," by either the "ordinary" or anyone he designates as his clerk.]

Those "clerks" then set up Gretna Green accommodations at strategic points just short of the Tennessee border, where they are open for business 24 hours per day. . . . With a license fee and a marriage honorarium at stake no instance is known to this committee wherein a license has been refused. . . .

. . . [I]t is easy to estimate the income of these Georgia justices of the peace in figures of tens of thousands of dollars annually.

Some other data relevant to the importance of a deliberative interval prior to marriage is provided in Burgess & Wallin, Engagement and Marriage 272-302 (1953). The authors found that in a study of 1000 engaged couples "at least a third of the young men and about half of the young women had one or more broken engagements" (id. at 273). The reasons assigned for the breakups include parental disapproval and cultural and religious differences; these are similar to factors we have already noted, page 230 supra, as disproportionately associated with divorce. Burgess and Wallin, supra, comment (at 302):

The existing high proportion of broken engagements indicates that many couples utilize the period of betrothal as a test of the soundness of their relationship. . . .

Broken engagements, which drew strong disapproval in the past, perform a useful function in the present. They prevent marriages which almost certainly would end in unhappiness and the majority of them in divorce. Further increase in broken engagements might very well result in decrease in the divorce rate.

If this conclusion is accepted, does it follow that an increase in the waiting period between license application and marriage would help reduce the incidence of unwise marriages? We have noted that American statutes vary from no waiting period to one of five days. Does tinkering within such a narrow range serve much purpose? Burgess and Wallin, dealing with long time periods, found that the proportion of broken engagements was higher where the couples had known each other less than eighteen months. Id. at 285-286.[79]

_____

[79] "In one of our larger counties in another state . . . while they had the law requiring a three day waiting period between the application for a license and getting it, 997 applications were not called for the third day. Some of the

Note also the relevance of this engagement data to the material immediately below.

C. ACTIONS FOR BREACH OF PROMISE AND SEDUCTION: A POLICY COUNTERWEIGHT

PAVLICIC v. VOGTSBERGER
390 Pa. 502, 136 A.2d 127 (1957)

MUSMANNO, J. George J. Pavlicic has sued Sara Jane Mills for the recovery of gifts which he presented to her in anticipation of a marriage which never saw the bridal veil. At the time of the engagement George Pavlicic was thrice the age of Sara Jane. In the controversy which has followed, Pavlicic says that it was Sara Jane who asked him for his hand, whereas Sara Jane maintains that, Pavlicic, following immemorial custom, offered marriage to her. We are satisfied from a study of the record that it was Sara Jane who took the initiative in proposing matrimony — and, as it will develop, the proposal was more consonant with an approach to the bargaining counter than to the wedding altar.

George Pavlicic testified that when Sara Jane broached the subject of holy wedlock, he demurred on the ground that he was too old for her. She replied that the difference in their ages was inconsequential so long as he was "good to her." Furthermore, she said that she no longer was interested in "young fellows" — she had already been married to a young man and their matrimonial bark had split on the rocks of divorce. Hence, she preferred an older man. George qualified. He was 75. Sara Jane was 26.

The May-December romance began on a very practical footing in April, 1949, when Sara Jane borrowed from George the sum of $5000 with which to buy a house, giving him a mortgage on the premises. In three and one-half years she had paid back only $449 on the mortgage. On the night of November 21, 1952, she visited George at his home and advanced the not illogical proposition that since they were to be married, there was no point in their having debts one against the other and that, therefore, he should wipe out the mortgage he held on her home. George said to her: "If you marry me, I will take the mortgage off." She said: "Yes," and so he promised to satisfy the mortgage the next day. To make certain that there would be no slip between the promise and the deed, Sara Jane remained at George's home that night; and on the following morning drove him in her automobile to the office of the attorney who was to

---

impatient ones went over the state line in all probability. But that three day waiting period took care of the 'gin marriage.' . . . It took care of marriages which result from parking and petting and sex desire which causes some people to jump into marriage. It took care of the 'dare marriages' where two couples are double dating and one couple dares the other to get married so they do." Ellzey, Marriage or Divorce?, 22 U. Kan. City L. Rev. 9, 17 (1953). But cf. Crouch v. Wartenberg and Lannamann v. Lannamann, at pages 181-184 supra.

make, and did make, arrangements for the satisfaction of the mortgage. . . .

[The court then recounted other instances which took place after
"George's bank book became Sara Jane's favorite literature" including his
purchase for her of a new Ford ($2200) which proved to be a "lemon" and
was traded for a new Oldsmobile ($1700 more), a watch ($140), rings
($800), and insulation of her house ($800).]

It is not to be said, however, that Sara Jane was completely lacking in
affectionate ante-nuptial reciprocity. In June, 1953, she bought George a
wedding ring for him to wear. . . .

George testified that when he wore the wedding ring people laughed
and asked him when he was to be married. He replied: "Pretty soon."
He tried to live up to the prediction and asked Sara Jane for the wedding date. She said she could not name the month. In view of what was
to develop, she could have added with truth that she could not name the
year either.

In October, 1953, Sara Jane [persuaded George to give her money to]
buy a cheap saloon outside of Pittsburgh. George gave her $5000. And
Sara Jane disappeared — with the $5000.

The next time she was heard from, she was in Greensburg operating
Ruby's Bar — with George's $5000. From Ruby's Bar she proceeded to
the nuptial-bower where she married Edward Dale Mills. Although she
had many times assured George she would marry him because she liked
the idea of an old man, the man she then actually married was scarcely a
contender for Methuselah's record. He was only 26 — two years younger
than Sara Jane.

When George emerged from the mists and fogs of his disappointment
and disillusionment he brought an action in equity praying that the satisfaction of the mortgage on Sara Jane's property be stricken from the record, that she be ordered to return the gifts which had not been consumed,
and pay back the moneys which she had gotten from him under a false
promise to marry. . . .

The defendant urges upon us the proposition that the Act of June 22,
1935, P.L. 450; 48 P.S. §171, popularly known as the "Heart Balm Act,"
outlaws the plaintiff's action.

[The principal provisions of this Act follow: "§171. All causes of action for breach of contract to marry are hereby abolished . . .

["§172. No act hereafter done within this Commonwealth shall operate to give rise, either within or without this Commonwealth, to any of
the causes of action abolished by this act. No contract to marry, which
shall hereafter be made within this Commonwealth, shall operate to give
rise, either within or without this Commonwealth, to any cause of action
for breach thereof. It is the intention of this section to fix the effect,
status, and character of such acts and contracts, and to render them ineffective to support or give rise to any such causes of action, within or
without this Commonwealth.

["§173. It shall hereafter be unlawful for any person, either as litigant or attorney, to file, cause to be filed, threaten to file, or threaten to

cause to be filed in any court in this Commonwealth, any pleading or paper setting forth or seeking to recover upon any cause of action abolished or barred by this act, whether such cause of action arose within or without this Commonwealth.

["§176. Any person who shall violate any of the provisions of this act shall be guilty of a misdemeanor . . ."]

This is the first time that the Act of 1935 has come before this Court for interpretation and ruling. Although the Act contains several sections, the heart of it lies in the sentence, namely, "All causes of action for breach of contract to marry are hereby abolished."

There is nothing in that statement or in any of the provisions of the Act which touches contracts subsidiary to the actual marriage compact. The Act in no way discharges obligations based upon a fulfillment of the marriage contract. It in no way alters the law of conditional gifts. . . .

The title to the gifts which Sara Jane received, predicated on the assurance of marriage with George, never left George and could not leave him until the marital knot was tied. . . .

The appellant in her argument before this Court would want to make of the Act of June 22, 1935, a device to perpetuate one of the very vices the Act was designed to prevent. The Act was passed to avert the perpetration of fraud by adventurers and adventuresses in the realm of heartland. To allow Sara Jane to retain the money and property which she got from George by dangling before him the grapes of matrimony which she never intended to let him pluck would be to place a premium on trickery, cunning and duplicitous dealing. . . .

The Act of 1935 aimed at exaggerated and fictional claims of mortification and anguish purportedly attendant upon a breach of promise to marry. The legislation was made necessary because of the widespread abuse of the vehicle of a breach of promise suit to compel overly-apprehensive and naive defendants into making settlements in order to avoid the embarrassing and lurid notoriety which accompanied litigation of that character. The legislation was intended to ward off injustices and incongruities which often occurred when, by the mere filing of breach of promise suits innocent defendants became unregenerate scoundrels and tarnished plaintiffs became paragons of lofty sensibility and moral impeccability. It was not unusual in threatened breach of promise suits that the defendant preferred to buy his peace through a monetary settlement rather than be vindicated by a trial which might leave his good name in shreds.

. . . [I]t had been demonstrated that the action of breach of promise had been so misemployed, had given rise to such monumental deceptions, and had encouraged blackmail on such a scale, that the Legislature of Pennsylvania, acting in behalf of all the people, concluded that the evil of abuse exceeded to such an extent the occasional legitimate benefit conferred by a breach of promise suit that good government dictated its abolition.

Thus the law of 1935 prohibited, but prohibited only the suing for damages based on contused feelings, sentimental bruises, wounded pride, untoward embarrassment, social humiliation, and all types of mental and emotional suffering presumably arising from a broken marital promise. The Act did not in any way ban actions resulting from a tangible loss due to the breach of a legal contract. . . .

It thus follows that a breach of any contract which is not the actual contract for marriage itself, no matter how closely associated with the proposed marriage, is actionable. . . .

Decree affirmed at appellant's costs.

NOTE

1. For an illustration of why the action for breach of promise was once so well regarded and a suggestion of why it has now fallen under attack, see Wightman v. Coates, 15 Mass. 1, 3 (1818), where the court said:

> We can conceive of no more suitable ground of application to the tribunals of justice for compensation, than that of a violated promise to enter into a contract, on the faithful performance of which the interest of all civilized countries so essentially depends. When two parties, of suitable age to contract, agree to pledge their faith to each other, and thus withdraw themselves from that intercourse with society, which might probably lead to a similar connection with another, — the affections being so far interested as to render a subsequent engagement not probable or desirable, — and one of the parties wantonly and capriciously refuses to execute the contract which is thus commenced, the injury may be serious, and circumstances may often justify a claim of pecuniary indemnification.
>
>   . . . A deserted female, whose prospects in life may be materially affected by the treachery of the man to whom she has plighted her vows, will always receive from a jury the attention which her situation requires . . . It is also for the public interest, that conduct tending to consign a virtuous woman to celibacy, should meet with that punishment which may prevent it from becoming common. . . .

2. Pennsylvania was one of seven states which in the same year (1935) suddenly moved to abolish actions for breach of promise of marriage. These statutes, which in varying forms now exist in a number of jurisdictions, have given rise to a variety of problems. The constitutionality of the abolition has been attacked on the grounds that it impairs contract rights, Fearon v. Treanor, 272 N.Y. 268, 5 N.E.2d 815 (1936), appeal dismissed, 301 U.S. 667 (1937) (although statute impairs obligation of contract, it is constitutional under police power to regulate marriage); that it violates other state constitutional provisions, e.g., Heck v. Schupp, 394 Ill. 296, 68 N.E.2d 464 (1946) (statute which did not explicitly abolish cause of action but made it unlawful to file complaint unconstitutional under Ill. Const. art. 2, §19, which secures a remedy for every wrong); and that a penalty provision against filing actions is unlawful, Pennington v. Stewart, 212 Ind. 553, 10 N.E.2d 619 (1937) (statute which abolished both

breach of contract and alienation of affections actions upheld in alienation of affections case despite remedy-for-every-wrong clause in constitution, but penalty for filing such actions is an unconstitutional attempt to
deprive courts of their power to pass on the constitutionality of legislation).   For a discussion of the constitutional issues, see Comment, Abolition of Breach of Promise in Wisconsin — Scope and Constitutionality,
43 Marq. L. Rev. 341 (1960).   As to conflict of laws questions, see Spiro,
Breach of Promise, 11 Int. & Comp. L.Q. 260 (1962).

Brockelbank, The Nature of the Promise to Marry — A Study in Comparative Law, 41 Ill. L. Rev. 1 (1946), deals with both the limited scope of
the breach of promise remedy in other legal systems and some of the interesting aspects of the traditional action in this country.   In addition to
limited ordinary contract defenses, courts have upheld defenses based on
unchastity or physical sexual incapacity; they have not, however, barred
the action when "all the facts may point realistically to the near certainty
that, if the marriage were ever solemnized, it would either be very unhappy or end in divorce."   Id. at 9.   Brockelbank also discusses (id. at 10-
13) the anomalous situation in regard to damages, whereby a plaintiff can
recover both on a contract theory of being put in the same position she
would have been in without the breach and also on tort theories, e.g., for
mental suffering, humiliation, or any aggravations such as seduction.

The most difficult problems have related to actions which are ancillary
to the promise to marry.   California makes explicit statutory provision for
the situation in the Pavlicic case, authorizing restitution of transfers in
contemplation of marriage if the donee refuses to marry or the marriage
is given up by mutual consent.   Cal. Civ. Code §1590.   New Jersey
and Indiana concurrently abolished the tort action of seduction, N.J.
Stat. Ann. §2A:1-23 (1952); Ind. Stat. Ann. §2-508 (1946).   Where the
statute explicitly deals only with the breach of promise action, the fate of
related actions is left to judicial interpretation.   Massachusetts and New
York initially took an extreme position, New York denying both fraud
actions and restitution of gifts, see 70 Harv. L. Rev. 1098, 1099 (1957),
and Massachusetts barring recovery for assault and deceit, Thibault v.
Lalumiere, 318 Mass. 72, 60 N.E.2d 349 (1945).   The Massachusetts court
said (318 Mass. at 75-76, 60 N.E.2d at 351):

> This statute . . . not only abolished the right of action for breach of
> promise but it went farther and abolished any right of action, what-
> ever its form, that was based upon such a breach. . . .   Actions in
> tort for fraud have been held to be within the prohibition of such
> statutes . . .   [The plaintiff] cannot circumvent the statute by
> bringing an action in tort for damages so long as the direct or under-
> lying cause of her injury is the breach of promise of marriage. [Cita-
> tions omitted.]

More recently, however, both Massachusetts and New York appear to
have retreated somewhat.   See De Cicco v. Barker, 339 Mass. 457, 159
N.E.2d 534 (1959) (restitution of engagement ring permitted; other gifts

held to be unconditional); Tuck v. Tuck, 14 N.Y.2d 341, 200 N.E.2d 554 (1964) (girl induced into going through what turned out to be void marriage permitted to recover in deceit).

In Thibault v. Lalumiere the court also stated that it would have barred a tort action of seduction if it had been alleged (the plaintiff merely raised the assault of caressing). The court's reasoning is traditional: the party seduced is barred as particeps criminis and, if she consented, she cannot maintain an action for seduction. See Morris, Torts 30 (1953). Only a father or master can recover directly for loss of services incident to seduction. The traditional evasion of this common law barrier whereby the party seduced could recover damages for seduction under the form of a breach of promise action was said to have been foreclosed by the heart balm statute.

PROBLEM

Your client tells you that after she became engaged to the very wealthy heir to a patent medicine fortune, she gave up a lucrative and responsible position as executive assistant to the president of a large corporation. Half an hour before the large and expensive wedding her fiance stated that he would not marry her because "I lied when I told you I loved you. I just felt sorry for you." Under pressure from her father, who wished to avoid acute embarrassment, he went through with the ceremony but left her at the altar and refused to cohabit with her. Soon thereafter she had the marriage annulled on the basis of this refusal. Now she wishes to recover for lost wages, the savings she put into the cost of the marriage reception, and her extreme mental anguish which has left her with assorted neuroses, a large bill for psychiatric care, and an inability to handle other than routine menial employment. Advise her, assuming that Pennsylvania law governs.

MACKEY v. COMMONWEALTH
255 Ky. 466, 74 S.W.2d 915 (1934)

STANLEY, C. The appeal is from a conviction of the crime of seduction under promise of marriage, carrying a penalty of one year in prison. The prosecutrix testified explicitly that the defendant had sexual intercourse with her at a certain time and place, and unequivocally, without any suggestion of affection or love, that she had yielded to him because of his offer and promise to marry her. There was no evidence of any artifice, beguilement, or blandishment exercised by him. He merely proposed that if she would indulge he would marry her. The letter of the testimony, strictly and technically construed, does present, as the appellant maintains, a simple barter. . . .

. . . The statute declares that "whoever shall, under promise of marriage, seduce and have carnal knowledge of any female under twenty-one years of age," shall be guilty of a felony. . . . The word "seduce," in its ordinary, general use, means to lead astray from the path of rectitude or duty and imports some species of artifice, beguilement, deception, or other seductive art. But the refinements of nomenclature for the sake of decency in speech may not be used to raise doubts and distinctions that obscure the real substance of a statute. The term has the specific meaning of inducing a female to surrender her chastity or to lead her from the path of virtue which she was following by such enticements or influences. Without the inducement by a false promise or the abuse of the simplicity and confidence of a virtuous woman by which her submission was obtained, the accomplished act would be purely meretricious and simple fornication or adultery.

In the statute under which the appellant was condemned, an essential element is the enticement or procurement of the consent of a girl under twenty-one years of age by means of or because of a promise to marry her. That unconditional promise must be the inducement or moving cause which prompted the woman to yield her chastity. That is the gist of the statutory offense, the elements of age and chastity being present. [Citations omitted.]

As thus measured, the evidence of the prosecutrix brought the case well within the terms and purpose of the statute, and, notwithstanding the defendant's vehement denials that he had ever carnally known her, it was sufficient to take the case to the jury and to sustain the verdict.

It was more than a year after the season of improper acts had closed, through the failure of the accused to visit the prosecuting witness, before an indictment was returned against him. On the day the case was set for trial the parties were married. The defendant upon this trial elaborately explained that he married the girl, with a complete consciousness of innocence, because his lawyer had insisted that in such cases the universal experience had been that the accused man was certain of conviction be his denials and protestations of innocence ever so clear and emphatic. He was further influenced by an effort to avoid the shame that would rest upon his six year old boy by a former marriage if he were sent to the penitentiary, and in the belief that if he treated the girl right she would become ashamed of her prosecution and confess his innocence of the charge.

The statute provides that where the person charged shall have married the girl seduced before final judgment any prosecution instituted shall be suspended, but it shall be renewed and proceed as though no marriage had taken place if the accused shall willfully and without such cause as constitutes a statutory ground of divorce to the husband abandon or desert his wife within three years after the marriage. The provision permitting marriage to avoid prosecution looks primarily to making the best reparation possible, the fulfillment of the pledge which the seducer made in order to accomplish his sinful purpose. If an immediate or present abandonment without just cause were allowed, the object would be frustrated and the wrong sought to be punished aggravated. . . .

[The court then found that on conflicting evidence there was sufficient support for the jury's finding of abandonment and affirmed the conviction.]

NOTE

For the prevalence of criminal statutes against seduction, see pages 114-116 supra. Some statutes are limited to cases where the female is young, and they differ as to whether or not the fraud must consist of a false promise of marriage.

Although the American Law Institute decided not to include in the Model Penal Code any provisions dealing with private consensual sexual activities such as fornication, adultery, or homosexuality,[80] it provides that a misdemeanor is committed when a male "has sexual intercourse with a female not his wife . . . if . . . the other person is a female who is induced to participate by a promise of marriage which the actor does not mean to perform." Model Penal Code §213.3(1)(d) (Proposed Official Draft, 1962). Under another provision of the Code a complaint must be filed within three months, and it is a defense to show that the complainant "had, prior to the time of the offense charged, engaged promiscuously in sexual relations with others." §213.6(4). The following Comments to an earlier version of this section are taken from Tentative Draft No. 4, pp. 260-262 (1955):

New Jersey's statute is the only one requiring that the woman become pregnant as a result of the seduction. . . .

. . . [T]he policy objective of the present section is to prevent imposition in sexual dealing. A discrimination between two equally deceitful seducers on the basis of the "accident" of pregnancy can hardly be justified, if the legislative intent is to prevent the deceit. The evidentiary value of pregnancy . . . would not justify the requirement, in view of the independent requirement of corroboration in subsection (5).[81] Moreover, the chief issue in the prosecution is likely to be deception, as to which the pregnancy furnishes no clue. . . .

Contrary to prevailing law the text does not make marriage a defense to criminal seduction. Where marriage bars prosecution it may be stipulated that it occur before the indictment (e.g., California), before plea (e.g., Texas), before the jury is sworn (e.g., Missouri), or before judgment (e.g., Colorado). The New Jersey statute even provides for discharge from imprisonment if the convict marries the complainant after sentence. A formally valid marriage is all that is required, and the defense has sometimes been held good even if the marriage was solely for the purpose of avoiding prosecution and is followed by desertion or annulment on grounds of duress.

The rational significance of marriage as a bar to prosecution for seduction might be that: (1) it indicates good faith in the promise of

[80] For a discussion of reasons behind this decision, see Model Penal Code, Tent. Draft No. 4, pp. 204-219 (adultery and fornication), 276-291 (sodomy) (1955).

[81] This reference is to an earlier version; the Proposed Official Draft §213.6(6) (1962) makes the corroboration requirement inapplicable to seduction. — Ed.

marriage (this view finds expression in statutes requiring the marriage to antedate the formal institution of the prosecution); or (2) it indicates a reformation of the defendant's character and a willingness to assume his responsibilities; or (3) regardless of good faith of the original promise, society should not wreck an incipient marriage by jailing the husband (cf. the New Jersey statute, mentioned above); or (4) the community desires to give the seducer a penal incentive to marry the girl. Furthermore, it is probable that only in the rarest cases will a complaint be filed or prosecuted after marriage, so that the consideration that the law should accurately represent our real determination to punish becomes applicable. Against the foregoing it may be urged that marriage between the victim and victimizer under threat of prosecution is very likely to work out badly and therefore should not be encouraged by law, particularly if the legitimacy of a child is not at stake. As on so many other questions of penal law, definitive studies of the impact of the law are lacking.

The situation in which the law is likely to be invoked must be considered. Regardless of what the law provides, the bulk of the seduction cases will be settled by marriage or otherwise, without being brought to the attention of the authorities. The complaints coming to the authorities will, then, consist of (1) a group of "first reaction" protests from parents, most of which should be referred to social agencies for resolution, or which will be withdrawn in a short time after private settlement; (2) a group of cases where the defendant persistently refuses to acknowledge responsibility or make amends; and (3) a small group of cases in which there has been a marriage, probably under duress, which has already collapsed. None of these situations calls for a legal nudge toward matrimony as the solution. Classes (2) and (3) had best go before a tribunal for a determination of guilt or innocence plus a discretionary disposition or probation. The objective of conforming the law to the actual enforcement operation contemplated can be achieved by express recognition of this offense as one resting on complaint of the injured person.

Would you support or oppose the inclusion of this section in a penal code?

5. *Eugenic and Health Regulation*

a.   MENTAL AND PHYSICAL DEFECTS

F.A. MARRIAGE LICENSE
4 Pa. D. & C.2d 1 (Orphans' Ct. 1955)

KLEIN, P.J. and LEFEVER, J. Application for a marriage license was filed by the applicants on April 30, 1955. It appears from the statements made by the female applicant (herein referred to as F.A.), that she was a mental patient in St. Mary's Hospital, Philadelphia, for a period of two months in 1951.

Mr. MacDonnell, assistant orphans' court clerk, . . . refused to issue the license and certified the matter to this court for hearing. . . .

. . . Section 15 of the Act of July 24, 1913, P.L. 1013, provided that:

". . . no license to marry shall be issued where either of the contracting parties is an imbecile, epileptic, of unsound mind, or under guardianship as a person of unsound mind."

The statute did not define the prohibited sicknesses nor give the court any discretion as to the manner in which the statute was to be administered.

The discovery of new drugs has dramatically reduced the ill effects of epilepsy. Enlightened medical opinion now regards the absolute bar to marriage of epileptics as harsh, unjust, and unnecessary. Tremendous strides have also been made in the care of the mentally ill, resulting in cures in many cases and substantial improvements in others. It is now possible for some of these people to marry without serious risk to themselves, their spouses, their offspring, or the community generally.

The Marriage Law of 1953 recognized these advances in medicine, and in a large measure, corrected these long existing, entrenched deficiencies in our marriage laws. . . .

The provisions of the old law, which forbade the issuance of a license to a person who "is an imbecile, . . . of unsound mind, or under guardianship as a person of unsound mind," has been substantially re-enacted in the new act.[82] However, the absolute prohibition against the issuance of a marriage license to an epileptic has been repealed. Under the 1953 statute a marriage license may be issued to a person who is suffering from epilepsy or who has been, within five years preceding the time of the application, an inmate of an institution for epileptics, but only if authorized by a judge of the orphans' court. Likewise, if the applicant has been an inmate of an institution "for weak-minded, insane or persons of unsound mind" within five years preceding the time of the application, the license may be issued only if authorized by a judge of the orphans' court.

The legislature has thus placed a great social responsibility on the orphans' court. It is our duty to determine whether "it is for the best interest of such applicant and the general public to issue the license." Yet, the statute contains no criteria, standards or rules for determining this fact; and no definition of crucial terms used in the statute. This is perhaps

[82] "Section 5. Restrictions on the Issue of Marriage License. — No license to marry shall be issued by any clerk of the orphans' court: . . .

"(d) If either of the applicants for a license is weak-minded, insane, of unsound mind, or is under guardianship as a person of unsound mind.

"(e) If either of the applicants is an epileptic, or is or has been, within five years preceding the time of application, an inmate of an institution for epileptics, weak-minded, insane, or persons of unsound mind, unless a judge of the orphans' court shall decide that it is for the best interest of such applicant and the general public to issue the license, and shall authorize the clerk of the orphans' court to issue the license." [Pa. Stat. Ann. tit. 48, §1-5 (1965) (as amended in 1957 to delete references to epileptics).]

necessary, for the broad discretion vested in the courts, will enable them, in true common-law tradition, to progress with the advances of science in this difficult and inexact field of law and medicine and decide each case on its own facts.

A vast, hazy shadowland exists between mental health and mental illness. The gradations of abnormalities are as varied and diffused as the merging colors of the rainbow. The most illustrious and respected psychiatrists often disagree radically in their opinions with respect to the sanity of an individual.

The following extract from the Encyclopaedia Britannica, vol. 12, p. 383 (14th ed.) points up the difficulty very sharply:

"INSANITY. This term ordinarily connotes more or less severe unsoundness of mind. Though its loose usage is almost synonymous with mental disease, scientifically the term should only be applied to the mental condition of an individual who, through socially inefficient conduct, has to be placed under supervision and control. The mind is the mechanism by means of which we adapt adequately to our environment and when, through its derangement, conduct is exhibited which the community looks upon as evidence of disease and as implying irresponsibility, the individual concerned is said to be insane and the law steps in to certify him as such. Strictly speaking, then, insanity is really a social and legal term and not medical. Mental illness is a broad concept which may include very efficient members of society. No satisfactory definition can therefore be arrived at, since it would be necessary to define what we mean by sanity, which would involve us in equal difficulties."

The phrase "an inmate of an institution for weak-minded, insane, or persons of unsound mind" is, likewise, subject to interpretation. Institutions for the insane are no longer regarded merely as places in which persons of unsound mind are confined as custodial cases to rid the general public of their troublesome presence. Today, great progress is being made toward curing the mentally sick and the establishments in which they are housed are usually called "hospitals." In fact, many general hospitals have departments set aside for the care of the mentally sick. Furthermore, in present day usage the word "inmate" has been generally replaced by the more charitable word "patient." The language of the statute is general, but we believe that the legislature intended to include all cases in which the applicant has been hospitalized for treatment of some form of mental illness or deficiency in any mental institution, including a general hospital which conducts a department for the care of the mentally sick.

Basically, the problem which confronts us is one for the medical profession. A diagnosis by judicial decree should not be made except with the advice, and upon the recommendation of, trained psychiatrists.

The statute does not in so many words state that an applicant who has been in a mental institution must be cured permanently at the time the application is made. However, because the issuance of a license to a person who is weak-minded, insane or of unsound mind is absolutely prohibited by the statute, the legislature must have intended that a license is to be issued only to a person who has been completely cured of his mental illness or whose condition has so improved that he can be expected to lead a normal life and to take his place in society without serious risk to himself or to the community generally.

Leading members of the medical profession freely admit that the science of caring for the mentally ill is in its infancy. Much research and investigation has been undertaken recently which has resulted in tremendously enhancing the chances of curing or, at least, improving the condition of persons suffering from mental sickness.

It seems clear that under no circumstances should a marriage license be issued to persons having a mental deficiency of severe degree, e.g., an idiot or imbecile. It is also apparent that persons suffering irremedial brain injury, or deteriorating organic brain syndromes which are of progressive or irreversible nature, e.g., senile dementia, should not be permitted to marry.

On the other hand, many persons who are unable to cope with the intense pressures of the modern age, suffer what is commonly designated as "mental breakdowns" and are institutionalized. Most of these people respond favorably to therapy; many are completely cured. These obviously are the persons whom the legislature intended to benefit primarily and furnish no serious problem when they apply for marriage licenses.

The real difficulties arise with respect to persons who suffer moderate mental deficiency or who have been hospitalized because of the more serious mental illnesses, such as manic-depressive psychosis, schizophrenia (dementia praecox), post-partum psychosis, and involutional melancholia. Although many of these cases are completely hopeless, a great number show marked improvement under modern therapy, such as shock treatment, psychotherapy, and the use of newly discovered drugs. Some of these persons are able to leave the mental hospitals and, at least temporarily, take their places in society as useful citizens. Some apparently have complete remission from their malady. Whether they have recovered sufficiently to assume the responsibilities of marriage presents an extremely delicate question.

No general rule can be handed down. Each case is sui generis and must be decided upon its own facts. The discretion vested in the orphans' court must be carefully exercised in order to protect not only the applicants and their issue, but the general public as well.

Three preliminary requirements seem to be indicated in every case before a license should issue: (1) Full disclosure must be made to both applicants of all of the details of the case history of the applicant who has been mentally afflicted; (2) the court must be satisfied that such applicant has recovered sufficiently to adjust normally to the problems of everyday living, particularly those arising from the marriage relationship, and (3) the court must be reasonably assured that if children are born of the marriage, such children will be normal, healthy children, free from the taint of mental illness or deficiency.

With these principles in mind, let us examine the factual situation existing in the present case.

No question is raised concerning the sanity of the male applicant. He was present at the hearing, fully cognizant of the history of F.A.'s mental sickness, and is, nevertheless, not only willing, but eager, to marry her.

F.A. is 30 years of age. She was graduated from a Catholic parochial grade school and attended Little Flower High School for two years. She left school when she was about 17 years old and took a job in a hosiery mill, "sewing on piece-work." She continued in the hosiery industry until, apparently, the pressure of "piece-work" caused her to have a mental breakdown. She was hospitalized at St. Mary's Hospital in Philadelphia for a period of eight weeks with a diagnosis of dementia praecox. While in the hospital she received a full course of electric shock treatments, following which she received treatments as an out-patient until December 1953, when she was pronounced well. It appears, further, from the testimony that since her discharge from the hospital she has managed the household of her invalid sister satisfactorily and efficiently and has given no evidence of any recurrence of her malady.

Dr. William L. Long, the physician who treated F.A., was the principal witness in her behalf. Dr. Long has specialized in neuropsychiatry since 1928 and is well and favorably known to the court. He is chief neuropsychiatrist at St. Mary's Hospital, and is on the psychiatric staff at Nazareth Hospital, Doctor's Hospital, and the Philadelphia General Hospital. Dr. Long examined F.A. shortly before the date of the hearing. He testified:

"I am satisfied that she is fully recovered from her illness and I think she now has a well-adjusted emotional life."

He testified further that, in his opinion, if she had children they would be normal. He recommended that the marriage license be issued.

Following the hearing, at the request of the hearing judges, F.A. was examined by Dr. Nicholas G. Frignito, neuropsychiatrist for the Municipal Court of Philadelphia. Dr. Frignito filed a written report in which he made a diagnosis of dementia praecox (recovered normal intelligence). This report concluded with the opinion that F.A. is now recovered from her mental illness and is competent to marry. . . .

This is a borderline case and we confess that we are beset with doubts. However, life at its very best is uncertain. Probably in a strictly disciplined society persons of defective mentality would be deprived of the blessings of matrimony. This, however, is an imperfect world. It is difficult to foretell the unhappy consequences which might result from our refusing to issue a marriage license in this case in view of the fact that the marriage banns have been posted, and all of the arrangements for the marriage have been made. The applicants are obviously in love with each other. If they cannot be married in this State, they may be tempted to live together without the benefit of marriage, or to seek a marriage license in another State where the restrictions are less stringent. Under all of the existing circumstances, we are of the opinion that it is for the best interest of the applicants and the general public to issue the marriage license. . . .

NOTE

1. Would the result of the F.A. case have been different or would different standards have been applied if the certification to the Orphans' Court by the marriage license clerk had been as follows:

I have refused to issue a marriage license to F.A. because of the following facts developed at the time of application. [The clerk then summarizes F.A.'s history up to the time of her breakdown under the pressure of piecework.] She was immediately put under the care of a psychiatrist and for two years received intensive psychiatric treatment, including shock therapy, on the basis of four or five office visits a week. She has responded to treatment and her psychiatrist, who states that her disease is now in remission, is seeing her only once every two weeks. While this case is not in terms covered by subsection (e) in that applicant has never been in an institution, it seems doubtful and is certified accordingly.

2. Dementia praecox is a term for the diseases which today are included within the label schizophrenia. The following definition may be helpful:

Schizophrenia does *not* mean what the word has come to mean in newspaper editorials: an inner conflict, a dilemma. A schizophrenic person has broken with reality over a considerable area of life; i.e., broken both in the sense of a major impairment of perception or judgment of reality, inaccessible to the corrective influence of experience, and of emotional estrangement from people, sometimes to the degree of complete withdrawal and inaccessibility. Angular mannerisms of bodily movement or rigid bodily immobility are often part of it. The illness proceeds usually in episodes after each of which there may be a far-going, though not quite complete, restoration of the preceding state. The more schizophrenic episodes a patient has incurred, the greater is the likelihood of an outcome in intellectual deterioration (demence). . . .[83]

3. The legislatures have done little to modify Vernier's critical description of statutory policies a quarter century ago. See 1 Vernier 190:

The totally unscientific character of the statutes dealing with a scientific subject in this modern age of scientific enlightenment is revealed in connection with the inconsistent . . . statements defining the classes of incompetents . . . . There are all degrees of mental incapacity, and many varieties of insanity, some curable, some incurable; some acquired and some hereditary. Perhaps these defy legal description or definition, but it is certain that their different degrees and characteristics have hardly been recognized at all by the legislation of the Nation in dealing with the marriage problem. . . .

[83] Waelder, Psychiatry and the Problem of Criminal Responsibility, 101 U. Pa. L. Rev. 378, 380 n.2 (1952).

OREGON REVISED STATUTES (Supp. 1963)

106.071 Mental and physical prerequisites to marriage license. (1) Before any county clerk issues a marriage license, each applicant therefor shall file with the clerk a medical certificate for marriage license signed by a physician licensed by the State Board of Medical Examiners . . . In the certificate the physician shall certify that:

(a) The applicant was given an examination and laboratory test on dates specified in the certificate.

(b) In the opinion of the physician, the applicant is not infected with syphilis in a communicable stage and is free from other communicable venereal diseases, feeble-mindedness, mental illness, drug addiction or chronic alcoholism.

(2) Before issuing a medical certificate for marriage license, the physician shall apply or, in a laboratory approved by the State Board of Health, have applied a recognized blood test approved by the State Board of Health for the determination of syphilis. . . .

(3) The confidential record of premarital examination shall consist of the following:

(a) The applicant's sworn statement of medical history.

(b) The laboratory report which shall be certified by the laboratory, indicating the dates and results of the laboratory tests.

(c) The physician's report of mental and physical examination; and

(d) When required, the countersignature of the health officer or State Board of Eugenics. The confidential record of premarital examination shall be filed by the examining physician with the State Board of Eugenics within three days after completion and shall not be open to public inspection. . . .

(6) If, at the time of the examination, the physician decides that the applicant is ineligible for a medical certificate for marriage license because of any present communicable venereal disease, feeble-mindedness, mental illness, drug addiction or chronic alcoholism, he shall delay issuance of the certificate and shall refer all pertinent information to a committee of three appointed by the State Board of Eugenics together with any other or additional evidence the applicant may wish to submit. If, in the opinion of this committee, the applicant should not marry, its decision is final, unless appealed, as provided in ORS 106.074 to the circuit court.

106.074 Appeal from denial of medical certificate. (1) . . . The circuit court shall try such appeals summarily, without a jury, upon the evidence contained in the confidential record of premarital examination and any other pertinent evidence presented. . . .

NOTE

In a few states marriage rights are denied to persons suffering pulmonary tuberculosis in its advanced stages, e.g., Wash. Rev. Code Ann.

§26.04.030 (1961), and occasionally to habitual drunkards and narcotics addicts, e.g., Delaware, page 194 supra. The only prevalent restrictions which go beyond mental health to physical condition concern contagious venereal disease. Although Wisconsin required a medical test as early as 1913,[84] most legislation stemmed from a nationwide campaign against venereal disease launched in the mid-thirties, and was given impetus by the wartime draft law's discovery of the high incidence of the disease. Almost every state now requires some form of premarital serological blood tests; Washington requires the groom to submit an affidavit stating that he is not infected,[85] and only a few states have no legislation on the subject. For an example of the commonest form of the requirement, which bars marriage until the disease is no longer contagious, see Delaware, page 199 supra. Compare Va. Code Ann. §20-4 (1960), providing that the parties are merely to be informed if the test is positive and, if they marry, requiring under penal sanction that they take treatment until cured, §20-5.

While untreated syphilis during pregnancy often has disastrous consequences for the child,[86] nonetheless, there was heated opposition, particularly from physicians, to premarital blood test legislation on the grounds of inadequacy and unreliability of blood tests, the liberty of the individual, and secrecy for the physician. Shafer, Premarital Health Examination Legislation, 69 Pub. Health Rep. 487 (1954). For a discussion of and citation to opposition to the requirement by Maryland public health officials, see Jacobson, American Marriage and Divorce 53-54 (1959). The argument was that the public health educational value of the premarital regulation is slight and that a piecemeal concentration on venereal disease is unsound.

> There is no question but that everyone should try to determine, before marriage, whether he is fit to marry. Do I have tuberculosis? Am I mentally sound? Are we compatible in all essential relationships? Can I make an adequate living for a family? Do I have syphilis or gonorrhea, or any other condition which would make me unsuitable for marriage? There is, however, no legal process by which the answers to these questions can be forced. People must learn to want to know whether they are fit to marry. . . .[87]

As in the case of other marriage law restrictions, evasion of the blood test requirement by migratory marriage has posed serious problems. The

[84] Wis. Sess. Laws 1913, §2339m, pp. 1607-1608.

[85] For the ineffectiveness of an earlier comparable Virginia statute, see Note, 37 Va. L. Rev. 339, 340 (1951).

[86] Note, Virginia's Pre-Marital Blood Test Act, 37 Va. L. Rev. 339, 340 (1951), cites statements such as the fact that "[a] mother with untreated syphilis will bear a dead or diseased baby five times out of six, whereas, if treatment is begun before the fifth month of pregnancy, ten out of eleven children will be born with no harmful effects."

[87] Why Is a Pre-Marital Blood Test Law Unsound Legislation?, 24 Baltimore Health News 131 (Baltimore City Health Dept., May, 1947), as quoted in Jacobson, American Marriage and Divorce 53 (1959).

spread of the legislation now makes such evasion impracticable in many parts of the country.

ERTEL v. ERTEL
313 Ill. App. 326, 40 N.E.2d 85 (1942)

RIESS, J. A suit in chancery was filed in the circuit court of Adams county by D. L. McNeall, conservator of Elmer Ertel, to annul a marriage which had been entered into at Palmyra, Missouri, on October 3, 1940, between the allegedly feeble-minded ward, Elmer Ertel, and the defendant appellee, Inez Casley. Trial was had before the court, and upon submission of certain questions of fact to a jury, there followed a verdict and decree finding that Elmer Ertel at the time of such marriage had "sufficient understanding to know the nature of the contract of marriage and the duties and responsibilities which it created," and the complaint was dismissed for want of equity. From such decree, the conservator has appealed to this court. . . .

The principal and controlling assignment of error discussed in the respective briefs of the plaintiff conservator on the one hand and of the guardian ad litem and appellee on the other concerns the construction and application of a Missouri statute . . . in effect at the time of the marriage, which provides in part as follows: "All marriages — between persons either of whom is insane, mentally imbecile, feeble-minded or epileptic, are prohibited and declared absolutely void." . . .

The medical testimony included that of the managing officer of the Lincoln State School and Colony, who testified concerning Ertel's mental capacity, habits and ability to work and stated that in his opinion, Ertel was not insane but was graded as a high class mental defective.

Certain allegedly eccentric conduct of Ertel in childhood was detailed by some witnesses, among them being an incident wherein certain school children had ridiculed Ertel, resulting in resentment and a fight between him and another boy or boys. The incident is construed in opposite ways by different witnesses. The testimony by his school teachers and some of the students tended to show that he was unable to entirely carry on the required school work; that he had been unable to satisfactorily accomplish the course of study required of average children to advance beyond the fifth grade. . . .

On his behalf, it was shown that he had raised and marketed certain small crops in a satisfactory manner while on the farm with his late father; that he drove an automobile for a number of years and worked as a farm hand in the neighborhood in a satisfactory manner to a number of his employers; that at the time of his marriage he was aged thirty-two years and that his wife was a widow with two children; that he had inherited an interest in lands and some personal assets from his father and subsequent to his marriage, had acquired the interest of a sister in the 120-acre farm upon which he and his wife now reside. From the mass of testimony offered by respective parties, the jury arrived at its affirmative answer to the written interrogatory submitted as hereinabove indicated.

It is conceded by the respective parties that the validity of the marriage depends upon the provisions of the Missouri statutes and that a construction thereof by the Courts of Review of Missouri, the place of the contract, is relevant herein. . . .

While the parties to a marriage contract must have sufficient mental capacity to enter into the status, and proof of feeble-mindedness will render such contract void under the provisions of the Missouri statute [citations omitted], such proof of lack of mental capacity must be clear and definite. Slais v. Slais, 9 Mo. App. 96. It was held to be sufficient in Illinois if the contracting party has sufficient mental capacity to "understand intelligently the marriage contract into which he entered and the obligations which it imposed upon him." Hagenson v. Hagenson [258 Ill. 197, 201-202, 101 N.E. 606, 608 (1913)]. A mere weakness of intellect is not deemed sufficient to invalidate a marriage if the parties are capable of comprehending and understanding the subject of the contract, its nature and probable consequences. [Citations omitted.]

[The court then dealt with the allegation that it was error to refuse to admit in evidence the adjudication of another court on October 22, 1940, that Ertel was a feeble-minded person. It held that this] collateral finding in the county court as to his mental status or alleged feeble-mindedness was neither competent nor controlling. . . .

In Illinois, less mental capacity is required to enable a person to enter into the marriage contract than is required for the execution of ordinary business transactions. [Citations omitted.] There was testimony before the court and in the record tending to establish that Ertel was capable of transacting and did engage in numerous ordinary business transactions and did perform work and labor in an acceptable manner to his employers.

It is a matter of common knowledge that many married men or women continue in a satisfactory marital status although they may not possess high grade mentality or be successful in the conduct of business ventures and that many of them are acting with the aid of conservators. . . .

A question was asked Dr. Graff, managing officer of the Lincoln School, to which objection was sustained and concerning which plaintiff complains, as follows: "State whether or not in the case of a mental defective such as you found Elmer Ertel to be, whether it is probable or improbable that any child he might have by this marriage would be mentally defective?" The court properly sustained objection thereto and committed no error therein. The issue was one of the validity of a contract entered into pursuant to certain statutory provisions, and this question was not material or relevant to the issues herein.

We find no reversible error in the record and are in accord with the holding of the learned trial court upon both the facts and his construction of the law in all material matters in issue, and the decree of the circuit court of Adams county will therefore be affirmed.

Decree affirmed.

NOTE

1. Would the judges who decided the F.A. case (page 247 supra) have decided Ertel as the Illinois court did? If there are two standards of capacity — one where the issue is premarital permission as in F.A., and another where the issue is postmarital annulment as in Ertel — which standard should be more "rigorous"?

2. The Pennsylvania statute construed in the F.A. case also included restrictions on the marriages of epileptics; these have since been eliminated, Pa. Laws 1957, No. 201, §1, p. 378. See also other recent repeals of comparable restrictions, e.g., Ind. Acts 1957, c. 83, §1, p. 143; N.H. Laws 1959, c. 99, §1, p. 109; Ore. Laws 1959, c. 377, §1, p. 578.

The harsh provisions against epileptic marriages, including some severe criminal sanctions, which formerly were common and which still persist in some states, are reviewed by Fabing & Barrow, Medical Discovery as a Legal Catalyst: Modernization of Epilepsy Laws to Reflect Medical Progress, 50 Nw. U.L. Rev. 42 (1955). See also Fabing & Barrow, Epilepsy and the Law (1956); Fabing, Epilepsy and the Law, Harper's, Sept. 1960, p. 55.

In a marriage license application case prior to the change in the Pennsylvania law, E.P. Marriage License, 8 Pa. D. & C.2d 598, 601-602 (Orphans' Ct. 1957), the court summarized the problem as follows:

Epilepsy may be either acquired or idiopathic. The acquired type may be brought on by various known factors, namely, brain injury, intracranial tumors, chemical and metabolic disorder, infections of the nervous system such as encephalitis, hypertension and diabetes. Many persons, who have an acquired type of epilepsy, go through life without any overt signs of the malady. "Idiopathic" or "essential" epilepsy encompasses all other cases which may or may not be definable, viz., congenital, inheritable or epilepsy springing from no known cause; it is a "catch all" in a field of medical science which is still in the pioneer stages. The proportion of idiopathic cases decreases as knowledge of the causes of epilepsy places more cases in the acquired category.

"There is no positive answer" as to whether "epilepsy is transmissible." Many physicians are of the present opinion that epilepsy is not *inheritable,* although a predisposition to the disorder may be inherited, as a recessive trait. The tendency to convulsions among descendants of patients who have had attacks is about one in forty. The children of parents having "idiopathic" seizures are about five times as likely to have attacks as children of apparently normal parents. However, the likelihood of occurrence of grand mal in the epileptic's issue is greater, particularly where the epilepsy is idiopathic; but the modern view is that the transmissibility does not follow an exact Mendelian or genetic pattern. Consideration must also be given to the fact that "carriers" outnumber those who have exhibited seizures, by a ratio of ten to one. A marriage of two carriers may produce offspring with a greater tendency to seizures than offspring of a marriage between one person who has had seizures and one who is completely free of the malady. Yet, there is no practicable way for either the applicant for a marriage license or the issuing official to detect this latent condition.

Happily, all forms of epilepsy usually respond to modern medication. The customary treatment is a combination of barbiturates with dilantin, tridione, mesantoin or other recently developed anticonvulsants. Ordinarily where the epileptic responds to one of these drugs, there is likelihood that other of the drugs will be efficacious when a tolerance develops to the first drug. However, there are certain cases of epilepsy which do not respond to these drugs. In such cases, eventual brain deterioration is common, and the prognosis is guarded at best. By use of anticonvulsants, over 50 percent of those subject to seizure gain complete control, while another 30 percent have fewer seizures. Still others respond to surgery. Therefore, the group which does not respond to any treatment is small, and epilepsy remains a disabling disorder in less than 20 percent of cases.

3. A variety of legislative restrictions have been devised to control the marriages of persons with mental or emotional disorders. A recent survey reports that in nine states "mentally disabled persons are permitted to marry when sterilization has been performed or when the woman is over forty-five years of age." The Mentally Disabled and the Law 198 (Lindman & McIntyre eds. 1961). The Minnesota Probate Code provides that the Commissioner of Public Welfare can be made the personal guardian of any person who is "so mentally defective as to require supervision, control, or care for his own or the public welfare." Minn. Stat. Ann. §525.749(6) (Supp. 1964). Feeble-minded wards of the Commissioner cannot marry without their guardian's consent. The Commissioner's discretion is broad; he may grant consent "if it appears from his investigation that such marriage is for the best interest of the ward and the public." Minn. Stat. Ann. §517.03 (Supp. 1964).[88] No ward has contested the Commissioner's exercise of discretion. The Commissioner is authorized to approve sterilization of any institutionalized ward if his nearest kin consents. If no near relative can be found, "the commissioner . . . , as the legal guardian of such feebleminded person, may give his consent." Minn. Stat. Ann. §256.07 (1959). An institutionalized ward who wants to marry could be required to exchange his agreement to sterilization for the Commissioner's consent to the marriage. Moreover, since the Probate Code provides no judicial review of the Commissioner's decision to institutionalize a feeble-minded ward, a ward who wants to marry could easily

---

[88] Of course, the requirement of consent is easily evaded if the licensing clerk makes no investigation of the applicants or of the state registry of feeble-minded wards. As is the case with other premarital regulations, many wards have obtained licenses despite the regulatory provision. In addition, couples can easily travel to another state and marry. See pages 263-265 infra. Once a ward is married, the absence of the Commissioner's consent is no guarantee that the marriage can be annulled. See Ertel v. Ertel, page 255 supra.

be required to consent to sterilization simply to purchase his release from an institution.[89]

b. COMPULSORY STERILIZATION

It seems clear that marital prohibitions aimed at the mentally or emotionally disabled were designed, at least in part, to promote eugenic goals.[90] Compulsory sterilization statutes, which became popular in the late 1920's, expressed similar values. A brief examination of these statutes may be instructive. Although accurate figures cannot be obtained, the total number of sterilizations under state sterilization statutes has been reported as 63,678; 33,374 of these were performed upon the mentally deficient, 27,917 upon the mentally ill, and 2387 upon "others," e.g., epileptics.[91] Use of the legislation appears to be falling off markedly in many states; California has reported over 20,000 sterilizations since the enactment of its statute in 1909, but for 1962 there were only 26, and for 1963 only 17. See Sterilizations Performed in the United States through December 31, 1963 (Human Betterment Assn., N.Y., Feb. 1964).

The ultimate question posed by the materials which follow is whether compulsory sterilization legislation is scientifically and socially justifiable. The answer to this question is important in several ways to sound marriage policy: should marriage restrictions be interpreted so as to provide an exception for feeble-minded persons who are sterile? Are the marriage prohibitions unconstitutional to the extent that they are premised upon scientific theories which are incapable of rational proof? Can the prohibitions be justified on noneugenic grounds?

BUCK v. BELL
274 U.S. 200 (1927)

HOLMES, J.   This is a writ of error to review a judgment of the Supreme Court of Appeals of the State of Virginia, affirming a judgment of

[89] Not too many years ago, the Commissioner often institutionalized wards when it seemed likely that a marriage was in the offing. Sterilization frequently followed. Note the following comments by the former director of Minnesota's program for the retarded: "By 1925 . . . sterilization appeared to be at least a tool for meshing the concept of decreasing some social problems by preventing procreation by the feebleminded with the newer concept that the feeble-minded capable of self-support should be in the community under supervision. . . .

". . . This [Commissioner's consent to marriage] provision was designed primarily to permit wards to establish homes when, with guidance, they could function satisfactorily, provided there were no children." Thomson, Prologue 57, 224 (1963).

[90] See page 253 supra. The Mentally Disabled and the Law 198 (Lindman & McIntyre eds. 1961): "In nine states eugenic considerations are apparently at the core of the law." The same is true of consanguinity prohibitions. Wisconsin's 1959 Family Code permits marriages "between first cousins where the female has attained the age of 55 years." Wis. Stat. Ann. §245.03 (Supp. 1965).

[91] The total may include a very small number of voluntary sterilizations where such are authorized by state sterilization statutes. See page 626 infra.

the Circuit Court of Amherst County, by which the defendant in error, the superintendent of the State Colony for Epileptics and Feeble Minded, was ordered to perform the operation of salpingectomy upon Carrie Buck, the plaintiff in error, for the purpose of making her sterile. 143 Va. 310. The case comes here upon the contention that the statute authorizing the judgment is void under the Fourteenth Amendment as denying to the plaintiff in error due process of law and the equal protection of the laws.

Carrie Buck is a feeble minded white woman who was committed to the State Colony above mentioned in due form. She is the daughter of a feeble minded mother in the same institution, and the mother of an illegitimate feeble minded child. She was eighteen years old at the time of the trial of her case in the Circuit Court, in the latter part of 1924. [The Court then described the Virginia statute under which institutionalized mental defectives can be sterilized on petition of an institutional superintendent, the statute reciting that many defectives in institutions could be discharged if sterilized and that] experience has shown that heredity plays an important part in the transmission of insanity, imbecility, &c. . . .

. . . There can be no doubt that so far as procedure is concerned the rights of the patient are most carefully considered, and as every step in this case was taken in scrupulous compliance with the statute and after months of observation, there is no doubt that in that respect the plaintiff in error has had due process of law.

The attack is not upon the procedure but upon the substantive law. It seems to be contended that in no circumstances could such an order be justified. It certainly is contended that the order cannot be justified upon the existing grounds. The judgment finds the facts that have been recited and that Carrie Buck "is the probable potential parent of socially inadequate offspring, likewise afflicted, that she may be sexually sterilized without detriment to her general health and that her welfare and that of society will be promoted by her sterilization," and thereupon makes the order. In view of the general declarations of the legislature and the specific findings of the Court, obviously we cannot say as matter of law that the grounds do not exist, and if they exist they justify the result. We have seen more than once that the public welfare may call upon the best citizens for their lives. It would be strange if it could not call upon those who already sap the strength of the State for these lesser sacrifices, often not felt to be such by those concerned, in order to prevent our being swamped with incompetence. It is better for all the world, if instead of waiting to execute degenerate offspring for crime, or to let them starve for their imbecility, society can prevent those who are manifestly unfit from continuing their kind. The principle that sustains compulsory vaccination is broad enough to cover cutting the Fallopian tubes. Jacobson v. Massachusetts, 197 U.S. 11.[92] Three generations of imbeciles are enough.

[92] How valid is this comparison? See the following construction by the Supreme Judicial Court of Massachusetts of the statute upheld in Jacobson: "If a person should deem it important that vaccination should not be performed in his case, and the authorities should think otherwise, it is not in their power

But, it is said, however it might be if this reasoning were applied gener-ally, it fails when it is confined to the small number who are in the insti-tutions named and is not applied to the multitudes outside. It is the usual last resort of constitutional arguments to point out shortcomings of this sort. But the answer is that the law does all that is needed when it does all that it can, indicates a policy, applies it to all within the lines, and seeks to bring within the lines all similarly situated so far and so fast as its means allow. Of course so far as the operations enable those who otherwise must be kept confined to be returned to the world, and thus open the asylum to others, the equality aimed at will be more nearly reached.

Judgment affirmed.

MR. JUSTICE BUTLER dissents.

NOTE

1. The Supreme Court has had one other occasion to deal with compul-sory sterilization. In Skinner v. Oklahoma ex rel. Williamson, 316 U.S. 535 (1942), the Court struck down an Oklahoma statute which provided for the sterilization of certain habitual criminals. The Court's opinion, while noting that the act was challenged as an impermissible "exercise of the police power, in view of the state of scientific authorities respecting inheritability of criminal traits" (id. at 537-538), rested on a violation of equal protection because the statute unreasonably provided for steriliza-tion of larceny offenders but did not apply to such a closely allied crime as embezzlement. In a concurring opinion (id. at 543) Chief Justice Stone found the vice of the statute in its failure to provide a habitual criminal with some opportunity to show that his criminal tendencies are not of the inheritable type. Mr. Justice Jackson concurred on both due process and equal protection grounds and also said (id. at 546-547):

> There are limits to the extent to which a legislatively represented majority may conduct biological experiments at the expense of the dignity and personality and natural powers of a minority . . . But this Act falls down before reaching this problem, which I mention only to avoid the implication that such a question may not exist be-cause not discussed. . . .

2. For a review and evaluation of the current status of compulsory ster-ilization legislation, see The Mentally Disabled and the Law 183-197 (Lindman & McIntyre eds. 1961). They report (id. at 184-185):

> In the ten years following this Supreme Court decision [Buck v. Bell], twenty states passed sterilization statutes, most of them closely resembling the Virginia law. During the last thirty years, thirty-two

---

to vaccinate him by force, and the worst that could happen to him under the statute would be the payment of the penalty of $5." Commonwealth v. Pear, 183 Mass. 242, 248, 66 N.E. 719, 722 (1903), aff'd sub nom. Jacobson v. Massa-chusetts, 197 U.S. 11 (1905). — Ed.

states and the Commonwealth of Puerto Rico have had sterilization statutes, five of which have been declared unconstitutional. The controversy over the merits of this legislation still continues. . . .

Twenty-seven states identify the class subject to sterilization as the mentally deficient, and with few exceptions the mentally ill are similarly identified as being within the scope of the statutes. Only eighteen states include epileptics in their designation of the classes of persons subject to such laws. Other classifications or groups not considered in this chapter, such as "hereditary criminals," sex offenders, and syphilitics, are also included in many of the compulsory sterilization statutes.

3. The scientific evidence for and against the use of compulsory sterilization was analyzed in Cook, Eugenics or Euthenics, 37 Ill. L. Rev. 287 (1943). He suggests that compulsory sterilization or marriage restrictions such as Oregon's (page 253 supra) will have little impact in reducing the incidence of mental deficiency. Not all feeble-mindedness is hereditary and the genetic process in those cases which are is extremely complicated. Most hereditary mental deficiency is perpetuated by normal persons who carry a recessive defective gene, so that even if all feeble-minded persons both in and out of institutions were sterilized, the reduction in the number of mental defectives in the next generation would be very small.

Concerning the appearance of a feeble-minded person before a eugenics board established under a compulsory sterilization statute or under a statute like Oregon's for reviewing marriage licenses, Cook concludes (id. at 302):

The most that present-day biological theory can say is that some of the children of the particular person under examination *may* be mentally defective; that what the probability of such a result is can not be accurately computed; but that it will be greater, to an unknown degree, if the person in question mates with another mentally defective individual. This, of course, does not of itself show that sterilization would have no effect; such a procedure if applied would reduce somewhat (but to an unpredictable amount) the production of feebleminded persons and of normal-minded persons who carry recessive genes for "feeblemindedness." It does show, however, that the "procedural" due process called for [by the courts] provides for a hearing to answer a question which biological science is not yet prepared to answer.

As to the mentally ill, The Mentally Disabled and the Law 186 (Lindman & McIntyre eds. 1961) summarizes present views as follows:

The sterilization of the mentally ill is on even more precarious scientific ground than the sterilization of the mentally deficient. Little is known of the organic pathology of the two major mental diseases, schizophrenia and manic-depressive psychosis. Since the hereditary mechanisms by which these diseases may be transmitted are unknown and the separation of environmental factors from hereditary factors is most difficult, the American Neurological Association Committee for the Investigation of Eugenical Sterilization concluded that compulsory sterilization could not be advocated.

4. The Report of the Task Force on Law of the President's Panel on Mental Retardation (1963), discussing the causes of retardation, commented (at 7-8):

> In addition, the deprivation of adequate opportunities for learning in infancy and early childhood, and severe emotional disturbances and psychotic disorders which may interfere with learning, are factors which are known to create or accentuate mental retardation.
>
> The prognosis for a mentally retarded person and the indicated direction for treatment . . . are as dependent upon the underlying mechanisms responsible for the mental retardation as upon the present level of functioning of the retarded person. It is worth emphasizing, too, that . . . the greatest number of mentally retarded are persons in whom no [central nervous system] pathology has been identified but who suffer from poor socio-economic and socio-cultural conditions. . . .

The Task Force suggested that the "social argument" in favor of sterilization of the mentally retarded "addresses itself to the right of every child to be born to parents who can give him at least minimum opportunities, and conversely to the right of a mentally retarded adult not to be deprived of marriage when the complications of child rearing would tip the balance against him in a marginal case." Id. at 22. The Task Force did not take a position "on whether sterilization can ever be ethically justified. Our recommendations are limited to urging that the operation not be allowed to result from misjudgment as to its scientific need or from inadequate opportunity for administrative and judicial review." Id. at 23.

6. *Enforcement of Marriage Law Regulation*

The locality which has given its name to marriage law evasion is Gretna Green, a Scottish village near the English border, which became a haven for English couples after common law marriage was abolished in England in 1753. Even after Scotland introduced a three weeks' residence requirement in 1856 and in 1939 abolished common law marriage, Gretna Green retained some of its migratory marriage business because, contrary to the situation in almost all surrounding countries, in Scotland minors over the age of sixteen could be married without parental consent. See Runaway Marriages in Scotland, 74 Scot. L. Rev. 213 (1958); Anton & Francescakis, Modern Scots "Runaway Marriages," 3 Jurid. Rev. (n.s.) 253 (1958).

A list of American "Gretna Greens" for the year 1948 has been compiled by Jacobson, American Marriage and Divorce 50-51 (1959). During that year 1,811,155 marriages were contracted in the United States, a national rate of 12.4 per 1000 population. Jacobson classified as a "Gretna Green" a county with at least 1000 marriages a year where the marriage rate was at least four times greater than the national average. Heading the list were Washoe County (Reno), Nevada (with 24,511 marriages at a rate of 495 per 1000 resident population), Clark County (Las Vegas), Nevada (19,197, rate 404), Yuma County, Arizona (15,460, rate 570), and Cecil County (Elkton), Maryland (12,602, rate 378). Forty-six other counties with 7500 or fewer marriages, mostly in the South or West, also met Jacobson's standards.

Even allowing for the facts that Nevada's gambling and vacation facilities and the remarriage of persons divorced in Nevada would tend to give it more marriages than the average, it seems clear that differences in marriage laws account for most of these abnormally high rates. We have already noted that Maryland does not require a premarital examination (page 254 supra) while Nevada requires neither premarital examination nor waiting period. The requirement in both California and Arizona that divorce litigants wait one year following divorce before they can be remarried probably also contributes to the high marriage rates in Nevada and in some New Mexico counties bordering on Arizona. Jacobson reports that Arizona marriage rates plunged downward in 1956 after legislative enactment of a blood test and a two-day waiting period. Jacobson, supra, at 52. He also cites numerous instances from the period when premarital health examination laws were slowly spreading from state to state; in each instance where a particular state enacted a blood test requirement, its marriage rate declined and the rates in neighboring states without the requirement rose sharply. Id. at 46-49.

Some states have made sporadic efforts to discourage nonresident marriage business. See, e.g., the second section of the Uniform Marriage Evasion Act, page 209 supra; §107(a) of the Delaware statute (imposing a longer waiting period on nonresidents), page 195 supra; Sweigart v. State, 213 Ind. 157, 12 N.E.2d 134 (1938) (enjoining marriage license clerk from issuing licenses in violation of an Indiana statute, later repealed, limiting the issuance of licenses to the county where the female applicant resided). Maryland has attempted to control the commercial and fraudulent aspects of its Elkton traffic. E.g., Hopkins v. State, 193 Md. 489, 69 A.2d 456 (1949) (affirming conviction of minister for violation of statute prohibiting advertising to solicit marriage business); Greenwald v. State, 221 Md. 235, 155 A.2d 894 (1959) (affirming three-year prison sentence for doctor convicted of issuing fraudulent certificates of pregnancy under Maryland statute waiving requirement of parental consent where minor female is pregnant).

All the foregoing data apparently relate to attempts to evade restrictions which are relatively easy to enforce in the domiciliary state, e.g., blood tests, waiting periods, or post-divorce restrictions on remarriage. There is no data on the extent of the attempts, if any, to enforce other kinds of marriage restrictions within the domiciliary state. See, for example, the general and apparently unverified deposition required of Delaware applicants, page 197 supra (last paragraph immediately above the applicants' signatures). There are no reported prosecutions for making false statements on a license application, see §127, page 199 supra.

PROBLEM [93]

A colleague on a legislative commission of which you are a member has proposed the following statute for enactment. Do you agree with the premises in the introductory purpose clauses? If the commission accepts those premises and wishes to utilize all practicable methods to restrict marriage evasion, can you improve upon this statute? How efficacious would you predict that it could be?

Whereas the present licensing restrictions are largely ineffective; and
Whereas it is of the gravest importance to society that marriage only be entered into by those who are fit to assume its profound responsibilities and who are sensible of the seriousness of their undertaking;
Now therefore, be it enacted that after this date marriages may be validly contracted by a resident of this state only after the following procedure shall have been complied with:

1. Upon application for a marriage license, each applicant shall submit proof of date of birth and one of the following: (a) if the applicant has never before been married, a sworn affidavit to that effect; (b) if the applicant is widowed, proof of death of the former spouse; (c) if the applicant is divorced, a certified copy of any prior final judgment of divorce.
2. After application has been filed, each applicant shall be examined by a physician whose qualifications are acceptable to the marriage license clerk and who shall submit a written report of his examination to the marriage license bureau upon a form prescribed by the bureau.
3. After receipt by the bureau of the medical forms, each applicant shall be interviewed by a Marriage License Hearing Examiner. The Examiner may require further proof as to the validity of any alleged divorce and, if he has doubt as to the physical or mental fitness of an applicant, may require that the applicant be examined by a panel of physicians selected by the bureau.
4. If the Examiner is satisfied that each of the applicants meets all the prerequisites for a valid marriage set forth in our marriage law, and furthermore, that such marriage is consonant with the objectives set forth in the preamble hereto, he shall direct the issuance of the license to marry.

Any marriage entered into by residents of this state either within or

[93] Compare Bradway, The Family Watchdog, 86 U. Pa. L. Rev. 823 (1938), reprinted in Selected Essays on Family Law 230.

without this state in respect to which no license pursuant to this Act was issued shall be totally null and void, and each of the parties thereto shall be guilty of a felony, subject to imprisonment of one year or a fine of $1000, or both.

7. De Facto Families

Up to this point we have discussed two kinds of family formation. In Chapter 1 we considered the mother-and-child family which results from transitory sexual intercourse outside of any stable relationship of mother and father, and we noted some of the problems of families which are fatherless from the outset. In this chapter we have been concerned with families that have come into being through the orthodox method of a licensed, ceremonial marriage. There remains for examination a third common type of family where a man, woman, and often their children live together with at least some degree of permanence but where there has either been no attempt at a licensed ceremonial marriage or a purported ceremonial marriage was legally defective. As we examine the legal consequences of this kind of de facto family existence, it will be helpful to distinguish four variants of the situation in which parties may live together:

1. A man and a woman who have not attempted a ceremonial marriage and neither of whom is married to anyone else may live together with their children (if any), cohabiting and holding themselves out as husband and wife. Formation of such a family may come about in a wide variety of ways. At one extreme is the classic instance of common law marriage: those presumably rare couples who, out of a desire to be different, privately exchange marriage vows in words of the present tense in advance of any act of intercourse. Second, there are couples who have consciously decided to live together for a while for the fun of it, who intend to remain unencumbered by marriage but who purport to be married merely to silence the gossip which their relationship would otherwise invite. Between these extremes are the "marriages" which one would suppose would be more common than either of the foregoing. Starting out either with the meretricious intention not to be married or without any conscious intention either way about marriage, the couple become accustomed to one another and gradually become what they started out merely to purport, a family with the intention of remaining together indefinitely. The subculture to which the family belongs may be an influential factor in the method by which the relationship is created. A woman's insistence on a legally binding wedding band is doubtless much stronger in some strata of society than in others. For an extreme example of class and racial variants, see Patchett, Some Aspects of Marriage and Divorce in the West Indies, 8 Int. & Comp. L.Q. 632 (1959). He reports that mother-and-child family groups and de facto unions with some permanency but without legal status are very common and taken together

account for nearly as large a figure as the category of legal marriage. To the sociologist, how the relationship came about will be of less interest than the fact that a family now exists; to the lawyer, who may have to try to establish a common law marriage, the method and place of formation will be of critical importance.

2. A second category of informal marriage differs from the first in the critical fact that one or both of the parties is already married to someone else, so that a ceremonial marriage would be bigamous prior to the termination of the earlier marriage(s) by death or divorce. In societies where divorce is impossible or very difficult to obtain, this situation may be very common. See, e.g., Mueller, Inquiry into the State of a Divorceless Society, 18 U. Pitt. L. Rev. 545 (1957). How prevalent it is in the United States is unknown, but it is certainly not uncommon. In other countries limited legal rights may be extended to concubines, e.g., in India until 1956, see Mulla, Principles of Hindu Law 705 (12th ed. 1959).

3. A couple neither of whom has ever been married before may create a de facto family after contracting a ceremonial marriage which is either void or voidable, e.g., for nonage, consanguinity, or lack of requisite mental capacity. But even if there is a subsequent action for avoidance, there is a trend in many jurisdictions to fasten upon the parties some of the incidents of a lawful marriage, see, e.g., the Delaware statute, page 195 supra, legitimating the children.

4. A couple may set up a de facto family after going through a ceremonial marriage despite the fact that at least one of the parties is still validly married to another. This raises some of the most complicated problems for the lawyer and is undoubtedly a common category of de facto but defective marriage. Such a marriage is absolutely void and constitutes the crime of bigamy, usually even where the defendant has acted in good faith. Compare State v. De Meo, 20 N.J. 1, 118 A.2d 1 (1955) (defendant guilty even though he disclosed his invalid Mexican mail order divorce to marriage license clerk and was issued license), with Long v. State, 44 Del. 262, 65 A.2d 489 (1949) (fact that defendant was advised by an attorney that he could remarry after invalid Arkansas divorce was a defense). Here the chances of disclosure are greater than in the preceding category, where only a disgruntled spouse would raise the defect. In the void remarriage situation the state has standing to act in a bigamy prosecution and the other lawful spouse may have an incentive to act — for example, to obtain support. Yet bigamy prosecutions are extremely rare, and the statistical odds are high that the other spouse will also remarry or take on a new "common law" liaison and thus will have a comparable interest in preserving the status quo.

In many instances of void remarriage there has been no attempt to obtain a valid divorce from the prior spouse. Both Foster, Common Law Divorce, 46 Minn. L. Rev. 43 (1961), and Weyrauch, Informal and Formal Marriage — An Appraisal of Trends in Family Organization, 28 U. Chi. L. Rev. 88, 103-104 (1960), have noted the high incidence of de facto or "poor man's" divorces. In regard to divorce by desertion without court action, Weyrauch states:

Every year in the United States thousands of husbands abandon their wives, even though their marriages were formal, and a great many of them are never located again. . . . The more or less fictitious presumption that somewhere he obtained a valid divorce may be impossible to overcome. As a result of this, the poor man's divorce is frequently more effective than, let us say, a formal Nevada divorce decree. . . .

In those segments of society where social acceptability is an important consideration, the void remarriage is likely to follow even a dissolution which may be patently illegal (such as a Mexican mail order divorce) or one which is at least known from the outset to be subject to attack.

a. COMMON LAW MARRIAGE

MEISTER v. MOORE
96 U.S. 76 (1878)

[Action of ejectment. Plaintiff introduced evidence that in about 1845 one William Mowry went from Pennsylvania to Michigan and there married and lived with Mary, an Indian girl. Seven years later Mowry died intestate, survived by his mother and one child of the marriage, Elizabeth. The latter ultimately conveyed the property in issue to plaintiff. Defendant, who obtained his title from Mowry's mother, asserted that the marriage was invalid for failure to comply with the Michigan statutory requirements. The jury rendered a verdict for defendant.]

STRONG, J. The learned judge of the Circuit Court instructed the jury, that, if neither a minister nor a magistrate was present at the alleged marriage of William A. Mowry and the daughter of the Indian Pero, the marriage was invalid under the Michigan statute; and this instruction is now alleged to have been erroneous. It certainly withdrew from the consideration of the jury all evidence, if any there was, of informal marriage by contract per verba de praesenti. That such a contract constitutes a marriage at common law there can be no doubt, in view of the adjudications made in this country, from its earliest settlement to the present day. Marriage is everywhere regarded as a civil contract. Statutes in many of the States, it is true, regulate the mode of entering into the contract, but they do not confer the right. Hence they are not within the principle, that, where a statute creates a right and provides a remedy for its enforcement, the remedy is exclusive. No doubt, a statute may take away a common-law right; but there is always a presumption that the legislature has no such intention, unless it be plainly expressed. A statute may declare that no marriages shall be valid unless they are solemnized in a prescribed manner; but such an enactment is a very different thing from a law requiring all marriages to be entered into in the presence of a magistrate or a clergyman, or that it be preceded by a license, or publication of banns, or be attested by witnesses. Such formal provisions may be construed as merely directory, instead of being treated as destructive of a common-law right to form the marriage relation by words of present assent. . . . In most cases, the leading purpose is to secure a registration of marriages, and evidence by which marriages may be proved; for example, by certificate of a clergyman or magistrate, or by an exemplification of the registry. In a small number of the States, it must be admitted, such statutes have been construed as denying validity to marriages not formed according to the statutory directions. . . .

As before remarked, the statutes are held merely directory; because marriage is a thing of common right, because it is the policy of the State to encourage it, and because, as has sometimes been said, any other construction would compel holding illegitimate the offspring of many parents conscious of no violation of law.

The Michigan statute differs in no essential particular from those of other States which have generally been so construed. It does not declare marriages void which have not been entered into in the presence of a minister or a magistrate. It does not deny validity to marriages which are good at common law. The most that can be said of it is, that it contains implications of an intention that all marriages, except some particularly mentioned, should be celebrated in the manner prescribed. . . .

It is unnecessary, however, to pursue this line of thought. If there has been a construction given to the statute by the Supreme Court of Michigan, that construction must, in this case, be controlling with us. And we think the meaning and effect of the statute has been declared by that court in the case of Hutchins v. Kimmell (31 Mich. 126), a case decided on the 13th of January, 1875. There, it is true, the direct question was, whether a marriage had been effected in a foreign country. But, in considering it, the court found it necessary to declare what the law of the State was; and it was thus stated by Cooley, J.: ". . . Whatever the form of ceremony, or even if all ceremony was dispensed with, if the parties agreed presently to take each other for husband and wife, and from that time lived together professedly in that relation, proof of these facts would be sufficient to constitute proof of a marriage binding upon the parties, and which would subject them and others to legal penalties for a disregard of its obligations. This has become the settled doctrine of the American courts: the few cases of dissent, or apparent dissent, being borne down by the great weight of authority in favor of the rule as we have stated it"; citing a large number of authorities, and concluding, "such being the law of this State." [Court's quotation abbreviated by Eds.] We cannot regard this as mere obiter dicta. It is rather an authoritative declaration of what is the law of the State, notwithstanding the statute regulating marriages. And if the law in 1875, it must have been the law in 1845, when, it is claimed, Mowry and the Indian girl were married; for it is not claimed that any change of the law was made between the time when the statute was enacted and 1875. . . .

Judgment reversed, and new trial ordered.

NOTE

1. Suppose that the statute to be construed by the Court in Meister v. Moore had been Section 126 of the Delaware statute, pages 198-199 supra. Would the result have been different? Compare Wilmington Trust Co. v. Hendrixson, 31 Del. 303, 114 Atl. 215 (1921).

2. Would the introduction into the marriage laws of most states in the last thirty years of compulsory blood testing warrant a changed interpretation from that enunciated in Meister v. Moore, in which the Court found that usually "the leading purpose" of marriage legislation was "to secure a registration of marriages"? See Fisher v. Sweet & McClain, 154 Pa. Super. 216, 226, 35 A.2d 756, 760 (1944), where shortly after the passage of Pennsylvania's blood test act the court reasoned that "the legislature never intended that such an important hygienic statute could be circumvented by the simple device of the parties entering into an informal marriage contract in verba de praesenti" and announced that "a valid common-law marriage cannot *hereafter* be entered into in this Commonwealth without first complying with the Act of 1939 and securing a marriage license."   In view of the fact that that Act also stated that "Nothing herein contained shall be construed to change the existing law with regard to common law marriage," Pa. Stat. Ann. tit. 48, §1-23 (Supp. 1964), this was a remarkable holding, and it was repudiated three years later in Buradus v. General Cement Products Co., 159 Pa. Super. 501, 48 A.2d 883 (1946).

3. As Meister v. Moore indicates, most American states in the nineteenth century preserved common law marriage despite its abolition in England in the previous century, but the number of states in which such marriages remain valid has been declining. A useful summary of current statutory and case law will be found in Common Law Marriage — A Bibliography, 6 Prac. Law., Jan. 1960, p. 87; only about fifteen jurisdictions continue to recognize common law marriages.[94] In the course of the past forty years, almost a dozen states have abolished it. Compare Koegel, Common Law Marriage 164-166 (1922). But in light of the nomadic tendencies of the American people and the fact that under the usual conflicts rules a common law marriage valid where contracted is valid everywhere, lawyers in abolition states are not likely to be altogether rid of the institution.

4. The history of common law marriage is useful in untangling the confusion which now surrounds the subject. Maitland, Magistri Vacarii Summa de Matrimonio, 13 L.Q. Rev. 133, 135-136 (1897), traces the legal rules which continue to govern its operation back to the medieval church:

> Gratian (circ. 1139-42) made a determined endeavour to obtain a consistent theory out of the materials that he collected. He holds that the sponsalia, the agreement to marry hereafter, constitute an

---

[94] In a few other states at least some forms of common law marriages may be valid for some purposes. See pages 289, 294 infra.

"initiate marriage," which however only becomes a "consummate marriage" at the moment of physical intercourse. Were we to translate his doctrine into modern terms, we should say that really there is no marriage until such intercourse has taken place, though from this principle he would not draw all the inferences that would be drawn from it by modern law. About the same time Peter Lombard was developing a new distinction, the famous distinction between sponsalia de futuro and sponsalia de praesenti. Espousals by words of present time, which are contracted if man and woman express their agreement to be from henceforth husband and wife, constitute a perfect marriage, though the copula carnalis is necessary to introduce into the union the sacrament of Christ and His Church. On the other hand, espousals by words of future time are no marriage; they are but an agreement that there shall be a marriage hereafter.

Thenceforth there were two main theories before the world. . . . [Pope Alexander III] went over to Peter's side, and in the course of his long pontificate settled the law of the Church by a series of decisions that were promulgated in decretal letters. . . .

One of the decretals of Pope Alexander III to which reference is made is quoted in 2 Pollock & Maitland at 371 and summarizes the doctrine as it has continued in American law to this day:

"We understand from your letter that a certain man and woman at the command of their lord mutually received each other, no priest being present, and no such ceremony being performed as the English church is wont to employ, and then that before any physical union, another man solemnly married the said woman and knew her. We answer that if the first man and the woman received each other by mutual consent directed to time present, saying the one to the other, 'I receive you as mine (meum),' and 'I receive you as mine (meam),' then, albeit there was no such ceremony as aforesaid, and albeit there was no carnal knowledge, the woman ought to be restored to the first man, for after such a consent she could not and ought not to marry another. . . ."

Pollock and Maitland comment (id. at 368-369):

The scheme at which they thus arrived was certainly no masterpiece of human wisdom. Of all people in the world lovers are the least likely to distinguish precisely between the present and the future tenses. In the middle ages marriages, or what looked like marriages, were exceedingly insecure. The union which had existed for many years between man and woman might with fatal ease be proved adulterous, and there would be hard swearing on both sides about "I will" and "I do." . . .

The Catholic Church, of course, went on from this position at the twenty-fourth session of the Council of Trent in 1563, thereafter requiring that a marriage be solemnized in the presence of a priest before witnesses, and a normal rule in Catholic countries is that informal marriages are not valid. But by the time of the Council, England was in the middle of the Reformation and the English common law marriage was not invalidated until Lord Hardwicke's Act of 1753, 26 Geo. 2, c. 33.

In the present century American critics of common law marriage have frequently reasoned that, e.g., "with the ready means of transportation everywhere available, common-law marriage may be an anachronism in the present day — born as it was of the exigencies of pioneer life." Buradus v. General Cement Products Co., 159 Pa. Super. 501, 504, 48 A.2d 883, 885 (1946). However, what was probably the first and certainly the most influential early American case involved parties resident in New York City. See Fenton v. Reed, 4 Johns. R. 52 (N.Y. 1809), whose per curiam opinion may well have been written by the court's famous Chief Justice, Chancellor Kent. Plaintiff claimed a pension as the widow of her second husband, Reed, whom she had married in 1792 after the disappearance and reputed death of her first husband, Guest. She continued to live with Reed after Guest reappeared later that year. Guest died in 1800 and Reed in 1806. The court found that the 1792 marriage was void but that there was a common law marriage after the first husband's death in 1800. The English cases upon which the court relied in finding a valid common law marriage may have been misconstrued, see Kirkpatrick, Common-Law Marriages: Their Common Law Basis and Present Need, 6 St. Louis U.L.J. 30, 32-34 (1960), who suggests that Kent "constructed the opinion of his own preconceptions." Id. at 34.

PROBLEM CASE

You are a judge on a three-judge court sitting en banc before which the following case, Estate of George, has been tried without a jury. Your brothers Contract and Status have agreed on a common statement of facts and issues, but are in disagreement on the law. Your vote will therefore determine the court's decision. With which opinion do you concur? How would you want to change this opinion? Why?

1. JOINT STATEMENT OF FACTS AND ISSUES

This is an action by Annie to take a widow's intestate share against the will of George. George's will, which was admitted in evidence over objection, left most of his property to two sisters, but included a modest bequest to his son and a provision for Annie in these terms: "To Mrs. Annie Myerson, my housekeeper, $2000 for services rendered." The only issue is whether George and Annie were ever lawfully married.

Twenty-two years ago in Delaware, Annie, then age thirty-four, met George Hapstrum, then age forty-five, and after a time George came to live in Annie's house, ostensibly as a roomer. Annie was married at the time, but her husband, Myerson, was in the merchant marine and was away from home for long periods of time. After two months Annie and George moved out and took an apartment in the name of Mr. and Mrs. George Hapstrum. Soon thereafter she was served with divorce papers, about which she did nothing. A year after they had started cohabiting, she and George were married in Delaware, obtaining a license on Annie's assertion that she had never previously been married. Two years thereafter Annie gave birth to a son, she and George moved to Pennsylvania where they lived for a year, and for the last eighteen years they have been domiciled in this state.

It is conceded that Myerson's divorce from Annie did not become final until two months after the date of her ceremonial marriage to George in Delaware, and that neither George nor Annie took any steps to ascertain the status of the divorce action before they married. That marriage is therefore bigamous and void. As neither this state nor Delaware recognizes common law marriage, the case turns on whether or not there was a common law marriage during the year in which they were domiciled in Pennsylvania.

The principal witness against Annie's claim was the lawyer who drew George's will four years before his death. Over objection he testified that George told him that he was unmarried; that "Mrs. Myerson" was his housekeeper; that, although he had gone through a marriage ceremony with her and had had a son by her whom he recognized, the marriage was invalid because she was then married to someone else; and that he had never subsequently married her.

Annie produced abundant evidence that, not only in Pennsylvania but ever since they moved from Myerson's house, she and George cohabited, held themselves out as husband and wife, and had the general reputation of husband and wife. In addition, Annie took the stand and testified to the following event:

Q. What happened after you moved to Pennsylvania?

A. Well, just after we settled in Philadelphia, George came home one night all upset. He said he saw Myerson, and Myerson told him my divorce wasn't good until after we'd been married, and that we weren't married.

Q. Then what did he say?

A. He said, "We can get married right now. We don't need another ceremony."

Q. What did you do then?

A. He said, "I, George, take you, Annie, as my lawful wedded wife."

Q. What did you reply?

A. I said the same thing, "I take you, George, as my lawful wedded husband."

On cross examination, Annie could not precisely date this occurrence and admitted it might have taken place just before they moved from Delaware, although she thought it was just after they arrived in Pennsylvania. She was also asked the following:

Q. At that time had you ever heard of common law marriage?

A. No.

Q. Your lawyer told you about it?

A. Yes.

Q. He explained it all to you before this hearing?

A. Yes.

Q. Tell us again exactly what was said that night, after George told you you weren't lawfully married.

A. Well, we agreed we were man and wife.

Q. But what was said?

A. He said, "I will take you for my lawful wedded wife because we're not validly married," and I said, "Well, if that's the way it is, you are my husband always."

2. OPINION OF JUDGE CONTRACT

Unlike either this state or Delaware, Pennsylvania recognizes informal marriages contracted without license or ceremony, provided there was an agreement to marry in words of the present tense between persons with capacity to marry. E.g., Blecher Estate, 381 Pa. 138, 112 A.2d 129 (1955). If a common law marriage was entered into in Pennsylvania which would be lawful in that commonwealth, it would generally be accorded recognition elsewhere, although there are holdings the other way. See Taintor, Marriage in the Conflict of Laws, 9 Vand. L. Rev. 607, 609-610 (1956), and cases cited therein. In a case such as this, where a relatively brief sojourn in a common law marriage jurisdiction is claimed to give rise to a common law marriage, particularly careful scrutiny of the evidence is indicated.

Pennsylvania has long applied the common presumption of marriage from proof of cohabitation and reputation. Richard v. Brehm, 73 Pa. 140 (1873). Were no other evidence available, common sense would dictate the inference that a couple so generally believed to be married as was true in this case were in fact married, for the law presumes morality. But the Supreme Court of Pennsylvania has emphasized that: "Cohabitation and reputation are not marriage; they are but circumstances from which marriage may be presumed, but such presumption may always be rebutted and will wholly disappear in the face of proof that no marriage in fact had taken place." Bisbing's Estate, 266 Pa. 529, 531, 109 Atl. 670, 671 (1920). The presumption is inapplicable in this case for two reasons.

First, it is conceded that the relationship of George and Annie was illicit during the first year in which they were holding themselves out as husband and wife. In Pennsylvania as in other common law jurisdictions a relationship meretricious in inception is presumed to continue to be meretricious, Pierce v. Pierce, 355 Pa. 175, 179, 49 A.2d 346, 348 (1946), and there must be "clear and convincing evidence" that the transformation from illicit to licit actually took place, Commonwealth ex rel. Drebot v. Drebot, 199 Pa. Super. 439, 441, 185 A.2d 617, 618 (1962). Second, the claimant here testified to an actual alleged contract and her case must stand or fall on that testimony. If the contract evidence shows an actual marriage, "resort to proof by habit and reputation is not necessary; it is mere cumulation," McGrath's Estate, 319 Pa. 309, 315, 179 Atl. 599, 602 (1935), whereas if claimant's testimony itself proves that no valid contract was entered into, "evidence as to cohabitation and reputation is worthless." Nikitka's Estate, 346 Pa. 63, 65, 29 A.2d 521, 522 (1943). In this last case the court rejected a claim of marriage based on cohabitation and reputation because the claimant, attempting to take an intestate share, "was available to testify to the precise form of the alleged marriage contract between her and the decedent but this she did not do, from which it may properly be assumed that no contract was in fact entered into." Ibid. (alternative holding).

As concerns the alleged contract, claimant's evidence is unsatisfactory and is far removed from that "clear and convincing" proof required to rebut the presumption of meretriciousness. Her testimony on direct examination is unworthy of belief, for the unexpected precision of this verbal exchange is an instance of the "disgusting spectacle," referred to by a Pennsylvania Bar Association committee, in which "people hardly able to enunciate their own names clearly, and quite unable to make themselves understood on simple propositions . . . testify to the common law marriage status in the pure language used by our appellate courts." Report of Special Committee on Workmen's Compensation, Pa. B. Assn. Q. No. 20, pp. 93, 98 (1934). If the alleged conversation ever took place, which we doubt, it was probably in some such terms as those elicited on cross examination. Such a garbled mixture of the mere conclusions of the witness ("we agreed we were man and wife"), a promise to marry in the future ("I will take you . . ."), and a reference to the past void contract ("you are my husband always") is insufficient to show a present intent to marry at that moment. Finally, it is far from clear that this event took place in Pennsylvania at all; if it occurred in Delaware, it is of no avail to claimant. Even if the evidence is viewed favorably to her, it is evident that claimant has failed to sustain her heavy burden of proof.

In Baker v. Mitchell, 143 Pa. Super. 50, 54, 17 A.2d 738, 741 (1941), a case in which language at least as persuasive as that exchanged here was held not to constitute a common law marriage, the Pennsylvania Superior Court stated:

> The law of Pennsylvania *recognizes* common law marriages. But they are a fruitful source of perjury and fraud, and, in consequence, they are to be *tolerated, not encouraged;* the professed contract should be examined with great scrutiny, and it should plainly appear that there was an actual agreement entered into, then and there, to form the legal relation of husband and wife [citation omitted].

This language has been approved as recently as Collings Estate, 405 Pa. 280, 281-282, 175 A.2d 62, 63 (1961). We are convinced under Pennsylvania law that no common law marriage is established by these facts, and accordingly Annie's claim must fail.

3. OPINION OF JUDGE STATUS

The presumption of marriage from proof of cohabitation and reputation is familiar enough, and in this case that proof is legally undisputed over a period of many years. The evidence to the contrary provided by the will and the testimony of the lawyer who drafted it will be entirely disregarded because both are clearly self-serving declarations and therefore inadmissible. For a strong holding that the rule against admissibility of such declarations will not be relaxed in common law marriage cases lest one be enabled "to cast [marriage] obligations and duties aside at will" and impose the stigma of illegitimacy, see Horton Estate, 357 Pa. 30, 38, 52 A.2d 895, 899 (1947). Furthermore, in a case like this where a claim is made against a dead man's estate, evidence of cohabitation and reputation will normally be the only kind of evidence available, for as the Pennsylvania Supreme Court observed in Wagner Estate, 398 Pa. 531, 536, 159 A.2d 495, 498 (1960):

> In the instant case the decedent is dead and the claimant's lips are sealed by the Dead Man's Act, May 23, 1887, P.L. 158, 35(e), 28 PS §322. To deny the status of marriage, let alone a remarriage, because words in the present tense cannot be proved, would be a clear injustice. . . .

As this state has an identical Dead Man's Act, Annie could not have testified to her conversations with decedent over objection and could not have been forced to testify concerning them. For reasons best known to himself, however, counsel chose to open the subject; there was no objection and the contract evidence is therefore properly before us. In our opinion it supports the inference raised by the evidence of cohabitation and reputation that the parties intended to live together as husband and wife.

In the much cited Pennsylvania case where the danger of fraud was stressed and the court dissected the language of the parties with a finely honed knife, the court had before it an alleged secret marriage about which the claimant had not even told her parents, with whom she continued to live until the alleged husband was killed a few months later. Baker v. Mitchell, 143 Pa. Super. 50, 17 A.2d 738 (1940). In such a case judicial skepticism is certainly warranted, and, despite repeated dicta that it is possible, we have found no case in recent decades which has upheld a common law marriage despite such a total absence of evidence of cohabitation and reputation. It is usually only where reputation evidence is unsatisfactory and the fact of marriage therefore suspect that we find hard lines being drawn around the language of the participants. Where, as here, the parties have lived together for nineteen years, and until the death of one of them enjoying an unblemished reputation of respectability, we are less prone to engage in semantic niceties. "Unlettered persons frequently become confused in the use of tenses," Caddy v. Johnstown Firemen's Relief Assn., 129 Pa. Super. 493, 499, 196 Atl. 590, 592 (1938), and language used by the parties is to be "[t]aken as a whole" to see if it meant "that the parties intended to live with each other as man and wife until death did them part." Rager v. Johnstown Traction Co., 184 Pa. Super. 474, 480, 134 A.2d 918, 922 (1957). Both these cases found a common law marriage despite ambiguous language that did not comport with Oxford usage; in Rager the decedent merely said, "Come and live with me and make a home" and "Between the eyes of God we are husband and wife," (184 Pa. Super. at 478, 479, 134 A.2d at 921) and the wife's only assent was the fact that she accepted his invitation. It is significant that in both these cases there was ample evidence of cohabitation and reputation extending over many years.

That it is uncertain whether the agreement was made in Delaware or Pennsylvania is not controlling so long as cohabitation and reputation in Pennsylvania in the light of all the circumstances show an intent to be man and wife at that time. We think that Travers v. Reinhardt, 205 U.S. 423 (1907), applying New Jersey law at a time when that state allowed common law marriage, states the proper rule. The initial ceremonial marriage in Travers was invalid because of a formal defect, the parties lived for eighteen years in states which did not recognize common law marriage, and they moved to New Jersey less than a year before Travers's death. There was no evidence of any contract in New Jersey, but the Court said (id. at 440):

> Their conduct towards each other in the eye of the public, while in New Jersey, taken in connection with their previous association, was equivalent, in law, to a declaration by each that they did and during their joint lives were to occupy the relation of husband and wife. Such a declaration was as effective to establish the status of marriage in New Jersey as if it had been made in words of the present tense after they became domiciled in that State.

We are not impressed with the technically contractual dissent of Mr. Justice Holmes, who reasoned (id. at 442, 443-444) that there must be proof of a contract in New Jersey:

> To live in New Jersey and think you are married does not constitute a marriage by the law of that State. . . . When a void contract is acted upon, the remedy, when there is one, is not on the contract, but upon a quasi-contract, for a quantum meruit. There is no such alternative when a marriage fails.

Compare In re Foster, 77 Idaho 26, 32, 287 P.2d 282, 285 (1955):

> [Even if] the marriage was consented to and consummated in the state of Washington [whose law holding common law marriage invalid was not proved in the case], consent is a continuing thing, and it follows that the parties also consented to and consummated the marriage in Idaho upon their return. [Citation omitted.]

We come finally to the question of whether the admittedly meretricious inception of this relationship is to deny Annie a widow's share after twenty years of faithful performance of the role of a wife. Abstract analysis of presumptions is of little help where, as here, the proof of cohabitation and reputation raises a presumption of marriage, and proof of meretricious inception raises the presumption of no marriage. We see little value in trying to determine whether the first presumption, because "one of the strongest presumptions known to the law," Hynes v. McDermott, 91 N.Y. 451, 459 (1883), should be accorded the greater weight. Even if all presumptions are disregarded, the most reasonable factual inference from the totality of these facts is one of a continuing intent to be married.

In Wagner Estate, 398 Pa. 531, 159 A.2d 495 (1960), a couple who had been divorced went on a second honeymoon two years later without formal remarriage and lived together for ten more years before separating a second time. There was ample evidence of holding out and reputation, but the lower court found against the common law remarriage because the reputation might have stemmed from the first marriage. Reversing, the Supreme Court said (398 Pa. at 533-534, 159 A.2d at 497):

> In such case [of alleged common law remarriage] we think that the law's role of mere toleration of the common law relationship should be reversed and the status of remarriage favored, even if acquired with common law informality. If the law allows a spouse . . . to establish by divorce that the marriage was a mistake, it should be at least equally eager to let both spouses discover that their divorce was also a mistake. We regard it better to encourage remarriage than to leave such parties under judicial edict that they were living sinfully together for ten years. If children had been born of this relationship, the wisdom of regularizing it if possible would be all the more apparent.

Here the evidence is convincing that Annie and George attempted to rectify their earlier meretricious mistake. Their marriage in Delaware, while void in legal effect, is relevant in showing their intent to change their status, and the evidence of the ensuing years demonstrates that in fact they had transformed concubinage into wedlock. We think that Pennsylvania, in the liberal spirit of Wagner Estate, would see in this relationship "the wisdom of regularizing it if possible." We find that a valid common law marriage was created in Pennsylvania.

NOTE

Consider also whether the result or any of the legal problems or policies involved would be affected if, instead of an action to take against a will, this was:

a. an action by Annie for workmen's compensation benefits after George had been killed in the course of his employment;

b. an action by Annie two years after George had deserted her in which she sought a divorce and alimony and George's defense was no marriage;

c. a prosecution of George by the state for bigamy, charging that two years ago he had left Annie and contracted a licensed, ceremonial marriage with another woman without first obtaining a divorce from Annie.

b. OTHER CURATIVE DEVICES FOR DEFECTIVE MARRIAGE

TATUM v. TATUM
241 F.2d 401 (9th Cir. 1957)

BARNES, J. Appellant appeals from a judgment entered by the District Court, sitting without a jury, disallowing her claim to the proceeds of a policy of life insurance issued to and upon the life of Erwin . . . Tatum under the provisions of the Federal Employees Group Life Insurance Act, and awarding the proceeds thereof to appellees, the decedent's three surviving children by his first marriage.

This action was originally brought against the United States of America and the Metropolitan Life Insurance Company, the insurer. Metropolitan counterclaimed interpleading appellees as defendants. The United States was later dismissed as a party.

On August 29, 1954, group life insurance policy No. 17000-G was issued to the United States Civil Service Commission covering certain Federal employees including the decedent, a postal clerk, Erwin Tatum [who] was insured in the amount of $4000 upon his life with double indemnity coverage in the event of accidental death. He died by accidental means on December 7, 1954.

The enabling statute and the group policy provide that:

"Any amount of group life insurance and group accidental death insurance in force on any employee at the date of his death shall be paid, upon the establishment of a valid claim therefor, to the person or persons surviving at the date of his death, in the following order of precedence:

"First, to the beneficiary or beneficiaries as the employee may have designated by a writing received in the employing office prior to death;

"Second, if there be no such beneficiary, to the widow or widower of such employee;

"Third, if none of the above, to the child or children of such employee and descendants of deceased children by representation." 5 U.S.C.A. §2093.

The decedent did not designate a beneficiary. Appellant claims the proceeds as the widow. The sole issue before the trial court and on appeal is whether appellant is Erwin Tatum's widow. . . .

[Decedent Erwin Tatum and Mattie Tatum, appellees' mother, were married in Texas in 1927, had four children, and separated in 1935. On May 19, 1943, while serving in the Army, Erwin married appellant in Arizona. Both before and after this marriage Mattie received Army allotments as Erwin's wife, and appellant's application for allotments was denied on the ground that she had not proved dissolution of the prior marriage. After Erwin's discharge in 1945 he cohabited with appellant until 1948, briefly resumed marital relations with Mattie in that year, and from later in 1948 until his death cohabited with appellant, all in California. Mattie obtained an interlocutory default divorce decree in 1948 and a final decree in 1949.]

On various occasions between 1949 and 1954, the decedent and appellant made trips together to Texas where Erwin unsuccessfully sought employment in the postal service. These sojourns were combined business and vacation trips and were all of short duration. No stay extended beyond one month and neither Erwin or appellant relinquished their California jobs. Appellant readily concedes that no domicile was established in Texas on any of these journeys.

The trial court found that at the time of the ceremonial marriage in 1943, Erwin's first marriage was subsisting and undissolved. Since this impediment rendered Erwin's second marriage bigamous and hence void, the court concluded that appellant could not claim the insurance proceeds as the ceremonial wife of the decedent. The court further found that Erwin and appellant did not enter into any agreement to be husband and wife during their brief stays in Texas, and therefore appellant was not entitled to the proceeds under an asserted common-law marriage. The court also held that appellant was not a putative spouse. . . .

We must first consider what meaning should be given the word "widow" as used in this Act, and what law should be looked to in determining whether plaintiff is the widow.

The word "widow" is not defined in the statute, and we have found neither judicial nor administrative construction of it. However, it has been interpreted frequently, under the analogous National Service Life Insurance Act, 38 U.S.C.A. §802(g), to mean lawful widow. The court below so construed the instant statute. We agree with that interpretation. Accordingly, appellant was required to prove that she was the lawful widow of Erwin Tatum.

The parties have assumed without discussion that the question of appellant's marital status is to be determined by the law of California. The answer is not that crystal clear. . . .

. . . One point of unanimity is that state law will govern. But there exists little agreement as to what state law is applicable. . . .

. . . Conceivably, this court could refer to the law of either Arizona, Texas, or California to determine this question. However, an analysis of the authorities in each state leads us to conclude that regardless of which law is applied, appellant cannot prevail. . . .

We turn next to a consideration of the Arizona ceremony and the presumptions arising thereunder. It is a rule of almost universal acceptance that when a person has contracted two successive marriages, a presumption arises in favor of the validity of the second marriage, and the burden is upon the party attacking the validity of the second marriage to establish existence of the first marriage, and that such marriage has not been dissolved by death, divorce or annulment at the time of the second marriage. [Citations omitted.] This presumption supersedes the presumption of subsistence that attached to the prior marriage. [Citations omitted.] It is a presumption not founded in logic but in public policy. The purpose is not only to preserve the relationship of the parties and prevent the stigmatization of offspring as illegitimate, but also to protect and strengthen the social and moral standards of the community.

However, the presumption, not being conclusive, is simply a rule of evidence, not one of law. It may be rebutted. . . . Thus the critical question on this issue is whether the evidence is sufficient to support the trial court's finding that a valid marriage existed between Erwin and

Mattie at the date of the former's ceremonial marriage to appellant Bertha.

There is ample evidence to establish at least prima facie existence of the first marriage. The duly certified marriage certificate was introduced in evidence; Mattie's testimony and Erwin's declarations corroborate the existence of the marriage. It is further argued that appellees were required to negative all possible defects which would render the first marriage invalid. However, no reference is made to California authority compelling the imposition of this heavy burden. Indeed, it appears that the California rule is just the contrary; that is, despite the strength of the presumption of the validity of the later marriage, it merely requires the advocate of the prior marriage to establish by competent evidence a prima facie case of a regularly solemnized prior marriage. Hunter v. Hunter [citation omitted]. This appellees did. Then with two presumptively valid marriages in existence, the ultimate burden rests on the party who advocates the second to prove the invalidity of the first. [Citations omitted.] Moreover, even in the absence of a ceremonial marriage, the appellees could rely on a common law marriage formed during Mattie and decedent's eight years of cohabitation as husband and wife in Texas. Against the evidence to the contrary, there is not a scintilla of evidence impugning the existence or validity of the prior marriage.

Obviously, since Mattie testified, the marriage was not terminated by death. Only divorce or annulment remain as possibilities. Here again, there is substantial evidence that the marriage was subsisting in 1943. Mattie testified that she was served with no summons or complaint for a divorce prior to October, 1948; that she, not appellant, received the Army allotments; that appellant discussed prosecuting Erwin for bigamy with her; and that except for an abortive attempt in 1938, she made no endeavor to dissolve the marriage. There is also the 1949 divorce judgment and the property settlement agreement negotiated pursuant thereto. This agreement refers to Erwin and Mattie as "Husband" and "Wife" and they signed as *Erwin Tatum*, Husband, and *Minnie Tatum*, Wife. (Defendants Exhibit "A.") Furthermore, Erwin declared that he had not gotten a divorce because he did not need one. Once again, appellant did not produce any evidence to support the bare presumption.

. . . While we may grant appellant her contention that each item is not per se sufficient, it can hardly be doubted that cumulatively the evidence, viewed in its entirety, supports the trial court's finding. On the basis of the evidence, we cannot hold that its finding is clearly erroneous. Due respect should have been, and we assume, was paid the presumption, but it could not stand in light of the overwhelming evidence to the contrary. . . .

Appellant next predicates her claim on an asserted common-law marriage. In California, where appellant and Erwin were domiciled from 1945 until his death, only ceremonial marriages may be contracted. However, California does recognize common-law marriages validly created in states which allow such marriages. Texas is one of those states. . . .

[The court then reviews the lower court's finding that there was cohabitation, reputation, but no proof of agreement to marry during the parties' brief sojourns in Texas.]

To summarize Texas law, it appears that an agreement is necessary, but that in the case of Texas residents, particularly where the relationship is not meretricious, mere continuance of marital relations suffices to show such agreement. On the other hand, in cases involving out-of-state residents, particularly where the relationship is meretricious, it is essential to prove a new agreement. . . .

. . . Here no domicile in Texas was found. It is true that none was necessary, but in the absence thereof, it was incumbent on appellant to prove an agreement. She did not carry that burden. Therefore, she cannot avail herself of the status of common-law wife. . . .

The third and final basis of appellant's claim is that of putative spouse. At the outset it should be observed that we entertain serious doubt as to whether a putative spouse qualifies as a lawful "widow." By hypothesis, the putative spouse is *not* the lawful wife, but rather a person who because of a good faith belief in the existence of a valid marriage, is viewed by state law to be the equivalent of the lawful wife for some purposes. We reiterate that the word "widow," as employed in this Federal statute, presents a Federal question of interpretation. Lembcke v. United States [citation omitted]. Under the similarly phrased National Service Life Insurance Act, it has been held that the putative spouse does not come within the scope of the statute.[95] But we need not finally determine this issue, since it is clear that appellant is not a putative spouse.

It may well be that appellant engaged in the Arizona ceremony in good faith;[96] but from her own lips comes the admission that she subsequently learned of the continuing existence of the prior marriage. . . . Despite her knowledge of the overlapping marriages, appellant did nothing to rectify the situation . . . .

In Vallera v. Vallera, 21 Cal. 2d 681, 134 P.2d 761, the Supreme Court of California held that the sina qua non of a putative marriage is a good faith belief in the validity of the marriage at its inception. Appellant refers us to no California case nor could diligent research discover any, which would permit a person to claim the rights of a putative spouse when such person, after acquiring knowledge of the infirmity in his or her marriage, continues to live under the same conditions, without undertaking any action to perfect the marital status. Although this question is

---

[95] Muir v. United States [93 F. Supp. 939 (1950)]. The case cited by appellant to support award of the proceeds to the putative spouse, Speedling v. Hobby, D.C., 132 F. Supp. 833, 836, is not in point. There the Social Security Act, 42 U.S.C.A. §401 et seq., was involved, and the same District Judge who decided the Muir case, supra, specifically noted that "claimant does not have to be the lawful widow of the decedent, but rather must have the same status relative to taking intestate personal property as a widow."

[96] The only evidence on this point was appellant's own statements. The trial court was not required to accept as true her uncontradicted testimony. United States v. Fotopulos, 9 Cir., 180 F.2d 681.

evidently novel in California, we feel certain that the courts of that State would, consonant with the decision in the Vallera case, supra, deem it essential that the good faith belief continue throughout the life of the marriage. The courts in other jurisdictions which have considered the question have so held. Accordingly, when appellant discovered the subsistence of the first marriage she ceased to occupy, if she ever had, the status of putative spouse.

We are not unaware that our resolution of the instant case may entail hardship to the appellant. It is an unfortunate turn of circumstances that she is embroiled in a legal contest against the children of the man with whom she lived for over eleven years. It is all the more unfortunate that in this "winner take all" conflict, she receives nothing. Yet, we note, if the decedent had definitely desired that the proceeds of the policy should go to appellant, he could easily have fulfilled that wish by naming her beneficiary. This is indeed a hard case, but that fact does not permit this court to heed the old saw and make what we consider to be bad law.

The decision of the District Court is affirmed.

NOTE

1. As to the presumption of the validity of a subsequent marriage, compare, e.g., Troxel v. Jones, 45 Tenn. App. 264, 322 S.W.2d 251 (1958), where in a wrongful death action an alleged widow relied on a common law marriage subsequent to her prior ceremonial marriage to another. She had testified that she had not obtained a divorce and stated (45 Tenn. App. at 274, 322 S.W.2d at 256): "Charles Hutchson married another woman and he was supposedly divorced from me and I didn't think I needed to bother with that." An attack on the presumption that the second marriage was valid was unsuccessful because of failure to meet the burden of "showing that no divorce decree is disclosed by the records of any of the divorce courts in any of the counties where either of the spouses might have obtained such divorce." 45 Tenn. App. at 277, 322 S.W.2d at 257. But see Di Giovanni v. Di Giovannantonio, 233 F.2d 26 (D.C. Cir. 1956), where the court says that it is doubtful if the presumption arises where the subsequent marriage is at common law. In that case the same facts alleged to rebut the presumption also cast doubt on the validity of the common law marriage which was alleged as the basis of the presumption.

2. The Louisiana Civil Code provides specifically for putative spouses (La. Stat. Ann. arts. 117, 118 (1952)):

Art. 117. The marriage, which has been declared null, produces nevertheless its civil effects as it relates to the parties and their children, if it has been contracted in good faith.

Art. 118. If only one of the parties acted in good faith, the marriage produces its civil effects only in his or her favor, and in favor of the children born of the marriage.

These are literal translations of Articles 201 and 202 of the French Civil Code of 1803, and Louisiana courts have drawn heavily from French precedents. For applications finding sufficient good faith, see, e.g., Funderburk v. Funderburk, 214 La. 717, 38 So.2d 502 (1949) (marriage void for bigamy because prior divorce fraudulent, but wife relied on divorce judgment and there was no proof that she knew of fraud); Kimball v. Folsom, 150 F. Supp. 482 (W.D. La. 1957) (divorced adulterer married his partner in adultery, a union declared by La. Civ. Code art. 161 to be bigamous, but wife alleged she was ignorant of this law); and Succession of Marinoni, 183 La. 776, 164 So. 797 (1935) (good faith belief of putative spouse in validity of actually invalid informal marriage without license or ceremony).

While California does not extend the full civil effect of marriage to a putative spouse, in that state the

> courts have progressively equated the rights of the putative spouse to those of the legal wife. She is entitled to share in the putative property upon death or divorce; she is entitled to recover a workmen's compensation award and to bring an action for wrongful death. She has, however, no right to permanent alimony. And, since a putative spouse is said not to be entitled to a right to support, she is probably not entitled to either a family allowance or a probate homestead. . . .[97]

The meretricious spouse is in a far worse position, since she can "recover the reasonable value of services rendered or a share of property accumulated during the relationship only if there exists an express agreement to that effect." Comment, Rights of the Putative and Meretricious Spouse in California, 50 Calif. L. Rev. 866, 879 (1962). This Comment summarizes the case law on California putative marriage as follows, id. at 866:

> A putative marriage is one in which at least one of the parties has a good faith belief that the relationship existing between them is a valid marriage. Only a party having such a belief is a putative spouse. No marriage ceremony is necessary. Even a good faith belief that a common law marriage was valid is sufficient to make the believer a putative spouse.
>
> A person incapable of contracting a valid marriage is not thereby barred from becoming a putative spouse. For example, assume that A's divorce from B is, without A's knowledge, invalid. If A and C, in good faith, enter into a purported marriage, both A and C are putative spouses. That A was incapable of contracting a valid marriage with C is merely a factor considered in determining A's requisite good faith belief. The court looks to the facts in the particular case. The education, intelligence, and experience of the one claiming putative status are considered.
>
> Knowledge of the invalidity of the marriage cuts off any rights the

[97] Comment, Rights of the Putative and Meretricious Spouse in California, 50 Calif. L. Rev. 866, 873 (1962).

person may have gained thereafter as a putative spouse. It does not, however, destroy rights already acquired. . . .

3. The existence in some Latin-American countries of what appears to be a discretionary form of common law marriage has been noted by Eder, A Comparative Survey of Anglo-American and Latin-American Law 122-123 (1950), e.g., a provision of the Cuban Constitution of 1940, art. 43, par. 6: "The courts shall determine the cases in which, for reasons of equity and in view of its stability and security, a union between persons legally capable of entering into matrimony, shall be deemed equivalent to a civil marriage." Noting that opposition to American common law marriage rests in part on the dangers of fraud and blackmail, Eder comments that "The Cuban Law, with the words 'for reasons of equity,' seems to eliminate partly the danger." Eder, *supra*, at 123.

ARCAND v. FLEMMING
185 F. Supp. 22 (D. Conn. 1960)

SMITH, C.J. This is an action brought under Section 205(g) of the Social Security Act, as amended, 42 U.S.C.A. §405(g), for review of a decision of the Secretary of Health, Education and Welfare denying plaintiff's claim for Children's Insurance Benefits under the Old Age and Survivors Insurance provisions of the Social Security Act, 42 U.S.C.A. §401 et seq. This action for review is brought by Lois Arcand, individually and on behalf of her children, Marilyn and Ronald Arcand who claim benefits as children of the deceased wage earner, Maurice A. Arcand. It is the latter claim with which we are concerned here. The claim was denied after a hearing before the Referee on the ground that the children would not be entitled to inherit intestate personal property from the deceased wage earner, Maurice A. Arcand, under Connecticut law and therefore are precluded from receiving benefits under the Act as children of the insured. It was decided that the children were illegitimate under Connecticut law for the purposes of intestate succession since the mother of the children and Maurice A. Arcand, the putative father, were never legally married.

The facts are not in dispute and can be stated as follows: Maurice A. Arcand married one Rosina L'Ecuyer on February 1, 1930 in New York. On March 10, 1940, Maurice married the plaintiff in this action, Lois Arcand, in Vermont. At this time the first wife, Rosina, was still alive and the marriage between her and Maurice had not been dissolved. Lois, however, was unaware of the prior marriage. Shortly after their marriage in Vermont, Maurice and Lois moved to Connecticut where they established a permanent residence. They lived together in this state as man and wife and two children, the present claimants, were born of this relationship. Marilyn was born in 1940 and Ronald in 1944. Later, Lois learned of her mate's prior marriage and insisted that he obtain a divorce so that they could validate their marriage. Maurice agreed and instituted divorce proceedings in the Probate Court of Hampden County, Massachusetts, and on December 16, 1953 was granted a divorce by decree nisi to become absolute on June 17, 1954. On February 24, 1954, before the expiration of the interlocutory period under the Massachusetts decree and while the first wife, Rosina was still living, Maurice and Lois had a second marriage performed by a Justice of the Peace in Darien, Connecticut. It was Lois' belief at this time that no impediment existed and that she and Maurice were free to enter into a valid marriage. The parties continued to reside together until April 24, 1956 when Lois obtained a divorce from Maurice in Connecticut. Maurice subsequently died on November 17, 1956 in Connecticut which was his place of domicile at the time of his death.

The question in this action for review of the decision of the Referee is whether the claimants, Marilyn and Ronald Arcand, are children of the insured within the meaning of the Act so as to make them eligible for Child Insurance Benefits under 42 U.S.C.A. §402(d). Title 42 U.S.C.A. §416(h)(2) provides that in determining whether an applicant is a child of the insured, the law applied shall be the same as would be applied in the courts of the state where the insured was domiciled at the date of death to determine the devolution of intestate property. We must look to the body of law on this subject in Connecticut since the insured was domiciled here at the time of his death.

Although an illegitimate child is allowed to inherit from the mother in Connecticut, Brown v. Dye, 1795, 2 Root, Conn., 280; Heath v. White, 1824, 5 Conn. 228; Dickinson's Appeal, 1875, 42 Conn. 491; Eaton v. Eaton, 1914, 88 Conn. 269, 91 A. 191, there is no corresponding right of a child with such a status to inherit from the putative father or succeed to the devolution of the father's intestate property. Heath v. White, supra. A child born out of wedlock may acquire rights of inheritance from and through the father if the parents are later joined in a legal marriage. Section 7058 of the General Statutes of Connecticut (1949 Revision), in effect at the time of the insured wage earner's death, provided in part:

> "Children born before marriage whose parents afterwards marry shall be deemed legitimate and inherit equally with other children."

It follows that the children's right to benefits in the instant case can be established only if it is found that Lois and Maurice Arcand were legally married so as to legitimize the children born of this relationship. At the time of the Darien marriage on February 24, 1954, an impediment unquestionably existed since the Massachusetts divorce decree did not become absolute until June 17, 1954. There is a Massachusetts statute which provides for the validation of a marriage which takes place at a time where an impediment exists but where one of the parties acts in good faith and where the impediment is later removed. Chapter 207, Section 6 of the General Laws of Massachusetts (Ter. Ed.) provides as follows:

> "If a person, during the lifetime of a husband or wife with whom the marriage is in force, enters into a subsequent marriage contract with due legal ceremony and the parties live together as husband and wife, and such subsequent marriage contract was entered into by one

of the parties in good faith, in the full belief . . . that the former marriage had been annulled by a divorce . . . they shall, after the impediment to their marriage has been removed by the death or divorce of the other party to the former marriage, if they continue to live together as husband and wife in good faith on the part of one of them, be held to have been legally married from and after the removal of such impediment, and the issue of such subsequent marriage shall be considered as the legitimate issue of both parents."

The Referee, relying on Commonwealth v. Stevens, 1907, 196 Mass. 280, 82 N.E. 33, held that the Massachusetts statute could not be applied to validate the marriage and legitimize the children when the parties to the marriage were residing outside of Massachusetts at the time the decree nisi became absolute. We think that his reliance on such a broad holding in the Stevens case was misplaced. Commonwealth v. Stevens, supra, was a case involving a criminal prosecution for polygamy. The defendant obtained a divorce from his first wife by decree nisi in Massachusetts. Before the decree became absolute, the defendant removed to Georgia and after residing there for four months married Minnie Tourtelotte who was unaware that an impediment existed at the time of the marriage. The parties set up residence and remained in Georgia until after the interlocutory period under the Massachusetts divorce decree expired. They later came to Massachusetts but had no further marriage ceremony performed. Thereafter, the defendant married one Jennette H. Smyth and was prosecuted for polygamy on the ground that he was legally married to Minnie Tourtelotte at the time of the Smyth marriage. The State argued that the statute which is now Chapter 207, Section 6, operated to validate the Georgia marriage and made the later marriage polygamous. The Massachusetts Supreme Judicial Court refused to apply the statute in this criminal prosecution and held that a Georgia statute (Civ. Code 1895, §§2412, 2416) which made the Georgia marriage void was controlling. The court ruled that the Massachusetts statute had no extraterritorial effect and that since the parties were not in Massachusetts when the interlocutory period expired, it could not be applied.

There are two significant aspects to the Stevens case which are important here. First, there were no children involved and no question of legitimacy was before the court. The Massachusetts cases have made it quite clear that the statute is a remedial statute intended for the protection of persons who marry innocently in good faith and to avoid the stigma of illegitimacy for innocent children when one parent is blameless of any conscious transgression of the laws regulating marriage. Vital v. Vital, 1946, 319 Mass. 185, 190, 65 N.E.2d 205; Gardner v. Gardner, 1919, 232 Mass. 253, 258, 122 N.E. 308; cf. Commonwealth v. Ross, 1924, 248 Mass. 15, 142 N.E. 791. The objectives to be attained through application of the statute were not present in the Stevens case and it is plain to see why there would be a reluctance to bring the statute into such a case. There is a second point which is of prime importance here. The Stevens case presented a situation where a Massachusetts court was called upon to apply the Massachusetts statute to the marital status of parties at a time when they were residing in another state. In such a case it was the State of Georgia which had the paramount interest in determining the status of the parties. It was entirely proper that a Massachusetts court would apply the statute in effect in the foreign state where the parties were married and where they resided during the period of time in question rather than to apply a Massachusetts statute to an internal matter of a foreign state which Georgia would desire to regulate. This is especially true where criminal responsibility is sought to be imposed as a result of what occurred in another state. In the present case, we sit just as a Connecticut forum would sit in determining the marital status of persons who were married and domiciled in Connecticut and to determine the legitimacy of offspring born here. In such a case we feel that it would be a matter of choice for a Connecticut court to apply Chapter 207, Section 6 if it saw fit to do so. The same kind of comity considerations which were present in the Stevens case do not appear in the instant case. Here we have a case where a Connecticut forum would be called upon to pass on a matter in which the forum state has the major interest — the status of children residing here who were born of parents who were residents of this state and who were married here. In giving full faith and credit to the interlocutory nature of the Massachusetts divorce decree, we feel that there is no prohibition against a similar recognition by a Connecticut court of Chapter 207, Section 6, which operates on the force of the transitory impediment under this decree. There is no interest of the State of Massachusetts which would be prejudiced through application of the statute by a Connecticut court and the standards prescribed by the statute do not require any peculiar procedural devices of a Massachusetts forum.

It is our view that Chapter 207, Section 6 of the Massachusetts General Laws could be applied by a Connecticut court in deciding a question of legitimacy under the succession statute under these facts. . . . There is no policy in this state against the restoration of illegitimate children to a status of legitimacy in order to afford them the full enjoyment of the rights of legitimacy and this is especially true where only the rights of the innocent child are involved. Connecticut has always been more liberal and considerate than other jurisdictions in its treatment of the illegitimate. . . . With this background, it is our view that a Connecticut court would probably apply a statute such as Chapter 207, Section 6 which has a primary purpose of legitimizing blameless children.

The saving force of the statute takes effect if Lois Arcand entered into the Darien marriage "in good faith in the full belief that the former marriage had been annulled by divorce" and further that Lois and Maurice "continue(d) to live as husband and wife in good faith on the part of (Lois)." In applying these standards, the Massachusetts courts have taken a liberal view in order to effectuate the essential purpose of legitimizing blameless children. See Hopkins v. Hopkins, 1934, 287 Mass. 542, 192 N.E. 145, 95 A.L.R. 1286. The good faith required in the statute does not require that a person be diligent or prudent but that there be an actual honesty of purpose. Gardner v. Gardner, 1919, 232 Mass. 253, 122

N.E. 308. There is testimony in the record that Lois Arcand fully believed that she and Maurice were free to enter into a valid marriage on February 24, 1954 due to the Massachusetts divorce and that this belief on her part continued as they lived together as husband and wife.

Plaintiff's motion for summary judgment is granted and defendant's cross motion for summary judgment is denied. The plaintiff may submit for entry an appropriate judgment on notice to the defendant.

NOTE

Pennsylvania has given a liberal interpretation to its similar statute, both in the interpretation of good faith, Jones v. Jones, 19 Pa. D. & C.2d 209 (C.P. 1959), and in applying it to a good faith marriage contracted outside the commonwealth by Pennsylvania domiciliaries. Commonwealth v. Wenz, 195 Pa. Super. 593, 171 A.2d 529 (1961) (alternative holding). With the Massachusetts and Pennsylvania statutes, compare N.H. Rev. Stat. Ann. §457:39 (1955): "Persons cohabiting and acknowledging each other as husband and wife, and generally reputed to be such, for the period of three years, and until the decease of one of them, shall thereafter be deemed to have been legally married." Despite the seemingly broad thrust of this statute, the New Hampshire Supreme Court in Hilliard v. Baldwin, 76 N.H. 142, 80 Atl. 139 (1911), held that it did not have the effect of validating a polygamous or otherwise void marriage.

In addition to such statutes of general applicability, a number of states have enacted special validating provisions. See, e.g., Wis. Stat. Ann. §245.035 (1957) (all epileptic marriages contracted prior to a certain date declared valid, provided they were lawful in other respects). Cf. Mich. Stat. Ann. §25.15 (1957), validating all out-of-state marriages which are valid under the law of the place where contracted.

The curative statutes considered above operate automatically; if the impediment is in fact removed at a time when the other prerequisites have been met, the validation is automatic. There are occasional situations, however, where either by express statutory delegation or by reason of its general powers to enter divorce decrees with retroactive effect (so-called nunc pro tunc decrees) a court may achieve the same purpose without benefit of a curative provision such as exists in Massachusetts. R.I. Gen. Laws Ann. §15-1-6 (1956) provides that a marriage void at its inception because of a remarriage bar arising from a previous divorce "may be declared valid and binding upon the parties thereto by decree of the superior court, if such marriage was in all other respects [valid]." For the equivalent operation of the nunc pro tunc divorce decree power of the courts (pursuant to, e.g., Cal. Civ. Code §133), see Kelley v. Kelley, 210 Ore. 226, 310 P.2d 328 (1957), in which an invalid marriage contracted between W and H-2 during the interlocutory period of W's divorce from H-1 was retroactively validated by a decree entered after H-2's death.

Where none of the powers described above has been provided for by the legislature, however, and where common law marriage has been abolished, harsh consequences may be unavoidable, despite judicial eagerness to salvage the effects of the marriage wherever possible. See, e.g., Dacunzo v. Edgye, 19 N.J. 443, 117 A.2d 508 (1955); but cf. Thompson v. Monteiro, 58 N.J. Super. 302, 156 A.2d 173 (1959), the latter representing a commendable though not altogether satisfying attempt to avert serious hardship despite the attitude of the New Jersey Supreme Court evinced in the Dacunzo case.

DANES v. SMITH
30 N.J. Super. 292, 104 A.2d 455 (1954)

FRANCIS, J. Appellant sought an annulment of his marriage to respondent, a partition of real estate which they owned ostensibly as tenants by the entirety, discovery with respect to moneys entrusted to her, and an accounting. . . .

After a number of hearings respondent received a favorable judgment and this appeal followed.

The parties were married on May 30, 1942 in Newark, New Jersey, by a minister of the gospel. Thereafter they lived together as man and wife, except for three years when the husband was in the armed forces. . . . Upon the termination of his military career they resumed living together and continued to do so until December 1950, when he separated from respondent. He claimed that the separation took place because he discovered then for the first time that she was already married when she went through the ceremony with him. Some months later this annulment action was instituted.

It appears without dispute that on October 12, 1926 the wife went through a valid ceremonial marriage in North Carolina with one John Smith and that he was still alive at the time of the marriage under consideration.

The testimony is in conflict as to whether Danes was aware that respondent had a husband in North Carolina when he married her. She said he knew about it and in fact assisted her in the making of false statements about her marital history in the application for a marriage license at the bureau in Newark, New Jersey. He denied it.

Smith died on October 23, 1944, while Danes was overseas, and Mrs. Danes testified that she wrote advising him of the fact. Danes admitted receiving the letter which he said simply told him of the death of John Smith. He knew a number of John Smiths and was not aware that she was referring to another husband.

There is further conflict in the testimony as to whether there was conversation between them about the elimination of the impediment to their marriage upon Danes' return to this country and after his discharge from service. In any event, as already indicated, they continued living as man and wife until December 1950 when according to her he left, saying he had another woman.

After considering the facts recited and all the circumstances in the case, the trial court concluded that Danes knew his wife had a living husband when he married her and was therefore estopped to question the validity of their marriage. . . .

. . . [W]here a person enters into a ceremonial marriage with another, knowing of the existence of an impediment to lawful wedlock and thereafter cohabits with the spouse thus acquired, he will be barred from questioning the legality of the union under the doctrine of estoppel or unclean hands. In our judgment the factual conclusion reached here amply justified the application of the doctrine so as to deny the claim for annulment.

The trial court decided additionally that even if Danes found out for the first time that his wife was under the disability of an existing marriage when he married her, his cohabitation with her in New Jersey after the removal of the impediment, matrimonially meant, made them man and wife. . . .

No case has yet been decided in our state courts as to the effect of [the statute abrogating common law marriage] on a situation where the parties complied with the formal requisites of license and ceremony in good faith unconscious of an obstacle in the path of a valid marriage, and then continued to live together as man and wife after the removal of the bar. Is the union of these persons void, regardless of their belief and conduct? Has the strong public policy manifested by the statute completely overcome the strong public policy of the common law in favor of recognition of marriage in such cases? Unquestionably the Legislature has the authority to abrogate the common-law doctrine completely if it sees fit to do so.

Strangely enough, a holding that a common-law marriage is barred by the statute in the instance described would bring about a most anomalous situation from a public policy standpoint. When, as here, parties to a ceremonial marriage enter into the relation with knowledge that an impediment exists, they are barred by estoppel or unclean hands from asserting its invalidity, *and their status is unaffected by the statute.* Yet where two persons in good faith undergo a ceremonial marriage unaware of an invalidating obstacle and that obstacle is subsequently removed, continuance of cohabitation matrimonially meant will accomplish nothing for them; their state will still be concubinage. It has been suggested that in such cases there is social and legal justification for the recognition of common-law marriage. . . .

. . . In view of the state of the record here, it is not necessary to decide the question and it is reserved until the issue is directly presented. . . .

Title to the rooming house premises was acquired in the names of the Danes as husband and wife. Thus in form at least they became tenants by the entirety. The purchase was made in 1948 after the death of the first husband, Smith, and while the parties were living together.

As set forth above, appellant's complaint sought partition of the realty on the ground that there being no valid marriage, the title was held as tenants in common. Since the trial court concluded that Danes was estopped to deny the marriage and also that the continued cohabitation after the removal of the impediment created a valid marriage, he denied partition. More specifically, the denial was predicated upon the conclusion that the marriage having been validated prior to the acquisition of title, the conveyance created a tenancy by the entirety; and since an incident of such a tenancy is the right of survivorship, the compulsory partition sought could not be granted. As is the case with the annulment action, it is not necessary to pass upon the validation of the marriage through the death of Smith; the estoppel theory seems an adequate solution of the issue.

The law is clear that if the parties to a deed are not actually husband and wife, their designation as such even in the honest belief that they are married establishes a tenancy in common and not a tenancy by the entirety. . . .

Research has revealed no case involving the effect of an estoppel or the application of the doctrine of unclean hands in such a situation in a controversy between the immediate parties. Here the law has precluded Danes from denying that he and his wife are lawfully married. Should not the same bar be applied in any civil controversy, the determination of which involves the validity of the marriage? Certainly to have consistency, an object much to be desired in the law, it should operate in every controversy *between them and those in privity with them.* Thus where the effect of a deed to them as husband and wife is in dispute between them, since they cannot be heard to say they are not lawfully married they ought not be permitted to deny that they are tenants by the entirety. This conclusion does not do violence to the traditional notions of such a tenancy. It does not permit an invalid marriage to create a tenancy by the entirety; it simply prevents a denial of the existence of that type tenancy — again a result to be desired in the interest of land title stability. Accordingly no error was committed in refusing to order partition. . . .

JAYNE, J. (dissenting in part). It is in only one particular that my conception of the applicable law constrains me to disagree with the conclusions expressed by my learned associate Judge Francis.

The plaintiff sought, inter alia, a judgment authorizing the partition of the real estate conveyed to the parties by a deed of conveyance in which they are represented to be husband and wife. That measure of relief was denied the plaintiff in the Chancery Division and Judge Francis expresses in his opinion the conviction that the denial should be affirmed. I cannot concur.

The conclusion that the judgment should be affirmed in that respect appears to be produced by a functional rationale of consistency and homogeneity that since the plaintiff will not be awarded a judgment nullifying the void marriage, the ownership of the realty is that of tenants by the entirety. I think that in the law that cannot be so.

Initially, let me state that I have always entertained the belief that the inability in certain circumstances of a spouse to obtain a decree annulling a void marriage is more responsive in equity to the doctrine of unclean hands than appropriately attributable to the doctrine of estoppel. Vide, Tonti v. Chadwick, 1 N.J. 531, 536 (1949). I decline to suppose that there is any type of estoppel that permits bigamy. The refusal of the court to anul a void marriage under equitable principles certainly does not validate the unlawful marriage. . . . Whether the policy of invoking in the present day the doctrine of unclean hands in these sui generis nullity cases is conducive to the public welfare is at least debatable, but in the disposition of that branch of the present case I am obedient to existing precedents.

I have been taught to understand that a tenancy by the entirety arises only from a conveyance or devise to a man and a woman who are husband and wife at the time of such transfer. . . .

It is evident that the parties to the present action who were the grantees in the deed were not husband and wife at the time of the conveyance of the real estate to them. I cannot agree that the doctrine of unclean hands has the legal potency to procreate a tenancy by the entirety between unmarried grantees of real estate. If the doctrine cannot bestow validity upon a void marriage or justify an award of alimony to an unmarried woman, I am unable to perceive by what legitimate process it can synthetically construct a tenancy by the entirety. [Citation omitted.] I would not extend the doctrines of unclean hands or estoppel to in effect metabolize a tenancy in common into one by the entirety or artificially engraft upon the former the qualities of the latter.

. . . The plaintiff should have been granted the right to a partition of the property. The judgment under review should in that respect be reversed.

I am authorized by Judge EASTWOOD to state that he unites with me in this dissent.

NOTE

1. Since there were only three judges on the court, the "dissenting" opinion of Judge Jayne in which Judge Eastwood concurred was dispositive on the partition issue. On what basis do they distinguish between the parties' invulnerable marital status and their vulnerable property status? Some inherent limitation in the concepts of estoppel or unclean hands? Or is this yet another example of the fragmentation between status and incidents that we have already encountered, see page 31 supra, and that we shall encounter repeatedly throughout these materials?

Be that as it may, their dictum that the doctrine of unclean hands "cannot bestow validity upon a void marriage or justify an award of alimony to an unmarried woman" has not been uniformly recognized. See, e.g., Sears v. Sears, 293 F.2d 884 (D.C. Cir. 1961), holding that where H went through a concededly invalid Mexican mail order divorce in order to marry W-2, H would be barred from asserting the invalidity of the Mexican divorce and the ensuing marriage as a defense against W-2's support claims. See also Krause v. Krause, 282 N.Y. 355, 26 N.E.2d 290 (1940), a case in which the New York Court of Appeals reached a similar result.

The enactment of N.Y. Civ. Prac. Act §1140-a (now dealt with in N.Y.

Dom. Rel. Law §236) made it possible for the court in annulment actions to make such direction for support of the wife by the husband as "justice requires," so that the economic rationale for Krause was eliminated. In 1950 the New York Court of Appeals denied an estoppel in an action to annul a marriage that was alleged to be void because it antedated the final decree dissolving the wife's prior marriage. Landsman v. Landsman, 302 N.Y. 45, 96 N.E.2d 81 (1950). The very brief opinion did not mention Krause, which could be distinguished because Krause involved a foreign divorce, but included the following sweeping language (302 N.Y. at 48, 96 N.E.2d at 82):

> the attempted marriage here in question was wholly without validity from its beginning; it created neither right nor duty; it gave neither scope for recrimination nor room for any counteractive estoppel. Hence . . . the plaintiff was free to bring this annulment action though he did not come to the court with clean hands. . . .

On the general question of estoppel to challenge a prior divorce, see page 746 infra.

2. Compare the more limited doctrine of estoppel to deny the validity of what amounts to a common law marriage based on proof of cohabitation and reputation. This doctrine has been applicable at least in theory in Tennessee despite the state's rejection of common law marriage. See Note, Informal Marriages in Tennessee — Marriage by Estoppel, by Prescription and by Ratification, 3 Vand. L. Rev. 610 (1950). In Smith v. North Memphis Savings Bank, 115 Tenn. 12, 89 S.W. 392 (1905), the court reiterated the state's rule that it would not recognize as a common law marriage an informal, secret agreement under which a couple had lived together as man and wife for twenty-five years. The court held, however, that the deceased husband's personal representative was estopped to controvert the surviving spouse's rights as widow, reasoning that were the husband alive he would be estopped to deny liability for, e.g., any contract she might have made which would have bound a lawful husband. The force of such precedents, however, has been greatly weakened by subsequent decisions. See, e.g., Crawford v. Crawford, 198 Tenn. 9, 277 S.W.2d 389 (1955), which denied an estoppel on facts very similar to those of Smith and expressly repudiated some of the language on which the estoppel doctrine rested. This curious analogy to common law marriage now appears to be limited to service as a curative device for certain types of void or voidable ceremonial marriages.

PROBLEM

A state commission for the revision of the marriage law has recommended the abolition of common law marriage. The commission believes that in the past common law marriage has sometimes enabled courts to reach a just result in hardship cases and that its abolition should be accompanied by a statutory enactment to afford protection for deserving women and children of de facto families whose legal status is defective.

Five members of the commission have recommended adoption of the following curative statute:

§300. Persons cohabiting and acknowledging each other as husband and wife, and generally reputed to be such, for the period of three years, and until the decease of one of them, shall thereafter be deemed to have been legally married.

§301. If a person, during the lifetime of a husband or wife with whom the marriage is in force, enters into a subsequent marriage contract with due legal ceremony and the parties live together as husband and wife, and such subsequent marriage contract was entered into by one of the parties in good faith, in the full belief that the former marriage had been annulled by a divorce or death they shall, after the impediment to their marriage has been removed by the death or divorce of the other party to the former marriage, if they continue to live together as husband and wife in good faith on the part of one of them, be held to have been legally married from and after the removal of such impediment.

§302. Children of void or voidable marriages shall be deemed to be legitimate.

Two members of the commission regard the foregoing proposals as entirely inadequate and have recommended the adoption of the following statute:

§1. Proof that persons have cohabited and acknowledged each other as husband and wife and have generally been reputed to be such for a period of one year shall:

(a) create a presumption that they are formally married; and
(b) if that presumption is rebutted, shall be sufficient to establish the relationship as an informal marriage.

§2. An informal marriage shall produce the same effects as a formal marriage, and the child, spouse or surviving spouse of an informal marriage shall legally be regarded for all purposes as a lawful child, spouse or surviving spouse, except as provided in sections 3 and 4 of this act.

§3. In any action for benefits or involving claims arising out of the death of a spouse where more than one surviving formal or informal spouse is involved, the court shall make an equitable division of the benefits or proceeds.

§4. In any action for support or alimony in which it appears that a husband is legally obligated to more than one present or former formal or informal spouse, the court shall make an equitable award or awards.

Which of these alternatives do you prefer? Do you have some other solution you would recommend in their place?

PART II

The Going Family

CHAPTER 3

Legal Relations of the Family

A. INTRODUCTION

Since the earliest phases of the common law, the courts have often been asked to order the daily affairs of members of families and to determine their relations with outsiders. The rules have been developed and applied in a host of contexts: H dies and W and H's brothers cannot amicably settle the ownership of H's cattle and lands; W purchases food and the seller seeks the purchase price from H; C is injured by X's negligence and C's parents sue X for C's medical expenses and lost earnings. The issues have been of extraordinary variety — one can find "law" relating to every aspect of family life and to all the common transactions between family members and outsiders. This chapter examines the history, the current scope, and the wisdom of some of these doctrines.

At common law an unmarried adult woman was a fully competent person who could sue, be sued, and hold property. In the very early periods of common law development, the postnuptial ownership right of either spouse in the property of the other posed largely academic questions. "Such questions will become important so soon as the marriage is at an end; but in the meanwhile the husband has everywhere a very large power of dealing as he pleases with the whole mass of property." [1] After some hesitation, English judges began to state that at marriage a married woman's personal chattels vested in her husband; the husband's dominion of his wife's real property, while not absolute, was substantial.[2] In

---

[1] 2 Pollock & Maitland 400. This discussion relies upon the work of Pollock and Maitland; 3 Holdsworth, History of English Law 520-533 (6th ed. 1934); 1 American Law of Property §§5.50-5.56 (Casner ed. 1952); A Century of Family Law (Graveson & Crane eds. 1957); 3 Vernier §§149-173 (1935).

[2] "So long as coverture lasted, the husband was entitled to the usufruct of her real property. He could alienate his interest therein, and the same was

time, a notion (more appropriately, a fiction) of the legal identity of husband and wife emerged.   Blackstone observed: "By marriage, the husband and wife are one person in law: that is, the very being or legal existence of the woman is suspended during the marriage, or at least is incorporated and consolidated into that of the husband." [3]   A less serious commentator suggested: "The Creator took from Adam a rib and made it Eve; the common law of England endeavoured to reverse the process, to replace the rib and to re-merge the personalities." [4]   The sources of what eventually became the concept of legal identity were disparate: social conditions in feudal England;[5] jurisdictional disputes between ecclesiastical and common law courts; pressures for free alienability of interests in land; the tendency to avoid complexity in a primitive legal system; an unstated but nonetheless significant principle that the husband was entitled to a profitable guardianship of his wife.

We cannot explore the historical development in detail; it must suffice to indicate that over the centuries the fiction of husband-wife identity progressively became the major premise of a series of doctrinal syllogisms whose conclusions influence the outcome of lawsuits even today.   At common law, for example, the wife could neither make a contract nor incur a debt.   The husband was entitled to his wife's earnings.   Since the wife's choses in action were part of her property (if "reduced . . . to possession during coverture" [6]), and thus would belong to her husband, he had to be joined as plaintiff in the wife's actions claiming damages for the tortious conduct of a third party.   Because the husband was also entitled to his wife's society and services, he was permitted to sue anyone who deprived him of that right.   He also had a cause of action " 'per quod consortium amisit,' as it is expressed, for injuries to her which render her less able to perform services." [7]   Neither spouse could contract with or sue the other. The husband's dominance was not confined to economic affairs.   According to Kent, the husband was entitled to put "gentle restraints" on

---

subject to execution against him.   If the wife had an estate of inheritance, and if during coverture issue capable of inheriting such estate was born alive, his interest became enlarged to a life estate."   3 Vernier 167.

[3] 1 Blackstone, Commentaries *442.

[4] de Montmorency, The Changing Status of a Married Woman, 13 L.Q. Rev. 187, 192 (1897).   Compare Petruchio's description of the wife's position:

> She is my goods, my chattels, she is my house,
> My household stuff, my field, my barn,
> My horse, my ox, my ass, my anything.

Shakespeare, Taming of the Shrew, Act III, Scene 2.   Another common sally is: "At common law husband and wife were one, and the husband was that one." Sayre, Property Rights of Husband and Wife, 6 Marr. & Fam. Liv. 17 (1944).

[5] "We can not be certain that for long centuries the presiding tendency [underlying the husband's right to his wife's property] was not one which was separating the wife from her blood kinsmen, teaching her to 'forget her own people and her father's house' and bringing her and her goods more completely under her husband's dominion."   2 Pollock & Maitland 403.

[6] Madden, Persons and Domestic Relations 158 (1931).

[7] Id. at 161.

his wife's liberty.[8] Blackstone stated that despite some doubt about such power by the husband, "the lower rank of people, who were always fond of the old common law, still claim and exert their ancient privilege: and the courts of law will still permit a husband to restrain a wife of her liberty, in case of any gross misbehaviour." He concludes his discussion with the masterful euphemism that the wife's disabilities "are for the most part intended for her protection and benefit. So great a favourite is the female sex of the laws of England." [9]

The most ludicrous doctrines might have been avoided even if they were logical corollaries of the legal identity fiction. During the early stages of common law evolution individual doctrines were apparently more intelligently constructed:

> If we look for any one thought which governs the whole of this province of law, we shall hardly find it. In particular we must be on our guard against the common belief that the ruling principle is that which sees an "unity of person" between husband and wife. This is a principle which suggests itself from time to time; it has the warrant of holy writ; it will serve to round a paragraph, and may now and again lead us out of or into a difficulty; but a consistently operative principle it can not be. We do not treat the wife as a thing or as somewhat that is neither thing nor person; we treat her as a person. Thus Bracton tells us that if either the husband without the wife, or the wife without the husband, brings an action for the wife's land, the defendant can take exception to this "for they are quasi one person, for they are one flesh and one blood." But this impracticable proposition is followed by a real working principle: — "for the thing is the wife's own and the husband is guardian as being the head of the wife." . . .[10]

Even with respect to the property doctrines which originated and nurtured the fiction, legal identity of husband and wife was not inevitable:

> we can not . . . explain the marital relationship as being simply the subjection of the wife to her husband's will. He constantly needs her concurrence, and the law takes care that she shall have an opportunity of freely refusing her assent to his acts.[11] To this we must add that . . . there is a latent idea of a community between husband and wife which can not easily be suppressed.[12]

[8] 2 Kent, Commentaries 181 (12th ed. 1873). "It is a sickly sensibility which holds that a man may not lay hands on his wife, even rudely, if necessary, to prevent the commission of some unlawful or criminal purpose." Richards v. Richards, 1 Grant's Cases 389, 392 (Pa. 1857).

[9] 1 Blackstone, Commentaries *445.

[10] 2 Pollock & Maitland 405-406.

[11] The comment apparently refers to the practice which barred the wife's right to dower in land sold by the husband during coverture — the levy of a fine. This practice, since it involved a lawsuit, required that the wife be examined in open court and her concurrence in the conveyance obtained. Id. at 411-413. — Ed.

[12] Id. at 407.

In any event, the fiction was never monolithic: "The English judges were too reasonable to be logical, if they could possibly help it." [13]   Thus, many wives were not completely at their husband's mercy:

> by basing the incapacities of the married woman rather upon the fact that she has no chattels of her own than upon the principle that she ought to be subject to her husband, they were leaving open the possibility that a third person should hold property upon trust for her and yet in no sort upon trust for him. In course of time this possibility became a reality, and by means of marriage settlements and courts of equity the English wife, if she belonged to the richer class, became singularly free from marital control. . . .[14]

It is not impossible that reforms were delayed so long at least in part because the trust device was available.

Since the middle of the nineteenth century, in response to changing social conditions and increasing de facto social and economic emancipation of women, legislation in England and in most American jurisdictions has drastically transformed the legal status of married women.[15] As the materials that follow indicate, however, these statutes, known as Married Women's Property Acts, were not so much concerned with adapting the legal relations of husbands and wives to contemporary social conditions as with correcting specific disabilities of married women at common law.[16] Thus, the District of Columbia statute, enacted in 1901, read:

> Married women shall have power to engage in any business, and to contract, whether engaged in business or not, and to sue separately upon their contracts, and also to sue separately for the recovery, security, or protection of their property, and for torts committed against them, as fully and freely as if they were unmarried; contracts may also be made with them, and they may also be sued separately upon their contracts, whether made before or during marriage, and for wrongs independent of contract committed by them before or during their marriage, as fully as if they were unmarried, and upon judgments recovered against them execution may be issued as if they were unmarried; nor shall any husband be liable upon any contract made by his wife in her own name and upon her own responsibility, nor for any tort committed separately by her out of his presence without his participation or sanction: *Provided,* That no married woman shall

----

[13] de Montmorency, The Changing Status of a Married Woman, 13 L.Q. Rev. 187, 192 (1897).

[14] 2 Pollock & Maitland 433. See also the discussion of the wife's "equity to a settlement" in 1 American Law of Property §5.54 (Casner ed. 1952).

[15] The first English statute was enacted in 1857. See Graveson, The Background of the Century, in A Century of Family Law 1, 4 (Graveson & Crane eds. 1957). The earliest American provision was adopted in 1844. See 3 Vernier §149.

[16] See Kahn-Freund, Inconsistencies and Injustices in the Law of Husband and Wife, 15 Mod. L. Rev. 133, 135 (1952).

have power to make any contract as surety or guarantor, or as accommodation drawer, accepter, maker, or indorser.[17]

The legal attributes of infancy were apparently never affected by notions of legal identity of parent and child. An infant could sue to protect his interest in land, and "must answer for his own wrongdoing, for example, a disseisin that he has perpetrated, and he may not have any guardian either in law or in fact." [18] The disparity between the treatment of married women and infants is in part attributable to the "deep reverence for seisin which characterizes medieval law" [19] and to the financial concomitants of feudal tenures. Certainly the father's prerogatives as guardian of his infant child were not ignored: he was entitled to the child's services and earnings — a right reciprocal to the father's obligation of support; and he was entitled to compensation for tortious conduct which injured the child, so long as the injury resulted in loss of the child's services. Indeed, because the notion of guardianship for the benefit of the ward came much later, the early common law was obliged

> to have recourse to a ruder expedient. The guardian will manage the infant's property during his minority; but during that minority the status quo must as far as possible be maintained. . . . All claims by or against the infant must await the infant's majority for settlement. All actions to assert those claims will therefore be suspended. . . . It was this conception which was the basis of the common law doctrine as to infants . . . .[20]

But no notion of a parent-child identity emerged. An infant had many legal disabilities and was entitled to special privileges; "but the legal capacity of the infant is hardly, if at all, affected by the life or death of his father, and the man or woman who is of full age is in no sort subject to paternal power." [21]

If an infant was emancipated, at least some, and perhaps all, of the concomitants of the father-child relationship were eliminated. But emancipation — a doctrine of much later vintage — did not modify the infant's general incapacities. All disabilities of infancy were abolished only when the child reached majority. Early English law set no single age of majority:

> The young burgess is of full age when he can count money and measure cloth; . . . the tenant by knight's service when he is twenty-one years old. . . . That prolongation of the disabilities and privileges of infancy, which must have taken place sooner or later, has been hastened by the introduction of heavy armour. But here again we have a good instance of the manner in which the law for the gentry be-

[17] D.C. Code Ann. §30-208 (1961), as amended in 1926 to delete concluding proviso. For a discussion of the several varieties, see 3 Vernier 24-29.

[18] 2 Pollock & Maitland 442.

[19] Id. at 443.

[20] 3 Holdsworth, History of English Law 513 (3d ed. 1923).

[21] 2 Pollock & Maitland 438.

comes English common law. The military tenant is kept in ward until he is twenty-one years old; the tenant in socage is out of ward six or seven years earlier. Gradually however the knightly majority is becoming the majority of the common law. . . . Coke tells us of the seven ages of a woman; but the only line of general importance is drawn at the age of one and twenty; and *infant* . . . stands equally well for the new-born babe and the youth who is in his twenty-first year.[22]

We will refer to the powers and disabilities of the infant only to provide counterpoint. The infant's "legal capacity does not directly concern the family as such." [23]

Whether or not they are deduced from fictions, legal doctrines must be devised, judicially or by legislation, to order the affairs of members of families. Duties and rights among the members must be articulated; relationships between members and outsiders must be clarified. It is easy enough to state the major concern of the sections which follow: under contemporary social conditions, to what extent and for what purposes should the family be considered a unit? Since the answers depend, or certainly should depend, on the legal issues to be decided, we have posed not one, but many questions. If the answers to these questions are left to the judiciary, history will obviously be influential. But other considerations should be equally important.

PROBLEM

In response to the continuing drive for the removal of all legal discriminations against women, a number of countries have recently adopted constitutional amendments which provide that men and women shall be equal before the law. See, e.g., Article 3, Paragraph 2 of the German Constitution (Federal Republic). A similar amendment has been introduced in each Congress in the United States since 1923. In the version presented to the 88th Congress the amendment read as follows: "Equality of rights under the law shall not be denied or abridged by the United States or by any State on account of sex." S.J. Res. 45. The amendment was approved by the Senate both in 1950 and 1953, albeit with the so-called Hayden rider, which provided that the amendment "shall not be construed to impair any rights, benefits, or exemptions now or hereafter conferred by law upon persons of the female sex." [24]

As you examine the materials presented in this chapter, consider whether you would favor this amendment. With or without the Hayden rider? What would the amendment accomplish? What would it *not* accomplish? What problems would it create?

Compare §703 of the Civil Rights Act of 1964 which prohibits discrimi-

---

[22] Id. at 438-439.

[23] Morrison, Contract, in A Century of Family Law 116, 139 (Graveson & Crane eds. 1957).

[24] 96 Cong. Rec. 870 (1950), 99 id. 8973 (1953).

nation in private employment on account of "race, color, religion, sex, or national origin" unless "religion, sex, or national origin is a bona fide occupational qualification reasonably necessary to the normal operation of that particular business or enterprise."   42 U.S.C.A. §2000e-2(a), (e) (1964).

B. SUPPORT AND PROPERTY RIGHTS

McGUIRE v. McGUIRE
157 Neb. 226, 59 N.W.2d 336 (1953)

MESSMORE, J. The plaintiff, Lydia McGuire, brought this action in equity in the district court for Wayne County against Charles W. McGuire, her husband, as defendant, to recover suitable maintenance and support money, and for costs and attorney's fees. Trial was had to the court and a decree was rendered in favor of the plaintiff.

The district court decreed that the plaintiff was legally entitled to use the credit of the defendant and obligate him to pay for certain items in the nature of improvements and repairs, furniture, and appliances for the household in the amount of several thousand dollars; required the defendant to purchase a new automobile with an effective heater within 30 days; ordered him to pay travel expenses of the plaintiff for a visit to each of her daughters at least once a year; that the plaintiff be entitled in the future to pledge the credit of the defendant for what may constitute necessaries of life; awarded a personal allowance to the plaintiff in the sum of $50 a month; awarded $800 for services for the plaintiff's attorney; and as an alternative to part of the award so made, defendant was permitted, in agreement with plaintiff, to purchase a modern home elsewhere.

The defendant filed a motion for new trial which was overruled. From this order the defendant perfected appeal to this court.

For convenience we will refer to the parties as they are designated in the district court.

The record shows that the plaintiff and defendant were married in Wayne, Nebraska, on August 11, 1919. At the time of the marriage the defendant was a bachelor 46 or 47 years of age and had a reputation for more than ordinary frugality, of which the plaintiff was aware. She had visited in his home and had known him for about 3 years prior to the marriage. After the marriage the couple went to live on a farm of 160 acres located in Leslie precinct, Wayne County, owned by the defendant and upon which he had lived and farmed since 1905. The parties have lived on this place ever since. The plaintiff had been previously married. Her first husband died in October 1914, leaving surviving him the plaintiff and two daughters. He died intestate, leaving 80 acres of land in Dixon County. The plaintiff and each of the daughters inherited a one-third interest therein. At the time of the marriage of the plaintiff and defendant the plaintiff's daughters were 9 and 11 years of age. By working and receiving financial assistance from the parties to this action, the daughters received a high school education in Pender. One daughter attended Wayne State Teachers College for 2 years and the other daughter attended a business college in Sioux City, Iowa, for 1 year. Both of these daughters are married and have families of their own.

On April 12, 1939, the plaintiff transferred her interest in the 80-acre farm to her two daughters. The defendant signed the deed.

At the time of trial plaintiff was 66 years of age and the defendant nearly 80 years of age. No children were born to these parties. The defendant had no dependents except the plaintiff.

The plaintiff testified that she was a dutiful and obedient wife, worked and saved, and cohabited with the defendant until the last 2 or 3 years. She worked in the fields, did outside chores, cooked, and attended to her household duties such as cleaning the house and doing the washing. For a number of years she raised as high as 300 chickens, sold poultry and eggs, and used the money to buy clothing, things she wanted, and for groceries. She further testified that the defendant was the boss of the house and his word was law; that he would not tolerate any charge accounts and would not inform her as to his finances or business; and that he was a poor companion. The defendant did not complain of her work, but left the impression to her that she had not done enough. On several occasions the plaintiff asked the defendant for money. He would give her very small amounts, and for the last 3 or 4 years he had not given her any money nor provided her with clothing, except a coat about 4 years previous. The defendant had purchased the groceries the last 3 or 4 years, and permitted her to buy groceries, but he paid for them by check. There is apparently no complaint about the groceries the defendant furnished. The defendant had not taken her to a motion picture show during the past 12 years. They did not belong to any organizations or charitable institutions, nor did he give her money to make contributions to any charitable institutions. The defendant belongs to the Pleasant Valley Church which occupies about 2 acres of his farm land. At the time of trial there was no minister for this church so there were no services. For the past 4 years or more, the defendant had not given the plaintiff money to purchase furniture or other household necessities. Three years ago he did purchase an electric, wood-and-cob combination stove which was installed in the kitchen, also linoleum floor covering for the kitchen. The plaintiff further testified that the house is not equipped with a bathroom, bathing facilities, or inside toilet. The kitchen is not modern. She does not have a kitchen sink. Hard and soft water is obtained from a well and cistern. She has a mechanical Servel refrigerator, and the house is equipped with electricity. There is a pipeless furnace which she testified had not been in good working order for 5 or 6 years, and she testified she was tired of scooping coal and ashes. She had requested a new furnace but the defendant believed the one they had to be satisfactory. She related that the furniture was old and she would like to replenish it, at least to be comparable with some of her neighbors; that her silverware and dishes were old and were primarily gifts, outside of what she purchased;

that one of her daughters was good about furnishing her clothing, at least a dress a year, or sometimes two; that the defendant owns a 1929 Ford coupé equipped with a heater which is not efficient, and on the average of every 2 weeks he drives the plaintiff to Wayne to visit her mother; and that he also owns a 1927 Chevrolet pickup which is used for different purposes on the farm. The plaintiff was privileged to use all of the rent money she wanted to from the 80-acre farm, and when she goes to see her daughters, which is not frequent, she uses part of the rent money for that purpose, the defendant providing no funds for such use. The defendant ordinarily raised hogs on his farm, but the last 4 or 5 years has leased his farm land to tenants, and he generally keeps up the fences and the buildings. At the present time the plaintiff is not able to raise chickens and sell eggs. She has about 25 chickens. The plaintiff has had three abdominal operations for which the defendant has paid. She selected her own doctor, and there were no restrictions placed in that respect. When she has requested various things for the home or personal effects, defendant has informed her on many occasions that he did not have the money to pay for the same. She would like to have a new car. She visited one daughter in Spokane, Washington, in March 1951 for 3 or 4 weeks, and visited the other daughter living in Fort Worth, Texas, on three occasions for 2 to 4 weeks at a time. She had visited one of her daughters when she was living in Sioux City some weekends. The plaintiff further testified that she had very little funds, possibly $1500 in the bank which was chicken money and money which her father furnished her, he having departed this life a few years ago; and that use of the telephone was restricted, indicating that defendant did not desire that she make long distance calls, otherwise she had free access to the telephone.

It appears that the defendant owned 398 acres of land with 2 acres deeded to a church, the land being of the value of $83,960; that he has bank deposits in the sum of $12,786.81 and government bonds in the amount of $104,500; and that his income, including interest on the bonds and rental for his real estate, is $8000 or $9000 a year. There are apparently some Series E United States Savings Bonds listed and registered in the names of Charles W. McGuire or Lydia M. McGuire purchased in 1943, 1944, and 1945, in the amount of $2500. Other bonds seem to be in the name of Charles W. McGuire, without a beneficiary or co-owner designated. The plaintiff has a bank account of $5960.22. This account includes deposits of some $200 and $100 which the court required the defendant to pay his wife as temporary allowance during the pendency of these proceedings. One hundred dollars was withdrawn on the date of each deposit.

The facts are not in dispute. . . .

[The court then reviewed a series of cases from Nebraska and other jurisdictions which held that where the spouses are living separate and apart, or where the husband is guilty of such abusive conduct as to entitle the wife to move out, or where the husband has deserted the wife, she may maintain an action for separate maintenance.]

It becomes apparent that there are no cases cited by the plaintiff and relied upon by her from this jurisdiction or other jurisdictions that will sustain the action such as she has instituted in the instant case.

With reference to the proposition that the parties are living under the same roof, [the cases have held] that while a wife had no right to the interference of the court for her maintenance until her abandonment or separation, there might be an abandonment or separation, within the sound construction of the statute, while the parties continued to live under the same roof, as where the husband utterly refused to have intercourse with his wife, or to make any provision for her maintenance, and thus he might seclude himself in a portion of his house, take his meals alone or board elsewhere than in his house, and so as effectively separate himself from his wife and refuse to provide for her as in case of actual abandonment, although in whatever form it might exist there must be an abandonment. . . .

In the instant case the marital relation has continued for more than 33 years, and the wife has been supported in the same manner during this time without complaint on her part. The parties have not been separated or living apart from each other at any time. In the light of the cited cases it is clear, especially so in this jurisdiction, that to maintain an action such as the one at bar, the parties must be separated or living apart from each other.

The living standards of a family are a matter of concern to the household, and not for the courts to determine, even though the husband's attitude toward his wife, according to his wealth and circumstances, leaves little to be said in his behalf. As long as the home is maintained and the parties are living as husband and wife it may be said that the husband is legally supporting his wife and the purpose of the marriage relation is being carried out. Public policy requires such a holding. It appears that the plaintiff is not devoid of money in her own right. She has a fair-sized bank account and is entitled to use the rent from the 80 acres of land left by her first husband, if she so chooses. . . .

Reversed and remanded with directions to dismiss.

YEAGER, J., dissenting. . . . There is and can be no doubt that, independent of statutes relating to divorce, alimony, and separate maintenance, if this plaintiff were living apart from the defendant she could in equity and on the facts as outlined in the record be awarded appropriate relief. . . .

If relief is to be denied to plaintiff under this principle it must be denied because of the fact that she is not living separate and apart from the defendant and is not seeking separation.

In the light of what the decisions declare to be the basis of the right to maintain an action for support, is there any less reason for extending the right to a wife who is denied the right to maintenance in a home occupied with her husband than to one who has chosen to occupy a separate abode?

If the right is to be extended only to one who is separated from the husband equity and effective justice would be denied where a wealthy husband refused proper support and maintenance to a wife physically or mentally incapable of putting herself in a position where the rule could become available to her.

It is true that in all cases examined which uphold the right of a wife to maintain an action in equity for maintenance the parties were living apart, but no case has been cited or found which says that separation is a condition precedent to the right to maintain an action in equity for maintenance. Likewise none has been cited or found which says that it is not.

In primary essence the rule contemplates the enforcement of an obligation within and not without the full marriage relationship. The reasoning contained in the opinions sustaining this right declare that purpose.

In Earle v. Earle [27 Neb. 277, 281, 43 N.W. 118, 119 (1889)], it was said: "The question is, whether or not the plaintiff shall be compelled to resort to a proceeding for a divorce, which she does not desire to do, and which probably she is unwilling to do, from conscientious convictions, or, in failing to do so, shall be deprived of that support which her husband is bound to give her." . . .

I think however that the court was without proper power to make any of the awards contained in the decree for the support and maintenance of the plaintiff except the one of $50 a month.

From the cases cited herein it is clear that a husband has the obligation to furnish to his wife the necessaries of life. These decisions make clear that for failure to furnish them the wife may seek allowances for her support and maintenance. However neither these decisions nor any others cited or found support the view contended for by plaintiff that the court may go beyond this and impose obligations other than that of payment of money for the proper support and maintenance of the wife.

There is no doubt that plaintiff had the right to charge her husband with her necessaries of life and that recovery could be had therefor. No award of a court of equity was necessary to establish this right. Nothing was accomplished by the declaration of that right. The provision relating thereto therefore had no proper place in the decree. . . .

As pointed out the district court made an allowance of $50 a month. In the light of generally well-known present day economy the conclusion is inevitable that this award is insufficient for the maintenance of the plaintiff. The record before us however does not supply adequate information upon which this court could make a finding as to what would be sufficient.

. . . [A]ccordingly this phase of the case should be remanded to the district court for the taking of evidence in order that finding may be made as to what would be adequate for plaintiff's suitable maintenance. . . .

NOTE

1. Compare a report describing the operations of the Jewish Conciliation Board of America, a private body set up for the purpose of resolving family disputes according to Jewish law and custom. The matters dealt with by the Board pertain to such subjects as demands for increased support, interfering in-laws and child-parent controversies. The parties are

required in advance of the hearing to sign an arbitration agreement which stipulates the judicial enforceability of the award. Tolchin, Jewish Family Problems Are Settled Out of Court, N.Y. Times, Aug. 24, 1962, p. 28, col. 7. But see page 809 infra concerning the difficulties posed by judicial enforcement of such awards. See also page 327 infra for a consideration of husband-wife support contracts.

2. Although factual situations like that depicted in McGuire are probably not uncommon, there is a dearth of reported decisions. Why is this so? This dearth of decisions, coupled with the results of cases like McGuire, helps to explain why it is so difficult to determine the precise scope of a man's legal duty to support his wife and children while the family is united. Such support statutes as there are are characteristically unhelpful, and the extent of his obligations is commonly inferred from the results in other types of litigation, such as divorce proceedings,[25] parents' suits under Dram Shop statutes for a child's death or injury, wrongful death actions, and criminal prosecutions or allied proceedings for nonsupport. Another indirect enforcement device is the ancient doctrine alluded to in the dissenting opinion which holds a man responsible to the supplier for "necessaries" furnished to his wife. The types of items generally encompassed by this doctrine are clothes, household supplies, furniture, certain jewelry, and medical or dental services; the specific application of the doctrine usually depends upon the husband's "station in life." The fact that the wife has sufficient independent income or earning capacity normally does not absolve the husband. However, he does have a variety of defenses available to him in such actions, e.g., that he has already adequately provided his wife either with the items or with money to purchase them, that the merchant intended to extend credit to the wife alone, or that the wife has abandoned the family home without good cause. Compare the so-called "Family Expense" statutes enacted by approximately twenty-five states which are sometimes quite detailed and often extend to items beyond mere "necessaries." See, e.g., Conn. Gen. Stat. Ann. §46-10 (1958). These statutes were passed primarily for the benefit of creditors and make both husband and wife jointly liable; the husband, however, normally has a duty to indemnify the wife. See 3 Vernier 102-108. Note finally that in many cases the husband is liable to the supplier simply because his wife is found to have been his agent.

In line with the prevailing world-wide trend towards legal equality of men and women, some states have made the wife secondarily liable for the family's support where she has sufficient means and the husband does not. See, e.g., Ohio Rev. Code Ann. §3103.03 (Page 1960). Some of the family expense statutes have even gone so far as to make the property of both husband and wife jointly or severally liable for the "reasonable and necessary expenses of the family and the education of the children," without any right of indemnification by the wife against the husband. Iowa Code Ann. §597.14 (1950). The last step toward complete equality would be a statute which would require the wife to contribute part of her earnings, either from her employment or perhaps from any property

[25] See Chapter 10.

which she owned, toward the support of the family. In a state which still looks solely to the husband for the family's support, which, if any, of these alternatives would you favor? Before coming to a final conclusion on this matter, consider the note on matrimonial property regimes (page 317 infra) which seeks to put the problem of support into the broader context of husband-wife property relationships.

In general, see Paulsen, Support Rights and Duties between Husband and Wife, 9 Vand. L. Rev. 709 (1956); Annot., 60 A.L.R.2d 7 (1958).

3. Although the early common law, and even fairly recent English decisions, posit only a "moral obligation" in the parent to provide support for children, the current rule in most American jurisdictions is that the father is liable for "necessaries" purchased by an unemancipated child living with the family.[26] See 4 Vernier §234; Greenspan v. Slate, 12 N.J. 426, 97 A.2d 390 (1953). This liability provides a counterpart to the parent's right, up to emancipation, to the child's earnings. A number of jurisdictions impose liability by statute beyond twenty-one if the child is disabled. See, e.g., N.Y. Dom. Rel. Law §32. The mother, too, is liable for the child's necessaries upon the death of the father or when she otherwise comes into custody and control of the child, as are other persons who are found to be in loco parentis. 4 Vernier 56. The courts in several states, either by statutory interpretation or in reliance on their own equitable powers, have permitted children to obtain direct enforcement of the parents' duty of support. See id. at 57-58; Annot., 13 A.L.R.2d 1142 (1950). Compare also page 918 infra with respect to child support issues raised in divorce proceedings.

4. Where there are insufficient resources within the immediate family, public support programs such as ADC come into play. See page 67 supra, note 43. In this connection, keep in mind the so-called "poor laws" which impose support liability on various relatives of the indigent family member, and sometimes even require such relatives to reimburse the state for financial assistance or institutionalization supplied to the indigent. See Mandelker, Family Responsibility under the American Poor Laws, 54 Mich. L. Rev. 497, 607 (1956); tenBroek, California's Dual System of Family Law: Its Origin, Development, and Present Status, 16 Stan. L. Rev. 257, 900 (1964), 17 id. 614 (1965).

PROBLEM

Laws in other areas sometimes make specific reference to the laws of support. For example, §677 of the Internal Revenue Code of 1954 taxes

[26] Although infants are themselves held liable for their purchases of "necessaries," they may usually disaffirm other contracts prior to or within a reasonable time after reaching majority. See 2 Williston, Contracts §§222 et seq. (3d ed. 1959). The scope of the protection afforded infants has been criticized because the interests of tradesmen are largely subordinated. See New York Law Revision Commission, Report for 1938, Act, Recommendation and Study Relating to Infancy as a Defense to a Contract 105-161, reprinted in Selected Essays on Family Law 647.

As regards the concept of emancipation, see page 344 infra.

the settlor of a trust on the income of the trust if the trustee may and actually does use such income to discharge the settlor's obligation to support his dependents as determined by applicable state law. Suppose H, a resident of Georgia, with an annual income of $20,000 a year, has set up a trust, the income of which is to be accumulated for the benefit of his children, subject to a power in the trustee to apply it for W's "needs." H now wants the trustee to purchase W a new Buick convertible, and the trustee is willing to do so. H asks you to give him an opinion whether this will result in the income being taxed to him. Ga. Code Ann. §53-510 (1961) provides: "The husband shall be bound to support and maintain his wife, and his consent shall be presumed to her agency in all purchases of necessaries suitable to her condition and habits of life, made for the use of herself and the family. This presumption may be rebutted by proof." What will you advise him?

FLAGLER v. FLAGLER

94 So.2d 592 (Fla. 1957)

Luckie, J. Harold Flagler secured a divorce from Nellie Flagler in January, 1949, obtaining service on her by publication. At the time of the divorce Nellie Flagler was alleged to be a resident of Wisconsin. Also, at the time, she was pregnant and was delivered of a female child on September 4, 1949. On November 19, 1949, Harold Flagler executed his will in which he made no reference to the minor child or to his former wife, but left the bulk of his estate to his then wife, Juanita Flagler. In January of 1950 Nellie Flagler petitioned the court to have the divorce decree set aside and to compel Harold Flagler to support the child. In the latter proceeding Harold denied the paternity of the child and objected to any allowance for the child's support. The court denied Nellie's petition to set aside the divorce, but held that Harold did not overcome the legal presumption that he was the father of the child. Harold was ordered to pay $300.00 per month for the support of the child. He made all payments until his death on January 6, 1955. Juanita Flagler has been duly appointed as administratrix of Harold's estate in Illinois and is now the ancillary executrix in Florida of Harold's last will and testament and of his estate, which is valued in excess of $400,000.00.

Thereafter, Nellie Flagler, claiming that neither she nor the minor child have any funds whatever, petitioned the lower court to substitute Juanita Flagler, as ancillary executrix, for Harold Flagler as the obligor under the support decree, and for a decree requiring the ancillary executrix to continue to make payments for the support of the child until the child reaches her majority. The lower court ruled against Nellie Flagler and followed an earlier decision of this court in the case of Guinta v. Lo Re, 159 Fla. 488, 31 So.2d 704, holding that the obligation of the father to support the minor child terminated upon the death of the father. . . .

We readily agree that minors in divorce cases are wards of the court and should receive every protection consistent with the law. But we cannot agree that courts of equity have any right or power under the law of

Florida to issue such order it considers to be in the best interest of "social justice" at the particular moment without regard to established law. This court has no authority to change the law simply because the law seems to us to be inadequate in some particular case. The right of a parent to disinherit his children seems to be firmly rooted in our law, subject only to the provisions of the Probate Act or such other laws as the legislature may enact.

This court does not necessarily *prefer* to protect the father's power of testamentary disposition rather than the welfare of the child, but the court does feel that only the legislature has the authority to enact laws dealing with this problem. It is significant that at the next session of the legislature following our decision in Guinta v. Lo Re, supra, Section 733.20, Florida Statutes, was amended to provide for the support of any dependent minor child from the estate of a parent dying testate, when there is no legally responsible surviving natural or adoptive parent, such amendment being "designed to afford reasonable protection to any dependent minor child who has been excluded from the provisions of the parents' will under circumstances which deprive it of an effective legal substitute for the continuing obligation of the parent, while living, for support and maintenance during the period of its minority." Chapter 25274, Laws of Florida, Acts of 1949, §733.20(j), Florida Statutes 1955, F.S.A. Apparently it was not the intention of the legislature to place a dependent minor child in whose favor a support decree was in existence at the time of a parent's death in a preferred position over a dependent minor child not having the benefit of a support decree. . . .

Affirmed.

TERRELL, C.J., and THOMAS and O'CONNELL, JJ., dissent. [Opinion omitted.]

NOTE

1. Whether or not it is desirable that the support and property rights of family members during the marriage be more strictly defined by the legislature and enforced by the courts, the instant case illustrates that these problems are unavoidably thrust before the courts and legislatures upon dissolution of the marriage by death or divorce. In Chapter 10 we will examine more closely the rights of wives and children upon dissolution of the marriage and in particular the question whether support orders survive the death of the husband. Here we are more concerned with the fact, noted in passing by the court, that in our legal system a parent is free to disinherit his minor child.[27] In most civil law countries, a child (minor or otherwise) is entitled to a certain statutory share of the parent's estate. The precise share and the method of enforcing it vary from country to country. Interestingly enough, in France an "unworthy child" (defined

[27] As noted previously (page 32 supra), pretermission statutes generally establish a presumption that the mere omission of a child in the parent's will was unintentional. But the Florida statute only covers children born after the execution of the will. Fla. Stat. Ann. §731.11 (1964).

as one who has attacked or slanderously accused the decedent or who has refused to denounce his murderer) is denied participation in the estate. Code Civil, art. 727 (57th ed. Dalloz 1958). Yet another approach that is utilized by New Zealand and a number of other countries is to provide wives and children with a right to continued maintenance but according to a discretionary grant by the probate court rather than a statutorily fixed share. See Laufer, Flexible Restraints on Testamentary Freedom — A Report on Decedents' Family Maintenance Legislation, 69 Harv. L. Rev. 277 (1955). In view of our traditional concern for the welfare of the child, is there any rational explanation for this seeming disregard of its welfare in this regard? Would you favor a change in the Florida law to permit a child to share in the estate? How should such an amendment be worded?

2. The wife has fared somewhat better. At common law she enjoyed the right of dower, which entitled her to a life estate in one third of the real estate which the husband owned at any time during coverture. See 1 American Law of Property, pt. 5 (Casner ed. 1952). Although the wife's dower rights arguably gave her sufficient protection at a time when land was the major form of wealth, in recent times a number of jurisdictions have substituted for dower (or occasionally provided as an alternative option to dower) a so-called statutory forced share which, generally speaking, entitles the wife to so much of the husband's property (both real and personal) as she would have been entitled to if he had died intestate.[28] Note, however, that the statutory forced share usually only applies to property actually owned by the husband at the time of his death. Thus, in those jurisdictions which have altogether abolished dower and substituted the statutory forced share, there naturally arises the question whether the husband, by judicious inter vivos transfers, can so deplete his estate as effectively to deprive the wife of her statutory share.[29] In the vast majority of states an outright, absolute transfer would successfully withstand attack by the widow. A few jurisdictions invalidate such transfers where fraud or an intent to deprive the surviving spouse of her inheritance rights can be established. See Dunnett v. Shields, 97 Vt. 419, 123 Atl. 626 (1924); Mo. Ann. Stat. §474.150-1 (Supp. 1964). Others have struck down only those transfers which are "illusory." Newman v. Dore, 275 N.Y. 371, 9 N.E.2d 966 (1937) (where settlor retained income for life as well as power of revocation and right to control trustee, trust held illusory). A third approach is in terms of retention of excessive control over the transferred property. See Pa. Stat. Ann. tit. 20, §301.11 (Supp. 1964)

---

[28] The husband had a comparable right of "curtesy" at common law, and is usually also entitled to a statutory forced share in those states which have provided such.

[29] The analogous problem can arise with respect to surviving husbands in those states which have abolished curtesy and have given the husband instead a statutory forced share.

Under a recent Massachusetts statute enacted at the behest of the conveyancers, even dower and curtesy can be claimed only with respect to property owned at death. Acts 1965, c. 165. Thus, similar possibilities of inter vivos avoidance transfers are presented.

(where grantor retains power of appointment or revocation or right to consume principal, transfer treated as testamentary, but provision inapplicable to insurance). But compare National Shawmut Bank v. Cummings, 325 Mass. 457, 91 N.E.2d 337 (1950) (validity of trust upheld against surviving spouse despite fact that husband was co-trustee and retained income for life as well as power of revocation and right to demand principal). See 1 Scott, Trusts §57.5 (2d ed. 1956); Annot., 49 A.L.R.2d 521 (1956). The significance to be attached to the donor's control is most sharply put in issue by the so-called Totten Trust, an informal trust of a savings bank account for the benefit of a named person, with the depositor retaining complete power of disposition over the account through retention of the savings book. See In re Jeruzal's Estate, 269 Minn. 183, 130 N.W.2d 473 (1964) (in the absence of a contrary enactment by the legislature, Minnesota courts will henceforth apply the Restatement rule recognizing a Totten Trust insofar as the beneficiary is concerned but allowing the surviving spouse to include such transfer in the estate for purposes of computing her statutory share). New York, following earlier judicial recognition of the Totten Trust, recently provided (effective with respect to wills executed after August 31, 1966) that the following types of transfers will be deemed "testamentary" and hence includible for the purpose of determining the wife's statutory share: joint bank accounts, property held in joint tenancy or tenancy by the entireties, Totten Trusts, gifts causa mortis, and transfers as to which the decedent retained a power to revoke, consume, invade, or otherwise dispose. Pension plan benefits, life insurance, and government bonds are specifically exempted. N.Y. Sess. Laws 1965, c. 665, §1, amending Decedent Estate Law by adding §§18-a and 18-b.

3. Other, less significant, benefits of the surviving spouse include the so-called homestead exemptions which protect the spouses' residence up to certain statutory limits against attachment by creditors or transfer without the wife's consent. However, the statutory limits were set many years ago and have remained fixed "in disregard of economic and other social changes." [30] Many jurisdictions also provide for temporary allowances to the widow while the estate is in administration. In general, see 3 Vernier §228.

McCLELLAN ESTATE
365 Pa. 401, 75 A.2d 595 (1950)

BELL, J. . . . The widow of the decedent duly filed her election to take against his will. Eight months later the executors filed a petition praying that the election to take against the will should be stricken from the records because the widow and the decedent had entered into an antenuptial agreement specifically fixing the amount or share of decedent's estate to which the widow should be entitled. The court dismissed the petition on the ground that the provision for the widow was unreasonable

---

[30] 1 American Law of Property §5.82, p. 828 (Casner ed. 1952). Some states have raised the limits in recent years. Ibid. and id. at n.32 (Supp. 1962).

and grossly inadequate and that the decedent had not made a full and fair disclosure to his fiancee of his worth.

Dr. McClellan, the decedent, was married to the respondent on May 15, 1943, and they lived together for four years and five months until the decedent's death. At the time of the marriage the Doctor was 80 years old and the respondent 58. Each of them had been married before, the Doctor having several children and the respondent one child by a prior marriage.

Decedent by his will gave his wife $5000. pursuant to said ante-nuptial agreement; as well as household furniture and effects, and the right to live in their apartment without payment of any rent or taxes (in connection with said premises) as long as his wife remained his widow. The $5000. legacy and the furniture and effects were bequeathed free of tax. Decedent gave respondent at some undisclosed time prior to his death, securities worth approximately $15,000.

Respondent and her first husband rented the Doctor's home for $40. a month and the Doctor paid respondent $50. a month for an apartment in said home and for board and lodging. This arrangement continued for several years. A year after the death of respondent's first husband she and the Doctor entered into the aforesaid ante-nuptial agreement which provided in the first paragraph thereof that his "Executors . . . shall pay to her the sum of $5000.00 in full satisfaction, payment, and discharge of any and all claims that the party of the second part may have under any and all laws as his widow or heir at law . . . ." The agreement also provided as follows: "Fifth: This agreement is entered into by each party with full knowledge . . . of the extent and probable value of all the property, or estate, of the other, ..." *Attached to the ante-nuptial agreement* and offered in evidence by the decedent's executors was a paper which was found in the possession of the decedent and was signed by the respondent and duly witnessed: ". . . He has bought and holds in his own name the following real estate," naming four properties valued at $68,000. "and bank stocks worth $15,000., Jersey and other stocks $20,000., and bonds worth about $90,000., but that for fear something was underestimated, or forgotten, we added $7000." The parties agreed that the actual value of the Doctor's real estate at the time was $70,100., so that he made a substantially correct disclosure of his real estate. However, at the time of the ante-nuptial agreement, the bank stocks had an actual value of $86,152.50; Jersey and other stocks $147,379.98; bonds $249,778.23; cash in banks $36,376.55. In other words the Doctor had disclosed personal property of $132,000., whereas the actual value of his personal property was $519,727. (less liabilities of $10,500). . . .

At the time of the Doctor's death, his assets . . . totalled $675,500., made up of securities and cash of $580,000. and real estate of $95,500. There was no evidence as to the testator's income during his life, but from accounts filed after his death it appeared that he had an annual income from securities and real estate alone of approximately $19,608.

At the time of the ante-nuptial agreement the respondent owned a house worth $6000. which had a gross annual rental value of $600. and household goods and cash aggregating $1000. After his death she received Social Security benefits of approximately $400. a year.

Ante-nuptial agreements depend for their validity upon the presence of one of two factors, namely: A reasonable provision for the wife, or in the absence of such provision, a full and fair disclosure to the wife of the husband's worth [citations omitted].

Where the provision made for the wife is grossly disproportionate to the value of the husband's estate, fraudulent concealment will be presumed and the burden of proof thrown on him to show that full disclosure had been made [citations omitted].

It is also well established that in considering the adequacy of the provisions for a wife in an ante-nuptial agreement, all of the relevant facts and circumstances surrounding the case must be considered; and the true test of adequacy is whether the provision for the intended wife is sufficient to enable her to live comfortably after her husband's death in substantially the same way as, considering all the circumstances, she had previously lived [citations omitted].

Considering all the facts and circumstances in this case, the provision for his future wife in the ante-nuptial agreement plus the decedent's gift to her of $15,000, was very unreasonable and grossly inadequate. Fraudulent concealment will therefore be presumed and decedent's executors had the burden of proving that decedent had made a full and fair disclosure of his worth at the time of the ante-nuptial agreement. The executors contend that such a disclosure was made because the agreement recites that it "is entered into by each party with full knowledge on the part of each of the extent and probable value of all of the property, or estate, of the other . . . ." Such a provision is prima facie evidence that a full and fair disclosure had been made by the husband to the wife of his worth [citations omitted]. However, this statement in the agreement is rebutted and completely overcome by the facts which appeared in detail in said agreement, namely, that the Doctor had unintentionally or intentionally materially misrepresented the value of his personal property in that he disclosed said property had a value of $132,000., whereas its value was $519,000. . . .

This agreement was entered into and executed by the Doctor's fiancee under unusual circumstances. Dr. McClellan's attorney prepared the agreement and brought with him and paid his office attorney or assistant to represent the Doctor's fiancee. No disclosure or explanation was made to her at that time and no inquiry was made as to decedent's worth except what was set forth in the ante-nuptial agreement and in the aforesaid paper which was attached to and became a part of the ante-nuptial agreement.

It is obvious that Dr. McClellan stood in a confidential relationship to his fiancee and that she did not have independent counsel or independent advice. Moreover, a very material misrepresentation, wittingly or unwittingly, was made to her by the Doctor as to the value of his property. There is no doubt that she was overreached and that the agreement was voidable at her election. . . .

NOTE

1. Would the result of the McClellan case have been different if the doctor had made full disclosure?

2. Section 587 of the Restatement of Contracts (1932) provides that "A bargain between married persons or persons contemplating marriage to change the essential incidents of marriage is illegal." In view of the long history of protection for widows through dower and the statutory forced share, why should courts permit women to forego this minimum protection which the law has afforded them? Why is the widow's share not an "essential incident" of the marriage? Compare, by way of contrast, the traditional nonenforceability of antenuptial agreements which wholly or partly purport to relieve the husband of his duty to support his wife during the marriage or which provide for specific alimony and property divisions upon separation or divorce. Note also that some state statutes expressly provide that the surviving spouse shall not be entitled to a statutory share where he or she has received instead such property as was provided for in a written antenuptial agreement. See, e.g., Conn. Gen. Stat. Ann. §46-12 (Supp. 1964).

3. Full discussion of the problems involved in the drafting and enforceability of antenuptial contracts will be found in Lindey, Separation Agreements and Antenuptial Contracts, pt. 4 (1964).

4. Concerning postnuptial agreements (other than those entered into in contemplation of divorce, see Chapter 11) a distinction similar to that adverted to in Note 2 supra prevails. Except in those few states where husband-wife contracts pertaining to their property rights are altogether invalid, see, e.g., Iowa Code Ann. §597.2 (1950), a postnuptial agreement whereby one spouse waives his or her rights in the other's estate is generally held valid if it is supported by fair and adequate consideration. 1 American Law of Property §5.40 (Casner ed. 1952). The courts usually find consideration in the reciprocal waiver of dower and curtesy rights. See, e.g., Estate of Beat, 25 Wis. 2d 315, 130 N.W.2d 739 (1964). Postnuptial support agreements, however, are invalid. See pages 324-328 infra.

PROBLEMS

1. Your client is Richard Riley, a forty-five-year-old insurance salesman. He earns around $10,000 a year (with some considerable fluctuations), and he has no assets worth speaking of except for a small equity in a house, a car, and a small savings account.

Richard was married at age nineteen to his childhood sweetheart, Joan, and they had three children, who are now nineteen, fifteen, and eleven. Two years ago Joan was killed in an automobile accident. With means provided by Joan's parents, who are quite well off, Richard was able to get sufficient help to care for the children. Six months ago, Richard met and fell in love with an attractive thirty-nine-year-old divorcee, named Pamela, who was working as a salesgirl at a nearby department store. A few months ago he married her.

The problem which Richard is concerned about is the following. About six years ago and continuing up to Joan's death, her parents started to make fairly sizable annual gifts to her because they wanted her family to be able to live in a somewhat better style than Richard's modest income permitted. As of Joan's death, the net amount on hand was about $60,000. Recently, as a result of the settlement of Joan's will which left everything to Richard, this money has been paid to him. Now Joan's parents have begun to put considerable pressure on Richard to "put this money aside" for the children. They point out that they don't dislike Pamela, but that she does have extravagant tastes and that this money did, after all, come from "our side of the family." Richard is anxious not to hurt Pamela and "wants to do the right thing by everybody." He seeks your guidance as to what he should and could do to satisfy his in-laws. (Assume that your researches reveal no governing cases or authorities in your jurisdiction.)

2. Assume that you are in a state which presently permits a husband to transfer his property in trust, retaining substantial control over the property while at the same time successfully depriving his wife of her statutory share. You, as chairman of a bar association committee, are asked to formulate a remedial statute "to close this loophole." The following statute has been proposed: "All transfers made by a husband during coverture shall be included in determining the surviving spouse's statutory rights under §—." Would you favor its enactment? Why? If not, how would you modify it? Should the policy be different for Totten Trusts than for other types of transfers, as the framers of the Restatement of Trusts concluded? Compare Restatement (Second), Trusts §57, Comment *c*, with §58, Comment *e*.

MATRIMONIAL PROPERTY REGIMES [31]

The rights of support and inheritance which we have just examined present but two of the diverse problems which must be resolved in any legal system which purports to allocate property rights among family members. The initial task is to classify the various types of marital property and to assess the relative equities of the spouses in each. Frequently the husband and wife each owns some property which he or she brings into the marriage; under most circumstances, it would be difficult to make a strong case for creating an interest in such property in the other spouse

[31] In general, see Matrimonial Property Law (Friedmann ed. 1955); Legal Status of Married Women (United Nations 1958); Müller-Freienfels, Equality of Husband and Wife in Family Law, 8 Int. & Comp. L.Q. 249 (1959); Selected Essays in Family Law 503-574; Royal Commission on Marriage and Divorce, Report 1951-1955, Cmd. No. 9678, pp. 177 et seq. (1956). Except where otherwise indicated, the material which follows has been largely drawn from these sources.

solely because of the fact of marriage. A more persuasive argument might be made with respect to the income derived during the marriage from such separate property or with respect to extraordinary receipts (such as gifts or bequests) received by either of the spouses. Earned income received by the spouses in the course of the marriage undoubtedly presents the best case for some form of shared ownership; in the common situation where the husband obtains all or most of the earnings, the wife has materially contributed to its acquisition by her uncompensated services in the home. Yet even if marriage is to be regarded as an economic partnership — a view which has gained increasing recognition throughout the world — it does not necessarily follow that the wife must be given an immediate half interest in the husband's earnings. It may well be that the management of the marital property while the marriage is in full force and effect should be entrusted to the husband, because he is the one more generally versed in financial matters and because it is simpler to have one manager rather than to require joint action with respect to all property dispositions. Yet, as cases like McGuire (page 303 supra) suggest, the rights of management and control may be so crucial in some situations as to make almost academic other legal rights. Also, if management is to be separated from ownership, means must be devised for protecting one spouse's cointerest against improper dissipation or alienation of the property by the person who has possession and control of it. Still other issues are presented once the marriage is terminated by death or divorce, such as whether, absent an amicable division between the spouses, the marital property should be split 50-50, or according to some more flexible judicial allocation which seeks to take account of such factors as the needs of the parties and their respective contributions to the marriage. Finally, whatever be the rights of the parties inter se, the rights of third parties (such as creditors) who deal with either of the spouses must be established.

At the outset it may be well to note that most families do not appear to look to the law to allocate their available resources but work out a variety of arrangements which fit their particular means, personalities, and modes of living.[32] In one of the relatively rare empirical investigations in this area, Professors Jacobs and Angell in 1928 examined the relationship between law and custom respecting the allocation of the earnings received by the spouses. After studying over 1000 families in various parts of New York State, they concluded that in almost half of the families where only the husband worked, the wife in some way shared in the administration of the husband's earnings, and in an even higher percentage of the cases the spouses acted jointly with respect to important family expenditures above the "necessaries" level. This practice existed even though under the law of New York the wife had no legal rights in the husband's earnings (aside from her right to support). Similarly, in the vast preponderance of those families where the wife was gainfully employed, she retained her own earnings (sometimes using them for family expenses) and often even ob-

---

[32] Compare Crane, Family Settlements and Succession, in A Century of Family Law 227, 255 (Graveson & Crane eds. 1957): "In England sentiment, not law, continues to regulate the distribution of property among the family."

tained the husband's too. Again, decision with respect to important family expenses was usually joint.[33]

Despite such evidence of pervasive extralegal arrangements, a need for governing legal principles does arise in those cases where the parties are unable to come to a satisfactory agreement or where outsiders are involved. We shall turn now to a consideration of some of the existing regimes of matrimonial property.

At common law, as we have seen, upon marriage the husband obtained control of and a substantial ownership interest in all personal property possessed by the wife at that time. Her real property also passed to the husband under an estate by the marital right, and she retained only a right to support during his lifetime and to dower and a reversion of her own property upon the husband's death. Similar rules deprived the wife during the husband's lifetime of any claim to property accumulated during the marriage.

All this of course was drastically changed by the Married Women's Property Acts, by which typically property brought into the marriage by the wife, as well as that acquired by her during the marriage, is regarded as her separate estate subject to her separate control and power of disposition. On death, as we have seen, she is generally entitled to a specified statutory share of the husband's estate, and on divorce, as we shall see further in Chapter 10, the court may award her alimony or support, as well as (in many states) a share of the husband's property. But in spite of all these benefits, which, according to some commentators,[34] may sometimes even place modern women in a preferential position, neither the common law nor its modern statutory counterparts have as yet fully recognized the de facto community of property which prevails in most marriages. During the marriage each spouse has a legal claim only to that property which he or she can command, unless assets are voluntarily placed in some form of joint ownership.[35] Even upon death or divorce, there is often no attempt to divide up in a rational manner the property which has been accumulated through the spouses' joint efforts. Perhaps, in light of the increasing incidence of married women in the labor force,[36] this scheme arrives at some rough form of justice in those relatively few marriages where both spouses work and have approximately

[33] Jacobs & Angell, A Research in Family Law 469 et seq. (1930). Certain variations relating to economic status, nationality, and extent of urbanization have been omitted from this brief summary.

[34] See, e.g., the reference in Dean, Matrimonial Property Law in the State of New York, in Matrimonial Property Law 315, 363-364 (Friedmann ed. 1955).

[35] In some jurisdictions it has been held that despite the passage of the Married Women's Property Acts a wife's only rights in property held as tenants by the entireties are those of survivorship. See 2 American Law of Property §6.6 (Casner ed. 1952).

[36] One out of every three married women is now employed. President's Commission on the Status of Women, Report 27 (1963). In 21 per cent of those families where the wife works full time throughout the year, she contributes at least half of the total family income. The comparable percentage for all working wives is 10.8 per cent. U.S. Dept. of Labor, Bur. of Lab. Stat., Monthly Lab. Rev., Table W, p. A-23 (Feb. 1964).

comparable earnings. Indeed in those situations the pendulum may have swung too far if the wife is permitted to retain her own earnings while the husband must support the family entirely out of his. But while such cases may suggest the need for a reconsideration of the support obligations within the modern family, they hardly represent a satisfactory general solution to the allocation of matrimonial property.

By way of contrast, the system of community property which is in force in such states as Arizona, California, Idaho, Louisiana, Nevada, New Mexico, Texas, and Washington, as well as in a number of civil law countries around the world, purports to give legal recognition to marriage as an economic partnership. It does this by establishing a new class of property (community property) consisting in essence of the assets or income (other than gifts or bequests) received by the spouses during the marriage.[37]   This community property, in which each of the spouses has a legally defined interest, is normally managed by the husband,[38] subject to certain restrictions to assure the appropriate protection of the wife's cointerest. In addition, each spouse continues to own and manage his or her own separate property. Upon dissolution of the marriage by death or divorce, each spouse is theoretically entitled to his or her separate estate plus one half of the community. In practice, however, this rule is subject to a variety of exceptions and qualifications.[39]

Such an oversimplified statement of the essence of the community property system is misleading in that it fails to take account of the subtle variations between differing versions as well as the myriad complexities which necessarily arise within any particular system.[40]   In some states, for example, the income derived during the marriage from separate property is treated as community property; in others it is not. This rule has obvious significance in a case where a husband's wealth is largely inherited and he has little or no earned income. If this occurs in a state where the husband's unearned income is regarded as his separate property, the wife may be worse off than she would be in a common law state.

The complexities which commonly arise are such as might naturally be anticipated whenever a new type of property interest is given legal recognition. Suppose, for example, one of the spouses receives compensation on account of a personal injury. Or suppose new assets are purchased in part with separate property and in part with community property. How are such transactions to be viewed? Generally speaking, the answers are

---

[37] California has recently created an additional category known as quasi-community property consisting of property similar to community property but acquired while the recipient was domiciled outside California. 1 The California Family Lawyer §4.1 (California Practice Handbook No. 17, 1961). In many jurisdictions, the spouses may by antenuptial agreement elect to avoid community property treatment.

[38] In some states the wife is given control over her own earnings. 2 American Law of Property §7.21 (Casner ed. 1952).

[39] In some states the court has power upon divorce on the grounds of adultery or extreme cruelty to divide the community in such proportion as it may deem just; in others it has this power in any divorce proceeding. See id. §7.35.

[40] In general, see id., pt. 7.

arrived at by a weighty presumption that assets acquired during the marriage are community property — and by a host of technical rules and exceptions.

One of the most troublesome and confusing aspects of community property concerns the rights of creditors. In most of the community property states, the community is liable for all postnuptial debts incurred by the husband but not those incurred by the wife unless she was her husband's agent; a few states embark upon the hopeless task of distinguishing between community and separate obligations.[41] But even in the majority group, there are occasional exceptions, such as that community property consisting of the wife's earnings will not be subject to the husband's debts. The rules with respect to antenuptial debts of the spouses are, if anything, more complex.

Professor Moynihan has provided the following comparison between the common law and community property regimes:

> That the community system was far superior to the former barbarous common law system few would deny. Whether that superiority exists when comparison is made with the modernized common law system, with its ameliorative Married Woman's Property Acts, is a debatable question. To a large extent one's views will be shaped by his prejudices and judgments of marriage as a sociological institution. In favor of the community system it may be urged that it gives realistic recognition to the contributions made by both spouses to the material success of the marriage. Moreover, as a legal system it is, perhaps, more accurately reflective of actual marital customs and usages than its rival system. It has been asserted, with considerable justification, that the community idea exists extra-legally to a substantial degree in the common law states. Broadly speaking, the community system may be said to constitute a de jure recognition of a de facto marital partnership.
>
> It is true that neither system offers a completely satisfactory solution to the age-old problem of property rights of the married woman — a problem which Holdsworth accurately characterizes as one of the most difficult in the entire field of private law. The desire to afford protection to the wife and at the same time to protect third persons dealing with the husband necessarily involves a conflict of interests. By and large the community system may be said to favor protection of the wife. The common law system continues to be influenced by the theory of individualism despite legislation designed to protect the married woman's rights in the husband's property. Against the community system it may be contended that due to the husband's extensive powers of management the protection given to the wife during the marriage is largely theoretical and that in reality the protection begins when the community ends. Moreover, the

[41] Is it a community obligation, for example, if a tort judgment is entered against the husband for negligent operation of his automobile while driving to a dance without his wife? See id. §7.31.

price paid for this protection is a high degree of complexity in the law of marital rights, with a resultant heavy burden of litigation and controversy.[42]

The difficulties and disadvantages manifest in both the common law and community property regimes have led to a search for new systems which combine the familiarity and relative simplicity of separately held property with the economic partnership principle inherent in the community property regime. Such a hybrid system has been used for some time in some of the Scandinavian countries and was recently adopted by West Germany after a comprehensive review of the problem of matrimonial regimes.[43] In the German system, as in the common law system, each spouse owns and controls the property brought into the marriage as well as that acquired during the marriage. But, by analogy to the community property system, at the end of the marriage the gains made by the spouses in the course of the marriage are equalized. This is done by computing the amount by which each spouse's net assets at the end of the marriage exceed those at the beginning, coupled with an appropriate transfer from the spouse possessing the greater excess. Note, however, that no joint or community property is created; each spouse's equalization claim represents simply a contractual right in the marital property owned or acquired by the other spouse. The law also provides certain protections against improper waste or transfers.

Although normally the marital "excess" is divided equally, the rigor of the 50-50 rule is dispensed with where it would be "grossly unfair" to apply it in view of one spouse's culpable failure to fulfill his or her "economic obligations." In addition, upon death the surviving spouse is given an option to take a one-fourth additional share of the decedent's estate (on top of her statutory widow's allowance) in lieu of the equalization claim. This latter rule was apparently added to provide a simpler formula for the most common dissolution event (i.e., death of one of the spouses). Both of these departures from the rule of strict equality illustrate well the conflict between simplicity on the one hand and flexibility and refinement on the other that has pervaded so much of the work in this area.

A simplified illustration may serve to highlight the practical differences between the three property regimes which we have examined. Assume that neither the husband nor the wife owns any property at the time of their marriage. Thereafter H is employed at a salary of $10,000 per year; W remains in the home. In the common law jurisdictions W has no rights in H's earnings, apart from her claim to support. As long as she continues to live with H, she generally cannot even compel H to support her in accordance with his means nor prevent him from dissipating or transferring the funds so as to deprive her of any effective rights upon death or divorce.

42 Id. §7.5.
43 See Note, "Equality of the Spouses" under the New German Law, 7 Am. J. Comp. L. 276 (1958). For yet another variant, see Gorecki, Matrimonial Property in Poland, 26 Mod. L. Rev. 156 (1963).

In Germany, on the other hand, W immediately obtains a contractual right to equalization upon dissolution of the marriage. Similarly, in the community property states H's earnings constitute community property in which W has a recognized cointerest. Although in both of these regimes H will probably have full control over the funds, and W may therefore be as powerless against a niggardly husband as she is at common law, these systems do provide some protection against dissipation or improper alienation of the assets by H. Insofar as the rights of third parties are concerned, if W owed $1000 on a note at the time of her marriage to H, the creditor would most likely be unable to recover from H either in Germany or in the modernized common law jurisdictions. In the community property regimes, the community would normally be liable. California, however, has by statute exempted the husband's earnings from responsibility for the wife's antenuptial debts.[44]

It is evident that all three of the systems examined are working from very different origins and through very different devices to the same end: the development of a relatively simple, yet flexible, system which will provide maximum freedom of transferability while at the same time giving due recognition to the respective equities of the spouses and the rights of third parties. It is also evident that none of these systems has fully succeeded in this aim.

PROBLEM

In 1963, the Committee on Civil and Political Rights of the President's Commission on the Status of Women made the following recommendation:

> Marriage is a partnership to which each spouse makes a different but equally important contribution. This fact has become increasingly recognized in the realities of American family living. While the laws of other countries have reflected this trend, family laws in the United States have lagged behind. Accordingly, the Committee concludes that during marriage each spouse should have a legally defined and substantial right in the earnings of the other spouse and in the real and personal property acquired as a result of such earnings, as well as in the management of such earnings and property. Such right should survive the marriage and be legally recognized in the event of its termination by annulment, divorce, or death. This policy should be appropriately implemented by legislation which would safeguard either spouse against improper alienation of property by the other.[45]

Do you agree with the Committee's statement? If you were given the task of implementing the Committee's recommendation, how would you deal with the problems suggested by the foregoing materials?

[44] 2 American Law of Property §7.30 (Casner ed. 1952).
[45] Recommendation 14, p. 18 (1963).

C. Variations on the Family Harmony Theme

GRAHAM v. GRAHAM
33 F. Supp. 936 (E.D. Mich. 1940)

TUTTLE, J. This is a suit by a man against his former wife upon the following written agreement alleged to have been executed September 17, 1932, by the parties:

"This agreement made this 17th day of September, 1932, between Margrethe Graham and Sidney Graham, husband and wife. For valuable consideration Margrethe Graham hereby agrees to pay to Sidney Graham the sum of Three Hundred ($300.00) Dollars per month each and every month hereafter until the parties hereto no longer desire this arrangement to continue. . . .

"This agreement is made to adjust financial matters between the parties hereto, so that in the future there will be no further arguments as to what money said Sidney Graham shall receive."

The parties were divorced on July 11, 1933. While the writing itself recites no consideration but merely states that it is made to prevent future arguments as to the amount of money the husband is to receive from his wife, the complaint alleges that the plaintiff had quit his job in a hotel at the solicitation of the defendant who wanted him to accompany her upon her travels, she paying his expenses, and that he was desirous of returning to work but that the defendant in order to induce him not to do so entered into this agreement. The total amount claimed until November 7, 1939, is $25,500, with interest at five per cent per annum from the time each monthly installment of $300 became due. The defendant in her answer alleges that she has no recollection of entering into the agreement; and she denies that she ever induced plaintiff to give up his hotel work, alleging that on the contrary his abandonment of work and continued reliance upon her for support was always distasteful to her. The answer further alleges that at the time of divorce the parties entered into a written settlement agreement under which defendant (plaintiff in the divorce suit) paid plaintiff (defendant in the divorce suit) $9000 and each party surrendered any and all claims he or she might have in the property of the other.

Subsequent to filing her answer, the defendant filed a motion to dismiss the complaint on the grounds that her promise was without consideration; that the alleged contract was not within the power of a married woman under Michigan law to make; that, since under its express provisions it was to continue only until the parties no longer desired the arrangement to continue, it was terminated by the divorce and settlement agreement . . . . I . . . assume all of the allegations of the bill of complaint to be true. . . .

. . . As noted, the written contract itself does not recite any consideration. Plaintiff's counsel argues that consideration for defendant's promise is found in the oral agreement of the plaintiff "to give his wife his constant society, to travel with his wife wherever she wished and as frequently as she wished and not to return to work," all of which he was under no duty to do. . . . [I]t is unnecessary to decide this question, since I am convinced that . . . the contract was not a competent one for married persons to enter into.

In the first place, it is highly doubtful if the alleged contract is within the capacity of a married woman to make under Michigan law. The degree of emancipation of married women with respect to contract and property rights varies widely in the different states. However, it has been repeatedly stated by the Michigan Supreme Court that under the Michigan statutes a married woman has no general power to contract, but can contract only in relation to her separate property. . . . The limitation applies to contracts of married women with their husbands as well as with third parties. [Citations omitted.] In general, the Michigan Supreme Court in deciding whether an agreement is within a married woman's contractual capacity looks to the nature of the consideration, requiring it to be for the benefit of her separate estate. . . . Since the promise of the defendant here consists of a general executory obligation unrelated to specific property and since the consideration is not for the benefit of her separate estate, but if anything to its detriment, it would appear that the contract is beyond the capacity of a married woman under Michigan law to make.

However, I do not rest my decision on this ground, but rather upon the broader ground that even if the contract is otherwise within the contractual power of the parties it is void because it contravenes public policy. Under the law, marriage is not merely a private contract between the parties, but creates a status in which the state is vitally interested and under which certain rights and duties incident to the relationship come into being, irrespective of the wishes of the parties. As a result of the marriage contract, for example, the husband has a duty to support and to live with his wife and the wife must contribute her services and society to the husband and follow him in his choice of domicile. The law is well settled that a private agreement between persons married or about to be married which attempts to change the essential obligations of the marriage contract as defined by the law is contrary to public policy and unenforceable. . . .

Thus, it has been repeatedly held that a provision releasing the husband from his duty to support his wife in a contract between married persons, or those about to be married, except in connection with a preexisting or contemplated immediate separation, makes the contract void. . . . Even in the states with the most liberal emancipation statutes with respect to married women, the law has not gone to the extent of permitting husbands and wives by agreement to change the essential incidents of the marriage contract.

The contract claimed to have been made by the plaintiff and defendant in the case at bar while married and living together falls within this prohibition. Under its terms, the husband becomes obligated to accompany his wife upon her travels; while under the law of marriage the wife is obliged to follow the husband's choice of domicile. . . . The contract, furthermore, would seem to suffer from a second defect by impliedly releasing the husband from his duty to support his wife . . . The present contract does not expressly contain such a release, but if the husband can always call upon his wife for payments of $300 per month he is in practical effect getting rid of his obligation to support his wife. The plaintiff seems to place this construction on the contract since his claim makes no deduction from the promised $300 per month for support of his wife. . . .

The law prohibiting married persons from altering by private agreement the personal relationships and obligations assumed upon marriage is based on sound foundations of public policy. If they were permitted to regulate by private contract where the parties are to live and whether the husband is to work or be supported by his wife, there would seem to be no reason why married persons could not contract as to the allowance the husband or wife may receive, the number of dresses she may have, the places where they will spend their evenings and vacations, and innumerable other aspects of their personal relationships. Such right would open an endless field for controversy and bickering and would destroy the element of flexibility needed in making adjustments to new conditions arising in marital life. There is no reason, of course, why the wife cannot voluntarily pay her husband a monthly sum or the husband by mutual understanding quit his job and travel with his wife. The objection is to putting such conduct into a binding contract, tying the parties' hands in the future and inviting controversy and litigation between them. . . .

The case is also to be distinguished from a group of cases which hold that a married woman can properly contract with her husband to work for him outside the home and be compensated by him for her services (although it appears that this is contrary to the weight of authority). See annotations in 14 A.L.R. 1013 and 23 A.L.R. 18. The ground on which the contract has been upheld in those cases is that it covered services outside the scope of the marriage contract; the promises did not, as here, involve the essential obligations of the marriage contract, and no question of public policy was therefore involved. . . . Admittedly, it is difficult to draw the line in cases not so extreme between contracts involving the personal rights or obligations of the marriage contract and those which involve matters outside its scope; but it is unnecessary here to decide exactly where the line is to be drawn, since in my opinion the promises made in the contract in the case at bar clearly attempt to alter essential obligations of the marriage contract. . . .

[Complaint dismissed.]

NOTE

1. Compare the judicial approach to antenuptial agreements, pages 313–316 supra, and to separation agreements, Chapter 11. Balfour v. Balfour, [1919] 2 K.B. 571 (C.A.), involved an agreement by the husband to give his wife £30 a month while she recuperated from an operation in Eng-

land and he returned to his employment in Ceylon. The Court of Appeal refused to enforce the agreement; Lord Atkin commented (id. at 579):

> To my mind it would be of the worst possible example to hold that agreements such as this resulted in legal obligations which could be enforced in the Courts. It would mean this, that when the husband makes his wife a promise to give her an allowance . . . for the maintenance of the household and children, and she promises so to apply it, not only could she sue him for his failure in any week to supply the allowance, but he could sue her for non-performance of the obligation, express or implied, which she had undertaken upon her part. All I can say is that the small Courts of this country would have to be multiplied one hundredfold if these arrangements were held to result in legal obligations. . . . Agreements such as these are outside the realm of contracts altogether. The common law does not regulate the form of agreements between spouses. . . . The parties themselves are advocates, judges, Courts, sheriff's officer and reporter. In respect of these promises each house is a domain into which the King's writ does not seek to run, and to which his officers do not seek to be admitted. . . .

In Garlock v. Garlock, 279 N.Y. 337, 18 N.E.2d 521 (1939), the Court of Appeals refused to enforce an agreement by the husband to pay his wife $1250 a month; the agreement was made while the parties were living together harmoniously because they wanted to reduce to a stated sum the amount which the husband would be obligated to pay for his wife's support. The court held the contract void because it violated N.Y. Dom. Rel. Law §51 (now Gen. Obligats. Law §5-311): "but a husband and wife cannot contract to alter or dissolve the marriage or to relieve the husband from his liability to support his wife or to relieve the wife of liability to support her husband provided that she is possessed of sufficient means and he is incapable of supporting himself and is or is likely to become a public charge." [46]

"Domestic services" agreements have been enforced if the parties were separated at the time the agreement was made and the wife had grounds for divorce. The courts have found consideration for these contracts in the wife's promise to refrain from bringing suit for divorce; morever

> the law, always favoring the settlement of controversies and especially desiring the reconciliation of husband and wife, does not forbid a husband or wife to forgive the other spouse for wrongs committed and to enter into an agreement for re-establishment of the family. . . . In the absence of proof, it may be presumed that the wife's grievance was substantial. . . .[47]

[46] The concluding clause of the statute, relating to wives, was added in 1960. Acts 1960, c. 132.

[47] Young v. Cockman, 182 Md. 246, 253, 34 A.2d 428, 432 (1943). But see Lacks v. Lacks, 12 N.Y.2d 268, 189 N.E.2d 487, 14 Syracuse L. Rev. 681 (1963).

Graham involved a dispute about an express contract. But many of the suits claiming compensation for "domestic services," whether the parties were husband and wife or other members of the family, have relied either on an oral promise by the beneficiary of the services, an "implied contract," or simply a quantum meruit theory. It is not surprising, therefore, that the courts have also been concerned with the serious problems of proof posed by these suits. See Gorrell v. Taylor, 107 Tenn. 568, 64 S.W. 888 (1901) (presumption that services rendered by a child for a parent while living in the family home were intended to be gratuitous in the absence of proof of an express contract or exceptional facts and circumstances); Key v. Harris, 116 Tenn. 161, 92 S.W. 235 (1905) (alternative holding) (sister permitted to recover for services rendered an incompetent sister prior to her death).

2. When the "contract" has not involved domestic services, the wife's claim for the value of her services has often been successful. In Hull v. Hull Bros. Lumber Co., 186 Tenn. 53, 208 S.W.2d 338 (1948), the wife recovered for office work she had performed for her husband's partnership business during the years prior to their divorce; without an express agreement she had worked full time and had replaced an employee who had been paid $75 a month. In Woods v. Fifty-Third Union Trust Co., 54 Ohio App. 303, 6 N.E.2d 987 (1936), however, the court dismissed an adult son's suit to recover for personal services he had rendered in the management of his mother's property ($80,000 in securities) for the six years prior to her death. Although he did not live in his mother's home, and the mother "had a complete legal right to entirely disinherit him, and his neglect of her might have caused her to exercise that right" (54 Ohio App. at 307, 6 N.E.2d at 989), there had been no "express promise made under such circumstances as to manifest an intention of contracting." (54 Ohio App. at 305, 6 N.E.2d at 988.) The court pointed out that the plaintiff had never made a demand for payment during his mother's lifetime, although he had managed her estate for twelve years; in addition, at his mother's death he had received half the estate, sharing it with his only sister.

Note also the following statutory provision: "Husband and wife shall not contract with each other, so as to entitle the one to claim or receive any compensation from the other for work and labor, and any contract between them whereby one shall claim or shall receive compensation from the other for services rendered, shall be void." Miss. Code Ann. §454 (1956). Compare this provision with Hull, above, and with the materials which follow.

EGGLESTON v. EGGLESTON
228 N.C. 668, 47 S.E.2d 243 (1948)

SEAWELL, J. The plaintiff brought this suit against her husband for alimony without divorce under G.S., 50-16, joining with this cause of action . . . a cause of action to have herself declared a business partner with her husband and to have her rights under the partnership adjudicated and an account taken . . . .

. . . The case then proceeded to trial, the issues being answered as to both causes of action unfavorably to the plaintiff . . . .

The plaintiff sought to show the existence and nature of the alleged partnership between herself and her husband by evidence of dealings inter partes for a long period of years and her contributions to the joint undertaking; and by introducing the joint partnership income tax returns for the year 1945 made by herself and husband to the Federal and State taxing authorities, respectively, with other evidence pertinent to this transaction.

More particular reference to these returns will be made further on. For clarity we may say here that in both of the returns it is declared that a partnership existed between the plaintiff and the defendant for the calendar year 1945, manifesting partnership on equal shares as to the net income. After this suit was brought the defendant filed "amended" or "corrected" returns, in point of fact *individual* returns, eliminating the partnership feature.

The evidence by which plaintiff sought to show the alleged partnership may be summarized as tending to show the following facts and conditions:

When they first moved into the filling station on the Draper road and started business she helped display the stock; while defendant went out into the "territory" plaintiff was in charge of the filling station, worked there with no assistance except casual help from little boys to whom plaintiff paid small sums; plaintiff had access to the funds, taking in the money and keeping it in the cash drawer; she put her "inheritance money," about $125.00, in the business at this early stage; she sometimes bought, but buying was mostly done by defendant. As more filling stations were added plaintiff went and put up signs in the windows, displayed stock and helped them get set up in the business. She worked regularly during this period, living in the service station for 15 years, and except for a short period of time and vacations in the summer, was there continually, often being compelled to let her housework go. She had often gone without food all day except what she could pick up at the filling station. She sold things out of stock, serviced cars, putting in gas and oil; carried water from the pump in tubs, as there was, for a long time, no running water; washed cars, often making $5.00 a day in this way. Plaintiff handled the paid and unpaid bills, made out statements and sent them out. Later plaintiff took a bookkeeping course and learned to type, and thereafter kept books for the business. After plaintiff and defendant moved into the new home in 1940 until 1946, while plaintiff did not go to the filling station every day because of her illness, the help came to her to inquire about the business and for direction in matters with which she was familiar, and she continued in charge during Mr. Eggleston's absence. Between 1940 and 1946, when they separated, she went down and did book work. During 1945 plaintiff and her brother, Pickett

Parker, did the book work together. Plaintiff took part in the conduct of the tire business . . .

All this proffered evidence was rejected upon objection made seriatim by defendant, and in the same manner plaintiff excepted.

The plaintiff then testified that during the year 1945, she was not certain of the date, defendant came into the kitchen where she was cooking supper, put his arm around her, started kissing her and told her she was his business partner. "I asked him what he meant and I said I had been his business partner for twenty years. He said I had always been worried about losing a great deal of the business at his death, and he had fixed it so I would not even have to pay inheritance tax on my part of the partnership. He talked to me about it and ten days or two weeks later he signed — he said of course I would have to pay income since I was a partner in the business and he brought some papers in for me to sign. I signed three different sheets, I think, income papers and different papers, and a blank check."

After identification, plaintiff then introduced in evidence copies of the joint partnership income tax returns made by herself and husband for the calendar year 1945 to the Federal and State taxing authorities, respectively. These returns manifest a taxable net income for that year of $20,801.29 and indicate that Mattie P. Eggleston, the plaintiff, and Frank Eggleston, the defendant, were partners upon equal shares in the business, entitling each to one-half of said net income. The partnership appears as "Eggleston Brothers Filling Station." Accompanying these returns there was a partnership return of estimated tax for the year 1946. . . .

. . . [I]t is necessary to turn to the evidence of the plaintiff as above noted — principally her own testimony — of the dealings between herself and husband with relation to the business in which she claims partnership.

This evidence was excluded apparently upon the theory that her complaint setting up the creation of the partnership restricts her to the transactions involved in the filing of the income tax returns, and especially to its organization on January 1, 1945. . . . Its exclusion was error. But we do not mean by this to limit its effect to the function of supporting evidence for a partnership subsequently created. In our view of the case the whole evidence directed to the existence of the partnership must be taken together, and so taken was competent to be submitted to the jury for their consideration and evaluation.

Under the common law as a consequence of the fictional merger of husband and wife into one person, and other disabilities of the wife incident to coverture, there could be no contract and, therefore, no business partnership between husband and wife. [Citations omitted.] That incapacity has been removed in many states by the enactment of "Married Women's Acts," — statutes directly or impliedly giving them the power or the right to contract. The broad general powers of contract given under most of these statutes has in many instances been extended by judicial interpretation to authorize the formation of partnerships with the husband. . . .

"A contract, express or implied, is essential to the formation of a partnership." 40 Am. Jur., Partnership, p. 135, sec. 20, see notes 14, 15.   But we see no reason why a course of dealing between the parties of sufficient significance and duration may not, along with other proof of the fact, be admitted as evidence tending to establish the fact of partnership provided it has sufficient substance and definiteness to evince the essentials of the legal concept, including, of course, the necessary intent. . . .

Not only may a partnership be formed orally, but "it may be created by the agreement or conduct of the parties, either express or implied," Sterman v. Ziem, 17 Cal. App. (2d), 414, 62 P.(2d), 160, 162. . . .   Of significance on this issue is the statement of the plaintiff, "We divided the profits," and that when they came to a temporary separation the defendant agreed to keep her interest intact. [Citations omitted.]

Where the fact at issue is the existence of partnership the admissions against interest of the person denying the partnership are significant in establishing it.   The use and the function of the partnership tax returns as evidence was not per se to create the partnership but, together with other evidence directed to the fact, to establish its existence. . . .   While we doubt the propriety of admitting the evidence of the amended or corrected returns, because of their self-serving nature, the hasty effort of the defendant to regain his lost status did not cancel out the evidence afforded by the original returns or such legitimate inferences as the jury under proper instructions might have drawn from them as evidence of the existence of the contract . . . .

It is proper to say here that the services rendered by the wife to her husband are presumed to be gratuitous. [Citations omitted.]   The presumption is not conclusive [citation omitted] and may be overcome by evidence tending to show that the services were not gratuitous. [Citation omitted.]   That was a matter for the jury. . . .

. . . [I]t is not necessary to a partnership that property or capital involved in it should belong in common to the parties to the contract.   On the contrary, a familiar type of partnership, as indicated by the evidence in this case, occurs where the services of the one party [are] balanced against the capital furnished by the other; . . . while in partnership, as in any other kind of contract, there must be an intent, it was error to instruct the jury that before they could find for the plaintiff they must be satisfied by the greater weight of the evidence that the defendant, by the making and filing of the partnership income tax returns in evidence, intended to make his wife a partner.   The instruction to that effect has a further infirmity that the plaintiff has not contended and could not contend that the partnership was created by these documents, but only introduced them as evidence of its existence.

A further instruction to the jury to the effect that they were not concerned with the question whether the defendant made and filed the partnership income tax returns for the purpose of defrauding the Government, as that was a matter between defendant and the Government, was calculated to impress the jury that such a thing, if true, need not reflect upon his credibility, and to relieve him from the most damaging situation he had to confront on this issue. . . .

New trial.

NOTE

1. The court also ordered a new trial of Mrs. Eggleston's request for "alimony without divorce" — the North Carolina equivalent of separate maintenance. North Carolina apparently has no statutory provision authorizing a property settlement between the spouses upon dissolution of the marriage. As to the extent to which an alimony award may be a covert substitute for a property distribution to the wife, see Chapter 10. Both Graham and Eggleston were decided after the effective dissolution of the parties' marital relationship. Professor McDowell has estimated that seventy per cent of the noncommercial husband-wife contract disputes have reached the courts either after the death of one of the parties or following their separation or divorce. McDowell, Contracts in the Family, 45 B.U.L. Rev. 43, 52 (1965). Is this an important datum in understanding these cases? Suppose that while the marital relationship continued, Mrs. Eggleston had sought an accounting with respect to her partnership interest. Would she have been successful? Cf. McGuire v. McGuire, page 303 supra.

See also McGehee v. McGehee, 227 Miss. 170, 85 So.2d 799 (1956), in which the court held, without explanation, that Miss. Code Ann. §454 (1956) (quoted at page 328 supra) had no application to a partnership agreement between husband and wife. If it is true, as the opinion in Eggleston indicates, that a partnership may contemplate the services of one partner and the capital of the other, why did not the McGehee partnership entitle the wife to "receive . . . compensation from the other for work and labor"? Similarly, if neither Mrs. Eggleston nor Mrs. McGehee would have been permitted to recover for cleaning the family home and preparing her husband's meals, why should either be permitted to claim a financial return (pursuant to an "implied contract" of partnership) for "pulling an oar" with her husband in the family business? Consider once more the holding in Hull v. Hull Bros. Lumber Co., described at page 328 supra.

2. Analogous problems of sorting out the spouses' respective interests have often arisen subsequent to interspousal transfers of property. The judicial effort in these cases has produced, by and large, no more than a bizarre collection of presumptions. If the husband purchases property in his wife's name, it is presumed that a gift was intended; a resulting trust in favor of the husband will be created only if the evidence of a contrary intent is "clear, explicit and unequivocal — though not necessarily uncontradicted." Lapayowker v. Lincoln College Prep. School, 386 Pa. 167, 171-172, 125 A.2d 451, 454 (1956). On the other hand, in Van Inwegen v. Van Inwegen, 4 N.J. 46, 71 A.2d 340 (1950), an aging wife, dissatisfied

with her second husband's substantial expenditures, contended that funds she had deposited in their joint bank account were loans to her husband. Most of the withdrawals had been made by the husband for improvements to houses owned by each of the parties and for current housekeeping, entertainment, medical, and personal expenses. The wife sued for $19,000. The New Jersey Supreme Court reversed a judgment for the wife and remanded for a more adequate trial as to how the money had been spent. The court indicated that the trial court should be guided by the following legal principles:

> Transactions between husband and wife, by reason of the confidential relationship, are closely scrutinized [citation omitted]; and gifts by a wife to her husband are examined "with an anxious watchfulness and caution and dread of undue influence." [Citations omitted.]
>
> It has long been established in this State that where a wife advances money from the principal of her separate estate to her husband there is no presumption that such a transaction constituted a gift; on the contrary, the presumption is that the advancement is a loan or a deposit for safekeeping and the burden of proving the transaction . . . to be a gift is upon the husband or the person who asserts it to be a gift. . . .
>
> The rule appears to be equally established that where a husband receives the rents and income, as distinguished from the principal, of his wife's separate estate and expends it with her knowledge and without her dissent, there is acquiescence from which a gift will be presumed. . . .
>
> Moreover, advances by the wife for use in the payment of ordinary current family expenses, during the time the parties are living together as husband and wife, are not recoverable in the absence of an agreement for reimbursement. . . .[48]

Oates v. Oates, 127 W. Va. 469, 471, 33 S.E.2d 457, 458 (1945), concerned a seventy-eight-year-old bachelor, who was "lonely and desired the companionship of a woman"; Mrs. Oates, a thirty-three-year-old schoolteacher, "was in need of money to pay her debts and to assist ailing relatives." After two years of connubial, albeit unconsummated, bliss, Mr. Oates conveyed his farm to his wife, reserving a life estate for himself. The deed, prepared by Mrs. Oates when her husband executed a new will devising the farm to a nephew, recited as consideration the payment of $10 and Mrs. Oates's promise to provide a home for her husband. The court held that the conveyance lacked consideration, but dismissed Mr. Oates's petition to set it aside: Mr. Oates had made only a "mistake of law," and in any event, a court of equity should not assist one wrongdoer against another. 127 W. Va. at 476, 33 S.E.2d at 460.

Intrafamily property transactions have also been subjected to close judicial scrutiny at the behest of creditors of either the husband or the wife.

---

[48] 4 N.J. at 51-52, 71 A.2d at 343-344. See also Note, Transfers from Wife to Husband: A Reexamination of Presumptions in Illinois, 53 Nw. U.L. Rev. 781 (1959).

The intricacies of creditors' rights under community property regimes are mentioned at page 321 supra. In common law states generally, in the absence of a fraudulent conveyance, the husband's creditors may not attack the wife's assets, nor may the wife's creditors attack the husband's, for postnuptial debts; this is true regardless of the source of the assets. See Dean, Matrimonial Property Law in the State of New York, in Matrimonial Property Law 315, 332-339 (Friedmann ed. 1955). Of course, agency principles may play an important part in deciding these cases. Note the following statutory formulation (Miss. Code Ann. §454 (1956)):

> all business done with the means of the wife by the husband shall be deemed and held to be on her account and for her use, and by the husband as her agent and manager in business, as to all persons dealing with him without notice, unless the contract between the husband and wife which changes this relation, be evidenced by writing . . . and filed with the chancery clerk of the county where such business may be done . . . .

Suppose the husband, with savings from his salary, buys stock in his wife's name; thereafter he negligently injures a third person without fault on the part of his wife. Should the third person be able to claim this stock to satisfy a judgment against the husband?

SELF v. SELF
58 Cal. 2d 683, 376 P.2d 65 (1962)

PETERS, J. The sole problem involved in this case is whether California should continue to follow the rule of interspousal immunity for intentional torts first announced in this state in 1909 in the case of Peters v. Peters, 156 Cal. 32 [103 P. 219]. Because the reasons upon which the Peters case was predicated no longer exist, and because of certain legislative changes made in recent years, we are of the opinion that the rule of the Peters case should be abandoned. . . .

In the instant case, the problem arises under the following circumstances: The complaint for assault and battery was filed on May 5, 1961. It charges that the defendant husband on July 14, 1960, "unlawfully assaulted plaintiff and beat upon, scratched and abused the person of plaintiff," and that as a result plaintiff "sustained physical injury to her person and emotional distress, and among other injuries did receive a broken arm." The answer consists of a general denial, except that it is admitted that plaintiff's arm was broken. . . . Thereafter, defendant filed a notice of motion for a summary judgment on the ground that a wife cannot sue a husband for tort in California. This motion was supported by an affidavit averring that the parties had been married on November 2, 1954, and, on the date of the affidavit (May 18, 1961), were still married, although an action for divorce was pending. The motion for summary judgment was granted, and judgment for defendant entered.

The common-law rule of interspousal immunity for either intentional or negligent torts is of ancient origin. It was fundamentally predicated on the doctrine of the legal identity of husband and wife (1 Blackstone, Commentaries, *442; 2 Blackstone, Commentaries *433). This rule precluded actions between the two as to either property or personal torts. As long as this doctrine existed, the rule prohibiting a tort action between the spouses was logically sound. As Prosser points out (Prosser on Torts (2d ed. 1955) p. 671): "If the man were the tort-feasor, the woman's right would be a chose in action which the husband would have the right to reduce to possession, and he must be joined as a plaintiff against himself and the proceeds recovered must be paid to him; and if the tort involved property, the wife had no right of possession to support the action. If the wife committed the tort, the husband would be liable to himself for it, and must be joined as a defendant in his own action." But the social order upon which this concept was predicated no longer exists. Early in the 19th century married women's emancipation acts were passed in all American jurisdictions. These were designed to confer upon women a separate legal personality, and to give them a separate legal estate in their own property. . . .

From an early date it was recognized that a primary purpose of these statutes was to free the wife's property from the control of her husband. As a result, most American jurisdictions agreed that inasmuch as these statutes destroyed the legal identity of husband and wife, one spouse could recover against the other for a tort, intentional or negligent, committed against his or her property. (See discussion, Prosser on Torts (2d ed. 1955) p. 672.) But this emancipation was not generally extended to the field of personal torts, most of the courts rationalizing that personal tort actions between husband and wife, if permitted, would destroy the peace and harmony of the home, and thus would be contrary to the policy of the law. . . .[49]

. . . Since [1910], the number of "majority" states adhering to the old rule has steadily dwindled, until today at least 18 jurisdictions [permit interspousal suits]. . . .

California has several cases adhering to the old rule. The first case to discuss the problem in California was Peters v. Peters, supra, 156 Cal. 32, decided in 1909 . . . In Peters the action was by the husband against the wife for assault and battery. The wife, without justification, seriously wounded her husband by willfully shooting him in the leg. The court held (p. 34) that ". . . we are satisfied that, under the law in this state as it is, an action cannot be maintained by one spouse against the other for a battery committed during the continuance of the marriage relation . . . ." [Court's quotation abbreviated by Eds.]

The court squarely based its conclusion upon the reasoning that California had adopted the common law, and that at common law no such

---

[49] See Ritter v. Ritter, 31 Pa. 396, 398 (1858): "The flames which litigation would kindle on the domestic hearth would consume in an instant the conjugal bond, and bring on a new era indeed — an era of universal discord, of unchastity, of bastardy, of dissoluteness, of violence, cruelty, and murders." — Ed.

action existed. The court recognized that under the married women's emancipation acts (p. 34) "it is now generally held that an action at law concerning property may be maintained between them." . . .

The Peters case has been cited with approval and followed . . . but . . . in the cases following the Peters case the rule of Peters was simply accepted by both parties, the litigants contending that the rule was or was not applicable to a particular factual situation. . . .

Paulus v. Bauder, 106 Cal. App. 2d 589 [235 P.2d 422], was a negligence case growing out of an automobile accident. Both parties accepted the rule of the Peters case, the injured party claiming that the rule did not apply when the tort was committed after the interlocutory, and the case was tried after final divorce. The court held that because the marital bonds existed when the tort was committed, the rule of Peters applied.[50]

[The court then reviewed a number of judicially created exceptions to the general rule.]

That brings us to the case of Spellens v. Spellens, . . . 49 Cal. 2d 210, . . . in which Justice Schauer wrote a concurring and dissenting opinion . . . The case involved primarily the rights of the parties growing out of a Mexican divorce. The majority opinion was entirely, and the concurring and dissenting opinion mainly, involved with these divorce problems. . . .

Justice Schauer . . . pointed out that a possible justification of the marital immunity rule as announced in Peters is that the law as it existed then provided that the recovery by the wife in most such tort actions would be community property [citations omitted] and held that such justification did not exist in the instant case, because (49 Cal. 2d at p. 242): "Plaintiff acquired the judgment for abuse of process after she and defendant had finally separated. It was, therefore, her separate property . . . ." . . .

From this analysis of the California cases it appears that the basic reasons given by the Peters case for adopting the rule no longer exist . . . The rule of the Peters case is definitely out of line with the general policy of the law of this state. Of course, the general rule is and should be that, in the absence of statute or some compelling reason of public policy, where there is negligence proximately causing an injury, there should be liability. Immunity exists only by statute or by reason of compelling dictates of public policy. Neither exists here. That being so, these are sufficient reasons alone to justify this court in overruling the Peters case and in adopting the more modern, intelligent, and proper rule. . . .

. . . [T]he contention that the rule is necessary to maintain conjugal harmony — one of the reasons given in the Peters case — is illogical and

[50] Contra, Steele v. Steele, 65 F. Supp. 329, 332 (D.D.C. 1946): "[A] decree of absolute divorce does not take effect until the expiration of six months after its entry . . . . To be sure, in the meantime the marriage is not entirely dissolved. Nevertheless, the status of husband and wife lacks its original character." — Ed.

unsound. It would not appear that such assumed conjugal harmony is any more endangered by tort actions than by property actions — yet the latter are permitted. For these reasons alone the old common law rule should be abandoned. But there exists another and compelling reason why the rule of the Peters case is no longer the rule that should be followed in this state, and that is that in 1957 the Legislature saw fit to provide that "All damages, special and general, awarded a married person in a civil action for personal injuries, are the separate property of such married person." (Civ. Code, §163.5, added by Stats. 1957, ch. 2334, pp. 4065-4066, §1.) Prior to 1957, both the cause of action and damages recovered for personal injuries to either spouse were community property. [Citations omitted.] As a result, contributory negligence was imputed between the spouses to prevent a spouse guilty of contributory negligence from sharing in the amount received (Kesler v. Pabst, 43 Cal. 2d 254, 256 [273 P.2d 257]). . . . The hardships created by allowing the contributory negligence of one spouse to be a defense against the other caused criticism [citation omitted], and the injustice of that rule was undoubtedly the basic reason for the legislative change in 1957. But while these rules existed they constituted some justification for the continuance of the rule of the Peters case. Obviously, it would be incongruous for a wife to sue her husband for a personal tort as long as the recovery would be community property controlled and managed by the husband. (See 2 Armstrong, Cal. Family Law (1953) p. 1468.) Thus, the legislative change of 1957 by the addition of section 163.5 to the Civil Code removed the last bar to the adoption of the more modern rule in this field.

The arguments that permitting such actions will inundate the courts with trifling suits, and that to permit such action will encourage perjury, fraud and collusion, are not relevant in an intentional tort case. . . .

The judgment appealed from is reversed.

NOTE

1. In an accompanying case, the court held that a wife could sue her husband for a negligent tort as well, since "insofar as interspousal liability for tort is concerned there is no logical or legal reason for drawing a distinction" between intentional and negligent torts.[51] Klein v. Klein, 58 Cal. 2d 692, 693, 376 P.2d 70, 71 (1962). But Klein was not a unanimous decision. Justice Schauer's dissenting opinion (58 Cal. 2d at 696, 698, 376 P.2d at 73, 74) argued that interspousal liability for negligence should be left to the legislature:

Indeed, judicial interference in this sensitive area of substantive law may well have the opposite effect: e.g., within a few months after the Supreme Court of Illinois judicially abrogated in that state the common-law rule of interspousal immunity in an action based on "wilful

[51] Note that Mr. Self might have been subject to criminal prosecution (see page 363 infra), whereas negligently caused injury is less frequently made criminal.

and wanton" conduct resulting in an automobile accident (Brandt v. Keller (1953) 413 Ill. 503 [109 N.E.2d 729]) the Illinois Legislature reinstated the immunity rule as to all personal torts between spouses, enacting that "neither husband nor wife may sue the other for a tort to the person committed during coverture." (Ill. Rev. Stats. 1953, ch. 68, §1; see Hindman v. Holmes (1955) 4 Ill. App. 2d 279 [124 N.E.2d 344, 345].) Such legislative reversal of judicial declarations of "public policy" has not been unknown in California. . . .

With respect to the difficulties faced by insurance companies in situations like Klein, cf. Keeton, Ancillary Rights of the Insured against His Liability Insurer, 13 Vand. L. Rev. 837, 859-865 (1960). In 1961, the Australian Law Journal noted the report of a Law Reform Committee on marital tort immunity:

> If the Committee had been free to start with a clean slate it would have been attracted by either of two clear-cut solutions: to permit no actions at all between husband and wife, or to allow complete freedom of legal proceedings. Neither of these two extreme views finally commended itself, the former because it would not be acceptable to a substantial section of the community, the latter because it would be undesirable as a matter of general social policy.
>
> The Committee's proposals favour an enlargement of freedom of action in tort. The first proposal is that . . . in the case of torts, . . . husband and wife should be able to sue each other as if they were unmarried. A power would, however, be reserved to the Court to enable it, either of its own motion or on the application of the defendant, to stay the action if the complaint is one of no substance or if it would not be in the best interests of the parties that the action should be allowed to proceed. . . .
>
> The Committee makes it clear that the Court would not normally stay proceedings where the defendant appears to have a claim to indemnity or contribution from some other source, whether by means of insurance or otherwise. . . .[52]

2. As the Self opinion indicates, the tortious conduct may occur in a variety of marital contexts:

a. If the defendant and plaintiff marry during the course of the litigation, the usual holding in jurisdictions recognizing the common law immunity has been that the defendant's liability is extinguished. E.g., Kennedy v. Camp, 14 N.J. 390, 397, 102 A.2d 595, 599 (1954); Tanno v. Eby, 68 N.E.2d 813 (Ohio Ct. App. 1946) (action dismissed despite antenuptial agreement preserving wife's right to prosecute the action, since the agreement is against public policy and void).[53] Yet a number of

---

[52] 35 Aust. L.J. 62 (1961).

[53] Even in these states a parent is commonly permitted, despite the marriage of the child and the tortfeasor, to recover money expended for treatment of an unemancipated minor's injuries and for the child's loss of earnings. See page 353 infra; Meisel v. Little, 407 Pa. 546, 548, 180 A.2d 772, 773 (1962); Annot., 91 A.L.R.2d 910 (1963).

courts have permitted the wife to sue for antenuptial torts because the chose in action has been considered "property" within the meaning of the Married Women's Property Act.   E.g., Hamilton v. Fulkerson, 285 S.W.2d 642 (Mo. 1955).

b. Most of the decisions which recognize the common law rule treat interspousal immunity as a rule of substantive law and hold that it survives a divorce.   E.g., Lynn v. Gaskins, 212 F. Supp. 951 (N.D. Ind. 1963); Ensminger v. Campbell, 242 Miss. 519, 134 So.2d 728 (1961).   Yet a few courts have distinguished between divorce and annulment.   E.g., Henneger v. Lomas, 145 Ind. 287, 44 N.E. 462 (1896); contra, Callow v. Thomas, 322 Mass. 550, 555, 78 N.E.2d 637, 640 (1948):

> It is to be observed that this is not a case of a marriage prohibited by law such as a bigamous marriage or one prohibited by reason of consanguinity or affinity between the parties.   [Citation omitted.]   Such a marriage is no marriage at all . . . .   While it doubtless is true that a decree of nullity ordinarily has the effect of making a marriage, even one which is voidable, void ab initio, this is a legal fiction which ought not to be pressed too far.   To say that for all purposes the marriage never existed is unrealistic.   Logic must yield to realities. . . .   The better rule, we think, is that in the case of a voidable marriage transactions which have been concluded and things which have been done during the period of the supposed marriage ought not to be undone . . . .

c. Many jurisdictions which continue to accept the immunity doctrine have nonetheless permitted wrongful death actions against the spouse for the benefit of other members of the deceased's family.   These suits have been permitted although the typical wrongful death statute (e.g., Minn. Stat. Ann. §573.02(1) (Supp. 1964)) authorizes recovery only "if the decedent might have maintained an action, had he lived."   Johnson v. Peoples First Natl. Bank and Trust Co., 394 Pa. 116, 145 A.2d 716 (1958); Welch v. Davis, 410 Ill. 130, 101 N.E.2d 547 (1951).

d. Generally, the wife has been permitted to impose vicarious liability on a principal for injuries caused by her husband in the course of his employment; see Restatement (Second), Agency §217 (1958); Miller v. J. A. Tyrholm & Co., 196 Minn. 438, 265 N.W. 324 (1936); Schubert v. August Schubert Wagon Co., 249 N.Y. 253, 164 N.E. 42 (1929).   Dean Prosser finds it "difficult not to regard these decisions [imposing liability] as bites at the cherry, which will ultimately succeed in nibbling it away."   Prosser, Torts 884 (3d ed. 1964).

3. Husband-wife automobile cases have provided the basis for considerable disagreement about the appropriate conflict of laws doctrine.   Compare Shaw v. Lee, 258 N.C. 609, 129 S.E.2d 288 (1962) (despite a North Carolina statute which authorizes interspousal tort suits, wife residing in North Carolina may not sue because Virginia, where the accident occurred, does not permit such suits), with Thompson v. Thompson, 105 N.H. 86, 193 A.2d 439 (1963) (New Hampshire wife may sue her husband, although accident occurred in Massachusetts, which does not per-

mit interspousal tort suits, because the law of the domicile of the parties governs wife's right to sue). See Hancock, The Rise and Fall of Buckeye v. Buckeye, 1931-1959: Marital Immunity for Torts in Conflict of Laws, 29 U. Chi. L. Rev. 237 (1962); Ford, Interspousal Liability for Automobile Accidents in the Conflict of Laws: Law and Reason Versus the Restatement, 15 U. Pitt. L. Rev. 397 (1954).

BADIGIAN v. BADIGIAN
9 N.Y.2d 472, 174 N.E.2d 718 (1961)

Desmond, C.J. This is a negligence action brought by a mother on behalf of her three-year-old child against the father for negligently causing personal injuries to the child. The father, it is alleged, left the family car unlocked in a parking lot and the child released the brakes and was hurt when he tried to jump from the vehicle. There is no charge of misconduct which could be considered wanton or willful (see Siembab v. Siembab, 284 App. Div. 652). The complaint has been dismissed for insufficiency. We must affirm the dismissal unless we are to change the settled New York rule that an unemancipated minor child has no right of action against his parent for nonwillful injuries [citations omitted].

There is no decision in any American or English appellate court sustaining such a cause of action as is here alleged. The writers who attack the no-liability rule misunderstand its basis and purpose. It is a direct application of a concept that cannot be rejected without changing the whole fabric of our society, a fundamental idea that is at the bottom of all community life. The basic principle is that children and parents form a unique kind of social unit different from all other groups.

The courts have already provided different treatment for situations where the injury occurs outside the normal familial relationship such as where the injury is wanton and intentional or where the tort is committed in the course of the parent's business. Perhaps some other special provision should be made for cases where disability extends beyond infancy, but it would be a great oversimplification to attempt to deal with those instances by a simple reversal of the settled rule. Inquiry and planning for any such protection is beyond the competence of a court and belongs with the Legislature.

The statutory compulsion on all New York automobile owners to carry insurance against liability is hardly a sufficient ground for destroying our concept of the family unit. When New York State in 1937 changed the old rule of nonliability of a husband to a wife (or a wife to a husband) for personal injuries, it was done in the form of statutes (Domestic Relations Law, §57; Insurance Law, §167, subd. 3) which created a cause of action for the injured spouse but at the same time provided that automobile liability insurance policies would not cover such a liability unless express provision therefor was written into the policy. We are informed that no insurance company writes such "spouse coverage."

Automobile liability insurance premiums, like all other insurance premiums, are based on recent experience and, since there is no loss experience as to injuries to a child caused by its parent's negligence, the current rates do not contemplate such indemnity. Thus it is incorrect to say that the existence of automobile liability insurance provides a fund available for the payment of such a claim as is sought to be enforced in this suit.

The judgment should be affirmed, without costs.

FULD, J. (dissenting). If the present decision were necessary to preserve the integrity of the family, I would subscribe to it. But I do not believe that it is. In my opinion, the doctrine of family immunity, which under-lies the holding, is based on dubious prophecy and, at least when applied to deny redress in automobile negligence cases, is wrong in principle and at odds with justice and modern-day realities.[54]

The family immunity doctrine, without precedent in English common law [citations omitted], was first announced in 1891 in Mississippi. (See Hewlett v. George, 68 Miss. 703.) There the tort was willful. A minor daughter sued her mother for maliciously confining her in an insane asy-lum. Public policy, it was held, forbade the suit; to permit such an ac-tion would undermine parental authority and disrupt domestic harmony. . . . In Washington, a 15-year-old daughter sued her father who had ravished her. (See Roller v. Roller, 37 Wash. 242.) The court denied a right of action to the child. To allow a remedy in such a case would, it was said, open the door to one for injuries which were negligent, since in principle no distinction could be made between them. The peace of the family would be marred if the conduct of the parent could thus be chal-lenged in a civil court.

The immunity doctrine soon spread to cases involving negligently caused injuries without any change in the underlying reasoning. [Cita-tions omitted.] And in 1928, this court adopted the rule exempting par-ents from liability to an unemancipated minor for personal injuries caused by their negligence in operating an automobile . . . .

A rule which so incongruously shields conceded wrongdoing bears a heavy burden of justification. For me, the burden is not met either by the early rationale or by other arguments more recently advanced. A parent who by negligence injures his minor child surely commits a civil "wrong" in the sense that there is neither lawful right nor privilege to inflict the injury. . . .

There is a wrong, it may be said, but the remedy is withheld for reasons of fundamental public policy, namely, to prevent undermining parental authority and disrupting the peace of the family. That principle might be compelling in this case if consistently and evenhandedly applied when-ever a child sues his parent. But, since innumerable exceptions and qual-ifications to its application have evolved, it can no longer serve as a force-ful or valid basis for denying liability.

First, the doctrine does not apply if the child is of legal age. If filial

---

[54] And, I would add that, although the rule has been accepted by almost every court which has considered the problem, it has been "universally condemned in the thoughtful professorial and student writings on the subject." (Hastings v. Hastings, 33 N.J. 247, 254, per JACOBS, J., dissenting.) Many of these writings are listed in Judge JACOBS' opinion (33 N.J., at pp. 254-255).

duty or family peace is the test, it is impossible to understand why a distinction should be made between minor children and those who are adult. The Biblical command, "Honor thy father and thy mother," does not end at 21. Yet there is no doubt that the grown son or daughter, the emancipated minor, may sue the parent for negligent wrongs.[55] [Citations omitted.]

Nor is it solely to a child of adult years that the immunity yields. Even an unemancipated minor child may sue his parent for an injury to his property. [Citations omitted.] Indeed, the books are filled with cases in which children have litigated with their parents over contracts, wills, inheritances and settlements. . . .

It is likewise difficult to understand the other qualifications to the rule of parental immunity. Thus, there is no doubt today that an unemancipated minor may maintain an action for personal injuries willfully or intentionally inflicted. [Citations omitted.]

In addition, a child may actually, albeit indirectly, obtain redress from his parent for personal injuries resulting from an automobile accident if the child can find and sue a third person who in turn transfers his liability to the parent. . . .

And, finally, an infant may sue his parent directly for personal injuries caused by the father's careless operation of a car, provided only that it was being used in connection with the father's business. [Citations omitted.]

. . . I cannot believe that the peace of family life requires that the cripple go through life unaided by our law if he was hurt while under age. Nor can I believe that there will be a mad rush by children to extract money from their parents if once the barriers are down. The family life itself, the life to be preserved in all its communal solidarity, it seems to me, supplies the answer. Those parents who are worthy of affection will make provision for the crippled child to the extent of their ability without the spur of legal process. The child will be unwilling to sue, will have no need or thought to sue. What is right will be done, and it will be done out of a love that is stronger than the law. . . .

It is not too much to say that the broad and numerous qualifications and exceptions to the family immunity doctrine have almost swallowed the rule. [Citation omitted.] It is quite likely that this came about when the realization dawned that, when a child sues a parent, family harmony must already be at so low an ebb that it is grotesque to deny the child a remedy in the name of preserving that harmony. So far as the related argument that parental authority must be preserved by denying the child his right of action, I fail to see its applicability to a case such as the one before us. [Citation omitted.] Surely, causing a child harm by negligent operation or maintenance of an automobile involves no attribute of parental control or filial obedience.[56] . . .

---

[55] But see page 345 infra. — Ed.

[56] Although Borst v. Borst (41 Wn. 2d 642 . . .) differs somewhat from the present case in that the father's automobile was being operated in connection with his business, the court's statement is most pertinent (p. 651): ". . . The field of parental control and discipline covers such matters as the maintenance of the

New York now requires automobile liability insurance. I recognize that the presence of insurance does not create liability but, since it was fear that domestic peace and tranquility would be destroyed and the family disrupted which gave rise to adoption of the family immunity doctrine, its existence is a factor to be taken into account in considering whether or not the doctrine should be perpetuated. [Citations omitted.] It has ushered in new tendencies and habits which may not be ignored in any estimate of values. Insurance against accidents, once solely a contract of indemnity, a means of reimbursement for the doer of the wrong, has lost much of its ancient quality and has in effect become insurance for the protection of the sufferer. . . .

Certainly, where there is insurance, it becomes more difficult to justify the stock arguments advanced against recovery, to say that recognition of a right of action destroys our concept of the family unit. . . .

Since the insurer is the real defendant, it has been said that there is danger of fraud and collusion between parent and child. One may not, of course, deny the hazard, but such a danger, being present in all liability insurance cases, furnishes reason not for denial of a cause of action, but for added caution on the part of court and jury in examining and assessing the facts. The danger is precisely the same when the injury is to a child who has attained 21 or to a brother or sister or, to a less degree, to a friend. In Rozell v. Rozell (281 N.Y. 106), this court actually rejected just such an argument when it upheld the right of a 12-year-old youngster to sue his 16-year-old sister who had injured him while driving an automobile covered by liability insurance . . . .

The decision to be made herein has little, if anything, to do with a case where the child is injured in the kitchen or in some other room making up the family establishment. There may be injustice, as well as difficulty, in applying the standardized duty of the reasonable man in such a situation. Heed, it may well be, must be given to excuses to which the law declines to listen when the victim is a business visitor. The house or the apartment may be out of order or in need of repair, but, there is force to the query, what is the father to do if there is no money to repair it? . . .

I have remarked these problems but to exclude them. What concerns us now is not the parent's liability to his infant child for failing to put the house in order. . . .

. . . [I]t is urged that, if there is to be a remedy, it must be given by the Legislature, if there is to be change, it may not be effected by the courts. This court has heard such arguments before and has answered them by saying that, where the rule is court made, it may be court modified if reason and a right sense of justice recommend it. . . .

The problem, in short, comes to this: A child is seriously injured by his father's careless operation or maintenance of his automobile. As the law

---

home, chastisement, and no doubt other activities which need not here be delineated. But when the parental activity whereby the child was injured has nothing to do with parental control and discipline, a suit involving such activity cannot be said to undermine those sinews of family life." [Court's quotation abbreviated by Eds.]

now stands, the judgment recovered against the parent is more than likely, in the vast majority of cases, to be paid by an insurer. If the crippled child may have the benefit of this insurance, a fund will be supplied the family to provide for him. If the fund is cut off, cripple as well as parent will have to stagger beneath the load. To tell them that the pains must be endured for the peace and welfare of the family is something of a mockery.

I would reverse the summary judgment dismissing the complaint and give the child his day in court.

NOTE

1. Compare Goller v. White, 20 Wis. 2d 402, 122 N.W.2d 193 (1963), abolishing the parent-child immunity prospectively in all negligence actions except those based on an exercise of parental authority over the child or ones involving parental discretion with respect to the provision of food, clothing, housing, and similar services to the child. As is apparent from the Goller case, abolition of the immunity necessitates facing up to the problem of parental discipline. See proposed §147(1), Restatement (Second), Torts (Tent. Draft No. 1, 1957): "A parent is privileged to apply such reasonable force or to impose such reasonable confinement upon his child as he reasonably believes to be necessary for its proper control, training or education." Cf. id. §150 (listing factors for judging reasonableness of parental discipline). See also Cooperrider, Child v. Parent in Tort: A Case for the Jury?, 43 Minn. L. Rev. 73 (1958), for a critical discussion of the Restatement's position.

2. Appellate opinions commonly state that those who stand in loco parentis are not entitled to the immunity enjoyed by parents. For a discussion of the issues, see Prosser, Torts 886 (3d ed. 1964); Restatement (Second), Torts §147(2) and Comment *d* (Tent. Draft No. 1, 1957).

3. As Justice Fuld's opinion in Badigian indicates, the doctrine of "emancipation" is likely to be important in intrafamily tort cases. The standard formulation is:

> In modern law "emancipation of an infant" is used in two distinct senses: (1) to denote the release of the infant from parental control; (2) to describe the process of removing the disabilities of infancy by judicial decree. This latter use of the expression is entirely the outgrowth of statutes . . . At common law, emancipation denoted the release of a minor from parental control, and the acquisition by the minor of the right to dispose of his own earnings. . . . Although many courts have spoken of complete emancipation, actually a parent could not emancipate a child and thereby relieve himself of all parental obligations, nor could the parent preclude the child from rescinding the emancipation agreement and reclaiming his rights as child. . . .
>
> At common law, emancipation of a minor might be effected by the consent of the parent, or by operation of law. Emancipation was

effected by consent . . . when there was a written or oral agreement between parent and child, or when such consent could be implied from the facts of the case. . . . Emancipation by operation of law occurred generally only when a person attained the age of majority, but under certain circumstances even a minor might be emancipated by operation of law. Thus, common-law courts held that a minor who contracted a valid marriage, either with or without his parent's consent, was emancipated. Similarly, where the parent abandoned or failed to support the child, the parent lost his right to the earnings of the child . . .[57]

Whether the child is emancipated may be an important issue in a variety of contexts: Can the child recover from his parent in a negligence suit? Is the child's employer liable to the parent for the child's wages when the employer has already paid the child? Can the child maintain a separate domicile — for purposes, perhaps, of paying resident tuition at a school in a state where his parents do not reside, or for purposes of obtaining diversity of citizenship jurisdiction in a federal court? Is the parent liable for necessaries purchased by the child? Is the parent liable for the child's support under a separation agreement? Can the parent recover for the child's seduction? When the issues are so varied, it should not be surprising that the case law does not lend itself to precise formulation.

Despite Justice Fuld's remark in Badigian, at least one court has held, in a child's suit based on her parent's negligent operation of the family car, that the attainment of majority does not ipso facto emancipate the child. Goldstein v. Goldstein, 4 N.J. Misc. 711, 134 Atl. 184 (1926) (twenty-three-year-old daughter living at home and working for wages; emancipation for jury; denial of directed verdict affirmed). In another automobile negligence suit against a parent, Wurth v. Wurth, 313 S.W.2d 161 (Mo. Ct. App. 1958), the plaintiff was a nineteen-year-old girl who, while living at home, had independent employment, paid her own expenses, and gave her parents money for her board. The court affirmed a directed verdict for the defendant. The plaintiff's showing

> does not completely rebut the cautionary presumption with which the law protects the parent in the enjoyment of the normal parental relations. The preservation of the peace, harmony and security so vital to the family and home cannot so easily be accommodated to meet the ends of expediency.[58]

Compare Wood v. Wood, 135 Conn. 280, 63 A.2d 586 (1948) (twenty-year-old plaintiff, living in the family home and working independently for three years, paid her own expenses but no board to her parents; emancipation for the jury and directed verdict for defendant-father set aside).

Suppose that, after a jury verdict for Miss Wood in her suit against her father, a doctor sues her father for the value of medical services he performed for Miss Wood after the accident. Can he recover?

[57] 5 Vernier 240-241.
[58] 313 S.W.2d at 165.

4. In general, see McCurdy, Torts between Parent and Child, 5 Vill. L. Rev. 521 (1960).

PARKER v. GORDON
178 F.2d 888 (1st Cir. 1949)

Magruder, C.J. Charles Gordon filed in the court below a complaint in tort against Stanley W. Parker for loss of consortium. The amended complaint . . . was in two counts . . . [Count 1 alleged that the defendant had alienated the affections of plaintiff's wife; Count 2 alleged that defendant had "entered into adulterous relations" with plaintiff's wife and "was thereby guilty of criminal conversation."] Judgment was given for the plaintiff on a jury verdict, and defendant appeals.

Federal jurisdiction was invoked on the ground of diversity of citizenship, plaintiff being a citizen of Pennsylvania and defendant of Massachusetts. . . .

Plaintiff Gordon was born and raised in Pennsylvania. After their marriage in 1940, he and his wife Naomi made their home in Pittsburgh, where he had a job. In March, 1941, Gordon was called to active duty as a reserve officer in the U.S. Army, and sent to a post in Boston Harbor. During the ensuing months they lived together in an apartment in Winthrop, Massachusetts. Gordon left for overseas in March, 1942, and Mrs. Gordon went to Scottdale, Pennsylvania, to live with her husband's family. In December, 1943, Mrs. Gordon came back to Massachusetts to visit her former neighbors in Winthrop, and on this occasion she met the defendant Parker. It did not take long for that chance meeting to ripen into a warm friendship. Mrs. Gordon returned to Pennsylvania in February, 1944, but was back again in Winthrop for another visit in March, and saw Parker again. In May, 1944, Mrs. Gordon came up for a third visit, but this time she stayed at a hotel in Boston rather than with friends. Her last visit to Boston without her husband was over the July 4th weekend of 1944.

Starting shortly after their first meeting, and during all of Mrs. Gordon's above-mentioned visits to Boston, she and Parker had numerous dates together, swimming, bowling, dancing, dining out, or dining in Parker's apartment sometimes with no third person present. There were "going-away" kisses, "welcome-back" kisses, and "just regular" kisses. Parker rather grudgingly admitted to other occasional familiarities indicative of a less than discreet relationship between him and Mrs. Gordon. Both denied on the witness stand that they had ever had adulterous intercourse. Gordon, however, testified that during a meeting he had with Parker, after divorce proceedings against Mrs. Gordon had been instituted, Parker admitted that he had had "improper sexual relations" with Mrs. Gordon, but added: "The conversation goes between you and I only, and if you think you can prove it, go ahead. As far as I am concerned, you can see my attorney." This conversation was denied by Parker.

In the intervals between Mrs. Gordon's visits to Boston, Parker kept up his contact with her by long-distance telephone, and by correspondence. Mrs. Gordon thought she had destroyed Parker's letters, but Mr. Gordon's "meddlesome aunt," to use a phrase of the district judge, fished out from the incinerator and pieced together the torn fragments of three of these letters, which eventually were turned over to Gordon, and were introduced as exhibits at the trial below. The letters look silly in print, and would hardly be included among the classics of amatory writing. They are, however, sprinkled with terms of endearment and erotic allusions which betoken a relationship not casual and circumspect, but intimate indeed. From certain expressions in the letters, together with other evidence in the case, a jury would be warranted in inferring that Parker's intention was to break up the marital relationship between Mrs. Gordon and her husband, and to appropriate her for himself. We refer, for instance, to expressions such as "the speed of our pickup on loving"; "Come on quit haunting me and join me for good!"; "Were you today to join me for life we'd just sail right along on a breeze having fun, having fights, having love, having many friends. Gosh, do we click!"; "Gee this week how I wished I could spoil you again — but this time for life." Parker's explanation that he was merely trying to keep up Mrs. Gordon's morale during the period of her enforced separation from her husband might not unreasonably be discredited.

Gordon testified that he noticed a change in the tone of his wife's letters to him overseas, coinciding with the inception of her acquaintanceship with Parker. Mrs. Gordon met her husband in August, 1944, in Washington, D.C., upon his return from India. Gordon testified: "There was a complete metamorphosis in her reactions. My desires for her, of course, had been unchanged. But I say she was neurotic. The matter of sexual relations were entirely out of the question with her"; and further he said that there were no sexual relations between them from the time Gordon returned from abroad. Shortly after his arrival in Washington, he and his wife proceeded to Fort Harrison, Indiana, where they occupied an apartment together while he took a six-weeks training course. Upon their return to Scottdale, Pa., Gordon saw for the first time the three letters from Parker above referred to. Gordon consulted a lawyer with reference to a divorce. He decided to try for a reconciliation, and he and Mrs. Gordon embarked on what he described as a "second honeymoon." . . . After a short stay in Canada, during which it was evident, according to Gordon, that the reconciliation was not working out, they returned to . . . Scottdale, Pa. . . . In early spring of 1945 Gordon instituted a divorce suit against his wife, and the divorce was eventually granted.

According to Mrs. Gordon's testimony she had been faithful to her husband throughout, had not ceased to love him, and had had no desire to separate from him; she attributed the estrangement which developed after his return to this country in August, 1944, to his changed attitude, rather than to hers. She testified that "all the time" during the period after his return, up to the filing of the divorce suit, they had lived together and had had relations "as husband and wife"; that at or about the time of the filing of the divorce suit her husband had peremptorily ordered her to remove her things from the home of Mr. Gordon's parents; and that after that she moved out and did not live with her husband thereafter.

When the evidence was all in, defendant filed a motion for a directed verdict on both counts. The motion was denied. In this there was no error, if for no other reason than that there was certainly sufficient evidence to warrant a finding of criminal conversation, and this, admittedly, would have made out a cause of action under the Massachusetts law.

Defendant then presented certain requests for rulings. So far as appears, the district judge did not expressly rule on these requests one by one. . . . The jury retired to consider its verdict, but subsequently returned for further enlightenment from the judge, at which time the court gave the jury certain additional instructions which we shall refer to at a later point.

The jury brought in a verdict for the plaintiff on Count 1, in the sum of $5000, but found for the defendant on Count 2. . . .

Thereafter, defendant moved to set aside the verdict for the plaintiff on Count 1, and the judgment entered thereon, and for the entry of judgment for the defendant notwithstanding the verdict. This motion was denied, for the reasons stated in a memorandum reported in D.C., 83 F. Supp. 45.

The legal wrong here in question, as recognized by the Massachusetts courts, is sometimes inaccurately described as the tort of "alienation of affections." Dow v. Bulfinch, 1906, 192 Mass. 281, 283, 78 N.E. 416. However, the Supreme Judicial Court of Massachusetts has repeatedly stated that alienation of affections alone is not a substantive cause of action, but merely aggravates the damages where the wife is debauched or enticed away. [Citations omitted.] The gist of the action is a "loss of consortium," brought about by the unprivileged acts of the defendant — i.e., acts done "with malice or improper motives" [citation omitted] — as distinguished, for example, from the mere giving of honest advice having in view the welfare of both spouses [citation omitted]. The interest of the husband expressed by the term "consortium" is defined in Bigaouette v. Paulet, 1883, 134 Mass. 123, 124, 45 Am. Rep. 307, as "the right to the conjugal fellowship of the wife, to her company, cooperation and aid in every conjugal relation." If criminal conversation between the defendant and the wife is proved, nothing further need be shown to make out a cause of action, for this is an obvious trespass upon one of the basic rights of consortium, an invasion of the husband's "exclusive right to marital intercourse with his wife, and to beget his own children"; and so it is said that "loss of the consortium is presumed" from the fact of criminal conversation. Bigaouette v. Paulet, supra, 134 Mass. at page 125.

But under the Massachusetts cases it is clear that the tort of loss of consortium may be established by proof of acts other than criminal conversation. Thus in Gahagan v. Church [239 Mass. 558, 132 N.E. 357 (1921)] the defendant, by a campaign of love-making evidently designed to break up the marital relationship, enticed the wife to leave her husband's home and thus to withhold performance of her conjugal duties.

The court held that a verdict for the plaintiff was warranted, though there was no allegation or proof of adulterous intercourse. . . .

Though we have found no square decision in any Massachusetts case on the point, we believe the Massachusetts courts would hold that an action for wrongful deprivation of consortium might in some circumstances be sustained even though the wife was not enticed and induced to abandon her husband's home, and though adulterous relations were not proved. Thus if the defendant's course of love-making, with the purpose of disrupting the marital relationship, has the effect of inducing a married woman to refuse sexual relations with her husband, there has been a tortious deprivation of an essential right of the consortium, even though the wife, in mockery of the conjugal relation, continues to live under the same roof with her husband until he turns her out and obtains a divorce. Such seems to be the law in other jurisdictions. [Citations omitted.] There is at least a negative implication to the same effect in McCracken v. Cohen, 1947, 322 Mass. 12, 75 N.E.2d 501. In that case the court upheld a directed verdict for the defendant, saying, 322 Mass. page 13, 75 N.E.2d page 501: "There was evidence that would have required the jury to find that the associations of the defendant and the plaintiff's wife were known to the plaintiff during the entire period . . . , but that notwithstanding he continued to live with her, *occupying the same bed with her and having sexual relations with her* even down to the time of the trial of the present case in the court below. [Italics added.] This being so, and since the jury would not have been warranted in finding that the plaintiff's wife had been debauched by the defendant, there could be no recovery for loss of consortium." . . .

With this statement of the Massachusetts law, we turn to the complaint in the case at bar. Count 2 charges criminal conversation, which, without more, would make out a cause of action, deprivation of consortium being presumed in that case, as we have seen. Paragraph II(b) of Count 1 also alleges criminal conversation, so in that respect the two counts overlap; that is, a finding for plaintiff on both counts would be warranted if criminal conversation were established. But [Count 1 was] apparently intended by the pleader to allege a cause of action for breach of consortium even in the absence of adulterous relations . . . At any rate, that is how the district judge construed Count 1 of the complaint, and that is the theory on which he submitted the case to the jury. . . .

. . . In the main charge, the judge told the jury that on Count 1, for the plaintiff to prevail, they "must find either adultery or that the defendant caused the wife to leave the husband." But after the jury had deliberated for a while, they came back to the court with the question "whether Mrs. Gordon's several visits to the Boston area constituted leaving home?". The judge then pointed out that this question need not bother the jury if they had found adultery, but that if they had come to the conclusion that there was no adultery, then the question would have to be dealt with. He proceeded to read to the jury the following quotation from Longe v. Saunders [246 Mass. 159, 140 N.E. 741 (1923)] . . . : "The plaintiff could recover . . . only by proof that the defendant with malice or improper motives persuaded and enticed his wife to leave his home; there could be no recovery so long as [they] lived together as *husband and wife* in their home and no adultery was committed with the wife."

The judge thus gave emphasis to the phrase "as husband and wife" . . . He then explained to the jury that if Mrs. Gordon came to Boston "with the intention of not thereafter having marital relations with her husband, she was enticed away"; and that they might so find if they believed Mr. Gordon's story, but not if they believed Mrs. Gordon's testimony. In other words, as the case was finally submitted to the jury, they were permitted to find for the plaintiff on Count 1 if they believed that Parker's acts, having the purpose of disrupting the marital relationship, had had the effect of inducing Mrs. Gordon to refuse sexual relations with her husband, even though adultery was not proved, and even though Mrs. Gordon continued to live under the same roof with her husband after his return from India until he ordered her to get out. As above indicated, we think that the charge to this effect was not in error under the Massachusetts law. . . .

. . . The district judge might, under his broad discretion in such matters, have set aside the verdicts and granted a new trial. He chose not to do so, and in fact the defendant never moved for a new trial. The only motion which the defendant made after verdict was a motion for judgment in his favor notwithstanding the verdict. There was certainly no error in denying that.

The judgment of the District Court is affirmed.

NOTE

1. Kinsey, Pomeroy, Martin & Gebhard, Sexual Behavior in the Human Female 413-415 (1953), state:

The anthropologists find that most societies recognize the necessity for accepting at least some extra-marital coitus as an escape valve for the male, to relieve him from the pressures put on him by society's insistence on stable marital partnerships. These same societies, however, less often permit it for the female. But most societies have also recognized that some restraint on extra-marital activities is necessary if marriages and homes are to be maintained and if the social organization is to function effectively. . . .

Most societies, in consequence, permit or condone extra-marital coitus for the male if he is reasonably circumspect about it, and if he does not carry it to extremes which would break up his home, lead to any neglect of his family, outrage his in-laws, stir up public scandal, or start difficulties with the husbands or other relatives of the women with whom he has his extra-marital relationships. . . .

In many of these societies [those which permit or condone extramarital intercourse for the male], extra-marital coitus is overtly forbidden for the female, although it may be covertly condoned if it is not too flagrant and if the husband is not particularly disturbed. As our later data may indicate, this seems to be the direction toward which American attitudes may be moving.

The Kinsey study suggests that underlying all of the moral and social reasons for prohibiting extramarital intercourse by females is a less rational substratum: "The arguments would be more impressive if they led to any resolution of behavior which does not appear in the unreasoned behavior of the males of the lower mammalian groups." Id. at 416. In Kinsey's sample, 26 per cent of the married females had had extramarital coitus by age forty. In the sample of males, 27-37 per cent of the married males in each age group admitted having some experience in extramarital intercourse. A 50 per cent rate was estimated because individuals in some groups were hesitant to cooperate; since the researchers had "every reason for believing that extra-marital intercourse is the source of the hesitance," the figures "must represent the absolute minimum, and it is not at all improbable that the actuality may lie 10 to 20 per cent above the figures now given." Kinsey, Pomeroy & Martin, Sexual Behavior in the Human Male 585 (1948).

For criticism of Kinsey's sample and statistical techniques, see Zeisel, Book Review, 21 U. Chi. L. Rev. 517 (1954); Wallis, Statistics of the Kinsey Report, 44 J. Am. Stat. Assn. 463 (1949).

2. See Prosser, Torts 896-898 (3d ed. 1964):

One type of interference with the husband's interests is variously called abduction, enticement or harboring of the wife. There was a very early writ "of ravishment" which listed the wife with the husband's chattels, and was available to him when she was taken away forcibly or eloped with another. In time this was replaced by the action of trespass for depriving him of a servant. Since there is an obvious loss of "consortium" when a wife is either compelled or induced to live apart from her husband, all courts are agreed that he may maintain a tort action against anyone who, without justification and for an improper purpose, influences or advises her to do so, or assists her to depart. It was said that the old law was so strict that "if one's wife missed her way upon the road, it was not lawful for another man to take her into his house, unless she was benighted and in danger of being lost or drowned"; but this gentle rule for the encouragement of chivalry is a thing of the past. It may still be a tort against the husband to "harbor" the wife, if it is coupled with persuasion or encouragement not to return to him; but a mere reception in good faith upon grounds of friendship, hospitality or common humanity will not result in liability. . . .

Criminal conversation, enticement and alienation of affections still are often treated as separate torts, but there is no good reason for distinguishing them. . . . There is now a decided tendency to confuse the three, or to lump them together, usually under the general name of "alienation of affections," without any attempt to distinguish the possible elements of the tort.

The Supreme Court of Louisiana held that the courts should no longer recognize actions for alienation of affections; such actions are against public policy because they are punitive and because no one has a property right to the company, care, or assistance of another human being. Moulin v. Monteleone, 165 La. 169, 115 So. 447 (1928). Legislative relief has been more common; see the discussion of heart balm statutes, page 357 infra. For another method by which the societal interest in marital harmony and fidelity is enforced, see State v. Fullen, 176 N.E.2d 605 (Ohio Ct. App. 1959). Defendant was convicted for violating a statute which read: "No person shall . . . aid, abet, induce, cause, or encourage . . . the neglect . . . of a child . . ."   The defendant, "knowing that one Lee Bernard Brown was the father of three very young children, set up a separate domicile with him and lived with him for over two months."   Id. at 606.

3. For the plaintiff to recover in an alienation action, the defendant's conduct must have been intentional rather than negligent (Prosser, Torts §103 (3d ed. 1964)) and must have been the "active and controlling cause" of the plaintiff's injury (McQuarters v. Ducote, 234 S.W.2d 433, 435 (Tex. Civ. App. 1950); Annot., 19 A.L.R.2d 462 (1951)). It is no defense to a cause of action for alienation that the spouses were estranged at the time the defendant's conduct occurred. See Fennell v. Littlejohn, 240 S.C. 189, 197, 125 S.E.2d 408, 413 (1962), permitting plaintiff to recover although (1) the action for criminal conversation is not favored, (2) the plaintiff had already filed for divorce alleging two prior acts of adultery by his wife, (3) the state's mandatory reconciliation procedure had been unsuccessful; "[t]he fact that the marriage . . . may have been dealt a mortal blow by her adulterous conduct with others did not license the defendant to join in its destruction." Neither the defendant's lack of knowledge that the woman was married (McGrath v. Sullivan, 303 Mass. 327, 21 N.E.2d 533 (1939)) nor the plaintiff's impotence (Bedan v. Turney, 99 Cal. 649, 34 Pac. 442 (1893)) is sufficient to bar an action for criminal conversation. Suppose the defendant could prove that the plaintiff had forgiven his wife her misconduct and reconciled with her; should the action be dismissed?

4. In a jurisdiction which has adopted a Married Women's Act, should a wife be permitted to seek damages for another woman's alienation of her husband's affections? For another woman's criminal conversation with her husband? For an affirmative answer, consult Karchner v. Mumie, 398 Pa. 13, 156 A.2d 537 (1959); Restatement, Torts §690 (1938). One of the early decisions refusing to recognize a protectible interest in the wife was Duffies v. Duffies, 76 Wis. 374, 45 N.W. 522 (1890); the court commented: "The wife is more domestic, . . . and her duties in the domestic economy require her to be more constantly at home . . . . She is purer and better by nature than her husband, and more governed by principle and a sense of duty and right, and she seldom violates her marriage obligations, or abandons her home . . . . With the husband the case is different. He . . . is charged with the duty of providing for, maintaining, and protecting his wife and family. He is engaged, for

this purpose, in the business and various employments of the outside world . . . . He is exposed to the temptations, enticements, and allurements of the world, which easily withdraw him from her society, or cause him to desert or abandon her." 76 Wis. at 383-384, 45 N.W. at 525. If the legislature were interested in establishing complete equality for women, should it recognize the wife's right to sue for alienation, or should it abolish the husband's cause of action?

5. At common law a female could not recover damages for her own "seduction" either because she had consented to the injury or because she was in pari delicto. But a parent could recover because the action was premised upon loss of the child's services, with the seduction merely enhancing the parent's damages. The importance of the daughter's service to the cause of action (once it became established) is illustrated by a comment in Carr v. Clarke, 2 Chitty 260, 261 (K.B. 1818): "Even making tea has been said to be an act of service." Moreover, it is presumed that an unemancipated minor daughter was performing such services at the time of the injury. See 4 Vernier §252. See the discussion of emancipation at pages 344-345 supra; note also the following *Caveat* to the treatment of seduction in §701 of the Restatement of Torts (1938):

> The Institute expresses no opinion as to whether one who, without the parent's consent, has sexual intercourse with an unmarried adult child who lives in her parent's home under the same conditions as though she were a minor and who renders service to a parent, is liable for the resulting loss of services or for the reasonable expenses incurred by the parent for medical treatment for the child.

Statutes in a number of states permit recovery by the victim. See, e.g., Tenn. Code Ann. §20-17 (1956); Ore. Rev. Stat. §30.720 (1963).

The parent's right to his child's services is also the source of the parent's right to recover expenses he has borne because of a defendant's negligent injury to the child. See Note, Judicial Treatment of Negligent Invasion of Consortium, 61 Colum. L. Rev. 1341, 1346 (1961). As we have seen, page 298 supra, the husband may recover his damages — including loss of his wife's services and society ("consortium") and his costs for her care — resulting from another's tortious injury to his wife. Id. at 1347-1357; 3 Vernier §158. Several jurisdictions have abolished the husband's right to recover for loss of consortium, either judicially (e.g., Lockwood v. Wilson H. Lee Co., 144 Conn. 155, 128 A.2d 330 (1956)) or by statutory interpretation (e.g., Clark v. Southwestern Greyhound Lines, 144 Kan. 344, 58 P.2d 1128 (1936)). A few jurisdictions have obtained equality by permitting the wife to recover for loss of her husband's consortium. Montgomery v. Stephan, 359 Mich. 33, 101 N.W.2d 227 (1960); Hitaffer v. Argonne Co., 183 F.2d 811 (D.C. Cir.), cert. denied, 340 U.S. 852 (1950); Annot., 23 A.L.R.2d 1378 (1952). In Best v. Samuel Fox Co., [1952] A.C. 716, as the result of defendants' negligence, plaintiff's husband was permanently disabled from engaging in sexual intercourse; the husband had recovered £4200 for his injuries. The wife's action for damages for loss of consortium was dismissed; the House of Lords pointed out that the decision would work no injustice on the wife since the damages normally recovered by the husband in actions of this kind compensate expenses normally incurred by him, while the wife normally does not incur such expenses when her husband is injured.

6. A child has never been permitted to recover for loss of "consortium" occasioned by negligent injury to a parent. See Note, 61 Colum. L. Rev. 1341, 1347 (1961). But a number of courts have recently permitted a child to sue a third party who has alienated the affections of one of his parents. See, e.g., Johnson v. Luhman, 330 Ill. App. 598, 71 N.E.2d 810 (1947) (suit by mother would have been barred); Daily v. Parker, 152 F.2d 174 (7th Cir. 1945); contra, Lucas v. Bishop, 224 Ark. 353, 273 S.W.2d 397 (1954); Taylor v. Keefe, 134 Conn. 156, 56 A.2d 768 (1947).

DEVINE v. DEVINE
20 N.J. Super. 522, 90 A.2d 126 (1952)

EWART, J. The plaintiff, daughter-in-law of the defendant, by her complaint seeks the aid of this court and demands a judgment "enjoining and restraining the defendant, Helen Devine, from the doing of any acts designed or having the effect of maliciously and improperly interfering with the marital relations between the plaintiff and her husband, or to in any wise do and perform any acts seeking to further alienate the affections of the plaintiff's husband or to do or perform any acts designed to harass and terrorize the plaintiff . . ." [Court's quotation abbreviated by Eds.]

The complaint alleges that plaintiff was married to John Devine, son of the defendant, on August 5, 1950; that she and her husband resided together happily until the latter part of June 1951; that on June 18, 1951 plaintiff's husband was inducted into the U.S. Army Air Force, and stationed at Langley Field at Virginia for training; that plaintiff was employed at Rutgers University in New Brunswick and could only see her husband on week-ends; and that her husband drove his car from Virginia to New Brunswick on a week-end at the end of June 1951 and invited her to return in the car with him to Virginia for the week-end, but that she was compelled to refuse because of the length of the trip and the necessity of her being at work at 9:00 A.M. on the Monday morning following. The complaint charges that the defendant took offense at the plaintiff's refusal to spend the week-end with her husband in Virginia and, shortly after the husband's departure, telephoned the home of plaintiff's parents and became noisy, threatening and abusive over the 'phone, accusing plaintiff's parents of interfering with her son and the plaintiff; made insulting remarks over the 'phone, and threatened to go to the home of the wife's parents "to straighten them out once and for all." . . . The complaint further charges that a short time after the occurrences above mentioned the defendant gave plaintiff's husband a false account of the foregoing occurrences and maliciously and falsely informed plaintiff's husband that she, the defendant, had been grossly insulted on the 'phone by the plaintiff and by the plaintiff's family; that they had sworn at her and treated her discourteously; . . . that the plaintiff was evading and not performing or fulfilling her obligations as a wife should; . . . that henceforth the defendant would not permit the plaintiff to come into her home and would not be recognized or treated by the defendant as the wife of her son; for all of which the defendant demanded satisfaction of her son. The complaint further charges that as a result of the foregoing statements and actions of the defendant, quarrels developed between the plaintiff and her husband and that the husband, on or about October 4, 1951, deserted and abandoned the plaintiff who by that time was pregnant, and that plaintiff's husband had refused to maintain, provide for and support her as he was legally obliged to do and otherwise disregarded her status as his lawful wife. . . . And the complaint further charges that by reason of the matters above recited, the plaintiff has been deprived of the support of her husband; has been receiving no financial help of any kind from him since October 1951 . . . ; and that the plaintiff's husband is now (at the time of filing of the complaint) in the U.S. Air Force stationed in Korea. . . .

The gist or gravamen of this suit, as I read the complaint, is for the loss by the plaintiff of her husband's consortium by which is meant loss of marital affections, comfort, society, assistance and services. . . .

The plaintiff has no adequate remedy at law since the enactment of the "Heart Balm" statute, L. 1935, c. 279, R.S. 2:39A-1. That statute, as a matter of public policy, has outlawed suits for damages for alienation of affections. . . . However, the statute is in derogation of a common law right; is to be strictly construed and not stretched to cover more than its plain language would justify; and there is nothing in the statute that would prohibit a suit for injunctive relief as distinguished from a suit for money damages.

This suit was filed March 29, 1952. The latest offensive act charged to the defendant in the complaint is during the month of October 1951. Injunction is primarily a preventive remedy intended to afford relief against future acts or conduct which are against equity and good conscience, and to preserve and keep a thing in statu quo, rather than to remedy what is past and done or to punish for wrongs already committed. [Citations omitted.]

Offensive acts alleged to have been committed by the defendant between June and October of 1951 cannot be remedied by a suit for injunctive relief filed on March 29, 1952.

Nor, where no breach of trust or of contract appears, will equity ordinarily enjoin libelous or slanderous statements injurious to the plaintiff. [Citations omitted.]

The extraordinary relief by injunction is not granted as a matter of course, but rather rests in the sound discretion of the court depending upon the facts and circumstances of each particular case. It is a remedy which should be exercised sparingly and cautiously and should be awarded only in clear cases reasonably free from doubt. . . .

Plaintiff does not ask, nor could she reasonably do so, that defendant be prohibited from communicating with her son by letters or other means of communication while he is stationed in Korea or by visits and conversations when he may be at home. Rather it appears that the plaintiff would have the court censor the written or verbal communications by the defendant to her son and restrain and enjoin the defendant from making adverse comment or criticisms of the plaintiff to her son, and from telling any false stories or disseminating any false information to the son of, about and concerning the plaintiff. Just how the court could enforce such an order, were an injunction granted, is not clear and the enforcement of such an injunction would appear to present insurmountable difficulties. . . .

Equity has always regarded the problem of enforcing its judgment or decree as an important factor in determining whether injunctive relief is appropriate. Such relief may be denied when, though otherwise appropriate, the judgment or decree would not be enforceable because of the inherent difficulties involved in the enforcement. [Citation omitted.] And injunctions against torts perpetrated wholly or in part by means of spoken or written words present special difficulties of enforcement and an injunction to prohibit words or conduct resulting in alienation of affections would probably only serve to add fuel to the flame. . . .

Under the facts and circumstances disclosed in the complaint, which for the purpose of this motion are to be taken as true, I feel constrained to grant defendant's motion to strike the complaint and dismiss the suit . . . .

Judgment will accordingly go for the defendant.

NOTE

1. See Comment, 38 Cornell L.Q. 255 (1953). For a description of the parental "privilege" to alienate affections, see Prosser, Torts 901 (3d ed. 1964). Some courts have approved a rebuttable presumption that a parent's advice is given in good faith and from proper motives. See, e.g., Worth v. Worth, 48 Wyo. 441, 49 P.2d 649 (1935). Gottlieb v. Gleiser, [1958] 1 Q.B. 267, [1957] 3 All E.R. 715, was a husband's suit for damages against his wife's mother. Denning, L.J., dismissing the action, commented ([1958] 1 Q.B. at 268-269, [1957] 3 All E.R. at 716-717):

I do not know that the rule has ever been extended so as to enable a husband to sue his mother-in-law for enticement. An action against parents-in-law has been allowed in America but, so far as I am aware, not in this country, and I do not think that it should be started now. When a man takes to himself a wife, he takes her parents to be his parents and they become his parents-in-law; he becomes part of their family. In this new situation the infirmities of human nature are such that stresses and strains are often set up without any malice on either side. The mother-in-law may be unduly possessive of her daughter and seek to protect her from the unkindness, as she regards it, of the husband. The wife may be immature and unduly reliant on her mother, instead of placing her trust in her husband, as she ought to do. These psychological defects may break up the marriage and cause the wife to leave the husband. But I do not think that this should be made the subject of an action for damages. It is altogether unseemly that families should bring these troubles into the courts of law. . . .

2. For additional material on heart balm statutes, see pages 239-244 supra, and compare Pa. Stat. Ann. tit. 48, §170 (Supp. 1964), expressly exempting from the scope of the act abolishing actions for alienation of affections "cases where the defendant is a parent, brother or sister or a person formerly in loco parentis to the plaintiff's spouse." See also Note, Avoidance of the Incidence of the Anti-Heartbalm Statutes, 52 Colum. L. Rev. 242 (1952). The narrow construction in Devine is not atypical. Consider the following:

a. Russick v. Hicks, 85 F. Supp. 281 (W.D. Mich. 1949), held that the prohibition against alienation of affections actions does not bar a suit by the children of the alienated parent. The court reasoned that since the only type of alienation action recognized in the jurisdiction prior to enactment of the statute was one to assert the wife's interest, the legislature could not have intended to bar suits by children. Accord, Johnson v. Luhman, 330 Ill. App. 598, 71 N.E.2d 810 (1947); contra, Katz v. Katz, 197 Misc. 412, 95 N.Y.S.2d 863 (Sup. Ct. 1950).

b. Antonelli v. Xenakis, 363 Pa. 375, 69 A.2d 102 (1949), held that Pennsylvania's heart balm statute, which prohibits actions for "alienation of affections," does not bar an action claiming damages for criminal conversation.

PROBLEM

Your client is Mary Sullivan; she is twenty-four years old and has been married for three months to John Sullivan, a twenty-four-year-old law student. John's parents are both deceased and he lives on the income from a $1 million trust of which his much older brother and sister are co-trustees. The trust provides that the trustees shall pay John such of the income of the trust as in their judgment is in his best interest and that the trust shall terminate and the corpus be paid to John when he becomes thirty-five "or sooner in the discretion of the trustees." Mary and her family are Baptists, having converted from Roman Catholicism; the Sullivan family is Roman Catholic, although John is not an active church member. Mary and John agreed to marry six months ago; their plan was to have a Baptist ceremony and, sometime later, to be married in a Catholic ceremony to please John's family. About three months ago they married secretly in a Baptist church and spent several weekends together without informing either family of the marriage. Two months ago Mary learned for the first time that a Catholic ceremony would require her to promise to raise her children in the Catholic faith; she refused to make such a promise or to lie to a priest (which would have satisfied John, since he had always been willing to raise their children as Baptists). They obtained their families' agreement to a civil marriage, went through the ceremony a month ago and left for a seven-day honeymoon. In their absence both families discovered their former marriage. Upon their return, John's brother and sister threatened to deprive John of any income from the trust unless he went through a Catholic marriage ceremony. Mary refused to accede to this demand. John's brother and sister told him that their parents would turn over in their graves if they knew of his conduct. John then decided not to risk the loss of support for his law school education and moved back to his brother's home.

Advise Mary as to her rights, if any, against John's brother and sister.

UNITED STATES v. DEGE
364 U.S. 51 (1960)

FRANKFURTER, J. This is an indictment charging husband and wife with conspiring to commit an offense against the United States in violation of §371 of Title 18 of the United States Code, which was enacted by Congress on June 25, 1948, 62 Stat. 683, 701, in connection with §545 of that Code, id., 716, in that they sought illicitly to bring goods into the United States with intent to defraud it. On authority of controlling decisions of its Circuit, Dawson v. United States, 10 F.2d 106, and Gros v. United States, 138 F.2d 261, the District Court dismissed the indictment on the ground that it did not state an offense, to wit, a husband and wife are legally incapable of conspiring within the condemnation of §371. . . .

The question raised . . . is clear-cut and uncomplicated. The claim that husband and wife are outside the scope of an enactment of Congress in 1948, making it an offense for two persons to conspire, must be given short shrift once we heed the admonition of this Court that "we free our minds from the notion that criminal statutes must be construed by some artificial and conventional rule," United States v. Union Supply Co., 215 U.S. 50, 55, and therefore do not allow ourselves to be obfuscated by medieval views regarding the legal status of woman and the common law's reflection of them. Considering that legitimate business enterprises between husband and wife have long been commonplaces in our time, it would enthrone an unreality into a rule of law to suggest that man and wife are legally incapable of engaging in illicit enterprises and therefore, forsooth, do not engage in them.

None of the considerations of policy touching the law's encouragement or discouragement of domestic felicities on the basis of which this Court determined appropriate rules for testimonial compulsion as between spouses, Hawkins v. United States, 358 U.S. 74, and Wyatt v. United States, 362 U.S. 525, are relevant to yielding to the claim that an unqualified interdiction by Congress against a conspiracy between two persons precludes a husband and wife from being two persons. Such an immunity to husband and wife as a pair of conspirators would have to attribute to Congress one of two assumptions: either that responsibility of husband and wife for joint participation in a criminal enterprise would make for marital disharmony, or that a wife must be presumed to act under the coercive influence of her husband and, therefore, cannot be a willing participant. The former assumption is unnourished by sense; the latter implies a view of American womanhood offensive to the ethos of our society.

The fact of the matter is that we are asked to write into law a doctrine that parrot-like has been repeated in decisions and texts from what was given its authoritative expression by Hawkins early in the eighteenth century. He wrote:

> "It plainly appears from the Words of the Statute, That one Person alone cannot be guilty of Conspiracy within the Purport of it; from whence it follows, . . . That no such Prosecution is maintainable against a Husband and Wife only, because they are esteemed but as one Person in Law, and are presumed to have but one Will." (Hawkins, Pleas of the Crown, 4th ed. 1762, Bk. I, chap. lxxii, Sect. 8, p. 192.)

The pronouncement of Hawkins apparently rests on a case in a Year Book of 38 Edward III, decided in 1365. The learning invoked for this ancient doctrine has been questioned by modern scholarship. [Citations omitted.] But in any event the answer to Hawkins with his Year Book authority, as a basis for a decision by the Supreme Court of the United States in 1960 construing a statute enacted in 1948, was definitively made long ago by Mr. Justice Holmes:

> "It is revolting to have no better reason for a rule of law than that so it was laid down in the time of Henry IV. It is still more revolting if the grounds upon which it was laid down have vanished long since, and the rule simply persists from blind imitation of the past." Holmes, Collected Legal Papers, 187 (1920), reprinting The Path of the Law, 10 Harv. L. Rev. 457, 469 (1897).

For this Court now to act on Hawkins's formulation of the medieval view that husband and wife "are esteemed but as one Person in Law, and are presumed to have but one Will" would indeed be "blind imitation of the past." It would require us to disregard the vast changes in the status of woman — the extension of her rights and correlative duties — whereby a wife's legal submission to her husband has been wholly wiped out, not only in the English-speaking world generally but emphatically so in this country.

How far removed we were even nearly a century ago when Congress passed the original statute against criminal conspiracy, the Act of March 2, 1867, 14 Stat. 484, from the legal and social climate of eighteenth century common law regarding the status of woman is pithily illustrated by recalling the self-deluding romanticism of Blackstone, whereby he could conscientiously maintain that "even the disabilities, which the wife lies under, are for the most part intended for her protection and benefit. So great a favourite is the female sex of the laws of England." Blackstone, Commentaries on the Laws of England (1765), Bk. I, ch. 15, p. 433. It would be an idle parade of learning to document the statement that these common-law disabilities were extensively swept away in our different

state of society, both by legislation and adjudication, long before the originating conspiracy Act of 1867 was passed. Suffice it to say that we cannot
infuse into the conspiracy statute a fictitious attribution to Congress of
regard for the medieval notion of woman's submissiveness to the benevo-
lent coercive powers of a husband in order to relieve her of her obligation
of obedience to an unqualifiedly expressed Act of Congress by regarding
her as a person whose legal personality is merged in that of her husband
making the two one.

Reversed.

MR. CHIEF JUSTICE WARREN, with whom MR. JUSTICE BLACK and MR.
JUSTICE WHITTAKER join, dissenting.

If the Court's opinion reflects all that there is to this case, it is astonishing that it has taken so many years for the federal judiciary to loose itself
from the medieval chains of the husband-wife conspiracy doctrine. The
problem, as the Court sees it, is almost absurdly uncomplicated: The basis
for the notion that husband and wife are not subject to a conspiracy
charge is that man and wife are one; but we know that man and wife are
two, not one; therefore, there is no basis for the notion that husband and
wife are not subject to a conspiracy charge. I submit that this simplistic
an approach will not do.

The Court apparently does not assert that if the husband-wife conspiracy doctrine was widely accepted when the conspiracy statute was passed
in 1867, 14 Stat. 484, and therefore was presumably within Congress' understanding of the reach of that statute, nonetheless this Court should
now reject the rule because it finds it nonsensical. Instead, the Court's
position is that

> "It would be an idle parade of learning to document the statement
> that these common-law disabilities [of women] were extensively
> swept away in our different state of society, both by legislation and
> adjudication, long before the originating conspiracy Act of 1867 was
> passed."

But, however rapidly nineteenth century jurisprudence moved toward
a recognition of the individuality of women in other areas, it is wholly
inaccurate to imply that the law of conspiracy changed apace. In fact,
the earliest case repudiating the husband-wife doctrine which the Government has been able to cite is Dalton v. People, 68 Colo. 44, 189 P. 37,
which was decided, as the Government puts it, "[a]s early as 1920." And
if the doctrine is an anachronism today, as the Court says, its unusual
hardiness is demonstrated by the fact that the decision of the Court represents a departure from the general rule which prevails today in the
English-speaking world. As recently as 1957, the Privy Council approved
the husband-wife doctrine, and other Commonwealth courts are in accord. For American decisions, see Annot., 4 A.L.R. 266, 71 A.L.R. 1116,
46 A.L.R.2d 1275.

Thus it seems clear that if the 1867 statute is to be construed to reflect
Congress' intent as it was in 1867, the Court's decision is erroneous. And
I believe that we must focus upon that intent, inasmuch as there is no

indication that Congress meant to change the law by the 1948 legislation which re-enacted without material variation the old conspiracy statute. Surely when a rule of law is well established in the common law and is part of the legislative purpose when a relevant statute is passed, that rule should not be rejected by this Court in the absence of an explicit subsequent repudiation of it by Congress. Consequently, I would be compelled to dissent whether or not I believed the rule to be supported by reason.

But more, I cannot agree that the rule is without justification. Inasmuch as Mr. Justice Holmes' observation that it is "revolting" to follow a doctrine only "from blind imitation of the past" is hardly novel, the tenacious adherence of the judiciary to the husband-wife conspiracy doctrine indicates to me that the rule may be predicated upon underlying policies unconnected with problems of women's suffrage or capacity to sue. The "definitive answer" to the question posed by this case is not to be found in a breezy aphorism from the collected papers of Mr. Justice Holmes, for "[g]eneral propositions do not decide concrete cases."

It is not necessary to be wedded to fictions to approve the husband-wife conspiracy doctrine, for one of the dangers which that doctrine averts is the prosecution and conviction of persons for "conspiracies" which Congress never meant to be included within the statute. A wife, simply by virtue of the intimate life she shares with her husband, might easily perform acts that would technically be sufficient to involve her in a criminal conspiracy with him, but which might be far removed from the arm's-length agreement typical of that crime. It is not a medieval mental quirk or an attitude "unnourished by sense" to believe that husbands and wives should not be subjected to such a risk, or that such a possibility should not be permitted to endanger the confidentiality of the marriage relationship. While it is easy enough to ridicule Hawkins' pronouncement in Pleas of the Crown from a metaphysical point of view, the concept of the "oneness" of a married couple may reflect an abiding belief that the communion between husband and wife is such that their actions are not always to be regarded by the criminal law as if there were no marriage.

. . . One need not waver in his belief in virile law enforcement to insist that there are other things in American life which are also of great importance, and to which even law enforcement must accommodate itself. One of these is the solidarity and the confidential relationship of marriage. The Court's opinion dogmatically asserts that the husband-wife conspiracy doctrine does not in fact protect this relationship, and that hence the doctrine "enthrone[s] an unreality into a rule of law." I am not easily persuaded that a rule accepted by so many people for so many centuries can be so lightly dismissed. But in any event, I submit that the power to depose belongs to Congress, not to this Court. I dissent.

NOTE

1. In Commonwealth v. Jones, 1 Pa. D. & C.2d 269, 274-275 (Leh. County Ct. 1954), a wife was convicted of drunken driving despite her

reliance upon the "presumption of compulsion" resulting from her husband's presence in the car. There was ample evidence that Mrs. Jones
had been intoxicated (as was her husband) while driving the automobile.
The trial judge denied the defendant's motion for a new trial even
though it held that she was entitled to take advantage of a rebuttable
presumption of compulsion:

> We recognize that many jurisdictions have abandoned the rule,
> some by legislation, others by statutory construction, but we are not
> impressed by the reasons given. . . . Granting that the original ac-
> tual reasons for the rule are no longer valid, the rule would not have
> survived so long had it not appealed to some new reason, which we
> are convinced is human experience of the wife's tendency to follow
> her husband's bidding.
>
> The rule is not founded on . . . public policy to promote domes-
> tic [tranquility]. . . . The rule is based upon human experience and
> therefore its continuing validity is not affected by any change in a
> wife's property or personal rights.
>
> While . . . instances could possibly be found where a wife may
> dominate her husband . . . , we have not yet reached the point
> where we decry the nobility, dignity or grace of a wife's deference to
> her husband's desires. Chivalry alone would call for this explana-
> tion of a married woman's participation in her husband's crime.
>
> The rule of a rebuttable presumption is flexible enough to accom-
> modate itself to woman's rising independence and to a realistic in-
> quiry whether or not coercion actually exists in any particular case
> and in a more enlightened age. . . .
>
> We have found no reason to exclude the crime of drunken driving
> from the operation of the rule, although there is a strong public pol-
> icy that would dictate its inapplicability to that situation.

Perkins reports that the presumption is still the orthodox view, but
"the trend against it is so obvious and so persistent as to forecast its eventual disappearance." Perkins, Criminal Law 801 (1957).

2. The existence of a family relationship may be important in determining the criminality of particular conduct. For example, many statutes provide that subsequent marriage to the victim precludes conviction
of such diverse crimes as seduction or contributing to the delinquency of a
minor. Subsequent marriage is generally not a defense to statutory rape.
See Foster & Freed, Offenses Against the Family, 32 U. Mo. K.C.L. Rev.
33, 46 (1964). "Although in many such cases where there has been a marriage, the prosecution is quashed or if the defendant has been convicted,
he is given a suspended sentence or placed on probation, there are numerous cases where the strict letter of the law has been followed and marriage
did not relieve the man from imprisonment." Id. at 46-47.

As we have seen (page 299 supra), the common law rule was that a
husband could "chastise" his wife. The husband no longer has this freedom in any jurisdiction; perhaps more important, the law has apparently
been modified judicially, even in the absence of terminological changes in

the substantive criminal statutes.   In The Queen v. Jackson, [1891] 1 Q.B. 671, 678-679, a husband's conviction for assaulting his wife was affirmed.   Lord Halsbury commented:

> I confess that some of the propositions which have been referred to . . . are such as I should be reluctant to suppose ever to have been the law of England. . . .   [S]uch quaint and absurd dicta as are to be found in the books as to the right of a husband over his wife in respect of personal chastisement are not, I think, now capable of being cited as authorities in a court of justice in this or in any civilized country. . . .

Compare the doctrines as to rape.   Coercion of a wife to submit to sexual intercourse is not rape under existing law.   See Mendes da Costa, Criminal Law, in A Century of Family Law 165, 181 (Graveson & Crane eds. 1957); Annot., 84 A.L.R.2d 1017 (1962).   The most common explanation is Hale's: "by their mutual matrimonial consent and contract the wife hath given up herself in this kind unto her husband, which she cannot retract."   1 Hale, Pleas of the Crown 628 (1800).   But a husband can be convicted as an accomplice in his wife's rape.   See Perkins, Criminal Law 564 (1957).   The Model Penal Code (Proposed Official Draft, 1962) codified these common law rules.   See §§213.1, 213.6(2).   The nonculpability of husband-wife conduct applies "to persons living as man and wife, regardless of the legal status of their relationship," unless the spouses are "living apart under a decree of judicial separation."   Ibid. See generally Note, The Effect of Marriage on the Rules of the Criminal Law, 61 Colum. L. Rev. 73 (1961).

The criminal process is not the only way of dealing with such delicate intrafamily disputes.   See the discussion of family courts in Chapter 9. As of 1962, the New York Family Court "has exclusive original jurisdiction . . . over any proceeding concerning acts which would constitute disorderly conduct or an assault between spouses or between parent and child or between members of the same family or household."   N.Y. Family Ct. Act §812.   Intrafamily crimes "are to be treated as civil proceedings with the aims of help and rehabilitation rather than punishment."   Oughterson, Family Court Jurisdiction, 12 Buffalo L. Rev. 467, 491 (1963).   The Family Court may transfer the case to the appropriate criminal court (N.Y. Family Ct. Act §814) or, after the offense is proved, may suspend judgment, place the respondent on probation, or make an "order of protection."   Id. at §841.

Parents have not been considered immune from criminal sanctions for mistreatment of their children; prosecutions have not been uncommon where "unreasonable" disciplinary methods have resulted in the child's death or serious injury.   In recent years, however, the focus has been on nonpunitive corrective methods.   See Am. Humane Assn., Protecting the Battered Child (1962); An Act for the Mandatory Reporting by Physicians and Institutions of Certain Physical Abuse of Children, in U.S. Children's Bureau, The Abused Child 3 (1963).   See the discussion of parental neglect, pages 405-417 infra.

3. At common law, neither the husband nor the wife could be guilty of larceny of the other's property. See Mendes da Costa, Criminal Law, in A Century of Family Law 165, 184 (Graveson & Crane eds. 1957). The Married Women's Acts were interpreted to authorize the wife to bring a civil suit against her husband in order to protect her separate property. See 3 Vernier §180. If a jurisdiction's larceny prohibition were phrased in general terms ("Every person who . . .") and had not been modified after passage of the jurisdiction's Married Women's Act, could the husband be prosecuted for theft of his wife's property? Compare People v. Morton, 308 N.Y. 96, 123 N.E.2d 790 (1954) (husband's conviction affirmed), with State v. Arnold, 182 Minn. 313, 235 N.W. 373 (1931), 30 Mich. L. Rev. 622 (1932) (wife's conviction reversed).

Model Penal Code §206.13 (Tent. Draft No. 4, 1955) read:

(1) . . . Where the property involved is that of the actor's spouse, no prosecution for theft may be maintained unless:
   (a) the parties had ceased living together as man and wife prior to the alleged theft; or
   (b) the alleged theft was committed when the actor was leaving or deserting or about to leave or desert his spouse; or
   (c) the actor entered into the marriage within 6 months prior to the alleged theft with the purpose of committing theft; or
   (d) the property involved exceeded $500 in value exclusive of household belongings.

(2) . . . [No prosecution for theft may be maintained against any member of the household where the property involved consists of household belongings.] . . .

(4) . . . No prosecution for theft may be maintained against a spouse or member of the household . . . unless the victim or someone acting on his behalf complains to public authority within six months after learning of the offense and the probable identity of the offender.

(5) . . . Member of the household means a relative who regularly lives in the household of the victim. Household belongings means furniture, personal effects, vehicles, money or equivalent in amounts customarily used for household purposes, and other property usually found in and about the common dwelling and accessible to its occupants. . . [59]

4. In Hawkins v. United States, 358 U.S. 74 (1958), the Supreme Court held that the federal courts must continue to recognize the common law rule of evidence permitting a criminal defendant to exclude the adverse testimony of his or her spouse. See 8 Wigmore, Evidence §§2227-2245

---

[59] Brackets in original. The Proposed Official Draft (1962) substituted for this "much broader and more complicated provision" (id. at 167) the following: "It is no defense that theft was from the actor's spouse, except that misappropriation of household and personal effects, or other property normally accessible to both spouses, is theft only if it occurs after the parties have ceased living together." §223.1(4).

(McNaughton rev. ed. 1961). Most of the commentators have criticized the common law rule. See, e.g., McCormick, Evidence 145 (1954):

> [F]amily harmony is nearly always past saving when the spouse is willing to aid the prosecution. The privilege, in truth, is an archaic survival of a mystical religious dogma [quoting Coke's statement of the family unity concept] and of a way of thinking about the marital relation, which are today outmoded. So generally is this recognized that one may expect the federal courts in the future to . . . [declare] that the privilege has no place in common law as interpreted by present-day courts . . . .

Only two years after Hawkins, in Wyatt v. United States, 362 U.S. 525 (1960), the majority relied upon an exception to the rule: the wife may testify when the husband's prosecution is for an offense committed against her. The majority held that the privilege ordinarily belongs to the wife-witness as well as to the husband-defendant. See 8 Wigmore, Evidence §2241 (McNaughton rev. ed. 1961). Nonetheless, the majority held that Mrs. Wyatt could be *compelled* to testify since her husband was charged with violating the Mann Act by transporting Mrs. Wyatt in interstate commerce for purposes of prostitution. "It is a question in each case, or in each category of cases, whether, in light of the reason which has led to a refusal to recognize the party's privilege, the witness should be held compellable." 362 U.S. at 529. The Mann Act rests on a legislative judgment that women are weak and need protection from unscrupulous men; therefore (id. at 530),

> it [is] not an allowable choice for a prostituted witness-wife "voluntarily" to decide to protect her husband by declining to testify against him. For if a defendant can induce a woman, against her "will," to enter a life of prostitution for his benefit — and the Act rests on the view that he can — by the same token it should be considered that he can, at least as easily, persuade one who has already fallen victim to his influence that she must also protect him. To make matters turn upon ad hoc inquiries into the actual state of mind of particular women, thereby encumbering Mann Act trials with a collateral issue of the greatest subtlety, is hardly an acceptable solution.

The three dissenters objected to this "facile" equation of the "legislative judgment involved in fashioning a criminal statute with the judgment involved in the Court's restriction of the husband-wife privilege." 362 U.S. at 531, 534. Pointing out that in the Mann Act Congress had chosen between the interest in prohibiting the transportation of prostitutes and the interest of women in voluntarily engaging in prostitution, the dissenters added (ibid.):

> [I]t is hardly surprising that Congress passed the Mann Act and made consent [of the female] entirely immaterial . . . The testimonial privilege, however, presents questions of quite a different order, since

there is a significant interest traditionally regarded as supporting the privilege, as we recognized in Hawkins — the preservation of the conjugal relationship. And where the wife refuses to testify, there is strong evidence that there is still a marital relationship to be protected.

In most jurisdictions the husband and wife are fully competent and may be compelled to testify for or against a party-spouse in civil actions. The statutes abolishing the disqualification of spouses almost uniformly contained provisions disabling spouses from testifying to confidential communications between them. There is a learned dispute as to the existence of a "husband-wife privilege" for confidential communications at common law. See 8 Wigmore, Evidence §§2332-2341 (McNaughton rev. ed. 1961); Hutchins & Slesinger, Some Observations on the Law of Evidence: Family Relations, 13 Minn. L. Rev. 675 (1929); McCormick, Evidence 168-172 (1954). To be privileged, the communication must be intended to be confidential and made during the marriage; there are several types of controversies in which the privilege cannot be claimed. See id. at 172-179.

CHAPTER 4

State Intervention in the Parent-Child Relationship

Regardless of the lengths to which a particular jurisdiction may pursue the policy of respecting "family privacy," circumstances often demand that the state exercise supervision of the affairs of individual family members. Both parents of a child may die or disappear; when other relatives cannot amicably arrange for the child's care (or even when they can, if the child has an estate of his own), judicial supervision of the child's personal and financial affairs is customary. If a parent becomes incompetent, the court which supervises the parent may incidentally make some disposition of the child. See In re Edwards' Estate, 197 Misc. 396, 98 N.Y.S.2d 369 (Surr. Ct. 1949). But even if no such traumatic event has disrupted the family, it has become customary for the juvenile court to interfere with family privacy to safeguard the welfare of children. This chapter explores a spectrum of the reasons for state interference with parents' control of their children and the methods by which that intervention is usually accomplished.

We begin with the common probate court jurisdiction to appoint guardians of the person for minors.[1] Guardianship jurisdiction — commonly traced to the ancient notion that the state, as parens patriae, is responsible for safeguarding all children — is an important aspect of state regulation of relationships which are similar to the relationship of parent and child. In addition, guardianship doctrines are themselves helpful in understanding judicial limitations on other forms of state intervention.

A. GUARDIANSHIP

COMERFORD v. CHERRY
100 So.2d 385 (Fla. 1958)

DREW, J. and PARKS, J. The County Judge of Palm Beach County, after hearing the testimony of the parties, appointed Joseph R. Cherry and his wife, Aleese S. Cherry, guardians of the person and property of William Chester Comerford, Jr., and James Russell Comerford, minor sons of William Chester Comerford, deceased. The guardians are the

---

[1] We will not examine the problems of estate guardianship. Guardians are generally subject to the rules which govern trustees. See generally Model Probate Code §§221-226 (A.B.A. Section of Real Property, Probate & Trust Law). reprinted in Problems in Probate Law 205-209 (Mich. Legal Studies 1946).

maternal grandparents of the children, whose mother predeceased their father. Upon appeal the circuit court affirmed the order of the county judge and this appeal from his judgment was duly taken by George C. Comerford, paternal uncle of the minors . . .

The will of William Comerford executed about one week before his death, provided:

> "*Third:* I do hereby nominate, constitute and appoint my brother, George E. Comerford, to be the legal guardian, and have the custody of my two minor children hereinabove named."

. . . By the will appellant was also appointed executor, and trustee of a trust for the boys during their minority. The executor qualified and was issued letters testamentary. . . .

On December 17, 1954, the grandparents petitioned the county judge for appointment as guardians of the persons and property of the children. They alleged their relationship to the boys, ages five and four years; . . . that the boys were residing with their paternal grandmother (mother of appellant) . . .

Appellant moved to dismiss the petition on the ground that he had been appointed guardian of the boys by the will of his deceased brother, as set forth supra. The motion was denied . . . [T]he uncle [then] petitioned the county judge that he be appointed guardian of the person and the property of the boys. . . .

It will be noted that neither the grandparents nor the uncle alleged that the other was not qualified to act by reason of unfitness or for any other reason which might affect the general welfare and proper upbringing of the children.

. . . The record shows that a prior will of decedent, executed about six weeks before his death and five weeks before the probated will, was received in evidence, by which decedent named appellee, Aleese S. Cherry, executrix of his estate and provided that she, or anyone she should name, should be guardian or guardians of the boys during their minority and trustee of the estate assets for their benefit.

The record of the evidence is not brought here on this appeal.

The pertinent part of the order of the county judge . . . is:

> ". . . having given due consideration to the appointment of one of the next of kin of said minors and likewise to any person designated as guardian in any will in which the said minors are beneficiaries, the court finds that . . . it is to the best interest and welfare of said children that Joseph R. Cherry and Aleese S. Cherry be guardians of the person and property of said minors . . ." [Court's quotation abbreviated by Eds.]

Appellant advances one point for determination which is that the "appointment" of a testamentary guardian of the person of a minor is binding upon the court until such guardian becomes disqualified. . . .

On the record it appears that this case presents to the Court for interpretation two provisions of the Florida guardianship law . . . :

"F.S. 744.14. Testamentary guardian. A surviving father or a surviving mother may by will name a guardian for the person of his or her minor child to serve during such child's minority or any part thereof. Such guardian shall be subject to the provisions of law in the same manner as other guardians."

"F.S. 744.35. Preference in appointment. In the appointment of a guardian the county judge shall give due consideration to the appointment of one of the next of kin of said incompetent who is a fit and proper person and qualified to act, and likewise to any person designated as guardian in any will in which the incompetent is a beneficiary. The county judge may in his discretion appoint any person who is qualified to act as guardian, whether related to the ward or not."

Appellant concedes that under the provisions of Sec. 744.14, supra, a testator has no power to appoint a guardian of the property of a minor. By its specific terms, which are free of any ambiguity, the statute confers on a surviving parent the right to name a guardian of the person only.

This leaves the question of whether, as a matter of law, the county judge, under the provisions of Sec. 744.35, supra, has the power in the exercise of his discretion to appoint some other qualified person to act as guardian of the person of the minor, notwithstanding the provisions of the will. . . .

The legislature defined certain pertinent words in the guardianship law:

(1) "A 'guardian' is one to whom the law has entrusted the custody and control of the person or of the property or of both, of an incompetent. . . ." (F.S. §744.03[1], F.S.A.)

(2) "An 'incompetent' is any person who, because of minority, senility, lunacy, insanity, imbecility, idiocy, drunkenness, excessive use of drugs or other physical or mental incapacity, is incapable of either managing his property or caring for himself, or both." (F.S. §744.03-[5], F.S.A.)

(3) "A 'testamentary guardian' is one appointed for the person of a minor child by the will of its parent." (F.S. §744.03[4], F.S.A.)

Considered in the light of these definitions the language of Sec. 744.35, quoted supra, . . . applies to both guardians of the person and guardians of the property. The legislature was careful to designate specifically a guardian as being a guardian of the person or guardian of the property when specific provisions of the act apply solely to one type or the other. . . .

Appellant argues that if a county judge must only give consideration to the "testamentary guardian" in making the appointment, along with the next of kin, then Sec. 744.14 becomes meaningless because, if so interpreted, a surviving parent in fact does not have the power to "appoint" a guardian of the person of a minor child by will. . . .

Appellees rely solely on . . . Sec. 744.35, and contend that when a surviving father or mother by will "names" a guardian for a minor child, this designation serves only as a "guide" to the county judge . . . . While it seems clear to us, as above stated, that the last cited section covers appointment of guardians of both property and person by the county judge, this would not preclude the creation of testamentary guardianships of the person under Sec. 744.14, supra. The entire Sec. 744.35 having specified applicability to appointments by the court as opposed to appointments by a testator, the quoted language would encompass only the situation where a testator, lacking power to appoint a guardian of property, might yet indicate his preference by "designating" a person to so serve; or, similarly, where a will names a guardian for an incompetent (other than a minor) to whom the testamentary guardianship provision does not apply. The fact that the statutory direction under consideration is limited to cases involving wills "in which the incompetent is a beneficiary" would further indicate that this particular clause relates to guardianships involving property interests, and not to testamentary guardianships of the person. . . .

Florida has by statute provided for testamentary guardians since 1828. The first statute gave the father power to appoint a guardian by deed or will, but limited the guardian to an exercise of power over the person only. . . . In 1921 the legislature . . . provided for the naming of both guardians of the person and the property in the will of the surviving parent. This statute remained in effect until 1945 when Sec. 744.14 was enacted. . . .

Testamentary guardians being unknown to the common law and creatures of statute only, there is a wide divergence of opinion in other jurisdictions as to the function and power of the probate courts when guardians are appointed by will. These opinions range all the way from the view that such appointment is without legal standing until the guardian is appointed by the court, to the view that a testamentary appointment ousts the jurisdiction of the Court. See 39 C.J.S. Guardian and Ward §13, p. 24.

Our legislature saw fit to define a "testamentary guardian" as one "appointed" by will. F.S. §744.03(4), F.S.A. . . . [W]e think that whatever may be required of a testamentary guardian in the way of qualification before the court, he derives his powers by appointment of the testator and not by appointment of the court.

The courts have always seen to it that the property of a testator was received by those whom the testator intended. The upbringing of minor children is a matter which concerns every thoughtful human being more vitally than the disposition of his worldly possessions when he has passed on. No person is in a position to know as well who should have the custody of children as the surviving parent. They are his flesh and blood. He has observed them throughout their lives. By daily contact he knows their temperaments and habits, and by observation he knows those who have evidenced the greatest interest in his children, and those whose moral and spiritual values are in his judgment conducive to the best interests of his children. A judge treads on sacred ground when he overrides the directions of the deceased with reference to the custody of his children.

Accordingly, the issue before the court, upon petition by a third party for appointment as guardian of the person, is not one for the exercise of its free discretion vel non as in the choice of a guardian in the first instance, but rather involves the propriety of an ouster. We are of the opinion, therefore, that the motion by appellant to dismiss a petition entirely lacking any allegations in this respect should have been granted . . . and the burden placed upon the moving parties to overturn the testamentary guardianship by proper allegation and proof. F.S. §§746.03, 746.04, F.S.A.

This Court has, of course, consistently held that the welfare of the child is the final test in determining who should ultimately be appointed guardian or given custody. . . . We conclude that this sound rule applies equally to testamentary guardians.

The judgment appealed from is affirmed in part and reversed in part, and the cause remanded for the entry of an order in conformity with the principles above stated.

NOTE

1. Many state statutes impose no other jurisdictional requirement than the minority of the person for whom a guardian is sought. But see Cal. Prob. Code §1405, authorizing appointment of a guardian of the person only "whenever necessary or convenient." In re Guardianship of Kentera, 41 Cal. 2d 639, 262 P.2d 317 (1953), involved a fourteen-year-old boy's petition to have his paternal grandmother appointed his guardian. The boy's parents were divorced, and he was living with his mother, stepfather, a stepbrother, and two half brothers; he claimed that his stepfather discriminated against him in settling disputes among the children. Despite a statutory provision giving minors over fourteen an absolute right to nominate their guardians (Cal. Prob. Code §1406), the California Supreme Court affirmed the trial court's refusal to appoint a guardian. Since the mother and stepfather were giving the boy adequate care, a guardian of the person was not "necessary or convenient." The majority commented: "The statutory provisions were not intended to upset the normal relationship of parent and child or to disrupt normal family discipline by allowing the 14-year-old minor to withdraw from the family circle at his whim." 41 Cal. 2d at 643, 262 P.2d at 319. The court distinguished cases involving appointment of guardians of estates: "Where a minor owns property, that fact is ordinarily sufficient to support a finding that the appointment of a guardian of the minor's estate is 'necessary or convenient.'" Ibid.

2. If a parent is alive and otherwise qualified, a number of statutes provide that he should be given preference when a guardian is to be appointed for a minor. See, e.g., Cal. Prob. Code §1407; Minn. Stat. Ann.

§525.54 (1947).[2] In re Guardianship of Smith, 42 Cal. 2d 91, 265 P.2d 888, 42 Calif. L. Rev. 514 (1954), involved a father's effort to obtain custody of his two illegitimate daughters, aged eight and six. The girls had lived with their mother until her death; an adult half sister, also illegitimate, had petitioned to be appointed their guardian. Three members of the California Supreme Court believed that the father was entitled to custody because "[o]n the death of the mother the natural father is entitled to the custody of an illegitimate child if he is a fit person." 42 Cal. 2d at 93, 265 P.2d at 890. The three dissenting Justices would have affirmed the trial court's decision granting the sister's petition. Justice Traynor wrote a separate concurring opinion (42 Cal. 2d at 94, 265 P.2d at 891):

> The objection to the rule that custody must be awarded to the parent unless he is unfit carries the harsh implication that the interests of the child are subordinated to those of the parent when the trial court has found that the best interests of the child would be served by giving his custody to another. The heart of the problem, however, is how the best interests of the child are to be served. Is the trial court more sensitive than the parent to what the child's best interests are, better qualified to determine how they are to be served? It would seem inherent in the very concept of a fit parent that such a parent would be at least as responsive as the trial court, and very probably more so, to the best interests of the child. The rule requiring that custody be awarded to such a parent in preference to a stranger does not operate to subordinate the interests of the child to those of the parent; it merely serves to define the area of the parent's responsibility for the welfare of the child. . . .
>
> One gains perspective by recalling that families are ordinarily allowed to function without outside interference though their wisdom in the upbringing of children may vary as widely as the physical heritage or economic advantages they give their children. . . . It is generally understood that the stability of established family units would be jeopardized by outside interference.
>
> It is only when the family is dissolved by death, divorce or separation that conflicting claims to custody are likely to arise. . . .
>
> Ordinarily in any of these circumstances the determination of what course will best serve the interests of the child will involve the consideration of numerous imponderables. All things being equal, it is clear that the parent should have custody. All things are ordinarily not equal, however. The outsider may be able to offer the child greater material advantages. . . . On the other hand, the importance of preserving the relationship between a natural parent and his child cannot be gainsaid. Even in a case where the foster parent treats the child as his own, the child may still suffer from the lack of a natural parent . . . .

---

[2] A number of statutes also contain a provision similar to the one construed in Comerford v. Cherry, requiring acceptance of the parent's testamentary nominee. See, e.g., Minn. Stat. Ann. §525.541 (1947).

Psychology is not an exact science. If expert testimony were introduced in cases such as this in all probability it would be in conflict. The ordinary judge as well as the ordinary parent lacks the omniscience accurately to evaluate all the conflicting considerations that may enter into a custody problem. . . .

Cases may arise in which the child's interests would be seriously prejudiced by awarding custody to his parent. In such cases, however, the parent's insistence on his right to custody despite the harm that would clearly result to his child will itself be evidence of his unfitness. [Citations omitted.]

. . . It bears emphasis . . . that the father of an illegitimate child comes before the court in at best a questionable light.

Although past indiscretions do not necessarily demonstrate present unfitness [citations omitted], such a father should be required to explain why he has not legitimated his child. . . . On the other hand, a desire to secure custody may be the outgrowth of a moral rehabilitation reflected in an effort to undo a past wrong by legitimating the child.

A father may legitimate his child . . . "by publicly acknowledging it as his own, receiving it as such, with the consent of his wife, if he is married, into his family, and otherwise treating it as if it were a legitimate child." (Civ. Code, §230.) . . . At the present time the father is married. . . . On retrial the father must establish that the children will be legitimated as a minimum prerequisite to establishing his fitness for appointment as guardian.

3. The Model Probate Code §§219-220 (A.B.A. Section of Real Property, Probate & Trust Law), reprinted in Problems in Probate Law 204-205 (Mich. Legal Studies 1946), states the functions of a personal guardian as follows:

It is the duty of the guardian of the person to care for and maintain the ward and, if he is a minor, to see that he is properly trained and educated and that he has the opportunity to learn a trade, occupation or profession. . . .

The guardian of the person shall be entitled to the custody of the ward . . .

Nonetheless, the probate court's appointment of a personal guardian does not necessarily determine who should have physical custody of the ward. In the Comerford case, for example, Mr. and Mrs. Cherry might have obtained physical possession of the children. If they had refused to turn the children over to Mr. Comerford, his right to physical custody could have been tested, in most states, by a habeas corpus petition; the outcome would have turned on "the best interests" of the children, despite the fact that Mr. Comerford had been appointed their guardian. Yet most of the personal guardianship cases implicitly involve consideration of the ward's future physical custody. As a result, judges must face social and psychological issues similar to those presented when divorcing or divorced parents dispute custody of their children.

Appellate opinions often contain discussions of the powers of personal "guardians" when there has been no appointment by a probate court. These discussions may pertain to the custodian of a child — because of divorce, or as the result of a proceeding in a juvenile court freeing a child from his parent's control, etc. The term "guardian" has been used with abandon in decisions involving a wide range of legal issues.

In re GUARDIANSHIP OF WOODWARD
102 N.Y.S.2d 490 (Surr. Ct. 1951)

WITMER, Surr. Philip J. Sweeney, the stepfather, and Mr. and Mrs. Courtney Cooke, the maternal grandparents of Diane Reid Woodward, the infant involved in this proceeding, have joined in a petition asking for the appointment of Mr. Sweeney as guardian of the person of said infant. The paternal grandparents, Donald Woodward and Florence S. Woodward, his first wife, oppose the application and ask for the appointment of their daughter, Barbara Woodward, the paternal aunt of the infant. The need for a general guardian of the person grows out of the death in December 1944 of the infant's father, Reid T. Woodward, while serving in the armed forces of the United States, and the death of her mother, Dona Cooke Woodward Sweeney, in May 1950. Diane, the infant herein, was born June 1, 1942, and is now about $8\frac{1}{2}$ years old.

Various factors are urged by each side as reasons why the nominee of the other should not be appointed guardian of the person of Diane. The question is not one of law, but is one of fact addressed to the Court's sound discretion concerning the welfare of the child. . . .

Diane's father was in the service of his country during most of the time from her birth until his death, and as a consequence Diane spent most of the time in this period at the home of her maternal grandparents in New Haven, Connecticut, her mother also being there generally . . . Diane's maternal aunt, Beverly Cooke, was living in the home of the maternal grandparents during this period and became well acquainted with Diane. In May 1946, when Diane was nearly four years old, her mother, Dona, married the petitioner, Philip J. Sweeney of Livonia, N.Y., and lived with him thereafter in Livonia until her death four years later. Diane lived with her mother and stepfather during this same period. On July 1, 1947 a daughter, Phyllis, was born to Diane's mother and Mr. Sweeney. Since the death of Diane's mother last May, Diane and Phyllis have continued to live in the home of petitioner, Philip J. Sweeney, in Livonia; and during most of this time Beverly Cooke, maternal aunt, has lived in the household, employed by Mr. Sweeney, caring for the children and doing the necessary housework.

Reid T. Woodward, Diane's father, was a member of the Presbyterian Church, as are the paternal grandmother, Florence S. Woodward, and paternal aunt, Barbara Woodward. Dona Cooke Woodward Sweeney, Diane's mother, was a Methodist, [as] are the maternal grandparents, Mr.

and Mrs. Courtney Cooke, and the maternal aunt, Beverly Cooke. Diane's paternal grandfather, Donald Woodward, is divorced from the paternal grandmother, has re-married, and is taking steps to become a member of the Roman Catholic Church. Diane's stepfather, Philip J. Sweeney, is a Roman Catholic, and so is her half sister, Phyllis Sweeney. Mr. Sweeney attends his church in Livonia, and Diane is sent . . . to the Methodist Church in Livonia . . . [A]ll agree that in any event Diane shall be reared as a Methodist or Presbyterian, and there is no suggestion that she be reared as a Roman Catholic. Hence the question of religion enters into the matter only as the difference of church attendance, forms of worship and particular church decrees and doctrines of Mr. Sweeney and Phyllis on one hand and Diane on the other may affect Diane's attitude toward religion and her relations with her stepfather and half sister.

A particularly important factor in this case is that of Diane's property. There is held in guardianship and in trust for her about a half million dollars, with income accumulating thereon in excess of $13,000 annually. Provided she outlive her paternal grandfather and paternal uncle, she will receive three-fourths of a million dollars more. These assets all originated from the Woodward side of the family. In addition, if Diane is kept in close relationship with her father's family, she presumably will inherit or receive through inter vivos gifts substantial additional property therefrom. Her paternal grandfather is a very wealthy man. Likewise, her paternal grandmother, Florence S. Woodward, is a wealthy woman in her own right, and has only one son (married with children) and one daughter (Barbara, unmarried) besides the granddaughter, Diane. Similarly, her paternal aunt, Barbara, has substantial assets in her own right, with an annual income therefrom of between $15,000 and $20,000.

Petitioner, Philip J. Sweeney, has assets in excess of $100,000 with an annual earned income of approximately $10,000. . . . Both Mr. Sweeney and Barbara Woodward have assured the Court that they have no interest in Diane's property nor the income therefrom, and that either, if granted the guardianship, will rear Diane without any encroachment upon the corpus of or income from her property, except that Mr. Sweeney limited his offer in this respect to the normal needs of Diane, not to include extra expenses which her financial status might warrant being made in her behalf.

. . . After [Dona's] death Mr. Sweeney instituted a proceeding to adopt Diane. The proceeding was dismissed. Mr. Sweeney assures the Court that he has given up all thoughts of adopting Diane, and does not seek the guardianship in order to facilitate such adoption. It appears that the antipathies evidenced between the parties since said proceeding grew out of that application.

Petitioners . . . point out that Phyllis is Diane's closest relative, and urge that Dona would not like to have her two daughters separated, that it is best for Diane and Phyllis to be reared together, that it is their right . . . .

Mr. Sweeney recognizes that he has no duty beyond what he chooses to assume as a moral obligation toward Diane, and no right to the guardianship except through the wishes of the maternal grandparents and the Court's consideration of the welfare of Diane. Barbara Woodward, paternal aunt, and Beverly Cooke, maternal aunt, stand in an equal position with respect to Diane. Beverly is twenty-six years old, unmarried, and states that she has no forseeable expectations of marriage. . . . Barbara, thirty years old, is likewise unmarried and without present expectations of marriage. . . . Barbara is a trained artist (drawing and painting), and has travelled widely. She has had less experience than Beverly in caring for young children, and is much less acquainted with Diane; but the latter fact is in no way the fault of Barbara and may not weigh against her herein.

The Court, with counsel, has visited the respective homes of the proposed guardians . . . Either home is completely adequate for Diane.

. . . [W]here a decision rests upon judicial discretion, to some extent the parties are at the mercy of the court's background and experience. And that is something very difficult for the parties, through their counsel, to meet. They cannot cross-examine the Court on his life history and personal biases and prejudices, many, if not most, of which he himself may not realize he possesses. Nonetheless, in some measure in matters of this sort the background and experience of the Court affect his decisions . . . .

The Court has had considerable family experience and has observed a great comradeship between the children of a family. . . . The Court knows of families having two daughters only, with from two to eight years' difference in the daughters' ages, and they get along admirably. Indeed, difference of age is virtually inherent in the makeup of a family. By the time Diane's greater age and property may combine possibly to give rise to friction between her and Phyllis, Diane will be ready for separate training. From observing Diane and Phyllis the Court is satisfied that the matter of age difference has no important bearing on its decision herein at this time. The same may be said for the difference in the girls' temperaments. . . .

The matter of religion is more difficult. We all deplore the evils of religious differences. But we have to deal with the fact that religious differences exist amongst us. The situation cannot be improved by building up the barriers. People can respect each other's beliefs and live together while retaining their respective views. . . . Tolerance is a virtue to be cultivated. . . . There are many instances of differences of religion within families, which still live together in complete harmony. The difference of religion does not seem sufficient justification for separating Diane and Phyllis.

The remaining principal difference is that of property and the results flowing therefrom. It is an important difference. Diane is a Woodward. It is no fault of hers that her father died in the service of his country; nor was it the fault of her father as a result of which his daughter should be denied her rightful Woodward heritage (association and culture, as well as property). There are decided benefits which Diane may receive from close association with her paternal relatives, which otherwise she may miss. She must be protected in this respect.

On the other hand, Diane is equally a member of the Cooke family. They have equal claim to her, and Diane is entitled to the benefits which she may have from continued association with her half sister and maternal aunt and grandparents. Her mother did not make a will naming Philip J. Sweeney as guardian of the person of Diane; but it is not unreasonable to suppose that had she considered the matter she would have done so and that she would want him to act in such capacity while the two girls are young, thus keeping them together.

. . . Moreover, the Court, as a man and father, cannot repress his view that the presence of a father in the home is important to young children. Reid T. Woodward cannot be replaced. But his widow's choice of a successor mate, Mr. Sweeney, with whom Diane has lived since she was four years old and upon whom she looks as a second father, is an honorable man and earnestly requests the privilege and obligation of fathering Diane along with his daughter Phyllis. I know of no reason why for the most part he should not be granted such privilege and duty for a limited period of years, during which Diane will enjoy the advantages of having a "father" . . . .

Try as they may, adults cannot take the place of a brother or a sister in childhood play. By placing Diane principally in Mr. Sweeney's custody Diane will have the benefit of close association with her sister Phyllis during her early years when she normally would be at home. This will result in as little change for Diane as is possible in view of the death of her mother. . . . Through her thirteenth year the property differences between Diane and Phyllis will not be of great significance, and if Diane does have some unusual benefits during this period, it will not be amiss for her to learn how to share them with Phyllis. Diane in turn will gain from this relationship with Phyllis as much as will Phyllis. Thereafter, Diane in her station would be expected to go to private schools, and she may then be placed in more exclusive custody with Barbara, who is particularly well fitted to supervise her from that time forward. Diane will then be old enough to appreciate her earlier life with Phyllis . . .

Subject to review upon the application of any party hereto in the event that Mr. Sweeney re-marry or Beverly Cooke leave his household, or either guardian should die, and in any event subject to review when Diane attains fourteen years of age, a decree may be presented appointing both Philip J. Sweeney and Barbara Woodward as co-guardians of the person of Diane Reid Woodward. [Citations omitted.] Diane shall be in the exclusive custody of Philip J. Sweeney as such guardian from Labor Day of each year until her school work ends the following June. This shall also apply to the balance of the present school year. One week-end per month on Friday after school Barbara may take Diane to her home in Le Roy and return her on the following Sunday afternoon before eight o'clock P.M. From the time school is "out" in June of each year until Labor Day, Diane shall be in the exclusive custody of Barbara Woodward as such co-guardian. . . .

The guardian in whose custody Diane may be during a particular period shall supply her wants and needs at such guardian's own expense; but if unusual but proper purchases are to be made for Diane, her own funds may be used therefor upon the consent of both guardians of her person.

. . . If events prove that this plan is impracticable, upon the application of any party hereto the Court may then make other disposition of the matter. [Citation omitted.]

Submit decree accordingly.

NOTE

Cal. Prob. Code §1400 provides: "In the management and disposition of the person or property committed to him, a guardian may be regulated and controlled by the court." Most guardianship statutes contain some such provision. See Weissman, Guardianship, A Way of Fulfilling Public Responsibility for Children 101 (U.S. Children's Bureau Pub. No. 330, 1949). Unless the parties complain, how could the probate judge in Woodward supervise his orders? After studying the practice in two local jurisdictions in each of six states, Weissman concluded:

Although the law provides a framework for supervising the guardian of person, regular procedures have not been devised for this purpose at any of the courts visited. None of the courts of study maintains supervisory contact with guardians of person or in any way requires them to account for their stewardship. To all practical intents and purposes the guardian of person is left to his own devices.

Complaints serve as the court's chief source of information concerning the functioning of the guardian of person. But these are usually made at a point when the inadequacy of the guardian has become so patently serious as to necessitate formal petition for his removal. . . .

Where the complaints are made informally, most courts refer them to the attorney to evaluate and to decide on the need to initiate formal court action. . . .[3]

Compare the frequency with which the propriety of the estate guardian's conduct is litigated. Since the estate guardian must make regular financial reports to the court, the issues are, by comparison at least, difficult to avoid. Moreover, the estate guardian's fee must be approved by the court, and this responsibility may dispose the judge to supervise more carefully.

The guardianship statutes of West Germany make use of an institution known as the Jugendamt to aid in the supervision of personal guardians. Jugendamter (representatives of the Jugendamt) act as local counsel for orphans. They propose suitable guardians to the court, act as an advisory agency for guardians, and are charged with informing the court if the

[3] Weissman, Guardianship, A Way of Fulfilling Public Responsibility for Children 102 (U.S. Children's Bureau Pub. No. 330, 1949).

guardian is not adequately caring for a ward. The Jugendamt, which is automatically appointed guardian of all illegitimate children, may be appointed the guardian of other children as well. In addition to these safeguards, all guardians must obtain the court's approval of important decisions affecting their wards, e.g., consenting to or seeking to invalidate the ward's adoption, permitting the ward to marry, determining the ward's religious education, or changing his name. See generally Beitzke, Familienrecht 132 (10th ed. 1962); 4 Enneccerus, Kipp & Wolff, Lehrbuch des Burgerlichen Rechts (Familienrecht) 548-554 (1931).

Weissman, supra, at 179, suggests that American probate courts use social service personnel to supervise the activities of personal guardians.

B. THE LIMITS OF PARENTAL PREROGATIVES

PEOPLE ex rel. SISSON v. SISSON
271 N.Y. 285, 2 N.E.2d 660 (1936)

[Mrs. Sisson sought a writ of habeas corpus to free her daughter Beverly from Mr. Sisson's custody. The writ alleged that Mr. Sisson, a member of the Megiddo sect, "aided and abetted by other Megiddo adherents, places so much emphasis on the study and practice of the Megiddo teachings that Beverly is kept from home to an unreasonable extent, alienated in some respects from her mother, thereby destroying the natural relationship which should exist between them and tending to make her peculiar and perhaps fanatical, rather than normal." Sisson v. Sisson, 156 Misc. 236, 237, 281 N.Y. Supp. 559, 560 (Sup. Ct. 1935). The trial court could find nothing immoral in Megiddo teachings, but characterized their beliefs as ultrareligious and strict. Pointing out that "all frivolity is disapproved" (156 Misc. at 238, 281 N.Y. Supp. at 560) and that "normal activity and the innocent pleasures of childhood are limited" (156 Misc. at 239, 281 N.Y. Supp. at 562), the trial court granted the petition despite the fact that Mr. and Mrs. Sisson had not separated. The Appellate Division modified the trial court's order to award the parents joint custody, but enjoined some of Mr. Sisson's methods of assuring that Beverly would accept Megiddo teachings. Sisson v. Sisson, 246 App. Div. 151, 285 N.Y. Supp. 41 (1936). Nonetheless, the Appellate Division had no praise for Mr. Sisson's behavior: "the course pursued here by the appellant . . . has been extreme and unreasonable . . . and such as the court may not approve, nor ignore. . . . It seems to the court that it would be difficult for the average man of sound mental balance, education and clear understanding of the nature and necessity of family unity, to dissent from this conclusion." 246 App. Div. at 155, 285 N.Y. Supp. at 44-45.]

PER CURIAM. A Special Term, by its order sustaining a writ of habeas corpus, deprived the father of a ten-year old daughter of his right to control the child jointly with the mother and awarded exclusive guardianship, custody and control to the mother. The Appellate Division modified by returning the child to the joint guardianship, custody and control of both parents with the limitations that the father should not take the child from the town in which she resides without the consent of the mother nor from her home for a longer period than two hours at a time and then only after personal notice to the mother of the purpose and the place of the proposed visit.

The family consists of the father, Howard Sisson, the mother, Blanche Sisson, and the daughter, Beverly. They live together at their home in Sherburne, N.Y. Except for the difficulty over the education to be given the child, the family life appears to be much above the average despite the illness which has afflicted the mother. The father, a graduate of Cornell University, has built up a prosperous produce business. The mother had suffered somewhat from arthritis before the marriage and afterward the condition became progressively worse. As the condition became acute the father spared no expense or trouble in attempting to effect a cure, sending her to the Mayo brothers in Rochester, Minn., and other like places. All to no avail. For the past six years the mother has been bedridden. The child, Beverly, is above the average, both physically and mentally.

Disagreement between the parents has arisen over the education of the child. In no way does it appear that the health or welfare of the child is in danger.

In proceedings for the custody of children the courts have reiterated that their sole point of view is the welfare of the child. The parents of this child are obviously interested only in her welfare. When they realize that for the good of the child it is necessary for them to repress to some extent the natural desire of each to have the child educated solely according to his or her point of view, the remaining sources of difficulty doubtless will disappear.

The court cannot regulate by its processes the internal affairs of the home. Dispute between parents when it does not involve anything immoral or harmful to the welfare of the child is beyond the reach of the law. The vast majority of matters concerning the upbringing of children must be left to the conscience, patience and self restraint of father and mother. No end of difficulties would arise should judges try to tell parents how to bring up their children. Only when moral, mental and physical conditions are so bad as seriously to affect the health or morals of children should the courts be called upon to act.

The writ of habeas corpus must be dismissed.

The order of the Appellate Division and that of the Special Term should be reversed and the writ of habeas corpus dismissed, without costs.

Matter of SEIFERTH
309 N.Y. 80, 127 N.E.2d 820 (1955)

VAN VOORHIS, J. This is a case involving a fourteen-year-old boy with cleft palate and harelip, whose father holds strong convictions with which the boy has become imbued against medicine and surgery. This proceeding has been instituted by the deputy commissioner of the Erie County Health Department on petition to the Children's Court to have Martin declared a neglected child, and to have his custody transferred from his parents to the Commissioner of Social Welfare of Erie County for the purpose of consenting to such medical, surgical and dental services as may be necessary to rectify his condition. The medical testimony is to the effect that such cases are almost always given surgical treatment at an earlier age, and the older the patient is the less favorable are likely to be the results according to experience. The surgery recommended by the plastic surgeon called for petitioner consists of three operations: (1) repair of the harelip by bringing the split together; (2) closing the cleft or split in the rear of the palate, the boy being already too late in life to have the front part mended by surgery; and (3) repairing the front part of the palate by dental appliances. The only risk of mortality is the negligible one due to the use of anesthesia. These operations would be spaced a few months apart and six months would be expected to complete the work, two years at the outside in case of difficulty. Petitioner's plastic surgeon declined to be precise about how detrimental it would be to the prognosis to defer this work for several years. He said: "I do not think it is emergent, that it has to be done this month or next month, but every year that goes is important to this child, yes." A year and a half has already elapsed since this testimony was taken in December, 1953.

Even after the operation, Martin will not be able to talk normally, at least not without going to a school for an extended period for concentrated speech therapy. There are certain phases of a child's life when the importance of these defects becomes of greater significance. The first is past, when children enter grade school, the next is the period of adolescence, particularly toward the close of adolescence when social interests arise in secondary school. Concerning this last, petitioner's plastic surgeon stated: "That is an extremely important period of time. That child is approaching that age where it is very important that correction, that it is very significant that correction made at this time could probably put him in a great deal better position to enter that period of life than would otherwise. Another thing which is difficult is that we have very excellent speech facilities at the Buffalo Public Schools through grade level. At secondary school level and in higher age groups speech training facilities are less satisfactory, so that it is important that it be done at this age. However, the most important thing of all is this gradually progressive with time. The earlier done, the better results. Normally the lip is repaired in early infancy, one to three years of age. Speech training would begin at school or earlier. Every year lost has been that much more lost to the boy. Each year lost continues to be lost. The time to repair is not too early." He testified that in twenty years of plastic surgery he had never encountered a child with this boy's defects who had not been operated upon at his age. Nevertheless, he testified that such an operation can be performed "from the time the child is born until he dies." In this doctor's view, the consideration bulked larger than the quality of postoperative results, that the boy's increasing social contacts required that he be made to look and to speak normally as he approached adolescence.

Everyone testified that the boy is likeable, he has a newspaper route, and his marks in school were all over 90 during the last year. However, his father did testify that recently the boy had withdrawn a little more from his fellows, although he said that "As soon as anyone contacts Martin, he is so likeable nobody is tempted to ridicule him. . . . Through his pleasantness he overcomes it."

The father testified that "If the child decides on an operation, I shall not be opposed," and that "I want to say in a few years the child should decide for himself . . . whether to have the operation or not." The father believes in mental healing by letting "the forces of the universe work on the body," although he denied that this is an established religion of any kind stating that it is purely his own philosophy and that "it is not classified as religion." There is no doubt, however, that the father is strong minded about this, and has inculcated a distrust and dread of surgery in the boy since childhood.

The Erie County Children's Court Judge caused the various surgical procedures to be explained to Martin by competent and qualified practitioners in the field of plastic surgery and orthodontia. Photographs of other children who had undergone similar remedial surgery were exhibited to him showing their condition both before and after treatment. He was also taken to the speech correction school where he heard the reproduction of his own voice and speech, as well as records depicting various stages of progress of other children. He met other children of his own age, talked to them and attended class in speech correction. Both the boy and the father were given opportunity to ask questions, which they did freely not only of the professional staff but of the different children.

On February 11, 1954, Martin, his father and attorney met after these demonstrations in Judge Wylegala's chambers. Judge Wylegala wrote in his opinion that Martin "was very much pleased with what was shown him, but had come to the conclusion that he should try for some time longer to close the cleft palate and the split lip himself through 'natural forces.' " After stating that an order for surgery would have been granted without hesitation if this proceeding had been instituted before this child acquired convictions of his own, Judge Wylegala summed up his conclusions as follows: "After duly deliberating upon the psychological effect of surgery upon this mature, intelligent boy, schooled as he has been for all of his young years in the existence of 'forces of nature' and his fear of surgery upon the human body, I have come to the conclusion that no order should be made at this time compelling the child to submit to surgery. His condition is not emergent and there is no serious threat to his health or life. He has time until he becomes 21 years of age to apply for financial assistance under County and State aid to physically handicapped children to have the corrections made. This has also been explained to him after he made known his decision to me." The petition accordingly was dismissed.

The Appellate Division, Fourth Department, reversed by a divided court, and granted the petition requiring Martin Seiferth to submit to surgery.

As everyone agrees, there are important considerations both ways. The Children's Court has power in drastic situations to direct the operation over the objection of parents (Matter of Vasko, 238 App. Div. 128, 129). Nevertheless, there is no present emergency, time is less of the essence than it was a few years ago insofar as concerns the physical prognosis, and we are impressed by the circumstance that in order to benefit from the operation upon the cleft palate, it will almost certainly be necessary to enlist Martin's co-operation in developing normal speech patterns through a lengthy course in concentrated speech therapy. It will be almost impossible to secure his co-operation if he continues to believe, as he does now, that it will be necessary "to remedy the surgeon's distortion first and then go back to the primary task of healing the body." This is an aspect of the problem with which petitioner's plastic surgeon did not especially concern himself, for he did not attempt to view the case from the psychological viewpoint of this misguided youth. Upon the other hand, the Children's Court Judge, who saw and heard the witnesses, and arranged the conferences for the boy and his father which have been mentioned, appears to have been keenly aware of this aspect of the situation, and to have concluded that less would be lost by permitting the lapse of several more years, when the boy may make his own decision to submit to plastic surgery, than might be sacrificed if he were compelled to undergo it now against his sincere and frightened antagonism. One cannot be certain of being right under these circumstances, but this appears to be a situation where the discretion of the trier of the facts should be preferred to that of the Appellate Division (Harrington v. Harrington, 290 N.Y. 126).

The order of the Appellate Division should be reversed and that of the Children's Court reinstated dismissing the petition, without prejudice to renew the application if circumstances warrant.

FULD, J. (dissenting). Every child has a right, so far as is possible, to lead a normal life and, if his parents, through viciousness or ignorance, act in such a way as to endanger that right, the courts should, as the legislature has provided, act on his behalf. Such is the case before us.

The boy Martin, twelve years old when this proceeding was begun, fourteen now, has been neglected in the most egregious way. He is afflicted with a massive harelip and cleft palate which not only grievously detract from his appearance but seriously impede his chances for a useful and productive life. Although medical opinion is agreed that the condition can be remedied by surgery, that it should be performed as soon as possible and that the risk involved is negligible, the father has refused to consent to the essential operation. His reason — which is, as the Appellate Division found, entirely unsubstantial — was that he relies on "forces in the universe" which will enable the child to cure himself of his own accord. He might consent to the operation, he said, if the boy "in a few years" should favor one.

It is quite true that the child's physical life is not at peril — as would be the situation if he had an infected appendix or a growth on the brain — but it may not be questioned, to quote from the opinion below, "What is in danger is his chance for a normal, useful life." Judge Van Voorhis does not, I am sure, take issue with that, but he feels that the boy will benefit, to a greater extent, from the operation if he enters the hospital with a mind favorably disposed to surgery. Therefore he counsels delay, on the *chance* — and that is all it is — on the *chance* that at some future time the boy may make his own decision to submit to plastic surgery.

It would, of course, be preferable if the boy were to accede to the operation, and I am willing to assume that, if he acquiesces, he will the more easily and quickly react to the postoperative speech therapy. However, there is no assurance that he will, either next year, in five years or six, give his consent. Quite obviously, he is greatly influenced by his father, quite plainly a victim of the latter's unfortunate delusions. And, beyond that, it must be borne in mind that there is little if any risk involved in the surgery and that, as time goes on, the operation becomes more difficult.

Be that as it may, though, it is the court which has a duty to perform (Children's Court Act, §24), and it should not seek to avoid that duty by foisting upon the boy the ultimate decision to be made. Neither by statute nor decision is the child's consent necessary or material, and we should not permit his refusal to agree, his failure to co-operate, to ruin his life and any chance for a normal, happy existence; normalcy and happiness, difficult of attainment under the most propitious conditions, will unquestionably be impossible if the disfigurement is not corrected.

Moreover, it is the fact, and a vital one, that this is a proceeding brought to determine whether the parents are neglecting the child by refusing and failing to provide him with necessary surgical, medical and dental service (Children's Court Act, §2, subd. 4, cl. e).[4] Whether the child condones the neglect, whether he is willing to let his parents do as they choose, surely cannot be operative on the question as to whether or not they are guilty of neglect. They are not interested or concerned with whether he does or does not want the essential operation. They have arbitrarily taken the position that there is to be no surgery. What these parents are doing, by their failure to provide for an operation, however well-intentioned, is far worse than beating the child or denying him food or clothing. To the boy, and his future, it makes no difference that it may be ignorance rather than viciousness that will perpetuate his unfortunate condition. If parents are actually mistreating or neglecting a child, the circumstance that he may not mind it cannot alter the fact that they are guilty of neglect and it cannot render their conduct permissible.

The welfare and interests of a child are at stake. A court should not place upon his shoulders one of the most momentous and far-reaching decisions of his life. The court should make the decision, as the statute contemplates, and leave to the good sense and sound judgment of the public authorities the job of preparing the boy for the operation and of getting him as adjusted to it as possible. We should not put off decision

---

[4] A "Neglected child," the Children's Court Act (§2, subd. 4) recites, "means a child . . . (e) whose parent, guardian or custodian neglects or refuses, when able to do so, to provide necessary medical, surgical, institutional or hospital care for such child."

in the hope and on the chance that the child may change his mind and submit at some future time to the operation.

The order of the Appellate Division should be affirmed.

[Desmond and Burke, JJ., concur in this dissent.]

NOTE

1. How might the majority have dealt with the language of the Children's Court Act (see footnote 4) which so impressed the dissenters?

2. In re Hudson, 13 Wash. 2d 673, 677, 126 P.2d 765, 768 (1942), involved an eleven-year-old girl afflicted with abnormal growth of her left arm. The arm was a useless, giant appendage; it was also a menace to her health and made her a social recluse. Although the examining physicians indicated that there was a "fair degree of risk of life involved in the operation," they uniformly recommended that the arm be amputated. The girl's parents refused to consent to the surgery; the mother was afraid that the operation was too dangerous. The Supreme Court of Washington held that the Juvenile Court had no statutory authority to order the operation since the parents were not "neglecting" the child.

3. Much of the litigation concerning medical care has been occasioned by members of the Jehovah's Witnesses religion — who, because of their strict interpretation of the Bible, object to blood transfusions for their children even if the child's life is threatened. When there has been time to appeal one of these cases (on occasion the courts have disposed of the issue even if it was "moot"), the courts have uniformly held that an order compelling a blood transfusion when the child's life is endangered is a proper exercise of the state's power as parens patriae and is not an invasion of the child's or the parents' freedom of religion. See Wallace v. Labrenz, 411 Ill. 618, 104 N.E.2d 769 (1952); State v. Perricone, 37 N.J. 462, 181 A.2d 751, cert. denied, 371 U.S. 890 (1962); In re Clark, 185 N.E.2d 128 (Ohio C.P. 1962).

See also Ore. Rev. Stat. §419.500 (Supp. 1963): "The practice of a parent who chooses for himself or his child treatment by prayer or spiritual means alone shall not be construed as a failure to provide physical care within the meaning of [the Juvenile Court Act]." How would Wallace v. Labrenz have been decided if Illinois had had such a statute? If the New York Children's Court Act had contained such a provision, would it have compelled the majority's decision in Seiferth?

In one of the recent blood transfusion cases, the Juvenile Court Act provided for a waiting period between the filing of a neglect petition and the hearing. The parents refused to waive the waiting period and the child died before the hearing could be held. See Larson, Child Neglect in the Exercise of Religious Freedom, 32 Chi.-Kent L. Rev. 283, 287 (1954). If you had been the parents' lawyer and a representative of the welfare department had asked you to waive the waiting period, what would you have done?

4. Some child welfare experts believe that the religious objectors are

really anxious to have medical care for their children — especially when their lives are at stake — so long as religious principles need not be compromised. Cf. Judge Wright's comments in Application of President and Directors of Georgetown College, 331 F.2d 1000, 1006-1007, 1009 (D.C. Cir.), cert. denied, 377 U.S. 978 (1964) (in chambers):

> I thereupon proceeded with counsel to the hospital, where I spoke to Mr. Jones, the husband of the patient. He advised me that, on religious grounds, he would not approve a blood transfusion for his wife. He said, however, that if the court ordered the transfusion, the responsibility was not his. I advised Mr. Jones to obtain counsel immediately. He thereupon went to the telephone and returned in 10 or 15 minutes to advise that he had taken the matter up with his church and that he had decided that he did not want counsel. . . .
>
> . . . If the law undertook the responsibility of authorizing the transfusion without her consent, no problem would be raised with respect to her religious practice. Thus, the effect of the order was to preserve for Mrs. Jones the life she wanted without sacrifice of her religious beliefs.[5]

Can a judge determine whether the parents "really" favor the blood transfusion? Cf. United States v. Ballard, 322 U.S. 78 (1944) (truth or falsity of defendant's religious belief not an issue which government can examine and determine in criminal mail fraud prosecution).

5. See also Raleigh Fitkin-Paul Morgan Memorial Hospital v. Anderson, 42 N.J. 421, 201 A.2d 537, cert. denied, 377 U.S. 985 (1964), in which the court relied on cases like Wallace v. Labrenz to approve an order authorizing a blood transfusion for an adult pregnant woman because it was necessary to save the life of the foetus. In Application of President and Directors of Georgetown College, 331 F.2d 1000 (D.C. Cir.), cert. denied, 377 U.S. 978 (1964) (in chambers), Judge Wright issued an emergency order authorizing a transfusion to save the life of an adult woman suffering from a bleeding ulcer "to maintain the status quo and prevent the issue respecting the rights of the parties in the premises from becoming moot before full consideration was possible." 331 F.2d at 1007. Judge Wright indicated that the applicant was likely to prevail on appeal because: the woman was "hardly compos mentis" (id. at 1008) when she refused a transfusion, and it might have been the duty of the court to appoint a guardian to authorize treatment to save her life; the state, as parens patriae, "will not allow a parent to abandon a child," and the woman's death would have been the "most ultimate of voluntary abandonments" of her child (ibid.); she might have been committing a crime by attempting to commit suicide; the hospital might be exposed to the risk of criminal liability for her death; and finally, the woman did not want to die. The court denied the petition for a rehearing en banc. But see In re Brooks' Estate, 32 Ill. 2d 361, 205 N.E.2d 435 (1965) (appointment

---

[5] Judge Wright also pointed out that none of the parties had sought a hearing on the temporary order until the series of transfusions had been completed and the woman was out of danger. 331 F.2d at 1003.

of guardian for purpose of consenting to transfusion on behalf of unwilling adult Jehovah's Witness who had expressly exculpated hospital from potential liability for failure to give transfusion is unconstitutional).

PROBLEM

Mr. and Mrs. Lane are the parents of four-year-old identical twins, their only children. One of the twins, James, has been afflicted with a chronic kidney ailment for the last year. The doctors have given the Lanes the following information: the malfunction appears to be permanent since it has not responded to any drug therapy; radioisotope tracings indicate that one of James's kidneys has already been destroyed and the other has been seriously weakened; James is likely to live no more than another year if the present course of the disease continues; there is a very small chance that continued drug therapy will correct the malfunction. The doctors, however, are reluctant to risk James's general health further by administering more drugs. The doctors believe that James can be cured if a new kidney can be transplanted into his body, and they recommend that the Lanes consent to using one of the twin brother John's kidneys for this purpose. Although voluntary kidney donors can be found, only very few transplants involving nonsiblings have ever been successful — and these were performed within the last three years, so that the doctors have little experience on which to base a judgment of the long-term effectiveness of such a procedure. Since human bodies tend to reject strange issue, transplantation requires the administration of massive doses of toxic drugs to blunt the production of antibodies. The amount of drugs given must be precisely accurate; in several transplant cases the patient to whom the new kidney was given has died as a result of overdosage.

The Lanes discover in the medical literature that in the decade preceding February 1964, 244 kidney transplants had been attempted: of the 28 identical twins who had received transplants, 21 had survived; of the 91 patients who received kidneys from blood relatives, only five had survived for more than a year; of the 120 patients who received kidneys from living, unrelated donors or from cadavers, only one had survived for more than one year.[6]

Although there is no special risk to John in the surgery to remove one of his kidneys, any major surgery to a four-year-old child entails risk and occasionally can be fatal. One kidney is sufficient to perform kidney functions. John's resistance to other diseases will not be lowered by the operation. He will simply have less protection in case he ever contracts a kidney ailment.

If the transplant is successful, James can expect to lead a completely normal life; there is no indication that the disease will strike a new kidney or that the malfunction is hereditary and might later strike John.

The doctors recommend the surgery; the hospital's chief of psychiatry

6 See Elkinton, Moral Problems in the Use of Borrowed Organs, Artificial and Transplanted, 60 Annals Int. Med. 309, 311 (1964).

suggests that if the operation were not performed and James dies, the experience would have a "grave emotional impact" on John.

Mr. and Mrs. Lane cannot agree. Mr. Lane wants to have the operation performed. Mrs. Lane, on the other hand, refuses to consent to the surgery. She feels that the chances are slim that the operation will be successful; that there can be no guarantee that the surgery required to remove John's kidney will not harm or kill him, and then they will have lost both their children; that James's kidney ailment may clear up without surgery; and that it would be immoral for them to make such an important decision for John. Finally, she admits to a feeling of distrust for surgeons because they seem to urge surgery on many occasions when it turns out not to have been necessary.

In desperation, Mr. Lane consults the welfare department and, with the agency's consent and assistance, files a petition in the juvenile court alleging that James is a neglected child because Mrs. Lane refuses to consent to the transplant. If you were the juvenile court judge to whom this evidence was presented, how would you decide this case under the New York Children's Court Act, page 384 supra, note 4?

PEOPLE v. DONNER
199 Misc. 643, 99 N.Y.S.2d 830
(Dom. Rel. Ct. 1950) [7]

DELANY, J. This prosecution for violation of the Compulsory Education Law (Education Law, §3212) presents a grave constitutional question. The case was presented to the court for determination upon an agreed statement of facts. . . .

. . . [R]espondents are the fathers of children of school age who do not now attend any public, private or parochial school in which secular subjects are taught; instead they attend a small religious school maintained by persons of the Jewish faith in the borough of Brooklyn, city of New York, which is not registered with nor recognized by the Jewish Education Committee of New York which supervises secular instruction in Hebrew parochial schools. It functions as an entirely independent organization.

The only instruction received by the children who attend this school is in the Bible, the Talmud and elementary Jewish law. Time is allotted to them for supervised play. They receive some physical training. Attendance is from 9:30 A.M. to about 4:00 P.M. at least five days a week. No record of attendance is kept. The sole instructor admittedly does not possess the minimum qualifications of a teacher for secular instruction required by the board of education of the city of New York.

The children do not receive any formal or systematic instruction in the ten common branches and other courses of study required by section 3204 of the Education Law. English is not the language of instruction. Such

---

[7] Aff'd, 278 App. Div. 705, 103 N.Y.S.2d 757, aff'd, 302 N.Y. 857, 100 N.E.2d 48, appeal dismissed, 342 U.S. 884 (1951) (Justices Black and Douglas would have noted probable jurisdiction).

textbooks as are used in the school are not written in English. The children receive a certain amount of instruction (in the Hebrew language)
informally, in arithmetic, geography, civics, hygiene and physical education, but only as an incident to their instruction in the Bible, the Talmud
and the Jewish law. Such information as they may acquire in the remaining common branch subjects, namely, reading, spelling, writing English language and United States history, they have obtained through
other, informal contacts outside the school.

It is conceded by the parties hereto for the purpose of this case that in
the course of their instruction, these children are taught and trained in
the different concepts of moral and religious behavior and respect for and
loyalty to the laws of our country generally and the rights of others, suited
in content, method and objective to their years, and that, particularly as a
result of the mental discipline derived from the nature of their instruction in this religious school, these children are mentally alert.

It is further conceded by the parties hereto that it is the religious belief
of the parents of these children that all systematic, secular education is
prohibited as a matter of Jewish law. They believe that where the provisions of the Compulsory Education Law of the State of New York are in
conflict with these provisions of the Jewish law, the latter must prevail.

The court can take judicial notice that practically all Jewish children
of school age in the United States receive secular instruction in the public
schools, except some who attend Hebrew parochial schools in which they
receive both secular and religious instruction. It seems obvious that respondents' interpretation of the fundamental Jewish law is not in accordance with the normal interpretation of almost all Americans of the Hebrew faith. The court does not question the bona fides of respondents'
belief in this case in their interpretation of the Jewish law of their particular sect . . . .

In the case at bar respondents contend, and it cannot fairly be contested, that in view of their deep religious convictions, enforcement of the
Compulsory Education Law against them infringes upon their religious
liberty. Whether this infringement violates respondents' constitutional
rights is the underlying question involved in this case.

. . . The First Amendment of the Federal Constitution prohibits any
"law respecting an establishment of religion, or prohibiting the free exercise thereof." While this amendment refers specifically only to Congress,
it is now well settled that the prohibitions imposed upon Congress by the
First Amendment have been incorporated into the Fourteenth Amendment as prohibitions against the States. [Citations omitted.]

Pierce v. Society of Sisters (268 U.S. 510) held unconstitutional a statute that sought to prohibit the operation of parochial or private schools.
The Pierce case did not hold that the State could not compel children to
receive secular education. Rather did it hold that the State could not
prescribe the place where, or the auspices under which, secular education
was to be obtained. The court expressly stated: "No question is raised
concerning the power of the State reasonably to regulate all schools, to
inspect, supervise and examine them, their teachers and pupils; to require

that all children of proper age attend some school, that teachers shall be of good moral character and patriotic disposition, that certain studies plainly essential to good citizenship must be taught, and that nothing be taught which is manifestly inimical to the public welfare." (P. 534.) . . .

In Meyer v. Nebraska (262 U.S. 390) the Supreme Court invalidated a State law prohibiting the teaching in any private, denominational, parochial or public school of any modern language other than English to any child who had not passed the eighth grade. The court held that the statute interfered with the constitutional right of the parent "to bring up children, [and] to worship God according to the dictates of his own conscience." (P. 399.) The court, however, expressly stated that "the power of the State to compel attendance at some school and to make reasonable regulations of the schools, including a requirement that they shall give instructions in English, is not questioned." (P. 402.)

Public education laws are the outgrowth of social legislation designed to give equality of opportunity to all children in a society dedicated to the democratic ideal. Without equality of opportunity in education there is no equality among the children of our democratic society. . . . Moreover, our State and our society [have] an interest in seeing to it that every child receives a basic secular education since the kind of education our children receive has substantial bearing upon the kind of citizens they will become when they grow into maturity. The kind and quality of education our children receive have like bearing upon whether they will in later life be able to take their rightful place in civil society or whether they may, by reason of a lack of equal educational opportunities, become frustrated delinquents or frustrated adults who continually run afoul of our criminal statutes. . . . Since equality of education has a direct bearing upon the economic resourcefulness of our country in times of peace and directly affects the civil and military manpower resources of our country in times of war, every citizen has an interest in whether all of our children receive a basic secular education. . . .

The finding of fact that there has been an infringement of the religious liberty of respondents, does not necessarily require a determination by the court that their constitutional rights have been violated. The constitutional guaranty of religious liberty "embraces two concepts — freedom to believe and freedom to act. The first is absolute but, in the nature of things, the second cannot be. . . ." [Court's quotation abbreviated by Eds.; citation omitted.] Respondents' failure to act — i.e., failure to obtain public or private secular education for their children as prescribed in section 3204 of the Education Law of the State of New York constitutes conduct which is subject to regulation for the protection of society. . . .

. . . In all cases where an individual seeks to invoke the protection of the constitutional safeguards of religious liberties the court is faced with the responsibility of weighing the interest of our total society in compelling compliance, as against the interest of our total society in permitting noncompliance.

In this case, therefore, the issue is whether it is more important to our total society, that all children . . . shall receive a basic secular education in the English language as prescribed in section 3204 of the Education Law, than that parents whose religious convictions preclude compliance with our secular education laws, shall be permitted to rear their children exclusively in conformance with their religious conviction. If the answer were in the negative, it might leave the door open to all sorts of abuses against society in the name of religion. . . .

It seems clear . . . that the religious convictions of respondents herein must yield to the total public interest. Compulsory education laws constitute but one of many statutes of a government, dedicated to the democratic ideal, which are universally enacted for the benefit of all the children within the realm of government. . . .

In Prince v. Massachusetts (321 U.S. 158 . . .) the United States Supreme Court held that a statute forbidding children to sell magazines in public places and penalizing the parents of children who permit them to sell magazines in public places is not an unconstitutional abridgement of religious liberty when applied to a member of a religious sect who furnished religious periodicals to a child and permitted her to sell them on the streets. In language which is particularly appropriate here, the court stated (pp. 166-167, 168-169): "But the family itself is not beyond regulation in the public interest, as against a claim of religious liberty. . . . Acting to guard the general interest in youth's well being, the state as parens patriae *may restrict the parent's control by requiring school attendance,* . . . and in many other ways. . . . *It is too late now to doubt that legislation appropriately designed to reach such evils is within the state's police power, whether against the parent's claim to control of the child or one that religious scruples dictate contrary action.*" (Emphasis added.) . . . [Court's quotation abbreviated by Eds.]

Since this court finds, for the foregoing reasons that the constitutional rights of respondents herein have not been violated, it follows that they and each of them are guilty of having violated section 3212 of the public Education Law. . . .

NOTE

1. The issue in Donner can arise in other contexts as well. A juvenile court may assert jurisdiction over the child because of his truancy; see In re Marsh, 140 Pa. Super. 472, 14 A.2d 368 (1940), and see page 421 infra. Note that some religious groups have successfully sought modifications of state public schooling policies. Although N.Y. Educ. Law §3204, which prescribes curricular prerequisites for accreditation, includes courses in health and hygiene, a provision was included, at the instance of the Christian Science Church, which excuses students from these courses if the study conflicts with the religion of their parents.

2. As recently as 1890, at least some professional educators saw the problem in a quite different perspective. The Superintendent of Schools of Texas argued:

Yet there are not wanting evidences of a drift toward the breakers of socialism . . . . I hold that compulsory education is contrary to the dominant idea which has pervaded the development of American institutions, and further, that it is perilous to one of the most vital and essential of the institutions on which civilization rests — the family. . . . Education I hold to be a right inherent in the family and the parent. . . .

This provision for the education of the children by the state should be sure and as ample as the means of the people will justify. So far the state may and should go, but no further. Universal education is one of the greatest of blessings; but I would not imperil, even for universal education, the integrity of the family. The dangers to the welfare of society resulting from a great mass of illiteracy are appalling, but the evils of illiteracy are less perilous than those which result from the destruction of parental authority and the loosening of family ties. . . .[8]

3. The Illinois compulsory education law exempts "[a]ny child attending a private or a parochial school where children are taught the branches of education taught to children of corresponding age and grade in the public schools." Ill. Ann. Stat. c. 122, §26-1(1)(1962). In People v. Levisen, 404 Ill. 574, 90 N.E.2d 213 (1950), Seventh Day Adventists were prosecuted and convicted for refusing to send their children to public school. The father was a college graduate and a minister; the mother had had two years of college training in "pedagogy and educational psychology." The Levisens believed that

the child should not be educated in competition with other children because it produces a pugnacious character, that the necessary atmosphere of faith in the Bible cannot be obtained in the public school, and that for the first eight or ten years of a child's life the field or garden is the best schoolroom, the mother the best teacher, and nature the best lesson book.[9]

The child received five hours of instruction each day at home; moreover, her achievement level was concededly comparable to what it would have been in public school. The parents' convictions were reversed because the child was attending a "private school" within the meaning of the exempting provision. The dissenting judge argued that parents would construe the decision as a license to keep their children at home:

This will do violence to the letter and spirit of the law. True, the opinion says in substance that parents may not, under a pretext of instruction by a private tutor or by themselves, evade their responsibility to educate their children. . . .

If the compulsory attendance school law is not enforced may not

---

[8] Journal of Proceedings and Addresses of the National Education Association, 1890, pp. 186-187, quoted in 1 Abbott, The Child and the State 310-311 (1938). (All but second omission by Eds.)

[9] 404 Ill. at 575-576, 90 N.E.2d at 214.

parents withdraw their children from school at any time desired, even in the middle of a term or semester so as to teach them at home? Thereafter, should they change their minds, could they not again, under the law, return their children to the same school? Schools may thereby be disrupted and certainly will lose the power, prestige and jurisdiction which is now theirs. . . . We should not permit so salutory a statute to be thwarted by the whim and caprice of the many who, I fear, will take advantage of the situation under authority of this case.[10]

Contra, Washington v. Counort, 69 Wash. 361, 124 Pac. 910 (1912). In People v. Turner, 121 Cal. App. 2d 861, 867, 263 P.2d 685, 688 (1953), appeal dismissed, 347 U.S. 972 (1954) (Justices Black and Reed would have noted probable jurisdiction), the parents were convicted despite a claim that their home instruction was at least as good as the instruction available in public or private schools in the state; although children taught by "private tutors" were not required to attend school, the parents could not be considered "private tutors" since they did not "hold a valid State credential for the grade taught."

If the doctrine of People v. Levisen, supra, is accepted, how should the quality of the home instruction be measured — by comparing the parents' intelligence with that of average public school teachers? By comparing their children's progress with the progress of public school students in the same age group? By assessing their children's progress in relation to the children's potential? Do you think these cases present a constitutional issue?

4. The universal education movement in the United States was closely associated with efforts to eliminate the evils of widespread employment of children in American industry. Poverty-stricken parents had often been willing to consign their children to unscrupulous employers — for long hours, under abominable conditions, in return for minimal wages. "Child labor legislation had for its object the prevention of the withdrawal of children from school to work in factories." 1 Abbott, The Child and the State 405 (1938). Although many states passed statutes setting minimum age limits for employment, they were largely unenforced:

> Parents and mercenary and corrupt notaries alike connive at the employment of children under the statutory age. A parent who is willing to permit its child to work in a factory at an age under 14 is ordinarily just as willing to perjure himself as to the age of the child. . . .[11]

According to Miss Abbott, the problem gradually became less serious during the twentieth century: "the number of children gainfully employed, including those in agriculture, per 1000 of the total number of children

[10] 404 Ill. at 579-580, 90 N.E.2d at 216 (dissenting opinion).
[11] Report and Testimony Taken before the Special Committee of the Assembly Appointed to Investigate the Condition of Female Labor in the City of New York, New York Assembly Documents, 1896, Vol. 23, No. 97, Part I, quoted in 1 Abbott, The Child and the State 424, 426 (1938).

ten to thirteen years of age had dropped from 121 in 1900 to 24 in 1930, and of those fourteen and fifteen years of age from 309 to 92 per 1000 of that age group." Id. at 267. The Fair Labor Standards Act, 29 U.S.C.A. §§201-219 (Supp. 1964), prohibited employment in manufacturing establishments of any person under the age of sixteen. The Chief of the Children's Bureau was instructed to provide by regulation that employment of a child between fourteen and sixteen, in occupations other than manufacturing or mining, was permissible if it would not interfere with the child's schooling and so long as physical conditions would not constitute a hazard to the child's health. There was a general exemption for agricultural endeavors during periods when the child was not required to attend school. See generally Livengood, The Federal Wage and Hour Law 162-164 (1952).

C. THE DYSFUNCTIONAL FAMILY

1. Introduction

Community interventions in family affairs are currently accomplished, or attempted, largely under the auspices of a juvenile court. When the first juvenile court was created in Illinois, on July 1, 1899,

> [t]his socio-legal invention was enthusiastically hailed and widely copied. Almost at birth, its cause became a part of the era's wide-ranging movement toward social reform. The concept of the juvenile court took institutional form with dramatic rapidity. Such courts now exist in every state of the Union, and in much of the rest of the civilized world as well.[12]

The origins of the modern juvenile court movement cannot be traced with certainty.[13] But it is clear that the movement was given impetus not only by widespread distaste for subjecting children to the harshness of the criminal process, but also by broadly based endeavors to protect children who had not committed criminal acts:

> The streams of reform . . . sprang from such apparently disparate headwaters as the activity of philanthropic associations on behalf of street urchins, waifs, and wayward misdemeanant youngsters; the growth of laws preventing cruelty to children and rescuing the dependent and neglected; and developments in the criminal law and in

[12] Shireman, Foreword, in Justice for the Child v.

[13] See Custer, Historical Evolution of the Doctrine of Parens Patriae (unpublished manuscript on file in Biddle Law Library, University of Pennsylvania), suggesting that the doctrine that the state acts as parens patriae of all children — the common justification for juvenile court jurisdiction and juvenile court interventions — originated in the medieval practice of recognizing that the king was entitled to a profitable guardianship of the property of all "natural fools," "idiots" and "madmen." Custer reports that the doctrine was applied to children because of a printer's error — in Lord Coke's discussion of an early case involving an "ideot," the word "enfant" was substituted in one place for the word "ideot." The error was corrected in a subsequent edition, but by that time the assertion of jurisdiction over children by courts of chancery was a commonplace.

equity. Indeed, scholars have sometimes debated whether . . . the Juvenile Court Act was a "consolidating statute," so to speak, or instituted a significantly new approach to children. . . .[14]

Juvenile courts are usually given jurisdiction over any child adjudicated "delinquent," "neglected," or "dependent." The materials which follow explore the statutory and judicial meanings these terms have acquired in a number of states. The issues cannot be adequately examined, however, without recognizing that juvenile courts influence, actually or potentially, an extraordinary number of American families. Although accurate statistics are difficult to obtain because of the disparities in statutory definitions and the lack of any standardized reporting procedure,[15] Perlman estimated that 1.1 million persons under eighteen years of age were arrested in 1962; almost one half of the arrests were for minor offenses and were handled by the police without referral to a juvenile court. In the same year the juvenile courts processed an estimated 555,000 delinquency cases, involving an estimated 478,000 children. This number represented 1.8 per cent of all children between the ages of ten and seventeen. The reasons for referral, at least in urban centers,[16] are shown on page 396.

The measurement of delinquency rates poses problems similar to, perhaps more difficult than, those presented when illegitimacy rates are assessed. See page 77 supra. Nonetheless, most students of delinquency seem to agree that delinquency rates are rising. The national rate of reported delinquency doubled in the decade 1948-1958.[17]

Nor have the juvenile courts ignored their jurisdiction over neglected children. The Children's Bureau estimated that there were 140,000 dependency and neglect adjudications in 1961; with the exception of 1956, the number of adjudications has grown larger every year since 1951. Adjudications aside, many child welfare experts believe that a great many parents in fact neglect their children. Bishop reported that of a sample of 50,000 children, chosen from a total child population of 377,080 receiving public child welfare services, "for 36 per cent of the children, the principal problem was 'neglect, abuse or exploitation.' . . . The same study found in a sample of voluntary agencies that 13 per cent of the children served

[14] Rosenheim, Perennial Problems in the Juvenile Court, in Justice for the Child 1-2.

[15] The figures most frequently utilized are the arrest data collected by the Federal Bureau of Investigation and the data on court referrals of delinquents collected from a national representative sample of 502 juvenile courts by the Children's Bureau. The data which follow are based upon information reported by Perlman, Statistical Aspects of Antisocial Behavior of the Minor in the United States (U.S. Children's Bureau 1963). See also Tappan, Juvenile Delinquency (1949); Perlman, Reporting Juvenile Delinquency, 3 N.P.P.A.J. 242 (1957).

[16] Courts in urban areas handled more than two thirds of all delinquency cases. Other figures indicate that the general trend to increasing urbanization has particularly affected youths in the juvenile court age range. See Perlman, Statistical Aspects of Antisocial Behavior of the Minor in the United States 15 (U.S. Children's Bureau 1963).

[17] U.S. Children's Bureau, Report to the Congress on Juvenile Delinquency 3 (1960).

REASON FOR REFERRAL TO COURT IN DELINQUENCY CASES, 1962 [18]

Offense	Percent		
	Both sexes	Boys	Girls
All	100.0	100.0	100.0
Applicable to both juveniles and adults			
Criminal homicide[19]	0.1	0.1	—
Forcible rape	0.1	0.1	—
Aggravated assault	1.9	2.1	1.0
Other assault	3.4	3.7	2.1
Robbery	2.0	2.4	0.5
Burglary	11.7	14.0	2.3
Larceny — theft (except auto)			
Under $50	15.9	17.0	11.4
$50 or more	2.0	2.2	1.2
Vandalism	4.1	4.9	1.1
Auto theft (unauthorized use)	8.4	10.1	1.7
Auto theft (other)	0.7	0.8	0.2
Sex offenses (excl. forcible rape)	3.9	2.5	9.4
Violation of narcotic drug laws	0.1	0.1	0.1
Violation of other drug laws	0.2	0.2	0.3
Weapons (carrying, possessing)	1.0	1.1	0.3
Disorderly conduct	4.4	4.8	3.0
Driving while intoxicated	0.1	0.1	[20]
Drunkenness	2.4	2.5	2.1
Hit and run	0.3	0.3	0.2
Driving without a license	4.0	4.3	2.8
Other	6.1	6.6	4.2
Applicable to juveniles only			
Ungovernable behavior	7.5	5.0	17.8
Truancy	4.7	3.9	7.9
Running away	10.0	6.2	25.3
Curfew violation	2.4	2.4	2.2
Other	2.6	2.5	2.9

had neglect as a primary problem." [21] These figures are not very helpful, of course. In the first place, no meaningful base has been provided against which to measure the number of problem children. Moreover,

[18] Monthly reports to Children's Bureau for the year 1962 from 22 of the 30 courts serving the larger cities in the United States. U.S. Children's Bureau Stat. Series No. 73, Table 5 (1963). Traffic offenses are excluded except for driving while intoxicated, hit and run, and driving without a license.

[19] Includes murder and manslaughter with or without negligence.

[20] Less than 0.05 percent.

[21] Bishop, Helping Neglectful Parents, 355 Annals, Sept. 1964, pp. 82, 85.

the sample is obviously biased; it was chosen from a total population of all those who were receiving public or private child welfare services — a group likely to include a disproportionately large share of neglectful parents.   Finally, even if we ignore the possibility of differing definitions of neglect among caseworkers who described the "principal problem," it is obvious that caseworkers as a group are likely to define neglect more expansively than would either judges or lay members of the community.[22]

Nonetheless, the statistical data almost certainly understate the extent of both "delinquency" and "parental neglect."   The Children's Bureau's figures report either adjudications or court referrals.   But we know that about half of the court referrals in delinquency cases are handled "unofficially" without petition or adjudication;[23]   there is good evidence that the police handle approximately one half of the juvenile arrests without referring the matter to the juvenile court.   Finally, most juvenile delinquency never becomes a matter of official record.   A report on the Cambridge-Somerville Youth Study (see page 448 infra) concluded:

> At our conservative estimate, these boys had committed a minimum of 6416 infractions of the law during the five-year period; while only 95 of their violations had become a matter of official complaint.   In other words, authorities took official action in less than $1\frac{1}{2}$ per cent of the infractions.   Approximately 1400 of these infractions were violations of city ordinances, none of which became a matter of court complaint.   Of 4400 minor offenses, only 27 (.60%) were prosecuted.   Of 616 serious offenses, 68 (11%) were prosecuted.[24]

Thus, it is clear that the juvenile court exercises jurisdiction over a very small sample of "delinquent," "neglected," and "dependent" children.[25]   Perhaps more important, it is likely that juvenile courts do not deal with a representative sample of either delinquents or neglectful parents.   Goldman gave the following summary of the available literature:

1. There is much undiscovered delinquency among juveniles.

2. The number of delinquents dealt with by the police is much greater than the number recorded in the juvenile court. . . .

5. The degree of organization of child welfare services in a community will affect the rate of court referral of juvenile offenders by police.

[22] Cf. Boehm, The Community and the Social Agency Define Neglect, 43 Child Welfare 453, 457 (1964).

[23] See Perlman, Statistical Aspects of Antisocial Behavior of the Minor in the United States 7 (U.S. Children's Bureau 1963).   See also page 444 infra.

[24] Murphy, Shirley & Witmer, The Incidence of Hidden Delinquency, 16 Am. J. Orthopsychiatry 686, 688 (1946).

[25] Appellate review of juvenile court adjudications is less frequent than in other areas: lawyers are seldom provided (see page 418 note 45 infra); most of the families involved in juvenile court matters have neither the money nor the social sophistication to hire their own attorney (cf. pages 442-443 infra). As a result, appellate opinions do not provide an accurate picture of juvenile court law "in action."   The material which follows includes the transcript of a delinquency hearing in the New York Family Court.   See pages 417-440 infra.

6. Reporting by police is variable and may depend on a number of factors such as police department facilities and philosophy, the attitude of the police toward certain offenses, the court calendar, the degree of cooperation given by the parents and the child, etc.

7. Race, nativity, and nationality of the child or his parents determine to some extent the offender's liability to be arrested and referred to the court.

8. There is a preferential treatment of juveniles of socially important or influential families, or those living in the more select residential areas of a community.

9. Various offenses are differentially reported, with serious [?] offenses often unreported and relatively large numbers of minor [?] offenses reported to the juvenile court.[26]

Goldman studied police arrest and reporting data in four disparate communities in the greater Pittsburgh metropolitan area; his study conclusions paralleled the data reported in the existing literature:

Offenses seem to be differentially treated with respect to court referral. Some offenses were always reported to the court, while others were reported relatively infrequently. . . . [O]f the ten cases of robbery, all were referred for official action. Ninety-one per cent of the arrests for the larceny of a motor vehicle and 90 per cent of the arrests for riding in a stolen car were reported to the juvenile court. Eighty-three per cent of the sex offenses and 80.9 per cent of cases in the delinquent and incorrigible group were made known to the court. . . . On the other hand, the relatively frequent offenses of gambling, violation of a borough ordinance, violation of the motor vehicle code, mischief, property damage, and drunkenness are relatively infrequently made the bases of an official or unofficial report to the court. . . .

The high arrest rates of Manor Heights [a well-to-do residential area] and of Mill Town [an industrial community with a high percentage of foreign-born laborers, clerical workers, and operatives] are largely a result of arrests for trespassing, disorderly conduct, mischief, violation of a borough ordinance, property damage, etc. These are offenses which are, to a large extent, usually overlooked by citizens and police in other communities. The police chief in Manor Heights was frequently called by citizens to complain of children who took short-cuts across their lawns, or children who damaged prized shrubbery, or who were annoyingly noisy on the street or in the public busses. On the other hand, Trade City [a residential and commercial area, with a low percentage of foreign-born residents, whose major occupational groups are clerical, craftsmen, and foremen], with the lowest rate of arrest and the highest rate of arrests for

[26] Goldman, Differential Selection of Juvenile Offenders for Court Appearance 21-22 (N.C.C.D. 1963). See also Piliavin & Briar, Police Encounters with Juveniles, 70 Am. J. Soc. 206 (1964).

serious offenses, had very few recorded arrests for vagrancy, violation of a borough ordinance, mischief, etc.

Thus it appears from these data that the communities with the highest rates of arrest have the lowest proportions of arrests referred to the juvenile court. This seems to a large extent to be the result of the differential handling of minor offenses, although there seem to be also some relatively slight differences in the treatment of serious offenses. . . . This suggests possibly a more critical weighing of the offense on the part of police in Manor Heights and Mill Town than in the other two communities. It seems that in Steel City and in Trade City, the nature of the offense itself, in terms of seriousness may not always be the basic determinant of case disposition.[27]

The belief is widespread that children of the poor are overrepresented in juvenile court delinquency populations. Consider, for example, Lelyveld, The Paradoxical Case of the Affluent Delinquent, N.Y. Times, Oct. 4, 1964 (Magazine), p. 13:

Usually, it is not just the reputations of the parents and their children that are shielded, but the reputations of the towns themselves. . . .
. . . Often parents manage to keep the matter out of court by promising to send an offending youth to a boarding school — not infrequently a military school — or to a psychiatrist. It is very unusual for a teen-ager from a well-off family to be sent to a state correctional institution. . . .
There are many ways of covering up, including that of the officer on the beat who knows he is likely to be rewarded if he takes a delinquent youngster directly home rather than to the station house. . . .

There is some basis for believing that "parental neglect" petitions also concern predominantly poor families. Although anyone can file a neglect petition, by and large the child welfare agencies determine which children will be brought to the official attention of the court, and these agencies serve a clientele which is not evenly distributed among all socioeconomic groups. To some extent, of course, agencies which extend "protective service" to children[28] rely upon complaints from the community. Boehm, The Community and the Social Agency Define Neglect, 43 Child Welfare 453, 459 (1964), reports the results of a survey of neglect complaints received by two urban, public welfare agencies during a two-month period:

[T]his focus [of social work on personality disturbance of parents] would make it logical to assume that such disturbances would occur

---

[27] Id. at 37-39, 87-88.
[28] For a discussion of "protective service," see page 416 infra. The term refers to an agency's authority to give casework counsel to a family prior to intervention by a juvenile court.

among families regardless of social class or other demographic characteristics. . . .

Further analysis of the characteristics of the families involved in neglect complaints, however, [shows] that the assumption of random distributions does not hold up and that the educated, economically independent family is the rare exception among the neglect referrals. . . .

In the general population, only 3 percent of families are dependent upon general relief or public assistance; in the neglect families, 42 percent receive assistance. . . . [T]he proportion of nonwhites among neglect families is almost three times the proportion found in the general population. . . . In the general population, fewer than 10 percent of the husbands are in unskilled labor or service occupations; in the neglect families more than 50 percent are in this occupational group. In the general population, approximately 17 percent of families live in high delinquency areas; in the neglect families, approximately 50 percent live in these areas.

In the communities in which a public agency's "protective service" endeavors have been integrated with public assistance, it is much more likely that "neglect" by parents receiving assistance will come to the attention of child welfare personnel. Although no data are presently available, it seems appropriate to hypothesize that a family which comes to the attention of a social agency for any reason is much more likely to be the subject of a neglect petition.

Obviously not every child to whom an agency extends casework services becomes the subject of a neglect petition. Yet little is known as to the factors which determine whether a neglect petition will be filed. Some empirical data, as yet unreported, have been gathered. See Boehm, An Assessment of Family Adequacy in Protective Cases, 41 Child Welfare 10 (1962).

As you examine the materials below, consider whether these data are relevant in determining what jurisdiction a juvenile court should exercise, what case selection techniques it should adopt, how "informal" its procedures should be, and what dispositional authority it should possess.

2. Jurisdiction of the Juvenile Court

In re SIPPY
97 A.2d 455 (D.C. Mun. Ct. App. 1953)

CAYTON, C.J. Camille Sippy reached her eighteenth birthday on February 3, 1953. A little over a month before that birthday her mother, a widow, filed a complaint in the Juvenile Court charging that Camille was habitually beyond the control of the mother. Code 1951, §11-906(a)(2).[29]

[29] This charge is one of several, enumerated in the same Code section, which may be made against a "child" under the age of 18 years.
[D.C. Code §11-1551 (Supp. 1965) gives the Juvenile Court original and exclusive jurisdiction of cases concerning a child:

After a hearing, and six days before her eighteenth birthday, the court ordered her committed to the Board of Public Welfare "for an indefinite period" to be sent to a school near Philadelphia, where in addition to educational courses she would receive psychiatric treatment. She appeals from the order of commitment. In view of the rulings we are about to make, the evidence need not be recited at this point.

At the outset of the proceedings a gentleman addressed the court and identified himself as a member of the Bar representing the interests of the mother, the complaining petitioner. According to the transcript, "The Court permitted his presence as friend of the Court and directed him to file an appearance for the purpose of the record." The attorney thereupon entered his appearance "for defendant . . . at the request of her mother." In view of the fact that appellant had already engaged the services of Mr. Leimbach, who had filed a formal appearance as attorney for defendant two weeks earlier and was then in the courtroom representing his client, we think it was irregular and improper to permit or invite another attorney to enter an appearance for the [daughter]. It has been held that when a defendant appears by counsel of his own choice the court has no power to assign another attorney to him. [Citations omitted.] That ruling is directly applicable where, as here, the second attorney was admittedly not in sympathy with the position taken by respondent. We offer no criticism of the attorney, who made the frank statement that he represented the interests of the mother. Those interests were antagonistic or at least sharply opposed to the expressed wishes of the daughter: the mother was urging that the daughter be committed to a psychiatric school, while the daughter was protesting against the necessity or propriety of such commitment.[30] The error was by no means merely procedural and was certainly not harmless. The prejudicial nature of the ruling is emphasized by the fact that the second attorney was permitted to make a hearsay statement as to a conversation with the girl's personal

---

"(A) who has violated a law, or has violated an ordinance or regulation of the District of Columbia;

"(B) who is habitually beyond the control of his parent, guardian, or custodian;

"(C) who is habitually truant from school or home;

"(D) who habitually so deports himself as to injure or endanger himself or the morals or safety of himself or others; . . .

"(H) who associates with vagrants, or vicious or immoral persons;

"(I) who engages in an occupation, or is in a situation, dangerous to life or limb or injurious to the health or morals of himself or others. . . ."

[The D.C. Code is one of the statutes which does not use the labels "delinquent" and "neglected." The Standard Juvenile Court Act is drafted in a similar fashion. See 5 N.P.P.A.J. 323-391 (1959); Rubin, Legal Definition of Offenses by Children and Youths, 1960 U. Ill. L.F. 512, 513. The Standard Act does differentiate types of behavior for purposes of describing the court's dispositional alternatives. For example, the Standard Act's "beyond the control of his parent" provision authorizes disposition which other statutes make appropriate for "neglected" children. See also the New York definition of "person in need of supervision," page 421 infra.]

[30] An assistant corporation counsel who is regularly assigned to serve in the Juvenile Court was present throughout the proceedings but took no part therein and was not asked by the judge to participate.

physician, divulging information of a privileged nature, suggesting "that the court should give great weight to the doctor's recommendation" . . . All this, we are satisfied, operated to the prejudice of the respondent, throwing onto the scales against her matters which had no proper place in the proceedings.

Separately assigned as error is a ruling permitting Miss Ryder, an employee of the Social Service Department of the Juvenile Court, to read an ex parte report she had prepared, which contained a resume of her own conversations with respondent's physician and which included privileged matter — specifically an interpretation of the doctor's prognosis and his recommendation that respondent should "enroll" in the Devereux School in Pennsylvania. This report was received over the specific objection of respondent's attorney who protested that his client had never authorized the doctor to divulge information concerning her case nor discuss her case or its details with anyone . . . .

All these objections were valid. The statements and conclusions attributed to the physician were hearsay of the plainest sort. Just as plainly it was a violation of respondent's rights under our Code 1951, §14-308, to receive without her consent information of a confidential nature which the physician had acquired from her in his professional capacity. The Corporation Counsel says, accurately enough, that the privilege may be waived; and the trial judge held that the mother had in fact waived it. Aside from the fact that the record shows no formal waiver by the mother we are not persuaded that so solemn and important a privilege may be waived by an antagonist in a court proceeding, and such the mother clearly was in this case. We think there is no escaping the conclusion that respondent's statutory right of privilege was improperly invaded.

But even if we put aside the question of privilege there still remains the basic fact that respondent's rights were adjudicated and her liberty taken from her on the basis of the alleged professional opinion of a medical man whom her counsel had no opportunity to cross-examine. The doctor was described as a psychiatrist,[31] but there was nothing in the record about his professional status except his name. Respondent had no opportunity to cross-examine him as to his experience or qualifications, as to the nature and extent of his professional contact with respondent, as to the basis for his opinions, or whether commitment for an indefinite period (three years in this case) was the only sound medical solution of the frictions and problems which had arisen between mother and daughter. . . .

Appellant also asks us to rule that the trial court committed error in conducting the hearing and deciding the case on the basis of unsworn statements. While no objection seems to have been made at the time, the matter is serious enough to require discussion. The Juvenile Court Act provides that "The court may conduct the hearing in an informal manner," Code 1951, §11-915, and there are no doubt many cases . . . which may resolve themselves into conciliation hearings and in which unsworn

[31] This description without more created unfavorable implications against respondent.

statements may form a proper basis for disposition. But in a case like this where liberty is involved, we think a respondent is entitled to insist that the facts be presented by witnesses who are under the solemnity of an oath. Our Code, dealing with "Evidence in General" provides that "All evidence shall be given under oath according to the forms of the common law. . . ." Code 1951, §14-101. It is true, as we have said, that a proceeding of this nature is statutory . . . But the requirement that evidence shall be given under oath is not limited to any particular proceeding; it applies to all courts. . . . It is clear that the hearing prescribed by statute, though it may be informal, is nevertheless a judicial hearing resulting in a final judgment. Therefore in taking testimony the rule as to swearing of witnesses should apply there as well as in any other judicial proceeding. [Citations omitted.]

The Corporation Counsel takes an entirely different approach to the situation. His view is that "the minor was not entitled to advance or adopt a position separate from or adverse to that of the parent and society, and that the minor had no vested right to be heard in the proceeding." . . . He relies on Rule v. Geddes, 1904, 23 App. D.C. 31 . . . That litigation arose fifty years ago under a 1901 statute, at a time when there was no Juvenile Court. A more or less automatic extrajudicial procedure then prevailed under which the Reform School for Girls was authorized to receive into its custody any girl under seventeen on application or complaint of a parent that the girl was "incorrigible or habitually disregards the commands of her father, mother or guardian." . . . Far different is the situation today, governed as it is by the comparatively elaborate provisions of the Juvenile Court Act as amended in 1938. . . . [The] Rule decision is no longer applicable.

If the position taken by the Corporation Counsel were correct then only the parent or guardian of an infant could complain of a failure to follow the prescribed statutory procedures. So that in a case like this where the parent not only consented but instigated the proceedings as complainant and assumed a position hostile to the desires of the child, the child would be left completely without a remedy, and even without the right to be heard, either in the Juvenile Court or on appeal. That such was not the Congressional intent is plain from the Code . . . It is beyond question that this appellant was a party — the real party in interest — and the one most seriously affected by the order of the court below. . . .

What we have already said disposes of the appeal. But we think we should also discuss appellant's contention that the evidence did not support the charge that she was habitually beyond the control of her mother. Certain it is that without the incompetent hearsay evidence above-recited there was not enough left to support the charge, and nothing to justify the order removing appellant from her employment and committing her for an indefinite period to a school where psychiatric treatment was to be the principal objective. There was no suggestion that appellant was morally delinquent in a sexual way. It was true, as the appellant admitted, that there had been friction between her and her mother and some disobedience and spiteful conduct on her part (not necessary to be detailed here). But it was also true, as the judge commented, "that the situation probably was not respondent's fault alone, indicating that some responsibility was with the petitioner [mother]." (The mother had been receiving treatment from a psychiatrist of her own.)

We do not think the proof established that appellant was *habitually* beyond the control of her mother. Perhaps the key to the situation is in statements by appellant herself, not denied by her mother, that the mother said she had never been able to evaluate her own problems but was determined that appellant would be required to do so, and that "both she and her mother had strong tempers and wills and that both had difficulty in avoiding clashes." Appellant concluded her statement to the court thus: "She said that she did not want to be put in an institution with unusual or problem children and that she got along well with normal children and people."

We are of the opinion that neither the welfare of the minor nor the safety and protection of the public justified the order entered in this case.

Reversed.

NOTE

1. Many delinquency petitions, of course, are concerned with conduct which is clearly criminal. See the statistics at page 396 supra. For discussion of a variety of delinquency issues, ranging from age limitations to the circumstances under which the juvenile court can waive its jurisdiction in favor of the criminal process, see, e.g., Tappan, Juvenile Delinquency (1949); Justice for the Child; Pirsig, Juvenile Delinquency and Crime: Achievements of the 1959 Minnesota Legislature, 44 Minn. L. Rev. 363 (1960).

2. For discussion of the many procedural issues raised by juvenile court proceedings, see, e.g., Elson, Juvenile Courts & Due Process, in Justice for the Child 95; Antieau, Constitutional Rights in Juvenile Courts, 46 Cornell L.Q. 387 (1961); Paulsen, Fairness to the Juvenile Offender, 41 Minn. L. Rev. 547 (1957); Note, Employment of Social Investigation Reports in Criminal and Juvenile Proceedings, 58 Colum. L. Rev. 702 (1958); Note, 79 Harv. L. Rev. 775 (1966). The usual justification for relaxing procedural safeguards is that delinquency proceedings are not "criminal." Cf. pages 394-395 supra. The extent to which constitutional procedural safeguards are applicable to juvenile proceedings may be clarified by Kent v. United States, 343 F.2d 247 (D.C. Cir. 1964), cert. granted, 381 U.S. 902 (1965) (No. 104, 1965 Term).

3. In re Hook, 95 Vt. 497, 115 Atl. 730 (1922), held that a thirteen-year-old girl could not be adjudicated delinquent solely because of her marriage, since she had "a legal right" to marry. The court also held that her marriage did not oust the juvenile court's pre-existing jurisdiction founded on a prior adjudication of neglect. See also page 234 supra. In Richardson v. Browning, 18 F.2d 1008 (D.C. Cir. 1927), a fifteen-year-old girl sought release from the District of Columbia Training School on

grounds that her commitment as "incorrigible" was improper because she was validly married. The appellate court reversed a judgment granting her petition (id. at 1012):

> The underlying reason for statutes such as [the District of Columbia Probate Code provision terminating guardianship of the person at majority or marriage], as well as for the various court decisions [to the same effect], is based upon the public policy that the control by the husband of his wife's property ought not to be denied, or interfered with, or, under some jurisdictions, that the wife, having assumed the marital relation, is of right entitled to control her own property. But such reason does not at all apply to cases where the physical or moral welfare of the child is involved, and where the government has intervened, as parens patriae, to secure such physical or moral well being.

In re DOUGLAS
164 N.E.2d 475 (Ohio Juv. Ct. 1959)

YOUNG, J. This matter first came to the attention of this court late in January, 1959, when Carol Douglas, the mother of the children involved, came to the court and complained of her husband's conduct toward her. . . . She was advised that her domestic problems should be brought into the Common Pleas Court . . . , and that she should seek the advice of an attorney.

Some time thereafter, Charles Ray Douglas, the father of the children, came to this court complaining that his wife would not obey him, but had taken employment contrary to his wishes, and was neglecting the children. He also was told that he should see his attorney about the problem.

These two preliminary matters do not appear in the records of this matter, as the record commences with the official proceedings on April 16. However, they are part of the unofficial or informal proceedings of this court in this matter, and as such will be judicially noted by the court. . . .

On the evening of April 15, 1959, the mother of the children called the police of Monroeville and complained that the father of the children had driven her out of her home and had taken the children, who were ill, and gone away with them. The police called and reported the complaint to the judge of this court. A juvenile probation officer, Mrs. Miller, accompanied by a police officer, was sent to locate the children and take them into custody. She found them at the home of the father's parents, and took them to the Fisher-Titus Memorial Hospital, where they were examined by Dr. John Blackwood and admitted to the hospital. Mrs. Miller testified that she found the children ill and dirty, the younger one having a woman's underslip on for a diaper. Dr. Blackwood testified that the children were very dirty, when he examined them, and both were suffering from an upper respiratory infection. He also found that the younger child was anemic, and the older had some iron deficiency, although the blood chemistry was within normal limits. He attributed the anemia to nutritional deficiency.

The following morning a formal complaint was filed in this court alleging that the children, Christine Jodine Douglas, age two years, and Cynthia Rae Douglas, age one year, were dependent and neglected children, in that they lack proper care because of the faults or habits of their parents and their condition or environment is such as to warrant the state in the interest of said children in assuming their guardianship. An order was entered . . . reciting that it appearing that the children were in such condition that their welfare required that their custody be immediately assumed by the Court, it was ordered that . . . the children be temporarily placed in the Fisher-Titus Hospital . . . Later in the day, the court was advised by Dr. Blackwood that the children were sufficiently recovered to be discharged from the hospital. Thereupon, another order was entered upon the Journal of the Court placing the children temporarily in the custody of their mother, Carol Douglas, until the time of hearing. . . .

At the time set for hearing, both parents appeared, each represented by counsel. Hearings occupied parts of several days, spread over a period of six months. . . .

During the pendency of the proceedings, a divorce action, which had been filed in the Court of Common Pleas by Carol Douglas on April 15th, was certified to the Juvenile Court on April 18th. Papers filed with the divorce petition indicated that Mrs. Douglas had filed an action for divorce in Crawford County on January 29th, but the action was later dismissed.

Some time after the hearing on May 11, the parties to the divorce action resumed their marital relationships. This reconciliation lasted about two or three weeks. On July 23, 1959, Charles Ray Douglas filed another action for divorce in the Court of Common Pleas. This was also, on October 8, 1959, certified to the Juvenile Court, and is presently pending therein.

A large number of witnesses testified in this case, and from the testimony a most unpleasant picture emerges. Mr. Douglas was born January 19, 1924. Mrs. Douglas was born March 1, 1940. They were married May 5, 1956. Christine, the older child was born January 30, 1957 and Cynthia was born March 13, 1958. Thus at the time of the marriage, Mrs. Douglas was sixteen years old, and her husband was thirty-two years old.

"Husband twice as old as wife, argues ill for married life," W. S. Gilbert.

The testimony shows that during the time he was courting the present Mrs. Douglas, Mr. Douglas, who had been previously married and divorced, was carrying on an adulterous relationship with his former wife. Some time after the marriage, when Mrs. Douglas asked him about this affair, Mr. Douglas said that he had spent a week with his former wife while her husband was on a fishing trip; that he had done this to prove to her husband that he could get her back if he wanted her.

Mr. Douglas became acquainted with Mrs. Douglas through one of her brothers whom he had impressed with his fancy automobile. Mrs. Douglas's mother tried to discourage the courtship, but although she ordered Douglas to stay away, he refused to do so. Finally, he and Mrs. Douglas ran away to Indiana and stayed over night. He then asked the mother's consent to marriage. Mr. Douglas's mother also came and asked her not to prosecute him for running away with the girl, so she finally consented to the marriage which took place in Indiana. . . .

One witness testified that on one occasion after his marriage, Mr. Douglas had made advances to her.

Mrs. Douglas testified that for some time prior to their divorce actions Mr. Douglas had been unemployed. He had lost his job because his wages had been garnished by the Federal Government as the result of some income tax difficulty. She stated that whenever they would quarrel, Mr. Douglas would take the children and run off with them; that he threatened her that if she contested his divorce action, she would never get to see the children. On one occasion, he told her that he was anxious for the children to grow up, so he could tell them what a whore their mother was. There was other evidence of improper conduct on the part of Mr. Douglas. . . .

Mrs. Douglas, according to testimony, has two brothers who have served time in the Mansfield Reformatory for such offenses as breaking and entering, statutory rape, and forgery. One of them was returned to the Reformatory for parole violation because he operated Mr. Douglas' car without permission.

During the pendency of this matter, after one quarrel with her husband, Mrs. Douglas ran off with a young man named Sammy Lemon, and spent one or two nights out at the Norwalk reservoir with him. There was also evidence of other improper conduct on her part.

It should be recalled that this court had the dubious privilege of seeing and hearing the witnesses who testified in this matter. Some of them are well, and unpleasantly, known to the court as the result of criminal charges against them. Without going any further into the details of the testimony, it is sufficient to say that this court must necessarily conclude that both Mr. and Mrs. Douglas have been guilty of serious marital misconduct; that Mr. Douglas is a conscienceless, selfish monster, whose main interest in the children is to use them as clubs to beat his wife into submission; that Mrs. Douglas is without either morals or good sense, and is also more concerned with gratifying her desires of the moment than the welfare of her children.

In this state of facts, what is the law? Revised Code, §2151.03, in part defines a neglected child as follows:

"As used in section 2151.01 to 2151.54, inclusive, of the Revised Code, 'neglected child' includes any child:

. . .

"(B) Who lacks proper parental care because of the faults or habits of his parents, . . . ;

"(C) Whose parents . . . neglects or refuses to provide him with
. . . other care necessary for his health, morals, or well-being;

"(D) Who . . . associates with vagrant, vicious, criminal, notorious, or immoral persons; . . . ."

Section 2151.04, Revised Code, in part defines a dependent child as
follows:

"As used in sections 2151.01 to 2151.54, inclusive, of the Revised
Code, 'dependent child' includes any child:

. . .

"(C) Whose condition or environment is such as to warrant the
state, in the interests of the child, in assuming his guardianship." [32]

The record shows clearly that these children have been kicked back and
forth between their parents like a football; that at the time the court
intervened, the children were sick and dirty. Perhaps, as the parties tried
to convince the court, this was a temporary condition that resulted from
the father's habit of climaxing his quarrels with their mother by snatch-
ing up the children and running off to his parents with them, but does
that make it proper parental care? . . .

. . . The record clearly shows that the children involved in this matter
have not had proper, or really any, parental care since the first of this
year, at least. It is clear also that such lack of proper parental care is
entirely the result of the faults of the parents, which are many, and of the
extremely bad habits of the parents.

It seems equally clear that parents to whom adultery is a normal course
of life, who are selfish and childish far beyond any reasonable limits, and
whose ideas of proper upbringing are to tell the children how vile each
other has been, are neglecting or refusing to provide them with care necessary for their morals or well-being.

There can be no doubt whatsoever that the parents, and at least some
of their friends and relations are vicious, criminal, or immoral persons,
and these children, young as they are, already are in almost constant close
association with these vicious, criminal and immoral persons.

This court therefore has no hesitancy in finding that upon the facts
disclosed by the evidence in this case, the children, Christine and Cynthia
Douglas, are neglected children under the Ohio statute.

[32] "Dependent" is more commonly used to describe a child whose condition
or circumstances is not attributable to his parents' fault. Thus subsection (A)
of the Ohio statute reads: "Who is homeless or destitute or without proper
care or support, through no fault of his parents, guardian, or custodian." Ohio
Rev. Code Ann. §2151.04(A) (Page 1954). See Herman, Scope and Purposes
of Juvenile Court Jurisdiction, 48 J. Crim. L., C. & P.S. 590 (1958). A child
may be adjudicated "dependent" if he needs some specialized medical care
which his parents are willing, but financially unable, to provide. For an interpretation of subsection (B) of the Ohio statute which is consistent with a nonfault theory of dependency, see In re Larry and Scott H——., page 410 infra.
— Ed.

The question of whether the children are also dependent children is somewhat more difficult to resolve. The only applicable portion of the statutes defining dependent child is paragraph C of the section 2151.04, R.C., set forth above. . . .

. . . [T]he Supreme Court, for over one hundred years, has been entirely clear and consistent in its expressions. For reasons best known to themselves, the Courts of Appeal, in considering problems arising under this statute, have rarely referred to the decisions of the Supreme Court, but have gone off on tangents of sentimental nonsense about the "sacred tie which exists between parents and children." In re Konneker, 30 Ohio App. 502, at page 510, 165 N.E. 850, at page 852.

The Supreme Court, with a much better grasp both of the facts of life and the fundamental and ancient legal principles which underlie the juvenile court law, has held:

"Neither of the parents has any rights that can be made to conflict with the welfare of the child." Gishwiler v. Dodez, 4 Ohio St. 615. . . .

It seems quite apparent that the welfare of the children here requires something better than that they be made the instruments of the childish, spiteful, and immoral purposes of their parents. . . .

Under the evidence in the present case, and the authorities cited, the court concludes that the children, Christine and Cynthia Douglas, are dependent children.

Having found the children here involved both neglected and dependent, the final question that arises is what disposition should be made of them[.] Section 2151.35, R.C. provides in part as follows:

". . . If the court finds that the child is . . . neglected or dependent, it may by order entered proceed as follows: "(A) Place the child on probation, under supervision in its own home, in the custody of a relative, in an institution, or in a certified foster home, wherever situate, upon such terms as the court shall determine; . . .

"(B) Commit the child temporarily or permanently . . . to a county department of welfare which has assumed the administration of child welfare, . . . or to any institution, or to any agency in Ohio or in another state authorized and qualified to provide or secure the care, treatment, or placement required in the particular case; . . . ."
[Court's quotation abbreviated by Eds.]

. . . It is the conclusion of this court that the welfare of these children requires that they be permanently committed to the Huron County Welfare Department. These children are of sufficiently tender years that if taken permanently and completely from the strife and immorality of their parents, they may lead happy and normal lives, and grow to responsible adulthood. This court cannot decide cases in a vacuum, and without reference to what experience with hundreds of cases of delinquent, neglected, and dependent children reveals. This court is now dealing with the fourth generation of some families whose cases are in its files and records. . . . It is almost certain, it is unquestionably highly probable, that if these little children are left with their families, by the time they reach adolescence, the courts will have to deal with them as delinquents; as adults they will have no better habits or morals than their parents, creating problems for the divorce court and the criminal courts. There are only remote possibilities of their growing up to be decent and honorable adults in an atmosphere of hate, lust, spite, and wickedness. Courts must deal with probabilities, not possibilities, and this court will so act. . . .

In re LARRY AND SCOTT H——.
192 N.E.2d 683 (Ohio Juv. Ct. 1963)

WHITLATCH, J. This cause came on for hearing on the petition of Mary E. Forbes, case worker for the Cuyahoga County Welfare Department, alleging that Larry and Scott H——, minors, ages five and four years, are dependent children, "in this that the condition or environment of the children is such as to warrant the State in the interest of the children in assuming their guardianship and that said children lack proper care by reason of the mental condition of their mother."

Larry and Scott H—— are the illegitimate children of Norma H——; they live with her in a three-room apartment in the Central area of Cleveland. The paternity of the children has not been legally established and the whereabouts of Mr. J——, the alleged father, is unknown. Mrs. H—— divorced her husband in 1954 and subsequently lived illicitly in Kansas City, Missouri with Mr. J——, who moved with her to Cleveland in 1956. Their association was discontinued in 1958; since that time, Mrs. H—— has apparently led a moral life. The petitioner testified that the housekeeping standards of Mrs. H—— were "fair." Witnesses for Mrs. H—— testified that her home was clean, that she took good care of the boys and that they were generally neat and clean. The court interviewed the two boys who gave the appearance of being healthy, happy, out-going children.

The only suggestion of improper care was the testimony of the petitioner that the mother had told her that on occasions, as punishment, she had sent the boys to bed without their dinner and that on these occasions she had given the boys vitamin pills in lieu of their meal. The mother also admitted that she had whipped the boys with a small strap; but this does not appear to have been excessive. Larry's school report card shows him to be a well adjusted boy who is receiving better than average grades.

Three psychiatrists testified as to the mother's mental condition. Dr. L——, the Court's psychiatrist, testified that from his examination and from the records of the Mount Sinai Hospital Psychiatric Clinic that the mother was "a chronic paranoid schizophrenic and she should be considered as completely and totally inadequate and incapable of handling the two children now with her." Dr. G——, who had seen the mother when she was in psychotic episode in November 1961, likewise diagnosed the mother as a chronic paranoid schizophrenic. At the time of his examination, the mother manifested delusional symptoms. She said, among other things, that Scott had been a fetus in the time of Moses and that he was aborted in the fourth month and his soul was imprisoned until released in her womb. She further said that Larry came from a camel tribe and was destined to do great things in the world. At the hearing in June of 1962, the mother was apparently free from these delusions and denied that she had ever had them. When asked if the mother's mental condition would prevent her from giving the children proper care, Dr. G—— answered that he did not know. Dr. G—— further testified that if the children were removed from the mother it might be necessary to hospitalize her since she might then become "an acute schizophrenic."

The third psychiatrist, Dr. D——, who examined the mother at the request of counsel for the mother, originally reported that he found "no evidence of a psychosis, a character disorder or a neurosis which would make it physically or emotionally unsafe for her children to be reared by her." However, after examining the medical records of Mount Sinai Hospital and conferring with Dr. L—— and Dr. G——, he reexamined the mother and found her partially recovered from a schizophrenic psychotic reaction[.] Dr. D—— testified that many who recover from such a psychosis are quite capable of caring for children but from his examination of the mother he had reason to doubt her capability. The mother did not take the witness stand but, with consent of counsel, the Court conferred with her privately. During this interview, the mother was completely rational although she did exhibit considerable tenseness. She denied ever having experienced the delusions reported by Dr. G——. The Court was unable to determine whether she was controlling enough not to mention the delusions, although possessed of them, or whether she was now free of the delusions and had no memory of ever experiencing them.

The Court also had available for consideration the recommendations of two professional social workers who were completely familiar with the psychiatric opinions related above and the social investigation relative to Mrs. H——'s background. They were poles apart in their conclusions. One recommended immediate removal of the children from the mother's home, maintaining that the mother's mental condition made it dangerous for a social worker to visit her home. The other social worker advised leaving the children with the mother, with a social worker making periodic visits in the home to supervise the mother's care of the children and to protect them from her if necessary.

The petitioner contends that in the best interest of the children they should be removed from their mother and since the mother's condition is claimed to be "chronic" it is clearly implied that the separation should be a permanent one. . . . [T]he Court has the authority [citation omitted] to commit them to the permanent custody of the County Welfare Department or another certified child-caring agency, which agency in turn would then be authorized to surrender them for adoption [citation omitted].

. . . The Court is required by law to act in the best interest of the child but this requirement applies *only* to the child who has been legally determined to be within the Court's jurisdiction. . . .

Are Larry and Scott H—— dependent children?

Sect. 2151.04 Revised Code in so far as applicable provides as follows: "As used in sections 2151.01 to 2151.54, inclusive, of the Revised Code, 'dependent child' includes any child:

"(A) . . .

"(B) Who lacks proper care or support by reason of the mental or physical condition of his parents, guardian, or custodian;

"(C) Whose condition or environment is such as to warrant the state, in the interests of the child, in assuming his guardianship";

. . . The mother has never been adjudged mentally incompetent and we do not suggest that such a proceeding is a necessary prerequisite to a finding of dependency under (B) above. However, it would seem that at least the same degree of proof would be necessary to prove mental incapacity to care for children as would be necessary to prove mental illness or deficiency. Moreover, under this dependency provision, it would appear to be necessary for the petitioner to produce not only evidence of the mother's mental incapacity, but also evidence showing that the children lacked *"proper care"* because of the mental incapacity. Here the evidence of lack of proper care is meager almost to the point of being non-existent. We would not consider the mother's means of punishing the children either cruel or unusual. While the law will not countenance unconscionable physical chastisement, the mother's use of the small strap does not fall in that category. Certain are we that in many American homes children are occasionally sent to bed without their dinner as punishment for misbehavior.

Is the "condition or environment" of the children such as to warrant the state, in the interest of the children, in assuming their guardianship. The Court's psychiatrist was of the opinion that the mother's mental condition made her actions unpredictable and that she could be a source of danger to her children, especially so since her children were involved in her delusions. One doesn't need special training in psychiatry to know that the mental illness of a mother could [effectively] destroy the parent-child relationship and could greatly impair the mother's ability to nurture and rear her children . . . .

In the case at bar, we are asked to take the children from their mother and place them with strangers. The mother has not been adjudged incompetent, she is not a patient in a mental hospital. Although her condition is described as "chronic," the psychiatrists are divided in their opinions as to the curability of her condition. . . .

As in no other Court, the judge in the Juvenile Court must take under consideration the opinions of psychiatrists, psychologists and social workers. But this is not to say that they are charged with the responsibility of making the judge's decision. The distinction between the role of the judge and the clinician must not be blurred. It is the clinician's job to make findings and recommendations; it is the judge's job to make the decision after careful consideration of the clinical reports and the evidence in the case. [Citation omitted.]

. . . Here the expert opinion is divided and while it is most helpful to the Court in accentuating the gravity of the Court's problem it is not immediately helpful in formulating a final decision. It is the opinion of the Court that a longer period of observation both by psychiatrists and social workers is necessary for the final disposition of this case. The diagnosis of all three psychiatrists was based to a large extent on the mother's mental condition when examined at the Mount Sinai Clinic six months before their testimony was adduced in Court. . . . It would seem that the existence of the condition of dependency must [as in the case of neglect] be made as of the time of the hearing on the charge. The court must have expert advice on the mother's mental condition as of the time his decision is made.

The Court therefore arranged for Mrs. H—— to be seen at the Fairhill Psychiatric Hospital at weekly intervals for further evaluation of her mental condition and for supervision of the children in Mrs. H——'s home by an experienced social worker who was to make frequent unannounced calls in the home. With the consent of counsel, the Court's decision was postponed pending final reports from the psychiatrist and the social worker.

At the conclusion of a seven-month period, the hospital psychiatrist, Dr. R——, reported that Mrs. H——'s "adjustment appears to be entirely satisfactory" and that the "case can be discontinued." The social worker reported that the mother was giving the children "excellent care," that continued close supervision of the case was no longer necessary and that the County Welfare Department would continue to see the family as an incident of relief administration.

Upon full consideration of all the evidence including the testimony of the lay and expert witnesses, the clinical reports and the Court's conferences with Mrs. H—— and her children, we conclude that there is not sufficient evidence to sustain the petition. Thus, the processes of psychiatry and social work coupled with due process of law permit the children to remain with their mother, when to remove them could result in traumatic maternal deprivation for the children and an acute schizophrenic breakdown for the mother. Larry and Scott H—— are found not to be dependent children.

NOTE

1. "Emotional neglect" refers to parental conduct of any kind which denies a child the love and affection he supposedly needs to become a healthy, emotionally stable, productive member of society. See, e.g., Cheney, A Suggested Statute and Policy for Child Welfare Protective Services in Connecticut: A Report for the Legislature 57-64 (1964) (unpublished manuscript on file at Yale Law School):

Statutory protection of a child's psychological welfare is . . . equally necessary. The healthy development of a child's personality is as essential to his ability to live in society as is his physical health. Judge Gill has expressed the hope that "future statutory draftsmen will acknowledge emotional neglect forthrightly," and they have done so in Minnesota[33] and Idaho.[34] Social workers and psychiatrists have also argued that judges and laws which do not recognize emotional neglect . . . are archaic. . . .

Translating this principle into action founders on the rock of uncertainty in psychiatric knowledge. Thus the U.S. Children's Bureau believes that at this point "more needs to be known about the emotionally disturbed child in terms of causation, treatment, etc." before a separate category of emotional neglect is made the basis of neglect jurisdiction. . . . The Bureau is fearful that caseworkers and courts in joint ignorance will act and damage a child when inaction would be more to his benefit. . . . [If] the psychological disturbance of the child manifested itself in symptomatic delinquent behavior, . . . the court would have authority to act under present law. The court could then make a disposition in view of the child's emotional situation. . . .

. . . [S]ince psychological welfare is so important to the child, and since a caseworker may intervene in cases of physical neglect and treat for emotional neglect, and since the juvenile court recognizes emotional neglect de facto, it would be a wise policy for the legislature to legitimize the situation and at the same time exert control. . . . The most essential element for mental health is an affectionate relationship between mother and child. Without this relationship in early life there can be no adequate development of the ego, and hence little capacity for abstract thought, which can lead to the child developing an unintegrated personality.[35] Following this in importance is the necessity for continuity of relationship between the mother or mother substitute and the child. Without a continuous relationship a stable, integrated personality probably will not develop . . . .

Thus the object of legislation designed to protect a child's psychological development can be met by establishing the denial of a continuous affectionate relationship as the criterion for intervention. . . .

The U.S. Children's Bureau fear of premature action can be met within this standard also. . . . Waiting for symptoms . . . is the only way to be sure that state intervention is based on reasonable

[33] Minn. Stat. Ann. §260.015(10)(c) (Supp. 1964): " 'Neglected child' means a child: . . . Who is without proper parental care because of the emotional, mental, or physical disability, or state of immaturity of his parent . . ." — Ed.

[34] Idaho Code Sec. 16-1625j (1963) "Emotional Maladjustment" means the condition of a child who has been denied proper parental love, or adequate affectionate parental association, and who behaves unnaturally and unrealistically in relation to normal situations, objects and other persons.

[35] Bowlby, Maternal Care and Mental Health 53 (1952) . . .

cause. Moreover, the symptoms should be of a severe nature, not only to protect the rights of the parents . . . , but because psycho-analysis has not yet developed truly predictive tools. . . . Accordingly absence of a continuous affectionate relationship should not support state interference until it has resulted in some objective abnormal development in the child.

Do you agree with this standard for emotional neglect? If not, how would you formulate a substitute? Compare Paulsen, The Delinquency, Neglect, & Dependency Jurisdiction of the Juvenile Court, in Justice for the Child 44, 67.

2. Professor Paulsen suggests that "the parent who 'neglects' falls below the very minimum of acceptable parental behavior." Id. at 74. Boehm, The Community and the Social Agency Define Neglect, 43 Child Welfare 453, 455-456 (1964), reports an attitude survey of a representative sample of "community leadership groups" in urban and rural areas of Minnesota. The 1400 respondents were presented with case vignettes involving a range of problems of varying seriousness. They were asked to decide in each case whether (A) the problems should be left to the family, (B) the family should be encouraged to seek help from a social agency, or (C) a social agency should intervene regardless of the family's wishes:

[F]airly clear patterns of opinion and conviction emerged. . . . [T]he *strongest support* for protective action (alternative C) was found in Case 2, the situation of the children with impetigo whose mother did not carry out medical recommendations. More than 80 percent . . . agreed that protective action was necessary. A *fairly strong support* (58 percent) for protective action was found in Case 1, the situation involving physical abuse in which the child was beaten and burnt as punishment for stealing.

. . . Community support for protective intervention in the situation of the promiscuous mother [who takes good physical care of her children] (48 percent) was stronger than for intervention in the case of the mildly delinquent boy [who has stolen from neighbors' yards] (40 percent).

The remaining two situations are those describing emotional neglect; in these situations, we find not only less community support for protective action, but a strong consensus of opinion *opposed* to protective intervention. In Case 5, the situation of the seriously withdrawn child whose parents refuse to seek psychiatric help, [73 per cent were opposed to intervention]. In Case 3, where the child's mother refuses to permit her any social contacts because of phobic reaction to disease, we find almost unanimous agreement [96 per cent] that protective intervention is not needed . . .

Less than 20 per cent of the respondents chose alternative A for Case 5. The study indicated that "social work respondents were substantially in agreement with the attitudes expressed by the other community groups and did not assign greater latitude or responsibility to the protective agency than did members of other occupations." On the other hand, occupation was significantly related to opinions concerning the need for help from a social agency on a voluntary basis. Id. at 457.[36]

3. Even though there has been no adjudication of neglect, of course, a family can obtain casework help from a public or private social agency. The term "protective service" is now widely used to describe agency contacts with a family which result from a complaint from a member of the community. The Child Welfare League's Standards provide:

> The agency providing protective service must have certain defined powers and responsibilities derived from law, . . . which require it to receive reports of and inquire into possible neglect, and in the interest of the child to enter into situations where its services have not been requested, and to remain in them until the child is receiving care he needs.[37]

But parents can certainly refuse to accept the agency's offer of help, and the Standards would not permit an agency to remove the child without either parental consent or a court order.[38] "Protective service," therefore, may involve no more than statutory recognition of the agency's responsibility to investigate family situations which may be harmful to children. Yet many descriptions of the concept seem to contemplate an extensively broadened, if vaguely defined, role for the agency:

> [The social worker] should have the right and responsibility
> * to offer help, although it may or may not be wanted and accepted
> * to make clear that the community cannot allow a situation harmful to a child to persist
> * to help carry out a treatment plan . . .
> * to decide whether neglect has ceased and the service may be terminated
> * to initiate action (even without the cooperation and consent of the parents, where necessary) to remove the child from the parents and obtain adequate care for him.[39]

The Standards also urge a broader definition of neglect for purposes of "protective service" than the legal definition — one that would not be limited by community standards of child care.[40] Considering the very real possibility that some parents may be coerced by an implied threat of juvenile court action if they refuse to cooperate with the agency,[41] the

[36] Another aspect of Dr. Boehm's study is described at page 399 supra.

[37] Child Welfare League of America, Inc., Standards for Child Protective Service 12 (1960).

[38] Ibid.

[39] Id. at 13.

[40] Id. at 6-7.

[41] See Cheney, A Suggested Statute and Policy for Child Welfare Protective Services in Connecticut: A Report for the Legislature 14 (1964) (unpublished manuscript on file at Yale Law School).

concept may contemplate a substantial enlargement of state authority to intrude upon family privacy.[42]

4. The Supplement to this casebook contains a complete report of the case of Gerry Cohen — a problem of "emotional neglect." The report includes excerpts from the social agency's file, psychiatric reports, a transcript of the several juvenile court hearings, and the decision of the state supreme court.

3. *The James Barr Case*: *Trial Transcript and Probation Officer's File*

a.   INTRODUCTION

The material which follows includes the entire file of a delinquency case decided in New York City under the provisions of the New York Family Court Act. The names and dates have been changed in order to preserve the anonymity of the persons involved. Items normally separated — such as the probation officer's entries and the psychiatric reports — have been arranged chronologically. The file has been edited only to delete repetitions.

The Act provides three jurisdictional categories: "neglected" children (§312), "delinquent" children (§712(a)), and "persons in need of supervision" (§712(b)). The pertinent provisions are set out below in the order in which they appear in the Act.

b.   GOVERNING STATUTES

§312.   "Neglected child"
A "neglected child" means a male less than sixteen years of age or a female less than eighteen years of age

(a) whose parent or other person legally responsible for his care does not adequately supply the child with food, clothing, shelter, education, or medical or surgical care, though financially able or offered financial means to do so; or

(b) who suffers or is likely to suffer serious harm from the improper guardianship, including lack of moral supervision or guidance, of his parents or other person legally responsible for his care and requires the aid of the court; or

---

[42] See, e.g., de Schweinitz & de Schweinitz, The Place of Authority in the Protective Function of the Public Welfare Agency 2 (Child Welfare League of America Bull. No. 7, Sept. 1946) ("[The social worker] must take from the parents what every man cherishes most of all, his right to live in privacy within his own walls. . . . The parents have lost their independence.") The statement is quoted by Cheney, note 41 supra, at 70. The 1962 amendments to the Social Security Act encourage the states to coordinate child welfare services with federally supported financial assistance programs. See Bell, Aid to Dependent Children (1965). It is not unlikely that "protective service" — whatever it means — will soon be a common public agency function.

(c) who has been abandoned or deserted by his parents or other person legally responsible for his care.[43]

§322.   Temporary removal on order of court before petition filed

(a) The family court may enter an order directing the temporary removal of a child from his home before the filing of a petition under section three hundred thirty-one, if

(i) the parent or other person legally responsible for the child's care is absent from home or, though present, was asked and refused to consent to the temporary removal of the child and was informed of an intent to apply for an order under this section; and

(ii) the child appears so to suffer from the neglect of his parent or other person legally responsible for his care that his immediate removal is necessary to avoid imminent danger to the child's life or health; and

(iii) there is not time enough to file a petition and hold a preliminary hearing under section three hundred twenty-eight to determine whether removal is required, pending final disposition of the petition.

§346.   Evidence

Only competent, material and relevant evidence may be admitted in an adjudicatory hearing; only material and relevant evidence may be admitted in a dispositional hearing.[44]

§347.   Sequence of hearings

(a) Upon completion of the adjudicatory hearing, the dispositional hearing may commence immediately after the required findings are made.

(b) Reports prepared by the probation service or a duly authorized agency for use by the court at any time prior to the making of an order of disposition shall be deemed confidential information furnished to the court which the court in a proper case may, in its discretion, withhold from or disclose in whole or in part to the law guardian,[45] counsel, party

---

[43] The statutory definitions of neglect vary widely from state to state.   Compare the Ohio provisions, page 407 supra, which are based on the Standard Juvenile Court Act (5 N.P.P.A.J. 323 (1959)).   Many of the neglect definitions purport to provide greater specificity; see, e.g., Minn. Stat. Ann. §260.015(10) (Supp. 1964).   But these definitions seldom circumscribe to any significant extent the scope of the juvenile court judge's discretion.   Cf. In re Douglas, page 405 supra. — Ed.

[44] Most Juvenile Court Acts simply provide that the hearings shall be "informal."   See, e.g., Ohio Rev. Code Ann. §2151 (Page 1954).   See also the authorities cited page 404 supra.   Sections 744 and 745 of the N.Y. Family Ct. Act include similar instructions for delinquency and "person in need of supervision" (hereinafter PINS) hearings; §744(b) requires that a jurisdictional determination be based on "a preponderance of the evidence.   For this purpose, an uncorroborated confession made out of court by a respondent is not sufficient."

Section 346 was amended in 1963 to substitute the words "a fact finding hearing" for "an adjudicatory hearing."   See N.Y. Laws 1963, c. 529, §3.   The same change is made in §347.   See N.Y. Laws 1963, c. 529, §4. — Ed.

[45] The New York Family Court Act includes provision for the appointment of a permanent staff of attorneys, called "law guardians," to represent minors appearing in the court, at their request or at the request of their parents. N.Y. Family Ct. Act §§241-249.   Not all juvenile courts provide counsel to alleged delinquents.   Even when the state's statute requires appointment of counsel on request, minors are usually not informed that they have the right to request counsel.   Many juvenile court judges feel that lawyers do not under-

in interest, or other appropriate person. Such reports may not be furnished to the court prior to the completion of an adjudicatory hearing, but may be used in a dispositional hearing.

§351. Order dismissing petition

If the allegations of a petition under this article are not established, or if the court concludes that its aid is not required on the record before it, the court shall dismiss the petition.

§352. Disposition on adjudication of neglect

At the conclusion of a dispositional hearing on a petition to determine neglect, the court shall enter an order of disposition:

(a) suspending judgment in accord with section three hundred fifty-three;

(b) discharging the child to the custody of his parents or other person responsible for his care in accord with section three hundred fifty-four; or

(c) placing the child in accord with section three hundred fifty-five.

§353. Suspended judgment

(a) Rules of court shall define permissible terms and conditions of a suspended judgment. These terms and conditions shall relate to the acts or omissions of the parent or other person legally responsible for the care of the child.

(b) The maximum duration of any term or condition of a suspended judgment is one year, unless the court finds at the conclusion of that period that exceptional circumstances require an extension thereof for an additional year.[46]

§354. Discharge to custody of parent or other person responsible for care; supervision or order of protection

(a) If the order of disposition discharges the child to the custody of his parent or other person responsible for his care, the court may place the person to whose custody the child is discharged under supervision of the probation service or may enter an order of protection under section three hundred fifty-six or both.[47]

(b) Rules of court shall define permissible terms and conditions of supervision under this section. . . .

§355. Placement

(a) For purposes of section three hundred fifty-two the court may place the child in the custody of a relative or other suitable person, or of the commissioner of public welfare or to such other officer, board or department as may be authorized to receive children as public charges, or a duly authorized association, agency, society or in an institution suitable for the placement of a neglected child.

---

stand, and therefore undermine, the court's purposes and methods. See generally Isaacs, The Role of the Lawyer in Representing Minors in the New Family Court, 12 Buffalo L. Rev. 501 (1963); Furlong, The Juvenile Court and the Lawyer, 3 J. Fam. L. 1 (1963). — Ed.

[46] New York Family Court Act §755 contains a nearly identical provision for delinquency and PINS dispositions. — Ed.

[47] This section was amended by N.Y. Laws 1963, c. 979, §3 to insert after "probation service" "or of a public welfare official or duly authorized agency." — Ed.

(b) Placements under this section may be for an initial period of eighteen months and the court in its discretion may at the expiration of that period make successive extensions for additional periods of one year each. The place in which or the person with which the child has been placed under this section shall submit a report at the end of the year of placement, making recommendations and giving such supporting data as is appropriate. The court on its own motion may, at the conclusion of any period of placement, hold a hearing concerning the need for continuing the placement.

(c) No placement may be made or continued under this section beyond the child's eighteenth birthday if male, or twentieth birthday if female, without his or her consent and in no event past his or her twenty-first birthday. . . .[48]

§356. Order of protection

The court may make an order of protection in assistance or as a condition of any other order made under this part. The order of protection may set forth reasonable conditions of behavior to be observed for a specified time by a person who is before the court and is a parent or a person legally responsible for the child's care or the spouse of the parent or other person legally responsible for the child's care, or both. Such an order may require any such person

(a) to stay away from the home, the other spouse or the child;

(b) to permit a parent to visit the child at stated periods;

(c) to abstain from offensive conduct against the child or against the other parent or against any person to whom custody of the child is awarded;

(d) to give proper attention to the care of the home;

(e) to refrain from acts of commission or omission that tend to make the home not a proper place for the child.

The court may also award custody of the child, during the term of the order of protection to either parent, or to an appropriate relative within the second degree. Nothing in this section gives the court power to place or board out any child or to commit a child to an institution or agency. In making orders of protection, the court shall so act as to insure that in the care, protection, discipline and guardianship of the child his religious faith shall be preserved and protected.[49]

§712. "Juvenile delinquent" and "person in need of supervision"

(a) "Juvenile delinquent" means a person over seven and less than sixteen years of age who does any act which, if done by an adult, would constitute a crime.[50]

---

[48] New York Family Court Act §756 contains a similar provision for delinquency and PINS dispositions. In §756, however, placement can be in the child's home, to the custody of a relative or other suitable person, or to "an authorized agency, or a youth opportunity center." For a criticism of the serious shortage of foster family and institutional care facilities for neglected children in New York, consult Polier, A View from the Bench 37-38 (N.C.C.D. 1964). And see pages 459-464 infra. — Ed.

[49] New York Family Court Act §759 contains an identical provision for delinquency and PINS dispositions. — Ed.

[50] Compare the D.C. provision, page 400 note 29 supra. For a description

(b) "Person in need of supervision" means a male less than sixteen years of age and a female less than eighteen years of age who is an habitual truant or who is incorrigible, ungovernable or habitually disobedient and beyond the lawful control of parent or other lawful authority.

§753. Disposition on adjudication of juvenile delinquency

Upon an adjudication of juvenile delinquency, the court shall enter an order of disposition:

(a) Suspending judgment in accord with section seven hundred fifty-five;

(b) Continuing the proceeding and placing the respondent in accord with section seven hundred fifty-six;

(c) Putting the respondent on probation in accord with section seven hundred fifty-seven; or

(d) Committing the respondent in accord with section seven hundred fifty-eight.

§754. Disposition on adjudication of person in need of supervision

Upon an adjudication of person in need of supervision, the court shall enter an order of disposition:

(a) Discharging the respondent with warning;

(b) Suspending judgment in accord with section seven hundred fifty-five;

(c) Continuing the proceeding and placing the respondent in accord with section seven hundred fifty-six; or

(d) Putting the respondent on probation in accord with section seven hundred fifty-seven.[51]

§757. Probation

(a) Rules of court shall define permissible terms and conditions of probation.

(b) The maximum period of probation in the case of a person adjudicated a juvenile delinquent shall not exceed two years and in the case of a person adjudicated in need of supervision shall not exceed one year. If the court finds at the conclusion of the original period that exceptional circumstances require an additional year of probation, the court may continue probation for an additional year.

§758. Commitment

(a) For purposes of section seven hundred fifty-three, the court may commit the respondent to the care and custody of an institution suitable for the commitment of a delinquent child maintained by the state or any

---

and analysis of the varieties of delinquency definition, see Herman, Scope and Purposes of Juvenile Court Jurisdiction, 48 J. Crim. L., C. & P.S. 593-595 (1958). — Ed.

[51] Although the original Act had created the PINS adjudication to preclude the use of delinquency dispositional powers for a child who was simply "incorrigible," the Family Court judges soon held that they had authority to "place" a PINS child in a state institution under §756 (see page 420 note 48 supra) even if they could not "commit" him to an institution under §758. See Matter of "Doe," 36 Misc. 2d 611, 232 N.Y.S.2d 715 (Family Ct. 1962). The legislature then amended the Act to give the Family Courts temporary authority to place PINS children in institutions. N.Y. Laws 1963, cc. 698, 810, 811. — Ed.

subdivision thereof or to an authorized agency, subject to the further orders of the court.[52]

(b) Upon an adjudication of delinquency of a person who is fifteen years of age at the time of the commission of any act which, if committed by an adult, would be assault in the first degree, as defined in section two hundred forty of the penal law, . . . commitment may be for males to Elmira reception center and for females to the care and custody of an association, agency, society or private religious institution such as: The Wayside Home School for Girls at Valley Stream, . . . or to any other appropriate institution authorized by law to receive such persons or to the care and custody of a suitable institution maintained by the state or any subdivision thereof, such as, Westfield state farm.

(c) No commitment under this section may exceed three years.

§764. Petition to terminate placement or commitment

Any parent or guardian or duly authorized agency or next friend of a person placed under section seven hundred fifty-six or committed under section seven hundred fifty-eight may petition to the court for an order terminating the placement or commitment. The petition must be verified and must show:

(a) that an application for release of the respondent was made to the duly authorized agency with which the child was placed or to the institution to which the respondent was committed;

(b) that the application was denied or was not granted within thirty days from the day application was made; and

(c) the grounds for the petition.

C.   PROBATION OFFICER'S FILE (1) [53]

Petition (Juvenile Delinquent)

> CHILD'S NAME ....James Barr, b. 11/10/54 NYC PS 3rd gr.
> ADDRESS ....1152 Apple Street
> FATHER'S NAME ....John Carter, address unknown
> MOTHER'S NAME ....Barbara Barr

8/15/63

Intake Section Report: Indicates that complainant, Mrs. H. Dolan, of 1144 Apple Street, in behalf of her daughter, Toni, age 8, alleges that

---

[52] This subdivision was amended by N.Y. Laws 1963, c. 477, §2, to insert after "subdivision thereof" "to a commissioner of public welfare." — Ed.

[53] The probation officer's file contains notes of his interviews with the persons involved and provides short descriptions of the papers and reports filed with the court. Some of the entries in the file are not included.

In New York, all delinquency matters are originally referred to an Intake Section. The intake worker is authorized "to confer with any person seeking to file a petition [and] the potential respondent . . . concerning the advisability of filing a petition" and may "adjust suitable cases before a petition is filed over which the court apparently would have jurisdiction." N.Y. Family Ct. Act §734(a). The intake worker may not prevent the filing of a petition by someone who demands access to the court. Most juvenile courts have some informal procedure for settling cases without adjudication. See Sheridan, Juvenile Court Intake, 2 J. Fam. L. 139 (1962), and page 444 infra. — Ed.

James stabbed Toni in the back on 8/2, and subsequently, during the week of 8/12, again chased after Toni, and threatened her with a knife.

Also in intake was Det. Allen, who indicated that he found James and sister in the home on occasions unsupervised. Report further indicated that mother was accompanied by her sister, and was very intoxicated, and barely able to give information.

James admitted the allegations, stated that he got the knife from the mother's key ring, and went after the girl since Toni and her sister always got after James and his sister. Delinquency petition filed.

Petition: Petitioner, Harriet Dolan, the mother of the person injured, alleges that on or about 8/2/63 at about 10 P.M. at 1144 Apple Street, New York, resp. did without just cause or provocation, chase petitioner's daughter, Toni, aged 8 yrs., and did stab her in the back with a pen-knife; that on 8/8/63 at about 2 P.M., he again chased Toni and threatened her with a knife.

d. FIRST HEARING

BEFORE: HON. ALLAN MAINE

Present:

JAMES BARR,	Respondent
MRS. HARRIET DOLAN,	Petitioner
TONI DOLAN,	Daughter of Petitioner
MRS. BARBARA BARR,	Mother of Respondent
MISS JANE CARSON,	Law Guardian for Respondent
HENRY ALLEN,	Det., Shield #1
MR. G. WHITE,	Court Reporting Probation Officer

THE COURT:	Officer, are you ready to proceed in this case? [54]
DET. ALLEN:	Yes.
THE COURT:	Madam, what is your name and address?
MRS. BARR:	Barbara Barr; 1152 Apple Street.
THE COURT:	How old is your son?
MRS. BARR:	Eight.
THE COURT:	Miss Carson, is there any statement you want to make?
MISS CARSON:	No.
COURT OFFICER:	State your name and address.
MRS. DOLAN:	Harriet Dolan, 1144 Apple Street.

BY THE COURT:

Q	Now, Madam, you have a daughter?
A	Yes, Toni Dolan.
Q	How old is she?
A	Eight.

[54] In many juvenile courts, whether or not the child has an attorney, no "prosecutor" presents the evidence of the delinquent act. As a result, the judge and the probation officer question the witnesses. — Ed.

Q	Did anything happen to her on August 2nd?
A	Yes.
Q	About what time of day was that?
A	Around — it was ten o'clock at night.
Q	Where?
A	It happened — it really happened between my house and the next house, on the sidewalk.
Q	And were you there when it happened?
A	No, I just came — I wasn't there.
Q	Somebody told you what happened?
A	No, Toni came in. I just left her out there and came —
Q	Where were you at the time?
A	I was in my room ironing.
Q	Is that a rooming house?
A	No, I have a home.
Q	I see. Now, I suppose she told you something?
A	Yes.
Q	Did you look at her and examine her?
A	After she told me she pulled down the back of her dress, that is when I saw.
Q	What did you see, Madam?
A	She was bleeding.
Q	Did she have a mark?
A	She had a mark.
The Court:	Come here. (Indicating) (Girl approaches Judge's bench.)
The Court:	What is your name?
Toni Dolan:	Toni Dolan.
The Court:	Now, show it to me. Where? (Petitioner displaying mark on daughter's back.) Did you see this, Miss Carson? (Indicating mark on girl's back.) Did you call a doctor? (To Mrs. Dolan.)
A	No, I called the police to get an ambulance.
Q	Did you have some medical assistance for this girl?
A	Yes, I did.
Q	Where?
A	Lincoln Hospital.
Q	Any stitches taken?
A	Yes, two stitches taken.
Q	Has she been back to the hospital?
A	Yes.
Q	How many times did she go to the hospital altogether?
A	Twice.
Q	Did she give you the name of some person who did that to her?
A	Yes.

Q	Now, do you know this boy here? (Indicating)
A	No, I don't know him. I have seen him on the street but I don't know him.
Q	Did you see him August the 8th?
A	No, I didn't. I did not see him.
Q	Did you talk to him at all?
A	No, I haven't talked to him. I haven't.
Q	You don't know who did that to your daughter?
A	No, I don't know.
Q	Now that happened on August 2nd and you say that on August 8th something else happened?
A	Yes.
Q	Now what happened that day at 2:00 P.M.?
A	Well, I sent her and my other daughter to the store and she claims that the boy —
MISS CARSON:	Object.
Q	Don't tell me what she said. State what you saw.
A	I did not see anything.
Q	But after she told you, did you talk to him?
A	No, I didn't.
THE COURT:	Any questions?
MISS CARSON:	No questions.
	HENRY ALLEN, Detective, New York City Police Department.
COURT OFFICER:	Your name, Shield Number and assignment.
THE WITNESS:	Detective Henry Allen, Shield Number 1, 1st Squad.

BY THE COURT:

Q	Officer, did you detain this boy?
A	I did.
Q	How old is this boy?
A	He is eight years old.
Q	Well, will you tell us what happened?
A	As a result of information I went to the Barr home last night.
Q	Last night?
A	Yes, at about 9:30 P.M. and I asked him if he cut Toni Dolan and he said yes. I asked him why did he do it and he said because she was chasing him. I asked him did you have any trouble with her, and he told me yes. And he also stated that he was protecting his sister because Toni Dolan beat her up one time with her fists.
Q	Did you ask him what he used to cut her up?
A	Yes, I did. He said a pocket knife. He told me his mother has the knife. His mother gave me this pocket knife. (Displaying pocket knife)

THE COURT:	Exhibit 1 deemed in evidence. (White pocket knife deemed marked Petitioner's Exhibit 1 in evidence.)
Q	Did he say he used this knife to cut her? (Indicating)
A	Yes.
Q	Where did he cut her?
A	He said he cut her in the back. I asked him how many times. He said once.
Q	Where was she at the time?
A	She was on the sidewalk in front of her house, according to the boy.
Q	Do you know anything about the incident on August 8?
A	All I know is the allegation.
THE COURT:	Any questions?
MISS CARSON:	Did you ask the boy if anything happened on August 8th?
A	Yes, I did. I asked him if he chased Toni Dolan on August 8th. He said, no, she was chasing him.
MISS CARSON:	I have no further questions.
THE COURT:	When did you learn about this cutting?
A	On the 12th, Your Honor. My partner knew about it on the second. I was on vacation.
THE COURT:	Anything else?
BY MISS CARSON:	
Q	Did you see James' sister?
A	Yes, I did.
Q	How old a girl is she?
A	About six years old.
Q	Did you ask her any questions about what happened that day?
A	Yes, she said that all the kids in the neighborhood picked on her and her brother, chased them.
Q	Did she say that the petitioner's girl here was picking on her that day?
A	Yes, she did. She didn't say that day, she said picks on her.
Q	Did you ask her whether the little girl had ever hit her?
A	No, madam, I didn't.
THE COURT:	Is the sister here today?
MISS CARSON:	She was just here. I have no further questions.
THE COURT:	Do you have any other witnesses?
COURT OFFICER:	The girl. Do you wish to swear her in?
BY THE COURT:	
Q	How old are you, Toni?
A	Five —

Q	Five?
A	Eight.
Q	Eight; do you go to school?
A	Yes.
Q	What grade are you in?
A	The second.

THE COURT:　　　We have to take her testimony without an oath.

MISS CARSON:　　All right.

BY THE COURT:

Q	Toni, do you know this boy?
A	Yes.
Q	What is his name?
A	Jimmie.
Q	Do you play with him sometimes?
A	Yes.
Q	And you play with his sister?
A	Yes.
Q	Did anything happen between you and Jimmie?
A	Yes.
Q	And what happened?
A	One day I was going to school and then I saw him. And then I said, "Hi Jimmie," and he said, "Hi." And then I said, "Jimmie, what grade are you in?" He said in the second. And then I said, "Where is your sister?" And he said, "In the house sleeping."
Q	What is that?
A	He said, "In the house sleeping." And then I went on to school.
Q	And then what happened after that?
A	Then I came home from school and then I saw him. I said, "Bye Jimmie," and I went into the house.
Q	Anything else happen that day?
A	No.
Q	Did anything happen about two weeks ago?
A	No.
Q	Did you see him on the sidewalk?
A	I saw him in the street.
Q	And do you remember when that was?
A	No.
Q	What happened that day?
A	I saw him in the street yesterday.
Q	Do you know what this is? (Indicating)
A	A knife.
Q	Now, did you ever see this knife in his hands?
A	Yes.
Q	When was that?
A	One day I was going to the store. And then he

said, "I am going to cut you."

Q	Did he cut you?
A	No.
Q	Did he cut you at any time?
A	No.
Q	Now, do you have a mark on your back here?
A	Yes.
Q	How did you get that?
A	He did it.
Q	He did it. And how did he do it?
A	See, I told him that I was sorry. Then I ran after him and I said, "Jimmie, I am sorry." He said, "Leave me alone." And as soon as I got up to him our mothers came and the next door neighbor came. And he had a knife and he did it and he shoved me.

By Miss Carson:

Q	Why were you running after him?
A	I ran after him and told him that I was sorry.
Q	Sorry for what?
A	Because I was bothering him.
Q	You were bothering him. How were you bothering him?
A	Then he said, "Leave me alone."
Q	Were you bothering his sister also?
A	No.
Q	What were you doing to him to bother him?
A	I just was making friends with him.
Q	You were making faces?
A	I was making friends with him so he wouldn't bother me.
Q	What were you sorry for?
A	That I was beating up his sister.
Q	And he just wanted you to leave him alone, is that right?
A	Yes.
Q	Did you leave him alone?
A	Yes, and then when I was running to my house then he took the knife and then he shoved it.
Q	Weren't you running to the house after you got hurt?
A	Yes.
Miss Carson:	No further questions.
The Court:	Madam, did you want to say anything here about this case?
Mrs. Barr:	Yes.
Miss Carson:	Your Honor, she is the mother of the boy; therefore

	it would be for the respondent. I want to make a motion first.
MRS. BARR:	I have nothing more to say. She said enough.
MISS CARSON:	I would like to ask the girl one more question.

BY MISS CARSON:

Q	Did you ever miss any time in school?
A	Yes.
Q	You had to do the first grade all over again?
A	No.
Q	Was it kindergarten you did over again?
A	No.
Q	Shouldn't you be in the third grade?
A	Yes.

MISS CARSON:	I have no further questions. I make a motion to dismiss the case. The petition alleges "without cause or provocation," that the boy stabbed the girl. I think by the girl's own testimony she has been beating up the sister you saw in court who is much smaller than herself, and the boy did stab her slightly. He was protecting his sister. I feel it is self-defense of the sister.
THE COURT:	I don't see how it is self-defense. Motion denied. (Whereupon, the respondent took the stand and the following occurred:)

BY MISS CARSON:

Q	James, how old are you?
A	Eight.
Q	Do you want to tell us what happened that night, the night you had the fight?
MRS. BARR:	Tell what happened.
THE COURT:	Quiet.
A	Me and my sister were playing in the yard and Toni came down and threw a rock and hit her. And then our mother said to stay in the house. When she went in the house then she started throwing things in the window and then she went and got her big sister. And then they all started saying bad words.
Q	How old is Toni's sister, do you know?
A	No.
Q	Is she much bigger than Toni?
A	Yes.
Q	Does she go to school?
A	Yes.
MRS. BARR:	They are outside. She must be about thirteen.
COURT OFFICER:	Quiet, madam.

Q	You say this bigger sister of Toni's was hitting your sister?
A	Yes.
Q	Was her hand open or closed?
A	It was closed. And then after that the next day she wrenched my sister's arm, and then she couldn't use it until a couple of days.
Q	Now, were you afraid for your sister when they were hitting her?
A	Yes.
Q	Did your sister ask you to help her?
A	Yes, she told me could you go out there and tell Toni to leave me alone? And I went out there to tell Toni. She ran and when they came back out the next time she threw a can at me.
Q	Did you have the knife with you then?
A	No.
Q	Where did you get the knife from?
A	From my mother's key ring.
Q	Did you tell Toni if she didn't leave her alone you were going to do something?
A	No.
Q	What was she doing when you used the knife?
A	Ah, when I was going to the store for my mother then she was sneaking up behind me. She punched me in my back with her fist. And then I turned around and I told her to leave me alone but she kept on running closer.
Q	Is that how it happened with the knife?
A	Yes.
Q	Did you run after her with the knife?
A	Yes.
Q	And before that she wouldn't leave you alone?
A	Yes.
Miss Carson:	No further questions.

By the Court:

Q	You ran after her with the knife?
A	Yes.
Q	And then you stabbed her in the back?
A	(Nodding)
Q	Is this the knife you used? (Indicating)
A	(Nodding)
Q	What did you do after you stabbed her?
A	I just went into the house.
Miss Carson:	I have no further questions. Your Honor, I still say that it is not without just cause or provocation. We are dealing with a girl who is evidently retarded.

	She is bigger than the boy and throwing cans and beating up his sister. This boy is only eight years old. I feel that both parties here are equally at fault and this case should be dismissed.
THE COURT:	Motion denied. The Court finds that this boy committed the acts alleged in the petition.
MR. WHITE:	Sir, there is no prior record on this boy at all. Intake seems to feel that a remand is necessary and an emergency psychiatric.[55] They feel this boy is seriously disturbed. They feel there might be some neglect in this family.
MISS CARSON:	I am sorry. I would like a little more information why they feel he is disturbed. There was a street brawl. He was protecting his little sister. It is not uncommon. The mother is drunk.
THE COURT:	Where is the father of this boy, madam?
MRS. BARR:	I don't know.
THE COURT:	How many children do you have?
MRS. BARR:	Two.
THE COURT:	Do you work?
MRS. BARR:	No, I am on welfare.
THE COURT:	How long have you been on welfare?
MRS. BARR:	About nine months. I was working last year.
THE COURT:	Were you drinking?
MRS. BARR:	Yes, I had a couple of drinks.
THE COURT:	Today?
MRS. BARR:	Last night. I haven't drunk nothing today.
THE COURT:	What did you drink last night?
MRS. BARR:	I drink whisky.
THE COURT:	You have your own apartment?
MRS. BARR:	Yes.
THE COURT:	How many rooms?
MRS. BARR:	A room and a half.
MISS CARSON:	I would still like to know how the boy is disturbed?

[55] Apparently, the intake worker discussed the case with the probation officer; the worker's file does not indicate that such a recommendation was made. "Remand" refers to the practice of placing the child in a temporary detention center pending an investigation used to determine the disposition which should be made of the case. Most juvenile court acts do not specify the circumstances under which the child can be detained. In New York, however, the judge's discretion to detain prior to an order of disposition can be exercised only if he finds that "unless the respondent is detained: (a) there is a substantial probability that he will not appear in court on the return date; or (b) there is a serious risk that he may before the return date do an act which if committed by an adult would constitute a crime." N.Y. Family Ct. Act §739.

For some data on, and trenchant criticism of, the frequency with which juvenile court judges use temporary detention — "a relic of an antiquated retributive penological thinking in much of its usages" — see Tappan, Juvenile Delinquency 185-187, 385-399 (1949). — Ed.

	Officer, has he given you any indication of being disturbed?
DET. ALLEN:	That is hard to say. When I first spoke to the boy, he was reluctant to answer, then later on he did.
MISS CARSON:	Has he shown any behavior that would seem to indicate something mentally wrong with him?
DET. ALLEN:	I wouldn't know.
THE COURT:	Miss Carson, it seems to me from the mother here —
MISS CARSON:	The mother may be disturbed and should be put away. They made a statement about the boy and I want to know whether he has shown any other behavior?
MRS. BARR:	He was scared.
THE COURT:	In the condition of this lady, I can see —
MISS CARSON:	I don't know why he should be remanded to Youth House.[56] His aunt is here, maybe he can go home with her. He is in his right grade in school. I don't see any evidence of it. If there's an investigation and if you feel he shouldn't go home with his mother, his aunt is here. She is apparently interested.
RESPONDENT'S AUNT:	I room with my sister, my twin sister.
MISS CARSON:	Do you have a place to keep this boy?
RESPONDENT'S AUNT:	Nothing like that.
THE COURT:	She can't take this boy. Remanded to where?
MR. WHITE:	Youth House, sir, for psychiatric examination, to September 12th.
THE COURT:	So ordered.

e. PROBATION OFFICER'S FILE (2) 9/12/63

Family History: P.O. obtained history regarding family from mother at office visit. Mother was born 26 yrs. ago in Penn., had 11th grade grammar school education. She came to N.Y. in 1953. She lived in a common law situation with Mr. John Carter until 1956 when he deserted her when she became pregnant with their 2nd child, Sally. Mother states that she did general factory work for awhile after the birth of Sally, and children were kept during the day by her sister. Mrs. Barr relates freely, and verbalized an interest in both children, did not accept that they are left unsupervised except for a few moments. Mrs. Barr admits that she was

---

[56] Youth House is the temporary detention facility of New York City. In 1949 Tappan described it as "an unusually fine institutional facility" and indicated that it had proved "that a shelter of considerable size can be managed . . . with effective results." Tappan, Juvenile Delinquency 408 (1949). More recently, however, the facility was seriously overcrowded — until the 1962 intake procedures began to reduce substantially the number of delinquency petitions. See Polier, A View from the Bench 9 (N.C.C.D. 1964). In 1961, 46.7 per cent of the children adjudicated delinquent on new petitions in New York City were remanded pending disposition. Id. at 2. — Ed.

intoxicated at the date of the last court hearing, but states she was very much upset over the court involvement. Mother insists that drinking is not a problem and is sure that it has not had any adverse effect on the children or her ability to care for them. P.O. did not interview Mrs. B. until the date of the return to court on 9/12/63, since she did not respond to letters sent to the home, and P.O. was unable to find her at home. Mother indicated that she had moved to her current address 1525 Jones Street a few days after the court hearing. Youth House Social Worker report indicated also the failure of mother to cooperate with social workers who had requested appts. with her. On the day of the 9/12 interview mother appeared completely sober.

Father: John Carter, age 28 was born in the Virgin Is., was employed as a porter, had 7th grade education. Mother states she does not know his whereabouts. Father was said to have provided very poor support for his children.

Siblings: James Barr, subject of this petition. Sally, age 6, attends PS 93, 1st grade, doing well. Mother states that Sally has not had a behavior problem in school.

Home: From June to mid-Sept. family lived at 1152 Apple St., but because of trouble with the Dolan children, family moved 2 weeks ago. $20 weekly rent is paid for the new 3 room accommodation. Mother states that James and his sister sleep in the one room, and she uses another room for a bedroom.

Religion: Mother claims to be of Protestant faith, Baptist denomination. There has been no baptism or church affiliation.

School: James attends PS 93, the 3rd grade. School report not yet received.

Child's History: Mother states that James weighed 7 lbs. 14 oz. at birth. Boy is said to have walked at 13 months, talked when 2. He had all shots. No serious illnesses or accidents. He was toilet trained early, but became enuretic later and still has the problem. He sleeps soundly, and eats well. Mother took him to a clinic about 2 yrs. ago. Mother describes boy as being quiet, timid, and not the type of child that she thought would hurt anyone.

Psychological report from Youth House, 9/12/63, that boy was seen on 8/19/63 and achieved a borderline intellectual functioning level on Wechsler I.Q. Tests. His potential was thought to be within dull-normal to average range, but probably handicapped by emotional problems. He tested as a non-reader. Projective test revealed that he was an extremely emotionally deprived individual, who is markedly rejected by peer and adult.[57]

P.O. interviewed James twice in the detention room. He was observed to be crying in the detention room on 8/15, and was brought back for interview at which time he seemed more relaxed and in a pleasant mood. J. was very playful during the interview, and though he attempted to

[57] The psychologist's report was not included in the file. The psychiatrist's report on James also summarizes the psychologist's findings. See page 436 infra. — Ed.

relate freely, his attention span appeared to be very short. He said he likes to watch baseball on T.V. He assured worker that he behaves himself in school and at home and in the community. He stated he was expected to be in the home by 7 or 8 every night. He liked going to the movies every Sat. with his sister. At the 2nd interview it is to be noted that the boy indicated he had a good time at Y.H. and did not mind returning there at all. He admitted the allegations of the petition, but did not appear to realize the seriousness of his act. No remorse whatever was indicated. He stated that the girl hurt and picked on him and his sister several times.

f.   YOUTH HOUSE ADJUSTMENT REPORT 9/12/63

James is a small slim boy who appears more immature than his chronological age. He is basically a happy-go-lucky child in his usual manner of passivity despite his occasional aggressive action. From the begining of his remand he quickly adjusted without serious homesickness or crying. He related fairly well with his group and was very interested in our recreational program particularly swimming and games. He described his first experience in Youth House as pleasant although he wants to go home.

During the interviews, James was very playful and he often moved from one position to another. His attention span seemed to be very short. His memory for recent, past or remote events is fairly reliable except for some confusions. James' intellectual functioning would also appear to be somewhat lower than boys of his age. His emotional deprivation is probably contributable, at least in part, to his limited intellectual functioning.

James has a problem of enuresis. His group supervisor reported that almost every night James wets his bed. His mother also stated that he has been having the same difficulty while he was at home. He was examined by a physician on 9-6-63, and the doctor indicated that there was no sign of an organically based condition.

During his detention period James was able to identify himself with his group, especially the boys of his size and age. He does manage to get along with his peers and is obedient to his group supervisors. One of his dormitory supervisors reported that James is talkative and playful. Yet this does not belie the fact that he is obedient. His mood is usually serious not without sporadic occasions of laughter. However, his general behavior pattern is favorable and commendable. He has made much progress in adjusting to group and dormitory living.

Mrs. Barr did not keep her appointments with us although we wrote her twice for a personal interview. She visited James three times and I have seen her on a visiting day. Mrs. Barr was a well developed young woman and was dressed properly. She impressed me as being very emotional. Her capacity to look at herself would appear to be somewhat weak.

During the short interview the mother stated that James' detention was entirely the blame of her neighborhood. With a talkative manner she made a quite lengthy statement about her neighborhood children's faults. She seemed somewhat upset with the detention. She is seeking a new place to live believing that James can adjust better in a new community. She is obviously concerned about his staying at the present address.

In describing James' behavior at home, Mrs. Barr said that he is passive, timid and tending to withdraw from his peers. She seemed anxious to make her son active. Although James has had difficulties with other children in the community he has no difficulty in establishing relationships with members of his group here.

I think that this boy can be helped by providing adequate supervision and emotional security and to interpret to the mother the boy's underlying problems and assisting her in handling him better.

We were unable to complete the psychiatric study for this boy because of not obtaining P.O. investigation report.

g.　PROBATION OFFICER'S FILE (3)

Court Action 9/12/63　P.O., boy, mother and law guardian present. Case adjourned to 9/30/63. (P.O. explained that he not been able to interview Mrs. Barr until that day and that she had moved to a new address. James kept in Youth House for psychiatric examination.)[58]

h.　YOUTH HOUSE PSYCHIATRIST'S REPORT 9/30/63

James Barr is an 8 year old boy remanded to Youth House for the first time.

Background information is certainly pertinent insofar as the youngster comes from a broken home. He lives with the mother and younger sister. Evidently the father deserted the family a long time ago. The father was never married to the mother.

There seems to be considerable evidence that the mother is a rather irresponsible individual who is not particularly cooperative in her dealings with interested agencies. For example we have documentation that the mother was intoxicated in court. She also did not prove cooperative in keeping appointments either with the probation officer or with the Youth House social worker. Appointments were repeatedly made and broken. It would probably be helpful to obtain a psychiatric evaluation of this mother.

Psychiatric Examination　James was seen on September 20, 1963. He is a small well developed superficially pleasant and cooperative boy. If one discusses unimportant matters with him he is pleasant, affable and cooperative. However this youngster's strong negativism and intense resentment is amply displayed when discussing other matters with him. The youngster actually refused for a long time to discuss the matter which brought him to Youth House. At first he said he did not remem-

---

[58] The transcript of the hearing indicates that no request was made to parole James to the custody of his mother. See page 431 note 55 supra. — Ed.

ber. Later on he blocked considerably and even attempted to falsify information. When all these tactics proved to no avail he simply blocked and refused to speak at all. In other words this is a youngster who has been enraged for a long period of time and has attempted to handle his overwhelming rage by repression and assuming a facade of affability and pleasantness. Beneath however this youngster is an extremely resentful boy who has been frustrated and therefore angered for a long time. His relationship to the mother must be a source of continuous anxiety and frustration to him. His relationship to his younger sister likewise seems to be a source of tension, anxiety and resentment.

The enragement this youngster feels is affecting his ability to function. He attempts to cover his feelings of anger by a rather naive, docile pleasant slightly retarded facade. His intellectual functioning is repressed because of his severe consequent constriction.

Psychotic mental content was not elicited. The youngster was able to think clearly and rationally provided that he could be encouraged to verbalize his thoughts. When he discussed inconsequential matters he was quite spontaneous and verbal but when he was encouraged to discuss charged material he would withdraw, become constricted, sullen, negativistic and uncooperative.

Undue depression, hallucinatory experiences or delusional preoccupations were not observed.

Intellectually this youngster is functioning far [below] his capacity at the present time. As mentioned previously the youngster's intellectual retardation is secondary to severe emotional problems, particularly his resentment which he is unable to deal with adequately.

Psychological Examination Psychological examination indicates that this youngster is presently functioning in the borderline category with a full scale I.Q. of 77. However his potential is estimated to be much higher, perhaps in the dull normal to average range. At the present time his performance scale I.Q. is 82.

Projective material indicates extreme emotional deprivation, rejection and confusion regarding his psychosexual role.

Diagnosis Adjustment reaction of childhood with the development of a passive aggressive personality pattern.

Summary James Barr comes from an unsatisfactory home situation which is deprived and barren. The father deserted many years ago. The mother seems to be far less than adequate, uncooperative and has been observed to be intoxicated during the present investigation.

James is not psychotic. However he is unable to deal with tremendous rage and resentment, presumably towards the inadequate mother figure, possibly also towards the younger sibling. Interestingly enough he assaulted a girl slightly younger than himself.

Our feelings are that this youngster is retarded because of emotional problems primarily.

Recommendations This youngster would be helped most adequately if admitted to a residential treatment center where intensive psychotherapy is available to him.   It would also be highly valuable if the mother could be evaluated psychiatrically.

i.   PROBATION OFFICER'S FILE (4)

9/30/63 P.O. discussed recommendations of psychiatrist with mother who promised cooperation and indicated willingness to see psychiatrist.

Court Action 9/30/63 P.O., boy, and mother present.   His Honor ordered clinic study on mother and exploration of placement facility for James.   Boy paroled in custody of parent to 10/29/63.[59]

10/4/63 Referral sent to Wiltwyck School.   Referral sent for psychiatric on Mrs. Barr.

10/6/63 Material returned from Wiltwyck indicating boy's I.Q. is too low.   Material forwarded to Children's Village.[60]

Court Action 10/29/63 Adjourned to 11/21 for placement and psychiatric reports.   Mother reported late for hearing and was reminded of appointment at Court Clinic on 10/31/63.

11/18/63 P.O. contacted Court Clinic.   Mother did not keep appointment.   New one given for 11/28/63.

11/20/63 P.O. made home visit at 1525 Jones Street.   The apt. is dark and dingy but is adequately furnished.   There is a toilet and bath inside the apt.   Mrs. Barr indicated that she forgot to keep clinic appointment. P.O. stressed importance of keeping next appointment and indicated failure to cooperate would result in more drastic court action.   Mother states boy is no problem in home or community but still doing poor work in school.

Court Action 11/21/63 Parole continued to 12/10/63.

12/5/63 Rejection letter from Children's Village indicating boy not suitable for their program.

12/6/63 Psych. Report dated 11/25/63 rec'd on Mrs. Barbara Barr:

Summary: Mrs. Barbara Barr, aged 29, appears to be of dull normal intelligence and not psychotic.   She intends to lead a life where somebody would support her.   At the present, she is fully satisfied living on Department of Welfare assistance.   She is an immature, inadequate woman who tries to avoid facing her problem by indulging in drinking.   Basically she is a depressed woman.   Her self-esteem is quite low and her sense of responsibility is inadequate.

Diagnostic Impression Passive-Dependent Personality With Tendency to Alcoholism.

Recommendation for Probation Record Mrs. Barbara Barr is trying to shed off the responsibilities and she herself would like to be taken care of.

[59] At the request of the probation officer, the judge specifically ordered referral to Wiltwyck School, a residential treatment center for emotionally disturbed boys, aged eight to twelve, with minimum I.Q. of 80: "THE COURT: This is pending placement referral?   MR. WHITE: I would like placement to be ordered now in order that I may be able to explore placement facilities.   THE COURT: Order exploration of placement facilities." — Ed.

[60] Children's Village is a residential treatment center for emotionally disturbed boys between the ages of nine and fifteen. — Ed.

She is willing to place her son, but wants to keep her daughter at home. Mrs. Barr should be referred to a family agency for counselling and she should be encouraged to attend AA Meetings that would prevent her from becoming an alcoholic. The Court should continue supervising this family.

j. SECOND HEARING 12/10/63

THE HONORABLE PETER SULLIVAN, JUDGE, PRESIDING[61]

MR. WHITE: The boy is here with his mother. A psychiatric report was ordered as to the mother and we were to get a report as to placement referrals. We have the report on the mother, your Honor, and we have a report from the school, indicating that they are unable to work with the boy.[62] This boy is nine years of age. There is a question as to whether the mother could accept this type of situation. I feel that she might, but then there is also the question of her condition. She admits to the problem as outlined in the psychiatric report. There is a girl, seven years old. I think, with some support from a case worker, that the mother might care for this one child. I feel that this boy, however, is too much. I feel that it would be in the best interests of the boy to go to Highland.[63] I have spoken to Mrs. James of the Protestant Big Sisters. She feels that they can help this family.

THE COURT: Have you discussed this placement planning with the mother?

MR. WHITE: Yes. There will be the parole worker at Highland who will be working with the mother once the boy is in the institution. The consideration of foster placement, even after the boy has been treated, is a possibility. I think the mother might recognize this. The rejection from Wiltwyck was based on the boy's I.Q. I pointed out to them that the examination indicated that he was —

MISS CARSON: I would like to ask the Court for a short adjournment. I would like to give some thought to this recommendation.

---

[61] It is not uncommon in New York City, especially where the probation officer's investigation is delayed, for the dispositional hearing to be conducted by a judge who did not hold the initial hearing. See Polier, A View from the Bench 12-14 (N.C.C.D. 1964). — Ed.

[62] A summary of the school report was not included in the probation officer's file. — Ed.

[63] Highland State Training School is described as an institution for delinquent boys, "12 to 13 years old, and those under 12 who are in need of placement and cannot be placed in any private institution, with a minimum IQ of 70, and no severe physical handicaps or psychosis." N.Y.C. Legal Aid Society, Manual of Residential Child-Care Facilities 10 (June 1963) (unpublished, on file in University of Minnesota Law Library). Highland holds 240 boys and provides group casework services. — Ed.

	I would like to discuss this with Mr. White. I think, in view of the age of this boy —
THE COURT:	How long an adjournment do you want?
MISS CARSON:	Sometime this afternoon.
THE COURT:	Will you be here this afternoon, mother?
MRS. BARR:	Yes.
THE COURT:	All right, two-fifteen.
MISS CARSON:	We feel that the mother might be amenable to case work service.

(Whereupon, the hearing was adjourned to 2:15 P.M., this date.)

(Respondent and mother of respondent before the Court.)

MR. WHITE:	Referral to Protestant Big Sisters for the mother and placement at Highland for the boy. I have explained all the recommendations to the mother and she is willing to accept the services of the Protestant Big Sisters and placement.
MISS CARSON:	There are a great many factors here and, of course, the fact that the boy is nine years old is a very big factor. I talked with the mother and she told me that if possible she would do whatever she could for James. I would like to ask the Court for a further adjournment for the purpose of looking into some other possible placement here, or treatment. I have made some preliminary inquiries, but I have not had sufficient time.
THE COURT:	What are the alternatives?
MISS CARSON:	One, the possibility of out-patient treatment; two, the possibility of placement, of course, in some setting other than Highland.
THE COURT:	What are those possibilities?
MR. WHITE:	There are some elements of neglect here which I did not pursue, because it was really an academic question because of placement, regardless of the category. What I had in mind was getting something started immediately. Highland is a good place —
THE COURT:	Yes, and we can get started immediately on this case work for the mother.
MISS CARSON:	The case work for the mother could get started immediately, anyway. That has —
THE COURT:	What are the alternatives?
MISS CARSON:	I would like to make inquiries.
THE COURT:	Do you have any objection to sending this boy to Highland State Training School?
MRS. BARR:	No.
THE COURT:	Placed at Highland.
MISS CARSON:	This boy is nine years old. I think there might be a possibility of getting him into another place. His mother would not care if he went to a Catholic school. I am only asking for an adjournment to look into these things.

MR. WHITE: Is the law guardian going to make referrals —
MISS CARSON: You said you were not able to contact the Astor Home.
THE COURT: I am informed that Astor Home has a waiting list of nine
                 months. I am not going to keep this boy out for nine
                 months. Placed at Highland with referral of mother to
                 Protestant Big Sisters.
MISS CARSON: Objection.[64]
THE COURT: Certainly.

NOTE

1. Was James Barr a "juvenile delinquent" within the meaning of the New York Family Court Act? Was he "neglected"? On which ground do you think the judge based his adjudication? His disposition?

2. What do you think Miss Carson viewed her role in the hearing to be? If you had been the Law Guardian representing James Barr, would you have done anything which Miss Carson failed to do? Compare Alexander, Constitutional Rights in the Juvenile Court, in Justice for the Child 82, 89:

> Good lawyers . . . are unquestionably of tremendous value to child
> and family. The honesty and intelligence of these lawyers generally
> enable them to see matters in true perspective and to employ their
> wisdom to advise their clients to seek what is best for the child in the
> long run; such lawyers do not attempt to . . . obtain what the cli-
> ents want but perhaps should not have. . . .
>   When, however, a lawyer appears who possesses no social con-
> science . . . , he seems impelled to earn his fee by putting on a show
> for his client. He must win his case by hook or by crook, "spring the
> kid," and get for his clients what they want regardless of ultimate
> consequences to child or family. Since, as a rule, there is no counsel
> to oppose him, he frequently succeeds — but to what end? So that
> the child can further pursue his delinquent ways? . . .

3. What was the judge's role in the Barr case? Should he have been playing any other role? What do you think the judge expected to accomplish by sending James to the Highland State Training School? If you had been the judge, would you have conducted the adjudicatory or the dispositional hearing in any other fashion? How would you have dealt with the problem presented by the case?

[64] See Polier, A View from the Bench 57 (N.C.C.D. 1964): "Aside from the question of responsibility to his client, the law guardian finds it almost impossible to play a constructive role at the dispositional hearing at this time because the sheer volume of cases and his lack of knowledge of community and placement services reduce his function to one of urging probation or accepting whatever placement is recommended by the probation officer or ordered by the court." See also page 450 infra. — Ed.

4. *Dispositional Powers of the Juvenile Court* [65]

a. SCOPE OF DISCRETION

YOUNGHUSBAND, THE DILEMMA OF THE JUVENILE COURT
33 Social Service Review 10-18 (1959)

. . . [A] great deal of human behavior is molded by the carrot in front of the donkey and the stick behind him. Progress no doubt consists in increasing the size of the carrot and decreasing the size of the stick. . . . Some idealists have dreamed of all carrot and no stick. But, as far as our present knowledge of human motivation goes, there seems to be no escape from an admixture of the pleasure principle and the reality principle. . . .

This leads to one of the basic dilemmas of juvenile courts. The delinquent children who come before these courts have ipso facto been accused in one way or another of breaking the law, of putting themselves, so to say, in a stick situation. Yet this in itself gives rise to a dilemma which Bernard Shaw expressed vividly when he said, "To punish a man you must injure him: to reform a man you must improve him: and men are not improved by injuries." It is for this reason that all enlightened juvenile court systems tend to concentrate on the offender rather than on the offense. . . .

It gives us a nice warm feeling to talk about treating persons rather than punishing offenses; but do not let us delude ourselves about it. It is comparatively easy, straightforward, precise, and measurable to punish offenses — an eye for an eye and a tooth for a tooth — whereas to understand and treat persons presupposes that we do in fact know how to diagnose and treat them and that we have the necessary facilities available. This is not a valid assumption. . . .

Thus what progressive societies have in fact done is to embark on juvenile court programs based on humane and enlightened motives, without knowing or having what it takes to produce the results which we feel should follow as a result of our humane intentions. In other words, our juvenile court systems are in one sense experimental laboratories in which we try to discover, empirically for the most part, the things we need to know in order to achieve the objectives of the system. They are, of course, Alice-in-Wonderland laboratories if we are thinking in scientific terms, but in this they do not differ from many other respected social institutions.

The issues are further complicated by interwoven strands which yet bear no immediate causal relation to each other, for example, holding the

[65] Space limitations preclude any effort to deal in depth with the many legal and social issues raised by these topics. Nor can we mention more than a small sample of the substantial literature. A similarly small sample of the relevant empirical research is described in the material which follows.

balance true between the interests of the offender and the interests of society and facing the further complication introduced by moral condemnation of delinquent acts. The necessity not to condemn and not to condone is . . . a concept that requires a high degree of maturity to accept, and still more to practice. . . .

. . . [T]here is the further problem that over the centuries we have evolved a highly sophisticated legal system, while our diagnostic and treatment systems are at a quite different, even rudimentary and fragmentary, stage of development. Moreover, those who serve in juvenile courts have varying degrees of competence to do so, coupled with widely differing views about the function of courts as social institutions and, therefore, of their responsibilities and aims in relation to individual offenders. . . . The result is that we are abandoning the certainties of a rigid legal system without yet being able to substitute another kind of certainty based upon scientifically determined diagnosis and treatment. This creates not only a dilemma but also a real danger in view of the unique characteristics of courts as social institutions — the fact that society intrusts to them the ultimate sanction of compulsion.

. . . Here is power, enforceable coercion, over people's lives: the power to order their lives, to make devastating mistakes sometimes, without their having the freedom to accept or reject the proposed solution to a problem. Power is always in its very nature dangerous. . . .

This power aspect of the courts — and therefore of the juvenile courts — is often forgotten or minimized or glossed over, or we comfort ourselves by thinking about our good intentions, as if they alone somehow guarantee the constructive use of power. . . . [W]hatever name we give to things — and we have a touching belief that we can alter the nature of something by changing its name — the fact of this ultimate sanction of coercion remains. . . .

The real heart of this dilemma is that there is no escape from this exercise of power . . . It is generally agreed to be necessary to take forcible steps to protect some children from some parents. It is also agreed to be necessary to restrain young people who break the rules of society. But, given the recognition of this need to coerce, the parallel necessity for safeguards immediately becomes apparent. . . .

. . . The advance we have made is to recognize that we, society, have got to go beyond limit-setting in order to try to discover why individual young people do not respond to the social controls which most observe. This understanding is necessary in order to be able to help them positively rather than negatively to accept these controls — in other words, to make their position better rather than worse as a result of a court appearance. This is the heart of the matter. . . .

There are, of course, several other complexities associated with limit-setting. One of these is that unless the limitations are part of the offender's own cultural assumptions they will merely be, in his eyes, arbitrary rules to be observed only if he cannot get away with breaking them. . . .

Generally, those who come before courts are some of the least law-abiding, the most frustrated and hostile, members of any community. Their attitudes are destructive, condemning, and punishing, for others if not for themselves. Add to this what courts have symbolized through the long centuries in which their role has been to find guilty, to sentence, and to punish. . . .

. . . [I]n general, the more treatment-centered the court, the greater the gulf between it and the assumptions of those who come before it, and therefore the greater the skill required to establish some basis for communication. Moreover, unless the court succeeds in establishing some real communication with the young people who come before it and with their parents, it will widen the gap between such families and society and so make the larger society, with its demands, controls, and rewards, even more remote, incomprehensible, and undesirable. . . .

Here, then, is a further dilemma of juvenile courts, in that if we set out to deal with persons and situations rather than with offenses and restitution we are introducing complexities which people themselves do not grasp. In this, to them, confused situation, those who come before the courts may feel lost and powerless against authority, not understanding what it is all about, and thus may be threatened as persons just because the aim of the courts is to treat them as persons. This is indeed no argument for going backwards in our juvenile court practices; it is an argument for trying to understand, as clearly as we are able, what courts mean to delinquent youth, and for trying to establish some basis of common understanding which will be more constructive than the old common understanding of finding guilty and punishing. . . .

. . . Inevitably, people appear before courts because decisions must be made. There is no evading decision-making — the use of power. This is why it is essential that the binding decision should be based as far as possible on knowledge. . . . Some of these decisions themselves are very much like surgery, in that they are often major interventions in the complex biological, psychological, and social web of relationships which constitutes human life. In actually making the decisions which comprise this social surgery on individual young people and their families, one is equally oppressed by power and powerlessness. Those who serve in the court have power to change the setting of people's lives, to sever them from their roots, but in making these drastic decisions they grope in darkness and ignorance of much that needs to be known in order to make a sound social diagnosis and prognosis. Although having negative power, they have very little positive power to give damaged young people what they really need — to be wanted in a happy home, to find socially acceptable satisfactions in the neighborhood, to get along well in school and work, and to have friends. Nevertheless, it is possible sometimes, primarily through good casework by probation officers, to set off a chain reaction that makes these desirable things begin to happen and thus reverses a destructive process.

NOTE

1. The scope of discretion available to juvenile courts is very broad. Fradkin, Disposition Dilemmas of American Juvenile Courts, in Justice for the Child 118, 126-127, lists the following "frequently encountered" dispositions:

1. Dismissal or discharge, with or without warning, and with or without restitution
2. Probation, . . . with or without conditions imposed by the court, and with or without restitution
3. Foster home placement, with or without probation . . .
4. Commitment to a state training school or to a religious or charitable institution
5. Adjudication and release on suspended sentence, with or without time limit, or imposition of sentence and suspension or execution of judgment . . .
6. Fines (Colorado only)
7. Commitment or transfer to a penal institution after initial placement in a juvenile institution
8. Commitment to a mental institution
9. Extension of probation upon the child's reaching majority when the case warrants additional supervision . . .
10. Temporary detention awaiting final disposition or prior to commitment to a state institution
11. Termination of probation prior to release from court jurisdiction
12. Revocation of probation and . . . institutional commitment.

See also N.Y. Family Ct. Act §§352-356, 753-758, pages 419-422 supra.

In addition, many cases are dealt with by what is euphemistically called "informal supervision," or "unofficial handling." This refers to juvenile court action which is not preceded by a petition alleging, or an adjudication finding, delinquent behavior. Although the juvenile courts in larger cities seem to prefer official disposition, the Children's Bureau estimated that, nationally, approximately 50 per cent of all delinquency matters are handled unofficially. Perlman, Statistical Aspects of Antisocial Behavior of the Minor in the United States 7 (U.S. Children's Bureau 1963). Fradkin, supra, at 123-124, explains the practice as a product of the judges' efforts to achieve a low delinquency rate to please the public and a high case volume to make appeals for additional funds less difficult. Fradkin adds that "[m]ost students of the juvenile court regard unofficial handling . . . as an unmitigated, unconstitutional evil." Id. at 124.

2. In many of the statutes no distinctions are made between neglected and delinquent children in describing the judge's dispositional alternatives. The discussion below is organized by types of disposition, not according to the type of adjudication. Nonetheless, the source of the court's jurisdiction does place some limits on the available disposition

alternatives. We have already seen that the New York legislature decided initially that the court should not be able to commit a PINS child to a state training school; some statutes prohibit placement of a neglected child in an institution used for "care . . . of delinquent children." See, e.g., Ark. Stat. Ann. §45-222 (1964). If delinquency institutions are designed to "treat" a child's "problems," why is it improper to provide the benefits of such a setting to neglected children? See pages 453-460 infra. Since a delinquency adjudication focuses on the child's behavior rather than the parents', in most states delinquent conduct would not be sufficient grounds for terminating a parent's "parental rights." See pages 464-471 infra. Of course, a juvenile court might adjudicate a child neglected by finding that his delinquent conduct is attributable to a lack of "proper parental care because of the faults or habits of his parents." See the Ohio statute, quoted page 407 supra. See also Minn. Stat. Ann. §260.015(10)(i) (Supp. 1964), defining as a neglected child one "[w]ho comes within the [definition of delinquent child], but whose conduct results in whole or in part from parental neglect."

3. Younghusband suggests (page 441 supra) that the juvenile court's dispositional authority "presupposes that we do in fact know how to diagnose and treat" delinquents. Yet social and behavioral scientists have reached no consensus as to the causes of delinquency by children or neglect by parents. Thus, although a "number of factors associated with delinquency have been identified in a fairly complete way," many of these "factors are part of broad social and economic problems which are themselves as difficult to control as is delinquency." U.S. Children's Bureau, Report to the Congress on Juvenile Delinquency 5 (1960). Matza, Delinquency and Drift 14-22 (1964), describes three major theories as to the causes of delinquency, and criticizes each of them:

> Biological theories seek the origins of delinquency in the physiological constitution of the offender. Most often these theories have stressed inherited characteristics . . . .
> The passing of biological theories of crime — from a period when they were dominant to contemporary times when, rightly or wrongly, a belief in them is used as an index of authoritarian personality — was part of the general decline of the biological explanation of human behavior. . . .
> . . . By contrast, the central thesis of personality theories is that a certain organization of personality developed in intimate interpersonal surroundings will result in criminal behavior. Like their biological predecessors, few personality theorists deny the relevance of other factors. Thus, the argument is framed in probabilistic terms — delinquency is a necessary or almost necessary outgrowth of a particular personality pattern. But the probabilistic construction is *not* a compromise with the belief in the constrained delinquent. Rather, it is . . . another promissory note in the form of the humble confession that all is not yet known. . . .
> . . . [T]he specific factors . . . are many and diffusely described.

Delinquency results from an aggressive or antisocial personality arising out of parental neglect, or perhaps overindulgence, or perhaps inconsistency; from a delinquent self-image arising out of criminal or delinquent role models, or perhaps an overbearing maternal figure . . . ; from specific neurotic syndromes . . . ; from the failure of parents to adequately socialize their children . . . ; from an attenuation of the ego culminating in an inability to fathom the realistic consequences of transgression . . .

The distinguishing feature of sociological theory . . . lies in the prominence of the social situation. . . . Social theory begins with the observation that there are gross differences in the rate of delinquency by class, by ethnic affiliation, by rural or urban residence, by region, and perhaps by nation and historical epoch. From these gross differences, the sociologist infers that something beyond the intimacy of family surroundings is operative in the emergence of delinquent patterns; something in the cultural and social atmosphere . . . .

. . . [T]he delinquent as portrayed in sociological theory is constrained through commitment to an ethical code which makes his misdeeds mandatory. The delinquent . . . is a rather normal youngster — except that he belongs to what is essentially a different though related culture. Instead of learning our precepts, he learns others. . . .

. . . It is quite fair to say that subculture is *the* central idea of the dominant sociological view of delinquency. . . . The carrier of the delinquent code is a group of peers or perhaps a neighborhood . . . [whose] function is merely to transmit to the individual neophyte a set of beliefs that are traditionally implanted in a certain section of society — by general consensus, the slum. . . .

The forces . . . vary depending on the sociological observer. Some posit one or another frustration or resentment as the source of delinquent beliefs; inflexible scholastic standards which favor middle-class youth; the inability of working class youth to effectively compete for status with better-trained boys in more privileged sectors of society . . . . Other theories focus on the delinquent consequences of disorganization in certain neighborhoods; the breakdown of community and family organizations; the corruption of legal authority . . . .

[These theories account] for too much delinquency. Taken at their terms, delinquency theories seem to predicate far more delinquency than actually occurs. If delinquents were in fact radically differentiated from the rest of conventional youth . . . , then involvement in delinquency would be more permanent and less transient, more pervasive and less intermittent than is apparently the case. . . .

Given the assumptions of constraint and differentiation, the frequency with which delinquents more or less reform is most perplexing. . . . Anywhere from 60 to 85 per cent of delinquents do not apparently become adult violators. Moreover, this reform seems to occur irrespective of intervention of correctional agencies and irrespective of the quality of correctional service.

Most theories of delinquency take no account of maturational reform; those that do often do so at the expense of violating their own assumptions regarding the constrained delinquent. . . .

Current knowledge as to the causes of "parental neglect" is not much more adequate. Consider, for example, the observations of psychiatrists who have tried to study the parents who subject their children to physical abuse. Kempe, et al., The Battered-Child Syndrome, 181 A.M.A.J. 17, 18 (1962):

> Psychiatric knowledge pertaining to the problem of the battered child is meager . . . .
>
> . . . In some of these published reports the parents, or at least the parent who inflicted the abuse, have been found to be of low intelligence. Often, they are described as psychopathic or sociopathic characters. . . . They are immature, impulsive, self-centered, hypersensitive, and quick to react with poorly controlled aggression. Data in some cases indicate that such attacking parents had themselves been subject to some degree of attack from their parents in their own childhood.
>
> Beating of children . . . . also occurs among people with good education and stable financial and social background. However, from the scant data that are available, it would appear that in these cases, too, there is a defect in character structure which allows aggressive impulses to be expressed too freely. There is also some suggestion that the attacking parent was subjected to similar abuse in childhood. . . .

Note also the comments on "emotional neglect" by Cheney, A Suggested Statute and Policy for Child Welfare Protective Services in Connecticut: A Report for the Legislature 57-64 (1964) (unpublished manuscript on file at Yale Law School) quoted at pages 413-415 supra, and the analysis of the "maternal deprivation" syndrome in Yarrow, Maternal Deprivation: Toward an Empirical and Conceptual Re-Evaluation, in Maternal Deprivation 3 (Child Welfare League of America, Inc. 1962); finally, consider the continuing debate as to the nature of parental neglect and as to the most appropriate method of treating it. See page 452 infra.

4. That knowledge about the causes of delinquency is scanty is well illustrated by the lack of consensus as to proper methods of preventing its occurrence. During the last thirty years, varied efforts, large scale and small, have been made to establish effective delinquency prevention programs. These programs, commonly dissociated from the processes of the juvenile courts, have utilized a variety of community action and therapeutic methods. Since both "prevention" and "delinquency" can be defined either very broadly or very narrowly, many of these programs cannot be compared — or even, perhaps, individually evaluated — with any ac-

curacy. Moreover, because many of the programs reflect differing causation theories, their methods may not be consistent. For an excellent description and tentative assessment of a number of these endeavors, and a review of the enormous volume of literature they have engendered, see Witmer & Tufts, The Effectiveness of Delinquency Prevention Programs (U.S. Children's Bureau Pub. No. 350, 1954).[66]

Probably the best known of these efforts is the Cambridge-Somerville Youth Study. It was unusual because it hypothesized that many potentially delinquent youths could be helped to avoid delinquency "if they were provided with the continued friendship and wise counsel of adults who were deeply interested in them and who could secure them access to whatever community services . . . they needed." Id. at 27.

Teachers, policemen, and settlement workers chose boys from two underprivileged areas who were presenting "difficulties" (e.g., showed delinquent tendencies). Data were gathered on the boys, and they were paired into two groups of 325 — a treatment group and a control group. For seven years the Study's counselors worked with the boys in the treatment group, but had no contact with boys in the control group. The Study was unique in providing an opportunity for empirical testing of the success of its methods.[67] The final report concluded that for some 21 per cent the treatment had been "definitely beneficial," and for another 16 per cent the counseling had been of "slight benefit" (10 per cent) or "temporary benefit" (6 per cent) in improving "social adjustment"; nonetheless, the Study's method could not be considered successful in preventing "official" (that is, apprehended) delinquent behavior:

At the end of the Study's service program, the police and court records of the treatment and control groups were compared. It was found that the two series of boys had nearly identical records. This was true whether the comparison was made on the basis of number of

[66] In recent years, the suggestion has often been made that minimum age requirements be lowered to permit some delinquent or delinquency-prone youths to work full time. Cohen and Rosenblum, Will Relaxing Child Labor Laws Help Prevent Delinquency?, 23 Fed. Prob., March 1959, p. 44, conclude that we do not have enough information to determine whether work would significantly reduce delinquency. Of course, permitting some fourteen- and fifteen-year-olds to work full time requires that they be permitted to drop out of school. See page 393 supra.

[67] The Study is evaluated in Powers & Witmer, An Experiment in the Prevention of Delinquency (1951). See also Teuber and Powers, Evaluating Therapy in a Delinquency Prevention Program, 21 Proceedings of the Assn. for Research in Nervous and Mental Disease 138-147 (1953), who report that treatment gradually became similar to more orthodox child guidance centers and to reflect principles of psychiatric social work. Staff attitudes were apparently divided as to the more appropriate treatment method. Teuber and Powers suggest that, without the control group and the objective indices of behavior, the Study would have resulted in "merely another report on eminently successful therapy." Id. at 145. At the end of the treatment period, the counselors believed that they had "substantially benefited" about two thirds of the boys, and slightly more than half the boys reported to interviewers that they had been helped. Id. at 140.

boys and frequency of appearance before the crime prevention bureau of the police department or the juvenile court, on the basis of seriousness of offense, or on the basis of commitment to correctional institutions for juveniles or for older offenders. . . .[68]

Perhaps equally important, the number of boys who became seriously delinquent was not large:

In all, less than 200 of the total 650 boys in the treatment and control groups ever appeared in juvenile court, and only 52 of these were sent to correctional institutions. By the time they were 17 to 22 years old about 10 percent had become serious, chronic offenders.[69]

Witmer and Tufts state that, if the aim is reduction of official delinquency, the Study's findings "provide some justification for the narrowing of attention to children already committing unlawful acts or clearly headed in that direction." [70]

Other types of action programs have included intense psychiatric therapy with individual children, neighborhood "cohesiveness" and group recreational facility programs, and work with delinquent gangs by adult "infiltration" of the membership. Witmer and Tufts conclude that recreational services, although liked by many of the boys, do not seem to deter delinquency; psychiatric treatment has not been sufficient to overcome seriously inadequate social conditions; group work services have not had much effect in deterring delinquency.[71] On the other hand, "a start toward identifying the kinds of measures that are likely to lessen the delinquent acts of particular types of children has been made"; "child guidance . . . has been found to be helpful to youngsters who suffer from mild personality disorders and to those whose problem behavior stems primarily from distortions in the parent-child relationship"; neighborhood associations have helped some youths in slum areas.[72]

If preventive efforts are to be feasible and successful, there should be some method of identifying children who are likely to become delinquent while they are still young enough for preventive treatment. After extensive longitudinal studies of delinquent youths, Sheldon and Eleanor Glueck devised an instrument to be used for this purpose. See Glueck & Glueck, Predicting Delinquency and Crime (1959). The Gluecks' studies have excited considerable controversy. Compare McCord, Book Review, 13 Stan. L. Rev. 210 (1960), with Herzog, Identifying Potential Delinquents 1 (U.S. Children's Bureau, Juvenile Delinquency Facts & Facets No. 5, 1960).

[68] Witmer & Tufts, The Effectiveness of Delinquency Prevention Programs 29 (U.S. Children's Bureau Pub. No. 350, 1954).
[69] Ibid.
[70] Id. at 4.
[71] Id. at 50.
[72] Ibid.

b. CASEWORK SERVICES FOR DELINQUENT AND
NEGLECTED CHILDREN

Of the extraordinarily broad range of alternatives open to the juvenile court judge in fashioning a dispositional order, "probation" for delinquents and "casework supervision" for neglected children are the most frequently utilized. Perlman estimated that in 1962 forty-nine per cent of all delinquency dispositions following a petition ordered probation.[73] Probation may be used only as a form of leniency for first offenders or as a method of policing the future conduct of the delinquent. In theory, however, it is conceived as a therapeutic experience — reforming the delinquent by providing accessible and nonjudgmental counsel for his problems of social and psychological adjustment. Thus the Guides for Juvenile Court Judges, promulgated by the National Probation and Parole Association in 1957, state (at 77):

> [W]hatever the intensity of the treatment program, the great advantage in using this disposition is that the youngster receives help with his problems while living in the very community in which he must learn to get along. . . . To be fully effective, however, leaving a youngster in the community assumes that there is available to the court a probation officer . . . capable of giving or of procuring the kind of treatment that will enable the child to work through his problems and achieve a satisfactory adjustment.

Unquestionably, for many delinquents the probation experience is in fact therapeutic. Nonetheless, whether assessed independently or in relation to other possible methods of treatment, very little is known about the efficacy of probation as either a rehabilitative or a recidivism-preventive device. Many of the empirical studies of probation have had serious research flaws. Moreover, most of the studies have used as an evaluative measure only recidivism rates — referring simply to new delinquency adjudications. Despite the inadequacies of such a measure[74] most investi-

---

[73] Perlman, Statistical Aspects of Antisocial Behavior of the Minor in the United States 10 (U.S. Children's Bureau 1963). The figures are based on monthly reports from 22 of the 30 courts serving the largest cities in the United States. Traffic offenses are excluded except for driving without a license. Ibid. For a variety of statistical analyses of delinquency and dispositional problems, see Lunden, Statistics on Delinquents and Delinquency (1964).

[74] See generally Schreiber, How Effective Are Services for the Treatment of Delinquents? 20-23 (U.S. Children's Bureau, Juvenile Delinquency Facts & Facets No. 9, 1960). Many delinquents are never apprehended, or, if apprehended, may not be referred or adjudicated delinquent. Much "recidivism" may be for violation of probation — quite a different matter from the kind of conduct which may result in an initial adjudication. Many of the studies do not indicate in what sense recidivism is used; few try to take account of the possible differences in training or methods of probation officers, etc. For these and other reasons, the results of discrete studies provide little basis for comparison. See id. at 4. Studies of institutional care "success" suffer from the same and similar difficulties. Ibid. See id. at 10-12.

gators have concluded that no better one can currently be devised. A recent review of the literature concluded:

> . . . [T]he failure rates during supervision ranged from 15 percent to 22 percent . . . [T]he post-probation rates, although they vary widely, tend to show higher failure and lower success rates. This is hardly surprising. . . . In the post-probation studies we have found success rates as low as 43 percent . . . and more success rates under than over 70 percent. We have found no claim that fewer than 15 percent "fail" during probation; and a majority report that more than 30 percent backslide after probation. . . .[75]

"Outcome" need not, and perhaps should not, be the ultimate criterion for assessing the adequacy of probation services. Nonetheless, the picture is not a bright one. Judge Polier remarked:

> In no area of the Juvenile Term's work is there a wider discrepancy between principle and practice than in the staffing of probation. . . .
>
> [A Mayor's Committee, appointed to study the probation system,] . . . acknowledging that the cost of replacing "inadequate and at times meaningless . . . services" with a sufficient number of competent personnel would be substantial, urged action on the ground that "failure to act promptly would augur consequences too distressing to contemplate." [Quotation abbreviated by Eds.]
>
> The report included a staff survey which found that so much time was spent on investigations that staff could not carry through on the supervision and treatment required. Probation officers were able to render only a meager amount of counseling; surveillance . . . was their major activity. . . .[76]

Consider also the data developed in the course of several statewide studies of juvenile courts:

> In another [state] less than 25 per cent of the chief probation officers and 50 per cent of the probation officers have a college degree. Over 60 per cent of the chief probation officers . . . have a high school education or less. In a field in which a case load of fifty is considered an absolute maximum by national authorities, 40 per cent of these probation officers were carrying caseloads ranging from 100 to 200, and 20 per cent had caseloads of over 200. One officer was "supervising" over 800 probationers.[77]

[75] Id. at 9.

[76] Polier, A View from the Bench 41-42 (N.C.C.D. 1964).

[77] McCrea, Juvenile Courts and Juvenile Probation, 3 N.P.P.A.J. 385, 390 (1957). See also Tappan, Juvenile Delinquency 315-316 (1949). A more recent survey, reported in Krueger, Survey of Probation Officers, 1959 (U.S. Children's Bureau, Juvenile Delinquency Facts & Facets No. 15, 1960), was considerably more optimistic: 85 per cent of the probation officers were college graduates; one out of ten had a graduate degree in social work, but almost 80 per cent had case loads over 100, 13 per cent over 300. The survey was of a "selected group" of 502 courts (id. at 1); the responses therefore may not include a representative sample.

No one knows how often juvenile court judges attach "conditions" to their probation orders, or what types of conditions are most common. Certainly issues involving probation conditions are not frequently brought to the attention of appellate courts. The Guides for Juvenile Court Judges mention a curfew, reasonably and realistically designed, as one possibility. N.P.P.A., Guides for Juvenile Court Judges 90 (1957). The Guides also advise the judge:

> Many youngsters . . . are confused because of contradictory or widely fluctuating limits at home. The court has an opportunity to provide a sense of security to each delinquent child through wise and sound design of the conditions it establishes . . . Good conditions of probation strengthen, rather than replace or undermine, family authority and responsibility. . . .

In re Trignani, 148 Pa. Super. 142, 24 A.2d 743 (1942), held improper a revocation of probation because the condition violated by the delinquent should not have been imposed. In compelling the youth to pay more than $1000 restitution to a woman he had injured with his car, the juvenile court had been primarily interested not in reforming the boy, but in determining his civil liability and in compensating the injured woman. See also Jones v. Commonwealth, 185 Va. 335, 38 S.E.2d 444 (1946) (juvenile court cannot, consistently with first amendment, order delinquent to attend Sunday school and church every Sunday for a year).

The most common initial disposition following an adjudication of neglect is to permit the child to remain with his family, under the supervision of a caseworker. The objective is to protect the child and to influence the parents to modify the behavior which led to the adjudication. Caseworkers commonly make use of the "authority" of the juvenile court to "set limits" for neglectful parents.[78] Very little is known about the success of casework with parents following an adjudication of neglect; it does seem to be true, however, that some families — often identified as "hard core" problem families — fail to make progress no matter how much casework or judicial attention is paid to their problems. Leontine Young studied a small group of public welfare agency files on parents who neglect or abuse their children; as to one category of parents she concluded:

> If the behavior of the parents in this sample is true generally for severely abusing parents, then the goal of casework must be permanent removal of the children from the home. . . . [S]hould not ameliorative measures always be attempted first? Are there not methods yet untried to alter or at least mitigate this kind of parental behavior? To the first question one can only say that always the facts must be known, studied, and documented, but beyond that amelioration can be attempted only for a limited time when the price of fail-

[78] See Young, Wednesday's Children 124-125 (1964), recommending that caseworkers treat "moderate neglect" parents as children: "they respond to strength . . . that makes the everyday rules within which they can find some direction." Cf. Standards for Child Protective Service 23-29 (Child Welfare League of America, Inc. 1960).

ure may be the suffering or death of a child. As for the second question, there can be no doubt that to seek new and effective means of mitigating parental behavior is of primary importance. The amount of human suffering that would be prevented is tremendous. What has to be faced at the present is the fact that we are not accomplishing enough with existing methods.[79]

Casework "success" in neglect cases will not be measurable until there is consensus as to the meaning of neglect; moreover, if the judge and the casework staff define neglect to include parental behavior or child-rearing practices which are common, and perhaps accepted, in the parents' milieu, it is very likely that casework supervision will be unsuccessful. The juvenile court judge's task becomes most difficult, and his responsibility most onerous, of course, when casework supervision has not ameliorated the causes of the original adjudication.

C. INSTITUTIONALIZATION

STATE v. MYERS
74 N.D. 297, 22 N.W.2d 199 (1946)

BURKE, J. The appellant, Frank Myers, was adjudged a delinquent minor in juvenile court of Cass County and committed to the State Training School. Both he and his mother, Eva Myers, have appealed from the order of commitment and have asked a trial anew in this court upon the entire record in the case. Appellants' request for a trial de novo is a proper one. . . .

There are two questions in the case. 1. Does the record establish that Frank Myers is delinquent in the degree which the statute requires as a jurisdictional basis for an order with respect to his custody? 2. The jurisdictional basis being established, was the order of commitment to the State Training School for the best interests of Frank Myers and the State of North Dakota?

The record discloses that Frank, who was 16 years old on November 7, 1945, is one of four sons of Eva Myers. When he was two years old the Myers' home was broken by divorce and Frank and his brothers were given into the mother's custody. Mrs. Myers worked as a cook in the Fargo Bus Depot and at other jobs. She kept her family together until 1941, when all four boys were committed to institutional care at the Lake Park Children's Home because of their mother's inability to provide for their support. In 1943, Mrs. Myers secured employment as a waitress in the Waldorf Liquor Store which has been described in the record and argument in the case as a "cocktail lounge" and "night club." She is still so employed. Her wages are twenty-five dollars a week and she testified that her tips average about the same amount.

In the spring of 1944, at the close of the school year, Frank left the

<hr/>

[79] Young, note 78 supra, at 116-117.

Children's Home at Lake Park with the approval of all interested parties. He secured employment at Hope, N.D., as a farm hand. He worked the entire summer in this employment and earned $125.00. In the fall he came to Fargo to live with his mother. He entered the ninth grade at the Roosevelt Junior High School. After school hours he worked at odd employments including the setting of pins in bowling alleys. He completed his school work with satisfactory grades and was promoted to the tenth grade. As soon as school was out in the summer of 1945, he found employment doing odd jobs of yard work. In July and August he worked for the Northern States Power Company doing a man's work as an ordinary laborer. He worked an eight hour day and was paid $73\frac{1}{2}$ cents an hour. His employer has testified to his ability and dependability. At the beginning of the current school year, he left this employment and entered the tenth grade at Fargo High School. In addition to his regular school work, he became a member of the football squad and continued to engage in gainful employment after school hours.

During all of the time after he left the Children's Home at Lake Park, Frank has purchased all of his clothes with his own earnings. At all times he has given his mother money to help defray their living expense and during the time he worked for the Northern States Power Company he paid her twenty dollars a month. At the time of the hearing in this case, on September 17, 1945, he had a balance of $185.00 in his savings account with the Northwestern Savings and Loan Assn., he had $200.00 in war bonds which he had purchased with his own savings and a $50.00 war bond which his mother had given him.

It appeared, however, that in March 1945, Frank was invited by two girl acquaintances to attend a party at the home of a Mrs. Selstrom, a place which later achieved scandalous notoriety. Frank attended this party and thereafter became one of a group of boys and girls who frequented this home. Mrs. Selstrom is a vicious woman. She is 24 years of age and while her husband was away in the army, made her home a rendezvous where boys and girls who were scarcely more than children might gather to engage in practices condemned both by the moral law and the law of the land. There they learned to drink intoxicating beverages purchased by Mrs. Selstrom for the most part with money they contributed for the purpose. There, some of them at least, learned and were afforded an opportunity to engage in sex delinquency. No doubt, their hostess was preceptress as well for she took one of the boys as her own paramour.

It is not contended that Frank was a participant in these immoral practices to the extent that others were. He stated that for the most part he just sat around and listened to the phonograph. He drank some of the whiskey and beer that were provided and on one occasion "loaned" Mrs. Selstrom two dollars with which she purchased intoxicating liquor. On another occasion he slept all night on the floor at the Selstrom home while Mrs. Selstrom and her particular friend occupied a bed in another room. The juvenile commissioner who investigated the affair thoroughly stated "as far as I know there is no question of sex delinquency in which he (Frank) was involved." Nevertheless, there is no question but that Frank was aware of what took place at the Selstrom home, and knowing it, he continued to go there until an automobile accident early in August 1945, focused official attention upon the disgraceful situation.

Section 27-1608, Rev Code 1943, provides:

"Except as otherwise provided by law, the court (juvenile) shall have original jurisdiction in all proceedings:

1. Concerning any child residing in or who is temporarily within the county:

  a. . . .

  b. . . .

  c. Who habitually associates with dissolute, vicious, or immoral persons, or who is leading an immoral or vicious life. . . ."

Clearly Frank's conduct was such as to bring him within the provisions of subsection c, supra, and the juvenile court therefore had jurisdiction to make an order with respect to his custody.

We thus reach the second question. Was the order committing Frank to the State Training School for his best interests and for the best interests of the State of North Dakota? The order of the juvenile judge makes it clear, that in reaching his decision he took into consideration the scandalous nature of the Selstrom affair as a whole, Frank's individual delinquency, the commitments that he had ordered in the cases of other participants in that affair who had been before him, the moral atmosphere of the City of Fargo, the fact that Frank's mother's working hours, which were from 6 o'clock p.m. until 1 o'clock a.m. made his supervision by her difficult, and the deterrent effect which the commitment would have upon other juveniles.

We realize that proper disposition of cases of juvenile delinquency requires a delicate balancing of mixed considerations and that even the most careful weighing of pertinent factors can only result in conclusions that are speculative to the extent that they attempt to predict the course of future events. Confidence that a correct conclusion has been reached must of necessity rest upon hope founded in experience, rather than on certainty. We think therefore that the problem should be approached in a spirit of optimism and that drastic remedies should not be invoked where we can have reasonable hope that lesser ones will have an equal if not a complete success.

What then are the factors to be considered and what relative weight is to be given to each? To what extent is the welfare of an individual delinquent to be counterbalanced by the good of the state? In one sense, a decision, which will help quiet public indignation over a scandalous condition which has arisen in a community, or which, because of its severity, will act as a forbidding example to other youngsters, may be said to be for the good of the state. But we do not think that, as used in the juvenile act, the phrase can be given such a broad interpretation. Considerations of expediency, the satisfaction of public indignation, or example are contrary to the whole spirit of the juvenile act. They are dependent on publicity to be effective for any purpose and all proceedings in juvenile court are declared by statute to be "confidential." Section 27-1606, Rev Code 1943. We therefore hold that the good of the State requires a child to be removed from a community only when his delinquency is such that he has become a danger to society either because of his own conduct or his influence upon others.

Whether Frank's influence will be detrimental to others depends largely upon what his future conduct will be. The question of what is best for the State is therefore inextricably intertwined with the question of what is best for Frank. The record shows that Frank has need for supervision. It also shows that he has not had proper supervision at home and that because of her working hours it will be difficult for his mother to give him the kind of supervision he needs. This situation, however, does not of necessity require a commitment to the State Training School. That institution is not without its disadvantages. Certainly if we can have reasonable hope that other measures will suffice, we should not resort to a commitment to the Training School. In this case we have that hope. The record does not disclose that Frank is incorrigible but rather that he has respect for parental authority. There is nothing in the record to indicate that Mrs. Myers, his mother, is not a fit person to exercise that authority. It is true, that in the past that authority was not sufficient to keep Frank from being led astray. But circumstances have changed. The source of Frank's contamination has been removed. His more vicious associates are no longer in Fargo. It is only at the State Training School that he could continue those associations. Mrs. Myers had not been aware of the nature of all of her son's activities. The evening he slept all night at the Selstrom home she thought that he was staying at the home of one of his school friends. It was not disclosed to her that his intimates were other than what they should be. Nevertheless, when he stayed out late nights she punished him by not permitting him to go out at all for a stated period. Now both Frank and his mother have undergone a difficult experience and we think the record shows them both to be people who will profit by that experience. . . .

After a full consideration of all the evidence we have concluded that it is not for Frank's best interests to commit him to the State Training School. We think that he has demonstrated traits of character that entitle him to another chance to show he can accommodate himself to the normal healthy life society requires of a sixteen year old boy. We think this end may be obtained under the mother's supervision if she has the full and friendly cooperation of the juvenile authorities. The order committing Frank Myers to the State Training School is therefore reversed and the case remanded to the Juvenile Court of Cass County.

BURR, J. (concurring specially). The statement in the foregoing decision, regarding the acts of the juvenile concerned, is to say the least, as favorable to him as is warranted. But the serious situation in which this boy finds himself is a matter of his own choosing, as well as that of home and social environment. Thus this court, as well as the juvenile court, is convinced he is a delinquent.

The record shows that some of the others involved in the same transactions were committed to the training school by the juvenile court. He is not being singled out, though some others were not committed. The juvenile court which had the whole sordid matter before it — and it is a situation which the opinions herein do not adequately describe for reasons quite obvious — has not completed its adjustment.

There is intimation that disposition of some more seriously involved had not yet been determined. The problem here, however, is what to do with *this* boy. The juvenile court was confronted with a condition and not a theory — an extremely serious situation involving numerous people.

The boy is shown to be industrious and thrifty. The situation in which he is involved centers around drinking parties in which he participated, drinking associations and the consequent results that promote immorality. He is in bad company of his own choosing and with evidence, patent to him, which should have caused him to avoid it.

The record shows considerable effort to find a place where he could be sent for proper supervision. Nothing came of this, except, apparently, a choice between commitment to the training school, or of leaving the boy in the custody of his mother. These seem to have been the alternatives left to the juvenile court, and the court states the boy should not remain in Fargo.

The juvenile court, far better acquainted with the actual state of affairs than we, felt the mother was not a fit person to have supervision. I can not subscribe to the assumption in the opinion that he should be left under the influence of his mother. I see nothing in the record which suggests any improvement in him under her supervision. Confessedly she is engaged in the very business of promoting such a situation. For over two years she has been a barmaid in a liquor store serving intoxicating liquor to customers; and this very business of hers is an inducement for her son to do as others are doing. She seems to think that because she earns $25 a week with an average of $20 per week tips in addition, and is thus employed she said from "after supper" until 1 A.M. for six days in the week, this shows she is capable of taking care of him and excuses the lack of good example and care.

The usual excuse "others are doing it" is given as justification of the mother's dereliction and of the boy's. When a mother engages in the very acts which are the cause of the downfall of her son and seems to think this is respectable, it is difficult for me to see how she can be considered a fit influence to direct his moral conduct. There is no indication in the record she intends to abandon the business in which she is engaged, and one can readily see how little good influence she would have with him when she herself is actively promoting the very situation which has contributed to her son's present state. The mother says the boy "is a very good student if he wants to work." She admits he did not do very well and gives as a reason, "I suppose he was running around at the Selstrom place and was not studying; that is what he told me himself."

The record [shows] definitely that arrangements had been made permitting him to enlist in the Merchant Marine. He has a brother in the Navy. In the record is the statement of his counsel that if the boy joined

the Merchant Marine "he will receive four years of instruction and training which will train him for life if he wishes to stay in the Navy."

It does not appear the juvenile court gave any consideration to this
possibility. While concurring in reversal and remand I believe it wise,
before the boy is committed to the training school for the crucial years
before him, to require the juvenile court to investigate this contingency,
and make further efforts to find a proper place for this boy so that he be
away from these evil influences which surround him.

NOTE

1. In theory at least, the reasons for institutionalizing a delinquent are
clear. The judge should be convinced

> that the youngster does not possess the resources to cope with the
> demands of community living, or that his aggressive impulses are so
> out of control that he constitutes a real and constant threat to the
> safety of the community. . . .
>
> The child for whom there is little hope of rehabilitation in the
> community is not easy to identify, but is usually characterized by the
> total deterioration of the relationships between himself and his par-
> ents or parent substitutes, often also of his teachers. . . .
>
> The child whose impulses are completely out of control is usually
> easy to identify by the violence and frequency of his acts of aggres-
> sion. The impulse-ridden child may not profit too much from insti-
> tutional life; but he is placed there in the first instance as a matter of
> protection to the community and while under the external controls
> of the institution may develop sufficient self-control to make possible
> return to the community under close supervision.[80]

The available statistics indicate that juvenile court judges have not always used institutional commitment as a "last resort." It has been estimated that in 1962 some 350 public and private institutions housed about
50,000 delinquents. "In any one year approximately 100,000 juveniles
are committed to or released from these schools." [81] One commentator
claims that "incorrigibility" charges result in a substantial number of
commitments,[82] but satisfactory statistics — showing either the judge's
reasons for ordering commitment, or even the offenses with which institutionalized delinquents were charged — seem to be unavailable. In recent
years apparently, commitments have represented a smaller percentage of
total juvenile court dispositions.[83] Yet the number of institutions has in-

[80] N.P.P.A., Guides for Juvenile Court Judges 77-78 (1957).

[81] Lunden, Statistics on Delinquents and Delinquency 245 (1964).

[82] Rubin, Legal Definition of Offenses by Children and Youths, 1960 U. Ill.
L.F. 512, 515.

[83] See Tappan, Juvenile Delinquency 426-427 (1949); Polier, A View from the
Bench 31 (N.C.C.D. 1964).

creased substantially, and requests are regularly made for additional institutional space with a greater variety of treatment facilities.[84]

The sincere desire to "individualize" treatment and rehabilitate the offender is of no great aid in the difficult, if not impossible, task of isolating those delinquents for whom a period in a "structured environment" may be profitable. It is not impossible, in fact, that the "parens patriae philosophy" may mask the difficulty of the task:

> [U]nder the dominance of the rehabilitative ideal, the language of therapy is frequently employed, wittingly or unwittingly, to disguise the true state of affairs that prevails in our custodial institutions. . . . In short, the language of therapy has frequently provided a formidable obstacle to a realistic analysis of the conditions that confront us. And realism in considering these problems is the one quality that we require above all others.[85]

2. No assessment of institutionalization can be attempted without a brief, albeit inadequate, glance at the institutions themselves. It is generally conceded that institutional facilities and programs, especially those financed and administered by the states, have been improved tremendously in the last decade. Yet additional efforts would apparently not be wasted:

> There are still institutions in which a modern Dickens could find abundant material for an up-to-date Dotheboys Hall. There are institutions in which the size of the population makes individualization a joke; there are institutions in which brutality (labeled "corporal punishment") is a sanctioned routine; there are institutions in which other humiliating physical punishments . . . are accepted. . . . That is the low-water mark, but it is far from the whole story. There are other institutions in which a skilled and devoted staff is rendering service in accord with the latest scientific procedures. . . . [N]o national survey of institutions . . . has been made. My guess, however, would be that as a whole, and conspicuous and well-known exceptions to the contrary, the picture is not one in which we can take much pride.[86]

The Children's Bureau reported to the Congress that institutional staff turnover in 1958 was more than 20 per cent; many of the staff were inexperienced and inadequately trained. Less than one out of every four social workers had completed graduate training; less than half the cottage personnel (the delinquents' immediate supervisors) had attended college;

[84] See, e.g., id. at 31-36. Although commitment is usually for an indefinite term, juveniles average about nine months in the institution. See Lunden, Statistics on Delinquents and Delinquency 258 (1964). Since almost half the institutions are overcrowded, to some extent the length of a delinquent's stay is determined by the pressure of new commitments. Id. at 258-259.

[85] Allen, The Borderland of Criminal Justice 33-34 (1964).

[86] Shaw, Juvenile Institutions and Juvenile Parole, 3 N.P.P.A.J. 404, 406 (1957).

three out of ten state training schools had no full- or part-time psychologists.[87]

The empirical studies of the value of commitment as a delinquency preventive, to the extent any inferences may be permissible, are equally discouraging. Schreiber's review of the literature concluded:

[T]here may be more doubt about success rates than about failure rates. Despite a certain number of misleading entries due to unjustified or purely formal arrests, . . . the failure rates probably represent minimal figures. On the other hand, we know that a considerable proportion of delinquencies go undetected. It may be assumed, therefore, that success rates based on official non-recidivism probably represent maximum figures. . . .

It seems reasonable to conclude, then, that more than . . . 40 percent probably "fail" after a period in a training school.

These figures do not tell us which programs produce the best results with which boys; but they do tell us that the record of adults in helping juvenile delinquents is far worse than the record of juveniles with regard to becoming delinquent. . . .[88]

d.   FOSTER CARE FOR NEGLECTED CHILDREN

In 1962, 256,000 children were in foster care, some 31 per cent of them in institutions of all varieties. See Wolins & Piliavin, Institution or Foster Family, A Century of Debate 37 (Child Welfare League of America, Inc. 1964). Foster-family care is

the child welfare service which provides substitute family care for a planned period for a child when his own family cannot care for him for a temporary or extended period . . .
The distinctive component of foster family care is the development and use of the foster family home to provide substitute family life experiences, together with casework and other treatment services for both the child and his parents.[89]

[87] U.S. Children's Bureau, Report to the Congress on Juvenile Delinquency 43 (1960).

[88] Schreiber, How Effective Are Services for the Treatment of Delinquents? 12-13 (U.S. Children's Bureau, Juvenile Delinquency Facts & Facets No. 9, 1960). See also Weeks, Youthful Offenders at Highfields (1958), describing an effort to compare the results achieved by an open, work-oriented, group therapy institution with those of a more traditional "training school." One difficulty with the comparison was that juvenile judges seemed to assign less difficult youths to the open institution.

[89] Lewis, Foster-Family Care: Has It Fulfilled Its Promise?, 355 Annals, Sept. 1964, pp. 31, 32, quoting Standards for Foster Family Care 5 (Child Welfare League of America, Inc. 1959).

Foster-family care has been utilized as a treatment method for delinquents as well. See Fradkin, Disposition Dilemmas of American Juvenile Courts, in Justice for the Child 118; Kellar, Court Foster Home Program, 4 N.P.P.A.J. 57 (1958); Hunt, Foster Care for Delinquent Girls, 9 Children 183 (1962). But foster-family care is not a common delinquency disposition — because foster

Utilization of foster-family care involves some assumptions in addition to belief in the reliability of diagnostic and prognostic judgments in individual cases. To believe that foster-family care has therapeutic efficacy, one must place

> great emphasis upon the nuclear family as the preferred setting for the basic socialization experiences of youth in general and foster children specifically. Secondly, the therapeutic adequacy of parent surrogates . . . [must be] believed to be determined by the presence of more or less well-defined attributes that typically have been associated with mature parents and healthy families.[90]

Even if only the "protective" nature of foster-family placement is emphasized, placement assumes in each case that any damage, to the child or to the family, caused by the placement is less harmful than is the damage being caused by the child's present circumstances.

In recent years, these assumptions have been questioned and the general quality of foster-family care deplored. Eisenberg, reporting a study of children in foster-family care referred for psychiatric consultation, commented on the

> rather persuasive, if still incomplete, evidence that throughout the United States children in foster care are experiencing high rates of psychiatric disturbance.
>
> Is foster care to be held responsible for this psychiatric morbidity? Might it not be an irreversible consequence of what had happened to these children before they came into care? It is widely agreed that emotional and intellectual neglect in early childhood, the syndrome known as maternal deprivation, can result in defects in intelligence and personality. Many foster children have experienced deprivation; many exhibit symptoms interpretable as the sequelae of such an experience. However, the clinical characteristics displayed by the child subjected to deprivation are related to the adequacy of replacement measures as well as to the severity and duration of the deprivation and, perhaps, to individual vulnerability. . . . Certainly, there is little reason to anticipate favorable change when the care provided is marginal, let alone grossly inadequate, as our findings emphasize. Indeed, our data and those presented by Boehm suggest the possibility that symptoms of emotional disorder may be more prominent after a period in foster care than upon entering it.[91]
>
> If we must admit that we cannot yet offer decisive evidence as to

---

families have been difficult to find and because child welfare personnel have not supported their use.

[90] Wolins & Piliavin, Institution or Foster Family, A Century of Debate 4 (Child Welfare League of America, Inc. 1964).

[91] Careful examination of this disturbing possibility will require data obtained by a prospective longitudinal study of a representative sample of cases; conclusions obtained from a retrospective record search of a selected sample can be misleading (and I hope they are in this matter).

the reversibility of the psychopathology in children who enter foster care, we can also agree that its irreversibility has not been demonstrated. . . . It is painfully evident that, if they are to be helped, they require a great deal more than currently is offered to them.

In the midst of a nation whose affluence is unparalleled in the history of the world, welfare agencies are not being granted the public funds necessary to provide adequate casework services and to recruit enough foster homes. Many children languish in uncovered caseloads, their course unknown until a crisis arises. Those fortunate enough to have a caseworker may not keep her long enough to develop ties that might have insulated them against the vicissitudes of foster care. The urgency of the need for homes and the shortage of skilled casework result in insufficient study of prospective homes and the overutilization of those homes that are available. . . .

Agencies, harassed by overwhelming numbers, continue to employ euphemistic definitions that fail to reflect the reality of daily work. Children, left in "temporary" care for as long as two or three years for lack of other provisions, may suddenly be moved, after they have formed a meaningful attachment to the shelter home, in order to provide what is called a "permanent" home. Permanence is the fiction of foster care. . . .

Is it not time that we re-examine the very nature of foster care itself? The instability of foster homes, the shortage of adequate homes, the inability to provide continuity of worker, supervisor, and foster parent — all these factors combine to suggest that group homes deserve to be given more weight in planning. For some children, group homes are clearly preferable and always will be. But even for the child who might have settled into a foster home (if and when we had one for him), may not a durable group home be a better solution than a procession through a series of inadequate foster homes? [92] . . . [T]he insistence on foster care as the only method may be anachronistic in an era in which the institution of the family itself is undergoing rapid change.

Once we recognize the harsh realities of contemporary foster care, it becomes relevant to wonder whether we are not too ready to remove children from their homes. Might we not do more for children by enriching A.D.C. programs, public housing, health services, marriage counseling, and family agencies so as to preserve the family of origin? [93]

[92] For a discussion of this relatively new concept in foster care, consult Gula, Group Homes — New and Differentiated Tools in Child Welfare, 43 Child Welfare 393 (1964). Eisenberg's figures indicate a disproportionate number of foster-family replacements among the children referred for psychiatric consultation. Maas and Engler, Children in Need of Parents (1959), studied the children in foster care in nine representative communities. In six of them 25 per cent or more of the children in public foster care had experienced not less than four moves following removal from their parents. — Ed.

[93] Eisenberg, The Sins of the Fathers: Urban Decay and Social Pathology, 32 Am. J. Orthopsychiatry 5, 14-15 (1962). See also Lewis, Foster-Family Care: Has It Fulfilled Its Promise?, 355 Annals 31. 36-41 (1964).

Although the data required for comparative evaluation have been scarce, institutional care facilities and services have received just as much criticism as has the quality of foster-family care. See, e.g., Fraiberg, A Therapeutic Approach to Reactive Ego Disturbances in Children in Placement, 32 Am. J. Orthopsychiatry 18, 29 (1962) ("in . . . most . . . institutions that provide custodial care . . . we have no clinical facilities and the houseparents ordinarily have little training to equip them to understand the complexities of child behavior following placement"). It is possible, of course, that the child's development will not be affected in any fashion by the type or quality of foster care he receives. See Maas, The Young Adult Adjustment of Twenty Wartime Nursery Children, 42 Child Welfare 57 (1963), excerpts of which appear at pages 157-158 supra. Maas compared the adjustment of fifteen English children who had been placed in three different nurseries during World War II. The nurseries differed in several respects: in the numbers of children and staff; in the children's relationships with their parents during their time in placement; in the staff orientation to the children and their needs; and in staff methods of handling the children. Maas concluded:

> Examination of these ratings by nursery group reveals that the graduates of the somewhat firm, if not stern, and suppressive small Welsh Nursery E appear as young adults to be essentially no better or worse adjusted than the graduates of the psychologically sophisticated and much larger Nursery N. The group that is clearly the best off is the one from the day nursery school evacuated as a unit — Nursery S, with its faith in God, King, and denial and its rather inspirational, repressive, and possessive approach to the children.[94]

Maas also found that, as a group, the children's young adult adjustment had not been significantly affected by their placement experience.

The most important issues posed by foster care — issues that cannot be examined without assessing the quality of available foster-care facilities and their efficacy as therapeutic devices — concern the scope of judicial discretion to remove a child from his home against his parents' wishes. Obviously the problem is quite different if the parents consent to placement, but it seems likely that some juvenile court placements to which the parents agree should not be considered consensual. If Dr. Bowlby's "maternal deprivation" thesis is valid (see page 150 supra), in any given case the risks to the child which placement entails may well outweigh any disadvantages the home has, or any possible therapeutic value of a foster home. Dr. Witmer indicates that child welfare workers take such risks into account in recommending placement:

> Practitioners . . . have long recognized that "separation" may be for the best in some cases, and they have tried to lessen the deprivation this may entail. They have become more questioning, however, about the criteria for determining whether and when separation should take place. They have come to suspect, too, that for some

---

[94] 42 Child Welfare at 69.

children, even a depriving home may be a home for [all] that — possibly better than even a fairly good foster arrangement.[95]

Very little is known of the decision-making process which precedes an agency request that a particular neglected child be placed in foster care. The few research efforts, if they can be considered reliable, suggest that petitions requesting placement should receive careful judicial scrutiny.[96] On the other hand, the appellate opinions (and the juvenile court decisions they affirm or reverse) hardly inspire confidence in the ability of judges to formulate and apply consistently criteria appropriate to such a delicate responsibility.[97]

e. TERMINATION OF PARENTAL RIGHTS

STATE OF UTAH, in the Interest of L.J.J.
11 Utah 2d 393, 360 P.2d 486 (1961)

WADE, C.J. Mr. and Mrs. B——, petitioners in the juvenile court, appeal from the decision of that court refusing to allow a hearing of their petition for the custody of eight minor children. The appellants are the father and mother of six of the children, and Mrs. B—— is the mother of the two older children who were born to her by previous marriages.

On account of excessive drinking by the appellants, on June 20, 1959, the juvenile court made an order declaring all of the children neglected and placed them . . . under the protective supervision of the State Department of Public Welfare, but returned them to the custody of the appellants, the natural parents, upon condition that such parents would not drink intoxicating liquor or frequent taverns. Appellants resumed their drinking and a petition was filed in the juvenile court to take the custody of the children from them, and appellants were served with notice to appear . . . [T]hey took the children and left the state. In December of 1959, the appellants returned with the children to this state, upon which

---

[95] Witmer, Introduction, in Maternal Deprivation 2 (Child Welfare League of America, Inc. 1962).

[96] See, e.g., Briar, Clinical Judgment in Foster Care Placement, 42 Child Welfare 161, 168 (1963), concluding, inter alia, that "although there was a high degree of consensus among the social workers . . . regarding their diagnostic assessments . . . , consensus was very low for their prognoses and their placement formulations." But see Fanshel, Commentary, id. at 169, severely criticizing Briar's methodology and conclusions. See also Wolins & Piliavin, Institution or Foster Family, A Century of Debate 29 (Child Welfare League of America, Inc. 1964) ("Wolins, in research on selection of foster parents, shows that a worker is more likely to designate as 'good' those mothers with characteristics similar to his own, rather than those who are different from him"). Wolins's methods and conclusions are severely criticized in Gershenson, Book Review, Social Work, Jan. 1965, p. 117 ("the book cannot be taken seriously"). See also Wolins's response, id. at 117-118.

[97] See, e.g., Booker v. Cameron Cy. Child Welfare Unit, 320 S.W.2d 150 (Tex. Civ. Ct. App. 1959); Galloway v. State, 249 Ala. 327, 31 So.2d 332 (1947).

the children were immediately taken into custody by the juvenile court;
. . . the court amended its findings of fact and decree to contain the
following provision:

> "*That all the parental rights of the father . . . and the mother
> . . . be and are hereby terminated and said parents are hereby de-
> prived of the custody, control and guardianship of said children.*
> That the . . . Utah State Department of Public Welfare . . . *be
> and are hereby authorized to place said children for the purpose of
> adoption.* That said children shall remain under the continuous
> jurisdiction of this court until said adoption is granted by a court
> having jurisdiction. That said Utah State Department of Public
> Welfare . . . shall submit to this court for its approval, a report re-
> garding the character and social background of said proposed adop-
> tive parents . . ." (Emphasis ours.) [Court's quotation abbrevi-
> ated by Eds.]

On May 23, 1960, the appellants filed a petition for the restoration of
the custody of their children to them on the grounds of changed conditions . . . Such petition alleged that the parents had conquered their
alcoholic problem . . . The State answered this petition alleging (a)
that the court has no jurisdiction to grant the petition; (b) that the
mother has had insufficient time to overcome her alcoholic problem; (c)
that suitable homes and adoptive parents have been found for the two
sets of twins; (d) that the other children were adjusting well in foster
homes and asked that the petition be denied. On July 12, 1960, the juvenile court entered an order denying further hearing on these matters
. . . [A]fter the notice of appeal was filed, the juvenile court ordered a
stay of all proceedings to adopt the children.

On July 13, 1960, the juvenile court entered a memorandum of decision. Therein it pointed out that since July 6, 1951, there had been various petitions and proceedings in the juvenile court with reference to the
neglect of one or more of these children, and that almost constantly since
that time the mother, and later the father, had been before the juvenile
court promising to refrain from drinking and to take care of the children;
that these promises had invariably been broken . . . The court further
pointed out that . . . only about seven months had elapsed since the
parents were deprived of the custody of their children, which it pointed
out was a rather short period in which to determine whether or not the
parents had actually permanently stopped drinking.

Appellants urge that had they been granted a hearing they would have
shown that soon after being deprived of the custody of their children,
they were inducted into Alcoholics Anonymous and thereupon they had
both completely refrained from drinking alcoholic beverages; that they
had rented and furnished a home in a good residential area; that the
father was steadily employed at a base pay of $88 per week and that they
were in a position to furnish their children with good parental care and
sustenance. They also claimed that they could produce testimony of a

psychiatrist and an AA worker that in their opinion these parents would continue in their sobriety and be good parents to their children.

Section 55-10-41, U.C.A. 1953 provides:

"A parent, guardian or next friend of a child who has been committed to any children's aid society or institution . . . *may at any time file with the clerk of the juvenile court a petition . . . asking for the return of such child to its parents* or guardian, *for the reason that they have reformed or the conditions have changed and that they are fit and proper persons to have its custody and are able to support and educate it. . . If . . . the court is of the opinion that a hearing and further examination should be had, it may . . . proceed to hear the facts and determine the question at issue.* The court may thereupon order such child to be restored to the custody of its parents or guardian, or to be retained in the custody of the children's aid society or institution, . . . or the court may make a further order of commitment as the interest and welfare of such child may demand." (Emphasis ours.) [Court's quotation abbreviated by Eds.]

From the foregoing section it is clear that it was proper for the parents to file this petition, and that it was within the sound discretion of the juvenile court whether it would grant a hearing or not. . . .

Section 55-10-32, U.C.A. 1953, provides that no child shall be taken from the custody of its parents without their consent "unless the court shall find from all the circumstances in the case that public welfare or the welfare of a child requires that his custody be taken from its parents . . ."

This section, although not determinative in this case because the juvenile court had previously on ample evidence entered an order depriving the parents of the custody of the children here in question, does emphasize and point out that it is the policy of the law not to deprive the natural parents of the custody of their children without careful consideration of the welfare of the children involved.

Furthermore, this court has repeatedly recognized that there is a presumption that it will be for the best interests of the child to be raised under the care, custody, control and supervision of its natural parents. . . . [T]his presumption is based on logic, and experience shows generally that parents have more love, devotion and regard for their own children than do other people. . . .

Also, it is very unusual for a court to attempt to determine facts without hearing all of the evidence available which has a bearing on that question. . . .

Here the petition is based on changed conditions. . . . If this were only a question of the parents reaffirming their vows to overcome their alcoholic problem, which they have broken many times in the past, then the trial court would be well within its discretion in refusing to hear further evidence. But this is not the case. The plaintiffs claim that they have joined the AA society and with its help have completely overcome their drinking habits. . . .

It is not unusual for a person who has for a long period of his life had an uncontrolled drinking habit to completely overcome such habit during the rest of his life. Such a reformation often occurs with the aid of the AA society, which was established for that purpose. In view of these facts, the juvenile court abused its discretion in refusing to allow a hearing on this question. The contention that sufficient time had not elapsed . . . has now been eliminated by the lapse of time . . .

Whether some or all of these children shall be returned to the parents is a question for the juvenile court to decide after hearing all of the evidence and determining what will be most beneficial to each child. . . .

Decision reversed with directions that the juvenile court proceed with such hearing . . . .

HENRIOD, J. (concurring). I concur and believe that under the circumstances of this particular case the order denying a hearing on the petition for restoration of custody represented an abuse of discretion . . .

On May 23, 1960, petitioners filed their petition, asserting that they had won their bout with alcohol and were prepared to give the children proper care and attention. In what appears to this writer a rather unusual move, the juvenile court, the very next day, on May 24, 1960, while the petition was pending, and before the authorities who had custody of the children had made a reply to the petition . . . , signed an order authorizing the welfare department to procure the adoption of two of the children and to report back to the court after the adoption was consummated. This, in and of itself, seems to have violated the letter and spirit of the statute . . . [which] required the welfare authorities to reply to the parents' petition within five days. These authorities did not comply with the statute, but chose to reply to the petition, not within five days, but 16 days thereafter on June 8, 1960. . . . [The statute] obviously was designed to provide a quick hearing and a quick decision, but the court in this case made its decision denying a hearing on July 12, 1960, fifty days after the filing of this petition.

. . . [T]he juvenile court, in its order depriving the parents of custody, specifically retained continuous jurisdiction "until said adoption is granted by a court having jurisdiction." Having done so, without specifying the precise purpose therefor, I am of the opinion that in this particular case inherently was included in such reservation of jurisdiction, a requirement that the least that could be done . . . would be to hear the natural parents out in an eleventh hour hope that it could be established that a sincere effort had been made on the part of the parents to preserve the relationship of parent and child . . .

CALLISTER, J. (dissenting). I dissent. The majority opinion concedes that the juvenile court had "previously on ample evidence entered an order depriving the parents of the custody of the children here in question." . . .

Thus, the sole question presented to this court is whether or not the juvenile court in the instant case abused its discretion in refusing to grant [another] hearing. . . . In order to properly resolve this question, the following chronological summary of the record should be considered:

(a) In July, 1951, the juvenile court determined the children (two in number at that time) to be neglected and dependent because of the mother's constant use of alcohol and frequenting of taverns. The court retained jurisdiction of the children, but allowed the mother to have custody upon her promise to reform her ways.

(b) In August, 1957, the mother and her children (six in number at this time) again appeared before the juvenile court. It appeared that the mother had married Mr. B—— . . . , but they were separated and living apart. The court again determined that the children were neglected and dependent because of the mother's frequent intoxication, sometimes in the presence of the children. Again the court . . . permitted the mother to retain custody of the children upon her promise to mend her ways.

(c) In April, 1958, a probation officer petitioned the juvenile court for a rehearing of the matter, because the mother was continuing her drinking habits . . . This petition was dismissed upon the grounds that the mother was pregnant, not drinking, and was reunited with Mr. B——.

(d) In June, 1959, . . . another hearing was held (this time the children were eight in number). Again, the court determined the children to be neglected and dependent; this time, because of the drinking of Mr. and Mrs. B——, oftentimes in the presence of the children, their frequenting of taverns, the lack of medical care for the children, and the unkempt and unsanitary conditions of the children. . . . Again the court retained supervision of the children . . .

(e) On August 4, 1959, the Welfare Department again petitioned . . . , but Mr. and Mrs. B——, . . . absented themselves and the children from the state of Utah.

(f) Mr. and Mrs. B—— returned to this state and a hearing was held on December 1, 1959. At this hearing it was ascertained that Mr. and Mrs. B—— had failed to live up to their promises . . . and that Mrs. B—— had been discovered nude, in an intoxicated condition in the presence of two of her children . . . and . . . her brother-in-law. . . . [T]he juvenile court entered its order depriving Mr. and Mrs. B—— permanently of the custody of the children . . . .

From the foregoing, it is difficult, to say the least, to conclude that the juvenile court acted arbitrarily or abused his discretion in refusing to grant a hearing. For a period of almost nine years the mother and the children had been under the supervision of the court and the Welfare Department. The court . . . had the benefit of the advice and reports of trained social workers. It had experienced time and again the broken promises of the mother and Mr. B——. . . .

The juvenile judge filed a memorandum at the time of denying the petition for a hearing. After reviewing the history of the matter, he stated, among other things: "Even assuming that the mother during the requested hearing proved that she had not been intoxicated since the last hearing, it is doubtful that it would be in the best interest of the children that they be returned to her. . . . It would be in the best interest of the children that others be given the responsibility and privilege of rearing the children. Any longer delay would be injurious to the children."

If the circumstances here disclosed do not constitute sufficient justification for the denial of a hearing by the juvenile court, then I am made to wonder wherein is its discretion, and under what circumstances could such a denial be justified. . . .

This court should take a realistic view of such situations and recognize that unless the juvenile court is in fact allowed some latitude of discretion, it will be practically helpless in placing children found under such unfortunate circumstances . . . On the other hand if the juvenile judge is clothed with some discretion and authority, the children can be placed . . . where they may have a more wholesome well-adjusted life with a promise to build lives of that character for themselves and their families . . . .

CROCKETT, J., concurs in the dissenting opinion of Mr. Justice CALLISTER.

NOTE

1. Maas and Engler, Children in Need of Parents (1959), focused attention on the large numbers of children who grow up in a foster care limbo. According to Keith-Lucas, Maas and Engler only confirmed

> what was already patent — that far too many children were being reared in foster care with very tenuous relationships to their own parents and none of the protection of adoption. The situation was seen to be due to unrealistic indulgence of parents, and one writer suggested that "the field should review the concept of parental rights with greater attention to the rights of the child." Yet the report had made clear that all too often these parents had been left without agency assistance of any kind. They were not so much indulged as ignored.
>
> The report certainly gave impetus to a number of adoption statutes which permitted agencies to petition for permanent custody of children where parents had failed, during placement, to fulfill their responsibilities. Yet these laws . . . did not require that the responsibilities of the parent be spelled out at the time that temporary custody was given to an agency. . . . [M]any a parent must find himself deprived of rights he never knew that he had.[98]

Terminations of parental rights have not often received sympathetic appellate review. See, e.g., In re Baby Girl Larson, page 159 supra. In State v. Grady, 231 Ore. 65, 371 P.2d 68 (1962), termination of an unwed mother's parental rights was reversed although she had been in prison for seventeen months prior to the decision of the Supreme Court and would not be eligible for parole for at least another month. The opinion commented:

> What better inducement can she have for redemption than the assurance that she may have again her little girls in one united family?

[98] Keith-Lucas, Child Welfare Services Today: An Overview and Some Questions, 355 Annals 1, 6-7 (1964).

. . . To destroy the great human tie between her and those she bore would, under the circumstances present here, approximate a species of unintended vindictive justice which might well undo all of the reformation expected from her present incarceration. On the other hand, the very remission of the order of permanent custody may . . . encourage her in her striving to attain a new and better way of life, and we hope that it will.[99]

A number of statutes impose more rigorous requirements for terminations of parental rights than for adjudications of neglect. See, e.g., Wis. Stat. Ann. §48.40 (1957). Compare the definition of neglect in the N.Y. Family Ct. Act, page 417 supra, with the definition of a permanently neglected child in the same statute, page 168 supra. It is not unlikely that the appellate courts may accomplish the same result without legislative aid. See Paulsen, The Delinquency, Neglect, & Dependency Jurisdiction of the Juvenile Court, in Justice for the Child 44, 71. Note, however, that the Minnesota provision authorizes termination if the court finds "[t]hat following upon a determination of neglect or dependency, reasonable efforts, under the direction of the court, have failed to correct the conditions leading to the determination." [100]

Consider the following recommendation:

In our opinion, a situation should not be permitted to exist wherein parents may essentially abandon their children in foster care and yet retain legal control over them. Certainly one of the first priorities is to clarify each child's legal status and to sever parental rights in all situations where it is obvious that the parents will never take responsibility for the child. . . .[101]

It is clear, however, that not every child who has been "abandoned" in foster care will be adopted.[102] Under these circumstances, what does the termination accomplish? Should a court terminate parental rights only if the welfare agency proves that it can place the child in an adoptive home?

PROBLEM

We have noted at pages 378-379 supra that under probate court administration of guardianship of the person there is no effective supervision of the guardian. To remedy this defect, it has been proposed that exclusive jurisdiction for the appointment of guardians of the person be transferred from the probate court to the juvenile court. Proponents of

---

[99] 231 Ore. at 70, 371 P.2d at 70. Of course, the appellate courts have not always accepted the arguments of parents. See In re Douglas, page 405 supra; In re Black, 3 Utah 2d 315, 283 P.2d 887, cert. denied, 350 U.S. 923 (1955); In re M — L — J —, 356 S.W.2d 508 (Mo. Ct. App. 1962).

[100] Minn. Stat. Ann. §260.221(b)(5) (Supp. 1964). See page 169 supra.

[101] Reid, Action Called For — Recommendations, in Maas & Engler, Children in Need of Parents 378, 383 (1959).

[102] Id at 389.

this change argue that the juvenile court already has adequate probation and social service facilities to enable it to supervise and regulate the guardians.

In light of the preceding materials, would you support this proposal?

In life of the preceding matter it would not appear this proposal

CHAPTER 5

Augmentation of Children

A. ADOPTION

1. *Alternative Methods of Securing a Child for Adoption*

a. INDEPENDENT PLACEMENT

ASHTON ADOPTION CASE
374 Pa. 185, 97 A.2d 368 (1953)

JONES, J. Richard W. Kubach and Helen R. Kubach, his wife, filed their joint petition in the Orphans' Court of Montgomery County for a decree of adoption of an infant child identified in the petition as Baby Boy Ashton. At a hearing on the petition, the child's natural mother, Mildred Elaine Ashton, who was unmarried, appeared personally and by counsel to protest the adoption. During the progress of the hearing, she filed in the Court of Common Pleas of Montgomery County a petition for a writ of habeas corpus to obtain custody of the child. [That court transferred the custody action to the Orphans' Court for consideration along with the adoption proceeding.]

The petition for adoption averred the written and signed consent of the child's mother which was attached to the petition as was also a writing, signed and acknowledged by her, wherein she purported to assign, transfer and set over to .... "all my right, title and interest of, in and to a child about to be born to me." The places for the names of the proposed adopting parents in the written consents were likewise blank when the consents were signed by the mother; and such persons were actually unknown to her. The legal inefficacy of the incomplete consents, as well as the so-called assignment, having been properly pronounced by the court during the course of the hearing, counsel for the petitioners in the adoption proceeding sought to rest their claim to a decree of adoption on the alleged abandonment of the child by its mother for a period of over six months in which event, if proven, the mother's consent to the adoption would be unnecessary [citation omitted].

[The controlling statute, Pa. Stat. Ann. tit. 1, §§1(a), 2(b), 2(c) (1963), provided as follows:

§1. Definitions . . .

(a) As used in this act, unless the context clearly indicates otherwise, the following words and phrases shall have the meanings ascribed to them in this subsection:

"Abandonment" means conduct on the part of a parent which evidences a settled purpose of relinquishing parental claim to the child and of refusing or failing to perform parental duties. . . .

§2. Consents necessary to adoption

Consent to the adoption is necessary as follows: . . .

(c) Of the parents or surviving parent of the person proposed to be adopted, if such person shall not have reached the age of eighteen years. . . . In the case of an illegitimate child, the consent of the mother only shall be necessary. The consent of a parent who has been adjudged a person of unsound mind, of whose unsoundness of mind competent medical testimony presents a prognosis of incurability, or habitual drunkard, or who has abandoned the child, for a period of at least six months, shall be unnecessary, provided such fact is proven to the satisfaction of the court or judge hearing the petition, in which case such court or judge shall so find as a fact . . . .

§4. Decrees of court . . .

In no case shall any decree of adoption of a minor be made or entered unless the person proposed to be adopted shall have resided with the petitioner for a period of six months prior thereto . . . If satisfied that the statements made in the petition are true, and that the welfare of the person proposed to be adopted will be promoted by such adoption, and that all the requirements of this act have been complied with, the court or judge shall make a decree so finding . . . ; but otherwise shall make a decree refusing the adoption and dismissing the petition. . . .]

The Orphans' Court ultimately filed an opinion wherein it held that the averments of the adoption petition (treating the mother's alleged abandonment as substituted for the consent pleaded) had been sustained and therewith entered a decree adjudging the child to be the lawful child and heir of the adopting parents to whom, by decree of even date, the custody of the child was awarded. This appeal by the natural mother followed.

The primary question for review is whether the evidence justifies a finding of the mother's abandonment of the child. The learned court below correctly apprehended the legal situation to be as follows: ". . . The purported consents appended to the petition are absolutely worthless and of no effect. The only question, therefore, is, as to whether she has abandoned the child, rendering her consent unnecessary." [Court's quotation abbreviated by Eds.]

For a proper appraisal of the mother's attitude toward, and her actions with regard to, the expected child (she never had possession of it in being), a recital of the material findings by the hearing judge as well as other undisputed and corroborated facts of record becomes necessary.

In the summer of 1950, Mildred Elaine Ashton, then twenty-five years old, became acquainted with a man who, representing himself as single, kept company with her. He asked her to marry him and, during what appeared to her to be a courtship, they had sexual relations in August 1950. In the exact words of the hearing judge, the man "turned out to be a deceiver, . . . he at that time was a married man in the process of getting a divorce, and subsequently got a divorce and married another woman." Late August or early September, Miss Ashton suspected that she was pregnant. She confided her secret to her widowed mother with whom she lived; and, together, they consulted her married sister. The sister advised her to go to a reputable obstetrician whom she named and who had delivered her of her two children. Miss Ashton visited the suggested doctor toward the latter part of September. His examination confirmed that she was pregnant.

The doctor, upon hearing of the circumstances prior to and attending the relations responsible for her enceinte condition, advised her to see an attorney about compelling the father of the unborn child to contribute to the anticipated obstetrical and lying-in expenses. He also counselled her that in her unmarried state it would be less embarrassing to her and better for the child if she would agree in advance of its birth to place it for adoption. He said that he knew a married couple without children of their own who had already obtained a child through him, which they had adopted, and who were desirous of adopting another, and that he thought they would be glad to adopt hers. She told him that she "couldn't see giving the child up for adoption" and would rather keep it herself. The doctor, however, insisted that she should permit it to be adopted. He suggested that "people would talk about [her], and, if [she] did keep the child, no one would marry [her]." As she expressed it, — "He just gave me all the disadvantages." He explained to her that she "couldn't ask any questions as to where the child would go, or the sex of the child, and [she] was to know nothing about it. And, he said he wouldn't handle the case any other way." The doctor freely admitted at the hearing that it was he who proposed adoption for the child. As to an attorney, she told the doctor that she did not have one whereupon he recommended one to her whom she consulted in early October. The attorney's services at that time consisted of the making of an information against the father for fornication and bastardy and the negotiation with the father's counsel of a money settlement which, incidentally, the father never fully performed.

During the prenatal period, the doctor ascertained that the married couple he had in mind were willing to adopt Miss Ashton's child upon its birth. They agreed with the doctor to pay for his prenatal and postnatal care of her and for all obstetrical and lying-in expenses which were to include a private room for the mother in the Pennsylvania Hospital in Philadelphia. Except for some hearsay from a pediatrician who never saw or talked with the mother, there is nothing in the record to indicate that Miss Ashton had any knowledge of these financial arrangements between the doctor and the Kubachs. She herself paid the doctor ninety dollars. The private room was the doctor's idea in order that the mother could be more conveniently separated at birth from her baby whom it was the doctor's plan she should never see. As he explained in his testimony at the hearing, — "Well, it was a matter of protecting a patient. Unless a patient can go in a private room, they have to be delivered in the ward, and, it is not very pleasant for a girl who has just had a baby, to have babies brought to mothers all around her, and not get one herself. I mean, she could best be protected and be isolated by herself in a private room." The Kubachs also put the doctor in touch with their lawyer to whom the doctor sent the data, concerning the natural parents of the expected child, for future use in an adoption petition and the lawyer in turn sent to the doctor two consents to an adoption and the proposed assignment of the child, all in blank, for Miss Ashton's execution.

When she went to see the doctor the night of April 22, 1951, on one of her regular prenatal visits, he handed her the blank consents and the assignment and instructed her to take them to her attorney (the one he had originally recommended to her, naming him) "tomorrow morning and have it signed at his office." He said the papers must be signed before she was admitted to the hospital and that she would be going there "within a few days." She took the papers to the attorney's office the next day, as directed, and there, in the attorney's presence, she signed the two consents and the so-called assignment. She acknowledged the assignment before one of his secretaries, who was a notary public, while his other secretary witnessed the signatures to the consents which the attorney dated April 23, 1951. The attorney transmitted the signed consents and the assignment direct to the doctor by mail with a covering letter identifying the enclosures. The record plainly reveals that Miss Ashton signed the consents and the assignment with great reluctance and only after much questioning, but, in the circumstances, she felt compelled to do so. This appears in the cross-examination of Miss Ashton by petitioners' counsel at the hearing: "Q. . . . When [the doctor] told you, just prior to your entry, into the hospital, that you could not go into that hospital unless you executed this particular paper, did you do anything about that? Did you go to your mother? A. Yes, my mother —. Q. What? A. My mother said, suggested that I didn't sign it; she said I didn't have to. Q. What did you tell your mother on that occasion? A. well, I was so upset, and I said, 'Well, he told me it had to be signed before I am admitted to the hospital.'" Four days later (April 27, 1951), she was admitted to the hospital where the following day her baby was born and immediately taken from her. The doctor testified in direct examination by petitioners' counsel as follows, — "Q. She didn't see the baby, then, after it was born? A. No, sir. Q. It was taken away from her immediately then, was it? A. Yes, sir. Q. And she never saw it? A. To my knowledge, no, sir."

After the mother left the hospital the doctor gave her customary postnatal attention, seeing her three or four times, over a period of approximately six months. He testified that during that time she had no conversation with him nor did she make any inquiry as to the whereabouts of the child. However, as the opinion for the court below states, "She explains this silence on her part 'because he had told me from the beginning that I wasn't to ask any questions about it, and he wouldn't give me any information' and that she thought that she had to abide by that." According to her testimony, she inquired of the doctor concerning the welfare of the child up to her last visit to his office in the latter part of October 1951 and that he had assured her that the child was with a nice family and was being well taken care of. It is not open to dispute that she was intentionally and effectively kept in the dark as to the whereabouts of the child. She asked the attorney if he knew who had the child or where it was and he told her that he did not know. Her continued anxiety for the child and its well-being stands out too clearly in the record to be gainsaid.

It was not until November 24, 1951, when Miss Ashton was served with notice of the hearing (scheduled for December 19th) on the petition for adoption, which had just been filed in court, that she first learned the names of the proposed adopting parents and their residence address. They had maintained and cared for the child from the time it was handed over to them by the doctor following its birth and have since continued so to do until the present time. Miss Ashton has never seen her child except once casually at one of the hearings in court on the adoption petition, the first of which hearings was held on December 19, 1951, and the other on January 8, 1952. Upon receipt of the notice of the adoption [hearing], she at once consulted the attorney who had theretofore been representing her. She told him of her desire to have the custody of her child and of her intention to resist the proposed adoption. He endeavored to dissuade her, saying that what had been done was for her own and the child's best interests. When he found that she was adamant in her determination to thwart the adoption and gain possession of the child, he informed her that he could not represent her. Thereupon, in early December, she obtained other counsel who appeared for her at the hearing in the adoption proceeding on December 19th, filed her petition for a writ of habeas corpus for the custody of the child and has since represented her in all phases of the matter.

It is readily apparent from a reading of the material facts that there is bound to be tragedy in this case no matter what the ultimate decision is. The petitioners, who have acted in good faith and have done nothing improper in furthering their desire to adopt another child, have no doubt developed a deep affection for the baby whose care and nurture have been their responsibility for the two years since its birth. Nor are the doctor's motives to be questioned. He undoubtedly acted in what he thought was for the best interest of both the natural mother and the child. . . . On the other hand, the sincerity and depth of the mother's desire for her child is equally not open to question. It represents an expression of perhaps the strongest natural instinct known to man which is especially encouraged by and has become highly developed in our civilization. . . .

Unless the finding by the court below of the mother's abandonment of her child for a period of more than six months is justified by the evidence, the decree of adoption necessarily falls. As already appears, there was no legally valid consent. . . .

The fact that Miss Ashton signed the consents (which proved to be worthless) is some evidence of a willingness at the time to surrender the care and support of her child [citation omitted], but, standing alone, it is far from being sufficient to establish abandonment. Indeed, in the circumstances of this case, the fact of her signing is devoid of any relevant probative value [citation omitted]. As defined in Schwab Adoption Case [355 Pa. 534, 538, 50 A.2d 504, 506-507 (1947)], abandonment "imports any conduct on the part of the parent which evidences a settled purpose to forego all parental duties and relinquishes all parental claim to the child: Weinbach's Appeal, 316 Pa. 333, 175 A. 500" . . . Abandonment "requires an intent to escape parental responsibility, and conduct in effectuation of such intent" [citations omitted].

There is no evidence in this case of a self-conceived intent on the part of Miss Ashton to escape parental responsibility nor any voluntary conduct on her part to carry out such an intent. From the time she submitted to the obstetrician's care, she gave no indication that she wished to be relieved of the responsibility of the child. On the contrary, her every independent expression was a desire to retain her child. Admittedly, it was the doctor, and not she, who suggested and urged adoption of the child yet to be born. And, while the doctor is not to be censured for his zeal in doing what he thought was best in the circumstances . . . , the adoption plan was the doctor's and cannot justly be used to prove wilful abandonment by the mother. The evidence shows that she asked the attorney a number of times prior to the birth of the child whether it would not be possible for her to keep it. He testified at the hearing that her inquiries concerning the possibility of her keeping the child began in early October 1950 when she first consulted him at the instance of the doctor. . . . Yet, it was not until four days before her admission to the hospital on April 27, 1951, that she was called upon to execute the consents and assignment, when, as she understood, unless she signed them, she could not enter the hospital for the delivery of her baby or have the obstetrician's further services. . . .

In reality, the circumstances of the case did not admit of abandonment by the mother at any time. She never had possession of the child from the moment of its birth . . . No case in this State has been cited, and we know of none, where there has been abandonment by a mother who did not have actual possession of the child at some time or ready access to it and, being so situated, exhibited, by her conduct, an intent to be relieved of her parental responsibility for which she was willing to surrender her claim to the child. While proven abandonment renders unnecessary the abandoning parent's consent to adoption of a child, the two things are not synonymous and are not to be confused. In the instant case the petitioners' proofs, at best, show no more than that a prenatal arrangement for the adoption of Miss Ashton's child at birth was entered into which appeared to be consensual. It turned out not to be such, however, so far as the mother was concerned; and the formal consent executed by her proved to be legally ineffectual. . . .

. . . In this case, just as in Schwab Adoption Case, supra, the court below mistakenly "gave considerable attention to the desirability of the proposed adoption [and] concluded that the proposed adoption was beneficial to the child. Consideration of what is beneficial for the child is vital in custody cases, but cannot be regarded as evidence of abandonment."

As the decree of adoption cannot be sustained, we come to the question of custody raised by the petition for a writ of habeas corpus. The natural mother has a presumptive right to the care and custody of her child. Beyond that, as found by the court below, "It can not be said . . . that the home of the natural mother would be an unfit place for the child. She and her mother share and maintain a home in Drexel Hill, well located, and, though modest, with every modern convenience conducive to health and comfort." However, the paramount consideration upon a question of custody is the child's best interests [citation omitted]. The court below concluded that the mother could not give the child the advantages and afford him the future security that the petitioners can. . . . But, that is neither a legally nor socially valid reason for separating children from their parents.

The court further said that "The more important factor is that this child has been with these petitioners practically since birth and the strong tie of parent and child has grown up between them" and that "To uproot it from this home and break this domestic tie would be devastating to its emotional development and hence to its future welfare." There can be little doubt that a change now in the custody of the child, who is two years old, and in its living conditions and environment may have some emotional effect upon it. But, the continued presence of the child in the family of the petitioners has resulted from the inordinate delay in the disposition of the adoption proceeding which cannot justly be charged against the mother. When the adoption proceeding was instituted on November 13, 1951, the child was then but seven months old. The hearing on the petition was concluded a month and a half later on January 8, 1952, but the matter was not argued by counsel and taken under advisement by the court until July 15, 1952, and the court's opinion and decree were not filed until November 15, 1952, in all, a year after the institution of the proceeding. It should have been evident at the conclusion of the hearing that the petitioners had failed to make out a case of abandonment by the mother persisted in for over six months . . . It is to be hoped that any emotional disturbance to the child resulting from the change in its situation because of the order which must necessarily be made in this case will be but temporary and of no serious consequence.

The decree of the court below is reversed at the costs of the appellees and the custody of the child is awarded to the natural mother.

NOTE

1. A mother's consent to the adoption of her child is invalid if it was "coerced," e.g., In re Baby Girl Larson, page 159 supra, or obtained fraudulently, e.g., Ill. Ann. Stat. c. 4, §9.1-11 (Supp. 1964). See Barwin v. Reidy, 62 N.M. 183, 196, 198, 307 P.2d 175, 184, 185 (1957) (dictum) ("duress of circumstances," such as the natural parents' poverty, should not be considered sufficient to vitiate their consent); Lambert v. Taylor, 150 Fla. 680, 682, 684, 8 So.2d 393, 394, 395 (1942) (mother's consent invalid because she was not informed that the paper she was signing was a consent to adoption; adoption set aside seven years after decree because adoptive parents had waived a claim of laches by failing to raise the issue in the trial court). Cf. Arnold v. Howell, 98 Cal. App. 2d 202, 207, 219 P.2d 854, 858 (1950) (father's consent to adoption by sister-in-law obtained fraudulently because he was told that the adoption would protect the child while he was overseas in the army, and because adoptive parents promised he could have the child back when he returned).

Consents signed shortly before or after the child's birth have been particularly susceptible to attack although the evidence of actual coercion may have been sketchy. One explanation often given for the judicial penchant for holding that the mother's consent was involuntary is as follows:

> [I]n a great many instances the consent is given by an immature mother oftentimes in the depth of humiliation, in fear of scandal and condemnation and in desperate worry concerning her future and the future of her child. Often, too, this situation finds the mother not only in mental stress but in a delicate physical condition, in extreme financial difficulties and sometimes subject to freely given advice and entreaties of relatives, friends, doctors and upon occasions nurses and agents of maternity homes and child-placement agencies. . . .[1]

To the same effect, see Note, 28 U. Chi. L. Rev. 564, 570 (1961). In addition, in many of the cases the judges seem to be influenced by a desire to deter independent placement adoptions. In State ex rel. Nelson v. Whaley, 246 Minn. 535, 75 N.W.2d 786 (1956), the trial court found that an obstetrician had convinced the divorced mother that welfare department personnel might take custody of her two legitimate children if they discovered that she was pregnant out of wedlock. The Supreme Court, ordering the child's return to the mother although it had been in the adoptive parents' home for over eighteen months, remarked:

> If we are not to be controlled by the sentimental or ethical aspects of this transaction, considerations of public policy require that we realistically appraise its social implications. We disapprove of the methods by which [the adoptive parents] acquired custody of the child.

[1] Adoption of McKinzie, 275 S.W.2d 365, 372 (Mo. Ct. App. 1955) (dictum).

We cannot escape the conclusion that no real consent was given by the mother. . . .

A physician should not let his zeal for a patient's interests prompt him to use the opportunities of his profession to effectuate the transfer of a child to nonrelatives. . . . While we do not impugn the integrity of the attorneys who represented the [adoptive parents], this case demonstrates that, no matter how keen a lawyer's sense of social obligation may be, his training is inadequate in dealing with the imponderables of this kind of human conflict. This field of service should be left to the established social agencies with personnel trained to avoid the grave emotional toll which has resulted here.[2]

2. Even if the mother has executed a seemingly valid consent, it may be set aside on a variety of grounds: (a) the jurisdiction may be one which by statute or judicial doctrine refuses to recognize certain types of consents or consents given under specified circumstances; (b) the jurisdiction may allow the mother to withdraw her consent under certain conditions. These possibilities are explored below.

a. A number of states have statutes which declare invalid any consent executed by a mother before the birth of the child. See, e.g., Nev. Rev. Stat. §127.070 (1957); Mass. Gen. Laws Ann. c. 210, §2 (1958). Compare the British Adoption Act of 1958, which absolutely voids any consent unless the infant is at least six weeks old on the date of the execution of the document. 7 Eliz. 2, c. 5, §6(2). The Report of the Departmental Committee on the Adoption of Children, Cmd. No. 9248, par. 56 (1954), commented as follows on this provision:

[W]e found little disagreement with the view that it is preferable for a child not to be taken away from his mother before the age of six weeks. Most witnesses agreed that a mother needs about six weeks to recover physically and psychologically from the effects of confinement, and that it would be wrong to alter the provisions relating to the date of consent. Many organisations, including those specially concerned with unmarried mothers, deplored the making of adoption arrangements before birth, since their experience has shown that a large number of mothers who before the birth decide on adoption change their minds completely when the child is born. A few witnesses expressed the opinion that where a mother has had skilled help to enable her to arrive at a firm decision an earlier placing may be advisable, and one medical organisation said that ante-natal arrangements could sometimes be successful . . . .

Can it be argued, on the contrary, that the law should not encourage the tendency of unmarried mothers to procrastinate concerning the disposition of their children? Compare An Act to Amend the Adoption of Children Acts, Act No. 5851 of 1954, 3 Eliz. 2 (Victoria, Austl.) (consent

[2] 246 Minn. at 548-549, 75 N.W.2d at 794-795. The fact that an agency arranged the adoption does not guarantee that the unwed mother will not try to reclaim the child. See page 498 infra.

must be executed promptly after birth but may be revoked without reason within thirty days of its execution).

The Massachusetts statute, supra, also provides that any consent executed within one year after birth must be notarized or executed before a Justice of the Peace. Compare Cal. Civ. Code §226.1(a): "In all cases in which consent is required, the consent of the natural parent or parents to the adoption by the petitioners must be signed in the presence of an agent of the State Department of Social Welfare or of a licensed county adoption agency on a form prescribed by such department . . ."

Even if the mother's consent has been obtained at an appropriate time and with all necessary formality, the Ashton case indicates that consents executed without disclosure of the adoptive parents' identity may be considered invalid. Consents in blank commonly stem from attempts by attorneys involved in independent placement adoptions to duplicate the anonymity characteristic of adoptions handled through agencies, where the adoptive parents' identity is usually not disclosed to the natural mother. See page 498 infra. The courts have split with respect to the validity of consents in blank. Occasionally the decision has been based on a precise reading of the relevant statutory provision. In In re Adoption of a Baby Girl, 248 Iowa 619, 80 N.W.2d 500 (1957), for example, the statute required that the "consent shall refer to and be applicable only to the specific adoption proposed by such petition." 248 Iowa at 623, 80 N.W.2d at 503. The court held the blank consent invalid and reversed the adoption order, stating (248 Iowa at 625, 80 N.W.2d at 504):

> The attorney who procured the consent without doubt was sincere in his good intentions . . . Yet such a practice, if sanctioned, is capable of great abuse. A consent to adoption by unspecified parties makes possible a real "black market" in babies. We think there has been little of this in Iowa. The legislative provision above referred to, if observed by the courts, will go far toward preventing any development of this evil practice. . . .[3]

Compare Barwin v. Reidy, 62 N.M. 183, 191, 307 P.2d 175, 181 (1957) (since the purpose of the consent statute is only "to indicate the willingness of the parents that the natural relationship be swept away and a new one created in its stead," and since the court is not bound by the consent to permit only the petitioners to adopt, the fact that the consent did not name the prospective adoptive parents does not invalidate it). See generally Annot., 24 A.L.R.2d 1127 (1952).

After the decision in the Ashton case, the Pennsylvania legislature amended the adoption act as follows (Pa. Stat. Ann. tit. 1, §2.2 (1963)):

> A consent to a specific proposed adoption which meets all the requirements of this act but which does not name or otherwise identify

[3] Following this case the statute was amended to provide that no consent executed prior to January 1, 1957, and with respect to which no judicial proceeding was pending or commenced prior to July 1, 1957, could be declared illegal or void for failure to disclose the name of the adopting parents. Acts of 1957, c. 257, §1.

the adopting parent or parents shall be valid, provided that such consent shall contain a statement, by the person whose consent it is, to the effect that such person voluntarily executed the consent without disclosure of the name or other identification of the adopting parent or parents.

If this provision had been in effect at the time of the Ashton case, do you think it would have changed the result?

b. Jurisdictions take differing attitudes on the question whether a consent, once validly executed, may be withdrawn or revoked by the mother prior to the final decree of adoption. The traditional view is that a consent can be revoked until the decree is entered. See, e.g., In re White, 300 Mich. 378, 1 N.W.2d 579 (1942) (natural mother permitted to revoke consent during ninety-day period following entry of adoption decree since any person aggrieved could petition for a rehearing during this period). But see In re Adoption of Morrison, 260 Wis. 50, 49 N.W.2d 759 (1951) (consent may be revoked until adoptive parents have "acted upon" the consent by petitioning to adopt). See generally Annots., 138 A.L.R. 1038 (1942), 156 A.L.R. 1011 (1944). Other jurisdictions have adopted, either by statute or judicial doctrine, a more flexible rule, allowing withdrawal of the consent in the discretion of the court. See, e.g., Ellis v. McCoy, 332 Mass. 254, 124 N.E.2d 266 (1955); Rhodes v. Shirley, 234 Ind. 587, 129 N.E.2d 60 (1955) (governing consideration is best interest of child). The cases are collected and the considerations exhaustively analyzed in Adoption of McKinzie, 275 S.W.2d 365 (Mo. Ct. App. 1955). See also Note, 28 U. Chi. L. Rev. 564 (1961).

3. Even if the state's juvenile court act has a specific provision for terminating parental rights (see page 169 supra), many adoption statutes specify that the mother's consent is unnecessary if the child has been "abandoned." The term has frequently been left undefined; see, e.g., Minn. Stat. Ann. §259.24 (1959); N.M. Stat. Ann. §22-2-6 (Supp. 1963). As the Ashton case indicates, the legislative efforts to define "abandonment" have not always been very helpful. The New Jersey provision, N.J. Stat. Ann. §9:6-1 (1960), is unusually specific:

> Abandonment of a child shall consist in any of the following acts by any one having the custody or control of the child: (a) willfully forsaking a child; (b) failing to care for and keep the control and custody of a child so that the child shall be exposed to physical or moral risk without proper and sufficient protection; (c) failing to care for and keep the control and custody of a child so that the child shall be liable to be supported and maintained at the expense of the public, or by child caring societies or private persons not legally chargeable with its or their care, custody and control.

But see In re Mrs. M., 74 N.J. Super. 178, 187, 181 A.2d 14, 18 (1962): "Although it might have been argued that plaintiff *technically* abandoned her daughter, in the light of R.S. 9:6-1 . . . , counsel for Mrs.

R. . . . forthrightly conceded that there was no *actual* abandonment under the statute or common law."

As Ashton indicates, consent to the adoption, by itself, is usually held insufficient to constitute abandonment. See also People ex rel. Anonymous v. Anonymous, 19 Misc. 2d 441, 195 N.Y.S.2d 1009 (Sup. Ct. 1959). In all other respects, however, the cases are in hopeless disarray. In Ashton, for example, the appellate court was sharply at odds with the trial judge, who had remarked (69 Montg. Cy. Rep. 1, 11-12 (Pa. Orph. Ct. 1952)):

> It is not convincing that the natural mother actually believed the adopting parents would take this child for a period of over seven months, pay all the prenatal, postnatal, lying-in, and pediatrician expenses, and completely support and maintain the child, with the possible expectation that they would have to give it up if she changed her mind within a period of seven months or even a year. It must be borne in mind that these petitioners were not in the position of foster parents who had agreed to take the child simply to maintain it and to be paid for the maintenance of it while in their possession and be subject to delivering it back to those that had legal custody of it.
>
> . . . Certainly no man and his wife would accept this responsibility and relieve the natural mother of that responsibility except with such a distinct understanding, and it is not convincing that an intelligent young woman of twenty-seven years of age could have believed or contemplated otherwise. . . .

Compare Stone Adoption Case, 398 Pa. 190, 156 A.2d 808 (1959). The child was born in December 1957, and was placed with adoptive parents when the mother was discharged from the hospital; although the mother consulted an attorney in January and again in February 1958, the supreme court held that she had abandoned the child because she made no effort, in the subsequent nine months between her second visit to the attorney and the filing of the adoption petition, to locate or obtain custody of the child.

In Barwin v. Reidy, 62 N.M. 183, 307 P.2d 175 (1957), the parents consented to the adoption of their youngest child and, through intermediaries, received $400 to defray previously incurred "hospital and medical expenses" for the child's birth. When they decided to place their two older children with the same, unidentified parents, they received another $400 which was given without the knowledge of the adoptive parents' attorney and against his specific instructions. The court held the parents' first consent, although compensated, was valid because a child's welfare is enhanced if the mother receives adequate medical attention. But their consents to the older children's adoption were void because of the financial arrangement. Nonetheless, "the act of selling children constitutes abandonment of them as a matter of law." 62 N.M. at 196, 307 P.2d at 184. See generally Note, Child Abandonment: The Botched Beginning of the Adoption Process, 60 Yale L.J. 1240 (1951); Annot., 35 A.L.R.2d 662 (1953).

4. Some adoption statutes provide that a parent's "unfitness" makes his consent to the adoption unnecessary. E.g., Miss. Code Ann. §1269-09 (1942); N.M. Stat. Ann. §22-2-6 (1953). These provisions are often separate from those authorizing termination of parental rights by the juvenile court. Compare pages 464-470 supra. Thus, Ill. Ann. Stat. c. 4, §§9.1-1(D), 9.1-8 (Supp. 1964), provides that consent shall not be required of a parent whom the court finds to be an "unfit person" on any one of the following grounds:

a. Depravity;
b. Open and notorious adultery or fornication;
c. Habitual drunkenness for the space of one year prior to the commencement of the adoption proceeding;
d. Extreme and repeated cruelty to the child; . . .
g. . . . provided that in making a finding of unfitness the court hearing the adoption proceeding shall not be bound by any previous finding, order, judgment or decree affecting or determining the rights of the parents toward the child sought to be adopted in any other proceeding except such proceedings terminating parental rights as shall be had under either this Act or the Family Court Act.

See also State ex rel. Anonymous v. Anonymous, 19 Misc. 2d 441, 195 N.Y.S.2d 1009 (Sup. Ct. 1959) (mother's fitness relevant in determining whether to permit her to withdraw consent, but birth of two children out of wedlock not sufficient evidence of unfitness).

There are, in addition, a variety of other provisions authorizing an adoption without the natural parent's consent. See, e.g., N.Y. Dom. Rel. Law §111 (consent not required of a parent "who is insane or who has been judicially declared incompetent or who is a mental defective as defined by the mental hygiene law"). See generally Katz, Judicial and Statutory Trends in the Law of Adoption, 51 Geo. L.J. 64, 81-83 (1962).

5. As the Ashton case indicates, denial of an adoption petition does not necessarily require that possession of the child be returned to the natural parent. See Re F., 121 J.P. 270 (Ch. 1957) (although adoption denied owing to absence of valid consent, judge implies natural parents could not regain custody of seven-year-old child who has been living with petitioners since the age of six months). See also State ex rel. Nelson v. Whaley, 246 Minn. 535, 75 N.W.2d 786 (1956) (trial court had denied the adoption but continued custody with petitioners). Even if the mother's unfitness does not eliminate the need for obtaining her consent, such fitness will clearly be relevant to the custody determination.

PROBLEM

You are a judge who has heard testimony on the petition of Major and Mrs. John Bright to adopt a four-year-old boy. Miss Shirley Parr, conceded to be the mother of the child, has appeared, opposed the adoption, and filed a habeas corpus petition for custody. Both petitions were consolidated for trial.

Miss Parr testified that her baby was kidnaped shortly after she had taken him home from the hospital four years ago. A person who claimed to be a member of the hospital staff came to her home and told her that the child's blood tests had never been completed; he disappeared with the child after she accompanied him to the hospital. Miss Parr enlisted the aid of the police and hired private detectives, to no avail; the police suspected that the kidnaper might have been a member of a "black market" outfit which had previously approached her, without success, to use their services to place the child for adoption. Two years ago she resigned herself to the child's loss. She discovered the child only because the Brights' attorney contacted the welfare department two months ago, when the petition was filed, since the Brights had never been given a birth certificate. The welfare department notified Miss Parr when its record check produced unquestionable finger- and footprint identification of the child. You have no reason to doubt the mother's story.

The Brights testified that they obtained the child from a person who claimed to be an obstetrician; shortly after they had made inquiries of several adoption agencies, he had contacted them, indicating that he could get them a child quickly. They paid him $800 — a sum which they believed to be the amount of the mother's hospital and surgical expenses — and have not heard from him since. The child was one month old when the Brights received him; they delayed adoption proceedings because Major Bright was transferred from his local post to Germany shortly after placement. The Brights returned to the Major's former post six months ago. Testimony established that they have a fine reputation, have given the child excellent care for four years, and are comfortably situated financially.

Miss Parr claimed that she had neither consented to the adoption nor abandoned the child. If she obtains custody of the child, Miss Parr plans to establish a home with her widowed mother, who will baby-sit while she works. Except for the affair which led to her pregnancy, there was no evidence adverse to Miss Parr's reputation. She makes a good living as a secretary.

In addition to the common consent and waiver of consent provisions, the adoption statute in your jurisdiction contains the following: "The court may grant a petition for adoption without any of the consents required by this act if, after a hearing, the court finds that such consent or consents are withheld contrary to the best interests of the child." [4]

How would you decide the petitions?

[4] See Md. Ann. Code art. 16, §74 (1957). See also the British Adoption Act of 1958, 7 Eliz. 2, c. 5, §5, which gives the court authority to dispense with any required consent if the person whose consent is normally required "is withholding his consent unreasonably."

In re ADOPTION OF A MINOR
338 Mass. 635, 156 N.E.2d 801 (1959)

CUTTER, J. This is a petition filed April 6, 1956, for the adoption of a minor boy, born in February, 1956. The department of public welfare eventually[5] filed a report disapproving the proposed adoption. The natural parents of the child were not married to each other at the time of the child's birth or when the petition was filed but were married November 30, 1956, some seven and one half months after the filing of the petition. They opposed the adoption, although the mother had consented in writing to the adoption before the filing of the petition for adoption. The probate judge by final decree on October 31, 1957, approved the adoption. The natural parents have appealed. The evidence is reported.

The facts are stated upon the basis of the judge's findings of material facts which are plainly justified by the evidence. The unmarried mother of the child, discovering that she was pregnant, went with the father of the child, in September, 1955, to consult a doctor. The doctor urged marriage. The father, a student then receiving G.I. aid of $110 a month, said that "under no circumstances" could he "possibly get married." The mother said she did not want to use the baby to force marriage then or in the future. She declined to deal with the usual State agencies and asked that the "doctor . . . refer the baby to some private family."

The doctor discovered that the petitioners, married for eight years and childless, were going to Sicily in the hope of finding a child there to adopt. The doctor discussed this with the child's mother while she was still in the hospital following the child's birth. . . . On her discharge from the hospital, the mother and "the child's father left the new born baby at the home of the male petitioner's brother." . . . The confinement expenses of the mother were paid by the petitioners. The "child's mother assented to the" adoption petition after being told that the paper she was signing was "the adoption paper," although the attorney did not want her to "see the names of the adopting parents." [Citation omitted.]

The natural father and mother now live in a somewhat unsatisfactory apartment in a congested area. The father testified that he would plan to live for a time with his parents in a suburb of Boston, if the adoption should be in fact refused and if they should gain custody of the child. The father's income, while he remains a student and when first starting work, will be small compared to that of the petitioners.

The petitioners live in Winthrop and have adequate income and suitable facilities to enable them to give the child good care. Besides caring for the child, the female petitioner "keeps house for her husband, and a

[5] General Laws, c. 210, §5A . . . requires that the department "shall submit to the court not later than thirty days after receipt of . . . notice [of the petition], or within such further time as the court may allow, such written report as will give the court full knowledge as to the desirability of the proposed adoption." Partly because of the illness of the investigator originally assigned, a final report was not made until August 28, 1957, nearly a year and a half after the filing of the petition.

fourteen months old baby boy placed [there] . . . by the Catholic Charitable Bureau." They are happily married, "regular church attendants and highly respected in their community."

The department's psychologist examined the child in the petitioners' house. She stated that the female petitioner "is to be commended for her loving and wise care of . . . [the child] when she had two babies to care for at one time," that the child "shows by his splendid development and contentment that he is secure in this home," and that the male petitioner "is . . . devoted to the children." Counsel for the natural parents conceded that he did not "know anything ill or bad about the" petitioners. There was testimony of a psychiatrist from the Children's Medical Center that "any child who has developed very nicely in a family in which he has lived for nineteen months suffers a severe set back to be changed in [sic] any other situation."

The judge concluded "that it is for the best interest of this little boy to be the adopted son of the petitioners, not merely for security but also for the moulding of character."

Relevant statutes governing adoption are set out in part in the margin.[6] Various questions are raised by these provisions and by G.L. c. 190, §7 . . . which provides that an "illegitimate child whose parents have intermarried and whose father has acknowledged him as his child . . . shall be deemed legitimate and shall be entitled to take the name of his parents to the same extent as if born in lawful wedlock."

1. The failure of the department of public welfare . . . to consent to the petition presents no obstacle to the adoption. Under G.L. c. 210, §2A(E) . . . an appeal to the Probate Court lies from the department's action. . . .

2. The judge's finding . . . in a minor respect differs from the evidence, for the mother testified that she left the child at the doctor's office. This inadvertence is immaterial, for the judge would have been amply justified in finding that the doctor was the mother's agent to transfer the child to the petitioners. As the placement of the child for adoption thus was by both natural parents, the provisions of G.L. c. 119, §6 . . . were satisfied.

3. The probate judge's conclusion, that the adoption was for the best

[6] General Laws c. 210, §2 . . . reads: "A decree for such adoption shall not be made . . . without the written consent . . . of the lawful parents or surviving parent; of the mother only of the child, if illegitimate . . . " [Court's quotation abbreviated by Eds.] Section 2A . . . reads: "No decree of adoption shall be entered for the adoption of a child below the age of fourteen until one of the following conditions has been met: . . . (E) The petition for adoption has been approved in writing by the department of public welfare. . . . Any petitioner aggrieved by the refusal of the department . . . to approve such petition after being requested to do so, may appeal such refusal to the probate court . . . which court shall make final determination as to the allowance or dismissal of the petition." . . . Chapter 119, §6 . . . reads in part: "No person other than a parent . . . shall place any child under sixteen years of age of whom he is not the legal guardian in the care or control of any other person not related to such child by blood or marriage for purposes of giving such child a home, or for board, or for adoption. . . ."

interests of the child, was justified. We must consider, however, an issue of law which does not appear to have been argued to the probate judge.

An illegitimate child acknowledged by the father becomes legitimate under G.L. c. 190, §7, as amended, upon the intermarriage of the natural parents at least "from and after the time when the intermarriage becomes valid under the law." [Citations omitted.] The father acknowledged this child on various occasions . . . Because the child became legitimate about eleven months before the final decree, we must decide whether that decree could be entered without the father's written consent, in view of G.L. c. 210, §2 . . . If the persons whose consent to the decree of adoption is required under §2 are to be determined at the date of the decree, the consent of the natural father at that time may have become necessary. If the persons who must consent to the decree are to be determined at the date of the petition or upon the return of an order of notice under c. 210, §4,[7] then the result may be different. . . .

Sections 3, 3A, 4, and 5 of c. 210 provide some exceptions from the requirements of such consent laid down in §2. Sections 3 . . . and 3A . . . do not directly cover the present situation, although §3 does indicate that the date of the petition, in certain cases at least, determines the persons to whom notice is required under §4 and whose consent is necessary except as provided in §5 . . . .

It may be argued that G.L. c. 190, §7, has no necessary relation to adoption proceedings because it appears in a chapter of the General Laws relating to descent and distribution and because the section is usually thought of only in that connection. See e.g. 38 B.U.L. Rev. 299, 311-312. Section 7, however, has been applied in cases not involving the devolution of property. . . . There has been brought to our attention no indication whatsoever that the Legislature in framing the adoption provisions found in c. 210 has ever given any thought to the provisions of c. 190, §7. We recognize, however, that §7 carries out a broad legislative policy of relieving an illegitimate child, whose parents subsequently marry and whose father acknowledges him, from all the disabilities of birth out of wedlock and of placing the child on a parity with legitimate children for all purposes.

No prior Massachusetts case appears to decide the precise question here presented. [Citation omitted.] In other States, however, the question has been considered under statutes which vary somewhat from ours. See Annotation, 51 A.L.R.2d 497, 503-509. Some jurisdictions hold that the consent of the natural father to adoption is required where there has been legitimization of a child by the marriage of his natural parents and the

---

[7] Section 4 . . . reads: "If the written consent required by sections two and three is not submitted to the court with the petition, the court shall . . . order notice by personal service upon the parties of an order of notice . . . ." [Court's quotation abbreviated by Eds.] Section 5 provides: "If, after such notice, a person whose consent is required does not appear and object to the adoption, the court may act upon the petition without his consent, subject to his right of appeal, or it may appoint a guardian ad litem with power to give or withhold consent."

acknowledgment of the child by the father.[8] Decisions in other jurisdictions are consistent with the view that legitimization by intermarriage subsequent to the giving of consent to adoption by a mother, then unmarried, does not retroactively operate to make the father's consent necessary.[9]

In Wyness v. Crowley, 292 Mass. 461, 463-464, this court held that the consent of the natural mother, given before the filing of a petition under c. 210, §2, could not be withdrawn after the filing of the petition without the consent of the probate judge. [Citations omitted.] The effect of the Wyness case was thus to treat the date of the petition, with the prior consent of the natural mother upon it, as determining her consent . . . .

In the present case, the natural father participated in placing the child for adoption. This probably does not impose an absolute estoppel upon him to oppose the adoption for the probate judge in his discretion could certainly permit him to oppose an adoption as not in the best interest of the child. [Citation omitted.] At the time the mother's consent was given she alone had authority to speak for the natural parents under c. 210, §2, and did so. The father's consent then was not necessary. [Citations omitted.] The natural father's participation in the placement ought fairly to put him on no better basis, as of right, than the natural mother, who would not be allowed to withdraw her earlier consent except with the permission of the Probate Court. Her consent, conclusive when given, should be treated as binding on him as the other natural parent. Permission to withdraw that consent should be given by the probate judge only when the best interests of the child so dictate.

We give great weight to the considerations mentioned in the testimony (quoted above) of the psychiatrist from the Children's Medical Center. . . . When a child is placed by its parent for adoption in a good family the inevitable consequence will be that firm bonds of affection and confidence will rapidly arise on both sides. The damage to the child, who cannot understand what is happening, from breaking these bonds is something which even competent psychiatrists may be unable to predict. In the absence of compelling statutory command, such a breach should not be permitted lightly at the request of either of the natural parents who had their chance to take care of the child themselves and who themselves have created the unfortunate situation. The interests of the natural parents in such a case must be completely subordinated to the paramount interest of the child. . . . In the absence of any indication that the Legislature has ever had G.L. c. 190, §7, specifically in mind when dealing with c. 210, §2, we hold that the consent of a father who was not a

---

[8] Adoption of Anderson, 189 Minn. 85, 86 (but see Adoption of Anderson, 235 Minn. 192, 198-199). Adoption of Doe, 231 N.C. 1, 8-9. Sklaroff v. Stevens, 84 R.I. 1, 6-7. Harmon v. D'Adamo, 195 Va. 125, 128-129. [Further citations omitted.]

[9] Ex parte Combs, 150 N.E.2d 505. Davis v. Sears, 35 S.W.2d 99, 102-103 (Tex. Commn. App.). Adoption of Morrison, 260 Wis. 50, 63-65. [Further citations omitted.]

lawful parent at the child's birth . . . is not required by §2, as a condition precedent to adoption. . . .

Decree affirmed.

NOTE

1. A number of states either require or give the judge discretion to order an investigation by the welfare department when an adoption petition is filed. See, e.g., the Massachusetts provision quoted at page 486 note 5 supra; Neb. Rev. Stat. §43-107 (1960); Fla. Stat. Ann. §72.15 (1964). When an agency licensed by the state places a child, the investigation is usually pro forma. Whether judges frequently make use of discretionary investigations in independent placement cases is unknown. Forty-seven per cent of the Nebraska judges responding to a questionnaire indicated that they never order an investigation, and 22 per cent indicated that they do so only occasionally. See Broeder & Barrett, Impact of Religious Factors in Nebraska Adoptions, 38 Neb. L. Rev. 641, 651 (1959). Many caseworkers believe that the judges too often ignore welfare department recommendations. It does seem likely that many judges disagree with at least some of the standards agencies often use in assessing prospective adoptive parents;[10] moreover, since adoption agencies and the social work profession have usually supported efforts to ban independent placement adoptions,[11] some judges may believe that "social workers might tend to be more stringent in their evaluation of homes of independently adopted children than they would be of homes in general." [12]

Little is known about the quality or the results of welfare department investigations in independent placement adoption cases. The California Department of Social Welfare conducted a study, apparently unpublished, which reported that the agency recommended denial of 683 independent adoption petitions, or 20 per cent of the total filed, in 1951. Of the 683 adverse recommendations, 200 involved natural parents who had refused or withdrawn their consent to the adoption; in 62 of the cases, the adoptive parents had changed their minds; 41 of the homes were found to be unsuitable; the remaining cases involved unexplained "legal technicalities, some of which could be resolved at a later date." 1 Schapiro, A Study of Adoption Practice 110 n.3 (Child Welfare League of America,

---

[10] See generally the Broeder and Barrett study, excerpts from which are reprinted at page 508 infra.

[11] See, e.g., A Guide for Collaboration of Physician, Social Worker, and Lawyer in Helping the Unmarried Mother, 43 Child Welfare 304-305 (1964). See also pages 540-564 infra.

[12] Witmer, Herzog, Weinstein & Sullivan, Independent Adoptions, A Follow-Up Study 363, 366-367 (1963) (separate analysis of Professor Weinstein). Note the suggestion made by Jelks, Evaluating Adoptive Parents in Unprotected Adoptions, 41 Child Welfare 369, 372 (1962): "Recommendations that the adoption be granted may often have to be made despite some rather unfavorable findings, simply because the possible alternatives [e.g., the trauma of removing the child] would be more damaging to the child than the adoption."

Inc. 1956). See also Witmer, Herzog, Weinstein & Sullivan, Independent Adoptions: A Follow-Up Study 321-326 (1963).

2. One of the most striking features of most contested adoption cases is the time required for investigation and litigation. In Adoption of a Minor, three and a half years passed before the case was finally settled in the Massachusetts Supreme Judicial Court. In Sklaroff v. Stevens, 84 R.I. 1, 120 A.2d 694 (1956), cited in note 8 of the principal case, the petition was filed when the child was six months old, but the proceedings at the trial court level consumed two years and the appeal nearly another two years. The Sklaroffs, who had had the child since birth, refused to hand him over, and the natural mother, using her married name, sought and obtained a writ of habeas corpus. Skeadas v. Sklaroff, 84 R.I. 206, 122 A.2d 444, cert. denied, 351 U.S. 988 (1956). Delay can be tactically useful — the longer a child remains in the adoptive parents' home, the less chance there is that the adoption petition will be denied. Note the time lapse between the hearing and the trial judge's decision in the Ashton case, page 478 supra. Is there any way of dealing with this situation? For analogous problems occasioned by undue delay, see pages 518-532 infra.

3. The Report of the Departmental Committee on the Adoption of Children, Cmd. No. 9248, par. 104 (1954), suggested that the unwed father, even if he is unwilling to marry the natural mother, should not be totally ignored:

> [A] father who has taken a genuine interest in his [illegitimate] child should have an opportunity of making representations as a respondent to any application to adopt the child. This should not, of course, involve bringing the father (or alleged father) before the court as a general rule. We *recommend* that it should be for the guardian ad litem to ascertain and report to the court whether the father has taken sufficient interest in the child to warrant his being made a respondent to the application.

Most adoption statutes provide, expressly or by implication, that the consent of the natural father of an illegitimate child is unnecessary. See, e.g., the Massachusetts statute, page 487 note 6 supra; N.Y. Dom. Rel. Law §111. Although North Dakota has such a consent provision, the statute requires that notice of the adoption proceeding be given "to the father of an illegitimate child who has acknowledged paternity or against whom paternity has been adjudicated, unless the father has disclaimed in writing all parental rights with reference to the child." N.D. Cent. Code §14-11-10 (Supp. 1965). See also page 137 note 157 supra.

Suppose that the natural father has acknowledged the child without marrying the mother and that the jurisdiction provides for legitimation by acknowledgment alone. See page 33 supra. Would the natural father's consent to the child's adoption be required? See Embick, The Illegitimate Father, 3 J. Fam. L. 321, 327 (1961).

In re Brennan, 270 Minn. 455, 134 N.W.2d 126 (1965), involved an effort by an unwed father to obtain custody after the mother had surrendered the child to an agency for adoptive placement. During the trial, the father offered to marry the mother; the mother refused the offer and was opposed to his obtaining custody. The agency contended that although the father might appear and assert a claim to the child in a proceeding to terminate the mother's parental rights,[13] he could not interfere when the agency received the child by means of the mother's direct surrender. The appellate court did not agree, and it affirmed the trial court's refusal to dismiss the complaint (270 Minn. at 461-464, 134 N.W.2d at 131-132):

> The situation with which we are here presented was not specifically provided for by the legislature. It would appear that because disputes of this kind are not common, the right of the out-of-wedlock father to notice and to be heard has either been overlooked or intentionally omitted. This may be explained by historical experience from which it is assumed that the overwhelming percentage of fathers of out-of-wedlock children are not interested in their children, in recognizing them, in supporting them, in legitimating them, or especially in seeking their custody. . . .
>
> But . . . the expressed fears of the welfare agencies are not entirely warranted. . . . [I]t clearly appears that courts will hesitate to upset an adoptive placement at the behest of the out-of-wedlock father.
>
> But . . . courts express a natural and understandable willingness to listen to a natural parent who asserts a sincere interest in and concern for his child. . . . Even though the out-of-wedlock father does not appear before the court in the most favorable light, he should nevertheless be given an opportunity to express his interest when the mother has relinquished the child. . . . Although this policy may present some risk for the adoption process, it should nevertheless be permitted where the claim is asserted promptly and under circumstances to minimize the risk of trauma to the child or to the adoptive parents which would accompany judicial acceptance of his assertion.
>
> It should be conceded that by the procedure he followed, respondent here has tried to minimize these risks. . . . If he had failed to start this proceeding, his rights would have been jeopardized. Had the child been placed in an adoptive home, the rights of the prospective parents would have to be considered, which might greatly diminish the father's rights. To say that he must wait until proceedings are instituted to terminate parental rights, would imply that the rights are without remedies.

Subsequently, following the agency's withdrawal from the case, Mr. Brennan was awarded custody of the child. Sadden v. Brennan, Hennepin Cty. Dist. Ct. (Juv. Div.), Minn., June 23, 1965.

Suppose that a legislature, disagreeing with the decision in the Brennan case, makes it quite clear that the unwed father cannot claim custody

---

[13] See In re Zink, 264 Minn. 500, 119 N.W.2d 731 (1963).

of the child. In light of the responsibilities imposed on unwed fathers in most states, see page 49 supra, could the legislation be attacked as unconstitutional?

WITMER, HERZOG, WEINSTEIN, and SULLIVAN, INDEPENDENT ADOPTIONS: A FOLLOW-UP STUDY
109-118 (1963)

[Florida is one of the few states in which most adoptions are arranged by independent placement. The Florida Department of Public Welfare makes an investigation when an adoption petition is filed and reports to the court. See page 490 supra. This study, other excerpts from which are reprinted at pages 551-564 infra, was made during 1956 and 1957 under the direction of staff members of the Children's Bureau, Department of Health, Education, and Welfare, and was published by the Russell Sage Foundation, which supplied funds for the field work and gave consultation on various phases of the research. The investigators chose at random approximately one third of all adoption petitions granted in Florida during the years 1944-1947. Families which could not be found (some 27 per cent of the original group plus alternates) were replaced with alternates also chosen at random. The investigators interviewed a parent or both parents and checked the child's school records and adjustment, etc. The study was designed to examine the outcome of independent adoptions after approximately ten years; answers were sought to a number of questions (Witmer et al., supra, at 15):

> How well satisfied were the adoptive parents with the children they received? How often did they encounter difficulties with the natural parents? How well did the children develop? How good were the homes in which they were placed? By what signs, if any, can good homes be identified before the adoption petition is granted?

The excerpts below report the investigators' comments on the second question.]

All adoptions (like all parenthood) involve risk. One of the most frequently cited risks of independent adoptions is that adoptive parents may have difficulties with the natural parents. Gellhorn[14] mentions "possible legal conflicts, and even the possibility of attempted extortion." An article in the Yale Law Journal [15] warns that adoptive parents may be "harassed by a mother who has changed her mind and wants her child back." Yet, although much is said about this sort of risk, there has been little systematic evidence about the actual frequency of problems with natural parents, the kinds of problems involved, and the circumstances under which they occur.

In our sample, the proportion of adoptive parents who were "harassed"

[14] Gellhorn, Walter, Children and Families in the Courts of New York City. Dodd, Mead and Co., New York, 1954, p. 247.
[15] "Moppets on the Market: The Problem of Unregulated Adoptions," Yale Law Journal, vol. 59, March, 1950, pp. 715-736.

by the natural parents was rather small. Thirty of the 484 adoptive couples had told the Welfare Department's investigators during the period 1944 to 1947 that they were having or had had difficulties with the natural parents, and six others told our interviewers at follow-up in 1956 and 1957 of having had such problems. Together, such cases constitute 7 per cent of all that were studied.

The post-adoption experience of the 46 couples who refused to be interviewed by our staff might increase that proportion, but this seems rather unlikely. Only three of these couples had had difficulties before adoption. . . . Since none of the couples who were interviewed had problems with the natural parents that began after adoption, it is doubtful that many, if any, of the parents who refused to be interviewed had that experience.

For a complete count of this sort of risk among independent adoptions in Florida, there should also be added the adoptions that were not completed because the natural parents revoked consent or because they raised other obstacles to adoption after the children were in the adoptive homes. Analysis of the uncompleted adoptions during the 1944 to 1947 period suggests that such cases would raise the total would-be adoptions that involved difficulties with the adoptive parents to about 8 per cent of the whole.[16]

In addition to these cases, there may, of course, have been some in which problems with the natural parents prevented even an initial petition from being filed. There are no figures on this point, but the accounts of placements reported in the State Welfare Board records suggest that the number was slight.

We conclude, then, that the risk of interference and "harassment" by natural parents is probably something less than a one in twelve chance. The seriousness of such a chance will, of course, be rated differently by different individuals. . . .

The problems raised by the natural parents took a variety of forms. The majority were such as to arouse fear that the child would be taken away, either by legal means or by abduction. In 16 cases, natural parents threatened to revoke consent and in nine they actually did. In ten cases they threatened to take the child and in four they actually took him away from the adoptive parents for a period of time. . . .

Since the threats were made before the adoption petition had been granted, they were very disturbing to the adoptive parents, whether or not they were followed up. For the most part it was the natural mother who made threats or moves toward reclaiming the child. . . .

---

[16] During 1944 to 1947, there were 1534 independent petitions filed in Florida for the adoption of white children, unrelated to the petitioners. Forty-eight of these were not completed, 12 of them being withdrawn because the natural parents decided not to go through with the adoptions. Since the sample we studied represented something less than one-third of all the adoptions completed in Florida during the study period and since it was a random sample, it seems reasonable to add to the 36 cases already described an estimated four others (a third of the 12 mentioned above) for whom difficulties with the natural parents were known to have prevented adoption.

A number of natural parents vacillated between wanting the child back and wanting the new parents to keep him. . . .

A different kind of problem, usually associated with threats of undoing the placement, was the insistence of a natural parent — usually the mother — on visiting the adoptive home and seeing the child. In some instances the visits were friendly and wistful. In some they were associated with weeping and pleas to have the child returned. . . .

. . . Five adoptive families experienced problems of a different order. Three of these involved attempts to get money. . . . A different kind of problem, reported only once, was the unsuccessful attempt of a natural mother to force the adoptive parents to assume custody of an older child as the price of keeping the one originally placed with them. . . .

For the most part, difficulties with natural parents persisted less than a year. In more than half of the cases (22), the difficulty was resolved by the end of ten months, usually within six. In a few cases the period of overt difficulty was very brief. In 11 cases, however, the problems lasted between twelve and eighteen months; in 6, they persisted for more than four years, and in one they were still continuing at the time of the study.

What the tension or bickering between adoptive and natural parents meant for the children is a matter of speculation. Four-fifths of the children were under three years old at the time the problems with their natural parents were resolved. Moreover, the majority of these problems were worked out without direct involvement of the child — in six of the 36 cases with no direct contact between natural and adoptive parents. On the other hand, in a few cases the child was directly involved at an age when he must have been aware of the tension and conflict centering on him. . . . Actually, very few natural parents created problems after the adoption became final, but the adoptive parents could not be certain that this would be the case. . . .

. . . [One hundred fifteen] placements (24 per cent) [were] arranged directly by the natural parents . . . In all, 186 (38 per cent) of the adoptive couples had direct contact with natural parents at some time before the adoption was completed. . . . [I]t may be assumed that some natural parents who knew the identity of the adoptive parents did not approach them. . . .

As would be expected, difficulties seldom occurred unless there had been direct, personal contact between natural and adoptive parents. Sixteen per cent of the 186 adoptive couples who had contact, as compared with 2 per cent of those who did not have contact, had severe difficulties with the natural parents. . . .

. . . [T]he reverse of the coin is also worthy of notice. Eighty-four per cent of the adoptive families who had contact with the natural parents did not report it as a source of problems.

The importance of known identity probably accounts for the fact that difficulties with natural parents were most likely to occur when placement was arranged by the natural parent or some close relative or friend. They were much less likely to arise when placement was arranged by a doctor, a lawyer, a social worker, or some other professional person.

The less "personal" the arrangers were, of course, the more likely it was that the identities of the respective parents would not become known to each other. Again and again the adoptive parents informed the study interviewer that the physician who arranged the placement had told them only that the health history and educational status of the natural mother were favorable. A professional person arranged about half (53 per cent) of the placements in the total sample, but only four (11 per cent) of those followed by problems with the natural parents. On the other hand, natural parents or close relatives arranged not quite one-fourth of the adoptions, but over half of those in which problems developed. The difference between these proportions is statistically significant.

. . . A third factor making for difficulties was the manner in which the adoption came about. The placements that were attended by problems with natural parents fell into three approximately equal groups with respect to decision to adopt:

a. Adoptive parents had no prior thought of adopting and just happened into it   13
b. Wanted to adopt but had not made any move to do so   10
c. Planned to adopt and had taken steps toward that end   13

Six of the 13 impromptu placements developed from baby-sitting or boarding arrangements, or from some sympathetic acquaintance having told the couple that a baby in a foster home was available for adoption. . . .

Of the ten placements in which the adoptive parents had thought about adoption but taken no steps toward it, nine grew out of hearing by chance that a child was available. . . .

Decisions to adopt that were made on an impromptu basis were the most likely to be associated with problems with the natural parents. We do not have exact figures . . . but thorough acquaintance with the records leaves little doubt that most of the adoptive parents took a child after considerable thought. Thus, the proportion of impromptu arrangements among the parents who had difficulties was far out of line with what was usual. . . .

. . . The children in the 36 placements involving problems with natural parents tended to be placed at a somewhat later age than average. . . . While three-fourths of the children in the whole series were placed when they were less than a month old, three-fourths of those about whom problems with the natural parents developed were older at placement, a considerable proportion of them being a year or older.

In a striking number (12) of the 36 cases, the children were born in wedlock . . . compared with the 22 per cent of the total sample born in wedlock. . . . [This proportion] suggests that conditions likely to be associated with "parent problems" are also likely to exist when a married couple decides to place a child for adoption. . . .

The anxiety of the adoptive parents was not necessarily in direct proportion to the nature or duration of the difficulties with the natural parents. . . . The differences in reactions appeared to relate more to the individual than to the problem itself. . . .

. . . [T]he adoptive parents who had had problems with natural parents were no more likely to make such suggestions [that a person should adopt through an agency] than those who had not experienced such problems. About the same proportion of the others recommended using an agency or making sure that legalities were well taken care of. And a somewhat larger proportion recommended arranging the placement through a professional person.

Apparently, then, the adoptive parents who had had problems with the natural parents were unlikely to regard these problems as an argument against independent adoptions. This suggests that most of them took the problems in stride and, at least on a conscious level, relegated them to the past once they ceased to be a present danger.

NOTE

1. The Florida study also dealt with another risk commonly associated with independent placements — that the adoptive parents "may accept responsibility for a child physically or mentally incapable of maturing into a healthy human being." Gellhorn, Children and Families in the Courts of New York City 247 (1954). The authors concluded that "the chance of getting — especially of unwittingly getting — a handicapped child through the independent adoption process was small, and that even when such was the case, most parents rated the adoption as successful in spite of the handicap." Witmer, Herzog, Weinstein & Sullivan, Independent Adoptions: A Follow-Up Study 129 (1963). No information is available concerning the numbers of handicapped children placed by adoption agencies.

2. Adoption agencies claim that their placements afford better protection to adoptive parents than do independent placements against subsequent claims by the natural parent. See, e.g., Comment, 28 U. Chi. L. Rev. 564, 570 (1961):

> When an agency arranges an adoption the mother is given professional guidance and counseling to help her realize that adoption is the best solution for her and for her child; she is not urged to sign a consent unless and until she is validly convinced of its wisdom. In the private placement and "black market" adoption the mother may be exploited for financial gain and in any event is not given necessary counseling prior to signing the consent. As a result she may not be psychologically prepared to consent and later may have misgivings and attempt to revoke. . . .

See also State ex rel. Nelson v. Whaley, 246 Minn. 535, 545 n.3, 75 N.W.2d 786, 792 n.2 (1956) (reporting trial court's belief that welfare department would have convinced mother, "through gentle persuasion," that adoption would be in the best interests of the child and of the mother and her other children.) There are no data which would permit a comparison of the frequency with which revocation attempts occur following agency and independent placements. Although the appellate cases are not numerous, some children placed by agencies have been reclaimed by their parents. See, e.g., In re Baby Girl Larson, page 159 supra. Moreover, a number of statutes give the judge discretion to permit withdrawal of consent following a "voluntary surrender" of the child to an agency. But see La. Rev. Stat. Ann. tit. 9, §404 (1965) (surrender of illegitimate child is irrevocable). See Katz, Judicial and Statutory Trends in the Law of Adoption, 51 Geo. L.J. 64, 87-91 (1962). Nonetheless, the courts have been very unwilling to interfere with agency adoptions at the mother's behest. See, e.g., In re Surrender of Minor Children, 344 Mass. 230, 181 N.E.2d 836 (1962); Smith v. Welfare Department, 144 Colo. 103, 355 P.2d 317 (1960); Gonzalez v. Toma, 330 Mich. 35, 46 N.W.2d 453 (1951).[17]

3. A statutory (or perhaps constitutional) requirement that the natural parent be given notice of the adoption proceeding may increase the risk that the natural parent will delay or block the adoption. With respect to the possibility that notice is constitutionally required, consult Armstrong v. Manzo, 380 U.S. 545 (1965) (failure to notify divorced natural father of adoption proceeding initiated by stepfather denies natural father due process of law). Most statutes contain some notice requirement; those who oppose notification usually recommend that the natural parent's parental rights be terminated prior to the initiation of adoption proceedings. See Katz, Note 2 supra, at 67-69. If an agency formally terminates the natural mother's parental rights, she will not have to be notified of the adoption proceeding. See U.S. Children's Bureau Pub. No. 394, Legislative Guides for the Termination of Parental Rights and Responsibilities and the Adoption of Children (1961). But many private agencies would rather not compel the unwed mother's appearance in court.[18]

In the absence of a prior proceeding to terminate parental rights, some states apparently provide for notice in all cases; others either dispense with the notice requirement if a valid consent has been executed or permit the natural parent to waive the requirement, e.g., Mass. Gen. Laws Ann. c. 210, §4 (1958), quoted at page 488 note 7 supra; Minn. Stat. Ann. §259.26(1) (1959). Some states provide for notice to the natural parent

[17] With the Gonzalez case compare In re White, 300 Mich. 378, 1 N.W.2d 579 (1942), page 482 supra. Agencies have occasionally been urged to insure that the surrenders they obtain are in fact voluntary. See Heiman, Motivating the Resistive Client, Child Welfare, Nov. 1961, pp. 14, 15. For a suggestion that insensitive casework with the unwed mother may lead to another pregnancy out of wedlock, see Blatt, Intensive Casework with the Unmarried Mother with Her First Pregnancy, in Brief and Intensive Casework with Unmarried Mothers 8-9 (Child Welfare League of America, Inc. 1963).

[18] But see U.S. Children's Bureau Pub. No. 394, Legislative Guides for the Termination of Parental Rights and Responsibilities and the Adoption of Children 42 (1961): "Notice and appearance [in a termination proceeding] may be waived by a parent in writing before the court or in the presence of, and witnessed by, a clerk of court or social worker attached to and designated by the court, provided that such parent has been apprised by the court or by such person of the meaning and consequences of the termination action."

only if the child has not been surrendered for adoption to a licensed agency, e.g., Pa. Stat. Ann. tit. 1, §§1.1, 2.1 (1963); N.J. Stat. Ann. §9:3-23 (1960). If jurisdictions like Pennsylvania that discriminate, for purposes of notice, between agency and independent placements do not permit waiver, the agency placement provides more protection against an unwed mother's ambivalence. In some such states, however, protection may be afforded to the independent placement by a provision that the notice need not name the adopting parents. N.Y. Dom. Rel. Law §111. Whether such a provision can insulate the adoptive parents from subsequent harassment probably depends upon how the hearing is conducted and how determined the natural mother is. In states like Minnesota that explicitly permit waiver of notice by the unwed mother, the agency process is no more anonymous than are independent placements provided that consents in blank are permitted. An attorney or physician who arranges an independent placement can then simply include a waiver clause in the consent the mother signs. For discussions of the problem of notice, see Maxwell, Right of Natural Parents to Notice in Adoption Proceedings, 24 N.D. Bar Briefs 192 (1948); Note, 60 Yale L.J. 1240, 1248 n.27 (1951).

b. AGENCY PLACEMENT

PROBLEM

You are a law clerk to a judge of the United States Court of Appeals for the Eleventh Circuit. The judge is particularly troubled by the case of Morris v. Dept. of Child Welfare that has just been heard by a three-judge panel of which he is the senior member. He hands you the following opinion by the district judge and tells you that the oral arguments and briefs were not very helpful. You are to give him a detailed memorandum analyzing the issues and advising him how to dispose of the case.

(You will need to read through page 540 infra in order to handle this assignment properly.)

OPINION

John and Mary Morris
v. } Civ. No. 6236
State Dept. of Child Welfare

UNDERWOOD, J. This case presents an issue that is as novel as it is unmeritorious. Plaintiffs are husband and wife, residing in Charleston. They are members of a religious sect which forbids smoking, drinking, movies, dancing, television, card playing, and other kindred social activities. Their complaint alleges that nineteen months ago they first applied to the State Department of Child Welfare for a child whom they might adopt. After an extended waiting period, they, as well as numerous friends and neighbors, were visited repeatedly by an investigating officer of the Department. Finally, two months ago they were told curtly that they would not get a child. All subsequent efforts by plaintiffs to obtain a formal statement of the reason for the denial were unsuccessful. The complaint alleges, however, that plaintiffs believe the reasons for this action of the Department to be (1) their religious affiliation, (2) Mrs. Morris's part-time work as a kindergarten teacher which is said to violate the agency's desired qualifications for adoptive parents, and (3) the fact that their one other child was obtained through a nonagency placement. The relief requested is an order enjoining the defendant from engaging in its "arbitrary, capricious, and unconstitutional" conduct, including but not limited to its refusal to give plaintiffs any reasons for its action or a hearing thereon; a judicial declaration to the effect that plaintiffs are entitled to have their application for an adoptive child approved by defendant; and "such other relief as may be appropriate."

Defendant filed a motion to dismiss on the ground that the complaint failed to state a cause of action. Although the Department has therefore never directly controverted the facts alleged by plaintiffs, which on a motion to dismiss must be taken as true, counsel at the oral argument on the motion, in response to questions from the court, did assert his belief that the real reason for the denial of plaintiffs' application was that the Department became convinced, on the basis of its experience, that plaintiffs were too rigid and self-conscious about their religious beliefs, and that this made them emotionally unsuitable as adoptive parents. However, since the Department did not want to tell this to plaintiffs, it gave no official reason for its action.

This court has jurisdiction of this action under 28 U.S.C.A. §1343(3) (1962). We may assume for present purposes that plaintiffs have a sufficient interest to bring this action, and that adequate relief appears to be unavailable in the state courts. But that still leaves plaintiffs a long way from prevailing in this action, for they have completely failed to establish any tenable basis on which the requested relief can be granted. Indeed it would be a sad day for all the thousands of children awaiting adoption — not to speak of the agencies who patiently try to carry out the thankless and delicate task of placing these children in suitable homes — if the courts were to inject themselves into each and every decision made by these agencies that are charged with the responsibility for decision. The courts are simply not equipped to deal with this kind of problem.

Plaintiffs rely on the case of Rockefeller v. Nickerson, 36 Misc. 2d 869, 233 N.Y.S.2d 314 (Sup. Ct. 1962), which involved a somewhat similar type of action. There it was alleged that petitioners (white persons) were improperly denied the right to adopt a Negro child. But the court, after a hearing, summarily rejected petitioners' claim on the ground that the denial was based on other grounds, and that "the department's action in refusing to consider further petitioners' application was [not] arbitrary or unreasonable." 36 Misc. 2d at 870, 233 N.Y.S.2d at 315. Thus that case is certainly scant authority for the relief sought here.

Plaintiffs also cite a number of more remotely relevant decisions. In Niemotko v. Maryland, 340 U.S. 268 (1951), the Supreme Court invalidated the refusal to grant a park permit to a Jehovah's Witness. And in Hornsby v. Allen, 326 F.2d 605 (5th Cir. 1964), the court held that an applicant for a liquor license that was refused without reason, allegedly on an arbitrary basis, made out a prima facie case under 42 U.S.C.A. §1983 (1964), the provision that gives a remedy to anyone who was deprived of his constitutional rights by any person under color of state law. But there is quite a difference between an application for a liquor license or a park permit and an application to be permitted to receive a child for adoption. The choice of the most suitable parent for a particular child among several applicants is an extremely difficult and delicate task in which the courts cannot play any useful role. Moreover, plaintiffs have no constitutional right to adopt a child, and hence it is difficult to see how the cited statutory provision comes into play here.

Finally, plaintiffs cite the case of Dixon v. Alabama State Board of Education, 294 F.2d 150 (5th Cir.), cert. denied, 368 U.S. 930 (1961), which held that a Negro student expelled without reason from a state university was entitled to a notice of the charges against him and a hearing. This decision might be more apposite if the defendant here were trying to take away plaintiffs' child, or otherwise deprive them of some accrued benefit.

In conclusion, even if it be assumed for the moment that plaintiffs had made out their case, what relief should be given? Clearly this court cannot order the Department to turn a child over to them; yet that is the only relief that will give plaintiffs what they really seem to want.

For the reasons stated, the motion to dismiss is granted.

NOTE ON AGENCY METHODS FOR SELECTING ADOPTIVE PARENTS

In 1962 approximately 40,000 children were placed for adoption by public and private social agencies. See U.S. Children's Bureau Stat. Series No. 75, Child Welfare Statistics — 1963, p. 20 (1964). Many, but not all, of the private agencies are sectarian — handling adoptions only for members of the religion with which they are affiliated. See page 509 infra. Most agencies have a standard procedure for handling applications. Although methods differ from agency to agency, the process described below is fairly typical. When a couple seek information from any agency or express an interest in adopting a child, they are invited to attend a group meeting. At the group meeting an agency staff member discusses the agency's policies, how couples are chosen, and a range of other topics concerning adoption and adopted children. If the couple are still interested, they complete an application which includes questions about their marriage, their income, the likelihood that they will have children of their own, their reasons for wanting to adopt a child, etc. The couple, and each spouse individually, participate in an "intake interview" with a member of the professional staff, after which the intake worker and her supervisor decide whether to pursue the application further. If they are approved at intake, another caseworker undertakes the "home study," which includes a number of interviews with the couple and contacts with other persons who know them. Upon completion of the home study the applicants are informed if they are approved as adoptive parents; if so, their names are put on a roster which the agency — or perhaps all the agencies in a community or area — uses to "match" the children available for adoption with the approved applicants. Whether "matching" is important to good adoption practice has been the subject of continuing controversy in the child welfare literature,[19] but there is little doubt that it is a part of the process in most agencies. When a child is chosen for an approved couple, they are usually given an opportunity to meet the child and to decide whether he is acceptable to them. If they want the child and the agency responsible for the child agrees that the child should be placed with the couple, placement is made. The agency then supervises the child in the applicants' home for a probationary period which varies from state to state — usually six months or a year[20] — after which the adoption petition is filed by the couple's attorney.

Although the number of agencies charging a fee for placement services is growing rapidly, some 30 per cent — including many of the public agencies — charge no fee at all. Private agency fees vary from community to community — from a minimum of about $50 to a maximum of $2000 demanded by a New Jersey agency of couples with incomes of more than $20,000 a year. Many of the agencies which do charge for placement scale their fees in accordance with the couple's income. See generally Fradkin, A Study of Adoption Fees (Child Welfare League of America, Inc. 1961). Agency applicants are not charged for the mother's hospital costs, of course, but they must pay their attorney's fees and court costs incident to the adoption proceeding.

The decision to place a child, according to one observer, is "a step which can be fraught with such awful finality that it would make humble all but the calloused and case-hardened creature." [21] The Child Welfare League has promulgated standards for selecting adoptive parents which, although very general, give some indication of the factors agencies supposedly consider in studying applicants. The most important criterion, according to the Standards, is "capacity for adoptive parenthood":

> The study and evaluation of adoptive applicants should take into consideration the following characteristics which are presumed, on the basis of present knowledge, to indicate the capacity for adoptive parenthood: total personality functioning, emotional maturity, quality of marital relationship, feeling about children, feeling about childlessness and readiness to adopt, and motivation.

[19] See, e.g., Standards for Adoption Service 23 (Child Welfare League of America, Inc. 1959) ("Similarities of background or characteristics should not be a major consideration in the selection of a family, except where integration of the child into the family and his identification with them may be facilitated by likeness, as in the case of . . . some children with distinctive physical traits, such as skin color"). Compare 1 Schapiro, A Study of Adoption Practice 83-86 (Child Welfare League of America, Inc. 1956).

[20] See, e.g., N.J. Stat. Ann. §9:23A(4) (1960) (six months); Conn. Gen. Stat. Ann. §45-63 (Supp. 1964) (one-year interlocutory decree period).

[21] Lukas, Babies Are Neither Vendible Nor Expendable, 5 Record of N.Y.C.-B.A. 88, 104 (1950).

TOTAL PERSONALITY OF APPLICANTS. It is difficult to know what kind of parents people will be before they have the opportunity of actually being in a parental role. However, experience has shown that the way they have dealt with previous life situations, how they get along with their own families (particularly their attitudes toward their parents, brothers and sisters), their marriage, their work adjustment, relationships with friends, activity in the community, and the satisfactions they have experienced, have a bearing on a couple's capacity to meet the needs of an adopted child.

EMOTIONAL MATURITY. Adults who are emotionally mature will generally have a capacity to grow into parenthood as they experience a relationship with a child; and are likely to be able to give children the care they need. Some of the characteristics to consider in evaluating emotional maturity are: the capacity to give and receive love; acceptance of sex roles; ability to assume responsibility for the care, guidance and protection of another person; reasonable emotional stability; flexibility and ability to change in relation to needs of others; capacity for relationships; self-respect; ability to cope with problems, disappointments and frustrations; ability to accept normal hazards and risks.

QUALITY OF MARITAL RELATIONSHIP. The marriage should be one that could continue successfully even without a child. The emotional climate should be satisfying for the parents as well as for a child. Each should have respect for the other. . . .

FEELING ABOUT CHILDREN. Applicants should have a basic love for children and be able to have a relationship with and enjoy a child, as evidenced by experiences with children of relatives and friends, or other experiences with children. They should have a capacity for satisfaction from contributing to the development of a child and for allowing a child to develop and grow in his own way and at his own pace, ability to deal with development problems, and sensitivity, understanding and tolerance for children's difficulties. . . .

FEELING ABOUT CHILDLESSNESS AND READINESS TO ADOPT. The applicants should be able to deal with their feelings about childlessness, and should have arrived at a mutual decision to adopt. It is important to find out about possible feelings of inferiority and doubts about masculinity or femininity, whether there is a feeling of guilt toward the spouse, and whether they will be able to tell the child that he is adopted or have a need to deny this. . . .

MOTIVATION. The decision to adopt should be based on emotionally healthy needs, such as the desire to have a more nearly complete life, to accept parental responsibility, to contribute to the development of another human being, to love and be loved. Applicants may have a great variety of motives of which they may or may not be conscious. Any stated reason for wishing to adopt must be evaluated in the light of the total personality and maturity of the individual. Adoption as a means of strengthening an unstable marriage or merely acquiring an heir, or as treatment of emotional or mental illness, including grief over the death of a child, should be disapproved.[22]

The Child Welfare League's Standards are quite flexible in outlining agency "eligibility requirements" relating to such matters as age, religion, childlessness, the presence of natural children, working mothers, and the fact that the applicants have been providing foster care for a particular child.[23] But the Standards do not necessarily reflect casework practice in the private and public social agencies. Indeed, what little evidence there is suggests that although there is little uniformity, many of the League's principles are honored as much in their breach as in their observance. See, e.g., Broeder & Barrett, Impact of Religious Factors in Nebraska Adoptions, 38 Neb. L. Rev. 641 (1959), excerpts from which appear at page 508 infra; Brown, Positive Aspects in the Current Situation, 43 Child Welfare 292, 294 (1964): "Although many agencies agreed with [the Child Welfare League's age standard], some continued to have rigid age limitations"; Comment, Moppets on the Market: The Problem of Unregulated Adoptions, 59 Yale L.J. 715, 722 (1950).

No attempt has yet been made to determine empirically the standards different agencies have in fact applied in accepting or rejecting adoptive applicants. Nonetheless, any effort to assess the agency adoption process must take into account the fact that in many public and private agencies evaluations of adoptive applicants may not be carried out by trained social workers. (Employees in the better private agencies in large metropolitan centers are more likely to be trained.) In Massachusetts, for example, the rules governing licensing of private agencies handling adoptions establish the following requirements for staff education and training:

> Rule 6. All personnel shall possess good character and wholesome personality and shall have such additional qualifications as good health, emotional maturity, understanding of children, ability and desire to learn, flexibility, true appreciation of spiritual values, intelligence and competence in the function assigned.[24]

Brieland, An Experimental Study of the Selection of Adoptive Parents at Intake (Child Welfare League of America, Inc. 1959), reports a reliability study designed to test how trained agency caseworkers select adoptive parents. The study examined only the preliminary phase of the

----

[22] Standards for Adoption Service 38-39 (Child Welfare League of America, Inc. 1959).

[23] Id. at 35-38. Thus the age standard reads: "Adoptive parents should be within the same age range as that of the natural parents of the children whom the agency serves." Id. at 35. As to working mothers, the Standard reads: "A baby or recently placed child of any age needs the continuous care of his mother. Where a woman who is otherwise suitable as a mother for a particular child plans to continue to work, consideration should be given to her capacity to provide the mothering and care that the child needs, and to her ability to make adequate plans for him while she is at work." Id. at 37-38.

[24] Mass. Dept. of Public Welfare, Minimum Standards for Children's Foster Care Agencies 8 (1957).

agency process — the decision made following the intake interview whether to accept the applicants for further study or to reject them forthwith. Recordings were made of one caseworker's intake interviews with five different couples; these recordings were then played in random order to 184 trained caseworkers in 28 different agencies in 13 states. After hearing each interview, the caseworker-judges (1) indicated whether they would accept the couple for further study or reject them, giving a summary of their reasons, (2) rated the couple for strengths and weaknesses on a check list, and (3) ranked the couple's desirability as adoptive parents on a hundred-point scale. The results hardly inspire confidence in the agency process. With respect to acceptance or rejection, the average for all couples was 73.6 per cent agreement, which, while statistically significant, is not very high. None of the 25 agencies with two or more caseworkers participating in the study could claim uniformity among its workers as to acceptance or rejection of any of the couples or in the relative desirability rankings. Brieland's analysis of the reasons noted by the caseworkers for their decisions led him to conclude that the differences seemed to relate to differences in the caseworkers' personal experiences and value orientations. He added (id. at 58-59):

> Interviews that are directed specifically to competence in the parental role seem preferable to more projective interviews based on a diagnostic therapeutic model. Great differences in interpretation are evident when workers, with the limited evidence provided by one interview, use [the] client's responses to make depth-oriented evaluations. . . .
>
> Perhaps adoption agencies have been pushed into trying to achieve more diagnostic skill than is realistically possible at our present stage of knowledge. An agency should have two goals — first, to find good homes for the children for whom it is responsible and second, to eliminate from consideration those couples who would seriously damage children placed with them. . . .
>
> . . . [T]he sample of five couples did not include one with apparent serious psychopathology. No doubt workers can spot with more accuracy disturbed persons who would harm children.

Fanshel, Research in Child Welfare: A Critical Analysis, 41 Child Welfare 484, 497 (1962), criticized Brieland's study on a number of grounds, e.g., that agencies do not commonly make decisions on the basis of one interview and that the reliability data might have been more favorable if the cases, rather than approximating a random sample, had been widely distributed along a spectrum of desirable and undesirable parental attributes.[25] Whether or not one concludes that Brieland's study reflects ad-

---

[25] Fanshel also criticized the study because the use of tape recordings does not duplicate the face-to-face contact of real interviews. For purposes of reliability of the caseworkers' judgments, however, this was probably not a significant factor since all the caseworkers were subjected to identical conditions. On the other hand, since all the judges in the study had had graduate casework training, one would expect reliability to be greater than a representative sample of adoption agency personnel might attain.

versely on agency evaluations of adoptive applicants, Professor Fanshel's subsequent reflections on the subject merit careful consideration:

[There is a] need for conceptual clarity about the nature of adoption practice. To my mind, the so-called screening process in adoption has been overly emphasized, when, in fact, the major contribution of the adoption agency may lie elsewhere, namely, in the work that is undertaken with couples in preparation for a demanding parent role. In addition, misconceptions abound about the nature of the skills claimed by the caseworker . . . A number of recent research projects have been based upon the assumption that adoption workers must pass the test of being able to make quite subtle judgments about the varying parental capacities of adoptive applicants. . . . It is my view that caseworkers would be foolhardy to lay claim to this skill.

The present state of research-based knowledge in the behavioral sciences generally would hardly permit *any* profession to lay title to such magical perceptiveness. Examination of the child development literature reveals that the issue is still relatively open with respect to what constitutes the ingredients of a good parent or a bad parent. . . . Much more work is required for the development of predictive instruments that can make possible fine distinctions among parents whose children do *not* become delinquent or mentally ill or show some other form of overt mental disturbance. These middle-range parents constitute the great bulk of American parents.

I would maintain that all we can expect of caseworkers . . . is that they will be able to spot the manifestly poor risks among adoptive applicants. We would expect that they would be able to lop off the extreme shoulder of the curve, e.g., the psychotics and overt neurotics, and not to discern differences within the parent group of children who constitute the middle range.[26]

In recent years child welfare experts have often commented on the rapid growth in the number of children available for adoption and the decline in the number of applications to adopt relative to children available. See, e.g., Brown, Positive Aspects in the Current Situation, 43 Child Welfare 292 (1964). Hylton, Trends in Adoption, 1958-1962, 44 Child Welfare 377 (1965), reports the results of a national survey of public and private agencies conducted by the Child Welfare League. Although the survey took no account of the possibility that responding agencies had included Negro and other hard-to-place children in their data,[27] Hylton concluded:

The Supplement to this book contains (1) part of a transcript of one of the interviews used in the Brieland study and some sample caseworker responses to it and (2) a substantially shortened casework record of an agency investigation of adoptive applicants.

[26] Fanshel, Approaches to Measuring Adjustment in Adoptive Parents, in Quantitative Approaches to Parent Selection 18, 24-25 (Child Welfare League of America, Inc. 1962).

[27] See Herzog & Bernstein, Why So Few Negro Adoptions?, 12 Children 14 (1965); Fanshel, A Study in Negro Adoption 9 (Child Welfare League of

[E]ven a ratio of 146 applications to each 100 children available (the high in 1959) does not appear to be a comfortable one. Despite the increase in applications in 1961 and 1962, it has not been enough to counter the growing number of children available for adoption, and this ratio has gradually lowered to 122 applications for each 100 children.[28]

From 1958 to 1962, responding agencies had a net gain of 38.5 per cent in homes approved and a net gain of 44.5 per cent in placements made. Moreover, during 1960-1962, responding agencies "were apparently making nearly maximum use of their approved homes." Id. at 379. Nonetheless, the ratio of homes approved and placements made to children available was less than one to one for each of the years studied. Id. at 384. Since some eligibility rules were established when the belief was widespread that agencies received ten applications for every child available for adoption[29] — and at least in part reflected the agencies' desire to limit the number of applicants — the agencies have recently been urged to modify their rules and to encourage more couples to adopt. See, e.g., Brown, supra at 293-294; Letter from Edward J. Power, Exec. Sec., Diocesan Bureau of Social Service, Hartford, Conn., 41 Child Welfare 508, 509 (1962).[30]

Many of the agencies responding to the Child Welfare League survey indicated either that their eligibility requirements were being modified or that in individual cases the requirements could be waived. Most caseworkers believe that agency standards have in fact become less rigid during the last ten years because more children have been available for placement.

Even if we cannot be sure of the actual ratio of children available to applicants, there is no doubt that applicants are being rejected. Yet little mention can be found, in either the legal or the child welfare literature, of the interests of childless couples. Many caseworkers take the position

---

America, Inc. 1957): "As in other large urban centers throughout the country, the Pittsburgh community has had to look squarely at the fact that there are more Negro babies available for adoption than couples seeking such infants through social agencies." As to other minority group children and those with mental or physical defects, see Brown, Adoption of Children with Special Needs (Child Welfare League of America, Inc. 1959).

[28] Hylton, Trends in Adoption, 1958-1962, 44 Child Welfare 377, 379 (1965). The private agencies' ratio was consistently higher; the public agencies had a lower than one to one ratio of applications to children available in every year but 1959. Ibid.

[29] See, e.g., Comment, 59 Yale L.J. 715, 720 (1950). Of course, if most applicants are not interested in a large group of the children available for adoption, see note 27 supra, the agencies may still have to limit the number of applicants for the children who are in demand.

[30] Mr. Power argued that adoption agencies should provide a broad range of services to childless couples; he urged "a rethinking of that part of section 1.1 of Child Welfare League of America Standards for Adoption Service that reads as follows: 'An Adoption service should not . . . be expected to provide help for many of the problems associated with childlessness. Medical, psychiatric and casework services should be made available in the community to those whose needs cannot be met through adoption and who want such help.'"

that no one has a "right" to adopt a child and that, in any event, the agency's sole obligation is to insure the best possible home for the children it is seeking to place. Whether agency decisions to approve or reject applicants in fact further this objective is difficult to discover. Rejected applicants are not always given the "real" reasons for the agency's decision;[31] they can apply to another agency or, in many states, obtain a child by independent placement. Agency standards commonly receive judicial scrutiny only in the unusual case where a couple providing foster family care for a child while the agency seeks an appropriate adoptive home for him petitions to adopt the child despite the agency's opposition. Almost all the appellate cases which are reproduced in this section are such cases.

BROEDER and BARRETT, IMPACT OF RELIGIOUS FACTORS IN NEBRASKA ADOPTIONS
38 Nebraska Law Review 641, 644-683 (1959)

. . . As a matter of fact, we know precious little, almost nothing, about the relation of religious training to good citizenship and the good life and our social scientist friends have not yet done much to enlighten us.[32] Perhaps they never can; the problem of the relationship may be [insoluble]. . . .

The paucity of social science studies on the relation of religious training to behavior is paralleled on the legal side by an almost complete lack of statutes and caselaw concerning the importance of religion in adoption. There are, to be sure, the religious protection statutes . . . , and these have spawned some litigation. Petition of Goldman, in which the Massachusetts Court refused to permit the adoption by a Jewish couple of infant twins they had cared for almost from birth solely because the twins' mother, though consenting to the adoption, was nominally a Catholic, is perhaps the most famous recent example.[33] But such statutes and the cases they engender, while doubtless of importance, deal after all with

---

[31] See 1 Schapiro, A Study of Adoption Practice 82-83 (Child Welfare League of America, Inc. 1956): "[M]ore than four out of every five agencies explained the reasons for rejection. Although the most common reason was the disproportionate number of couples wanting to adopt healthy, Caucasian infants, agencies indicated that . . . there is a proportion of applicants who are considered unsuitable for adoptive parenthood because of psychological factors. . . .

"Social workers need to determine in each case whether they can really be constructive and helpful if they share the reasons for rejection. . . . It is important that applicants leave with the feeling that it is their application for a child and not they themselves who are being rejected. For this reason agencies attempt to relate the decisions about these applications to the children available."

[32] "Claims regarding the alleged . . . value of religious training and commitment . . . are the subject of considerable controversy in social work circles. The controversy continues without satisfactory resolution chiefly because too little research and documentary evidence have accompanied the frequent assertions of the value of social control and 'social adjustment.'" Hager, Race, Nationality and Religion, [3 N.P.P.A.J. 129 (1957),] at 133. [Further citations omitted.]

[33] Petition of Goldman, 331 Mass. 647, 121 N.E.2d 843 (1954), cert. denied,

only one religious factor in adoption, the question of crossing religious lines between the child's mother and the adoptive parents. . . .

While Nebraska has ten licensed adoption agencies three of them . . . together annually handle less than 2% of all adoptions and for this reason are here excluded from study. Of the seven remaining agencies, four, the Lutheran Children's Service, the Immanuel Children's Home and the Catholic agencies of Lincoln and Omaha ordinarily at least only handle applicants for adoption one or both of whom are members of their respective faiths or denominations — Catholic or one or the other of the two branches of the Lutheran church.[34] The Nebraska Child Welfare Department, on the other hand, considers applicants of all faiths while the Nebraska Children's Home and the Child Saving Institute consider all except Lutherans, Catholics and Jews all of whom they refer to their own respective agencies. Jewish applicants, it would appear, as a practical matter have no place to go except the State agency since their own agency has not had any children available for adoption for several years. The various agencies, together with the number of their completed adoptions [of] non-related petitions for 1957 . . . are as follows:

Name	No. of Cases	Percentage of Cases
Nebraska Children's Home Society	92	28.19
Office of Child Welfare (State)	60	18.34
Child Saving Institute	48	14.67
Catholic Social Service Bureau of Omaha	48	14.67
Catholic Social Service Bureau (Lincoln)	34	10.39
Lutheran Children's Home Society	29	8.86
Immanuel Children's Home	11	3.36
. . .		
	[322]	[98.48]

348 U.S. 942 (1955). Approximately twenty jurisdictions make some mention of religion in their adoption statutes. As of 1960, however, only a few states had provisions comparable to Mass. Gen. Laws Ann. c. 210, §5B (1958): "In making orders for adoption, the judge when practicable must give custody only to persons of the same religious faith as that of the child. In the event that there is a dispute as to the religion of said child, its religion shall be deemed to be that of its mother."

In Petition of Goldman the court held that the "when practicable" clause was satisfied by evidence, elicited by a Catholic adoption agency, and a trial court finding that there were many Catholic couples in the community equally qualified as adoptive parents who had already filed applications to adopt. 331 Mass. at 650, 121 N.E.2d at 844. The court brushed aside the contention that the statute, as construed, violated the first amendment as incorporated in the fourteenth. 331 Mass. at 652, 121 N.E.2d at 846. For a similar interpretation of N.Y. Dom. Rel. Law §113, see Matter of Santos, 278 App. Div. 373, 105 N.Y.S.2d 716 (1951), appeal dismissed, 304 N.Y. 483, 109 N.E.2d 71 (1952), 65 Harv. L. Rev. 694 (1952). See also page 515 infra. — Ed.

[34] Agency restriction of their services to applicants of a given faith is by no means solely a Nebraska phenomenon. A 1954 national survey of adoption agencies revealed that over half of the 270 responding agencies limited their services to persons of specified religions. This, of course, is accounted for by the sectarian nature of many of the agencies. 1 Schapiro, [A Study of Adoption Practice (1956),] at 78.

It should be noted at the outset that all of the agencies ask numerous questions concerning religious connections and either require or at least normally expect supporting references from clergymen. . . . Furthermore, all agencies check on the reliability of the information given . . . . [A]ll recognize and likewise always search for an "overemphasis" on religion. Getting the agencies to define "overemphasis" however was another matter . . . Nearly fruitless also was our effort to determine how often during the past five years applicants had been turned down on account of religious factors. However, something was learned. Several agencies indicated that they had frequently rejected applications where the applicants were of different religions and all admitted that they sometimes did so. . . .

While the study was initially intended only to cover agencies it soon appeared that a questionnaire survey of the county judges would also be useful. . . . [T]here is an unreal quality about all of the cases and literature dealing with the legal relevance of religion in adoption. Agency practice in screening out the "religiously undesirable" generally keeps religious factors out of court adoption cases . . . Nor at least in Nebraska is there legislation on the subject . . . . It must be recognized that our county courts in adoption cases are often in practice required to act in an almost administrative capacity. As the child has already been placed in the custody of the petitioners for six months and as no one else is usually available to take custody the county judges are not normally in any position to deny a petition . . . .

Again, there is the matter of independent placements. If adoption statistics for the nation as a whole are any criterion, Nebraska's adoption agencies handle just over 50% of all adoptions to non-related petitioners; the remainder, handled independently, are generally in Nebraska scrutinized solely in the county courts. . . .

The data of course must be taken with a certain amount of salt . . . [Q]uestionnaires are at best but a poor vehicle for obtaining information of the type desired . . . . [S]ome important matters had for practical reasons to be left out . . . Furthermore, the questionnaire took no account of the fact that many of the county judges would be personally acquainted with most of their adoptive petitioners and thus would have no need for asking questions about religious matters. . . .

. . . The 64 judges responding . . . granted 1458 petitions in the two years prior to the study and denied only 14.[35] Of the total number of petitions ruled on by these judges during this period approximately 44% involved step-parents, 33% were cases other than step-parent cases involving infants and 22% were non-step-parent cases involving children old enough to have received religious training. . . .

The first case considered is that of an infant *not dedicated* to any faith by a ritual such as baptism who is sought for adoption by persons of a faith different from that of the child's natural mother. . . .

---

[35] The small number of denials reflects the national pattern. The number of adoption petitions annually denied in the United States is "negligible." [Id.] at 26.

. . . [T]hree of Nebraska's seven major adoption agencies, representing 34% of all 1957 agency adoptions, automatically refuse an adoption in any case where the infant's natural mother and the adoptive applicants do not possess the same major basic faith. And this is apparently true though the natural mother would not object to or would even favor a placement of her infant across religious lines. A fourth agency, handling 15% of the cases, regards a lack of religious identity as "unfavorable" while a fifth, handling 3% of the cases, though checking "only slightly unfavorable," indicated that it had sometimes refused placement in part on this ground. On the other hand, the State agency and the Nebraska Children's Home, handling 18% and 28% of the cases respectively, attach no importance to the question normally though the latter would do so should a specific request be made by the natural mother. . . .

On the whole the judges seem to attach considerably less importance to the matter. Thus only 37% of the judges always (21%) or generally (16%) inquire about it as compared with 62% who only occasionally (10%) or never (52%) inquire. No judge would bar an adoption on this ground and 65% indicated that a lack of religious identity between the infant's natural mother and the petitioners would either have no effect (45%) upon them or only a slightly unfavorable effect (20%). On the other hand, 35% of the judges thought that a lack of such identity was either extremely unfavorable (14%) or unfavorable (21%). . . .

Closely allied to the case just considered is that of an infant who *has been dedicated* to some major basic faith by a ritual such as baptism who is sought for adoption by persons of a different basic faith. . . .

So far as the agencies as a whole are concerned baptism does add something. The dedicated infant is somewhat less likely to be placed across religious lines. The State agency, for example, handling 18% of Nebraska's agency adoptions, while attaching no importance to crossing religious lines in the case of non-dedicated infants, regards it unfavorably in the case of baptised or dedicated infants. . . .

Baptism likewise adds something for the judges. While none would automatically bar the adoption of a baptised infant across religious lines, 57% looked upon the practice with extreme disfavor (17%) or disfavor (40%) . . . .

The case now to be considered is quite different, that of a child old enough to have received religious instruction who is sought for adoption by persons of a faith different from the one in which the child has been instructed. Adopting a baby across religious lines is one thing; only the natural mother's religion and perhaps sometimes the natural mother's feelings can be hurt here. Uprooting a child previously grounded in the [tenets] of one faith and exposing him to another, on the other hand, may in some cases create serious psychological conflicts. And this is one point at least where psychologists and social workers concur. . . .

. . . Five of the six major agencies servicing such children would automatically bar the adoption while the sixth, the smallest, . . . thought such a situation to be "unfavorable" and indicated that it had sometimes refused to make a placement in such a case. The judges, on the other hand, were considerably more lenient. 43% said that the situation would either have no effect (30%) upon them or but a slightly unfavorable effect (13%) with 52% regarding it as unfavorable (31%) or extremely unfavorable (21%) and 5% holding it to be an automatic bar. . . .

Perhaps a more interesting dimension of the study involves the religiously mixed marriage. Two situations were examined, both involving infants as distinguished from children old enough to have received religious training. In the first the adoptive parents have different major basic faiths . . . and each regularly attends his own church. The second poses a couple belonging to different branches of the Protestant faith . . . with each parent again regularly attending his own church.

Religiously mixed marriages of both types . . . are very numerous. One recent writer, for example, using figures derived from Catholic sources, thinks "it . . . conservative to say that today, each year, at least one-half of all Catholics marrying find their mates outside of the Roman Catholic Church["][36] . . . Averaged in five year periods, the percentages of Lutherans marrying outside of their church are 46% in 1936-1940, 57% in 1941-1945, and 58% in 1946-1950.[37] . . .

. . . Unless one of the adoptive parents is a Catholic, couples whose basic faiths are different stand a very poor chance in Nebraska of securing a child through an agency. Three of Nebraska's seven major agencies, representing 52% of all annual agency adoptions, regard the situation as creating an automatic bar to placement. A fourth agency, handling 3% of the cases, views it as extremely unfavorable to placement and has sometimes refused placements on this ground while a fifth agency, the State, handling 18% of the cases, regards it unfavorably but not extremely so. The two Catholic agencies, however, handling 25% of the cases, have no objection whatever to making a placement with a couple whose basic faiths are different provided only that one of the parents is a Catholic in good standing. . . .

The judges, while again proving much less concerned with religious problems than the agencies, were nevertheless sharply divided in their reactions. . . . [A] large percentage of the judges, in contrast to the agencies, do not make the inquiries which would apprise them that a couple of basically different faiths is even before them. Thus in cases involving infants, for example, 42% of the judges never inquire concerning the names of the adoptive parents' basic faiths and another 13% do so only occasionally. . . . Two percent of the judges would automatically bar the adoption, 44% regard it as a factor extremely unfavorable (17%) or unfavorable (27%) to the adoption while 17% thought it was only slightly unfavorable. Thirty-seven percent, on the other hand, said that it would have no effect upon them one way or another.

. . . [Where] the adoptive parents are both Protestants but belong to different denominations . . . [the agencies' responses were] exactly the

---

[36] Bossard and Boll, One Marriage Two Faiths, 55 (1957). [See also page 801 infra.]

[37] Id., at 59.

same . . . . The judges, on the other hand, thought that the two cases were quite different. No judge would automatically bar an inter-Protestant type adoption and only 14% thought the situation to be either extremely unfavorable (2%) or unfavorable (12%). Eighty-seven percent of the judges said that it would either have no effect upon them (50%) or only a slightly unfavorable effect (31%). . . .

This portion of the study asks about the importance attached by Nebraska's adoption agencies and judges to such matters as the adoptive parents' church memberships, the regularity of their attendance at church . . . Such inquiries, and they are of course made, do more than just . . . raise policy questions of the most difficult character. The basic assumption of the inquiries, of course, is that participation in organized religion is essential to a good home and to the good life or at least helps make for them. But the assumption has not gone unchallenged and indeed has been a major point of controversy in adoption practice literature.[38] . . .

Now, what degree of interest do we as a population exhibit in religion? Approximately 49% of us belong to a church but doubtless many of our affiliations are little more than nominal.[39] Using the latest available national sample figures and taking our own statements in all cases as true, 36% of us, mostly women, went to church last Sunday while 64% of us did not.[40] Indeed, 42% of us have not attended church in the past month and another 11% attended only once. Only 19% of us attended each week during the past month and most who attended were Catholics. . . . "Never in the religious history of the United States is there much evidence to show that more than about one-third of the population ever went regularly to any place of worship, and sometimes the proportion has been probably much less." [41] . . .

. . . The general nature of the findings is readily predictable. The agencies on the whole were rigorously insistent upon church connections

[38] At the 1955 National Conference on Adoption, for example, "(t)here was . . . no agreement on the desirability of formalized religion in the adoptive home. Opinion here probably reflects a cross-section of opinion in the United States. It varied from those who believed that no home could be adequate for the nurture of a child unless parents were devoutly religious, to those who believed that ethical, moral parents, though they observed no formal religion, could provide a desirable home for a child." 1 Schapiro, [A Study of Adoption Practice,] at 59. . . .

[39] According to a recent survey, there are 74,125,462 church members in the United States, including 39,310,840 Protestants, 29,688,058 Roman Catholics and 5,112,024 Jews. Using 1950 census figures as a basis (150,697,361 total population) this means that 49.1% of us belong to a church. . . . Churches and Church Membership in the United States, Bureau of Research and Survey, Series A, No. 2, National Council of the Churches of Christ in the U.S.A. (1956). . . .

[40] Cantril, Public Opinion 1935-1946, at 700 (1951) (based on national sample in November, 1944).

[41] Hall, Religious Background of American Culture, quoted in Bultena, [Church Membership and Church Attendance in Madison, Wisconsin, 14 Am. Soc. Rev. 384 (1949),] at 388. . . .

while the judges or at least many of them were not. There is also the usual caveat in connection with the judges. Many of them simply do not ask the questions which would apprise them of the existence of the various situations. . . . 56% of the judges make it a practice always (31%) or generally (25%) to inquire concerning petitioners' church memberships . . . On the other hand, 43% of the judges only occasionally (10%) or never (33%) ask about church membership . . . .

. . . As would be expected, the adoption agencies uniformly make all inquiries necessary to learn of the various situations . . .

Where neither adoptive parent is a church member, five of the State's seven major agencies, representing 52% of all agency adoptions for 1957, would automatically refuse placement and several indicated that they had sometimes done so on account of this factor. The two major remaining agencies, representing 47% of all adoptions, would doubtless also do so as a practical matter. Both noted their extreme disapproval. Nor was it much different for the agencies when one of the applicants belonged. . . . When either the father or the mother did not belong, three of the seven agencies, handling 27% of the cases, would still automatically bar the placement, a fourth agency, the State of Nebraska, viewed it as extremely unfavorable while the remaining three agencies check the "unfavorable" category. In view of the large number of applicants for adoption in relation to the number of available children[42] probably every major adoption agency in the State must be regarded as closed to any couple both of whom do not belong to a church. With 47% of the state's population not belonging, this is a considerable exclusion.

The judges as a whole likewise attached considerable importance to church membership though by no means as much as did the agencies. Where neither adoptive parent belongs 2% of the judges would automatically bar the petition, 52% viewed the situation either as extremely unfavorable (19%) or unfavorable (33%) with 47% checking "only slightly unfavorable" (19%) or "no effect" (28%). . . .

The judges, unlike most of the agencies, thought the situation quite different where one of the parents belonged . . . Where the mother belongs and the father does not no judge would automatically bar the adoption, only 25% were extremely unfavorable (7%) or unfavorable (18%) while 76% said "only slightly unfavorable" (37%) or "no effect" (39%). . . .

. . . [B]oth the agencies and judges were less affected by non-church going than by lack of church membership though the agencies were still very much affected. Where neither parent regularly attends, two Protestant agencies, handling 24% of the cases, would automatically refuse placement though one indicated that the situation would only be unfavorable if it was impossible to regularly attend . . . . Three other agencies, representing 53% of the cases, viewed the situation as extremely unfavorable while the two remaining agencies, handling 22% of the cases, regarded it unfavorably. . . .

---

[42] But see the data reported at pages 506-507 supra. — Ed.

Furthermore, it was not too different for the agencies where one parent regularly attends and one seldom attends. . . .

So far as most of the judges were concerned regularity of church attendance was not particularly important. Where neither parent regularly attends no judge would automatically refuse his consent and only 3% thought the situation to be extremely unfavorable. 28% on the other hand thought it unfavorable but this is against 68% who thought it only slightly unfavorable (34%) or said that it would have no effect (34%). The judges were even less impressed when one parent regularly attended. . . .

All seven of Nebraska's major adoption agencies would automatically refuse placement where both adoptive parents have no belief in God . . . Nor is it much different for the agencies where only one adoptive parent does not believe. . . .

The judges, while on the whole definitely opposed to allowing atheists to adopt, were again considerably more liberal than the agencies . . . 22% would automatically bar the petition and 63% were extremely opposed (51%) or opposed (12%). 15% however said that the situation would either have no effect (12%) or only a slightly unfavorable effect (3%). . . . [T]he judges viewed the situation where one parent did not believe as about the same as where neither parent believed. There was some movement in favor of granting the petition but not much. . . .

NOTE

1. The religious protection statutes mentioned by Broeder and Barrett have received considerable attention and excited heated judicial and academic controversy. See, e.g., Ramsey, The Legal Imputation of Religion to an Infant in Adoption Proceedings, 34 N.Y.U.L. Rev. 649 (1959); 1 Proceedings, Institute of Church and State 61-126 (Villanova University 1958); Pfeffer, Religion in the Upbringing of Children, 35 B.U.L. Rev. 333 (1955); Note, Religion as a Factor in Adoption, Guardianship and Custody, 54 Colum. L. Rev. 376, 396-403 (1954); List, A Child and a Wall: A Study of "Religious Protection" Laws, 13 Buffalo L. Rev. 9 (1963). The statutes have been applied in independent placement adoptions, e.g., Petition of Goldman, 331 Mass. 647, 121 N.E.2d 843 (1954), cert. denied, 348 U.S. 942 (1955), as well as to placements by agencies, e.g., Cooper v. Hinrichs, 10 Ill. 2d 269, 140 N.E.2d 293 (1957) (children placed by court probation officer following judicial declaration of dependency).

2. With the cases mentioned at page 509 note 33 supra, compare Cooper v. Hinrichs, 10 Ill. 2d 269, 273, 140 N.E.2d 293, 295 (1957). The court held that the Illinois religious protection statute (Ill. Rev. Stat. c. 4, §4-2 (1953)) should be interpreted, in accord with "[t]he prevalent judicial attitude, . . . as advisory and discretionary, whereby the religious faith of the adopting parents is a matter for consideration, among all the circumstances of gradational significance in promoting the welfare of the child." The court added (10 Ill. 2d at 275-276, 140 N.E.2d at 297):

On the other hand, we do not imply that religious affiliation is no more significant than it would be in the absence of such a provision as section 4-2. This section . . . indicates a legislative intention to stress the religious factor and to direct the court to give preferences to persons of the same religion as the child to be adopted, where they are otherwise qualified to promote the welfare of the child. It does not, however, bar adoption irrespective of all other factors merely because the adopting parents are of a different religious persuasion than the child.

The court remarked that the Catholic Charities Bureau should not have been permitted to intervene in the proceeding, but refused to determine whether the trial court's allowance of the agency's intervention was prejudicial error.

3. Are the religious matching provisions designed to protect a mother's right to have her child raised in her own religion? If so, does this parental right theory require that if Protestant parents who have adopted a Protestant child are converted a year later to Catholicism, they must nonetheless continue to raise the child as a Protestant? Compare N.Y. Dom. Rel. Law §118-a (petition may be filed to abrogate adoption on ground that attempt has been made to change religion of adopted child). See also In re Doe's Adoption, 197 A.2d 469 (Del. Orph. Ct. 1964), page 533 infra. Or do the statutes rest on the assumption that the adoption is likely to be more successful if the religion of the adopted child and the adoptive parents is the same?

Religious protection statutes can lead to complicated religious and practical problems. Note the statement of Edward Terner, a New Jersey practitioner, quoted in 1 Proceedings, Institute of Church and State 125-126 (Villanova University 1958):

In a case in which I was involved, it seems that the child was born to Protestant parents who temporarily surrendered the child for custody to the State Board of Child Welfare. Lacking sufficient Protestant homes at that particular time, they placed the child in a Catholic home. It was an infant. These Catholic parents proceeded to have this child baptized. . . .

Later the custody of the child was transferred into a Protestant home and eventually it turned out that the child became available for adoption. The Protestant home in which the child was then placed proposed to adopt the child.

However, the State Board of Child Welfare said the child is now a Catholic, and before the Board would consent to the adoption of this child an agreement must be made to continue to give this child a Catholic education and bring this child up as a Catholic. . . .

See also N.Y. Times, Oct. 11, 1959, p. 1, col. 2, at p. 82, cols. 1-3:

This requirement [that the natural parent state a religious preference] recently threw a large nonsectarian agency into a minor crisis. An unwed mother in its care declared vehemently that she was an atheist, and refused to say anything else on the release form for her newborn child. . . .

. . . [F]inally she consented to list as her religious preference the denomination of her parents — Methodist. . . .

. . . The religion of ["true foundlings"] found in the city is listed as Protestant, Catholic or Jewish in rotation. . . .

However, if there is any indication of the child's religion, the child will be so designated. For instance, if the child is left on the steps of a Protestant church, the child will be designated Protestant. . . .

The problem arises when a foundling designated as Jewish in the rotational system happens to be a Negro, and when a dark-skinned child is born out of wedlock to a Jewish woman and a Negro man.

4. In Petition of Goldman, page 508 note 33 supra, the court did not indicate the ratio of agency-approved Catholic applicants to Catholic children available for adoption. One might argue that placement with Catholic adoptive applicants is not "practicable" if the Catholic children available outnumber the approved applicants. See Colby, Problems and Procedures in Adoption 38-39 (Children's Bureau Pub. No. 262, 1941), quoted in Note, Religious Factors in Adoption, 28 Ind. L.J. 401 n.2 (1953): "[R]epresentatives of both Catholic and nonsectarian child-placing agencies reported difficulties in finding enough Catholic adoptive homes to meet the needs of Catholic children available for adoption." The Note argues that religious protection statutes and agency religious identity policies encourage black market adoptions. On the other hand, most Catholic agencies claim that they have difficulty finding adoptive homes only for hard-to-place children, and with respect to this group, Catholic agencies are no worse off than other sectarian, nonsectarian, and public agencies. See, e.g., Buck, Children for Adoption 92-97 (1964) (reporting interview with Catholic agency executive).

5. Some of these controversial cases have not terminated with the appellate court's denial of the adoption. In Goldman, page 508 note 33, for example, the petitioners finally gave up their home and business and left Massachusetts in order to be able to keep the twins. See 1 Proceedings, Institute of Church and State 85 (Villanova University 1958). In Ellis v. McCoy, 332 Mass. 254, 124 N.E.2d 266 (1955), a petition for adoption was denied after the natural mother withdrew her earlier consent to the adoption of her child by a Jewish couple. The Ellises took the child to Florida; although they were later indicted for kidnaping in Massachusetts, the Governor of Florida refused to authorize their extradition. See N.Y. Times, July 9, 1957, p. 33, col. 1. The adoption was then approved by a Florida court despite objection by a representative of the State of Massachusetts. See id., July 11, 1957, p. 52, col. 1.

6. Caseworkers report that in some states agency practices with respect to religious considerations are far less rigid, and that some nonsectarian agencies are now actively seeking unwed mothers' consent to adoption by couples of religious persuasions other than their own. No data are available to evaluate these reports.

CRUMP v. MONTGOMERY
220 Md. 515, 154 A.2d 802 (1959)

PRESCOTT, J. This is an appeal by the petitioners below, Lloyd R. and Dorothy V. Crump, (the Crumps) from a decree entered by the Circuit Court for Wicomico County, dismissing the petition of the Crumps for the adoption of a minor child and decreeing the adoption of said child by Arthur P. and Blanche P. Montgomery, (the Montgomerys), who had also petitioned the court for the adoption of the child.

The child, Johnnie, was born in May of 1957 to an unwed mother. When he was seven days old, he was placed by the Montgomery County Welfare Board (Montgomery Board), which later received from his mother a written right to consent to his adoption, in the home of the Crumps, in Montgomery County, for foster care and pre-adoptive study. The Crumps had received five other foster children from the Montgomery Board and cared for them satisfactorily — not more than two being in their home at any one time. When first placed with the Crumps, it was thought Johnnie would be placed for adoption within three to six months. However, they were notified in a few months by a welfare worker that he was not adoptable, because of his showing in his early psychological tests. In later psychological tests, the child showed such improvement (his rating was then slightly below average) that he was rated as eligible for adoption and the Crumps were informed of this fact in September of 1958. During the intervening months (about 15) that Johnnie had been in their home, the Crumps had become very much attached to him and strongly desired him to be their adopted son. Oral requests concerning the adoption of Johnnie were frequently made by the Crumps to the Montgomery Board worker, but they were told, as they had been before, that they were not eligible as adoptive parents, due to the fact that they were foster parents, and also because the Montgomery Board had "closed its adoption list." [43]

Following the determination that Johnnie was adoptable, his name was placed on the roll of children in that category with the State Welfare Department in Baltimore, which roll is designated as a child "Pool." The testimony does not make the method of operation of this "Pool" certain, but it seems that the children's names (probably minus their surnames), together with their backgrounds, are sent to Baltimore, where they are, in turn, sent to the various Welfare Boards throughout the state to be considered for adoption by prospective adoptive parents who have made application to them. Johnnie's name came to the attention of the Wicomico County Welfare Board (Wicomico Board), which had such an application from the Montgomerys, who had already adopted one child through that Board. The Wicomico Board notified the Montgomerys,

---

[43] There was nothing in the testimony to show how many applicants were on the list before it was closed, or that Johnnie was ever considered by any of them. The adoption work of the Montgomery Board is but a small portion of their over-all business.

who, after consultation with the Board, consideration of Johnnie's background and an interview with him in Montgomery County, decided they would like to have him as their adopted son.

Much time was consumed and testimony taken below concerning the conduct of the Montgomery Board in taking Johnnie from the Crump home and transferring him to Wicomico County; but . . . in this class of cases the welfare and best interests of the child should be the paramount considerations of the Courts . . .

The Montgomery Board, over the protests of the Crumps, placed the custody of the child in the Wicomico Board for adoption, and thereafter, without any independent investigation of their own of the Montgomerys and without investigating the Crumps as possible *adoptive* parents, joined the Wicomico Board in consenting to the adoption of Johnnie by the Montgomerys.

Petitions for adoption were filed in the Wicomico County Circuit Court by both the Montgomerys and the Crumps. The Montgomery Board requested, and was granted, leave to intervene in the Montgomerys' petition; and, thereafter, the suits were consolidated for trial.

The testimony disclosed that Mr. and Mrs. Crump were 34 and 32 years of age, respectively, and had been married 12 years; they had one natural daughter, aged eleven, who was living with them; Mr. Crump had been an orphan himself and stated he desired to give some of the things that he had missed as a child to Johnnie; for the last six years they had lived in a modern brick bungalow in a desirable residential neighborhood in Silver Spring, Maryland; that Mr. Crump had been employed by the United States Government for nine years and was a scientist and engineer, receiving a salary of $7200 per year, which was supplemented by approximately $5000 per year, from his publications, inventions and private enterprises; one witness said that he was a "brilliant scientist"; that he was a steady, reliable and industrious worker; that Mrs. Crump was unemployed and spent her time in the care of the home, her child and the foster children; that neither Mr. nor Mrs. Crump indulged in alcoholic beverages and they were a compatible and congenial couple; and that the children in their home were receiving proper religious instructions.

In summary, the learned Chancellors below found that the testimony of "all of the witnesses who were familiar with the situation shows the Crump home to be an excellent one, . . . the care given to little Johnnie was all that could be desired, and no one, certainly not this Court, offers the slightest criticism of their conduct while the little boy was in their custody," but "[o]n the contrary, we wholeheartedly commend their conduct and what they have done for this little boy."

The testimony also disclosed that the Montgomerys are splendid people and maintain a nice home. Mr. Montgomery was 41 years of age — his wife 31 — and they had been married about 15 years. They were living in a "comfortable, modest and attractive" home in a wholesome residential community on the outskirts of Salisbury, with one daughter — 4 years of age — whom they had previously adopted. His home and automobile were fully paid for and he had money in the bank. The wife was a high school graduate, while the husband had stopped his formal education when through the eleventh grade, but had taken several vocational courses when in the armed services during the war. Mr. Montgomery had been employed by the Eastern Shore Public Service Company since 1948, starting as a member of a line crew and his "job," at the time of the hearing below, was "maintenance and utility." He received $2.18, per hour, from which he derived about $5000 yearly. He and Mrs. Montgomery were, also, a compatible couple, who were attentive to, and mindful of, their children's welfare. She was unemployed and spent her time in the care of her home where she saw that the children were receiving proper religious training. The Chancellors expressed their "complete approval and satisfaction with Mr. and Mrs. Montgomery as well as with the home they maintain."

The Montgomery Board objected to the Crumps as adoptive parents for Johnnie on two grounds: first, that in their opinion the child would be "over-placed"; and, second, it had not investigated their home for adoptive purposes *in accordance with their policies.* The Montgomery Board, while it advocated the wisdom of its established policy (not consistently applied) of not considering foster-care parents as eligible to become adoptive parents, concedes that this policy is not binding upon a court, which has the final authority to approve or disapprove a proposed adoption.

The "over-placed" objection was based upon the fact that Mr. Crump was a well-educated, highly intelligent young man, who might, because Johnnie was slightly "below average" in his psychological tests, become dissatisfied with the boy and exert "pressure" upon him if the child were unable to exhibit a very high degree of intellectual ability.[44] The Chancellors expressed serious doubt upon this point, stating: "We are not altogether in agreement with the position that an intelligent man should be penalized by being prohibited from adopting a child whose home and background is not apparently up to his standard, and especially is this so when the child is only 18 or 20 months old, and any determination of the capacity of the child to grow in intelligence must be speculative at this stage of his life. . . . On the face of the situation as we see it, without the ability to look in the future, it might well be that the possibilities offered in a home [such] as the Crumps . . . might indicate that the young boy could and would approach the future and manhood and man's responsibilities better educated and better prepared to successfully meet the competition which all young men must meet eventually. *We would be inclined to say that such a home would be more beneficial to him."* (Emphasis supplied.) [Court's quotation abbreviated by Eds.]

With reference to the fact that the Montgomery Board did not investigate the Crumps as adoptive parents (a fact which, of itself, could have

---

[44] This objection is based on one of the elements that comes under a general heading usually termed "matching." Rule 517.1 of the Board of Public Welfare calls for "likeness in temperament, intelligence and racial heritage." 1 Schapiro, A Study of Adoption Practice, p. 84, lists ten factors considered as important in "matching."

little, if any, bearing upon the outcome of the case), there can be little doubt that the Director and, at least, some of his workers knew the Crumps wanted to adopt Johnnie; and the Board's failure to make an adoptive investigation was due to its general policy not even to consider foster parents as prospective adoptive ones.

Had the matter of alleged over-placing been fully explored, it may have satisfied the Chancellors that their opinion, quoted above, was sound. It will be noted that the only testimony regarding the child's intellectual potentiality was the psychological tests given when very young. There was no other testimony concerning his background, other than that his mother was unwed. There was little of the hereditary background of any of the prospective parents given in evidence. And there was no professional investigation of the Crump home as an adoptive home, either by the Wicomico or Montgomery Boards or by an independent investigation directed by the court.

The results of Johnnie's early psychological tests would possibly be a matter of real concern as to his "over-placement" if they disclosed some serious impediment in his mentality, or if they could be correlated to his mental potential at any time in the future. However, while such tests are valuable in the ascertainment of a young child's current development, when given at the ages Johnnie's were, the text-writers and agencies seem to agree that they have small predictive value and bear little, if any, relation to a person's later or ultimate level of mental attainment; and there is no reason to conclude that a very young child, who shows slightly below average in such tests, will develop only a prosaic type of mind rather than one of keenness and alertness. Director Boyd R. McCandless, Ph.D., of the Iowa Child Welfare Research, sums the matter up as follows: "In summary, there is at this time no wholly satisfactory evidence that [psychological] tests given babies before the age of, at the earliest, eighteen months will predict later intellectual status in any useful sense." [45]

In considering further the relative intellectual powers of the prospective adoptive father, Mr. Crump, and the boy, it was noted above that it was suggested that because Mr. Crump is a well-educated, intelligent man he might, if permitted to adopt Johnnie, become dissatisfied with the union and exert undue pressure upon the boy if he failed to attain a high level of mental development. In order to give this its proper relative importance, it should be noted that the intellectual feature of matching is only one of many factors, such as race, religion, physical likeness, etc., that should be considered under the general heading of "matching adoptive parents with adoptive children." J. Richard Wittenborn, University Professor of Psychology and Education, Rutgers University, deals with the subject on pp. 131, 132, 133 of his book, The Placement of Adoptive Children (1957). He states that in the tests that he had conducted, . . . if a congruence between the ability of the child and the educational-occupa-

[45] McCandless, Psychological Assessment in Infancy and Very Early Childhood, p. 3. See also, Anderson, "The Predictive Value of Infancy Tests in Relation to Intelligence at Five Years," Child Development, pp. 202-210 [further citations omitted].

tional status of the home be important, we should find evidence for the ability of the adoptive father to accept the child easier in the families where there is a congruence than in the ones where there is an incongruence. He, therefore, divided his testing families into four groups: two where there presumably was a congruence between the children's Binet IQ and the educational-occupational status of the adoptive father, and two where there was an incongruence. He describes the result as follows:

> "We had argued that we might expect that the families in which there was congruence would be the most satisfied. Actually, this expectation was not fulfilled. We found no differences among our four groups with respect to parental satisfaction as indicated by such criteria as criticism of the child, desire that the child should be different in some respects, time spent with the child, etc.
>
> Thus our analysis fails to show any relationship between the pattern of congruence and the acceptance of the child."

Schapiro, [A Study of Adoption Practice], Vol. 1, p. 84, . . . points out there is "no one rule for appraising the qualitative contributions that any single factor can make to the general atmosphere of a home, as [t]here is no unanimity of opinion on what constitutes sound matching," and "matching has become more flexible because agencies have begun to recognize that some adoptive parents are frequently able to accept differences." [Citation omitted.]

Thus, we have two families that have been passed as eligible for adoptive purposes — both desiring to adopt the same child. The Child Welfare League of America Standards for Adoption Service, p. 23, says the selection of a family for an adoptive child should be made on the basis of an appraisal of their suitability for each other, and suitability "should be appraised in terms of the capacity of adoptive parents to meet the individual needs of the particular child . . ." [Court's quotation abbreviated by Eds.] . . .

In making short qualitative analyses of the two families involved herein, we make no reference to the qualifications where they seem to be equal . . . The Crumps have the better educational-occupational status (unless it is ultimately determined that the mental attainments of Mr. Crump will probably interfere with his accepting the child, or that he is likely to exert undue pressure upon the child to attain a level of mental development of which the child is incapable); they have a larger income, $12,200, per year, as compared to $5000; they have a slightly better residence; and Mr. Montgomery demonstrated in his testimony that he does not speak grammatically in simple, ordinary statements of speech. On the other hand, the daughter of the Montgomerys was nearer the age of Johnnie than the daughter of the Crumps (4 years as compared to 11), and Mr. Montgomery's mental development is not such as to raise any question about his accepting the child.

Another matter that the Chancellors should have thoroughly considered and weighed is that the adoption of Johnnie by the Montgomerys involved a change from the home, locality and environment in which he had been, practically, since birth.

. . . [The Chancellors] stated that they hesitated "to ignore these carefully considered opinions of the Welfare Board and *act upon our feelings in the case.*" They then stated: "As opposed to that [their own opinion that the Crump home would probably be more 'beneficial' to Johnnie than the Montgomerys'] we have what we are certain is the conscientious opinion of people who are long experienced in welfare work, . . . and who must be considered by us to be better prepared *to make a decision for this boy in this case* for his future welfare. . . . We hesitate to put *our opinion against theirs*. . . ." (Emphasis supplied.) [Court's quotation abbreviated by Eds.]

Thus, it is plainly seen that the Chancellors adopted the decision and judgment of the Montgomery Board . . . , although clearly intimating that their conclusion was contrary to the Board's. Code (1957), Article 16, Section 68, places the responsibility for the granting of adoptions in the counties of this State upon the Circuit Courts, and, in granting adoptions, it is the duty of said courts to determine what will best promote the welfare and interests of the child. Of course, the Chancellors were at liberty in this case to receive reports and recommendations . . . ; but . . . it was the function, duty and responsibility of the court ultimately to decide what was for the best interests of the child; and this duty and obligation cannot be abnegated in favor of any board or person.

. . . [W]e have decided, under Maryland Rule 871a, to remand the case without affirmance or reversal so that the court below may take such additional testimony as it desires, have an independent investigation made of the prospective adoptive parents and the infant if it deems the same necessary or desirable, and render a final and definitive finding, insofar as that court is concerned, as to what will best serve the welfare and best interests of Johnnie. . . .

The natural mother has filed a petition in this Court which may be considered in the nature of a petition to permit her to intervene. At the time of the trial below, her consent to adoption given to the Montgomery Board was over one year old, and she alleges that she had no actual notice of the proceedings below. As the cause is being remanded, she may petition the trial court for any relief to which she feels she is entitled.

Cause remanded without affirmance or reversal for further proceedings in accordance with this opinion . . .

NOTE

1. Following a complete restudy of the home situations of the Crumps and the Montgomerys, as well as psychiatric and psychological evaluation of the various parties, the Chancellors permitted the Montgomerys to adopt the child. They expressed their regret that "the transfer of Johnnie from the Crumps' home to the Montgomery home was inefficiently managed and badly handled"; "had the Montgomery County Welfare officials used some tact and diplomacy in dealing with the Crumps

. . . the transfer of the child could have taken place in orderly fashion, avoiding this lengthy and expensive litigation." Crump v. Montgomery, 224 Md. 470, 473, 168 A.2d 355, 356 (1961), affirming the decision of the Chancellors.

2. All couples with whom children are placed for supposedly temporary foster care pending adoptive placement are investigated and must possess qualities thought necessary to their specialized task. See generally Standards for Foster Family Care (Child Welfare League of America, Inc. 1959). Yet many foster parents may not meet the more rigorous agency standards for adoptive parents. One of the major differences between the two sets of eligibility criteria relates to the couple's age; because "agencies fear that younger couples without children may not be able to bear separation from a foster child, most select older boarding parents." N.Y. Times, March 9, 1960, p. 27, col. 1.

Only two years prior to the Crump decision, the Maryland Court of Appeals had affirmed dismissal of an adoption petition filed by foster parents. Ex parte Frantum, 214 Md. 100, 133 A.2d 408, cert. denied, 355 U.S. 882 (1957). The child was in poor physical condition when placed with the Frantums, but they nursed him back to health. Although the court's probation division investigated and recommended that the petition be granted, the welfare department refused to consent to the adoption on the ground that the foster father and mother were fifty-three and forty-seven years old. The opinion cited adoption literature urging the importance of flexibility in determining maximum age criteria; nonetheless, the court concluded (214 Md. at 106, 133 A.2d at 412):

> One cannot read even the printed record . . . without a feeling of sympathy for the foster parents who have done so much for this child . . .
>
> Primarily because of the inexorable fact of their age and its probable (though concededly not certain) effect ten or fifteen years hence, . . . an adoption by a younger couple would be better for the child . . . .

The dismissal was without prejudice to the filing of another petition if the child was not placed with a younger adoptive couple within six months. The dissenting judge, arguing for a distinction between foster parents who have cared for a particular child and couples who simply file an application with an agency, pointed out that the Frantums' daughter and son-in-law, who lived in an apartment in their home, would assume responsibility for the child if the Frantums became unable to care for him. 214 Md. at 107, 108, 133 A.2d at 412, 413 (dissenting opinion). For a similar result, see Convent of the Sisters of Mercy v. Barbieri, 200 Misc. 112, 113, 105 N.Y.S.2d 2, 3 (Sup. Ct. 1950) (foster child ordered returned to private agency "even though the respondent . . . is in every way a fit person to adopt [the child] except that . . . she does not qualify as to the age requirements" that neither foster parent be over forty years of age). Compare the Child Welfare League's age standard, page 504 note 23 supra; Annot., 56 A.L.R.2d 823 (1957). It seems likely that agency age restrictions lead some couples to seek a child for adoption by independent placement. Compare also the German law (BGB §§1744-1745) which provides that unless a special dispensation is obtained from the appropriate court, adoptive parents must be *at least* thirty-six years of age, and the adopted person must be a minor.

Of the 93 public and 111 private agencies responding to a Child Welfare League survey, "a large percentage" reported that they would waive or adjust the restrictions about maximum age, but only one public and one private agency reported the adoption of children by their foster parents. See Hylton, Trends in Adoption, 1958-1962, 44 Child Welfare 377, 385, 386 (1965).

3. See Eggleston v. Landrum, 210 Miss. 645, 50 So.2d 364 (1951), which held that foster parents, otherwise qualified to be adoptive parents, could not be refused permission to adopt the foster child simply because they were adherents of the Christian Science religion, one of the tenets of which is faith healing. The court relied upon evidence that the petitioners had given the child all necessary medical attention while he was in their foster care and that they had stated under oath their willingness to continue providing for the child's medical needs.

4. In re Adoption of a Minor, 228 F.2d 446 (D.C. Cir. 1955), involved a Negro stepfather's petition to adopt his white wife's illegitimate child. The trial court had denied the petition because "The boy when he grows up might lose the social status of a white man by reason of the fact that by record his father will be a negro," 228 F.2d at 447, and because both parents had received notice of eviction from a municipal housing development after refusing to sign the required "loyalty declaration" that they were not members of any organization listed as subversive by the Attorney General. The Court of Appeals reversed and ordered the district court to grant the petition, holding: (1) refusal to sign a loyalty oath cannot be considered an adverse reflection on the petitioner's character; (2) although race may have relevance in adoption proceedings, it cannot be considered decisive. The case concerns two separate problems: (a) stepparent adoptions and (b) racial criteria.

a. The Court of Appeals remarked (228 F.2d at 448):

> The child is living in the happy home of its natural mother and stepfather, receiving the same loving care they give to the two children born of their marriage. That it is in the best interests of the child to live in that home with the natural mother is obvious. It is equally plain that the child will continue to live there no matter what disposition is made of this case. Hence denial of adoption could only serve the harsh and unjust end of depriving the child of a legitimatized status in that home.

Estimates of the number of stepparent petitions usually range between 30 and 40 per cent of all adoptions. See, e.g., Broeder & Barrett, page 508 supra; U.S. Children's Bureau Stat. Series No. 75, Child Welfare Statistics — 1963, p. 17 (1964). Should a welfare department, exercising its statutory obligation to make an investigation and report to the court on the qualifications of adoption petitioners, utilize its normal criteria in stepparent cases? See Cal. Civ. Code §§226, 227a for an all too rare recognition of this differentiation. Why should the welfare department be given any investigatory responsibility in stepparent cases? Note that the adoption may affect relationships between the child and his divorced, noncustodian, natural parent — relieving him of any support obligation, perhaps depriving him of visitation rights. With respect to the circumstances under which a court may grant the stepparent's petition despite objection by the divorced spouse, see page 854 infra.

b. Most adoption statutes make no mention of race. In Louisiana petitioner(s) can only propose to adopt "any child of his or their race," La. Stat. Ann. §9:422 (1965),[46] while in Texas no Negro can adopt a white person or vice-versa, Tex. Rev. Civ. Stat. Ann. art. 46a, §8 (1959). Some of the southern states require that the investigation include consideration of the suitability of the racial affiliations which the adoption would create, e.g., Ga. Code Ann. §74-411(6) (1964). A few northern jurisdictions require the petition to note the race of the adopted child, e.g., Ind. Stat. Ann. §3-116 (1946); N.H. Rev. Stat. Ann. §461:2 (Supp. 1963). As might be expected, it is difficult to find litigation testing the validity of the statutes which do exist. There is no doubt that it is difficult to place Negro illegitimate children for adoption. See page 506 note 27 supra. See also Buck, Children for Adoption 115 (1964) (reporting interview with executive director of Protestant adoption agency). In recent years efforts have been made in some states to increase the number of interracial adoptions. See, e.g., PAMY's Progress: Report of Recent Campaign by Parents to Adopt Minority Youngsters (Minn. Dept. Public Welfare 1963) (reporting 11 Negro children adopted by white parents during first two years of program and forecasting increasing numbers of such adoptions in the future); Sheperd, Adopting Negro Children, New Republic, June 20, 1964, p. 10.

---

[46] The difficulties to which such prohibitions may lead are illustrated by Green v. City of New Orleans, 88 So.2d 76 (La. Ct. App. 1956). A child was born to a white unwed mother who died shortly thereafter. Without inquiry, the Bureau of Vital Statistics applied the presumption that the father of a white woman's baby is white and accordingly recorded the child as white. Three months later the child was turned over to the Department of Public Welfare because she was "growing darker day by day." Id. at 79. The Negro family with whom the child was placed, having been denied permission to adopt because of the child's recorded racial designation, brought a mandamus action to compel a change in the birth certificate. The principal evidence, aside from the child's "medium brown color" and the fact that the mother had worked "as a barmaid in a Negro saloon," was the testimony of a Tulane University anthropologist. Id. at 77, 78. He found a concurrence of "three characteristics which are distinctly Negro," but would only say that it was "extremely probable" that the nonwhite blood included "some degree of Negro blood . . . no matter how small." Id. at 79. Noting that it "is well recognized that anthropology is an inexact science" and that "all the methods presently in use to determine race are precarious," the court ordered the plaintiffs nonsuited and suggested they try again "when the child was more developed and mature." Id. at 80, 81.

COMMONWEALTH ex rel. CHILDREN'S AID
SOCIETY v. GARD
362 Pa. 85, 66 A.2d 300 (1949)

MAXEY, C.J. In habeas corpus proceedings the Court of Common Pleas of Allegheny County awarded custody of a female child, Betty Jean Tuttle, to the Children's Aid Society of that county. On appeal, the Superior Court reversed the judgment and awarded the child to Mr. and Mrs. W. Russell Gard, who have had custody of the child since June 28, 1945.

The child was born out of wedlock on January 19, 1944. Her mother, being unable to care for her, placed her in the Rosalia Foundling Asylum in Pittsburgh where she remained until May, 1945, at which time the Society requested the mother to remove the child because of its age. The mother then sought the assistance of the Children's Aid Society to arrange for the child's care. In May, 1945, Mr. and Mrs. Gard answered the appeal of the Children's Aid Society for foster homes for children then in the Society's custody. Mr. and Mrs. Gard sought to file an application for the adoption of a child but the Society discouraged it because of the large number of such applications they had already received. The Society's agent informed the Gards that there was need of "foster homes" for children. Being willing to provide such a home, the Gards on May 23, 1945, signed a "boarding home contract" in which they agreed "to accept any child so placed with us subject to the conditions laid down by the Society which we recognize has custody. We agreed to hold any such child subject at all times to the call of the Society." It was also provided that the Gards should be paid for "board, clothing, medical care," etc., for the child. They declared therein that they understood that "any child entrusted" to them was not "for placement and adoption," and they covenanted "not to do any act or thing with a view toward adoption."

On June 28, 1945, the child was taken to the Gard home and she has been there from that date to the present time. In August, 1945, the child's mother advised the Society that she had an opportunity to marry and she asked the Society to arrange to have the child adopted by suitable persons. On December 20, 1945, Mr. and Mrs. Gard expressed to the Society their desire to adopt the child. On June 28, 1946, the mother executed a formal release of her claim to her child and granted authority to the Society to arrange for the child's adoption. Three days before this, the Society advised the Gards, without stating any reason therefor, that the Society desired the return of the child. Appellees refused the demand. On June 28, 1946, without notice to the Gards, the Orphans' Court appointed the Society as Guardian of the child. On July 2, 1946, the Society filed with the Orphans' Court its petition for the child's custody. On July 29, 1946, the Orphans' Court directed the Gards to deliver possession of the Child to the Society. Upon appeal to the Supreme Court it was held that the Orphans' Court was without jurisdiction to decide the question of the custody of the child and that the parties seeking possession must proceed by writ of habeas corpus in the Court of Common Pleas.

On July 8, 1947, the Society filed its application for writ of habeas corpus averring, inter alia, its appointment as guardian by the Orphans' Court of Allegheny County, that custody of the child by it was necessary ". . . in order to perform the duties of its appointment," that "appellants presently have custody by virtue of the agreement referred to but have, after demand, refused to surrender the child," that "the Society pursuant to the wishes of the natural mother, has arranged for a permanent placement and selected an appropriate adoptive home," that "the immediate and permanent welfare of the infant requires that it should be in the custody of the Society" . . . On July 23, 1947, the mother of the child joined with the Society and refused to consent to the adoption of the child by Mr. and Mrs. Gard.

The Gards admitted the existence of the Agreement of May 23, 1945, and the receipt of the sum of $801.31 for the maintenance and support of the child. They averred that on May 12, 1947, they made a tender to the Society of all the money received by them for the care of the child, which tender was refused. They also averred that the Agreement was ineffective as "against public policy" and that "the best interests of Betty Jean Tuttle are best served by her remaining with the respondents." They denied that the Society had a permanent placement selected for the child in accordance with the desires of the natural parent, and demanded proof thereof. They declared that information concerning this matter "has been consistently denied to the respondents by the petitioners" and that they "have become attached to said child . . . and that they desire to raise and adopt this child as their own . . ." [Court's quotation abbreviated by Eds.] . . .

After a hearing on July 30, 1947, Judge ADAMS ordered the child returned to the Society. . . . Near the close of his opinion he said: "It is likely that adopting parents seeking a child — not to be boarded for a price, but to be their own — will develop a relationship more nearly like that of natural parents and child than exists now. The child's identity will be new in her new surrounding." In making this conjecture as to the child's future, Judge ADAMS overlooked the harm that would be done to her by the sundering of the close and affectionate relationship which has been formed between this child and the man and woman who have stood in a parental relationship toward her for more than three years. At the hearing, neighbors testified that Mr. and Mrs. Gard "have both been excellent parents, that they gave the child love and security," and that "they are very affectionate with her and she with them." One neighbor testified that "she never saw such a haunted face on a child" as this child had when she first came to the Gards' home, that the "sad look" on her face was "indescribable," and that "her appearance now spells happiness."

Witnesses described the community of Crescent Hills where the Gards reside as "very high class" and the reputation of Mr. and Mrs. Gard as being "the very highest." . . .

This Court is now asked to order the removal of this child from its present nurturing and pleasant environment, . . . into an utterly strange environment where it will be under the complete control of persons whose identity the Society has never disclosed to this or any other court . . .

. . . [W]hen in the oral argument before the Superior Court counsel for the Society was asked regarding the nature of the circumstances in which the Society desired this minor to be reared and cared for, he replied: "We decline to go into that. It is a secret of the Society." As to that Judge FINE, speaking for the Court, pertinently observed: "There are no secrets where the welfare of a child is concerned. For a court to award custody of a minor on a mere statement by the relator . . . would be to delegate the judicial function in such matters to the relator. . . ." [Court's quotation abbreviated by Eds.]

In reference to the agreement which the Society made on May 23, 1945, with Mr. and Mrs. Gard the Superior Court correctly said: ". . . contracts as to the custody of children are voidable agreements . . . and are subject to being set aside by the courts in the best interests of the child."

The basic error in the argument made in behalf of the claim of the Society for custody of this child because of the Society's "rights" under the contract of May 23, 1945, is that the child is treated as a chattel without any rights in respect to its own happiness and physical well-being. That a child cannot be made the subject of a contract with the same force and effect as if it were a mere chattel has long been established law.

An infant is the ward of the state and the latter may take the custody of the child away from even its own parents when the welfare of the child so demands. . . .

[A habeas corpus petition seeking custody of a child is decided] ". . . upon the court's view of the best interests of those whose welfare requires that they be in custody of one person or another; and hence a court is in no case bound to deliver a child into the custody of any claimant or of any person, but should . . . leave it in such custody as the welfare of the child at the time appears to require." 12 R.C.L., Section 34, p. 1215. [Court's quotation abbreviated by Eds.] . . .

It must not be forgotten that such a contract as the one on which the Society relies came into being *not* for the Society's benefit *but for the child's benefit,* and, therefore, it will be given only such legal effect as will serve the purpose of its creation. No guardianship is ever for the benefit of the guardian.

A child of two years of age or under will form new attachments quickly if treated kindly by those into whose care it is given. In that respect it resembles a young tree whose roots have not yet taken deep hold in the nourishing earth, but when a child is much beyond the age of two years, it becomes strongly attached to those who stand in parental relationship to it and who have tenderly cared for it. Its bonds of affection have become so strong that to sunder them suddenly may result not only in the child's unhappiness, but also in its physical injury. Even dogs which have been separated from masters to whom they are attached have been known to go into physical decline and sometimes to die as a result of that separation.

To take this nearly 65 months old girl, Betty Jean Tuttle, away from the only parents she has known since she was an infant of eighteen months would be exactly the same in its effect on her and on the man and woman who have stood in a parental relationship to her for nearly four years as would the separation of any well cared for child from its own parents. . . . [N]o judge can do justice without considering the human aspect of his problem.

The contention made in this case, that it would be better for the child to be taken from its present home and given into the hands of persons it does not know and whose identity has never been revealed, because of the so-called "illegitimacy" of this child's birth, is an argument of such little weight as to require no refutation. It is well known that Nature . . . never discriminates against the so-called "illegitimate," and the circumstances of their birth has been no blight upon their careers. . . . Now to separate this little girl from Mr. and Mrs. Gard would cause her far more anguish than any possible future malicious taunt as to the circumstances of her birth. . . .

The judgment of the Superior Court is affirmed.

PATTERSON, J., (dissenting). The majority opinion makes it appear that the order of the court of common pleas was based on the Society's rights under the contract, irrespective of the child's welfare. Such is not the case. On the evidence, including testimony given by the Society's supervisor and its trained and experienced case worker, and the testimony of the physician who has attended the child at regular intervals since placed with the Gards, Judge ADAMS found that "the child's best interest will be served by returning her to [the Society]," and based his decision thereon. His opinion states: ". . . The mutual rights and obligations of the parties growing out of the signed writing and [the Gards'] continued custody were considered only insofar as they throw light upon the basic issue." [Court's quotation abbreviated by Eds.] . . .

. . . Had the Gards released the child to the Society, upon request, as agreed, they would have no standing to maintain habeas corpus to regain custody. Their position would be that of a "mere stranger or volunteer who is in no way entitled to the custody, or responsible for the welfare of the child," and the question of the best interests of the child would not be considered in such proceeding: Commonwealth ex rel. Ebel v. King, 162 Pa. Superior Ct. 533, 537, 58 A.2d 484. By its decision that a different status can be acquired through the simple expedient of deliberate violation of the contract, the majority places a premium on disrespect for written obligations, solemnly entered into, and jeopardizes the effective operation of the Society and other similar agencies throughout this State. In the one case, as in the other, orderly procedure requires that the boarding home contract be enforced according to its terms, and, if the party or parties who have temporarily taken care of the child, for a consideration, under such a contract, should desire permanent custody or adoption, the question of their fitness can be determined upon a proper application for the purpose, as in other cases. . . .

MR. JUSTICE DREW joins in this dissent.

NOTE

1. The reason for the agency's refusal to approve the Gards as adoptive parents does not appear in the reports. Suppose the agency believed that although the Gards were suited for short-term foster care, they would make inadequate adoptive parents. What should it have done? What, exactly, is the status of Betty Jean after this decision?

Agencies can avoid the problem presented by the Gard case if they make sure that no child remains in a foster home long enough for the foster parents to establish strong ties with him. But the agencies would then run the risk that children like Betty Jean would be subjected to a series of traumatic "maternal deprivations." For a sample of the criticism leveled at current public agency foster care programs, see page 461 supra. Consider the following varied approaches to the problem posed by the Gard case:

a. The Angel Guardian Home, a private agency in New York, required all foster parents to agree that the child would be returned to the agency on request. In Convent of the Sisters of Mercy v. Barbieri, 200 Misc. 112, 113-114, 105 N.Y.S.2d 2, 4 (Sup. Ct. 1950), the foster parents were ordered to return to the agency a child whom they had given excellent care for several years. The court indicated that upon the record the best interests of the child would clearly be served by refusing the agency's request; nonetheless, the basic issue was whether such a decision would impair "the effectiveness of the placement and adoption programs established by public and private welfare agencies" by giving "a boarding parent the right to substitute her discretion and judgment for that of the public welfare officials and authorized agencies as to what is best for the welfare of the child." On the other hand, in a very similar case, Mary I— v. Convent of Sisters of Mercy, 200 Misc. 115, 121, 104 N.Y.S.2d 939, 945 (Sup. Ct. 1951), the foster parents were permitted to keep the child:

> The placement system in these particular proceedings must yield to the welfare of the individual child. This court refuses to sacrifice this infant's interests because of a claim that the interests of children, not before the court, will be affected by a possible impairment of a placement system, nor is the fact that the result reached may be operative as a precedent in future cases of any great moment. Each case will require an approach with respect to the facts therein presented and weighed accordingly. . . .

b. Some states have enacted statutes designed specifically to deal with the foster parent problem. See, e.g., Wis. Stat. Ann. §48.82(4) (Supp. 1965):

> Although otherwise qualified, no foster parent who has entered into a written agreement with the placing agency waiving his right to petition for adoption of a child placed in such foster home by the agency shall be eligible to petition to adopt such child except with the express written consent of its guardian.

For a similar provision, see Cal. Civ. Code §224n. Foster parents who are anxious to adopt might seek their own appointment as the child's guardian by the appropriate juvenile or probate court. In rural areas a court with county-wide jurisdiction might respond favorably to such an effort by local residents. In the Gard case, of course, the agency was appointed the child's guardian. See page 527 supra.

c. Wash. Rev. Code Ann. §26.32.030(5) (1961) provides:

> Written consent to such adoption must be filed prior to a hearing on the petition, as follows: . . .
> If the person to be adopted is a minor and has been permanently committed . . . to an approved agency, then by such approved agency . . . : *Provided,* That if the approved agency refuses to consent to the adoption, the court, in its discretion, may order that such consent be dispensed with.

See Adoption of Reinius, 55 Wash. 2d 117, 346 P.2d 672 (1959), a case similar to Gard, in which the adoption decree was vacated because the trial court had not given the agency an adequate opportunity to prove that it would not be in the foster children's best interests to dispense with its consent.

2. The difficulties occasioned by agency opposition to the adoption are not limited to the foster parent cases. A number of statutes require that the child's guardian, if he has one, consent to the adoption; often these provisions apply (or have been construed to apply) to private or public agencies to which the child has been consigned solely for adoptive placement. See, e.g., the Washington statute quoted in Note 1(c) supra; Minn. Stat. Ann. §§259.24(1)(f), 260.241 (Supp. 1964); Iowa Code Ann. §600.3 (Supp. 1964). In In re Adoption of Zavasky, 241 Minn. 447, 453, 63 N.W.2d 573, 578 (1954), 39 Minn. L. Rev. 567 (1955), a private agency placed two children in the home of approved applicants. Six months later, when the applicants petitioned to adopt, the agency refused to consent, claiming — without explanation — that the adoption would not be for the best interests of the children. The appellate court affirmed denial of the petition:

> We can only conclude . . . that the legislature intended to deprive the district court of jurisdiction to pass upon the merits of a proposed adoption if the guardian of the child refuses to give his consent, even though such refusal to consent is unsupported by any evidentiary showing that the proposed adoption is not for the best interests of the child.

But see Fleming v. Hursh, — Minn. —, 136 N.W.2d 109 (1965) (prospective adoptive parents who received child from welfare department entitled to hearing as to best interests of child when, eighteen months later, agency refused to consent to adoption and tried to remove child from home). Compare Adoption of McDonald, 43 Cal. 2d 447, 274 P.2d 860 (1954), which permitted a widow to adopt an agency-placed child; the agency refused to consent to the adoption because the plaintiff's husband had committed suicide eight months after the agency had placed the child pursuant to an agreement with the parents that the placement was probationary for one year and that the agency had the right to remove the child at any time prior to adoption.[47] The court held that the agency's consent was not required. Although Cal. Civ. Code §224n, added to the Code the year before, specifically entitled the agency "to the custody and control of the child at all times until a petition for adoption has been granted," the agency's relationship to the child is analogous to that of a guardian of the person to his ward — a status which "falls short of the close approximation to the relationship of parent and child . . . attainable through actual adoption." 43 Cal. 2d at 459, 274 P.2d at 867. The legislature then amended the statutory provision by adding (Cal. Civ. Code §224n (Supp. 1964)):

> After the petition for adoption has been filed, the agency may remove the child from the prospective adoptive parents only with the approval of the court, upon motion by the agency . . . , supported by an affidavit or affidavits stating the grounds on which removal is sought. If an agency refuses to consent to the adoption of a child by the person or persons with whom the agency placed the child for adoption, the superior court may nevertheless decree the adoption if it finds that the refusal to consent is not in the best interest of the child.

In re DOE'S ADOPTION
197 A.2d 469 (Orph. Ct.), aff'd per curiam, 210 A.2d 863
(Del. 1964)

McNEILLY, J. This matter arises by reason of a Motion filed by an Adoptive Agency of the State of Delaware in the following words, to wit:

> "The Adoptive Agency (name of Agency deleted) moves the Court to set aside the Decree of Adoption entered on July 26, 1963 and to deny the said Robert Doe and Mary Doe adoption of the said John Doe, a minor, on the grounds that the said Robert Doe and Mary Doe did fraudulently fail to reveal and did misrepresent certain material facts as to their qualifications to properly maintain, care for and educate the said minor; and that as a result of said fraudulent conduct it is not in the best interest of said child to be adopted by the said Robert Doe and Mary Doe . . . ." [Court's quotation abbreviated by Eds.]

In support of this Motion an Affidavit was attached thereto made by the Director of the Agency in the following language, to wit:

> "(1) I am the Director of . . . (Adoptive Agency) and among my duties am charged with overseeing the adoption policies, investiga-

---

[47] A common stipulation to which the agency and the prospective adoptive parents agree is quoted in In re Doe's Adoption, page 536 *infra*.

tions and recommendations made by the Agency, an authorized Agency under 13 Del. C. Ch. 9.

"(2) Social workers under my supervision prepared the customary investigation into the background and fitness of Robert Doe and Mary Doe, husband and wife, who wished to adopt an infant child through an Adoptive Agency of the State of Delaware.

"(3) No information was discovered which indicated that the Does were not morally and economically fit to be adoptive parents prior to July 26, 1963 by the Adoptive Agency or its Agents.

"(4) However, it has later been discovered that Mary Doe left the marital home on or about August 21, 1963 and on information and belief Mary Doe took up residence in Dover, Delaware with a Mr. Richard Roe, a former neighbor of Mary Doe.

"(5) On information and belief the home life represented to the Social Workers of the Adoptive Agency by the Does was deliberately falsified for the Does put on a display of domestic tranquility when in fact their home was not stable or conducive to proper adoption.

"(6) On information and belief the moral conduct of Mary Doe prior to the Final Decree and after the Final Decree makes her an unfit person to be an adoptive parent.

"(7) In light of the information obtained the Adoptive Agency would not have consented to the adoption of John Doe by Robert Doe and Mary Doe, his wife."

The Respondents, Robert Doe and Mary Doe, were married on May 18, 1957 and at the time of the hearing in this matter Mr. Doe was thirty-two years of age and Mrs. Doe was twenty-five years of age. . . .

Following the [Does'] marriage they attempted on many occasions to have children, but it was learned early in their married life that Mrs. Doe was unable to have children . . . Mr. and Mrs. Doe were so disappointed that they could not have children and so desirous of having children that she spent almost three years having medical tests and going through medical treatment in an effort to correct the unhappy situation. All of this was to no avail, however, and on February 4, 1960 Mrs. Doe first contacted the Adoptive Agency, a licensed Adoptive Agency in the State of Delaware, concerning the possibility of adopting a child. Since the present Petition is based upon fraud on the part of Mr. and Mrs. Doe in obtaining the ultimate consent of the Adoptive Agency to the adoption in question it becomes pertinent to quote a part of this letter as follows:

"My husband and I will be married three years May 18, 1960. To some people this doesn't seem like such a long time, but to us it is an eternity. We hoped we would be able to start a family right away. We didn't stop to think that we would ever have any trouble. It seems, as the time goes by, we just grow a little more disappointed. We talked about adopting a baby, and have decided that an adopted baby can make us as happy, as if we had our own. . . . We are both very fond of children, that is why it is so important for us to have a family. We are buying a new home, and plan to move in

April. A home is for a family to share, so we feel we cannot be entirely happy in one, unless children can share this happiness with us. . ."

Following this initial contact and subsequent communications Mr. and Mrs. Doe made a formal application on November 28, 1961 . . . In due course Mr. and Mrs. Doe attended a pre-adoptive meeting at which . . . time Mr. and Mrs. Doe were told by the Assistant [Director], in the words of Mrs. Doe, that now was the time prior to entering into the actual adoption proceedings to shake the skeletons out of the closet and take inventory of whatever problems they might have. No information was forthcoming at that time concerning any difficulties that might have existed between Mr. and Mrs. Doe, and there is nothing in the record to substantiate any thought that there were any differences at that time. In fact, the Social Worker who performed the background and pre-adoptive study para-phrased very well her conclusions of the actual marital status of this couple during and at the conclusion of her study in the following words:

"They like doing things together but with her working three nights a week and his attending school the two nights she is at home they do not have much opportunity for this except over weekends. Then they visit relatives and friends in Wilmington and Philadelphia, go to the movies, shows, chaperon C.Y.O. dances, help with other Church activities and enjoy romping with their poodle and collie. Mr. Doe likes to read and both attend the Albertson Civic Club once a month.

"Mrs. Doe likes to cook and try out new recipes. He likes to eat what she makes, he likes to build things for the house and she likes to sew.

"When they have disagreements they talk them out. He laughs at her when she gets going and this breaks her up. Both learned long ago not to argue. Mr. Doe said you win nothing by arguing. In a disagreement the emotional components get out of hand. So their sense of humor comes into their disagreements and then they talk them out.

"It is clear to see that this couple have a mutual love and respect for each other and that his strong pull is for his wife and his home while hers is to achieve the home life both want. Yet one is aware that children will enrich this home not because something is lacking in this marriage, but because there is in this marriage and this couple's attitude the awaiting of their complete fulfillment with the advent of their own children."

. . . [T]he Case Worker stated in this instance that it was her duty to make a study of the family but that it was not her duty to act in the capacity of an Investigator to uncover hidden facets of the prospective adoptive parents' lives. In making her study she felt that it was clearly understood by all parties concerned, as a result of preliminary interviews and lectures, that all matters pertaining to the family and family life of those who were being considered as adoptive parents should be held out to the Worker in an open and aboveboard manner. At no time during her study was any dissension between Mr. and Mrs. Doe noted, and according to the evidence before me it appears that no serious dissension did in fact exist at that time.

On March 23, 1962 the child who was then ten days old was placed for adoption with Mr. and Mrs. Doe, and thereafter another member of the Adoptive Agency took over the supervision of the child and parents in the adoptive home during the required ensuing year. Immediately following the placement of this child, . . . Mr. and Mrs. Doe signed an Agreement with the Adoptive Agency in which they agreed among other things as follows:

"We shall work closely with the Adoptive Agency during the supervisory year, keep the Agency advised of any significant changes in our family situation, permit its representative to visit our home, and attend Agency meetings designed to assist us with the adoption."

In the same text the Adoptive Agency through its Director agreed as follows:

"The Adoptive Agency placed a child with Mr. and Mrs. Robert Doe for the purpose of adoption and intends to allow them after a period of supervision to adopt the child legally and thus have the child become the same as their own natural child. We agree to consent to the legal adoption if, after the period of supervision, the above conditions have been filled and if we feel that the adoption will serve the interest of the child.

"We reserve the right to withdraw the child prior to legal adoption if, in our judgment, such removal is warranted and if we feel that the adoption will not be in the best interest of the child." . . .

Obviously, this was a happy couple living a fine and normal married life at that time, but the future was to bring forth insurmountable differences between them. During the course of the following year and prior to the obtaining of the consent of the Adoptive Agency this family was subjected to the normal supervision by the Agency Social Worker who was assigned to that particular case. Several home visits were made, and, according to the testimony, there were numerous phone calls and some office visits. At no time during this supervisory period was the Social Worker or anyone else connected with the Adoptive Agency advised of any marital difficulties in the Doe home. There were difficulties, however, which, according to Mrs. Doe, were small ones and which remained small until June of 1963 when, according to her, they all became one big problem. The basis for the difficulties and dissension which arose between them need not be hung on the family clothes line to air. The fact is that there were problems which Mr. Doe contends were caused by his wife and which Mrs. Doe contends were caused by her husband. . . . [T]he Adoptive Agency was in no way advised of the disagreements between them which ultimately led to their separation in August of that same year. This was the month following the signing of the Final [Decree] of Adoption on July 26, 1963 which was recommended and consented to by the Adoptive Agency on the basis of all studies and information which they had in hand.

This couple still remains separate and apart although after the institution of these proceedings efforts of reconciliation were made. According to the testimony of Mrs. Doe, she no longer loves her husband and states that whatever love she did have for him prior to June of 1963 was killed by him during the period between that time and August of 1963 when she left him. Her husband on the other hand, claims he still loves his wife and is desirous of a reconciliation. Such a reconciliation appears remote and improbable at this time . . .

Mr. Doe . . . has taken the position that he does not oppose the Petition of the Adoptive Agency although his testimony reveals that in fact he has every desire to be reconciled with his wife and to give this child a home wherein he would be raised to maturity by them as a true Father and Mother.

According to Mr. Doe's testimony he considered informing the Adoptive Agency of their marital difficulties prior to the signing of the Final Decree but did not do so because he still loved his wife, did not want to lose their child, and when he asked his wife about discussing the problem with a Priest she objected and stated that she would leave him if he did so.

Mrs. Doe on the other hand, does object to the Petition and very strongly asserts that at no time did she intentionally conceal the difficulties which existed between her and her husband. Mrs. Doe felt that their problems were normal family problems which they could cope with and which they should keep to themselves. . . .

At the present time Mrs. Doe and the child are living with her parents in Philadelphia, Pennsylvania, and it should be noted that the child has been in Mrs. Doe's custody since their separation . . .

The Respondent, Mary Doe, has moved to dismiss the Petition . . . First, it is her contention that the Adoptive Agency has no standing in this Court since it is not the real party in interest. This position I regard as being [untenable] since the Adoptive Agency did have the parental rights in this child during the entire period involved and since the consent of this Organization was required and relied upon by the Court in entering the Final Decree . . . Secondly, it is her contention that neither she nor her husband defrauded nor misrepresented material facts to the Adoptive Agency . . . .

The power of a Court to review and vacate an Adoption Decree on the ground of fraud is almost universally recognized. . . .

. . . [I]n the unreported decision in the Orphans Court of the State of Delaware, in and for Sussex County, . . . the Court in its Letter Opinion dated January 30, 1953 stated in part as follows:

"The Petition for revocation of the adoption is based upon fraud and misrepresentation. Our present statute is silent as to the Court's power to grant an annulment. . . . The authorities are uniform in holding that fraud practiced upon a Court is always ground for vacating a judgment. . . .

". . . [T]he Court's determination that the child was suitable for adoption in this home was based upon the report made to the Court by the State Board of Welfare. It then appeared, and still appears, that this report was based almost entirely upon the investigations and reports made by the Case Worker of the Kentucky Agency. These were accepted by our agency with little investigation on its own part.

"In the Report made to this Court in June 1948, there appear these statements: 'The psychological report stated that he is mentally above the average . . . James and his sister have become well adjusted in the home and are gaining real security and a feeling that they really belong. . . . The children are happy and free, well mannered and respond readily to gentle but firm discipline.' The statement concerning the child's mentality was apparently based upon the psychological test given in January 1947. Nothing was brought to the Court's attention at that time concerning the two previous psychological examinations in 1946 . . . . It will suffice to say that, had the Court known of those two prior tests and the results thereof, it no doubt would have suggested further tests and study before entering a final judgment. . . .

"More important, to my mind, is that part of the report which indicates that the child was adjusting so nicely in its new home and was responding readily to gentle but firm discipline. Uncontradicted evidence now before me shows this statement to have been untrue at the time it was made, that the child was actually not responding to discipline at the time, that it was not adjusting nicely in the home, and that the investigator had been informed of this condition and had seen some of the effects of it on a visit to the home in New Orleans. . . . Whatever the reason may have been for failure to do so, the facts should have been brought to the Court's attention. Had this been done, the Court would definitely have declined to sign a final decree until it was satisfied that the situation had been corrected. Concealment of these vital facts . . . constituted misrepresentation and fraud upon the Court.

"If the placement had worked out for the best interests of the child, perhaps the Court would be justified in refusing the present application. . . ." [Court's quotation abbreviated by Eds.]

In deciding the case before me at this time I adopt the same reasoning set forth by the Court at that time. In my opinion, the failure on the part of the Respondents to disclose their marital difficulties after they became major ones during the summer of 1963 prior to the signing of the Final Decree of Adoption would have caused the Adoptive Agency to withhold its consent . . . The consent of the Adoptive Agency was a prerequisite to the Court's issuance of its Final Decree, and, therefore, the failure on the part of the Respondents to disclose information which they knew or should have known would have caused the withdrawal of the consent by the Adoptive Agency constitutes fraud sufficient to cause this Court to revoke its Decree.

The question then which is of most importance is whether the best interest of the adopted child, John Doe, would be best served at this time by revoking or not revoking the Adoption Decree.

After listening to the testimony of the Doctors who are both known and respected authorities in the State of Delaware in infant psychology, and after listening to the testimony of the maternal Grandmother in whose home the child is now residing and the testimony of all other witnesses I cannot help but feel that the love of Mrs. Doe for this child and, in fact, the love of Mr. Doe as well is very strong. I also consider the evaluation of the child's progress as an indication that this child has been extremely well cared for and that he might very well continue his growth toward maturity in a perfectly normal and positive manner. The decision as to what is in the best interest of the child is a most difficult one and, in any event, must be based to some degree on conjecture and speculation as to what the future might hold in store for this child. Were this an older child my feeling might be contrary to my present feeling, but at this time I am of the opinion that it would be to the best interest of this child to revoke the adoption and to return the child to the Adoptive Agency for replacement in an undivided home . . .

An Order will be entered accordingly.

NOTE

1. The Sussex County Orphans' Court decision upon which the judge in Doe relied was apparently the result of a petition by the adoptive parents to have the adoption set aside. This issue is considered at page 565 infra. Are the relevant considerations the same when the agency is the moving party?

2. A number of adoption statutes deal with the problem presented by the Doe case. See, e.g., N.D. Cent. Code §14-11-12 (1960), which provides that after an adoption decree has been entered, proceedings to attack the validity of an adoption "must be commenced within one year from the date of entering the decree of adoption." See also Cal. Civ. Code §227d (action to set aside a decree on the ground of any defect or irregularity of procedure must be commenced within three years; on any other ground, action must be commenced within five years); D.C. Code Ann. §§16-310, 16-311 (Supp. 1965) (attempt to invalidate adoption decree "by reason of a jurisdictional or procedural defect" must be filed within one year after decree becomes final; records in adoption proceedings sealed after petition is filed and inspection permitted by any person only upon order of court "when the court is satisfied that the welfare of the child will thereby be promoted or protected"). See In re Wells, 281 F.2d 68 (D.C. Cir. 1960) (natural mother may not search records three years after adoption decree, which followed termination of mother's parental rights by juvenile court, since she makes no showing that the welfare of the child would

be served and no showing of fraud on the face of the record). Note that these statutes may apply to independent placement adoptions as well as agency placements.

C.   CONTROL OF CHILD PLACEMENT — AN EVALUATION OF LEGISLATIVE ALTERNATIVES

PROBLEM

In response to increasing concern about black market adoptions, the following bill has been proposed for enactment by the United States Congress.[48] In light of the material in this and preceding sections, would you favor enactment of this legislation? What modifications would you suggest? Alternatively, would you favor a similarly worded statute (subject to deletion of the "interstate commerce" phrases) for enactment by the states as a Uniform Adoptive Placement Act?

§1181. PLACING CHILD FOR PERMANENT FREE CARE OR FOR ADOPTION FOR COMPENSATION

(a) Whoever, either by himself or through any agent or employee, or other person, directly or indirectly solicits, collects, or receives any money or anything of value, or the promise thereof, in any manner whatsoever, for placing or arranging for the placement of any child in any home for permanent free care or for adoption, under circumstances requiring or resulting in such child being transported in interstate or foreign commerce, shall be fined not more than $10,000 or imprisoned not more than five years, or both.

(b) The provisions of this section shall not apply in the case of (1) money received by or paid to a child-care or adoption agency in any State, either public or private, which is authorized or licensed by said State to provide permanent care for children or to place children for adoption, as reimbursement for providing services by said agency; (2) reasonable fees received solely for professional legal services; or (3) reasonable fees received solely for professional medical services directly in connection with the prenatal care of the natural mother or delivery, examination, or treatment of the child.

(c) Nothing in this section shall be construed to penalize (1) any person for placing or arranging for the legal placement of any child in any home for permanent free care or adoption, if such person is the natural parent of such child; or (2) any person who legally arranges, or seeks to arrange, for the placement in his home of a child for the purpose of adopting such child or providing him with permanent free care.

§1182. COERCION OR ENTICEMENT OF NATURAL PARENT OR ADOPTIVE PARENTS

---

[48] Compare S. 1541, 88th Cong., 1st Sess. (1963); Interstate Compact on the Placement of Children, N.Y. Soc. Welfare Law §374a.

(a) Whoever, by himself or through any agent or employee or other person, whether in return for the payment or receipt of money or anything of value, or the promise thereof or without any such payment or receipt, in any manner whatsoever, persuades, induces, coerces, or arranges for a parent of a child (including a child in ventre sa mere) to travel from or to another place in interstate or foreign commerce to place said child for permanent free care or for adoption when the placement is made or will be made in return for the payment of money or anything of value, shall be fined not more than $10,000 or imprisoned not more than five years, or both.

(b) Whoever, by himself or through any agent or employee or other person, whether in return for the payment or receipt of money or anything of value, or the promise thereof, or without any such payment or receipt, in any manner whatsoever, persuades, induces, coerces, or arranges for a prospective adoptive parent, or prospective adoptive parents, to travel from or to another place in interstate or foreign commerce to obtain a child for the purpose of adopting such child or providing him with permanent free care, when the placement is made or will be made in return for the payment of money or anything of value, shall be fined not more than $10,000 or imprisoned not more than five years, or both.

(c) The provisions of this section shall not interfere in any manner with arrangements for the transportation of a natural mother in interstate or foreign commerce by (1) any child-care or adoption agency in any State, either public or private, which is authorized or licensed by such State to provide permanent care for children or to place children for adoption; (2) any licensed or authorized maternity home or shelter; or (3) any person who legally arranges or seeks to arrange for the placement in his home of a child for the purpose of adopting such child or providing him with permanent free care.

§1183. DEFINITIONS

As used in this chapter —

(1) The term "child" means any individual who has not attained the age of sixteen years; and

(2) The term "permanent free care" means the care given to any child on a permanent basis by any person who is not receiving compensation therefor, and is not either related to the child nor standing in such relation to the child or its mother as to create a legal interest in the child's welfare, but such term does not include the free care provided to any child by any licensed or authorized child-care agency or juvenile court.

GOODMAN v. DISTRICT OF COLUMBIA
50 A.2d 812 (D.C. Mun. Ct. App. 1947)

CAYTON, C.J. Appellant, who is a practicing lawyer, was found guilty of violating the so-called Baby Broker's Law. Code 1940, §§32-781 to 32-789. He appeals.

Appellant was associated as counsel for a woman who was separated from her husband and who was being sued for divorce in Rhode Island on the ground of adultery. She was eager that the divorce be granted and so she was advised to let the case go by default. At their first conference she revealed that she was pregnant by a man other than her husband, and asked appellant to find someone who would provide a good home for her child when born, and adopt it. He advised her to go to a welfare agency or to a certain infants' home of her religious denomination. She rejected this advice because she had herself been in an orphanage and did not wish her child brought up in such an institution; she insisted on having it placed in a private home.

Appellant told her that if he heard of any suitable potential foster parents he would let her know. She phoned him persistently at his home and office several times a week to inquire if he knew of anyone who would take her child. Finally when she called him about two months before the child was born he told her that he had learned of a couple interested in adopting the child, and he would have them contact her; she told him she preferred to remain anonymous and did not want to know the names of the prospective parents. Thereupon, as the transcript recites, appellant "offered to talk to the prospective adopters, report to her, and to otherwise conclude the matter for her so that the parties would not have to meet face to face." And so it was agreed that appellant should come to the hospital after the confinement and arrange for the transfer of the child. The mother had in the meantime instructed the hospital to permit the couple to see the child. The couple had through their own physician obtained from the mother's physician a satisfactory report as to her physical condition. After the child was born appellant took a release agreement to the hospital which he read to the mother in the presence of two of her friends and which she willingly signed. When she was ready to leave the hospital, appellant went there, took the child from her, and physically delivered it to the adopting father who was waiting at the front door of the hospital, while the mother left by a side door. The couple later adopted the child through court proceedings in Maryland.

Appellant charged the mother nothing in the divorce case and refused to accept any fee for his services in connection with placing the child for adoption. He did, however, accept about one-third of $294.90, which he had collected from the adopting couple to cover the mother's medical expenses.

The mother later changed her mind and sought appellant's services in regaining custody of the child. He refused, saying that he "could not accept such an assignment in good conscience and that the child had probably been adopted." Not long afterwards a complaint was filed against appellant with the Board of Public Welfare on the ground that he had no license to place children for adoption. Such complaint resulted in the prosecution and conviction which are here under review.

The Act under which appellant was prosecuted was passed early in 1944 and was the culmination of many years of struggle on the part of social agencies and others to put an end to the unregulated transfer, placing and brokerage of babies and the social evils which resulted therefrom. Until that time this was one of the very few jurisdictions in which there was no control over such activities.

The Act is comprehensive in nature and expresses the purpose of Congress to secure for children under sixteen who are placed in family homes other than their own or those of relatives, the best care and guidance, so as to serve the welfare of such children and the best interests of the community. To accomplish that purpose Congress prohibited the operation of any child-placing agency by anyone not specifically licensed for that purpose by the Commissioners. It authorized the Board of Public Welfare to investigate applicants for licenses and if found to meet certain requirements set out in the statute, to recommend them to the Commissioners. To prevent "careless placement of babies for adoption, without adequate consideration of the interests of the parents, the children, and the adopting parents," Congress wrote into the Act this provision:

"Any person, firm, corporation, association, or public agency that receives or accepts a child under sixteen years of age and places or offers to place such child for temporary or permanent care in a family home other than that of a relative within the third degree shall be deemed to be maintaining a child-placing agency." Code 1940, §32-782.

and followed it with this later provision:

"No person other than the parent, guardian, or relative within the third degree, and no firm, corporation, association, or agency, other than a licensed child-placing agency, may place or arrange or assist in placing or arranging for the placement of a child under sixteen years of age in a family home or for adoption." Code 1940, §32-785.

The purpose of Congress in enacting this legislation is of course our first point of inquiry, for that purpose is traceable to the evils it sought to correct. It was brought to the attention of Congress in hearings before committees of both the House and Senate, that a flourishing business was operating in the District, supplying the demand for children wanted for adoption. At the hearings it was emphasized that the placement of children for adoption could not be expected to succeed without a careful investigation by established social agencies with trained personnel, of the physical and social background of all the parties before the child was placed, followed by continuing investigation and supervision until the formal adoption was consummated.[49]

Congress therefore decreed that commercial agents, baby brokers, and even the best-intentioned citizens serving upon a non-commercial basis

[49] One of the regulations approved by the Commissioners pursuant to the statute provides that "a supervisory period of at least six months during which the child resides with the prospective adoptive parents shall be required before legal adoption is consummated." (Regulation VII, 2). This regulation was obviously designed to prevent hasty action or later change of mind on the part of either the natural or adoptive parents. And it is plain that the prescribed supervision cannot be expected when the adoption is arranged by other than a licensed placement agency.

and from the most humane motives, must none of them be permitted to place children for adoption unless previously investigated, found qualified, and licensed. This was to protect children and parents not only from corrupt or irresponsible intermediaries but also from the careless and untrained.

To emphasize that purpose Congress in the plainest language made it unlawful for anyone not licensed to "place or arrange or assist in placing or arranging for the placement" of a child.

What the appellant did is very clear. He "arranged" and "assisted" in placing and personally consummated the placement of the child. He was the intermediary who produced the prospective adopters and arranged contact (indirect though it was) with the mother. He it was who presented to the mother the document for release of her child and obtained her signature. He it was who arranged for the presence of the adopting parents at the hospital. And he it was who performed the final act of placement by accepting the child from the arms of its mother and physically handing it over to the adopting father. It would be difficult to imagine a more clear-cut infraction of the letter as well as the spirit of the law.

That appellant did these things without compensation, that he was animated by the most humane motives, that he was perhaps imposed upon by the mother or yielded in sheer pity to her cries of distress — all this we may concede. And all this appeals to our sympathy for him; but it cannot justify us in holding that his acts were within the law.

If appellant were proceeding on the assumption that he, as a lawyer, had a right to place the child for adoption, though he was unlicensed for that purpose, he was mistaken. We look in vain for any token of intention within the statute that the placing of babies by lawyers should be in any different or forgiven status than such placing by citizens in any other class. No court has said that such statutes do not apply to lawyers. No scrutiny of the sections involved can yield up such an exemption by mere process of judicial construction. If it could, the courts might just as properly create a whole series of exemptions; and before long the process of erosion by judicial construction would be complete and the Act ineffective.

We are told that if defendant is not absolved, no lawyer can feel safe when he is called on to advise or act in an adoption case. Even if that were so we could not help it; we would have to apply the statute as it is written. But we think the careful lawyer will have little trouble in determining what he may lawfully do in such situations. We think even a cursory reading of the statute will tell him how far he may go and where he must stop.

We think it plain that so long as the lawyer gives only legal advice; so long as he appears in court in adoption proceedings, representing either relinquishing or adopting parents; so long as he refrains from serving as intermediary, go-between, or placing agent; so long as he leaves or refers the placement of children and the arrangements for their placement to agencies duly licensed, he is within his rights under the statute. If that were all this appellant had done his conviction could not stand. It is plain he has done much more. Blameless though he is by ordinary standards of professional ethics, he has run afoul a statute which declares his actions malum prohibitum.

Affirmed.

NOTE

1. The various state laws concerning child placement pending adoption cover the spectrum — from the absence of any regulation to detailed legislative programs providing complete monopolies to public and licensed private agencies. Although a number of states have adopted more than one method of regulation, e.g., Mass. Gen. Laws Ann. c. 119, §§4, 6, 11, 36; c. 210, §§2A, 5A, 11A (Supp. 1964), the following paragraphs indicate the common types of statutory provisions:

a. Some jurisdictions, e.g., Arkansas, appear to have no legislative restrictions on child placement.

b. Some statutes are apparently designed primarily to deter "black market" placements — those which are arranged by a middleman for his own profit and those which involve commercial elements. See, e.g., Fla. Stat. Ann. §72.40(2) (1964):

> It shall be unlawful for any person:
>
> (a) Rendering any service in connection with the placement of a child for adoption, or in connection with the placement of a child with one other than its parents, to charge or receive from or on behalf of either the natural parent or parents of the child . . . from or on behalf of the person or persons legally adopting, or accepting, such child any compensation or thing of value whatsoever for the placement service, other than that now or hereafter allowed by law; but this shall not be construed to prohibit the payment by any interested persons of reasonable charges or fees for hospital or medical services, . . . or for legal services, or costs of court for an adoption suit or proceeding.
>
> (b) To sell or surrender a child to another person for money or anything of value; . . . provided, that nothing herein shall be construed as prohibiting any person, who is contemplating adopting a child not yet born, from paying necessary, actual prenatal care and living expenses of the mother of the child to be adopted, nor of paying necessary, actual living and medical expenses of such mother for a reasonable time, not to exceed thirty days, after the birth of the child. . . .

c. Some statutes require that any person who receives a child in contemplation of adoption give prompt notice to a court or public agency. See, e.g., Pa. Stat. Ann. tit. 1, §1(c) (1963).

d. A few statutes require that permission be obtained from a public agency or court before a child is placed by anyone. E.g., Wash. Rev. Code Ann. §26.36.010 (1961).

e. Several jurisdictions prohibit all placements for adoption which are not accomplished by a licensed agency. See, e.g., the District of Columbia statute construed in the Goodman case. These statutes usually exempt placements with relatives. See, e.g., N.J. Stat. Ann. §9:3-19 (1960): "this prohibition shall not apply to the placement of a child for the purpose of adoption with a brother, sister, aunt, uncle, grandparent or stepparent of such child." As to unrelated adoptions, these statutes at first glance seem designed to authorize public and private agencies to monopolize adoption practice. But many of them, either expressly or by judicial construction, exempt placements by a parent or other close relative. See, e.g., N.J. Stat. Ann. §9:3-19 (1960); Adoption of Moffett, 5 N.J. Super. 82, 68 A.2d 479 (1949) (construing prior New Jersey statute); Rogers v. Olander, 47 Wash. 2d 207, 286 P.2d 1028 (1955). Is it significant that Rogers v. Olander and a number of the other decisions which have narrowed broad legislative language concerned natural mothers' attempts to oppose the adoption petitions? Note that in In re Adoption of a Minor, page 486 supra, the court stated that although the natural mother's doctor actually transferred possession of the child to the prospective adoptive parents, the placement did not violate the Massachusetts prohibition because, for this purpose, the doctor was the mother's agent. Why was Mr. Goodman not considered the natural mother's agent for purposes of the District of Columbia statute?

The lack of legislative uniformity among the states reflects the apparent lack of consensus as to appropriate legislative policy. As the Goodman case indicates, social agencies have usually supported absolute prohibitions. But if the purpose of such statutes is to protect children "from the careless and untrained" persons who might otherwise make placements (page 544 supra), why does the District statute exempt parents from its prohibitions? Compare N.J. Stat. Ann. §2A:96-7 (Supp. 1964) (prohibition of placements involving commercial elements applies, inter alia, to a "natural parent or parent by adoption").

2. There have been few reported prosecutions — even in states which have adopted very broad prohibitions. In addition to Goodman, see Anderson v. District of Columbia, 154 A.2d 717 (D.C. Mun. Ct. App. 1959); State v. Segal, 78 N.J. Super. 273, 188 A.2d 416 (1963); State v. Wasserman, 75 N.J. Super. 480, 183 A.2d 467 (1962). Yet studies in several states have shown widespread violation of independent placement prohibitions. See Comment, 59 Yale L.J. 715, 733 n.94, 734 (1950). One explanation for this phenomenon may be that state attorneys general have often interpreted the statutes very restrictively. See page 549 infra. Are there other reasons for the lack of effective enforcement? See U.S. Children's Bureau Pub. No. 354, Protecting Children in Adoption 19-20 (1955), reporting the consensus reached by a discussion group which represented several disciplines concerned with adoption practice:

[T]he conferees recognized that there are "many groups opposed to any laws which although they may be aimed at the so-called black market, actually also affect the interests of professional groups . . . .

Rather than looking at laws we first have to look at ethics — and unless we can get a common agreement as to what is desirable and ethical in terms of the professional groups involved, we will get nowhere in terms of laws." [Quotation abbreviated by Eds.]

3. Using figures provided by 38 state welfare departments, the Children's Bureau estimated that in 1962, 62,900 children were adopted by unrelated petitioners. Some 64 per cent of these children were placed with the adoptive parents by public or private social agencies; 11 per cent were placed by the child's parent or other relative; 25 per cent were placed by someone else — either a nonprofessional person or a member of a profession such as a physician. U.S. Children's Bureau Stat. Series No. 75, Child Welfare Statistics — 1963, pp. 2, 20 (1964). The proportion of unrelated adoptions for which agencies made the placement has risen steadily in recent years; in 1951, for example, agencies placed only about 50 per cent of the total. Ibid. As one would expect, the proportion varies widely from state to state. These figures are the only ones available, but they are not very useful for making value judgments. For example, the data do not distinguish the kind of placement involved in the Goodman case — often described as a "gray market" adoption — from placements which may have been the result of black market operations.[50]

Although occasional publicity, e.g., N.Y. Times, Sept. 25, 1959, p. 12, cols. 3-4, and the sometimes lurid testimony before the Kefauver Committee, Hearings on S. Res. 62 Before the Subcommittee on Juvenile Delinquency of the Senate Committee on the Judiciary, 84th Cong., 1st Sess. 50-63, 202-203 (1955), document the existence of the black market, the extent of the practice is unknown. Senator Kefauver estimated that interstate sales of babies for adoption involved sums totaling $15,000,000 annually. N.Y. Times, Jan. 15, 1957, p. 18, col. 4. A report which appeared in 193 Economist 241-242 (1959) described two black market operations:

> Recently the New York police rounded up a group of people engaged in the illicit but extensive trade of buying and selling babies. This particular syndicate, complete with its own high-cost money-lenders and strong-arm collectors, was thought to be operating a $1 million a year business; the price of a baby can be as much as $10,-000. . . .

[50] For an unusual illustration of the distinction between "black market" and "gray market" adoptions, see Las Vegas Sun, Inc. v. Franklin, 74 Nev. 282, 329 P.2d 867 (1958). Mr. Franklin, an attorney in Las Vegas, responding to the insistent requests of an unmarried mother, arranged for the placement of her child. He received a fee of $100 from the adoptive parents. Shortly thereafter the Las Vegas Sun had the following headline: "Babies for Sale. Franklin Black Market Trade of Child Told." Franklin obtained a $190,000 libel verdict. On appeal, the court agreed that Franklin's conduct was prohibited by the Nevada placement statute but nevertheless held that the paper's characterization of Mr. Franklin was not protected by the defense of truth. The judgment was reversed, however, on procedural grounds, and the case was ultimately settled for a lesser amount.

. . . The black market does not overlook religious refinements; at one time French Canadian babies were mysteriously equipped with Jewish birth certificates before being smuggled across the border into New York. . . .

Some Americans, particularly those who face a religious barrier at home, have adopted children from Italy, Greece, Germany, Korea and Hong Kong, often choosing the country of their own ethnic origin. The Director of the International Social Service puts the number at between 8000 and 10,000 in a recent four-year period.[51] Many of these deals are innocent, if unwise in by-passing the responsible organizations which handle such cases. But others involve the purchase of children abroad and their resale at a profit. A New York City magistrate will come up for trial shortly on the charge of selling Greek children in the black market.[52]

On the other hand, a thorough survey of adoption problems reported that profit-making placements were not common. Comment, 59 Yale L.J. 715 (1950). See also Report of the New York Joint Legislative Committee on Matrimonial and Family Laws 17 (N.Y. Legis. Doc. No. 44, 1959); Witmer, Herzog, Weinstein & Sullivan, Independent Adoptions: A Follow-Up Study 95-96 (1963):

[T]wo-thirds of the adoptive couples reported that they had not paid the mother's medical expenses and that they had paid no fees other than routine legal costs. Though these people may have concealed facts, it seems rather unlikely . . .

A third of the adoptive couples . . . [said] that they had paid the medical expenses of the natural mother, a contribution most frequent in placements arranged by physicians. Some others paid for more than medical expenses, in an effort to help the mother. . . . Only 19 records reported expenses that appeared to be fees for the arrangement of the adoption.[53]

Most of the physicians placed children with couples who were their patients. . . . There were a few physicians, however, whose names appeared rather frequently in the records and whose charges for

[51] On the problems raised by intercountry adoptions, see, e.g., Graveson, The Tenth Session of the Hague Conference of Private International Law, 14 Int. & Comp. L.Q. 528, 532-538 (1965). — Ed.

[52] People v. Scopas, 11 N.Y.2d 120, 181 N.E.2d 754 (1962), affirmed by a 4 to 3 vote a lower court order that the grand jury's information against Judge Scopas be dismissed. He was held not guilty of "placing out" children since that term was statutorily defined as placing a child in a family other than that of its parents, and hence presumed placement prior to adoption. The defendant, on the other hand, customarily showed photographs of the Greek children to prospective applicants; following selection of a child, he would arrange for its adoption by proxy in Greece and its transportation to the United States. The statute was subsequently changed to deal specifically with foreign adoptions. See N.Y. Dom. Rel. Law §115-a. — Ed.

[53] There is currently no basis for comparing the cost of an independent placement adoption to an agency placement. The costs of independent placements vary with the person who arranges the placement. No data are available. — Ed.

"medical" expenses seemed high. About 30 children in the sample were placed by these doctors. . . .

All in all, the proportion of "black market" babies in our sample seemed rather small. The only sure statement that can be made on the subject, however, is "insufficient information."

Buck, Children for Adoption 205-206 (1964), suggesting that the black market "is almost out of existence" because of the efforts of social agencies, indicates the price that may have to be paid when independent placements are curtailed by statutes like the one in the District of Columbia:

[T]he effect of such a law is illustrated by the case of Connecticut, where in 1959 there were 1092 adoptions, of which 58% were independent or private placements. After the passing of the law prohibiting all but agency placements, in 1960 agencies placed 96% of all adoptions, but only 573 adoptions were made, and of these almost half were made the year before. Similar circumstances occurred in Delaware, where the number of adoptions fell from 254 in 1959 to 144 in 1960, and 128 in 1962.[54] . . .

OPINION OF THE ATTORNEY GENERAL
OF WISCONSIN
37 Ops. Wis. Atty. Gen. 403 (1948)

July 24, 1948.

A. W. BAYLEY, *Director,*
State Department of Public Welfare.

You have requested an opinion with reference to the interpretation of secs. 48.37(1) and 48.45(1), Stats., which provide as follows:

"48.37(1) No person, other than the parent or legal guardian, and no firm, association or corporation, and no private institution shall *place, assist, or arrange for the placement* of any child in the control and care of any person, with or without contract or agreement, or place such child for adoption, other than a licensed child welfare agency."

"48.45(1) No person conducting or in any way connected with the conduct of any maternity hospital shall in any way directly or indirectly offer to dispose of any child or hold himself out as being able to dispose of children in any manner."

These sections are part of the children's code originally adopted in 1929. The code contemplates that the care and placing of children in homes other than their own be undertaken by the state, acting through your department and the juvenile courts, and by certain private charitable agencies licensed as child welfare agencies by your department. . . .

The state having undertaken to perform the function of child place-

---

[54] See article by [Rael] Jean Isaac in The Atlantic Monthly, November, 1963. [Miss Buck cites no other source for her data.]

ment itself or through licensed private agencies, it is necessary to prohibit unlicensed persons from intermeddling therein. Provisions similar to the statutes above quoted are found in the children's codes of a number of other states, but we have found no court decisions construing them.

Experience has shown that so-called "irregular" placements do immeasurable harm in many respects. . . . The purpose of the above quoted statutes is to prevent such consequences, and they must be construed with that purpose in mind.

Section 48.37 prohibits not only the irregular "placing" of children but also "assisting" in or "arranging" for the placement. This must be construed as prohibiting unauthorized persons from "assisting" parents and legal guardians (even though the latter may lawfully make the placement) or "arranging" for placements by them. Otherwise practically every irregular placement could be justified by claiming that the actual placement was made by the parent or guardian and the intermeddler merely "assisted" in or "arranged" for a lawful placement. This would emasculate the law and rob the words "assist" and "arrange" of any meaning . . . .

You have submitted a number of types of cases of irregular placements and inquire in each case whether the facts show a violation of one or the other of the above statutes.

A. The physician who confined Miss A, an unmarried mother, learned that she had expressed a wish to place her child for adoption. He therefore informed Mr. and Mrs. Y, who were patients of his, that he knew of a child that would be available for adoption. He gave the name of the adoptive parents to the mother. They made arrangements to transfer the child to them upon discharge from the hospital. The adoptive parents sent a relative to meet the mother outside the hospital and the relative transported the child alone to the prospective adoptive home.

B. The physician who confined Miss B, an unmarried mother, learned that she had expressed a desire to place her child for adoption. The physician told the mother that he knew a desirable adoptive home. He communicated with the proposed adoptive family, telling them about the child and suggesting that they employ an attorney. Subsequently the attorney visited the mother and obtained the mother's consent. Upon discharge from the hospital the mother and child were met by the adoptive parents who took the child to their home. . . .

E. Miss E informed her physician that she wished to place her child for adoption. The physician told Miss E that he knew of a good home for the child. Miss E stated that because of her confidence in the physician she would place the child with anyone he recommended. The physician then informed the prospective adoptive parents and suggested that they employ an attorney. They conferred with an attorney, informing him that they had received information from the physician about a child that was available for adoption. The attorney conferred with the mother and arranged through the physician's office to personally take the baby upon the mother's discharge from the hospital. Thereafter, the attorney personally took the baby from the mother and delivered it to the adoptive parents. The attorney justified his actions on the grounds that he deemed it a desirable service to his client to prevent the mother from learning the names of his clients and to prevent the clients from learning the name of the mother. It was the position of the attorney that the mother had made the placement and that he had nothing to do with the actual placement as distinguished from the adoptive proceedings. You inquire whether the attorney violates section 48.37(1) in that he "assists" in the placement.

In case A it is our opinion that on the narrow fact situation presented no successful prosecution could be maintained. While it could be argued that one who gives information gratuitously to the parties performs a material act of "assistance," it is our view that unless more could be shown it would be impossible to obtain a conviction. If the physician, in addition to informing the prospective adoptive parents of the existence of the child, actively promoted the placement, there would be a clear violation. But just passing on the information is insufficient in our judgement to warrant a prosecution. The doctor could always say that nothing he did prevented the parties from using proper channels in obtaining the placement. Nor was the act of the relatives in taking possession of the child for the adoptive parents, after the arrangements had been made, sufficient in our judgment to warrant prosecution.

In case B it is also our view that the physician should not be prosecuted for merely giving the information, particularly since he suggested employment of an attorney. The attorney, according to the facts stated, merely performed a legal service in obtaining the mother's consent and did not "assist" in or "arrange" for the placement in the sense meant by the statute.

It should be repeated, however, that in both cases A and B if additional facts were shown there might well be grounds for prosecution. . . .

In case E the physician knew that his recommendation would be followed because of the mother's confidence in him. It seems that he did more here than in either case A or case B. It would appear that he *recommended* the prospective foster home. If so he "assisted" the mother in placing the child by making such recommendation and by putting the parties in touch with each other, notwithstanding his suggestion that an attorney be employed. The attorney also clearly "assisted" in and "arranged" the placement. His attempted justification is not valid, since he did more than perform a legal service. His theory would result in exempting attorneys altogether from the application of sec. 48.37(1). Such exemption was not put in the statute by the legislature and cannot be read into it by implication.

WITMER, HERZOG, WEINSTEIN, and SULLIVAN, INDEPENDENT ADOPTIONS: A FOLLOW-UP STUDY
68-341 (1963)

[See page 493 supra for a summary of how this study was conducted and the sample upon which it is based.]

The interviews with parents were held in the adoptive homes and usually lasted two or three hours. As a rule it was the adoptive mother who was interviewed, although in about one-third of the cases the adoptive father was also present for all or part of the time. . . . [N]o attempt to interview children was made. . . .

. . . [A] topical outline of points to be covered was prepared. The interviewers were left free to follow their own methods of obtaining information and to use whatever sequence they (and their respondents) preferred . . . .

As soon as possible after the interview, the interviewer dictated a report, using a tape recorder. She also filled out a checklist containing factual information, such as family composition and father's occupation, and some items concerning parental attitudes. . . . [Pages 68-70.]

Early placement is characteristic of independent adoptions, and our sample ran true to form. Nearly three-fourths of these children were placed in their adoptive homes before they were a month old, 10 per cent of them during the first day of life. . . . [Page 77.]

. . . The great majority of the children (80 per cent) had adoptive parents who had been married at least five years when placement occurred, and 39 per cent had been married ten or more years. Only 19 of the children were placed with couples who had been married less than two years; half of these had been married less than one year. . . .

. . . About a third of the children were placed in homes in which at least one of the marital partners had previously been divorced. A history of previous divorce was most frequent among couples who had been married less than five years. . . .

. . . The relatively long duration of a large proportion of the marriages is reflected in the average age of the adoptive parents at the time the child was placed in their home: 34.3 years for the mothers and 38.3 for the fathers. . . . [Seventy] children had mothers who had reached or exceeded the forty-year age limit often recommended by child placement agencies. Sixty-nine had fathers who were at or beyond the forty-five usually set as the top age at which agencies consider adoption of an infant desirable. Even so, the majority of the adoptive parents were within the limits usually recommended by agencies. . . .

[One fourth of the children were in families in the upper three occupational groups, but a majority of the fathers were engaged in skilled labor, sales, and white collar work. Almost 20 per cent of the fathers were "working class." The adoptive parents' median income was about $1000 higher than the national and the state figure for the years in question.] [Pages 83-86.] . . .

. . . To what extent were these homes the sort in which children would be expected to develop well? How many of them, if any, were "unsuitable"? How many lay between the two extremes? . . . . .

There are two main ways by which the questions can be answered. They can be answered directly by summating judgments made case by case by competent observers — judgments that are based on conceptions as to what parental and other characteristics promote or hinder children's

development. The questions can also be answered indirectly by determining (1) how well the children's development appeared to be proceeding . . . ; (2) what characteristics of the home were associated with good
adjustment; and (3) how many homes had such characteristics. The first
of these methods assumes . . . that we know what kinds of homes are
good and what are poor, and that dependable judgments about home
quality can be made in individual cases. The second makes no such assumption . . .

[The major part of the book, and the material included below, concern the first method mentioned. The authors next discuss the "tough
problem" of assessing home quality.]

In our present state of knowledge, there is no assurance that the criteria
chosen for judging the homes were "right" in the sense that they are precisely the characteristics that make homes best (or worst) for children.
What we have, in the conceptions that guided the evaluation of homes,
are not wholly verified criteria but rather some present-day ideas, partially substantiated by research, as to what makes homes good or poor for
children. . . .

Four aspects of the home were given special consideration in the overall
rating: the relationship between husband and wife, the parent-child relations, mental health of the parents (especially the mother), and social-
economic factors. Qualitative differences within these aspects served as
the major criteria by which homes were judged.

1. The relationship between husband and wife was regarded as the major characteristic to be considered in judging the emotional climate of a
home and its likelihood of favoring or impeding a child's development.
Excessive conflict or coldness between husband and wife, reluctance or
emotional inability of one or the other to assume marital and parental
responsibilities, usurpation by one of the partners of both father and
mother roles — these and other severe failures in role functioning were
regarded as unfavorable for children . . .

. . . The presence of divorce did not automatically put a home in a
low category, but divorce was seriously taken into consideration in rating
a home. If the home situation improved after the divorce, it was assumed
that a child's bad experiences during a period of severe marital disharmony were not likely to be wholly compensated by later favorable experiences with a stepparent. . . .

2. The quality of the parent-child relations (which, in this study, was
limited largely to mother-child relations) was another aspect of the home
that was thought to be highly important for children's well-being. The
degree of warmth, consistency, control, and regard for the child as an
individual were the aspects of that relationship that were particularly
stressed in assessing homes. [Interviewers rated the mothers on a five-
point scale for each "component" of the mother-child relation: "manifest
anxiety in the maternal role"; "emotional response to the child"; "control
of the child's behavior"; "regard for the child as an individual."] . . .

3. The third home aspect that was examined in the study of home
quality was the personality and mental health of the parents, especially

the mother. These broad and elusive categories could hardly be overlooked . . . .

. . . [A]t the lower end of the mental health scale [we looked for]: strikingly eccentric behavior, excessive rigidity, overwhelming anxiety, lack of feeling for other people . . . At the healthy end of the scale [we looked for such traits as]: "independent behavior," "self-determination," "perception of other people and the environment in a way that is free from distortion by one's own personality needs," "empathy or social sensitivity" (the ability to perceive situations and behavior from another person's point of view), and "mastery of the environment." . . .

4. [Initially the investigators posited "social and economic factors and those relating to health care and moral training" as the final aspect; this was to be given weight only if conditions were clearly disadvantageous. After all the ratings were made, however, the field director reread all the records to test consistency and to refine the assessment criteria. The fourth aspect was the only one substantially modified; it became: "father's functioning as a family member." See page 154 of the Study.] . . .

The overall home ratings, like the ratings of "components," were made on a five-point scale, running from high to low, A to E. They took into account both the number of areas in which conditions seemed favorable or unfavorable to a child's well-being and the degree of maladjustment, if any, that was present. The balance of favorable and unfavorable determined the rating on the scale from A to E:

A. Home seemed favorable in all aspects under consideration: personality and behavior of parents, marital relations, parent-child relations, social-economic conditions.
B. Home somewhat less than good in some ways but the balance was preponderantly favorable.
C. "Good" and "poor" were about in balance.
D. Home was preponderantly unfavorable psychologically (and in some cases, socially and economically also).
E. Home seemed unfavorable in all the above aspects except, in some cases, the social-economic.

Each category was conceived as representing a range, so that within each there was some variation from best to worst. . . .

. . . [T]he interviewer met with the field director, who meanwhile had studied and analyzed the record independently. The material on each case was reviewed jointly, in detail . . . [and joint decisions were made for] "components" and the overall home rating. . . .

In making the home assessment, neither the field director nor the interviewers had any information about the results of the various tests given to the adopted children in school . . . . They were instructed to base their ratings on the parental traits and behavior revealed in the interview, not on how well the child appeared to be adjusting.

Even for clinical ratings, our categories are far from precise. The nature of the classifications required, and the multiplicity of the possible indicators, appeared to us to preclude precise definition. . . . Accordingly, we settled for broad and "nonoperational" categories and attempted to "build in" as much consistency as possible.

. . . As a result of [the field director's final] review, 28 of the 438 home ratings were revised upward or downward. In no instance was a change of more than one half step (for example, from C+ to B−) found to be needed. . . .

[The final ratings were as follows:]

TABLE 23. RATINGS GIVEN TO ADOPTIVE HOMES AT FOLLOW-UP

Home rating	Children		Homes	
	Number	Per cent	Number	Per cent
Excellent to good				
A	91	21	91	21
B	109	25	106	25
Fairly good to questionable				
C	108	25	107	25
Poor				
D	62	14	61	14
E	68	15	66	15
Total	438	100	431	100

. . .

The confidence with which each rating was made was indicated on a three-point scale. Second-degree confidence was recorded for the majority (301) of the overall home ratings. . . . [T]he uncertainty was likely to involve a half-step difference rather than doubt as to whether the home was favorable or unfavorable. . . . There was no case in which it was thought that further observation would change an E to a C, or a C to an A. . . .

In order to check whether our confidence in the consistency of these ratings was justified, two sets of data were obtained.[55] First a reliability test, based on a small number of records, was made by the interviewers themselves during the course of the study. . . . A correlation of .42 was found between these ratings and the original conference judgments. . . .[56]

[Because it was thought that the reliability coefficient was affected by "re-rating anxiety," a larger group of records was given to two trained and experienced caseworkers not connected with the study; they read the interview summaries, rated them individually, and then made a conference judgment in a fashion similar to that employed in the study. The correlation between these ratings and those of the study was ".74 — a fig-

[55] . . . The validity of our definitions is either a matter of opinion and values or a question to be answered by the use of criteria that have not yet been determined. It has been suggested that the children's adjustment might be used as a criterion. This, however, does not seem feasible until (a) adequate measures of adjustment are developed and (b) the usual relation between home and adjustment is much better established than at present.

[56] See page 81 supra with respect to the discussion of reliability. — Ed.

ure much like those found in other investigations based on somewhat analogous ratings made by caseworkers."] . . .

In attempting to generalize about independent adoptions from these findings, at least two facts must be kept in mind. First, the study refers to a particular place and period of time and to all the conditions peculiar to that place and time. Among the latter are the nature of Florida's independent adoption system in the years 1944 to 1947 and the nature of the adoptive clientele in a state that had a few voluntary adoption agencies. Second, the study refers to a sample . . . .

Whether [the outcome record in Florida] is good or poor as compared with that of independent adoptions in other states is not known except for the findings of a rather small study in one state, Connecticut.[57] In that study proportions of good, fair, and poor adoptions almost identical with those of the present study were reported. As to adoptions arranged by social agencies, the proportions of adoption outcomes judged to be good or fairly good has ranged between 75 per cent and 90 per cent.[58] In such studies (which include the Connecticut one just mentioned) the samples were usually small, and neither the standards used in making ratings nor the methods of investigation employed were strictly comparable with ours. . . . [Pages 130-145.]

When the A homes were reviewed as a group, the characteristic that stood out most prominently was the clarity and comfort with which these adoptive couples fulfilled their roles as parent and as spouse. In these homes, each parent had specific duties that he carried out appropriately and without evidence of "working at it," while in areas of shared responsibility they simply and harmoniously performed as a team. Each had status, both in his own eyes and in the eyes of his spouse. The naturalness and ease with which family life was carried on were most impressive. . . .

The parents' emotional needs were not such that they made excessive demands on the children or attempted to hold them too close. Each parent was pleased when a child identified himself with the other parent, and did not interfere in the relationship. . . .

The parents were proud of their children and warm in their feelings about them. They did not push them unduly for academic or other achievement but did help them over discouragements and shared with them in the joy of accomplishment. If the children had social or emo-

[57] Amatruda, Catherine S., and Joseph V. Baldwin, "Current Adoption Practices," Journal of Pediatrics, vol. 38, February, 1951, pp. 208-212.

[58] See, for example: Brenner, Ruth, and others, A Follow-Up Study of Adoptive Families, Child Adoption Research Committee, New York, 1951; Davis, Ruth Medway, and Polly Bouck, "Crucial Importance of Adoption Home Study," Child Welfare, vol. 34, no. 3, 1955, pp. 20-21; Morrison, H. S., "Research Study in an Adoption Program," Child Welfare, vol. 29, July, 1950; Simon, Abraham Joseph, "Social Agency Adoption — A Psycho-Sociological Study in Prediction," unpublished doctoral dissertation, Washington University, St. Louis, Mo., 1953; Theis, S. Van S., How Foster Children Turn Out, State Charities Aid Association, New York, 1924.

tional difficulties, the parents described the problems without undue emotion and had taken appropriate steps (which included ignoring minor difficulties) to deal with them. . . . [Pages 146-147.]

[The authors next reprint an interviewer's summary of a home rated in the A category.] . . .

. . . [M]ost of the mothers in A homes received a Group 1 rating on marital relations, mother-child relations, and so on, while most of those in E homes received a Group 5 rating for these characteristics. . . .

All the mothers in Group 1 were positive in their feelings about their husbands, frank about how much emotional support they received from them, and appreciative of the part they played in the children's lives. . . . [The following case summary illustrates the diverse ways in which these traits were displayed:]

> One mother, who had talked considerably about her husband in a way that recognized the value of his affection and support, commented with pleasure on the close relation existing between him and their adopted son. She felt that their son was lucky to have such a good father. She was proud of father's activities in the community and expressed pleasure in their quiet evenings at home together. . . .

[The authors provide ratings for A families in each of the other components, e.g., 85 per cent of the A mothers were rated 1 in personality makeup, 85 per cent of the fathers were rated 1 in family functioning. Other examples of the authors' use of case summaries to illustrate the reasons for numerical ratings on each component have been included here in the authors' analysis of D and E homes.] . . . [Pages 155-161.]

Nearly all the homes rated E were seriously unfavorable with respect to the first three of [the components], somewhat less frequently with respect to the fourth, and occasionally with respect to [the presence of "factors classified as social-pathological"]. The homes rated D were somewhat less unfavorable, qualitatively or quantitatively. . . . Even so, the characteristics of these D homes seemed to justify classifying them with the E group as seriously unfavorable to the emotional development of children. . . .

All the homes rated E and all but three of those rated D were so classified partly because they failed to provide the experience of a childhood spent with parents whose marriage was at least fairly sound and stable.

. . . [T]he field director rated most of the marriages in D homes as belonging to Group 4 and most of those in E homes as Group 5 . . . .

For 19 families (16 D and 3 E homes) the quality of the marital relationship could not be determined adequately enough for classification. Nevertheless, if only by omission of detail, there was no evidence that the marriage was one that would be helpful to a child. These marriages were rated as belonging to Group 4.

In seven of these homes the mother was so emotionally involved with the adopted child that she gave the interviewer practically no information about her husband or her marriage. These women did not specifically disparage their husbands and, if questioned directly, made some conventional remark about them, such as "he's a good man." But it seemed clear that their husbands meant little to them. . . .

The interviews that elicited so little information about the husbands and the marriages were not briefer than the others, nor did the mothers seem suspicious or stand-offish. It was rather that these women either seemed completely absorbed in themselves and, in some cases, in their children, or appeared to be cold, reserved individuals who had little to give to either husband or child. Whether the husbands were dissatisfied with this state of affairs could not be determined. . . .

In 6 D and in 17 E homes there was either open conflict between the parents or such belittling and exclusion of the husband by the wife that the marriage was essentially a broken one. . . .

> One wife bitterly expressed her dissatisfaction with her marriage, saying that her husband thought only of his business; that she had no real relation with him; and that, from time to time, she threatened to leave. She added, however, that she knew which side her bread was buttered on and would probably never get a divorce, in spite of their numerous quarrels.

The sort of home in which the father was relegated to an inferior position and was much disparaged is illustrated by the remark of one adoptive mother who, when asked whether her husband liked the child, said abruptly that, of course, he had no interest in the child — his only duty in the family was to hand over his pay check.

Except for two D homes that were rated 4 because the marital discord was chronic but not overtly severe, the homes in this category were put in Group 5. . . .

. . . "Marital skew," in contrast, provides some satisfaction to one or both spouses. This satisfaction is achieved, however, in ways that create an unhealthy or unnatural environment for a child.

. . . [In] 32 families (33 children) . . . the marriage appeared to be skewed. Thirteen of these were D homes, 19 were E.

One type of skewed marriage (18 homes) was that in which a husband apparently accepted his wife's abnormal behavior as natural or in which an emotionally disturbed husband was permitted by his wife to have the kind of marriage he wanted. Marriages of this sort were rated as belonging to Group 5. . . .

> A marriage skewed to fit the emotional needs of a disturbed husband was seen in a family in which a patently eccentric woman, once divorced, was married to a very passive man, many years her junior. This husband spent most of his spare time sleeping and took no responsibility in the family except to give the wife his pay check. This arrangement, as far as the interviewer could discover, was satisfactory to both marital partners.

In all these families the wife had a severe personality disorder. Four mothers had symptoms that could only be described as psychotic. Others had had a nervous breakdown and were still erratic in their attitudes and relations with people. Some were very eccentric, and the rest highly "nervous" or hysterical.

Most of the husbands were less obviously disturbed than their wives, and a few of them seemed to be fairly adequate individuals. They apparently had made a personal adjustment to their wives' peculiarities and showed some affection for the children, but the children's position was insecure and unhappy nevertheless. . . .

The third type of skewed marriage (nine homes) was one in which both parents seemed to be affectless, insensitive people. This type, too, was put in Group 4. These people said nothing that would indicate dissatisfaction with each other, and they were apparently in agreement in their handling of the children and in other matters. Yet when parents of this sort were seen together, one sensed an emotional sterility in their marriage and in their capacity for human relations. . . .

In 35 families (36 children) [rated 5] there had been divorce or separation following severe marital discord. Fifteen of these were homes rated D; 20 were homes rated E. Not only was there considerable disorganization in these families just prior to the divorce but most of the marriages had been quarrelsome, unsatisfactory ones, even at the time of adoption. Alcoholism was a factor in a number of the divorces, in conjunction with other personality problems. Marital infidelity and family neglect were other reasons given for divorce. . . .

Twenty of these 36 children were living with their adoptive mothers at the time of our study. Only four of these mothers had remarried. All these adoptive mothers, remarried or not, were emotionally disturbed women, whose treatment of the children ranged from neglect to extreme overprotection and emotional dependence on the child. . . .

Nine homes rated D and three rated E (containing 13 adoptive children) had been broken by the death of the mother (five cases) or father (seven cases). Four of the mothers and five of the fathers died when the children were less than six years old. . . . If the marriage had been an especially unhappy one before the death of the parent and/or the subsequent situation was especially hard on the children, the marital situation was rated as belonging to Group 5. Otherwise, it was rated 4.

Little is known concerning the home situations before the five mothers died, but in each case the death of the mother brought the adopted children very unhappy experiences with caretakers. For instance, one child was sent to live with her elderly, ill grandmother. For another, there was a series of housekeepers interspersed with attempts by the father, a neurotic, difficult person, to do the housework and look after the child himself. . . .

The seven homes in which the father died had never been very satisfactory for the children, though several of the mothers said they had been happy with their husbands. Six of these seven fathers were twenty or more years older than their wives. In several of these homes the wife had apparently had a rather childlike relationship with her husband. . . .

With one exception, the mothers who did not remarry seemed to be excessively dependent on the adopted children and made great demands on them. They had apparently always been individuals who looked to their husbands for support and guidance, even if the men were old and ill. In the absence of their husbands they had great difficulty managing the children and their own affairs. . . .

. . . Five degrees [of the mother's "capacity in interpersonal relations"] were recognized, ranging from "emotionally healthy" to "seriously impaired . . . ," [deletion by Eds.] a category that included the psychotic and the very eccentric.

All the original adoptive mothers in homes rated D or E were judged to belong to one or the other of the two lowest categories, 41 of the 53 in D homes being classified as belonging to Group 4, and all 61 in E homes as belonging to Group 5. . . .

Group 4 was described by the field director as being composed of women who had little capacity for adult functioning but who had at times some ability to give and receive affection, and to be aware of the feelings and desires of others. . . .

In the first subtype of Group 4 were placed three women (four adopted children) who were extroverted, talkative individuals with little anxiety in the parental role. They regarded themselves as perfect, all-giving mothers and were controlling and dominating. Nevertheless, they had some warmth for people and some slight understanding of their feelings.

One mother, who had had many foster children in her care, spent most of the time telling the interviewer that many people turned to her for advice and guidance, and that she had been very successful in helping them. She felt that she could make any child perfectly healthy and happy. She said she thought of the adopted child as "my baby" and refused to let him play with rough boys or have much time alone with her husband because he was too easy with the child. She was apparently a benign despot, controlling every aspect of the lives of her husband, her own daughter, and the adopted child but she was probably fairly warm, though insensitive, in her relation with the child. . . .

A second subtype in Group 4 consisted of eight women who combined physical and psychological symptoms with a great deal of neurotic behavior. Some of these mothers had had a nervous breakdown, either before adoption or shortly after. Nevertheless, they were able to carry out some of their responsibilities fairly adequately and to be moderately effective in their personal relationships.

One of these mothers was extremely tense and anxious and had many physical complaints, among them migraine headaches. She was quite dependent on her own mother, who lived with her and her husband. Because she was so nervous, she found it impossible to stay at home, she said. She had taken a job and left to her mother all responsibility of homemaking and care of the child. . . .

The third subtype contained the largest number of women — 24 in all. These were very dependent, anxious individuals whose chief difficulty lay in their incapacity for assuming adult responsibilities. They were childlike people, both in appearance and in the way they conducted themselves during the interview. They had great difficulty in expressing themselves and were very uncertain about the ideas they did express.

These women showed great anxiety in relation to most aspects of their functioning as adults and parents. They disliked responsibility and had no idea how to deal with problems. Their inability to make mature judgments often led to impulsive and unrealistic decisions. They were exceptionally dependent on others in their environment, even on their young children. . . .

In spite of many differences in personality makeup, the 63 women (64 children) whose emotional adjustment was classified as of the first subtype of Group 5 had several traits in common. All of them were markedly narcissistic and self-centered. They did not express normal affection, and they seemed unusually insensitive to the needs and feelings of other people.

The majority of these women were superficially friendly and outgoing and talked freely with the interviewers. . . . Even when describing serious problems they did not seem to be worried. Serious illness on the children's part did not upset them greatly. Bad behavior and poor performance in school they took with equanimity, being concerned neither with what it meant to the children nor with what it implied for themselves.

. . . The statements they made about their husbands or their children, although expressed in the words others would use, did not carry the feeling one would normally expect. There were great discrepancies between what they said and what they did.

> One mother, a divorced woman, seemed to the interviewer to behave more like an adolescent than a grown-up. This mother seemed wholly unconcerned about her children, even though one was in a correctional school. On her own initiative and with little feeling, she described intimate details of her marriage and her problems in sexual relations. She cut the interview short because she had "a date with Daddy." . . .

In contrast, a few of the women in this subcategory, instead of being open and seemingly unconcerned, were guarded and suspicious in their talk with the interviewers and presumably in their relations with other people. These women had many of the characteristics of the mothers just described, but differed in that they presented a perfect picture of the children and could not admit that they had any problems. They tried to keep their children very close to them and to control every facet of their lives. Apparently they did this, not out of deep affection but because they felt that they and their children were one unit against the world. . . .

The second subtype in Group 5 consisted of four mothers (five children) in homes rated E who displayed such peculiar behavior, made such confused statements, or were so unable to communicate with the interviewers that it seemed likely they were psychotic.

One of these mothers spoke in a cautious, restrained manner about people and forces that were hostile to her. She was especially paranoid in describing her husband, alluding mysteriously to the terrible things he had done to her and the children. From time to time her statements were more lucid, and she would say that families like hers should not be allowed to adopt children.

Another of these mothers was so withdrawn that she was almost unable to speak. She responded to all questions in monosyllables and seemed unaware of the presence of the interviewer or of the reason for the interview. . . .

In no D or E home did the mother feel about the child and behave toward him in a way that could be regarded as healthy and helpful. On the contrary, the mother-child relation in every case seemed to be one that would seriously handicap the adopted child in his personality development sooner or later.

When the field director analyzed what the adoptive mothers said about the children and about their own actions toward the children, and their feelings concerning them, a division into the following two broad types of mother-child relationship seemed warranted:

Group 4   Mother overpermissive and ineffectual or insensitive and inconsistent

Group 5   Mother greatly involved with child or very rejecting or highly ambivalent . . . . [Pages 196-212.]

Did being in the homes we rated poor affect the children adversely? To answer this question we had to assess that elusive, sprawling cluster of elements known as "adjustment." Fallible as our measures may be, they are at least the same for the adopted children in the sample and the control group of "own" children. And they indicate that the adopted children were getting along nearly as well as their controls.

Taken as a whole, the adopted children showed no significant difference from the control group with regard to I.Q. or school achievement. According to these measures, they were equally bright. On the measures of adjustment, however, they were slightly below the control group — and the differences, though small, were statistically significant. When the adjustment measures were combined to produce overall adjustment ratings, the same slight difference in favor of the control group appeared.

The picture changed, however, when the children placed at later than one month of age (25 per cent of the sample) were removed from the group, along with their nonadoptive controls. When this was done, only one of the differences between the adopted and the control children remained statistically significant. The one exception was a slight indication that the adopted children may have been more "aggressive" than the natural children.

It may be argued — and sometimes is — that adoption should improve upon nature in the chance it gives a child for development. If this is true, and feasible, then the comparison just reported leaves much to be desired. On the other hand, there are at least suspicions that the fact of being adopted — a fact known to 90 per cent of our children — imposes problems that may tend to interfere with emotional adjustment. . . .

The correlation between home and adjustment ratings was not as high as might have been expected, however, being .45 for the children as a whole. It may be that the range of homes in each of the rating categories somewhat depressed the correlation coefficient. Possible defects in the measures used is another explanation. Even so, the small size of the correlation suggests that the development of adopted children has considerable independence of the home situation. Whatever independence there is, however, is more marked when the home is poor than when it is good. [Pages 339-341.]

NOTE

1. Part II of the Study, entitled "Some Methodological Problems and Their Implications," was written separately by Professor Weinstein. It contains three chapters (id. at 367):

> The first discusses the logical and empirical problems with the overall home rating as a measure of adoption outcome. The relationships between the home ratings and more specific child-rearing attitudes and practices are then presented in order to give a more systematic picture of the major influences on these ratings and the influences of such factors on the adjustment of the child are explored. In the last chapter an attempt is made to sort out some of the complex interrelationships among the variables and establish empirically based dimensions of outcome by means of factor analysis.

Weinstein's statistical analysis of the caseworkers' numerical component ratings suggests to him that some of the ratings show a strong "halo effect" — these components were not perceived differentially from the general perception of the home. He comments (id. at 384):

> As interpretations at increasing levels of generality enter into the ratings, the possibility of overlapping interpretations with a consequent "halo effect" is increased. . . . Is the home rated poor because of substantial evidence that the marriage is poor? Or is the marriage seen as poor because the mother is interpreted as neurotic and constricted in her capacity for human relationships in general? Examination of the interview records and evaluation summaries indicated that this type of "reasoning backwards" occurred but not frequently on an explicit basis. There is a strong possibility that it did occur frequently on an implicit level.

Perhaps more important, Weinstein questions the two major assumptions of the research method employed in the study: "(1) that the characteristics of homes conducive to healthy development in the child are known; and (2) that our rating procedures reliably and validly assess these characteristics." Id. at 365. He suggests that the caseworkers' assessments were four levels removed from "true" home quality: the parent's comments about her behavior might not reflect her actual behavior in the home, or the interviewer's selective perception could distort the information provided; error could occur in the interviewer's interpretation of cues given by the parent, e.g., in assuming that the parent's manner of relating to the interviewer accurately portrays the parent's general capacity for interpersonal relationships; the relative weight given individual components in the home ratings might fluctuate from interviewer to interviewer or from case to case for the same worker; the psychodynamic theory underlying the ratings may itself be in error. Id. at 369-370. Weinstein also objects to the study's failure to provide data on the homes of the nonadopted children used as controls in testing adjustment of the children in the sample; such data would have been useful for a number of purposes, among them (id. at 366-367): "[T]he data could have served as a check on possible bias in the home ratings. It is possible that social workers might tend to be more stringent in their evaluation of homes of independently adopted children than they would be of homes in general."

2. Fanshel, Book Review, Social Work, July, 1964, p. 119, praised the study and its methods. However, prior to its publication Professor Fanshel had reported that the Child Welfare League was unwilling to secure a control group of children who had been adopted through social agencies. Fanshel, Approaches to Measuring Adjustment in Adoptive Parents, in Quantitative Approaches to Parent Selection 18, 23-24 (Child Welfare League of America, Inc. 1962). He explained (id. at 24):

> The League declined to participate even though it held the researchers who would be conducting the study in very high regard. It was anticipated that the findings of such a study would have to be extremely guarded because of the methodological difficulties entailed in such studies. . . . Yet, the emotional climate was such that equivocal findings, no matter how tentatively stated, would become grist for the detractors of social work practice with uncertain contribution to be achieved in the way of added knowledge of patterns of adaptation of adoptive families with respect to the issue of independent-versus-agency adoption. This noncooperation may seem a strange stance to maintain in a field that constantly refers to the need for evaluative research as part of its obligation of accountability to its supporting public. Yet, cogent arguments could be mustered against *premature* evaluative efforts that cannot really fulfill the ambitious goals to which they aspire.

2. *Termination of Adoption by Adoptive Parents*

Matter of ANONYMOUS
29 Misc. 2d 580, 213 N.Y.S.2d 10 (Surr. Ct. 1961)

BENNETT, S. This is a motion to dismiss a proceeding to abrogate an adoption on the ground that the court lacks jurisdiction of the subject matter, and that the petition fails to state facts sufficient to constitute a cause of action.

The petitioner in this proceeding is the foster father of the adopted child and the second husband of the natural mother. The infant is a child of the natural mother's former marriage to the respondent. The infant, at the time of the natural mother's remarriage in 1945, was a little over a year old. Since that time, and continuing after the petitioner's adoption of the child in 1957, the infant has resided with his foster father and natural mother. The child is now 17 years of age and attending a highly specialized school in connection with which he receives psychiatric treatment for an alleged mental illness.

The petitioner asserts that although he has been strongly advised by [psychiatrists] to continue the child's attendance in such school, the tuition of $9800 is "beyond the ability of your petitioner to provide." He claims, however, that the natural father is a man of wealth and presumably well able to afford the requisite tuition were the adoption abrogated. Additionally, the claim is made that the adoption was brought about by the fraud of the natural father in concealing from petitioner the hereditary strains of mental illness present in the former's family. Also petitioner alleges that the child has willfully deserted him on many occasions and has behaved in a most disrespectful manner.

Although this is ostensibly an abrogation proceeding, the allegations of fraud relate more specifically to applications to vacate and set aside adoption orders under section 114 of the Domestic Relations Law, which grants to this court the power to vacate orders of adoption "for fraud, newly discovered evidence or other sufficient cause" to be exercised in "like manner as a court of general jurisdiction exercises such powers." The petitioner has commingled allegations relating to abrogation, a proceeding which treats the adoption as valid but seeks to set it aside because of subsequent events, and allegations relating to vacating or setting aside the adoption itself because of alleged invalidity.

Taking the aspect of setting aside the adoption, the petition alleges a concealment of hereditary strains of mental illness present in the family of the natural father. There is no allegation in the petition as to inquiry being made by the foster father of the natural father concerning mental illness in the family, nor any other facts which would place the natural father in the position of being required to disclose such information. There is nothing to suggest any inquiry or concealment about the infant who was adopted, and the allegations refer only to concealment of mental illness in the family of the father of such infant, with no allegation that such information was ever requested or sought by the foster father.

Had there been an allegation in the petition that an inquiry as to the mental condition of the infant in question had been made, and material facts concealed, this court would have granted a hearing to determine the facts in relation thereto. Even in such a situation, however, the fraud which will suffice to vacate an order or judgment must be fraud in the very means by which the judgment was procured . . . .

The order of adoption and the papers upon which it was granted are in all respects proper and the statutory requirements fully satisfied. The court, at that time, determined on all the facts then before it, that the adoption was for the best moral and temporal interests of the child. There is no justification to now upset this formal adjudication based upon an alleged failure of the natural father, at the time of the adoption, to delineate the alleged mental aberrations of his family. Accordingly, that portion of the petition which predicates the relief requested upon allegations of fraud, is dismissed.

The remaining portions of the petition may more properly be said to deal with matters of abrogation. Abrogation, similar to an adoption itself, is purely statutory (Matter of Eaton, 305 N.Y. 162, 165). Specifically, sections 116 to 118 of the Domestic Relations Law grant such jurisdiction to this court. Section 116 deals with abrogation by consent and section 118 relates to abrogation of adoptions from authorized agencies. The latter section provides that a foster parent may apply for abrogation because of the "wilful desertion of such foster parent by such foster child or because of any misdemeanor or ill behavior of such child." There is no corresponding ground in section 117, the sole remaining section dealing with abrogation. Since this proceeding does not deal with abrogation from an authorized agency, those allegations of desertion and general misbehavior on the part of the infant are dismissed. In any event, such desertion and misbehavior must be "wilful" according to the statute, and the petition is replete with indications that the acts of this child are far from rational or willful.

Section 117 of the Domestic Relations Law provides that a proceeding to abrogate may be brought by the foster child or any person on the ground of "(a) cruelty, (b) misusage, (c) inability or refusal to support, maintain or educate such child, (d) an attempt to change or the actual making of change of or the failure to safeguard the religion of such child or (e) any other violation of duty on the part of the foster parents or parent toward such child." While in Matter of Anonymous (185 Misc. 962), the Surrogate held that a foster parent could initiate such a proceeding under section 117, the dominant tenor and tone of a petition under this section would necessarily involve violations and derelictions of duty on the part of a foster parent. This is clear from the legislative intent of this section (Draftsman's note, L. 1938, ch. 606). Petitioner seeks not to bring to this court's attention any dereliction or violation of duty by himself as the foster parent, but merely his own alleged financial inability to properly provide for the child. The law has seen fit to raise the relationship of adoption to no less an elevated stature than that of the flesh and blood ties of parent and child (Domestic Relations Law, §115), and the law surrounds this relationship with the strongest of safeguards from intrusion (Domestic Relations Law, §114). To allow a foster parent to now retrace the steps he has taken toward culmination of this relationship on the ground of lack of financial means to properly support the child would be to set to naught the creation of law and establish a dangerous precedent.

Even if it be assumed that this court would have such jurisdiction, the affidavit of the respondent, which petitioner's attorney stipulated could be considered on this motion, states that the natural mother has very substantial financial means of her own, and the child himself is one of the beneficiaries of a relatively large trust fund. This affidavit stands uncontradicted by the petitioner or the natural mother. The court's prime concern in an abrogation proceeding is the welfare of the child. The special guardian reports that the petitioner's attorneys furnished him with a copy of a letter written by a psychiatrist which states that the child can be helped by a combination of educational environment, psychiatric treatment, and contact with *parents*. This child has resided with his mother and foster father for most of his life, and obviously the contact with parents refers to them and not to the respondent. Undoubtedly, foisting upon the child at this late date a "new" father could lead to a host of disturbing elements, even more so in the mind of a child who is mentally ill.

For all of the above reasons, together with the court's conviction that the welfare of this child dictates that he remain a part of the only family group he has known, the petition is dismissed.

NOTE

1. The statutes of a number of jurisdictions provide for revocation at the suit of the adoptive parents. See, e.g., Ark. Stat. Ann. §56-110 (1947) (revocable within five years because of feeblemindedness, insanity, epilepsy, any psychosomatic or mental disturbance, venereal disease, or any incurable disease as a result of condition existing prior to adoption unknown to the adopting parents); Ky. Stat. Ann. §199.540 (1962) (only if child "reveals definite traits of ethnological ancestry different from those of the adoptive parents" and they had no prior knowledge of the ancestry). Compare Uniform Adoption Act §17 (9 U.L.A. 28 (1957)), made optional by the Commissioners, which provides for annulment within two years if the child "develops any serious and permanent physical or mental malady or incapacity as a result of conditions existing prior to the adoption and of which the adopting parents had no knowledge or notice . . ."

The New York provisions quoted in the principal case (now renumbered as Dom. Rel. Law §§118, 118-a, 118-b, and 118-c) are among the most permissive of the abrogation statutes. See, e.g., Adoption of Souers, 135 Misc. 521, 525, 238 N.Y.S. 738, 743-744 (Surr. Ct. 1930) (adoption abrogated after ten years because stealing, delinquencies, and desertion suggested that "[t]here was evidently something wrong in the child's make-up"); Adoption of Anonymous, 8 Misc. 2d 155, 167 N.Y.S.2d 472 (Surr. Ct. 1957) (abrogation permitted after thirteen years and over vigorous protests of special guardian, where adopted boy's poor school work, culminating in his expulsion from high school, caused adoptive parents to lose affection for him and boy displayed no particular affection for them). The provision has been severely criticized by the New York Joint Legislative Committee on Matrimonial and Family Laws. See N.Y. Legis. Doc. No. 26, p. 27 (1958), and N.Y. Legis. Doc. No. 44, pp. 29-31 (1959).

2. A few cases suggest that in the absence of legislation adoptive parents cannot abrogate the adoption. See, e.g., Coonradt v. Sailors, 186 Tenn. 294, 209 S.W.2d 859 (1948); In re Bell's Estate, 310 Mich. 394, 17 N.W.2d 227 (1945). Estoppel has occasionally prevented attacks by adoptive parents based on jurisdictional defects in the original proceedings. See, e.g., Presley v. Presley, 77 Ga. App. 99, 47 S.E.2d 647 (1948); Rogers v. Baldridge, 18 Tenn. App. 300, 76 S.W.2d 655 (1934). But see McKenzie's Adoption, 44 Pa. D. & C. 86 (Orph. Ct. 1942) (adoption of older child abrogated on petition of all parties in state despite absence of relevant provision in adoption statute). The British attitude toward the problem was expressed in Report of the Departmental Committee on the Adoption of Children, Cmd. No. 9248, par. 21 (1954):

> [T]he adopters should know all that can be told them about the physical and mental health of the child for whom they are assuming responsibility and should appreciate the difficulties which may arise. All who adopt children at a young age, whether the child is apparently healthy or not, should be warned that his mental and physical development cannot be predicted or assessed beyond the possibility of doubt, even by the most expert. . . . [B]ut there can be no question of annulling the adoption. Adopters, who have voluntarily assumed the responsibilities of natural parents, must not expect to be able to give them back again at will, any more than they could relieve themselves of their responsibilities if the child had been born to them.

3. Consequences of Adoption

Matter of UPJOHN
304 N.Y. 366, 107 N.E.2d 492 (1952)

FULD, J. Frederick Lawrence Upjohn died in December of 1917. By paragraph Seventh (A) of his will, executed some eleven months before his death, he directed that the income of one half of his residuary estate be paid to his wife during her life, and then, during the life of his grand-nephew, Robert Redpath, to the beneficiaries named in Seventh (B). By the latter provision, the testator created seventeen separate trusts — in favor of nephews, nieces, grandnephews, grandnieces, and other persons

— out of the remaining one half of the residue, and directed that the income of each be paid during Redpath's life to the designated beneficiary. Mrs. Alice Childs, the testator's niece, was one of those beneficiaries. After making provision in Seventh (B) for the disposition of the corpus of the several trusts therein created, the testator provided in Seventh (C) that, if any beneficiary named in (B) was to die before the termination of the trust, the income payable to that beneficiary was to be paid, during the existence of the trust, "to his or her lawful issue or descendants, if any . . . and in default of such issue or descendants surviving" to the other designated beneficiaries; and, if any of the latter were then dead, to their "lawful issue or descendants," in the same proportions as provided for the original shares.

In 1905, Mrs. Childs and her husband, who never had any children of their own, adopted a two-month-old baby, Alice Elizabeth (now married, she is the appellant Mrs. Lake). The testator knew of the adoption, though with other members of the family he kept it secret. Upon Mrs. Childs' death in 1950, the trustees petitioned the Surrogate's Court to "construe the provisions of Paragraph SEVENTH (C) . . . and determine" whether or not Alice Elizabeth is the "issue" or "descendant" of Mrs. Childs, "as such words are contained in said Paragraph SEVENTH (C)." The surrogate held that she is not, and the Appellate Division . . . agreed with that conclusion.

Embodied in our adoption statute is the fundamental social concept that the relationship of parent and child, with all the personal and property rights incident to it, may be established, independently of blood ties, by operation of law, and that has been part of the public policy of this state since 1887 [citation omitted]. The statute unequivocally ordains that "The foster parents or parent and the foster child shall sustain toward each other the legal relation of parent and child and shall have all the rights and be subject to all the duties of that relation including the rights of inheritance from each other." (Domestic Relations Law, §115, 3d par.). By reason of that provision, we have held, "the adopted child, in a legal sense, became the natural child of the adoptive parent." (Carpenter v. Buffalo Gen. Elec. Co., 213 N.Y. 101, 108.) . . . In harmony with the legislative policy thus expressed, the adoption statute has been most liberally and beneficently applied. It has been held that, where property is devised or bequeathed to a brother, sister, child or descendant of the testator, and that person dies in the lifetime of the testator survived by a foster child, the devise or legacy does not lapse, but vests in the foster child — for the latter is a "child" or "descendant" of the legatee or devisee within the meaning of section 29 of the Decedent Estate Law. (See Matter of Walter, 270 N.Y. 201.) By the same token, a foster child, adopted subsequent to the execution of its foster parent's will, has a right, as a "child born after the making of a last will," to an intestate share of the parent's estate if no reference is made to him in the instrument. . . .

Wills, too, must be read and construed in harmony with the legislative policy of placing adopted children on a level with natural born offspring. . . .

The limitation under consideration does not, contrary to respondents' contention, contain "language that has acquired, through judicial decision, a definite and established significance." (Matter of Krooss, 302 N.Y. 424, 428.) Terms such as "issue," "lawful issue," "descendants" — and the word "children," as well — may or may not include adopted children; read alone, and apart from context, those words are ambiguous. . . . It has been said that the terms "issue" and "descendants" "probably carry a stronger connotation of blood relationship than the word 'children' " (Oler, Construction of Private Instruments Where Adopted Children Are Concerned, 43 Mich. L. Rev. 705, 727; see, also, 3 Powell, Real Property [1952], p. 132), but that is not normally a factor of weight, in view of the known frequency with which testators employ "issue" and "descendants" as essentially synonymous with "children" and, certainly, in a sense no more restrictive or narrow. [Citations omitted.]

What the testator meant when he used the words "issue" and "descendants" is not to be decided in vacuo. It is impossible for a court to ascertain the meaning with which they were employed in a particular will without considering the context of the entire instrument and the background of facts and circumstances existing when the will was made. [Citation omitted.] The rule in this state, declared in New York Life Ins. & Trust Co. v. Viele (161 N.Y. 11, 20), is that the limitation will be construed to designate only those related to the named ancestor by blood if "there is nothing to the contrary to be found in the context of the instrument or in extraneous facts proper to be considered." In other words, in the absence of any indication of the testator's intent, it will be assumed that the testator did not envisage adopted children taking under the limitation. That, though, is a rule of construction and nothing more. Where the testator's design to include an adopted child is clear, the limitation will be construed to effectuate that intention. In our view, the present is such a case.

Of surpassing significance is the fact that, when the testator drew the will, he had full knowledge of the adoption that had taken place eleven years earlier when Alice Elizabeth was two months old. . . . Where it appears that [the testator] knew of the adoption, he is taken, therefore, to have intended inclusion of the adopted child, and his will is so construed, unless other language in the will or other circumstances reflect a different or contrary intention. . . .

In the present case, the testator knew that Alice Elizabeth had, by force of the adoption, become his niece's child, her issue and descendant. Indeed, in view of Mrs. Childs' age — she was over forty years old — and her failure to have any natural born children during twenty years of marriage, the testator must have realized — even assuming that he did not know that his niece was physically incapable of bearing children — that Alice Elizabeth would in all probability be Mrs. Childs' *only* descendant. [Citations omitted.] The designation "issue" and "descendant," therefore, adequately and sufficiently identified the adopted Alice Elizabeth as a possible beneficiary of his bounty. Had he desired that she be excluded, he could and would have indicated that intention plainly and expressly.

Moreover, in view of the evidence of the testator's relationship with Alice Elizabeth and her foster parents, it is manifest that he could not have harbored a design to exclude her. The proof establishes that he was on intimate terms with his niece and her family. They often were house guests for extended periods at his Long Island home, and he was a frequent visitor of theirs. . . . And the uncontradicted evidence — consisting largely of the testimony, against interest, of a grandniece of the testator, a childhood companion of Alice Elizabeth — reveals numerous instances of the testator's affection and generosity toward his niece's foster daughter and demonstrates that he regarded and treated her at least as favorably as the children of his other nieces and nephews. . . .

Nor may the exclusion of Alice Elizabeth be predicated upon section 115 of the Domestic Relations Law. The fourth paragraph of that section — which follows the clause, quoted above, declaring that foster parent and child "shall sustain toward each other the legal relation of parent and child" — provides: "As respects the passing and limitation over of real or personal property dependent under the provisions of any instrument on the foster parent dying without heirs, the foster child is not deemed the child of the foster parent so as to defeat the rights of remaindermen."

The motivation for this provision and its underlying rationale are clear. Designed to assure that the testator's intention be effected, it mandates that, where the testator has designated remaindermen to share in his estate in the event that a named individual dies without children or descendants, an adopted child of the latter may not, by force of the adoption law, be held to come within the class and thus defeat the remainders. The legislature was particularly concerned about the perpetration of fraud on the rights of remaindermen "through an adoption for the very purpose of cutting out a remainder." (Matter of Walter, supra, 270 N.Y. 201, 206.) . . .

As we have seen, Frederick Lawrence Upjohn's intent to include Alice Elizabeth as "lawful issue" and "descendant" of Mrs. Childs is exceedingly clear and, for that reason, the statute — designed "to safeguard the intention of a testator," not to defeat it — does not apply. (Matter of Walter, supra, 270 N.Y. 201, 206.) And the possibility of fraud, it must also be marked, is entirely absent. When he made his will, the testator knew full well of Alice Elizabeth's adoption years before. . . . The danger of fraud arises where the adoption takes place without the testator's knowledge, especially when it occurs after his death. . . .

The order of the Appellate Division and the decree of the Surrogate's Court should be reversed, and the matter remitted to the Surrogate's Court for further proceedings not inconsistent with this opinion . . .

NOTE

1. Should it make any difference that the testator used terms such as "birth"? Compare Uihlein v. Uihlein, 11 Wis. 2d 219, 105 N.W.2d 351 (1960) (permitting adopted child to take), with Vaughn v. Vaughn, 161 Tex. 104, 337 S.W.2d 793 (1960) (denying claim of adopted child).

Compare Mass. Gen. Laws Ann. c. 210, §8 (Supp. 1964) (adopted child treated like natural born child for purpose of construing "[t]he word 'child,' or its equivalent" in trusts, etc., "unless the contrary plainly appears by the terms of the instrument"). But see Peirce v. Farmers State Bank of Valparaiso, 222 Ind. 116, 51 N.E.2d 480 (1943). The testator left his son a life estate, after which, "If my son Joseph shall have married and leave, surviving him, a child or children, then . . . to such child or children." The will was executed on August 29, and the testator died on October 24. Joseph (then forty-four) married a widow on November 20 and subsequently adopted his wife's twenty-five-year-old son by a former marriage. There was evidence that the testator knew of the forthcoming marriage and proposed adoption and was pleased at the prospect of someone to "carry on my name." The court ruled against the adopted son because of the absence of anything in the will to show testator's intent to include adopted children. "The fallacy in the appellant's theory is that the extraneous circumstances upon which he relies are not calculated to supply deficiencies in an ambiguous will, but rather to change the legal effect of a will that is unambiguous." 222 Ind. at 118-119, 124, 51 N.E.2d at 482, 483.

Approximately half of the states permit the adoption of adults. See Merrill & Merrill, Toward Uniformity in Adoption Law, 40 Iowa L. Rev. 299, 323-324 (1955). But see, e.g., Idaho Code Ann. §16-1501 (Supp. 1963) (only a minor child can be adopted unless adoption did not occur during minority by inadvertence and adopting person has acted as parent for at least fifteen years); Mass. Gen. Laws Ann. c. 210, §1 (1958) (no person can adopt his or her husband). Bedinger v. Graybill's Executor, 302 S.W.2d 594 (Ky. 1957), held that a fifty-six-year-old man could adopt his forty-five-year-old wife so as to allow her to take under a testamentary trust which provided that upon his death the property was to be distributed to his "heirs at law." The court pointed out that the Kentucky adoption statute expressly provided for the adoption of adults; under Kentucky inheritance law an adopted child is regarded as an heir with full rights of inheritance unless a contrary intent is evident in the will. The majority conceded that the settlor (the mother of decedent) doubtless intended the property to go to her son's lineal descendants, but felt that the result followed ineluctably from the statutory scheme. Three justices dissented on the ground that the recognition of such an adoption was against public policy and created uncertainty because the wife might be able to claim a wife's share of the estate, a child's share, or both.

See generally 5 American Law of Property §§22.34-22.36 (Casner ed. 1952); Halbach, The Rights of Adopted Children under Class Gifts, 50 Iowa L. Rev. 971 (1965); Annots., 86 A.L.R.2d 12, 115 (1962).

2. Despite the tendency to view an adoption as a complete severance of the relationship between the child and his natural parents, many states expressly permit an adopted child to inherit from his natural parents. See, e.g., Vt. Stat. Ann. tit. 15, §448 (Supp. 1963); Mass. Gen. Laws Ann. c. 210, §7 (1958). Consider the following statement taken from the Report of the Joint Legislative Committee on Matrimonial and Family Laws 25 (N.Y. Legis. Doc. No. 26, 1958):

Social agencies oppose the present system of inheritance by adopted children. Many times, it is said, the disclosure necessarily made for the sake of a small inheritance may do more harm than good. In addition, if the natural parents are cut off from the child and the foster parents assume all parental duties and responsibilities, there seems little use in retaining involved rights of inheritance. The change of relationship should be "for better or worse." The only exception to this is the suggestion that the adopted child may inherit from his natural parents only when his foster parents are next of kin of the natural parents. In this situation, he has not left his natural family.

The New York provision permitting inheritance from natural parents was repealed in 1963. Dom. Rel. Law §117.

For the few cases allowing adopted children to share in settlements for the wrongful death of a natural parent, see Annot., 67 A.L.R.2d 745 (1959). If the relevant measure of damages is the plaintiff's pecuniary loss, can an adopted child recover? See Smelser v. Southern R.R., 148 F. Supp. 891 (E.D. Tenn. 1956), aff'd, 244 F.2d 719 (6th Cir. 1957).

3. An adopted child is generally treated like a natural child insofar as intestate inheritance rights against the adoptive parents are concerned. But the right to claim against kindred relatives of the adoptive parents is less clear. Section 12(1) of the Uniform Adoption Act, enacted in only two states, provides (9 U.L.A. 35 (1957)):

After the final decree of adoption is entered the relation of parent and child and all the rights, duties and other legal consequences of the natural relation of child and parent shall thereafter exist between such adopted child and the adoptive parents adopting such child [and the kindred of the adoptive parents]. From the date of the final decree of adoption, the child shall be entitled to inherit real and personal property from [and through] the adoptive parents in accordance with the statutes of descent and distribution, and the adoptive parents shall be entitled to inherit real and personal property from and through the child in accordance with said statutes. [Brackets in original.]

The draftsmen would have omitted the brackets, but their recommendation proved to be so controversial that the Commissioners decided to authorize local choice of policy. What arguments can be made for and against the bracketed language? See Merrill & Merrill, Note 1 supra, at 318. For a collection of cases on this issue, see Annot., 43 A.L.R.2d 1183 (1955). In general, see Note, Property Rights as Affected by Adoption, 25 Brooklyn L. Rev. 231 (1959).

4. In Anderson v. French, 77 N.H. 509, 93 Atl. 1042 (1915), the court allowed an adopted daughter to take an intestate share of her adoptive uncle's estate. The adoption decree had been entered in Massachusetts, whose statutes provided that an adopted child could not take from collateral kindred of the adoptive parents; the New Hampshire law permitted such inheritance. The court held that status as an adopted child is deter-

mined by the law of the state of adoption, but the consequences of that status are determined by the law of the domicile of the deceased. This view is now generally accepted. See Restatement (Second), Conflict of Laws §143 (Tent. Draft No. 4 (1957)) (law of situs in the case of immovables; law of decedent's last domicile in the case of movables); Annot., 87 A.L.R.2d 1240 (1963). But see Mass. Gen. Laws Ann. c. 210, §9 (1958) (inheritance rights governed by law of jurisdiction where adoption decree granted unless such rights exceed those granted by forum). Although a decree of adoption by a state having the requisite jurisdiction[59] is entitled to full faith and credit, a sister state is free to bar the adopted child from inheriting local land. Hood v. McGehee, 237 U.S. 611 (1915). Compare the doctrine of divisible divorce, page 936 infra. In general, see Taintor, Adoption in the Conflict of Laws, 15 U. Pitt. L. Rev. 222 (1954); Lipstein, Adoption in Private International Law: Reflections on the Scope and the Limits of a Convention, 12 Int. & Comp. L.Q. 835 (1963).

5. An adoptive couple may obtain a child from the natural parents upon the express or implied understanding that they will adopt it. The child will usually live with the couple as if it were their own, but the adoption may never take place. Upon the death of the adoptive parents, can the child claim an intestate share as an adopted child? A number of courts have so held, generally upon a theory of "equitable adoption" or "adoption by estoppel." See, e.g., Cubley v. Barbee, 123 Tex. 411, 73 S.W.2d 72 (1934); Comment, 47 Mich. L. Rev. 962 (1949). But cf. Heien v. Crabtree, 369 S.W.2d 28 (Tex. 1963) (doctrine not recognized to permit inheritance by heirs of adoptive parents upon intestate death of child).

PROBLEM

James Johnson, a sixty-eight-year-old bachelor of considerable wealth, seeks your legal help. He tells you that with the exception of a few specific bequests, he plans to leave his entire estate to his twenty-three-year-old niece, Jane, whose parents are deceased. Recently, in going over some estate planning literature sent him by his bank, he discovered that under the state inheritance tax, a bequest to a "lineal descendant" is taxed at 2 per cent of value, whereas all other bequests are taxed at 5 per cent. He tells you that he has always been very fond of Jane and has recently helped her through college. He now wants you to file the necessary papers permitting him to adopt Jane. (A check by you reveals that the jurisdiction permits the adoption of persons who are above twenty-one.)

The state statute pertaining to adopted children reads in part as follows: "The adopting parents shall be treated in all respects as though the adopted child had been their natural child, and, following the promulga-

---

[59] There is considerable dispute concerning the proper jurisdictional basis for adoption proceedings. See Goodrich, Conflict of Laws 228-290 (4th ed. Scoles 1964); Comment, The Inadequacy of Domicil as a Jurisdictional Base in Adoption Proceedings, 17 Rutgers L. Rev. 761 (1963).

tion of a final decree of adoption, there shall be no distinction whatsoever between the rights and duties of natural children and adopted children."

What will you advise Mr. Johnson?

B. ARTIFICIAL INSEMINATION

MacLENNAN v. MacLENNAN
[1958] Sess. Cas. 105, [1958] Scots L.T.R. 12
(Sess. Ct. Outer House)

LORD WHEATLEY. The pursuer seeks decree of divorce from the defender on the ground of her adultery, and prima facie his case is essentially simple. The parties were married on 25th August 1952, and it is a matter of agreement that they have not lived together or had marital relations since 31st May 1954. On 10th July 1955 the defender admittedly gave birth to a female child in Brooklyn, New York, and on that historical narrative of events the pursuer asks the Court to find proven facts, circumstances and qualifications from which an inference of the defender's adultery can be drawn. In the uncomplicated days before science began to innovate on the natural processes of procreation, the lapse of time between the last act of marital intercourse and the birth of the child would have led to the inevitable inference that the defender had been guilty of an adulterous act with another man by means of the normal and natural physiological mechanism, as a result of which the child was conceived. The defender, however, has tendered an explanation by way of defence, which is unique in the annals of our law, and which seeks to establish that she conceived the child not as a result of sexual intercourse with another man, as that phrase is commonly understood, but as a result of artificial insemination from a donor. She does not aver, however, that the pursuer was a consenting party to such an artificial process of conception, and the pursuer maintains that he never agreed to the defender adopting it, if in fact it ever took place. The defender submits that artificial insemination by a donor, even without the consent of the husband, is not adultery as the law understands and has interpreted that term, and that proof of conception by such means would rebut the inference which would otherwise be raised from the fourteen months' period of non-access followed by the birth of a child.

The issue comes before me as a matter of relevancy, since the pursuer has submitted that such a general defence is irrelevant, on the ground that artificial insemination by a donor without the consent of the husband is adultery in the eyes of the law, and I am accordingly obliged to accept the defender's averments pro veritate at this stage. It should be noted, however, for the purposes of the record, that, while the defender does not aver that the artificial insemination by a donor was without the consent of her husband, the whole argument proceeded on the basis that there was no such consent. [The court then discussed the objectionable vagueness of defendant's plea in failing to give details as to the time.

place, and circumstance of the alleged insemination. Although this omission may have been traceable to defendant's desire not to divulge unnecessarily the details of the operation, it fails to give fair notice to the plaintiff and compels the court in effect to render a declaratory judgment.]

Before turning to examine the legal arguments on the major issue, it is desirable that I should set forth to the best of my ability what is involved in artificial insemination. Although this is a unique and novel case in our Courts of law, the term "artificial insemination by a donor" is glibly used without any explanation of the process in the pleadings, it being apparently assumed that such unusual practices and interference with the natural processes of procreation fall within that omniscience on all worldly matters which is described, sometimes euphemistically and sometimes with a complimentary but quite unjustified faith, as "judicial knowledge." My own particular knowledge of this subject is culled from the articles thereon in some of the journals to which I was referred in the course of the debate, but fortunately my comprehension of the process, thereby derived, seems to square with that of counsel when they were addressing themselves to the subject at the Bar.

Artificial insemination is the process whereby the seed of the male is extracted from the male body, enclosed in a receptacle, and subsequently inserted into the female sexual organ, presumably by means of a syringe, thereby reproducing the same end-result as follows from the natural and unrestricted act of full sexual intercourse. This scientific innovation on the natural processes substitutes a syringe containing male seed for the male sexual and reproductive organs, and the act of conception, if the seed eventually fertilises, is achieved without the presence of the male body. Technically, although I have no particular knowledge of this, I presume that the woman could acquire the seed and operate the syringe herself, thereby excluding the presence of any other person during the actual insertion. There are apparently three recognised systems of artificial insemination. The first is A.I.H., which is insemination in the manner indicated by seed extracted from the husband. The second is A.I.D. which is effected by the introduction into the female organ of seed extracted from a male known as the "donor," and who in practice seems to be a man unknown to the recipient, although there would appear to be no reason why the donor should not be known to or indeed selected by the recipient, if the latter preferred it that way and the donor was agreeable. This method may be employed either with or without the consent of the husband. If such a practice constitutes adultery on the part of the wife, the fact that the husband has consented would not prevent the act from being adultery, but it would not be adultery on which the husband could found, since he had connived at it. The third method is somewhat cynically known as C.A.I. or confused artificial insemination, wherein there is used for the impregnation of the woman a mixture of the seed of the husband and the seed of a donor.

There are manifestly grave moral, ethical, social, and personal considerations involved in the practice of artificial insemination in its various forms which will no doubt be fully deployed elsewhere. It is almost trite to say that a married woman who, without the consent of her husband, has the seed of a male donor injected into her person by mechanical means, in order to procreate a child who would not be a child of the marriage, has committed a grave and heinous breach of the contract of marriage. The question for my determination, however, is not the moral culpability of such an act, but is whether such an act constitutes adultery in its legal meaning. A wife or a husband could commit an act of gross indecency with a member of the opposite sex which would be a complete violation of the marital relationship, but which could not be classified as adultery. It would indeed be easy according to one's personal viewpoint to allow oneself to be influenced by the moral, ethical, social, and personal considerations to which I have referred and to reach a conclusion based on these considerations, but this problem which I am called upon to solve must be decided by the objective standard of legal principles as these have been developed and must be confined to the narrow issue of whether this form of insemination constitutes adultery in the eyes of the law. If it is not adultery, although a grave breach of the marriage contract, that is a matter for the Legislature if it be thought that a separate legal remedy should be provided.

In determining whether the marital offence (which I opine it to be, whatever view one takes of its nature) of being impregnated by the seed of another man without the husband's consent constitutes adultery in its legal sense, one naturally seeks a solution from the definitions of "adultery" in the works of our leading legal writers or in reported decisions. Some of our great legal writers, however, do not even seek to define it, while others, in referring to it, use terms which are more descriptive than definitive. This may be due to the fact that in earlier days, when life was regulated by the natural rather than the scientific order of things, people knew what was meant by adultery and what its concomitants were. Where, however, attempts were made to describe adultery, if not to provide an exhaustive definition of it, the idea of conjunctio corporum seems to be an inherent concomitant — a conception of the process which incidentally can likewise be found in the Book of Deuteronomy, the writings of St Paul and the works of the Canonists. The idea that adultery might be committed by a woman alone in the privacy of her bedroom, aided and abetted only by a syringe containing semen, was one with which the earlier jurists had no occasion to wrestle. Certainly this form of perpetuation of the species does not conform to the common conception of adultery. None-the-less the argument advanced in support of the contention that it does constitute adultery was powerfully advanced. I accordingly turn to consider the views of the earlier jurists on the meaning of the term "adultery." . . .

Taking a line through these various definitions or descriptions of what constitutes adultery, there runs the basic conception that adultery involves sexual intercourse or carnal connexion. . . . What is sexual intercourse or carnal connexion, and, in particular, can artificial insemination fall within such a definition? . . .

In the normal and natural method of performing an act of sexual intercourse there is a mutual surrender both of the sexual and reproductive organs. While the primary purpose of sexual intercourse is procreation, in the eyes of the law surrender of the reproductive organs is not necessary to consummate the act of intercourse. Expedients may be used by the parties to secure birth prevention, or the woman may have previously undergone an operation by which her reproductive organs were removed, or they may have ceased to function from natural causes; and yet the conjunction of the sexual organs, involving at least some degree of penetration, would constitute intercourse and, in the circumstances under consideration, adultery. Thus impregnation per se cannot be a test of adultery, since in the eyes of the law the act of intercourse can be consummated without impregnation, either as a result of natural causes or by the parties resorting to artificial expedients (cf. Baxter v. Baxter, [1948] A.C. 274). It would seem therefore that, in determining such questions as consummation of marriage or adultery, the law looks at the act and not at the result. . . .

. . . Impregnation, therefore, may be the result of sexual intercourse, may be evidence of sexual intercourse, may be causally connected with sexual intercourse, but it is not necessarily a concomitant of sexual intercourse. It was submitted by senior counsel for the pursuer that, while impregnation could not be the sole test of adultery, any definition of adultery which excludes the impregnation of woman by seed would not be complete. I understood him to mean thereby impregnation by seed by any method. Although not presented in syllogistic form, the pursuer's argument seemed to be that in the given circumstances, while undoubtedly all cases of penetration of the female organ by the male organ were adultery even if impregnation did not take place, so too all cases of impregnation were adultery even if there was no such penetration. This, to my mind, is a legal non sequitur. The argument seems to me to confuse the method with the result. Impregnation may be the result of sexual intercourse, but is not necessarily an essential part of it, and, if it is achieved by other means which do not involve the physical presence of the male and his sexual organ, it is difficult to see how such other means can be classified as sexual intercourse or, to use the more significant phrase, "carnal connexion." . . .

The physical act in sexual intercourse is presumably the same whether it be carried out during the normal marital relations of spouses, in adultery or in fornication. It is of interest to note, therefore, that in two English cases the fact that a child had been born to a wife by her husband did not preclude the Court from holding that the marriage had not been consummated. In R.E.L. (otherwise R.) v. E.L., [1949] P. 211, Pearce, J., decided that artificial insemination by a husband, resulting in the birth of a child, did not consummate the marriage, and in Clarke (otherwise Talbott) v. Clarke, (1943) 112 L.J. (P.) 41, Pilcher, J., held that a marriage had not been consummated when in the endeavours to achieve sexual intercourse there had been no penetration, although a child had been conceived by the wife as a result of fecundation ab extra by the husband. I have quoted these English cases at some length, since it seems possible to derive therefrom the following propositions, according at least to the law of England: — 1. For adultery to be committed there must be the two parties physically present and engaging in the sexual act at the same time. 2. To constitute the sexual act there must be an act of union involving some degree of penetration of the female organ by the male organ. 3. It is not a necessary concomitant of adultery that male seed should be deposited in the female's ovum. 4. The placing of the male seed in the female ovum need not necessarily result from the sexual act, and if it does not, but is placed there by some other means, there is no sexual intercourse. . . .

I can find nothing to persuade me that the law of Scotland is not the same as the law of England so far as the legal propositions above enunciated are concerned (although non-consummation of the marriage is not a ground of nullity in the law of Scotland), and, in my opinion, these propositions are equally valid in our law. To me they seem to consist with the traditional Scottish views on adultery which I have canvassed *supra*. Just as artificial insemination extracts procreation entirely from the nexus of human relationships in or outside of marriage, so does the extraction of the nexus of human relationship from the act of procreation remove artificial insemination from the classification of sexual intercourse. If my views be correct, then it follows logically that artificial insemination by a donor without the consent of the husband is not adultery as the law interprets that term. The only case cited to me wherein a contrary view was reached was the unreported American case of Doornbos v. Doornbos, which was a declaratory form of action unknown to our procedure. Not having had the benefit of the judgment on which the decision was based, I cannot comment on it, but, for the reasons which I have given, I must express the view that the decision is one which cannot be followed or supported in our law. It is perhaps not inappropriate, however, to consider the implications of the contrary view. If artificial insemination by a donor without the husband's consent is to be deemed adultery, the first question which seems to call for a decision is whether the donor whose seed has been used has himself been guilty of adultery. If the answer is in the affirmative, the further question arises, at what point of time has he done so? If it be at the point when the seed is extracted from his body, certain interesting considerations would arise. I gather that seed so obtained can be retained for a considerable time before being used, and in some cases it may not be used at all. If the donor's seed is taken merely to lie in retentis, it surely cannot be adultery if that seed is never used. Thus, if his adultery is to be deemed to take place at the time of the parting with the seed, it can only be an adultery subject to defeasance in the event of the seed not being used. Such a statement need only be stated for its absurdity to be manifested. If, on the other hand, his adultery is deemed to take place when the seed is injected into the woman's ovum, this latter act may take place after his death, and in that case the woman's conduct would constitute not only adultery but necrophilism. Such a proposition seems to me to be equally absurd. The third alternative is that the whole process should be regarded as an act of adultery, but as this might in certain cases result in the act covering a period of say two years, and be committed partly during the lifetime and partly after the death of the donor, I cannot distinguish between the absurdity of such a proposition and the absurdity of the other alternatives. Senior counsel for the pursuer appreciated the illogicality and absurdity of these consequences of the proposition that the donor had committed adultery, and accepted that he had not. This then forced him to argue that the wife could commit adultery by herself. One need not consider the interesting point whether the administrator could be said to commit adultery, because the administrator might be a woman or the seed might be self-injected by the wife herself operating the syringe. The idea that a woman is committing adultery when alone in the privacy of her bedroom she injects into her ovum by means of a syringe the seed of a man she does not know and has never seen is one which I am afraid I cannot accept. Unilateral adultery is possible, as in the case of a married man who ravishes a woman not his wife, but self-adultery is a conception as yet unknown to the law. The argument of pursuer's counsel was that adultery meant the introduction of a foreign element into the marital relationship. That, however, seems to me to beg the question, because what has still to be determined is what is the foreign element? For the reasons which I have already explained, that foreign element is the physical contact with an alien and unlawful sexual organ, and without that element there cannot be what the law regards as adultery. . . .

It accordingly follows, in my opinion, that artificial insemination by a donor does not constitute adultery according to our law. It is no part of my task in this case to animadvert on the moral, ethical and social aspects of the practice. That it constitutes a grievous marital offence against a non-consenting husband I have no doubt. The law, however, lays down certain grounds upon which divorce may be obtained, one of which is adultery, and if artificial insemination by a donor is not adultery in law, then proof of such insemination may rebut the inference which might otherwise be inevitably drawn from the birth of a child following a long period of non-access. In such circumstances the onus would undoubtedly be upon the defender to establish that the child was so conceived, and failure to do so would result in the primary inference of adultery being applied. If it be that science has created a *casus improvisus*, the remedy is not to be found in fitting such a case into one of the existing grounds of divorce on arguments which cannot logically or physiologically be supported.

I accordingly find that the pursuer's plea to the relevancy of the defences based on the general argument is ill-founded, but I shall not repel it in hoc statu, since it must be kept open in view of the admitted lack of specification in the defender's pleadings. I shall accordingly continue the cause to enable the defender, if so advised, to table such amendments as she thinks fit.[60]

[60] On 29th January 1958, after counsel for the defender had intimated that the defender declined to provide the information necessary to cure the defective specification, the Lord Ordinary sustained the pursuer's first plea in law, and remitted the case to the undefended roll.

On 28th February 1958, after proof, he granted decree of divorce in terms of the conclusion of the summons.

NOTE

1. It is surprising that counsel in the MacLennan case did not direct Lord Wheatley's attention to the elaborate dictum on the subject in the opinion of the Supreme Court of Ontario in Orford v. Orford, 49 Ont. L.R. 15, 18, 58 D.L.R. 251, 253, 254 (1921). Mrs. Orford sued for alimony; the defense was adultery, based on the fact that she had given birth to a child in England after more than three years of separation from her Canadian husband. The wife explained that her marriage had never been consummated because of her inability to have intercourse and that her husband urged her to go to a doctor to be cured. The doctor told her, she said, that "the only thing to do was to bear a child, and that it might be done artificially." She then met a man who knew "quite a little about insemination," who offered to help her, paying all the expenses and agreeing to adopt the child. She went to his flat where he introduced her to a physician whose name she did not remember, went to bed, was put under an anaesthetic, and when she woke up was told by her friend that she had been inseminated artificially.

The court refused to believe this story and found her guilty of adultery "in the ordinary, natural way" (49 Ont. L.R. at 19, 58 D.L.R. at 254), but then proceeded to discuss her alleged justification at great length. It concluded that "the essence of the offence of adultery consists, not in the moral turpitude of the act of sexual intercourse, but in the voluntary surrender to another person of the reproductive powers or faculties of the guilty person; and any submission of those powers to the service or enjoyment of any person other than the husband or the wife comes within the definition of 'adultery.'" 49 Ont. L.R. at 22-23, 58 D.L.R. at 258.

2. The unreported Doornbos case referred to in MacLennan is discussed in Johnston, Family Law, 31 N.Y.U.L. Rev. 368, 373-374 (1956). It involved an action by the wife for divorce and custody of a son conceived by A.I.D. with her husband's consent. The court held that the child was illegitimate and that the husband had no right or interest in the child, not even that of visitation. The wife's conduct was treated as adultery. The continued validity of the decision as regards the status of the child is open to question since on appeal by the State of Illinois as intervenor, the court intimated that a child would not be bound by a declaration of illegitimacy in a proceeding in which it was not represented. Doornbos v. Doornbos, 12 Ill. App. 2d 473, 139 N.E.2d 844 (1956) (abstract only). On the adultery issue, the court's decision squarely conflicts with a 1945 unreported Illinois lower court decision, Hoch v. Hoch, referred to in Johnston, supra, at 374. See also Strnad v. Strnad, 190 Misc. 786, 78 N.Y.S.2d 390 (Sup. Ct. 1948) (husband who consented to A.I.D. entitled to visitation rights upon divorce; child not illegitimate); Gursky v. Gursky, 39 Misc. 2d 1083, 242 N.Y.S.2d 406 (Sup. Ct. 1963) (although child born through A.I.D. with husband's consent is illegitimate, husband is still liable for its support on grounds of implied contract or equitable estoppel).

3. It has been stated that there are between 5000 and 7000 children born by artificial insemination in the United States each year and that

the number is increasing. See Note, 64 Colum. L. Rev. 376, 377 (1964). Does this warrant legislation to deal with the principal legal problems presented? What form should such legislation take? Should the insemination procedure itself be subject to detailed regulation? What are the relevant considerations? See, e.g., Comment, 9 Vill. L. Rev. 77 (1963); Tallin, Artificial Insemination, 34 Can. B. Rev. 166 (1956); Symposiums in 7 Syracuse L. Rev. 96 (1955) and 34 U. Det. L.J. 383 (1957); St. John-Stevas, Life, Death and the Law c. 3 (1961); Report of the Human Artificial Insemination Committee, Cmd. No. 1105 (1960).

CHAPTER 6

Limitation of Children

A. Family Limitation and Population Growth

This chapter deals with family limitation through the use of birth control, abortion, and voluntary sterilization. While at first glance these might appear to be subjects more pertinent for the gynecologist or the religious counselor than the lawyer, serious legal problems are involved.

Individual and societal attempts to limit family size are of great antiquity. Although no longer a significant factor, infanticide has been widely practiced among primitive peoples and in many earlier civilized cultures (see pages 13-15 supra). Abortion has been extensively utilized and practiced in probably all primitive and civilized cultures and remains a major birth limitation device at the present time. Prohibition of sexual intercourse by married couples during taboo periods for up to four years following childbirth have been very common among primitive peoples and likewise have served to limit the size of families; doubtless abstinence from intercourse, even if no longer regulated by taboos, continues to be employed as a means of limitation today. Mechanical or chemical methods of contraception have also been in existence for centuries, but organization of birth control movements did not occur until the latter part of the nineteenth century in Great Britain and the period of the First World War in the United States. The development of more reliable techniques of contraception is still continuing. Most recent has been a change in emphasis on voluntary sterilization. Originating in compulsory measures to deal with supposedly defective elements of the population,[1] voluntary sterilization today has become more and more a method of family limitation. Despite these far-reaching developments and growing use of at least some methods of family limitation, the only major evidence that the law is beginning to come to grips with these problems has been Griswold v. Connecticut, 381 U.S. 479 (1965), holding unconstitutional a state statute forbidding use of contraceptives. As is true in other areas of family law, the law is now seriously out of step with much current social practice, and an uneasy accommodation of the conflict has been achieved by the dubious practice of minimal enforcement.

Before reviewing these legal problems it is important to set them against the perspective of revolutionary changes in the social situation which are only now emerging into public consciousness. Sir Charles Darwin predicted that the population of the world would double to five billion in

[1] See, e.g., Buck v. Bell, 274 U.S. 200 (1927), and discussion at pages 259-263 supra.

the next fifty years and stated that the population of the world is now increasing at the rate of 100,000 persons a day.[2] (This would mean that during the class hour at which these materials are discussed there will be a net increase of more than 4000 persons in the world.) The primary factor in this astounding growth is the marked reduction in death rates, achieved first in technologically developed areas and then passed along to underdeveloped areas. Former high death rates were predominantly due to famine, epidemics, and diseases which have now been largely brought under control. While war has also influenced world population control, its importance is far outshadowed by the food and disease factors and the improvement in medical skills. Sir Charles stated:

> There is an urgency in the matter. When our numbers are doubled fifty years hence, what is to stop their doubling again in the following fifty years? . . . [O]ne main consequence of having no Natural Selection seems to be a doubling of numbers in fifty years. Does this not imply that there will be ten billion of us a century hence, a figure which would make the world distinctly crowded? I do not say that this crowded life would be impossible, but that is not the point since it only postpones the evil day. As a mere matter of arithmetic — which you can find stated in The Origin of Species — if man were to continue to multiply at the present rate for a thousand years, which is not a long time in human history, there would then be just about standing room for us on the land surfaces of the earth.[3]

Some of the implications of this population growth and the difficulties of control methods are elaborated in the following excerpts.

1. The Population Explosion

THE FUTURE GROWTH OF WORLD POPULATION

United Nations Population Study No. 28, pp. 19-23 (1958)

[This study gives the following estimates, in rounded millions, for the world's population, using high, medium, and low figures (Table I(B) at 70):

	1975	1985	2000
High	3860	4770	6900
Medium	3830	4660	6280
Low	3590	4110	4880

The differences between the estimates depend upon differences in assumptions about fertility: "Fertility will: (*a*) remain constant until the year 2000 (high assumption), (*b*) decline at rates observed previously in some areas after 1975 (medium assumption), or (*c*) decline forthwith, and continuously until 2000, at such rates (low assumption)." Id. at 20.]

---

[2] U.S. News & World Report, Nov. 23, 1959, pp. 80, 82.
[3] Address by Sir Charles Darwin, Brown Univ., Oct. 1959, in Man's Contracting World in an Expanding Universe 31 (Bagdikian ed. 1960).

In appraising the value of these results it is necessary, first of all, to recognize that they have been obtained by methods of demographic projection. In other words, it has been assumed that future population growth will be the outcome of an orderly development of past and current trends in mortality and fertility. The record of the past shows that, in modern times, and for large populations, this has generally been the case. Wars, famines, epidemics and economic depression have caused various disturbances of trends but their effects, for the most part, have been quite transitory. . . .

Aside from this matter of general principle, the value of the detailed figures remains to be considered. All future estimates are affected by errors in current estimates, in the estimated current trend, and in assumed future changes therein. Some of these errors affect the short run and others the long run. . . .

. . . Errors are probably involved in each step of the procedure. Those arising from inaccurate current population estimates affect future estimates mainly in the short run. Errors in the estimated current rates of population growth, caused by comparing estimates for 1950 and 1955 which are not strictly comparable, have cumulative effects on estimates for a more distant future. Future changes in rates of growth depend on explicit assumptions, which have been made on the basis of plausible interpretation of demographic situations. But expectations which now seem plausible can be upset in the future as new events and improved observations affect the picture. . . .

Decreases in fertility may, and perhaps will, occur in various parts of the world at different times. It is quite improbable that they will occur simultaneously from 1975 onward in all areas of presently high birth rates. But in view of the length of the period and the intensity with which, apparently, population pressure is already being felt in some areas, it is rather probable that fertility decline will occur in at least certain regions before the year 2000.

The most probable estimates of future world population for the year 1975, therefore, would seem to fall slightly short of the high estimates and for the year 2000 to lie anywhere in the range between the high and medium estimates. It can therefore be stated that, barring either a catastrophe, or a deterioration of social conditions for progress in health, of global proportions, a world population of between 6000 and 7000 million by the end of the century should now be expected almost as a matter of practical certainty. . . .

It would be absurd, at this time, to carry detailed calculations forward into a more remote future. It is difficult to imagine the conditions in a world inhabited by more than double the number of people now in existence. And it is most debatable whether the trends in mortality and fertility can continue much longer with the degree of inertia which has characterized them in the past. Factors other than the slow secular changes in fertility and mortality may eventually bring population growth to a halt. Otherwise, even if it is conceded that population growth, after its peak near the end of our century, might diminish gradually and cease within another century, world population would not stop growing until it had reached between 10,000 and 25,000 million. One cannot say that such further growth is utterly impossible, but the vast changes in human organization required to sustain it can hardly be conceived at the present time. . . .

Consideration of such numbers immediately raises the problem of determining at what point the earth would reach its maximum carrying capacity. Despite many attempts to find an answer to this question, the problem cannot be solved by scientific reasoning. Because of his powers of reflection man adapts himself to ever changing circumstances, and his eventual adjustment to a new situation cannot be predicted before that situation has arisen. Different technical and organizational responses to a given environment, evidently, will permit different numbers of human beings to exist on earth.

Couched in more conditional terms, the question can be formulated as follows: given the present store of knowledge and organizational techniques, and assuming them to be applied to an extent which is consistent with human endurance, what is the maximum number of individuals who can draw their sustenance from the earth's resources? The frailty of human nature and the rigidity of social structures impose limits on the most effective uses of known methods, and practical achievement always falls short of what would seem technically feasible. Therefore the question, even if made contingent on specific conditions, cannot be answered independently of some subjective appraisal of human powers. Some of the more serious answers to this question, subject to particular assumptions made in each instance, have resulted in figures varying from 5000 to 16,000 million.

In view of current scientific progress, conditional estimates of the world's population-carrying capacity may now have to be revised upward. Recently our attention has been drawn to vast unused resources of vegetable substance in the sea, the possible uses of solar energy, and the likelihood that atomic energy will become widely available as a source of power in the near future. Other scientific discoveries may yet yield surprising results in terms of a more intensive use of the gifts of nature. But it is doubtful whether the limit to human numbers depends on technological progress alone.

Elaborate techniques in the intensive utilization of resources depend to an ever-increasing extent on a specialization of human activities which can be accomplished only by virtue of a high degree of social organization. This, in turn, requires individual discipline and restraint; things which human beings can scarcely tolerate beyond a certain point. A major disruption of the social fabric can nullify many of the gains which scientific progress has rendered technically feasible. It is questionable whether previous conditional estimates of the world's capacity can now be adjusted upward. If at all, by how much?

More disturbing than the projected figure of a population amounting to 6000 or 7000 million is the fact that it will probably be attained so soon. At the time of writing, the year 2000 is no further in the future than the year 1914 is in the past. Not only technical achievement but progress in international co-operation and organization will have to be more effective than during the past 43 years if the expected numbers of mankind are to be organizationally and technologically accommodated to the minimum conditions required for human dignity. . . .

A dichotomy now widely recognized is the division of the world into regions where intensive use is made of new technological methods, and others where this is not done to any comparable extent. Industrialization, urbanization, comparatively high incomes, and high degrees of literacy are some of the seemingly inevitable concomitants of technological development. Low mortality and low or moderate fertility likewise prevail in the developed areas, but are rare elsewhere. These various features are correlated in varying degrees, and a precise dividing line between developed and under-developed areas cannot be drawn. It has been generally agreed, however, that world regions can be classified in two categories, as follows:

1. *Technologically developed areas:* Northern America, Temperate South America, Japan, the three regions of Europe, Australia and New Zealand, and the USSR;

2. *Technologically under-developed areas:* The three regions of Africa, Central America, the Caribbean, Tropical South America, the four Asian regions other than Japan, and the Pacific Islands. . . .

To sum up, the technologically advanced areas contain now slightly more than one-third of the world population. This share, according to the seemingly most plausible expectations, will drop to less than one-quarter by the end of the century. Under extreme assumptions, before this century is ended, it may fall to only slightly below one-third, but it may also dwindle to one-fifth.

Relative economic conditions in different parts of the world will change. The gulf in living conditions, separating the two groups of regions may be reduced, but it may also widen. One of the factors which militate against a narrowing of this gap is the expected rapid growth of population in areas whose technological equipment is still deficient. Incomes there are low, and a considerable part of the portion of these incomes that might be saved is continuously absorbed in the maintenance of a constant level of living for a growing population. The problem involved in raising the capital needed for technological improvements is likely to persist for a long time to come.

2. *Experiments in Population Control*

HILL, STYCOS, and BACK, THE FAMILY AND POPULATION CONTROL: A PUERTO RICAN EXPERIMENT IN SOCIAL CHANGE
(1959)

[The excerpts that follow are drawn from the Introduction, which sets out the method of study (pp. 1-4), and the concluding chapter on research implications (pp. 366, 370-372, 375-377). With the exception of one item of data (from pp. 134-136) which is interpolated where it is relevant, considerations of space preclude full exposition of the careful research design and inclusion of the extensive data which support the conclusions.]

Puerto Rico is one of the countries of the world in which rising living standards accompanied by improved health facilities have brought about a marked decline of the death rate without comparable changes in the birth rate. The resulting gap has led to a rapid increase in population which has endangered economic development, strained existing physical facilities, and caused migrations that have affected Puerto Rico's relations with other countries. Since Puerto Rico is now one of the world's most densely populated areas, and since the population is still increasing, the possibilities of widespread fertility control have been the concern of government planners, population scientists, other experts, and civic-minded citizens.

Facile explanations of the failure of Puerto Ricans to control fertility come quickly to mind. Close to ninety percent of the population is Catholic, and until recently the country was overwhelmingly agricultural. These two facts alone have led many to the conclusion that large families are desired, that knowledge of methods of contraception is minimal, and that the use of these methods is virtually proscribed. None of these popular explanations can be accepted. Puerto Rico has government supported clinics where advice on birth control and contraceptive materials are available without cost. Female sterilization is well known, is widely used, and can be performed at many public hospitals for a minimal fee or for a blood donation by a relative. As far as the objective conditions for widespread fertility control are concerned, few countries in the world provide more favorable settings for action. Yet actions to limit family size by individual family heads have been at best sluggish and irregular. . . . It is this double paradox — that the popular explanations for high fertility can be easily contradicted, but fertility is still so high that natural increase of the population remains a critical problem — which makes Puerto Rico a crucial place to study the conditions of incipient population decline. . . .

In this volume several methods will be used to depict the workings of the family in controlling fertility. . . . The research design consisted of three interlocking steps: a pilot study employing a small number of depth interviews; a large scale survey which selected a number of hypotheses from the pilot study to be tested [references omitted]; and a field experiment which tested the conclusions of the survey by translating them into a series of educational programs . . . . [In one chapter we] describe an action experiment in which change in the variables extracted from the model did lead to change in contraceptive practice in a new set of families specifically selected to conform to the rigors of a controlled experiment. . . .

In pursuing different methods to determine the position of the family as the center of fertility control, we have uncovered conditions which facilitate and inhibit the effective use of contraception. We can now understand why favorable conditions for low fertility take so long to lead to an actual drop in the birth rate. Chapter 12 shows how the existing institutions for communication of knowledge and the present attitudes toward contraception are insufficient to produce rapid change in fertility behavior. In the course of the research we have learned how this process can be speeded up through a broad scale program of formal and informal education, through expanded pre-maternal health services, and through public discussion of the basic issues of family size and family limitation. Chapter 13 lists the principles such a program must observe and sketches out a list of objectives and services within the framework of present Puerto Rican facilities. Searching methods and theoretical model building lead thus to substantive results and practical applications. . . . [Pages 1-4.]

. . . [In Puerto Rico t]he phenomenal increase in population density due to increasingly effective mortality control accompanied by only modest progress in fertility control has been held within tolerable limits only by mass emigration to the mainland of the United States. Evidence is provided, moreover, that the small decline in the insular birth rate in recent years is due to the withdrawal by migration from the population of thousands of young people of the childbearing ages, since there is little evidence that age specific birth rates in the non-migrating age groups have declined. Puerto Rico's population is ripe for substantial declines in the birth rate both ideologically and technically, since the people now accept the three child family as ideal (with reservations and ambivalence to be sure) and the means of family limitation are freely available on the island. This study has been undertaken to ascertain why the expected equalization of birth rates and death rates has not occurred. To make possible suggestions for educational and medical agencies we have taken the individual nuclear family as the unit of study, viewing population control as a summation of family limitation practiced by the 450,000 childbearing families on the island. . . . [Page 366.]

Insofar as our various surveys have been able to capture them, the consequences of the one major primary program of the pre-maternal clinics of the Department of Health and the many massive secondary programs of formal economic, medical, agricultural, and educational agencies have been to induce people to think about, and to some extent to start to use, birth control methods. The programs have been quite unsuccessful in making families systematic, regular, and efficient in their use of contraceptives.

With respect to family size preferences, the ideal size is small, but the attitude is weakly held and often characterized by ambivalence. The motivations are not strong enough to carry families into effective action, often because of ambivalence and often because husband and wife are in disagreement or imagine they are in disagreement about how many children are best. The crystallization of an attitude about optimum family size tends to come late in the marriage.

With respect to knowledge of the means of fertility control, it is clear that most people know at least one method, but women, especially, learn about methods too late for them to be useful in implementing a small family ideal. The most effective non-surgical methods are learned latest, usually long after the family has already had more children than it wanted. Again, knowledge is unevenly shared within the family, the husband knowing methods his wife is not aware of and vice-versa, making the utilization of these methods unlikely. Present programs of dissemination of information reach women too late to be maximally useful, and reach men through unreliable channels of friends and neighbors. Fifty-five percent of men so learned the first method used, whereas only 18 percent utilized the more reliable professional and clinical channels for their information.

Although objections to the use of birth control are minimal in this population, not more than half the families in a representative sample of Puerto Rico have ever tried a method. Although men report wanting smaller families than their wives, they show less enthusiasm for using birth control methods than their wives. Women who do not use birth control cite "husband objects" more frequently than any other reason for not using. Yet husbands are as likely as wives (38 percent compared to 33 percent) to assert that "everyone has the right to use birth control," not just those who are in ill health or economically impoverished. Fewer than 7 percent said "No one has the right." Men have apparently been won over to small families and to the appropriateness of birth control, but most do not actually incorporate birth control as a regular part of their sexual life.

Present formal and informal programs can take credit for pushing about half the population into testing a birth control method at least once, but the distance in family planning terms from the testing of a method to systematic regular use of contraceptives is great. For a variety of reasons only a minority of those who have ever used birth control are currently practicing family limitation. Thirty percent have quit all attempts at limitation but may resume again. Forty percent have been sterilized after trying out birth control, 70 percent were irregular users while practicing. Of those who have defected, 75 percent were irregular users. Thus a high proportion of families which the present programs induced to start using birth control were occasional users who were never effective family planners. It is no wonder the difference in total pregnancies between those who have used methods and those who have not is only 0.7 after ten years of marriage. The effectiveness of use is low because it is irregular, short term, and experimental (shifting from one method to another). The present educational and medical programs are not achieving the hoped for results.

We have suggested earlier that the conditions of effective fertility planning are four: high motivation, adequate knowledge of the means, accessibility and acceptability of the means, and family organization adequate to implement action. The programs we have described above have placed their accent on the first three conditions while largely ignoring the fourth, the family action potentials. Families need training in problem solving, communication, and action taking as a team. Basic to effectiveness in problem solving is mutual understanding, concurrence on goals and means, and communication and empathy. These do not occur automatically in families where men and women are reared as strangers to each other. . . . [Pages 370-372.]

Two barriers which are often cited by officials and mainlanders as reasons for going slow in programs of persuasion in family planning are the alleged opposition of the Roman Catholic population and the deep-seated opposition to birth control based on the virility drives described elsewhere as *machismo*. We find scant evidence that either of these sources of opposition [exists] except in the minds of the officialdom of the island.

At the grass roots level of individual parishioners the religious opposition to [programs] of family limitation is negligible. The lack of objections stems not only from ignorance of the church's official position, but from opposition to it as well. The opposition by the church, moreover, is to the means employed, not to the objective of small families, and the clinics could very well prescribe methods of birth control in keeping with a family's religious convictions. The research has adequately documented that affiliation with the Catholic Church and attendance at church do not inhibit the regular and long term practice of family limitation. . . . [Page 375.]

[Data reported earlier and interpolated here] indicate that among 54 percent of the island's urban Catholic families and 35.5 percent of its rural Catholic families birth control has at some point been used. The figures are even more striking when we compare them with similar figures for non-Catholics: only 54 percent of the urban non-Catholic families and 27.5 percent of the rural non-Catholic families have practiced birth control. Thus, in the urban area no difference by religion was found, and in the rural area the incidence of birth control is somewhat higher for Catholics than for non-Catholics.

However, the Catholic Church does not forbid all methods of birth control, and it is possible that Catholics are practicing approved methods of contraception. . . . [But] only a minority of the Catholics who have used birth control have ever used abstinence or rhythm.

It has been suggested that sterilization is popular in Puerto Rico because it involves sinning only once. If this were true we would expect that among contraceptors, Catholics would be more likely to have used this method than non-Catholics. We find, however, that no difference exists. Among those who have ever practiced birth control, 36.4 percent of the Catholic and 37.5 percent of non-Catholic women are sterilized. However, it is true that somewhat more Catholics have been sterilized without previous experience with other methods. Seventy-seven percent of the sterilized Catholic women, but only 66.8 percent of the sterilized non-Catholic women, have never used other methods. . . . [Pages 135-136.]

Closely allied with the fear of the church's opposition is the mistaken idea that Puerto Ricans regard family planning as a private matter not open for public discussion or legitimate treatment in the schools. Our experiences in interviewing thousands of parents in the surveys and in the field experiment tell us that Puerto Ricans are as likely to talk about these matters publicly as any other people. Indeed, it is quite possible that there are fewer inhibitions in discussing these topics publicly than privately between husband and wife because of the respect and modesty barriers.

Finally, the alleged masculinity drives, which are supposed to lie behind the Puerto Rican male's opposition to family limitation, appear largely the figment of novelists and others who have stereotyped all Puerto Rican men with the *macho* stamp. In Puerto Rico men are authoritarian, dominant, and distant, but not virility obsessed. . . .

Although there is little organized opposition, the formal and informal agencies of Puerto Rico have not had the impact on the families of the island which they are capable of delivering because they have been operating under wraps, fearful of an opposition which our research would suggest is largely fictional. A number of trends are under way which are ready to be utilized, favorable conditions for a speeding up of the processes of change toward a society with birth rates and death rates in reasonable balance. A crash program promoted by the Commonwealth government and its major agencies is both possible and necessary to transform the composition of the family population from 15 percent current use to a maximum of effective planners. . . .

The supporting evidence for the evaluation of Puerto Rico's programs of action has been drawn . . . largely from the several sample surveys of the verification stage of the research. The field experiment was an attempt to validate these findings in an actual program of persuasion. The experiment was not designed as a model to be followed in a crash program as the most efficient and direct way to influence most of the families of the island, but as an intricately designed experiment to suggest which methods and what content work best for what types of families. A second auxiliary purpose of the experiment was to discover whether health educators could be trained in minimum time to be effective discussion leaders and pamphlet writers in this somewhat new area of health education. Our affirmative findings on this point, provided in detail in Chapter 10, are most heartening for future work on the island.

Perhaps the most important conclusions to be drawn from the experiment is that educational techniques are successful in promoting birth control use among Puerto Ricans of the lower income group. When it is realized that the subjects were exposed only to a few pamphlets or meetings, it is encouraging that as many as 50 percent of the non-users began to use birth control methods. The implication is that if such techniques and others were employed continuously, the response would be greater. [Pages 375-377.]

NOTE

Compare with the Puerto Rican material and with each other the following excerpts, the first earlier and pessimistic, the second recent and cautiously optimistic.

1. Woodside, Sterilization in North Carolina 104-105 (1950), in a sub-section entitled "Limitations of Contraception":

The early advocates of birth control, influenced by the rational and utilitarian philosophy of their time, believed that once the value of this population check had been demonstrated and the practical knowledge made available, man in his own interest would apply it in intelligent and responsible manner. . . .

Experience, however, does not bear out this optimistic view. . . . As a general rule, efficient practice [of contraception] is directly related to intelligence and intensity of motivation, and therefore no great success would be expected from the introduction of birth control knowledge to the unintelligent and socially irresponsible persons who make up the social problem or subnormal group.

For a decade now, the material conditions for achievement of a neo-Malthusian utopia have existed in North Carolina. Incorporated as part of the public health service, contraceptive advice and supplies are provided free of charge at almost all the city and county health departments throughout the State, and public health nurses are encouraged to inform their patients about the advantage of planned pregnancy. Yet (as we shall show in the next chapter) the program fails to reach many women of normal intelligence or seriously to affect their reproductive behavior, and has had practically no success with women of borderline or subnormal mentality. Workers in the contraceptive service are unanimous about the difficulty of persuading such persons to attend clinics, of instructing them in procedures, and ensuring that advice is carried out. There is further difficulty in that many are bad contraceptive risks, due to neglected gynaecological conditions following frequent childbearing, and no method available is likely to guarantee adequate protection.

2. Bogue, The Demographic Breakthrough: From Projection to Control, 30 Population Index 449, 449-450 (1964):

The years 1963-1964 very probably will go down in demographic history as one of the great landmarks of social-science research progress. In twelve months from June 1963 to June 1964 researchers in fertility control began to get a string of successes that left no doubt that by planned intervention they had induced a downward change in the birth rate in high-fertility populations. Experiences in Taiwan and Ceylon now are quite well documented. Other research, for which the data are only now being assembled, gives every evidence of showing similar results. . . .

It would be easy to disparage the "successes" as being too little in their impact, and too costly to be of practical use. In no case yet, with the exception of Taiwan, can it be clearly demonstrated that the birth rate of a population of major size in an underdeveloped nation has been genuinely slackened by a fertility-control program. (Let me add that there are several cases where such a decline probably has taken place; we merely lack the methodology to measure it quickly.) . . .

Even if we were to accept this minimization of the accomplishments of the past twelve to eighteen months (and to admit that actual support for fertility control is smaller than the nominal support), it would still permit us to declare that a truly tremendous demographic "breakthrough" has taken place. Two or three years ago demographers tended to hold the gloomy view that only a small miracle could save many nations from disaster because of rapid population growth. The picture now is completely different. If we make generous use of the word "if," we now find a basis for a cautious optimism.

The smallness of the impact in these first few successes should not deceive us into thinking that this is all that is to come. The history of science shows that a first breakthrough success tends to be crude and clumsy. Once the basic principles necessary for success are learned, progress and refinement come rapidly. There is much reason to expect that this will happen with the new discovery of fertility control. This discovery, and the refinements that will be made in the next five to ten years, may well lead to social-engineering work that will have as great an impact upon the course of human history as any of the major inventions or discoveries in the physical sciences.

DAVIS, THE THEORY OF CHANGE AND RESPONSE IN MODERN DEMOGRAPHIC HISTORY
29 *Population Index* 345, 345-347, 349-351 (1963)

My purpose here is to try to encompass some of the complexities in an overall analysis of demographic change in the industrialized countries. To do this, I prefer to start with Japan. Not only does Japan, the sole fully industrialized non-Western country, furnish a perspective that no other country can furnish, but some phases of its population change are statistically better documented. . . .

The phenomenon most discussed — and one commonly regarded as peculiarly Japanese — is the rapid rise of the registered abortion rate from 11.8 per 1000 women aged 15-49 in 1949 to a peak of 50.2 per 1000 in 1955, although at the latter date the registration of abortions is estimated to have been only 50 to 75 per cent complete. The resort to abortion has been the leading cause of probably the fastest drop in the birth rate ever exibited by an entire nation, births per 1000 women aged 10-49 falling by 41 per cent between 1950 and 1957. Westerners profess to be astonished by this phenomenon, but they should not be. The behavior of the Japanese is essentially the same in kind as the behavior of West Europeans at a similar time in their social and demographic history. The main difference is that Japanese tolerance permits the abortion rate to be reasonably well known, whereas in the past of Europe the abortion rate has never been known and, for this reason, is usually ignored in population theory.

Yet there is indirect and approximate evidence that in the late nineteenth and early twentieth centuries in Western Europe abortion played a great role. David Glass, who in 1940 summarized the findings for eight northwest European countries, cited the records of women under a German sickness benefit fund which show a gradual climb in abortions from 38 per 100 births in 1908 to 113 per 100 in 1932. . . . In fact, one gets the impression that the attitude toward abortion in West European society was much less intolerant between 1900 and 1935 than it is today. . . .

Finally, in five of the People's Republics in Eastern Europe, which have legalized abortion, the subsequent history of the rise of registered abortions, as summarized by Tietze, is amazingly like that of Japan. In Hungary, for example, medical boards were established about 1953 for authorizing therapeutic abortions. "That these boards progressively liberalized their policies is reflected in the growing numbers of legal abortions from 1953 onward." After the decree of 1956 permitting "the interruption of pregnancy on request, the number of legal abortions increased rapidly until in 1959 it exceeded the number of live births." Not only did the legal abortion rate rise rapidly in all four countries but also, as in Japan again, there was a substantial non-legal rate. The number of abortions per 100 births in 1961 was in Hungary, 145; Czechoslovakia, 55; Poland, 35; and Yugoslavia (1960), 34.

If, then, abortion was once a widespread practice in the most advanced countries of Western Europe, if it is now widespread in Eastern Europe, where it is legal and subject to record, and where economic development is behind that of Western Europe, there is no reason to regard the resort to abortion as peculiarly Japanese. It is not an outgrowth of ancient tradition in Tokugawa times; not an outgrowth of the absence of Christian ideology. It is a response to social and economic conditions arising in country after country at a particular time in the process of modernization. The fact that abortion was not safe earlier in the century shows how determined the people of northwest Europe were in their reproductive control. Now that it is reasonably safe when legalized, it is an effective means of family limitation for Hungary and Poland as well as for Japan. . . .

If Western prudery and Oriental realism have led to an exaggeration of the role of abortions in Japan, this tendency has been helped by a statistical illusion. Not only have abortions increased as births have fallen, but the sum of births and registered abortions for each year yields a combined rate per 1000 population that has changed little during the big fertility drop (Table 1).[4] This seems to say that an abortion was responsible for each birth [prevented]. Actually, of course, abortions can and do occur much more frequently than births can.[5] Other factors must therefore have played a role in Japan's falling birth rate.

[4] The combined rate would doubtless remain even more unchanging if the number of unregistered abortions were known.

[5] According to surveys in 1949-50 and 1953-54, the gestation preceding abortions in Japan lasted between 9 and 11 weeks, depending on the order of the abortion. Kimura, [note 6 infra], pp. 3, 9.

[Apparently the author's text statement refers to the fact that several abortions

TABLE 1. BIRTHS AND ABORTIONS IN JAPAN[6]

Annual totals (000's)

	Births	Abortions	Sum	Sum per 1000 Population
1949	2,697	102	2,798	34.4
1950	2,338	320	2,658	32.1
1951	2,138	459	2,596	30.8
1952	2,005	798	2,803	32.8
1953	1,868	1,067	2,935	33.9
1954	1,770	1,143	2,913	33.1
1955	1,727	1,170	2,897	32.6
1956	1,665	1,159	2,825	31.4
1957	1,563	1,122	2,686	29.6
1958	1,653	1,128	2,781	30.4
1959	1,626	1,099	2,725	29.5

[The author discusses, e.g., increased use of contraception and data showing that reported sterilization] operations, totaling 5695 in 1949, averaged 42,843 per year during 1955-59, at which time they equalled 3.8 per cent of the reported abortions. . . . [Pages 345-347.]

What, then, is the picture that Japan presents? It is the picture of a people responding in almost every demographic manner then known to some powerful stimulus. Within a brief period they quickly postponed marriage, embraced contraception, began sterilization, utilized abortions, and migrated outward. It was a determined, *multiphasic response,* and it was extremely effective with respect to fertility. . . .

. . . Obviously the demographic response of the Japanese is not to be explained in terms of spreading poverty or diminishing resources. Nor were the people influenced in their behavior by concern about national "overpopulation," for they let their government proclaim a policy of population expansion during the "Co-prosperity" era. In short, an explanation of the vigorous Japanese response to sustained natural increase must account for the antagonism between such increase and prosperity, in terms of behavior prompted by personal rather than national goals.

. . . Since the northwest European countries, years ahead of Japan, also had a sustained natural increase, did they manifest a similar multiphasic response? The answer is undeniably yes. Although generally overlooked because of our preoccupation with the contraceptive issue, the fact is that every country in northwest Europe reacted to its persistent excess of births over deaths with virtually the entire range of possible responses. Re-

---

could result in the prevention of only one live birth. A woman could conceive in January, abort nine weeks later, and repeat this pattern following subsequent conceptions in April and August. This would increase the number of abortions by three but reduce the number of live births by only one.]

[6] Sources: Kimura, Masabumi. "A Review of Induced Abortion Surveys in Japan." Paper No. 43 in mimeographed proceedings of the 1961 conference of the International Union for the Scientific Study of Population. P. 1; United Nations Demographic Yearbook 1960.

gardless of nationality, language, and religion, each industrializing nation tended to postpone marriage, to increase celibacy, to resort to abortion, to practice contraception in some form, and to emigrate overseas. The timing and relative importance of the reactions were not identical in the various countries, and of course methods could not be used that were not then technically feasible for the public at large (e.g., harmless sterilization); but the remarkable thing is that all of the northwest European countries reacted, that they did so in each case with the reappearance of the whole range of responses, and that virtually the entire panorama was later repeated in Japan. [Pages 349-351.]

[The author's theory is that in Europe and later in Japan industrialization provided opportunities for migration out of agriculture at the same time that declining mortality rates were causing rapid population increase, resulting in increased competition for a constant supply of farmland. For both those who migrated to a new urban occupation and those who stayed in agriculture, smaller families were required — for the migrants, in order that they could "maximize their new opportunities," and for both urban and agricultural populations, "to avoid relative loss of status" (p. 362).]

3. *The Legal Implications of Population Control*

Some of the demographic responses which affect the birth rate through deliberate efforts to reduce the number of children, e.g., postponement of marriage, have no legal consequences. Nor are any legal problems presented by some of the methods that may be utilized by spouses who mutually agree not to have children. One state court has suggested that if a couple cannot have children without endangering the wife's life or health, they can always follow the "positive and certain" method of "absolute abstention" from intercourse. Tileston v. Ullman, 129 Conn. 84, 92, 26 A.2d 582, 586 (1942), aff'd on ground that appellant doctor had no standing to litigate his patient's constitutional rights, 318 U.S. 44 (1943). But see Griswold v. Connecticut, reproduced below. Likewise a couple is legally free deliberately to restrict marital relations to definite periods in the menstrual cycle in order to avoid pregnancy; this is the so-called rhythm method of birth control. For a discussion of the methodology and morality of this practice and the moral distinctions drawn by Catholic theologians between it and mechanical contraceptive devices (but query the status of birth control pills), see Thomas, Marriage and Rhythm 79-81, 103-104, 118-119 (1957).

To the extent, however, that the population control experiments and proposals we have examined depend upon contraception, abortion, or sterilization, they pose a variety of legal questions. These are considered in the remaining sections of this chapter.

B. CONTRACEPTION

GRISWOLD v. CONNECTICUT
381 U.S. 479 (1965)

DOUGLAS, J. Appellant Griswold is Executive Director of the Planned Parenthood League of Connecticut. Appellant Buxton is a licensed physician and a professor at the Yale Medical School who served as Medical Director for the League at its Center in New Haven — a center open and operating from November 1 to November 10, 1961, when appellants were arrested.

They gave information, instruction, and medical advice to *married persons* as to the means of preventing conception. They examined the wife and prescribed the best contraceptive device or material for her use. Fees were usually charged, although some couples were serviced free.

The statutes whose constitutionality is involved in this appeal are §§53-32 and 54-196 of the General Statutes of Connecticut (1958 rev.). The former provides:

"Any person who uses any drug, medicinal article or instrument for the purpose of preventing conception shall be fined not less than fifty dollars or imprisoned not less than sixty days nor more than one year or be both fined and imprisoned."

Section 54-196 provides:

"Any person who assists, abets, counsels, causes, hires or commands another to commit any offense may be prosecuted and punished as if he were the principal offender."

The appellants were found guilty as accessories and fined $100 each, against the claim that the accessory statute as so applied violated the Fourteenth Amendment. The Appellate Division of the Circuit Court affirmed. The Supreme Court of Errors affirmed that judgment. 151 Conn. 544, 200 A.2d 479. We noted probable jurisdiction. 379 U.S. 926. . . .

. . . We do not sit as a super-legislature to determine the wisdom, need, and propriety of laws that touch economic problems, business affairs, or social conditions. This law, however, operates directly on an intimate relation of husband and wife and their physician's role in one aspect of that relation.

The association of people is not mentioned in the Constitution nor in the Bill of Rights. The right to educate a child in a school of the parents' choice — whether public or private or parochial — is also not mentioned. Nor is the right to study any particular subject or any foreign language. Yet the First Amendment has been construed to include certain of those rights.

[Some earlier cases which are then discussed by Justice Douglas] suggest that specific guarantees in the Bill of Rights have penumbras, formed by emanations from those guarantees that help give them life and substance.

See Poe v. Ullman, 367 U.S. 497, 516-522 (dissenting opinion). Various guarantees create zones of privacy. The right of association contained in the penumbra of the First Amendment is one, as we have seen. The Third Amendment in its prohibition against the quartering of soldiers "in any house" in time of peace without the consent of the owner is another facet of that privacy. The Fourth Amendment explicitly affirms the "right of the people to be secure in their persons, houses, papers, and effects, against unreasonable searches and seizures." The Fifth Amendment in its Self-Incrimination Clause enables the citizen to create a zone of privacy which government may not force him to surrender to his detriment. The Ninth Amendment provides: "The enumeration in the Constitution, of certain rights, shall not be construed to deny or disparage others retained by the people."

The Fourth and Fifth Amendments were described in Boyd v. United States, 116 U.S. 616, 630, as protection against all governmental invasions "of the sanctity of a man's home and the privacies of life." We recently referred in Mapp v. Ohio, 367 U.S. 643, 656, to the Fourth Amendment as creating a "right to privacy, no less important than any other right carefully and particularly reserved to the people." . . .

The present case, then, concerns a relationship lying within the zone of privacy created by several fundamental constitutional guarantees. And it concerns a law which, in forbidding the *use* of contraceptives rather than regulating their manufacture or sale, seeks to achieve its goals by means having a maximum destructive impact upon that relationship. Such a law cannot stand in light of the familiar principle, so often applied by this Court, that a "governmental purpose to control or prevent activities constitutionally subject to state regulation may not be achieved by means which sweep unnecessarily broadly and thereby invade the area of protected freedoms." NAACP v. Alabama, 377 U.S. 288, 307. Would we allow the police to search the sacred precincts of marital bedrooms for telltale signs of the use of contraceptives? The very idea is repulsive to the notions of privacy surrounding the marriage relationship.

We deal with a right of privacy older than the Bill of Rights — older than our political parties, older than our school system. Marriage is a coming together for better or for worse, hopefully enduring, and intimate to the degree of being sacred. It is an association that promotes a way of life, not causes; a harmony in living, not political faiths; a bilateral loyalty, not commercial or social projects. Yet it is an association for as noble a purpose as any involved in our prior decisions.

Reversed.

MR. JUSTICE GOLDBERG, whom THE CHIEF JUSTICE and MR. JUSTICE BRENNAN join, concurring.

I agree with the Court that Connecticut's birth-control law unconstitutionally intrudes upon the right of marital privacy, and I join in its opinion and judgment. . . .

[Justice Goldberg proceeds to place great emphasis on the ninth amendment, finding that] as the Ninth Amendment expressly recognizes, there are fundamental personal rights such as this one, which are protected from abridgment by the Government though not specifically mentioned in the Constitution. . . .

The logic of the dissents would sanction federal or state legislation that seems to me even more plainly unconstitutional than the statute before us. Surely the Government, absent a showing of a compelling subordinating state interest, could not decree that all husbands and wives must be sterilized after two children have been born to them. Yet by their reasoning such an invasion of marital privacy would not be subject to constitutional challenge because, while it might be "silly," no provision of the Constitution specifically prevents the Government from curtailing the marital right to bear children and raise a family. While it may shock some of my Brethren that the Court today holds that the Constitution protects the right of marital privacy, in my view it is far more shocking to believe that the personal liberty guaranteed by the Constitution does not include protection against such totalitarian limitation of family size, which is at complete variance with our constitutional concepts. Yet, if upon a showing of a slender basis of rationality, a law outlawing voluntary birth control by married persons is valid, then, by the same reasoning, a law requiring compulsory birth control also would seem to be valid. In my view, however, both types of law would unjustifiably intrude upon rights of marital privacy which are constitutionally protected.

In a long series of cases this Court has held that where fundamental personal liberties are involved, they may not be abridged by the States simply on a showing that a regulatory statute has some rational relationship to the effectuation of a proper state purpose. . . .

. . . The State, at most, argues that there is some rational relation between this statute and what is admittedly a legitimate subject of state concern — the discouraging of extra-marital relations. It says that preventing the use of birth-control devices by married persons helps prevent the indulgence by some in such extra-marital relations. The rationality of this justification is dubious, particularly in light of the admitted widespread availability to all persons in the State of Connecticut, unmarried as well as married, of birth-control devices for the prevention of disease, as distinguished from the prevention of conception, see Tileston v. Ullman, 129 Conn. 84, 26 A.2d 582. But, in any event, it is clear that the state interest in safeguarding marital fidelity can be served by a more discriminately tailored statute . . . .

[Justice Harlan's concurring opinion restated the position more fully elaborated in his dissenting opinion in Poe v. Ullman, 367 U.S. 497, 522 (1961). The Court in that case found the constitutional questions nonjusticiable because they were raised in a declaratory judgment action and state nonenforcement of the birth control statute "deprives these controversies of the immediacy which is an indispensable condition of constitutional adjudication." Id. at 508. At that time Justice Harlan concluded that the case was justiciable and that the statute represented an unconstitutional invasion of privacy under the due process clause.

[The concurring opinion of Justice White and the dissenting opinion of Justice Black are omitted.]

MR. JUSTICE STEWART, whom MR. JUSTICE BLACK joins, dissenting.

Since 1879 Connecticut has had on its books a law which forbids the use of contraceptives by anyone. I think this is an uncommonly silly law. As a practical matter, the law is obviously unenforceable, except in the oblique context of the present case. As a philosophical matter, I believe the use of contraceptives in the relationship of marriage should be left to personal and private choice, based upon each individual's moral, ethical, and religious beliefs. As a matter of social policy, I think professional counsel about methods of birth control should be available to all, so that each individual's choice can be meaningfully made. But we are not asked in this case to say whether we think this law is unwise, or even asinine. We are asked to hold that it violates the United States Constitution. And that I cannot do.

In the course of its opinion the Court refers to no less than six Amendments to the Constitution: the First, the Third, the Fourth, the Fifth, the Ninth, and the Fourteenth. But the Court does not say which of these Amendments, if any, it thinks is infringed by this Connecticut law.

We *are* told that the Due Process Clause of the Fourteenth Amendment is not, as such, the "guide" in this case. With that much I agree. There is no claim that this law, duly enacted by the Connecticut Legislature, is unconstitutionally vague. There is no claim that the appellants were denied any of the elements of procedural due process at their trial, so as to make their convictions constitutionally invalid. And, as the Court says, the day has long passed since the Due Process Clause was regarded as a proper instrument for determining "the wisdom, need, and propriety" of state laws. . . .

As to the First, Third, Fourth, and Fifth Amendments, I can find nothing in any of them to invalidate this Connecticut law, even assuming that all those Amendments are fully applicable against the States.[7] . . .

The Court also quotes the Ninth Amendment, and my Brother GOLDBERG's concurring opinion relies heavily upon it. But to say that the Ninth Amendment has anything to do with this case is to turn somersaults with history. The Ninth Amendment . . . was framed by James Madison and adopted by the States simply to make clear that the adoption of the Bill of Rights did not alter the plan that the *Federal* Government was to be a government of express and limited powers, and that all rights and powers not delegated to it were retained by the people and the individual States. Until today no member of this Court has ever suggested that the Ninth Amendment meant anything else, and the idea that a federal court could ever use the Ninth Amendment to annul a law passed

---

[7] The Amendments in question were, as everyone knows, originally adopted as limitations upon the power of the newly created Federal Government, not as limitations upon the powers of the individual States. But the Court has held that many of the provisions of the first eight amendments are fully embraced by the Fourteenth Amendment as limitations upon state action, and some members of the Court have held the view that the adoption of the Fourteenth Amendment made every provision of the first eight amendments fully applicable against the States. See Adamson v. California, 332 U.S. 46, 68 (dissenting opinion of MR. JUSTICE BLACK).

by the elected representatives of the people of the State of Connecticut would have caused James Madison no little wonder.

What provision of the Constitution, then, does make this state law invalid? The Court says it is the right of privacy "created by several fundamental constitutional guarantees." With all deference, I can find no such general right of privacy in the Bill of Rights, in any other part of the Constitution, or in any case ever before decided by this Court.[8] . . .

NOTE

This case apparently terminates the long controversy engendered by American legislation restricting contraception practice and the devices employed in its practice. Although the Connecticut statute invalidated in the Griswold case is the only one flatly prohibiting all use of contraceptives, many states have legislation regulating the sale, distribution, and advertising of contraceptives. See the compilation of state statutes in Comment, 70 Yale L.J. 322, 333-334 (1960). See also St. John-Stevas, Life, Death and the Law (1961). In the absence of specific legislation, some states have reached the same result under the terms of a general obscenity statute. Lanteen Laboratories v. Clark, 294 Ill. App. 81, 13 N.E.2d 678 (1938). Even more sweeping, at least in its literal language, is federal legislation stemming from the Comstock Act of 1873, 17 Stat. 598, which prohibited the importation, mailing, or introduction into interstate commerce of contraceptive devices. See, e.g., 18 U.S.C.A. §1461 (Supp. 1965) (nonmailable matter includes every "article or thing designed, adapted, or intended for preventing conception" and any kind of writing "giving information, directly or indirectly, . . . how or by what means conception may be prevented").

Long before the Griswold case, however, minimal enforcement, coupled with common statutory exceptions for distribution by physicians or druggists and permissive court interpretations, had undermined the effectiveness of this legislation. Thus the very restrictive Massachusetts statute was construed in Commonwealth v. Corbett, 307 Mass. 7, 29 N.E.2d 151 (1940), to permit the sale of a condom in a package marked "Sold for prevention of disease"; as the dissenting judge noted, "The construction adopted by the opinion leaves the statute as a whole without practical effect." 307 Mass. at 14, 18, 29 N.E.2d at 155, 156. Similar implied exceptions were read into 18 U.S.C.A. §1461. See, e.g., Consumers Union of United States, Inc. v. Walker, 145 F.2d 33, 35 (D.C. Cir. 1944) ("Congress did not intend to exclude from the mails properly prepared information intended for properly qualified people"; hence mass mailing of booklet about contraception to married persons lawful). Compare Judge Learned Hand's "doubts" expressed in one of the earlier cases: "There seems to me

---

[8] . . . The Court does not say how far the new constitutional right of privacy announced today extends. See, e.g., Mueller, Legal Regulation of Sexual Conduct, at 127; Ploscowe, Sex and the Law, at 189. I suppose, however, that even after today a State can constitutionally still punish at least some offenses which are not committed in public.

substantial reason for saying that contraconceptives were meant to be forbidden, whether or not prescribed by physicians, and that no lawful use of them was contemplated." But he nonetheless concurred in a holding that the statutory language barring importation of "any article whatever for the prevention of conception" is to be read as excepting importation where the articles are to be used for legitimate medical purposes. United States v. One Package, 86 F.2d 737, 740 (2d Cir. 1936) (concurring opinion).

The contrast between the earlier restrictive legislation and the opinions in the Griswold case apparently mirrors a rapid change in public opinion and policy. In 1958, a controversy over the availability of birth control assistance in New York City hospitals was resolved in a cautiously worded resolution permitting birth control treatment when "there are clearly defined medical conditions in which the life or health of a woman may be jeopardized by pregnancy." N.Y. Times, Sept. 18, 1958, p. 1, col. 2. Seven years later the federal government began to make funds available under the Poverty Program for birth control clinics, N.Y. Times, June 20, 1965, p. 1, col. 2, and several states agreed to provide birth control assistance to individuals on relief, e.g., N.Y. Times, March 17, 1965, p. 28, col. 1 (Michigan). See also N.Y. Times, Nov. 5, 1965, p. 25, col. 3, for the recommendations of the White House Conference on Health to make available birth control devices to all American families who desired them, particularly the poor, and to promote the widest possible discussion of responsible parenthood.

Perhaps the most interesting question raised by the Griswold case is what, if anything, the concept of "family privacy" may portend for the future. See, e.g., the last footnote in Justice Stewart's opinion, and Justice Goldberg's discussion of "totalitarian limitation of family size." If the federal government at some future time found it necessary to limit family size, could it constitutionally do so? Are the decisions of married persons to use other methods of family limitation such as those discussed below also protected by the new "zone of privacy"?

C. ABORTION

THE KING v. BOURNE
[1939] 1 K.B. 687 (1938), [1938] 3 All E.R. 615

MACNAGHTEN J. Members of the jury, now that you have heard all the evidence and the speeches of counsel, it becomes my duty to sum-up the case to you and to give you the necessary directions in law, and then it will be for you to consider the facts in relation to the law as laid down by me, and, after consideration, to deliver your verdict. . . .

The charge against Mr. Bourne is made under s. 58 of the Offences Against the Person Act, 1861, that he unlawfully procured the miscarriage of the girl who was the first witness in the case. It is a very grave crime, and judging by the cases that come before the Court it is a crime by no means uncommon. This is the second case at the present session of this Court where a charge has been preferred of an offence against this section, and I only mention the other case to show you how different the case now before you is from the type of case which usually comes before a criminal court. In that other case a woman without any medical skill or medical qualifications did what is alleged against Mr. Bourne here; she unlawfully used an instrument for the purpose of procuring the miscarriage of a pregnant girl; she did it for money; 2l. 5s. was her fee; a pound was paid on making the appointment, and she came from a distance to a place in London to perform the operation. She used her instrument, and, within an interval of time measured not by minutes but by seconds, the victim of her malpractice was dead on the floor. That is the class of case which usually comes before the Court.

The case here is very different. A man of the highest skill, openly, in one of our great hospitals, performs the operation. Whether it was legal or illegal you will have to determine, but he performs the operation as an act of charity, without fee or reward, and unquestionably believing that he was doing the right thing, and that he ought, in the performance of his duty as a member of a profession devoted to the alleviation of human suffering, to do it. That is the case that you have to try to-day. . . .

. . . The protection which the common law afforded to human life extended to the unborn child in the womb of its mother. But, as in the case of homicide, so also in the case where an unborn child is killed, there may be justification for the act. . . .

[The court then notes that under another statute proscribing "child destruction" during delivery at birth there can be no conviction] ". . . unless it is proved that the act which caused the death of the child was not done in good faith for the purpose only of preserving the life of the mother." It is true . . . that this enactment provides for the case where a child is killed by a wilful act at the time when it is being delivered in the ordinary course of nature; but in my view the proviso that it is necessary for the Crown to prove that the act was not done in good faith for the purpose only of preserving the life of the mother is in accordance with what has always been the common law of England with regard to the killing of an unborn child. No such proviso is in fact set out in s. 58 of the Offences Against the Person Act, 1861; but the words of that section are that any person who "unlawfully" uses an instrument with intent to procure miscarriage shall be guilty of felony. In my opinion the word "unlawfully" is not, in that section, a meaningless word. I think it imports the meaning expressed by the proviso in s. 1, sub-s. 1, of the Infant Life (Preservation) Act, 1929, and that s. 58 of the Offences Against the Person Act, 1861, must be read as if the words making it an offence to use an instrument with intent to procure a miscarriage were qualified by a similar proviso.

In this case, therefore, my direction to you in law is this — that the burden rests on the Crown to satisfy you beyond reasonable doubt that the defendant did not procure the miscarriage of the girl in good faith for the purpose only of preserving her life. . . .

What then is the meaning to be given to the words "for the purpose of preserving the life of the mother." There has been much discussion in this case as to the difference between danger to life and danger to health. It may be that you are more fortunate than I am, but I confess that I have found it difficult to understand what the discussion really meant, since life depends upon health, and it may be that health is so gravely impaired that death results. . . .

. . . There are cases, we are told, where it is reasonably certain that a pregnant woman will not be able to deliver the child which is in her womb and survive. In such a case where the doctor anticipates, basing his opinion upon the experience of the profession, that the child cannot be delivered without the death of the mother, it is obvious that the sooner the operation is performed the better. The law does not require the doctor to wait until the unfortunate woman is in peril of immediate death. In such a case he is not only entitled, but it is his duty to perform the operation with a view to saving her life.

Here let me diverge for one moment to touch upon a matter that has been mentioned to you, the various views which are held with regard to this operation. Apparently there is a great difference of opinion even in the medical profession itself. Some there may be, for all I know, who hold the view that the fact that a woman desires the operation to be performed is a sufficient justification for it. Well, that is not the law: the desire of a woman to be relieved of her pregnancy is no justification at all for performing the operation. On the other hand there are people who, from what are said to be religious reasons, object to the operation being performed under any circumstances. That is not the law either. On the contrary, a person who holds such an opinion ought not to be an obstetrical surgeon, for if a case arose where the life of the woman could be saved by performing the operation and the doctor refused to perform it because of his religious opinions and the woman died, he would be in grave peril of being brought before this Court on a charge of manslaughter by negligence. . . . I mention these two extreme views merely to show that the law lies between them. It permits the termination of pregnancy for the purpose of preserving the life of the mother.

As I have said, I think those words ought to be construed in a reasonable sense, and, if the doctor is of opinion, on reasonable grounds and with adequate knowledge, that the probable consequence of the continuance of the pregnancy will be to make the woman a physical or mental wreck, the jury are quite entitled to take the view that the doctor who, under those circumstances and in that honest belief, operates, is operating for the purpose of preserving the life of the mother.

These general considerations have to be applied to the particular facts of this case; the verdict of the jury must depend on the facts of the case proved before them. The girl in this case was under the age of fifteen, for she has attained that age within the last ten days. It is no doubt very undesirable that a young girl should be delivered of a child. Parliament has recently raised the age of marriage for a girl from twelve to sixteen, presumably on the view that a girl under the age of sixteen ought not to marry and have a child. The medical evidence given here confirms that view; the pelvic bones are not set until a girl is eighteen, and it is an observation that appeals to one's common sense that it must be injurious to a girl that she should go through the state of pregnancy and finally of labour when she is of tender years. Then, too, you must consider the evidence about the effect of rape, especially on a child, as this girl was. Here you have the evidence of Dr. Rees, a gentleman of eminence in the profession, that from his experience the mental effect produced by pregnancy brought about by the terrible rape which Dr. Gorsky described to you, must be most prejudicial. You are the judges of the facts and it is for you to say what weight should be given to the testimony of the witnesses; but no doubt you will think it is only common sense that a girl who for nine months has to carry in her body the reminder of the dreadful scene and then go through the pangs of childbirth must suffer great mental anguish, unless indeed she be feeble-minded or belongs to the class described as "the prostitute class," a Dolores "marked cross from the womb and perverse." [9] You will remember that the defendant said that if he had found that this girl was feeble-minded or had what he called a "prostitute mind" he would not have performed the operation, because in such a case the pregnancy would not have affected her mind. But in the case of a normal, decent girl brought up in a normal, decent way you may well think that Dr. Rees was not overstating the effect of the continuance of the pregnancy when he said that it would be likely to make her a mental wreck, with all the disastrous consequences that would follow from that.

. . . The case is a grave case, and no doubt raises matters of grave concern both to the medical profession and to the public. As I said at the beginning of my summing-up, it does not touch the case of the professional abortionist. As far as the members of the medical profession themselves are concerned — and they alone could properly perform such an operation — we may hope and expect that none of them would ever lend themselves to the malpractices of professional abortionists, and in cases of this sort, as Mr. Bourne said, no doctor would venture to operate except after consulting some other member of the profession of high standing. . . .

Verdict Not Guilty.

COMMENTS ON PROPOSED ABORTION LEGISLATION
Model Penal Code 146-150 (Tentative Draft No. 9, 1959)

. . . Although abortion and even infanticide at the will of the parents were lawful in some ancient civilizations, religious influence and the gradual shift of authority from the family to the state have led to legislation almost everywhere more or less severely restricting the practice.[10] In the

---

[9] "Dolores" (Swinburne), stanza 18.

[10] Major sources of information on abortion include: Calderone, Abortion in the United States (1958); Gebhard and others, Pregnancy, Birth and Abortion, chap. 8 (1958); Rosen, Therapeutic Abortion (1954); The Abortion Problem (1944); Taussig, Abortion, Spontaneous and Induced (1936); Williams, The Law

United States, England, and Canada, the prevailing pattern is absolute prohibition, except for the purpose of saving the mother's *life*. Only half a dozen states go so far as to recognize preservation of *health* as an independent justification. In Japan and the Soviet Union abortion is substantially unrestricted, if performed under authorized medical auspices.[11] In Scandinavia, Twentieth Century legislation has authorized abortion upon application to a public body which must be satisfied of the existence of one or more medical, humanitarian, eugenic and social considerations.

The salient features of American experience under relatively severe repressions of abortion may be summarized as follows:

(1) Estimates of the yearly number of abortions vary from 333,000 to 2,000,000, of which the proportion of illegal abortions has been put at anywhere from 30% to 70%.[12]

(2) 8000 women died annually as a result of abortion, according to one authority, basing his estimate as of 1935 on approximately 700,000 abortions a year and a death rate of 1.2%.

(3) In contrast to the abortion mortality rate of over 1% in the United States, the Russians are said to have achieved a rate as low as one hundredth of 1% during the period of liberal abortion, performed by skilled physicians under asceptic hospital conditions.

(4) 90 to 95% of pre-marital pregnancies are aborted; but the illegal abortion problem is not primarily a problem of the unmarried. "The vast majority of all abortions equalling 90 per cent occur among married pregnant women, especially those between 25 and 35 years of age who have had several children." [13]

(5) Over half the illegal abortions are performed by physicians, one-fifth by midwives, about one-fourth by the mother. Many physicians who, out of moral scruple or caution, do not perform illegal abortions, do not hesitate to refer cases to less inhibited colleagues. . . .

Abortion is opposed by some on the ground of physical or psychic danger to the woman, or as an inhibitor of population growth. But it is clear that the main factor accounting for laws against abortion is ethical or religious objection. As the fetus develops to the point where it is recognizably human in form (4-6 weeks), or manifests life by movement per-

---

of Abortion, 5 Current Legal Problems 128 (1952) and the same author's chapter on the Law of Abortion, in his book, The Sanctity of Life (1957); Davies, The Law of Abortion and Necessity, 2 Modern L. Rev. 126 (1938); 1 Encyc. Soc. Sci. 372 (1927); 2 Encyc. Soc. Sci. 559-65 (1937); Westermarck, The Origin and Development of the Moral Ideas 413-17 (2d ed. 1912).

[11] See Calderone, [note 10 supra], at 200-210. In Russia strict control was relaxed after the 1917 revolution, reimposed in 1936, and relaxed again in 1955.

[12] Pollak, The Criminality of Women 43-44 (1950); cf. Dunn, Frequency of Abortion: Its Effect on Maternal Mortality Rates, The Abortion Problem 10 (1944): Per 1,000,000 annual births, 330,000 abortions, 20.5% of which were induced, with 1% total fatality, or about 3000 annual deaths from all kinds of abortion; Whelpton, Frequency of Abortion: Its Effects on the Birth Rates and Future Population of America, The Abortion Problem 19 (1944): Survey of 3795 pregnancies showed 9.3 to 9.9% total abortions, 0.7% therapeutic abortions, and 1.0 to 1.9% criminal abortions.

[13] Taussig, [Abortion, Spontaneous and Induced 387-388 (1936)].

ceptible to the mother ("quickening": 14-20 weeks), or becomes "viable," i.e., capable of surviving though born prematurely (24-28 weeks), it increasingly evokes in the greater portion of mankind a feeling of sympathy as with a fellow human being, so that its destruction comes to be regarded by many as morally equivalent to murder.[14]   Moreover, abortion is opposed by many on moral grounds not directly related to the homicidal aspects.   For some it is a violation of the divine command to be fruitful, from which has been inferred also the sinfulness of homosexuality, contraception, masturbation, and in general all sexuality which is "unnatural" in the sense of not being procreative.   Furthermore, legalizing abortion would be regarded by some as encouraging or condoning illicit intercourse, although this factor can hardly be a significant influence on the rate of illicit sexuality in a society where contraceptives offer reasonable assurance against need for the unpleasant and expensive prospect of abortion.   Finally, discussion of abortion techniques, with its necessary reference to female sex organs, becomes for some a shocking violation of the conventions of communication, to be dealt with as "obscenity."

Despite the foregoing, the weight of critical and public opinion probably favors much more restricted application of criminal sanctions than present law contemplates.   A number of arguments are advanced favoring a relaxation of the repressive laws.   Economic and social conditions are said to be the primary cause of abortion.   Economic distress, or a desire to maintain a higher living standard, is at the root of the largest number of induced abortions.[15]   The great movement of women into industry and

[14] In the second century, Tertullian voiced the early Christian view, when he said, "Murder being once for all forbidden, we may not destroy even the fetus in the womb.   To hinder a birth is merely a speedier homicide; nor does it matter whether you take away a life that is born or destroy one that is coming to birth." Taussig, Abortion, Spontaneous and Induced 398 (1936); cf. reported approval by Plato and Aristotle of abortion as an alternative to infanticide in Greek society where parents were legally privileged to take the lives of their unwanted children. 1 Westermarck, The Origin and Development of the Moral Ideas 415 (2d ed. 1912). Early Roman Law drew a distinction between abortion or feticide and infanticide.   Abortion was regarded as an offense against the parents rather than against the unborn life, and it was no offense at all if done with the consent of the parents.   Davies, The Law of Abortion and Necessity, 2 Modern L. Rev. 126, 131 (1938).   Modern Protestantism adheres generally to the early Christian disapproval of abortion, but recognizes exceptions for therapeutic purposes at least. Catholic dogma, however, proscribes all induced abortion.   In England in 1953, Cardinal Griffin opposed therapeutic abortion as, inter alia, introducing "the principle that an individual may decide which life is the more valuable."   The Cardinal and the Woman, 45 New St. & Nation 193 (1953).   Fundamental to the Catholic Church is the doctrine of inherent sin, that unless a man be absolved through the intervention of Jesus by means of Baptism, his fate is eternal residence in Limbo.   From the Catholic viewpoint, therefore, death without Baptism counts more heavily than the destruction of the fetus.   Taussig, Abortion, Spontaneous and Induced 399 (1936); see also Curran, Religious Implications, in Rosen, Therapeutic Abortion 153-172 (1954).

[15] Taussig, Abortion, Spontaneous and Induced, c. 24 (1936).   But cf. Whelpton, Frequency of Abortion: Its Effects on the Birth Rates and Future Population of America, The Abortion Problem 20 (1944): In a study of 1980 women, among all income groups below $2200.00 annually, the rate of criminal abortions was fairly uniform, but in income groups above that figure, a higher proportion was evident.

professional careers inclines them toward abortion when confinement or parenthood would interfere with these pursuits. Prospective illegitimacy of offspring, with its unfavorable consequences for both the mother and child, furnishes another powerful social incentive toward abortion. There are unsatisfactory family situations, in which the father is alcoholic, cruel, or unable or unwilling to support his children. There are normal families in which the parents, having had a number of children, believe that further additions will so dilute the family's resources that all the children will suffer unfairly. It has been argued that a society which insists that children be born must be prepared to support those children out of the community treasury. The restrictions which society places on the distribution of contraceptives and birth control information are themselves contributors to the abortion problem.

As to the "homicidal" aspects of abortion, the answer of those who would favor liberalization would be as follows: most abortions — those which occur naturally as well as induced abortions — occur prior to the fourth month of pregnancy, before the fetus becomes firmly implanted in the womb, before it develops many of the characteristic and recognizable features of humanity, and well before it is capable of those movements which when felt by the mother are called "quickening." There seems to be an obvious difference between terminating the development of such an inchoate being, whose chance of maturing is still somewhat problematical, and, on the other hand, destroying a fully formed viable fetus of eight months, where the offense might well become ordinary murder if the child should happen to survive for a moment after it has been expelled from the body of its mother. This difference, it is urged, should be recognized at least to the extent of permitting a broader justification of abortion than of homicide. Proponents of liberalization would add that criminal repression of abortions which are widely regarded as permissible can only lead to the illicit performance of the operation by quacks under conditions much more likely to kill the mother. On this hypothesis, abortion law purporting to be based on the morality of saving life actually results in more deaths. On the other hand, if all legal restraint on abortion were removed, so that it could be performed under the best conditions, it is possible that the absolute number of abortions might so increase that even with a lower death *rate* a larger number of deaths would have to be anticipated.

NOTE

One of the most interesting developments in recent American abortion practice is the hospital committee that passes upon proposed operations by members of the hospital's medical staff. For a detailed description of the formation, procedure, and practice of such a committee in one hospital, see Boulas, Preucel & Moore, Therapeutic Abortion, 19 Obstetrics & Gynecology 222 (1962). They state (id. at 223):

Alarmed by the increased incidence of therapeutic abortions in 1954, the department of obstetrics and gynecology of the Hospital of the University of Pennsylvania formed a plan to govern this procedure in January 1956. A member of the departmental staff who wishes to obtain approval for a therapeutic abortion must present a letter summarizing the patient's medical history, physical findings, and laboratory results. The letter must also contain the indication for therapeutic abortion and the recommendation of one or more consultants. A letter from the patient and her husband requesting the operation must be submitted.

For each request, a committee of 3 is then appointed by the chairman of the department. None of these physicians may have acted as consultant in the case under consideration. If the principal indication for the abortion falls within a specialty other than obstetrics and gynecology, a member of the staff from that specialty is included on the committee. The composition of the committee remains anonymous, except to the departmental chairman, unless personal interview and examination of the patient is necessary to arrive at the final opinion. A written opinion is submitted by each member of the committee to the chairman, who then grants or refuses the request, depending upon the findings of the majority of the committee.

Following initiation of this plan, during the years 1956 through 1959, forty-five applications were submitted, of which forty-two were granted, id. at 226; the ratio of abortions performed to number of deliveries ranged from a low of 1:339 to 1:168. Id. at 223.

The following two excerpts set out the abortion law of California and the administration of abortion by hospital committees in the San Francisco and Los Angeles areas.

CALIFORNIA PENAL CODE

§274. Every person who provides, supplies, or administers to any woman, or procures any woman to take any medicine, drug, or substance, or uses or employs any instrument or other means whatever, with intent thereby to procure the miscarriage of such woman, unless the same is necessary to preserve her life, is punishable by imprisonment in the State prison not less than two nor more than five years.

PACKER and GAMPELL, THERAPEUTIC ABORTION: A PROBLEM IN LAW AND MEDICINE
11 Stanford Law Review 417 (1959)

[The authors submitted a two-part questionnaire to twenty-nine hospitals having obstetrical services in the San Francisco Bay and Los Angeles areas, of which twenty-six responded at least in part. The first section of the questionnaire elicited information about the number of therapeutic abortions (TA's) performed and their ratio to deliveries during the years 1952 through 1956.]

The obstetrical services of the twenty-six hospitals which responded to the questionnaire delivered 224,823 babies during the five-year period 1952-1956 covered by the questionnaire. During the same period 538 TA's were performed in these hospitals. The over-all TA rate for the twenty-six hospitals during the five-year period was 418:1. . . .

The five-year TA rates for each respondent hospital varied from a low of 7616:0 to a high of 126:1. In other words, there was one hospital which performed 7616 deliveries without performing any TA's, while another performed one TA for every 126 live births. . . .

The question which undoubtedly put the heaviest strain on the respondents' candor called for an expression of opinion as to whether the hospital had authorized the performance of any TA's which did not fall strictly within the exception prescribed by the California Penal Code (which was quoted, without explanation). It was made clear that the question did not call for a legal opinion but rather for a statement of what the words meant to a nonlawyer. Of twenty-four hospitals answering this question, eighteen voiced the view that they had authorized the performance of TA's which did not strictly conform to what they understood the legal standard to be. Only six took the view that they had not done so. In short, 75 per cent of the hospitals polled considered that their practices did not strictly conform to the legal norm, as they understood that norm.

[The second part of the questionnaire posed eleven hypothetical case histories, "each one presenting a possible indication for performance of a TA, and each one containing as much data as a hospital TA committee might have before it." Id. at 425. The eleven cases are reproduced or summarized below. Where necessary for evaluation, a brief summary in brackets following a case abstracts some of the authors' discussion of the medical problems posed. In each instance their analysis of the legality of the proposed abortion is omitted. The reader may want to make his own evaluation of legality and estimate the likelihood that the patient would be able to find a hospital willing to perform the abortion. He can then compare his estimates with the results which are summarized in the table that follows the cases.]

CASE No. 1

[A twenty-six-year-old married woman, pregnant with her third child, has a severe heart condition resulting from childhood rheumatic fever. To allow the pregnancy to continue would create a substantial risk of hastening her death.]

CASE No. 2

Mrs. C. is a thirty-eight-year-old woman referred for consultation by Dr. D. because of depression following a diagnosis of pregnancy of approximately two months duration. She has had six children in the past ten years and has reacted with depression with the last three.

Mrs. C. has been "nervous" and "afraid" of things all her life. She describes herself as having had "the blues" many times since her adolescence, not having many friends, except a few close ones, usually one at a time.

She describes her childhood as "not happy," being dominated by a strict father, not feeling particularly close to her mother who was always "tired and sick." She is the fifth of eight siblings in her family and always felt that she was a burden to her parents. She lived at home "helping mother" until she married at age twenty-seven a boy she had known in high school. She feels she married to "get away from home" and felt quite happy "for the first time in her life." This did not last after the first three years when she began feeling tired, worried and overwhelmed with household and child care. She feels her husband doesn't love her anymore, that he gets angry with her and the children, feels that she's not a good mother or housekeeper. Following the birth of her third child she "became sick" and went to bed for a period of one month. She has repeated this pattern with her following pregnancies and deliveries. During her last pregnancy one year ago she spent most of the time in bed, vomiting a great deal, unable to eat. It was felt that this was on a hysterical basis and she was hospitalized when dehydration and weight loss alarmed her obstetrician. This was successfully handled in the hospital, but the situation recurred on discharge and she was finally hospitalized for the last month before delivery. She was in bed at home for a period of time following delivery and continued chronically depressed, listless, with multiple physical complaints. The patient presents an apathetic, listless, depressed appearance. She complains of being tired, not caring, wanting to rest and sleep most of the time. She states she can't eat, vomits anytime she tries. She appears emaciated, underweight, hollow-eyed. She appears fairly well in contact with reality and situation, but unable to face the prospects of a seventh pregnancy. A diagnosis of severe anxiety neurosis with hysterical physical manifestations (vomiting, dehydration) is indicated.

Mrs. C.'s personality limitations and reality situation is such that she is suffering from severe emotional and physical symptoms endangering her life and emotional stability. It is recommended that the pregnancy be terminated.

Case No. 3

Mrs. A. is thirty-two. She has three healthy children, aged six, four and one. She is now eight weeks pregnant. There is conclusive evidence that she had an attack of rubella two weeks ago.

[Rubella, or three-day German measles, is of itself an inconsequential disease, but its occurrence during the first three months of pregnancy increases the chances of major congenital defects in the newborn. In 1952 the incidence of such defects was believed to be as high as 70 per cent, but more recent evidence places the incidence at between 10 and 12 per cent.]

Case No. 4

Miss C. is a fifteen-year-old of good up-bringing, the daughter of a local minister. Eight weeks ago she was raped, while on her way home from school, by an escapee from a state institution for mental defectives. She has become pregnant. There is a psychiatric opinion that describes her emotional distress and which recommends an abortion.

Case No. 5

[This case is similar to No. 2 except that the psychiatric indication is more severe, posing the threat of regression from a neurotic into a previously existing and completely disabling psychotic state which would require prolonged institutionalization of the patient.]

Case No. 6

Mrs. B. is thirty-four. She and her husband are both Jews. Her first child is now seven years old and is apparently healthy. Her second child was born five years ago. It was diagnosed as having amaurotic family idiocy (Tay-Sachs Disease) and died aged two. Her third child is now one and one-half years old and has been diagnosed as having Tay-Sachs Disease. She is now eight weeks pregnant.

[This congenital disease is characterized by progressive mental impairment and progressive diminution of sight, ending with total idiocy and blindness before death by the third year. The first child is rarely affected, but when one child has had the disease, subsequent children seldom escape.[16]]

Case No. 7

[A twenty-two-year-old married woman expecting her first child is suffering from diabetes, which was first diagnosed at age ten and is now in an advanced stage. Without pregnancy her life expectancy is three years, but the changes associated with pregnancy make her treatment vastly more difficult and pose an immediate threat to her life. Diabetes has a marked adverse effect on the fetus, the infant death rate being up to five times higher than in the nondiabetic group.]

Case No. 8

[The patient is Rh negative, her husband Rh positive; their first child was born healthy, the second required extensive transfusions after birth, and the third was stillborn. Once damage has appeared from Rh incompatibility, subsequent children are likely to be affected, but its manifestation will not necessarily become increasingly severe; there is about a 10 per cent chance that the pregnancy could produce a live infant.]

[16] Compare the situation presented by the famed thalidomide scandal. Mrs. Sherri Finkbine, one of a large number of persons who had taken the drug during early pregnancy, sought to obtain an abortion in Arizona after learning that a deformed infant would probably be born. After dismissal on the ground of nonjusticiability of her action seeking a declaration that an abortion was justified in her case under Arizona law, she went to Sweden, where, although fetal deformity was not then a statutory ground of abortion, the abortion was nevertheless approved and the law subsequently changed to authorize abortions in this type of case. See N.Y. Times, July 31, 1962, p. 9, col. 2; Hall, Thalidomide and Our Abortion Laws, 6 Colum. U. Forum, Winter 1963, pp. 10, 12.

CASE NO. 9

[The thirty-two-year-old patient has just been diagnosed as suffering from Hodgkins disease, which is always fatal. She has a life expectancy of two to three years. Treatment can only be palliative, either by X-ray therapy or by injection of an agent, e.g., nitrogen-mustard, into the blood stream. X-ray therapy is likely to result in fetal abnormality; the effect of nitrogen-mustard on the fetus is not known. Aside from effects of treatment on the fetus, pregnancy does not affect the course of the maternal disease.]

CASE NO. 10

Mrs. C. is thirty-two years old and is the mother of three children, aged seven, four and three.

Following the birth of her last child, she had what was diagnosed as a post partum depression in which she became completely withdrawn. She was hospitalized in a state hospital for six months during which time she had electro shock therapy with some improvement. She has remained under psychiatric care since then but she still becomes depressed very easily and talks freely about committing suicide, saying that her family will be better off without the burden of her care.

Four weeks ago, it was diagnosed that she was approximately four weeks pregnant. The news of this precipitated a severe emotional crisis. This has been manifested by vomiting, spells of uncontrollable crying lasting for hours at a time, at which time the patient locks herself in her room. She threatened suicide several times in the last four weeks, saying that she could never be a "good mother" and that she was a "useless member of society."

Last night Mrs. C. was found unconscious on the floor of her living room. There was an empty bottle, which should have contained approximately eighteen sleeping pills, in her bedroom. She was taken to the hospital and has apparently responded to vigorous therapy for her barbiturate overdose.

As the committee will see from the consultation, it is the opinion of the psychiatrist that these suicide threats are genuine.

[If the patient is kept under restraint in a mental institution, the possibility of successful suicide may be greatly decreased.]

CASE NO. 11

Mrs. A. is thirty-seven years old. She has five children, aged twelve, eleven, nine, seven and six. Her husband who is forty-two years old is a truck driver. Four years ago he was found to have pulmonary tuberculosis in the right lung. He had a thoracoplasty on that side and the collapse is maintained by regular refills at the county hospital. He has, however, not been able to hold any sort of steady job since he has no skill other than as a driver. Two months ago an early tubercular lesion was detected in the left apex and he is to be re-admitted to a sanatorium next week.

As soon as her husband became ill, Mrs. A. went to work on the production line at an electronics plant. She has done well at this job and has also tried with reasonable success to maintain the home for her husband and children. In the last two years, however, they have gone heavily into debt, since at that time the six-year-old child was found to have fibrocystic disease. The drug bills for this child average more than $50.00 per month.

Mrs. A. is now eight weeks pregnant. With the discovery of this present pregnancy she has become extremely tense and apprehensive. She cries a great deal and she is sure that the enforced cessation of her work will cause the collapse of the family unit which she has worked so very hard to hold intact.

Dr. B., her family physician, strongly recommends a therapeutic abortion. As her obstetrician, I am willing to do this procedure if the therapeutic abortion committee will approve.

TABLE II

RESPONSES TO HYPOTHETICAL CASE HISTORIES

1	2	3	4	5	6	7	8	9
				(a)		(a) + (b)		*Individual*
Case No.	Type	Legal?	Yes	No Percent	Yes	Percent	Yes	No Percent
1	M	yes	21	1 95	21	95	31	0 100
2	P	no	10	12 45	17	77	4	27 13
3	F	no	6	16 27	10	45	7	24 23
4	P	no	15	7 68	18	82	27	4 87
5	P	no	8	13 38	14	67	11	20 35
6	F	no	8	14 36	15	68	8	21 28
7	M	yes	17	4 81	19	90	30	1 97
8	F	no	5	17 23	12	55	2	29 6
9	M	?	10	11 48	16	76	14	13 52
10	P	?	17	4 81	19	90	19	6 76
11	P	no	1	20 5	4	19	2	29 6

Table II presents in highly condensed form the results obtained from part II of the questionnaire. The first three columns identify, respectively, the case number, the type of indication presented (medical, fetal, or psychiatric), and our conclusion as to its legality. Column 4 presents the Yes and No answers submitted on behalf of the hospitals to question (a): "Would you approve a therapeutic abortion?" Column 5 expresses the Yes answers to question (a) as a percentage of total hospital responses to the case. Column 6 cumulates the Yes answers to question (a) and the Yes answers to question (b): "If the answer is in the negative, do you think that this case stands a good chance of approval at some other reputable hospital?" Column 7 expresses this cumulated figure as a percentage of total hospital responses to the case. Column 8 presents the Yes and No answers submitted by individual physicians. Column 9 expresses the Yes answers as a percentage of total individual responses to the case.[17]

[17] The authors state at page 426 that three hospitals "furnished the judgments of each individual member of the hospital's obstetrical staff but did not furnish a 'hospital' ruling." This is apparently the source of the data in columns 8 and 9 of Table II. — Ed.

An example may facilitate reference to Table II. Case No. 3 presents a woman who has contracted German measles in the first three months of pregnancy, a fetal indication which in our view is plainly illegal under the current standard. Six hospitals would perform an abortion while sixteen would not (column 4), an affirmative response of 27 per cent of the hospitals replying to this case (column 5). In addition to the six hospitals which would themselves authorize performance of an abortion in this case, four more hospitals thought that, while they would not themselves authorize performance, the case would stand a good chance of approval in another reputable hospital. Put another way, there were ten hospitals which would not regard the performance of a therapeutic abortion in this case as being beyond the pale (column 6). Expressed as a percentage of total hospital responses, 45 per cent of the hospitals regarded a therapeutic abortion for German measles as being consistent with professional standards (column 7). Of the individual obstetricians who expressed an opinion, seven would approve a TA while twenty-four would not (column 8), an affirmative response of 23 per cent (column 9). . . .

NOTE

1. Consider also one additional case: A twenty-one-year-old married woman is eight weeks pregnant. Employed as a receptionist, she is the sole support of her husband, a second-year law student. She and her husband wish to have children, but not until he is settled in his career, and they request an abortion.

In this connection, compare the following report by Simms, Abortion — A Note on Some Recent Development in Britain, 4 Brit. J. Criminology 491, 493 (1964):

> At the Annual General Meeting of the Abortion Law Reform Association in October 1963, the President, Dr. Glanville Williams, the eminent Cambridge jurist, delivered a challenging address, which forced members into a reappraisal of their fundamental attitudes to this question. Arguing that the traditional aims of the Association, to legalise abortion on a limited number of medical and eugenic grounds, were far too narrow to come to grips with the major public health problem of criminal abortion in this country, Dr. Williams suggested that the aims of the Association ought to be essentially simpler. Any registered medical practitioner should be permitted to terminate a pregnancy, at the mother's request, up to the thirteenth week of pregnancy, if he considered this to be in the interests of his patient. He should be guided by the same considerations that would apply to other operations, without, as at present, wondering "whether he can get an acquittal by judge and jury if he operates."
>
> In the controversy this opened up within the Association, it became clear that the membership was divided into two fairly clearly defined groups, that might be labelled the "Moderates" and the "Fundamentalists." The "Moderates," who probably included much of the re-

ligious opinion within the Association, were in fact only concerned with "hard cases," medical grounds, psychiatric grounds, and sexual assault. The "Fundamentalists" took their stand on the inalienable right of a woman and her husband and doctor to make decisions of this sort for themselves, asserting that this was the area of private life into which, in a democratic society, the long arm of the law has no moral right to reach. Despite the fact that it is the "Fundamentalists" who provide much of the impetus for the abortion law reform movement as a whole, the final consensus of opinion came down on the side of preserving the Association's traditional and more limited aims.

In a later article, The Legalization of Medical Abortion, 56 Eugenics Rev. 19, 23-24 (1964), Williams notes and responds to one criticism of his position:

> In my book called The Sanctity of Life and the Criminal Law I devoted two chapters to the problem of abortion, in one sentence of which I remarked that the legislation in Sweden and Denmark allowing medical abortion on stated grounds had not, unhappily, substantially reduced the number of illegal abortions. Commentators upon my book who were critical of my point of view seized upon this one sentence as destructive of the argument for legalizing abortion. . . .
>
> . . . How is it, then, that in Sweden with its liberal laws there are still illegal abortions? [18] The answer is obvious: their law is not sufficiently liberal. We are told that in Sweden the special hospital boards which hear applications for abortions allow only 40 per cent of the applications. In addition to the 60 per cent who are turned down, there is the unknown number of women who do not apply for legal abortions, either because they realize that their case does not fall within the rules, or because they cannot tolerate the formality and even humiliation of applying to a hospital board in a matter which they regard as being uniquely their own affair. These are the women who go to illegal abortionists . . . .

2. Simms, Note 1 supra, also noted the controversy created in Britain by the publication in a medical journal of an article asserting that there are "no psychiatric grounds for the termination of pregnancy" and that abortion was essentially a socioeconomic problem with the "psychiatrist being exploited, for he at present provides the most convenient way round the legal situation." 4 Brit. J. Delinquency at 492.[19] Compare the finding of Dr. Edwin M. Gold, obstetric consultant to the New York City Health Department, that the proportion of therapeutic abortions based

[18] The Swedish law, in addition to more conventional eugenic grounds, includes justification of termination of pregnancy "[i]f, taking into account the living conditions of the woman and other factors, there is reason to believe that her physical or mental strength would be seriously impaired by the birth and care of the child." Model Penal Code 166 (Tent. Draft No. 9, 1959). See also page 613 note 16 supra. — Ed.

[19] The article to which Simms refers is Sim, Abortion and the Psychiatrist, Brit. Medical J. 145-148 (July 20, 1963).

on psychiatric indications had increased from 8 per cent in 1943 to 40 per cent in 1953 and to about 65 per cent in 1960-1962.[20] Gold's study also showed that the TA rate apparently varies sharply according to the patient's economic class; it was 3.9 per 1000 live births in private hospitals, 2.4 for private-room patients in voluntary nonprofit hospitals, 0.7 for ward patients in voluntary hospitals, and 0.1 in municipal hospitals.[21] See also Schur, Crimes Without Victims 21-22 (1965): "The private patient almost invariably receives greater consideration than the clinic patient, even though the former has the money to secure a relatively competent and safe illegal abortion should that need arise."

PROBLEM

The following proposal of the Model Penal Code (Proposed Official Draft 1962), typifies the kind of reforms being advanced in this country.[22] Would you support its adoption in your jurisdiction? By what criterion should its adequacy be judged, e.g., as a compromise of conflicting moral opinion, as legalizing what hospitals are already doing, as solving the public health problem of deaths caused by illegal abortions?

Section 230.3. Abortion.

(1) *Unjustified Abortion.* A person who purposely and unjustifiably terminates the pregnancy of another otherwise than by a live birth commits a felony of the third degree or, where the pregnancy has continued beyond the twenty-sixth week, a felony of the second degree.

(2) *Justifiable Abortion.* A licensed physician is justified in terminating a pregnancy if he believes there is substantial risk that continuance of the pregnancy would gravely impair the physical or mental health of the mother or that the child would be born with grave physical or mental defect, or that the pregnancy resulted from rape, incest, or other felonious intercourse. All illicit intercourse with a girl below the age of 16 shall be deemed felonious for purposes of this subsection. Justifiable abortions shall be performed only in a licensed hospital except in case of emergency when hospital facilities are unavailable.

(3) *Physicians' Certificates; Presumption from Non-Compliance.* No abortion shall be performed unless two physicians, one of whom may be the person performing the abortion, shall have certified in writing the circumstances which they believe to justify the abortion. Such certificate shall be submitted before the abortion to the hospital where it is to be performed and, in the case of abortion following felonious intercourse, to the prosecuting attorney or the police. Failure to comply with any of the requirements of this Subsection gives rise to a presumption that the abortion was unjustified. . . .

[20] See Shaffer, Abortion in Law and Medicine, 11 Editorial Research Rep. 723, 732 (1965).

[21] Id. at 735.

[22] For a summary of recent state reform proposals and of the formation of two new associations to press for changes in abortion law, see id. at 724-727.

D. VOLUNTARY STERILIZATION

We are no longer living in the day when every sexual contact carries with it the threat of pregnancy. Why resort to the radical method of surgery when there exists the simpler method of preventive conception? [23]

Is sterilization permissible simply as a stringent form of birth control? Does the case for voluntary contraception extend this far? I would doubt it. The case for contraception rests on the voluntary having of children. It is quite another matter to foreclose altogether one's choice in these matters. . . .[24]

[Because of the uncertainty of the legal status of sterilization] no surgeon will feel safe without explicit statutory regulation. Havelock Ellis disputed that.[25] He maintained that legal regulation was no more needed for sterilization than for any other surgical operation or for a haircut. . . .[26]

CHAMPLIN and WINSLOW, ELECTIVE STERILIZATION

113 University of Pennsylvania Law Review 415 (1965)

The desire for family planning has become a prevalent and widely accepted attitude in American marriage. Sterilization is a surgical procedure which offers a married couple a permanent means of limiting their family to its present size. However, it has significant moral and religious overtones for many members of the community, and the law in most jurisdictions has not provided the medical profession with any standards for a legally acceptable sterilization policy. The first half of this Note is the product of field research among doctors and hospitals in the Philadelphia area to discover whether sterilization is readily available for the purpose of family limitation and upon what grounds doctors tend to restrict its use for this purpose. . . .

. . . The method of field research consisted of interviews with thirteen obstetricians or gynecologists and six urologists, who were all hospital staff members or chiefs of service of their respective departments. Since most of the doctors were affiliated with at least two hospitals, the survey represents an extensive cross-sampling of the larger metropolitan and suburban hospitals.[27] . . .

[23] Frohman, Vexing Problems in Forensic Medicine: A Physician's View, 31 N.Y.U.L. Rev. 1215, 1219-1220 (1956).

[24] Kalven, A Special Corner of Civil Liberties: A Legal View I, 31 N.Y.U.L. Rev. 1223, 1231 (1956).

[25] Sex in Relation to Society (1937), p. 486.

[26] Mannheim, Criminal Justice and Social Reconstruction 20-21 (1946).

[27] No interviews were conducted with staff members of Catholic hospitals because preliminary inquiries revealed that these hospitals would not permit sterilizations of convenience. . . .

When used in this Note, "elective" sterilization or "sterilization of convenience" designates surgical sterilization performed for the purpose of family limitation motivated solely by personal or socio-economic considerations. "Therapeutic" sterilization, on the other hand, is employed to protect the physical or mental health of the patient. "Voluntary" sterilization, performed with the consent of the patient, is used to distinguish the elective and therapeutic procedures from those operations performed pursuant to state statutes providing for compulsory eugenic sterilization of mental defectives and habitual criminals. . . .

In female sterilization, called salpingectomy or tubal ligation, the abdominal cavity is opened and the fallopian tubes are cut and tied to prevent the uniting of sperm and egg. The operation requires general anesthesia and is generally designated as major surgery. Hospitalization is always required, but when a tubal ligation is done post partum, after delivery, a woman's hospital confinement is not appreciably lengthened. . . . In either case there is some risk of death as an immediate result of the operation.[28]

Male sterilization, vasectomy, is a simpler procedure which may be performed in the physician's office under local anesthesia. The vas deferens, the tube connecting the testes with the urinary canal, is severed and tied, preventing the sperm from thereafter passing into the urinary canal. . . . There may be some discomfort or a possibility of slight infection following the operation, but usually the patient is not inconvenienced for more than a few days.

The permanence of surgical sterilizations is qualified by the possibility either of recanalization or a surgical reversal of the operation. Recanalization, which is more common in the case of vasectomy, occurs when the cut tubes grow together to permit the passage of sperm or egg. Due to the use of improved surgical techniques, this possibility has been greatly reduced. Surgical reversal is a difficult operation and is only successful in a small percentage of cases. Therefore, a patient contemplating undergoing the operation must consider it as a permanent, irreversible procedure. . . .

In view of the reasonably effective contraceptive devices presently available, it would seem unlikely that many people would undergo elective sterilization. However, recent studies on the effectiveness of contraceptive

---

There are sixteen non-Catholic hospitals with over two hundred beds in the Philadelphia area, and the doctors interviewed included staff members of thirteen of these hospitals. Most of the doctors were also affiliated with smaller hospitals and familiar with their sterilization policies.

Because vasectomy is usually an office procedure, each individual physician may determine his own standards for performing elective sterilization. For this reason a broadly representative sample of vasectomy practice would have necessitated a greater number of interviews than the resources of the research project permitted. However, the urologists interviewed indicated that their attitudes and practices reflected the approach of most of the Philadelphia urologists.

[28] There was some disagreement among the doctors interviewed as to the seriousness of the risk to the patient. Some doctors reported that the danger of mortality was about one per thousand. However, other doctors indicated their belief that it was substantially lower.

methods indicate that these devices do not completely eliminate the risk of accidental pregnancy. In one group composed of 5788 couples who used several different methods of contraception, there were 1437 accidental pregnancies.[29] Experts in the area of family planning suggest that the lack of complete success in the use of contraceptives is caused not by any technical failure of the devices, but rather by the individual couple's inability to employ them properly and consistently — primarily because of the inconvenience accompanying their use.[30] Although contraceptive pills are not subject to this objection, they may produce side effects of nausea and vomiting, and they are as yet so new that many women are afraid to use them.[31] . . .

In many areas of hospital practice, the Joint Commission on Accreditation of Hospitals promulgates certain procedural and substantive rules which a hospital must follow if it wishes to be accredited. In December 1961 the commission responded to several inquiries from member hospitals on the proper procedure to be followed for sterilization operations and issued a bulletin on this subject. The commission did not attempt to establish substantive criteria to be applied to requests for sterilizations. However, they did decide that certain minimal procedures should be followed "for the protection of the patient, hospital, and physician." The commission requires that each hospital set and enforce its own substantive rules, with the approval of the governing board of the hospital and its legal counsel. Moreover, the hospitals' rules must conform to applicable state law and contain a requirement that another doctor be consulted before the operation is performed.

Despite the freedom from regulation by the commission and the absence of Pennsylvania statutes on the subject, obstetricians and gynecologists in the Philadelphia area have established rules for their hospitals which greatly restrict the number of elective sterilizations. Three of the eighteen hospitals investigated will not perform sterilizations of conven-

[29] Freedman, Whelpton & Campbell, Family Planning, Sterility and Population Growth 421 (1959).

In a compilation of studies on the rate of pregnancies of women using the diaphragm and jelly methods, the average pregnancy rate in fourteen reported studies was about 14%. Agarwala, Population Control in India: Progress and Prospects, 25 Law & Contemp. Prob. 577, 590 (1960).

[30] . . . In a recent study of vasectomy, fear of contraceptive failure and contraceptive interference with sexual pleasure were major reasons for seeking sterilization. Poffenberger & Poffenberger, Vasectomy as a Preferred Method of Birth Control: A Preliminary Investigation, 25 Marriage & Family Living 326, 327 (1963).

[31] The intrauterine coil, a new device which was being used experimentally by a few doctors interviewed, can be removed by a doctor when pregnancy is desired and may make sterilization obsolete once it is perfected. However, the medical profession is still unsure of the reason for its effectiveness and whether it may have any reaction on internal body tissue. Moreover, if the effectiveness of the coil is due to the fact that it produces an abortion of a fertilized ovum, rather than simply preventing fertilization of the ovum, it may incur the serious objection of both the Catholic and Protestant religions. See Medical World News, Nov. 6, 1964, pp. 110-11. And it might be held to be a device for procuring an abortion within the terms of many abortion statutes.

ience; they require a showing of medical necessity to justify the operation. In one of these hospitals, the committee which passes upon every application for sterilization often strains to find a therapeutic indication when there are already several children in the family. Where voluntary sterilizations are permitted, most hospitals have required that a woman have either conceived (gravity) or delivered (parity) a certain number of children at the time the operation is performed.[32] Age, too, is a determinative factor; there is much more hesitancy to sterilize a younger woman, regardless of the number of children she has.

In order to accommodate both of these considerations, some hospitals have established age/parity formulae based upon the standards promulgated by Mount Sinai Hospital in New York. Under this formula a tubal ligation will be done at the request of a couple that has six living children. However, the required number is varied with reference to the age of the patient. If a woman is thirty to thirty-five years old with 5 living children, or over thirty-five with four living children, a sterilization can be obtained.[33]

The hospitals in Philadelphia generally apply more liberal standards. . . . The most liberal standard is three living children without any fixed-age requirement. . . .

Two serious medical objections to female sterilization, the use of general anesthesia and the opening of the abdominal cavity, are not present in male sterilization. Since the cutting and tying back of the vas deferens can be done under local anesthesia in the doctor's office, male sterilization generally is not regulated either by the hospitals or their departments of urology to the same extent as female sterilization. . . . In spite of the ease of the operation and the discretion in the individual doctor, the interviews suggested that urologists have imposed even more severe substantive restrictions on vasectomy operations than are present in female sterilization.

Five out of seven urologists interviewed reported that they will only perform sterilizations when therapeutic indications exist. Another doctor said he would relax the requirement of medical justification in cases of severe economic hardship, but suggested that in the past these exceptions have been very rare. Only one doctor said that he performed vasectomies on the basis of the number of children a couple had. He would sterilize a man, upon request, if he had three living children. However, this is not his sole criterion because he excludes Catholics, who may have adverse psychological reactions, and those applicants [who] he feels are emotionally unstable. This doctor and the other members of the staff of the department of urology of the hospital with which he is affiliated do not

[32] The requirement that a certain number had been delivered or conceived seems to show more concern for the health of the mother, because after a certain number of conceptions or deliveries, future pregnancies become more complicated. A rule which requires that there be a certain number of living children reflects a greater concern for the possibility that a woman will change her mind or circumstances so that she desires additional children.

[33] Guttmacher, The Influence of Fertility Control Upon Psychiatric Illness, 116 American J. Psychiatry 683, 685 (1959).

perform vasectomies of convenience in the hospital because of the elaborate procedure that must be followed there. . . .

The primary emphasis of the field research interviews was placed on the reasons by which doctors justify the imposition of restrictive standards on elective sterilization. Many of the considerations which may dissuade an individual from undergoing sterilization were also suggested as justifications for a restrictive policy. Each doctor interviewed was primarily concerned with the permanent nature of the operation and the possibility that something might happen to one or more of the couple's children or that the party to be sterilized might remarry and desire children by the second spouse.[34]

Another important consideration, which significantly affects the practice in female sterilization, is the possibility of mishap during surgery. Since the procedure is purely elective, doctors do not like to take even a small chance with the patient's life, especially in view of the availability of other reasonably effective contraceptive methods.

Finally, some doctors considered the possibility that vasectomy may produce adverse psychological reactions, such as diminution of pleasure in the sexual act or even functional impotence.[35] . . .

The fear of community disapproval of a liberal sterilization practice may be a major reason for adopting a restrictive policy. . . .

When asked about sterilization, doctors would invariably bring up the subject of abortion, and it seems that the legal and moral prohibitions against abortion affect their attitudes towards sterilization. One doctor felt that this close identification of abortion with sterilization is one of the major reasons why the medical profession has restricted the availability of sterilizations. Moreover, the common association of the two problems has led hospitals to establish similar procedures for passing upon applications for sterilizations and therapeutic abortions. . . .

The practice of recommending or even requiring that a woman be sterilized in some cases when a therapeutic abortion is performed indicates that doctors are willing to perform sterilizations where they feel that public opinion would not be unfavorable. This practice is reason-

[34] We have already had occasion to note the growing practice of sterilization in Puerto Rico, page 591 supra. Compare Ridgeway, Birth Control by Surgery, 151 New Republic, Nov. 14, 1964, pp. 9, 11: "Twenty percent of the women between 15 and 45 [in Puerto Rico] have been sterilized. This has given rise to a difficult situation in New York City hospitals which receive requests from young Puerto Rican girls who, having landed in a new home and fallen in love, wish to have the operation reversed." — Ed.

[35] Although there is relatively little evidence to support the validity of this belief, . . . it might be desirable for the doctors to refer certain applicants to a psychiatrist for his advice on whether the operation should be performed. . . . [In their footnote 10 the authors had cited two studies: "[T]he most extensive study on the sexual and psychological effects of sterilization indicates that it produced exhilarating or at least no depressive effects on sexual activities in about 95% of the cases studied. Koya, Sterilization in Japan, 8 Eugenics Q. 135, 139 (1961).

["Of 235 women sterilized in Stockholm in 1951, 54% reported no change in capacity for sexual satisfaction, 33% improved and 13% reduced. 2 Excerpta Criminologica 735, 736 (1962)."]

able when the therapeutic justification for the abortion indicates that the woman's life would be endangered by future pregnancies, because doctors do not want to be forced to perform repeated abortions. However, it may be objectionable when the indication for therapeutic abortion is an emotional disorder, because psychiatric care could enable many women to withstand the emotional strain of childbirth and parenthood.[36] . . .

A comparison between legal regulations and medical practice in the fields of abortion and sterilization suggests that the medical profession attempts to reflect a consensus of community values in its attitudes toward controversial procedures. Although doctors recognize the legal and moral restraints on abortion, they have felt that the law is unnecessarily restrictive in light of prevalent public opinion, and there is evidence that the practice of therapeutic abortion is much broader than the law would seem to permit. On the other hand, there are no statutory restrictions on sterilization in most states and most doctors do not have rigid ethical objections to this procedure. However, doctors have invariably imposed their own restrictive standards for the operation, which have substantially reduced its availability. . . .

Although some individuals may object to elective sterilization on ethical or moral grounds, there appears to be no strong opposition among Protestant or Jewish theologians to contraception in general, nor to sterilization in particular. According to present Catholic doctrine, however, sterilization is subject to the prohibition against artificial birth control and is not permitted in Catholic hospitals unless sterility is induced as the result of a necessary primary procedure. . . . When asked about the hospital's sterilization practice, the administrator of one Catholic hospital in Philadelphia responded that sterilization is contrary to natural law and facilitates licentious living, undisciplined habits, and venereal disease. Because sterilization involves a surgical interference with natural bodily functions, a liberalization of Catholic doctrine on the subject of birth control would probably not affect the attitude toward sterilization. At present this attitude not only affects the practice in Catholic hospitals, but has wide ramifications throughout the medical profession as a whole. The large percentage of Catholics among the total population has a significant effect on society's consensus as to the morality of a sterilization operation. Several doctors interviewed stated that the Catholic position was a definite inhibiting factor for individual practitioners, including non-Catholics. Although the same Catholic prohibition on other contraceptive devices does not affect most doctors, sterilization is distinguished because it may require major surgery and is usually irreparable. . . .

Almost all of the doctors interviewed expressed a fear of the possible legal consequences to themselves and to their hospitals of performing elective sterilizations. Among urologists this fear was a major factor in restricting sterilizations of convenience; gynecologists and obstetricians did

---

[36] One psychiatrist has stated that the insistence that a sterilization accompany a therapeutic abortion of a youthful patient must have certain punitive aspects, because her psychiatric condition may improve greatly. Laidlaw, Discussion, 115 American J. Psychiatry 689. 690-91 (1959).

not feel it was as significant a deterrent. . . . Most of the doctors interviewed did not think that they would be criminally prosecuted. . . .

Doctors and hospitals were primarily concerned with the possibility of civil tort actions by the patient founded upon the theory that the operation was performed without his consent. They believed that the consent which they always required before they would proceed may be held invalid, because a court might find that the operation is against public policy. One doctor suggested that the same public policy that underlies laws to prevent criminal abortion applies to sterilizations, even though that policy had not produced a statute specifically forbidding such operations. Another theory on which the consent might be invalidated is that the patient did not fully understand the serious and permanent consequences of the operation.[37] This claim would be particularly common in situations where the patient had later become dissatisfied with the permanent results of the operation. . . .

Three states have enacted statutes declaring the performance or promotion of salpingectomy or vasectomy a criminal offense unless performed under the provisions of the compulsory eugenic statutes or by a private physician where there is a "medical necessity." [38] One of these statutes expressly extends the criminal liability to any person who knowingly submits to the operation.[39] The test of "medical necessity" applicable under these statutes is a novel one in the criminal law. The only analogous standards are those established by statutes prohibiting abortion except when necessary to preserve the life or, under some statutes, the health of the mother. It would seem that if the legislatures wished to limit the availability of sterilization to the same extent, they would have employed the more definite language of the abortion statutes. Their failure

[37] Compare Kelly, The Physician, The Patient, and the Consent, 8 Kan. L. Rev. 405, 426-427, 430 (1960): "Without discussion it may be assumed that a nontherapeutic abortion is condemned by society and its laws. Its performance has been made a crime under the criminal statutes of all the states. The consent of a woman to the abortion will of course not be a defense to criminal prosecution. Is the consent a bar to a civil action for damages by the woman involved? The affirmative and negative answers to this question are about evenly divided. . . .

". . . The Restatement of Torts contains the following illustration: 'A, at B's solicitation, performs a criminal abortion upon her. The operation is skillfully performed. A is not liable to B.' In the 1948 supplement to the Restatement, a comment to this section was added which stated there may be liability for any negligence in performing the operation, as in the case of the use of unsterilized instruments."

"Insofar as civil liability for a battery is concerned, the performance of a nontherapeutic sterilization has been compared to the performance of a nontherapeutic abortion, but this writer has been unable to find a single reported case in which a person who consented to a sterilization operation sued the physician for an assault and battery." See also Turiel v. Benveniste, 30 U.S.L. Week 2203 (Cal. Super. Ct. 1961), 14 Stan. L. Rev. 901 (1962), holding that a husband can maintain an action against a physician who performed an abortion on his wife with her consent since the operation constituted an unjustifiable interference in the husband's relationship with the unborn child. — Ed.

[38] Conn. Gen. Stat. Rev. §53-33 (1958); Kan. Gen. Stat. Ann. §76-155 (1949); Utah Code Ann. §64-10-12 (1961).

[39] Conn. Gen. Stat. Rev. §53-33 (1958).

to do so indicates that the "medical necessity" test may allow doctors more discretion. Whether this test will prove broad enough to permit volun-tary sterilization for eugenic purposes or to protect the health of the pa-tient's spouse must be determined by judicial construction as the cases arise.

With the exception of two other states which have granted doctors a statutory immunity from criminal liability for elective sterilization done under certain procedures, no state has legislation dealing specifically with elective sterilization. . . .

. . . Virginia in 1962 and North Carolina in 1963 . . . enacted stat-utes expressly negating civil or criminal liability of physicians for the nonnegligent performance of surgical sterilizations in accordance with prescribed procedures. Neither statute purports to restrict the purposes for which the operation may be performed. To come within the protec-tion of these statutes the doctor must perform the operation pursuant to the written request of the patient and, if married, of his or her spouse,[40] in a licensed hospital, after giving the patient a full and reasonable medical explanation of its nature and consequences. He must obtain the concur-rence of at least one consulting physician and may not operate until thirty days after the request. Although these statutes would seem to preclude any action based upon the illegality of a properly documented operation, they do not automatically insure that the physician will not incur civil liability just because the operation is not negligently performed. He must continue to protect himself against the claim of a warranty of permanent sterility. Another source of uncertainty is the failure of the statutes to specify where the burden of establishing the nonexistence of a spouse shall lie. The statutory requirement of the consent of both spouses may lend support to a claim that sterilization of the patient without such consent was an actionable wrong as to the nonconsenting spouse.[41] However, in the absence of circumstances which would reasonably place the doctor on notice to the contrary, it would seem that he would be found justified in relying upon the patient's representation that he or she was unmarried.

Each physician interviewed during the field research was asked his opin-ion on various provisions of the Virginia and North Carolina statutes, as well as the probable effect of a similar statute upon sterilization practice in Pennsylvania. The reactions of obstetricians and gynecologists were generally favorable; the primary objection expressed was directed at the

---

[40] But see Woodside, Sterilization in North Carolina 73 (1950): "Where the client is married, the requirement of the husband's or wife's consent presents the spouse with a right of veto which may be — and in practice often is — unfairly exercised. It happened that of the 48 sterilized women who were interviewed, 9 of them reported that their husbands had at first completely refused to agree to the operation or had required a great deal of persuasion and pleading before they would give consent. Many people feel that such control by one individual over another is hardly to be thought desirable, however orthodox it may appear to the legal mind; and it is frequently criticized by health and social workers who are thus prevented from giving a constructive service to mentally or physically handi-capped clients." — Ed.

[41] Compare Turiel v. Benveniste, note 37 supra. — Ed.

requirement of a thirty-day waiting period. Some physicians pointed out that most salpingectomies are performed post partum, and that the decision to undergo the operation often is not made until late in pregnancy. . . . Some urologists interviewed expressed dissatisfaction with the statutes' requirement that the operation be performed in a hospital. Since vasectomy may be performed as an office procedure, they felt that hospitalization would only add expense and inconvenience for the patient and place the doctor under the substantive restrictions imposed by his hospital.

Both urologists, obstetricians, and gynecologists objected to the requirement of consultation in nontherapeutic cases. Since the physician is not required to exercise any medical judgment in such cases, any limitations upon the availability of the operation will be those imposed by the hospital or by the individual doctor based upon their own interests and social values and an estimation of what is in the patient's best interest. . . .

When asked about the probable effect of a Pennsylvania statute similar to those passed in Virginia and North Carolina, the doctors interviewed expressed differing opinions. About half of the doctors thought that a statute would liberalize present standards . . . .

On the other hand, the doctors who felt that a statute would not influence the existing practice suggested that the reason why sterilization had been restricted was not the fear of incurring legal liability or an uncertainty about public policy. In their own practice they were more concerned with the irreparable nature of the operation and the militant opposition of religious groups. In view of these factors and the availability of other contraceptive means and the possibility of mortality in female sterilization, they would continue to impose the same restrictive policy, regardless of the passage of such a statute. . . .

NOTE

1. On possible criminal liability for sterilization on a theory of either mayhem or assault and battery, see Glanville Williams, The Sanctity of Life and the Criminal Law 104-107 (1957):

It is sometimes said that a person cannot effectively consent to the commission of a maim (mayhem) upon himself, and the question then resolves itself into whether sterilization is a maim. In principle, a maim was some injury that lessened a person's ability to fight and defend himself, such as cutting off a hand or even knocking out a tooth (which would impair his power to bite an adversary); and castration was also held to be a maim, because it was thought to diminish bodily vigour or courage. Sterilization has no effect upon mental or muscular vigour and so should not be held to be a maim. Also, vasectomy is not a maim because the legal meaning of a maim (as contrasted with a wound) is that it is permanent; the possibility of a reversal operation means that the prosecution cannot prove that vasectomy is permanent. Again, the law of maim seems historically to have no application to women. Even if all these difficulties are surmounted, it may be questioned whether the antiquated law of maim affords a satisfactory basis for a conclusion as to the defence of consent. It seems unlikely that a person would today commit a criminal offence by having his teeth extracted without adequate reason.

However, to decide that sterilization is not a maiming does not, perhaps, end the question. In Rex v. Donovan, where a sex pervert had caned a girl for the purpose of sexual gratification, the English Court of Criminal Appeal held that the girl's consent was not necessarily a defence, even though the injury to her did not amount to a maim. Mr. Justice Swift, speaking for the court, said that if an act is malum in se, so that it is in itself unlawful, consent cannot convert it into an innocent act. . . .

It used to be said that hard cases make bad law — a proposition that our less pedantic age regards as doubtful. What is certain is that cases in which the moral indignation of the judge is aroused frequently make bad law. Donovan's case is an example. . . .

. . . [I]t seems to be much too wide to say that a person cannot effectively consent to any hurt calculated to interfere with his comfort. For one thing, this proposition wrongly omits reference to the question of countervailing advantage. Every surgical operation temporarily interferes with comfort, but is not for that reason illegal. Even if the hurt is consented to for some reason that a court does not regard as adequate, this does not mean that it is illegal. Human beings are usually the best judges of their own interest, and if they consent to damage, there is generally no reason why the law should protect them further. . . .

Returning to the specific matter of sterilization, it may be taken as reasonably certain that the courts would uphold a voluntary sterilization submitted to on eugenic grounds. . . .

The troublesome area is the "sterilization of convenience." The only possible evil that can be discerned even in these sterilizations (there is no evil, but only good, in eugenic sterilizations) is that the power of procreation is removed. Some writers argue that this is against public policy because it imperils the future of the race. This appears to be an unrealistic attitude . . . .

These arguments are advanced in full consciousness that they are quite likely to be rejected by some judges, who may decide, when the question arises, that "sterilization for convenience," at least if the medical evidence is that it is irremediable, is a criminal offence. It may be of some importance, in this connection, that judges belong to the male sex, since, as has been shown, males have a stronger instinctive reaction against sterilization than females. . . . A psychologist might predict that a male judge would tend to look with a kindlier eye upon female sterilization than upon male vasectomy; he does not feel the former as such an immediate threat to his own security. . . .

2. "About 100,000 people in America have themselves sterilized each year, and while some of these operations are for health reasons, the great

bulk are done for persons, half of them men, who seek a permanent method of contraception." Ridgeway, Birth Control by Surgery, 151 New Republic, Nov. 14, 1964, p. 9. No source is stated for these figures.

3. Compare the German prosecution of Dr. Axel Dohrn, who was alleged to have performed 1300 sterilizations on consenting women between 1947 and 1961; the indictment was limited to 419 "selected cases." Dr. Dohrn, part Jewish and persecuted under racial laws by the Nazi regime, was charged with violating, inter alia, a law which "stems from Nazi racial legislation that made it illegal for a healthy 'Aryan' woman to submit to sterilization." N.Y. Times, Nov. 20, 1963, p. 10, col. 4.

SHAHEEN v. KNIGHT
11 Pa. D. & C.2d 41 (C.P. 1957)

WILLIAMS, P.J. Plaintiff, Robert M. Shaheen, is suing defendant physician because of an operation. He alleges defendant contracted to make him sterile. According to the complaint, the operation occurred on September 16, 1954, and a "blessed event" occurred on February 11, 1956, when plaintiff's wife, Doris, was delivered of a fifth child as a result of marital relations continued after the operation.

Plaintiff in his complaint does not allege any negligence by defendant. The suit is based on contract.

Plaintiff does not claim that the operation was necessary because of his wife's health. He claims that in order to support his family in comfort and educate it, it is necessary to limit the size of his family, and that he would be emotionally unable to limit his family's size by reason or will power alone, or by abstention.

Plaintiff claims damages as follows: "That the Plaintiff, as a result, despite his love and affection for his fifth (5th) child, as he would have for any other child, now has the additional expenses of supporting, educating and maintaining said child, and that such expense will continue until the maturity of said child, none of which expense would have been incurred, had the Defendant, Dr. John E. Knight, fulfilled the contract and undertaking entered into by him, or fulfilled the representations made by him."

Defendant has filed preliminary objections to the complaint . . . .

We are of the opinion that a contract to sterilize a man is not void as against public policy and public morals. It was so held in Christensen v. Thornby, 192 Minn. 123, 255 N.W. 620. Also see 93 A.L.R. 570. It is argued, however, that in the Christensen case the operation was for a man whose wife could not have a child without hazard to her life, whereas in the instant case claimant has contracted for sterilization because he cannot afford children.

It is only when a given policy is so obviously for or against the public health, safety, morals or welfare that there is a virtual unanimity of opinion in regard to it, that a court may constitute itself the voice of the community in declaring such policy void: Mamlin v. Genoe, 340 Pa. 320. . . .

. . . There is no virtual unanimity of opinion regarding sterilization. The Superior Court, in Wilson v. Wilson, 126 Pa. Superior Ct. 423, ruled that the incapacity to procreate is not an independent ground for divorce where it appears that the party complained against is capable of natural and complete copulation. This case so held whether or not there was natural or artificial creation of sterility, and recognized that in some cases there was artificial creation of sterility. It would appear that an exception would have been made had there been recognized any public policy against sterilization.

Defendant argues that there is no "warranty of cure" by physician in Pennsylvania. He also argues that the duty of a physician or surgeon does not arise from contract and suggests that it is against public policy for such a contract to be upheld.

It is true that there is no implied "warranty of cure" in Pennsylvania: McCandless v. McWha, 22 Pa. 261. An action against a physician for malpractice can only be sustained by proof of his negligence: Nixon v. Pfahler, 279 Pa. 377. . . .

A doctor and his patient, however, are at liberty to contract for a particular result. . . .

In the instant case plaintiff is suing, according to his claim, under a special contract in which defendant agreed to make him "immediately and permanently sterile and guaranteed the results thereof." Defendant's "warranty of cure" argument therefore does not apply to this case. . . .

Defendant argues, however, and pleads, that plaintiff has suffered no damage. We agree with defendant. The only damages asked are the expenses of rearing and educating the unwanted child. We are of the opinion that to allow damages for the normal birth of a normal child is foreign to the universal public sentiment of the people. . . .

To allow damages in a suit such as this would mean that the physician would have to pay for the fun, joy and affection which plaintiff Shaheen will have in the rearing and educating of this, defendant's fifth child. Many people would be willing to support this child were they given the right of custody and adoption, but according to plaintiff's statement, plaintiff does not want such. He wants to have the child and wants the doctor to support it. In our opinion to allow such damages would be against public policy.

Order

And now, March 15, 1957, it is ordered and decreed that plaintiff's action be dismissed, costs on plaintiff.

PART III

Dissolution of the Family

CHAPTER 7

Termination of Marital Status

A. Law, Administration, and Ethics

PROBLEM

After his client Wendy had left his office, her lawyer wrote the following memorandum of the conference for his files:

Wendy is twenty-eight, attractive, intelligent, a Wellesley graduate. Four years ago she married Hal, thirty-four; her second marriage, his fourth. No children. She is now employed as a secretary; Hal works with a construction firm. Wendy says that soon after the marriage she realized she had made a mistake; she should have known better than to have married someone with so much less education (Hal didn't finish high school).

Wendy says she and Hal had nothing in common, nothing to talk about. His only interests were baseball, boxing, and other women. Hal would go for days without speaking to her. He had a habit of insulting her in front of other people, several times apologizing to guests for the food she had prepared, adding that she "can't even cook." Hal had a habit of dropping his dirty clothes all over the house and he would expect her to pick them up for him. He refused to help around the house — "he never washed a single dish; if I was away he'd pile up the dirty dishes and leave them for me." Once Wendy got so mad at Hal that she threw a carving knife at him. She missed.

After two years of this they separated. Hal soon started living with Bertha, a married woman. Six months ago, however, Hal and Wendy were reconciled. Wendy soon found it was as bad as ever; he continued to insult her and refused to help in the house. So a few weeks ago they separated again and Wendy now wants to get a divorce as soon as possible so that she can marry Joe. She discussed the possibility of divorce

with Hal, who said he didn't care one way or the other. Wendy is sure
he is bluffing, for she thinks Hal wants to marry Bertha, who has now
obtained her divorce. Hal told Wendy he would be willing to give her
a divorce if she would pay the costs involved, agree not to ask for any
alimony, and agree to allow him to keep their new car and their joint
savings account. Wendy was furious with Hal about this and told him
that as she had given Hal "the best years of my life" she was certainly
entitled to something. Besides, she told me that Joe is still a medical
student, her earnings are modest, and she needs some help.

In response to persistent questioning, Wendy finally revealed that during the first separation she had had an affair with Joe, when she lived
with him for several months.

She also said that during their last reconciliation Hal became depressed
because of his inability to maintain a lasting relationshp with any woman.
At Wendy's urging, Hal consulted a psychiatrist whom he has since been
seeing weekly. The psychiatrist contacted Wendy and explained that
she should be tolerant of Hal's immature conduct because he had always
identified his wives with his mother and was rebelling against her authority.

How would you deal with Wendy's case?

(For this problem you will need to read through page 711 infra.)

1. *The Conceptual Framework: Grounds and Defenses*

MINNESOTA STATUTES ANNOTATED (1947)[1]

§518.01 What marriages void

All marriages which are prohibited by law on account of consanguinity,
or on account of either or both parties being under the age of 15 years,
or on account of either party having a former husband or wife then living, if solemnized within this state, shall be absolutely void, without any
decree of divorce or other legal proceedings; provided, that if any person
whose husband or wife has been absent for five successive years, without
being known to such person to be living during that time, marries during
the lifetime of such absent husband or wife, the marriage shall be void
only from the time that its nullity is duly adjudged.

§518.02 What marriages voidable

When either party to a marriage is incapable of assenting thereto for
want of age or understanding, or when the consent of either has been
obtained by force or fraud, and there is no subsequent voluntary cohabitation of the parties, the marriage may be annulled at the suit of the
injured party, and shall be void from the time its nullity is adjudged.

§518.03 Action to annul

When the validity of a marriage is disputed for any of the causes mentioned in section 518.01 or 518.02, either party may begin an action in

[1] For teaching purposes this statute is reproduced as it existed in 1947;
some sections have been amended since that date.

the district court of the county where either resides, to annul the same. In such action the complaint shall be filed and proceedings had thereon as in actions for divorce and, upon due proof of the nullity of the marriage, it shall be adjudged null and void.

§518.04   Insufficient grounds for annulment

No marriage shall be adjudged a nullity on the ground that one of the parties was under the age of legal consent if it appears that the parties had voluntarily cohabited together as husband and wife after having attained such age; nor shall the marriage of any insane person be adjudged void after his restoration to reason, if it appears that the parties freely cohabited together as husband and wife after such restoration.

§518.05   Not at suit of party capable

No marriage shall be adjudged a nullity at the suit of the party capable of contracting, on the ground that the other party was under the age of legal consent, or was idiotic or insane, if such idiocy or insanity was known to the party capable of contracting at the time of such marriage.

§518.06   Grounds for divorce

A divorce from the bonds of matrimony may be adjudged by the district court for any of the following causes:

(1) Adultery;

(2) Impotency;

(3) Cruel and inhuman treatment;

(4) Sentence to imprisonment in any state or United States prison or any state or United States reformatory subsequent to the marriage; and in such a case a pardon shall not restore the conjugal rights;

(5) Wilful desertion for one year next preceding the commencement of the action;

(6) Habitual drunkenness for one year immediately preceding the commencement of the action;

(7) Incurable insanity, provided that no divorce shall be granted upon this ground unless the insane party shall have been under regular treatment for insanity, and because thereof, confined in an institution for a period of at least five years immediately preceding the commencement of the action; in granting a divorce upon this ground, notice of the pendency of the action shall be served in such manner as the court may direct, upon the nearest blood relative and guardian of such insane person and the superintendent of the institution in which he is confined; such relative or guardian and superintendent of the institution shall be entitled to appear and be heard upon any and all issues; the status of the parties as to the support and maintenance of the insane person shall not be altered in any way by the granting of the divorce;

(8) Continuous separation under decree of limited divorce for more than five years next preceding the commencement of the action, and continuous separation under an order or decree of separate maintenance for a period of two years immediately preceding the commencement of the action.

§518.07   Residence of complainant

No divorce shall be granted unless the plaintiff has resided in this state one year immediately preceding the filing of the complaint, except for adultery committed while the plaintiff was a resident of this state.

§518.11   Service; publication

Copies of the summons and complaint shall be served on the defendant personally, and, when such service is made out of this state and within the United States, it may be proved by the affidavit of the person making the same, with the certificate of the clerk of the court of the county to the identity of the officer taking the affidavit, and when made without the United States it may be proved by the affidavit of the person making the same, taken before and certified by any United States minister, charge d'affaires, commissioner, consul or commercial agent, or other consular or diplomatic officer of the United States appointed to reside in such country, including all deputies or other representatives of such officer authorized to perform their duties; or before an officer authorized to administer an oath with the certificate of an officer of a court of record of the country wherein such affidavit is taken as to the identity and authority of the officer taking the same, but, if personal service cannot well be made, the court may order service of the summons by publication, which publication shall be made as in other actions.

§518.13   Failure to answer; reference

If the defendant does not appear after service duly made and proved, the court may hear and determine the action at a general or special term, or in vacation; provided, that the court or judge, upon application, may refer the action to a referee to take and report the evidence therein. When issue is joined, like proceedings shall be had as in civil actions.

CALIFORNIA CIVIL CODE

§111.   Denial; grounds

DIVORCES DENIED, ON SHOWING WHAT.   Divorces must be denied upon showing:

1. Connivance; or,
2. Collusion; or,
3. Condonation; or,
4. Recrimination; or,
5. Limitation and lapse of time.

§112.   Connivance

CONNIVANCE, WHAT.   Connivance is the corrupt consent of one party to the commission of the acts of the other, constituting the cause of divorce.

§113.   Corrupt consent; manifestation

CORRUPT CONSENT, HOW MANIFESTED.   Corrupt consent is manifested by passive permission, with intent to connive at or actively procure the commission of the acts complained of.

§114.   Collusion

COLLUSION, WHAT.   Collusion is an agreement between husband and wife that one of them shall commit, or appear to have committed, or to be represented in Court as having committed, acts constituting a cause of divorce, for the purpose of enabling the other to obtain a divorce.

§115. Condonation

CONDONATION, WHAT. Condonation is the conditional forgiveness of a matrimonial offense constituting a cause of divorce.

§116. Condonation; requisites

REQUISITES TO CONDONATION. The following requirements are necessary to condonation:

1. A knowledge on the part of the condoner of the facts constituting the cause of divorce;
2. Reconciliation and remission of the offense by the injured party;
3. Restoration of the offending party to all marital rights.

§117. Condonation; implied condition

CONDONATION IMPLIES WHAT. Condonation implies a condition subsequent; that the forgiving party must be treated with conjugal kindness.

§118. Condonation, evidence of

Where the cause of divorce consists of a course of offensive conduct, or arises, in cases of cruelty, from excessive acts of ill-treatment which may, aggregately, constitute the offense, cohabitation, or passive endurance, or conjugal kindness, shall not be evidence of condonation of any of the acts constituting such cause, unless accompanied by an express agreement to condone.

§119. Condonation; time of making

In cases mentioned in the last section, condonation can be made only after the cause of divorce has become complete, as to the acts complained of.

§120. Condonation; concealment of facts; effect

CONCEALMENT OF FACTS IN CERTAIN CASES MAKES CONDONATION VOID. A fraudulent concealment by the condonee of facts constituting a different cause of divorce from the one condoned, and existing at the time of condonation, avoids such condonation.

§121. Condonation, how revoked

CONDONATION, HOW REVOKED. Condonation is revoked and the original cause of divorce revived:

1. When the condonee commits acts constituting a like or other cause of divorce; or,
2. When the condonee is guilty of great conjugal unkindness, not amounting to a cause of divorce, but sufficiently habitual and gross to show that the conditions of condonation had not been accepted in good faith, or not fulfilled.

§122. Recrimination

RECRIMINATION, WHAT. Recrimination is a showing by the defendant of any cause of divorce against the plaintiff, in bar of the plaintiff's cause of divorce.

§123. Condonation as bar to recriminatory defense

Condonation of a cause of divorce, shown in the answer as a recriminatory defense, is a bar to such defense, unless the condonation be revoked, as provided in section one hundred and twenty-one, or two years have elapsed after the condonation, and before the accruing or completion of the cause of divorce against which the recrimination is shown.

§124. Denial of divorce; limitation of actions

A divorce must be denied:

One — When the cause is adultery and the action is not commenced within two years after the commission of the act of adultery, or after its discovery by the injured party; or,

Two — When the cause is conviction of felony, and the action is not commenced before the expiration of two years after a pardon, or the termination of the period of sentence.

Three — In all other cases when there is an unreasonable lapse of time before the commencement of the action.

§125. Presumptions from delay

LAPSE OF TIME ESTABLISHES CERTAIN PRESUMPTIONS. Unreasonable lapse of time is such a delay in commencing the action as establishes the presumption that there has been connivance, collusion, or condonation of the offense, or full acquiescence in the same, with intent to continue the marriage relation notwithstanding the commission of such offense.

§126. Presumptions from delay; rebuttal

PRESUMPTIONS MAY BE REBUTTED. The presumptions arising from lapse of time may be rebutted by showing reasonable grounds for the delay in commencing the action.

NOTE

While the eight grounds for divorce and seven for annulment provided in Minnesota include all those which are of common incidence, there is a wide range of miscellaneous other causes of action in scattered jurisdictions, e.g., crime against nature, incompatibility, public defamation of spouse, sterility, or vagrancy of husband. Other states specify grounds, e.g., pregnancy at marriage by another man, for which most jurisdictions provide under the rubric "fraud." Different labels are also used to describe similar conduct, e.g., compare desertion with abandonment or nonsupport; cruelty with indignities to the person, violent and ungovernable temper, or attempted murder of spouse. The doctrinal trappings of the more common grounds are sketched in the materials which follow.[2]

In addition to absolute divorce, most states make provision for a limited form of divorce variously known as divorce a mensa et thoro or legal separation. See page 646 Note 2 infra.

Tables 1-3 which follow provide some data about dissolution practice and the relationship between the legal grounds and alleged "real" causes of marital dissolution.

[2] A chart showing for all fifty-one American jurisdictions what grounds are available for divorce, annulment, and separation, together with some items on procedure, is published annually by the National Legal Aid and Defender Assn., American Bar Center, Chicago 37, Ill.

TABLE 1. THE GROUNDS OF DIVORCE — FOUR APPROACHES

1. Legal Grounds Alleged, Divorces and Annulments in 13 States, 1958		2. Opinions of Idaho Lawyers as to "Real" Causes of Divorce		3. "Main Cause of My Divorce" as Stated by Detroit Divorcees		4. Opinions of Domestic Relations Judges as to Causes of Divorce (Rated in Decreasing Order of Importance)
Cruelty	59.9%	Finances, nonsupport	19%	Finances, nonsupport	21%	Drinking
Desertion	25.0%	Adultery	18%	Authority clashes	12%	Financial problems
Drunkenness	1.6%	Drunkenness	17%	Drinking	12%	Infidelity
Adultery	1.6%	Incompatibility	13%	"Drinking, gambling, helling around"	12%	Unsatisfactory sexual relations
Nonsupport	0.8%	Irresponsibility	6%	Personality clashes	11%	Desertion
Bigamy	0.6%	Immaturity	5%	No real home life	9%	In-law problems
Conviction of crime	0.6%	Sexual incompatibility	5%	Value conflicts	8%	Wife beating
Fraud	0.4%	Cruelty	5%	The triangle	6%	Lack of social activity
Insanity	0.1%	Cultural differences	4%	Desertion	3%	Immaturity
Under age	0.1%	Desertion	2%	Relatives	2%	Lack of communication
Other (mostly variations of cruelty, nonsupport)	5.8%	In-laws	2%	Misc.	4%	Difference in education
Not stated	3.4%	Misc.	3%			Separation because of job requirements
						Improper care of children
						Interfaith problems
						Gambling
						Sickness
						Incompatibility
						Frequent changes of dwelling

Source: 1 Vital Statistics of the United States 1958, p. 2-26, Table 2-X.

Source: Harmsworth & Minnis, Non-Statutory Causes of Divorce: The Lawyer's Point of View, 17 Marr. & Fam. Liv. 316, 320, Table III (1955).

Source: Adapted from Goode, After Divorce 123 (1956).

Source: Quenstedt & Winkler, What Are Our Domestic Relations Judges Thinking?, Monograph No. 1, A.B.A. Sect. of Fam. L., July 1965, p. 1.

TABLE 2. DIVORCES AND ANNULMENTS BY LEGAL GROUNDS FOR DECREE (STATISTICS FOR 24 STATES, 1954)

Area	Total	Adultery	Bigamy	Conviction of crime	Cruelty	Desertion	Drunkenness	Fraud	Insanity	Non-support	Under age	Other[3]	Not stated
Total	146,554	2,016	611	681	71,102	21,894	2,910	480	169	1,191	68	43,895	1,537
Div.[4]	142,150	1,923	230	671	69,181	21,239	2,753	130	124	1,188	1	43,596	1,114
Annul.[4]	1,528	2	342	3	43	4	7	336	25	3	67	273	423
Alabama	8,916	369	27	12	4,264	—	341	37	17	27	7	3,792	23
Arkansas[5]	7,917	67	20	—	1,079	1,068	59	42	29	99	—	5,400	54
Connecticut	2,876	91	39	7	1,878	651	150	14	20	—	—	26	—
Delaware	655	66	17	2	150	383	27	2	4	—	—	4	—
Florida	19,387	184	99	—	12,986	4,526	932	55	6	—	4	515	80
Georgia[5]	7,041	34	—	32	4,558	1,290	360	15	14	—	—	4	734
Idaho	2,523	5	—	21	2,021	130	15	5	2	35	7	105	177
Iowa	5,217	36	19	61	4,736	280	58	1	8	2	8	8	—
Kansas	5,324	38	25	26	3,513	—	20	11	14	—	—	1,677	—
Maine	2,093	9	—	—	1,836	100	43	—	—	89	—	—	16
Michigan[5]	16,281	17	—	26	14,953	648	28	82	—	373	—	119	35
Mississippi	5,001	348	36	43	2,431	1,748	323	—	6	—	—	13	53
Missouri[5]	11,705	99	15	45	140	1,401	99	—	—	143	—	9,610	153
Montana	1,966	19	17	19	1,527	199	10	64	7	—	7	97	—
Nebraska	2,427	45	29	6	1,604	162	312	30	7	222	7	3	—
New Hampshire	1,067	47	8	5	415	171	11	13	2	17	7	371	—
North Dakota	554	3	3	6	370	78	8	2	3	21	3	57	—
Ohio	21,665	55	78	124	1,548	742	—	75	—	—	—	19,022	21
Oregon	6,130	7	—	46	5,319	562	9	2	13	4	—	14	154
South Dakota	954	2	3	7	771	93	19	6	3	46	2	—	2
Tennessee	7,866	143	49	77	4,573	918	82	—	—	—	—	1,989	35
Vermont	542	8	1	1	302	20	—	—	3	80	—	128	—
Virginia	7,262	324	127	102	—	6,632	—	24	3	—	11	39	—
Wyoming[5]	1,185	—	—	13	128	92	4	—	8	33	5	902	—

³ Specified grounds included in "Other," which formed 10 percent or more of the total number of divorces and annulments in a State, are shown separately below:

Alabama: Abandonment	3,669
Arkansas: Indignities	4,797
Kansas: Gross neglect	1,180
Missouri: Indignities	9,610
New Hampshire: Treatment injurious to health and/or reason	369
Ohio: Gross neglect and extreme cruelty	7,652
Gross neglect and neglect of duty	10,751
Tennessee: Abandonment	1,945
Vermont: Living apart 3 years	128
Wyoming: Intolerable indignities	860

Grounds that are similar to those reported separately have been grouped together with them (e.g., "infidelity" has been included with "adultery").

⁴ Excludes data for Connecticut. Divorces and annulments not tabulated separately.

⁵ Incomplete.

TABLE 3. DISTRIBUTION OF DIVORCES AND ANNULMENTS BY PARTY
TO WHOM GRANTED (STATISTICS FOR 12 STATES, 1958)

Area	Total	Decree granted to			
		Husband	Wife	Other[6]	Party not stated
Total	100.0	23.8	66.3	8.2	1.6
Alabama	100.0	19.9	52.3	27.1	0.7
Georgia	100.0	24.7	56.4	14.5	4.4
Idaho	100.0	26.6	71.1	0	2.3
Iowa	100.0	20.5	79.2	0.0	0.3
Montana	100.0	26.1	73.4	0.5	0
Nebraska	100.0	21.2	78.8	0	0
Oregon	100.0	23.7	75.0	0	1.3
S. Dakota	100.0	26.1	73.8	0.2	0
Tenn.[7]	100.0	23.2	76.5	0.0	0.3
Utah	100.0	14.7	60.4	0.1	24.9
Virginia	100.0	32.9	67.1	0	0
Wyoming	100.0	28.3	71.6	0	0.1

Source: 1 Vital Statistics of the United States 1958, p. 2-26, Table 2-Y.

Whether on a particular ground the cause of action will be annulment
or divorce varies widely from jurisdiction to jurisdiction. Only for
cruelty and desertion is the remedy exclusively divorce. Impotence, for
example, is a ground for divorce in Minnesota and in many other states.
In at least as many more, however, the proper remedy is annulment,
while a third group of jurisdictions permits either procedure. In regard
to the fragile distinction between annulment and divorce, see pages 173-
179 supra.

CROSBY v. CROSBY
186 Kan. 420, 350 P.2d 796 (1960)

PARKER, C.J. This case was commenced on September 15, 1958, by
Thomas M. Crosby against his wife, Marjorie Rosen Crosby, by the filing
of a petition in the district court of Shawnee County wherein he prayed
for a divorce on grounds of habitual drunkenness and gross neglect of
duty. The wife answered denying the charges and in a cross-petition asked
for a divorce against her husband on grounds of extreme cruelty and gross
neglect of duty. Thereafter both plaintiff and defendant furnished the
trial court with Bills of Particulars containing detailed charges of alleged
misconduct. . . .

After hearing evidence on the divorce issue the trial court on April 14,
1959, found that the defendant had been guilty of gross neglect of duty
and for that reason plaintiff should be granted a divorce and that the
relief sought in the defendant's cross-petition should be denied. Thereupon judgment was rendered accordingly, effective as of the date last
mentioned. Two days later defendant gave notice of her intention to
appeal from the divorce decree.

[6] Parent, guardian, cross-complainant, or both husband and wife.
[7] Data incomplete.

Subsequently, the remaining issues in the case [alimony and property division] came on for trial and after the introduction of evidence relating to those issues the court, on May 26, 1959, rendered a judgment with respect thereto which, for present purposes, may be said to have been favorable to the plaintiff and wholly unsatisfactory to the defendant.

Thereafter, and upon the overruling of proper motions for a new trial on the issues as tried, defendant perfected an appeal . . . .

. . . [T]he vital and all important question involved in this case is whether, in view of the uncontradicted evidence of record relating to the appellant's mental status on all dates in question, our decisions preclude the upholding of the judgment granting the appellee a divorce from appellant on the ground of gross neglect of duty. . . .

Appellee and appellant were married on June 1, 1928. He was twenty-two years of age and she was nineteen. She had no assets or property of her own but he had a one-fourth interest in some business properties in Topeka which he had inherited from his father. For the first two years following their marriage they lived in a rented house at Fifth and Topeka Blvd. Then they built a new house and for the next twenty-seven years lived in a spacious sixteen room home located at 1545 Stratford Road in Topeka. Indeed it may be stated that during their entire marriage they were financially independent and in their every day walk of life conducted themselves accordingly.

The parties concede that for the first twenty years of their marriage they had a very happy, if not ideal, marital relationship. Two lovely daughters were born of the marriage. Each was reared in the home and grew to womanhood in Topeka. Both are happily married and have children of their own. At the time of the trial one daughter was thirty years of age and the other was twenty-eight.

In 1948 appellant and appellee commenced to have marital difficulties. Obviously, some of their differences were attributed to a disturbed mental condition on the part of appellant. In any event it appears from the record, and is not denied by either party, that between 1948 and 1955 appellant was treated at Robinson's Neurological Hospital, Kansas City, Missouri, for a considerable period of time for mental illness, where she was given thirteen shock treatments and her illness classified as hyper manic-depressive psychosis; and that during portions of the same period she received treatments at the Menninger Foundation, Topeka, Kansas, for her mental condition.

Sometime in 1955 appellant filed an action for a divorce against appellee in the district court of Shawnee County. Following joinder of issues in that action and the furnishing by appellee to the court of a Bill of Particulars, *to which we shall presently refer,* the parties became reconciled. Thereafter, but not until execution of a postnuptial agreement containing certain reciprocal provisions, which we pause here to note must be classified as more advantageous to appellee than appellant, appellant dismissed the divorce action and they again resumed their marital relationship in the home on Stratford Road. Notwithstanding they continued to have marital differences but lived in the Stratford Road home until February, 1957, when it was sold. Shortly thereafter they moved into a rented house at 1528 Oakley and lived there until Saturday, September 13, 1958, when appellee left the home and two days later commenced the instant action.

Turning now to evidence pertinent to the disposition of the decisive question, . . . it is to be noted:

1. That in his 1955 Bill of Particulars, which it should be pointed out is attached to and must be considered as a part of his Bill of Particulars in the instant case, appellee makes the following statement:

". . . ; that the defendant has tried his level best to help plaintiff in every way for the reason that this defendant honestly believes the plaintiff to be a very sick and mentally ill person, incapable of taking care of herself for a sustained period of time, with a craving and almost insane desire to hurt this defendant, all of which this defendant believes is a result of plaintiff's sickness . . ."

2. That while testifying as a witness in his own behalf appellee stated in substance (a) that all allegations set forth in his present Bill of Particulars were true; (b) that based on his own observation and what the doctors told him he believed that appellant's mental sickness was a recurring disease; (c) that at the time of the 1955 reconciliation he was familiar with his wife's mental condition and knew she was mentally disturbed; (d) that after he went back to live with her he kept a daily record of her activities because he was aware of some mental disturbance (these it may be noted were all listed in his Bill of Particulars as supporting his petition for divorce); (e) that since 1951, up to the time of bringing the instant case, he had often discussed appellant's mental illness problem with her and wished that she would take treatment for it; (f) that at those times he looked upon her as needing psychiatric help and treatment; (g) that he had discussed appellant's mental sickness during the period from January 1956 to the present time with Dr. Karl Menninger and Dr. Cooper, psychiatrists.

3. That Dr. Herbert C. Modlin, a physician, specializing in the practice of psychiatry, whose qualifications are not challenged and who was the only expert medical witness produced by either party during the trial, was called as a witness for the appellant. That while on the witness stand he was asked if he had examined a document containing appellee's 1958 Bill of Particulars, which set out in detail facts related in 1956, 1957 and a portion of 1958; and a document, also attached thereto, likewise called a Bill of Particulars, which set forth detailed facts pertaining to Marjorie Crosby and things and occurrences during the existence of the marriage between Marjorie and Tom Crosby up to and including the year 1955. Upon answering such inquiry in the affirmative, and having stated that he had read such documents, Dr. Modlin then testified as follows:

"Q. Now, Doctor, assuming all of the facts set forth in all of those documents which you stated you have read and examined to be true, do you have an opinion as to whether or not Marjorie Crosby during the time embraced by the documents was suffering from any mental illness or disturbance?

"A. Yes, I do.

"Q. Will you state that opinion?

"A. The evidence included in these documents is suggestive of well-recognized mental illness.

"Q. Will you describe what type or form you would classify it?

"A. The 1955 bill of particulars gives a very good description of what is ordinarily thought of as Maniac Depressive reactions, Hyper Maniac type [sic].

"Q. Could you elaborate a little on what that means?

"A. Yes, maniac depressive reaction is a phrase used to describe people who have rather wide variations in moods, from depression to elation. These variations in moods being partial at times but at other times not at all under their conscious control. The kind of behavior described there suggests recurrence periods of mild elation which we usually call Hyper Maniac which means something less than severe mania, the over activity, the suggestive findings of poor judgment at times, the evidence of excessive drinking, again periodically. The suggestions of deterioration in social manners and habits are all characteristic of this particular kind of illness. The other documents from '55 to the present time are not as clear in describing this particular illness but it gives evidence of a recurrence problem of drinking. As far as abnormal behavior it is based on some sort of psychological depression."

4. That as a witness in her own behalf appellant, without subsequent refutation of any kind on the part of appellee, testified she had been receiving medical treatment at the Menninger Foundation within the last few weeks preceding the trial.

In the face of the foregoing evidence, which for all purposes of this appeal must be regarded as incontrovertible, we are convinced this case comes squarely within the scope of our ruling and decision in Lindbloom v. Lindbloom, 177 Kan. 286, 279 P.2d 243, where, in connection with a factual situation somewhat different but nevertheless so similar the case must be regarded as a precedent controlling our decision of the decisive question here involved, we held:

"It is the duty of a husband to provide and care for his wife in her illness as well as in her health.

"The fact that the wife, in the intervals between temporary hospitalization, and with three small children, ages 3, 2 and 1, and without help the husband was able to provide, did not keep her house or the children as clean as they should have been, did not constitute 'gross neglect of duty' justifying the granting of a divorce to the husband upon that ground." (Syl. ¶¶ 1, 2.)

And in the opinion said:

"In this court counsel for appellant present three questions for our determination. They read:

"'1. Was it error to grant the appellee a decree of divorce from his wife on the ground of gross neglect of duty when the evidence disclosed that appellant had been hospitalized for mental illness in the fall of 1951; in the winter of 1952-1953, and in July of 1953, and when the acts complained of took place between her hospitalizations?' . . .

"With respect to the first question presented we think the answer should be in the affirmative. When parties are married they take each other for better or worse. If the wife should become ill of tuberculosis, cancer, or any other disease, and be unable to perform her household duties as well as she ordinarily would perform them, we would not be willing to say that the husband was entitled to a divorce because of that situation. . . .

"While in this case plaintiff was never adjudged insane, we think the rule stated in the authority last quoted is applicable. What she had was an illness which affected the 'emotions and the moods' for which she was treated as necessity therefor arose." (pp. 296, 297.)

And so here, based on what is said and held in the Lindbloom case, we have little difficulty in concluding that the uncontradicted evidence in this case relating to appellant's mental status on all dates in question was sufficient to preclude appellee from obtaining a divorce from appellant on the ground of gross neglect of duty. It follows the trial court's action in granting him a divorce on that basis is erroneous and cannot be upheld. This, we may add, is so even though the record discloses some testimony which, absent evidence of the mental illness, might otherwise be sufficient to uphold a judgment of that character. Here, according to the record, following a concededly normal, if not ideal, marital relationship of more than twenty years duration, what appellant had was a mental illness affecting her emotions and moods, so serious she received treatment in well-known mental institutions, which was the real cause of the acts of misconduct relied on by appellee as constituting gross neglect of duty during the later years of the marriage. In that situation we do not believe appellee was entitled to a divorce on that basis and refuse to so hold.

Appellant contends the trial court erred in denying her claim she was entitled to a divorce by reason of appellee's extreme cruelty and gross neglect of duty. We are not disposed to labor arguments advanced on this claim of error. It suffices to say the testimony on the subject is conflicting and that the record discloses substantial competent evidence to sustain the trial court's finding and conclusion the divorce prayed for by appellant in her cross-petition should be denied. This, under our decisions, requires an affirmance of that ruling and judgment. See, e.g., Paul v. Paul, 183 Kan. 201, 326 P.2d 283.

In conclusion it should be stated that appellant also appeals from the judgment entered on May 26, 1959, making provision for permanent alimony, division of property and final allowance of attorneys' fees. These rulings, as we read the record, were all made by the trial court subject to the outcome of the evidence upon the grounds for divorce. In other words, when made, they were based upon the premise the appellee (husband) was entitled to a divorce for the fault of the appellant (wife). Under this court's decision, as heretofore announced, the parties now find themselves in a situation where neither is entitled to a divorce and the trial court is placed in a position where its orders, with respect to the matters now under consideration, should be reconsidered and determined on that basis. Under these circumstances we believe all such orders should be set aside and that, after complying with this court's decision directing a reversal of the divorce decree, the trial court should make such further and additional orders in connection with such matters, including the allowance of reasonable attorneys' fees, as it may deem necessary and proper, under the then existing conditions and circumstances.[8]

The judgment effective April 14, 1959, granting appellee a divorce from appellant is reversed with directions to set it aside; the judgment, effective as of the same date, denying appellant a divorce on grounds set forth in her cross-petition is affirmed; and the orders made by the court in its judgment, effective May 26, 1959, are set aside with directions to proceed as heretofore indicated. . . .

NOTE

1. Compare, e.g., Rice v. Rice, 332 Mass. 489, 125 N.E.2d 787 (1955) (insanity a defense to cruelty, citing cases for proposition that this is consensus of American authority); Fansler v. Fansler, 344 Mich. 569, 75 N.W.2d 1 (1956) (apparently applying M'Naghten test). But cf. Nunes v. Nunes, 62 Cal. 2d 17, 396 P.2d 37 (1964), 38 So. Cal. L. Rev. 713 (1965) (insanity no defense). In Manley v. Manley, 193 Pa. Super. 252, 264-265, 164 A.2d 113, 120 (1960), the court made the following distinction:

> [I]nsanity is a defense to an action for divorce brought against a wife on the ground of adultery if it affirmatively appears . . . that at the time the defendant committed adultery she did not know the nature and consequences of her acts, or have the ability to distinguish between right and wrong. . . .
>
> Care must be taken not to confuse the mental or physical ill-health which we have held to be a defense to indignities, with the insanity which . . we here hold to be a defense to adultery. A wife's neglect of her home and her husband have been listed among indignities recognized in Pennsylvania, but if she fails to cook her husband's

---

[8] On remand, the trial court dismissed the divorce but ordered a property division in accordance with a separation agreement entered into by the parties, and awarded $2000 attorney's fees. The appellate court again reversed, holding that the agreement was not enforcible against the wife because of her mental illness at the time of its execution, and that the award of attorney's fees, though normally within the discretion of the trial court, was clearly insufficient. Crosby v. Crosby, 188 Kan. 274, 362 P.2d 3 (1961). — Ed.

meals, and wash his clothes and clean his house, and if she neglects him generally because she is physically or mentally unable to do otherwise, of course, the neglect does not constitute an indignity. . . . [S]he is excused . . . *on the theory that such conduct lacks the spirit of hate, estrangement and malevolence which is the heart of the charge of indignities.* [Citations omitted.]

Upon what principles does this distinction rest — relief for the plaintiff, protection for the ill defendant, or some other value? For an illuminating discussion of the difficulties in applying criminal insanity rules in the field of divorce, see Goodhart, Cruelty, Desertion and Insanity in Matrimonial Law, 79 L.Q. Rev. 98 (1963).

Confusion in English law on the insanity defense in divorce was resolved in 1963 by a 3 to 2 decision of the House of Lords holding that insanity is not a defense to a divorce action based on cruelty. Williams v. Williams, [1964] A.C. 698 (1963), [1963] 2 All E.R. 994. The dissenting lords stressed the element of blameworthiness in the concept of cruelty: "[I]t is right to view a charge of cruelty as a 'grave accusation.' Opprobrium is involved . . . It is described as a matrimonial 'offence.' " ([1964] A.C. at 733, 737, [1963] 2 All E.R. at 1010, 1013, Lord Morris.) "I do not attempt to define cruelty, but would assert that it involves mercilessness and delight in or indifference to pain and suffering"; "to say of a man that he is merciless is to stigmatise him and cannot be justified if he is out of his mind." ([1964] A.C. at 743, 747, 748, [1963] 2 All E.R. 1017, 1019, 1020, Lord Hodson.) The majority opinions were more circumspect in stating the grounds upon which they rested, but Lord Pearce referred to the demands imposed by "the practical nature of the court's function" ([1964] A.C. at 762, [1963] 2 All E.R. at 1029), and Lord Reid, after noting that "Some [judges] think there cannot be cruelty without some kind of mens rea and some think there can" ([1964] A.C. at 721, [1963] 2 All E.R. at 1003) continued: "Surely it is much more satisfactory to accept the fact that the test of culpability has broken down and not to treat entirely differently two people one of whom is just short of and the other just over the invisible line which separates abnormality from insanity." [1964] A.C. at 723, [1963] 2 All E.R. at 1004. See also the companion 3 to 2 decision of the House of Lords in Gollins v. Gollins, [1964] A.C. 644 (1963), [1963] 2 All E.R. 966 (intention not essential element in divorce based on cruelty).

2. The pervading influence of the concept of fault in American divorce law goes back to the same historical roots to which reference has already been made. See pages 172-174 supra. For many centuries prior to 1857, exclusive jurisdiction in matrimonial matters in England was in the ecclesiastical courts, and before that date the only judicial decree which was available was separation a mensa et thoro, without right of remarriage. 1 Holdsworth, A History of English Law 622-624 (6th ed. 1938). Although for a brief period after the Reformation these courts took the position that they could grant an absolute divorce, in 1602 this opinion was overruled, and for the next two and one-half centuries the only

method of divorce granting the right of remarriage was by a prolonged and very expensive procedure culminating in a private act of Parliament. See generally id. at 621-625. During this period, although the ecclesiastical courts were no longer subject to Rome, they applied the principles of canon law in which they had been steeped for many centuries. Because of the continuing force of these principles in the evolution of modern civil law, a brief review of the major canon law provisions is necessary.

While under canon law the Church has power to dissolve certain unconsummated or nonsacramental marriages, these rules apply only in exceptional circumstances, and the underlying doctrine is that a "valid and consummated marriage of baptized persons can be dissolved by no human power and for no cause other than death" (Canon 1118). Marriage involves, moreover, the duty that "Spouses must live together unless a justifying reason excuses them from doing so" (Canon 1128). For a discussion of the strict construction given to this and other relevant canons, see Genuario, Rotal Criteria for Granting Separations, 22 Jurist 333 (1962). The Sacred Roman Rota, highest judicial authority in the Church, has been quoted as stating (id. at 344):

> "It has been the constant jurisprudence of this Sacred Tribunal . . . that great caution should be used in granting separations from bed and board, because separation is directly opposed to the very purpose and ends of marriage; it gives rise to scandal; it destroys the family; it exposes the consorts to the danger of incontinence; and it inflicts a severe loss on children, if there are any. . . . There is no one who does not know that if *divortium semiplenum* is easily granted, the way is made easy for *divortium plenum*. For matrimony exists also as a remedy for concupiscence and, if common life is dissolved by separation, immediately it opens the door to adulterous amours and illicit associations."

Permanent separation can be granted only for adultery, with the proviso that the spouse granted the right to live separately has not "given consent to the offense, caused it, or expressly or tacitly condoned it, or has himself also been guilty of the same offense" (Canon 1129). A temporary separation, good only until "the reason for the separation ceases to exist," is available if "one of the spouses joins a non-Catholic sect, or procures the non-Catholic rearing of the children, or leads a criminal or disgraceful life, or creates for the other a serious threat to the latter's soul or body, or makes the common life unduly burdensome by cruelty" (Canon 1131).

Under canon law, therefore, separation is relief for the innocent spouse from the duty of cohabitation because of the guilt of the other spouse. For the offending spouse it is a punitive measure, and for neither is there any possibility of remarriage. This is the seedbed from which our civil law has sprung. With respect to the abolition in 1857 of the ecclesiastical courts and the establishment of absolute divorce a vinculo matrimonii for adultery, Holdsworth quotes with approval the observation.

"Not the least part of the merit and success of the Act of 1857 is due to the skill which, while effecting a great social change, did so with the smallest possible amount of innovation." 1 Holdsworth, History of English Law 624 (6th ed. 1938). This minimum of innovation was accomplished by incorporating into the law of absolute divorce the jurisprudence which had grown up around separation.

In America both the assertion of civil jurisdiction and the utilization of canonical principles for separation as grounds for absolute divorce came much earlier than in England. Haskins has noted that in Massachusetts "the absence of a separate ecclesiastical court in the colony almost necessarily entailed its taking jurisdiction over divorce." He continues:

> [T]he colonists appear to have abandoned the conception of the divorce a mensa et thoro and to have granted divorces a vinculo in the same types of situations in which the bishops' courts issued a mensa decrees. A decree of separation was incompatible with colonial ideas, constantly expressed in the legislation and court records, that the unattached individual was a potential danger to the community. If a marriage was effectively to be dissolved for practical purposes, it was thought wiser both for the parties and for the community that they be free to settle themselves in new marriages than to pose continual threats to the stability of other households. . . .[9]

But even with this earlier and more radical development, the thread of a common history is apparent to anyone comparing current American legislation with canon law and the jurisprudence of the English ecclesiastical courts.

Should the grounds and defenses developed for governing the right of separation under an "indissoluble marriage" legal system be transferred to a system which permits absolute divorce? If they are, is it appropriate that the transfer be accomplished "with the smallest possible amount of innovation"?

3. How, within the traditional fault structure of divorce, can the relatively recent nonfault grounds be accommodated? A majority of the states explicitly provide for divorce (or occasionally annulment) on the grounds of postnuptial insanity. The Kansas statute is fairly typical; it requires

> confinement in an institution for five years because of insanity and a unanimous finding by three physicians, appointed by the judge before whom the action is pending, that the insanity is incurable, but a decree granted on this ground shall not relieve the plaintiff from contributing to the support and maintenance of the defendant.[10]

---

[9] Haskins, Law and Authority in Early Massachusetts 195 (1960).

[10] Kan. Stat. Ann. §60-1601 (1964). In 1965 the word "insanity" was changed to "mental illness." Kan. Sess. Laws c. 354, §14(7). See also the Minnesota statute, page 633 supra.

In Katz v. Katz, 191 Kan. 500, 382 P.2d 331 (1963), plaintiff surmounted the difficult obstacle of obtaining the requisite expert testimony that the defendant's disease was "incurable." He was then faced by the fact that although defendant had been "in mental institutions and under psychiatric care in excess of five years," she had not been in continuous residence in any one hospital for that period. The court granted the divorce, noting that: "Under modern methods of treatment of mental illness, it would be a most severe case where the patient was confined during all of the first five years." 191 Kan. at 502, 382 P.2d at 334. For references to varying holdings on these facts in other jurisdictions, see Comment, 12 U. Kan. L. Rev. 454 (1964).

How does the Kansas provision for divorce on grounds of incurable insanity square with the Crosby holding that insanity is a defense to a divorce based on fault? Are the underlying principles distinguishable, or does Kansas law exhibit a fairly common effort to effect an uneasy compromise of irreconcilable values? Similar and equally difficult questions are presented by other nonfault grounds for divorce. Should traditional defenses, premised on the fault principle, be applied to new legislative experiments with nonfault divorce?

CLARK v. CLARK
54 N.M. 364, 225 P.2d 147 (1950)

SADLER, J. The question for decision is whether recrimination affords a valid defense in a suit for divorce sought on the ground of incompatibility since the decision of this court in Pavletich v. Pavletich, 50 N.M. 224, 174 P.2d 826.

The issue is squarely put in the case before us. The parties were married in September, 1926, and lived together as husband and wife for many years. However, for a short time before July 23, 1949, when the husband filed his complaint seeking a divorce, he and his wife had been living separate and apart. The divorce was sought upon the ground of incompatibility. There are no children of the marriage and on this appeal the wife, who defended unsuccessfully the husband's suit for divorce, makes no complaint against the division of property ordered, nor objects to the award of attorney's fees and alimony as being too small. In addition to a general denial the wife pleaded recrimination as an affirmative defense to the husband's complaint. . . .

At the trial the wife, as defendant, tendered and offered to prove that the plaintiff had committed repeated acts of adultery with a named co-respondent, registering with her as man and wife at hotels and tourist cabins in various towns and cities in New Mexico, and that any incompatibility existing between the parties to the suit had resulted "solely and entirely and directly from the insistence of the plaintiff upon his pretended right to engage in extra-marital adulteries" with the corespondent named. The plaintiff objected to the tender upon the ground that it was incompetent and immaterial . . . .

Thus it is that we are asked to review our decision in the case of Pav-letich v. Pavletich, supra, holding that since the legislature added incompatibility as a ground of divorce in 1933, L.1933, c. 54, §1, a court of equity is no longer required to treat recrimination as a valid defense to a divorce suit if the parties are so irreconcilable as to be incompatible. The writer dissented in the Pavletich case and still entertains the view, shared by Mr. Justice McGhee as well, that this first opportunity for doing so should be taken advantage of to overrule that decision outright, a view not shared by another justice concurring in this opinion.

. . . If, as the trial judge seemed to think, incompatibility once established entitles a plaintiff to a decree of divorce, whatever may have occasioned the incompatibility, then the judgment is correct and should be affirmed; otherwise not.

It is obvious from a reading of the Pavletich case that it does not go so far as to hold that a finding of incompatibility imposes upon the trial court, sitting as a chancellor, the mandatory duty of granting a divorce where the defense of recrimination has been pleaded and fully established. The decision in that case does not hold, as the trial judge seems to have felt and as counsel for appellee (plaintiff) insisted below and maintains here, that the chancellor *must* ignore the defense of recrimination, even though irreconcilable differences exist between the parties. Note this language from the closing words of the opinion in the case of Pavletich v. Pavletich, supra . . . : "If the chancellor believes the parties are reconcilable, he will, no doubt, endeavor to bring about a reconciliation. But where the parties are irreconcilable we believe that the public policy of this state as expressed by the legislature, is against denying a divorce on the doctrine of recrimination. Chavez v. Chavez, 39 N.M. 480, 50 P.2d 264, 101 A.L.R. 635, in so far as it holds it to be the imperative duty of the chancellor to deny a divorce upon a showing of recrimination, should no longer be followed."

True enough, the court expressed as its opinion a belief that ". . . where the parties are irreconcilable we believe that the public policy of this state . . . is against denying a divorce on the doctrine of recrimination." But such language is followed immediately by that overruling Chavez v. Chavez, 39 N.M. 480, 50 P.2d 264, 101 A.L.R. 635, *only "in so far as it holds it to be the imperative duty* of the chancellor to deny a divorce upon a showing of recrimination." (Emphasis ours.)

It would be absurd to say that "incompatibility" itself could be pleaded by way of recrimination as a defense to a divorce sought upon the ground of incompatibility. But as to other defenses traditionally employed by way of recrimination, if pleaded, established and found to have resulted from acts of the plaintiff, there resides in the trial judge the discretion to say whether, notwithstanding such incompatibility, it shocks the conscience to hold such plaintiff entitled to a divorce by reason thereof. [Citations omitted.] When exercised, discretion so residing in the trial judge as in the case of an exercise of discretion by him in other matters, is subject to review in this court for abuse.

We think we have accurately appraised the holding in the Pavletich case. So viewed, it is apparent that the trial court erred in declining to receive evidence tending to show that such incompatibility as exists arose from adulteries committed by the husband both before and subsequent to his separation from the wife. When this proof is received, if satisfying the trial judge of its truth, he will then exercise his discretion to determine whether, notwithstanding the incompatibility shown, a divorce should be denied. He may feel that he should so hold. At the former trial he considered he had no choice but to grant the divorce. In this view of the matter, he erred.

The judgment will be reversed and the cause remanded with a direction to the trial court to set aside its judgment and award a new trial. The appellant will recover her costs of the appeal.

It is so ordered.

LUJAN and COMPTON, Justices (dissenting).

In our opinion the case of Pavletich, 50 N.M. 224, 174 P.2d 826, properly appraised and understood, completely removes recrimination from consideration in divorce suits except for such weight as proof of it may have on the issue of incompatibility as a ground for divorce.

To elucidate our views, adultery on the part of the plaintiff is set up as a defense by the wife against his suit for divorce on the ground of incompatibility. We do not say proof of such adultery may not be shown in evidence. We think it can be but only and solely for the purpose of determining whether the incompatibility alleged as a ground of divorce in fact exists. If the trial judge makes a finding that incompatibility does exist that ends the matter and a decree of divorce should be entered. If this result may seem harsh in individual cases the problem is one for the legislature. We feel convinced that such is the effect of this court's holding in the Pavletich case. . . .

NOTE

1. The Court of Appeals for the Third Circuit, interpreting the ground of incompatibility in the Virgin Islands divorce statute, refused to permit the defendant to claim the plaintiff's cruelty as a recriminatory defense. Burch v. Burch, 195 F.2d 799 (3d Cir. 1952). The court relied in some measure on Pavletich, commenting as follows on the defense: "It may be conceded that a majority of the decisions in the various states have held that the defense of recrimination will bar a plaintiff from obtaining a divorce if knowingly and without connivance or justification he has committed an offense which itself would amount to a ground for divorce. . . . But the doctrine of recrimination in divorce has been much criticized in recent years. . . . From a social point of view it is hard to defend the rule that recrimination is an absolute bar to the granting of a divorce for it requires that parties who are guilty of conduct which makes their marriage impossible of success shall continue their impossible marital relationship as a sort of punishment for their mutual guilt. For this reason the application of the doctrine has been relaxed as an absolute bar to divorce in a number of jurisdictions. . . ." Id. at 809.

2. The applicability of the defense of recrimination also poses problems with respect to another nonfault divorce ground found in a number of states, e.g., Va. Code Ann. §20-91(9) (Supp. 1964), providing that divorce may be granted

> [o]n the application of either party if and when the husband and wife have lived separate and apart without any cohabitation and without interruption for two years. A plea of res judicata or of recrimination with respect to any other [ground of divorce] shall not be a bar to either party obtaining a divorce on this ground.

The policy underlying this ground for divorce has been described as a preference that "spouses who have been living separate and apart for the statutory period and have found reconciliation to be hopeless . . . have an opportunity to remarry and reestablish the family relationship." Otis v. Bahan, 209 La. 1082, 1087, 26 So.2d 146, 148 (1946). It is usually held that the defense of recrimination is inconsistent with this policy. See, e.g., Matysek v. Matysek, 212 Md. 44, 128 A.2d 627, 17 Md. L. Rev. 268 (1957); Annot., 21 A.L.R.2d 1267 (1952). In Smith v. Smith, 54 R.I. 236, 239, 172 Atl. 323, 324 (1934), the court said:

> It is evident that the conjugal life and the family life of the parties are permanently disrupted. There is no inclination for and no prospect of a reconciliation. Nothing is left of the marriage relation but the legal tie. Respondent contends that, regardless of these facts, petitioner should be punished for his misconduct by a refusal of the trial justice to dissolve the marriage. If it appeared that there was any advantage to the family or to the State in continuing the marital status, the divorce might well be denied. But no such advantage is apparent. On the contrary it is plain that to compel the parties to continue in their present status would be prejudicial to the parties and to their children. . . .

In North Carolina, however, an exception has developed by which a wife who has been wilfully abandoned by her husband can successfully defend against his action for divorce under the two-year living apart ground provided for in N.C. Gen. Stat. §50-6 (1950). See, e.g., Pickens v. Pickens, 258 N.C. 84, 127 S.E.2d 889 (1962).

CHAFEE, SOME PROBLEMS OF EQUITY
73-75, 81-84 (1950)

It was an evil day when the first American judge to speak of clean hands[11] had the bright idea of injecting the maxim into the very place where it would work its greatest mischief. In dealing with a marriage, judges have an especially strong duty to look at the total situation, and not let the result turn on the ethical behavior of a single individual. Marriage does not involve just one person. Indeed, most of its difficulties as well as its delights come from the basic fact that it takes two to make a

[11] Mattox v. Mattox, 2 Ohio 233 (1826).

marriage. And besides the other spouse, whose appearance as defendant rather than plaintiff may be somewhat fortuitous, many more persons are interested in the formation, continuance, and termination of the relationship. . . . Over and above this host of citizens, the community has all sorts of vital interests, which are not altogether consistent. For instance, as against the policy preferring a permanent family to barnyard matings, there are practical advantages in replacing one hopelessly unhappy childless marriage by two happy and fruitful marriages, as sometimes happens, rather than condemning each spouse to celibacy or sin. And if the discordant couple have children, statistics cannot demonstrate whether they will suffer more from a broken home or from a nominal home full of hatred and contempt. When society cannot make up its mind how to reconcile all these competing interests and policies, we ought not to blame judges for being bewildered. I am certainly not qualified to say which considerations ought to prevail in any case, but what I do say is that a judge has enough to do if he forces himself to be aware of all these interests and policies and do his best to evaluate them with reference to the whole family. He cannot afford to waste his efforts on deciding how to punish one person who happens to be the plaintiff. He is asked to reorganize the family, and not to try an offender. If an equity judge is engaged in reorganizing a corporation which is proved to be in dire straits, he does not devote his main attention to the moral conduct of the particular creditors who have put the enterprise under his charge. Instead, he endeavors to keep it going on new terms, or else distribute the assets so that they can be used in different enterprises with hopes for better fortune. The judge's task is much the same when the failure of a family is before him. The clean hands maxim is an impertinent intrusion on a very difficult and important judicial job. . . .

If courts would forget the clean hands doctrine and consider only the policies involved, they might start asking how much actual good is accomplished by the substantive defense of recrimination. Let us see how it worked in an English case.[12]

Mr. Pullen was married in 1912, enlisted in 1915, and was sent with his battalion to Egypt. In July, 1917, he received a letter from his wife, stating that she had committed adultery and had gone away with her paramour. The next January she bore this man's child. When Pullen returned from Egypt he could not find his wife. She had left their only child in the care of Pullen's mother. In 1919 when he was demobilized, he met Miss Greatorex. In August, he sued for a divorce. Immediately afterwards, he committed adultery himself with this young woman, his first infidelity to his vanished wife. The court found that Miss Greatorex was apparently a respectable young woman "apart from her conduct with the petitioner." She and Pullen went on living together as man and wife. She became pregnant. They were eager to get married.

Justice McCardie had statutory discretion to set Pullen free from the dead marriage. Yet he held that "the requirements of public morality,"

[12] Pullen v. Pullen & Holding, 123 L.T.R. 203, 36 T.L.R. 506 (1920). See Judicial Wisdom of Mr. Justice McCardie, edited by Crew, 140 (1932).

as embodied in the precedents, compelled him to deny relief. "I must administer the law as it stands"; reform of the law must come from Parliament.[13] Parliament did nothing at all about divorce until 1937, which was too late to help Pullen and Miss Greatorex, and even then on this point it did not do much.[14]

To do justice to the Justice, he made a handsome apology to the unlucky couple for leaving them in the lurch.

> "The result of refusing a decree in this suit may seem strange indeed. For if the wife alone had committed adultery, then the husband could at once have dissolved the marriage. Adultery is presumed to render further married life impossible. But inasmuch as the husband himself has here committed adultery also, and married life is therefore doubly impossible, the decree must, in accordance with the existing law, be refused. The marriage bond must continue. I regret this result, but I must administer the law as it stands." [15]

Still, this apology was a poor substitute for a marriage license. As Lord Macnaghten said, "Thirsty folk want beer, not explanations." [16] . . . What good did this decision do anybody on earth except the barrister[17] who reprinted it as an example of "The Judicial Wisdom of Mr. Justice McCardie"?

Divorce exists, not only to enable the spouses to rebuild their lives, but also to avoid the social consequences of adultery and discordant personal relations. A decision like this loses the opportunity to substitute a happy and fruitful new marriage in place of a dead marriage and a liaison. Society gained nothing whatever from the continuation of Pullen's first marriage.

Naturally, a divorce should sometimes be refused when both parties are at fault. The law does not wish to make couples think that they can get out of a marriage by the simple process of each violating his vows. Marriage is not a contract which can be terminated by mutual discord and dissatisfaction. . . . [J]udges ought to have some discretion about denying a divorce when the petitioner is unfaithful, but discretion means the ability to use a practical judgment in shaping the decision so as to fit the facts and the needs of the particular situation.

NOTE

1. How seriously does Chafee's last paragraph undercut the position he had previously taken on recrimination? Compare the views of the California Supreme Court in De Burgh v. De Burgh, 39 Cal. 2d 858, 250 P.2d 598 (1952), in construing Cal. Civ. Code §§111, 122, reproduced at

---

[13] Pullen v. Pullen & Holding, 123 L.T.R. 203 at 206 (1920). The English cases on discretion are reviewed by Lord Merrivale in Apted v. Apted and Bliss, [1930] Pro. D. 246.

[14] 1 Edw. VIII & 1 Geo. VI, c. 57, §4 (Matrimonial Causes Act, 1937).

[15] Pullen v. Pullen & Holding, 123 L.T.R. 203 at 206 (1920).

[16] Montgomery v. Thompson, [1891] A.C. (H.L.) 217 at 225.

[17] See Judicial Wisdom of Mr. Justice McCardie, edited by Crew, 140 (1932).

pages 634-635 supra. The majority reasoned that the last clause of §122 created not an absolute defense but instead placed upon the trial judge a discretion similar to the English discretion noted by Chafee. A vigorous dissent to this application of the statute argued that the court was in effect repealing the statute and that the phrase "in bar of the plaintiff's cause of divorce" modified "showing" and not the words "any cause of divorce." The dissent also stressed the use of the word "must" in §111 and the fact that only three of thirty-two states providing by statute for the defense of recrimination specify such discretion.

The most interesting feature of De Burgh is the court's analysis of how the discretion should be exercised in cases where the evidence establishes that each party has committed a statutory offense entitling the other to divorce:

> There can be no precise formula for determining when a cause of divorce shown against a plaintiff is to be considered a bar to his suit for divorce, for the divorce court, as a court of equity (Sharon v. Sharon, 67 Cal. 185 [7 P. 456, 635, 8 P. 709]), is clothed with a broad discretion to advance the requirements of justice in each particular case. In general, however, certain major considerations will govern the court's decision:
>
> *1. The prospect of reconciliation.* The court should determine whether the legitimate objects of matrimony have been destroyed or whether there is a reasonable likelihood that the marriage can be saved. It should consider the ages and temperaments of the parties, the length of their marriage, the seriousness and frequency of their marital misconduct proved at the trial and the likelihood of its recurrence, the duration and apparent finality of the separation, and the sincerity of their efforts to overcome differences and live together harmoniously.
>
> *2. The effect of the marital conflict upon the parties.* If a continuation of the marriage would constitute a serious hazard to the health of either party, as in the case of physical brutality, the court should be reluctant to deny divorce. Although financial considerations can play only a minor role in determining the propriety of divorce, even these may not be entirely ignored if the evidence indicates that marital conflicts are destroying the livelihood of the parties.
>
> *3. The effect of the marital conflict upon third parties.* In every divorce case in which children are involved, their interests are of the utmost concern to the court. The disruptive effect of divorce upon children is to be deplored, but in a given case it may be preferable to violence, hatred, or immorality when these are present in the home. The community as a whole also has an interest. Adultery, desertion, or cruelty, for example, can only discredit marriage; their perpetuation is not lightly to be decreed.
>
> *4. Comparative guilt.* In many ways the guilt of the parties may be unequal — in the gravity of the misconduct involved, in the frequency of its occurrence, or in its effect upon children and others.

Moreover, one spouse may demonstrate substantially greater repentance and reform. Marital offenders, therefore, are not necessarily in pari delicto before the chancellor. Their comparative guilt may have an important bearing upon whether or not either one or both should be granted relief. . . .

Upon remand of the case for application of the clean hands doctrine as herein indicated, the trial court may decide that one of the parties should be granted a divorce. In that event, alimony and more than half of the community property may be awarded to the prevailing spouse as in any other case. It is also possible, however, that a divorce will be granted to both parties [citations omitted], and it seems advisable to indicate here the rules that should govern the granting of alimony and the apportionment of community property under such circumstances. When a divorce is granted to both, alimony may be awarded to either, for the basis of liability for alimony is the granting of a divorce against the person required to pay it. (See Civ. Code, §139.) Section 146 of the Civil Code provides that if the divorce is granted for extreme cruelty, the court may apportion community property as it deems just, but that statute has been interpreted to permit an award of more than half of the community property only to an innocent spouse. (Eslinger v. Eslinger, 47 Cal. 62, 64.) When a divorce is granted to both parties, neither is innocent within the meaning of this rule, and the community property must be equally divided.[18]

In light of these considerations, under what circumstances would recrimination properly be applied to bar a divorce to either party?

2. Many states continue to reaffirm the defense of recrimination in one form or another despite strong criticism of the doctrine. E.g., Rothwell v. Rothwell, 219 Ore. 221, 347 P.2d 63 (1959). In some jurisdictions the defense has been abolished by judicial opinion, e.g., Hendricks v. Hendricks, 123 Utah 178, 257 P.2d 366 (1953), or by legislation, Nev. Rev. Stat. §125.120 (1957), Wis. Stat. Ann. §247.101 (Supp. 1965); both these statutory provisions expressly incorporate the doctrine of comparative rectitude.

3. Is the doctrine of recrimination limited to acts of the plaintiff which would justify a divorce to the defendant? This appears to be the general rule, e.g., Reddington v. Reddington, 317 Mass. 760, 59 N.E.2d 775 (1945). The Michigan Supreme Court has set forth three prerequisites for recognition of a recriminatory defense: (1) the plaintiff's alleged offense must have constituted legal cause for divorce; (2) that offense must have been the actual cause of marital discord; and (3) the act must not have been excusable as provoked by the defendant. Sovereign v. Sovereign, 347 Mich. 205, 209, 79 N.W.2d 460, 462 (1956). Many courts would be less strict than this, particularly with respect to the second requirement. As to the third element, some courts would allow the defense of recrimination for an act provoked by the defendant where the plaintiff retaliated with

[18] 39 Cal. 2d at 872-874, 250 P.2d at 606-607.

excessive force. Cf. Schmidt v. Schmidt, 51 Wash. 2d 753, 321 P.2d 895 (1958).

4. With the California statute, page 634 supra, compare the case of Peck v. Peck, 16 Ill. 2d 268, 157 N.E.2d 249 (1959), in which the Illinois court espoused the view that only the plaintiff's adultery would bar his action based upon the defendant's adultery, and that other recriminatory acts such as physical and mental cruelty were defensively irrelevant. Of the states whose statutes contain some express provision for the defense of recrimination, a substantial number limit to adultery those offensive acts of the plaintiff which will preclude granting a divorce for the defendant's extramarital relations.

5. Should the fact that the "defense" of recrimination is considered a bar to divorce affect the decision of a lawyer whether or not to take a case in which he knows that his client has engaged in recriminatory conduct? If he takes the case, does he have a duty to disclose his client's conduct? See Rosengren v. Rosengren, 17 Ill. App. 2d 415, 149 N.E.2d 798 (1958) (divorce denied if it appears that both parties have committed adultery, even though the plaintiff's adultery has not been pleaded as a defense); pages 702-710, 754 infra.

6. Extensive scholarly consideration has been given to problems of recrimination and comparative rectitude. Samples of this commentary may be found in Fair, A Comparison of Recrimination and the Doctrine of Comparative Rectitude and Their Incidents, 3 Baylor L. Rev. 55 (1950); Malkan, Petitioners' Fault in Matrimonial Actions, 106 U. Pa. L. Rev. 52 (1957); Raskin & Katz, The Dying Doctrine of Recrimination in the United States of America, 35 Can. B. Rev. 1046 (1957). See also Annot., 63 A.L.R.2d 816 (1959).

HECHTER v. HECHTER
12 D.L.R.2d 326 (Manitoba C.A. 1957)

SCHULTZ, J. This is an appeal from a judgment of Maybank J. in which he found adultery had been proved between the respondent and the co-respondent and that the petitioner had not "connived at, or had corruptly acquiesced in, the adultery." . . .

Considering first the question of the alleged adultery, certain facts are clearly proved. The petitioner, Gerald Morley Hechter, lawfully married Marge Hechter in Los Angeles, California on February 18, 1945, some 10 days after she had been granted a divorce in Illinois from one Joseph Kaufman. They lived and cohabited together in Winnipeg until July 12, 1956. The marriage was a normal happy one in the beginning but for several years, in its later stages, unhappy differences arose, chiefly over Mrs. Hechter's drinking habits. Mrs. Hechter, who claimed she drank moderately, stated her husband seldom drank; that he had "an obsession about drinking"; that he accused her of being an alcoholic "even to the point he had my mother convinced in July" (1956) "that I was ready for a sanatorium." There were repeated quarrels on this subject and as early as April 1956 she was pressing for a separation with alimony. A tentative separation agreement was drawn up early in July but was not signed due to the fact the financial terms were not satisfactory to Mrs. Hechter. She admitted that in July 1956 she had no love for her husband and was interested only in obtaining the best possible financial settlement from him.

Then as to her relations with the co-respondent: prior to the crucial date of July 13th it is evident that the Hechters and Cohen belonged to the same social set and had known each other for several years. It is to be noted that for some time Mrs. Hechter had been meeting Cohen without the knowledge of her husband and without informing him of such meetings. . . . In regard to the events of the early morning of July 13th, the learned trial Judge concisely and correctly sums up the evidence on the basis of which the petitioner claims that adultery was committed. He says: "Undisputed facts relating to the alleged adultery are that the female respondent left her apartment which was the home of her and the petitioner at about 1:00 o'clock in the morning of said July 13th, and proceeded in her automobile to the suite which was the male respondent's home, with the intention of seeing him there. The female respondent knew that the man she was going to meet might not be at home but that if he were absent he would arrive home soon."

Arriving at his suite she found it in darkness and sat in her car awaiting his return until asked to move by a policeman for being wrongly parked. She stated she drove around and, returning, found the Cohen suite with the lights on and, in her words: "I parked the car and I went in, on my own." Continuing, I quote from the reasons for judgment:

"They then (Mrs. Hechter and Laurie Cohen) sat together in the suite not far from its front windows. The lights of the suite were on and thus the parties were in full view of anyone on the street; and, as a matter of fact, they were observed. At about 2:00 o'clock they both left the suite and got into their respective automobiles and they drove to the home of the female respondent a couple of miles away. There she left her auto, and she then walked to a nearby street corner, and got into the automobile of the male respondent who had been following her. They returned to his suite. Arrived there, she got out of his automobile and entered his suite, unlocking the door with a key he had given her. He drove a few city blocks further to a restaurant; purchased some food there; and returned to the suite. The couple then sat as before, in a lighted room near the windows, the blinds of which were up, in full view of anyone on the street, and consumed the food the male respondent had bought.

"Some slight differences are to be found in the evidence of the parties and the witnesses from this time onwards. However it would seem clear that the suite was properly illuminated and the positions of the respondents as stated up to about 2:30 a.m., because the petitioner and his friend were observing them. The petitioner left the location at about 2:30 a.m., to telephone detectives he had engaged. He went a mile or so away and the telephone call was made at 2:45. He then returned to the suite and found it in darkness. His detectives arrived at the place at 3:10 a.m., and found it the same way. Within 5 or 10 minutes thereafter the petitioner and one of his detectives knocked on the door, rang the bell and called out to the occupants of the suite intermittently until 4:50 a.m. During this time the suite remained dark. The female respondent then came out and after a short time went home. The co-respondent admitted the detectives to his suite. The evidence of the detectives is that one of the beds in the suite was disarranged but otherwise the bedroom was tidy. This evidence was not denied. The respondents, then, were alone together in the suite with the lights turned out most of the time between 2:30 and 4:50 a.m. They were in undisturbed occupation for a period of 40 minutes or 20 minutes depending upon the exact time when the lights were put out."

The learned trial Judge examines with some care the explanations given by Mrs. Hechter and Laurie Cohen in regard to these events. . . .

The fatal flaw in the explanation of the respondents is their inability to explain, with any degree of plausibility, their actions from 2:00 a.m. onward — that being the time they left Cohen's suite to park Mrs. Hechter's car at the rear of her home. Up until that time, however indiscreet their conduct, there was no evidence of misbehaviour, although admittedly on an earlier occasion there had been opportunity. But from that time forward almost every action they took is suspicious, compromising, and for the purpose of concealing the fact they were together. . . . Finally, when Hechter and the detectives arrived at the door of the suite and requested admittance, Cohen delayed opening the door for almost two hours although he and Mrs. Hechter knew her husband was at the door demanding entrance and asking that his wife be sent out. Were these the actions of people who had nothing to conceal; was this the conduct of people innocent of wrongdoing? . . .

On appeal, counsel for the female respondent argued that the behaviour of Mrs. Hechter and Laurie Cohen must be looked at in the light of modern day manners and present day social customs, which accept, as not unreasonable or improper, freedoms formerly considered with grave suspicion. But both respondents admitted, by the steps they took to avoid detection, that they realized their actions placed them in a most equivocal position. The learned trial Judge found the explanations they gave of their conduct to be untruthful and impossible of acceptance, and I think it may be observed that, however much social standards may vary, the biological urge remains constant. In the instant case one would have to be incredibly naïve to believe that Mrs. Hechter's car was parked at her home at 2:00 a.m.; that she returned to the co-respondent's suite at 2:30 a.m.; that the blinds were lowered and the lights turned out, in order that the respondents might continue a discussion regarding the possibility of Mrs. Hechter exchanging an automobile. . . .

In the instant case the learned trial Judge found that the explanations given by the respondents were unconvincing; he found that as witnesses the respondents were "not veracious"; he found that they had committed adultery on the date specified in the petition. I am in agreement with the conclusion he reached and believe it is fully justified by the evidence.

The question of connivance remains for consideration. In general, it may be said that the defense of connivance is a weak one in that it is an admission of adultery, and, to prove it, intention on the part of the petitioner must be shown. What the trial Judge had to determine was

whether or not the petitioner in the instant case had the corrupt intention of promoting or encouraging the adultery of his wife on which he
based his petition, or whether, having some suspicion that she might be
committing adultery, he took the action he did to ascertain whether or
not his suspicion was justified and without the corrupt intention of encouraging or promoting her adultery. This poses a psychological problem
of great difficulty for the trial Judge: he must decide what was in the
mind of the petitioner, what motive influenced him. The learned trial
Judge in his reasons for judgment first states the relevant facts and then,
in his words, "presuming all facts against the petitioner," comes to the
conclusion he was not guilty of connivance. In no instance is he giving
the petitioner the benefit of any doubt. He says, in effect, that if the
facts are regarded in the light most unfavourable to Hechter, it is his considered opinion he is not guilty of connivance. . . .

"The charge that the petitioner connived at his wife's adultery rests
on a combination or a sequence of several acts and omissions on his part.
Presuming nothing in his favor the facts seem to be as follows:

"He and his wife had been living unharmoniously for several years.
Affection of one for the other was dead: in fact neither had respect for
the other. From April 1956 the two of them had been discussing formal
separation and during the week before her adulterous conduct they were
on the verge of entering into an agreement of that sort. Their respective
solicitors were negotiating or advising upon the terms. The only term
that stood in the way of the execution of an agreement was quantum of
alimony. She wanted all she could get: he desired the payments to be as
small as possible.

"He was suspicious of his wife's fidelity. On one occasion when the
two of them were quarrelling or bickering she said something that made
him suspect that she was interested in some other man. This suspicion
came to him later when he was thinking over what had been said during
the quarrel. While he became suspicious of her he could not settle in
his mind on any particular person as 'the man in the case,' although he
considered the co-respondent as a possibility. He had an interview with
his lawyer and after that he engaged detectives to watch his wife every
evening up until midnight.

"Next, he announced an intention to go fishing for a few days. He
told this to his wife and on the day he was to go he called the co-respondent for some information about a fishing camp and thus he apprised him
also of his intention. He got his gear ready, loaded his boat on his automobile, and prepared to leave Winnipeg for the fishing locale. In this
he was assisted by his friend Kenneth Jack Miklash. But he did not go
fishing. Instead he went to the home of Miklash and after a meal there
he and Miklash drove about the City of Winnipeg in the latter's car. In
presuming all facts against the petitioner it should be presumed that he
told his wife and the male respondent that he was going fishing when in
fact he never intended to go; and he gave them false information with
a view to lulling them into a sense of security. Indeed I may as well say
now that I would find as a fact that the petitioner's statements to the

other parties about him going on a fishing trip were merely a ruse. His actions after leaving his home as though to go fishing are consistent with him having attempted to lull the other parties into a sense of security; and also, a few days after the crucial incidents at the male respondent's suite, the petitioner averred to Mr. Havelock, a credible witness and a friend of both the petitioner and the female respondent, that as a matter of fact he, the petitioner, never had really intended to go on any fishing trip.

"At any rate the petitioner stayed in Winnipeg and drove about the City as stated. He and Miklash, several times, saw the female respondent's automobile parked in its usual place near her and the petitioner's home. Then in the neighbourhood of 1:00 o'clock they observed that it had been removed. They searched several places for it and eventually discovered it in front of the suite of the male respondent. They then saw the two respondents sitting together in that suite; saw them come out; saw her drive away to her home, park her car, and cross the street to where the male respondent was waiting for her in his automobile. They then saw the two of them go back to the male respondent's suite."

The learned trial Judge then concludes his summary of the evidence in regard to connivance by giving a brief account of what happened from that time forward. It should be noted, however, that one important and significant fact is overlooked in this summary, namely, that after Hechter telephoned the detectives and returned to Cohen's suite and found it in darkness, he then went back to his home to ascertain if Mrs. Hechter had returned there during his absence. This is not the action of a man conniving at adultery; it is the action of a distraught husband giving his wife the benefit of the doubt but endeavouring to ascertain the true facts of the situation. When he found she was not at their home he returned to Cohen's suite where he was almost immediately joined by the detectives. There was only a very brief delay before they knocked on the door of the suite demanding entrance. There is the further fact to be mentioned: that although Mrs. Hechter immediately recognized his voice the door was not opened until almost two hours later.

Two other points in the evidence deserve enlargement. First, I think the evidence shows that while Mrs. Hechter was thoroughly dissatisfied with the marriage and desired a separation, Hechter would have preferred the marriage to continue. Under cross-examination on the point of the separation she was asked: "Q. But there were occasions when he asked you to call it off? A. That is correct. Q. Would it be correct to say that you were the one that was pressing for the separation? A. Yes, it would be." Hechter himself said he was not anxious for a separation and Havelock's evidence corroborates him on this point for it indicates that even after the events of July 13th Hechter desired a reconciliation.

Second, the evidence supplies ample proof that Hechter was justified in having grounds for suspicion of his wife's fidelity. Referring to a discussion with his wife on July 8th, he states: "I said, 'What is this thing all about?' I still didn't want a separation particularly, and I said, 'There is no sense to this. We are both young and it is just a bunch of foolishness.' I said, 'I have nobody else that I am particularly interested in.' And I said, 'I am sure you haven't.' She looked at me and said, 'Haven't I?' I tried to pursue it further and she wouldn't pursue that any further with me." . . .

I think the learned trial Judge is correct in his statement of the law, that to find connivance on the part of a petitioner "his state of mind must be such that he *desires and intends* the consummation of a matrimonial offence." . . .

The necessity of having to prove intent to constitute connivance is put even more forcibly in the judgment of Denning L.J. in Douglas v. Douglas, [1951] P. 85 at p. 96, thus: "The principle on which connivance is founded is volenti non fit injuria. That was laid down by Lord Stowell in Forster v. Forster ((1790), 1 Hagg. Con. 144, 146) and by Sir John Nicholl in Rogers v. Rogers (3 Hagg. Ecc. 57) and has never been doubted since. Volenti is very different from scienti. It is not the knowledge of what may occur which bars a husband from complaining. It is his consent to it. A husband cannot complain of his wife's adultery if he has, theretofore, by his words or conduct, consented to it taking place. But the consent, to be a bar, must be a consent to the inception of the adultery."

There is ample legal authority for the view that it is not improper for a man or woman who suspects his or her spouse of infidelity to take steps to ascertain whether the suspicion is justified, and, if it is, to obtain the necessary proof to satisfy a Court to that end. Thus a husband may himself watch or employ others to watch his wife in an endeavour to verify a reasonably held suspicion; but unless he does this with the intention of facilitating the adultery such procedure does not constitute connivance. . . .

I think, therefore, it can be said that the question at issue in the present case, so far as connivance is concerned, is this: Did Hechter, having a suspicion that his wife was committing adultery, take the action he did to ascertain whether his suspicion was justified? Or did he intend that his wife should commit adultery with the co-respondent on the morning of July 13th? What has to be ascertained is his state of mind in regard to these matters. . . .

In the instant case the learned trial Judge made specific findings of fact that adultery had been committed and that the petitioner was not guilty of connivance. These findings are based on his assessment of the credibility of witnesses whom he had the opportunity of seeing and hearing, including both spouses and the co-respondent. In regard to the female respondent and the co-respondent, he definitely found they were not veracious witnesses and that they were guilty of adultery.

In regard to the issue of connivance, it is primarily the character and actions of the petitioner which come into question. Assessing the evidence against him in what is the most unfavourable light as far as he is concerned, presuming nothing in his favour, the learned trial Judge comes to the conclusion he was not guilty of any corrupt intention. In his carefully reasoned judgment the trial Judge summarizes the evidence and analyzes the cases with scrupulous fairness in regard to both adultery and connivance. I am in complete agreement with the conclusion he reaches in each instance.

I would dismiss the appeal with costs and allow a factum fee of $50.

TRITSCHLER, J. (dissenting). I accept the findings of credibility and fact made by the learned trial Judge. This disposes of the first ground of appeal against the finding that adultery had taken place.

There remains the question whether the inference of connivance should be drawn from the found facts of this particular case. . . .

The difficulty I feel about this case is solely because of the petitioner's communication to the male respondent of the story of the intended absence with the found motive of lulling him into a sense of security. The finding of the learned trial Judge shows that this communication was a deliberate seeking out by petitioner of the male respondent which had as its sole purpose putting into the mind of the male respondent a belief that the petitioner would be away — and consequently the field clear — at a certain time. Why did petitioner desire to lull the respondents into a sense of security? The state of the petitioner's mind is all-important upon the question of connivance.

Petitioner suspected his wife's fidelity. The learned trial Judge finds that petitioner "could not settle in his mind on any particular person as 'the man in the case,' although he considered the co-respondent as a possibility." The petitioner's evidence on the point is "I had some suspicion but the suspicion wasn't directed at Mr. Cohen." However this may be, the case is not within the principle suggested in Douglas v. Douglas, [1951] P. 85 by Denning L. J. (p. 98): "But when an innocent husband is only seeking to discover proof of an adulterous intrigue which he quite reasonably believes is already going on, the creation of an opportunity for it is not of itself connivance."

Petitioner did not believe an adulterous intrigue was going on between his wife and the male respondent and it is with his belief vis-a-vis the male respondent that we are concerned.

Connivance is often said to be present when a petitioner "desires or intends" the adultery. The test is sometimes put another way which I prefer for this occasion. Did petitioner have an intention of "promoting or of encouraging" the adultery which followed his communication with the male respondent? The adjective "corrupt" which usually is placed before "intention" seems unnecessary. We must consider petitioner's action in relation to the circumstances. The marriage was broken; affection of one for the other was dead; neither had respect for the other. They were negotiating a separation agreement but were in dispute about quantum of alimony. It was to be a substantial sum in any event. Petitioner was offering $2000 cash and $300 a month for 10 years, but the wife wanted $27,000 cash and $300 a month for 10 years. When petitioner got his evidence he said to a family friend, "I don't have to give her a cent now." Petitioner, who had nothing now to lose in terms of love or respect from his wife and whose marriage had already foundered, would benefit financially if his wife were caught in adultery. In these circumstances he communicated information to the male respondent with the found motive of lulling him into a sense of security. . . .

NOTE

1. What sort of conduct by the suspicious spouse amounts to connivance? A Massachusetts court has stated that the defense is based upon conduct that smooths "the path to the adulterous bed." Vinton v. Vinton, 264 Mass. 71, 73 (1928). From this point of departure it is generally agreed that mere acquiescence of the wronged spouse, or even acts which indirectly facilitate development of the adulterous relationship do not so "smooth the path" as to deprive the injured party of his lawsuit. See, e.g., Hayden v. Hayden, 326 Mass. 587, 96 N.E.2d 136 (1950). Thus merely keeping watch on the suspected spouse is not connivance, Bingenheimer v. Bingenheimer, 2 N.J. 284, 66 A.2d 327 (1949), on the theory that the suspicious spouse is entitled to employ any lawful means to procure evidence of a marital offense. If, however, the injured party employs detectives or other persons as agents provocateurs to lure the other spouse into infidelity, that is of the essence of connivance. See, e.g., Rademacher v. Rademacher, 74 N.J. Eq. 570, 70 Atl. 687 (1908); McAllister v. McAllister, 137 N.Y. Supp. 833 (Sup. Ct. 1912). Similarly if the plaintiff has guilefully placed the defendant in a position where prostitution becomes requisite to survival, it seems perfectly clear that his connivance should bar his suit. See Benson v. Benson, 102 So.2d 748, 752 (Fla. 1958) (dictum).

2. Connivance as a defense has received some statutory attention, though rarely beyond the mention of the term among a list of defenses, or through the type of definition supplied by Cal. Civ. Code §112, quoted page 634 supra. Several states have sought to define the defense with greater clarity, by disallowing a divorce "if the husband connived at his wife's prostitution, or exposed her to lewd company whereby she became ensnared to the offense." Ariz. Rev. Stat. Ann. §25-313(A) (1956). In the sense that this formulation limits the defense to the wife, it is probably narrower than the common law of connivance, though in fact the defense is usually raised by the wife, and almost invariably in extenuation of the plaintiff-husband's charges of adultery. In another sense, however, this statute goes beyond the common law in its "exposure to lewd company" corollary, which is not included in the nonstatutory concept of "smoothing the path to the adulterous bed."

3. Closely related to the defense of connivance is the defense, recognized by a few courts, of provocation. The rationale of this doctrine, applicable notably in Pennsylvania, is that one spouse may not obtain a divorce for conduct of the other, which he has incited or provoked, unless the response is excessive and unreasonable by comparison with the provocation. See Colin v. Colin, 181 Pa. Super. 564, 124 A.2d 184 (1956). This type of defense is sometimes treated as a matter of recrimination rather than of connivance or provocation, a classification which seems illogical in view of the fact that in this situation the defendant's act al-

ways follows rather than precedes the plaintiff's alleged counteroffense. See De Burgh v. De Burgh, page 654 supra; Schmidt v. Schmidt, 51 Wash. 2d 753, 321 P.2d 895 (1958) .

4. For further discussion of these problems, see Cartwright, Divorce — Connivance — Some Recent Decisions, 29 Can. B. Rev. 203 (1951); Note, A Survey of the Law of Condonation, Connivance and Collusion in New England, 35 B.U.L. Rev. 99 (1955); Note, Connivance, 95 Sol. J. 147, 829 (1951); Annot., 17 A.L.R.2d 342 (1951) .

WILLAN v. WILLAN
[1960] 1 W.L.R. 624 (C.A.)

APPEAL from Mr. Commissioner Constantine Gallop Q.C., sitting as special commissioner in divorce, Sussex Assizes.

The facts as stated in the judgment of Willmer L.J. were as follows: A husband petitioned for the dissolution of his marriage on the grounds of his wife's alleged cruelty. The parties had been married in June, 1935, and there were two children of the marriage, one born shortly after the marriage and the other after the war in 1946. The husband was away on military service during the war, but cohabitation was resumed on his demobilisation, and he continued to live with his wife until the morning of September 29, 1958, when he left the matrimonial home and did not return to it.

The cruelty alleged in the petition and at the hearing was, inter alia, that throughout the marriage, and more particularly in the latter part of it, the wife frequently and persistently assaulted him and showed violence to him; that she was immensely jealous of his relations with other women; and that she habitually used offensive and obscene language, calling him by horrible names and so forth. It was also alleged that she frequently demanded sexual intercourse with him at times when he did not wish to have it, obliging him to conform to her wishes by indulging in various types of violence in order to bend his will to hers. In particular, it was said that she would pull his hair, catch hold of him by the ears, and shake his head violently to and fro; and, at any rate on one occasion, it was said that she kicked him on his injured leg, causing him great pain. She would also pester him far into the night to have sexual intercourse, so that eventually he was compelled to comply as the only means of getting his rest.

For some time before the final separation the parties were on bad terms, although sexual intercourse was continuing in the circumstances described. The husband at least was for some time in the hands of solicitors, and on or about August 13, 1958, the solicitors wrote on his behalf to his wife, complaining of her cruel conduct and informing her that the husband would be obliged to leave her. Even after that life went on very much as before, the husband continuing to reside in the matrimonial home with his wife, and continuing to share the same bed with her. He said in evidence at the hearing of his petition that two or three weeks before the final separation he voluntarily and willingly had intercourse with his wife. A distinction was drawn in the evidence between that occasion and certain others when he had intercourse with his wife, not because he wanted to, but for the sake of peace, in the circumstances described.

On the night of September 28/29 — the night before the husband left for the last time — an act of sexual intercourse took place between the parties. The husband said that that act, like many other acts previously, was induced by the wife pestering him far into the night, showing some degree of violence to him, pulling his hair and so forth and, finally, rolling on top of him, so that eventually, towards the small hours of the morning, and for the sake of peace, he did have intercourse with her. Thereafter, the parties appeared to have gone straight to sleep, and the next thing that happened was the alarm clock going off at a quarter to six in the morning. The husband promptly got up, dressed and left the house at six o'clock in order to go to work. He kissed his wife and said good-bye, all in accordance with his usual procedure, the wife saying good-bye to him.

The husband did not return to the matrimonial home but presented his petition for the dissolution of the marriage.

The commissioner, on October 14, 1959, found in his judgment that cruelty by the wife had been established, and in particular found the cruelty in relation to pulling his hair, gripping his ears and rocking his head to and fro, kicking his leg and so on; but he held that by the act of sexual intercourse on the final night the husband had condoned that cruelty since the act of intercourse on that occasion was a voluntary act; and he dismissed the petition. . . .

WILLMER L.J., giving the first judgment . . . .

. . . The only question is whether or not the husband, by having intercourse with his wife in the circumstances which I have described on the night of September 28/29, must be held to have condoned the prior cruelty found against the wife. . . .

. . . In the first place, it is said that this act of intercourse on the part of the husband could not be held to amount to condonation, because it was one and the same with an act which was of itself relied on as part of the cruelty alleged. It was contended that an act which the husband relied on as an act of cruelty cannot be said at one and the same time to be an act of condonation. . . . [That] contention is really the result of muddled thinking, because it confuses the actual act of sexual intercourse, which constitutes the evidence of condonation, with the prior conduct complained of on the part of the wife, whereby she induced the act of intercourse. I can well understand that pestering in such circumstances on the part of the wife, in such a way as to deny the husband sleep, more particularly if accompanied by the pulling of his hair, might very well be capable of amounting to cruelty. But, whether that be so or not, I find it impossible to say that the subsequent action of the wife in submitting herself to an act of sexual intercourse could in any circumstances amount to an act of cruelty against the husband. Therefore, I do not think it is possible to accept the argument that that which was relied on as condonation was itself one and the same with conduct alleged to amount to cruelty.

Then it was said that this act of intercourse was induced by duress on the part of the wife, and that the husband was not to be regarded as a free agent. It is well established that, whatever may be the position of a wife, in the case of a husband the fact of having intercourse with the wife, with full knowledge of the matrimonial offence of which complaint is made, is conclusive evidence of condonation by the husband of the wife. . . .

It is sought to say, however, that some other exception to the rule ought to be accepted, which would cover facts such as have arisen in the present case. The difficulty, as I see it, in the way of the husband is that the facts found by the commissioner will not support the argument which has been put before us. The commissioner towards the end of his judgment said: "But, having seen the two parties concerned in this case, and the husband not saying that he acted under fear or apprehension for his safety and had no alternative, I cannot help thinking that the reason why he had intercourse with her on that particular occasion was that he was so tired and exhausted and knew that his prospect of rest and sleep was very small, if it existed at all, until he had done that which his wife required of him." Later the commissioner expressed this view: "Leaving aside questions of hysteria or hypnotism, or other such matters, if a man, through whatever blandishment or irritation, decides to have sexual intercourse, that must be a voluntary act, and I must hold that the act of intercourse in this case was a voluntary act." I agree with the commissioner, and I doubt whether the matter can be better stated than in the commissioner's own words.

All that has been proved in this case is that the wife used means, to which exception may well be taken, for the purpose of persuading her husband to have intercourse with her. He was free to submit or to resist. He was free, I suppose, to have run away; but in the end he decided that the best course to take was to submit to her wishes. I daresay he did show unwillingness, but to say that he showed unwillingness is not to say that he acted involuntarily. It might be otherwise in the case of a wife; but in the case of a husband who has sexual intercourse it can only be said of him that what he does he does on purpose, and that sexual intercourse with his wife must be a voluntary act on his part.

. . . In the absence of any evidence of revival afterwards . . . . in my judgment this appeal, which was always a difficult appeal, fails and must be dismissed.

[Concurring opinions of Harman, L.J., and Sellers, L.J., omitted.]

NOTE

1. American case law shows sharp divergence on two aspects of the law of condonation. First, does a single voluntary act of intercourse between the parties constitute condonation per se? Compare, e.g., Tarr v. Tarr, 184 Va. 443, 449, 35 S.E.2d 401, 404 (1945) ("It would be shocking

to the moral sense for a court of equity to grant a divorce to parties who, during the pendency of the suit, litigated by day and copulated by night"), with Henning v. Henning, 89 Ariz. 330, 362 P.2d 124 (1961) (intercourse must reveal intent to forgive; not condonation where none of normal marital affection was manifested). The application of the doctrine of condonation to cruelty or other causes of action which may rely on a continuing course of conduct raises particular difficulties. In Seiferth v. Seiferth, 132 So.2d 471 (Fla. Dist. Ct. App. 1961), the court held that resumption of cohabitation was not condonation per se of extreme cruelty where freely exercised intent to forgive is lacking. Courts may be reluctant to find condonation in course-of-conduct cases because of the strong public policy in favor of reconciliation where possible:

> The rule is that sexual cohabitation after acts of cruelty cannot be considered as condonation in the sense in which it would be after an act of adultery. The effort to endure unkind treatment as long as possible is commendable; and it is obviously a just rule that the patient endurance by one spouse of the continuing ill treatment of the other should never be allowed to weaken his or her right to relief. [Citation omitted.] [19]

Second, if a husband and wife reside together but one or both allege that they refrained from sexual relations, some but not all courts will infer that a condoning relationship existed because they remained together under the same roof. For an interesting discussion of this and the foregoing point, see Huffine v. Huffine, 74 N.E.2d 764 (Ohio C.P. 1947).

2. Royal Commission on Divorce and Matrimonial Causes, Report, Cmd. No. 6478, par. 375 (1912):

> [Condonation] is the blotting out of an offence, with knowledge of the facts, not by mere forgiveness, but by such conduct as amounts to a resumption of the married life. It is a complete answer to a charge, but if a subsequent marital offence is committed, it is held that the condoned offence is revived, the condonation being treated as conditional upon proper future conduct. . . .
>
> [While it has been suggested that there should be no revival of condoned offenses], in cases of cruelty, condonation of first acts is natural, and, if all proof of these acts be shut out, a culminating act of cruelty might not by itself be sufficient proof of cruelty. It might be productive of hardship in cases of cruelty, if the doctrine of revival were departed from.

The doctrine of revival was vigorously attacked by Vaisey, J., in his dissenting opinion in Beard v. Beard, [1946] P. 8, 25 (C.A. 1945), [1945] 2 All E.R. 306, 316. While Beard was a prisoner of war, his wife committed adultery. When they met again, she confessed, he forgave her, they lived together for three weeks, and the wife then deserted him. The husband was denied a divorce on the ground of adultery, the trial court

[19] Brown v. Brown, 171 Kan. 249, 252, 232 P.2d 603, 605-606 (1951).

holding that the condoned adultery could only be revived by a subsequent offense which in itself would constitute a ground for divorce; for this purpose under the English statute desertion must have continued for three years. In reversing, the Court of Appeal held that a difference in kind between the new and old matrimonial misconduct was not controlling and that subsequent misconduct which was a substantial breach of conjugal duty, even though insufficient by itself to justify a divorce, was enough to revive the condoned offense. In his dissenting opinion, Vaisey, J., said ([1946] P. at 28-30, [1945] 2 All E.R. at 317-318):

> Condonation appears to me to rest on sound legal, moral, and logical principles; to be entirely consistent with reason and fairness; and to be in the interest as well of the individuals immediately concerned as of the public. I find the doctrine of revival much less easy to explain and to justify, and I have sought in vain for its historical origin. . . . I do not doubt that condoned offences may be revived in cases of cruelty, and in other cases also, to complete a picture, but I do not think they can be revived to convict the offender by their own force, as is suggested on the present appeal. In my view the [principle] of revival exists, but has become of extremely limited application, and in any case does not apply here. . . .
>
> Some of the consequences which will follow the success of this appeal are, I think, surprising. I dare to suggest that when a wife or a husband condones the other's offence, and particularly the offence of adultery, by the resumption of sexual intercourse with full knowledge . . . . in the vast majority of such cases the intention and purpose of both is to re-establish the marriage as securely as it was established before. "Let us not refer to this again," would be their thought, "let things be as if it had never happened." Now I am quite aware that condonation does not lie in contract, but arises by operation of law, yet at least such a purpose as I have attributed to the parties would be praiseworthy, and I do find it very hard to believe that the law is compelled (with what seems to me to be incredible cynicism) to frustrate it. Must these people really be told that the law actually forbids them to re-establish their marriage on any other than a precarious basis; that they were mistaken in supposing that they had thrown into the sea — twenty years before, it may be — the hatchet that might then have severed their lives; and that the hatchet was in fact (without their knowledge and contrary to their wishes) buried in quite a shallow grave, and has lain there ready to be disinterred, for use with fatal results, on the happening of comparatively slight matrimonial misconduct in the future? I hope that I may be excused for the homeliness of the illustration of the buried hatchet. But the matter goes further still, for the revival of the ancient wrong would to-day leave the court no option. Given the act of adultery, however long ago, and given a month's desertion now, the court has no option or choice, or discretion, and the decree of divorce a vinculo must inescapably and automatically follow. I have

the greatest difficulty in persuading myself that this can be the law, and that the invariable consequence of, and penalty for, a condoned offence is a lifelong period of probation, rendering the offender liable to be called up for inevitable judgment thereon if he or she commits any other conjugal offence whatsoever at any time, however distant, thereafter. . . .

The Beard case was overruled by the Matrimonial Causes Act, 1963, 11 & 12 Eliz. 2, c. 45, §3, but the statute was limited to the specific situation involved in that case (i.e., the revival of condoned adultery). Section 1 of the same Act provided that resumption of marital intercourse constitutes merely rebuttable evidence of condonation; §2 specified that the resumption of cohabitation for the purpose of reconciliation for a period not exceeding three months shall not constitute condonation of adultery or cruelty nor serve to break the three-year desertion period required for divorce or separation.

PROBLEM

The husband brought an action based upon his wife's adultery with Edgar. His evidence established that the wife and Edgar lived together and repeatedly committed acts of adultery during the month of October. The wife did not defend, but upon further examination the court established that the husband first learned during the previous May that his wife was assertedly in love with Edgar, although at that time, he had had no evidence that she had committed adultery, and the husband and wife continued to live together. One night in June the husband came home to find his wife and Edgar seated on the sofa with their arms around each other. In what he described as "a drunken rage," the husband yelled at them: "If you two want to go to bed together, why the hell don't you?" The husband then stomped off to his boy's room, where he spent the night.

Upon arising in the morning, the husband found his wife and Edgar in bed together. After throwing Edgar out of the house, the husband tried to repair their marital state of affairs. He persuaded his wife to stay with him, if for no other reason than the best interests of their two small children, and for about a month they occupied the same bed, although the husband stated that his wife refused to have intercourse with him.

Late in July she left home with the children, going first to her mother's house. While she was there, the husband visited her on several occasions and wrote her numerous letters. The letters, which were submitted to the judge, made it clear that the husband was doing all he could to persuade his wife to return to him. She refused and in October, leaving the children with her mother, she went to live with Edgar, where she has since resided.

On these facts the court stated that, although it was with regret, a divorce must be denied. Cf. Godfrey v. Godfrey, [1964] 2 W.L.R. 981, [1964] 2 All E.R. 72 (C.A.). How would you argue the husband's appeal?

CHURCHWARD v. CHURCHWARD
[1895] P. 7, 64 L.J. Prob. 18 (1894)

[The President (Sir F. Jeune).] In this case the husband petitioned for a divorce, on the ground of his wife's adultery with the co-respondent. There was no defence, either by the respondent or the co-respondent, and at the hearing the adultery was clearly proved. I therefore granted a decree nisi; but, as the counsel for the petitioner gave me information of an agreement between the petitioner and the respondent, and of correspondence between their solicitors, I thought it right to direct that the papers should be laid before the Queen's Proctor, in order that he might intervene if he should be so advised.[20] He has intervened, alleging collusion between the petitioner and respondent.

With the exception of some evidence taken at the hearing of the intervention, the whole of the evidence consists of the agreement, of certain correspondence, and of the diary, or notes, of the petitioner's solicitor. I think, therefore, that it must be taken that, substantially, all the materials affording evidence of collusion were disclosed and offered to me at the trial of the petition by the petitioner's counsel.

The material facts are as follows. On June 4, 1893, the respondent left her home, no doubt accompanied, or soon afterwards joined, by the co-respondent. On the 5th she telegraphed to her husband's sister that she had left home for good. On the 6th she wrote a letter to her husband containing the following passages: "You are not surprised, I presume, at my leaving you. It had preyed on my mind for some time past, the fact that you did not want me; and that your opinion was that Poppie would be better looked after without me; and that everything I did was wrong. You have so often, over a mere trifle, told me 'to go'; and I have now done so; and I need not remind you of all the cruel things you have said to me since Poppie's birth." On June 10 she wrote: ". . . After all that has occurred, it is impossible for me ever to return, or matters to be

---

[20] 23 & 24 Vict. c. 14. The material words of section 7 are as follows: "Every decree shall, in the first instance, be a decree nisi, not to be made absolute till after the expiration of such time, not less than three months from the pronouncing thereof [now six months by 29 & 30 Vict. c. 32, s. 3] as the Court shall by general or special order from time to time direct; and during that period any person shall be at liberty, in such manner as the Court shall by general or special order in that behalf from time to time direct, to shew cause why the said decree should not be made absolute, by reason of the same having been obtained by collusion, or by reason of material facts not brought before the Court; . . . and at any time during the progress of the cause, or before the decree is made absolute, any person may give information to her Majesty's Proctor of any matter material to the due decision of the case, who may thereupon take such steps as the Attorney-General may deem necessary or expedient; and if from any such information or otherwise the said Proctor shall suspect that any parties to the suit are or have been acting in collusion for the purpose of obtaining a divorce contrary to the justice of the case, he may, under the direction of the Attorney-General and by leave of the Court, intervene in the suit. . . ." [Footnote appearing only in report of case in 64 L.J. Prob. at 19 n.6; brackets in original.]

mended. You had far better proceed with a divorce against me. . . . Had you only been different these last three-and-a-half years . . . , things would not be as they are." [Court's quotation abbreviated by Eds.] At that time, or at latest by June 14, the petitioner was aware that the respondent and co-respondent were living together.

It was stated by the petitioner's solicitor, Mr. King, that before June 19, the petitioner informed him, as a friend, of what had happened, and expressed a wish to sue for a divorce. . . . In Mr. King's notes the following entry occurs: "June 19. — Attending Messrs. Chester, who represented Mrs. Churchward, upon their call discussing this matter very fully with them, and explaining the position of the matter, and that Mr. Churchward was disposed to act in a reasonable way with regard to Mrs. Churchward's clothes and securities, provided he was fairly met, and we were, after conferring with you, to endeavour to make some proposal with a view to a settlement. Afterwards attending you, discussing matter very fully, informing you result of our interview with Messrs. Chester, and the admissions they were prepared to make, and conferring particularly as to taking proceedings in the Divorce Court, which under our advice you declined to do, at any rate for the present, and you requested us to see Messrs. Chester to-morrow and make the best arrangement we could by way of settlement for the benefit of the child."

Mrs. Churchward was possessed of about 2600*l.* in various investments, and also of a reversion expectant on the death of her father in about 1600*l.* This property was at her disposal, and could, of course, at any time have been expended or given away by her; and it must have been obvious that she might not improbably either give it to the co-respondent, or, if she could marry him, settle it on herself and him. Under date of June 20, in Mr. King's notes occurs this entry: "Attending Messrs. Chester, discussing matters fully, when we stated that you would be prepared to accept a scheme by which the whole of Mrs. Churchward's property should be settled for her exclusive benefit for her life, 2000*l.* on her death to be held in trust for the benefit of the child, and they promised to see her on the matter. . . ." [Court's quotation abbreviated by Eds.] [After further negotiations on] June 24 the respondent's solicitors wrote: "We do not for a moment suppose your proposals will be accepted in their entirety, but we shall advise that a proper settlement be made if you meet us in other ways, and, when we last saw the parties, there was a distinct disposition to accept our advice in that respect." This was followed by a letter from the respondent's solicitors on the 26th, in which the terms proposed are accepted, with modifications, and the following words follow: "The whole of the above suggestions are, however, contingent on this further term — viz., that Mr. Churchward at once commences and uses all due diligence to obtain a divorce, so as to enable Mrs. Churchward to marry Mr. Holliday as early as may be practicable."

Under date of June 27 Mr. King's notes state: "Attending Mr. Churchward, discussing the matter with him, but he declined to accede to the proposal, and insisted on some better terms being made for the benefit of the child" . . . On June 29 the respondent's solicitors wrote to the petitioner's solicitors, modifying the pecuniary proposals, and adding: "This is the very best we can do, and we believe, if it be not accepted, we shall have peremptory instructions to at once issue a summons that the property be made over to Mrs. Churchward." On July 3 it appears from Mr. King's note that Mr. Churchward "declined to take any proceedings until the terms were finally agreed on," and on the same day the petitioner's solicitors wrote: "With regard to the proceedings" (for a divorce) "our client will be prepared to act on your suggestion after settlement of the above matters, provided he be fully indemnified against all costs by a sum of money to be agreed on being deposited." On July 4 the respondent's solicitors, after referring to the pecuniary terms of the proposed settlement, wrote: "We do not think there is anything else in your letter to which any objection will be taken . . . and we think the matter of costs of suit may be met by a deposit of 50*l.* in joint names, the deed of settlement containing a proviso that, unless within twelve months from its date Mr. Churchward obtains a decree absolute, Mrs. Churchward may at her option avoid the deed. We think this proviso should be inserted, because we feel some fear that if the arrangement came to light, we might have trouble with the Queen's Proctor, and, although we are of opinion that the contemplated arrangement would not enable him successfully to intervene, it is quite possible a jury, at his instance, might take an adverse view."

Some further discussion took place between the petitioner's and respondent's solicitors, but on July 11 the latter sent to the former draft terms of agreement. The terms of this agreement as to the divorce proceedings appear from a letter composed by the petitioner's and respondent's solicitors jointly, and sent to counsel, in consequence of the strong objection of the petitioner's solicitors to any reference to the divorce proceedings. That letter, dated July 17, contained this passage: — "We are instructed in a matter between husband and wife, where the latter is now living in adultery, and terms are being arranged as to the wife's property, which at present remains in the physical custody of the husband. In these circumstances we, acting for the wife, have suggested that, in consideration of certain things to be done by the wife, the husband shall covenant at once to sue for a divorce, and prosecute his suit to completion, claiming no damages against the co-respondent, and the wife and co-respondent agreeing not to defend, and the husband agreeing to these terms on condition that the sum of 100*l.* is secured in the joint names of the solicitors in the case, to cover his costs." Counsel, thereupon, advised: — "I am of opinion that the proposed arrangement is, if not actually collusion, liable to the suspicion of collusion, and would, therefore, endanger the husband's decree, and I think his solicitor is very wise in refusing to enter into it. I do not think the terms as to costs so objectionable as the agreement not to defend. The wife and co-respondent may or may not have a good defence; if they have, such an agreement is, of course, ipso facto, collusion; and, if they have not, I do not see the necessity for any such agreement, and, if the Queen's Proctor intervened, the husband would have considerable difficulty in inducing the Court to believe that he did not enter into the agreement for the purpose of suppressing facts, which he would prefer were not brought to the knowledge of the Court." It was admitted by the petitioner's solicitor, in evidence given at the hearing of the intervention, that the terms of agreement stated in the letter to counsel represented the agreement then and now existing between the parties. An endeavour was made by the petitioner's solicitors in a letter, dated July 20, to leave the agreement as to divorce on an understanding; but eventually two agreements were settled and signed by the husband and wife on August 25, one settling the wife's property to some extent for the benefit of the child, and the other in [terms substantially those expressed in the July 17 letter except that no mention was made as to any defense to the suit.]

On August 7 Mr. Churchward wrote to his solicitor in these terms: "I think this week is the only chance before the Long Vacation of filing a petition, and I shall feel much more comfortable when it is done . . . . Please hasten the petition." At this time the terms of the arrangement were settled, except a question as to the persons to be named as trustees. It would appear, from an entry of October 21, that the petitioner's solicitors felt difficulties as to presenting a petition, but on November 1 this was done. . . .

From the evidence before me I draw the following conclusions: — 1. That the respondent and co-respondent were guilty of adultery.

2. That the petitioner did not connive at such adultery.

3. That there was no collusion to present to the Court false facts in proof of adultery.

4. That the petition was presented in accordance with, and in consequence of, the agreement come to between the parties. By this I mean that the petitioner would have been content with a separation, could he so have obtained the pecuniary settlement he sought; and he would not have presented the petition, if he could not have secured himself against the risk of his wife's property being diverted from his child. It was strongly urged on me, that the petitioner would in any case have presented a petition for a divorce; and that the unwillingness exhibited to the respondent's solicitor was a justifiable stratagem to secure a favourable settlement; and the letter of August 7 was relied on in support of the contention. I cannot accept this view.

5. That it was in fact part of the agreement that the wife and co-respondent should not defend the suit.

6. That it was not shewn that there were any specific facts, material to defence or recrimination, which might have been brought forward by the wife. But it appears to me impossible to say, especially having regard to the wife's letters of June 6 and 10, that it was proved that there were no material facts, which she could have brought forward, by way of defence or recrimination. The petitioner, the petitioner's solicitors, and the respondent's solicitors denied that they knew of any such facts; but such statements cannot, I think, be taken to be conclusive on the point.

The question is whether, under these circumstances, the claim of the petitioner for a divorce should be dismissed, by reason of his collusion with the respondent.

It was contended by Mr. Lawson Walton, in his very able argument for the petitioner, that the collusion necessary to be shewn was that described in the latter part of s. 7 of the Act of 1860, as "collusion for the purpose of obtaining a divorce contrary to the justice of the case," and he drew a distinction between such collusion and that referred to in s. 30 of the Act of 1857. It is, however, to be observed that the intervention of the Queen's Proctor is not under the latter, but under the earlier part of s. 7, where the phrase is simply "collusion." . . .

The contest raised in this case as to the meaning of collusion proceeds on clear lines. On the one hand, it was urged that collusion is agreement either, on the positive side, to put forward true facts in support of a false case, or false facts in support of a true case; or, on the negative side, to suppress facts which would prevent, or tend to prevent, the Court granting a divorce. It was insisted that, in a suit against a wife, unless it be shewn that the petitioner's charge of adultery was in fact unfounded, or was supported by false evidence, or that material facts in support of defence or recrimination were concealed, there can be no collusion. On the other hand, it was maintained that collusion has a wider scope, and that if there be an agreement to prosecute a suit which induces the petitioner to prosecute it, and, a fortiori, if such agreement contains terms providing for the petitioner's costs, and providing that the case shall not be defended and damages not asked, that is collusion, even though it be not shewn that adultery was not in fact committed, or any false facts put forward to prove it, and though no specific facts adverse to the success of the claim for divorce are shewn to have been concealed. . . .

In Crewe v. Crewe[21] Lord Stowell said: "Collusion may exist without connivance, but connivance is (generally) collusion for a particular purpose. Collusion, as applied to this subject, is an agreement between the parties for one to commit, or appear to commit, a fact of adultery, in order that the other may obtain a remedy at law as for a real injury. Real injury there is none, where there is a common agreement between the parties to effect their object by fraud in a court of justice. . . . However, it is no decisive proof of collusion that, after the adultery has been committed, both parties desire a separation; it would be hard that the husband should not be released, because the offending wife equally wishes it; she may have honest or dishonest reasons, innocent or profligate; an aversion to live with the man she has injured, a desire to live uncontrolled, or to fly into the arms of the adulterer; it would be unjust that the husband should depend upon her inclinations for his release; he has a right to it. . . . If the Court sees a fair case made out, what may be the inclination of the wife, be it corrupt or honest, is of little importance; the question is, whether the husband has received a real injury, and bonâ fide seeks relief."

. . . It is to be observed . . . how carefully Lord Stowell limits the

---

[21] 3 Hagg. 123, at p. 129.

case in which he excludes collusion, to that of a mere desire of both parties to obtain a separation, and does not deal with the results of such a common desire leading to an agreement relative to the suit, still less with those of the desire on the part of the husband being induced by extraneous considerations offered by the wife; and it is to be observed, further, that Lord Stowell insists that the husband must have received a real injury and be seeking relief bonâ fide. This leaves open the question, in what cases is relief sought bonâ fide?

[The Court then reviews various authorities at great length.]

On the whole, it appears to me that the authority of the House of Lords, as shewn by its practice, and of Sir Cresswell Cresswell, as well as of Byles and Wightman, JJ., is decidedly in favour of the position that, if the initiation of a suit be procured, and its conduct (especially if abstention from defence be a term) provided for by agreement, that constitutes collusion, although no one can put his finger on any fact falsely dealt with, or withheld; and I do not think that the authority of Lord Stowell, Dr. Lushington, Lord Penzance, or, though no doubt this is less clear, of Lord Hannen, can be invoked in favour of a contrary opinion.

It must always be remembered that, on grounds of public policy, second, perhaps, to none in importance, the marriage status cannot, however much the parties to it may otherwise desire, be altered, except on the fulfilment of certain conditions prescribed by law, conditions which relate to the conduct not only of the person against whom, but of the person by whom, relief is sought. Hence, it arises that in matrimonial proceedings, this Court has imposed on it, by the previous practice, and by the provisions of the Act of 1857, the peculiar duty of ascertaining for itself, so far as it can, whether in any case there exist bars, absolute or discretionary, to the petitioner's claim. . . . [W]hen the parties to a suit are acting in complete concert, the Court is deprived of the security for eliciting the whole truth, afforded by the contest of opposing interests, and is rendered unable to pronounce a decree of dissolution of marriage with sufficient confidence in its justice. If this be so, the expression in s. 7 of the Act of 1860, "collusion for obtaining a divorce contrary to the justice of the case," may be understood to indicate that, by such an agreement, justice is imperilled, but not to require that it must be affirmatively shewn that, having regard only to the matrimonial conduct of the parties, justice will not be, or has not been, done. No doubt the protection to the Court, afforded by the mutual watchfulness of hostile parties, often does not exist, because the petitioner and the respondent may, independently of each other, be of the same mind. Against results of that unanimity no legislation can guard. But it may well be worth while to prevent the parties to a suit from binding themselves by an agreement which, if there be anything to hide, renders it obligatory on both of them to keep the veil drawn. At least, if a petitioner makes the institution of his suit and its proceedings a matter of bargain, stifling defence and recrimination by a covenant of silence, he cannot wonder if the Court declines to be satisfied that it has before it all the material facts. Such a petitioner has mistaken his position. Pacem duello miscuit. He appears before the Court in the character of an injured husband asking relief from an intolerable wrong; but if, at the same time, he is acting in concert with the authors of the wrong, and is subjecting his rights to pecuniary stipulations, he raises more than a doubt whether, in the words of Lord Stowell, "he has received a real injury and bonâ fide seeks relief."

In the present case, being of opinion, as I have said, that the initiation of the suit was procured and its results as to costs and damages settled by agreement, I think it must be held that there was collusion. If it be necessary to constitute collusion that there should be a compact not to defend, that also was present in this instance. Further, if it be needful that suspicion of the concealment of some facts be entertained, I entertain suspicion (I do not wish to say more) as to the facts of the husband's conduct from the expressions used by the wife in her letters. But I do not think it has been shewn, nor in my opinion need it, that any specific facts of a material character exist which might have been brought before the Court.

I was much pressed by counsel with the hardship on the petitioner of dismissing his petition and of rendering the agreement of no effect. But I cannot assent to this view. As regards freedom from an adulterous wife, if the petitioner desires that, for its own sake, I see nothing to prevent his filing a petition without agreement with her. As regards the obtaining pecuniary advantage, for himself or his child, I must say that a divorce suit ought not, in my judgment, to be made the stipulated price of any pecuniary consideration.

The intervention of the Queen's Proctor must, therefore, succeed; but there will be no order as to costs. I was pressed to say that the disclosure of the agreement at the trial negatived collusion. I cannot follow that suggestion, because confession is not a defence. But I think that the conduct of the petitioner, in making this disclosure, entitles him to favourable consideration as to costs.

NOTE

1. For later developments in the English law of collusion, see Puxon, Collusion — I, 103 Sol. J. 686 (1959), who quotes Denning, L.J., in Teale v. Burt, [1951] P. 438:

> "Those arrangements (i.e., for maintenance, the ownership of the matrimonial home, costs, etc.) are not collusive so long as they do not tend to pervert the course of justice. They often have to be made of necessity. They amount to collusion only if one party or the other uses them as a bribe . . . (Parties) can compromise in claims for damages in divorce proceedings so long as the agreement does not tend to pervert the course of justice *and it is brought to the notice of, and sanctioned by the court*" (author's italics).

Compare the testimony of Professor Gower on current English divorce practice, in particular his discussion of collusion, page 697 infra. On American theories of collusion, see Drinker, page 706 infra.

2. Contrary opinions have been expressed as to the effectiveness of the Queen's Proctor in detecting collusion. In 1910 a judge of the Probate, Divorce, and Admiralty Division of the High Court testified that there was a great deal of collusion which could not be detected: "I speak not only of my own powers of detection, or my brother judge, but of the King's Proctor, who has every agency at his command. You hardly ever get a case of collusion established; perhaps two in the course of the year; not more, certainly." [22]

If Professor Gower's testimony before a later Royal Commission in 1952, page 696 infra, represents an accurate appraisal of English practice, it supports such a negative inference on the Proctor's work. The Commission itself, however, made the following appraisal of the Queen's Proctor's work:

951. The Queen's Proctor rarely intervenes of his own motion before decree nisi. The usual case is that in which the Queen's Proctor shows cause after decree nisi. A member of the public may have called the attention of the Queen's Proctor to matters which caused him to make enquiries; or the solicitors acting in the case may have given information to the Queen's Proctor of material circumstances which came to their knowledge after the decree. Additionally, it is the practice of the Queen's Proctor to select cases at random for investigation. In all these cases, if it is thought that cause should be shown against the decree, the directions of the Attorney-General are obtained and, if he so directs, the allegations of the Queen's Proctor are brought before the court.

952. Several witnesses suggested that the practice of pronouncing a decree nisi of divorce or nullity of marriage should be discontinued and that the office of Queen's Proctor would not then be required. These proposals depend to some extent on other proposals made by the witnesses for an extension of the grounds of divorce, as a result of which the incentive to bring a collusive action would largely disappear and it would become unnecessary to make collusion a bar to relief. Independently of these proposals, however, it was said to be in itself undesirable that there should be an official charged with such duties and powers. On the other hand, other witnesses supported the retention of the decree nisi and of the office of Queen's Proctor.

954. We have said elsewhere that we are not proposing to recommend any material change in the existing bars to relief. So long as the court has to be satisfied positively that these bars are absent, we consider that there must be some period of time before a decree of divorce or nullity of marriage becomes final. Moreover, this procedure constitutes one effective means of protecting the court against the presentation of a false case. It follows, therefore, that we are not prepared to recommend the abolition of the office of Queen's Proc-

---

[22] Testimony before the Royal Commission on Divorce and Matrimonial Causes, I Minutes of Evidence, Cmd. No. 6479, par. 1144 (1912).

tor. The fact that there is an officer of the court charged with the duty of investigating a case which is suspected to be false or collusive, in our opinion serves as a very useful deterrent and safeguard, besides being of great assistance to the court in the discharge of its duties.[23]

For a discussion of American experimentation with the use of the proctor device, with a reproduction of some of the statutes, see Connolly, Divorce Proctors, 34 B.U.L. Rev. 1, 10-12 (1954):

In the United States, twenty-four states have adopted legislation similar to that of England, but in no state is as much power given to the Divorce Proctor as is granted to the King's Proctor under the English Act. . . .

In the United States, the functions of officers doing the work of a Divorce Proctor vary greatly. In Hawaii, Probation Officers investigating the circumstances may, if in the public interest, call upon the Attorney General or other prosecuting officers, to present evidence in any divorce proceeding. Arkansas makes it the duty of the Standing Masters to serve as domestic relations attorneys in divorce suits, principally for purposes of investigation and enforcement of court orders. Delaware, Indiana, and Michigan allow or require the court to appoint an attorney or request the prosecutor to act for the purpose of defending uncontested cases. Wisconsin requires an official known as Divorce Counsel to appear, investigate, and defend such suits.[24] Massachusetts judges may appoint an attorney to investigate and defend the action, whether contested or not. In Oregon, the state is deemed to be a party defendant, and the plaintiff must serve the District Attorney whose duty it is to prevent fraud and collusion in the suit and control the proceedings on the part of the defense regardless of whether or not the suit is contested. In Utah, the County Attorney investigates, appears in and defends all cases where the defendant is insane, for the stated purpose of protecting the rights of the defendant and the state. Connecticut requires notice to the Commissioner of Welfare in all cases where the defendant is insane, absent, or incapacitated. The Delaware statute is somewhat similar to that of Connecticut. The rules of the state of Washington far exceed those of all other states as there the prosecutor is to be served in every default or uncontested hearing and to appear as a party, but in addition he shall have power to cause witnesses to be subpoenaed, to testify and even to take an appeal. This comes the nearest to the powers given to the English King's Proctor. These eleven jurisdictions have taken the strongest steps in the United States toward the eliminating of collusion in divorces and

[23] Royal Commission on Marriage and Divorce, Report 1951-1955, Cmd. No. 9678 (1956).

[24] The Wisconsin law has been changed and the duty to intervene lodged with the family court commissioner. See Wis. Stat. Ann. §§247.14, 247.15 (Supp. 1965). — Ed.

making it more probable that all the facts will be brought to the court's attention. Several other states have legislation on the subject which is considerably narrower.

Connolly gives no data as to the extent to which these procedures have actually been employed in practice; compare a report that in Oregon "experience has shown that as a practical matter district attorneys do not interest themselves in divorce suits." Note, 3 Ore. L. Rev. 344, 346 (1924). Connolly does suggest (34 B.U.L. Rev. at 16) that "it will be only in a small number of cases that the Proctor's services will be used," and the dearth of reported cases, particularly in recent decades, in which such an official has been involved suggests that this has also been true in the past.

In commenting on the frequency of divorce "by collusion and perjury," Vernier stated: "It is believed that this evil could be most effectively combated by the adoption of the divorce proctor system." [25] Do you agree with this? To what extent do the courts in their practices in uncontested divorce cases seem to operate on the assumption that the evil of collusion is one to be vigorously combated? See, e.g., pages 683-701 infra.

3. Puxon states that in England

> it is quite common for counsel to agree, during the hearing of a defended divorce, not to proceed with certain charges and to allow other charges to be made without challenge, provided that the judge is satisfied that "the proper course" is being taken in the interests of justice. This sort of arrangement is normally put before the judge in his private room and usually no difficulty arises and all concerned are contented with the result. It sometimes happens that the judge himself throws out the broadest of hints in open court that there may be "an unsatisfactory result for both parties" (a euphemism for "no decree for either party") if the case is allowed to take its natural course and to follow the pleadings. Counsel naturally take such hints, and the end of the matter is an agreement between counsel, a visit to the judge, a greatly shortened hearing and smiles all round.[26]

In Maimone v. Maimone, 90 N.E.2d 383 (Ohio Ct. App. 1949), plaintiff filed a petition for divorce and defendant filed a cross-petition. Upon plaintiff's withdrawal of his petition when the case was called for trial, defendant was granted a divorce on her cross-petition. After plaintiff changed counsel, he moved for a new trial, alleging that he had been confused and unwilling when, because of the trial's intervention, he had abandoned his petition in the case. The trial judge denied the motion for a new trial, stating that when the case was called for trial he had followed his usual practice in cases where each side was petitioning for divorce (id. at 384):

[25] 2 Vernier 8.
[26] Puxon, Collusion — II, 103 Sol. J. 705, 706 (1959).

"I asked [counsel] whether both parties wanted to be divorced and they told me that they did, and that there was no possibility of a reconciliation, and I told them that if the case went to trial the probability was, from my experience, that no divorce would be granted by me to either side, inasmuch as I do follow the law in contested cases and the law is that one side or the other must make out that the opposite side was the one who was the cause of the marital disagreement and that the other side was without fault and that evidence is very seldom produced. I said if a divorce was refused the parties would be in a very difficult situation, being married and unable to get along with one another, and suggested that they discuss the possibility — I asked them what the controversy was about, if both sides wanted a divorce and they informed me, that it was on the question of alimony and I suggesed that they retire and discuss that question and if that could be settled between them, then one side or the other could withdraw the petition or cross-petition and the divorce could be granted.

"They discussed the matter for at least an hour and then told the Court that they had arrived at a conclusion and the petition was withdrawn and the case was heard on the cross-petition. . . ."

In reversing and ordering a new trial, the appellate court said (id. at 386-387):

It is inconsistent with the duty of judicial vigilance against collusion for a trial court to advise or encourage the withdrawal of one of the parties to a contested action for divorce to permit the other party to obtain a decree in an ex parte hearing. It is not the business of courts to facilitate the procurement of divorce decrees. The function of a trial court in divorce actions is to hear all the evidence and determine whether a true case for divorce has been made upon one or more of the grounds set forth in the statute. This does not mean that a party to a divorce action may not withdraw a pleading where he or she is unable to support the allegations thereof by evidence, or for other proper reasons. Neither does it mean that a party may not refuse to assert a meritorious defense. The law cannot compel parties to defend actions. But . . . [a] husband and wife may not agree upon a divorce nor may they agree that either of them shall obtain a divorce upon a partial presentation of facts in an uncontested hearing. . . .

It has been suggested that the law against collusive decrees is more honored in its breach than in its observance. We are told in argument that the enormous number of divorce cases on the docket of the Common Pleas Court and the multitude of complex social problems arising therefrom make necessary the adoption of short cut measures to insure the efficient and prompt disposition of pending cases. We answer these arguments by asserting that it is our duty to declare and apply the law as we find it. Also, it is the duty of this court and of courts of original jurisdiction to uphold the public policy of the state as declared in the authoritative pronouncements of the supreme court. Any action of a trial court calculated to subvert that policy is an abuse of discretion.

For a contrary holding under apparently similar facts, see Schlesinger v. Schlesinger, [1959] 1 W.L.R. 92 (C.A. 1958), where a wife who implied that her counsel arranged the case in the judge's chamber without her consent was not permitted to impeach her counsel.

4. Alexander, The Follies of Divorce — A Therapeutic Approach to the Problem, 1949 U. Ill. L.F. 695, 702:

> [T]he availability of the defense of recrimination is often used as a threat or lever by either or both parties in negotiating for a settlement of alimony and property claims (not so often child custody or support, for the parents are not wholly free to bargain in these respects, and the court will do what is best for the child, regardless of the wishes of either or both parties). If the wife's demands appear exorbitant and the husband's offers niggardly, the well-grounded fear that a court battle will result in a draw and that each will leave the scene of battle exactly as he entered it (except for fresh wounds and salt for old ones) serves to bring into the arena a faint scent of sweet reasonableness so that a compromise is effected. There is some evidence that about five out of every six contested cases assigned for trial are thus settled at the eleventh hour, just as the parties are called to enter the ring. And since the settlement must be submitted to and approved by the court, there is very little danger that substantial justice will not be done.
>
> Thus the availability — not the application — of the defense of recrimination appears to be something of a boon to counsel, clients, and court, albeit an unwitting one.

5. In reading the materials which follow, consider these observations:

a. Hahlo, Can Law Reform Stop the Disintegration of Family Life?, 71 So. Afr. L.J. 391, 393 (1954):

> Experience at all times and in all countries has shown that, as long as divorce is permitted on any ground whatsoever, spouses who have agreed to part can obtain a divorce.

b. Selected Writings of Benjamin Nathan Cardozo 238 (Hall ed. 1947):

> Sooner or later, if the demands of social utility are sufficiently urgent, if the operation of an existing rule is sufficiently productive of hardship or inconvenience, utility will tend to triumph.

c. Ulman, A Judge Takes the Stand 173 (1933):

> [Divorce law is] a tool of society which actually works much better than one has a right to expect of it. That is because modern judges

have imitated an ancient practice which has served frequently throughout the centuries as a means to develop our legal system. They have shut their eyes in some directions, while in other directions they have been astute to see the invisible. In that way judges have created a legal fiction, by means of which a legal tool carves out socially desirable products, secures those results which society demands, without seeming to do so, sometimes pretending even that it does not do so.

d. O'Gorman, Lawyers and Matrimonial Cases 21 (1963):

When evasion becomes common practice among large numbers of law-abiding citizens, the determinants of such evasion are to be found, as Lincoln Steffens eventually realized, in institutional inconsistencies rather than in individual morality.   The extraordinary prevalence of evasion in matrimonial actions plainly points to a basic cultural conflict in which the legal norms . . . are incompatible with norms held by a large segment of American society.   The laws prohibit what the public permits.   Under these conditions patterns of evasive behavior have developed by which the law is obeyed in theory and denied in fact. . . .

e. Harter v. Harter, 5 Ohio 318, 319 (1832):

Perhaps there is no statute in Ohio more abused than the statute concerning "divorce and alimony."   Perhaps there is no statute under which greater imposition is practised upon the Court and more injustice done to individuals. . . .   The hearings are generally ex parte.   Witnesses are examined, friendly to the applicant, and it is almost if not utterly impossible for the Court in most instances to arrive at the real truths of the case.   I would not be understood that there are no meritorious cases.   That there are some such there can be no doubt.   But of the great multitude of cases which are before this Court I am confident that by far the greater number are not of this class. . . .

2.   *Judicial Administration and Lawyers' Ethics*

NOTE, THE ADMINISTRATION OF DIVORCE: A PHILADELPHIA STUDY
101 University of Pennsylvania Law Review 1204 (1953)

"In the whole administration of justice there is nothing that even remotely can compare in terms of rottenness with divorce proceedings." [27]

[27] Smith, Dishonest Divorce, 180 Atl. Monthly 43 (Dec. 1947).   "Practically all divorces today are uncontested. . . .   These uncontested cases are, in fact, agreed-to cases.   Everybody knows it.   Everybody must pretend not to know it."   Ibid.

This sweeping criticism, as startling as it may seem in light of the importance to the state of the legal dissolution of families, is in fact typical of indictments being directed at the entire divorce procedure by lawyers, judges, and sociologists. . . .

The bulk of the administration of the Pennsylvania divorce law is done by masters. A master is a member of the bar who may be appointed by the court on its own motion or after a motion of either party, to hear any case in which there is no petition for a jury trial, or where such petition is denied. If a case is contested, some judges hear it themselves as a matter of course on the ground that an inexperienced lawyer serving as master in a contested case may be taken advantage of by one or both of the attorneys representing the parties; other judges hear contested cases themselves except when they feel that they can appoint a master who is especially well qualified. Where an uncontested divorce develops into a contest the judge may withdraw the case from the master unless he feels that the master has special competence. An uncontested case in Philadelphia County, however, is almost invariably heard by a master. Since in Philadelphia, as elsewhere in the nation, the vast majority of divorce actions are uncontested, the importance of the mastership system is apparent.

Aside from being a member of the bar, a master need not have any special experience or training; each judge selects his masters according to his own standards.[28] The masters observed in practice varied from lawyers recently admitted to the bar to older practitioners both with and without much experience in divorce work. A number of attorneys in semi-retirement are occasionally appointed masters. Although a conscious effort to obtain an experienced master is usually made where the divorce is contested, this may not be true in many uncontested cases. . . .

In drawing up recommendations in uncontested cases, many masters feel that if the plaintiff has presented a fairly plausible story, there is no tenable basis for disbelieving it, because here the testimony is uncontradicted. Therefore, it is not surprising that the vast majority of masters' recommendations favor granting the divorce. The master's findings of fact and recommendations are only advisory and are not binding on the common pleas court; it has been repeatedly held that the appointment of a master does not relieve the court of the duty to examine the testimony independently and decide upon the merits of the case. It is clear, however, that the disposition of the case will depend in large part on the kind of record that has been made at the master's hearing. If the report indicates that the plaintiff has a plausible story and that all the elements required by the statute are present, the master's recommendation that divorce be granted will ordinarily be approved. The tendency of masters to approve any claim and judges to approve any record which are

---

[28] In some Pennsylvania counties other than Philadelphia, masters are appointed in alphabetical order or according to seniority, or from a board of standing masters, annually appointed. 2 Freedman, Law of Marriage and Divorce in Pennsylvania 1304 (1944).

prima facie plausible is evidenced by the very high proportion of actions filed which actually result in divorce.[29]

A major purpose of any system for administering divorce laws is to protect the interests of the state in the proceedings. . . . This need to protect the concerns of society is especially pressing in uncontested cases, where there is no adversary present to serve as a check on the plaintiff. The theory behind the mastership system is that the master through his hearing can, without consuming the time of the courts, serve both the function of a finder of facts and the quasi-judicial function of an impartial referee. To perform the first of these duties the master must not merely determine whether the plaintiff and his attorney have prepared and presented a case which satisfies the statute, but he . . . . has a duty to call as a witness anyone [who] he has reason to believe has knowledge of relevant facts, whether or not requested to do so by either party. In practice little effect is given to this rule, since most cases are disposed of in one hearing and the master has no knowledge of the case prior to this meeting. Any corroborating witnesses who are present are generally brought by plaintiff's attorney in recognition of the customary requirements of the particular judge who is to review the testimony. Typical testimony of a corroborating witness is described below. . . .

. . . [C]omparison of the grounds most commonly used in Pennsylvania as formulated by statute and appellate interpretation with typical handling by masters, illustrates the extent to which administration differs from legal doctrine.

Desertion. — Ground for divorce is established when it shall be judged "that the other spouse . . . [s]hall have committed wilful and malicious desertion, and absence from the habitation of the injured and innocent spouse, without a reasonable cause, for and during the term and space of two years." The willful and malicious character of the desertion is established by a mere finding that the desertion was intentional, for it has been held that "if the desertion is intentional it is willful; if willful it is malicious." It must be further established that the willful and malicious

29 Year	Number of Divorces Filed	Number Granted	Percent Granted
1938	2012	1713	85.14
1946	6590	5273	80.01
1947	4829	4576	94.76
1948	4255	3866	90.85
1949	3821	3380	88.47
1950	4198	3167	75.44
1951	4040	3266	80.84
1952*	2443	1859	76.09

* From January to July only.

The figures were supplied from unofficial records kept in the office of the Prothonotary in Philadelphia. Since many of the divorce actions filed are dropped before any judicial decision is reached, the difference between the number of cases filed and the number of divorces granted does not represent the number of cases in which a divorce was denied by the court. Thus, the proportion of cases decided which result in a grant of divorce is even higher than the percentages indicate.

character of the desertion persisted for the entire two year period. There must be an actual physical absence from the habitation and it must be shown that the abandonment of marital cohabitation was without consent or good cause. The mere failure by a husband to support the family properly does not constitute desertion and is not in itself a ground for divorce. The deserted spouse has no legal duty to seek a reconciliation or return of the deserting spouse — that is, the failure to attempt to effect a reconciliation will not be fatal to a divorce action. However, if the deserting spouse makes a bona fide offer to resume cohabitation, the desertion will be held to have terminated; furthermore, if such an offer is not accepted, the originally deserted spouse will be held to be a deserting spouse. It should be emphasized that a mere showing of a departure is not sufficient to prove desertion; surrounding circumstances must be shown which are indicative of the requisite intent.

The development of a desertion case in practice is illustrated by the following testimony taken in a typical case. On being asked to tell the story of the marriage and its difficulties the plaintiff answered:

"Well, we just simply had an argument and he just got up and walked out, and he didn't return for two days. . . .

"Q. And you didn't see him for two days?

"A. No I did not. He went to his mother's home, and I called and asked him if he was there, and they said yes. So I asked him if he was coming back, and he said that he wasn't ready. Naturally, I was worried about whether he was returning home or not. So he returned two days later and got his clothing.

"Q. When did your troubles with him first begin?

"A. Oh, when he was still in the service. . . ."

The testimony then becomes an account of all the unpleasant experiences that the plaintiff can remember of her married life. There is usually only perfunctory inquiry into the conduct of the plaintiff during the marriage which might have furnished provocation for the acts of the defendant. The master will often, however, inquire into the size and character of the living quarters in which the parties resided. The theory seems to be that if the living quarters are adequate it might negative justification for the defendant's leaving the home. . . .

It has been seen that an offer by the defendant to return terminates the desertion. An experienced master may cover this point in the following manner:

"Q. Did he on any occasion ever offer you a home?

"A. He did not.

"Q. Did he ever offer to return to the former place of residence?

"A. No, he did not."

The surrounding circumstances are relevant in a desertion case to show intent to desert, and also to show that the plaintiff is an injured spouse who has not provided any justification for the defendant's act. Invariably the defendant is made out to be completely in the wrong.

"Q. When you lived with your husband were you always a dutiful wife?

"A. Yes, I was.

"Q. Did you always provide for the means and care of your husband?

"A. Yes.

"Q. Did you always properly take care of his child and your child?

"A. Definitely.

"Q. Did you give your husband any reason for justification or excuse for leaving you?

"A. No.

"Q. Was it a question of money with you?

"A. No, I don't think it was; I'd say no it wasn't. . . .

"Excused."

One can only conjecture as to how the story would sound if told by the husband in this case.

It is common knowledge among members of the bar in Philadelphia who handle divorce cases that certain of the common pleas courts prefer or require corroboration in divorce cases where the ground alleged is desertion. To be safe, the plaintiff's lawyer brings in a friend or a relative to testify. Many masters make no attempt to question the witnesses called by the plaintiff. They merely ascertain the name and address of the witness and turn the examination over to the plaintiff's lawyer on the theory that this procedure will save time, since they do not know the purpose of the plaintiff's lawyer in calling the witness. The advantage of this method was demonstrated in some of the meetings observed, where the master attempted the initial examination and found that the witness professed to have no knowledge of the matters inquired about. Initial examination by the plaintiff's attorney seems to contravene the rule of court which requires that: "Neither party shall be allowed to examine any witness until after the master has finished his examination. . . ." A typical corroborating witness may testify as follows:

"Q. Do you know whether they separated?

"A. Yes. . . .

"Q. Do you know the reason for the separation?

"A. It was over an argument, and he left. . . .

"Q. Since January 10, 1946, do you know whether or not George B. __ has stayed any night at your mother's home?

"A. No, he hasn't.

"Q. Will you please tell the master how your sister treated her husband?

"A. She treated him very good.

"Q. What sort of housekeeper is she?

"A. Very good.

"Q. Does she take proper care of her child?

"A. Yes, she does.

"Q. At the time they lived together did she take proper care of her husband?

"A. Yes, she did.

"Q. Did she provide for his wants and comfort?

"A. Yes.

"Q. Do you know of any reason or excuse or justification that George B. __ might have had for leaving his wife?

"A. No, I don't.

"Excused."

Cruel and Barbarous Treatment and Indignities. — ". . . [I]t shall be lawful for the innocent and injured spouse to obtain a divorce . . . whenever it shall be judged, in the manner hereinafter provided, that the other spouse . . . [s]hall have, by cruel and barbarous treatment, endangered the life of the injured and innocent spouse." Actual personal violence or the reasonable apprehension of such violence is required to establish cruelty. While a single act, if sufficiently severe, may constitute cruelty, it must be such that the life of the innocent spouse is endangered. Some of the acts which have been held not to support a divorce on the cruelty ground are humiliating charges, refusal of sexual intercourse, indifference and neglect. However, much of the conduct which does not constitute cruelty is serious enough to meet the statutory standard for the indignities ground. To insure successful action many lawyers allege both cruelty and indignities or desertion in their complaint. Then, when the master's meeting stage of the proceedings is reached, the plaintiff's lawyer is apt to declare that the cruel and barbarous ground is not being pressed and he will proceed on the other ground alleged. It is felt that it is easier to make out a case on the grounds of indignities or desertion.

For indignities the statute requires that the defendant "[s]hall have offered such indignities to the person of the injured and innocent spouse, as to render his or her condition intolerable and life burdensome." The statute is vague in that it provides no definition of what constitutes an indignity. Vulgarity, unmerited reproach, habitual contumely, studied neglect, intentional incivility, manifest disdain, abusive language, malignant ridicule and every manifestation of settled hate and estrangement are some of the common judicial formulations of the acts sufficient to constitute indignities to the person. Unlike cruel and barbarous treatment, indignities cannot be established by a single act, no matter how severe. The evidence must disclose a course of conduct which indicates continued mistreatment. Causes which are not recognized as rising to the statutory standard for indignities are: incompatibility, lack of affection, habitual drunkenness per se and poor performance of household duties. In addition, as is the case with other grounds for divorce, if the conduct complained of takes place during a time when the defendant was insane or is caused by ill health, no divorce may be granted. This is because the requisite intent is negatived. Since the statute requires that the condition of the innocent spouse be rendered intolerable and his life burdensome, a great deal depends on the sensibilities of the individual plaintiff. Manifestly, a very sensitive person may find unbearable conduct which another might consider quite normal.

Where the grounds alleged are indignities the master has even less guidance from the complaint in his examination of the plaintiff than in a desertion case, where he at least knows that the plaintiff must prove a departure and an absence of two years. Also, since the definition of indignities is at best rather vague and uncertain, ordinarily the master will simply have the plaintiff tell the story of the marriage with emphasis on all the ill treatment and abuse inflicted by the defendant. An illustration from a case follows:

"Master: You charge the defendant with indignities to the person commencing in September, 1947, and continuing until June 12, 1951. Will you start from the beginning and in your own words relate for the record, the circumstances?

"A. The time we were married, when I moved to Newport, why, everything went all right for a while, and then she started going out, came in all late hours under the influence of drink, and any time I had any few friends up, like Mr. __ or Mr. __ and his wife, why, she would tell me how much she hated me and use all kinds of foul language and it kept continuing. . . .

"Q. Would you give us an example of the kind of language she used toward you?

"A. You _____ I don't like you and never did. I don't know why I married you in the first place. . . .

"Q. Did she keep house for you very well?

"A. No, the house always looked like a pig pen. I had to do all of the house work myself to keep the place clean. . . . And then finally she introduced me to this guy and she said he was in love with her. . . .

"Q. You tried to persuade her to change her mind?

"A. Oh, numerous times, it did no good.

"Q. Did she ever call you names or abuse you in front of your friends?

"A. Yes, many times.

"Q. And she would curse you at these times?

"A. She would curse me, rave and take off, start arguments, try to fight with me.

"Q. As far as you know was there any reasonable cause for these arguments?

"A. As far as I know, no. I tried to do my best.

"Q. Did you do anything to prevent the incidents? . . .

"A. No, I didn't.

"Q. What reason would you assign, if any, for your wife's conduct?

"A. As far as I could see, she was just out after the allotment she was getting from me. When she was first married she said she didn't love me or anything, all she wanted was what she was getting out of me, she was getting her support from me.

"Q. Mr.___ do you have any letters or statements from the defendant to substantiate your claims?

"A. No.

"Q. Is there anything else you would like to state in support of
your case?

"A. No.

"Q. How frequently, how many times a week would you say that
she called you these names that you refer to?

"A. Once or twice a week at least.

"Q. Was that a continuous course during the period commencing
with September, 1947, and going to the date of your separation in
June, 1951?

"A. Yes, sir.

"Q. Except the time that you were overseas?

"A. Except the time I was away."

Corroborating witnesses are frequently introduced in indignities cases,
but this depends a great deal on the judgment of the plaintiff's lawyer
as to the attitude of the reviewing court. In the case from which the
above extract was taken, the plaintiff who was in the Navy, called a shipmate to testify. It should be noted that the witness will ordinarily testify
after having heard the plaintiff's testimony. The shipmate testified as
follows:

"Q. How frequently would you say you went to their home?

"A. Oh, at least once a week, sir.

"Q. What did you observe with regard, first, to the manner in
which the home was being kept? Was it a tidy home?

"A. I wouldn't call it well kept. It looked like a man was taking
care of the place.

"Q. What, if anything, did you observe with regard to the behavior of the defendant in regard to the plaintiff.

"A. I say it was generally abusive.

"Q. Would you be a little more specific and tell us what you
heard and what you saw on your visit to this home?

"A. All I know, Mr. ___'s wife used extremely foul language at
times. It seemed every time we went over and played cards she
would start picking on him.

"Q. What, if anything, did she say to him in your presence?

"A. Well she called him nasty names.

"Q. Such as what?

"A. She called him a _____ several times and called him a _____,
that I know of.

"Q. In your presence?

"A. In the presence of my wife and myself. . . .

"Q. Did you observe the course of conduct, whether or not the
course of conduct by the defendant had any effect on Mr. ___?

"A. Yes, it hurt the man.

"Q. Did he appear to be nervous?

"A. Nervous and angry, and generally shook up you might say, irritable. . . .

"Q. Have you noticed any change in the condition of his health since then?

"A. Well, he is considerably more cheerful, more like his normal self.

"Lawyer: That is our case, Mr. Master."

As indicated above, neglect of household duties, bad temper, occasional quarrels are not in themselves sufficient to constitute indignities. It has been held, however, that such evidence may be considered in the general scrutiny of the defendant's conduct. While testimony in the form of general accusations and conclusions has repeatedly been held to have no evidentiary value, plaintiffs continue to utilize these generalities. Actually, much of the testimony presented to establish a ground for divorce is largely intended to show that the defendant was generally a disagreeable person and a poor spouse. This is true in both desertion and indignities cases. For example, mere claims by the plaintiff of nervousness and adverse effects on his health are supposedly valueless,[29a] yet this type of evidence is almost universally utilized. It is difficult to determine just how much effect this kind of evidence has, but interviews with masters immediately after they had heard the testimony indicate that many masters come away from the meeting with the general impression that the defendant is a completely unworthy person. This may be very important to the decision in the case, depending upon the attitude of the particular master toward the divorce law. . . .

The story of divorce administration in Philadelphia is essentially the story of the mastership system. The extent to which masters comply with and enforce the statute is more significant than appellate court decisions[30] in terms of the actual conditions under which the vast majority of divorces are granted. . . .

[29a] But compare Reed v. Reed, 340 Mass. 321, 163 N.E.2d 919 (1960) (W's insistence on keeping company with another man, resulting in adverse effects on H's health and weight loss, constitutes cruel and abusive treatment). — Ed.

[30]

Year	Number of Divorces Granted in Philadelphia*	Number of Appeals to Superior Court from Philadelphia Divorce Proceedings**	Number of Appeals to Supreme Court from Philadelphia Divorce Proceedings**
1938	1713	9	0
1944	2933	8	0
1948	3866	7	0

   * Figures taken from unofficial records in office of Prothonotary in Philadelphia.

  ** Figures compiled from official reports by writer.

NOTE

That the Philadelphia divorce practices did not change materially in the ten years following the publication of the above Note is borne out by Fonzi, Divorce Philadelphia Style, Greater Philadelphia Magazine 26, 79 (Feb. 1964):

> . . . Pennsylvania is a divorce mill. The only factor which keeps it from becoming a much-publicized mass production machine on the order of Nevada or Alabama is the ignorance of the general public in how quick and easy it is to break the marital knot here. There is a residence requirement of one year, but considering the lies and perjury which are a part of so much of the testimony anyway, the ethical bounds wouldn't be stretched much, if at all, by representing temporary addresses as long-time domiciles. . . .
>
> It usually takes between 12 and 15 weeks to get a divorce in Pennsylvania. It has been done in less than six. . . .
>
> . . . Total Court and filing costs come to about $210. Lawyers fees run an additional $300 to $500.
>
> Question: What does it take to get a divorce in Pennsylvania?
> Answer: Money.

VIRTUE, FAMILY CASES IN COURT
86-91 (1956)

A total of more than a hundred uncontested cases were heard in the two courts. The phrase "uncontested case" is used to designate those cases in which there was no observable controversy among litigants with respect to the granting of a divorce. . . . Except very rarely, controversy appears to be limited to financial and custodial matters, and to be thrashed out in pre- or post-decretal hearings on motions directed specifically to one or both of these problems. . . .

The presentation of decretal hearings has been reduced to such a universally applicable formula in Chicago that without conscious effort to do so, this writer memorized the formula. As recalled a month after observation, it goes roughly like this:

Q. What is your name?
Q. How long have you lived in Cook County?
A. More than a year before the filing of this petition.
Q. When and where were you married to _____?
Q. What are the names and ages of children born to the marriage?
Q. Are they now with you?
A. Yes.
Q. In the event the court sees fit to grant a divorce, do you want custody?
A. Yes.
Q. Calling your attention to such and such a date, what happened?

ALTERNATIVE 1:

A. He (she) left me.
Q. Did you give him (her) any cause or reason?
A. No.
Q. Have you seen him (her) since?
A. No.
Q. Have you, since that date, been living alone and as a single person?
A. Yes.

ALTERNATIVE 2

A. He (she) struck me.
Q. Did it leave visible marks?
A. Yes.
Q. Where did (she) strike you?
A. In the face.
Q. Did it cause you great pain and suffering?
A. Yes.

ALTERNATIVE 3

A. He (she) hit me again.
Q. Where?
A. In the face.
Q. Cause pain and suffering?

(end of alternatives)

Q. Did you give him (her) any cause?
A. No.
Q. How did you conduct yourself during your marriage?
A. As a good wife (husband) should.
Q. How did he (she) treat you?
A. (The answer to this question permits more leeway: "Cruel," "Bad," "Real Mean," "With a kind of an indifferent attitude, sort of," are all acceptable. The preferred response, however, is: "Terrible.")
Q. Would the court care to ask this witness any questions?

* * *

The number of cruel spouses in Chicago, both male and female, who strike their marriage partners in the face exactly twice, without provocation, leaving visible marks, is remarkable. It appears to be the generally accepted single conjugal rejection among widely variegated cultural, educational, and economic groups. . . .

Corroborative witnesses are almost without exception (1) the mother of the plaintiff, and (2) a sister or brother. Some attorneys bring along three or four siblings, if the supply is good. Plaintiff's father sometimes

appears; neighbors and business associates are brought in where necessary. . . .

CHATTANOOGA DIVORCE REPORT
19 Tennessee Law Review 944-958 (1947)

For a number of years a Chattanooga newspaper deplored the alleged
existence of a disgraceful divorce "racket" in Hamilton County. It alleged that a "divorce mill" in that city rivaled the one in Reno, and
prominently publicized alleged irregularities in the handling of certain
divorce cases involving men in the Armed Forces. As a result of these
charges, and because they seriously reflected against the bar as a whole,
the President of the Chattanooga Bar Association appointed a special
committee to investigate these charges. The scope of the committee's
investigation was subsequently broadened to include a comprehensive
study of all phases of the divorce situation in Hamilton County. . . .

". . . [W]e have actually studied approximately 1750 court files. . . .
Out of that number, for statistical purposes, 1000 filed in circuit court
have been selected at random and a complete tabulation made. . . .
The results of this tabulation are as follows:

"Judge L. D. Miller tried 985 (98.5 per cent) of these cases . . . .

"In 625 cases (65.2 per cent) [sic] no contest of any kind appears. Answers were filed in 348 cases (34.8 per cent) but the mere fact that an
answer was filed does not indicate an actual contest. It was found that in
only 177 cases (17.7 per cent) had attorneys appeared for the defendant and
it can be fairly stated that in less than 10 per cent was there a contest.
. . . [I]t was found that answers were signed by the defendants themselves in 171 cases, which means that in most cases these answers were
prepared and filed by the attorneys for the petitioner, usually for the
purpose of avoiding the necessity of process or to expedite the entry of
final decree. . . .

"Some lawyers, we feel, are not interested enough in preserving the
marriage ties of their clients. In this lack of interest they disregard a
basic principle of human relationship, viz., that dissolution of the marriage relation is not in the best interests of all the people in the community. This is not to say that relief should not be had in certain types of
cases wherein continued cohabitation might be detrimental both to the
individuals and to society. But the lawyer's duty is to apply this rule to
all cases coming before him. Generally speaking, if it is to the best interest of the individuals (husband and wife and children) that the parties be separated, the interest of society will likewise be best served. . . .

"This committee can't criticize too strongly the so-called 'one day
divorces' which have been brazenly flaunted before the public. They
not only do injury to the court and lawyers actually participating, but
they discredit the entire bar before the public. After a reasonable 'cool-
ing-off' period at least some of the marriages might be saved. Recently
the press has given wide publicity to the disgusting story of a Chatta-

nooga woman, 27 years old, who has been married and divorced 16 times in 11 years . . . .

"It is not to be inferred from anything said herein that this committee impugns the motives of Judge Miller whom we all know to be the very soul of honor. He is truly the friend of everyone and desires the respect of all. Inherently he is desirous of accommodating lawyers, litigants and the public and makes every effort to do so. As a result of his efforts to be accommodating, he carries an extremely heavy load of divorce litigation. A custom has developed, perhaps encouraged by other judges, whereby most lawyers direct their divorce cases to him and, as he states, the increasing number has become quite burdensome considering his other duties. He has a natural hesitancy toward questioning lawyers as to jurisdictional requirements, preferring to assume that they will not present him a case in which any elements are lacking. It is quite true that when a lawyer presents a matter to the court he thus impliedly represents that he has met all jurisdictional and procedural requirements insofar as he is advised.

"When interviewed by the committee, Judge Miller contended that he did not have the time to inspect the pleadings nor inquire into the jurisdictional aspects of the numerous cases and, therefore, had to rely on the lawyers to see that all these requirements were met. . . .

"Especially was this true as to men and women in the service. The Soldiers' and Sailors' Civil Relief Act provides that no decree shall be entered upon default unless it appears by affidavit that the defendant is not in military service. Less than 40 per cent of the uncontested divorce cases examined contained this affidavit. Judge Miller stated to the committee that he had instructed the clerk not to enter any pro confesso unless such affidavit had been filed. The clerk does not recall receiving this instruction. Such affidavits when filed were placed in the respective jackets and the presence or absence thereof was ascertainable by a mere inspection of the papers at the hearing. The clerk should not be blamed for a mistake, the avoidance of which is the primary duty of the court. . . .

"The laxity in procedure permitted by Judge Miller in divorce cases is accompanied by informality at the hearing of them. Far too many are heard in chambers. Trials from the bench are conducted with little more formality than those heard at chambers. The lawyer, client and witness merely appear before the bench and the case is over in a matter of two or three minutes. Frequently the trial of a criminal case is interrupted to accommodate lawyers in hearing divorce cases. This practice has occasioned much unfavorable comment. Instances are known in which husbands, desirous of obtaining a divorce, have, through their attorneys, been able to persuade their wives to sue them upon the assurance that the case would be privately heard in Judge Miller's chambers. It being common knowledge among lawyers and litigants alike that a decree is wellnigh automatic in uncontested cases, his chambers have become a mecca for divorce litigants. An instance known to have recently occurred forcefully illustrates our point. Finding Judge Miller out of his chambers, a certain lawyer carried his client before another judge. Upon inspecting the file this judge found that both the petition and answer, signed by the defendant, had both been filed the same day the case was presented to him for trial. This judge told the attorney that he would hear the case, but warned him in advance that he would deny the divorce on the grounds of collusion. The attorney promptly retrieved the file and departed.

"Judge Miller is equally lax in requiring sufficient proof in uncontested cases respecting jurisdiction and grounds for divorce. Seldom is any proof introduced to establish jurisdiction and much too little as to the grounds for divorce, with the result that uncontested cases are too speedily heard. On a recent Saturday morning a member of the bar observed the granting of 12 divorces in 17 minutes in Judge Miller's chambers. . . ." [Report abbreviated by Eds.]

THE ADMINISTRATION OF DIVORCE — GREAT BRITAIN

Testimony of Professor L. C. B. Gower of the University of London before the Royal Commission on Marriage and Divorce, Minutes of Evidence 18, 21, 23-26
(May 20, 1952)

[Professor Gower had submitted a memorandum advocating divorce by consent. At the start of our excerpt, he is being questioned by Mr. F. G. Lawrence, Q.C.]

184. . . . I think you told us that in your view it was quite easy for a couple to obtain a divorce by consent, even under our existing system? — Yes, indeed.

185. But that involves this, does it not, that they are not only deceiving the court, but deceiving their solicitor and their counsel? — Not really, you know, in a sense that is not quite true, necessarily. What happens is that the husband goes off, very often, and I imagine a discussion takes place beforehand — I am quite sure it does — and it is understood that the husband will supply the wife with evidence. The wife then receives a letter, normally drafted by the solicitor, in which the husband explains that he has met another woman who, he thinks, will make him happy, that they have slept together, and normally he encloses a hotel bill. The wife then goes to her solicitor; she certainly does not mention the discussions which have taken place, but otherwise it is quite above-board. I am not suggesting that people commit perjury in the Divorce Court, there is no need to; they are just asked a succession of leading questions, the evidence is produced, the evidence of the chamber maid is given, all is perfectly genuine, the only thing is that in fact the man has stayed at this hotel for a weekend with a woman, but it is highly unlikely that he committed adultery with her — indeed, he may have got her from an agency where he has agreed that he will not commit adultery with her.

186. I think we understand the process you mention, but the whole process is initiated upon the basis of agreement between the spouses that they wish for a divorce? — Yes.

187. You of course fully realise that there comes a stage when the petitioner has to swear an affidavit in support of the petition? — Yes, I do.

188. And one of the matters that have to be verified upon oath is the absence of collusion? — Yes. The trouble is that the borders between collusion and no collusion are very fine. If I and my wife have a quarrel and I say "It is no good, we had better part. I will go, and I shall send you evidence upon which, if you like, you can take a divorce," which I think is the normal sort of conversation, in law I do not think that is collusion. There is no definite agreement. I think my wife in those circumstances would be perfectly entitled to swear that the petition was not collusive. But it is so difficult to know where to draw the line.

189. Would you take the view that in those circumstances there was a divorce by consent? — Yes, frankly, and in reality, it is a divorce by consent, surely.

190. I take it that what you mean is that if the parties could go to the judge and ask for a divorce the husband would not have to go off and commit adultery with some woman with whom he otherwise would probably not commit it? — Yes, and indeed he probably does not commit it at all, he merely, as I say, goes to the hotel, and produces the hotel bill. I do not know which is worse, whether it is worse to commit adultery with someone with whom you would not otherwise commit it, or to pretend to commit adultery in order that your wife might persuade the court that you have committed it.

191. In your view as a practising solicitor, does the fact that the oath has to be taken that there is no collusion operate as a deterrent to collusive petitions? — Frankly, I should have thought that it acts as a very small deterrent, because, as I say, of the difficulty of knowing where to draw the line between collusion and no collusion. Every solicitor explains most carefully the meaning of it, but [it is difficult to decide] whether there is in law an agreement, when there is unquestionably a meeting of the minds, in the sense that both parties understand that there will be a divorce, which is I think the normal position at the moment . . . .

197. (*Mr. Mace*): Have you any information that you could give us, either in public or in private, of the names, addresses, cases, where you say that evidence has been manufactured? — I do not see how I could possibly do that. How can I? I am a solicitor, I cannot possibly do so. In so far as I have any actual knowledge, it is not what I am at liberty to reveal, even to this Commission, and, as I say, the trouble is that solicitors only know when they are acting for the respondent in an undefended divorce; then they frequently know a great deal but it does not matter that they should know, then. I know of cases, that I can assure you, but I do not see how I can possibly tell them to you, much as I should like to.

198. (*Mr. Maddocks*): Are you quite emphatic that today there is an abuse, and a widespread abuse, in the Divorce Court? — Yes. . . .

200. Did I hear you aright when you said that in the case which you visualise the letter is usually written by the husband's solicitor? — I did say that, Sir.

201. Seriously? — Seriously, very seriously.

202. Do you happen to be a Commissioner of Oaths? — I do not.

203. Thank you. — May I go back on that question? I do not quite follow my friend's question. If a client comes to me and says: "I want to give my wife evidence for a divorce, what do I do?," I say to him, and in my view this is perfectly proper: "When the offence has been committed you should then write a letter on the following lines to your wife." I have done that many times, and I know thousands of solicitors who have done likewise, and if you go to the Divorce Court you will hear these letters being read out. . . .

241. (*Mr. Justice Pearce*): I gather that you think genuine divorce cases are rare? — No, I would not go as far as that. I think that among the so-called upper classes, if I may use that word, although there often is a genuine matrimonial offence, probably very often it is not that genuine one on which the petition is based. There seems to be an extraordinary idea that if a man wants to marry someone after getting a divorce he should not drag her through the Divorce Court, but that it is better to obtain some other lady and allow her to be the woman named or the woman unnamed. . . .

244. I want you to see the point of what I am asking you. You have talked about the whole thing being a farce. Of course, if people were merely pretending to commit matrimonial offences, that would be so. I want to know whether you are saying that in fact there are a large number of people who arrange to commit a matrimonial offence and are then divorced for that offence? — There are certainly a lot of such cases, but there are a substantial proportion of cases where no matrimonial offence has been committed at all. The average London solicitor, I would say, dealing mainly with the non-legal aid type of case, meets a great many of those.

245. Your experience is what I want. — Yes, I have experience of both, I think. You see, I see the other side, I still sit on the certifying committee of the Legal Aid Scheme, and there we deal mainly with matrimonial applications. The impression I get there, so far as one can judge from the mere paper work one sees, is that the proportion of bogus cases, if I may call them that, is considerably lower than it is among the wealthier people.

246. In point of fact, the great bulk of divorce cases are of course of poorer people, because there are more of them, and those cases, you would agree, would you not, are generally cases where somebody has been genuinely deserted, or where one spouse has simply set up an establishment with someone else? — Generally, yes — by no means universally, but generally.

247. And that leaves a small number of divorces in respect of the well-to-do where you think that a matrimonial offence has been committed but the name of the lady is concealed? — No, I think that in some of those cases a matrimonial offence has been committed but the name of the lady is concealed. In a substantial proportion of cases no matrimonial offence has been committed at all.

248. And is it your view that the solicitor helps such a case forward? — No, if the solicitor knows that for a fact he does not help, but he does not know.

249. If a solicitor knows that or suspects it, would he consider it his duty, if he is a good solicitor, not to take any further part in the case? — Yes, in my view if a solicitor knew that for a fact, and was acting for the petitioner, he would take no further part in it — I should not.

250. So you are speaking, are you, of cases in which you have refused to go on? — No, a solicitor meets divorce cases partly when he is acting for the petitioner and partly when he is acting for the respondent. My experience of acting for respondents in undefended divorce cases has been that in a fair proportion of them the respondent has never committed a matrimonial offence at all. From that I deduce that the situation must in fact be much the same in those cases where I am acting for the petitioner but it is not for me to refuse cases merely because I am not satisfied that the other side has committed the offence which he pretends to have committed. That is for the judge; it is not for me to decide, I am not to set up my judgment.

251. I thought you were talking of cases where the husband's solicitor, say, drafts a letter. Would you expect a solicitor to do that if he knew that the thing was bogus, as you call it? — As I have said, what happens, in my experience, is that the husband comes along and says: "Look, I hope my wife will divorce me, what is the best way of supplying her with the necessary evidence?" To him I say: "What usually happens is that you take a lady along to a hotel, book a double room, make sure that the chamber maid recognises you — it is quite useful to upset a cup of coffee, or something like that, to draw her attention to you — and then write your wife a letter on the following lines, enclosing the hotel bill."

252. I do not think that is quite the answer to my question, which was whether the solicitor who knows it is bogus is content to go on acting in the case? — If the solicitor knows for a fact that it is bogus, my view is that he should not continue to act.

253. (*Chairman*): That puzzles me. There are two things that puzzle me in your answer to Mr. Justice Pearce. The first thing is, if a solicitor does not act when he knows there is good reason to suspect a case is bogus, how can you say there are thousands of bogus cases every year? — From my experience of acting for the respondents in similar cases, I am quite satisfied that in those cases, where I was acting for the respondent, the thing was completely bogus.

254. And, being satisfied with that, you acted for the respondent? — Certainly. . . .

274. (*Lord Keith*): I would like to ask a supplementary question: what you have been saying about dishonest divorce relates, I understand, to the pretence of adultery, is that right? — Not only adultery, there is also the pretence of desertion.

275. Yes, that is what I was really coming to. I may be on uncertain ground here. So far as desertion in English law is concerned, is it enough that the separation commenced against the will of one of the spouses, or

must it continue throughout the whole three years? — It must continue throughout the whole three years.

276. Against the will of one of the spouses? — Yes.

277. Then, when the spouse who is suing for divorce on the ground of desertion is giving evidence, is that spouse asked: "Were you willing throughout the three years to have your husband back if he were prepared to come back?"? — I think that I am right in saying he is not formally asked that question. The judge may happen to ask it. . . .

281. (*Lord Keith*): Your view is that a dishonest divorce may be obtained in desertion cases by the spouse who is claiming divorce putting forward a case that he or she has throughout been anxious for the other spouse to come back? — Yes.

282. And in some cases you think that that might not be the honest view of the spouse? — I am absolutely certain of it.

283. (*Chairman*): Did you give your example? — The example was this. When I was not in practice as a solicitor I was asked by a lady friend to give her some advice about divorce. She and her husband had been separated for a number of years. She showed me all the correspondence. It was perfectly clear to me that there was no desertion, they had obviously drifted apart. However, I said to her, "If you like to come back to-morrow I will try to give you a form of letter which I suggest you might write to your husband; that may do some good." I took some pains to prepare a letter, and I said, "Now, if you send this letter to your husband, and after a month or two there is no reply, I should then go to a solicitor and you may get a divorce." I gave her the form of letter which, with some misgivings, she wrote to her husband. I understand that a few months later she went to her solicitor. The solicitor went through all the correspondence and said, "There is no hope here." Then he came to this particular letter, and he said, "This puts an entirely different complexion on it, I think we might get a divorce on the basis of three years' desertion in view of this letter." In point of fact that lady was divorced on the grounds of desertion a few months later. Without the letter there would have been no divorce. As a result of the letter the court was satisfied that there had been desertion for the past three years.

284. In other words the lady, with your assistance, successfully deceived the court, is that right? — I suppose that is what it comes to. . . .

291. (*Mr. Mace*): I am a solicitor, and it is from a solicitor's point of view that I want to ask a supplementary question. Who comes to see you to ask you how to get a divorce, the petitioner or the respondent? — The respondent. The husband, for example, comes to see me and says, "I want to give my wife evidence upon which she can divorce me."

292. And would you feel that you were acting professionally if you entered an answer to that petition? — I should not enter an answer.

293. Not in respect of alimony? — What you are suggesting is that if I have given a man this letter to write I ought not any longer to act for him if he wishes to defend on the issue of maintenance.

294. I am making no suggestions at all. I want to know what your

views are as to your own professional conduct, because it will affect the general bearing of your evidence. — Yes.

295. If you have advised a man, rightly or wrongly, how to go about giving the evidence upon which his wife could launch a petition, and you have reason to believe that he is not going to commit a matrimonial offence or that he is doing so with the knowledge of his wife, do you think it professionally proper to put in an answer to that petition on the question of maintenance? — Yes, I think it perfectly proper.

296. If a petitioner comes to you and you see from the documents elements of this practice which you allege exists, would you make any enquiries before you took up the case? — Certainly. I should point out to the petitioner that she has to swear that there has been no collusion, and I should tell her what that meant, but belief in the commission of the matrimonial offence is not a thing which is any concern of either her or me.

297. You have said that this is a practice? — Yes, indeed. . . .

301. (*Mr. Maddocks*): Is it a fact that you have no particular firms of solicitors in mind when you make this accusation against London solicitors? — I do not regard it as an accusation at all. The unfortunate London solicitors are doing their best to make this absurd system work in as civilised a fashion as possible. We are the victims, and that is why I have come along today, because we are one of the worst sufferers of the present system. . . .

303. (*Mr. Young*): I want to get the English law of collusion a little more clearly in my mind. If a client comes to you and says, "I am away from my wife and I want to get a divorce; how do I go about giving her the evidence?" is there anything wrong in English law in your telling him that the way to do it is to go away and commit adultery and send her the hotel bill, and then hope for the best? — In my view, there is nothing wrong at all, but various people round this board seem to think that it is very wrong. In my view, it is not legally wrong. I think it is thoroughly objectionable that we should have to do it, but we certainly do do it and in my view it is perfectly proper professional etiquette. . . .

309. (*Mr. Lawrence*): If you knew that husband and wife had talked it over beforehand, and that the wife was expecting the hotel bill, and had agreed if she got it to institute divorce proceedings, the whole aspect of the matter would be different, would it not? — The whole aspect of the matter would be different.

310. Is it the duty of a reputable solicitor when he is asked by a client the question that you have postulated to go further and enquire whether there had been any such prior agreement? — In my view, the most one can be expected to do is to advise that there must not be any form of agreement, and that there will not be any divorce if there is and it is found out. . . .

In re BACKES
16 N.J. 430, 109 A.2d 273 (1954)

BRENNAN, J. The respondent is charged with a willful and knowing attempt to perpetrate a fraud upon the courts of this State in the initiation and conduct of a divorce action on behalf of one Earlin Dillard.

Dillard was living with one Lillian Dillard in 1946 when respondent sold Dillard a house in Vauxhall, Union County, through a corporation, Orange Land Company, solely owned by respondent. A purchase money mortgage for $4000 was taken by respondent in the name of the Company. Seven years later, in 1953, respondent, through the corporation, helped Dillard finance the purchase of abutting lots on each side of the house. Both the mortgage and the deed to the lots described Lillian Dillard as the wife of Dillard.

A few months after that purchase Dillard revealed to respondent that he had married Lillian in 1933 although not divorced from Viola whom he had married in 1922 in Virginia and from whom he separated in 1926. Dillard professed that he had married Lillian after a lapse of more than seven years following his separation from Viola because he had heard that Viola had been declared legally dead. Dillard gave respondent the address of a daughter of his marriage with Viola and respondent wrote to the daughter and learned from her that Viola was alive and living in New York City. Dillard shortly thereafter retained respondent to secure a divorce from Viola and paid him a fee of $350. He told respondent that he wanted the divorce so that Viola on his death could not "have anything belonging to me, insurance or nothing," and the respondent told him "he thought he could get it."

Respondent filed a divorce complaint, making no mention of Dillard's marriage to Lillian and charging Viola with desertion. Respondent entertained the hope that Viola would not contest the action. That hope was revealed in a letter he wrote Viola forwarding her a copy of the summons and complaint and requesting an acknowledgment of service. He stated in the letter:

> "Earlin Dillard has filed suit against you for divorce on the ground of desertion . . . *I am sure that you will agree with me, that after all these years, it is the proper thing to do.* . . . In order to facilitate matters, I would greatly appreciate it if you would acknowledge service . . . . If you will kindly do this it will avoid the necessity of my having to publish the same in the paper." [Emphasis supplied by court.]

Respondent's hope was not realized. Viola retained counsel who filed an answer pleading the defense of Dillard's adultery with Lillian, and a counterclaim for a divorce on that ground, asking alimony.

Respondent thought that Viola might still be discouraged. He reasoned, he says, that she was defending only to get her hands on some of

Dillard's property. He testified at the hearing before the Ethics and Grievance Committee:

> "I knew Viola Dillard was after an interest in the property and I wanted to impress upon the attorney representing the defendant that he had very little interest in the property, that there was a $4000 mortgage on it. I thought that would take the wind out of their sails. I knew the only interest they had in the suit was to see what they could get out of it."

The fact was, as he admitted in his testimony, "There was very little due" on the mortgage because of payments that Dillard had regularly made thereon over six and one-half years. Pursuing his strategy, however, he incorporated in the answer to Viola's counterclaim the wholly frivolous and untrue allegation that

> "The reason for his [Dillard's] instituting this suit for divorce was for the purpose of clearing the title of said property herein mentioned, at the behest of the Orange Land Co., who holds a certain purchase money mortgage on the said property in the amount of $4000.00."

Also in obvious pursuit of the same objective, he refrained in answering the counterclaim from suggesting a defense to the claim of recrimination by reason of the alleged good faith of Dillard in marrying Lillian in the honest belief that Viola had been declared legally dead. He chose the course which would avoid the necessity of spreading the true facts upon the record by equivocal responses to the counterclaim's allegations that "Plaintiff committed adultery with a woman whose first name is . . . Lillian," and "Plaintiff and co-respondent went through a pretended ceremony of marriage and . . . have been cohabiting as husband and wife." These were answered with the statements, "Plaintiff denies that he committed adultery with a woman whose first name is Lillian" and "denies that he and co-respondent went through a pretended ceremony of marriage."

But the hoped-for result did not materialize. Viola's attorney propounded interrogatories, answers to which as to Dillard's relations with Lillian forced the response that "Plaintiff believing his wife was dead married Lillian Dillard in New York." Thereupon a motion was made on Viola's behalf to dismiss Dillard's complaint as a "fraud upon the court" and to strike the frivolous allegation that Dillard's action was filed to clear the title to the property. Respondent filed no affidavits in opposition to the motion but at the oral argument contended that Dillard had married Lillian in good faith believing Viola had been declared legally dead. When the trial judge found no merit in that position respondent says he felt, "All right, I could not do anything about it." Such is the reason given for his assent as to form to the order dismissing the complaint, which order recites that plaintiff had "consented to the entry of an order" granting applications "(1) to dismiss plaintiff's complaint for divorce on the ground the same was filed in fraud of the court" and "(2) to strike that part of paragraph 5 of plaintiff's answer to counterclaim asserting that his reason for filing his complaint for divorce was to clear the title to the property."

The law regards divorce actions as imposing special responsibilities upon the court and attorneys as officers of the court. This is because in every suit for divorce the State is in fact if not in name a third party having a substantial interest. The public is represented by the conscience of the court, Duerner v. Duerner, 142 N.J. Eq. 759 (E. & A. 1948), and "The law regards these actions which tend to disrupt the marriage status with regret — certainly it does not encourage them." Shaffer v. Shaffer, 129 N.J. Eq. 42, 44 (E. & A. 1941).

Our rules of court governing matrimonial actions, R.R. 4:93 to R.R. 4:98, cast special burdens upon attorneys in the conduct of such actions, in purposeful reflection of the deep concern for the maintenance of the integrity of such proceedings to avert disservice to the public interest. The rules recognize that protection of the State's interest in particular cases necessarily lies with the attorneys in the first instance because of their superior knowledge of facts made known to the court ordinarily through their representations. It is implicit in our scheme of things that the lawyer who endeavors deliberately to prevent the revelation of facts which, revealed, may be destructive of his client's right to secure a divorce under our laws is faithless to his trust as an officer of the court to conserve and protect the state's interest and is deserving of severest censure.

It is argued on respondent's behalf that lawyers, even when aware of facts which, disclosed, would defeat the suit, cannot be and are not held to a duty to refrain from prosecuting an action for divorce or to anticipate a defense in pleadings filed on behalf of a client in the divorce suit. [Citations omitted.] It is further argued that at all events respondent might reasonably and honestly have believed that Viola's defense of recrimination could not be sustained if there was a showing that Dillard married Lillian under the honest belief that Viola had been declared legally dead and therefore that, the form of the denials in the answer to the counterclaim was entirely proper in the circumstances.

We have no reason to deal with these arguments as they are not germane to this case. From the outset, starting with the thinly veiled invitation to collusion contained in his letter to Viola, respondent, by his own admission, strove to prevent or discourage a defense of the action by Viola, and as a necessary and integral part of that plan refrained as long as it was within his power to do so from putting upon the record the facts of Dillard's relations with Lillian. That was not mere strategy in the conduct of the litigation, designed to put forward his best efforts in his client's behalf. His conduct can only be characterized as intentionally calculated to obtain a divorce for Dillard whatever the merit or lack of merit in Viola's defense of recrimination. That was conduct in flagrant disregard of his duty as an officer of the court not intentionally to frustrate, but, if anything, to aid, the court in the preservation of the integrity of divorce proceedings in the furtherance of the state's interest. Moreover, his inclusion of the frivolous and untrue defense to the counterclaim that Dillard wanted the divorce only to clear title to property is itself a ground for disciplinary action.　That was done, by his own admission, with knowledge of its lack of merit and truth and solely to discourage further resistance by Viola and her attorney to Dillard's suit, and thus was patently a willful violation of R.R. 4:11 which by its express terms subjects "to appropriate disciplinary action" an attorney who willfully violates that rule by filing a pleading not consistent with the representations read into his signature, "that to the best of his knowledge, information, and belief there is good ground to support it; and that it is not interposed for delay."　A willful violation of that rule, without more, is a fraud upon the court.

We thus cannot agree with respondent's contention and the finding of the Ethics and Grievance Committee that, at most, respondent's "manner of handling the matrimonial matter was stupid and incompetent, ..."　The majority of the court, the Chief Justice and Justices Oliphant, Wachenfeld, Burling and Brennan, find him guilty as charged of fraud upon the court in his willful violation of R.R. 4:11 and in the other particulars mentioned, contrary to Canons 15, 29, 30, 31, 32 and 41 of the Canons of Professional Ethics.

HEHER, J. (concurring in part).　The Essex County Ethics and Grievance Committee found that respondent's "manner of handling the matrimonial matter was stupid and incompetent," but not fraudulent.　There was a division of opinion "as to whether such stupidity and incompetence . . . were tantamount to unethical or unprofessional conduct"; and the Committee "resolved the doubt" in respondent's favor, "and determined that the charges which it preferred against him be dismissed." . . .

The respondent hitherto has borne a good reputation.　His professional conduct has been without blemish, so far as appears.　It would seem that under all the circumstances the suspension of respondent from the practice of law for a period of one year, and until the further order of the court, would constitute adequate discipline.

MR. JUSTICE JACOBS joins in this opinion.

For suspension for one year — Justices HEHER, WACHENFELD, BURLING and JACOBS — 4.

For disbarment — Chief Justice VANDERBILT, and Justices OLIPHANT and BRENNAN — 3.

NOTE

1. Compare In re Goodrich, 111 Vt. 156, 11 A.2d 325 (1940).　In preparing a libel for divorce on behalf of his client, attorney Goodrich had her swear to the allegation "That during said coverture the said libellant on her part has faithfully kept the marriage covenant and performed all the duties appertaining thereto."　111 Vt. at 157, 11 A.2d at 325.　The attorney had previously represented the same client when she had been convicted of adultery and sentenced to prison.　In the divorce action the

libellee entered an appearance by attorney but did not defend, and a divorce was granted. When the prior adultery conviction came to the attention of the court, the divorce was stricken and the attorney summoned for his participation in presenting the libel. In Vermont, it "has long been the law of this state that uncondoned adultery on the part of a libellant is a bar to the granting of a divorce brought on any ground." 111 Vt. at 159, 11 A.2d at 326. Accepting as mitigation the attorney's claim that he was ignorant of this rule, the court suspended him from practice for one year.

2. Especially in recent years there are very few cases such as Backes and Goodrich reporting disciplinary action against lawyers because of their conduct in matrimonial cases. New Jersey's enforcement appears to be unusual (see, in addition to Backes, Staedler v. Staedler, page 756 infra), and in that state there appear to have been no such cases since the death of Chief Justice Vanderbilt in 1957. Disciplinary action sometimes arises as a by-product of an investigation of publicized extreme abuses, as in Chattanooga, page 694 supra, or in Alabama, page 740 infra. In most reported decisions the lawyer's misconduct in the divorce case is linked with other serious derelictions of duty, e.g., In re Reinmiller, 213 Ore. 680, 325 P.2d 773 (1958), or involves participation in invalid proceedings concerning nonresidents, e.g., Louisville Bar Assn. v. Walker, 298 Ky. 877, 183 S.W.2d 26 (1944) (attorney disbarred for operating "divorce mill" for nonresidents).

DRINKER, PROBLEMS OF PROFESSIONAL ETHICS IN MATRIMONIAL LITIGATION
66 Harvard Law Review 443, 447-454 (1953)

The Manufacture of a Cause of Action. — No one would have any doubt of the gross impropriety of any participation by a lawyer in the hiring on behalf of one spouse of a co-respondent to seduce the other in order to give ground for a divorce. This, while not perhaps "collusion" in that there is no cooperation between the parties, would doubtless constitute a violation of the criminal code. There is observable no relaxation in its availability as a defense.

A somewhat different problem exists where the lawyer does not participate in the creation of a ground of divorce, such as adultery, but rather aids in the fabrication of evidence which makes such a ground appear to exist. Such are the "hotel divorces," based on the principle that intercourse will be presumed from apparently uninhibited opportunity. They have been or are most prevalent in jurisdictions like England and New York where adultery was or is the sole ground for divorce.

The temptation to a lawyer to countenance such a scheme is enhanced by its apparent success despite the fact that in many cases the court is probably not actually deceived, and by the further fact that the time consumed and the expense to the client, including the disservice fee of the familiar blonde in black silk pajamas, is so much less than that of a seven-week trip to Reno.

However, irrespective of a lawyer's honest belief in the desirability of

a relaxation of the restrictions on divorce, the clandestine participation
in such a shabby scheme is obviously unworthy of an honorable member
of the bar and derogatory of the dignity of the profession which it is the
lawyer's constant duty to uphold and maintain.[31]

Deliberately to Neglect to Allege or Prove a Defense. — Examples of
such cases are where a "deserted" spouse refrains from showing his entire satisfaction with the situation, or where the "deserting" spouse neglects to prove a rejected offer to return.   In cases of this type it is of
course apparent that both the parties want a divorce.   Any semblance
of a contest must of necessity be a mere fiction.   In an ordinary law suit
there is no obligation on the part of a party or his lawyer to set up what
might be a valid defense.   It is wholly proper to bring a suit which would
be barred by limitations or under the Statute of Frauds; nor is there any
obligation on the part of defendant's counsel to set up these defenses if
his client does not desire this.   Does the interest of the state in matrimonial status place divorce cases in a different category and make it incumbent on the lawyers on both sides, as officers of the court, to have no part
in a divorce case in which, if all the facts appeared, the divorce would
have to be denied?   Doubtless some lawyers may take this position.   The
great majority, however, would feel, it is believed, that in the year 1953,
they were not bound to do more than to see to it that no false or misleading testimony was offered on behalf of their clients.   Where neither
the master, the proctor, nor the court brings up the question and no
actual misstatement on behalf of their client is necessary, most lawyers
would, it is believed, allow the decree to be signed, on the theory that
it is not the function of a lawyer to prove the other side's case or to protect the state's supposed interest in preserving the matrimonial status of
spouses both of whom want a divorce.

A similar case is the concealment by one suing for divorce on the
ground of adultery of the fact that his client, the plaintiff, was also guilty
of adultery.   After a decision by the New York Appellate Division[32]
holding that plaintiff's adultery was by way of defense only, the Ethics
Committees[33] of the New York City and County Bar Associations held it
proper for a lawyer to accept employment to secure a divorce on the
ground of adultery though knowing that his client had also committed
adultery.[34]

A distinction might be drawn between cases in which defendant fails

[31] See Canon of Professional Ethics No. 29, 62 A.B.A. Rep. 1115 (1937).   In
Matter of Gale, 75 N.Y. 526 (1879), a New York lawyer (who himself played
the part of the "co-respondent") was disbarred for participating in such a
conspiracy, involving as it did the fabrication of a serious statutory crime.

[32] Thompson v. Thompson, 127 App. Div. 296, 111 N.Y. Supp. 426 (2d
Dep't 1908).

[33] The Committees on Professional Ethics of the Association of the Bar of
the City of New York and of the New York County Lawyers Association
render numbered opinions in answer to questions.   These opinions (for the
most part undated) are referred to throughout this article as in the following
footnote.   Complete copies are on file in the Bar Association Library, 42 W.
44th St., New York, N.Y.

[34] N.Y. City Nos. 726, 951; N.Y. County No. 365 (overruling N.Y. County
No. 106).

to interpose a possible defense solely because of a desire to have the divorce granted, and those in which this is the price of a satisfactory financial settlement. If, however, the settlement is fair and the defendant is properly advised by unbiased counsel, this factor would not seem to alter the problem.

The New York Committees have differed and have not, it is believed, been always consistent as to the propriety of an agreement by the lawyer for the defendant in a divorce case, in consideration of a satisfactory and reasonable settlement, not to make a defense. While in several cases they have flatly held that a lawyer should not countenance an agreement not to defend a matrimonial action, as "against public policy" of that state,[35] in other cases they have sanctioned such agreements "in the absence of fraud or collusion" or if the lawyer is "satisfied of his client's good faith and of the absence of collusion." In the opinions approving such agreements, the Committees have insisted that the agreement be disclosed to the court,[36] in order that the court may be "put on notice of all circumstances and make such inquiry as those circumstances may suggest — concerning, for example, the good faith of the parties, the absence of collusion, the credibility of the witnesses and the weight that should be given to the evidence."

The responsibility for protecting the supposed interest of the state is thus disclaimed by the lawyer and thrown on the court. For a lawyer who honestly believes that the state's interest in the matrimonial status of its citizens is a conception which is outmoded or at least well on the way out, this would not seem to be an unreasonable position.

Furnishing Evidence of Actual Facts Constituting Ground for a Divorce. — A distinction may well be drawn between conniving in or manufacturing facts constituting a ground for divorce, and facilitating the proof of acts constituting such grounds after they have unquestionably occurred. The latter would also appear to be even less open to question than the withholding of facts constituting a defense. The objective of the proceedings being the production of all pertinent evidence, it is difficult to see how it can be considered improper to further this, unless the lawsuit be considered a mere game. Even so, it is "cricket" to give up a pawn in order to take a queen, or to hit a long sacrifice fly to score a run. Realistically, the objective of the lawyer for a defendant who wants to be divorced is not to prevent the divorce, but to achieve it. This he must of course do only by legitimate means; but disclosure of the truth can hardly be considered otherwise. The danger, however, in sanctioning the production of vital evidence by the defendant of his own fault, is that it may be a temptation to fraud or perjury, particularly where such production is an essential part of an agreement by the producing party to make substantial and satisfactory provision in the event that a divorce is granted.

[35] N.Y. County No. 205; see also Sheehan v. Sheehan, 77 N.J. Eq. 411, 420, 77 Atl. 1063, 1066 (Ch. 1910).

[36] E.g., N.Y. County Nos. 192, 54; cf. N.Y. County No. 230; N.Y. City Nos. 139, 173.

Here again the decisions of the Ethics Committees have not on their face been entirely consistent. The New York County Committee has said flatly that a lawyer should not countenance a bargain to obtain necessary testimony in a divorce suit, this being "against public policy." In another opinion, however, a majority of the County Committee held it not improper for the wife's lawyer to accept the husband's agreement to furnish, in consideration of a satisfactory money settlement, witnesses to flagrant acts by him, the agreement being "fully disclosed to the court" and the parties being told that the court might not agree. In the case last cited, the opinion of the majority made it a point to say that "the attorney in a divorce case should regard with disfavor any offer by the adverse party to stipulate to furnish witnesses to the past offense charged in consideration of stipulations as to alimony, release of dower, etc. (see Train vs. Davidson, 20 App. Div. 577)." [37]

In view of the apparent differences of opinion on the part of the distinguished and experienced lawyers constituting these two Committees, what, then, may we conclude to be the proper course for the lawyer in such cases? As a practical matter it is believed that the propriety of the lawyer's conduct in sanctioning an arrangement for procuring essential testimony from the other side depends largely on the personalities of the litigants and the relations, past and present, between them. Where they and their lawyers are apparently reliable people, the offense asserted as ground for the divorce clear, flagrant, and indefensible, the proposed settlement between the parties fair and reasonable, and the stipulated cooperation by the defendant merely to eliminate nuisance value, the disclosure of all the facts to the court affords adequate protection against fraudulent "collusion." Where, however, the situation is such as to indicate the possibility that purchased evidence may be manufactured, the

---

[37] In a case where the husband gave the wife the names of witnesses to his adultery, which antedated her engaging of counsel, the Disbarment Committee of the Supreme Court of Louisiana advised counsel that it was proper to use such evidence, saying:
The fact that the act of the husband was committed long prior to the employment of counsel, precludes the idea of collusion on the part of either. What the law reprobates is consent divorces and any collusion between the principals or their attorneys to obtain them. This proceeds from considerations of public policy too obvious to mention. Any offer of assistance from opposing counsel in a divorce case is ordinarily to be regarded with disfavor. If the offer of assistance is conditioned on a consideration such as to limit the wife's right to alimony or to relinquish other valuable property interests, the situation is reduced to one of barter and sale and should not be countenanced. Where, however, the assistance offered has to do with giving names of witnesses to an act committed by the husband, as to which the wife neither condoned nor consented, and is not conditioned on the relinquishment of any of the wife's rights, the Committee thinks the attorneys, if satisfied with the wife's good faith, may proceed to submit the evidence; provided, the agreement so to do be in writing and be expressly made subject to the approval of the Court, and that the Court be fully informed of all the facts and circumstances at or before the trial, and the parties be advised that the Court may decline to confirm it.
4 Tulane L. Rev. 226, 228-29 (1930). This decision was rendered in 1930. It would seem questionable that all the qualifications represent the current consensus.

lawyer should resolve the doubt by declining to have any part in the arrangement. While the decisions by the two New York Committees are on their face difficult to reconcile, as a practical matter they may well have been influenced by the above considerations.

Arrangements for Defendant's Lawyer to be Designated by Plaintiff or by Plaintiff's Lawyer. — The American Bar Association, the Michigan, and the two New York Committees have held that the lawyer for one spouse should not recommend a lawyer for the other, or prepare the pleadings or papers or testimony for the other, or act for or give legal advice to the other in any respect, and that disclosure to the court, even before the decree, would not make this proper. . . .

Canon 6 . . . forbids the representation of "conflicting interests except by express consent of all concerned, given after a full disclosure of the facts." Where the public interest is involved, it has been held that the consent of the immediate parties is insufficient.

Apparently the decisions which would insulate the parties and their respective lawyers completely from one another are based on the fiction that the interests of parties to a divorce suit are necessarily and always antagonistic to one another, and on the further assumption that this is essential to secure proper protection for the supposed interest of the state in preserving their marital status. It would, however, seem very questionable as to whether such protection is needed in a clearly bona fide case, where it is clear that the wife honestly wants the divorce and is not coerced into it by an obviously dominant husband, where the allowance proposed by him is reasonable, and where the lawyer suggested to her by the husband or by his lawyer is thoroughly honest and reliable, has not theretofore represented the husband, and is therefore in a position to give the wife unbiased advice. It is manifest that such suggestion is but natural and occurs all the time in uncontested cases. To condemn it where it is openly disclosed would seem both futile and unnecessary.

Acceptance by Wife's Lawyer of Compensation from the Husband. — Where approved by the court it is not considered unethical or apparently as indicating "collusion" for the wife's lawyer to be paid by the husband. In fact, many divorce statutes provide for this, as well as for alimony. Where the relative affluence of the parties, the amount of the payment, and the other surrounding circumstances indicate the reasonableness of the arrangement, there would seem to be no impropriety in a bona fide agreement to this effect.

NOTE

How correct is Drinker's usage in referring to the restrictions of divorce law and jurisdiction as fictions? He was not the first to apply this label; compare Ulman, A Judge Takes the Stand 174-175 (1933):

> Should one suggest to a Maryland legislature that the time has come when legal recognition should be given to the fact that the best possible reason for granting a divorce is that both husband and wife

want it, that it is nonsensical to force such persons to pretend to have a bitter contest with one another, to call one another ugly names, and to titillate the public with a spicy story of scandal in the newspapers — should someone make this suggestion, no doubt he would be assailed as an enemy of the home and of religion, a dangerous radical fit only for instant deportation. Yet, though the forms of law remain essentially what they were in 1842, when they doubtless expressed the current social concepts, judicial administration of them has found a way to make them do what society wants them to do in 1932. A legal fiction, in the truth of which no one believes, the very existence of which some will deny, has taken the place of courageous modification of the letter of the law.

As a result, scientific investigators are able to report that in only two and one half per cent of all the divorce cases which go through the Maryland courts is there any actual contest over the granting of the decree. In the other ninety-seven cases out of every hundred, the court, by its decree of divorce, simply registers in legal form the fact that the parties have agreed to disagree. . . . Where, as in divorce litigation, legal theory is allowed to depart so widely from social practice, a hypocritical society may get the law it wants without putting itself on record as wanting it; but the price it pays is a weakened respect for its own law and the loss of moral fiber that always goes with self-deception.

B.   EVASIONARY DEVICES

PROBLEMS

1. When you arrive at your New York City office after an out-of-town trip, your secretary hands you the following letter from Donald Croft, adding that in response to the request in the last paragraph she has given the Crofts an appointment with you for that afternoon:

> Carol and I have finally reached the end of the road and want you to arrange the termination of our marriage. Carol hopes to take off for Italy in a few weeks for her annual long vacation, and we would like to get this matter settled as expeditiously as possible.
>
> In reality, of course, a divorce for us will only formalize what happened when we separated nearly two years ago. We both realize that our marriage was a mistake and that probably no one is particularly at fault. We just didn't get along together: things which are important to Carol irritate me, and vice versa. We have little basically in common, and we both feel we should be free while we are still young enough for another marriage. We want to be mature about this thing and settle it with a minimum of unpleasantness. We have agreed in a general way on the division of the property we have, and Carol has no interest in alimony. She has a good job and inde-

pendent income. Fortunately there are no children — Carol took care of that. I have always wanted children, but when we married, Carol told me that she didn't want to give up her job just then and that we would have to wait. I was always unable to change her mind, and I slowly came to realize she had never had any intention of ever having children.

I'll phone in a day or so to arrange a time in the near future when Carol and I can come in to talk with you.

You first met Croft, now in his middle thirties, through your general corporate practice when he took over his father's small business a number of years ago. His business has been very successful and has been a relatively easy and profitable client for you. You have also handled some personal matters for the Crofts, relating chiefly to taxation matters in connection with property inherited by Carol. Over the years you have come to know them socially as well as professionally; your wife is a member of the Board of Directors of the Settlement Art School where Carol teaches. Carol is also a talented sculptress. Both were born and raised in New York and, like you, love the big city.

2. Assume all the same facts as in Problem 1 except that the couple involved is Mr. and Mrs. Hudson, who live not in New York but in any state having a "typical" divorce law.

3. Suppose that your office were located in yet another state whose courts have not passed upon the validity of Mexican divorces and whose law interposes a one-year waiting period between an interlocutory and a final decree of divorce during which no remarriage can be contracted. Your clients are John and Martha Matson, both of whom want a quick divorce in order to facilitate their planned remarriages and whose problem is complicated because John is afraid that he has already gotten his future second wife pregnant. The Matsons come from very modest economic circumstances; John is a mechanic, and Martha is employed as a filing clerk. Like the Crofts in Problem 1, they have been separated for nearly two years for the same reasons and have the same attitude towards the termination of their status.

4. Assume the same jurisdiction and facts as Problem 3, except that your clients, Harold and Wilma Dorsey, are both unemployed and on relief, and you are employed by a legal aid agency.

(You will need to read through page 769 infra to handle this assignment.)

1. *Fraud, Deception, and Perjury*

WELS, NEW YORK: THE POOR MAN'S RENO
35 Cornell Law Quarterly 303 (1950)

In the sense that the grounds for divorce are severely limited, New York has the strictest divorce laws in the United States. New York courts can only grant a decree of divorce on the grounds of the defendant's adultery. . . .

To the lay mind divorce usually connotes any judicial action which dissolves a marriage. In that sense adultery is not the only available cause for divorce in New York, since the statutes permit marriages to be dissolved for other reasons. Thus, marriages may be annulled in New York where at the time of the marriage either party was under the age of consent, already married, an idiot or a lunatic, impotent, or otherwise lacked the capacity to enter into a binding marriage or agreement. Marriages may also be dissolved under New York law where the consent of one of the parties thereto was obtained by fraud, force, or duress. The distinction, of course, between such proceedings and divorce is that the court decree declaring the marriage annulled states that the marriage never validly existed, while the divorce decree pronounces that a marriage, once legally constituted, no longer exists. The effect of both, however, is precisely the same — it puts an end to a state of matrimony which is no longer desired. . . .

. . . On the surface, its retention of the ecclesiastical concept of awarding a divorce only for the cause of adultery lends New York law an apparent severity which it does not in fact possess, and has caused many critics to describe it as archaic. The acid test lies, however, not in statutory language but in the answer to the question of how difficult these laws have made it for New Yorkers to have their marriages dissolved. For those answers we must look not to the words of the statute themselves, but to the practices to which those words have given rise.

The present divorce statute was first enacted (substantially in its present form) in 1787. In establishing adultery at that time as the sole ground for divorce, the Legislature then intended to make divorce as difficult as possible for the purpose of preserving the family unit. For many years this result was attained, and the statute exercised a severe restraint upon divorce actions. Adultery, the only recognized cause for divorce, was a criminal offense which prosecutors could be counted upon to prosecute. In addition, it carried, when exposed, heavy social penalties. Social ostracism and extensive publicity were the lot of anyone upon whose brow a court of the State of New York placed the scarlet letter.

The twentieth century has brought with it, however, a profound change in the social and moral values of our community. In the judicial year ending June 30, 1947, some 7744 New Yorkers who were charged with adultery by their spouses in New York matrimonial actions did not defend themselves against the charge. Yet, except where the personalities involved were public figures or the evidence was particularly erotic or bizarre, few such cases were reported in the press. And, of course, not a single person in the state was criminally prosecuted for adultery by any of the sixty-four district attorneys. This is not because the District Attorneys are remiss in their duty. It is just that they are sufficiently sensitive to public opinion and public morals to know that the public does not sympathize with such prosecutions, and that convictions would be difficult to obtain. In our New York society of today, adultery is shrugged off as a commonplace affair which does not materially affect the social or community status of the persons involved.[38] . . .

The device which made it possible to transform New York into an easy divorce state, despite the severity of its divorce laws, and to establish there a divorce mill with the assistance of the bench and bar is the so-called undefended matrimonial calendar.

Our entire Anglo-American body of law is based on the theory that by cross-examination the truth will out and justice will be done. More than ninety per cent of all matrimonial actions in New York are uncontested. As a result, no one is present to test the testimony given by the

---

[38] In Schmidt v. United States, 177 F.(2d) 450, the petitioner appealed from an order of the United States District Court for the Southern District of New York denying his petition for naturalization on the ground that his admission that he had engaged in sexual intercourse with unmarried women established that he was not a person of good moral character. The Court of Appeals for the Second Circuit unanimously reversed the order of the District Court and granted the petition for naturalization. Chief Judge Learned Hand, writing the court's opinion, said: "It is true that in Estrin v. United States, 80 F.(2d) 105, we held that a single act of adultery, unexplained and unpalliated, was alone enough to prevent the alien's naturalization; but we refused to say whether under the "common standards of morality" there might not be "extenuating circumstances" for such a single lapse. In Petitions of Rudder et al., 159 F.(2d) 695, 698, the question arose as to what those circumstances might be. Each of several aliens had been living for years with a single woman in an adulterous union, which apparently had not been concupiscent. Either the alien or the woman had been unable, for one reason or another, to get a divorce. We admitted them all because we did not "believe that the present sentiment of the community views as morally reprehensible such faithful and long continued relationships under the circumstances here disclosed." . . .

. . . [I]t must be owned that the law upon the subject is not free from doubt. We do not see how we can get any help from outside. It would not be practicable — even if the parties had asked for it, which they did not — to conduct an inquiry as to what is the common conscience on the point. Even though we could take a poll, it would not be enough merely to count heads, without any appraisal of the voters. A majority of the votes of those in prisons and brothels, for instance, ought scarcely to outweigh the votes of accredited churchgoers. Nor can we see any reason to suppose that the opinions of clergymen would be a more reliable estimate than our own. The situation is one in which to proceed by any available method would not be more likely to satisfy the impalpable standard, deliberately chosen, than that we adopted in the foregoing cases: that is, to resort to our own conjecture, fallible as we recognize it to be. It is true that recent investigations have attempted to throw light upon the actual habits of men in the petitioner's position and they have disclosed — what few people would have doubted in any event — that his practice is far from uncommon; but it does not follow that on this point common practice may not have diverged as much from precept as it often does. We have answered in the negative the question whether an unmarried man must live completely celibate, or forfeit his claim to a "good moral character"; but, as we have said, those were cases of continuous, though adulterous, union. We have now to say whether it makes a critical difference that the alien's lapses are casual, concupiscent and promiscuous, though not adulterous. We do not believe that discussion will make our conclusion more persuasive; but, so far as we can divine anything so tenebrous and impalpable as the common conscience, these added features do not make a critical difference."

plaintiff's witnesses, and attorneys know that the prima facie case which they present will not be challenged either by the defendant or by someone representing the public interest.

Even the prima facie case which is presented is not required to be more than meagre in its quality or quantity. Essentially, all that is required is proof that the defendant was found in a room with a person of the opposite sex (who need not be identified beyond the positive fact that such person was *not* the husband or wife of the defendant), that both were found in a semi-undressed condition — and that is all. Under the New York law, as developed by the courts, the fact of adultery is customarily proved by circumstantial evidence of opportunity and inclination. As Mr. Justice Gaynor, speaking for the majority of the Appellate Division in Kerr v. Kerr said, seeking bedroom privacy was certainly strong evidence of inclination. And, he said, when a man and a woman who are not married are found together in a hotel bedroom, the courts will presume that the purpose of their visit was not "to say a paternoster." [39]

At least since 1907, that has been the judge-made law in New York. As disclosed by District Attorney Hogan of New York County in his recent exposé of divorce mills operating in Manhattan, the same unidentified woman served in many cases as the [corespondent]. In none of those cases was an act of adultery committed. In many she did not even undress, but merely arranged to be found in bed in the same room as the newly arrived defendant who had never seen her before, and presumably would never see her again. Yet the testimony of the persons who broke into the room by pre-arrangement and found her there with the defendant was sufficient, under the controlling decision of Kerr v. Kerr, to justify the New York courts to issue a decree of divorce. Not only sufficient, but where, as in the recent case of Slawinski v. Slawinski,[40] the justice at Special Term refused to grant a divorce on such evidence, he was reversed by the Appellate Division which inferentially held by its decision (without opinion) that such evidence required the court to make a finding of adultery and award a decree.

The facts in the Slawinski case are important only in that they are typical of the evidence which the Appellate Division today finds adequate for the granting of a divorce. In his opinion at Special Term refusing to confirm the referee's report, and dismissing the complaint, Mr. Justice Greenberg said:

> Plaintiff seeks a decree of divorce predicated on the testimony of one witness to the effect that on March 15, 1943, the female defendant occupied a room in his house and that he found her in bed with "her boy friend." The entire record on this pertinent issue is: "Q. During the year 1945 where did you live? A. 2501 Creston Avenue, Bronx. Q. Did the defendant, Rita Slawinski, have a room in your

[39] 134 App. Div. 141, 118 N.Y. Supp. 801 (2d Dep't 1909).
[40] 275 App. Div. 766 (1st Dep't 1949). The decision at special term appears in New York Law Journal January 3, 1949, p. 12, col. 1.

house? A. Yes, she did. Q. Can you recall the middle of January, 1943, what happened? A. On March 15, 1943, I woke up about five o'clock in the morning, and I had to walk to her room, and I found her and her boy friend in bed together. Q. Did you know him? A. I knew him for some time. Q. In what condition did you find them? A. I found them in bed together with their clothes on a chair. Q. Did you find how they were dressed? A. They were undressed. I seen their clothes on a chair there. They were undressed. Q. Was that man in bed at that time? A. He was in bed with her. Q. Was that man the plaintiff in this action? A. It was not." A recommendation that a decree should issue in favor of the plaintiff was made by the official referee on the basis of this testimony. This court finds the record woefully inadequate to justify a granting of relief to the plaintiff. In the first place the witness to the claimed act of adultery bears the same name as the plaintiff and there is no explanation what relationship, if any, is between the two parties. In the second place the witness did not indicate why he had "to walk to her room" at five o'clock in the morning. For all that appears from the record this witness walked into the room of the defendant where he had no right to be without knocking on the door and for no obvious reason. His entire testimony reeks with grave suspicion and indicates strongly that the facts were manufactured to suit plaintiff's objective. To countenance a divorce in such a situation would be to make a mockery of the law and to hold the courts up to ridicule and contempt. In such a situation the court obviously will not lend its assistance. . . .

Involving as they do only a question of fact (i.e., whether an act of adultery was committed by the defendant), such cases are customarily referred by the Supreme Court at Special Term to an Official Referee, normally a former judge who has reached the age of retirement. The Official Referees have followed the practice of disposing of these cases on a mass production basis. It is rare that the trial of a single case will take as long as fifteen minutes. Four witnesses are customarily heard by the court in each case — the plaintiff who testifies as to the marital status, the process server who has made service upon the defendant, and two persons who found the defendant and the co-respondent enjoying an opportunity and inclination for adultery. Such dignity as is normally expected in a court house is often dissipated by the handing of a card by the court clerk to the plaintiff's attorney. This card lists in order the questions which the court expects to be asked of the witnesses and which, if properly answered, will afford a basis for the award of a decree. If the attorney deviates from the pattern of questioning appearing on the card, he will normally be stopped by the Referee or the clerk, and cautioned to ask the questions, and only the questions appearing on the card. It is obvious from the attitude and comments of most Referees and court room attendants that they, together with the plaintiffs and their attorneys, are in on the big secret and are fully acquainted with the traffic that is indulged in before them.

Despite the ease with which divorces are granted from the undefended matrimonial calendar, many persons without the means of going to another state are reluctant to avail themselves of a New York divorce because of an unwillingness to have a judicial finding of adultery on their records. The New York courts have sought to be accommodating to such persons too, and have through this same uncontested matrimonial calendar been able to effect easy dissolutions of marriage without such findings. As noted supra, annulments of marriages can be granted by the New York courts on a showing that one of the parties to the marriage was fraudulently persuaded to enter the marriage state. Judge Desmond of the Court of Appeals has estimated that more than one hundred and fifty types of fraud have been judicially recognized by the Supreme Court as a basis for such annulments. These have covered a wide range, from a finding of fraud in a case where a husband was induced to marry by his wife's representation that spirits of the other world in which he believed had ordered their marriage to misrepresentation of status as an American citizen. In recent years, however, two bases for an annulment have been particularly recurrent and fashionable. One of these has been the defendant's strong representation before marriage that he or she desired a family and intended to have children. It has been a common occurrence for such an action to allege that it was only years after the marriage that the wife discovered that her husband had been using contraceptives throughout the marriage relation. And, oddly enough, there has been no dearth of witnesses to ante-nuptial conversations as to the parties' desire and intention to have children. . . .

Another recurrent state of facts which has been a common basis of actions for annulment in recent years has been an allegation, in cases where the parties were married in a civil ceremony, that the defendant had promised that this would be followed by a religious ceremony, and that, had it not been for this promise, the marriage would not have occurred. On such allegations, many annulments have been granted by our courts.

As each new type of fraud has been advanced, it has been at first accepted by the courts. As the bar has become acquainted with such acceptance and brought large numbers of actions grounded on such state of facts, the bench has tended to become jaundiced and to look at such actions with a certain amount of skepticism. At the appearance of such skepticism, the popularity of the particular type of fraud has dwindled and another has been developed to take its place. At the present moment, there has been a sudden increase in undefended matrimonial actions based on the Enoch Arden laws, and the New York Law Journal has been carrying almost daily advertisements directed to spouses allegedly absent for more than five years notifying them that such actions have been commenced. . . .

NOTE

An earlier investigation, based on Golluban's 1929 sample of 104 undefended divorce actions and 1275 consecutively filed undefended divorce actions in 1929-1933 collected by Jackson, noted as evidence of collusion in many cases that (1) in the great majority the corespondent was unnamed; (2) in most cases there was a close relationship between the defendant and witnesses for the complainant; (3) in many cases the period intervening between the alleged adultery and service of process was so short (sometimes the same day, often within three days) as to suggest a prearranged plan; and (4) there was a surprising state of undress of the defendant at the time the door was opened to permit the witness to enter. See Note, 36 Colum. L. Rev. 1121 (1936).

WELLS v. TALHAM
180 Wis. 654, 194 N.W. 36 (1923)

JONES, J. This is a suit to declare a marriage void on the grounds of fraud. The complaint alleged:

> "That plaintiff is seventy-eight years of age and a resident of Milwaukee county, Wisconsin; that defendant is upwards of sixty-four years of age and resides in Wakefield, Massachusetts.
>
> "That on the 7th day of February, 1921, at the city of Wakefield, Massachusetts, the plaintiff was in form married to the defendant, and that there is no issue of said marriage; that prior to and at the time of said marriage plaintiff was very infirm in physical health.
>
> "That at the time of and for many years prior to such marriage plaintiff was and still is a member of the Roman Catholic Church; that one of the canons or rules of said church prohibits the marriage of any member thereof to any person who had been divorced and whose divorced spouse is living, under penalty of excommunication from said church.
>
> "That defendant, prior to promising to marry the plaintiff and to her marriage to the plaintiff, knew the canon of the Roman Catholic Church above set forth, and knew that plaintiff was a member of said church, and knew that plaintiff would not have consented to marry the defendant had he known she was a divorced woman and that her divorced husband was living.
>
> "That defendant had been married previously to one Clemons and had been divorced from said Clemons prior to her marriage to plaintiff, and that said Clemons was living at the time plaintiff and defendant became engaged to marry and at the time of their marriage, and to the best of plaintiff's knowledge and belief is still living.
>
> "That for the purpose of inducing the plaintiff to consent to marry and to marry the defendant, the defendant falsely and fraudulently represented to him that she was a widow, that she would have the

marriage solemnized in the Roman Catholic Church after such ceremony had been solemnized in the Methodist Episcopal Church, well
knowing that such promise could not be carried out, and intending,
at the time she made such promise, not to carry it out . . . .

"That plaintiff would never have consented to marry the defendant
except for the false and fraudulent representations, promise, and
concealment made by the defendant, because at his advanced age and
in his weak bodily condition the consolations of his religion were
cherished by him in the highest degree.

"That shortly after the marriage of plaintiff and defendant the
plaintiff first learned that defendant was a divorced woman whose
divorced husband was living, and that plaintiff thereupon presented
the facts to the Roman Catholic priest of his parish and was advised
by said priest that said marriage would not be recognized as valid by
the Roman Catholic Church, and the plaintiff must repudiate said
marriage and separate from the defendant or suffer excommunication from the Roman Catholic Church; that thereupon plaintiff
separated from defendant and has not since cohabited with her."
[Court's quotation abbreviated by Eds.]

Plaintiff demanded judgment "that said marriage between plaintiff
and defendant be annulled and declared void, and for the costs of this
action." . . .

The contract of marriage was made in Massachusetts, and it seems
to be agreed by counsel that the validity of the marriage is to be governed by the law of that state and that there is no material difference in
the law of the two jurisdictions.

There is no doubt that under our statute a marriage may be annulled
for fraud, force, or coercion unless the marriage has been confirmed by
the acts of the injured party. Sub. (4), sec. 2351, Stats. The problem
consists in determining what acts or representations amount to fraud
which may authorize the courts to decree the annulment.

In England the law on this subject has long been well settled. In a
case decided in 1818 the court used the following language:

"The strongest case you could establish of the most deliberate
plot, leading to a marriage the most unseemly in all disproportions
of rank, of fortune, of habits of life, and even of age itself, would not
enable this court to release him from chains which, though forged by
others, he had riveted on himself. If he is capable of consent and
has consented, the law does not ask how the consent has been induced." Sullivan v. Sullivan, 2 Hagg. Cons. Rep. 238, 248.

In somewhat less emphatic language it was said in 1897:

"The result is that the English law of the validity of marriage is
clearly defined. There must be the voluntary consent of both parties. There must be compliance with the legal requirements of publication and solemnization, so far as the law deems it essential.
There must not be incapacity in the parties to marry either as re-

spects age or physical capability or as respects relationship by blood
or marriage. Failure in these respects, but I believe in no others (I
omit reference to the peculiar statutory position of the descendants
of George II.), renders the marriage void or voidable." Moss v.
Moss, L.R. [1897] Prob. Div. 263, 268.

In that case it was held that concealment by a woman from her husband at the time of her marriage of the fact that she was then pregnant
by another man did not render the marriage null and void.

In an early case in Massachusetts the court laid down the rule which
has been consistently followed in that state, that mere errors or mistakes
into which a person may fall concerning the character or qualities of a
wife or husband, although occasioned by disingenuous or false statements
or practices, will not afford sufficient reason for annulling an executed
contract of marriage; that in the absence of force or duress, where there
is no mistake as to the identity of the person, any error or misappre-
hension as to personal traits or attributes or concerning the position or
circumstances in life of a party is wholly immaterial and furnishes no
ground for divorce; and that no misconception as to the character, fortune, health, or temper, however brought about, will support an allegation on which a dissolution of the marriage contract, when once executed,
can be obtained in a court of justice; that these are accidental qualities
which do not constitute the essential and material elements on which the
marriage relation rests.

It was held in that case that misrepresentations as to antenuptial unchastity alone did not afford a sufficient ground for declaring a marriage
void; but that a marriage consummated on the faith of a representation
that the woman is chaste and virtuous, when it is afterward ascertained
that the statement was false, and that at the time of making it and at the
time of entering into the marriage relation she was pregnant with child
by another man, the marriage might be annulled for fraud.

This ruling was placed on the ground that such false representations
affected directly her actual present condition and her fitness to execute
the marriage contract; that in such a case the concealment and false
statements go directly to the essentials of the marriage contract and
operate as a fraud of the gravest character. Reynolds v. Reynolds, 85
Mass. 605.

In Smith v. Smith, 171 Mass. 404, 50 N.E. 933, a marriage was annulled where it appeared that the plaintiff, soon after the ceremony and
before the consummation of the marriage, on learning that the respondent was afflicted with a venereal disease, refused to live with and never
did live with him, and the judge found that he was constitutionally afflicted with syphilis, with which the plaintiff would become infected
in case of cohabitation, and that the disease would be transmitted to any
offspring which they might have. . . .

In the recent case of Chipman v. Johnston, 237 Mass. 502, 130 N.E. 65,
there was manifestly wicked deception perpetrated by the husband as to
his name, place of residence, business, property, relatives, and situation

in life. A few days after the marriage he deserted the plaintiff. But it did not appear that the man impersonated another or that the woman was mistaken as to his identity. The case quoted approvingly the Reynolds Case, supra [and denied the requested annulment].

There is a line of decisions in this country which have adopted a less rigorous rule for annulling marriage contracts than that which prevails in Massachusetts. This is illustrated by New York cases. In Di Lorenzo v. Di Lorenzo, 174 N.Y. 467, 67 N.E. 63, the defendant by a fraudulent representation and by a stratagem caused the plaintiff to believe that he was the father of defendant's child. It was said in the opinion of the court that the law considers marriage in no other light than as a civil contract; that it is a general rule that every misrepresentation of a material fact made with the intention to induce another to enter into an agreement, and without which he would not have done so, justifies the court in vacating the agreement; and that there is no valid reason for excepting the marriage contract from the general rule. It is held that the fraud must be material to the degree that, had it not been practiced, the party deceived would not have consented to the marriage. The theory of the court of appeals in this case has been adopted in numerous decisions of the supreme courts of New York on varying facts.

Of course it is well known that in New York there is only one ground for divorce. Owing partly to this fact, cases for the annulment of marriage have often presented to the New York courts instances of extreme hardship, and it is possible that the courts of that state have insensibly been affected by such situations. . . .

There is no doubt that the decisions of our court have adopted the rule prevailing in Massachusetts and most other states rather than that of the New York courts. . . .

It will be seen from the decisions that this court early adopted the view, which has been adhered to, that, although marriage is purely a civil contract, false representations which would set aside ordinary civil contracts are not necessarily sufficient to void the contract of marriage. This policy depends not alone on the vital importance of the dissolution of the marriage relation to the parties directly concerned. It rests on the deep concern of the state that the integrity of the marriage contract shall, so far as possible, be preserved. This is shown by the careful provision of our statute regulating marriage and divorce, including the statute providing for the appointment of divorce counsel in each county to represent the public, whose duty it is to appear and investigate the merits in such actions for the prevention of collusion, fraud, and imposition upon the court.

We are convinced that the general rule to be applied in actions of this kind, which was early adopted in Massachusetts and which has been followed in this state, may be said to be the rule which generally prevails in this country. [Citations omitted.]

Counsel for plaintiff place some reliance on the allegation that decedent was of advanced age and weak bodily condition. It will be observed that there is no averment that his intellect was impaired by age or that he was mentally unable to give his consent with full understanding of the obligation he assumed. There are cases in which marriages have been annulled by reason of gross frauds practiced on very young girls or upon aged persons mentally incompetent, but an examination of the cases shows that under the circumstances there was a failure or inability to give consent. We find no such element in the present case.

Plaintiff's counsel also rely on the promise to have a second marriage performed with the intention not to fulfil the promise, and several cases decided by the New York supreme court are cited where marriages were annulled because the husbands refused to fulfil promises to have a Jewish ceremony after the civil marriage. [Citations omitted.] But we believe them to be utterly at variance with the rule generally adopted in this country.

Even in ordinary civil cases it is the familiar rule that representations to be fraudulent must relate to a present or past state of facts and not to promises looking to the future, although there is some division of authority on the question whether an action for fraud may be based on a false statement of present intent which is material, made with intent to deceive and relied on by the other party. But this is not an ordinary civil contract, and we cannot agree that a marriage should be annulled on the ground of broken promises.

It is not claimed by counsel for plaintiff that as a general rule false representations that a party to a marriage has never been divorced constitute such fraud as will justify a decree nullifying the marriage contract. Such a fraud does not go to the essence of the contract. [Citations omitted.] The discovery by the party deceived might bring mental distress, but a divorce does not prevent entering into a new marriage relation or the performance of all its duties.

Counsel for respondent earnestly argue that owing to the age and the religious faith of decedent and the canons of his church the false representations did go to the very essentials of the marriage contract; that the marital relation under the facts stated in the complaint could only result in unhappiness to at least one of the contracting parties. This presents a new phase in actions to nullify the marriage contract, and no case from any court of last resort seems to have passed upon it. However, in Boehs v. Hanger, 69 N.J. Eq. 10, 59 Atl. 904, a somewhat similar situation was presented and the plaintiff was denied relief. The question is raised whether members of one church can succeed in nullifying a marriage upon false representations when the same representation would afford no cause of action to members of other churches. We are not inclined to give our sanction to such a proposition. . . .

In the opinion of many, the representations relied on in this case would be far less productive of marital unhappiness than falsehoods leading a sensitive and honorable man into marriage with a woman whose life had been sexually impure.

It is argued that if the facts had been known to the decedent he would not have entered into the contract and therefore the decedent never gave the consent necessary to the validity of the marriage contract. In other words, the question whether the complaining party would have entered into the contract if the real facts had been known is made quite controlling as to the materiality of the false representations. There is some basis for this argument in some of the New York cases, but it is a view which we cannot accept and which is out of harmony with the decisions of this court and the prevailing rule in America. Nor do we accept the view expressed in some of the quotations from decisions found in plaintiff's brief that the word "fraud" in statutes of this character means fraud as usually understood in its application to contracts generally.

The contract is "something more than a mere contract; it is rather to be deemed an institution of society, founded upon the consent and contract of the parties, and in this view it has some peculiarities in its nature, character, operation and extent of obligation, different from what belong to ordinary contracts." Story, Conflict of Laws, sec. 108, note.

There is no allegation in the complaint from which it can be inferred that the defendant is not able and willing to perform all the duties of the marriage contract, and we must hold that it appears on the face of the complaint that the essentials of the marriage contract, as construed by the great weight of authority, were complied with. It follows that the demurrer should have been sustained. . . .

NOTE

1. Compare Akrep v. Akrep, 1 N.J. 268, 63 A.2d 253 (1949), a case in which the New Jersey Supreme Court granted an annulment under rather similar circumstances. There the plaintiff was induced to go through a civil ceremony by the defendant's promise that he would subsequently go through a religious ceremony, which he later refused to do. Although the New Jersey courts generally appear to follow the majority or Massachusetts view discussed in the principal case,[41] the court in Akrep stressed the fact that the marriage there was unconsummated. "[A]n unconsummated marriage is little more than an engagement to marry and where effected with fraud which would render a contract voidable, is voidable at the option of the injured party if promptly disaffirmed before any change of status has occurred." 1 N.J. at 270, 63 A.2d at 254.

In accord with Akrep is Aufiero v. Aufiero, 222 App. Div. 479, 226 N.Y. Supp. 611 (1928), where the court intimated that the same result would follow even if there had been cohabitation. See also Brillis v. Brillis, 4 N.Y.2d 125, 127, 149 N.E.2d 510, 511 (1958) (on finding that defendant had never intended to follow civil with religious ceremony, annulment for fraud upheld "at least where, as in the present case, there has been no consummation by cohabitation"). But see Nilsen v. Nilsen, 66 N.Y.S.2d 204 (Sup. Ct. 1946) (promise to embrace Catholic faith after marriage is not one on which a reasonably prudent person would rely and its enforcement violates public policy).

2. In Masters v. Masters, 13 Wis. 2d 332, 108 N.W.2d 674 (1961), the

---

[41] See, e.g., Houlahan v. Horzepa, 46 N.J. Super. 583, 135 A.2d 232 (1957) (wife's failure to apprise husband before marriage of long history of serious mental illness not such fraud as would warrant annulment). Compare Holland v. Holland, 224 Md. 449, 168 A.2d 380 (1961) (annulment granted).

Wisconsin Supreme Court appeared to liberalize its attitude towards fraud annulments. In that case H was induced to marry W by her false claims that she was pregnant by him, supported by a certificate of pregnancy executed by a reputable physician. After the ceremony H discovered that W was not pregnant, and immediately thereafter he refused to cohabit with her. An annulment was granted since the representations of W were material, and but for them, H would not have married W.

According to a Comment on the case in 45 Marq. L. Rev. 447 (1961-1962), the only previous case supporting an annulment in such circumstances was the Di Lorenzo case in New York, which is discussed in the principal case. But the Wisconsin court indicated that it might not necessarily go along with some of the other New York cases.

3. Compare Shonfeld v. Shonfeld, 260 N.Y. 477, 184 N.E. 60 (1933), with Woronzoff-Daschkoff v. Woronzoff-Daschkoff, 303 N.Y. 506, 104 N.E.2d 877 (1952). In Shonfeld the Court of Appeals held that where the husband was induced to marry by his wife's false promise that she would provide the necessary funds for his new business, W's promise went to the essence of the marriage contract and therefore its breach was a proper basis for granting H an annulment. The wealthy Mrs. Woronzoff-Daschkoff, however, was refused an annulment from her husband who had represented himself as a Russian nobleman of great social position and reliability, whereas in fact he was a ne'er-do-well without social position whose principal aim seemed to have been to milk her of her money. One distinction between these cases is that the Shonfeld marriage had never been consummated, whereas the Woronzoff-Daschkoffs cohabited during a lengthy European honeymoon. Clark, Estoppel against Jurisdictional Attack on Decrees of Divorce, 70 Yale L.J. 45, 56 (1960), finds in these cases an expression of the New York courts' "ambivalence about the ultimate goals of its divorce laws," since judicial "adherence to contemporary sociological theories of divorce, at the expense of the 'conventional wisdom,' " is occurring "only reluctantly and with many a backward glance. This explains the confusion, the inconsistencies, the incomprehensible distinctions to be found in their decisions." See also Kober v. Kober, 16 N.Y.2d 191, 211 N.E.2d 817 (1965) (H's concealment of Nazi party membership and fanatic anti-Semitism threatening W with loss of her Jewish friends justifies fraud annulment) (4-3 decision).

4. A Note, Annulments for Fraud — New York's Answer to Reno?, 48 Colum. L. Rev. 900 (1948), studied all New York fraud annulment cases reported during 1943-1947. There were 142 reported opinions, more than two thirds denying annulment, and of these cases fourteen were appealed to the Appellate Division and two to the Court of Appeals. Id. at 901. During the same five-year period Jacobson reported that New York courts granted 24,740 annulments;[42] 91 per cent of the annulments about this

---

[42] Compiled from Jacobson, American Marriage and Divorce, Table 53, p. 113 (1959). These statistics are unofficial and the source listed is "Compiled by the author," who is with the Statistical Bureau of the Metropolitan Life Insurance Company. The 24,740 annulments compared with 54,500 absolute divorces for adultery in the same period. It will be recalled that these figures

time were in uncontested actions.[43]   Whether or not the doctrine of the reported cases bears any close relationship to actual practices before the referees is therefore uncertain.   The Columbia Law Review study concluded (id. at 901-903, 905-906):

[B]y 1942 there were enough appellate court decisions to establish a fairly definite set of principles governing annulments for fraud.   Any deliberate misrepresentation of fact or intention inducing consent was such fraud as to make a marriage voidable, provided the misrepresentation would be material to a reasonable man, and would deceive an ordinarily prudent person.   Any concealment or nondisclosure of facts or intention contrary to those normally implied by the mere assumption of the marital relationship stood substantially on the same footing with express misrepresentation of the same facts. That the marriage had been [consummated] before the bringing of the action was of no significance if there had been no cohabitation after discovery of the fraud.   In certain situations, however, the fact of consummation might be of evidentiary weight in determining the materiality of the alleged fraud as an inducement to a particular plaintiff's consent.   Likewise, as in an action for rescinding a contract, a showing of actual damage was not necessary, except insofar as it bore on the materiality of the alleged misrepresentation to the consent of a reasonable man.   In proving the cause of action, something more than the declaration or confession of either spouse was necessary as evidence of the fraud, but a defendant's course of conduct could constitute such evidence. . . .

[Of the 142 reported cases, 39 were] favorable and 103 unfavorable to the plaintiffs.   In seven of the former, there were express misrepresentations of existing facts.   These included misrepresentations of good health, chastity, professional status, and financial standing. Eleven involved concealment of facts contrary to those implied by entry into the marital relationship: mental illness; atrophy of private organs; criminal record; and illegal presence in the country.   In sixteen cases there were express misrepresentations of intention, including promises to establish a home; to preserve the harmony of the home of the wife and her children by a previous marriage; to have children; to love wife and forget another girl; to live a normal married life; to follow a civil ceremony with a religious one; to embrace and abide by the tenets of the spouse's religion; and to become a United States citizen.   Five cases arose from concealment of intentions contrary to those normally implied: not to consummate and cohabit normally; not to live permanently with the spouse; and not to bear children (wife), or cohabit without contraceptives (husband).

---

reflect the postwar dissolution boom; the numbers decline for later years and the proportion of annulments to all dissolutions increased.   E.g., for 1955 Jacobson reports 4800 divorces and 3750 annulments; for 1956, 4750 divorces, 3600 annulments.   Ibid.

[43] Id., Table 54, p. 115 (figures for 1946-1950).

Five decisions favorable to annulments for fraud did not indicate the facts.

5. Agreements between the spouses respecting their plans to have children have been the subject of an increasing number of annulment actions. Violation of an express understanding not to use contraceptives has generally been sufficient grounds for annulment. See, e.g., Zoglio v. Zoglio, 157 A.2d 627 (D.C. Mun. Ct. App. 1960). Indeed, in the absence of an express understanding to this effect, it will normally be implied. Ibid. The courts have surprisingly been less prone to recognize agreements to prevent or at least postpone the birth of children. See Frost v. Frost, 15 Misc. 2d 104, 181 N.Y.S.2d 562 (Sup. Ct. 1958) (annulment denied where H before marriage purported to be adherent of planned parenthood but subsequently desired to have five or six children). Cf. Baxter v. Baxter, [1948] A.C. 274 (wife's refusal to have intercourse unless contraceptive used is not willful refusal to consummate marriage so as to entitle husband to an annulment).

6. Jurisdiction to grant an annulment, like that for divorce (see Alton v. Alton, reproduced below), is generally based on domicile. See, e.g., Romatz v. Romatz, 355 Mich. 81, 94 N.W.2d 432 (1959) (Michigan can annul Ohio marriage of its domiciliaries); Perlstein v. Perlstein, 152 Conn. 152, 204 A.2d 909 (1964) (personal service on defendant within forum not necessary). But cf. Owen v. Owen, 127 Colo. 359, 257 P.2d 581 (1953). As indicated at page 176 supra, however, other considerations may bear on the lawyer's choice between annulment and divorce. Cf. also Wis. Stat. Ann. §§247.05(2), 247.05(3) (Supp. 1965) (two-year residence requirement for divorce; thirty days for annulment).

7. In general, see Vernon, Annulment of Marriage: A Proposed Model Act, 12 J. Pub. L. 143 (1963).

2. *Migratory Divorce*

ALTON v. ALTON
207 F.2d 667 (3d Cir. 1953)

GOODRICH, J. This case involves an important and novel question with regard to jurisdiction for divorce. The plaintiff, Sonia Alton, left her home in West Hartford, Connecticut, and went to the Virgin Islands, where she arrived February 10, 1953. After six weeks and one day continuous presence there she filed a suit for divorce on March 25, 1953. Her husband, David Alton, defendant, entered an appearance and waived service of summons. He did not contest the allegations of the complaint. The commissioner to whom the case was referred filed findings of fact and conclusions of law and recommended that the plaintiff be granted a divorce for "incompatibility of temperament." When the case came to the judge of the district court he asked for further proof on the question of domicile. This was not furnished. He thereupon denied the plaintiff the relief sought, and the case comes here on her appeal. The defendant has filed no brief and made no argument.

The core of our question is found in two acts of the Legislative Assembly of the Virgin Islands. The first is the Divorce Law of 1944, section 9 of which requires six weeks' residence in the Islands prior to commencement of a suit for divorce. In Burch v. Burch, 3 Cir., 1952, 195 F.2d 799, this court construed the words "inhabitant" and "residence" in that statute to mean "domiciliary" and "domicile." In 1953 the Legislative Assembly passed another act which must be stated in full in order to understand the specific problem involved in this case. It amends section 9 of the Divorce Law of 1944 by adding to it an additional subsection (a) which reads:

> "Notwithstanding the provisions of sections 8 and 9 hereof, if the plaintiff is within the district at the time of the filing of the complaint and has been continuously for six weeks immediately prior thereto, this shall be prima facie evidence of domicile, and where the defendant has been personally served within the district or enters a general appearance in the action, then the Court shall have jurisdiction of the action and of the parties thereto without further reference to domicile or to the place where the marriage was solemnized or the cause of action arose." . . .

. . . We approach the problem on review, therefore, as though the legislation in question had been passed by one of the States in this Circuit. . . .

We turn first to the opening clause of the statute. Continuous physical presence in the Islands for six weeks prior to the filing of a complaint in a divorce action is declared to be prima facie evidence of domicile. The question is whether such a declaration is within the legislative competence. The test to be applied is whether the fact or facts to be presumed are reasonably related or have some rational connection with the fact which creates the presumption. . . .

. . . The requirements for effecting a change of domicile by a person having legal capacity are clear and undisputed. There must be physical presence in the place where domicile is claimed and there must be the intent to make that place the home of the person whose domicile is in question. Restatement, Conflict of Laws, §15. If these two elements concur even for an instant the domicile is established at the new place. . . .

The statute in question jumps the difficult phase in the proof of domicile, namely, the intent to make a home in the place where domicile is claimed. It would not be denied that long continued residence in a place tends to show that one has made a home there although there are many decisions in which courts have struggled with the problem even in the face of long continued presence in a place other than the one which at one time was the domicile of an individual concerned.

A six-weeks' sojourn without proof of the intent with which one makes it, we think, tends to establish nothing but the fact of six weeks' physical presence. Thousands and thousands of people spend six weeks or more in a place every year on business, for pleasure, for reasons of health, to visit relatives and all the other different reasons which make Americans move about, without the faintest intention of making a change in their homes.

It is to be noted also that the statutory presumption in this case applies to the very thing on which jurisdiction is founded. We think it is much easier to support a presumption or prima facie rule which allows a conclusion such as negligence to be drawn from named operative facts than it is to support a conclusion lifting a court into jurisdiction over that which it would not otherwise have. Of course, it may be urged that in the first part of the statute this conclusion is not an irrevocable one and that the statute speaks in terms of "prima facie" only. But in considering all this we must open our eyes to the known facts about divorce litigation in this country. We know that while it is still conducted against a background of what appears to be ordinary contentious litigation in a great proportion of cases it is not this way at all. Thus, in the Virgin Islands for 1952 divorce litigation accounted for 343 cases concluded during that period; all other civil litigation amounted to only 272 cases. Of these divorce cases 342 were uncontested. Back as far as 1932 surveys conducted by The Institute of Law of The Johns Hopkins University showed that in Maryland, a state with almost no migratory divorce problem, only 80 cases were actually contested out of the 2090 actions filed in 1929 and disposed of by May, 1931. 41.3% of these actions were technically contested by the filing of an answer. Marshall and May, I The Divorce Court 206-208 (1932). . . .

In considering this statute we do not think that we can ignore the facts of life with respect to migratory divorce in America. It is well known to all of us that increasingly large numbers of persons who are dissatisfied with their marital lot are repairing to other jurisdictions, the Virgin Islands among them, where short residence requirements and liberal grounds for divorce appear to offer them the relief they desire. In very few of these instances do the parties intend to remain longer than necessary to obtain the decree sought. Consequently in these cases the court's finding of domicile usually is contrary to the fact and frequently is based upon evasive or even perjured testimony. The statutory presumption in the present case will doubtless eliminate the temptation to such perjury but the findings based upon it will still be contrary to the true fact in the great majority of cases. . . .

. . . The second part of the statute goes on to provide that the court shall have jurisdiction, after six weeks' residence by the plaintiff, where the defendant has been personally served or appeared, "without further reference to domicile." . . . The action, in other words, is to become a simple transitory action like a suit for tort or breach of contract where, the defendant being in court and the court competent to proceed in this type of action, all the requisites for jurisdiction are satisfied. Can divorce be turned into a simple, transitory action at the will of any legislature? . . .

. . . It is of significance upon the importance of domicile as the foundation for jurisdiction that the Supreme Court has recently held that a divorce action at the domicile of one of the parties is entitled to full faith and credit as a matter of constitutional compulsion even without the presence of the defending spouse.[44]　On the other hand, a divorce not at the domicile gives no protection against a prosecution for bigamy in the state of the domicile,[45] although if the defendant is in court he, himself, may be precluded from questioning the decree on the grounds of res judicata.[46]

We now go out beyond the place where legal trails end.　The Supreme Court has never had occasion to say what would happen in a case where two parties, being personally before the court, are purportedly divorced by a state which has no domiciliary jurisdiction, and the question of the validity of the decree comes up in a second state in a prosecution for bigamy, or in a suit for necessaries by a creditor, or in some other such fashion. . . .

We think that adherence to the domiciliary requirement is necessary if our states are really to have control over the domestic relations of their citizens.　The instant case would be typical.　In the Virgin Islands incompatibility of temperament constitutes grounds for divorce.　In Connecticut it does not.　We take it that it is all very well for the Virgin Islands to provide for whatever matrimonial regime it pleases for people who live there.　But the same privilege should be afforded to those who control affairs in Connecticut.

Our conclusion is that the second part of this statute conflicts with the due process clause of the Fifth Amendment and the Organic Act.　Domestic relations are a matter of concern to the state where a person is domiciled.　An attempt by another jurisdiction to affect the relation of a foreign domiciliary is unconstitutional even though both parties are in court and neither one raises the question.　The question may well be asked as to what the lack of due process is.　The defendant is not complaining.　Nevertheless, if the jurisdiction for divorce continues to be based on domicile, as we think it does, we believe it to be lack of due process for one state to take to itself the readjustment of domestic relations between those domiciled elsewhere.　The Supreme Court has in a number of cases used the due process clause to correct states which have passed beyond what that court has considered proper choice-of-law rules. . . .

The judgment of the district court will be affirmed.

HASTIE, J. (dissenting). . . .

. . . [I]t seems to me that the rational connection between six weeks continuous presence and domicil is substantial and very clear.　It proves one element of domicil and is relevant to the other.　In these circumstances it is difficult to see upon what basis the statutory presumption can be attacked unless it is argued that domicil must in logic be inferable from six weeks presence standing alone before the latter fact can by legislation

[44] Williams v. North Carolina (I), 1942, 317 U.S. 287.
[45] Williams v. North Carolina (II), 1945, 325 U.S. 226.
[46] Sherrer v. Sherrer, 1948, 334 U.S. 343 [further citation omitted].

be made prima facie evidence of the former. Apparently, this is the view of the majority. The difficulty with that position is that the Supreme Court seems to have settled the law the other way. . . .

The opinion of the court [seems to require] that this statute should be treated as if it embodied something different from the ordinary shifting of the burden of going forward with evidence because in so many jurisdictions, including the Virgin Islands, so few defendants elect to contest divorce actions. To me this circumstance is not relevant to the question of legislative power to make one fact prima facie evidence of another. I cannot see that the percentage of defendants who take advantage of the opportunity to rebut a presumption affects the genuineness or the essential fairness of the opportunity the legislature has given all defendants to eliminate the presumption entirely by merely offering evidence on the ultimate issue. And that, in my judgment, is the important consideration here. . . .

In striking down the second amendment of the statute, which provides for divorce where both parties are subject to the jurisdiction of the insular possession and its courts, this court now says that the Fifth Amendment requires that the exercise of legal power to grant divorce be restricted to those cases where one party at least is a local domiciliary. . . .

. . . The court reasons this way: "Because it [marriage] is a matter of public concern, the public, through the state, has an interest both in its formation and in its dissolution, and the state which has that interest is the state of domicile, because that is where the party 'dwelleth and hath his home.' " Accordingly, the court concludes "that adherence to the domiciliary requirement is necessary if our states are really to have control over the domestic relations of their citizens," and that any departure from the domiciliary rule would be a denial of procedural due process. This statement of social justification of a legal rule presupposes a stable and intimate attachment of both spouses to a single community which in fact and alone has a genuine interest in their relationship. But this picture is no longer characteristic of our society or of the conduct of estranged spouses in it. In their activities and their careers men are increasingly mobile. Community attachments tend to be less intimate and less lasting than heretofore. And when the unsettling factor of domestic estrangement is added there is considerable likelihood that the spouses will go their separate ways in different communities. One need not approve these patterns of behavior to recognize what doubt they cast upon the essentiality of a legal rule which must be justified by premising a single community which alone and intimately is concerned with each unsuccessful marriage.

Actually, the concept of domicil as a basis of jurisdiction is in practice elusive and very unsatisfactory for several reasons. It is a highly technical concept depending upon the proof of the mental attitude of a person toward a place. Whether in taxation or in divorce, the use of domicil as a jurisdictional base gives trouble when it is applied to people who really have no "home feeling" toward any place or, at the other end of the scale, to those who have more than one home. And, as already pointed out, in the divorce field difficulties are multiplied because the estranged spouses so often establish separate homes. Thus, when a court is asked to grant a divorce it very often finds that not one domicil but at least two — potentially more through refinements of the "marital domicil" concept — may be interested in the parties and their relationship. In these all too familiar situations of divided domicil, the jurisdictional requirement which the majority regards as so essential to fairness that it can not be changed is a troublemaker and a potential source of injustice. . . .

NOTE

1. On appeal to the Supreme Court of the United States, the Alton case was dismissed as moot, because one of the spouses had meanwhile procured a second divorce in another jurisdiction. Alton v. Alton, 347 U.S. 965 (1954). The Supreme Court did ultimately invalidate the Virgin Islands statute, but on the ground of the local legislature's lack of power under the grant given to it by Congress rather than on the ground involved in the Alton case. Granville-Smith v. Granville-Smith, 349 U.S. 1 (1955). Justice Clark, joined by Justices Black and Reed, dissented (id. at 16, 27-28):

"[The judge-made doctrine of domicile] creates strange anomalies. A married couple, both of whom desire a divorce, can obtain one in Nevada merely by having one spouse "reside" there uninterruptedly for six weeks, and claim an intention to take up permanent residence there. [Citation omitted.] Then, after divorce, though the divorcee immediately leaves Nevada, as was always intended, both sides here concede that regardless of how evident it is there was no domicile in the divorcing State, no other State can question the validity of the divorce so long as both parties appeared in the action. . . . Still the Court strikes down the Islands' law which avoids this judicial fraud.

"Divorce is an intensely practical matter, and if a husband and wife domiciled in any State want a divorce enough, we all know that they can secure it in several of our States. This being true, I see no sense in striking down the Islands' law. There is no virtue in a state of the law the only practical effect of which would be to make New Yorkers fly 2400 miles over land to Reno instead of 1450 miles over water to the Virgin Islands.

"The only vice of the Virgin Islands' statute, in an uncontested case like this, is that it makes unnecessary a choice between bigamy and perjury. I think the Court should not discourage this and I would reverse."

2. The issue posed by the Alton case does not often arise because most Anglo-American jurisdictions expressly base divorce jurisdiction on the domicile of one or both of the parties (or else so interpret terms such as "residence" in their jurisdictional statute). But see Wheat v. Wheat, 229 Ark. 842, 318 S.W.2d 793 (1958) (residence of three months sufficient); and see Crownover v. Crownover, 58 N.M. 597, 274 P.2d 127 (1954) (presumption that one year's continuous residence by serviceman stationed

in New Mexico constitutes domicile is valid). Moreover, as will be seen below, a divorce in which both parties participate is normally effectively immune from attack.

The more commonly litigated issue is under what circumstances an ex parte divorce must be given full faith and credit by other states. For many years under the rule of Haddock v. Haddock, 201 U.S. 562 (1906), such recognition was not compelled even if the plaintiff was in fact domiciled in the divorce forum, unless it was the "matrimonial domicile." [47] All this was changed by the landmark case of Williams v. North Carolina, 317 U.S. 287 (1942), which overruled Haddock and held that a divorce rendered by a state in which the petitioning spouse was domiciled must be given full faith and credit by every other state.

But this seeming shift of power from the home state to the migratory state was soon redressed when the Supreme Court held in the second Williams case that the essential jurisdictional finding of domicile[48] was subject to re-examination in the courts of the home state. Williams v. North Carolina, 325 U.S. 226 (1945). To be sure, the determination of the rendering state that the petitioning spouse was domiciled there is presumptively valid. Cook v. Cook, 342 U.S. 126 (1951). But if the absent spouse can persuade the courts of the home state that, despite the jurisdictional finding of domicile in the rendering state, the petitioner was not in fact domiciled there, then, subject to ultimate review by the Supreme Court of the United States, the home state is entitled to refuse recognition to the foreign divorce. See, e.g., Gregg v. Gregg, 220 Md. 578, 155 A.2d 500 (1959) (plaintiff not domiciled in Nevada although he was resident there several years and obtained employment there); Henry v. Henry, 362 Mich. 85, 106 N.W.2d 570 (1960) (registration for voting, real property ownership, rental of apartment on one-year lease, and payment of income tax in Nevada disregarded because substantial business and other ties remained with home state). Whether these decisions would have been upheld by the Supreme Court remains unclear. A related question which must await Supreme Court clarification is whether a divorce which is refused recognition for lack of domicile nevertheless remains valid in the rendering state. It was so held in Colby v. Colby, 78 Nev. 150, 369 P.2d 1019, cert. denied, 371 U.S. 888 (1962), 63 Colum. L. Rev. 560 (1963).

The right of the stay-at-home spouse thus to challenge a divorce decree procured by the other spouse is not the only available remedy. If jurisdiction can be obtained over the absent party before he or she becomes domiciled in the divorcing state, it may be possible to obtain an injunction against the foreign proceeding. Garvin v. Garvin, 302 N.Y. 96, 96 N.E.2d 721 (1951). But see Stultz v. Stultz, 15 N.J. 315, 104 A.2d 656 (1954). And see Developments in the Law — Injunctions, 78 Harv. L. Rev. 994, 1040 (1965). Moreover, even if the foreign divorce is valid insofar as the determination of marital status is concerned, it may not be

---

[47] For some other qualifications of Haddock, see Goodrich, Conflict of Laws 264 (4th ed. Scoles 1964).

[48] The Supreme Court has never decided whether anything less than domicile will bring the full faith and credit clause into play.

effective to cut off the support rights of the wife who remains at home. See page 935 infra. Similarly, any attempt by the divorcing jurisdiction to adjudicate custody rights to children in an ex parte proceeding will not be binding on the absent spouse. See page 899 infra.

3. As is made clear by the case which follows, none of the indicated infirmities are present if both parties participate (either personally or by attorney) in the foreign divorce proceeding. This fact undoubtedly explains why virtually all migratory divorces today are of the consensual variety.

SHERRER v. SHERRER
334 U.S. 343 (1948)

VINSON, C.J. We granted certiorari in this case and in Coe v. Coe, post, p. 378, to consider the contention of petitioners that Massachusetts has failed to accord full faith and credit to decrees of divorce rendered by courts of sister States.

Petitioner Margaret E. Sherrer and the respondent, Edward C. Sherrer, were married in New Jersey in 1930, and from 1932 until April 3, 1944, lived together in Monterey, Massachusetts. Following a long period of marital discord, petitioner, accompanied by the two children of the marriage, left Massachusetts on the latter date, ostensibly for the purpose of spending a vacation in the State of Florida. Shortly after her arrival in Florida, however, petitioner informed her husband that she did not intend to return to him. Petitioner obtained housing accommodations in Florida, placed her older child in school, and secured employment for herself.

On July 6, 1944, a bill of complaint for divorce was filed at petitioner's direction in the Circuit Court of the Sixth Judicial Circuit of the State of Florida. The bill alleged extreme cruelty as grounds for divorce and also alleged that petitioner was a "bona fide legal resident of the State of Florida." [49] The respondent received notice by mail of the pendency of the divorce proceedings. He retained Florida counsel who entered a general appearance and filed an answer denying the allegations of petitioner's complaint, including the allegation as to petitioner's Florida residence.

On November 14, 1944, hearings were held in the divorce proceedings. Respondent appeared personally to testify with respect to a stipulation entered into by the parties relating to the custody of the children. Throughout the entire proceedings respondent was represented by counsel. [50] Petitioner introduced evidence to establish her Florida residence and testified generally to the allegations of her complaint. Counsel for

[49] Section 65.02 of Florida Stat. Ann. provides: "In order to obtain a divorce the complainant must have resided ninety days in the State of Florida before the filing of the bill of complaint." The Florida courts have construed the statutory requirement of residence to be that of domicile. Respondent does not contend nor do we find any evidence that the requirements of "domicile" as defined by the Florida cases are other than those generally applied or differ from the tests employed by the Massachusetts courts. [Citations omitted.]

[50] It is said that throughout most of the proceedings respondent did not appear in the courtroom but remained "in a side room."

respondent failed to cross-examine or to introduce evidence in rebuttal.

The Florida court on November 29, 1944, entered a decree of divorce after specifically finding that petitioner "is a bona fide resident of the State of Florida, and that this court has jurisdiction of the parties and the subject matter in said cause; . . ." Respondent failed to challenge the decree by appeal to the Florida Supreme Court.

On December 1, 1944, petitioner was married in Florida to one Henry A. Phelps, whom petitioner had known while both were residing in Massachusetts and who had come to Florida shortly after petitioner's arrival in that State. Phelps and petitioner lived together as husband and wife in Florida, where they were both employed, until February 5, 1945, when they returned to Massachusetts.

In June, 1945, respondent instituted an action in the Probate Court of Berkshire County, Massachusetts, which has given rise to the issues of this case. Respondent alleged that he is the lawful husband of petitioner, that the Florida decree of divorce is invalid, and that petitioner's subsequent marriage is void. Respondent prayed that he might be permitted to convey his real estate as if he were sole and that the court declare that he was living apart from his wife for justifiable cause. Petitioner joined issue on respondent's allegations.

In the proceedings which followed, petitioner gave testimony in defense of the validity of the Florida divorce decree. The Probate Court, however, resolved the issues of fact adversely to petitioner's contentions, found that she was never domiciled in Florida, and granted respondent the relief he had requested. The Supreme Judicial Court of Massachusetts affirmed the decree on the grounds that it was supported by the evidence and that the requirements of full faith and credit did not preclude the Massachusetts courts from reexamining the finding of domicile made by the Florida court.

At the outset, it should be observed that the proceedings in the Florida court prior to the entry of the decree of divorce were in no way inconsistent with the requirements of procedural due process. We do not understand respondent to urge the contrary. The respondent personally appeared in the Florida proceedings. Through his attorney he filed pleadings denying the substantial allegations of petitioner's complaint. It is not suggested that his rights to introduce evidence and otherwise to conduct his defense were in any degree impaired; nor is it suggested that there was not available to him the right to seek review of the decree by appeal to the Florida Supreme Court. It is clear that respondent was afforded his day in court with respect to every issue involved in the litigation, including the jurisdictional issue of petitioner's domicile. Under such circumstances, there is nothing in the concept of due process which demands that a defendant be afforded a second opportunity to litigate the existence of jurisdictional facts. [Citations omitted.]

It should also be observed that there has been no suggestion that under the law of Florida, the decree of divorce in question is in any respect invalid or could successfully be subjected to the type of attack permitted by the Massachusetts court. The implicit assumption underlying the position taken by respondent and the Massachusetts court is that this case involves a decree of divorce valid and final in the State which rendered it; and we so assume.

That the jurisdiction of the Florida court to enter a valid decree of divorce was dependent upon petitioner's domicile in that State is not disputed. This requirement was recognized by the Florida court which rendered the divorce decree, and the principle has been given frequent application in decisions of the State Supreme Court. But whether or not petitioner was domiciled in Florida at the time the divorce was granted was a matter to be resolved by judicial determination. Here, unlike the situation presented in Williams v. North Carolina, 325 U.S. 226 (1945), the finding of the requisite jurisdictional facts was made in proceedings in which the defendant appeared and participated. The question with which we are confronted, therefore, is whether such a finding made under the circumstances presented by this case may, consistent with the requirements of full faith and credit, be subjected to collateral attack in the courts of a sister State in a suit brought by the defendant in the original proceedings. . . .

This Court has . . . held that the doctrine of res judicata must be applied to questions of jurisdiction in cases arising in state courts involving the application of the full faith and credit clause where, under the law of the state in which the original judgment was rendered, such adjudications are not susceptible to collateral attack. . . .

. . . [T]he requirements of full faith and credit bar a defendant from collaterally attacking a divorce decree on jurisdictional grounds in the courts of a sister State where there has been participation by the defendant in the divorce proceedings, where the defendant has been accorded full opportunity to contest the jurisdictional issues, and where the decree is not susceptible to such collateral attack in the courts of the State which rendered the decree.

Applying these principles to this case, we hold that the Massachusetts courts erred in permitting the Florida divorce decree to be subjected to attack on the ground that petitioner was not domiciled in Florida at the time the decree was entered. . . . It has not been contended that respondent was given less than a full opportunity to contest the issue of petitioner's domicile or any other issue relevant to the litigation. . . . If respondent failed to take advantage of the opportunities afforded him, the responsibility is his own. We do not believe that the dereliction of a defendant under such circumstances should be permitted to provide a basis for subsequent attack in the courts of a sister State on a decree valid in the State in which it was rendered. . . .

It is urged further, however, that because we are dealing with litigation involving the dissolution of the marital relation, a different result is demanded from that which might properly be reached if this case were concerned with other types of litigation. . . .

But the recognition of the importance of a State's power to determine the incidents of basic social relationships into which its domiciliaries enter does not resolve the issues of this case. This is not a situation in which a State has merely sought to exert such power over a domiciliary. This is, rather, a case involving inconsistent assertions of power by courts of two States of the Federal Union and thus presents considerations which go beyond the interests of local policy, however vital. . . . The full faith and credit clause is one of the provisions incorporated into the Constitution by its framers for the purpose of transforming an aggregation of independent, sovereign States into a nation. If in its application local policy must at times be required to give way, such "is part of the price of our federal system." Williams v. North Carolina, 317 U.S. 287, 302 (1942). . . .

It is one thing to recognize as permissible the judicial reexamination of findings of jurisdictional fact where such findings have been made by a court of a sister State which has entered a divorce decree in ex parte proceedings. It is quite another thing to hold that the vital rights and interests involved in divorce litigation may be held in suspense pending the scrutiny by courts of sister States of findings of jurisdictional fact made by a competent court in proceedings conducted in a manner consistent with the highest requirements of due process and in which the defendant has participated. We do not conceive it to be in accord with the purposes of the full faith and credit requirement to hold that a judgment rendered under the circumstances of this case may be required to run the gantlet of such collateral attack in the courts of sister States before its validity outside of the State which rendered it is established or rejected. That vital interests are involved in divorce litigation indicates to us that it is a matter of greater rather than lesser importance that there should be a place to end such litigation. And where a decree of divorce is rendered by a competent court under the circumstances of this case, the obligation of full faith and credit requires that such litigation should end in the courts of the State in which the judgment was rendered.

Reversed.

MR. JUSTICE FRANKFURTER, with whom MR. JUSTICE MURPHY concurs, dissenting. . . .

. . . I cannot agree that the Constitution forbids a State from insisting that it is not bound by any such proceedings in a distant State wanting in the power that domicile alone gives, and that its courts need not honor such an intrinsically sham proceeding, no matter who brings the issue to their attention.

. . . Nowhere in the United States, not even in the States which grant divorces most freely, may a husband and wife rescind their marriage at will as they might a commercial contract. Even if one thought that such a view of the institution of marriage was socially desirable, it could scarcely be held that such a personal view was incorporated into the Constitution or into the law for the enforcement of the Full Faith and Credit Clause . . . .

. . . To hold that [what Massachusetts has done in this case] contravenes the Full Faith and Credit Clause is to say that that State has so slight a concern in the continuance or termination of the marital relationships of its domiciliaries that its interest may be foreclosed by an arranged litigation between the parties in which it was not represented.[51]

Today's decision may stir hope of contributing toward greater certainty of status of those divorced. But when people choose to avail themselves of laws laxer than those of the State in which they permanently abide, and where, barring only the interlude necessary to get a divorce, they choose to continue to abide, doubts and conflicts are inevitable, so long as the divorce laws of the forty-eight States remain diverse, and so long as we respect the law that a judgment without jurisdictional foundation is not constitutionally entitled to recognition everywhere. . . . To attempt to shape policy so as to avoid disharmonies in our divorce laws was not a power entrusted to us, nor is the judiciary competent to exercise it. Courts are not equipped to pursue the paths for discovering wise policy. A court is confined within the bounds of a particular record, and it cannot even shape the record. Only fragments of a social problem are seen through the narrow windows of a litigation. Had we innate or acquired understanding of a social problem in its entirety, we would not have at our disposal adequate means for constructive solution. . . . The only way in which this Court can achieve uniformity, in the absence of Congressional action or constitutional amendment, is by permitting the States with the laxest divorce laws to impose their policies upon all other States. . . .

Fortunately, today's decision does not go that far. But its practical result will be to offer new inducements for conduct by parties and counsel, which, in any other type of litigation, would be regarded as perjury, but which is not so regarded where divorce is involved because ladies and gentlemen indulge in it. . . .

In considering whether the importance of the asserted uncertainties of marital status under existing law is sufficient to justify this result, it is important to think quantitatively, not dramatically. . . . The proportion of divorced people who have cause to worry is small indeed. Those who were divorced at home have no problem. Those whose desire to be rid of a spouse coincided with an unrelated shift of domicile will hardly be suspect where, as is usually true, the State to which they moved did not afford easy divorces or required a long residence period. . . . [In the divorce mill states of Nevada and Florida] only 16,375 divorces were granted in 1940, 6% of the total. [Citation omitted.] Some of these people were undoubtedly permanently settled in those States, and have nothing to fear. Others may have moved to those States, intending to make their permanent homes there, and have since remained. They were amply protected by the Full Faith and Credit Clause even before today's decision. The only persons at all insecure are that small minority who temporarily left

[51] Today's decision would also seem to render invalid, under the Full Faith and Credit Clause, a large proportion of the commonly encountered injunctions against a domiciliary prosecuting an out-of-State divorce action. [Citations omitted.] Since no State may enjoin its inhabitants from changing their domiciles in order to procure divorces, it would seem that henceforth a recital of domicile in the out-of-State divorce decree will render the injunction retroactively invalid if there has been any semblance of a contest in the divorce proceeding.

their home States for a State — one of the few — offering quick and easy divorce, obtained one, and departed. Is their security so important to the Nation that we must safeguard it even at the price of depriving the great majority of States which do not offer bargain-counter divorces of the right to determine the laws of domestic relations applicable to their citizens?

Even to a believer in the desirability of easier divorce — an issue that is not our concern — this decision should bring little solace. It offers a way out only to that small portion of those unhappily married who are sufficiently wealthy to be able to afford a trip to Nevada or Florida, and a six-week or three-month stay there.[52] . . .

NOTE

1. In a companion case decided the same day, the Supreme Court held that the Sherrer rule was equally applicable if the defendant conceded rather than contested the jurisdiction of the court. Coe v. Coe, 334 U.S. 378 (1948). But the Court has never ruled expressly on whether or not the Sherrer principle applies in the following situations:

a. Where the home state tries to attack the foreign divorce in a bigamy prosecution, where a state instrumentality questions the marital status, Hamilton v. Dillon, 110 Ohio App. 489, 167 N.E.2d 356 (1959), or where a federal agency seeks to invalidate a divorce in the course of a social security award, cf. Magner v. Hobby, 215 F.2d 190 (2d Cir. 1954), cert. denied, 348 U.S. 919 (1955).

b. Where the defendant enters a special appearance to contest the jurisdiction of the divorce court. See Davis v. Davis, 259 Wis. 1, 47 N.W.2d 338 (1951) (Sherrer inapplicable in such situations; decision seems questionable).

c. Where the defendant merely corresponds with the clerk of court or local attorney with respect to the action. Beardsley v. Beardsley, 144 Conn. 725, 137 A.2d 752 (1957) , and Jamieson v. Jamieson, 14 Ill. App. 2d 233, 144 N.E.2d 540 (1957) (held sufficient to bar later attack). But see Collins v. Collins, 175 Pa. Super. 214, 103 A.2d 494 (1954).

d. Where the record shows on its face that there was no compliance with the jurisdictional requirements of the rendering state and the proceeding there was a sham. Staedler v. Staedler, 6 N.J. 380, 78 A.2d 896 (1951) (Sherrer presupposed true adversary proceedings; hence instant divorce permitted to be attacked). Case seems of dubious validity. See Schlemm v. Schlemm, 31 N.J. 557, 158 A.2d 508 (1960).

e. Where the defendant's appearance or assent to jurisdiction was co-

[52] The easier it is made for those who through affluence are able to exercise disproportionately large influence on legislation, to obtain migratory divorces, the less likely it is that the divorce laws of their home States will be liberalized, insofar as that is deemed desirable, so as to affect all. See Groves, Migratory Divorces, 2 Law & Contemp. Prob. 293, 298. For comparable instances, in the past, of discrimination against the poor in the actual application of divorce laws, cf. Dickens, Hard Times, c. 11; Hankins, Divorce, 5 Encyc. Soc. Sci. 177, 179.

erced or obtained by fraud, the Sherrer rule is not applicable. Zenker v. Zenker, 161 Neb. 200, 72 N.W.2d 809 (1955); Winston v. Winston, 276 Ala. 303, 161 So.2d 588 (1964).

f. Where the defendant merely signs in the home state an acceptance of service and waiver of notice and answer. See, e.g., White v. White, 25 Conn. Supp. 235, 201 A.2d 662 (Super. Ct. 1963); Donnell v. Howell, 257 N.C. 175, 125 S.E.2d 448 (1962) (divorce invalid). But see Gessula v. Gessula, 34 U.S.L. Week 2215 (N.Y. Sup. Ct. 1965). See also Day v. Day, 237 Md. 229, 205 A.2d 798 (1965), 65 Colum. L. Rev. 924 (unauthorized use of W's waiver by H and fact that W had no attorney permits subsequent challenge by W).

2. Another troublesome aspect of the Sherrer decision is its effect on collateral attacks by third persons or "strangers" to the divorce decree. Johnson v. Muelberger, 340 U.S. 581 (1950), held that the full faith and credit clause applies equally in such situations and that the law of the rendering state must be looked to to ascertain whether the third party has standing to attack the decree. See Comment, 24 U. Chi. L. Rev. 376 (1957). Some of the states do not permit a third party to attack a decree on jurisdictional grounds unless he had an assertible interest at the time the divorce decree was rendered. See, e.g., deMarigney v. deMarigney, 43 So.2d 442 (Fla. 1949) (second spouse barred); In re Eglund's Estate, 45 Wash. 2d 708, 277 P.2d 717 (1954) (5-4 decision), 17 Hastings L.J. 317 (1956) (heirs of deceased second spouse cannot challenge validity of divorce so as to deprive party to divorce of marital interest). In many other states third parties are permitted to attack the decree regardless of when their interest accrued. See, e.g., Old Colony Trust Co. v. Porter, 324 Mass. 581, 88 N.E.2d 135 (1949); Ex parte Nimmer, 212 S.C. 311, 47 S.E.2d 716 (1948). Since most third party attacks arise as a result of a subsequent remarriage of one of the parties to the divorce and hence of necessity involve interests that accrued subsequent to the divorce, third party attacks are normally permitted only if the rendering jurisdiction follows the more permissive rule. It is interesting to note that most of the so-called divorce mill states do not do so. See, e.g., deMarigney v. deMarigney, supra; cf. Nev. Rev. Stat. §125.185 (Supp. 1963) (if divorce binding on parties, third parties barred). Closely related to and intertwined with the stranger doctrine is the concept of estoppel. Where the parties and their privies are estopped to attack what would otherwise be an invalid decree, the courts have split on whether the estoppel extends to strangers. Compare deMarigney v. deMarigney, supra (estoppel), with Ex parte Nimmer, supra (no estoppel). And see pages 746-751 infra. In general, see Annot., 12 A.L.R.2d 717 (1950).

3. As Justice Frankfurter indicated in his dissenting opinion in Sherrer, the incidence of migratory divorce is not great. Jacobson, American Marriage and Divorce 109 (1959), states that the statistics on migratory divorce are very inadequate and estimates that migratory divorces "probably account for no more than 3 to 5 per cent of the total divorces annually." But the figure is very much higher for New York (id. at 116):

In the absence of valid information we can only speculate on the true extent of divorce among New Yorkers. Generally, it has probably been about one third to one half greater than the number recorded in New York State; currently [1959], it may even be double, in view of the marked increase of Mexican divorces to Americans following the 1952 decision of the New York Supreme Court upholding the validity of certain Mexican decrees.

Most of the pressure to resort to migratory divorce in states other than New York comes in those jurisdictions, especially California, which impose restrictions on remarriage following divorce by entry of an interlocutory decree of divorce (or decree nisi in some states) which does not become final until some specified period of time has elapsed. Thus in California parties must wait for one year after obtaining an interlocutory decree before they can obtain a final decree, and remarriage is prohibited during the interlocutory period. See generally Note, Interlocutory Decrees of Divorce, 56 Colum. L. Rev. 228 (1956).

The states that have become most closely associated with the phenomenon of migratory divorce appear to fall into two categories: (1) those that have relatively short minimum residence requirements[53] but purport to base their divorces on domicile, thus effectively immunizing these divorces against attack when both parties enter an appearance, and (2) those in which some judges, often in violation of governing statutory law, grant so-called "quickie" or overnight divorces.[54] The most prominent recent example in the latter category has been Alabama. The divorce rate in that state almost doubled between 1954 and 1961, despite a population increase of only about 5 per cent. Almost half the 17,554 divorces obtained in Alabama in 1961 were obtained in only three of Alabama's 67 counties with a population of approximately 5 per cent of the state's total population. See Reese, Grounds for and Method of Setting Aside an Alabama Divorce, 11 Prac. Law., April 1965, p. 37. Indeed, the courts of one county in 1960 granted the equivalent of two divorces for every three families resident in the county. See Note, Migratory Divorce: The Alabama Experience, 75 Harv. L. Rev. 568, 569 (1962). The phenomenal growth of this divorce mill was slowed, if not altogether halted, as a result of nationwide publicity culminating in a sharp crackdown by the Alabama Bar Association, at whose instance the Alabama Supreme Court prohibited all attorneys admitted to practice in Alabama from filing a suit for divorce "with knowledge or reasonable cause to believe that neither party to such suit . . . is . . . a bona fide resident of the State of Alabama." Also instrumental may have been a number of decisions by other states refusing to recognize Alabama divorces obtained under such circumstances. See,

[53] Nevada and Idaho (6 weeks); Wyoming (60 days); Utah (3 months). Florida, since the Sherrer case, has increased its residence period from 90 days to 6 months. See the chart, Divorce, Annulment and Separation in the United States (1965), described at page 638 note 2 supra.

[54] It is noteworthy that several of the cases in Note 1 supra in which Sherrer was held to be inapplicable have been divorces of the second variety. Is there anything in the Sherrer case that would warrant such a differentiation?

e.g., Gherardi de Parata v. Gherardi de Parata, 179 A.2d 723 (D.C. Mun. Ct. App. 1962), and cases cited in Note 1.f supra. Characteristic of the rapid changes of scene in the drama of quickie divorce, the focus of attention is currently on Mexico as a result of the recent decisions which appear below.

ROSENSTIEL v. ROSENSTIEL
WOOD v. WOOD
16 N.Y.2d 64, 209 N.E.2d 709 (1965)

I. Rosenstiel v. Rosenstiel

BERGAN, J. The defendant wife's former husband Felix Ernest Kaufman in 1954 obtained a divorce from her in a district court at Juarez in Chihuahua, Mexico. Plaintiff and defendant were married in New York in 1956 and this action by the husband seeks to annul that marriage on the ground the 1954 divorce is invalid and that, therefore, the defendant wife was incompetent in 1956 to contract a marriage.

In seeking the divorce in Mexico Mr. Kaufman went to El Paso, Texas, where he registered at a motel and the next day crossed the international boundary to Juarez. There he signed the Municipal Register, an official book of residents of the city, and filed with the district court a certificate showing such registration and a petition for divorce based on [incompatibility] and ill treatment between the spouses.

After about an hour devoted to these formalities, Mr. Kaufman returned to El Paso. The following day his wife, the present defendant, appeared in the Mexican court by an attorney duly authorized to act for her and filed an answer in which she submitted to the jurisdiction of the court and admitted the allegations of her husband's complaint. The decree of divorce was made the same day. The judgment is recognized as valid by the Republic of Mexico.

The Divorce Law of the State of Chihuahua provides that the court may exercise jurisdiction either on the basis of residence or of submission. Article 22 provides that the Judge "competent to take cognizance of a contested divorce" is the Judge "of the place of residence of the plaintiff" and of a divorce "by mutual consent," the Judge "of the residence of either of the spouses."

For the purposes of article 22, the statute further provides that the residence "shall be proven" by the "certificate of the Municipal Register" of the place (art. 24). Article 23, which has application to Wood v. Wood, provides that judicial competence "may also be fixed" by express or tacit submission.

After a trial at Special Term in the present husband's action for annulment, the court, holding that New York would not recognize the Mexican decree, granted judgment for the plaintiff and annulled the marriage; the Appellate Division reversed this judgment and dismissed the complaint.

In the background of this problem is a long series of decisions over a period of a quarter of a century in the New York Supreme Court at Appellate Division and at Special Term recognizing the validity of bilateral Mexican divorces which we consider has some relevancy to the question before us. No New York decision has refused to recognize such a bilateral Mexican divorce.

It has been estimated that many thousands of persons have been affected in their family and property status by these decisions [citations omitted]. In this respect the problem in New York differs somewhat from that in New Mexico, New Jersey and Ohio which have as a matter of their own public policy refused to accept as valid such Mexican divorces (Golden v. Golden, 41 N.M. 356; Warrender v. Warrender, 42 N.J. 287; Bobala v. Bobala, 68 Ohio App. 63).

There is squarely presented to this court now for the first time the question whether recognition is to be given by New York to a matrimonial judgment of a foreign country based on grounds not accepted in New York, where personal jurisdiction of one party to the marriage has been acquired by physical presence before the foreign court; and jurisdiction of the other has been acquired by appearance and pleading through an authorized attorney although no domicile of either party is shown within that jurisdiction; and "residence" has been acquired by one party through a statutory formality based on brief contact.

In cases where a divorce has been obtained without any personal contact with the jurisdiction by either party or by physical submission to the jurisdiction by one, with no personal service of process within the foreign jurisdiction upon, and no appearance or submission by, the other, decision has been against the validity of the foreign decree [citations omitted].

Although the grounds for divorce found acceptable according to Mexican law are inadmissible in New York, and the physical contact with the Mexican jurisdiction was ephemeral, there are some incidents in the Mexican proceedings which are common characteristics of the exercise of judicial power.

The former husband was physically in the jurisdiction, personally before the court, with the usual incidents and the implicit consequences of voluntary submission to foreign sovereignty. Although he had no intention of making his domicile there, he did what the domestic law of the place required he do to establish a "residence" of a kind which was set up as a statutory prerequisite to institute an action for divorce. This is not our own view in New York of what a bona fide residence is or should be, but it is that which the local law of Mexico prescribes. . . .

The voluntary appearance of the other spouse in the foreign court by attorney would tend to give further support to an acquired jurisdiction there over the marriage as a legal entity. . . .

It is true that in attempting to reconcile the conflict of laws and of State interests in matrimonial judgments entered in States of the United States, where the Constitution compels each to give full faith and credit to the judgments of the others, a considerable emphasis has been placed on domicile as a prerequisite to that compulsory recognition [citation omitted]. But domicile is not intrinsically an indispensable prerequisite to jurisdiction [citations omitted].

The duration of domicile in sister States providing by statute for a minimal time to acquire domicile as necessary to matrimonial action jurisdiction is in actual practice complied with by a mere formal gesture having no more relation to the actual situs of the marriage or to true domicile than the formality of signing the Juarez city register. The difference in time is not truly significant of a difference in intent or purpose or in effect.

The State or country of true domicile has the closest real public interest in a marriage but, where a New York spouse goes elsewhere to establish a synthetic domicile to meet technical acceptance of a matrimonial suit, our public interest is not affected differently by a formality of one day than by a formality of six weeks.

Nevada gets no closer to the real public concern with the marriage than Chihuahua. New York itself will take jurisdiction of a matrimonial action without regard to domicile or residence if it happened, by mere fortuity, that the marriage was contracted here, even between people entirely foreign to our jurisdiction (Domestic Relations Law, §170, subd. 2; [further citations omitted]). . . .

A balanced public policy now requires that recognition of the bilateral Mexican divorce be given rather than withheld and such recognition as a matter of comity offends no public policy of this State.

The order should be affirmed, with costs.

II. Wood v. Wood

Although the Mexican decree of divorce in Wood v. Wood was entered under a provision of the Chihuahua Divorce Law (art. 23) which does not require proof of registration as a resident and which allowed jurisdiction to be taken by submission, the personal appearance in Chihuahua before the court of one party and the appearance through a duly authorized attorney by the other require that for the purposes of New York public policy decision in this case be consistent with that in Rosenstiel. . . .

Desmond, C.J. (concurring in part). Although for reasons hereafter stated I would not void past-granted Chihuahua divorces, I emphatically reject the proposition that New York State must continue to recognize these one-day decrees awarded to our residents in manner and on theories repugnant to our basic ideas.

There is no justification in positive law, public policy, natural justice or morals for a validation by this court of the practice of some of the citizens of our State of going to Mexico for divorces of the sort attacked on these appeals. My vote against recognizing them for the future is based on these self-evident propositions:

1. Divorce decrees rendered in foreign countries and purporting to

dissolve New York marriages are entitled to recognition and effect in New York State only when such recognition is consistent with the public policy of our State . . . .

2. Mexican "bilateral" divorces where one party crosses a bridge from El Paso, Texas, spends a day in Juarez and, by arrangement, the other appears by attorney, followed by a pro forma one-hour court appearance with no real hearing, or persuasive evidence or independent judicial determination lack almost all the elements which New York State considers requisites for a valid divorce. The residence requirements of the State of Chihuahua are minimal and inadequate to form a recognizable domiciliary jurisdictional base since in Mexico and contrary to our views neither spouse need have a true or real domicile in Mexico. . . .

3. No attention is paid in Juarez divorces to the principle, fundamental with us, that marriage is an institution in which the public as a third party has a vital interest [citations omitted]. The Mexican State does not concern itself with maintenance of the marriage or reasons for its dissolution. In these latter respects the one-day judgments here attacked differ in no essential respect from the mail-order writs described in Caldwell v. Caldwell (298 N.Y. 146).

4. Such decrees are blatantly and obviously the fruit of consensual divorce arrangements and as such are forbidden by New York public policy statute [citations omitted].

5. Although there is a line of lower court decisions in the State upholding these "Chihuahua" decrees (e.g., Leviton v. Leviton, 6 N.Y.S.2d 535, 254 App. Div. 670) they are, so we are told and so it would seem, refused recognition everywhere else [citations omitted]. Approval of these lower court decisions puts our State in the uneasy and inappropriate position of sole acceptor of Mexican "quickie" divorces. The suggestion in the majority opinion that these trial court and Appellate Division decisions, together with the fact that Mexico has issued numerous divorces to New Yorkers, plus the fact of advices by New York attorneys to their clients, force this court into a totally wrong public policy is a suggestion that answers itself. We are forgetting that the public policy of this State as to divorce "exists to promote the permanency of the marriage contracts and the morality of the citizens of the state" (Hubbard v. Hubbard, 228 N.Y. 81, 85).

Of course, it is in the modern manner to shrug off all this, to ask what is the difference between a one-day "domicile" in Juarez and a six weeks' "domicile" in Reno, to pile scorn and ridicule on New York's one-ground divorce law as archaic, cruel or worse. The approach is too facile. For 160 years New York as a State has recognized one cause only for divorce. . . . There can be no doubt that this speaks the public policy of our State to be changed only by the people through Constitution or statute. No court is licensed to write a new State policy, however attractive or convenient. As to divorces gotten in other States of the Union we are constrained to recognition by modern constructions of the Federal full faith and credit clause. But when asked to recognize divorces rendered in foreign countries we as a court have neither right nor need to look beyond our own declared and unmistakable State policy [citations omitted].

As to analogizing the one-day Mexican divorce to the six weeks' Nevada decree, the first and ready answer is that judgments from other States are given faith and credit here because the Federal Constitution so commands. The second answer is a substitution of the true analogy, that is, between one-day foreign divorces and post-card foreign divorces, as between which there is no logical or real difference at all (see Warrender v. Warrender, 79 N.J. Super. 114, affd. 42 N.J. 287 . . .

. . . Were we to give credit to these Mexican judgments we would as a court be turning our backs on New York's restrictive divorce policy and allowing the divorce of our own citizen-residents by a foreign government having no interest in the marriage res.

For these reasons I vote for a declaration that such divorces are void, but I am not bound to and do not vote to give this ruling any more than prospective effect. I cannot shut my eyes to the realities. Tens of thousands of such purported divorces have been granted to New Yorkers who acted on advice of attorneys who relied on 25 years of decisions by the New York lower courts. No social or moral purpose would now be served by ruling that marriages long ago dissolved are still in existence, and the result would be destructive to the present homes, marriage and lives of those who remarried on the strength of Juarez decrees. This court has a clear right to give our ruling prospective effect only [citations omitted] and justice and fairness dictate that we should do so and refuse to allow these plaintiffs or others to attack collaterally such past-rendered Mexican "one-day" divorces. . . .

In each case the order should be affirmed, with costs, but with the clear understanding that divorces of this sort granted after the date of the decision of these appeals will be void in New York State.

[Dissenting opinion of Scileppi, J., agreeing with Desmond, C.J., that bilateral Mexican divorces are not entitled to recognition in New York, but stating that even the present appellants should be entitled to take advantage of this principle, omitted.]

NOTE

1. In connection with the court's flat assertion that "The judgment [of the Chihuahua court] is recognized as valid by the Republic of Mexico," see Stern, Mexican Divorces — The Mexican Law, 7 Prac. Law., May 1961, pp. 78, 82-83 (questioning validity under Mexican law of typical Chihuahua divorces). The internal validity of the foreign divorce may become particularly relevant under statutes such as Cal. Civ. Prac. Code §1915 that purport to recognize only those foreign divorces that are valid in the rendering jurisdiction; it may also be a relevant factor in determining whether comity recognition should be given to the foreign proceeding. California has also enacted the Uniform Divorce Recognition Act (Cal. Civ. Code §150.1) under which foreign divorces obtained by local domiciliaries are refused recognition. Thus that state,

along with those referred to in the majority opinion in Rosenstiel, would probably refuse to recognize Mexican divorces of the Rosenstiel-Wood variety. See, e.g., 2 The California Family Lawyer §§33.16-33.48 (California Practice Handbook No. 17, 1963); Ehrenzweig, Conflict of Laws 247 (1962).

2. Although Mexican mail order divorces are almost universally regarded as legally ineffective to dissolve a valid marriage, they still appear to be used with an indeterminate frequency by those who do not have the money required for a personal appearance divorce and who are more concerned about the social than the legal status of their marriages. Moreover, these divorces may not be altogether devoid of legal effect. See, e.g., Matter of Rathscheck, 300 N.Y. 346, 90 N.E.2d 887 (1950) (wife who procured Mexican mail order divorce denied distributive share of husband's estate under statute barring spouse who obtains invalid divorce outside of New York). The article which follows further elaborates on the limitations imposed by the estoppel doctrine on the likelihood of successful challenge of an invalid divorce. But see page 765 infra concerning the ethical aspects of attorneys participating in the procurement of mail order divorces; see also Adams & Adams, Ethical Problems in Advising Migratory Divorce, 16 Hastings L.J. 60, 74-79 (1964).

CLARK, ESTOPPEL AGAINST JURISDICTIONAL ATTACK ON DECREES OF DIVORCE
70 Yale Law Journal 45 (1960)

One application of estoppel to divorce decrees is to be distinguished. Sherrer v. Sherrer held that if a state which granted a divorce would deny collateral attack upon it because the defendant had had an opportunity to raise and litigate the question of jurisdiction over the subject matter by having been made subject to the court's in personam jurisdiction, then other states must also refuse to entertain collateral attacks upon the same grounds. Sherrer thus announced a principle of full faith and credit whose application depends upon the rule of res judicata adopted in the state granting the divorce. The policy underlying this rule is that which demands finality in litigation after a person has had a chance to present his case. As will appear, the policy underlying the kind of estoppel presently under discussion is different. Both doctrines preclude attack on admittedly invalid divorces, but for different reasons.

Logically it would seem that if the full-faith-and-credit clause requires that a foreign state respect the doctrines of res judicata of the divorcing state, it should likewise require that the foreign state respect the various other rules of estoppel prevailing in the divorcing state. So, if on a theory of estoppel the divorcing state would exclude collateral attack upon its own decree by the party who obtained it, the full-faith-and-credit clause should forbid a similar attack in other states. But in spite of the apparently logical analogy, this is not the law. The reason lies in the difference between res judicata and the variation on equitable estoppel involved in divorce cases. The application of res judicata depends upon the conditions under which the divorce was granted and is really a function of the divorce decree itself. The estoppel under discussion here, however, is an equity principle dependent upon events which may have occurred after the divorce was granted or apart from the divorce action. It is not a function of the decree but a personal disability of the party attacking the decree. It is not a rule of jurisdiction. Therefore its application is not governed by the full-faith-and-credit clause. . . .

The [circumstance] which most obviously calls for application of the estoppel theory is that the divorce was obtained by the very party attempting to attack it. The divorce plaintiff is usually held estopped to question the decree. The courts which reach this result are careful not to say that such divorces are valid, but say rather that the attacking party is estopped to assert that they are invalid. In fact, one court held that a husband could not assert the invalidity of his divorce from his first wife even after an annulment suit brought by his second wife had established that the divorce was void. What is probably the utmost extension of the estoppel doctrine occurred in an Ohio case which held that a wife who falsely told her husband she had divorced him was estopped to deny that she had, after he had remarried on the faith of her statement. This is divorce by consent with a vengeance, but it does fit the usual requirements for technical equitable estoppel. Sometimes the defense of connivance may be used to reach the result ordinarily achieved through estoppel.[55]

Obtaining the decree does not estop the wife from questioning it, however, where she brought the divorce action as the result of the coercion, duress or fraud of her husband, or where for other reasons she cannot be held responsible for her actions.

Participation in obtaining the divorce, as by persuading a married person to divorce his spouse, or by financing a married woman's divorce with the intention of marrying her, also has been held to estop one from a later collateral attack on the decree. If participation takes the form of an appearance in the case as defendant, then of course the Sherrer rule would immunize the resulting divorce from attack on the basis of res judicata, although the cases occasionally use the language of estoppel here.

Estoppel may also rest upon acts or events occurring after the divorce in question. A long acquiescence in the divorce with knowledge of its jurisdictional defect will often foreclose an attack, whether the rationale of the defense is labeled estoppel or laches.

Acceptance of benefits, usually alimony, under the divorce has the same consequence. Remarriage after the defective decree, either by the person attacking it or by the other party, will usually raise an estoppel, as will

---

[55] Shilman v. Shilman, 105 Misc. 461, 174 N.Y. Supp. 385 (Sup. Ct. 1918), aff'd without opinion, 188 App. Div. 908, 175 N.Y. Supp. 681 (1919), aff'd without opinion, 230 N.Y. 554, 130 N.E. 890 (1920). Here the husband had obtained a Jewish divorce, after which the wife remarried. He then sued her for divorce on the ground of adultery and the court held him barred by his connivance. See also Langewald v. Langewald, 234 Mass. 269, 125 N.E. 566 (1920); Loud v. Loud, 129 Mass. 14 (1880).

reliance upon the decree by innocent third parties. At this point estoppel to attack a defective divorce begins to resemble estoppel to attack a defective marriage, since both arise from courts' reluctance to upset relationships formed (by one party at least) in good faith and in ignorance of any defect.

This summary of the kinds of cases in which courts have rejected attacks upon invalid divorce decrees is evidence of a broad acceptance of the estoppel doctrine. If a mere counting of cases were not irrelevant, or even misleading, one might sum up by saying that the majority of jurisdictions approve of estoppel in this context and let the matter rest there. Nevertheless, the cases which do not approve are numerous enough and of sufficient standing as authorities to require further discussion of the basis and extent of the doctrine. The confusion which is found within particular jurisdictions such as New York also demands some clarification. . . .

It is clear that New York has both applied and rejected estoppel in identical types of cases, thereby proving that no criterion based upon the nature of the lawsuit is determinative in the use of the estoppel doctrine. . . . [This] has at last begun to focus courts' attention on the real source of the difficulty, a profound conflict in policies, a conflict whose ultimate outcome depends upon the changing attitudes toward divorce of both the public and the courts.

The traditional nineteenth century attitude toward divorce, which is still reflected in the law and the official pronouncements of New York and some other states, views divorce as a remedy provided exclusively for an innocent person whose spouse has been guilty of a serious marital wrong. Divorce itself is looked upon as evil, to be tolerated only in circumstances which strictly meet the statutory standard both as to grounds and as to the court's authority to act. . . .

More modern authorities look upon divorce as a regrettable but necessary legal recognition of marital failure. It is recognized that very often, perhaps in most cases, the factors leading to breakdown of the marriage are not all on one side. Although the statutes rarely reflect this sociological view of divorce, the practice in trial courts and the opinions of some appellate courts do. The doctrine of estoppel as applied in many jurisdictions also reflects this view, since it recognizes, at least for certain purposes, that a marriage has ended de facto and adjusts the legal rights and obligations of the parties accordingly, notwithstanding the fact that the termination of the marriage was not accomplished pursuant to prevailing legal requirements. This has the effect, for most relevant purposes, of allowing the parties to end their marriage by consent, although courts often attempt to appease tradition by stating carefully that they are not validating a divorce without jurisdiction, but merely refusing to hear an attack upon it. This sort of distinction is of course familiar to lawyers, being similar to other ancient equity defenses, but we cannot expect laymen to understand it easily. It is therefore bound to create some confusion about the marital status of the parties, confusion which is highly undesirable. The uncertainty over whether parties are or are not married, or over whether they are married for some purposes, and if so, for what purposes, is a legitimate objection to the use of the estoppel theory. The refusal to rely on estoppel, however, may create even greater uncertainty. In any event, we are now so committed by the United States Supreme Court to a theory of "divisible divorce" that a large amount of uncertainty about the validity of divorces and ensuing marriages is inevitable.

One additional factor gives support to the estoppel doctrine. Protection of children is often said to be the strongest reason for a strict divorce law, and thus for what we have called the traditional nineteenth century attitude towards divorce. The assumption is that children are better off in the custody of two persons who remain married, albeit unhappily, than when they are placed in the custody of one or the other spouse upon the break-up of a marriage. In many of the estoppel cases, however, this harmful result is avoided, since one or the other of the parties has contracted a new marriage and the children can have a stable home, with both a mother and a father. This may be a further reason for the apparent willingness of courts to recognize a de facto marriage breakdown via the estoppel theory and to apply the analysis which we have suggested.

The estoppel doctrine thus represents an adherence to contemporary sociological theories of divorce, at the expense of the "conventional wisdom." . . .

Notwithstanding the confusion, a principle is emerging from the cases which, with allowances for differences of approach, offers an explanation for the results reached and gives insight into the operative policies. It turns upon the conduct of the parties rather than the type of action. Three factors seem to be involved: 1) The attack on the divorce is inconsistent with prior conduct of the attacking party. 2) The party upholding the divorce has relied upon it, or has formed expectations based upon it. 3) These relations or expectations will be upset if the divorce is held invalid. When either the first and third, or the second and third, of these factors exist, then one or the other or both of the parties have treated the marriage as at an end, and estoppel to attack the divorce amounts to recognition that such a marriage cannot be resurrected. All three factors will sometimes appear in a single case, making the nature of the situation particularly plain. . . .

Some cases have imposed an additional qualification on the use of estoppel. They reject estoppel where the party attacking the divorce was ignorant of the facts making the divorce invalid until a short time before bringing the suit to invalidate it. This qualification is based upon the traditional equity view of estoppel, rather than the social policy discussed in this article. It reflects some unwillingness to accept the implications of that policy and to that extent reveals a point of view opposed to the analysis advanced herein. . . .

. . . One fact of great importance to the application of estoppel is the remarriage of one or both of the parties to the void divorce. When this happens, the social purpose which has been advanced as the real basis for estoppel clearly demands recognition of the later marriage. . . .

The arguments supporting estoppel where there has been a remarriage are so strong that courts have been persuaded by them even where the divorce has been judicially held invalid, or where no final divorce had occurred at the time of the second marriage, or where the divorce was by mail-order, or where there was no judicial divorce at all. These cases (the most numerous class in which estoppel is applied) lend additional force to the foregoing analysis of the social purpose involved in estoppel. They furnish an analogy to the well-established presumption that the latest of several marriages is valid. The presumption, though rebuttable, imposes a heavy burden of persuasion on the proponent of the earlier marriage. Like the doctrine of estoppel, it fulfills the legitimate expectations of the parties, and recognizes that a de facto marriage is entitled in most instances to legal protection. . . .

Often, no second marriage follows the void divorce. Nevertheless, the courts will usually refuse to hear an attack on the divorce if one or both parties have by their conduct given objective evidence that the marriage is at an end. If the wife accepts alimony or property pursuant to the invalid decree, she may not later attack it. The only thing accomplished by upsetting the divorce in this situation would be to enable the wife to extract more support from the husband or his estate, a reconciliation being the last thing on earth the parties desire. As the wife has generally been given all the alimony she is entitled to by the decree to which she objects, there is nothing to be gained by attempting to revive the defunct marriage. . . .

It must be conceded that there are cases which flatly reject both the doctrine of estoppel and the social policy which underlies it. They can only be accounted for as vestiges of an obsolete legal approach to marriage and divorce. There are other cases allowing attacks upon invalid divorces, however, which can be reconciled with the analysis we have been advocating. . . .

When a divorce is obtained without jurisdiction of the subject matter, and one of the parties remarries, he may be prosecuted for bigamy or bigamous cohabitation. In such a case estoppel is properly rejected, since the state is not subject to estoppel. . . .

Estoppel is also inappropriate in . . . . actions for divorce brought by the party who had originally obtained the invalid divorce, so that granting the divorce merely confirmed the putative existing relationship of the parties. No later marriages had occurred, and no financial claims were being made or extinguished. . . . [T]he result reached by rejecting estoppel gave legal recognition to the fact that the marriage had ended, at the same time settling any possible doubts about the parties' status, all of this without upsetting any expectations of either spouse. The moral is plain. When the goals of a modern divorce law can be reached by refusing estoppel, it will be refused. The important thing is the end, not the means. . . .

. . . [S]hould the doctrine apply to a second "marriage," even though it was contracted before the parties had obtained any divorce, even an invalid one? . . .

. . . [O]ne may find authority both ways. The issue commonly arises when a woman remarries before her divorce or annulment from her first husband is final. The second husband understands the circumstances, and may even go to some lengths to persuade her that there is no need to wait until the decree is final. Later the husband grows tired of his bargain and sues to annul. In states where common-law marriage is recognized, this relationship might ripen into a valid marriage by the mere passage of time, but this would not happen in states like New York or California which have abolished common-law marriage. If no estoppel is raised on these facts the husband is entitled to his annulment, and the wife has no claims for support or property. In New York this harsh result has been prevented by a statute which authorizes support awards in annulment cases as justice may require, and this may explain New York's refusal to hold the husband estopped. In other states which do not have this salutary statute estoppel should be used as the rationale for protecting the wife. Denial of annulment would leave the parties, if their marriage had irretrievably broken down, to the remedy of divorce, in which the wife's financial claims could be honored. This same result is sometimes reached, even in New York, by imposing a heavy burden on the second husband to show that the first marriage has not ended in a divorce action brought by the first husband. Here again the desire to recognize the expectations of the parties, frustrated by one doctrine, is given vent by another.

There remains for discussion the question whether, assuming that estoppel would preclude attack on an invalid divorce by one of the parties to the divorce action, the same doctrine would stand in the way of an attack by third persons. . . .

This problem most commonly arises when a man persuades a married woman to divorce her husband so that she will be free to marry him. He may even finance the divorce, provide a lawyer, or take an active part in other ways. When he does so, or even when he merely marries her with full knowledge of the circumstances surrounding the divorce, he is estopped to question the validity of the divorce. He has engaged in conduct calculated to induce reliance on the divorce, and indeed, he has relied on it himself. Therefore, the reasons of policy which prevent attack by a party to the divorce action are equally persuasive here. Some cases have said, however, that if he marries without knowledge of the circumstances in which the divorce was obtained he is not estopped to attack it when he later learns the facts. These cases represent an adherence to the traditional view of equitable estoppel, and a reluctance squarely to face the social policies involved in this situation. Here, as in other cases where estoppel is asserted, the invalidity of the divorce is really irrelevant to the interests of the second spouse. But the force of the older notions of good faith and innocence inhering in all equity doctrines is so strong that it is not surprising to find cases which refuse to apply estoppel in these circumstances. . . .

3. *Ethics and the Lawyer's Choice*

O'GORMAN, LAWYERS AND MATRIMONIAL CASES
78-80 (1963)

[This important study of lawyers' work in family law is based on data gathered from interviews with 82 New York City attorneys. The lawyers interviewed were randomly selected from a list of all 595 attorneys who represented matrimonial clients before the State Supreme (e.g., trial) Court in New York County in December and January 1957-1958. O'Gorman discusses his interview technique at 174-177. His lawyers naturally represented a wide variety of practices. For 18 of them, matrimonial work constituted only a peripheral part of their practice, such cases being characterized as comparatively rare, with 10 handling about 4 cases a year, most of which were referrals by the attorney's regular (nonmatrimonial) clients; 46 had a "minor" matrimonial practice, of whom 25 had up to 11 cases a year, and 21 estimated 12 to 25 cases a year; for the remaining 18 lawyer-informants, "the legal problems attending separation, annulment, and divorce constituted a major part of their practices," in 8 instances the matrimonial work being almost exclusive and the number of cases handled annually ranging from 25 to 100. See id. at 65-71.]

. . . Confronted with clients who wish to obtain a divorce, attorneys usually have two alternatives: they can advise that residency be established and an action initiated in a jurisdiction outside of New York; or they can advise that the proceedings take place locally. If the foreign jurisdiction is chosen, the problems created by the cultural conflict are circumvented. If the action is local, then both lawyer and client must accommodate to the New York context. To be sure, this decision will rest, in part, on the evidence in each case. But, for our purposes, this factor can be ignored. We are more interested in any characteristic of law practice that might predispose an attorney, whatever the evidence may be, to advise consistently one jurisdiction rather than another.

The socioeconomic background of a legal clientele is precisely this kind of characteristic. Since the costs of travel to, and residence in, a foreign jurisdiction are greater than the costs of securing a local divorce, a client's financial resources probably determine, in most cases, where the divorce will be secured. Consequently, we would expect that the frequency with which a lawyer is involved in New York matrimonial actions is largely determined by his clients' class position.

We asked our informants where most of their matrimonial clients obtained their divorces. Many lawyers had difficulty in answering this question. Some claimed that it was impossible to classify their practices by jurisdiction. Others, curiously enough, took the position that since it was a violation of legal ethics to suggest a foreign divorce, the query was unfair. Among the forty-five informants who did describe their divorce cases by place of jurisdiction, we find the following patterns: only one out of fourteen peripheral practitioners, and only two out of nine major practitioners reported that their clients' divorce actions usually took place in New York; in contrast, fifteen out of twenty-two minor practitioners said that they handled most of their divorce cases in local courts. It would appear, then, that attorneys with minor matrimonial practices are more likely than other lawyers to be exposed directly to the New York cultural context. But who are these minor practitioners? As we indicated above, they are mostly general practitioners who . . . usually have working-class clienteles.

Further evidence bearing on the association between a minor practice and clients with relatively low socioeconomic status appears in a comparison of types of matrimonial practice with clients' class background. Almost three-fourths (74 per cent) of lawyers with minor matrimonial practices had working-class clienteles. In contrast, 22 per cent of those with major practices and only 11 per cent of those with peripheral practices normally had clients from the working class.

The tendency for minor practitioners to use local rather than foreign jurisdictions seems clearly to be related to a specific attribute of law practice: the working-class background of their clients. As one lawyer remarked about his matrimonial clients: "They all go through the local courts. They can't afford to travel." This selection of jurisdiction is supported by the economic function served by matrimonial cases in this type of practice. Several minor practitioners stated their preference for local actions on the grounds that their fees would be larger than in a foreign proceeding, where another lawyer would have to be retained. "I prefer that they go in New York," explained one attorney, "because I don't have to split the fee."

In a similar fashion, the jurisdiction chosen by lawyers with peripheral and major matrimonial practices is influenced by their clientele's class attributes. Since their clients come from comparatively high socioeconomic strata, there are normally fewer financial obstacles to obtaining divorces outside of New York. . . . A foreign divorce may be desirable, as the next excerpt indicates, as an expedient way of protecting clients against adverse publicity:

> Well, it's more expensive to go out of state, but . . . it's a matter of reputation. If it's local, the newspapers can get hold of the story and report it first hand. . . . A client may be a well-known businessman, and he doesn't want that kind of publicity. . . .

NOTE

"Judges handling [matrimonial actions in New York] do not emerge as paragons of consistency or staunchness." "But here again no human being is being victimized. The judge is permitting estranged spouses to do what their wealthier neighbors may accomplish by a trip to Nevada or Florida. Still, one wonders whether even the party who seeks the end result does not experience a certain disrespect for laws so easily circumvented." Botein, Trial Judge 300 (1952).

If a client is too poor to go to Nevada for six weeks or to Alabama or Mexico for a day, or to pay the costs and fees involved in retaining a lawyer to obtain a New York adultery divorce or fraud annulment, he may apply for legal assistance through a legal aid bureau. But sometimes the legal aid bureau will not handle cases of clients who have previously been divorced. We have noted that in Illinois it has been held that a divorce must be denied if it appears that both parties have committed adultery even though the plaintiff's adultery has not been pleaded as a defense. Rosengren v. Rosengren, 17 Ill. App. 2d 415, 149 N.E.2d 798 (1958) (abstract decision). See Ill. Ann. Stat. c. 40, §11 (1956). We have found no data indicating whether this decision affects private lawyers' conduct in deciding whether or not to accept clients whom they know to be guilty of recrimination; at least as divorce cases are handled in Chicago, see Virtue, page 692 supra, it would be improbable that the court on its own motion would discover the recrimination, so that the Rosengren rule would depend for whatever efficacy it may have (but see the possibility of migratory divorce) upon lawyers screening out cases by refusing to handle them. However that may be, the Chicago Legal Aid Bureau regards itself as bound by the rule:

> The poor may be subject to some discriminations when they seek divorce, but recrimination is not one of them. The Chicago Legal Aid Bureau "refuses" to represent clients guilty of adultery on the ground that under Illinois law they are not entitled to a divorce and a lawyer who proceeds, knowing the facts and concealing them from the court, is, in our opinion, guilty of improper practice. . . .
>
> Unfortunately, with the staff we have at present, we cannot accept all the divorce requests that come to us. Consequently, we have two arbitrary rules (subject to exceptions in proper cases) for controlling our case load. We do not accept cases where: (1) there are no minor dependent children living with the applicant, or (2) where there has been physical separation for more than five years. If this does not control case load within limits we can handle, then we make further limitation based on the urgency of the client's request.
>
> These are rules of expediency which some day we would like to eliminate so that all eligible persons might be served.[56]

[56] Letter to Robert J. Levy from Arthur K. Young, Director, Chicago Legal Aid Bureau, dated January 4, 1965. A device used by another legal aid society to bring caseloads within manageable proportions is to require potential divorce clients to get approval of the social welfare agency of which they were a client. In a case which may or may not be typical of actual administration, one agency, in refusing to approve a case, informed Legal Aid that "unless a man is a real danger to his family because of brutality due to drunkenness or insanity we do not feel it is the function of this agency to assist in divorce action." (This letter has been seen by the Editors, but the Bureau did not wish to be named.)

Do you agree with the first sentence of this excerpt?

If both parties are indigent, a legal aid society is faced with a problem of conflict of interest; one agency has "taken the position that we will represent the side that is able to convince us that they should have custody of the minor children involved." The agency sees no solution for this dilemma "in the absence of another facility for indigent persons." [57] Or an agency "may insist that anyone who wishes legal help to obtain a divorce must involve himself in an effort at marital reconciliation, employing a scheme prescribed by the agency." [58] Persons employing private counsel, of course, are under no such restriction. Professor Paulsen has commented:

> We cannot often offer the same kinds of remedies to the disadvantaged as to the wealthy, but here we can. It seems rather too bad to require something of indigents that is not required of those with means. Perhaps there is a feeling that those without money are likely to be poorer judges of their own best interests. This kind of notion, I believe, runs through a great many of the legal institutions which the poor must use. It's even a hard position to deny. To me, however, it is an unhappy thought because it contributes to what I believe to be one of the most difficult aspects of dealing with poverty: The existence of an attitude on the part of the poor that they are clients rather than citizens, an attitude unhappily reflected in the minds of many of those who deal with them.[59]

For a different approach, compare Theophilus, Determining Social Need, 22 Legal Aid Brief Case 211, 213 (1964):

> People may say that poverty prevents [the poor] from having the same right to get a divorce as a person with money, yet we must remember obtaining a divorce is not a right but a privilege. For most Legal Aid clients, a separation is just as useful and practical as a divorce.[60]

In dealing with illegitimacy, we raised the problem whether there was an implicit conflict between legal disabilities imposed on illegitimates and the equal protection clause of the fourteenth amendment. See page 72 supra. Is there a similar problem for New York divorce administration? We have seen that a Rockefeller can, notwithstanding New York State policy, obtain a divorce which for all practical purposes is unassailable provided he pays out the $1500 or more required by the Nevada procedure. We have seen also that the New York courts have similarly insulated from attack a Mexican bilateral divorce if one of the

---

[57] Letter to Robert J. Levy from Harlan E. Smith, Chief Counsel, Legal Aid Society of Minneapolis, dated January 11, 1965.

[58] Paulsen, The Legal Needs of the Poor and Family Law, in The Extension of Legal Services to the Poor 18, 19 (Dept. H.E.&W. 1964).

[59] Ibid.

[60] This factor would appear to set the poor apart from other Americans. See Jacobson, American Marriage and Divorce 82-87 (1959) (most divorced persons remarry soon after divorce). — Ed.

parties puts up the cost of a round-trip air ticket to El Paso, in order to spend an hour south of the border. Under these circumstances, does the refusal of New York courts to recognize Mexican mail order divorces where the parties cannot afford the plane ticket offend the equal protection clause?

STAEDLER v. STAEDLER
6 N.J. 380, 78 A.2d 896 (1951)

OLIPHANT, J. This is an appeal from a judgment nisi entered in the Chancery Division setting aside and declaring null and void a decree of absolute divorce granted the appellant by the Eleventh Judicial Circuit Court of the State of Florida, dated January 28, 1948, and granting a divorce to the respondent on the ground of adultery but denying alimony to the respondent. The appellant appealed to the Appellate Division from the judgment nisi on the question of jurisdiction, on the merits and the allowance and amount of counsel fee. The respondent cross-appeals from the denial of alimony. These appeals were brought here on our own motion.

The parties were married on June 20, 1937, in East Orange, New Jersey, and lived in Verona as husband and wife, later moving to Montclair, New Jersey, until the appellant left for Florida to obtain a divorce under circumstances related hereafter.

The appellant has been engaged for the last 25 years in the painting and decorating business . . . . [and] respondent was actively engaged with him in the business as secretary and bookkeeper . . .

There was considerable bickering during their married life and at various times the appellant asked the respondent for a divorce but the respondent always refused, whereupon he finally threatened to go to another state and procure one. In 1946, over one year prior to the Florida decree here in question, the appellant communicated with Morris G. Warner concerning a divorce in Florida. Warner is a member of the bar of this State and of Florida and later represented the appellant in the Florida proceedings. The respondent in the meanwhile had consulted with present counsel and when the appellant learned of this he threatened to leave the State, turn over his assets to a dummy corporation, get a divorce and leave her without anything. He said there was no need for two lawyers in the case, that his lawyer could take care of everything by an agreement.

Finally the appellant took the respondent to his lawyer Morris Rubin in Bloomfield and discussed with him their difficulties and affairs and Rubin drew an agreement which is the nub of this appeal. The agreement followed an oral discussion of the problems and a study of a preliminary draft thereof by both the parties. Rubin testified that he did not advise the wife as to her rights because she never asked him.

The written agreement was signed on October 17, 1947, and under its terms the appellant agreed to pay his wife $60 a week until the payments totaled $20,000. It further provided that, when and if their home on

Park Street, Montclair, New Jersey, was sold, title to which was apparently in both names, $10,000 from the proceeds of the sale would be deposited in a trust fund to be paid to the wife in weekly payments of $60, except that she could draw therefrom $1500 at any time. However, no weekly payments were to be made from this trust fund until the wife had been paid $10,000 in weekly payments of $60 as first mentioned above. In all the wife was to receive $20,000 to be secured by a non-interest bearing note signed by the appellant for $20,000. The wife also was to receive a 1946 De Soto car valued at $2500.

On her part she agreed to withdraw from the business and to waive, release, and bar herself of all right of dower or other claim in all real property the appellant then owned or thereafter acquired, if the appellant did not breach the agreement.

She also further agreed to the following terms and conditions which are pertinent here:

". . . 7. The party of the second part agrees promptly to execute any papers, and enter, or cause to be entered any appearance required in the divorce proceedings to be instituted by the party of the first part, without delay. Should the party of the second part oppose said divorce proceedings the said trust shall become inoperative, and the monies deposited thereunder shall be returned to the party of the first part.

11. . . . If the party of the first part shall hereafter obtain a decree of divorce against the party of the second part, nevertheless, this agreement shall continue in full force and effect. . . ." [Court's quotation abbreviated by Eds.]

The appellant testified that he left for Florida a few days after the agreement was signed, but the correspondence he engaged in with his wife and his associates indicates that he arrived in Florida in the middle of November, 1947. By his own direct admission and his testimony as to the dates of the discussions which led to the consummation of the above agreement, the appellant certainly was not in Florida on or about September 18, 1947, as he testified in the Florida proceedings or as testified to here by his Florida attorney.

All during the time he was in Florida he constantly directed the business through instructions sent to the respondent up to December 31, 1947, when she by agreement withdrew from the business, and thereafter through the manager, Richard Coutant, who testified he consulted with the appellant in Florida by letter and telephone as to all business decisions and policies. The appellant maintained bank accounts in the Verona Trust Company, Federal Trust Company in Newark, and the Bank of Montclair. All of these accounts were never closed and are open and in use at the present time. The testimony clearly shows that during the period in question, October 17, 1947, to May, 1948, the appellant directed and has been before and since actively associated with the business and has controlled all of its policies and activities.

About the time he left for Florida, the respondent wife finally consulted an attorney of her own choice, Charles E. Garrett. He testified she had read the agreement and knew what it meant and wanted to go through with it. Shortly thereafter the appellant, in early December, called the respondent from Florida and told her there was being sent to her a power of attorney authorizing one Maxwell Hyman to represent her in the Florida proceedings and asked her to execute it. Subsequently Rubin called her and told her he had received the power of attorney; he in turn sent it to Garrett, and in answer to a call from Garrett she went to his office, executed it and mailed it to her husband. At about the same time, at the suggestion of his Florida attorney, the appellant admits he paid $60 to Maxwell Hyman, a Florida lawyer, to represent the respondent in the Florida action. He protested paying this since he considered that the $750 he had paid Rubin would include all the costs, because he understood it was a "package deal" with everything taken care of by the one fee paid to Rubin.

With this attended to the appellant returned to the home in Montclair for the Christmas holidays. He and his wife attended a number of social functions together and apparently shared the same bedroom, although he denies the inference that they resumed marital cohabitation.

He returned to Florida after the holidays and on January 11, 1948, he wrote his wife asking her to send an authorization to Maxwell Hyman to represent her and enclosed a copy of such authorization in his handwriting dated November 28, 1947, which she was to sign, which among other things stated: "I am enclosing herewith your fee for taking care of this and representing me." This despite the fact that the appellant and Hyman knew he had already paid Hyman the fee. The respondent signed and mailed the letter to Hyman as required.

The Florida complaint for divorce was filed the next day, January 12, 1948. An answer was filed by Hyman on behalf of the respondent, wherein he admitted the jurisdictional allegations and residence of the plaintiff in Florida. The gravamen of the complaint was extreme cruelty. The proofs were taken before a master. There was minimal perfunctory cross-examination by Hyman, who did little more than offer and prove his power of attorney to appear for the respondent. On the report of the master, the Florida Circuit Court entered a decree of divorce a vinculo in favor of the appellant here. The fraudulent purpose of the appellant here was a fait accompli due to the culpable failure of the appellant and the attorneys of both parties, here and in Florida, to discharge their sworn duties.

The proof offered on the merits in the Florida cause was that respondent here was unjustifiably charging him with having illicit relations with other women, including a Mrs. Klinge, which was making a nervous wreck of the appellant. These charges of the wife evidently had more than a modicum of truth to them and though they may have been painful and distressing to the appellant, would not amount to extreme cruelty, here or in most jurisdictions. The appellant testified that Mrs. Klinge came to Florida, a few days after his decree became final, and that they shared a room together in Delray, Florida, until she obtained her decree in April, 1948, through the same attorney, Morris G. Warner, who represented this appellant, and that they entered into a common-law relationship which continued after they both returned to Bloomfield, New Jersey, in May, 1948, where they lived as husband and wife; that a child was born of this relationship but that they returned to Florida on March 10, 1950, and were married there, and they both shortly there-after returned again to Bloomfield. Presently another child is expected to be born of this alleged marriage.

The appellant made the payments under the agreement with respondent for seven months and in May, 1948, discontinued them because he claimed that he could not afford to continue them. After some discussion he finally suggested that the Park Street house be sold, but not for the purpose of establishing the trust fund set up by the agreement. This would have left the respondent without support. Instead of $20,000 she had received about $3200, which included a lump sum of $1500. The appellant then ordered the respondent to leave the Park Street home but she was able to arrange a mortgage on the property and out of the funds so raised she paid the appellant $8450 for his half interest in it, which he then sold and conveyed to her, and in return she gave a general release as to all claims against him. She was represented in this transaction by Garrett. She thus received only $3200 instead of the $20,000 agreed to be paid under the original agreement.

The trial court held that the appellant never intended to and did not establish a bona fide domicile in Florida, and that while the United States Supreme Court has held that where the defendant in a divorce proceeding appears and participates therein and has an opportunity to raise the jurisdictional issue, the decree of divorce is ordinarily entitled to full faith and credit, Sherrer v. Sherrer, 334 U.S. 343 [further citations omitted], the learned trial judge believed these cases do not go to the length of requiring that full faith and credit must be given to a decree where the plaintiff acknowledges that the decree was obtained by a fraud practiced on the court of the foreign jurisdiction, as well as upon the State of New Jersey. He held that the State of Florida certainly has no interest which is infringed by a refusal to recognize a decree, thus confessedly obtained by a fraud upon it, with respect to persons with whom that state had no domiciliary concern.

He therefore tried the divorce cause on the basis that the Florida decree was void and the marriage to the co-respondent invalid. He found that the proofs established adultery. The co-respondent, Mrs. Klinge, was represented by counsel and was present in court, but failed to take the stand. The trial court denied alimony or support to the respondent since she had taken all the steps she had after consideration, including the final settlement and general release given by her to the appellant at that time, and considered her right to support a matter of judicial discretion. He awarded a counsel fee of $3500 to the counsel for the respondent.

The basic question is the validity of the Florida divorce. . . . A mere reading of [the] agreement [of October 17, 1947] indicates that the basic consideration for it was the undertaking by the wife to facilitate the procurement of a divorce by the husband in this State or any other state and required that the wife would enter "any appearance required in the divorce proceeding," and that should she "oppose said divorce proceedings the said trust shall become inoperative and the moneys deposited thereunder shall be returned to the party of the first part."

All bargains which have for their object or tendency the divorce of married people are opposed to public policy. Bargains to bring suit for divorce or to make no defense to such suit, or having for their object such purposes, are unlawful. . . . This agreement is obviously contrary to the public policy of this State and is likewise contrary to the public policy of the State of Florida. [Citations omitted.]

The appellant admits that the purpose of the agreement was to suppress any inquiry that would disclose the fraud and make a mockery of any appearance by the respondent in the Florida proceeding, and that it was not intended that any divorce proceeding between the parties should be an adversary proceeding. Yet he contends that his Florida decree is protected by the full faith and credit clause of the Federal Constitution under the decisions by the United States Supreme Court . . . .

We have carefully considered these cases and we do not believe that the full faith and credit clause of the Federal Constitution was ever intended to be used as a shield for or to give validity to the type of contract here under consideration, or to approve the acts performed pursuant thereto in cases where the ultimate purpose was to commit a fraud upon the jurisdiction of a court of one of the several sovereign states. Jurisdiction depends upon the existence of basic facts and a bona fide finding that the necessary facts actually exist, and where they do not exist it cannot be conferred upon any court anywhere by consent of the parties or by fraud. It presupposes a bona fide examination by a court of competent jurisdiction of such facts before any judgment can be entered by such court. . . .

. . . No matter what others may perceive to be the recent trend in the decisions of the United States Supreme Court in causes of this type, we are constrained not to impute to that court an intent that . . . that court will acquiesce in a fraudulent scheme to use the principles of the Davis [305 U.S. 32 (1938)], Sherrer [334 U.S. 343 (1948)] and Coe [334 U.S. 378 (1948)] cases as a device to infuse constitutional virility into the judgment of a court of a sovereign state which has been deliberately deceived in proceeding to judgment in a cause over which in fact it had no jurisdiction. . . .

. . . We find as a fact, as the trial court did below, that the appellant here was not resident in Florida on September 18, 1947, and that he did not reside in Florida for 90 days next preceding the institution of his action in that state, a requisite jurisdictional requirement. . . .

We further hold that the appearance in the Florida proceeding by Maxwell Hyman ostensibly on behalf of the wife was an appearance by him as agent for the husband who paid for his services and controlled his actions, and that there was never any intention on his, Hyman's, part to enter a bona fide contest as to the jurisdictional elements of that court.

We are firmly of the opinion that the principles of the Sherrer and Coe cases, supra, only apply to a true adversary proceeding where the parties are represented by counsel of their independent choice and where there is an opportunity to make a voluntary decision on the question as to whether or not the case should be fully litigated either on the question of jurisdiction or the merits, and that once an election has been made by the defendant under such circumstances and conditions that then and then alone can the judgment of the court be res adjudicata and the full faith and credit clause operate for the advancement of justice rather than for the perpetration of a fraud. . . .

The appellant makes the further point that the Florida decree does not have to be held valid by this court and that the respondent can be estopped from challenging it without determining its validity. The point here made is that she willingly and knowingly participated in the fraud after she had the opportunity of fully considering the situation and obtaining independent legal advice. But at no time was she told that the original contract agreement was null and void as against the public policy of this State. Yet it is true she was a willing co-conspirator.

The argument made by the appellant in support of the estoppel is really an argument for the application of the doctrine of clean hands to the particular facts of this case. But the application of the doctrine of clean hands is purely discretionary and should not be applied where it will produce a result contra to the firm public policy of this State in a matter of such fundamental importance as the preservation of the dignity of the marital relationship. . . .

For the foregoing reasons we deem that the decree of divorce granted the appellant in Florida was null and void on the ground of fraud actually and deliberately perpetrated upon that court by the appellant, and that since the appellant admits cohabitating with his present wife during the period prior to the ceremonial marriage and even before she was divorced from her husband, a cause of action for divorce on the ground of adultery has been established.

[The court then modified the rulings below on counsel fees and alimony.]

The judgment of the Chancery Division is accordingly modified and as modified is affirmed.

A rule to show cause will forthwith issue as to why Morris Rubin, Esq., and Morris G. Warner, Esq., should not be disciplined for their conduct of and with respect to this cause.

In re RUBIN
7 N.J. 507, 81 A.2d 776 (1951)

PER CURIAM. The factual situation which gave rise to the issuance of the order to show cause in this matter is set forth in the opinion of this court in the case of Staedler v. Staedler, 6 N.J. 380 (March 5, 1951).

Canon 6 of the Canons of Professional Ethics provides in part as follows:

"It is unprofessional to represent conflicting interests, except by express consent of all concerned given after a full disclosure of the facts. Within the meaning of this canon, a lawyer represents conflicting interests when, in behalf of one client, it is his duty to contend for that which duty to another client requires him to oppose."

It is clear from the record in the Staedler case and from the depositions taken on this order to show cause that the conduct of the respondent at the time of the drawing of the agreement between Mr. and Mrs. Staedler was in violation of this canon.

Canon 31 provides:

"No lawyer is obliged to act either as adviser or advocate for every person who may wish to become his client. . . . The responsibility for advising questionable transactions, for bringing questionable suits, for urging questionable defenses, is the lawyer's responsibility. He cannot escape it by urging as an excuse that he is only following his client's instructions."

The conduct of the respondent in drafting the unenforceable and illegal agreement between Mr. and Mrs. Staedler constituted a violation of this canon.

For these reasons we find the respondent guilty of unprofessional conduct requiring disciplinary action. The judgment of the court is that the respondent be suspended from practice as an attorney-at-law for a period of one year and until the further order of the court.

NOTE

1. See page 706 Note 2 supra in regard to New Jersey disciplinary proceedings. For further consideration of the problems of lawyers in drafting separation agreements, see Chapter 11.

2. Compare Opinion 58, handed down in 1931, in A.B.A., Opinions of the Committee on Professional Ethics and Grievances 152-153 (1957):

It would be a violation of Canon 9 for a lawyer consulted by a client who desires to procure a divorce to confer with the adverse party in an attempt to get the adverse party to agree to the divorce. . . . [Such a conference] might easily lead to the giving of advice to the adverse party. Canon 9 provides that "it is incumbent upon the lawyer most particularly to avoid everything that may tend to mislead a party not represented by counsel, and he should not undertake to advise him as to the law."

The proper procedure for the lawyer representing a party seeking a divorce, and having occasion to communicate with the adverse party not represented by counsel, would be to limit the communication as nearly as possible to a statement of the proposed action, and a recommendation that the adverse party should consult independent counsel.

But the disapproval herein expressed should not be understood as condemning the laudable and proper efforts which an attorney may make to bring about a reconciliation between his client and an adverse spouse not represented by counsel, when such efforts involve no discussion of the facts which furnish, or might furnish, grounds for divorce.

See also Opinion 85, Committee on Professional and Judicial Ethics of the Michigan State Bar, Mich. State B.J., May, 1959, p. 112 (improper for plaintiff's attorney to prepare and file pleadings for divorce defendant).

DRINKER, PROBLEMS OF PROFESSIONAL ETHICS IN MATRIMONIAL LITIGATION
66 Harvard Law Review 443, 454, 458, 461-464 (1953)

. . . It is not, it is believed, professionally improper for a lawyer to advise a local client that by going to another state the client may take advantage of its more liberal divorce laws.

It is not his function to support the public policy of the state in which he practices to the extent of dissuading his client from taking proper advantage of the more accommodating laws of another state, any more than it is that of a doctor to urge his patient not to obtain the benefit of another more salubrious climate. It is the lawyer's duty to advise and act for what in his honest opinion he believes to be the best interest of his client. . . .

In 1932 the opinion of the American Bar Association Ethics Committee was asked as to "whether an attorney may properly advise a client, who desires a divorce, to leave the state of the matrimonial domicile and establish a residence in another state for the purpose of procuring a divorce, where such residence is not intended to be bona fide, but is for the sole purpose of obtaining the divorce." The unanimous opinion of the Committee, stated by Chairman Howe, was as follows:

> Any evasion or attempt to mislead the courts of another state regarding the facts as to residence, or any silence where good faith would require disclosure, would be a form of deceit and would be a fraud upon the court. An attorney cannot properly counsel his client to deceive or perpetrate a fraud upon any court, whether of his own or another state. Canons 22, 29 and 32.
>
> Where the statutes of a state require the establishment of a residence therein, as a prerequisite to the filing of an action for divorce, the word "residence" must be construed as referring to a bona fide residence and any bona fide residence is usually held to imply an intention that it be of other than a temporary or transitory nature. Therefore, under the circumstances stated in the question, a lawyer could not properly advise his client to institute action in a state requiring such a residence.

This opinion was issued prior to the recent decisions by the Supreme Court in Sherrer v. Sherrer, Coe v. Coe, Johnson v. Muelberger, and Cook v. Cook [see pages 733-741 supra] . . . .

Do these decisions modify the lawyer's duty in such cases?

When the American Bar Association opinion was rendered in 1932 the foreign divorce could have been upset in the state of matrimonial domicile by the non-appearing spouse. It might therefore have been said, as in the case of invalid Mexican divorces, that the client's purpose in obtaining the divorce was to misrepresent its validity. This is no longer the case. Also it did not there appear, as it now does, that the local judges were not in fact deceived by the allegations of proposed residence "for an indefinite time." Whether the present Committee (no members of which participated in the earlier decision) would now reach the same conclusion cannot be determined until another similar case is presented to it.

A wife consults a lawyer of her independent choice in the jurisdiction of matrimonial domicile, desiring to obtain a divorce. She tells him that her husband has recently left her permanently; that he is more than willing for her to secure a divorce and suggests that she go to Reno for the six weeks necessary to obtain it; that he will agree to appear by counsel and make no defense; and that he will make substantial and satisfactory provision for her, conditioned, however, on a prompt divorce.

[Mr. Drinker then discusses divorce practice in Nevada. See pages 777-778 infra.] Should the husband later change his mind and contest the decree, the Nevada Supreme Court will uphold it as based on substantial evidence and the husband's appearance in the proceedings. Under its recent decisions it would seem that the Supreme Court would also uphold it, under the Full Faith and Credit Clause, as against everyone except perhaps the state of domicile in a prosecution for bigamy or adultery in case either of them marry and live in their home state. Such a prosecution, however, would be most unlikely unless, like the Williams couple, they chose flagrantly to flaunt their new marriage before an indignant local community.

Under these circumstances there are many lawyers, including a number of high professional standing, who would not hesitate to advise the client to proceed with the suggested program provided she was willing, after a full explanation, to assume the slight risks involved. They would draw up the agreement with the husband's lawyer and send her to a reliable lawyer in Reno, advising her to make it easier for the Nevada judges by not buying a return ticket, by openly expressing delight in the Nevada climate, etc., and on her return to be as unobtrusive as possible and to do nothing to arouse or aggravate local public opinion. . . . These lawyers would consider that it was not their function to supervise or regulate the decisions of the local Nevada court, which, in their practical effect, amount to a fiction acquiesced in by all concerned, the result of which, under the latest United States Supreme Court decisions, is to make the divorce binding practically everywhere.

Some lawyers, unwilling to take any such active part in the proposed proceedings, would adopt the rather weak course of sending the client to another lawyer, believed to be less punctilious.

Others would consider it incompatible with the traditions and principles of their profession under any circumstances to advise a client, in order to succeed in a litigation, to swear to a misstatement of fact . . .

NOTE

1. Compare Opinion 248, handed down in 1942, in A.B.A., Opinions of the Committee on Professional Ethics and Grievances 495-496 (1957). Parts of the inquiry and of the Committee's answer follow:

> "1. Is it illegal, unethical, or reprehensible for a practicing attorney in the City of New York, to represent a client who seeks a Mexican decree of divorce after he or she has been fully informed of its invalidity in the State of New York, but who, nevertheless, insists upon the procurement thereof by mail, from a State in Mexico? . . ." [Quotation abbreviated by Eds.]

. . . There is no impropriety in the New York lawyer advising on Mexican Law, for a lawyer of one state may advise on the law of another state. For the correctness of such advice he assumes full legal responsibility. . . .

Participating and aiding in the procurement of admittedly illegal Mexican divorces for New York residents is another matter. To use the words of the submitted statement, it is illegal and unethical.

It is illegal because the state is a party to the matrimonial status of its citizens and insists that that status shall be dealt with only in a manner that will be recognized as according with the law of the state. (Maynard vs. Hill, 125 U.S. 190; Restatement of the Law of Conflict of Laws, §§54, 110, 111, 113.)

It is unethical because the participation of a lawyer in illegal proceedings violates the Canons of Ethics. "It is steadfastly to be borne in mind that the great trust of the lawyer is to be performed within and not without the bounds of the law." (From Canon 15.) "The responsibility for advising as to questionable transactions, for bringing questionable suits, for urging questionable defenses, is the lawyer's responsibility. He can not escape it by urging as an excuse that he is only following his client's instructions." (From Canon 31.) "No client . . . . nor any cause . . . . is entitled to receive nor should any lawyer render any service or advice involving disloyalty to the law whose ministers we are . . . . When rendering any such improper service or advice, the lawyer invites and merits stern and just condemnation." (From Canon 32.)

See also In the Matter of Anonymous, 274 App. Div. 89, 80 N.Y.S.2d 75 (1948) (New York lawyer who participates in procurement of Mexican mail order divorce through Mexican correspondent violates the law and public policy of the state but no disciplinary action imposed in this case because of novelty of proceeding).

2. Spellman, Successful Management of Matrimonial Cases 288-289 (1954):

Where it is the unwritten understanding of the parties that one of them will go to a foreign jurisdiction, establish the requisite residence, and then sue for a divorce, which will be regularized by the voluntary appearance through attorney by the other party, . . . [t]he ethical problem presented to the lawyer by such a set of circumstances is clear and should not be avoided by some legalistic type of self-delusion.

The solution is not simple. . . . [I]t is proper for the attorney to advise his client concerning the grounds and requisite period of residence for divorce in a foreign jurisdiction, and it is not improper for him to recommend a lawyer in such a jurisdiction. On the other hand, if part of the understanding between the parties involves simulated residence, the attorney must not only decline to be a party to the scheme, but must refuse to give any advice as to how it may be carried out and must decline to recommend a lawyer in the jurisdiction where the divorce is to be sought.

It is sometimes asked how the fact that a simulated residence is contemplated will come to the attention of the attorney unless he makes pointed inquiry covering this precise subject. Necessarily coupled with this query is the inferential suggestion that an attorney should "mind his own business" and not examine the motives or intentions of his own clients.

There is some validity to the proposition that a lawyer should not withhold the benefit of legal remedies from those who engaged him merely by reason of suspicion; but, in practice, an attorney who is asked for legal advice about a foreign divorce is often brought face to face with the bald statement of his client that he intends to simulate a residence and that he is seeking advice as to the methods to be employed best calculated to effectuate the deceit. Needless to say, an attorney who gives this type of advice even in the most general terms is a traitor to his profession.

If a husband or wife intends to go to a foreign jurisdiction to obtain a divorce, . . . there would seem to be no ethical impediment to the attorney for the other party advising his client about the regularizing effect of entering a voluntary appearance in the foreign jurisdiction. Recommending an attorney in that jurisdiction to enter the appearance and assisting in the preparation and execution of authority for that attorney to act are also beyond just criticism, provided there is no conspiracy as to the validity of the residence established by the party who has moved to the foreign jurisdiction.

3. Clad, Family Law 136-138 (1958), also states flatly that "It is unethical for a lawyer to counsel a change of domicile for the purpose of divorce." However, he appends to this statement a check list of twenty-

five things which a person can do "to make a record." Included are buying "a one-way ticket to the new domicile, not a round-trip, even though you may expect to return for a visit shortly"; if you must register at a hotel or boarding house, "do not register the old address, or at least make it 'formerly of' "; "sacrifice the modesty of strangers in order to make a record."

O'GORMAN, LAWYERS AND MATRIMONIAL CASES
27-34 (1963)

[For a description of the methodology and terminology used in this study, see page 752 supra.]

. . . Only four of the eighty-two lawyers in the sample expressed the belief that New York matrimonial laws are adequate. All the rest were sharply critical.

Our informants' comments on the state's laws focused on three main objections: the laws are unrealistic, they discriminate against poor people, and they produce deviant behavior. . . .

. . . One of five informants objected to the New York divorce law because it discriminates against the poor. "My main gripe," an informant told us, "is that it works only for the rich, or at least in their favor." What he had in mind, of course, was the extent to which the financial resources of matrimonial clients influence their ability to secure a migratory divorce. As we were repeatedly reminded, "The rich leave the state." That the solution to a client's legal problem is affected by his economic status is certainly not restricted to matrimonial cases. Nevertheless, it constitutes, in the eyes of many lawyers, a serious indictment of the state's divorce law. . . .

. . . [T]hey implicitly confirmed, on the basis of their experience, that evasion of the law is characteristic of most New York matrimonial cases. One informant gave this estimate of the prevalence of evasion: "You could throw a dart blindly and say, 'this one is phony,' and you'd be right most of the time."

. . . [M]ost significant is the idea that the evasion is a matter of common knowledge among lawyers and judges. "The amount of perjury is terrible," admitted an attorney, "I know it; the judges know it; we all know it." . . . Members of the legal profession *privately* recognize that they in fact share the knowledge that matrimonial laws are consistently broken; but this private knowledge is accompanied by institutional silence, for the courts proceed on the empirically unwarranted assumption that matrimonial cases are legally valid. The knowledge that the evasion is known to and permitted by the courts is especially important; it is interpreted by many lawyers to constitute judicial acceptance of illegal behavior. Thus, an informant concluded his description of collusion in these cases by saying: "It is done with the consent of the judges."

The fact that the evasion of law is known to officers of the court symbolically legitimatizes the behavior; it is given tacit institutional approval. No matter how much each lawyer or judge personally dislikes what he is a party to, the general absence of punitive action structurally stamps the evasion as acceptable. . . .

Attorneys who participate in matrimonial cases are faced with a dilemma: while they are obligated to uphold laws whose deficiencies they acknowledge and lament, they represent clients whose problems they are expected to solve without violating laws or professional ethics. . . .

The lawyers' dilemma in handling these cases involves a professional role conflict: lawyers are exposed "to conflicting sets of legitimized role expectations such that the complete fulfillment of both is realistically impossible." Attorneys may attempt to cope with this conflict in one of three ways. They can, of course, avoid matrimonial cases completely. If the cases are accepted, the conflict can be reduced by conformity to one of the two conflicting expectations. A lawyer may insist, for example, on strict adherence to legal requirements and refuse to accept a case in which such adherence is not possible:

> I, myself, refuse to touch a divorce case in New York where the evidence is not absolutely unimpeachable. For instance, where there is a case of open and flagrant adultery. But in any case where there is some doubt about the evidence, I won't take it at all.

Or a lawyer may give priority to the client's expectations and deliberately evade the law:

> Many lawyers, including myself, send [matrimonial clients] out of the state simply to avoid the adultery issue.
> I know where possible we resort to annulment proceedings rather than go through that adultery routine.

However the role conflict may be handled, it is a source of frustration for those who practice matrimonial law. Evidence of this frustration among our informants can be illustrated in three ways. The question asking for an informant's opinion of New York matrimonial laws evoked, in many instances, highly affective reactions. . . . Although many of them appeared to be deeply interested in the study, they generally kept their professional demeanor; their answers were expressed, for the most part, in a thoroughly detached way. However, when we requested their views of New York laws, many reacted in a much less impersonal manner. Some got up from their desks and walked around the office while replying. One attorney went to his office door, called in his partner, and with a snort, asked to have the question repeated. When this was done, both of them laughed. . . .

. . . Here is a sample of terms used by lawyers to describe the matrimonial laws of New York: "farce," "ridiculous," "stink," "terrible," "incredible," "asinine," "cockeyed," "stupid," "horror," "inhuman," "fantastic," "outrageous," and "puritanical." The repeated use of these and similar epithets in an otherwise calm interview may be interpreted provisionally to indicate (a) that the query tapped feelings of tension related to role conflict, and (b) that some of the tension was released through the use of highly affective language.

. . . Sometimes these feelings were expressed as the informants talked of their participation in undefended cases:

> Ninety per cent of the undefended matrimonials are based on perjury. They are all arranged. The raids are made with the consent of the defendant. We all know this. The judges know it. *It's embarrassing to go* [*to court*].
>
> [The laws] are a farce. . . . I have in mind especially the undefended matters before official referees. You have these black nightgown routines with the man in the blue shorts. *I tell you it's insulting to a lawyer.*

In other interviews the frustration was verbalized when attorneys discussed the problem of dealing with clients who have no grounds for a matrimonial action in New York: . . .

> I have a case now where the husband refuses to allow the wife to get a divorce in another jurisdiction. . . . Grounds of cruelty and nonsupport clearly exist . . . they should be divorced. In another state they would. *This kind of thing is very trying on a lawyer.* . . .
>
> The legal profession is caught: either they help their clients in a New York action where we have to act like blind monkeys, or we help them engage in the sophistry of an out-of-state divorce in Mexico or Alabama. Why they don't even give up their apartments or jobs as they establish residence in another state. *I know they're coming back. I feel very sensitive about it, but I don't know what else to do.*

C. DIVORCE REFORM: PROPOSALS AND PROSPECTS

1. *A Quadrilogue on Divorce Policy*

The time is late evening on a warm night in midsummer. The place is a small cafe in Opatija looking out over the moonlit Adriatic. The participants — the Judge, the Professor, the Doctor, and the Bishop — are American delegates to the First International Interdisciplinary Congress on Family Stability and the Rights of Children. They have just emerged from a frustrating session at which they tried to follow a Yugoslav interpreter's simultaneous translation into English of an address in Polish on Polish family law as an expression of Socialist morality.

BISHOP — Well, whatever else one may think about communism behind the iron curtain, at least they are doing something about divorce. When you compare the way their divorce rate is going down with how ours shoots up —

JUDGE — Ours is not "shooting up."

DOCTOR — I thought he said the Polish rate was rising.

BISHOP — No, it was down.

JUDGE — Professor, I noticed you switched to the French channel. Was that translation any better? Is divorce in Poland up or down?

PROFESSOR — The French was awful. I don't know. It doesn't make any difference anyway. Divorce rates prove nothing.

BISHOP — What do you mean, divorce rates prove nothing? It's humiliating to be here. Every time an American says anything about the sacredness of family life, these Europeans smile broadly because they know that we have the highest divorce rate in the world. Just today a German judge gloated as he told me that our rate was four times that of England or France, three times that of Germany, and twice Sweden's.[61] Sweden, mind you!

PROFESSOR — Bishop, the divorce rate in Italy is zero.[62] Do you think that proves that morality in Italian family life is so much better than ours, or haven't you seen any of Antonioni's movies lately?

JUDGE — The Bishop is right, though, that over the long haul our divorce rate has risen. I think there is cause for alarm. The divorce rate more than tripled between the Civil War and 1910, when it reached about one per thousand population, and now has more than doubled again to around 2.2.[63]

DOCTOR — That's per thousand total population?

JUDGE — Yes. And that ignores temporary fluctuations due to wars or depression.[64] It seems to have leveled off since 1950.[65]

DOCTOR — But those figures are misleading. Hasn't the proportion of adults who get married also risen since 1900?

PROFESSOR — Our statistics are inadequate, but apparently the higher marriage rate hasn't contributed very much to the increase in divorce. If you measure the number of divorces against a base of existing marriages, the results are still pretty much the same.[66]

---

[61] "The Swedish rate of 1960 was 1.2 per 1000 population, which is higher than the figure for England and Wales (0.51) or that for France (0.61) or Western Germany (0.83), but considerably lower than that for the United States [2.24 in 1959]." Schmidt, The "Leniency" of the Scandinavian Divorce Laws, in 7 Scandinavian Studies in Law 107, 118 (Schmidt ed. 1963).

[62] Like many other Catholic countries, Italy permits no absolute divorce. But cf. Professor Mario Berruti, of the Italian Court of Cassation, in a reported speech, Manchester Guardian Weekly, Dec. 10, 1964, p. 7, col. 1 ("De facto divorce is widespread in Italy. . . . The notorious 'divorce — Italian style' is a national shame"). See also Rheinstein, Trends in Marriage and Divorce Law of Western Countries, 18 Law & Contemp. Prob. 3 (1953).

[63] Jacobson, American Marriage and Divorce 90 (1959).

[64] Id. at 91-94 (in both world wars divorce rose sharply immediately after cessation of hostilities, falling off again but to a level higher than that existing before the war), 95-96 (divorce rate dropped during worst period of depression).

[65] "The consistent pattern of decline shown by both the crude and the marital-status-specific divorce rates indicates that the upward divorce trend ended a decade ago, but it seems too early to tell whether the present decline is the beginning of a long-downward trend." 1 Vital Statistics of the United States 1958, p. 2-10.

[66] Jacobson, American Marriage and Divorce 90 (1959), estimates the follow-

BISHOP — I've heard it said that in the immediate postwar years there was one divorce for every four couples who got married.[67]

PROFESSOR — True, but that statistic seems totally meaningless to me. The two figures don't involve the same people. The most adequate statistic, of course, would be to follow a large sample of marriages through life. One could take a sample of marriages contracted, say, in 1955, and by following this sample find out how many persons were being divorced in each succeeding year. Then, after all persons in the sample had either been divorced or died, the true divorce rate could be established.[68] As we don't have that kind of a study, a reasonably realistic alternative is to use as a base for any given year the average annual number of marriages over the preceding ten years. This at least means there is some relationship between the divorces and the particular marriages which are being dissolved by divorce. On this basis there were less than 10 divorces per 100 marriages around 1900. This rose pretty steadily to about 20 just before World War II, skyrocketed to nearly 40 in 1946, and has leveled off in the low twenties.[69]

JUDGE — So nearly one in every four marriages is going to end in the divorce court.

PROFESSOR — That's a frequently stated figure, but I don't think it is quite correct, if you limit it to first marriages. Persons who remarry after a divorce have a somewhat higher divorce rate,[70] so that if one counts first marriages alone it appears to be about one in five.

BISHOP — You fellows make it sound so urbane and lifeless with your figures. Do you realize the increasing moral instability and the rising numbers of children deprived of a normal home that lie behind this rise in divorce?

DOCTOR — But the proportion of children forced to grow up in a household that doesn't contain both his parents probably hasn't risen at all,

---

ing rates per 1000 existing marriages: 1860, 1.2; 1890, 3.0; 1900, 4.0; 1918, 5.4; 1920, 7.7; 1922, 6.6; 1929, 7.9; 1933, 6.1; 1940, 8.7; 1946, 18.2; 1950, 10.2; 1956, 9.3.

[67] "In the United States the number of divorces per 100 marriages occurring in the same year was estimated in 1867 to be 2.8; in 1890, 5.8; in 1910, 8.8; in 1930, 17.4; in 1949, 25.1; and in 1950, 23.1." Rheinstein, The Law of Divorce and the Problem of Marriage Stability, 9 Vand. L. Rev. 633 n.2 (1956).

[68] Jacobson, by using a hypothetical sample of 100,000 marriages, estimates that as of 1955, 24.9 per cent of these would be expected to end in divorce. As of 1948, the comparable figure was 29.1 per cent. Jacobson, American Marriage and Divorce 145-146 (1959).

[69] Blood, Marriage 230 (1962).

[70] See, e.g., Monahan, How Stable Are Remarriages?, 58 Am. J. Soc. 280, 287 (1952). Interpreting Monahan's and other data, Blood, Marriage 238-239 (1962), estimates that whereas the first marriage divorce rate is around 20 per cent, 30 to 40 per cent of first remarriages end in divorce; where the parties have had two or more previous marriages, the divorce rate rises sharply. "A conservative interpretation would be that a majority of first remarriages succeed whereas a majority of subsequent remarriages do not." Id. at 238. "Success" here is equated with lack of subsequent divorce, and the data are not further broken down according to remarriage status of each party (i.e.. single, widowed, or divorced).

Bishop. The death rate in 1900 for persons in the child-rearing stage of life — from the middle twenties to the middle thirties in age — was about eight per 1000 per year; now it's around one and a half.[71] The decline in the proportion of child-rearing families broken by death more than compensates for the rise in families broken by divorce.

PROFESSOR — And of course this declining mortality is one of the many factors which have contributed to the rise in the divorce rate. Because many fewer spouses die young, more marriages are exposed to the risk of divorce. Many unhappy marriages which used to be terminated by death may now end up in the divorce court.

BISHOP — This is entirely irrelevant to the point I'm trying to make. A family broken by the death of one parent represents an inevitable tragedy, and death is morally neutral. A family broken by divorce, however, is not only a needless tragedy but an index of moral failure.

JUDGE — Is it the divorce which is the moral failure, Bishop, or is it the failure to make a go of marriage and establish a stable, secure home for the children?

BISHOP — Both represent the same failure.

DOCTOR — But they're not necessarily the same thing at all. The decree of divorce is merely the law's recognition of a failure which occurred months or years earlier when the family was in fact broken by separation.[72] What I'd like to know is whether or not the underlying breakdown rate is going up. Are there really more separations today? We know that during the age of colonization in England, or when there was no divorce there,[73] or when our own frontier still existed, it was commonplace for an unhappily married man just to disappear. His family would never see him again, and the chances were that he would establish a new family.

PROFESSOR — It still happens. We have what is sometimes called common law divorce.[74] A couple separate, whether by agreement or by the desertion of one of them. One or both remarry, either formally or by starting a new household. Because they never appear on any divorce court records, we have no statistics on the incidence of this kind of breakdown — we never have had. But even in this day such poor man's divorce is probably far more frequent than we might guess. It would be interesting to take a random sample of people who hold themselves out as married and find out how many are in fact not legally married. I

[71] For persons aged 25-34 years the death rate per 1000 population has declined from 8.2 in 1900 to 3.1 in 1940 and 1.4 in 1960. Statistical Abstract of the United States, 1962, p. 63.

[72] See in particular the illuminating discussion by Rheinstein, The Law of Divorce and the Problem of Marriage Stability, 9 Vand. L. Rev. 633 (1956).

[73] E.g., Mueller, Inquiry into the State of a Divorceless Society: Domestic Relations Law and Morals in England from 1660 to 1857, 18 U. Pitt. L. Rev. 545, 577-578 (1957): "The moral of England's experience, as this writer sees it, can be summarized in two sentences: A divorceless law does not make for less divorces. Such a law has only one effect: it will create misery and immorality in any meaning and sense of these words."

[74] Foster, Common Law Divorce, 46 Minn. L. Rev. 43, 58-66 (1961); Jordan, Doctrine of Common Law Divorce, 14 U. Fla. L. Rev. 264 (1961).

suspect you'd find a surprising proportion of illegality — bigamists, people previously married who've remarried after a patently invalid divorce or after no divorce, and so forth.

DOCTOR — Wouldn't you agree that this sort of thing was much more common a hundred or two hundred years ago than today? It was much easier to run away and start again then, and going to law was financially out of reach of a much larger proportion of the population.

PROFESSOR — It was more common, yes, but how much more we just don't know and we can never know.

DOCTOR — All that may have happened in the last fifty or one hundred years is that changing customs, the increasing standard of living of the working classes, and things like the provision of legal aid for the poor have resulted in an increase merely in the proportion of breakdowns that are formally recorded by divorce. It would be quite possible, would it not, that the rate of family breakdown — and I'm not talking about death now, Bishop, but breakdown by separation — hasn't gone up at all?

PROFESSOR — It is possible, but not probable.[75] If we could hold morality constant, I would expect the breakdown rate as well as the divorce rate to have risen substantially in the last hundred years.

JUDGE — I agree entirely. We keep forgetting the profound changes in our way of life.[76] Imagine, for example, what the emancipation of women has meant to family life. Realistically, one hundred years ago divorce was a privilege reserved for men alone. Especially if she was burdened with young children, a woman with an unhappy marriage had virtually no recourse but to endure it. There was heavy stigma against a divorcee; she had much less chance to remarry and to support herself. Now she can be relatively independent of her husband economically, and her chances of achieving a remarriage are at least nine out of ten if she's still reasonably young.[77] Naturally some women are going to exercise their new equality by getting divorces.

PROFESSOR — I was thinking even more of the change in the family role brought about by the industrial revolution and all the trappings of modern urban life.[78] In the old days, marriage used to be much more

---

[75] "That . . . a shift from informal to formalized marriage breakup has been responsible for at least a part of the increase of the divorce rate, appears to be highly probable . . . It also seems probable, however, that there has also occurred an increase of the cases of factual marriage breakup." Rheinstein, The Law of Divorce and the Problem of Marriage Stability, 9 Vand. L. Rev. 633, 653 (1956).

[76] See Royal Commission on Marriage and Divorce, Report 1951-1955, Cmd. No. 9678, p. 9 (1956).

[77] The per cent of divorced females who ultimately remarry was estimated for 1948 at the given attained ages as follows: age 25, 99.4; age 30, 98.1; 35, 93.5; 40, 83.4; 45, 68.5; 50, 52.9; 55, 37.2; and 60, 23.4. Jacobson, American Marriage and Divorce 85 (1959). Compare Landis, Sequential Marriage, 42 J. Home Econ. 625 (1950) (divorcee's chances of remarriage 50-50 or better until she is 45 years old).

[78] Discussing the effects of the industrial revolution, Selznick, Legal Institutions and Social Controls, 17 Vand. L. Rev. 79, 80-82 (1963), says: "The loosening of social bonds, and the concomitant weakening of non-legal controls, is manifest in many ways. The most important, of course, is the decline of kin-

what it is today on an isolated farm — not only companionship and child-rearing, but also the basic economic unit providing livelihood, recreation, and often even education. To terminate your connection with the family then had much more drastic consequences. Psychologically and econom-ically, family breakup is simply a lot easier today. All the brakes that used to hold the family together have been relaxed. Isn't one of the ma-jor causes for our sense of dissatisfaction with the way divorce law oper-ates today a product of this change? Aren't we expecting entirely too much of law, as if it could step in and provide that stability which for-merly was the product of economic and cultural forces?[79]

DOCTOR — One more or less hidden aspect of this change which greatly concerns me is the role of the young mother in our new kind of family. It seems to me that we put young parents, especially the young mother, in an intolerable position.[80] In the old family there were maiden aunts and grandparents to help with the children, and the wife was often her husband's partner in the economic sphere, especially on the farm. Her life may have been hard, but at least it had meaning. The modern wife is cut off from her husband's career, isolated in her little apartment or home from the relatives who could share the burdens of child care, edu-cated as women have never been educated before, but then relegated to a role of house-cleaning and diaper-changing even more insignificant than that of her grandmother and great-grandmother.

---

ship as the major unit of social organization and therefore of social control. That the functions of the family have changed in recent history is a familiar sociological tale. What was once an enterprise and a nuclear community, a unit of production and an indispensable alliance against a forbidding external world, has now become a more specialized and limited institution. What it can do for its members, and what it may ask of them, have both been radically curtailed. . . .

"The weakening of the family as an agency of social control is only a phase, although a major one, of the broader trend toward a looser, less disciplined so-cial order. Thus another feature of our society is the steady decline of *fixed status* as a vehicle of social control. . . . We sometimes forget, I think, how much even our own society has depended on the proprieties of status, on the giving and receiving of deference. . . .

"It seems obvious to me that we are in no position to deplore this waning of non-legal controls. Dedicated as we are to personal autonomy and well-being, we cannot very well yearn for the submergence of the individual in family or community. . . ."

[79] See Pound, Foreword, A Symposium in the Law of Divorce, 28 Iowa L. Rev. 179, 181 (1943): "[We] are demanding more of the legal order in this matter of family law than we did in the last century. Progressive enfeeblement of domes-tic discipline, of neighborhood public opinion, and of the discipline of religious organizations, under conditions of modern urban life, has thrown an added and heavy burden on the legal order."

[80] E.g., Mead, Beyond the Nuclear Family, in The Future of the American Family: Dream and Reality, pp. C-13, C-15 (mimeo., Child Study Assn. of Amer-ica 1963): "It is not yet certain how we are going to solve the problem of the un-supported nuclear family, how we are going to alter the isolated, exposed posi-tion of two very young parents attempting to rear several children all by them-selves with no one to advise and comfort, no one to take over in emergencies, no one to rely on in the small day-by-day details of living. But it is perfectly plain that we are going to have to solve this problem, somehow."

BISHOP — I guess I'm just an old-fashioned conservative, but I'm mildly surprised to hear a psychiatrist characterize the role of a mother rearing children as insignificant.

DOCTOR — Bishop, you know what I mean.   Of course it is critically important.   All I'm saying is that our modern culture takes a young woman and throws her into this role without the help and reinforcement that the old-fashioned family used to provide.

BISHOP — Doesn't this just emphasize what I've been saying?   If the moral stamina were there, the family would not disintegrate.   I'll wager there isn't a woman in America who would willingly trade roles with her great-grandmother.   Both she and her husband have it a lot easier today, and they know it.   That they still can't make a go of it just points up the moral decline of our times.

PROFESSOR — I've recently had occasion to read a lot of colonial court records.   For all their preoccupation with moral values, I saw little indication that the Puritans had any superiority over us on that score.   Every third case was fornication or bastardy.   Even if a couple got married, if their first child arrived in less than nine months, they were haled into court to be fined and censured.[81]   If a man came over from England leaving a wife and children behind, he would be ordered to go back to his family or take the consequences.[82]

BISHOP — That strikes me as an admirable law.

DOCTOR — Come now, Bishop, you're kidding us.

BISHOP — I most certainly am not.   The state has a strong interest in the stability of the family.   Why shouldn't it take preventive measures?   Why should a married man be permitted to abandon his wife and children in England and come to America to make trouble and probably break up another marriage besides his own?   I think the colonists showed very good sense.

DOCTOR — Like most laws, it probably wasn't enforced.

BISHOP — That's just the point.   We've never given our legal structure half a chance.   We've never really exploited — or indeed explored — the state's power to take effective preventive measures to discourage the breakup of families.   I agree with the Doctor.   We need to help the

[81] See Colonial Justice in Western Massachusetts (1639-1702): The Pynchon Court Record 1, 104 (Smith ed. 1961): "[T]he commissioners . . . concluded, from the date of the birth of their child, that Samuel Terry and his wife 'did abuse one another before marriage' and accepted a four-pound fine in lieu of punishment of ten lashes apiece.   This offense was frequently punished on the county level by the courts of the Bay."

[82] "This Court taking into theire consideracion that Colonell William Crown hath Lived here a considerable time from his wife judge meete to Order that the saide Colonell do take passadge for England & return thither to his wife by the next oppertunity of Shipping . . . under the poenalty of twenty pounds according to Law."   Records of the Suffolk County Court 1671-1680, in 29 Pub. Colonial Soc. of Mass. 425 (1933) (reporting court hearing of April 28, 1674).   See also York County Court Records, Colony of Massachusetts Bay, in 2 Province & Court Records of Maine 434 (Libby ed. 1931) ("Wee Marke Roe" held for court "for his breach of the County Court order in not goeing home to his wife in due tyme").

young mother in her difficult role and use law to reinforce family morality.

Doctor — I don't mean that kind of help! Are you really proposing that law can compel man and wife to live together? Do you think the state can turn love into a command performance?

Bishop — I think the law can do a lot, yes. Take a typical situation today, a young man with his young wife and a couple of young children. They got married young; they weren't very mature about it; they acted precipitously. I'd do something about that, too, incidentally — tightening up our marriage laws would prevent a lot of divorces.[83] But they were permitted to get married and now there are the usual frictions. Marriage has not turned out to be the bowl of honey they anticipated. Of course it never is, but they don't know that. The baby cries all night; the two-year-old has a cough and fever; the wife doesn't get enough sleep; she's shut up in the house all day; she feels neglected and frustrated. When the husband gets back from work, home is far from the Utopia he's imagined. The house is a mess, dinner isn't even started, his wife forgot to get the vermouth for the martinis, and at the first rebuff she has a crying jag.

Doctor — You paint an idyllic picture, Bishop. What are you leading up to, a divorce for incompatibility?

Bishop — Now you've put your finger on it! If the depth of our moral bankruptcy can be epitomized by a single word in our divorce law, that's the one. Incompatibility, indeed! Of course they are incompatible. Every couple is. But a husband and wife with some maturity and some sense of responsibility for the innocent children they've brought into the world will do something about it. They will deliberately set out to strengthen their existing common interests and to develop new ones. Suppose the wife likes to bowl and the husband doesn't. Well, if he has any sense, he'll take his wife bowling once a week. Chances are he'll come to enjoy it too, and if he doesn't, she'll respond to his interest in her interests. It's a small thing to ask of him. In a petty matter he'll be demonstrating that love and marriage don't go together like a horse and carriage but are the product of give and take, self-sacrifice, and hard work.[84]

Professor — That's a fine sermon, Bishop, but it strikes me as bad law. Of course in a world peopled by saints we wouldn't have these problems. But law must operate in this world, with immature people. You yourself stipulated that your hypothetical husband and wife were silly and immature.

Bishop — But our law has a responsibility to help people develop the requisite maturity and responsibility. What happens now is that our di-

[83] See Redmount, An Analysis of Marriage Trends and Divorce Policies, 10 Vand. L. Rev. 513, 546 (1957) (suggesting, inter alia, a compulsory waiting period before issuance of the marriage license "so as to permit a course of instruction and counseling during which an opportunity for reflection may be given"). See also page 265 supra.

[84] See Royal Commission on Marriage and Divorce, Report 1951-1955, Cmd. No. 9678, par. 47 (1956).

vorce law encourages irresponsibility. Let's also suppose that our young husband meets an attractive young woman, and one thing leads to another. The new woman is always charming and attractive and never has irrational crying spells; indeed, under the circumstances, why should she? The husband draws from this contrast with his harried wife and tension-ridden home a distorted significance — that his wife doesn't understand him, whereas the other woman is sympathetic and builds up his ego. Our present divorce law literally invites this young fool to indulge his folly. It whispers to him, "Go ahead. It's easy. Everyone else does it, why not you? You owe it to yourself to find happiness and self-fulfillment."

PROFESSOR — But in this practical world, Bishop, what do you want? You can't have a legal action to compel the husband and wife to live together in misery while —

BISHOP — Not in misery, but to live together as they learn to love and respect and cherish one another.

JUDGE — Recently you typed yourself as a conservative, Bishop, but you're a wild-eyed radical if you really think that you can legislate that sort of thing. I happen to think the chances are high that the marriage you've described can be saved, and in my court we'd send them to the conciliation service for counseling.

BISHOP — Would you prevent them from getting a divorce?

JUDGE — No, but we'd delay and counsel.

PROFESSOR — Bishop, what you're describing is the problem of your profession, not the law's. It isn't the compulsion of law which makes people moral or immoral, prone to divorce or resistant to it. The community's basic moral and sociocultural and religious values are what determine conduct, not what the law says.[85] They are our only protections against further family breakdown.

BISHOP — Precisely. And the law can either strengthen these community values or it can subtly undermine them. Imagine what a moral tonic it would have been for the country if the district attorney in New York had done his duty and prosecuted Governor Rockefeller and his new wife for bigamy. I remember reading in The New York Times that in the morning Mrs. Rockefeller swore in court that she was going to make Nevada her permanent home, and in the afternoon she was flying back east. All the time both she and her husband knew perfectly well that they had made an agreement that she would be given an apartment on Fifth Avenue as her permanent home.[86]

DOCTOR — Wait a minute, Bishop. That divorce was perfectly valid under the law.

BISHOP — I know nothing about legal technicalities and neither do you, Doctor. Tell me, Professor, would it have been legal for the district attorney to have prosecuted Governor Rockefeller?

PROFESSOR — Well, as between the parties and their collaterals, since Mrs. Rockefeller was present in Nevada and her husband appeared by

[85] See pages 812-821 infra.
[86] N.Y. Times, March 17, 1962, p. 1, col. 3.

counsel, the divorce cannot be attacked. Whether the state can assert its invalidity through a bigamy prosecution is another question.[87]

BISHOP — You lawyers are all alike — unable to answer a simple question "Yes" or "No."

PROFESSOR — The Supreme Court has never ruled on the precise facts.

BISHOP — I take it the answer is "Yes."

PROFESSOR — The community would never have stood for such a prosecution.

BISHOP — The community would have applauded.

JUDGE — Bishop, don't you think it's significant that such prosecutions are never brought? Isn't it significant that the judge who gave Mrs. Rockefeller her divorce, who knew perfectly well what was going on, told the press that "[t]his is a great break for Reno" because he knew the publicity would bring more divorce clients to the state? [88]

BISHOP — The significance I see in what you've said is how desperately we need men of courage and responsibility who will act forthrightly to check the moral decline of our country. Imagine the effect on the young man in my story if, instead of offering him the prospect of easy divorce, the law were to say: "Look here, young fellow. You can never get a divorce from your wife" — for certainly there is nothing in the situation I described which gives any moral basis for his getting a divorce — "and if you try it and then try to marry your paramour, you'll go to jail for bigamy. If you try to live with her without marriage, you'll go to jail for adultery. And no matter what you do or where you go, we'll follow you and take from you the full measure of your obligation to support your wife and children and throw you in jail if you default." You know as well as I do that any young man would think five times before he took a step which would have such drastic consequences. It would be enough to make him take stock and try harder to make a go of his marriage.

DOCTOR — If the law were ever really to do that, it would be a great day for the jail construction industry.

JUDGE — Bishop, it's a lovely dream, but it just won't work. It's impossible for the law to say that and really be able to carry out its threat. Juries wouldn't convict, judges wouldn't impose the prison sentences. Take just the question of support. You can send a man to jail today for nonsupport under existing law, but are you aware that it doesn't work out that way in practice? Any husband, if he really wants to, can and does evade most of his obligations.

BISHOP — I've heard that, and it bears out Dickens's observation about the law. A child could do better than you lawyers. The FBI can find its man. Everyone has to have a social security number; he has to reveal it to get a job; he has to put it on his income tax return. They have these big machines now by which they can trace these things electronically. We could find almost all defaulting husbands and throw them in jail — if the lawyers and judges wanted to uphold the law.

JUDGE — Suppose you find a defaulting divorced husband after a couple

[87] See page 738 supra.
[88] Time, Mar. 23, 1962, p. 15.

of years. By now he's 2000 miles away and has a new wife and baby. This time he appears to be making a success of his marriage. He's earning just enough to support them. If you make him do much for his prior family, what happens to the second family? They're innocent too, and they deserve some consideration. If you throw him in jail, neither family's supported and the state foots the bills for both. Besides, it costs the state where his first family lives a lot of money to go that far to bring him back to jail.

BISHOP — If that's the state's policy, I can only characterize it as short-sighted economy and misguided sentimentality. In the long run strict enforcement would save countless marriages and millions of tax dollars.

DOCTOR — Bishop, you men who know what's best for other people and want to ram it down their throats fascinate me —

BISHOP — Look who's talking!

DOCTOR — What's so horrendous about what your young man is doing? You said it was a silly marriage and that they're both unhappy. Let them separate if they want to. They'll both remarry, and we may substitute two at least tolerable families for one unhappy one.

BISHOP — It was a member of your own profession, Doctor, who wrote a book prophetically entitled "Divorce Won't Help." [89]

DOCTOR — You amaze me! Did you read it?

BISHOP — Well, I skimmed it. I don't go in much for these theories that the reason why a man fights with his wife is because unconsciously he's getting even with his mother — or is it his father? Anyway, there's nothing very novel about the book's basic idea. Emerson said a long time ago that wherever a man goes, his shadow goes too, and that book proved what I've long suspected — that if you let a man out of one foolish marriage, he'll go out and make another just like it. You might as well stop him the first time, before he goes on creating family after family and wrecking each in turn.

DOCTOR — Bishop, tell me one thing. Would you prohibit all divorce?

BISHOP — I really think the Catholics are right. Theologically, I'm sure they are. Both Christ and Paul were very explicit, and my own church has become much too lax for my tastes. I suppose I would allow an innocent party to divorce and remarry in a very extreme situation like adultery.

PROFESSOR — You would approve, then, of those laws in a few states which prohibit the guilty party in an adultery divorce from remarrying the paramour during the lifetime of the innocent spouse? [90]

BISHOP — Of course. I wouldn't allow the guilty party to remarry anyone.

DOCTOR — We are back again to forcing people to live together.

BISHOP — Not necessarily. Where there is cause, I would permit the parties to live apart, as where there is cruelty that really makes it unsafe for the wife to continue to reside in the same house with her husband.

[89] Bergler, Divorce Won't Help (1948).

[90] See, e.g., Taintor, Marriage to a Paramour after Divorce: The Conflict of Laws, 43 Minn. L. Rev. 889 (1959).

That would be what the church calls divorce a mensa et thoro, but there could be no remarriage. The law provides for that, does it not?

JUDGE — Yes, in many states, but fortunately it's becoming obsolete and is now very little used.[91]

DOCTOR — Of what possible value is a procedure that recognizes that a marriage is finished but insists on retaining the empty shell?

PROFESSOR — It permits the wife to retain valuable inheritance and intestate rights for which alimony and property division upon absolute divorce is a very inadequate substitute.

DOCTOR — It still sounds like a punitive device to me. It leaves the spouses with a choice of lifelong celibacy or an illicit union.

BISHOP — Unlike you, my dear Doctor, I do not feel a need to make divorce as attractive as possible.

JUDGE — It's interesting that the system which the Bishop advocates is approximately that which exists in New York State, where the only ground for divorce is adultery but where there are broader grounds for legal separation.

DOCTOR — That's what happens when a legislature permits the Catholics to impose their dogma on everyone else.

PROFESSOR — Come, Doctor, that's one of those sloppy generalizations all you liberals are so fond of. If you will consider that such predominantly Catholic states as Massachusetts and Rhode Island have relatively liberal divorce laws, you may admit that blaming the Catholics for what you describe as the New York situation represents pretty loose analysis.

JUDGE — The point is that the New York law doesn't work anyway as the Bishop thinks it would. New York seems to have a higher rate of marriage disruption than the national average.[92] People just go to another state.

BISHOP — That's why I've always advocated a federal divorce law.[93]

[91] Most of the states grant divorces a mensa et thoro under various names. "Pragmatically speaking, almost the same result may be obtained [in the remaining jurisdictions] by a statutory provision for separate maintenance, or a criminal statute for non-support, which permit the court to tack on to its decree an order that the parties live separate and apart." Rappeport, Domestic Relations, 20 U. Pitt. L. Rev. 433, 444 (1958). It has been estimated that only about one legal separation or bed and board divorce is granted for every twenty-five annulments and absolute divorces. Dublin, The Facts of Life from Birth to Death 76 (1951). Even in New York, with its restricted divorce law, the ratio of separations to divorces and annulments has never exceeded 1 to 10. Jacobson, American Marriage and Divorce 113 (1959). Compare Clad, Family Law 120 (1958) ("Fortunately, this relic of an earlier day appears on its way to oblivion in most jurisdictions").

[92] "[A]lthough the recorded divorce rate in New York is the lowest in the country, it is likely that annulments, migratory divorces, separations and desertions raise the total disruptions above the national average." Jacobson, American Marriage and Divorce 118 (1959).

[93] "Proposals to create by constitutional amendment federal regulatory power over divorce were made as long ago as the 1880's. The chances of such an amendment appear today to be slimmer than ever." Rheinstein, The Law of Divorce and the Problem of Marriage Stability, 9 Vand. L. Rev. 633, 634 (1956). Compare 74 Harv. L. Rev. 424 (1960), for a discussion of the national divorce law enacted in 1959 in Australia.

DOCTOR — At last the Bishop and I have found common ground. Why slapping your wife is sufficient cause for divorce on one side of the Hudson River but not on the other is a mystery to me. I can't believe the moral beliefs of people change appreciably as you drive from New Jersey through New York City and on into Connecticut. For each state to have separate laws just invites hypocrisy and worse. Right, Bishop?

BISHOP — Obviously we can do nothing to cope with the divorce scandal until the federal government enacts a nationwide law. That would provide a means for curbing easy divorce.

DOCTOR — Then we could have a sensible divorce law which took reality into account and left morals to the clergy.

PROFESSOR — I suspect that the enthusiasm you gentlemen show for uniformity of law is dependent upon the uniform law being one that you agree with. Can you imagine Congress trying to find the national consensus about divorce where in fact no consensus exists? [94] Of course such a law would probably be invalid, for the Constitution gives the federal government no power to regulate domestic relations. If, in the alternative, you sought to have the states adopt a Uniform Divorce Law — assuming you could ever agree upon one — you can be sure that Nevada would not rush to adopt it.

JUDGE — Such uniform law proposals are just smoke screens anyway. What you called the scandal of divorce law is not caused by lack of uniformity but by loose administration. The law of Nevada is not substantially different from that of many other states insofar as the statutory grounds of divorce are concerned. There are plenty of divorce mills outside Nevada, including one in New York City. What creates laxity is loose administration. A national divorce law is not only politically and constitutionally unobtainable, but the idea that it would cure anything strikes me as absurd.

BISHOP — Then if you will permit me to be absurd for another moment, Judge, just let me say that I am totally unable to follow you. If we had a national law prohibiting divorce except for adultery and allowing remarriage only to the innocent party, and —

DOCTOR — My God, Bishop — pardon me, but — out of all the things that married people do to each other to make themselves and their partners unhappy, why do you single out adultery and grant relief there but nowhere else? A man can be an absolute monster to his wife, although he never sleeps with his secretary. If —

BISHOP — Just a moment, Doctor, let me finish, please. I want to pin

---

[94] Answers to public opinion polls have shown a majority in favor of divorce laws at least as strict as those now existing, but the questions asked are sometimes so vague (e.g., not differentiating among states) as to make the results almost meaningless. E.g., in 1945, in response to the question "Do you think the divorce laws in this state now are too strict or not strict enough?": too strict, 9 per cent; not strict enough, 35; about right, 31; undecided, 25. Compare a 1937 poll which asked: "Do you think that there should be easy divorce laws so that it would not be so expensive and troublesome to dissolve an unhappy marriage?": yes, 28.3 per cent; no, 54.3; no divorce should be allowed, 10.8; don't know, 6.6. Public Opinion 1935-1946, p. 172 (Cantril ed. 1951).

these lawyers down, for I now think I see clearly the crux of the whole problem. Judge, if we had such a national law, and that law was enforced vigorously, why wouldn't it be a total solution?

JUDGE — Because it couldn't be enforced.

BISHOP — That's just what I thought you'd say. The reason there was no bigamy prosecution in the Rockefeller case was because the district attorney lacked courage to do his duty and —

JUDGE — Oh come on, it wasn't his "duty" —

BISHOP — And the reason a national divorce law wouldn't work is because you judges announce in advance that you won't enforce it. If you don't like a law, or if clients are willing to pay big fees, the motto of the legal profession seems to be evasion.

DOCTOR — I'd chalk that one up to the lawyers' credit. Our divorce law reminds me of a situation that the anthropologist Ruth Benedict described concerning the Kurnai tribe in Australia, which had such strict rules restricting marriage choices that usually a young man would find there wasn't a single girl whom he could lawfully marry. Dr. Benedict pointed out that this didn't cause the Kurnai to reformulate their impossible marriage rules; instead, they institutionalized evasion. Those who wanted to get married would have to elope, and all the villagers would set out in pursuit, even though they too had been married in the same fashion. If the couple were caught before they reached a traditional place of refuge, they would be killed. But if they made it, they would then be accepted back into their tribe after the birth of a child.[95] Isn't this the sort of thing the lawyer does with our divorce law? We have a silly law, out of step with psychological reality and with the wishes of many people, and yet the lawyer manages to make it work tolerably well.

BISHOP — Tolerably well?!

DOCTOR — By that I mean that almost anyone who really wants a divorce can get one. My experience with patients who have marital difficulties is that the law is entirely irrelevant to the resolution of the case. If they can progress to the point where married life reaches a tolerable level, they stay together whether or not they have grounds for divorce. If their treatment reveals that there is really nothing left on which to base a marriage, they get a divorce whether or not they have legal grounds. The law is at most an irritant, a sometimes expensive nuisance, but it is never determinative of the result. People want and get a divorce for their own reasons, which may or may not be sound, but the law has nothing to do with it.

PROFESSOR — There's a great deal in what the Doctor has just said, Bishop. The trouble with your position of strict enforcement seems to me very simple: it would be a practical possibility only if there were a

---

[95] Benedict, Patterns of Culture 34-35 (1934). "The Kurnai meet their cultural dilemma typically enough. They have extended and complicated a particular aspect of behaviour until it is a social liability. They must either modify it, or get by with a subterfuge. And they use the subterfuge. They avoid extinction, and they maintain their ethics without acknowledged revision. This manner of dealing with the *mores* has lost nothing in the progress of civilization."

virtually unanimous consensus that what you propose is right. We can enforce laws against murder and robbery and rape because virtually everyone agrees on the wrongness of such conduct. But we've seen over and over again that if a substantial proportion of the population believes that prohibited conduct is in fact right and another segment of the population doesn't care about strict enforcement, then you just can't make such a law work. This happened in the twenties with prohibition, and I think it is happening today with gambling and divorce.[96]

BISHOP — I think we have just such a consensus. Most people agree that divorce is wrong. I'm shocked to hear you draw an analogy between taking a drink before dinner and divorcing your wife, as if people put those on the same plane.

PROFESSOR — But the ardent prohibitionists did just that, in part because they thought the one caused the other. I agree with you that probably most people think divorce is at least undesirable, that marriage should be for keeps. But that is a generality, and we start right off with perhaps a fifth of the population who did not apply that generality to their own lives.

BISHOP — Many of those may still feel what they did was wrong and despite their own conduct would support a strong law as the best thing for the community. In any event, your figure leaves four fifths, and that's a pretty strong majority.

JUDGE — The trouble is that people feel differently on the abstract question of what the divorce law should be than they do on whether divorce should be readily available to their relatives and friends who are trapped in unsatisfactory marital relationships. Suppose you see your own daughter in a desperately unhappy marriage. She made a mistake; you tried to stop her, but she went ahead anyway. Few people are going to take your position, Bishop, sitting back with a philosophic overview that tolerates the wreckage of a daughter's whole life so that her bad example can serve as a deterrent to future generations.

PROFESSOR — Bishop, if you will settle for a partial solution rather than total victory, I think we will find that there are at least some areas of agreement among the four of us. First, wouldn't we all agree that many divorces today represent cases much less aggravated than that of the Judge's hypothetical daughter — where the only alternative to divorce is lifelong misery? In many of the marriages that are terminated today the parties would have been better off if they had been kept together. In other words, at least some fraction of the existing divorce rate represents divorces that serve no real purpose either for the parties or society. Would you agree with that, Doctor?

DOCTOR — Yes.

PROFESSOR — The standard that ought to be applied, then, is one which would screen out these cases. I'm very much taken with the view of many of these Europeans that the proper test is not fault at all but a

---

[96] See Rheinstein, Our Dual Law of Divorce: The Law in Action versus the Law of the Books, in U. Chi. L. School Conf. on Div. 39, 45 (1952).

purely factual determination whether the marriage has irretrievably broken down.

DOCTOR — I would buy that.

BISHOP — That's no solution. That's worse than what we have now. All anyone would have to do would be to tell the judge that his marriage has broken down and he's free. That would encourage a change in the attitude towards marriage which would be disastrous for the nation. Before you know it, marriage would come to be regarded as nothing but a temporary institution and divorce would be normal.

PROFESSOR — No, no, Bishop, you misunderstand. This is not the same thing at all as divorce by mutual consent. The whole purpose is to prevent divorce for some trivial reason. But it would provide a dignified and blameless way out from a marriage where the breach is irreparable and due to a grave cause.

BISHOP — It is not the function of the state to make divorce blameless or dignified. If there is to be any divorce at all, it should be only to give relief where a wrong has been done.

PROFESSOR — But the existing grounds for divorce based on fault simply don't work, Bishop, and they invite the parties to scheme and manufacture causes of action. Moreover, these grounds are not really indicative of the true causes of the breakdown; they merely represent the symptoms. On the other hand, a fault system permits divorce where there is no reason why the marriage should not continue, as with an isolated act of adultery followed by repentance. The breakdown theory would cut through these fault fictions and permit divorce when, and only when, marriage has irretrievably broken down due to grave cause.[97]

DOCTOR — I guess I was a little hasty in my agreement with you. The rabbit in the hat is that phrase, "due to grave cause." What would constitute grave cause?

PROFESSOR — Certainly adultery, or desertion, or cruelty.

DOCTOR — Aren't these just the same "faults," the same moral judgments we have today, with the difference that each judge can apply his own personal standard?[98] If the Bishop here were a judge, grave cause would exist only where there was adultery.

PROFESSOR — No, there's a great difference. We would not be concerned with who is guilty of what or whether both parties are guilty, or with condemnation of guilty parties. We could put an end to the dis-

[97] This paragraph is based on the discussion in the report of the Royal Commission on Marriage and Divorce, Cmd. No. 9678, par. 58 (1956). Nine members of the Commission opposed "the introduction of the doctrine of breakdown of marriage, in any form, because they consider that it would be gravely detrimental to the well-being of the community." Id., par. 66. The nine members who favored the principle limited it by the extraordinary provision that the husband and wife must first have lived apart for seven years. Id., par. 67. See also Stone, The Matrimonial Causes and Reconciliation Bill 1963, 3 J. Fam. L. 87, 93 (1963), for a report on the unsuccessful attempt to implement even this modest recommendation.

[98] See Rheinstein, The Law of Divorce and the Problem of Marriage Stability, 9 Vand. L. Rev. 633, 640 (1956).

gusting spectacle of a ritualistic, name-calling public trial and permit the parties to bury their marriage with some sense of dignity. The judge would look at the total situation without regard to who was wrong, and if under all the circumstances it would be unreasonable to expect this marriage to continue, then that would constitute the requisite grave cause.

DOCTOR — Let me put you an example, and not an uncommon one in its basic manifestations.[99] Imagine a quiet, serious young man who has a good job. Behind these objective manifestations of success, however, he is desperately unhappy. He is so shy that meeting anyone is an acutely painful experience, and it is no accident that the career he has chosen keeps him in a research laboratory where he is left largely to himself. He buries himself in his work, and at night he reads books or listens to records, also by himself, for he rooms alone. He meets a girl just like himself — insecure, timid, and afraid. Somehow the ice is broken between them and they find in friendship a happiness neither has known before. After long deliberation they decide upon marriage. This is no hasty affair, and their families approve, noting how many common interests the young couple share. But unconsciously each longs for freedom from fear, to leave the books and music and to be able to venture out into the wider world. Each expects the other to be strong and to lead the way, for this is the unconscious demand that each requires of marriage. After they have been married for a time, they find nothing has changed except that the psychological deficiencies of each are now reinforced by the deficiencies of the other. Suddenly each one comes to the subconscious realization, "I have been cheated." But as they do not understand what is happening, they cannot explain their increasing dissatisfaction with one another. He only knows that he feels increasing irritation with the way she does almost everything, while each evening as he withdraws into a book, she realizes his love of reading is no longer a common bond but a growing annoyance.

JUDGE — They need therapy.

DOCTOR — Yes, but that's another issue. They may never get to a therapist.

JUDGE — They would in my court.

DOCTOR — Hold off just a minute — one thing at a time. What I want to know is what happens to them when they get to the Professor's divorce court. This couple represents a lot of cases — people whose marriages have failed because unconscious expectations which were taken into marriage have not been met. This is a profoundly grave cause of marital breakdown, but because they themselves don't understand what is happening, they are bewildered, and the manifestations of their unhappiness are apt to appear trivial to someone who doesn't understand what is really going on. What does your judge do when he explores the causes of the breakdown of this marriage, and all she can tell him is that her husband buries himself in a book, while the husband explains that he doesn't like the way his wife cooks scrambled eggs?

[99] See, e.g., Neurotic Interaction in Marriage (Eisenstein ed. 1956).

PROFESSOR — The judge would have to explore the possibilities of a reconciliation.

DOCTOR — Without therapy they are close to zero.

BISHOP — Nonsense. You were throwing statistics at me right and left earlier in our discussion. Do you have any statistics to back up your last statement? Is there any evidence that they won't be able to improve their situation without therapy, or even that therapy is particularly helpful in such cases? [100] All of us have unfulfilled expectations in marriage. A basic lesson in life is to learn to make do with what God has given you.

DOCTOR — I can't see that under the breakdown theory giving the judge discretion to grant or deny divorce according to his estimate of the gravity of circumstances is any improvement over what we have today. It seems to me a step backwards.

PROFESSOR — Of course you could establish an objective standard for determining the gravity of the breakdown. In Sweden, if the parties have separated, they can petition the court for a decree of separation and the court has virtually no discretion to deny it. Even if only one spouse wants the decree and the other is opposed, it will usually be granted if they are in fact living apart and one party wants the decree.

JUDGE — But that's only a separation decree, not a divorce.

PROFESSOR — That's right, but after one year under a decree of separation either party is entitled to an absolute divorce upon petition. The only proof required is that they have lived separate and apart during the year.[101]

DOCTOR — I would find that procedure acceptable, except that a year seems to me a little long.

PROFESSOR — Apparently some Swedes agree with you. About one in eight divorces are not under this procedure but are brought on the ground of adultery, which requires no such delay.[102]

DOCTOR — The only purpose of requiring any delay seems to me to be to make sure that the parties really want a divorce.

[100] Cf. Gurin, Veroff & Feld, Americans View Their Mental Health 318 (1960) (individuals receiving professional help with marriage problems find assistance less helpful than therapy for any other kind of personal problem).

[101] Schmidt, The "Leniency" of the Scandinavian Divorce Laws, in 7 Scandinavian Studies in Law 107, 109-110 (Schmidt ed. 1963).

[102] Id. at 113. Compare Rheinstein, The Law of Divorce and the Problem of Marriage Stability, 9 Vand. L. Rev. 633, 642 (1956): "In Denmark a divorce can be obtained either upon the ground of adultery or upon the fact that the parties have separated, that such separation has been officially noted by the decree of a court or an administrative agency, and that it has lasted for two years. No specific ground has to be shown where a divorce is sought on the second ground. While the total number of divorces annually obtained in Denmark has remained fairly stable, the number of adultery divorces has steadily increased while that of separation divorces has decreased in the same proportion. The reason is, of course, not that adultery would be on the increase in Denmark, but simply that an adultery divorce can be had immediately, while a separation divorce requires a waiting period of two years. The speedier divorce has proved to be more attractive, and the by-product of this development seems to be that the official certification of the commission of adultery is losing its terror as a social stigma."

PROFESSOR — You don't want divorce to be immediately available upon sudden impulse?

DOCTOR — No. But I would think the period of delay should be quite short, a matter of months at most. Any longer waiting period seems to me to be moralistic.

PROFESSOR — Almost half the states in the United States grant divorce now without showing fault, provided the parties have lived separate and apart for a requisite number of years.[103]

DOCTOR — Years? To make them wait for years after the factual dissolution of their marriage is punishment plain and simple.

PROFESSOR — The purpose is not to punish but to make sure they really want it and to facilitate the opportunities for reconciliation.

DOCTOR — Ha! Is that also the purpose of what I understand to be the procedure in California, where you get a first decree of divorce —

JUDGE — An interlocutory decree.[104]

DOCTOR — After which you have to wait for a year for the final decree that entitles you to remarry?

JUDGE — I'm opposed to that too, Doctor. It's a silly time to try to achieve reconciliation, for the divorce proceeding merely hardens the parties in their discord and makes treatment that much harder. The year's wait should come before the divorce action is tried.

DOCTOR — Judge, I suspect that reconciliation has nothing to do with such laws. It's just a penalty assessed on getting a divorce.[105] It reminds me of a parent who reluctantly gives in and allows his child to do something but who gives him a whack at the same time to express his displeasure.

JUDGE — What the law of my state does do, however, is to attack the problem of divorce at its root. Your case of the shy couple, Doctor, and the Bishop's case of the dissatisfied young man beautifully illustrate the deficiency of the Professor's breakdown theory. That theory takes the

---

[103] See pages 633, 652 supra. See also McCurdy, Divorce — A Suggested Analysis with Particular Reference to Dissolution for Living Separate and Apart, 9 Vand. L. Rev. 685 (1956).

[104] See generally Note, Interlocutory Decrees of Divorce, 56 Colum. L. Rev. 228 (1956). Only about ten states utilize the interlocutory divorce device. But quite a few jurisdictions have provisions imposing some sort of delay (commonly referred to as "cooling off" periods) between the initiation and the trial of the divorce action. See page 792 note 114 infra.

[105] Under such delay provisions the assumption that the marriage continues after the interlocutory decree until a final decree is rendered raises serious problems which illustrate the punitive aspects of divorce law. See, e.g., Linn v. Linn, 341 Mich. 668, 69 N.W.2d 147 (1955) (final decree of divorce set aside after proof that plaintiff became pregnant during six-month interlocutory period by man she had married after final decree rendered); Pakuris v. Pakuris, 186 A.2d 719 (R.I. 1962) (adultery during waiting period after decision for divorce but before final decree justifies denial of final decree). For the problems that have arisen in California with respect to couples who remarry after the elapse of the one-year period but without going through the formality of obtaining a final decree, see Comment, Nunc Pro Tunc — A Cure for Bastardy and Bigamy in California, 6 U.C.L.A.L. Rev. 298 (1959).

facts as it finds them and doesn't try to do anything to change them. What we would do with cases like those is to assign them for counseling.

PROFESSOR — If by that you mean compulsory counseling, I'm awfully skeptical, Judge. They have this here in Europe, where it's reported to be a complete farce; at least that's what some French and German judges have told me.[106]

JUDGE — If you'll give me a moment, I'll tell you what we do.[107] I can assure you there's nothing farcical about it. When a divorce case is filed, but before there is any action on the divorce petition itself, we send the couple to a trained marriage counselor.

BISHOP — This is the first sensible suggestion I've heard from any of you tonight. Does it work?

JUDGE — It certainly does. I have had no satisfaction in my career comparable to that represented by the marriages our court has saved. I guess I'm just sentimental, but when I meet a couple on the street strolling along arm in arm and they say, "Hello, Judge, do you remember us?" and they tell me they're one of our reconciliations, I get a real glow. Why, the very day I left for this conference I got a letter which is typical. It said, in effect: today is the second anniversary of our signing the conciliation contract in your office, and we just want to let you know that we are happier together all the time and eternally grateful to you.

BISHOP — What is a conciliation contract?

JUDGE — That's really the secret of our success. After the parties have worked things through with a marriage counselor and decided on a reconciliation, we get very formal and have them make a contract with each other and the court. It's a real contract and violation of it constitutes contempt of court.

DOCTOR — I don't understand.

JUDGE — The contract is a long, detailed document covering more than thirty pages which evolved out of the court's experience. The parties agree to reconciliation, may agree to accept long-term counseling from some agency, agree to look forward and forget the past —

DOCTOR — That would be some achievement.

JUDGE — And the contract covers all the matters which we have found to have caused difficulties — how to handle money, the division of re-

---

[106] Gower, Testimony before the Royal Commission on Marriage and Divorce, 1 Minutes of Evidence 24 (1952): "[I]n every country where [compulsory reconciliation] has been tried I understand that it has been proved a complete farce. It merely adds another step to the procedure. The parties are brought before a judge or some other court official and he pretends to try and reconcile them. . . . I have spoken to French and German judges about this, and they have all agreed that it is completely farcical."

[107] See generally Virtue, Family Cases in Court 206-212, 215-227 (1956); see also Pfaff, The Conciliation Court of Los Angeles County (litho., 1961), describing that court's procedures. The "Husband-Wife Agreement" used in Los Angeles is appended to Judge Pfaff's report. For an earlier account, see Burke, With This Ring (1958).

sponsibility in the home and in the family, mutual friends, in-laws, methods of speaking to each other, not bearing grudges, avoidance of late hours, sex, and so forth.   We also have special clauses to insert where appropriate, such as an agreement by one spouse to attend Alcoholics Anonymous.

DOCTOR — Could you be a little more specific?   For example, you mentioned sex.

JUDGE — The contract points out the importance of mutual respect in sexual intercourse and the importance of achieving a mean between excessive demands on the one hand and reluctance or uncooperativeness on the other.   The parties also agree not to ignore the important phase of leisurely love-making as a prelude to intercourse, with the husband agreeing to take his time and the wife agreeing to respond to his attentions.[108]

DOCTOR — So that if someone tries to have intercourse without the prelude he goes to jail for contempt of court?

JUDGE — Go ahead and ridicule us, Doctor.   We're used to having fun poked at us, although I hardly expected it from you.   You have no idea how often the couples use this agreement.   They tell us they read it over and over.   It gives them an anchor to windward, a standard to which they can hew.   The agreement concludes, incidentally, with a family prayer, because we recognize that God's help is needed if reconciliation is to be achieved.   Of course the contempt of court provision is largely a psychological weapon, although we have used it in extreme situations.[109]   That isn't the heart of the matter, however.   What we have done is to prove that reconciliation works and that most of these marriages can be saved.   Just come to my court someday and I'll let you read the mail received in a single week.   That will prove it to you.

PROFESSOR — I presume you hear only from those who reconcile and stay reconciled.   What is your over-all success rate?

BISHOP — Here we go again!   Don't let them sidetrack you with statistical sleight of hand, Judge.   You're obviously doing great work.   Just keep it up.

JUDGE — Never fear, Bishop, I'm ready for them.   I'll send you copies of our annual reports.   In round figures, 60 per cent of the cases that

---

[108] E.g., from the Los Angeles husband-wife agreement: "The wife agrees to respond to the husband's efforts in lovemaking and not to act like a patient undergoing a physical examination.   For the husband to acquire proficiency in making intercourse pleasurable to the wife, he must learn to relax physically and to take his time."   Pfaff, The Conciliation Court of Los Angeles County (litho., 1961), Exhibits §II, Husband-Wife Agreement, p. 19.

[109] In Los Angeles "in certain cases the plenary power of the court to enforce its Orders by Contempt proceedings is utilized, and in at least one instance in the history of the court the Judge sentenced a husband and a female third-party respondent to five days in jail for a flagrant violation of the Reconciliation Agreement."   Pfaff, The Conciliation Court of Los Angeles County 13 (litho., 1961).   "An interfering in-law or third party romantic interest may be joined as a party respondent in order to ensure the permanence of the reconciliation."   Id. at 14.

come to our court are reconciled and 75 per cent of those reconciliations last.[110]

DOCTOR — Psychiatrists are always being criticized for drawing generally applicable conclusions from the small unrepresentative sample of patients they see. Do you mean to tell me that 60 per cent of all divorce actions in your city are being reconciled?

JUDGE — No, I said 60 per cent of the cases in our Conciliation Court.

PROFESSOR — And the cases that come to your court come on petition of one of the parties, is that it?

JUDGE — Mainly, yes. It would be a physical impossibility for us to handle all the cases, or even just all those cases in which children are involved. We have inadequate facilities as it is, or our success rate would be even higher.

DOCTOR — So you deal with a self-selected and not a representative sample, just the way I do.

PROFESSOR — Judge, are you aware that about 30 per cent of all divorce cases filed in the United States are dismissed voluntarily by the parties or by the court for want of prosecution? [111] The most probable hypothesis is that most of these 30 per cent are reconciled without outside intervention and there is some evidence that this is so.[112]

[110] In 1960, reconciliations were achieved in Los Angeles in 59.7 per cent of the 3876 petitions filed in the Court of Conciliation; for the "past 5 years [publication date, May 1961] the average percentage has been 43 out of every 100 couples whose cases were heard. . . . A check made one year after each reconciliation is effected reveals that 3 out of 4 have remained reconciled." Id. at 1. It is difficult to evaluate these figures. The base against which the success rate is calculated apparently includes an unstated number of cases in which a reconciliation was effected before the parties came to the Conciliation Court. Where attorneys in a divorce case in which no conciliation petition has been filed appear in court to state that the parties have reconciled and to request attorney's fees, the court instead of dismissing the case apparently continues it for referral to the Court of Conciliation. See id. at 22; id., Exhibits §I, p. 15 (reproducing an extraordinary "Suggested Attorney's Letter to Parties Who Have Reconciled on Their Own, to Get Them into the Conciliation Court"). See also id., Exhibits §I, p. 8, reproducing the form letter sent one year after a reconciliation to determine whether the parties are still living together. This is apparently the only follow-up. As it is inconceivable that all respondents answered this questionnaire and the percentage not answering is not stated, the ambiguous statement that "3 out of 4" remain reconciled is not very helpful. Compare the results of a recent survey of domestic relations judges and similar hearing officers. In 133 courts (27 per cent of the total) there was some form of reconciliation procedure; in three out of four of these 133 courts the procedure was voluntary. In 59, or almost half of these courts, the responding judges estimated that reconciliations were achieved in less than 10 per cent of the cases referred for conciliation. Quenstedt & Winkler, What Are Our Domestic Relations Judges Thinking?, Monograph No. 1, A.B.A. Sect. of Fam. L., July 1965, p. 5.

[111] Foster, Procrustes and the Couch, 2 J. Fam. L. 85, 91 (1962) (30 to 50 per cent of divorce suits are abandoned); Alexander, The Family Court — An Obstacle Race?, 19 U. Pitt. L. Rev. 602, 608 (1958) (30 per cent).

[112] See Johnstone, Divorce Dismissals: A Field Study, 1 Kan. L. Rev. 245 (1953). He studied 47 randomly selected cases in which a divorce action had been dismissed between 1946 and 1952. In 21 of the cases the interval between dismissal and the study was less than one year; in 9 cases, one to two years; in 17, over two years. In 44 of the 47 cases the reason for the dismissal was recon-

JUDGE — It proves what I've always maintained — that it is never too late to try reconciliation.

PROFESSOR — It also may show that your success rate, as you call it, is meaningless as a purported justification of your elaborate and expensive court apparatus. These cases that give you such a glow may well be the very ones that would have reconciled themselves anyway.

JUDGE — But we know we are accomplishing a great deal.

PROFESSOR — With all due respect, you know nothing of the kind. Very probably you are accomplishing something, but what or how much is just not known. I have a suggestion for you. Next year, why not take all cases referred to your court and divide them by random methods into three groups. Treat the first group according to your usual routine, give the second your usual counseling but leave out the contract bit, and do nothing for the third group — you can tell them you're sorry but you don't have the facilities — and this will be your control group. This will leave you with some staff services left over, because you'll be treating a third less cases, and to fill up this time I suggest drawing a fourth group from cases not normally referred to your court. After a couple of years we can compare success rates. This will allow you to test the validity of your hypothesis that the conciliation contract is the key to your success, as you put it — which frankly I very much doubt. It will put my skepticism to the test by allowing a comparison of the treated group with the control group. And it will allow us to compare success with the self-selected group and the general run of cases.

DOCTOR — I don't like the way you two keep talking about success rates, as if every case which did not result in reconciliation was a failure. In some, perhaps many, of these cases there ought to be a divorce.

JUDGE — I agree that we don't "fail" with the cases that are not reconciled. Our counselors feel that even when no reconciliation is achieved, they often can reduce the bitterness of the divorce process and achieve better results for the children. Incidentally, Professor, if we make that study to which you referred, you should understand that when we talk about cases being self-selected, that doesn't mean all the parties come voluntarily. One party can initiate the process and then the unwilling spouse is compelled to come to an interview with the counselor. Many of our cases are of this kind.

PROFESSOR — We better have separate samples to compare cases where both parties are willing with those where one spouse resists. The available evidence seems to indicate that compulsory counseling has little success.[113]

---

ciliation, but only 30 of these couples were still living together at the time of the study. In 13 cases there had been a divorce subsequent to the dismissal. The data are inadequately reported, but it appears that a number of the reconciliations were short-lived.

[113] See, e.g., Bodenheimer, The Utah Marriage Counselling Experiment: An Account of Changes in Divorce Law and Procedure, 7 Utah L. Rev. 443 (1961); Committee on Reconciliation, New Jersey Supreme Court, Report (1960); New Jersey State Bar Assn., Special Committee on Divorce and Custody, Final Report (1956).

DOCTOR — What happens if the unwilling spouse refuses to be counseled?

JUDGE — Then we can issue a subpoena.

DOCTOR — There is something about that that really repels me. I'm not only a psychiatrist; I also happen to be a citizen of a democratic state who believes that the right to privacy is an important attribute of liberty. If someone wants help with the neurotic problems in his marriage and comes to me, I'll try to help him, but you can't force therapy. If a man and a woman decide they want a divorce, as far as I'm concerned they should get it and I don't care what their reasons are. I'm willing to delay a little, to make sure they're not acting on temporary impulse. I'm affirmatively anxious to make available counseling facilities, although I don't think they should be attached to the court.

PROFESSOR — What about a procedure whereby a party merely files a notice of intention to seek a divorce and the parties are then told where they can get free counseling services during the waiting period before any further steps are taken on the divorce action? It would be a kind of "cooling off" period, buttressed by the availability of counseling help.[114]

JUDGE — I repeat that in that way we'll miss the important cases. We get cases referred to us long before that when one spouse goes to a social agency for marriage counseling but the other spouse refuses to come in. Then they refer the case to us because we can use compulsion.

PROFESSOR — Let's withhold judgment on that until we see how successful your procedures are with that particular kind of case.

DOCTOR — I reject that kind of compulsion no matter what the results are. Damn it, marriage is a private affair. When I think of the Judge's court issuing orders telling people not to speak harshly to one another or how often to go to bed together or what technique to use in making love — well, it sickens me. It must be unconstitutional. Isn't there some amendment that prohibits that sort of prying into the intimacy of one's private life?

PROFESSOR — Judging by the Supreme Court's decision in the Connecticut birth control case, there are a lot of constitutional provisions protecting family privacy.[115] What really disturbs me about this current craze for counseling, however, is its motive. I have no objection to making counseling available, or even to the use of the minimal amount of compulsion employed in the Judge's court. But it is ridiculous to expect counseling to have much effect on divorce or dissolution rates. It is

---

[114] See, e.g., Mich. Stat. Ann. §25.89(6) (Supp. 1963) (except in desertion actions no proofs or testimony within 60 days of filing complaint, or within six months if there are minor children); Wis. Stat. Ann. §247.081 (Supp. 1965) (no complaint until 60 days after service of summons; summons must also be served on family court commissioner who "shall cause an effort to be made to effect a reconciliation between the parties"). For a description of the constitutional and other difficulties encountered upon the enactment of such a provision in Illinois, see Casenote, 1961 U. Ill. L.F. 336.

[115] See Griswold v. Connecticut, 381 U.S. 479 (1965) (holding state birth control law unconstitutional and citing amendments one, three, four, five, nine, and fourteen as creating "zones of privacy").

significant that in the Judge's city the regular courts are still open side by side with the Conciliation Court, and so long as the requirement for conciliation is not universal, people who want to avoid it will flock to the easy courts, just as they have always done. This process is what Rheinstein has called the application of Gresham's law to divorce.[116] But more important, even if you could overcome this problem of evasion, the implicit premise of the counseling approach seems to be that it is individual failure which causes our high breakdown rate. That is really the same basic error as that into which I feel the Bishop has fallen, the only difference being that the Bishop's root cause is immorality and the Judge's is psychopathology.

DOCTOR — I couldn't agree more. Kubie has pointed out that it is destructive social forces in our society and not individual psychopathology which threaten the family. It seems obvious to me that Kubie is right when he says that psychiatry — and by that I take it he also includes all forms of counseling help — can't roll a ball uphill when everything else in society is conspiring to roll it down.[117] The real danger I see in both the Judge's and the Bishop's approaches is that by their emphasis on false issues they keep us from tackling the basic problems of family life in modern society.

BISHOP — Gentlemen, the time has come to agree to disagree. I'm glad none of the Europeans has been here to see how deeply we are divided. Apparently the sanctity of the marriage relationship as I conceive it and as it has come down to us in our Christian heritage means very little to any of you. There is a sacredness about the permanence of marriage that is the essential foundation stone of our whole family structure. No statistics you cite me are going to persuade me otherwise. And believe me, if the family goes, God help our civilization.

PROFESSOR — Cheer up, Bishop, one of the more interesting discoveries of the statistical studies is that, contrary to all earlier hypotheses, the frequency of divorce has been found to vary inversely with occupational status and therefore, presumably, with education.[118] It is not wholly implausible that over the next half century the divorce rate may even decline. I see no evidence that the family as an institution is on its way out. It is changing, yes, but it will continue to provide the only vehicle for meeting very basic human needs.

DOCTOR — We may, indeed, end up with a family structure that offers

[116] See Rheinstein, The Law of Divorce and the Problem of Marriage Stability, 9 Vand. L. Rev. 633, 641 (1956).

[117] Kubie, New Forces Constraining the American Family, in The Future of the American Family — Dream and Reality, pp. C-1, C-2 (mimeo., Child Study Assn. of America 1963).

[118] "Numerous studies have shown that divorce proneness is . . . inversely related to husband's occupational rank." Levinger, Marital Cohesiveness and Dissolution: An Integrative Review, 27 J. Marr. & the Fam. 19, 23 (1965). As to education, there is some data that the "amount of the husband's education is higher for durable than for dissolved marriages." Ibid. Levinger's article is a useful compendium of the major investigations that have sought to isolate the factors that differentiate viable marriages from those that end in divorce. See particularly his table at 22.

a far more meaningful role to husbands and wives than has ever been true in the past.

BISHOP — I wish I could share your optimism. As I look at family disintegration and its concomitants — the frequency of delinquency, rising crime rates, more illegitimacy, more mental illness — the future seems to me very bleak. But I repeat, gentlemen, it is very late. I will have one more slivovitz, if my prohibitionist friend will permit me such an indulgence, and then to bed. Slivovitz is certainly not the least of Yugoslavia's attractions. What's on tomorrow's agenda?

JUDGE — There is a plenary session in the morning on the topic, "What is the Effect of Divorce on Children?"

PROFESSOR — I think I'll sleep late and then take a leisurely swim. Want to join me, Doctor?

BISHOP — I would have supposed that this topic would be of particular interest to you.

PROFESSOR — You know as well as I what we'll hear — a series of platitudes with which to mask our ignorance.

JUDGE — But the effect on children is the most appalling thing about divorce.[119] You should see them in my court, bewildered and hurt. They are the innocents, but they are the ones who have to pay.

PROFESSOR — Judge, you have just given us a headnote which summarizes the whole of tomorrow morning's session. When the program asks the wrong question, you can hardly expect to receive an enlightening answer.

DOCTOR — I agree with you, and I think I'll join you for that swim. I didn't need to come four thousand miles to Yugoslavia to find out that a child living in a home torn by dissension and strife is at a disadvantage compared to a child growing up in a happy, contented home.

PROFESSOR — Precisely. Everyone knows divorce hurts children, if the reference point for comparison is a happy home with both parents. But such a happy home is not in the cards for most of these children, unless perhaps through remarriage after divorce. What we need to know, but don't know, is which of the three realistically available alternatives is least damaging: continued residence with both parents in an unhappy home; separation without divorce, which usually means living in a household with the mother alone; or separation with divorce, which usually means remarriage and the introduction of a stepparent. There is one study of an adolescent population in a western urban setting that tends to support the hypothesis that children in unbroken unhappy homes are worse off than children in all forms of broken homes. When the home was broken, all the significant differences showed that there was less psychosomatic illness, less delinquent behavior, and generally better adjustment than in

[119] "The proportion of divorces affecting children under 18 years of age increased from approximately 41 per cent in 1932 to 60 per cent in 1959. . . . In recent years, the number of children under 18 affected by divorce has been increasing by approximately 20,000 annually." Burchinal, Characteristics of Adolescents from Unbroken, Broken, and Reconstituted Families, 26 J. Marr. & the Fam. 44 (1964).

unbroken unhappy homes.[120] When Goode studied 425 divorced mothers, he found that while almost all had worried about the possible effects
of divorce upon their children, more than 90 per cent thought their children were either better off or as well off as a result of the divorce.[121]
There are also some other studies which fail to support the hypothesis
that divorce harms children.[122] All of these investigations are inadequate, and at most they provide us with hints which need to be pursued
by further investigation. Until we have more data, however, I see little
value in the kind of speculation or unrepresentative clinical case studies
which will doubtless be presented tomorrow morning.

JUDGE — Well, I need to know all I can about this subject, so I'm going
to the session to see what I can find out. But I'm ready to call it quits for
tonight. Let's go, Bishop.

BISHOP — Good night, all.

2. *The Impact of Religious Diversity*

From the many factors adverted to in the Quadrilogue which bear
upon the formulation of divorce policy, two have been selected for more
detailed examination: the impact of religious diversity in the determination of a divorce law equally applicable to all (this section), and the influence of law upon the incidence of marital dissolution (Section 3 below).
The examination of religious attitudes towards divorce is in turn confined
to a brief survey of two major roots of the Judeo-Christian heritage: Roman Catholic and Jewish law. Between these essentially opposing positions there is a wide spectrum of Protestant opinion to which no reference is made. Less obvious but also relevant to law is the range

120 Nye, Child Adjustment in Broken and Unhappy Unbroken Homes, 19
Marr. & Fam. Liv. 356 (1957).

121 See Goode, After Divorce 307-329 (1956).

122 Burchinal, Characteristics of Adolescents from Unbroken, Broken, and Reconstituted Families, 26 J. Marr. & the Fam. 44 (1964), reporting his own study
and citing others. Burchinal studied 1566 families of seventh and eleventh grade
children in Cedar Rapids, Iowa, and concluded: "Inimical effects associated with
divorce or separation and, for some youth, with the remarriage of their parents
with whom they were living, were almost uniformly absent in the populations
studied. Acceptance of this conclusion requires the revision of widely held beliefs about the detrimental effects of divorce upon children. Many persons will
quarrel with the results of this study — and similar results from other studies as
well — by pointing to their obvious limitations. It is true that data were limited
to the type collected by questionnaires or obtained from school records. It is
also true that some children will suffer extreme trauma because of divorce or
separation and consequent withdrawal of one parent, and, for some, their development will be affected deleteriously. However, even in these cases it is difficult to assess whether the difficulty occurs because of divorce or whether it
reflects the conflict preceding the divorce and separation. Nevertheless, for the
adolescents in the seventh and eleventh grades in one metropolitan area, there is
no question that in terms of variables measured, family dissolution and, for
some families, reconstitution [with a stepparent], was not the overwhelming influential factor in the children's lives that many have thought it to be." Id. at
50. For a discussion of ways in which to minimize the trauma of divorce for
children, see Despert, Children of Divorce (1962).

of opinion concealed behind the authoritative sectarian statements of a particular religious position; as an example, some indication is given of the diversity of private action in regard to divorce among those who share the label "Catholic."

The difficulties posed for divorce law by the fact of religious diversity are not confined to policy formulation but also affect the practical daily counseling work of lawyers and reach into subsidiary areas, e.g., custody law. How far, for example, should the Catholic lawyer be influenced by factors of religious belief when he is consulted about absolute divorce by a Catholic or non-Catholic client? Is the situation different for a non-Catholic lawyer consulted by a Catholic client? When the parties to a mixed marriage make solemn agreements before marriage regarding religious doctrines such as the indissolubility of marriage or the religious upbringing of their children, to what extent should such provisions be legally enforceable? It is commonplace that in civil contract law parties are permitted to select the law which is to govern the application of the contract, and in Chapter 3 we noted the extent to which parties to a marriage are permitted to take their particular circumstances into account by modifying state policy regarding such matters as inheritance rights through the use of antenuptial contracts. Are the same policy considerations which underlie these rules applicable to antenuptial agreements which affect the right of divorce or its consequences?

CATHOLIC LAW ON DIVORCE

[The following excerpts are taken from two articles by the Rev. James P. Kelly, J.C.D., at the time of writing a judge of the Archdiocesan Tribunal of New York. The first selections, to the point noted in the footnote, are from his Divorce — Some Practical Canonical Considerations, 9 Jurist 187, 188-191, 196 (1949); the others are from Separation and Civil Divorce, 6 Jurist 187 (1946). Subheadings have been omitted.]

As is well known, it is the constant and age-old teaching of the Church that every marriage (between baptized or between unbaptized persons) is, by Divine Law, indissoluble, although, as Our Most Holy Father Pius XI, of happy memory, stated in his encyclical letter on Marriage, "not in the same perfect measure in every case." On this point His Holiness declared:

"And this inviolable stability, although not in the same perfect measure in every case, belongs to every true marriage, for the word of the Lord: 'What God hath joined together let no man put asunder,' must of necessity include all true marriages without exception, since it was spoken of the marriage of our first parents, the prototype of every future marriage. Therefore, although, before Christ, the sublimeness and the severity of the primeval law was so tempered that Moses permitted to the chosen people of God, on account of the hardness of their hearts, that a bill of divorce might be given in certain circumstances, nevertheless, Christ, by virtue of His supreme legislative power, recalled this concession of greater liberty and restored the primeval law in its integrity by those words which must never be forgotten, 'What God hath joined together let no man put asunder.' " [123]

It is evident from the words of the Holy Father that the Divine Law of Indissolubility admits of exception, and from the practice of the Church we know that these exceptions are two in number:

1) the dissolution of the unconsummated bond of marriage by religious profession or by Pontifical Dispensation; [124] and
2) the dissolution of the non-sacramental bond of marriage by the Pauline Privilege or by Pontifical Dispensation.[125]

Accordingly, The Code of Canon Law, in Canon 1118, states the matter as follows: "The valid and consummated marriage of baptized persons can be dissolved by no human power and for no cause other than death."

However, the power to dissolve these unconsummated or non-sacramental marriages does not belong to the civil authority. This power belongs *solely* and *exclusively* to the Church, for the Church of Christ alone has been established by God to be the Guardian and Interpreter of the Divine Law. Hence Pius XI, quoting his predecessor, Pius VI, continued:

". . . . 'Hence it is clear that marriage even in the state of nature, and certainly long before it was raised to the dignity of a sacrament, was divinely instituted in such a way that it should carry with it a perpetual and indissoluble bond which cannot therefore be dissolved by any civil law. Therefore although the sacramental element may be absent from a marriage, there must remain, and indeed there does remain, that perpetual bond which by divine right is so bound up with matrimony from its first institution that it is not subject to any civil power.' "

The civil authority, therefore, in every nation, has absolutely no competence to dissolve the bond of marriage existing between any man and woman, be they baptized or unbaptized. When the civil authority attempts to do this by granting a civil divorce, it violates the Law of God, it usurps the jurisdiction of the Church, and it performs a juridical action which is null and void in reality and before God. The Church of God alone, as the Guardian and Interpreter of the Divine Law, has exclusive competence and jurisdiction to dissolve both the natural contract of marriage between unbaptized persons and the sacramental but un-

[123] Pius XI, encycl., "Casti connubii," 31 dec. 1930 — AAS, XXII (1930), 539-592. Translation by the writer.

[124] Canon 1119.

[125] Canon 1120 and S.C.S. Off. 5 nov. 1924 (private to Bishop of Helena) in Bouscaren, The Canon Law Digest, I (Milwaukee: Bruce Publishing Co., 1934), 553. [The Pauline Privilege is derived from I Cor. 7:10-16, where in his discourse on marriage Paul deals with the case of the convert whose unbelieving husband or wife dissolves the marriage, under which circumstances the convert is not bound by the marriage.]

consummated contract of marriage between baptized persons. This is the clear and unequivocal position of the Church which has not changed one jot or tittle in twenty centuries from Peter to Pius XII.

Cognizant of this position, the Bishops of the United States gathered in Plenary Council in Baltimore in 1884 decreed:

> "It is manifestly evident that they are guilty of grave sin who seek to have their marriages dissolved by a civil magistrate; and that it is even a graver sin if, having obtained a civil divorce, they attempt to enter a 'new marriage' while the bond of their true marriage still exists, to which they are held before God and the Church. To curb these crimes, we impose the penalty of excommunication, reserved to the Ordinary, and incurred ipso facto on those who, after they have obtained a civil divorce, dare to attempt another 'marriage.' " [126] . . .

The Code of Canon Law, as well as the Council of Trent and the pronouncements of many Popes, places a grave obligation on married persons "to observe the communion of conjugal life." "Conjuges servare debent vitae conjugalis communionem," states the Code. This "communion of conjugal life" means not only actual cohabitation under the same roof but a mutual sharing in each other's lives and possessions. This "communion of conjugal life" cannot be broken except for the reasons and under the conditions stated in the Code. A permanent separation from bed, board and cohabitation therefore cannot be allowed to Catholics for any cause other than adultery, and then only under the conditions explicitly set down in Canon 1129. A temporary separation, to last only as long as the cause perdures, may be allowed for a variety of reasons but, again, only under the conditions stated in Canon 1131. Now all of these sacred canons on "separation from bed, board and cohabitation" presuppose that the local Ordinary makes the judgment on whether or not the requirements of the law have been fulfilled in the individual case. The parties may be the judge in their own case only when the crime of the consort "is certain and there is danger in delay." This danger, the Sacred Roman Rota has declared, must be a grave and urgent danger to soul or body. It is evident therefore, from the law and practice of the Holy See, that Catholics are gravely prohibited from separating by mutual agreement or on their own authority (except in an emergency) and that the local Ordinary is expected to pass judgment on the cases of Catholic consorts who wish to separate from each other.[127]

The question now arises whether, in view of the position of the Church on this matter, and in view of the direct prohibition of the Third Council of Baltimore, it is ever licit for a Catholic to approach the civil courts seeking the dissolution of his marriage. It is *certain* that a Catholic is

---

[126] Acta et Decreta Concilii Plenarii Baltimorensis Tertii, n. 124. Translation by the writer.

[127] This is the final excerpt from Kelly's article in 9 Jurist; the remainder are from 6 Jurist at the pages noted in the text. — Ed.

never permitted to approach the civil courts seeking the dissolution of his marriage without the permission of the Holy See or of the local Ordinary. But when may the local Ordinary grant this permission to a Catholic? It is also certain that a local Ordinary may permit a Catholic to seek a civil divorce, *after* his marriage has been declared null by canonical process, or *after* the bond has been dissolved by the Holy See, or *after* the Ordinary has declared that the requirements of the Sacred Canons are present for the use of the Pauline Privilege, provided that the Ordinary in these cases makes it clear that he is permitting this merely to protect the property rights of the Catholic against a consort who is not really his spouse, (or who is no longer his spouse), or to assure civil recognition of any future marriage he may enter, or to avoid the danger of the Catholic being charged with bigamy under the civil law, if and when he enters another marriage which he now has the right to do. If it is possible to obtain a civil annulment in such cases, this, it would seem, is to be preferred, for, although the State is also incompetent to annul the marriage of baptized persons, the granting of an annulment does not have the stigma of an attempted violation of the Divine Law on the part of the State which the granting of a civil divorce entails. This would seem therefore to be the lesser of the two evils, and to be preferred when it can be obtained.

But *when the bond of a valid marriage remains,* may the local Ordinary ever grant permission to a Catholic to seek a civil divorce? This question has been a burning issue since the time of the Protestant Reformation, and particularly since the time of the French Revolution, when the modern states began to usurp the authority of the Church on this matter. [6 Jurist at 219-220.]

[The author reviews some of the differences of opinion in the Church authorities and concludes that a Catholic can lawfully obtain a civil divorce, even if only for the protection of his property rights, when that protection can be achieved in no other way, he has already received an ecclesiastical decree of permanent separation, there is cause for approaching the civil courts beyond mere protection of civil rights, he declares under oath that he does not recognize the authority of the state to dissolve the bonds of marriage, and he solemnly promises not to attempt another marriage during the lifetime of his true spouse. 6 Jurist at 220-231.]

[Earlier, the author considers the problems of Catholic lawyers and judges in assisting clients seeking legal separation or divorce in the civil courts. The following excerpts from 6 Jurist at 210-212 refer to separation cases, but the same considerations apply to absolute divorce, see id. at 231-233.]

Juridically the lawyer is the same person as his client. Therefore, if it is lawful for the client to separate on his own authority, or to approach the civil courts for a separation, it is lawful for a Catholic attorney to act in his behalf. But is it ever lawful for a Catholic lawyer to represent a client who is *illicitly* separating from his spouse? This question is answered by invoking the principles regarding cooperation in the sin of another. Applying these principles, a Catholic lawyer may represent a client who is *illicitly* seeking a separation under two conditions:

1. The cooperation of the lawyer must not be formal cooperation in the sin of his client but merely material (i.e., he must not approve the evil intention of his client and must do everything possible to dissuade him from following his evil course — thus rendering his cooperation only material).

2. The Catholic lawyer may give even this material cooperation only when there is a grave reason for doing so, which is proportionate to the evil in which he is cooperating. The magnitude of the evil, in which he is cooperating, must be judged from the effects following upon the separation of consorts. Inasmuch as the evils which flow from separation are not only evils of a private nature (such as placing the consorts in the occasion of sin) but, inasmuch as they are also evils against the public good (such as the destruction of the family and the undermining of society), the reason which would justify a Catholic lawyer in cooperating in the illicit separation of a married couple must be a reason which would be proportionate to these evils. Therefore, this must be a reason of the public or supernatural order, and not merely a reason of a private nature. Therefore the mere fact that the Catholic attorney will lose a client, or that another less scrupulous lawyer will take the case if the Catholic lawyer refuses it, are not sufficient reasons to permit a Catholic attorney to undertake these cases, for such are not reasons of the public order. If all the Catholic lawyers were threatened with disbarment, or expulsion from the Bar Associations, these would constitute sufficient reasons for undertaking the case of a couple illicitly separating, for the public good would suffer from the disbarment or expulsion from the Bar Associations of all Catholic lawyers. If, by effecting this separation, even though it were done illicitly, the Catholic lawyer would prevent children being brought up as non-Catholics, or by an unworthy parent, this would be a sufficient reason of the supernatural order to permit him to act.

It is evident, therefore, that Catholic lawyers must seek the guidance and direction of their Pastor and Bishop before undertaking cases of this kind, for only thus can they be sure that they are acting with a good conscience.

The case of the Catholic judge of the civil court granting a separation a mensa et thoro manente vinculo differs from that of the Catholic lawyer seeking such in behalf of a client in one important aspect. The judge is obliged by his office to render sentence in accordance with the statutes of the State regardless of his own personal attitude toward these statutes, and he is obliged to hear those who come before him in accordance with these statutes whether he likes it or not, whereas the lawyer is ordinarily free to undertake the case or not as he chooses. With this difference in mind, the principles regarding cooperation in the sin of another apply.

Therefore, if a plaintiff is illicitly seeking a separation from his spouse before the civil court, a Catholic judge may cooperate in the sin of the plaintiff only:

1) If his cooperation in the sin of the plaintiff is not formal but merely material cooperation (i.e., he does not approve the evil action of the plaintiff, and does everything possible to dissuade him from instituting this action);

2) If he has a grave reason of the public order which justifies him in cooperating in this evil action. In the case of the Catholic judge this grave reason of the public order is almost always present inasmuch as if he did not act it would be necessary for him to resign his office, and if all Catholic judges were forced to resign, or were unable to accept the public office of magistrate, a grave and public harm would be done to both the Church and the State.

Therefore, it would seem that if the Catholic judge fulfills the first condition, by making sure that his cooperation in the sin of those who are unlawfully seeking a separation from the civil court is merely material cooperation, he may continue to act with a good conscience.

[The difficulty of obtaining compliance by American Catholics with this law is discussed at 6 Jurist 214-216.]

It is impossible to determine just how many Catholic marriages end in the divorce court, but if half of the marriages in this country end in divorce a goodly percentage of these must, of necessity, be Catholic marriages. Moreover, who of us does not know many Catholics who have already obtained civil divorces, and many more, especially as a result of hasty war marriages, who are about to do so. The best figures I have been able to find, in order to obtain some idea of the number of Catholics who are being affected by the plague of civil divorce, come from a very small suburban parish. The pastor of this parish has informed me that he has about 475 adult Catholics living in his parish, and, of these, more than 100 are now living in adulterous or concubinate unions. There are 96 invalid marriages in this parish. In 26 of these invalid unions, a Catholic has been civilly divorced in a previous marriage. In 29 a Catholic is living with a divorced non-Catholic after only a civil ceremony or a ceremony before a non-Catholic minister. This means that in 55 out of 96 invalid unions the reason for the nullity is directly traceable to the evil of civil divorce. If anything approaching this proportion exists in other parishes throughout the country, then the divorce evil has already made tremendous inroads into the ranks of the followers of Christ.

This pastor tells me that almost all of these bigamists still consider themselves Catholics. They attend Mass on Sunday, they make novenas and contribute to the Church and to charity. They feel that the only thing they are deprived of is the right to receive the Sacraments, but they console themselves with the thought that even this right will be accorded to them in danger of death (which would seem to be an excellent example of the sin of presumption). Many of these Catholics have obtained a civil divorce with no intention of attempting another union, but as time went on and they met someone with whom they fell in love, they felt that life had treated them badly, and that they were entitled to some happiness even in this life, and that God would understand and be more merciful to them than the Church, and thus they have salved their consciences sufficiently to enter another union. In the minds of these people the Divine Law has been reduced to the force of a directive rubric, for they have rationalized themselves into the conviction that they are violating only a Church regulation. They are not married "acccording to the Church," they will tell you, *but they are married."* They would seem to be almost oblivious of the seriousness of their crime and its consequences to themselves and to their illegitimate offspring. They are aided in the development of this mentality by the respectability which has been accorded to them by the civil law, and by the general let-down in moral standards which has marked this first half of the twentieth century. It is evident that divorced people, who remarry, are no longer regarded by their neighbors, even by Catholics, as people of loose morals or undesirable friends.

This situation is giving rise to a thoroughly secularist mentality among many Catholics in this country relative to marriage. More and more American Catholics seem to be ignoring or spurning the authority of the Church with regard to marriage and adopting the perverted position that the State has sole and exclusive jurisdiction over the marriage of all of its citizens. I daresay, that innumerable Catholics now no longer regard the dissolution of the marriage bond by the civil authorities as a usurpation of the jurisdiction of the Church and a violation of the Divine Law, but rather complacently accept this as a right belonging to the State. To these Catholics, the jurisdiction of the Church is confined to "blessing" a marriage, and the Church has no authority over marriage other than to confer such a "blessing."

Hence the problem for us has a twofold aspect. In the first place, it is a problem iuris publici: viz. when Catholics seek and obtain a civil divorce, even if this is done only to safeguard their civil rights, they thereby acknowledge the authority of the State to dissolve the bond of marriage, and their action in obtaining this civil divorce fosters in the minds of other Catholics the false impression, that the State has full authority over all the marriages of its citizens, and that the State has the right to dissolve the bond of marriage. Secondly, the problem is one iuris privati viz. Catholics who obtain a civil divorce, even if only with the intention of protecting the civil effects of the bond, place themselves in the proximate occasion of sin, for very many, if not most of them, as noted above, soon justify themselves and enter an adulterous union.

NOTE

For a discussion of procedure within the Catholic Church's judicial system, see Gest, Nullity of Marriage in Ecclesiastical Courts, 26 Pa. B. Assn. Q. 245 (1955). In each diocese there is a court of three judges which hears nullity cases, or more commonly these are determined in a summary procedure before the Bishop or his delegate.   Under either procedure an Auditor is appointed to report on the facts, and the Defender of the Bond is under the duty "to present all facts and argument in favor of the validity of the marriage."   Id. at 252.   If the decision is that the marriage is invalid, the Defender of the Bond is obliged to appeal to a higher (usually the Archbishop's) court, and a further appeal to the Roman Rota is discretionary.   Id. at 255.   The Rota is the highest court of appeal in the Church and consists of sixteen judges who hear cases in panels or en banc.   Certain advocates are entitled to practice in the Rota, and costs are eliminated or reduced for the poor.   Gest cites the following summary of the Rota's decisions in nullity cases in 1953 (id. at 257-258):

Affirmative decisions with fee..................................... 40
Negative decisions with fee.. 66
Affirmative decisions (nullity) without fee or costs.................... 25
Negative decisions (nullity not proved) without fee or costs........... 41

Total 172

The breakdown on the basis of averred causes of nullity was as follows:

Basis of Nullity	Affirmative (Nullity) (Proved)	Negative (Nullity) (Not Proved)	Total
Impediments:			
Bond of previous marriage..........	2	1	3
Consanguinity	—	1	1
Affinity...........................	—	1	1
Impotency	3	16	19
Defects of Consent:			
Force and Fear....................	21	33	54
Insanity..........................	1	1	2
Defect of Liberty.................	1	—	1
Simulated Consent	9	12	21
Conditions (Unspecified)...........	3	12	15
Intention or Condition			
Against Unity of Marriage........	3	4	7
Against Indissolubility...........	17	9	26
Against Procreation..............	23	36	59
Total	85	131	216

The total of 216 exceeds the total cases of 172 because more than one ground was averred in a number of cases, and the decision is simply that nullity is or is not proven on one of the claimed bases.

AMRAM, THE JEWISH LAW OF DIVORCE
22-123 (1896)

The origins of law are to be found in the constitution of the patriarchal family, and the fundamental principle of its government was the absolute authority of the oldest male ascendant, who was the lawgiver and the judge, and whose rule over his wives, children and slaves was supreme. . . .

The further back that we trace the history of institutions, and especially of domestic relations, the greater we find this power of the father and husband; not only affecting the legal status of the wife, but controlling her actions, her property and her person. At the very beginning, or, at least, as far back as the history of this institution can be traced, the husband's right to divorce was absolutely untrammelled, and it was only with the gradual breaking up of the patriarchal system, and the substitution of an individualistic for a socialistic state, that the woman acquired, at first merely negative rights, such as protection against her husband's acts, and, finally, positive rights, under which she could proceed against him.

This ancient right of the husband, to divorce his wife at his pleasure, is the central thought in the entire system of Jewish divorce law; and the Rabbis did not, nor could they, set it aside, although, as will be shown hereafter, they gradually tempered its severity by numerous restrictive measures. . . .

The view that has been above set forth, that the theory of the ancient Jewish common law considered divorce a private right of the husband, established by immemorial custom, is not generally accepted, and certain ethical dicta of the Old and New Testament are cited against it. It is commonly supposed that Moses permitted divorce because of his people's hardness of heart; and that from the beginning it was not so; that the pre-Mosaic law forbade divorce and did not attempt to put asunder what God hath joined together. In support of this view the words of Genesis are quoted. "And the man (Adam) said, This time it is bone of my bones and flesh of my flesh; this shall be called Woman (Ishah) because out of Man (Ish) was this one taken; therefore doth a man leave his father and his mother and cleave unto his wife and they become one flesh." But it is an error to suppose that these high ethical conceptions of the marriage relation were carried out in actual practice. Divorce was and is a necessary evil, so considered in all civilized society. Theoretically, men have always agreed that the lofty sentiments expressed both in the Old and the New Testament constituted the ideals that should govern a perfect marriage. But the practice of men, as well in the dim antiquity of the pre-Mosaic age as in the eighteen hundred years since the establishment of Christianity, has recognized the necessity of divorce, while regretting its nonconformity with the ideals that should govern the marriage relation. And, indeed, it will be observed on closer inspection that the sayings both of Hebrew and Christian moralists in condemnation of divorce are directed not against the exercise of this right, but against its abuse. Jesus himself felt obliged to recognize the validity of divorce, although he confined it to cases of the wife's fornication.[128] The Jewish law recognized the validity of divorce in all cases, and sought to prevent its abuse by moral injunction and judicial regulation. The Old Testament, written

[128] Matthew xix, 9.

at a time when the domestic law of the patriarchal family was in full vigor, accepted divorce as a matter of fact, as an institution that had existed since time immemorial. . . . [Pages 22-26.]

The old patriarchal theory was gradually modified; exceptions to the general unrestricted right of the husband gradually grew more numerous, and ere long we find the old rule practically abolished, by reason of the many exceptions to it which were recognized by the law.

But although the Rabbis did, in time, set a bar to the unlimited right of the husband, they did not seek to prevent divorce for cause or by mutual consent of the parties. The Hebrews are often somewhat maliciously called "a practical people." In no better manner did they show their practical common sense than in their divorce regulations. They did not foolishly sacrifice the realities of life to the ideal by which they were guided. They had a wholesome regard for human nature and were too practical to have false theories about it. The sacramental character that the Christian Church sought to give to marriage, and the concomitant theory of its indissolubility, never struck root among the Jews, because these theories were not in harmony with the demands of human nature and the realities of life.

The Rabbinical theory was sound and defensible. Indiscriminate exercise of the right to divorce was condemned, and moral grounds had to be given before the Rabbis gave their sanction to the proceeding. If the parties agreed to be divorced, the Rabbis could not oppose any objection, because the mutual consent of the parties was the highest moral ground for divorce. The modern legal barbarity which yokes together in matrimony persons who mutually agree to be separated, was not countenanced by the Jewish law. [Pages 39-40.]

. . . [The] numerous qualifications [by which the rabbis limited] the theoretical right of the husband to give the Bill of Divorce to his wife whenever it pleased him to do so, resulted in gradually eliminating from the popular mind the notion that such a right existed. Men had become so accustomed to go to the Rabbi, who was both spiritual leader and judge, when they wished to divorce their wives, that they eventually forgot that, by ancient common law, they were entitled to give the Bill of Divorce without the Rabbi's sanction.

In the beginning of the eleventh century of the Common Era, the theoretical right of the husband, which for centuries theretofore had ceased to exist in practice, was formally declared to be at an end. This was done by a decree issued by Rabbi Gershom ben Yehudah (about 1025 C.E.), who presided over a Sanhedrin convened at Mayence. The substance of this decree is thus stated: —

"To assimilate the right of the woman to the right of the man, it is ordained that even as the man does not put away his wife except of his own free will, so shall the woman not be put away except by her own consent." Always excepting the cases where good cause has been shown by either husband or wife why the marriage should be dissolved against the will of the other. . . .

That the Biblical law has neglected to make the rights as well as the duties of husband and wife entirely reciprocal, and to provide for the wife's right to sue for divorce, has been a source of frequent comment. The reason for the silence of the law on this question is, however, obvious. In a state of society where the husband and father was practically a sovereign in dealing with his own, the case of a wife suing for divorce could not have occurred to the lawgivers, because there was no forum in which she could obtain redress. . . .

The germ of the wife's right to sue for divorce does, however, exist in the Pentateuch. . . .

. . . By virtue of the position that the woman assumed in the husband's household, she obtained certain rights against him. He having taken her into his *manus,* the law imposed upon him certain obligations towards her. The next step probably was, the recognition of the wife as plaintiff before the Elders of the City or the Heads of the Houses, in case the husband failed in his duty towards her, and the infliction of some penalty for his transgression. This penalty very likely consisted of a fine or a levy on some of his property for her sustenance. Eventually (at first no doubt in flagrant cases) the judges compelled the husband to release her entirely by giving her a bill of divorce.

The right to compel the husband to give a bill of divorce to his wife, may well have appeared doubtful to these ancient judges who were ingrained with the theory of the absolute right of the head of the house to deal as he pleased with his own; and the judge or the Council of Elders who first exercised this right were no doubt looked upon as usurpers of authority. But the right existed at a very early period, and the courts had the power to compel the husband's consent to a divorce by the infliction of corporal punishment, usually thirty-nine stripes.

The objection to the Bill of Divorce thus given under order of the court was that it was given under duress. The law required that the husband should act as a free agent [but this objection was evaded] by a very neat bit of reasoning. [The courts] said, in substance, "We do not compel the husband to give this Get [bill of divorce] against his will. We assume that every man intends to act according to law. The law says that this woman shall receive a Get, and it therefore becomes the duty of the husband to give it to her. His refusal to do so, is the result of an evil disposition which prompts him to act contrary to law. . . . When he has been sufficiently punished, his evil disposition will leave him and he will be able, as a free agent, to give the divorce according to law." [Quotation abbreviated by Eds.]

This argument justified the Jewish courts in enforcing their decrees in divorce against the husband; but the Rabbis refused to apply it for the purpose of validating Bills of Divorce which were prepared in the courts of the Heathen (Romans). In all cases, where the non-Jewish Courts conducted the divorce proceedings of a Jewish couple, the Rabbis declared their act to be null and void. Although the Jewish authorities readily submitted all questions affecting civil rights and contracts to the courts of the Gentiles, they always refused to recognize their authority in religious matters. Divorce was a quasi-religious act among the Jews; the woman was said to be married and divorced "according to the law of Moses and Israel." The Bill of Divorce was peculiar to the Jews and other nations did not make use of it in divorce proceedings; for these reasons the interference of non-Jewish courts in matters of marriage and divorce was deemed a usurpation of authority even when both the parties voluntarily submitted to its jurisdiction. But in cases where the court of the Gentiles exercised merely an ancillary jurisdiction for the purpose of enforcing a decree of the Jewish court, its action was recognized as valid . . . .

Although in course of time the wife was recognized as a plaintiff in divorce proceedings and could obtain a decree of the Court to compel her husband to divorce her, the law always supposed that the husband was giving the divorce of his own free will and accord. By means of this legal fiction no violence was done to the letter of the old law, and the theory of the husband's exclusive right to give the divorce was apparently maintained; yet the divorce given by the husband under order of the court, at the suit of his wife, was as much a judicial divorce as any modern proceeding of such a nature. The woman was never entitled to divorce her husband at Jewish law. Such an act would have been in opposition to the fundamental theory that divorce was the exclusive right of the husband, and although, as was shown above, this exclusive right was modified in favor of the wife, the old forms were always used and the idea of the bill of divorce given by the wife to her husband was impossible to the Jewish legal mind. [Pages 52-60.]

While conceding the right of the husband to divorce his wife, and the right of the wife to sue for divorce from her husband, the law nevertheless sought to prevent divorce without cause by every means within its power, short of an absolute denial of the legal right. . . . The Rabbi was judge, legal adviser, spiritual guide and religious instructor. This combination of functions resulted in establishing a system of equitable rules among the Jews separate and apart from the Law. These equitable rules and maxims were merely hortatory, and represented the moral principle protesting against an inequitable application of purely legal rules. But as these equitable principles were expounded by the same Rabbis who laid down the law, they received the acknowledgment of the people and came in time to have almost the same force and effect as the law itself; so that in the Codes of Law will be found legal rules and equitable maxims and admonitions side by side.

The reconciliation of persons about to be divorced, or who had already been divorced, afforded a fair field for the application of these ethical precepts. Besides the legal safeguards against unreasonable and ill-advised divorces, moral suasion was a potent factor, and it was the duty of the judges or Rabbis to exercise their influence in checking the unrestrained passions that often prompted men to divorce their wives without cause. [Pages 78-79.]

[Amram also discusses another major brake upon hasty or ill-advised divorce. The Kethubah or] dowry given to the father upon the marriage of his daughter originally was the purchase money which the husband paid for her. Undeniable traces of the original commercial nature of marriage are to be found in the Bible, although the state of society which is therein described had already passed through the lower stage of matrimonial bargains. . . . The dowry was originally payable to the father of the wife, and late in Talmudic times this was still the law in cases where the wife was a minor or was divorced before the marriage had been consummated. Eventually, however, the dowry was given to the wife, remaining undivided in the estate of the husband, and being payable to her on her divorce, or on the death of her husband. As the heirs of the husband often defrauded the widow of her rights, it was ordained that the amount of the dowry should be deposited with the father of the wife, thus making it secure against the adverse claim of his heirs. But as it was the purpose of the institution of the dowry to act as a check upon the husband, so that "it shall not be easy in his eyes to divorce her," the deposit of the money with the father of the wife destroyed the effect intended. As the husband had no further payment to make, there were no financial considerations to hinder him from giving the divorce whenever he pleased, and telling his wife "to go to her dowry." It was then provided by law that the amount of the dowry should be invested in articles of value, and that these should remain in possession of the husband. This regulation, however, was found to give no greater satisfaction than the former one, for it was very easy for the husband to give the articles of value to his wife and tell her to go. The final remedy, the Kethubah, was provided by an ordinance of Shimeon ben Shetah. He ordained that the dowry should remain with the husband and not be separated from his estate; that it should be secured to the wife by a writing, whereby all his estate was charged with its payment.

. . . The Kethubah was, like the Common Law dower, a lien upon all real estate owned by the husband during his lifetime, and if after his death or when he divorced his wife he had no estate in possession, it could be collected out of the estate which he had formerly owned but which was now in the possession of third persons. This regulation was a very important check upon the freedom of divorce. The wealth of the people consisted chiefly of estate in lands, and as it was necessary that the Kethubah should be paid in coin, it was often difficult for a man to obtain so large a sum, and hence gave time for reconsideration of his intention to divorce his wife.

. . . The Kethubah was an inalienable right of the wife, and marriage without a Kethubah was unlawful. Rabbi Meïr (about 150 C.E.) was of the opinion that a man was forbidden to remain with his wife even one hour, unless she had a Kethubah, "lest it appear easy to him to divorce her." . . . The wife could not sell her Kethubah to her husband or release him from its obligation . . . [Pages 111-114.]

. . . The wife's right to claim the amount of her Kethubah depended on her good conduct, and she lost her right in certain cases if she failed in the performance of her duties as a wife. The cases of the adulteress, against whom the law was especially severe, and the woman who had been guilty of antenuptial incontinence, founded on the Biblical laws, were, very probably, the earliest cases in which the woman lost her claim to the Kethubah.

Following these, the Mishnah cites a number of cases in which the woman, by reason of her misconduct, forfeited her right. . . .

Generally speaking, the divorced wife lost her Kethubah if she had been guilty of an offense against ethical custom or usage, whether in the breach of some ritualistic prescription or in the violation of some social convention. In either case, however, the offense had to be one involving moral turpitude. [Pages 122-123.]

NOTE

1. As might be expected, the principal problem for Jewish divorce law in the United States concerns the husband who out of spite or malice refuses to give his wife a get or bill of divorce after one of them has obtained a civil decree of divorce. The conservative wing of American Judaism has attempted to resolve this dilemma by adding a clause to the Kethubah whereby the parties agree "as evidence of our desire to enable each other to live in accordance with the Jewish Law of Marriage throughout our lifetime" to recognize a religious court "as having authority to counsel us" in case of difficulty; the paragraph then concludes with the key provision: "We authorize the Beth Din [religious court] to impose such terms of compensation as it may see fit for failure to respond to its summons or to carry out its decision." This purports to give a religious body the same power to compel a husband to give a get as it would be able to exercise in a Jewish state. See Levin & Kramer, New Provisions in the Kethubah: A Legal Opinion (pamphlet, Yeshiva U., 1955).

Suppose you were consulted by a Jewish client who was about to be married and who wished to know whether the antenuptial assent to this contract clause by the man she was about to marry would make him liable in the civil courts for the enforcement of any "compensation" award which the religious court might enter against him. How would you advise her? On what theory might enforceable legal rights arise from the Kethubah? For a critical discussion of these issues, see Levin & Kramer, supra.

Compare Price v. Price, 16 Pa. D. & C. 290 (C.P. 1931), where complainant wife had obtained a secular divorce and then sought an equity decree to compel her former husband to appear before a rabbi and give her a religious divorce. The husband had signed an antenuptial agreement that he would submit all marital disputes to a rabbi and recognize his powers of "arbitration and jurisdiction" as "on a plane and footing coequal with powers exercised by civil and judicial authorities in like juridical matters." Ibid. The court held that it had no jurisdiction "to order one to follow the practices of his faith," id. at 291, and dismissed the bill. In Koeppel v. Koeppel, 138 N.Y.S.2d 366, 370 (Sup. Ct. 1954), defendant husband was denied summary judgment in an action by his former wife to enforce a clause in a postnuptial separation agreement in which he had agreed that he would "whenever the same shall become necessary, appear before a Rabbi . . . and execute any and all papers" necessary for a religious divorce. The court apparently viewed the clause as enforceable: "Complying with his agreement would not compel the defendant to practice any religion. . . . His appearance before the Rabbinate to answer questions and give evidence needed by them to make a decision is not a profession of faith." Id. at 373. Ultimately, however, the defendant prevailed; see Koeppel v. Koeppel, 3 App. Div. 2d 853, 161 N.Y.S.2d 694 (1957), affirming dismissal of the action for specific performance on the ground that as the wife had been remarried by a rabbi, a religious divorce was not "necessary" under the terms of the agreement. Neither the Price nor Koeppel opinions really examines the problems of secular enforcement of such agreements.

2. "Mohammed borrowed many of the provisions of the Jewish law, following it closely in many instances, and in others deliberately changing it to suit his purpose. . . . The important departure of the Mohammedan from the Jewish law is in the right given the wife to release her dowry to her husband." Amram, supra, at 115. For a discussion of the restraints upon the husband's unilateral power and modern reforms in, e.g., Egypt, to give the wife a cause of action for divorce, see Anderson, Islamic Law in the Modern World 53-58 (1959).

DUMAIS v. DUMAIS
152 Me. 24, 122 A.2d 322 (1956)

WILLIAMSON, J. On appeal. This is a bill in equity by a husband to enjoin his wife from proceeding further with a pending divorce action and to obtain custody of their minor children. The controversy centers upon the effect of antenuptial promises relating to divorce and the religious education and custody of the children. . . . The case . . . reaches us on appeal from a decree dismissing the bill. . . .

The plaintiff, a Catholic, and the defendant, a non-Catholic, both over twenty-one years of age, sought and obtained dispensation for their marriage from the Bishop of Cleveland. The application signed by the defendant reads in part:

"I, *not a member of the Catholic Church*, desiring to marry Joseph Alcide DuMais, a Catholic, promise on my conscience:
1. that I will ever adhere to the divine law that prohibits all divorce; . . .
3. that all children, boys and girls, that may be born of this union, shall be baptised and educated solely in the Catholic religion by me even in the event of death of my Catholic consort;
4. that all children in the event of dispute, shall be given to such guardians that will assure the faithful execution of my covenant and promise;" . . .

The plaintiff made a like "promise on my conscience," with suitable changes arising from the fact that he was a Catholic.

There are four children from 11 to 3 years in age. The two elder were baptized in the Catholic Church. The defendant has refused to have the two younger so baptized, although often requested by the plaintiff.

In July 1955 the defendant brought a libel for divorce, now pending in the Androscoggin Superior Court, in which she prays for the care and custody of the children. The bill in equity was commenced on November 7 and dismissed on November 23rd last, during which period the record indicates there was in effect a restraining order against proceeding with the libel. We have no official knowledge of what, if any, action has since taken place in the divorce case.

The first and decisive question is whether equity has jurisdiction of the controversy. We answer in the negative.

With respect to the libel for divorce, the plaintiff says in substance that the promises to "ever adhere to the divine law that prohibits all divorce" formed a binding contract between the parties; that only by preventing further proceedings on the divorce libel may the plaintiff be saved from irreparable loss; and that there is no plain adequate and complete remedy at law. In short, the plaintiff's argument is that by such promises a husband or a wife may forever close the door of the divorce court to the other.

Divorce by statute is placed within the jurisdiction of the Superior Court. R.S., c. 166, §55. "The law of divorce in this jurisdiction is wholly statutory." Wilson, Petr. v. Wilson, 140 Me. 250, 251, 36 A.(2nd) 774. Given cause, the libelant is entitled of right to a divorce. The decision does not lie within the discretion of the court. Kennon v. Kennon, 150 Me. 410, 111 A.(2nd) 695. The Equity Court has no jurisdiction to grant or deny divorce. The plaintiff husband does not indeed contend otherwise. His position is that the antenuptial promises are not available directly in defense of the divorce libel, and so he seeks indirectly through equity to reach for practical purposes a like result. There is, however, no necessity for the intervention of equity in the pending legal proceedings. The case differs widely from Usen v. Usen, 136 Me. 480, 13 A.(2nd) 738 in which the court restrained a Maine husband from proceeding further in Florida against his Maine wife with a divorce based upon false allegations of residence.

No authority has been called to our attention in which the point in issue has been raised. The subject matter — divorce — is entirely governed by the statutes, to which alone the courts may look for jurisdiction. Equity on this ground has no jurisdiction of the case insofar as divorce is concerned.

With respect to the religious education and custody of the children, there is no sound reason for equity to act. . . .

The rule is plainly and firmly established that the welfare of the child is the controlling fact in determining care and custody. . . .

The complete provision for care and custody cases in other courts is a sufficient denial of jurisdiction in equity. . . .

[Appeal dismissed.]

NOTE

For further discussion of mixed marriages and the full text of the agreement quoted in the DuMais case, which is required of every marriage in which a Catholic participates with a non-Catholic if the Church is to regard it as valid, see Blood, Marriage 80-84 (1962). For a review of "a fairly consistent body of data" that shows that Catholic-Protestant marriages have a substantially higher divorce rate than marriages where both parties are of the same faith, see Kephart, The Family, Society, and the Individual 610-611 (1961).

3. The Influence of Law on the Rate of Marital Dissolution[129]

RHEINSTEIN, DIVORCE AND THE LAW IN GERMANY: A REVIEW [130]
65 American Journal of Sociology 489 (1960)

This book constitutes a contribution to a major research project of the University of Chicago's Comparative Law Research Center. By investigating the relation between changes in the divorce law of Germany and in the actual stability of marriages as expressed in changing divorce rates, the authors try to shed some light on the problem to what extent, if any, the stability of marriages can be protected or promoted by the enactment and administration of laws dealing with the substantive and procedural law of divorce. . . .

By . . . instability of marriage which we regard as a danger to society, we cannot merely mean the issuance by the court of a comparatively great number of decrees of divorce, but a high frequency of actual cases of abandonment, desertion, or separation. It is by these events that homes are broken, children turned into "orphans," dependents thrown on the taxpayers, and expectations of love and security destroyed. The decree of divorce never causes, or even precedes, such collapse of a marriage: it is nothing but an official ascertainment of the fact that a marriage has gone to pieces and that to the parties thereto, or, occasionally to only one of them, the freedom of remarriage is officially restored: this

---

[129] On this question see also Kelly, page 796 supra, who in his discussion of the "ipso facto censure of excommunication reserved to the Ordinary on the . . . crime of attempting marriage after a civil divorce" notes that "from a practical viewpoint I do not think that this has deterred many Catholics from attempting another marriage after having obtained a divorce in the years which have intervened since 1886, when this censure was promulgated." Kelly, Divorce — Some Practical Canonical Considerations, 9 Jurist 187, 203 (1949).

[130] Scheidung und Scheidungsrecht: Grundfragen der Ehescheidung in Deutschland ("Divorce and Divorce Law: Basic Problems of Divorce in Germany"). By Ernst Wolf, Gerhard Lüke, and Herbert Hax. Tübingen: J. C. B. Mohr (Paul Siebeck), 1959. Pp. xii + 487.

is its essential feature. Frequently, it is true, a decree of divorce also takes care of additional issues: alimony, property settlement, and custody of children and their support. But none of these issues is essential to divorce: each calls for, and can receive, judicial regulation as soon as the marriage is actually broken asunder, whether or not the "tie" of marriage continues. The denial of a decree of divorce can prevent the petitioners from entering upon a new legitimate marriage, but it cannot reunite the spouses, who must have separated at the latest at the time of the filing of the petition for divorce; nor can it prevent them from entering into new factual unions. All the denial of the decree can do is deprive any such new union of the characterization as a legitimate marriage.

But this does not rule out the fact that the comparative ease or difficulty of obtaining a decree of restoration of the freedom of remarriage may have some influence upon the frequency of cases of actual marriage breakdown. This relationship is not, however, of the simple order of "no divorce, no family breakup." It is rather a psychological connection, in the sense that ease in entering upon a legitimate remarriage may actually encourage a person to destroy his present marriage, while the difficulty or impossibility of legitimate remarriage may serve as a deterrent. It is as a psychological force that there exists, or may exist, a cause-and-effect relationship between a society's divorce law, on the one side, and the actual state of its families' stability, on the other. If we wish to enact a divorce law which is to serve as a deterrent to family breakdown, we ought to know what this psychological relationship is; but as yet we have very little such knowledge. All we have are allegations either that "divorce breeds divorce" or that "absence of divorce breeds immorality." Both allegations are affirmed with equal fervor and with equal lack of evidence.

Evidence as to the facts of the psychological cause-and-effect relationship between divorce law and actual stability of marriage is, indeed, difficult to obtain, especially because we have few statistics of marriage breakdowns. In contrast to decrees of divorce which can, or should be, counted without too much difficulty, the fact of the actual failure of marriages is difficult to define, difficult to observe, and difficult to count. However, the obtaining of some insight into the relationship between divorce law and stability is not completely hopeless. The method must, of course, be statistical and comparative. Attempts must be made to assemble such statistical data about broken marriages as are available and then to see whether differences or changes in the laws on divorce can be correlated with differences in the statistics. The difficulty lies, of course, in the fact that differences in the frequency of actual breakdown may be due to differences in factors other than the state of the divorce laws. Is it at all possible to isolate that factor out of the seamless web of socially relevant factors, such as strength of religious commandment, strictness of neighborhood criticism, the social status of women, mobility of population, housing conditions, etc.?

A set of investigations aiming at the unraveling of these interconnections has been designed at the University of Chicago's Comparative Law Research Center, and some such investigations have been actually undertaken in co-operation with the International Association of Legal Science and the University of Chicago-University of Frankfurt Exchange Project. The book here under review is the product of the last-named co-operation. . . .

The idea of using statistical material from Germany was conceived because in that country considerable changes in the divorce law occurred twice within a period for which ample and detailed statistical materials are available. The first change occurred when on January 1, 1900, the new Civil Code for the German Empire, of August 18, 1896, replaced the numerous different laws which had been in effect in the country up to that day. The second change occurred under the National-Socialist regime, when, in 1938, the marriage and divorce law of the Civil Code was replaced by the new Marriage Law for Greater Germany. With slight modifications brought about in 1945 by Control Council Law No. 16, the provisions of the law of 1938 are still in effect in the Federal Republic of Germany.

Because of the diversity of the divorce laws preceding the Code of 1896, their effects were different in the different parts of the Reich. As far as the law of divorce is concerned, three major districts could be distinguished: (1) those of the Prussian General Code of 1791-94; (2) those of the Code Napoléon; and (3) those of the so-called common law of Germany.

The Prussian General Code, which was in effect in the state of Prussia in about one-half of its territory, but outside of Prussia in a few small territories, was the most liberal of these laws. As a product of the period of Enlightenment and decisively influenced by the secular thought of King Frederick II ("The Great"), it allowed divorce not only on the ground of misconduct but also, at least as a general rule, upon mutual agreement, and even upon the unilateral petition of one spouse based upon "insuperable aversion" to the other. The Prussian Code thus clearly followed the notion that a marriage might be terminated not only because of one party's guilt and misconduct but also where, without any party's fault, the marriage had become thoroughly disrupted beyond hope of repair. The Prussian Code was, indeed, the earliest of modern divorce laws in which there was embodied this "principle of disruption" that had been postulated by the thinkers of the Enlightment as a necessary concomitant of every individual's inalienable right to the pursuit of happiness but which has been consistently condemned by religious, especially Roman Catholic, conservatives as being incompatible with the ideal of Christian marriage.

These traditional Christian notions had found expression in the common law of Germany, which was, indeed, as far as marriage and divorce were concerned, identical with ecclesiastical law. It was, however, not the same for Catholics and Protestants. For Catholics the rule was simply that of the Canon Law: that marriage is a sacrament and indissoluble. In Protestant ecclesiastical law, too, marriage was, on general principles, regarded as concluded for life, but the concession was made that a marriage would be dissolved in certain cases of grave misconduct, viz., adultery, desertion, and cruelty of a particularly serious character.   In contrast to the "disruption principle" of the Prussian Code, the Protestant common law thus strictly followed the "guilt principle," while the Catholic common law adhered to the principle of complete indissolubility.

Similar to the position of the Protestant common law was that of the Code Napoléon.   Upon general principle, divorce was to be granted only in cases of guilt, but the definition of what might be called cruelty was less strict.   Furthermore, in addition to divorce for guilt, the code provided for divorce on the ground of mutual agreement of the spouses.   However, the procedure provided for the expression of the agreement was so cumbersome and time-consuming that divorces based on it were rare.

In the new Civil Code it was not easy to find a solution acceptable to the whole country.   The final result was similar to that of the Code Napoléon.   Any possibility of divorce on the ground of mutual agreement was abolished, however.   All traces of the disruptive principle were deleted.   Divorce was to be granted exclusively in the case of guilty misconduct.   The general tendency of the draftsmen was one of hostility toward divorce: in their report they stated that it was their intention to stem the rising tide of divorce and firmly to establish the principle of stability of marriage.

The changes brought about by the new code were considerable for the regions under the Prussian Code and those under the common law.   In the former, divorce became considerably more difficult; in the latter it was made somewhat easier for Protestants and available for the first time to Catholics.

What were the actual effects of the legislative change in the various parts of the country?   To what extent, if any, was the hope of the draftsmen of the code that it might stem the rising tide of divorce realized?   The answers to these questions [occupy] the major part of the book under review.

Three sets of statistics are used for the purpose; they are of: petitions for the initiation of the conciliation proceedings which under German law must precede the filing of an action for divorce; decrees of divorce granted as related to the total figure of divorce proceedings; and divorces granted per each 100,000 population.

Each set of figures is subdivided by appellate court districts, so as to correlate them to the different regions of pre-code law.   A further correlation is undertaken, relating the figures to the religious composition of the populace by region.   All three sets of statistics cover the period from 1881 to 1915, that is, nineteen years before and sixteen years after the new law went into effect.

The number of petitions for the initiation of conciliation proceedings is computed for each 100,000 population.   Changes in the figures indicate changes in the extent of the desire for divorce.   The authors are aware that, for the sake of reliability, the number of petitions per 10,000 marriages should be used rather than per 100,000 inhabitants. They believe, however, that the latter correlation may be used just as well because the percentage of married people among the total population not only was remarkably stable during the period of investigation but also showed no great differences between different regions of the Reich. In 1880 the percentage of married people in the total population was 34; in 1910, 35.8. In 1880 the regional differences varied between 38.1 and 31.2 per cent; in 1910 between 40.8 and 32.8 per cent.

The authors also state that, to learn the extent of the desire for divorce, it might be desirable to know the number of approaches made to their lawyers by persons considering divorce. However, no such figures are available, and thus the next best index is, indeed, provided by the figures for petitions for the initiation of conciliation proceedings.

Throughout the country the figures increased during the period under observation. For the country as a whole the figure for 1880 was 34.5 petitions for every 10,000 of the population; in 1913, the last normal year before World War I, it had risen to 61.5. The figures indicate, however, regional differences. In one region the upward trend does not show any increase or decrease at the time of the introduction of the new law; in a second region the upward trend is somewhat increased; and, in a third, the curve shows a downward break in 1900, which is reversed, however, after a very few years. These three regions coincide more or less with the region of the Code Napoléon and the predominantly Protestant parts of the North German region of the common law; the South German regions of the common law which have both a predominantly Catholic and a predominantly Protestant population; and the region of the Prussian Code.

The authors draw the following conclusions:

> The introduction of the Civil Code has not reduced the increase of the number of petitions for conciliation proceedings and has thus not reduced the extent of the divorce desire. Preponderantly the new law has not had any effect in this respect. In some of those regions in which the divorce law was liberalized one can observe a certain increase of the trend. It is by no means certain, however, whether this increase would not have occurred independent of the change in the law. Nowhere was the progressive trend retarded. Even in the regions of the Prussian law, where the divorce law was tightened, the trend did not change in any significant way [p. 13].

The authors properly observe that the increase in the years after 1900 was even greater than that shown by the figures of petitions for conciliation proceedings, because in these years the courts showed a steadily increasing willingness to grant permission to file an action for divorce without preceding conciliation proceedings. They are certainly justified in concluding that the draftsmen of the new code have failed in their expectation of reducing the desire for divorce. They do recognize, however, that the differences between the pre-code divorce may have had

a certain influence insofar as in the regions of difficult divorce the increase of the trend began somewhat later than in those of easy divorce.
This difference tends to be minimized, however, by the fact that in
those regions where the tide started earlier the curve also tended to
flatten out earlier.

The second set of figures indicates the numbers of decrees of divorce
per each 100 proceedings terminated, figures regarded as indicative of
the attitude of the courts. Has the introduction of the Civil Code rendered the courts more inclined to grant divorces? For the Reich as a
whole the change in the law is hardly reflected at all in the figures. . . .

The third set of figures, the number of divorces per 100,000 population, refers to what is commonly known as the divorce rate, changes in
which are regarded as indicative of the divorce trend of any given country. It was the professed intention of the makers of the new Civil Code
to stop the increase which the divorce rate had shown continuously over
the last decades. It was even more their intention to stop the upward
trend in those parts of the Reich where divorce had so far been comparatively easy. Did they succeed? The trend of the divorce rate gives
the most unmistakable answer. To ascertain the trend with greater
certainty than is obtainable from the raw figures, and particularly to
find out whether in 1900 the trends of the several districts were upward
or downward, the authors have computed for each year the median
height of the curve and the median rate of change, using the method of
least squares.

The figures thus computed demonstrate that before 1900 the trend
was rising in the districts of most and, since 1900, in those of all appellate courts. In a few court districts the trend shows a slight downward
break in 1900. The majority of the latter districts belongs to the region
of the Prussian Code, but there are among them also two districts of
Protestant common law. In all these districts the break is small, and
the trend rose continuously after 1900. While the break in the Prussian
law districts may be attributed to the change of the law, it was insignificant and without lasting effect. Nowhere did the change turn the
trend downward; and nowhere did it prevent its continuous rise.   In
many districts the curve was even steeper after 1900 than before.

The authors thus conclude that

the shape of the law of divorce was neither the cause of the divorce
wave nor even one of its essential conditions. In the face of other
circumstances, the influence of the law did not make itself felt at all.

Neither was it possible to prevent spouses ready to resort to divorce from actualizing such readiness, nor could the new Code influence their moral or religious attitudes with respect to their marital
lives.

The rising trend is regarded, in fact, to have been the result of changes
in the structure of society, especially of what is called the change of the
"old society" into modern mass society.

The insignificance of the factor, "divorce law," is also indicated by the figures for the period after 1914. The outbreak of the first World War resulted in a drop of the divorce rate of almost one-third. In 1916 and 1917 it began to rise again. In 1919 it reached twice the height of 1913. The total increase within the seven-year period from 1913 to 1919 was indeed twice that of the thirty-five years from 1881 to 1915. A small drop during the 1920's was reversed again in 1928. The rate of divorce per 100,000 population was 59.1 in 1920, 62.2 in 1921, 63.3 in 1930, and 65.0 in 1932.

In 1933, the first year of the National-Socialist regime, the rate was 65.1; in 1934, it was 81.9 (i.e., three times that of 1913, when it had been 26.6).

In 1939, the first year after the liberalization of the divorce law by the new statute of 1938, the rate reached 89.1. The drop to 70.5 in 1940, which followed the outbreak of World War II, was proportionately smaller than the drop that had accompanied the outbreak of World War I. For the war years no divorce statistics were collected. In 1946, the first postwar year, the rate already surpassed that of 1939; in 1948 it climbed up steeply; and in 1949 it reached the all-time peak of 188 (i.e., twice the figure of 1939 and seven times that of 1913). From 1949 to 1956 the rate steeply dropped to 82 in 1956, and the decrease seems to be continuing, although at a much lesser grade.

From these figures the authors draw again the conclusions that the effect of the factor "law" was insignificant in comparison with other factors by which the structure of society was influenced. Neither the strictness of the Civil Code of 1896 nor the liberalizing of the National-Socialists' divorce law appears to have influenced behavior in any but the most insignificant way. The vast changes which did occur must be regarded as the results of social circumstances other than the law.

This result is remarkable even though the analysis is concerned with the legal event divorce rather than with the ultimately relevant event of marriage breakdown. Theoretically, it is possible that the rise of the divorce rate reflects an increase not in breakdown but only in the frequency of its being made official by a decree of divorce. Perhaps the rate of breakdown was already 188 in 1881 and has remained static ever since, so that in 1881 only 8.7 divorces were sought for every 188 separations, in 1949 divorces were obtained in all cases of separation, and in 1956 in only 82, so that in every 100 separations no divorces were obtained. Such a situation, while theoretically possible, is highly improbable. Upon the basis of other observations it can be assumed, it is true, that the number of separations made official by divorce has increased, especially in consequence of the change of workers' attitudes from proletarian to bourgeois respectability. That proportion of the German population in which it is socially feasible, after the breakup of a marriage, to establish a new "free" union without divorce seems to have decreased among the lower classes. It may well have increased, however, at higher levels. However that may be, it is improbable that the changes in the divorce rate are due exclusively, or even preponderantly, to shifts from non-officialization toward increasing . . . official recognition of actual breakdowns of marriages. Even though divorce statistics do not directly reflect changes in actual breakdowns, the German statistics seem to allow the conclusion that changes in the number of breakdowns are to some extent reflected in the change of the divorce rate. It is highly probable that, if the changes of the law have failed to stop the increase of divorce, they have also failed to stop an increase in the breakdown of marriages.

The authors, nevertheless, believe that in one special respect the law has not remained quite ineffective. Before and after the changes of 1900 and 1938, German law has provided that, as a general rule, no action for divorce may be commenced until a reconciliation of the parties has been attempted by a judge. In addition to their analysis of the statistics of divorce in general, the authors have also analyzed the statistics of conciliation proceedings. By ascertaining the number of actions commenced per every 100 conciliation proceedings, they believe that they are able to learn the percentage of cases in which conciliation proceedings were successful in effecting reconciliations. The authors are, of course, aware that the figures do not allow any direct conclusions. On the one hand, parties may fail to follow up the conciliation proceedings with an action for divorce, while remaining unreconciled, and thus continue to live apart. On the other hand, the courts may allow the commencement of an action for divorce without preceding conciliation proceedings, where such proceedings appear to be hopeless, and the courts have shown a steadily increasing readiness to make use of such power of dispensation.

Even if these and other sources of possible error are considered, the figures throw some light upon the effectiveness of conciliation proceedings when carried out in a serious manner. In the period before World War I the percentage of cases in which conciliation proceedings were not followed by action for divorce was remarkably high. During the period from 1881 to 1899 it was 41.3 per cent for the country as a whole; in the districts of some courts it was above 50 per cent; in one-third of the districts it was above 40 per cent; and in one-half of the districts it was above 30 per cent. However, in other districts the figures were much lower: in one, the percentage of conciliations not followed by an action for divorce was as low as 3.1. These wide differences seem to indicate that the manner in which the conciliation preceedings were conducted varied greatly within the Reich and that they were generally conducted in a more serious manner in the eastern districts, with their traditionally paternalistic government, than in the western districts, where the tradition is liberal-democratic.

The period from 1900 to 1913 showed a slight drop in the rate of success of conciliation proceedings. For the Reich as a whole it was 36.6 per cent; in the district with the highest rate, Königsberg, it changed but imperceptibly, from 60.9 to 59.1, but in the district which now was that of the lowest rate, Munich, the percentage was −1.2 per cent. The negative figure indicates that the courts granted dispensations from the requirement of reconciliation proceedings in more cases than those in which such proceedings had taken place and had not been followed by an action for divorce.

After World War I the proportion of actions following conciliation proceedings increased rapidly. The figures, available for Prussia only, are as follows: 1917, 100.3 per cent; 1919, 87.5 per cent; and after 1920, continuously above 100 per cent. Owing to a number of circumstances extensively discussed by the authors, conciliation proceedings had ceased to be taken so seriously as they had been before 1914.

Two conclusions may be derived from these figures: (1) counseling activities can be helpful if conducted seriously and (2) the mere legislative command that an action for divorce must be preceded by conciliation proceedings does not guarantee their being carried on seriously and competently.

We have pointed out that the book originated in the current efforts of the University of Chicago's Comparative Law Research Center to assemble factual material for the purpose of possible legislative reform in the United States. Reforms of the divorce law are also being promoted in Germany. Criticism is rife in the circumstance that a marriage may be dissolved merely upon the objective ground of disruption. Roman Catholic writers are demanding, if not complete abolition of divorce, at least its limitation to cases of guilty misconduct, that is, in other words, that the principle of disruption in the Marriage Law of 1938 be abolished and the guilt principle of the Civil Code of 1896 be restored. It was natural for the authors of the present book to express their opinion of these German proposals, especially to analyze them in the light of their statistical data. Their well-reasoned conclusion is that a return to the principle of guilt could not be expected to reduce the divorce rate in any appreciable way, to say nothing of promoting the stability of marriage. The influence of social factors other than law is so much stronger, they find, that a statutory return to the principle of guilt would be of hardly appreciable influence.

> The attempt undertaken by the makers of the Civil Code to stem the divorce tide by strictly adhering to the guilt principle not only ended in total failure but actually helped to promote time conditioned dangerous tendencies in the society in general and in the administration of justice in particular. The limitation of the catalogue of statutory grounds for divorce could as little protect marriage as it was possible to stabilize the cost of living by the pronouncement of statutory maximum prices [p. 223].

In the decisive point, viz., that of the attitude of the spouses toward their marriage and toward each other, the statutory compulsion failed to have any effect. By far the larger number of persons desiring divorce was influenced neither in their marital conduct nor in their resolution to obtain the desired divorce. In large groups of the population, especially among parties to marriages disrupted without fault, the statutory limitation of the grounds for divorce was felt to be unjust. The authority of the law was thus weakened, and the parties and their attorneys were caused to believe themselves to be in a situation of morally justified self-defense. The rise and growth of collusive practices and the court's acquiescence therein appears to have been essentially caused by this state of fact.

The experiment made by the makers of the Civil Code refutes the [notion] that a limitation of the statutory catalogues of grounds for divorce to situations of guilt could result in a reduction of the number of divorces or even in their rate of increase. On the other hand, the present Marriage Law has refuted the apprehension that the introduction of the disruption principle would naturally result in an increase of divorce. No causal or even statistical connection exists in one direction or the other [pp. 225-26].

The authors' careful analysis thus confirms the observation made in this country by Willcox, who wrote in 1897 that "the immediate, direct and measurable influence of legislation is subsidiary, unimportant, almost imperceptible." American legislatures have conspicuously failed to take notice of this observation. . . .

PROBLEM

The following statute has been proposed. What factual and moral assumptions about marriage and divorce are implicit in it? Would you support its enactment?

SEC. 1.   When a marriage has heretofore or shall hereafter be contracted and celebrated, it shall be lawful for one of the spouses to obtain a divorce from the bond of matrimony whenever it shall be found that:

(a) the disruption of the marriage is irreparable and attempts at reconciliation would be impracticable or futile or not in the best interests of the family; and

(b) the other spouse enters an appearance in the action and consents to the divorce, provided that the parties have been living apart for at least three months prior to the filing of the complaint; or

(c) the parties have been living apart for at least one year.

SEC. 2.   In any divorce action filed under this act, notice of intention to file a divorce action must be given to the defendant spouse by registered mail to his or her last known address at least 45 days prior to the filing of the complaint.

SEC. 3.   At any time while a divorce action is pending and before a decree has been granted, the court of its motion or at the request of either party may stay the proceedings for six months if it finds that attempts at reconciliation are practicable and in the best interests of the family. During this period the parties shall be afforded an opportunity to consult a marriage counselor of their own choice. At the end of the period of six months, if no reconciliation has taken place the disruption of the marriage shall be deemed irreparable.

CHAPTER 8

The Role of the Lawyer in Counseling Divorce Clients

THE MATRIMONIAL CLIENT — PROBLEM CASE AND COMMENT [1]

This problem case concerns a hypothetical lawyer who, after twenty years of practice, has been both intrigued and frustrated by the occasional matrimonial cases that have come his way. He likes the challenge of working with such clients and trying to help them resolve their problems but is puzzled by the difficulties he has encountered. In response to a request for a detailed description of a "typical matrimonial case" he has handled, he submitted the problem case which appears below. It is followed by an interview with a psychiatrist who comments upon the lawyer's work and the general problems of lawyers in working with matrimonial clients.

1. PROBLEM CASE

Mr. Arthur is a fifty-six-year-old man who came to see me in regard to his getting a divorce. My law firm has done some legal work for the fairly large manufacturing concern in which Mr. Arthur is employed as vice-president in charge of sales. I have had dealings with Mr. Arthur directly, and these have always gone well, so I suppose that he came to see me about his divorce for that reason. In addition, we have had some social contacts because his youngest son and my oldest are good friends.

Therefore I knew some things about Mr. Arthur before he ever came to discuss the divorce. I knew he has three children: a boy, at present in his second-year residency in internal medicine, married with one child; a girl, married to a young lawyer in a good firm, also with one child; and a boy who is an engineering student in his senior year at college. I also knew that his wife is a few years younger than he and that it has been rumored that she has been in poor health for a number of years.

In addition I was aware that Mr. Arthur has the reputation of being a hard-driving man with considerable skill but one who somehow was not able to deliver the final 10 per cent of whatever it takes to make him as truly successful as everyone thinks he ought to have been. I knew that his name has just recently been dropped from consideration for promo-

---

[1] This form of teaching material was suggested to us by Professor Harrop Freeman's Legal Interviewing and Counseling (1964).

tion to the presidency of the firm in favor of a somewhat younger man, and that this undoubtedly meant that he would not be promoted beyond his present position of vice-president in charge of sales.

When he first came in, Mr. Arthur seemed rather uncomfortable, which I suppose was natural considering what he had in mind. At the outset he said that he had come to see me about getting a divorce, that he had given the matter a lot of thought, and that he didn't want anyone to try to talk him out of it. He said he'd been dissatisfied with his wife and with his life for some time. When I asked him to explain what he meant, he acknowledged that Mrs. Arthur had been sick for some time. But he added that "it really wasn't serious, just some sort of damn allergy" that kept her at home and in bed a good percentage of the time and prevented her "ever going anywhere or having any real fun." He admitted that he was "bored by it all" and "in desperate need for something new and exciting" to keep him from "just plain falling apart."

A little questioning soon revealed that he was thinking of remarriage. As he put it, he was "very interested in" and would "probably marry" the thirty-four-year-old widow of a young man who worked as one of his junior associates until he was killed in an airplane crash fourteen months ago. He said he was in love with this woman and was "sure she's in love with" him. He indicated that he had been seeing her with increasing frequency over the past eight months and found her "exciting, stimulating, interesting, and provocative." He liked playing with her young children (three boys aged ten, five, and three), helping them with their homework, and claimed that they had given him a "new outlook and interest in life."

I must admit that the whole thing struck me as rather silly. It seemed obvious that he had some sort of crazy idea about being rejuvenated by marrying a younger woman with her young kids. Obviously he would be a good catch for her since it didn't strike me as too likely that anybody except someone like Mr. Arthur would want to marry somebody thirty-four years old with three children. When I asked him if he didn't have his doubts about getting into such a marriage, he said that he did, adding that he often wondered if he'd "be able to satisfy" the younger woman and her children. I told him that I had to agree with these doubts and that if I were in his position, I certainly would have them too.

I asked him if he really was sure of what he was doing. He said that he wasn't absolutely sure but that he really couldn't see any other out. He said he was bored at home and with himself. He said his job didn't really interest or challenge him any more and that he felt as if he were "just playing out the string" at the company. From what I had heard, I suppose he was accurate in that observation.

He told me that he had discussed the "whole idea" any number of times with his wife and that she had agreed to give him a divorce, but that that didn't really satisfy him. He said he'd discussed it "some" with his children and that they'd been no help at all, just saying that they didn't see how he could divorce their mother when she was sick. When he told me that, he slammed his hand down on the desk and exploded that he felt as if he were in a "whipsaw" between "what I want" and "what I feel tied to and obligated to." I asked him how his wife had taken his announcement of wanting a divorce. He said his wife seemed "sort of depressed" since they had the talk in which she agreed to the divorce. He slammed the desk again with his hand and said "the whole damn situation makes me sore as hell" and sometimes "I just feel like telling them all to go to hell and do what I want to do," adding that this "of course" meant to get the divorce and marry the young widow.

Up to this point in our discussion I'd kept fairly quiet, trying only to ask questions to get him to tell me more of the story. It seemed quite clear by this time that Mr. Arthur was trying to ditch his sick wife, on whom he's probably blamed his failure to be promoted at the company, and then marry the younger woman. It even seemed as if he wanted everybody to go along with this: he wanted his wife to give her permission; he wanted his children to support his plan; he probably would want all of his colleagues to accept the new wife with no questions asked. I guess what I was supposed to be doing was just to pull the legal levers that would make all this come true.

And I certainly wasn't inclined to go along with it. What happened eventually just bore me out, but at this point I was so full of doubts as to the wisdom of what Mr. Arthur was doing that I'd have felt I hadn't done my duty or fulfilled my obligation to my client unless I pointed out how wrong I thought he was. You can't stop a man from making a fool of himself in this free country, but you certainly don't have to stand on the sidelines and cheer him on. My only problem was how to make this clear enough to him so that there could be no doubt where I stood and no doubt about what course I was counseling him to take.

So I asked him if he really thought his wife would stand by and let the divorce go through. He said he was sure she would; after all, they'd talked about it a number of times and she'd finally agreed to let him get the divorce. But I asked him if he didn't think that she'd feel she'd been treated unfairly if he divorced her. He said "No, why should she? After all, I've provided for her very generously and I'll make her a good settlement. What complaints could she have?" I asked him about the children. Wouldn't they be angry with him for leaving their mother high and dry? He said it was none of their business — they were grown up now and leading their own lives the way they wanted to. Why shouldn't he have the same privilege? After all, he said, he was only fifty-six, and with any luck he ought to live another twenty years, and why shouldn't they be happy years? Besides, he wasn't leaving their mother high and dry — he would provide for her very generously, and she could keep the house and the furniture and most of their possessions, so who could say that he was leaving her high and dry?

By this time he was getting pretty worked up about it, and he'd begun to pace up and down in the office. I could really tell I had him on the defensive and on the run, and I didn't want to let him off the hook, so I asked him if he really thought the widow loved him or if she wasn't just looking for a soft touch to help her out of her financial and social dilemma. That question really got him because he began to splutter and stammer, and it took him several minutes to come up with an answer. Even then it wasn't a very satisfactory answer or one that anyone with any intelligence could really believe.

Of course I raised all these doubts in his mind because I really was convinced that he was doing the wrong thing and that he was just letting himself in for disaster if he stayed on the course he'd set out on. I knew that if I could just get him thinking of the problems he was raising that he'd see the error of his reasoning and come back to his senses.

At this point I thought I'd let him think about it for a while and suggested that we get together to talk about it in a week. He said he thought he'd had enough for one day and thanked me, made another appointment for five days later, and left. I don't know what happened during those five days, but his secretary called me the morning of our appointment to cancel it, and I didn't see Mr. Arthur again. I suppose he talked it over with the widow, and I guess she convinced him to stop raising doubts and to just go to see another lawyer who wouldn't try to counsel him as I was trying to do but would just do what Mr. Arthur wanted him to do.

In any event, that's apparently just what happened. A couple of months later I learned that he had obtained a divorce and married the widow. He went to a lawyer who just pushes these cases through for the fees he gets out of them, no questions asked. Things have gone from bad to worse. Mr. Arthur used to get a lot of pleasure out of his children and grandchildren, but now he hardly sees them any more — the children are very cool. I've also learned through my son that he's doing a lot of drinking. Recently I heard that things aren't going too well for Mr. Arthur in his firm either; they are considering moving him over into some less important position.

2. COMMENT

[A psychiatrist, Dr. Richard G. Lonsdorf of the Law and Medical Schools of the University of Pennsylvania, was interviewed about this case; his comments follow.]

Q. Do you think the lawyer selected this case for discussion because he was satisfied with how he had conducted it?

A. I have the impression from what he said that what he hoped to achieve was to have the client continue on in his marriage. But it is hard for me to see how he really could be satisfied because obviously that didn't happen. I do suspect that he feels he did everything that he could do to bring this about and perhaps that's where his dilemma exists. He must recognize that he left the client with a feeling of dissatisfaction.

Q. In examining what happened, we might start by looking at the interview itself. How do you feel about the way the lawyer handled the interview process?

A. It would help to have an actual transcript, and even more to have a sound film, so we could sense the lawyer's tone of voice and see what kinds of nonverbal communication were taking place. Still, I think we have a pretty good picture of what went on. We don't seem to have many of the difficulties of interviewing which are so frequently encountered. One thing that is perfectly clear is that to a large extent the lawyer did keep himself out of the first part of the interview. He apparently asked relatively few questions, and one gathers those were only of the sort to move the story along. With a client who is willing to talk, who is in a sense bursting with his problem, one of the best things to do is simply to stand aside and let him spill it out. Not only is this most efficient, but also it gets out many of the ramifications that a question and answer method simply won't elicit. Far too many people have preconceptions of how an interview should run and cannot step aside and allow it to proceed on its own strength and in the way the client wants it to go. Such a structuring of the interview would clearly be a mistake with someone who is as willing to talk as this client seemed to be. With other clients who have more difficulty expressing themselves or in whom the problem is nowhere nearly as well defined or as close to the surface, the question and answer approach may be needed, at least to get things started.

Q. I suppose one test of an interview is whether or not the information necessary for initial planning for the case has been elicited. Would you regard this interview as successful on this score?

A. Obviously I can't answer that from the technical viewpoint of the lawyer. I don't know, since it isn't clearly stated, how long they spent together, but my guess would be that he probably got the basic information from the client in not much more than half or three quarters of an hour. There was an enormous amount of information gleaned in a very short period of time. So I would say that the lawyer really got off to a very fine start.

Q. But you said that something went wrong?

A. Yes, there's a sudden and dramatic shift in the middle of the interview. Somewhere after the client had told the main outlines of his story, our attorney began to get in there with both fists. It seems to me that that is when the trouble began. He obviously was being judgmental and allowing these judgments to interfere with his interview.

Q. But isn't it inevitable that the lawyer would have feelings?

A. Of course, not only lawyers — anyone who interviews.

Q. The case is not a very pretty one, is it?

A. No, and it's not hard to imagine what the lawyer was thinking. A wife who's being ditched after many years of marriage because she's sick and can't have fun with him any more, the alienation of the children — the lawyer's going to come to the view that the client is being what he called "silly."

Q. Silly?

A. I think he really meant bad, morally wrong, sinful, so that an element of condemnation comes into it too. It seems that when this feeling became clear to him, he began to give the client the third degree.

Q. Should he have suppressed these feelings?

A. Just as anyone who listens to a story makes judgments, our lawyer was obviously judging as he went along. It isn't his making judgments that produced the trouble; it is the fact that he let these judgments proceed to dictate the rest of the interview. This is what caused the problem. After he became a district attorney, he never again allowed any of the mixed feelings of the client to come forth. And in taking a strong stand himself, the lawyer forced the client into taking a stronger stand than the client had ever meant to take.

Q. How do we know that? Doesn't the fact that the client went ahead and got his divorce anyway show that he probably felt fairly strongly about it from the outset?

A. Yes, of course he did. But whether or not that would have been the outcome had this interview been handled more skillfully, I'm not at all sure. Of course we can only guess what might have happened if both sides of the client's dilemma had been brought out more skillfully than the lawyer was able to bring them out.

Q. Is it your view that the client was actually very uncertain of himself and that the lawyer in a sense pushed him into his course of action?

A. I certainly had the impression that the client was protesting too much, so to speak, about what he planned to do. His plan of divorcing his wife and marrying the widow seems quite in contrast with what we can infer about the rest of his life. It's as if a man has been a straight arrow for fifty-six years and suddenly decides to throw it all over and change his whole approach to life. This contrast should raise a question in the mind of the lawyer and should start him looking for clues to help explain the shift. Whatever clues were available were lost in this interview as conducted here. If the lawyer simply had given him more time, if there had been fewer judgments expressed or easily inferred in the comments the lawyer made, if he had allowed the client to expand upon his position and his dilemma a good bit more, the other side of the client's ambivalence would have come out far more strongly. Perhaps a different and more satisfactory ending of their interview might have ensued.

Q. And what prevented this different result?

A. When you attack someone in the way that the lawyer did, you force him to defend his stated position as best he can, and as a result that position simply becomes more entrenched.

Q. Is the lawyer aware of this now?

A. He doesn't seem to be. He blames the client, blames the second lawyer who got the client his easy divorce, and derives a certain amount of self-satisfaction from the fact that his judgment proves to be right in the long run because the client has really gotten into trouble by following the course of conduct of which the lawyer disapproved.

Q. What keeps the lawyer even now in retrospect from being able to see the mistake he has made?

A. Well, he has to be at some sort of peace with himself. I think he is convinced that he did absolutely the right thing, and in some ways he did. He really did look into the situation and see it as something far more complicated and dangerous than a straightforward job of doing what the client said he wanted. The lawyer's intentions were fine; it was his technique that was faulty. He stumbled and fell over his own moral judgments about the client's stated intentions.

Q. How does the lawyer develop an ability to walk this tight rope you've described: having the judgments but not allowing them to interfere with his work?

A. It takes a long time to develop these skills. But I don't think the beginning of the development is as difficult as you might think. Obviously the first step is to be aware that we are influenced by and judgmental of the stories our clients and patients tell us. Too often we think we are nonjudgmental in situations where in fact we are judging. To be aware of this fact is the first step toward learning how to deal with it. The second thing is to be aware that the judgments you are making and the conclusions you are drawing aren't necessarily valid for the person with whom you are dealing, no matter how well-intentioned or well-thought-out they may be. It isn't that you submerge the judgments; it's that you are as aware of them as you can possibly be. Any astute or sensitive client is going to be aware of some feelings on your part, and that in itself isn't necessarily bad. The problem comes in learning how to allow the client to develop his own answers to his own problems with nothing more on your part than a kind of general guidance.

Q. Of course, it was guidance that the lawyer was trying to provide.

A. If you want to call hitting the man over the head guidance, okay. As I said before, it isn't in what he was trying to do that he was so wrong; it was in the way that he tried to do it.

Q. So you could say that what the lawyer should have done was to point up to the client the strengths of his situation, where the client now is only oppressed by the negative aspects?

A. You can say this if you want, but it's not going to help much. That's not what I meant. The client is probably already doing this himself. It's like telling him, "You're making $20,000 a year; what are you complaining about?" That's really just another way of whamming him and doesn't help anyone. It is very important for a counselor to accept as real the way in which a client presents his problem even if it seems incredible to an outsider. Suppose you have a very bright guy who's just got his Ph.D. in physics and he comes to you and says in despair, "I don't know anything at all about physics." This is going to seem absurd to you, but you have to recognize that in a certain sense it must be true to the client; for example, he's probably thinking about his relationships with his peers in physics. It isn't going to help the client if you deliver the sermon he's given to himself a thousand times about accentuating the positive. He's got to work the thing through for himself.

Q. In other words, the problems you see in this interview arise as much from the lawyer's feelings as from the client?

A. Exactly. It's very interesting that the lawyer reacted so strongly against the client, whom he characterizes as silly and foolish. Of course we don't know much about the lawyer, either, but if he doesn't normally react with such intensity to the legal problems which come before him, it

should have given him a clue to watch out, that perhaps he was emotionally involved in the situation more than any objective examination of the
client's problem would have warranted. No lawyer, particularly no married lawyer, is likely to be "neutral" towards a client who brings him a
divorce problem. The lawyer's own relationships with his wife and his
attitude towards his marriage and what marriage should be like are going
to color his reaction.

Q. So that even if he can't help his own feelings —

A. I re-emphasize that it is not desirable that he block out his feelings,
but to the extent possible bring them up to awareness so he can make
some allowance for them. Thus if this lawyer had only recognized that
he was overreacting emotionally to the client, he could himself have re-
checked the validity of what he was proposing to do. With time one can
learn to perceive one's own symptoms of excessive reaction and to be
skeptical about the conclusions one draws under such circumstances.

Q. And if he had recognized this?

A. The most obvious things he could have done would be simply to
have allowed the client to talk a great deal more and to have raised his
questions in far more neutral ways. Ask the client if he has any doubts
about his course of action, ask him if he has any ideas of how this whole
situation developed, and ask such questions in a way that makes it easy
for the client to express his own dilemma in as sympathetic a way as he
possibly can. It seems clear that he has very mixed feelings about this
situation, and sooner or later he's going to give the lawyer the clues to
develop the opposite side of his stated feelings. Often he will even supply
the right words to use as an opener.

Q. Would you expect this all in the first interview?

A. No, I think not. Probably all that can be expected in the first interview is to let the client develop the story as far as it was developed. At
that point the lawyer might simply raise a few questions, say that it isn't
at all clear to him exactly how all this came about, that he'd like to think
about the situation and would like the client to think some more about it,
with a view to returning in two or three days. Most people would be
willing to do this, especially when they feel mixed up and when they
have already received some help just by finding a sympathetic listener.
On a second interview the lawyer will probably get the other side of the
coin.

Q. How many interviews would you expect the lawyer to go through
with this client?

A. Well, that depends on exactly what his goal is.

Q. What do you think his goal is?

A. I think one of his goals was to prevent the client from making what
the lawyer, apparently sincerely, believes would be a mistake for all persons concerned — not just for the client, but for his wife, his children,
and perhaps even the widow. But I don't think that's nearly all. The
lawyer is quite concerned about imposing his view of what he regards as
right conduct and right ethical standards upon the client. I think he's
aware of the first goal, but probably unaware of the second. And it is

this second goal which severely limits his ability to help the client to try to explore what the client wants to do.

Q. Do you think that a lawyer could really be expected to do the kind of a probing job that you are describing? What are his limits?

A. Anyone who is going to deal with people and their problems ought to have a sufficient amount of training to be able to recognize a situation in which an underlying problem exists behind the superficial one that is presented by the client. All psychiatrists and social workers are familiar with the so-called "calling card" concept, when the client or patient comes in with a stated complaint but in reality he wants to talk about something else that is very much more of a problem to him. The presenting complaint is just the "ticket of admission" to the professional.

Q. But why would this man go to a lawyer?

A. I suppose that in part it has to do with his previous dealings with the lawyer. As the lawyer himself said, these had gone well, and I suppose that in the course of them the client had learned to trust and like him and had some appreciation of his ability to deal with problems. The client came to him really as a problem solver, not as a divorce getter, no matter how directly he states the problem in terms that he knows the lawyer will find acceptable. If he'd come to a doctor, he might have presented a case of headaches or anxiety; if he'd come to a psychiatrist, he might have focused much more directly on what really troubled him. But in any case, he'll frame the problem in such terms as he thinks will fit the expertness of the person whom he has decided to consult.

Q. What sort of help do you think the client was really seeking?

A. I think he was seeking a way out of his entire life dilemma. Clearly this is more than simply getting a divorce. From the lawyer's own observations one can conclude that there are several things that have happened to this man — he was being turned down for promotion in his work; his children had grown up and left home; his wife had been sick; life was no longer as interesting or as challenging as once it had been. It's not fair to say that he wasn't a successful man, but he had reached the limits of his success. And at this point it must have seemed to him that life was somehow passing him by. Obviously he was looking for a way out, for something new, something to stimulate him, something to produce the interest that he once had in life. It is also clear that he was full of anger about what it was that was happening to him, and as so many people do when they are angry, he just struck out in whatever direction seemed to him to be at all plausible. Whenever you see this combination of events, you have to be very cautious about the underlying depression that exists. That the client was trying to solve a complex problem was clear; that he was solving it in a way that implied large elements of clinical depression is equally clear. What subsequently happened to the client just bears out an increasing amount of depression and an increasing inability to cope with the problems. Anyone who is going to deal with people ought to be able to elicit the clues and hints as to this outcome. This the lawyer did well at the start, but then he tripped over himself and botched it.

Q. Do you see this as a case that a lawyer could carry all the way through to completion?

A. I'm not sure. But I think that after two or three interviews the lawyer could have helped the client to clarify his dilemma to the point that the client might have been interested in developing and resolving it either himself or with some help more expert than it would be realistic to expect the attorney to provide.

Q. Is this the kind of case the lawyer should refer to a marriage counselor?

A. Well, this particular client doesn't really pose so much a problem with marriage as with himself. There are, of course, many cases in which the stresses are truly marital, with difficulties keyed to the interaction of both partners. Here, however, it seems to me that the client himself is the one who is having the difficulty and that everyone else is simply acting and reacting to him. I would think that this case would be better referred to a well-trained social worker, psychiatrist, or clinical psychologist, someone skilled in individual therapy and equipped to deal with what may be severe depression.

Q. Shouldn't the client's wife come into the picture too? Why do you seem to assume that she plays so small a role in the difficulties posed here?

A. I agree that you should get much more information about the wife and that there is a strong possibility that she has something more than a passive role in this marital breakdown. But the husband is the one who is the activist; he is the one who is most interested in doing something about the situation at the present time. So he has to be dealt with first. Until something of a preliminary nature is done with him, it would be a mistake to bring her into it. Later, yes. The more you talk with this client, the more he is going to talk about his wife — he can't avoid it. In due time you will find out more about his complaints about his wife.

Q. Let's go back a moment to your comment that this case is perhaps one you should refer for individual therapy rather than to a marriage counselor. What sort of case should be referred to a marriage counselor?

A. Marriage counselors can best deal with the kinds of cases in which both parties are motivators and actively involved, instead of where one appears to be wholly passive. That kind of therapy starts off on a different premise — a premise that I find quite acceptable — that the marital breakdown is due to the failure of both parties and both are aware of it. Further, typical marriage counseling assumes that neither of the parties is so neurotic as to be unable to work out individual problems which lie outside their mutual failure. Suppose you have a couple who are dissatisfied and angry with one another. Perhaps they fight over money, or the tension may come to a head in a sexual context or about child discipline or over some other aspect of their joint lives. Here a counselor would want to see both parties together first, to get some idea of their interaction, and then he might see each separately for a few sessions before bringing them back together again for a subsequent session or sessions. In the joint sessions the counselor may concentrate sometimes on the husband, sometimes on the wife, and sometimes on how they function as a unit. This is particularly useful where there is a chronic pattern of inability of husband and wife to communicate with one another.

Q. In our present case, isn't it also conceivable that without any expert therapy, either individual or joint, a lawyer might deal adequately with the problem?

A. Certainly. If the lawyer spent two or three or four hours with the client, he might be able to help him through this immediate crisis without any further help. You would know much better whether that was feasible after you'd had two or three interviews. It isn't always necessary that there be profound changes or that the dilemma be dealt with in profound terms. Simply to raise the right kinds of questions — different kinds of questions than the client himself has raised — is just as critical and just as important as actually providing the client with specific answers. I can imagine that this might well be the kind of case in which two or three skillful interviews might enable the client to go on and wrestle with the problem himself thereafter and not require a great deal of further treatment other than that which the lawyer had given him through those few interviews.

Q. On the other hand, isn't it even more probable that this client's problem will turn out to be insoluble no matter what kind of help he gets?

A. What do you mean by insoluble?

Q. After all that has happened so far, how can you expect him to go back to his wife and live happily ever after?

A. I don't. I guess it depends on what you mean by "happily." For instance, I can see as a realistic possibility some outcome like this: husband does not divorce his wife or marry the widow. The wife continues sick and perhaps deteriorates slowly and there isn't much basic improvement in the marital relationship, but they continue to live together. Maybe the husband will take up sailing and golf and get his pleasures out of them and out of occasional casual affairs. Is this a "happy" solution? The husband may see it as preferable to divorce and remarriage if he comes to an awareness that by acting out his frustration he will invite a disaster which damages or destroys his relationships with his children, friends, and business associates, and if he realizes that the likelihood of "success" for the second marriage is not too great. But he's not going to end up exuding happiness from every pore. The range of alternative outcomes for this kind of case is rather limited.

Q. So you do think it is within the range of practicality for a skilled lawyer to take this case and achieve an outcome considerably better than what has occurred?

A. Oh, yes.

Q. Then how does the lawyer develop the necessary skill? How is a social worker or psychiatrist trained?

A. I don't think that is really a germane question. It's not necessary to be a psychiatrist to be able to handle some of these cases. One simple fact that we are going to have to come to terms with is that there are never going to be enough psychiatrists to handle all of the human problems that come along. Any number of people — family doctors, attorneys, ministers, priests, rabbis, what have you — are going to have to have some knowledge of how to cope with these problems if we are ever going to come to any kind of solution.

Q. What, then, does the lawyer need?

A. The first requisites are some intellectualized concepts about how human beings behave — some appreciation of the way people react at different ages, of the kinds of dilemmas and problems that people face at different ages, and of the ways that they have of dealing with these. The lawyer must learn to recognize ways that they have of defending themselves against anxiety and of resolving dilemmas. This particular client is a fifty-six-year-old man. He is faced with the fact that he is now entering his declining years, although he doesn't feel this way yet. Up to this point he has probably been successful in life, but now suddenly he has run into a stone wall and must realize that he can't go any further. His response is one of anger, depression, and disappointment. He probably is angry with himself as well as with a number of people and with his environment for having produced this result, and he doesn't quite know what to do with it all. He wants to escape. He defends himself against having to come face to face with reality by trying to strike out anew with an entirely new family. What he has inadequately realized is the cost of cutting himself off from the family that he has already established. The lawyer needs to recognize that this kind of dilemma will produce depression, anxiety, and behavior that is often ill-designed to serve the purposes of the client who is going to go through with it. And as a lawyer will also see a variety of other clients, he needs knowledge about many different kinds of human behavior.

Q. You are talking about intellectual concepts?

A. Yes. The other side of the coin is simply a matter of practice. There is no way to learn clients, or to learn people, or to learn patients, without seeing clients, people, or patients under different kinds of circumstances. A law student is in a relatively unfortunate position in this respect. One of the most useful aspects of the education of psychiatrists or social workers is the supervision they get in clinical training. They see patients or clients and then discuss their cases with experienced, older practitioners who help them to understand not only what is going on with the client but also the reactions of the therapist himself and how these reactions can interfere with therapy. This kind of supervision is the heart of almost any training program, but presently legal education rarely provides it for lawyers.

Q. Wait a minute. Do you insist that training under supervision is indispensable?

A. It's hard to get what doctors call clinical judgment without a lot of clinical exposure.

Q. Most lawyers get the exposure; the question is whether there must be a period under supervision. Isn't it quite possible that a law student who likes people, has curiosity about them, feels rapport with them, can be helped a lot without any training under supervision simply by being alerted to the kind of intellectual concepts we have been discussing?

A. Yes, I'd buy that.

Q. Some people just naturally have a lot more interest in and empathy with other people?

A. Of course. Go to any cocktail party and observe the different ways people interact with one another.

Q. At the other extreme, are there people who just can't be taught counseling by any method?

A. I expect so. These are people who like to solve neat analytical problems and who are often not averse to making a lot of money. If they get into medicine, they head for some specialty like surgery, and in law I suppose they would be drawn to some aspect of practice that does not involve them with emotional problems. With such people, hopefully you can help them to recognize and accept this limitation. Perhaps the greatest benefit a person like that can derive from a family law course is to learn to avoid family law practice like the plague and to steer divorce or unwed mother clients to other lawyers.

Q. So at the two extremes we have law students who are so naturally good or bad in their dealings with people that they either don't need or can't profit from training. What about the middle?

A. The main difficulty for most of us comes from the blind spots in ourselves of which we are unaware but to which we could be alerted by a period of counseling under supervision.

Q. You mean a blind spot such as our lawyer's unconscious hostility to his client?

A. Not exactly. Hostilities are much easier to deal with because they're much easier to see. The person who has them feels them; they seem reprehensible to him; he is aware that he needs to get rid of them. Much more difficult are what you might call the loving kind of blind spots. There are people who are so full of the milk of human kindness that they are overwhelmed by a client's problems and are unable to bring reality to them, or they empathize so much with a client's sad situation that they lose perspective themselves as to what can and cannot be done. You might say this is the tender loving mothering type who overwhelms the client, really impeding him in gaining the independence he needs if he is ever to be able to solve problems on his own. These are the kinds of things that supervision can pick up and help a person to recognize in himself.

Q. Wouldn't a lawyer who had these kinds of blind spots need therapy himself?

A. Undoubtedly some do, but often just an understanding of their own personal blind spots will help. I think I might summarize it this way. Many law students can get substantial benefit just from increased intellectual awareness of the concepts on which successful interviewing and counseling are premised. But nothing can really replace the much deeper experience of clinical supervision while dealing with a series of cases.

O'GORMAN, LAWYERS AND MATRIMONIAL CASES
96-151 (1963)

[See pages 752-753 and 767-769 supra for other excerpts from this study and a description of its methodology and terminology.]

From a professional point of view, all clients are ignorant, although in varying degrees. . . .

. . . There is, however, another aspect to a marital client's ignorance that is not generally found in other types of cases. In matrimonial actions, clients are often ignorant of their own intentions. As one exasperated informant put it: "They don't know what they want, they change their minds, and consequently, you have to be careful with them." . . .

Marital clients have such changes of heart. Some months ago a woman called me and said she wanted a separation from her husband. Well, a week later she told me they were back together again. Then, three weeks later, she and he came in to draw up a separation, which I began to do. They called me last week: they're back together again. . . .

Aside from the possibility of reconciliation, the problem of client uncertainty is complicated further by another kind of behavior: some matrimonial clients hide from counsel their actual reasons for seeking legal help. A client, for instance, may hire an attorney ostensibly to contest an action for divorce when he is actually testing his spouse's determination to dissolve their marriage. One informant bitterly recalled the case in which he was asked by a young husband, who was "deeply in love with his wife," to oppose her attempt to divorce him. This was done successfully, and then, in the lawyer's words:

I called the young man and said that I thought his wife's case had fallen apart. So the next day he came into my office and told me that he loved his wife so much that if she wanted a divorce he'd let her have it. . . . Now I ask you, what am I [supposed] to do?

In other instances, we were told, clients ask lawyers to initiate separation or divorce actions with the hope — not communicated to counsel — that a reconciliation will be effected. This paradoxical maneuver was illustrated by another informant:

I had a recent case where I represented the wife and she really wanted me to go after her husband. . . . We pestered the guy continuously. Then I found out that she was sleeping with the guy. What she really wanted was to get her husband back and this was her way of doing it. She had no intention of divorcing the man. She fooled me. This turns up quite a bit in matrimonial cases. [Pages 96-99.]

[Two problems noted by O'Gorman's informants were those of dealing with female clients and of maintaining objectivity.] One informant
found women to be so emotional that he stopped accepting their cases.
He explained: "Women are impossible to deal with. . . . They're be-
reft of logic and reason. I don't represent wives anymore." Avoidance
is, of course, a well-known method of adjustment to a threatening situation. However, for many lawyers, it is an unrealistic one. For reasons
described in Chapter 4, they are under pressure to accept matrimonial
clients, male or female, even though the display of feminine emotion
may leave them — as the next excerpt indicates — "at a loss" . . . :

> Women get too emotional. They cry and carry on in here. When
> that happens, I keep wishing they were men. *I'm at a loss. What
> can I do?* The process of the law can't be explained to women when
> they act like that. [Pages 102-103.]

A norm common to all professions admonishes practitioners to remain
objective toward the problems brought to them by laymen. It is assumed
that if a professional loses his objectivity, if he gets personally involved,
he is less able to help his client. . . . Although the necessity of remaining objective was readily acknowledged, 17 per cent of the sample admitted that it was difficult to do so in [matrimonial cases]. . . .

. . . According to our informants, lawyers are more apt to become involved with a female than a male client. This is probably due, in part,
to the greater emotional demands made by many women clients. But
there is another contributing factor . . . "The woman client," said one
attorney, "will tend to rely on the lawyer. He becomes a kind of substitute husband. You feel sorry and don't want to hurt her." Thus,
given the intensely emotional context of these actions and its differential
effect on men and women, female clients often invest considerable affect
in their relationship with male counsel. Under these circumstances, as
an informant pointed out, "it can be tough not to get involved." The
same informant went on to say:

> The woman in many cases hasn't anyone else to talk to. The hus-
> band may have been the only man in her life, even though he was
> no good. You are her defender. She is grateful, lonely, and, if you
> are lucky, she's ugly. [Pages 109-112.]

[We have already noted O'Gorman's classification of his lawyer-informants according to type of practice, see page 752 supra. The author
also distinguishes them by the roles they see for themselves, both in their
general practice and specifically in matrimonial cases.]
. . . Thirty-six attorneys were classified as having problem orientations. These informants look for and obtain primary satisfaction
through the successful applications of their skills and knowledge to the
solution of problems arising in law practice. Although they appear to
share an image of the lawyer as a problem-solver, their sources of gratification and sense of accomplishment derive from different kinds of
problems. [Page 121.]

Of our thirty-six problem-oriented informants, seventeen were oriented as trial lawyers, fifteen as technicians, and four as business organizers. Conspicuously absent from these orientations is any significant reference to clients. Indeed, going over these interviews, we get the impression that clients are almost inconsequential to these attorneys as long as they have an opportunity to sink their teeth into problems.

. . . Twenty lawyers in our sample were classified as having an orientation toward people. Their descriptions of professional gratification were stated primarily in terms of the satisfaction received from interpersonal relationships. They like cases where "the development of human relations is paramount," where "people are directly involved." Problems, to these lawyers, mean people; and they emphasize the image of a lawyer as a helper. Said one: "After all, what is a lawyer? Someone who helps people." [Page 124.]

. . . Thirteen of our informants emphasized the importance of financial reward in their descriptions of work satisfaction. To them, a case is not primarily an opportunity to solve problems or to help clients, but a chance to earn a fee. "All legal work is satisfying," said one, "I get paid for it." We may assume that income is important to all lawyers but . . . these informants seem to give it greater priority than those with other orientations: . . .

> If you want the truth, I prefer the kind of work that pays me the most with the least amount of work. [Page 127.]

. . . We turn now to a related question: How do professionals describe their role . . . . in matrimonial cases?

[This] analysis . . . is based on our informants' responses to a direct query: "As you see it, what is the lawyer's basic job when he represents a matrimonial client?" Four lawyers gave answers that were either too vague or ambiguous for classification; five said that reconciliation was the lawyer's basic job. The answers provided by seventy-three attorneys were classified into two major role definitions: one is labeled the Counselor's role; the other, the Advocate's role.

. . . As defined by forty-seven informants, the job of an attorney in a matrimonial case is primarily to ascertain the nature of the client's problem and then to work toward a solution that is fair to both spouses. This role definition emphasizes the active part played by a lawyer in his relationship with a client. The Counselor participates in three important ways. First, he attempts to clarify, to his own satisfaction, the content of his client's problem. He tends not to accept at face value the client's version of marital difficulties; instead, he looks for . . . . the underlying problem, or "real story," [so that he can] arrive at an independent diagnosis of the client's case, which, in turn, permits him to distinguish between the client's opinion and his own professional judgment. As one informant explained: "Clients may come in here and tell you what they want when I know that is not what they need. . . . You keep listening and questioning until you feel that pang [sic], that pang that tells you what's underneath. . . . She may want a divorce but what sh:

needs is a separation. You have to keep in mind the distinction between the two."

Second, the Counselor attempts to discover what, in his opinion, would be the most beneficial solution for the client. As our informants so often expressed it: "You try and figure out what is best for the client." This, too, requires an independent judgment in which the lawyer weighs his view against the client's. He asks himself, in the words of one attorney, "Will the action which the client contemplates help her?"

Finally, the Counselor participates in an effort to work out a solution to the problem that is also fair to the opposing spouse: "We try for the best solution for all concerned." . . . [Pages 132-133.]

. . . [In contrast, in reading the interviews of those classified as Advocates, one gets] the impression that Advocates view their relationship with marital clients in a rather simple, straightforward — almost mechanical — manner. They seem to have a "tell-me-what-you-want-and-I'll-see-if-I-can-get-it" attitude. . . . [Page 137.]

. . . This position was summed up by one informant in this statement: "I tell clients what the facts are, what the law is, what the courts have done, and show them the alternatives. I tell them what the result of each alternative will be. Then I tell them they must decide." But what happens when the client cannot decide or seeks counsel's help? What is a lawyer's reaction to the situation described by one attorney? "After you lay out the facts and the alternatives, they immediately throw it back at you and say, 'You're the doctor.'" Our informants disagreed on how this problem should be dealt with. Two out of every three Advocates still insisted that they would not help the client to decide. . . .

> I don't help them to make decisions at all. They're the ones affected, not me. Besides, who is to say what a wrong decision is? What may be wrong for me or you, may be right for the client. I make them decide.

Counselors, on the other hand, are more inclined to aid the client; two out of every three said that they would attempt to induce the client to make what they thought was the right decision. "I try to persuade them," said one, "to do what is best for them." . . .

When an attorney describes what he tries to do with a legal problem, he is, if only by implication, stating how he expects a client to behave. And when he describes client-behavior as interfering with his job, he is basing his description on his own role conception. Another consequence of our lawyers' role definitions is found in their complaints about marital clients. The complaint most frequently cited by Counselors — it was mentioned by one out of three — was the reluctance of marital clients to compromise. This kind of behavior, generated by client-emotionalism, conflicts with the Counselor's view of his role; the client is angry and vindictive while the lawyer is looking for a fair solution to the problem. . . .

The unwillingness of marital clients to compromise was not consid-

ered by many Advocates to be much of an obstacle to their role performance; less than one out of ten referred to it.   Their major complaint
was directed to clients' indecisiveness.   One out of three Advocates felt
that client-uncertainty made it very difficult for a lawyer to do his job;
only one out of ten Counselors made this complaint.   An uncertain
marital client is particularly troublesome to an Advocate because, as we
reported, his role definition assumes that the client is certain.   In the
eyes of an Advocate, "a client must make up his mind before a lawyer
can help him." [Pages 140-142.]

[Most informants paid at least lip service to the goal of reconciliation.]
"As a human being," said one informant, "you hate to see a marriage
break up."   Because they share important values with matrimonial clients, lawyers can derive a deep gratification from their participation in
reconciliation.   This may prompt attorneys to make strong efforts to reunite estranged spouses.   Here is one lawyer's description of what he
called "the most satisfying thing that ever happened to me in practice":

> A couple had been married for thirty years and were going to break
> up. . . .   I kept after both of them, and it finally worked out. . . .
> I'd run into them on the street, walking to a movie arm in arm and
> I'd have a real glow, a tremendous sense of satisfaction.   I didn't
> get a penny for it.   He wanted to pay something, but how can you
> put a price on a thing like that?

. . . Even should a lawyer reject the norm of reconciliation on the
ground that it is not part of his role, or that it represents at best a futile
gesture, he may be forced into examining the problem simply to protect
his own interests.   When there is any likelihood that his client may be
reconciled with the spouse, he may be reluctant to devote his time to
the case.   He may therefore comply with the norm in order to be sure
that the marriage will be dissolved:

> We search the matter of reconciliation out as a possibility but really
> don't expect anything to come of it.   It's much too late by then.
> *But the important thing is that I don't want to go ahead and work
> on a matter if it isn't going through.   I don't want to work for
> nothing.* . . .

. . . Very few informants believed that a lawyer actually could successfully reconcile estranged spouses.   "My job should be to try and reconcile them," remarked one lawyer, "and I always see if it is possible,
but there's no chance as a rule."   His judgment was shared by most of
the informants whose experience with reconciliation attempts was largely
one of failure:

> I must report to you sadly that in thirty-two years, no matter how
> hard I tried, there were very few, only a very few reconciliations.

> It's a little too late by the time I see them.   In ten years I've had two
> reconciliations, but they didn't last.

The experience of failure would seem to be a strong pressure undermining the norm of reconciliation; and the reason why lawyers define their roles without including the norm is clear: men are not likely to give high saliency to a norm so far out of line with experience.

. . . Another pressure subverting the norm of reconciliation is the belief that identifies the presence of the marital client with the termination of his marriage. Slightly more than one out of five informants spontaneously asserted that if an individual sees a lawyer about his marital conflict, it is only a mattter of time before the marriage is dissolved: . . .

> By the time these people get to a lawyer, they have seen psychiatrists, they've talked to friends, counselors, rabbis, priests. Once they decide to see a lawyer, it's over.

The mechanisms employed by various segments of the public to obtain help with marital problems is a topic about which little is known. However, by assuming that such mechanisms are used, lawyers would seem to relieve themselves of some of the responsibility for effecting reconciliations: they become, in effect, professionals, who, through a division of labor, are responsible for burying legally what others have diagnosed as socially dead. There is also the possibility that, in an unknown proportion of cases, lawyers, by believing that their clients' marriages are beyond rehabilitation, may be contributing to the dissolution of those marriages. This is the familiar process of a "self-fulfilling prophecy": "A false definition of the situation" evokes "behavior which makes the originally false conception come true." . . .

. . . An attorney's attitude toward reconciliation is apt to be influenced by his sense of competency. There was no doubt in the minds of some informants that lawyers lack the necessary professional preparation: . . .

> We are not equipped to do it. We're not sociologists [sic] or marriage counselors. Reconciliation is a complicated business and lawyers are just not equipped to do it.

But this is more than a matter of inadequate training; as we pointed out earlier, the legal training that a lawyer receives and its application in the lawyer-client relationship tend to minimize the chances of reconciliation occurring. Not only does an attorney lack the skills of a psychiatrist or social worker, in his trained capacity as a lawyer he is expected to represent one side of a conflict. Thus, even when opposing counsel try to reconcile their clients, they do so without adequate professional preparation and within a context where each is held responsible only for his own client's interest. [Pages 147-151.]

NOTE

1. What is the significance for lawyers of O'Gorman's last sentence? To what extent is the fact that a lawyer is primarily concerned with the

welfare of only one spouse an impediment to counseling? Suppose the client, who after all has chosen to consult a lawyer and not a therapist, prefers not to deal with other counseling professions? What is the lawyer to do if his practice is located in a geographical area where other counseling facilities are unavailable?

Even in large cities trained social workers or psychiatrists are likely to be in short supply. It is also important to recall that in terms of professional academic training "social worker" is an ambiguous term; only a minority of those in practice, as distinguished from supervisors, have received the professional training which is the ideal of the profession.

The attitudes of O'Gorman's lawyer respondents merit critical reexamination. Compare, e.g., their complaints that many clients "don't know what they want" and "change their minds" with their reports that reconciliations rarely result. In this connection, consider Alexander, The Family Court — An Obstacle Race?, 19 U. Pitt. L. Rev. 602, 609 (1958):

> There is some evidence to indicate that about eight per cent of the lawyers handle about 80% of the divorce business in some cities. For them divorce is their rent, their stenographer's salary, their baby's shoes, sometimes their solid gold Cadillac. The simplest uncontested case is generally worth a couple of hundred dollars; a case involving even a moderately well-to-do husband accused (not necessarily guilty) of infidelity is ordinarily worth a few thousand to the lawyers. How unrealistic to expect them to forego anything like that for mere considerations of ethics or morals.

See also Annot., 92 A.L.R.2d 1009 (1963) (prevailing view that upon W's desire to discontinue matrimonial action, her attorney cannot continue the suit for the purpose of collecting his fee from H).

2. After becoming settled in a community, a lawyer should prepare himself in advance for the family client who will need to be referred for more expert counseling. He should make it a point to learn something about available social welfare, psychiatric, and marriage counseling facilities. Some lawyers, ministers, or family physicians who have had referral experience may be able to provide useful leads. The local family service agency can not only give information on the services which it provides but can also be helpful in suggesting competent private practitioners in psychiatry and marriage counseling. National agencies[2] can often provide the names of qualified local practitioners. For the especially difficult problem of arranging a satisfactory referral of a client to a psychiatrist, the chief of psychiatric service in a good hospital, the chairman of the psychiatry department in a medical school, a local mental health association, or one of a rapidly expanding number of out-patient mental health clinics are likely to know the community's resources. Redlich & Pines,

[2] American Association of Marriage Counselors, 9 E. 84th St., New York, N.Y.; Family Service Association of America, 44 E. 23d St., New York, N.Y.; National Association for Mental Health, 10 Columbus Circle, New York 19, N.Y.; National Council on Family Relations, 1219 University Ave., Minneapolis 14, Minn.

How to Choose a Psychiatrist, Harper's, March 1960, p. 33, is a helpful guide in distinguishing various kinds of psychotherapy and a sobering commentary on its cost and limited availability. Generally professional advice will be needed not only in making a specific referral but in giving guidance regarding the type of therapist most likely to meet the needs of a particular client.

3. Many different techniques are utilized in family and marriage counseling. For an account of the "separate but parallel lines" of development of marriage counseling outside psychiatry and family therapy within psychiatry, see Leslie, Conjoint Therapy in Marriage Counseling, 26 J. Marr. & the Fam. 65 (1964). The excerpt which follows is illustrative of one approach to such counseling. It not only gives an indication of the approach of some professional workers in the field but should also prove helpful to those lawyers who find themselves in the situation described by Pilpel, The Job the Lawyers Shirk, Harper's, Jan. 1960, pp. 67, 69, where the initial interview revealed

> only the top layer of deeper troubles that called for skilled psychological probing. But the couple refused to consult a marriage counselor or other expert on the grounds that they had neither the money nor the time. Besides, their minds were made up.
>
> Thus, as happens in so many marriage and family difficulties, the lawyer became the only outside adviser who had anything to do with the case. And he does the best he can with whatever knowledge of human beings he has gleaned over the years. In most cases, if he stops to think about it all, he wishes it had been more purposeful and scientific. . . .

WATSON, THE CONJOINT PSYCHOTHERAPY OF MARRIAGE PARTNERS [3]
33 American Journal of Orthopsychiatry 912 (1963)

Since the appearance in 1956 of Eisenstein's Neurotic Interaction in Marriage, publication of papers and books on the treatment of family and marriage problems has mounted. While for many years social workers and others have done "marriage counseling," psychiatrists only recently have started to work actively in this field, or at least to report their work in publication. The impact of psychoanalytic theory and practice on the concepts and techniques of psychotherapy tended to focus on the treatment of individual patients and has aimed at altering intrapsychic as well as external adaptation through manipulation of the psychological process This has brought excellent therapeutic results in certain categories of patients, but many others have not been treated or their treatment has failed. Frequently this has been accounted for by judging them as "untreatable," or by deciding that the psychotherapeutic method was poorly applied. It appears that many of these conclusions were arrived at largely by assumption, since there is not only little objective data to support such a view, but also . . . increasing evidence to the contrary. Clearly, adaptive

---

[3] References to the various studies discussed by Dr. Watson are omitted.

potential and versatility seem to be consistently underestimated by professionals. Likewise, the literature reveals that there is good reason to search further for causes of family disruption using the psychodynamic concept of homeostasis[4] as a launching point. In this paper, I will endeavor to explain and conceptualize my recent treatment efforts with family and marriage problems.

Several specific premises regarding the nature of marital unions will be utilized but not explicitly substantiated here. They are:

1. That marriage partners choose each other for highly specific, conscious and unconscious reasons. This selection represents the summation and gratification of normal and appropriate goals, as well as various neurotic and symbolic needs that must be met either intrapsychically or socially.

2. Both partners enter into a mutually "satisfying" interlocking homeostatic balance. Despite external appearances to the contrary, they reach a state of psychological equilibrium that "gratifies" both mature and neurotic needs for both partners. One of the treatment objectives in this kind of therapy will be to elucidate the details of this interlocking system, in order to open up the possibility for a different and more appropriate adjustment between them.

3. This homeostatic relationship may also be viewed as a mutually shared communication system involving many verbal as well as nonverbal communication devices. Therefore much characterological interchange will take place, and this will lead inevitably to the necessity for emphasizing the interpretation of character manifestations in this form of treatment.

4. Any therapeutic disruption in the psychological homeostasis of one partner in the marriage will inevitably force upon all other members in the family an alteration in their psychological adjustments. For this reason, it appears that often the most efficient way to impinge upon the interlocking adjustment of the partners is to have both participate in the insight-producing process. This would simultaneously tend to bring about revised homeostatic techniques for each. The family anxiety level may be kept closer to optimal limits than often occurs when individuals are treated separately and only one member has opportunity for, and access to, insight-producing experience.

These, then, are the premises on which this form of treatment is based. In addition, all the basic hypotheses of psychodynamic theory are utilized and woven into the treatment situation. . . .

In conjoint psychotherapy, both marriage partners are seen together and the strategic goal of the interpretive process is to work through the central neurotic distortions of their interlocking adaptive and communication systems. This involves interpretation of the multiple transferences, utilizing all the traditional psychoanalytic concepts of personality dynamics. Because of the more complex transaction in these sessions, several specific procedures are followed.

---

[4] Homeostasis is the process by which an individual or a family adopts and maintains a stable psychological balance in the face of change and conflicting drives. — Ed.

It will be clear to all sophisticated in the theory of psychotherapy that there is an extremely complex [situation] present in a therapeutic setting where three individuals participate. Because of this fact, it is essential at the very beginning of treatment to understand thoroughly the characteristics and etiology of each partner's psychological participation.

When the decision has been made to treat a couple conjointly, both parties will be interviewed separately for two or three sessions . . . . [A]n effort is made to isolate and formulate the core psychodynamic forces operating in each spouse and relate them to precise etiological data. Early memories are obtained; family backgrounds are explored with emphasis on recollections and thoughts about significant family members; dreams and other specific historical details needed to develop the diagnostic formulation are collected. By the time these interviews are concluded, the therapist should be able to make at least a well-educated guess about the meaning of the various communications that will be present during the course of treatment. . . .

Some may leap to the assumption that patients in this kind of treatment setting will not talk freely about the details of their fantasy life, but this has not proved true. It is my impression that freedom to communicate in such treatment is more often than not a function of the therapist's comfort and countertransference than it is of the patient's inhibition. As Ackerman has stated (p. ix), "These so-called secrets turn out not to be real secrets at all. Far more often they are common family knowledge surrounded by a tacit conspiracy of silence." I share this view, and, when the basis for the conspiracy is worked through, the participants have no further need to avoid free discussion, or free association.

As the exploratory sessions with each partner are drawing to a close, it is usually in order to make some general statement to each about specific adaptive techniques that appear to create their difficulty. Then, when both are brought back into the conjoint setting, they will have some anticipation about their own contribution to the marriage problems.

As in all psychotherapy, conjoint treatment starts where the patients want it to start. They may or may not talk about themselves, their children or a multitude of other problems. Material is not judged "good" or "bad" but as communication relating to the significant problems or resistances. Associations are interpreted in the same way as they are in any other form of psychotherapy. However, one factor controls the interpretive choice made at any given time: *All interpretations will focus on those aspects of the material and dynamics that relate to the process of communication between the spouses.* In other words, in selecting which of several alternative interpretations to make, the therapist will choose the one that is related dynamically to the cause of the communication distortion in the marriage. Material mainly relevant to only one partner will not be interpreted.

As material is brought up by one or the other partner and its meaning is interpreted in the presence of both, it helps the listening or observing spouse to impersonalize communications and progressively see them as a function of his partner's psychic problem. This distance-producing measure facilitates improvement in the ego's perceptive capacity, progressively decreases the narcissistic identifications between the partners, and thereby improves their capacity to communicate rationally and resolve mutual problems more objectively. For example, if psychological closeness is ego-threatening to a husband, any demonstration of closeness and intimacy by his wife will cause him to withdraw and she will usually interpret this as personal rejection. When this maneuver manifests itself and is interpreted in treatment, the husband can learn to understand why he "needs" to withdraw. At the same time, the wife is learning why she views such reactions as personal and, progressively, how to objectify the meaning of the withdrawal.

Another important aspect of this technique is that the therapist must observe strict strategic neutrality. He will interpret objectively whatever he sees in the behavior of both spouses, and from time to time will focus his attention on one more than the other. Over the course of treatment, however, he will not ally with one party more than with the other. This is especially important in the beginning phases of treatment, and it is essential to establish this fact clearly to both participants. For the first several hours, this necessitates shifting interpretive focus back and forth between the partners, so that hours end with each receiving approximately equal attention from the therapist. Interpretation should also balance in terms of their positive and negative implications to the partners. . . .

One of the principal tactical advantages of this kind of treatment lies in the fact that it is possible to make an interpretation to one spouse, though its main impact is directed toward the other one. If there is strong resistance or ego vulnerability in one, a correlated interpretation can be made to the other spouse, thus turning the interlocking nature of the marital neurosis to therapeutic advantage. For example, if there is a provocative-masochistic tendency in one, coupled with sadistic-criticalness in the other, either side of this emotional axis may be interpreted. Both hear the interpretation and perceive it in terms of their own dynamics. If they have a psychological need to do so, they may, temporarily at least, be permitted to view this as "the other person's problem." Such displacement-potential is useful for regulating the timing of interpretations . . . .

Another characteristic of this technique is the degree of participation in the process by the therapist. In most one-to-one psychotherapy, the therapist can remain essentially passive, only occasionally making interpretive or confronting remarks. In conjoint treatment, where interpretation often centers upon some character manifestation, the "action" is fast-moving and the therapist will by necessity bring himself more into view. . . .

[Dr. Watson then deals with some of the problems arising from the therapist's reactions to the treatment process which are referred to in psychoanalytic terminology as the transference-countertransference reactions.]

. . . Because of the presence of both marital partners and the more realistic presentation of problems, there is an increased risk of the therapist's unconsciously identifying with one or the other spouse. However, by being aware of this hazard and through more active involvement in the therapeutic process, there is greater opportunity for empathic identification and a quicker grasp of the problems unfolding before and with him. Under these circumstances it is neither possible nor effective to have long periods of silence nor to avoid finding answers to specific reality problems. This does not mean that the goal is simply to gratify. Rather, the exploration for answers is carried on in a way that impinges dynamically on the neurotic process of the couple. The *act* of mutual exploration is contrived to clarify the defensive maneuvers of each spouse in such a way as to increase insight and maturation even as a problem is being solved. . . . Defensive distortions are forced into sight where their current implications can be subjected to reality testing and possible revision.

Another common countertransference anxiety in conjoint treatment arises when the partners begin to make threatening remarks about getting a divorce, or some other offer to act out. Because both partners are present to witness the intense affect unleashed, and because it may readily be interpreted as more than mere transference, the therapist is likely to wonder if he may not have a tiger by the tail. These occasions may be turned to good therapeutic advantage, but only if the therapist is comfortable in taking them up and working them through. He may very easily assume that he has been the cause of such an upset. While this is obviously not true, the physical presence of both partners with their emotional reactions to the therapeutic situation makes this distortion easy to believe.

The therapist is also likely to react with deep concern to other kinds of highly charged material as it emerges and creates the specter of serious trouble between the partners. As noted above, such material is not truly secret, and its revelation presents an opportunity to clarify issues that have too long been hidden just deeply enough to prevent resolution and yet cause marriage difficulties. To date, there have been no instances in which truly damaging material has arisen. Rather, it has been confirmed that the information was "known" by both parties beforehand. . . .

[One] advantage I would like to comment on is economic. There is ample evidence that the decision of *who* gets psychotherapy depends to a large extent on economic status. Obviously, if the multiple parties to a marriage problem may be successfully and simultaneously treated, the saving of professional time will have at least two immediate and practical reverberations for this group of patients:

1. Therapy will become at least twice as available, which is important in the face of an absolute shortage of treatment personnel.

2. The cost of treatment to such a couple may be halved, which can extend the availability of treatment to many who cannot now afford it.

There are other economic effects in conjoint treatment. Several writers have commented on the speed with which this process works, and I concur fully with such observations. Psychodynamic elements that ordinarily take months to raise to awareness sufficient for their being re-examined and reality tested emerge and are effectively altered in a matter of four or five sessions. While these new insights are not fully integrated in such a short time, the improved adaptation that re-evaluation of attitudes and feelings carries with it begins and gains momentum. Patients can then return to their own reality testing and experience gathering with a likelihood for continued maturation. . . .

PROBLEM

Upon returning from an unexpected trip to Washington, you find the following note from your secretary:

One of your appointments for yesterday was with Mr. and Mrs. Wallace Tyson and their daughter, Mrs. Eleanor Tyson Jones. You will recall that Mr. Tyson was a college classmate of your father, and before your father's death he had handled a number of minor legal matters for him. As I was unable to contact the Tysons to cancel their appointment, they came to the office. When I said you weren't here, Mr. Tyson was quite upset and explained that his business was very urgent and that he had come to arrange for a divorce for his daughter. I explained that your calendar was crowded for the rest of the week, but he wishes you to phone him and give him an appointment as soon as possible. He said his daughter had been through hell and it was important for her well-being to get the divorce started as soon as possible. They insisted upon telling me their story, with Mr. Tyson doing most of the talking, while the daughter sat submissively, on the verge of tears.

I gather that she met Jones while in college, went with him for three years, and then married him four years ago despite her parents' objections. There are no children. At the time of the marriage Jones was a first-year law student, and ever since the marriage he has worked very long hours, while he was a student who also carried a half-time outside job as well as in his present position as an associate in a large law firm. This left little time for home life.

As nearly as I could determine, things came to a head a few weekends ago, when Jones came home with a briefcase full of work. His wife accused him of neglecting her, and according to Mr. Tyson, "He yelled at her that she was cold and frigid and didn't know how to love." At this point in his narrative Mr. Tyson said, "Tell her what he told you next, Eleanor." Eleanor collapsed in tears. "I'll tell you," said Mr. Tyson. "Eleanor has been suspicious, because on some of these long evenings of work at the office she's been unable to reach him on the phone. Now he told her to her face that she might as well know that he'd been spending his evenings in bed with another woman. Then he hit her and beat her." "It was awful," said Mrs. Tyson. "Naturally the poor girl was beside herself," Mr. Tyson continued, "so she phoned her doctor, and he told her to get right out of there and go home. So she came to us. I guess that's an open and shut case for divorce if there ever was one, isn't it?" I told Mr. Tyson that I couldn't give legal advice and he'd have to talk to you. He made me promise to put the facts before you so you could take action on them as quickly as possible.

CHAPTER 9

The Custody of Children on Divorce

A. CONSIDERATIONS RELEVANT TO THE CUSTODY AWARD

BUNIM v. BUNIM
298 N.Y. 391, 83 N.E.2d 848 (1949)

DESMOND, J. On the trial of this divorce suit the wife admitted numerous deliberate adulteries (with a man who was married and had children), attempted to rationalize and justify those adulteries, denied any repentance therefor, committed perjury in swearing to denials in her answer (see Civ. Prac. Act, §1148), and, as found by both courts below, testified to a deliberately false story as to consent by plaintiff (a reputable and successful physician) to the adulteries. With all that in the record, custody of the two children of the marriage (eleven and thirteen years old at the time of the trial) has been, nonetheless, awarded to defendant.

There is an affirmed finding below that the husband is a fit and proper person to have such custody, and no such finding as to the wife, but a finding that "the interests and welfare of the children, the issue of said marriage, will be best served by awarding the custody to the defendant." We see in this record no conceivable basis for that latter finding, unless it be the testimony of the two daughters that, though they love their father, they prefer to live with their mother. Unless that attitude of these adolescent girls be controlling as against every other fact and consideration (see, contra, People ex rel. Glendening v. Glendening, 259 App. Div. 384, affd. 284 N.Y. 598), this judgment, insofar as it deals with custody, is unsupported and unsupportable.

Of course, custody of children is ordinarily a matter of discretion for Special Term and the Appellate Division [citations omitted]. But that discretion is a judicial discretion, not an uncontrolled one, and its exercise must have sound and substantial basis in the testimony. Therefore, there can be no valid exercise of discretion in a judicial direction which is opposed to everything presented to the court. We hold that there was here such abuse of discretion as to be error of law, with consequent jurisdiction to review, and duty to reverse, in this court.

No decision by any court can restore this broken home or give these children what they need and have a right to — the care and protection of two dutiful parents. No court welcomes such problems, or feels at ease in deciding them. But a decision there must be, and it cannot be one repugnant to all normal concepts of sex, family and marriage. The State of New York has old, strong policies on those subjects . . . Our whole society is based on the absolutely fundamental proposition that: "Marriage, as creating the most important relation in life," has "more to do with the morals and civilization of a people than any other institution" (Maynard v. Hill, 125 U.S. 190, 205). Defendant here, in open court, has stated her considered belief in the propriety of indulgence, by a dissatisfied wife such as herself, in extramarital sex experimentation. It cannot be that "the best interests and welfare" of those impressionable teen-age girls will be "best served" by awarding their custody to one who proclaims, and lives by, such extraordinary ideas of right conduct.

The judgment should be modified by striking therefrom the provisions thereof dealing with custody and support, and the matter remitted to Special Term for further proceedings not inconsistent with this opinion.

FULD, J. (dissenting). This case involves a problem as perplexing as any in the field of human relationships, and, while a different result could, of course, have been reached below, I hesitate to stamp as an abuse the discretion exercised by the Special Term judge, and affirmed by four justices of the Appellate Division, only after the most painstaking and conscientious consideration.

Especially in a case such as this, the judge who sees and hears the witnesses, who is face to face with the children and the parents, is in a far better position to make a decision calling for the exercise of discretion than is the appellate judge whose only source of guidance is the cold print, the lifeless pages, of the record. No one can disagree with the statement of high principle in the opinion for reversal, but, on the other hand, no one can dispute that "The factors that made his [the Special Term judge's] duty clear to him can at this distance be seen by us only, as it were, through a glass darkly." (People ex rel. Herzog v. Morgan, 287 N.Y. 317, 322.)

The primary and paramount concern of the trial judge was the welfare and happiness of the children. Would it better serve their interests and their well-being to place them with their mother or with their father? Bearing directly on that issue was evidence that the father was inordinately preoccupied with his professional duties; that, as a result, he gave little of his time or of himself to the children; and that not infrequently he treated them brusquely, impatiently and even intemperately. Likewise pertinent was proof that the wife was ever a good and devoted mother; that her indiscretions were unknown to the children; that she was deeply devoted to the children and truly concerned with their welfare; and that, for their part, the children returned her affection with an attachment that was, in the language of the trial court, "almost Biblical" in its intensity.

With such evidence — and there was more of like import — in the record, the decision at Special Term and the judgment of the Appellate Division awarding custody to the mother cannot be said to be completely beyond the pale of permissible discretion.

I would affirm the judgment.

[Dye, J., concurs in this dissent.]

NOTE

1. See Casenote, 24 Notre Dame Law. 597, 599 (1949): "It is not logical to assume that a woman can be a good mother and an adulteress at the same time. The primary duty of any mother is to educate her children in basic moral principles. One who does not possess these principles can hardly be expected to teach them to others." Not unexpectedly there is a great diversity of judicial attitudes on the question of adultery as it bears on a woman's fitness to be a custodian; in view of the myriad factual variants in the cases, valid generalizations are difficult to draw. Compare Hild v. Hild, 221 Md. 349, 157 A.2d 442 (1960) (presumption against awarding custody to adulterous mother), with Grimditch v. Grimditch, 71 Ariz. 198, 225 P.2d 489 (1951) custody awarded to mother because children unaware of her indiscretions committed more than a year prior to the trial). See also Shrout v. Shrout, 224 Ore. 521, 356 P.2d 935 (1960) (mother's misconduct simply one of factors to be considered along with others relevant to determining what is best for child; woman who had children bring beer to her while she was in bedroom with paramour held unfit).

As indicated in Bunim, the guiding shibboleth used by the courts in custody disputes is "the best interests of the child." Besides unfitness and other more or less obvious criteria, such as the relative financial standing of the contestants, some of the factors looked to by the courts are:

a. *The age of the child.* Most jurisdictions give preference to the mother as a custodian for children "of tender years." See, e.g., Cal. Civ. Code §138(2). See also Ostergren v. Ostergren, 368 Mich. 408, 118 N.W.2d 245 (1962) (despite arguably mandatory statutory provision in favor of maternal custody for children under twelve, court refused to modify original award in favor of father; although mother had apparently recovered from emotional disturbance which was basis of original award, court felt it would be too disruptive to change custody of children now). The father is sometimes preferred for teen-age children (particularly boys).

b. *The preference of the child.* Ohio Rev. Code Ann. §3109.04 (Page 1960):

> Upon hearing the testimony of either or both parents . . . the court shall decide which of them shall have the care, custody, and control of the offspring, taking into account that which would be for their best interest, except that if any child is fourteen years of age or more, it may be allowed to choose which parent it prefers to live with, unless the court finds that the parent so selected is unfitted to take charge. The provisions permitting a child to choose the parent with whom it desires to live shall apply also to proceedings for modification of former orders of the court fixing custody. . . .

Surprisingly, this seemingly inflexible provision was enacted in response to a prior law (90 Laws of Ohio 186 (1893)) that was even more so, in that it required unfitness "by reason of moral depravity, habitual drunken-

ness or incapacity" in order to override the choice of a child ten years or
older. See also Watson v. Watson, 146 N.E.2d 443 (Ohio Ct. App. 1956)
(approval of trial court's dictum that under revised provision child's
choice not dispositive even if both parents are fit). Most other jurisdictions, either by statute or judicial decision, treat the child's preference as
simply another relevant factor.

c. *Race.* In Fontaine v. Fontaine, 9 Ill. App. 2d 482, 133 N.E.2d 532
(1956), a white mother, since remarried to a white second husband,
sought modification of an original award of custody to the Negro father.
The trial court had awarded the children to the father solely because of
their predominantly Negro characteristics. Pointing out that the mother
and her second husband resided in an integrated neighborhood, the appellate court reversed, instructing the trial court to consider race simply
as one of the many relevant factors. See Annot., 57 A.L.R.2d 678 (1958).

d. *Religion.* In Welker v. Welker, 24 Wis. 2d 570, 129 N.W.2d 134
(1964), a mother who was an agnostic was denied custody of her three-
year-old daughter, inter alia, because she had left the marital home and
because the trial court felt that the religious home of the father would be
preferable. The Supreme Court reversed, stating that the mother's marital fault should not be considered dispositive insofar as child custody was
concerned; since there was no evidence that the mother's beliefs would be
inimical to the welfare of the child, it was improper for the trial court to
give any weight to the religious factor. Cf. Smith v. Smith, 90 Ariz. 190,
367 P.2d 230 (1961) (Jehovah's Witness).

Religious issues also arise with respect to the validity of antenuptial
agreements concerning the religious education of children of the marriage. (See page 810 supra for the typical form of Catholic agreement.)
Such agreements are almost invariably held unenforceable even if they
have been embodied in a divorce decree.[1] See, e.g., Lynch v. Uhlenhopp,
248 Iowa 68, 78 N.W.2d 491 (1956) (5-4 decision) (violation of agreement
no contempt). But see Gottlieb v. Gottlieb, 31 Ill. App. 2d 120, 175
N.E.2d 619 (1961) (2-1 decision) (wife who deliberately violated decree
requiring child be raised in Jewish faith by enrolling it in parochial
school denied modification of decree in absence of showing that such was
in child's best interest). See 72 Harv. L. Rev. 372 (1958); 59 Colum. L.
Rev. 680 (1959).

e. *Mental illness.* In Bowler v. Bowler, 355 Mich. 686, 96 N.W.2d 129
(1959), a mother was deprived of custody of her three daughters, aged
fifteen, ten, and nine, on the basis of conflicting medical evidence concerning her mental illness which led her, among other things, to refuse
the husband visitation rights. Compare Galbraith v. Galbraith, 88 Ariz.
358, 356 P.2d 1023 (1960). A woman who had originally agreed to let her
husband have custody of their children was permitted by the trial court to
regain custody of two of the four children on the ground that she had

---

[1] A fortiori, separation agreement provisions concerning future custody arrangements will not necessarily be enforced, even if the agreement has been embodied in the divorce decree. See, e.g., Bastian v. Bastian, 160 N.E.2d 133 (Ohio
Ct. App. 1959). See also Chapter 11.

recovered sufficiently. The appellate court reversed, relying on the well-established principle that the moving party in a modification proceeding must show such a change of circumstance since the original award as would be sufficient to warrant an alteration of the original decree in order to protect the child's welfare. Here the children were adequately cared for by their father. See also Annot., 74 A.L.R.2d 1073 (1960).

In general, see Foster & Freed, Child Custody, 39 N.Y.U.L. Rev. 423 (1964).

2. The award of custody to one parent is normally counterbalanced by the grant of visitation rights to the other parent. But see Bowler v. Bowler, 355 Mich. 686, 96 N.W.2d 129 (1959) (mentally ill mother denied visitation rights); In re Two Minor Children, 53 Del. 565, 173 A.2d 876 (1961) (mother who had deserted her family and lived openly with paramour for period of two years not entitled to visitation rights since same considerations govern as with respect to custody; lower court decision in her favor reversed despite expert testimony that she had now become emotionally stable and had a sincere desire to see the children); Annot., 88 A.L.R.2d 148 (1963). The court's order will usually prohibit the custodian from taking the child out of the state without its permission, in order to preserve the court's control over the arrangement and to facilitate the noncustodial parent's visitation rights. Compare Grothendick v. Grothendick, 175 Neb. 726, 123 N.W.2d 646 (1963) (lower court warranted in modifying custody decree so as to permit custodial parent to take children out of state even though this would have practical effect of depriving other parent of visitation rights).

Occasionally courts will grant custody of a child to one parent for part of the year and to the other for the balance — so-called divided or joint custody. Where there are several children, they are sometimes "split" between the parents. See Annots., 92 A.L.R.2d 695 (1963), 98 A.L.R.2d 926 (1964). But these arrangements are not favored.

Concerning the relation between visitation rights and child support liability, see pages 923, 936 infra.

3. Upon the death of the custodial parent the surviving parent is frequently pitted against a third person, such as a stepparent. In this situation some courts adhere to a doctrine, apparently grounded on the maxim "blood is thicker than water," that the surviving parent is entitled to custody unless he or she is unfit. See, e.g., Ernst v. Flynn, 373 Mich. 337, 129 N.W.2d 430 (1964). But see Clifford v. Woodford, 83 Ariz. 257, 320 P.2d 452 (1957), where the court, by a vote of 3 to 2, granted custody to the deceased mother's second husband, primarily because the natural father had indicated little interest in the children after his divorce and because the children preferred their stepfather, with whom they had lived since infancy. See also Note, Alternatives to "Parental Right" in Child Custody Disputes Involving Third Parties, 73 Yale L.J. 151 (1963), suggesting that custody be awarded to the person with whom the child has the most viable "affection-relationship." And compare In re Guardianship of Woodward, page 374 supra.

4. Ordinarily a custody dispute asks the court to determine which of

the competing parties is entitled to custody. As we have seen above, if one of the parties is unfit, the other will normally be granted custody. But fitness is a relative concept. See, e.g., Williams v. Williams, 338 S.W.2d 689, 690 (Ky. Ct. App. 1960) (mother given custody although she was heavy drinker, moonshiner, and engaged in "other illicit activities" since father was even less fit). If the evidence and investigation disclose that neither litigant (usually the parents) is a fit person to have custody, custody may be awarded to a third party (such as a grandparent), or statutes may make it possible to refer the case to the juvenile court for disposition. See, e.g., Spade v. Spade, 6 Misc. 2d 170, 163 N.Y.S.2d 146 (Sup. Ct. 1957) (since both parents unfit, custody to Rochester Catholic Family Center); Hall v. Hall, 178 Neb. 91, 132 N.W.2d 217 (1964) (custody to juvenile court probation officer, with physical custody to mother, subject to court supervision, because both parties drank to excess). See also Chapter 4.

PROBLEM

Five years ago, as a result of a hotly contested custody proceeding challenging Marie Howell's fitness, she was granted custody of her then three-year-old son John upon her divorce from James Howell. The decree gave James visitation rights twice a week plus a right of temporary custody for a period of three weeks each summer. Subsequently, owing to James's move to another state, the original decree was modified to eliminate the weekly visitation rights and preserve only the three-week visitation period in the summer. James availed himself of this right each year except one, when he was on a trip abroad. At all other times the child has been with Marie. James has faithfully kept up the child support payments ordered by the court.

Recently James heard through some friends that Marie, who remarried shortly after her divorce, and her new husband have filed a petition to adopt John. James is greatly upset about this because he himself is planning to remarry shortly and would like to petition for a change of custody of John. He concedes, however, that Marie and her husband have made an excellent home for John.

What will you advise James? If you were the judge who was to hear James's petition for modification as well as the stepfather's petition to adopt, how would you decide the case?

Assume that the jurisdiction has the following statute:[2]

§101. All custody disputes shall be resolved according to the best interests of the child.

§102. No child shall be adopted without the consent of its parents, unless such child is illegitimate (in which case the consent of the

[2] Compare Minn. Stat. Ann. §259.24(1)(b) (Supp. 1964) (similar to provision cited in Problem); N.Y. Dom. Rel. Law §111 (no consent required if the parent has lost custody through divorce on grounds of adultery); Tex. Rev. Civ. Stat. Ann. art. 46(a)(6) (Supp. 1964) (no consent required of a parent who has abandoned the child or failed to give support commensurate with financial ability).

mother alone shall suffice); provided, however, that no consent shall be required of a parent who has abandoned the child or who has lost custody of the child through a divorce decree.

GOODE, AFTER DIVORCE
310-315, 322-323 (1956)

[This study was based on a sample of 425 mothers in Detroit.]

The Practical Choice of Parents in Conflict. To make the guess that *on the average* the life problems of the divorced child are slightly greater than those of the child in a separated home or one broken by death does not answer the practical problem many parents must answer: Are the effects of the divorce greater than those of continued conflict in the home? Most couples in a divorce process have only two choices. Until they know the answer to the above central question, most of the classic arguments about the bad effect of divorce on children will miss the point. We *can* make divorce so difficult that none will occur. Spouses *do* have the choice of *not* divorcing even when they are unhappy, and many do make this choice.

However, they do *not usually have the choice of creating a happy home for their children,* even when they are willing to avoid divorce "for the sake of the children." The couple has not, therefore, necessarily made a wise sacrifice in the interests of the child, when they decide to stay together.

Some small corroboration for these notions may be found in a study by Landis of adolescent adjustment among over 4000 high school seniors in the State of Washington. When these youngsters were asked about their problems in several main areas of life adjustment, it was clear that those from unbroken homes had fewer problems than those from broken homes. However, the data suggest that divorced children may not have on the average a higher number of such problems than children from separated homes, or even from homes broken by death. We have already seen that this conclusion also emerges from the Gluecks' study of juvenile delinquency. Indeed, these data suggest that the separated home perhaps creates slightly more problems for the child than does the home of divorce. . . .

In the cases involving children which went through the divorce courts of Cook County (Chicago) during 1940-1950, about 86% of the women obtained custody. Nine percent of the fathers obtained custody, and in 5% of the cases there was some other arrangement.[3]

This proportion was not greatly different in the Marshall and May studies of divorce in Ohio and Maryland, nearly a generation ago.[4] The wife is, of course, less likely to get custody if the husband is the plaintiff.

---

[3] Conference on Divorce, Conference Series, No. 9 (Chicago: University of Chicago Law School, 1952), remarks by Judge Edwin A. Robson, p. 4.

[4] Leonard C. Marshall and Geoffrey May, The Divorce Court (Baltimore: Johns Hopkins University Press, 1932), Vol. I, Maryland, pp. 31, 316; Vol. 2, Ohio, p. 346.

Since it is the ex-wife who answers, we would expect that she would maintain that this distribution was agreeable to both parents. Aside from this bias, however, there are many factors to make us believe that the father actually does approve the custody arrangement that gives care of the child to the mother. Most of these factors may be classified under the headings of (a) the social role of the father; (b) male skills; and (c) allocation of time to occupation. . . .

These factors operate to make husband custody neither easy nor very desirable (to husbands) in our time. Consequently, we are inclined to believe our respondents when four out of five wives claim that their husbands agreed to the custodial arrangements, which almost always gave custody to the wife. At least it seems safe to believe that in only a few cases did the father attempt to make a strong claim to custody. Both his own patterns of belief and action, and those of his friends and family, reinforce the social acceptance of the mother's claim. . . .

Various agreements are made between husband and wife, or their lawyers, regarding permissible visits. The court will not usually overrule such agreements. This is peculiarly an area in which the divorcee can expiate vague or sharp guilt feelings about previous treatment of the other spouse. By allowing visits, the divorcee can feel that he or she is not holding a grudge. This permission can be mentioned among friends as proof that the post divorce treatment of the other spouse is just. They may wonder why he or she is willing to be so kind, after hearing a recital of wrongs suffered, but this only accentuates the divorcee's apparent high-mindedness, or his or her willingness to "let bygones be bygones."

We would, then, expect to find that the husband has more rights to see the children than might appear in the simple phrase, "custody awarded to wife." These arrangements were as follows:

FREQUENCY OF PERMITTED VISITS BY PARENT TO CHILDREN

Frequency	Percent	
High frequency		
At any time	32	
Weekly	25	
Sub-Total		57
Low frequency		
Monthly	3	
Summers and/or holidays	2	
None arranged	19	
Husband away	18	
No answer	1	
Sub-Total		43
Total		100
		N = 425

There is a moderate association (Q = +.34) between predivorce talks about the children, and "high frequency of permitted visits." The above distribution suggests a rather close interaction between many wives and their former husbands after the divorce, through these visits to their children. However, these are predivorce arrangements, made prior to experience, and we have already analyzed at length the difficulty of making satisfactory arrangements prior to knowing what sort of life will be worked out after divorce. The husband is likely to have exaggerated notions about how much visiting he *can* do, and the wife may have equally unreal notions about how much visiting he *will* do. . . .

. . . Even when the husband has strong paternal feelings and maintains them undiminished, he will find that using all his visiting rights would occupy much of his time and money. This may not be the case when visits are only for summers or holidays, but this category is only 2% of our total. The more common patterns are "visits at will" and "weekly," the two together forming about 90% of the cases in which visits were at all *possible*. (1) If the father follows his first inclinations, and attempts to take the children to movies, parks, and playgrounds, buying them presents and sweets, he will find himself spending much of his surplus money (if any exists after support payments) on them, and this is especially so for the lower income groups. (2) *Time* allocation becomes a problem when he and his children are separated by any great distance in the city or between cities. He then has the alternative of frequent and long trips, with a consequent diminution of his own social activities, or of passing up some of his visiting rights.

(3) Even with the best of intentions to "be reasonable about the matter," few former mates are able to hand their children back and forth without tension. (4) Moreover, as we have noted, both spouses come to enter new circles, begin dating, or even marry again. The nonpaternal goals of such visits diminish, as both create new lives. Early in the postdivorce period, the husband may visit in order to find out about his former wife, in addition to seeing the children; later on, he has less desire to be informed about her activities. The visits, then, are not the unalloyed pleasurable experiences that had been anticipated, and they lose their importance as the side-goals of malice, punishment, or even love begin to fade. . . .

Effect of the Father's Visits. Half of these women thought that the children were no harder to handle after the father's visits. . . .

. . . [Twenty-five per cent] of these mothers thought that the child was harder to handle after the visits of the father, and only 2% thought that the child or children were easier to handle. An additional 14% said that the father never saw the child at all.

B. THE MEANS OF ADJUDICATION

KESSELER v. KESSELER
10 N.Y.2d 445, 180 N.E.2d 402 (1962)

[The parties were married May 3, 1950, it being the first marriage for defendant husband, a physician and surgeon, and the fifth for plaintiff wife, her four previous marriages having ended in divorce or annulment obtained by her. Heidi, the only child of the marriage, was born on July 15, 1951. Defendant left his wife and child on July 29, 1954, and on November 9, 1955, plaintiff wife obtained a judgment of separation from defendant on the ground of abandonment, defendant not having contested the action. Custody of Heidi was awarded to plaintiff wife with rights of visitation to defendant. On April 20, 1960, plaintiff obtained a judgment in the sum of $10,000 against defendant for having assaulted her.

On January 20, 1958, plaintiff, who then had custody of Heidi, gave defendant husband temporary custody of the child because she, plaintiff, was suffering from a back injury and was unable to care for her. The temporary custody was terminable at any time after February 2, 1958, on one week's written notice as set forth in a letter. Since that time plaintiff-wife has not regained custody of Heidi.

By court order dated February 10, 1958, Heidi was placed in a home for mentally disturbed children upon the recommendation of the court's psychiatrist, psychologist, and social investigator and released therefrom the end of April 1958, again by court order.

On June 2, 1958, the court, as a result of extensive psychiatric reports, ordered that custody be changed to the defendant, subject to plaintiff's right to have Heidi visit her each Saturday in her home from 10 A.M. to 6 P.M. On these visits Heidi was to be accompanied by a person to be designated by the defendant, who was to remain with Heidi at all times in order to safeguard the child's physical and emotional welfare. This order was subsequently affirmed by the Appellate Division and is now before this court for review.

The custody arrangement decreed by the court on June 2, 1958, remained in effect until spring of 1959, at which time plaintiff, through her attorney, stated that the visits with Heidi "in the presence of a guard" were intolerable. She did not see Heidi thereafter.

On July 3, 1959, defendant obtained a Mexican divorce from plaintiff and on July 13, 1959, married Sally DiGiovanni, night supervisor of nursing services at the Lenox Hill Hospital, New York City, in a civil ceremony at Arlington, Virginia, which was followed by a religious ceremony, Roman Catholic faith, also in Arlington, Virginia, on May 4, 1960. From about July 1959, defendant with his second wife has been living at No. 1 Gracie Square, New York City, together with Heidi, where she is being reared and cared for by her father and Mrs. Sally DiGiovanni Kesseler in the role of a mother.

On December 13, 1959, a judgment was rendered declaring the Mexican divorce invalid and that plaintiff is the lawful wife of the defendant.[5]

VAN VOORHIS, J. . . . The order directing the change in custody is challenged in this court mainly on the ground that Special Term erred as matter of law in considering the reports of a psychiatrist and of a psychol-

---

[5] These facts are taken in slightly modified form from the opinion on remand, Kesseler v. Kesseler, 236 N.Y.S.2d 473, 474 (Sup. Ct. 1963). For a more detailed account of this acrimonious custody battle, see the trial court opinion at 11 Misc. 2d 607, 178 N.Y.S.2d 160 (1958).

ogist concerning their examinations of the parties and their child, and in
the refusal of Special Term to allow the parties or their counsel to see
these reports or the report of the investigation made by the family counsellor of the court. The latter officer, named Mrs. Sylvia L. Golomb, belongs to the Family Counselling Unit, an advisory arm of Special Term,
Part XII, the Family Part of the Supreme Court, New York County, and
was authorized by a written stipulation of the parties to make any relevant investigation and inquiry which the court might deem appropriate,
including interviewing the parties and their child without further authorization from the attorneys, and this stipulation further provided:
"That the Family Counsellor is authorized to report to the Court concerning the investigation and inquiry conducted pursuant hereto."

As originally drawn, this stipulation contained a clause authorizing the
use of psychiatrists and psychologists, but by agreement of the attorneys it
was deleted from the stipulation. This clause which was thus eliminated
provided: "That said Family Counsellor may use psychological, psychiatric and other medical assistance in her inquiry and may require the
parties and the child of the parties to be examined by psychologists,
psychiatrists or other professional medical personnel, without the further
authorization of the attorneys for the parties."

Under this stipulation, Mrs. Sylvia L. Golomb, the family counsellor of
the court, was directed by the justice presiding at Special Term to make
an impartial, out-of-court evaluation of the factors bearing on the custody
of Heidi. She interviewed many persons having some knowledge of the
living conditions of these people whose hearsay declarations are recorded
in her report. In addition, as stated in the opinion by Special Term
written at the conclusion of the custodial hearing (11 Misc 2d 607, 608-
609): "In an endeavor to ascertain the best scientific and psychiatric information possible, this court availed itself of the services of a noted psychiatrist, a prominent psychologist and the court's family counsellor.
Careful investigation, study and interviews with all the principals, including the infant Heidi were initiated in the Spring of 1957. By agreement
of counsel (May 23, 1957) and in accord with the underlying necessity therefor, such reports have been held confidential. They are available to the appellate courts in a review of the instant decision. These
reports are, however, in complete agreement and strongly urge that the
welfare of the infant Heidi demands her removal from the household of
the mother and that she be placed in an appropriate school for disturbed
children."

In considering this independent investigation by means of a psychiatrist and a psychologist, the Special Term Justice went beyond what had
been agreed upon in the stipulation which, wisely or not, declined to
consent to psychological or psychiatric examinations and reports. The
stress which was placed by Special Term on all of these reports appears
from its opinion of April 2, 1958, adhering after reargument to its earlier
interim order directing the placement of Heidi in an institution for disturbed children known as St. Christopher's School at Dobbs Ferry, New
York. In that opinion (N.Y.L.J., April 4, 1958, p. 5, col. 3) it was stated:

"The ample reports of the psychiatrists and the court's family counsellor together with counsel's stipulation rendered wholly unnecessary oral testimony. These confidential reports will be available to the Appellate Division on its review of the proceedings. The record should include the papers on this motion for reargument and this determination thereof. Permanent custody is not changed, but the infant's welfare commands that the present school arrangements be carried out. Order signed."

The appellant mother complains not only that she received no notice of the ex parte order transferring [custody] to St. Christopher's School, which is now academic since Heidi is no longer there, but also and mainly that the court made an investigation on its own through these psychiatric and psychological studies of the parents and Heidi, which the stipulation had refused to authorize, and kept these reports from the parties and their attorneys as well as the report of the court's family counsellor, Mrs. Golomb. Appellant mother avers that she or her lawyers were entitled to inspect these reports and to have opportunity to cross-examine the psychiatrist and psychologist, as well as the family counsellor and the persons whose hearsay declarations are recited in her report. We are satisfied that appellant sufficiently raised these questions and is entitled to be heard upon them in this court.

Regarding the secrecy with which these reports were handled, Special Term said that "By agreement of counsel (May 23, 1957) and in accord with the underlying necessity therefor, such reports have been held confidential" (11 Misc 2d 608-609). The Appellate Division said: "Pursuant to stipulation of counsel these reports were held confidential and the contents thereof have not been revealed to the parties and their respective counsel." (10 AD2d 935.)

In construing the stipulation which has been mentioned above and to which these excerpts from these opinions referred, we consider that it lay within the power of the parties to stipulate that such reports could be made confidentially to the court, and that they did so in this instance respecting the investigation and report of the family counsellor, Mrs. Golomb. It is true that the stipulation does not state in so many words that the report of the family counsellor need not be disclosed to the parties or their counsel, but that appears to be the effect of their consent that the family counsellor report to the court concerning her investigation and inquiry. In trying and deciding questions concerning the custody of young children, the parties frequently stipulate that the Trial Justice may interview the child in chambers, and obtain whatever impressions or information the child may give privately to him. What is said by the child to the Justice under such circumstances is necessarily secret unless the Justice chooses to disclose it . . . If parties to matrimonial disputes are competent to stipulate that there may be confidential interviews between the Justice and the child without disclosure of what is said by the child, there is little further difficulty in arriving at the conclusion that the parties can stipulate that the probation officer or the family counsellor attached to the court or other qualified and impartial persons may make investigations and report to the court with similar confidentiality. . . .

. . . Custodial questions have sociological implications, and we are confronted here by a situation where common-law adversary proceedings and social jurisprudence are not entirely harmonious and where some reconciliation between them is necessary.

The parties did not have to stipulate that the report of the family counsellor, Mrs. Golomb, should be made to the court. The court could have directed Mrs. Golomb to make an investigation, to be sure, and then could have left her testimony to the parties to deal with under common-law rules in the absence of their consent. Even without their consent the report might have been used to furnish leads for the introduction of common-law evidence . . . Nor is there any reason which would prevent the court in the proper exercise of a judicial discretion from calling upon qualified and impartial psychiatrists, psychologists or other professional medical personnel, preferably under the auspices of the probation officer or family counselling unit connected with the court, to examine the infant or to examine the parents also if they will submit to such examination. In such case the psychologists, psychiatrists or other medical personnel could not report to the court in the absence of stipulation by the parties but would be available to be called as witnesses by either party subject to cross-examination by the other party under common-law evidence rules. No question is before this court concerning how such professional aid should be compensated, nor is it indicated that in the absence of consent the parties could be compelled to pay for their services.

[The court then reviewed various cases from other jurisdictions holding the consent of the parties to be the key element respecting the admissibility of custody investigations.]

Where, as here, a stipulation was made regarding the report of the family counsellor attached to the court, but not regarding the psychiatrist or psychologist, we consider, as above stated, that the court was authorized under the stipulation to consider the report of the family counsellor, even though the attorneys for the parties did not see it, just as it would have been competent for both sides to have stipulated that the Special Term Justice might interview the child in chambers and obtain whatever impressions or information might be imparted from such an interview. We believe that to have been the purport of the stipulation that the family counsellor should report to the court concerning the investigation and inquiry consented to be conducted by her without further authorization of the attorneys. They consented, in effect, that it should be dealt with by analogy to the use which is made in a criminal case of a probation report in imposing sentence. Were it otherwise, unnecessary technical issues would constantly present themselves where parties have stipulated in trials of this nature, that the court may make an investigation of its own directly or through the instrumentality of probation officers, family counsellors, welfare agencies and the like. The natural purport of such stipulations, unless they state otherwise, is that the common-law rules of evidence are suspended pro tanto in adapting to the social nature of the problem to be solved. In a case like the present, where this matrimonial dispute and custodial question were widely publicized in the newspapers, it may well be that the parties preferred a procedure of that sort to curtail somewhat the publicization of the intimacies of their lives.

The situation is otherwise, however, respecting the reports by the psychiatrist and psychologist. The stipulation which has been quoted specified that the person authorized to investigate and report to the court was "the Family Counsellor of this Court, Mrs. Sylvia L. Golomb." The parties refused to stipulate that she might use psychological, psychiatric and other medical assistance in her inquiry. Under our interpretation of the law, that did not prevent the Trial Justice from ordering a psychological and psychiatric inquiry (provided that arrangements were made concerning the expense) but, after they had been made, the reports of the psychiatrist and of the psychologist had to be dealt with under common-law rules since they were not covered by the stipulation. Either party could have called those expert witnesses, in that event, whose views regarding the parties and the custody of Heidi would then have become known immediately to the opposite side with opportunity of cross-examination. We do not go so far as to hold that the parties *could not* stipulate that such reports could be made confidentially to the court, but the fact is here that they did not so stipulate and expressly refused to do so. Therefore, the Special Term Justice erred in keeping confidential the reports of the psychiatrist and psychologist, and in considering them at all. . . .

[The court then rejects the view of the Appellate Division that the confidential consideration of the psychiatrist's and psychologist's reports was harmless error since there was ample other evidence to sustain the trial judge's conclusion.]

The orders of the Appellate Division should be reversed, we think, and the matter remanded to Special Term for a hearing de novo, at which the facts may be considered as of the present time after the child has been with the father about three years. One of the orders under review, it will be recalled, asked for a trial of custody de novo at the instance of the mother, and this was denied, as the opinion of Special Term shows (17 Misc 2d 498), mainly on the basis of a letter written to the justice presiding by an associate of Dr. Kesseler on the staff of the Lenox Hill Hospital, which was not exhibited to counsel for the wife nor its existence disclosed until after the decision. This is a two and one-half page, single-spaced typewritten letter, stating that Heidi had been under intensive psychiatric treatment by the author of the letter, that she is a seriously disturbed girl whose treatment has been made more difficult by her mother's attitude, and concludes that the mother's visitation should be limited to once per month so that her bad effect on Heidi can be minimized. No stipulation had been entered into concerning this letter. It was not brought to the attention of plaintiff or her counsel until they read about it in the Special Term opinion. The author of it was not even an appointee or attaché of the court, but was a colleague of Dr. Kesseler's on the staff at the Lenox Hill Hospital. It is quite clear that it should not have been received nor have entered into the decision.

. . . It is appropriate that there should be a hearing de novo both in view of the circumstance that three years have elapsed while Heidi has been in the custody of her father, and that the fact mentioned by the Special Term Justice did not come to pass that Dr. Kesseler's mother and aunt would be living with him and caring for Heidi. Instead he purported to marry again after obtaining a Mexican divorce from Mrs. Kesseler, and the child is now living with Dr. Kesseler and his new consort who are cohabiting as husband and wife. We do not intimate that this should necessarily preclude the awarding of custody to Dr. Kesseler, but it is a factor which has occurred since the decisions appealed from and goes counter to their rationale in certain respects. . . .

DESMOND, C.J. (dissenting). I see no reason for a retrial. In and out of the courts for six years, this sordid family squabble is now to be fought over again, not because of any doubt as to the essential rightness of the decision below, but because of a supposed error which was undoubtedly waived by appellant (if error it was) and which related to reports which, as both courts below assure us, did not affect the decision at all. All six of the Justices below agree (and I agree with them) that, with or without these psychiatric and psychological reports, the record is completely convincing that plaintiff should not have the child. Earnestly I ask: what right of a party or what rule of law or justice is vindicated by another lengthy, harrowing trial? . . .

I attach no importance to the use by the trial court of Dr. Luloff's letter on the motion for a new trial. Apparently appellant feels the same way about it, since her brief makes but passing reference to the matter. It was discretionary with the Trial Justice to grant or deny such a new hearing and it could not be a reversible error of law for him to take into account the contents of a physician's letter when the parties had stipulated for the receipt of similar opinions and the particular report was no more than cumulative.

The Appellate Division pointed to another sound, practical objection to a new trial when it held unanimously that the two-year delay in prosecuting the appeal to that court was the fault of appellant and made "appellate review of the custody order senseless as a practical matter" (10 AD2d 935). Court hearings as to this child's custody began more than five years ago. Orderly procedure requires that they come to an end. The question was always one of discretion for the Special Term and the Appellate Division and their decision in favor of the father was soundly based on the record evidence and the confidential reports, either or both.

The order should be affirmed.

[Dye, J., concurs in this dissent; Fuld, J., took no part in this decision.]

NOTE

1. On remand, a different trial judge, after hearing twenty-nine witnesses and interviewing Heidi in chambers, reaffirmed the original order of June 2, 1958, granting custody to the father in spite of his adulterous cohabitation with Sally DiGiovanni. The Saturday visitation arrangement for Mrs. Kesseler was also reaffirmed, subject to the possible removal of the condition requiring the presence of a third person when Heidi

attained the age of fourteen. Kesseler v. Kesseler, 236 N.Y.S.2d 472 (Sup. Ct.1963).

2. The general rule concerning the admissibility of custody investigation reports is as stated in Kesseler; in the absence of a governing statute, consent of the parties is essential if the ordinary rules of evidence and right to cross-examination are to be dispensed with. But, as in Kesseler, the courts do not always distinguish clearly between consent to the investigation and consent to the admissibility and confidentiality of the report. See, e.g., Onderdonk v. Onderdonk, 3 Wis. 2d 279, 88 N.W.2d 323 (1958). But see Commonwealth ex rel. Balick v. Balick, 172 Pa. Super. 196, 92 A.2d 703 (1952). Moreover, the parties may not always have an entirely free choice in the matter of consent. See Comment, 24 U. Chi. L. Rev. 349, 351 n.11 (1957):

> The requirement of the parties' consent may be a small obstacle for a court wishing to use reports and private interviews; when the judge indicates a desire to use these materials and asks for the parties' consent, counsel may often give it to avoid prejudicing their case. Consult, e.g., Withrow v. Withrow, 212 La. 427, 31 So.2d 849 (1947) (Trial judge stated that under the evidence neither spouse should get custody and requested consent to an independent investigation. On plaintiff's refusing consent, custody was awarded to defendant.).

Even if the report was held improperly admitted, some courts, like the intermediate court in Kesseler, refuse to reverse if there was sufficient admissible evidence to sustain the trial court's decision. But see Williams v. Williams, 8 Ill. App. 2d 1, 130 N.E.2d 291 (1955) (despite presumption that judge sitting without jury did not consider inadmissible evidence, trial judge's confidential use of investigation report which he requested from public welfare bureau contravenes due process).

Statutes in a number of states deal specifically with the matter of custody reports. Compare Va. Code Ann. tit. 16.1, §209 (1960) (report admissible even though not authorized by or disclosed to parties), with Mass. Gen. Laws Ann. c. 215, §56A (1958) (report must be made available to parties), and Cal. Code Civ. Proc. §263 (investigator must be subject to cross-examination). And see Fla. Stat. Ann. §65.21 (Supp. 1964), which authorizes social investigations in any case involving the custody of a minor and provides that the court may consider such a report despite "the technical rules of evidence"; however, in McGuire v. McGuire, 140 So.2d 354 (Fla. Dist. Ct. App. 1962), the court held that such a report must nevertheless be made a part of the record.

What are the relevant considerations here? Is it enough that the parties be furnished a copy of the report in ample time before the trial unless they have waived such right? Would it be desirable to require that all investigators must subject themselves to cross-examination, regardless of whether the parties have consented to the investigation? Would this be sufficient to meet all reasonable objections to such a report? See a typical sample of a custody investigation report, reproduced at page 866 infra. In general, see Foster & Freed, Child Custody, 39 N.Y.U.L. Rev. 615 (1964).

3. As indicated in Kesseler, a somewhat similar problem is presented by a trial judge's private interview with a child to determine its custodial preference. See Oakes v. Oakes, 45 Ill. App. 2d 387, 195 N.E.2d 840 (1964) (private interview upheld; in case of appeal, court should place in record substance of child's statement); Seelandt v. Seelandt, 24 Wis. 2d 73, 128 N.W.2d 66 (1964) (accord; court reporter should record interview but transcribe same only in case of appeal). Compare Callen v. Gill, 7 N.J. 312, 81 A.2d 495 (1951) (trial judge's failure to disclose in record expressed preference of child and facts upon which it was based was error). See Annot., 99 A.L.R.2d 954 (1965). Are the considerations here the same as with respect to custody investigations?

4. At least one state leaves the matter of custody determinations to the jury. See Tex. Rev. Civ. Stat. Ann. art. 4639(a) (Supp. 1964). A wholly different proposal calls for the parents upon divorce to agree to joint legal custody of their children and joint resolution of all custodial issues. In case of an impasse, a committee consisting of specialists (such as psychiatrists or educators) selected by the parties in advance will have the power to make a binding determination. See Kubie, Provisions for the Care of Children of Divorced Parents: A New Legal Instrument, 73 Yale L.J. 1197 (1964). Quite apart from its wisdom and feasibility, this proposal raises substantial legal issues in view of the questionable validity of any scheme that purports to oust the court of its jurisdiction in child custody matters. See, e.g., Fewel v. Fewel, 23 Cal. 2d 431, 144 P.2d 592 (1943) (judicial power cannot be delegated). These issues are fully explored in Note, 73 Yale L.J. 1201 (1964). See also Sheets v. Sheets, 22 App. Div. 2d 176, 254 N.Y.S.2d 320 (1964) (arbitration agreement respecting custody upheld).

5. The Kesseler case illustrates the difficulties that various types of family controversies pose for traditional courts with their traditional facilities and procedures. This has led some knowledgeable observers to support the increased use of family courts. See, e.g., Virtue, Family Cases in Court 234-241 (1956). The two principal advantages of family courts are (1) the centralization of all types of family controversies in one tribunal, so as to facilitate the integrated handling of a family's diverse problems and (2) the provision of adequate psychiatric, psychological, and social work facilities to aid the court and the litigants. See, e.g., Sheridan & Brewer, The Family Court, 4 Children 67 (1957). See also Gellhorn, Children and Families in the Courts of New York City 328-333 (1954), for a description of the method of handling custody investigations in various jurisdictions.

In view of the heat that is customarily engendered by proposals to reallocate the jurisdiction of established courts, it is not surprising that there has been far more controversy over the first characteristic of family courts than over the second. Thus, a recent survey of over 500 domestic relations judges and similar hearing officers revealed that almost 70 per cent of the courts have at least social workers assigned to them, in three fourths of the cases as full-time employees. Quenstedt & Winkler, What Are Our Domestic Relations Judges Thinking?, Monograph No. 1, A.B.A. Sect. of Fam. L., July 1965, p. 5. However, relatively few jurisdictions have as yet a truly unified and all-encompassing family court.

C. THE JONES CUSTODY CASE: CASEWORK
INVESTIGATION AND REPORT[6]

1. *Introduction*

After their separation in July, 1958, John Jones sued his wife Mary for a divorce on grounds of cruel and inhuman treatment. Mary, forty-one, and John, forty-two, were married in Minneapolis in April 1943. They had three children: Barbara (born June 1, 1945), Sally (born October 13, 1948), and James (born February 7, 1957). At the time of the initial hearing on the divorce complaint (May 20, 1959) the children were living with Mary. Because of a dispute concerning the future custody of the children, the referee decided that the Department of Court Services should make a custody investigation for the family court judge's use.

The Hennepin County, Minnesota, Department of Court Services was established pursuant to Minn. Stat. Ann. §487.03 (1959), which requires the Department, inter alia, "[t]o make investigations in divorce cases of children and home conditions when directed by a judge . . . and also to exercise supervision over children in such divorce cases as the court may direct." Typical of the many agencies that have been created as adjuncts to family and juvenile courts in recent years, it is staffed largely by social caseworkers, although psychiatrists and psychologists are available for consultation and are occasionally used to diagnose specific individuals.

The employee who was assigned to make the investigation in the Jones case was John Gibbs, a caseworker with a master's degree in social work. His first step was to send both parents a standard questionnaire. These documents may have given him leads to other information he wished to obtain; for example, in the Jones case, he secured a report from the Midwest Clinic where both Mr. and Mrs. Jones had been treated, and the Hibbing State Hospital, where Mrs. Jones had been a patient in 1952. He then interviewed all the members of the Jones family, obtained psychological evaluations of both parties and a psychiatric diagnosis of Mrs. Jones, and, as is indicated in his report which appears below, talked with a number of other persons such as relatives and neighbors.

All this information was incorporated into a file which was submitted to the family court judge, along with the caseworker's summary report, which is reproduced immediately below. The attorneys for Mr. and Mrs. Jones were also furnished a copy of the report.

---

[6] The materials that follow were drawn from an actual custody case in Hennepin County, Minnesota. Only the names and dates have been changed in order to preserve the anonymity of the persons involved.

2. *Report of the Department of Court Services*

John Jones, Plaintiff   [Filed on Sept. 19, 1959]
    vs.
Mary Jones, Defendant

TO: THE HONORABLE JOHN MARKSON

The above-named matter appeared before Your Honor on May 20, 1959, on an order for temporary relief in a divorce action. The plaintiff was to pay, in addition to attorney's fees, the amount of $7.50 per week alimony and $22.50 per week for support of the children. The custody of the children was awarded temporarily to the defendant, subject to reasonable visitation by the plaintiff and subject to a custody evaluation by the Department of Court Services. Defendant was awarded temporary use and possession of the premises and household goods, with plaintiff to pay reasonable household expenses and mortgage payments.

MARITAL STATUS

The plaintiff, 42, and defendant, 41, were married April 20, 1943, in Minneapolis. They were separated in July, 1958. Divorce action was commenced in May, 1959. There are three children born of this marriage: Barbara, 14 (born June 1, 1945), Sally, 10 (October 13, 1948) and James, 2 (February 7, 1957).

THE CHILDREN

The children are living with their mother in the family home. This is a modern brick-faced bungalow, but both the home and its modern furnishings have been allowed to deteriorate recently because of the defendant's emotional illness and resulting lack in housekeeping standards.

Barbara, 14, has assumed a certain amount of responsibility for the care of the house and the younger children although she recently has developed a flippant attitude and a forced indifference in the family situation since she has no way of living up to the expectations of this excessive responsibility. Ordinarily, she is a serious-minded young lady of average ability who drives herself beyond her abilities, especially in school.

Barbara was interviewed alone. She is rather non-committal in considering the family situation but she does view it objectively and she realizes that each of the parties has assets and liabilities as parents. She understands her mother's mental condition although she does not verbalize it directly. She states that her father gave the children as good care as he could during her mother's previous hospitalizations. She feels that her mother is kinder in manner than her father, who tends to be impulsive and does not allow for reasoning at times. She realizes that both parents love the children and do their best and that, by the same token, the children love both parents equally. She feels that her mother may have a better understanding of the girls, and her father of James, but she does not favor separating the children. Sometimes conflicts occur between herself and Sally, which are probably aggravated by the family disruption. The children try to avoid placing themselves in the midst of their parents' marital difficulties. Barbara's expression was that, whenever an argument began to brew, "we kids took to the hills." It is apparent that she feels something should be done about the total situation but she is uncertain as to what the outcome will or should be.

Sally, 10, is more shy than Barbara. She has handled the family situation by trying to avoid it. She wears an almost detached expression, accompanied by a wistful half-smile which seeks to draw attention and affection to herself. She is the most noticeably affected by the family situation and the school staff has been concerned about her difficulty in school adjustment. She has often gone to school unkempt, evidently disturbed, unable to concentrate and, apparently, unguided in the way in which she is going. The visiting teacher was not able to gain a working relationship with the mother and she therefore alerted the Welfare Board to the situation. Big Sister's has been active with Sally and has made it possible for her to attend summer camp.

James, 2, is a blonde, curly-haired youngster, who has responded favorably to the loving attention that he receives from everyone. He has not yet shown adverse effects from the negatives in his home environment except that he is lacking in any real training and discipline. His vocabulary is limited because his mothers and sisters anticipate his wants and provide them for him. He knows virtually no routine, no toilet-training, and no real limits.

Affection for the children is abundant, but there is no one in the home at present who is capable of assuming real responsibility for the care they need to grow and develop normally.

INTERVIEWS WITH PLAINTIFF, JOHN JONES

The plaintiff is a tense, impatient man whose judgment is sometimes warped by his inability to perceive a total picture. He is rigid and compulsive and attempts to fit people into his own pattern of thinking. However, he is interested and concerned for the children and does want to see the best things done for their welfare.

Plaintiff was an only child of an apparently weak father and domineering mother. After his marriage, he showed his ambivalent feelings about his parents by alternately dissociating himself completely for periods of time or by excessive association with them, in the pattern of a reactive formation. He seems to have responded, out of guilt, in the same ways in his marital situation. He has been alternately protective and alternately denying of his wife's mental illness. He gives the impression that he would like to be able to be understanding but that he is actually unable to do so and is therefore very much irritated by the situation but quite unable to cope with it. He chose a marriage partner whose superior intelligence and various competent skills he recognized. He apparently hoped to find solace in her strengths that would meet his own dependency needs. He has been frustrated in this hope because of his wife's emotional illnesses and resultant failures to function as the wife and mother that he envisioned.

However, it should be noted that some of plaintiff's own behavior through the years is certainly questionable in terms of reason and realism and must have done much to contribute to his wife's illness.

Plaintiff was educated in specific design and drafting skills. He states that he contracts his services to various companies for certain inventive projects that they require in their production. He has kept up his financial obligations to his family continuously since the separation.[7]

Plaintiff's description of their family life can best be given in his own words: "My wife lived a life alone from me and the children. I was forced to sleep in the basement and came up only to eat the evening meal which was served anytime between 6:30 and 9:30 P.M. which I know is too late for small children.

"She neglected the housework and spent most of her time reading, doing mathematics or playing [solitaire]. While she is doing this, she is apart from the world and not aware of what the children are doing. In order to be alone, she stays up to 2 or 3 A.M. and even later. In order for her to get enough sleep, it is necessary that she sleep late or during the day.

"My wife doesn't trust me, she believes me to . . . read her mind. She believes I have had newspaper articles written about her plus radio and television programs."

Mr. Jones relates his previous attempts to seek psychiatric help for his wife, who was treated for a three-month period in 1950 by Dr. Leon Kaufman and for a two-month period in 1952 at Hibbing State Hospital. During these times he cared for the two older children, with daytime care by a neighbor. He brought his wife home again upon her entreaties. Although she has had recurrent periods of obvious illness, he had promised never to recommit her to a hospital or to electroshock treatments. He feels bound by this, even though he realizes the unjudiciousness of such a promise. Therefore, when the marital situation became impossible, he left the home in July of 1958 and established a separate residence, although he visits the home periodically. In May of 1959, when he became concerned about the detrimental effects of the home conditions on the children, he initiated divorce proceedings. His plan would be to re-establish his residence in the family home with the children and a housekeeper. He believes, quite correctly, that defendant requires further psychiatric treatment and hospitalization. He is certain she will not physically harm the children and knows that she loves them but that she is incapable of their continued care.

PSYCHOLOGICAL REPORT ON PLAINTIFF, JOHN JONES

Plaintiff was administered psychological testing in the form of the Minnesota Multiphasic Personality Inventory, Shipley Hartford Scale, Incom-

---

[7] The financial aspects of the divorce were arranged by stipulation of the parties. The caseworker's materials on this subject have not been included. — Ed.

plete Sentence Test and the Bender-Gestalt by Mr. Keene on August 10th.[8] All validity scores were within normal limits. His intelligence is slightly above average. "The Bender shows evidence for a very expansive approach, a great deal of immaturity, anxiety and rather poor judgment." He is also a dependent, introverted man who "is quite depressed at the present time but the depression is felt to be situational rather than a permanent part of his personality make-up." His tendency to be critical, stubborn, and suspicious, and to hold himself blameless would make it difficult for him to reconcile two points of view. He has, however, a warm feeling for the children, noting the boy as his favorite. It is felt that he is interested in the children and that his personality pattern is not a grossly deviant one, although there are some conflicts.

INTERVIEWS WITH DEFENDANT, MARY JONES

Mrs. Jones is a tall, thin, blonde woman whose untidy grooming, childish speech, and flat accent immediately suggest the possibility of mental illness. She wears a continual half-smile, quite inappropriate for her feelings. Her home, on my three visits there, was just as slovenly and unattended as was her own personal appearance. Yet, her manner with the children was kind and warm.

Defendant was one of five children in a strict Lutheran family. She was an honor student in school but was unhappy in her family situation. She had some hesitation about her marriage, but both she and her husband, then in their late twenties, feel that they married to escape unpleasant home environments, even though they both had reservations about it. Plaintiff's mother resented their marriage and defendant felt she was never able to please either her husband or mother-in-law no matter how hard she tried, although references substantiate that she was an expert cook, seamstress and homemaker. Plaintiff insisted on their visiting his parents with the children every single weekend. Defendant's suggestions that they plan other things too resulted in a conflict where plaintiff found it impossible to choose between his mother and wife and would vacillate between them, sometimes strongly on one side and sometimes the other, but unable to settle on his own position. Shortly, after plaintiff's reconciliation with his mother, which followed a long period of absence from her, his mother suffered a stroke and died. Plaintiff apparently has not recovered from his guilt feelings over this and tends to project blame upon defendant in spite of the fact that she tried every reasonable approach to establish a comfortable relationship among the three. Plaintiff's father was apparently quite passive and did not appear to figure in the conflict.

Defendant apparently became increasingly unable to live up to the rigid demands of plaintiff. The events that precipitated defendant's first hospitalization centered around plaintiff's mother also. Plaintiff's mother was very fond and overly possessive of Barbara. She often kept her with her for periods of time, sometimes excessively, again causing conflict between the parties and herself. When Sally was born, plaintiff's

---

[8] See page 895 infra for a description of these tests and their evaluation. — Ed.

mother reportedly told the parties that since they now had another child, she would keep Barbara.   Although defendant was able to insist on her return, she became increasingly panicky, fearing that her husband and his mother would be plotting against her.   She became delusional and was placed under the care of Dr. Kaufman in 1950.   In 1952, she was committed to Hibbing State Hospital for two months with symptoms typical of paranoid schizophrenia.   She was returned home by her husband at her request and was discharged in 1953.   She has had periods of apparent illness and remission since that time.   Sometimes she appears to have insight into her condition; at other times she becomes delusional, with little understanding of her own illness except her belief that her husband is responsible for it.   Shortly before their separation in 1958, she left the home with sleeping pills, intending suicide.   She stayed away overnight in a motel, reconsidered and returned home.

At the present time, she is openly delusional, believing firmly that her husband has telepathic agents who are working with him to read her mind and transmit her thoughts.   She speaks of a "floating mind," tape recordings, and such extra-sensory perception in connection with her husband and sometimes her oldest daughter.

She is a kind, gentle person, who is keenly perceptive of her children and she loves them dearly, but her present condition makes it impossible for her to provide the type of parental guidance that would assure them of normal, wholesome rearing.

Psychological Report on Defendant, Mary Jones

Psychological testing in the form of the Minnesota Multiphasic Personality Inventory, the Shipley-Hartford Scale and the Incomplete Sentence Test were administered by Mr. Keene on August 11th.   Although Mrs. Jones shows superior intelligence, there is such a discrepancy in the two parts of the Shipley test as to suggest "either deterioration or the possibility of a schizophrenic process."   The Multiphasic "suggests a relatively high psychopathic deviate score that probably reflects her dissatisfaction at the disharmony in her home.   There is considerable elevation on the paranoid scale that seems to reflect the paranoid delusional system.   Although the Multiphasic does not seem compatible with the diagnosis of paranoid schizophrenia, nevertheless, there is strong evidence for paranoid thought processes.   During the interview, her behavior, mannerisms, facial expressions and speech content were strongly suggestive of paranoid schizophrenia.   On the Sentence Completion test, the same kind of thinking is evident along with uncertainty and depression."   There were frequent referrals to the telepathists and of her insecurity.   In summary, Mr. Keene felt that Mrs. Jones "seems sincerely interested in her children although she points out herself that, if she is not competent, then she should not have them.   She seems to be actively delusional and the suggestion is that of a paranoid schizophrenic."

Dr. Bell reviewed the records and testing and interviewed Mrs. Jones.   Mrs. Jones reiterated her delusions and she discussed her children and her situation.   Dr. Bell's summary and conclusions were: "Although the patient is quite sensitive to her children's feelings, I do not feel she is capable of taking care of them at this time. The diagnosis would be that of chronic paranoid schizophrenia active at this time. The treatment prospects are poor because it is such a chronic case and, secondly, because the patient is fully unable to accept that this is a delusional basis at all. Parts of her delusional system are well organized but other parts are very inappropriate, silly and poorly organized. The possibility of further treatment for Mrs. Jones should be thought of and one treatment plan might be to have the children reside with the husband temporarily while Mrs. Jones receives therapy. I know she will be very resistive to this but yet, something has to be done as it looks like she is gradually regressing more and more."

REFERENCES

Medical and Social Agencies

Supt., Hibbing State Hospital
Dr. Howell, Hennepin Clinic
Miss Forbes, psychiatric social worker, Midwest Clinic
Miss Jorgenson, Big Sisters, worker for Sally

PERSONAL REFERENCES

Mrs. Audrey Anderson, defendant's sister
Mrs. Joan Handler, former neighbor
Mrs. Elaine Peterson
Mrs. Ellen James
Mrs. Mary Karras

The medical history documents Mrs. Jones' hospitalization for psychiatric treatment. Her diagnosis was "very probably paranoid schizophrenic in basic structure," and her condition appeared to have a pattern similar to the one we see today with the exception that she has now regressed in her personal care and her ability to function realistically. It was noted, at that time, as now, that she is "exceedingly fond of her children." There are indications from relatives and neighbors at the time of her hospitalization and shortly thereafter that the plaintiff was aggravating his wife's illness by his own behavior. For example, a call from a neighbor on June 2, 1953, to the Midwest Clinic complained that there was continuous quarreling at the Jones' with screaming and crying on the part of the adults as well as the children. He was seen as "an emotionally unstable individual who was not able to get along with anyone." Suggestions on the part of psychiatrists that Mr. Jones also obtain professional help have met with rebuffs on his part to the extent that even professional people have found themselves in sympathy with the defendant in the marital situation.

Midwest Clinic saw Mr. and Mrs. Jones in a series of interviews in July and August, 1958, at which time Mrs. Jones was observed to have an "active paranoid delusional system, focused primarily on her husband" and his telepathic power. Both parties were seen in an effort to determine whether there were strengths in the mariage to build on. Few strengths were evident. "The only thing they have in common . . . is some love and concern for the children. Even this is diluted by their use of the children as pawns for the expression of hostility as well as the fact that the children represent some bonds to a marriage unwanted from the beginning and, more generally, some responsibilities for maturity which neither is able to provide." Mr. Jones was seen as an immature, dependent person, "more openly ambivalent regarding his family responsibilities than his wife and also not really able to look at the hostility and feelings of rejection he has for this entire situation." The parents, at that time, recognized the problems the children were having over this conflict. Barbara was reportedly showing temper tantrums and confusion. Sally had resorted to denial. Barbara had to assume maternal responsibilities far beyond what should be expected of a child her age. Mrs. Jones capitalized on this to make up for her own inadequacies and Mr. Jones avoided dealing with it, just complained and left the home. Both felt they were not being helped at the clinic and discontinued treatment.

Dr. Howell interviewed and tested Mrs. Jones in November, 1958. At that time testing "did not show any overt psychotic mentation," although "some of the residuals of the schizophrenic illness were evident in her dress, manner, vagueness, rambling and loose associations." She talked of having delusions and how difficult it sometimes was to maintain her grasp on reality. Dr. Howell found Mrs. Jones to be open and frank, however, while Mr. Jones was "unco-operative and vituperative."

The school became increasingly concerned about the children's adjustment and their conditions at home. A conference of the visiting teacher and representatives of the Welfare Board and Big Sisters was held in the spring of 1959, which resulted in direct case work with Sally through Big Sisters and the alerting of the parents to correct the home situation. After his conference with the Welfare Board, plaintiff commenced divorce action. He also became very agitated with the situation, misinterpreted information, and proceeded to charge that the children had to be removed within two weeks. Both parents then put the children in the difficult position of asking the children to choose between them. Both were surprised and shaken to find that the children were unable to choose and, as the children became more confused, the parents realized the error of their request.

Miss Jorgenson (Big Sisters) reports that, although Sally got along with the other children at camp, this month, she showed babyish behavior in wanting the counselor to carry her on hiking trips, etc. She ate very poorly and seemed quite unused to eating regular meals, particularly meat, indicating that they were used to snacking at home. She has expressed her confusion about the custody situation. She is feeling very lost at this point.

One personal reference, who was given by both parties, had had an opportunity to observe the family over a long period of time. She, and two other references, felt that the plaintiff's behavior was often more peculiar than the defendant's. He was described as argumentative and rigid. He was never satisfied with his wife's accomplishments even though she was an excellent homemaker in their early marriage. He was very critical of her. Several examples were given, including an incident that demonstrated his distorted methods of handling situations. Defendant found the electricity off one day after her husband had left for work. When she called her husband, he informed her calmly that he had cut off the electricity to prevent her from spending her time sewing or cooking, thereby forcing her to weed the garden as he had planned for her that day. He had given her no indication of his plan prior to that.

Another reference stated that he had one day given her a long list of auto parts that she must purchase for him that day. She reportedly exhausted herself unsuccessfully trying to obtain all the parts. She was fearful of going home to report this. When she called him from the home of the reference, he reportedly laughed coldly and said that he knew it would be impossible to get all those things even in a two-week period. He was just testing her to see if she would do it. References stated that he often set up similarly impossible things for her to do and then [upbraided] her if she could not accomplish them. They believe that this led to her breakdown. Since her hospitalization, he has allegedly reminded defendant continually that she is really "on probation" and his inferred threats of rehospitalization have left her in a state of constant insecurity. She maintained few friendships and withdrew more and more into herself.

All references attest to the kind and gentle manner of the defendant and most referred to the coldness and domineering manner of the plaintiff. Most references felt defendant had done the best she could under the circumstances. One was entirely non-committal. It was interesting to note that, although most of the references recognized the defendant's limitations by reason of her emotional difficulties, only one thought the children would be better off with the plaintiff. Most felt that his manner with the children was often overly severe and critical as it was with the defendant.

SUMMARY AND RECOMMENDATIONS

The defendant has a ten-year history of recurrent mental illness and emotional difficulties. She has the three children, ages 14 to 2, at the present time. Although she is a kind and gentle mother, loves the children dearly and is keenly perceptive to them, she is currently unable to cope with the actual responsibilities of parental care. Her home is grossly neglected. She is openly and actively delusional, believing firmly that her husband and his telepathic agents are plotting against her. Psychiatric evaluation at this time substantiates her current illness and regression. It was recommended that defendant should receive further treatment as soon as possible. One plan suggested by the court psychiatrist was that the children be placed temporarily with the plaintiff while the defendant receives therapy. The children are suffering emotionally from the confusion in their current environment. Excessive maternal responsibilities are being thrown upon the 14-year-old daughter.

The plaintiff shows a psychological pattern that is not grossly deviant. However, his past history of impatient, immature, and vituperative behavior and his distorted judgment in some [instances lead] one to pause before considering custody with the plaintiff as a permanent plan. In spite of her illness, defendant shows a good deal more understanding of the children and patience with them than the plaintiff does.

Neither of these parents has sufficient maturity to assume custody without continued supervision for a period of time. If custody is awarded the plaintiff, it would also be necessary to arange for competent homemaking services or foster home placement. If defendant receives custody, it should be joint custody with some responsible individual or agency, and, again, provision for homemaking assistance or foster home placement. In either instance, defendant should be encouraged to place herself under psychiatric treatment.

Whenever custody is awarded, it is recommended that the Department of Court Services continue supervision of custody, and that assistance be given to plan for living arrangements, home-making, foster-home placement, psychotherapy, or whatever practical aspects are necessary.

> Respectfully submitted,
> John Gibbs
> Domestic Relations Counselor

3. *Questions*

a. If you were counsel for the plaintiff, and as is customary in Hennepin County, received only the summary report which appears above without the underlying file, how would you use it in preparation for the custody hearing? What parts of it are particularly vulnerable? How would you bring them out in the course of the hearing? What additional evidence would you seek to obtain? Is there any way in which you could obtain all or part of the underlying file?

b. Suppose you did obtain the underlying file which is reproduced below (pages 875-894 infra), what use would you make of it?

c. Consider questions a and b on the assumption that you are counsel for the defendant.

4. *The Custody Investigation File*

a. Mary Jones's answers to the Department's Custody Investigation Questionnaire, dated June 18, 1959.

b. John Jones's answers to the Department's Custody Investigation Questionnaire, dated June 17, 1959.

c. Letter, dated July 9, 1959, from Dr. Albert Howell, a psychiatrist on the staff of the Hennepin Clinic, to Mr. Gibbs; attached to this letter, a copy of a letter, dated December 4, 1958, from Miss Ellen Forbes, a psychiatric social worker with the Midwest Clinic, to Dr. Howell.

d. Letter, dated July 15, 1959, from Dr. William Rogers, Superintendent of Hibbing State Hospital.

e. Psychological Report on Mrs. Jones, by Mr. Keene, Department of Court Services Psychologist, dated August 11, 1959.

f. Psychiatric Evaluation of Mrs. Jones, dated August 11, 1959, made by Dr. Bell, Department of Court Services Psychiatrist.

g. Psychological Report on Mr. Jones, dated August 12, 1959, made by Mr. Keene.

h. Report describing Sally's camp experiences, dated September 3, 1959, made by Miss Jorgenson, a caseworker with Big Sister Association.

i. Copy of a letter, dated September 16, 1959, from Dr. Howell to Will Meyer, Esquire, Mrs. Jones's attorney.

a. MARY JONES'S ANSWERS TO THE DEPARTMENT'S CUSTODY INVESTIGATION QUESTIONNAIRE

NAME Mary Jones   DATE   June 18, 1959   SEX Female

1. Describe the problems in your marriage or marriages that caused the present divorce action or past divorces.

You may by now have read the reports from the psychiatric clinic at which both Mr. Jones and I had interviews last fall. I cannot add anything important to the statements I made there.

I believe that the telepathist exists. That there may in fact be two or for that matter any number of these persons concerned. In any case my husband does at times know my thoughts which he receives by some extrasensory power, and I am convinced that if there are other sensitives involved, he is in communication with them. Some person, somewhere, has in turn relayed some of the messages so received to a number of persons to whom I would never personally have communicated them. I have protested time and again this invasion of my privacy only to be met with accusations that I suffer from delusions. I can think of no valid reason for these activities. And I think that for Mr. Jones to attempt to convince the children, as he did, their mother was suffering from hallucinations was cruel almost beyond belief. It disturbed Barbara terribly because she understood and had no way of knowing what the truth was.

In any case quarrels over this matter and other so called proofs of my derangement drove us so far apart that I finally refused to have sexual relations, a step for which I do not apologize. With our marriage in jeopardy it would have been criminal to have had another child, and if my health were as poor as my husband claimed it would have been worse.

Toward the end of our life together Mr. Jones took a position at which sometimes he was required to work evenings and on some days he stayed at work until he was finished, on others he came home for dinner and returned to work in the evening. When he was at home he was almost uniformly bad tempered. One evening he broke the vacuum cleaner I was repairing because I had supposedly taken it apart the wrong way. A while later he began working from either eight in the morning until twelve at night. There were even a few shifts which last until three and four A.M. On these nights, I called the plant several times but there was never any answer. When he was discharged shortly thereafter he asked me about my plans and I told him I was leaving, so he took a fishing trip with unknown companions at an unexplained destination and stayed another night at another. The time seemed convenient, Mr. Jones' being out of work meant that he would have time to make arrangements so I left on my little trip with a bottle of sleeping pills for company.

The floating mind went with me and when I left the cabin I rented for the night for a cup of coffee someone entered and removed the cover of my hat box in which I had placed notes for the children and which I had covered just before leaving.

The following day I returned to our house and found my husband in the kitchen drinking beer, as he had been for hours with his new housekeeper, whom he had called at twelve P.M. after the children were sent to bed, and brought back a little later to sleep in my room. He has never offered any explanation as to how he selected her or what their relationship was. During the afternoon she made several statements implying a rivalry between herself and me. When she called the next afternoon she made the remark that I could have him back again. Mr. Jones has not lived in this house since that time. He has never told us where he could be reached.

2. What did your spouse (or former spouse) feel were your problems? How did they contribute to the divorce and/or the present situation?

I am not sure which of our problems my husband felt were important. He has at various times made so many accusations. I feel that he must have known that many of them were false or grossly exaggerated. Some of those which he may have believed and thought were important I will list below.

That I did not love him when we were married and have never loved him. Our sexual adjustment has never I think been satisfactory to him. He felt and rightly that I sometimes rejected his advances. I could never make him understand that to me closeness is more than a matter of physical contact, and that we could not resolve a problem or a quarrel or erase the sting of his contempt by having intercourse.

That I am overcritical of myself. All people I think have periods when they feel inadequate, but I have never been as critical or expected as much of myself as he has demanded of me.

That I am oversensitive to his tone of voice. A person may sometimes, I believe, be very angry and speak quietly or kindly but it seems inconsistent to me to contend that one expresses love or affection with an habitual snarl.

That I am impractical and extravagant. Mr. Jones' salary has usually been modest but we have never had any large debts except those for mortgages on houses. He has given me just thirty dollars a week to pay for food, clothing, entertainment and miscellaneous expenses. As of today we have no outstanding bills. I never had any money except such sums as I asked for for a specific purpose.

That I treated him like a dog and made him sleep in the basement. He slept in the basement as is obvious because of his size and weight because he desired to do so. He was cruel, deliberately malicious, disinterested in the children and me, and I was tired and afraid of him and refused to have sexual relations. When he moved into the amusement room, I offered to make up a bed for him.

That I would not make his meals. For weeks he deliberately found some controversy about the children's or my own behavior to discuss each night at the dinner table. After I had first suggested, then demanded on several occasions that he wait to discuss these matters so that we could eat in peace I refused to eat at the same table or time as he did, hoping that he and the children could then have dinner quietly. Then he refused to have dinner at home.

That I am a poor housekeeper.

That I am not a fit mother. I wish very much that I were a better mother. I love my children very much and want them to have a happy home. They are all good healthy, sweet children and deserve the best that I can give them.

That I do not understand him. I am perfectly sure that this claim is entirely accurate.

3. Describe your spouse as a person. What are his or her strengths and weaknesses? What do you like and dislike about him or her? What did you like about him or her when you married? What has changed?

John is an able draftsman or engineer. He does not like his work but I know of none that he would like better. He has been an adequate if sometimes begrudging provider and he had been until the last few years faithful, that is sexually.

He is very critical of other people and seldom expresses admiration or approval. He has little sympathy with weakness of any sort and less for most illness, most of which he treats as imaginary. He is as inconsiderate of his own health as of that of others, and has never consulted a physician about his health. He was rejected for service in the army due to high blood pressure. I doubt that he has even a vague idea of what his present blood pressure is and know that he would regard any attention paid to it as neurotic. When I was in the hospital he was very kind. He brought the children to see me every week. But when our children were born he never offered a bit of assistance.

He is also an obstinate man and refused for some months, shortly after we were married to see his family because I said I was tired and asked him to go alone. His father finally met him at work and pleaded with him to visit. After that time he was equally determined that we must do so every Sunday.

He is seldom physically aggressive.

When we were dating John was invariably courteous and he had a shy flattering manner which I found attractive. He also had a delightful impish sense of humor which seemed to say he shared a special secret with you. He still has both. He also has what he himself calls a perverted sense of humor which is sometimes embarrassing sometimes malicious.

He was wonderfully kind during the early months of our marriage about my sexual ignorance, my inexperienced cooking, and he never mentioned housework at all.

Even then whenever we had a difference of opinion or a problem to be settled he would retreat into a shell. Each year that we have been married that shell has become a little larger not harder because it was always impenetrable. The shell is covered with thousands of prickly barbs, one for each hurt. The shell grew. We didn't.

4. Describe each child in the family. What are his or her strengths and weaknesses? What do you like about him or her?

Barbara is fourteen and the oldest of our children. Because she has more understanding of the problems, both past and present, that we have and must face she has been the most deeply affected. She does not feel any deep resentment toward either of us, and I think she realizes that many of her father's unjust criticisms were aimed primarily at me, and meant to convince [me] of my own inadequacies as a mother, or merely an outlet for his resentment.

She is a slightly better than average student and does most of her home work without being prompted. At home she is not very helpful with housework or routine assignments, but she sews well and is beginning to sew some of her own and her sister's clothes. She is also generally a willing and competent baby sitter for the younger children.

There is between Barbara and Sally some rivalry and resentment. Barbara has a tendency to be bossy and a little aggressive dealing out what she feels is needed discipline. While she may rebel at doing the dishes or dusting a floor, Barbara accepts my right to know where she is at all times and she always asks for permission before making any firm commitments to go anywhere out of the immediate neighborhood. She does not date and has had no opportunity.

I like Barbara though occasionally the temper tantrums she has when asked to do some small thing are quite severe, and I think she uses them to release tension. Some of these tensions are due to her own sense of inadequacy; she wishes that she were prettier, had a special talent, or was more competent generally. Don't we all? The failure of our marriage is of course a far more serious disturbance.

Sally is nine. She has the [temperament] of an elf. This may explain in part why the visiting teacher had the idea she lived in a dream world. Nothing could be farther from the truth. She's a very practical little girl. When she wants someone to love her she crawls into his or her lap and embraces the object of her affections. If she wants an object, she throws a temper tantrum, charges a small fee for any work she does to earn money to buy it, or waits for a good time to charm you into giving it to her.

She doesn't like housework and arranges to be busy when it should be done. She is not suffering from malnutrition but from a picky appetite accompanied by a strong resistance to foods she does not at the moment like.

She loves her father and would like to have him come home to live but knows now that she is not unbearably happy without him and that as she puts it she would rather stay with me because she loves me a bit more than she does her father.

I know that she is [a] willful child and is not as honest nor as conscientious as Barbara. She is also a very out-going friendly little girl, and I'm very fond of her.

Jimmie is two. He's a sweetheart. Both of the girls love him almost excessively. He is healthy, happy, and handsome. He finds things he shouldn't be able to reach. We've hidden the most dangerous items where he can never get them. He eats well, sleeps well, and loves so much. Whatever his problems are they lie in the future. Sally to whom I read this thinks I should add that even if he is only a baby he helps by bringing us the mail and the newspaper.

5. What do you feel are the points in favor of your spouse having custody of the children?

Mr. Jones would be able, because he is a man and has more skill and experience than I to provide more and better things and opportunites for the children than I can. Jimmie needs a father. It will be quite difficult to raise a normal boy in such a female household as ours. I think Mr. Jones loves the children. When I was in the hospital he took his responsibilities to them very seriously. In my absence their father would undoubtedly be kinder and more considerate of the children. I am certain that many of his criticisms of them were motivated by his dissatisfaction with me.

The children would not be further disturbed by my "delusions and accusations" that he reads my mind. The words in quotes are Mr. Jones' and while I know them to be an inaccurate description, the quarrels and doubts which resulted were very real and disturbing.

6. What do you feel are the problems involved in your spouse having custody of the children?

It would be difficult for Mr. Jones to find a housekeeper who could or would provide the interest and understanding that the children need.

The girls would, on the whole, rather remain in my custody. In discussing the pros and cons, Barbara said that "mother could provide more understanding."

I don't think their father has maintained the personal contact with the children which would make it possible to help them with their problems.

I would like to add that I love the children very much and consider that, whatever your recommendation may be I have been fortunate in having such sweet children.

7. What are your plans in the event you gain custody?

I plan to sell the house in which we are now living. It is much too expensive for our present income. I should like very much to be free to leave the state, as I am not fond of Minnesota winters. It would also simplify the problem of relations between my husband and myself.

Once relocated, I would look for employment on either a part time or a full time basis. Jimmie could be sent to a nursery school or approved home while I work and, during the school year, Barbara could supervise Sally during the few hours when they would not be in school and I would be at work. I should like when the children are a bit older and Barbara has matured enough to handle the responsibility of caring for Jimmie during the summers to buy a small business.

I do not plan to separate the children from their father entirely. He could, of course, see them during any of the school holidays, if he desired to provide transportation and reasonable care and living conditions. I am sorry that these terms are so harsh, but believe them to be important to our future.

b. JOHN JONES'S ANSWERS TO THE DEPARTMENT'S CUSTODY INVESTIGATION QUESTIONNAIRE

NAME John Jones   DATE June 17, 1959   SEX Male

1. Describe the problems in your marriage or marriages that caused the present divorce action or past divorces.

My wife lived a life alone from me and the children. I was forced to sleep in the basement and came up only to eat the evening meal which was served anytime between 6:30 P.M. and 9:30 P.M. which I know is too late for small children.

She neglected the house work and spent most of her time reading, doing mathematics, or playing solitaire. While she is doing this, she is apart from the world and not aware of what the children are doing. In order to be alone she stays up to 2 or 3 A.M. and even later. In order for her to get enough sleep it is necessary that she sleep late or during the day.

My wife doesn't trust me, she believes me to be a mind reader and read her mind. She believes I have had newspaper articles written about her plus radio and television programs.

I know the children are not properly being brought up. This is also known by the school, traveling teacher, and Big Sisters.

2. What did your spouse (or former spouse) feel were your problems? How did they contribute to the divorce and/or the present situation?

I read her mind she thought.

She thought I had strangers check up on her.

She thought I was unreasonable in asking her to keep regular hours for eating and sleeping and care of the children.

3. Describe your spouse as a person. What are his or her strengths and weaknesses? What do you like and dislike about him or her? What did you like about him or her when you married? What has changed?

My wife is a person who hates housework, but does a good job when employed outside the home. She has no friends and trusts not even her own father. She is very intelligent. She is a very good cook. She does an excellent job at sewing.

I most dislike my wife discussing mind reading, her suspicion of the press, radio, and television in front of the children.

I also dislike the fact that my wife refused to agree to any routine for the benefit of the children.

4. Describe each child in the family. What are his or her strengths and weaknesses? What do you like or dislike about him or her?

Barbara: Age 14. Doesn't have many friends. Really a very good child. Occasionally believes the world against her. Studies very hard (school believes her to be working above her capabilities). She doesn't advertise her home problems or thoughts to other people. Loves her baby brother very much and insists they not be separated. I do wish she would do more work about the house and be neater (care of her bedroom).

Barbara has told me that she would like very much for me to care for her and her brother and sister.

Sally: Very confused about the entire home situation. Would very much like her home life to be like her friends. Needs guidance which the Big Sister is very helpful. Has no trouble with school studies. Like Barbara she also loves her brother and doesn't want to be separated. She and Barbara do not get along too well. Make friends very easy and has many. I am very much afraid for her if her home life is not changed soon. I also wish she would do more work about the house and be neater (care for her bedroom).

Jimmie age 2: A very loving little boy who is not being brought up properly. His mother finds it more convenient to change diapers at her leisure than to train him. He is backward in learning to talk. He is very mechanically minded. He loves his two sisters very much as is very dependent upon them.

5. What do you feel are the points in favor of your spouse having custody of the children?

I have proven that I am able to care for the children as I did so when my wife was at the state hospital.

I love all three of the children and they love me.

I believe I know most of the three children's problems and how to help them solve them.

I know definitely that if I am granted custody of the children, I will be able to bring the girls closer together. Without marital differences, I will have much more time to knit the family in a single unit working toward a common goal.

6. What do you feel are the problems involved in your spouse having custody of the children?

She is their mother. She definitely would not physically hurt the children. She has proven she is not capable of caring for the children. I do not want what happened to my wife as a child to also happen to my children. Doctor Kaufman said it was definitely my wife's childhood that did much to contribute to her present mental condition.

My wife thinks she will not have any problems if she leaves Minnesota. I hate to think what will happen when she discovers that running away doesn't always solve problems.

7. What are your plans in the event you gain custody?

Move back into house and provide the three children with the love and care they have been deprived of. If the children so desire we will move to another neighborhood where they can have a new start. I really do not believe this to be necessary.

The most important thing is that more than just food, clothing and lodging is provided these three wonderful children.

C. LETTER FROM PSYCHIATRIST ON STAFF OF
HENNEPIN CLINIC, WITH LETTER FROM MIDWEST
CLINIC ATTACHED

HENNEPIN CLINIC
July 9, 1959

John Gibbs, A.C.S.W.
Domestic Relations Counselor
Court House
Minneapolis, Minnesota

Dear Mr. Gibbs:

I am in receipt of your letter regarding John and Mary Jones and Mrs. Jones' authorization to release medical information to you.

I first saw Mrs. Jones in the offices of the Hennepin Clinic upon the referral of Dr. Bart on November 12th. At that time she told me that she was considering a divorce and wanted an independent psychiatric evaluation to counteract any information which her husband might have in his possession to use against her. She stated that her husband said that he will take the children because "I am not emotionally sane because of being in mental hospitals." Her past history was relatively noncontributory with the exception of a number of hospitalizations for mental disorder.

I found her, on psychiatric examination, to be quite vague, somewhat rambling, and a poor historian. I further felt that some of the residuals of the schizophrenic illness were evident in her dress, manner, vagueness, rambling, and loose associations. She spoke very frankly of some of the delusions that she had once held, and told me how difficult it was sometimes to maintain her grasp on reality. At that time I asked that the husband come in so that I could see him, and I found him to be a most uncooperative individual; whereas I had found Mrs. Jones to be quite open and frank, he was vituperative, abusive, and uncooperative, and tried to start an argument with her and with me right here in the office. While it is certainly obvious that it has been trying for him to make a home for his children and to deal with a wife who at times has been mentally ill, I certainly felt that my sympathies lay with Mrs. Jones after seeing him.

I did give Mrs. Jones an MMPI and saw her on a follow-up visit. Furthermore, I obtained information from the Midwest Clinic which I have enclosed. The MMPI did not show any overt psychotic mentation. The validity scales were within normal limits. The T scores were as follows: Hs 50, D 64, Hy 61, Pd 79, Mf 41, Pa 68, Pt 52, Sc 62, Ma 59, Si 50.

I hope this information will be of some assistance to you, and if I can be of further assistance, please do not hesitate to call.

Sincerely,
Albert Howell, M.D.

MIDWEST CLINIC
December 4, 1958

Dr. Albert Howell
Hennepin Clinic
Minneapolis 22, Minnesota

Dear Dr. Howell: Re: Jones, Mary

Mrs. Jones was first seen in our clinic on July 29, 1958, and her husband on August 14, 1958. Following separate interviews, they were interviewed jointly by Dr. Bart and myself for three sessions and then seen individually again.

Mrs. Jones has an active paranoid delusional system, focused primarily on her husband. In both individual and joint interviews, she openly expressed her ideas that her husband could read her mind, was having her followed, that he had radio and television talking about her, and various recording machines inside and outside the house. These ideas are quite fixed in her thinking so that as far as she is concerned any discussion around their relationships begins with these as given facts. She has at times included her elder daughter in this delusional system. Since she has spent most of her time complaining about her husband and a possible divorce action, we saw them jointly in an attempt to learn whether there are any strengths in the marriage which could be built upon. These joint interviews revealed there were very few strengths from the beginning of this marriage. It would seem the only thing they have in common at this time is some love and concern for the children. Even this is diluted by their use of the children as pawns for the expression of hostility as well as the fact that the children represent some bonds to a marriage unwanted from the beginning and, more generally, some responsibilities for maturity which neither is able to provide.

Mr. Jones was seen as a very inadequate, dependent person. He is more openly ambivalent regarding his family responsibilities than his wife but he also is not able really to look at the hostility and feelings of rejection he has for this entire situation. Both Mr. & Mrs. Jones stated in individual interviews they wanted a divorce. Although they want to fight for the custody of the children, it was our feeling neither really wanted custody. Mr. Jones' plan did not include his taking care of the children. He felt a foster home with support from him was preferable.

From the reports of both parents, the responses of the children have been that Barbara, the eldest, has shown temper tantrums and expressed a good deal of confusion. Sally has resorted to denial. Barbara appears to be the most upset as she has had to assume maternal responsibilities far beyond what should be expected of a child her age. Mrs. Jones capitalizes on this to make up for her own inadequacies.

We hope this information will be useful in making your evaluation of this case.

Very truly yours,
(Miss) Ellen Forbes
Psychiatric Social Worker

d.   LETTER FROM SUPERINTENDANT OF HIBBING
STATE HOSPITAL

State of Minnesota
Hibbing State Hospital
Hibbing, Minnesota
July 15, 1959

John Gibbs, A.C.S.W.
Court House
Minneapolis 15, Minnesota

We are writing in reply to your request that we supply information regarding [Mary Jones]. Mrs. Jones was admitted to this hospital on 10-17-1952, provisionally discharged 12-20-52 and fully discharged 12-20-53.

A lengthy 23-page history from the patient's sister, Audrey Anderson, states that the patient was reared in a strict religious Lutheran home and that prior to her hospitalization she attended church regularly. Indications are that the patient's husband, John, was not interested in church activities and attended seldom. According to this history, the patient was a national honor student while in high school and a steady and conscientious worker.

The family history indicates that the patient received private psychiatric care for a three month period in 1950 under the supervision of Dr. Leon Kaufman, because of some paranoid ideas, and during this treatment she received electroshock treatment. There is also some indication that the patient [had] an inferiority complex prior to the disorder that led to her hospital commitment in 1952.

During her hospitalization, the patient informed the ward physician that she had never been happy during her childhood or even following her marriage in 1943. The patient had no realization that she was mentally ill and blamed her marital difficulties on the fact that her husband was a mama's boy and an only child. Patient's sister reported that the patient's mother-in-law was unhappy with the marriage, as she felt the patient came from a poor family; however, conditions improved as time passed.

Our patient stated that even when she was employed and had two children, her husband would not help her with the housework. During her hospitalization, it was frequently noted that the patient appeared to be very attached to her children but appeared to be quite indifferent toward her husband. There also appeared to be some suicidal tendencies.

The patient was described as a neat and attractive individual who was very cooperative with both the patients and ward personnel, and was quite congenial. She willingly participated in ward activities and duties on the ward. She had a good interest in her surroundings and was very kindly toward other patients.

Patient received nine electroshock treatments from 11-26-52 to 12-15-52, and showed a satisfactory remission. She regarded her former delusions as silly and was released as improved, with instructions to receive follow-up care at the Midwest Clinic. On October 22, 1952, the ward physician recommended some psycho-therapy for the patient's husband, probably based on the patient's statements.

Prior to her discharge, the patient attended three sessions of group therapy, conducted by our hospital psychologist, during which she spoke of her illnesses and reasons for hospitalization. On these occasions, the patient sounded quite immature in her thinking and even childish to some extent. For a more complete psychological report, we are enclosing a copy of the psychological examination conducted on the date that the patient was admitted to this hospital. It is interesting to note that in the reports received from the Midwest Clinic, dated January 22, 1953, it is mentioned that the patient is exceedingly fond of her children. On that date, the five year old daughter had accompanied the patient to the clinic and it was stated that she was an exceedingly well mannered and behaved child. In another clinic report dated 6-2-53, a neighbor of the Joneses had telephoned to complain that the Joneses had been quarreling continually and that there was screaming and crying on the part of the adults as well as the children. This neighbor at the time expressed sympathy for the patient's condition, but stated that she felt Mr. Jones was responsible for the patient's illness. She had characterized him as an unstable individual who was not able to get along with anyone.

We are sorry that we are not able to supply you with more helpful information. Should we be able to assist you further on this case please do not hesitate to call on us.

Yours truly,
William Rogers, M.D.
Superintendent

Hibbing State Hospital
Psychological Examination

Initial   (x)   Re-evaluation: 1 ( )   2 ( )   3 ( )   x Routine
                                                                  Referral

Name: Mary Jones   Admission date: Oct. 17, 1952
Age: 34   No. of Admissions: One
Education: High School   Testing dates: Oct. 17, 1952
Civil Status: Married
Tests Administered:
The MMPI: T-Scores; ?-54, L-43, F-55, K-44, Hs-50, D-40, Hy-53, Pd-64, Mf-47, Pa-56, Pt-60, Sc-67, Ma-65.

Although all of the scores in this test fall within normal limits there are a number of rather salient characteristics in this profile which are worthy of comment.

The depression scale is much *lower* than we usually see in patients in a mental hospital. In fact it is lower than what we usually obtain from "normal" people. This would indicate a complete lack of concern about her present condition. She apparently has no worries, no conflicts and hence very probably no insight into her difficulties. Coupled with this low depression score is also a general lack of somatic concern. There is apparently no evidence of any psychoneurotic complaints at the present time.

The schizophrenic scale is mildly elevated indicating perhaps a strong tendency to withdraw and be rather seclusive in social situations. The patient apparently experiences some difficulty in relating to other people and can perhaps be labeled as "schizoid" in nature. We also find a slight elevation in the psychopathic deviate scale. This very probably reflects her difficulties in her family situation. It is apparent from the commitment history that she has been having a considerable amount of difficulty with her husband and the high scores in psychopathic deviate may be largely due to those difficulties in inter-personal relationships.

Because all of the scales in the profile are reasonably well within normal limits we cannot make any clinical diagnosis on the basis of this profile alone. We would only indicate the evidence of strong schizoid trends coupled with some rebelliousness and a complete lack of insight.

THE INCOMPLETE SENTENCES TEST

Again the lack of insight is perhaps a salient characteristic of this test. She sees no reason why she is in the hospital and feels that everything that caused her to get into the hospital was a "lie." She shows evidence of some marital difficulties together with some hyper-suspiciousness perhaps of the paranoid variety in completing other items. Examples: "She worried because — they followed her.", "She is often at a loss when — eerie or unnatural events occur.", "My biggest problem — is my husband."

SUMMARY: We are dealing here with an individual who is very probably paranoid schizophrenic in basic structure but at present is showing no extreme characteristics of this illness. She is perhaps still in good contact with reality and has her mental illness at least verbally fairly well under control.

e.   PSYCHOLOGICAL REPORT ON MRS. JONES

8/11/59

Mary Jones is a 40 year old, white, married female who was referred for psychological testing by the Domestic Relations Counselor as a part of a custody action.

TEST DATA

The tests administered were the Minnesota Multiphasic Personality Inventory, the Shipley-Hartford Scale, and the Incomplete Sentences Test. On the Multiphasic Mrs. Jones attained a profile code of 4'62-17. The MF scores were within acceptable limits. On the Shipley Mrs. Jones attained a mental age of 20.6 on the vocabulary part of the scale, a mental age of 14.9 on the abstract part of the scale, for a total mental age of 17.9 and an estimated I.Q. of 119. There is a large discrepancy in this test with Mrs. Jones' estimated I.Q. derived from the vocabulary part of the scale being at 137 and her estimated I.Q. derived from the abstract part of the scale would be approximatly 99. This would seem to argue for either deterioration or the possibility of a schizophrenic process should be considered.

TEST INTERPRETATION

Mrs. Jones is a tall, thin, rather untidy person who laughs, smiles and giggles quite frequently and inappropriately. Her use of words is excellent and her description of her children seems to be sensitive and understanding. She verbalizes a good deal of concern for them and her descriptions of them appear to be quite accurate.

She talks about her inability to "solve the puzzles" of her husband and describes him on the one hand as being a rather brutal, punitive, rejecting and cold man and at the same time as being rather impish, humorous and sensitive. She points out that they began having marital difficulties early in their marriage and feels that her husband makes no effort to understand at all.

She considers that he has some mysterious control over her mind and considers that he has "telepathic" powers. By this she means that he is frequently able to read her thoughts and repeats back to her whole sentences that she is alleged to have previously thought of. She reports further that he is able to transmit this power to other people so that they in turn are able to read her mind or to say things that are already in her mind. She discusses a "floating brain" and considers that her husband is able to influence people far removed from him in ways that are calculated to bring her distress. In discussing these incidences, again her affect is most inappropriate, typified mostly by giggling and laughter.

Mrs. Jones has been hospitalized at Hibbing where it was considered that she showed symptoms typical of paranoid schizophrenia. She was discharged in remission and at the time of her discharge it was felt that she understood that her previous symptoms were delusional in nature. She has been seen by Dr. Leon Kaufman. In addition to this, she had been seen in the Midwest Clinic. It was considered that she had a paranoid delusional system that sometimes included her eldest daughter. Nevertheless it was felt that she sincerely cared for her children and was sensitive to them and that her husband was a rather inadequate, dependent person.

The Multiphasic at this time suggests a relatively high psychopathic deviate score that probably reflects her dissatisfaction at the disharmony in her home. There is a considerable elevation on the paranoid scale that seems to reflect this paranoid delusional system. Although the Multiphasic does not seem to be compatible with the diagnosis of paranoid schizophrenia but nevertheless there is strong evidence for paranoid thought processes. During the interview her behavior, mannerisms, facial expressions and speech content were strongly suggestive of paranoid schizophrenia. On the Sentence Completion Test the same kind of thinking is evident along with uncertainty and depression. She said such things as: "If it were possible, I would banish the telepathists"; "I like my friends but the telepathists build a wall between us"; "My biggest trouble is insecurity"; "My fears sometime force me to retreat"; "Compared with others I am an introvert; reasonably intelligent, and usually competent most of the time"; "I fail to solve the riddle of my husband."

In summary then it is felt that Mrs. Jones should be seen by Dr. Bell for psychiatric evaluation, relative to her fitness as a mother. She seems sincerely interested in her children although she points out herself that if she is not competent, then she should not have them. She seems to be actively delusional and the suggestion is that of a paranoid schizophrenic.

Allen Keene
Psychologist

f. psychiatric evaluation of mrs. jones

Hennepin County
Department of Court Services

Memorandum

To: Domestic Relations Counselor   Re: Mary Jones
                                        Date: August 11, 1959

On this date I had the opportunity to read the past history concerning Mrs. Jones and also go over Mr. Keene's psychological report. The past history reveals that Mrs. Jones has been in Hibbing State Hospital and had a diagnosis of paranoid schizophrenia. A report on Dr. Howell's examination of Mrs. Jones on November 12, 1958, revealed that although she was not actively psychotic at that time, she still showed many vestiges of her former schizophrenic condition.

The present psychological test tends to suggest a paranoid delusional system and of a very poorly functioning intellectual ability, both of which would be compatible with paranoid schizophrenia.

The clinical evaluation: Mrs. Jones readily talks in a somewhat confused, rambling, inappropriate type of affect and speech. She admits to believing in mental telepathy but is quite poorly organized and systematized in her explanation of it. She states that this mental telepathy began when she married her husband and that she feels her husband has some mysterious control over her mind by these telepathic powers. She feels that her husband is able to transmit these powers to other people and talks very vaguely about something like a floating brain. This telepathic power has occurred even when she has been out of town and at this point she states that it must be that her husband calls other people on the phone near where she is. It does not strike her as unrealistic at all that he may not know the people near her or that this just is not accepted by people at this time. Mrs. Jones states that her husband and others know what she is thinking about and that they repeat to her the things that she is thinking about before she has a chance to say them. She feels that sometimes this is done to irritate her and is quite resigned to the fact that this is going to occur for the rest of her life and thus is moderately depressed by it. She has even included her 14-year-old daughter in this delusional system, stating that her daughter at times will be able to know what she is thinking before she herself mentions it.

The history reveals that this patient is not functioning well as a mother. Her house is very poorly taken care of, her children are mainly taken care of by her 14-year-old daughter; although the patient is quite sensitive to her children's feelings, I do not feel she is capable of taking care of them at this time. The diagnosis would be that of chronic paranoid schizophrenia active at this time. The treatment prospects are poor because it is such a chronic case and secondly because the patient is fully unable to accept that this is a delusional basis at all. Parts of her delusional system are well organized but other parts of it are very inappropriate, silly and poorly organized. The possibility of further treatment for Mrs. Jones should be thought of and one treatment plan might be to have the children reside with the husband temporarily while Mrs. Jones receives therapy. I know she will be very resistive to this but yet something has to be done as it looks like she is gradually regressing more and more.

The last thing that is of concern to me is that Mrs. Jones is talking of leaving town with the children to get away from most of the telepathic powers of her husband. She, in a very rambling, ineffectual way, states that she will go to Texas, California or someplace and live with little reasoning behind it that she needs money, a job and a home for the children. Basically, she feels she can just take off and find these things as she goes along.

Aaron Bell, M.D.

g. PSYCHOLOGICAL REPORT ON MR. JONES

8/12/59

John Jones is a 42 year old, white, married male who was referred for psychological testing by the Domestic Relations Counselor as a part of a custody action.

TEST DATA

The tests administered were the Minnesota Multiphasic Personality Inventory, the Incomplete Sentences Test, the Shipley-Hartford Scale and the Bender-Gestalt. On the Multiphasic, Mr. Jones attained a profile code of 4'268. The MF score was at a T score of 53. A is at 12 and R at 18. All validity scores were within acceptable limits. On the Shipley Mr. Jones attained a mental age of 16.2 on the vocabulary part of the scale, a mental age of 18.1 on the abstract part of the scale, for a total mental age of 17.5 and an estimated I.Q. of 116. The Bender shows evidence for a very expansive approach, a great deal of immaturity, anxiety and rather poor judgment. There is some evidence for depression although the major indication seems to be a rather poor control that tends to loosen up as Mr. Jones gets more involved in situations. There is no clear evidence for organic deterioration. The major indications seem to be of emotional instability.

TEST INTERPRETATION

Mr. Jones is a very immature-appearing, petulant man who feels that testing is useless because his wife was able to become employed in spite of her performance on the Multiphasic. He points out that she has been hospitalized many times for psychiatric condition and that he considers her in the past and at the present time as being seriously disturbed. In spite of her emotional disturbance, however, he points out that he considers her to be a very intelligent person and it is to be noted that he is quite correct in this assumption.

Initially, during the interview, Mr. Jones was very nervous. He couldn't remember his age, laughed in a silly manner and generally acted quite nervous and tense. He was rejected from the service in 1942 at the age of 24 because of "high blood pressure." He was later told by someone to forget that he ever had high blood pressure or else he would die. He did this and proclaims now that he is feeling all right. The circumstances surrounding this situation should certainly be reviewed for whatever possible light it can throw upon Mr. Jones' past history of emotional adjustment.

Mr. Jones' approach was quite strongly to point out the illnesses of his wife and at the same time he attempted to portray himself as being absolutely blameless. The test suggests that Mr. Jones is a very immature, dependent, inadequate man who would generally be rather introverted. He is quite depressed at the present time but the depression is felt to be situational rather than a permanent part of his personality make-up. He is inclined to be somewhat suspicious, critical, and would be a somewhat stubborn man who would find it difficult to reconcile two points of view very smoothly. His Sentence Completion Test suggests a warm feeling toward his children. However, it is to be noted that he considers the favorite one to be the boy. There is evidence for some conflict and strain in the relationships between he and his own parents. However, generally the testing does not suggest grossly deviate patterns, the major features being immaturity, dependence and anxiety with a strong need to appear as adequate as possible. However, even in this attempt Mr. Jones has considerable anxiety. It was felt that he is interested in the children and it is not felt that his personality pattern is a grossly deviate one.

Allen Keene
Psychologist

h. REPORT FROM BIG SISTER ASSOCIATION RE SALLY

The Big Sister Association, Inc.
September 3, 1959

John Gibbs, A.C.S.W.
Court House
Minneapolis, Minnesota

Re: Sally Jones
Date of birth: 10-13-48

Dear Mr. Gibbs:

Enclosed please find a copy of our camp report concerning Sally. She is quite a fragile child. She was usually so preoccupied at meal time she would scarcely eat, meat particularly. She seemed to want to avoid meals. She was often docile, listless, inclined to stare off into space and was extremely slow in her movements.

She is a very intelligent, sensitive child who in office interviews has been stimulating and quite self-reliant.

We have been working with Sally since March, 1959. We feel we have made progress in gaining her confidence and would be happy to continue working with her.

Very truly yours,
(Miss) Carole Jorgenson
Caseworker

BIG SISTER ASSOCIATION COUNSELOR'S REPORT

August 18, 1959
Date
Sally Jones
Name of Child

I. Describe this girl briefly, as she appeared to you this camp session.

Sally was a quiet, likeable girl, always quite friendly. She wasn't particularly strong physically and this might have hindered enjoyment of some activities. She was neat about her personal appearance, although not too tidy around her bed and surrounding area. She was usually cooperative and followed most of our suggestions.

II. Describe her relationship to her cabin group. What role did she take? (Did the make-up of the group intensify this role?) Describe her relationship to campers in other cabins.

Sally wasn't too well accepted by her cabin group except for about three girls of like personalities. She wasn't a leader and usually had to be encouraged to participate in the various activities. A few of the girls were jealous of her, particularly because of her clothes. When she found some of them ripped one day, she took the situation very well, naturally disappointed, however. Several articles disappeared from her suitcase but she never accused any particular person of taking them. She usually went around by herself, either sitting in the cabin or on the steps. She seldom started activities or even participated in them unless one of us was along. When really angry she would stand up for her own rights, usually on the verge of tears.

III. What was her relationship to her counselor or counselors? Other Staff?

She particularly desired the company of the counselors or any older person. She always wanted to sit on our laps and have our arms around her. She desired this attention from the older campers also.

IV. What traits or characteristics seem to you to need attention and/or development? Describe any unusual behavior patterns.

It wasn't until the last few days that certain personality traits seemed to come out. One was evidenced when we took a hike. All of a sudden she wanted me to carry her; she started to demand that I pick her up. This was quite a surprise as it was the first time she had ever reacted in such a manner. No amount of explanation or talk would change her mind and she started to scream and cry. She soon began to complain that her legs hurt and wanted to turn back. We started singing and she soon forgot her desire to be carried.

Another situation developed while cleaning the dining-room. It was Sally's turn to help and she had always been most co-operative. But this time she positively refused to sweep, which was most unusual. She cried and cried but would not do her duties. However, she was soon persuaded that we all have our jobs, and did her remaining part.

V. What strong points in personality and behavior have you observed during this period? (Cooperation, friendliness, sense of humor, patience, etc.)

Sally was friendly to most of the girls in the cabin. She had a sense of humor not so much in evidence around the campers but with the counselors. I think one of her strong qualities was her quiet patience, especially when so many "accidents" were happening to her belongings.

VI. In what skills and areas did she display interest and/or ability — swimming, crafts, music, etc.

She especially enjoyed her swimming and also showed an interest in crafts. She wasn't too enthused about singing.

VII. Did she enjoy camp? Give examples. If you think she did not, why not? (Was she homesick? Did she make friends? Was she interested in activities?)

I'm not sure whether or not she really enjoyed camp. She never appeared to be homesick. She was by herself a lot of the time and had only one close companion.

VIII. As her counselor do you feel that she had gained or lost from this camp and group experience? Explain.

Many times it seemed that she was quite different and didn't quite fit in with the type of girls in our cabin or in the camp. I'm sure many things were a disappointment to her, particularly the destruction to her clothes. Had she been more accepted by some of the girls she might have enjoyed herself more.

IX. To what types of approach did she seem to respond best?

Sally enjoyed the love and affection of the counselors and always responded well to us. She could also be reasoned with and was capable of understanding difficult situations.

X. State here any further comments, suggestions for follow-ups.

I think probably she could be helped to develop an interest in other children and not be quite so dependent upon an older person for enjoyment and pleasure.

Carole Jorgenson
Counselor writing report

i. LETTER FROM DR. HOWELL TO MRS. JONES'S ATTORNEY[9]

Hennepin Clinic
September 16, 1959

Will Meyer, Esquire
Minneapolis, Minnesota

Dear Mr. Meyer:

Following our conversation of September 15th, I thought I would confirm in writing some of the things we discussed.

As you remember, I prefaced my thoughts with the statement that I felt it was extremely difficult to predict performance of a given individual without long experience with that given individual, and felt further that no one has had a long period of time in which to view Mrs. Jones' behavior. However, it does seem that the period of time in which she has had the sole custody of the children, and I understand that to be approximately eight months, would be a reasonably good measure of her adequacy as a mother.

I further stated that it followed sound psychiatric principles, as far as the health of the mother and the children are concerned, to work for a compromise arrangement where Mrs. Jones could have custody of the children for a trial period of about a year. It would be understood that she would have some household help, moral, spiritual, and financial assistance from members of the family, and close supervision by the Welfare Board. I further feel that if this compromise arrangement, which I favor, is approved that the husband should be enjoined from harassing this woman during the compromise period.

Sincerely,
Albert Howell, M.D.

[9] It is not clear whether Mr. Gibbs had Dr. Howell's letter at the time he prepared the report. Although the letter was part of the formal file in this case, it is possible that it might have been solicited by Mrs. Jones's attorney after he received a copy of Mr. Gibbs's report, which would normally have occurred five days prior to its filing with the court on Sept. 19, 1959. — Ed.

5. *Questions*

a. If you were the judge before whom the Jones case was to be heard and no evidence apart from that reproduced above (i.e., Mr. Gibbs's report and the underlying file) was introduced, how would you decide the case?

b. Should the judge be given the entire file on which the report was based or only the report itself? Should the report contain a recommendation as to how the judge should dispose of the case?

c. If you were a legislator in a state that presently had no provision for court-ordered custody investigations and the following statute were proposed, would you favor the statute? Could you suggest any amendments that would improve the proposal?

> In all child custody proceedings, the court shall direct the Department of Court Services (as hereinafter established) to make an appropriate investigation and to report its conclusions and recommendations to the court within sixty days.

6. *Description and Utilization of Psychological Tests*

NOYES and KOLB, MODERN CLINICAL PSYCHIATRY *131-133 (6th ed. 1963)*

BENDER-GESTALT TEST

This is a drawing test consisting of nine geometric designs chosen by Lauretta Bender from patterns first devised by Wertheimer in his study on perception. The nine patterns are presented to the patient one at a time and he is asked to copy what he sees. A frequent modification in the administration of this test is, after a short interval, to ask the patient to recall as many patterns as he can. The organization of the drawings, the page placement, the distortions and elaborations in the form of the individual drawings, any relative differences in pattern size, and other miscellaneous factors are used by an experienced interpreter to make inferences about personality functioning. Because of its dependence on visual-motor functions, the test is often helpful in detecting organic pathology. Although it was conceived of by Bender as a "maturational" test, many workers have in recent years found it more useful as a general projective technique and assign certain symbolic meanings to individual patterns. . . .

SENTENCE COMPLETION TEST

This test consists of giving the subject an incomplete sentence and of allowing him to complete it after his own fancy. It explores various life areas and attitudes of the patient about himself and toward others. Among the areas tapped are fears, worries, aspirations, and regrets.

MINNESOTA MULTIPHASIC PERSONALITY INVENTORY

This test is a questionnaire of 550 items designed to provide scores on all the more important phases of personality and personality adaptation. As such, it ranges across the areas of investigation explored in the psychiatric interview. The patient is given a box containing the questions printed on separate cards. He is asked to separate these cards into one of three categories, "true," "false," or "cannot say." The questions are distributed into some 26 different categories. From this usage, nine clinical scales have been developed. These are: hypochondriasis, depression, hysteria, psychopathic deviate, masculinity-femininity, paranoiac, psychasthenic, schizophrenic, manic.[10] This questionnaire has the special feature of additional validating scales which identify the test-taking attitude of the individual and provide an index of the degree to which the subject has been guarded and evasive, or overly frank and self-critical; a "lie scale," and finally, a set of items infrequently answered in the score directions by the standardization group and thus indicative of gross eccentricity, carelessness in respondent, or deliberate simulation.

Other studies, empirical in nature, have provided additional scales for social introversion, academic achievement, social satisfaction, and social tolerance. When used, a careful study of the item analysis in conjunction with the patterning scales may yield many unexpected insights concerning the individual.

CLINICAL USAGE OF PSYCHOLOGICAL TESTS

While the various techniques of personality diagnosis are of considerable assistance in determining whether the basic personality pattern is one of dependence, submissiveness, self-depreciation, ingratiation, arrogance, grandiosity, resentment, aggression, or other type, it must be recognized that the tests alone are not diagnostic procedures and that they do not form the basis for a formulation of the personality structure and its psychogenesis. The information secured through psychiatric examination, in addition to that yielded by the projective tests, should, among other disclosures, enable the psychiatrist to acquire a diagnostic understanding of the patient's attitudes and relationships to others. As the data from the psychiatric history, the psychiatric examination, and the projective tests are assembled and surveyed, one may discover that a meaningful pattern of the personality of the patient has been reconstructed and that its parts and features fall into place like pieces in a jigsaw puzzle. It is well to recognize that the information derived from

[10] The results are normally reported in the form of "T scores" which have the effect of adjusting the raw scores to a scale with a mean of 50 and a standard deviation of 10. See Good & Brantner, The Physician's Guide to the MMPI 8 (1961). However the process of translating the T scores into a diagnostic profile of the patient necessarily involves a large measure of judgment and discretion. — Ed.

initial interviews is seldom adequate to answer all the questions in regard to personality organization. Areas in which information is lacking and a satisfactory account may not be found for certain aspects of the personality should be noted. Here the psychological test may give information not initially available through the psychiatric history or psychiatric interview. Alone, the psychological test is not an adequate diagnostic tool.

D. INTERSTATE ASPECTS

STATE ex rel. FOX v. WEBSTER
151 So.2d 14 (Fla. Dist. Ct. App. 1963)

HORTON, J. The appellant husband was the petitioner in a habeas corpus proceeding in the Circuit Court of Dade County, Florida, in which he sought the custody of two minor children born to the parties during their marriage. This appeal is from an order discharging the writ of habeas corpus and continuing custody of the children in the appellee. We affirm.

This action arose out of the following facts. The appellee obtained a divorce from the appellant in the State of Ohio on May 18, 1960. The final decree incorporated the terms of a property settlement and custody agreement between the parties. By its terms, the appellee, inter alia, was awarded custody of the minor children of the parties on the express condition that she did not change the residence of the children without the approval of the appellant or the court. The appellant was granted reasonable rights of visitation.

On June 1, 1960, the appellee remarried, and on July 20, 1960, she filed a motion with the Ohio court requesting permission to remove the children to California. Hearing on the motion was scheduled for August 5, 1960. On July 28, 1960, the appellant filed a motion for change of custody, alleging that the appellee had never intended to live up to her undertakings in the separation agreement and had always intended to remove the children from the State of Ohio. A copy of this motion was personally served on the appellee.

On the day preceding the hearing on her motion to remove, the appellee moved to California, taking the children with her. The appellant's petition for change of custody and appellee's motion for permission to remove were heard by the Ohio court after an extensive investigation by the Department of Domestic Relations. The appellee did not make an appearance. Based upon the appellee's apparent violation of the separation agreement and the final decree of divorce, the court, on October 8, 1960, entered an order which denied her motion for permission to remove the children from Ohio and ordered her to return them to the State of Ohio on or before October 4 [sic], 1960. The order further provided:

". . . [I]n the event she fails or refuses to return said children . . . the custody of the minor children . . . be and is hereby granted to the defendant who is ordered to return the children to the jurisdiction of this court.

". . . [I]n the event the plaintiff fails or refuses to return the minor children to the jurisdiction of this court . . . the orders heretofore made for the support of said children shall be and are hereby terminated until further order of this court."

Armed with this order, the appellant followed the appellee to California where he brought a habeas corpus proceeding. The California court granted the writ solely on the basis of comity, indicating that it considered the Ohio order dated October 8, 1960 to be valid. No inquiry was made into the fitness of either party to have custody of the children. Following an unsuccessful appeal, the appellee and her husband took the children to San Juan, Puerto Rico. In July 1961, the appellee brought the children to Miami, Florida, where the appellant instituted the habeas corpus proceeding which culminated in the order appealed.

It should be noted at the outset that prior to the proceedings in the case at bar, only the final decree of divorce rendered by the Ohio court on May 18, 1960, purported to adjudicate the issue of the fitness of the parties to have custody of the children and determine where custody should be placed for the best interests and welfare of the children. The Ohio decree of October 8, 1960, was coercive in nature and, though it had the effect of changing custody, it did not purport to do so on the basis of fitness or welfare. The subsequent California decree merely placed the stamp of approval on the Ohio decree of October 8, 1960.

Though he tacitly concedes that the Ohio decree of October 8, 1960, is not ipso facto entitled to full faith and credit, the appellant contends that both it and the California decree recognizing its validity should, in this case, have been accorded full faith and credit, or at least comity. We find this contention to be without merit.

When jurisdiction vests in a custody case, the court has a duty to determine from the evidence where the minor child should be placed for its own best interest. DiGiorgio v. DiGiorgio, 153 Fla. 24, 13 So.2d 596. The court should not refuse to exercise jurisdiction or be deterred in the discharge of this duty by what it might be convinced is the bad faith of one parent in removing the child from a sister state. DiGiorgio v. DiGiorgio, supra; see also Williamson v. Osenton, 232 U.S. 619, 34 S. Ct. 442, 58 L. Ed. 758. Further, a foreign decree involving the issue of custody is required to give way to a Florida decree based on the best interests and welfare of the minor involved. This is so because decrees affecting the custody of minor children are not considered final but may be modified from time to time should the circumstances and changed conditions indicate that the best interests and welfare of the minor require a change of custody. [Citations omitted.]

As to the rule of comity, a court is not required to accord comity to a foreign custody decree but may, within its discretion, do so where practical convenience and expediency make it desirable. [Citations omitted.]

Reverting to the case sub judice, it is true that the appellee apparently acted in bad faith in ignoring the orders of the Ohio and California courts. However, it was the duty of the trial court to base its determination of where the custody of the children should reside on their best interests and welfare and not on the good or bad faith of the parties. Further, the trial court was not required to give full faith and credit to the orders of the Ohio and California courts, nor, we conclude, did it abuse its discretion in refusing to accord them comity.

Appellant further contends that the record does not support the trial court's conclusion that custody of the two minor children should continue with the appellee. We hesitate to sit in judgment of the trial court's view of the facts and since it has not been made to appear that it was guilty of an abuse of discretion in this regard, we must reject this contention.

What is said here is not intended to prejudice any rights of visitation the appellant has under the final decree of divorce or any right he might have in the future to seek a change in custody upon a showing that the best interests and welfare of the minor children require such a change. Nor do we condone the actions of the appellee. However, we must recognize the principle that in a case such as this, the paramount consideration is the best interest and welfare of the minor children.

The decree appealed is hereby affirmed.

PEARSON, C.J. (dissenting).

It is my view that a respect for law is an essential qualification for one seeking custody of a child. Bourn v. Hinsey, 134 Fla. 404, 183 So. 614, 616. I think that this record reveals a studied defiance of the courts of two states.

I would reverse.

NOTE

Results such as that reached by the Florida court have been made possible by two lines of decision in the United States Supreme Court. In May v. Anderson, 345 U.S. 528 (1953), the Court held that a decree rendered by the state of marital domicile awarding custody to the father was without proper jurisdictional foundation and hence was not entitled to full faith and credit in other states since the other spouse was not personally served in the rendering state. Justices Jackson and Reed, dissenting, felt that the child's domicile should be a sufficient basis of jurisdiction. But even if, as in Webster, the divorce court has personal jurisdiction over both parties, the original decree may still be modified by another state as a result of a subsequent change of circumstance if, as is usually the case, the decree was similarly modifiable in the rendering state. See Note, 73 Yale L.J. 134 (1963). Thus, although the Supreme Court has never squarely so ruled, the full faith and credit clause appears to be essentially a dead letter insofar as child custody decrees are concerned. See Ratner, Child Custody in a Federal System, 62 Mich. L. Rev. 795, 815 (1964), for a thorough exploration of the issues and a proposal that only the state of the child's "established home" (i.e. "the last place where the child has lived with a parent for sufficient time to become integrated into the community") should have original and modification jurisdiction in child custody cases; Ratner, Legislative Resolution of the Interstate Child Custody Problem: A Reply to Professor Currie and a Proposed Uniform Act, 38 So. Cal. L. Rev. 183 (1965).

There has been a trend, however, in the direction taken by the California court referred to in Webster, namely, to give comity recognition to foreign custody decrees, at least where there has been no significant change of circumstance since the original decree. Compare Brazy v. Brazy, 5 Wis. 2d 352, 92 N.W.2d 738 (1958), 58 Mich. L. Rev. 125 (1959). The wife was granted custody in a Wisconsin divorce proceeding and was permitted to remove the children to California subject to her duty to honor the husband's visitation rights. While visiting in California one summer, the husband was personally served in an action by the wife to obtain sole custody. Upon his return to Wisconsin, he petitioned that court to grant him exclusive custody. Pending a hearing on that petition, the Wisconsin court enjoined the wife from further proceeding in the California action, and sent her a personal notice of this order in California. Nevertheless the wife obtained the sought-for modification in California. The Wisconsin court then found that she had wilfully violated its order and instructed the clerk not to forward further alimony payments to her until she complied with the court order. The Wisconsin Supreme Court reversed, holding that both states had jurisdiction, but that since the California proceeding came first, the Wisconsin courts should have abstained. But see Stout v. Pate, 120 Cal. App. 2d 699, 261 P.2d 788 (1953), cert. denied, 347 U.S. 968 (1954), involving a Georgia divorce decree that also gave custody to the wife and visitation rights to the husband and was likewise followed by the wife's remarriage and authorized removal of the children to California. Here, however, the husband, while visiting in California, abducted the children and took them back to Georgia. The wife followed him there and brought an action in the Georgia court to gain sole custody. While the proceeding was pending, the wife obtained physical control of the children and took them back to California, where she initiated another proceeding for sole custody. The Georgia court refused to grant her subsequent request to dismiss her action there and modified its original award so as to give the husband exclusive custody. Stout v. Pate, 209 Ga. 786, 75 S.E.2d 748 (1953), cert. denied, 347 U.S. 968 (1954). The California court, though informed of the pendency of the Georgia action but apparently not of its result, rendered its own modification granting sole custody to the wife. As indicated above, the United States Supreme Court denied certiorari in both cases. See Ehrenzweig, Conflict of Laws 293 (1962), suggesting that the "clean hands" of the parties is a factor of "predominant significance" in custody proceedings.

See also Zaine v. Zaine, 265 Minn. 105, 120 N.W.2d 324 (1963). Following her third marriage to a man living in Michigan, respondent petitioned the Minnesota court which had twice previously granted her a divorce to permit her to remove the children of these two marriages to Michigan. Her first two husbands, who had been granted visitation rights, opposed the petition and requested that custody be granted to them because of the respondent's unfitness. At the hearing, respondent's counsel advised the court that she had meanwhile taken the children to Michigan. Respondent complied with the court's subsequent order to return the children, but she then sought to challenge the jurisdiction of the court on the ground that the domicile of respondent as well as the children was in Michigan. When the trial court sustained respondent's argument, the Supreme Court reversed and issued a writ of mandamus, holding that (1) the Minnesota court had continuing jurisdiction of the case following the initial custody decree[11] and (2) respondent could not oust the court of jurisdiction by her abduction of the children. Suppose respondent now again removes the children to Michigan and refuses to permit their fathers to exercise their visitation rights. What, if anything, can the latter do? Compare Rosefield v. Rosefield, 221 Cal. App. 2d 431, 34 Cal. Rep. 479 (1963) (mother and child have cause of action under Cal. Civ. Code §49 against grandfather who aided his son in abducting the child; implication that father might also be liable if there had been an outstanding court order against him).

[11] But compare Parks v. Parks, — Iowa —, 135 N.W.2d 625 (1965) (continuing jurisdiction of divorce court terminates upon death of custodial parent; in subsequent dispute between noncustodial parent and surviving spouse of custodial parent, neither of whom resided in divorce forum, that state lacks jurisdiction and must therefore abstain).

CHAPTER 10

Economic Consequences of Dissolution

A. SUPPORT AND PROPERTY RIGHTS OF THE SPOUSES

BRANDT v. BRANDT
36 Misc. 2d 901, 233 N.Y.S.2d 951 (1962)

MARKOWITZ, J. The parties in this separation action were married on July 29, 1934. There are two children of the marriage, a son who is now 26 years of age and a daughter of 13. Sometime prior to October 9, 1961, defendant obtained a Mexican decree of divorce from plaintiff, and on that date went through a marriage ceremony with a person he currently holds out to be his wife. Plaintiff thereupon obtained an adjudication from this court declaring that she was still the wife of the defendant and that the purported divorce was of no force and effect. In light of these events, plaintiff's right to a decree in this action was not challenged by defendant at the trial. The entire testimony and evidence introduced related almost exclusively to the question of fixation of alimony. Even in this regard there was little disagreement as to the material facts.

Except for the first few months of the marriage when the parties resided in the District of Columbia, they lived either in east side luxury apartments or in a cottage on an estate in Sands Point, Long Island, belonging to plaintiff's parents. They intermittently employed household help — sometimes having a full-time staff of three, other times utilizing only part-time help. Their children were sent to the finest private schools and they almost always maintained two automobiles.

This standard of living is far from commensurate with defendant's earning record, and can only be explained by the fact that help was received from other sources, particularly plaintiff's family. If any occupational description can be tagged onto the defendant it is that of "insurance agent." He was set up as such by his then father-in-law early in his marriage with the idea that he could establish himself with the impetus of business sent to him by his father-in-law and his associates. He obviously did not apply himself in this vocational pursuit, and again with his father-in-law's intercession, he tried the advertising field as an account executive, with almost guaranteed accounts but apparently would not convert these advantages into a profitable career. There is testimony that for a time he tried going into the business of operating a bowling alley, speculating in oil leases, and promoting a certain type of toy, all to no avail, as none of such ventures showed any profitable results. He claimed that he spent the major portion of each day for several years in search of new insurance clients and was chauffeured in such a venture by the woman whom he claims to be his current wife. He claims that his current income and income for many years past is only nominal and has been solely from insurance renewals, which did not require any current services or work on his part. He maintains a token office for his insurance business which he visits "once or twice a year." Currently he claims his occupation is that of a "farm supervisor" managing the Turkey Hollow Farm in Amenia, New York, which belongs to his "current" wife and which is where they both live. He says he hopes to put it eventually on a sustaining basis, but thus far derives no income from it. The court finds it incredulous that the amount of effort the defendant asserts he made in attempting to earn a living should produce absolutely no results.

His personal finances, however, did not deter him from living even up to the present in what must be characterized as playboy fashion. Expensive restaurants, night clubs and theatres, Jaguar automobiles, hunting, fishing and tropical vacation trips, golfing, high-stake poker games and even dating, while living with plaintiff, are but a few symbols of the life he has accustomed himself to. Even his current existence, which he tries to pass off as that of an impoverished farm worker, can more accurately be described as that of a country gentleman. He goes "cubbing" with the Milbrook Hunt Club which he describes as riding with hounds "in the nature of a fox hunt" and engages in the sport of "beagling" which Webster describes as hunting with beagle hounds, but which he says "is in the way of being a walk through the country following beagles, who are supposed to chase rabbits." These activities are here described not for the purpose of ridicule or condemnation but rather to show that defendant's activities are not those of the average man but of the wealthy, that his contacts are not with ordinary people but with the influential, that the circles he has always travelled in were such that had he seriously applied himself to any of the callings he undertook he would have met with [considerable] financial success. The court observed him during the trial to be a poised, suave, cultured, self-assured and fashionably well-dressed individual with an air of the educated and worldly wise, having varied interests extending even to creative writing and producing for television.

Accordingly, the court finds that plaintiff is entitled to judgment on her causes of action grounded on abandonment, nonsupport and adultery. A further cause of action based on cruelty was withdrawn at the trial. There remains only the question of alimony.

Alimony is an award by the court upon considerations of equity and public policy which is founded upon the obligation which grows out of the marriage relation that the husband must support his wife and family. This support must be measured by the husband's ability to earn a living (De Brauwere v. De Brauwere, 203 N.Y. 460), and by the manner in which the parties are accustomed to live. (Tirrell v. Tirrell, 232 N.Y. 224.) This measure of ability to support, however, is not based on what an irresponsible husband deigns to earn, but what he is potentially able to earn in light of his established physical and mental capabilities. (See Vought v. Vought, 22 Misc 2d 356.)

Defendant in the instant case has maintained a standard of gracious living, leaving to others the execution of responsibilities he undertook. While he idles, plaintiff is forced to live in her mother's apartment sharing a room with her daughter. The fact that plaintiff's mother is well to do is no factor here. It has been established that plaintiff's personal resources consist of an allowance for clothing, gratuitously given to her by her family since she was 16 years of age.

The figure of the penniless playboy might make an amusing and colorful caricature in the fanciful folklore of Hollywood movies, and might be acceptable within the established mores of the so-called "international set." He is not so amusing and acceptable in real life, where he has assumed the obligations of husband and father but refuses to live up to them. It is not the function of a court, not even a court of equity, to dictate to a party before it the standards of morality he should pursue. However, where a moral attitude amounts to a deliberate disregard of legal obligations, the court, under such circumstances, can and must see to it that the legal obligations are enforced.

In assessing defendant's earning potential, it is the opinion of the court that with proper application he is capable of earning sufficient moneys to enable him to maintain himself and also to adequately provide for his wife and infant child as hereinafter provided. The court has also considered the fact that the person he regards as his current wife thus far has never been supported by him and undoubtedly does not need his support and that his own personal needs are apparently absorbed in the overhead of Turkey Hollow Farm. The sum of $200 a week is awarded for the maintenance of his wife and support of their daughter. Counsel fees, in addition to the amount heretofore awarded, are awarded in the sum of $1300, payable within 20 days of entry of judgment. Custody of the infant child is awarded to the plaintiff, with visitation rights to the defendant as agreed upon by the parties.

MacDONALD v. MacDONALD
120 Utah 573, 236 P.2d 1066 (1951)

CROCKETT, J. Plaintiff brought this action for a divorce; defendant counterclaimed for separate maintenance; her counsel asked at the trial to amend to ask for a divorce also. Judgment was for plaintiff, defendant appeals.

The numerous points she relies on for reversal fall generally under these two main contentions: (1) that the evidence does not support the judgment granting the plaintiff a divorce, but to the contrary requires judgment for her on her counterclaim; and (2) that the decree was inequitable and unjust to her. . . .

The parties married at Oakland, California, June 15, 1922; they have one child, Barbara Ann, age 25, who is now in a convent. About 1941, while the parties were still residing in California, the defendant began to drink intoxicating liquor excessively. By the time the parties moved to Salt Lake City in 1946, her drinking had gone to such excesses as to present a considerable family problem. In 1948, a divorce action was filed by plaintiff which was thereafter dismissed and the parties reconciled. In June, 1949, the defendant spent a short period in the State hospital for observation and was released as being without psychosis. The trial court found that she had been guilty of habitual drunkenness for a period of at least four years; the evidence supports that finding.

The fact that the 1948 complaint was dismissed and the parties reconciled does not condone her prior conduct so as to wipe it out from consideration at the time of this trial; where the defendant's misconduct is resumed, the law permits the injured party to assert all the prior misconduct, as well as that occurring subsequent to the condonation. . . .

The assets possessed by the parties were as follows: Their home, valued at $13,000, less a $6000 mortgage, net value $7000; household furniture and equipment valued at $2000; 1949 Hudson automobile valued at $1400, less a lien of $212; a bank account of $6948.25 in defendant's name — which was the balance of an inheritance of $8000 which she had received in 1950. Defendant also has an expectancy in the estate of her mother who was 82 years of age at the time of the trial. The plaintiff has been employed by the Chicago, Milwaukee, St. Paul & Pacific Railroad Company at a good salary for many years; he is at present general agent for that company at Salt Lake City at a gross salary of $481.80 per month, or a net of $387.56 after all deductions. The court awarded the defendant all of the assets except the automobile; ordered the plaintiff to pay her attorney's fees in the sum of $250 and $378.10 payments in arrears. Except for the award of the assets just mentioned, the court made no allowance to the defendant for alimony except the sum of $10 per year which he awarded as a nominal sum. He stated,

"Such assets are sufficient to care for defendant . . . and should keep her in such fashion that she will not become a charge upon public authorities. Should defendant's financial condition become such that she is in danger of becoming a public charge, the duty of support should fall upon the plaintiff and not upon the public authorities . . . ."

Defendant complains that the court abused its discretion in not awarding her substantial alimony; in not imposing a higher duty upon plaintiff than merely to see that she does not become a public charge. She states pointedly,

"After 29 years of marriage which almost totally wrecked my life physically and mentally, how magnanimous of the court to decree that I may use my own money to live on."

She makes the valid contention that where there are sufficient assets and income to do so, she is entitled to be provided for according to her station in life and as demanded by her condition of health and lack of ability to work; that she should not be cast aside in her helpless condition to "sink or swim" or depend on others. With this argument, we agree. . . .

The trial judge awarded the divorce to the plaintiff and we do not question the correctness of his decision in that regard. Although the question of fault is not by any means to be entirely disregarded in determining the rights to property and alimony, it is settled that a spouse against whom a divorce is granted may under some circumstances be awarded adequate alimony. Alldredge v. Alldredge, 119 Utah 504, 229 P.2d 681. However, there is very little likelihood that all of the fault was on one side. There is evidence that the plaintiff associated freely with another woman; that he has seen her seven or eight times a month; that he drank with her and took her to parties; that he went to her apartment and she to his; and that he bought her a gift. Just how this conduct on his part is related by way of cause or effect to Mrs. MacDonald's excessive drinking we are not able to divine. . . .

From the point of view of adjusting property rights to best serve the social needs of the parties involved, a spouse who is at fault may be in greater need of alimony than a more innocent one. This case is an excellent illustration. If Mrs. MacDonald were not suffering from the disability of uncontrollable alcoholism, she might readjust her life, seek gainful employment and assist in sustaining herself. She is in such a sorry plight that both parties conceded that she cannot be expected to do so. It certainly does not comport with good conscience to turn such an unfortunate individual out to fend for herself after having given 29 years to this marriage, good or bad as her conduct may have been.

The problem of attempting to do justice to parties in a divorce action as to the division of property and the awarding of alimony is undoubtedly one of the most perplexing situations ever to confront a court. The longer the period of marriage, the greater the difficulties. It would be a wise judge indeed who could accurately apportion the weight of all factors and arrive at the one correct solution, if there be such. The problem is of such a nature as not to be susceptible of solution by any exact formula; indeed the authorities frequently say that for that reason each case must be determined upon its own facts. . . .

[The court then proceeds to enumerate a number of relevant factors such as the situation of the parties prior to marriage, their respective contributions (both tangible and intangible) to the marriage, their present needs and resources, etc.]

If we keep clearly in mind the fact that the decree was based upon the conditions which existed at the time of the divorce, we do not see that the decree is unjust to the defendant. The court awarded her much the larger share of the family assets, and in view of the fact that she had $6900 in cash immediately available, saw no necessity to decree that she be paid substantial alimony immediately. True, this cash is hers, but it was properly taken into account in appraising the entire financial situation of the parties and adjusting their property rights. Although the plaintiff does have a very good income, he was at the time of trial in debt to the extent of about $400 payments in arrears; $200 on his car; $250 to defendant's attorneys and whatever his own attorneys' fees were.

In making the decree awarding defendant only the nominal sum of $10 per year alimony, which was based on the then circumstances, Judge Van Cott expressly recited that it was for the purpose of preserving her right to alimony and directed that if danger of dependence appeared, the burden of her support would fall upon plaintiff and not upon others. . . . This may entail a future application to the court but that is what is contemplated by the decree.   Defendant expresses a number of forebodings of future possibilities: the plaintiff's retirement, remarriage, illness of the parties, etc. "Sufficient unto the day is the evil thereof."   If there is a substantial change in circumstances, a review and revision of the decree to meet them may be had.   The court's decree works no serious injustice as conditions now exist. . . .

HENRIOD, J. (concurring).   I concur, although reluctantly as to the alimony award.   It is difficult to yield to an award of $10 a year to a wife, even though she may have assets of her own sufficient to see her through for a limited time.   Such an award fails to anticipate the possibility that her husband may have died during or near the time of exhaustion of her assets.   Here the better part of appellant's life has been devoted to her husband, and she now arrives, in an atmosphere of misfortune, at a bourn of incapacity with an uncertain future, where current monthly contributions from the husband could aid in insulating against the day when this appellant well might need assistance most. However, the decision here leaves the door open for future application to the court for assistance if the respondent is available and able to contribute.

McDONOUGH, J.   I concur in the opinion of Mr. Justice CROCKETT and also in the observations of Mr. Justice HENRIOD relative to the alimony award.

NOTE

From the vantage point of logic it may be difficult to understand why once a marriage has been terminated by divorce, the husband continues to be responsible for the wife's support.   Initially, permanent alimony was a discretionary grant of support awarded to the wife in a divorce a mensa et thoro (see pages 172-173 supra).[1]   Since this decree did not dissolve the marriage, recognition of the husband's continued duty to support the wife was not without basis in logic.   Among the factors looked to by the ecclesiastical courts in making the award were the financial ability of the husband, the needs of the wife, and the relative fault of

[1] Traditionally the award encompasses not only the wife's support needs but also her attorney's fees.   See Annot., 56 A.L.R.2d 13, 115 (1957).   It should be noted that a contingent fee agreement between the wife and her attorney is generally regarded as against public policy.   See, e.g., Committee on Professional and Judicial Ethics, Opinion 72, Mich. State B.J., May 1959, p. 95.

Permanent alimony should be distinguished from temporary alimony (often called alimony pendente lite).

the spouses for the marital breakup (a "guilty" wife was not entitled to alimony since the husband's duty of support lasted only so long as the wife cohabited with him or lived apart from him through no fault on her part).

The transfer of these doctrines to the modern divorce a vinculo matrimonii was accomplished without much apparent thought.[2] In the United States today, alimony is a creature of statute,[3] but since the typical statute simply gives the trial judge authority to make such an award as "the circumstances of the case may warrant," [4] the judges must of necessity develop their own guides to aid them in the discharge of their statutory discretion. Generally speaking, they have tended to look uncritically to the rules fashioned by the ecclesiastical courts in a different context and a different time.

But there have been gradual departures from the common law doctrines. As indicated by the MacDonald case, in some jurisdictions even a guilty wife can now obtain alimony. See Mueller v. Mueller, 44 Cal. 2d 527, 282 P.2d 869, 9 Vand. L. Rev. 104 (1955); Annot., 34 A.L.R.2d 313 (1954). Concomitantly the wife's separate assets and earning capacity are now generally taken into account (albeit not always expressly) in making the award. See, e.g., Tenn. Code Ann. §36-821 (1955); compare Tonjes v. Tonjes, 24 Wis. 2d 120, 128 N.W.2d 446 (1964) (where H granted divorce against W, W required to use income from own resources to meet support, but abuse of discretion for trial court to require her also to utilize corpus).[5] Husbands are sometimes permitted, under appropriate circumstances, to collect alimony from wives. See, e.g., Annot., 66 A.L.R.2d 880 (1959). And a few states, recognizing the practical indistinguishability between divorce and annulment (see pages 174-178 supra), permit an award of alimony incident to an annulment. See, e.g., N.Y. Dom. Rel. Law §236.

In spite of some of these changes — or perhaps because of them — there remains considerable controversy over the proper scope of alimony in modern times.[6] Compare the following:

[2] In legal separation cases like Brandt the common law doctrines may be more readily applicable.

[3] Almost all states permit the award of permanent alimony. A notable exception is Pennsylvania.

[4] See, e.g., Colo. Rev. Stat. Ann. §46-1-5(1)(a) (1964). But compare N.C. Gen. Stat. §50-14 (1950) (alimony limited to one third of H's income).

[5] It is generally held that a wife must disclose her assets. Phillips v. Phillips, 1 App. Div. 2d 393, 150 N.Y.S.2d 646 (1956).

[6] Alimony appears to be waived in a large percentage of the cases. See Quenstedt & Winkler, What Are Our Domestic Relations Judges Thinking?, Monograph No. 1, A.B.A. Sect. of Fam. L., July 1965, p. 3 (one of the judges estimated that waiver occurs in 90 per cent of the cases). See also page 936 infra for further data on the incidence of alimony awards. And see page 946 infra concerning the possible invalidity of such a waiver. The reason for this may be that waiver is often the price exacted by the husband for his noncontest of the divorce. Also, in many cases, property divisions or child support are substituted for alimony. A wife who waives alimony initially may not be able to claim any later. Warner v. Warner, 219 Minn. 59, 17 N.W.2d 58 (1945). But see Blaufarb v. Blaufarb, 9 App. Div. 2d 86, 191 N.Y.S.2d 785 (1959), 26 Brooklyn L. Rev. 308 (1960).

a. Astor v. Astor, 89 So.2d 645 (Fla. 1956) (twenty-six-year-old girl who had earned $65 per week prior to her six-week-long marriage to John Jacob Astor, a multimillionaire, awarded $250 per week support and $12,500 attorney's fees).[7]

b. Doyle v. Doyle, 5 Misc. 2d 4, 7, 158 N.Y.S.2d 909, 912 (1957):

If a woman has contributed however indirectly to her husband's career and helped to increase his substance she may rightfully be regarded as entitled to a share of his gain. . . .

But the same considerations do not operate in the case of a young woman who in all but form has remained alien to her husband's interest. Why should ex-wives and separated women seek a preferred status in which they shall toil not, neither shall they spin. Alimony was originally devised by society to protect those without power of ownership or earning resources. It was never intended to assure a perpetual state of secured indolence. It should not be suffered to convert a host of physically and mentally competent women into an army of alimony drones.

c. N.H. Rev. Stat. Ann. §458:19 (1955):

Upon a decree of nullity or divorce, the court may restore to the wife all or any part of her estate, and may assign to her such part of the estate of her husband, or order him to pay such sum of money, as may be deemed just, provided that in cases in which no children are involved, or in which the children have reached the age of majority, said order shall be effective for not more than three years from the date thereof, but such order may be renewed, modified or extended if justice requires for periods of not more than three years at a time . . .[8]

d. Le Roy-Lewis v. Le Roy-Lewis, [1955] P. 1, 3 (1954), [1954] 3 W.L.R. 549, 551:

It has been suggested that because she was working before the marriage and is still young, and as there are no children of the marriage, she ought at once to go back into the position she was in before the marriage and start earning her living, with as far as I can see only one object, to reduce the amount of money which the husband should pay to her, his wife. I do not accept that view. She may have been lucky, or, at any rate thought that she was lucky at the time, in marrying someone who brought about an improvement in her financial and possibly her social position; but it has been through no fault of hers that their married life together has come to an end, and I see no reason whatever why the wife should go back to earning in order to reduce the husband's liability to maintain her. . . .

[7] See also Royal Commission on Marriage and Divorce, Report 1951-1955, Cmd. No. 9678, par. 495 (1956) (so long as H can afford it, W should be permitted to continue the same standard of living that she enjoyed during the marriage).

[8] But see id. at par. 492, recommending against a limited duration for alimony awards.

In general, see Symposium, Alimony, 6 Law & Contemp. Prob. 183 (1939); Paulsen, Support Rights and Duties between Husband and Wife, 9 Vand. L. Rev. 709 (1956); Brown, Family Maintenance and Its Enforcement in the United States, 13 Int. & Comp. L.Q. 139 (1964).

ANDERSON v. ANDERSON
68 N.W.2d 849 (N.D. 1955)

Morris, J. This is an action for divorce instituted on October 5, 1953, by the plaintiff against the defendant upon the grounds of wilful neglect and extreme cruelty. The plaintiff also sought custody of a three year old daughter born to the marriage.

The defendant answered denying the allegations of the complaint and counterclaimed for a divorce in his behalf upon the ground that the plaintiff had committed adultery with two men named in the complaint and asked that custody of the daughter be awarded to him.

The trial court made findings of fact setting forth in some detail plaintiff's conduct with respect to one of these men from which he drew the conclusion of law that the plaintiff had been guilty of the commission of adultery. He awarded custody of the child to the defendant and decreed that the defendant be divorced from the plaintiff. The plaintiff does not question these findings. The trial court also decreed that the defendant pay the plaintiff the sum of $2000 "as and for her services and property settlement in full."

The defendant appealed from the judgment entered pursuant to the court's conclusions of law and demanded a trial de novo. He challenges the award of $2000 to the plaintiff. This award constitutes the only question in issue on this appeal. . . .

The parties were married June 20, 1949. The defendant was then a bachelor owning and operating a farm of 240 acres, all but 35 acres being under cultivation. The plaintiff had previously been married and divorced. She brought to the home three children by her former marriage, a teen aged daughter and two boys aged about eight and six years respectively. The children were not adopted by the defendant but joined the family circle. The daughter went to Billings, Montana, in the spring of 1951. The boys remained on the farm until some weeks after the plaintiff left and went to Billings on February 14, 1953. Testimony concerning the circumstances surrounding her departure is conflicting. The plaintiff claims the defendant forced her to leave. The defendant testified that she left voluntarily to go to the home of her daughter who was then married and was about to be confined. The defendant's version appears to be the more reasonable one and the trial court so expressed himself in his memorandum opinion. Plaintiff took Jane, the baby daughter of the parties, with her. On February 17, 1953, she wrote the defendant as follows:

> "I am writing to let you know that Jane is just fine and everything is O.K. here and how is the Boy's come along by now hope they are O.K."

The relationship between the parties had been far from cordial for over a year due to the plaintiff's indiscreet actions with respect to other men.

On February 19 the plaintiff wrote a friend stating that she had a job in Billings and liked it fine. She said she came on the train and would have stopped but didn't have time and "I had to come at once and I couldn't even tell O.B. so I don't know how he will feel about it." She also said:

> "I am going to stay and after while I am comeing after the car and the too Boys. I share miss them and I like it hear just fine and I will like it better when O.B. get here for I share miss him like everything."

O.B. was a middle aged neighbor and a source of part of the difficulty between the plaintiff and her husband. O.B. was later supplanted in the plaintiff's affections by one C.M.L. who is the man with whom the trial court found the plaintiff committed adultery. Plaintiff's language as well as her conduct was indecent. She frequently used a crude but not uncommon expression attributing canine ancestry to the objects of her wrath. The record discloses that in October 1953 the plaintiff and her two boys were occupying a small apartment in Billings with a man who had two small daughters. This is the man referred to in the record as C.M.L. At the time of the trial in December 1953 the plaintiff testified she was supporting herself and two boys by working as a dishwasher in a Billings cafe.

The evidence clearly shows that the plaintiff voluntarily left the home of the parties and thereafter chose to live with a paramour rather than return to her lawful husband. It is the rule that under such circumstances a wife is not entitled to permanent alimony. [Citations omitted.] The plaintiff contends that this rule has no application to the award made by the trial court in this case. It is pointed out that Section 14-0524, NDRC 1943, provides that:

> "When a divorce is granted, the court shall make such equitable distribution of the real and personal property of the parties as may seem just and proper, ..."

It is argued that the court made the award of $2000 to the plaintiff "as and for her services and property settlement in full" and that it was just and proper that he do so under the provisions of Section 14-0524, supra.

In Ruff v. Ruff, 78 N.D. 775, 52 N.W.2d 107, 108, Syllabus Paragraph 4, we said:

> "In acting pursuant to the provisions of Section 14-0524, NDRC 1943, providing that 'When a divorce is granted, the court shall make such equitable distribution of the real and personal property of the parties as may seem just and proper,' the court may consider the respective ages of the parties; their earning ability; the conduct of the parties during the marriage and its duration; their station in

life; their health and physical condition; the necessities of the parties and their circumstances, financial and otherwise; the value and income-producing capacity of the property, and whether it was accumulated before or after marriage, and the efforts and attitude of the parties toward its accumulation."

The question here is not whether the court had power under the statute to make the award but whether under the facts and circumstances he abused his discretion in doing so.

In Heath v. Heath, 103 Fla. 1071, 138 So. 796, 797, the court upheld an award to an adulterous wife where it appeared that the wife's services and her invested capital contributed to the value of the husband's business properties. But in doing so, the court said:

"Such an allowance is not alimony and should never be made in any case unless shown to be warranted by special facts and circumstances which support a finding of an equity in the husband's property arising in favor of the wife from contributions of funds and services made by her toward its accumulation over, above, and beyond the performance of ordinary marital duties toward the husband."

[The court then points out that the plaintiff contributed no extraordinary services here; nor could the services performed by her two boys enhance her claim.]

The record contains no evidence of the value of defendant's property or the amount of his annual income. It shows that at the time of the marriage the defendant owned a farm of 240 acres on which there was a house he had started to build in 1948. The size of the house is not given. At the time of trial he still owned the same amount of real estate. He had nine head of cattle acquired or raised after the marriage. He owned some farm machinery with his brother. The size of the unit would indicate a farm income somewhat less than the average. . . .

The plaintiff brought to the home her daughter and two sons by a former marriage, where they became a part of the family. The daughter left and married some two years later. The boys stayed with the defendant until several weeks after the plaintiff left. There is no contention that she brought anything with her except her family. She still has the family but her responsibility has been lightened in the intervening time by the marriage of her daughter and the growth of her sons. On the other hand, the responsibility of the defendant has been materially increased. He now has a small daughter to care for and educate. His mother is assisting him in meeting that responsibility by assuming the duties of housekeeping and caring for the child in his home. It would seem unjust and improper that his responsibility should be further increased by requiring him to pay any sum to the plaintiff as or in lieu of a division of property. The judgment appealed from is modified by striking [the $2000 award].

NOTE

1. Many states have statutory provisions similar to that of North Dakota giving the divorce court discretion to make an equitable division of the individually owned property of the spouses.[9] But frequently neither the enabling statute nor the awarding decree differentiates clearly between property division and support payments. In some states the wife's separate property is included in the pool of divisible property only to the extent that it was derived from the husband. See, e.g., Wis. Stat. Ann. §247.26 (Supp. 1965). Even where there is no explicit statutory authority for property divisions, some courts have asserted an inherent equitable power. See, e.g., Johnson v. Johnson, 137 Mont. 11, 349 P.2d 310, 21 Mont. L. Rev. 230 (1960) (W had special equity on account of money advanced to H's business).[10]

2. Should the wife be entitled to an award only where her contributions to the marriage were "over, above, and beyond the performance of ordinary marital duties"? Compare Farrand v. Farrand, 246 Iowa 488, 67 N.W.2d 20 (1955) (wife who materially helped her husband to acquire and operate hotel is entitled to one half of its value on divorce, in addition to alimony). Is the purpose behind giving the wife some of the husband's property different from that underlying an award of alimony to her? Should the considerations applicable to each of the two types of award be the same, as the court's quotation from the prior North Dakota case of Ruff v. Ruff implies? Compare the Note on Matrimonial Property Regimes, page 317 supra. See also Daggett, Division of Property upon Dissolution of the Marriage, 6 Law & Contemp. Prob. 225 (1939), criticizing the flexible, discretionary rule for property divisions that prevails in most common law states and praising the 50-50 split made, regardless of fault, under Louisiana law, albeit not in some of the other community property states (see, e.g., page 656 supra).

3. Whatever the conceptual differences between support payments and property divisions, important practical consequences turn on this distinction. If and only if the payments are for support, they may be subject to modification (or indeed may be terminated altogether) upon a change of circumstances such as the death or remarriage of the wife (page 916 infra); they will be enforceable by contempt proceedings (page 924 infra); they will not be dischargeable by bankruptcy;[11] and they may qualify for special federal income tax treatment (page 956 infra).

---

[9] The partition of any jointly held property involves materially different considerations. See 2 American Law of Property, pt. 6 (Casner ed. 1952). Also to be distinguished are private agreements of the parties (sometimes confusingly referred to as property settlements). See Chapter 11.

[10] Such equitable power to decree a division of the spouses' jointly accumulated property is sometimes asserted also in the case of an annulment, where statutory authority is generally lacking. But compare the New Hampshire statute, page 909 supra.

[11] 11 U.S.C.A. §35(a)(2) (Supp. 1964). Compare Yarus v. Yarus, 178 Cal. App. 2d 190 (1960) (property settlement held discharged in bankruptcy).

This is a basic distinction that will recur throughout this chapter and the next. It assumes particular importance in the community property states where a divorced spouse's principal claim is on account of his or her rights in the community.

In view of these drastically different consequences it becomes important to determine what portion of an undesignated payment or series of payments represents support and what portion is on account of rights in the marital property. To judge the payments by their predominant characteristics often involves an element of circularity. Thus, if payments are to terminate on the wife's death, a court may conclude that they must be on account of support since this is a common characteristic of alimony. But obviously there is no such necessary relationship. Other courts have said that one must look at what the wife gave up. But in most cases she gives up both support and property claims. Some courts undoubtedly determine the character of the payments by the end result sought to be achieved. See, e.g., Lacy, Family Law, 29 N.Y.U.L. Rev. 720, 730 (1954), pointing out that in spite of a Florida statute expressly making all support orders modifiable, the Florida Supreme Court in a series of cases substantially emasculated the statute by treating the payments as a property division whenever nonmodifiability was desired. In the last analysis, although the labels attached are clearly not dispositive, the best assurance of achieving the results desired by the parties lies along the line of getting the divorce court to make a specific allocation between support and property rights that corresponds to the realities of the particular situation.[12]

WARREN v. WARREN
218 Md. 212, 146 A.2d 34 (1958)

BRUNE, C.J. The appellee wife was granted a decree of divorce a vinculo matrimonii on August 13, 1956, on the ground of adultery against the appellant husband. The appellant was required, by stipulation incorporated in the divorce decree and subject to the further order of the Court, to pay to the appellee the sum of twenty-five dollars a week as permanent alimony and fifteen dollars a week for the support of their minor child. This is an appeal from an order passed on February 28, 1958, dismissing appellant's petition for modification of the alimony and support portions of the decree.

One month after the divorce, the appellant married the co-respondent, who was then pregnant with his child, and since that time they have had a second child. It is conceded that the appellant's income is substantially the same now as it was when the alimony and support payments were originally agreed to and incorporated in the decree. This appeal therefore raises, first, the issue of whether his remarriage and the birth of two children in and of themselves constituted such a change of

[12] The desirability of distinguishing clearly between support and property rights underscores the importance of a negotiated separation agreement as a means of settling the rights of the parties. See Chapter 11.

circumstances as to justify a modification of the decree, and, secondly, whether the trial court abused its discretion in refusing to allow evidence to be introduced to show the various demands presently being made upon appellant's income. We will consider these questions in the order mentioned.

It is not within the province of this Court, in considering a petition for modification, to review the propriety or sufficiency of the original award. Our inquiry is limited to determining whether or not the Chancellor was clearly in error in finding that the appellant has shown no such change in the circumstances of the parties since the alimony and support decree as would warrant its reduction. Langrall v. Langrall, 145 Md. 340, 345, 125 A. 695.

The appellant admitted that his income has remained substantially the same since the divorce, and he offered no evidence to controvert the appellee's contention that a reduction in payments would work a hardship upon her and the infant child of the parties. He alleged that "circumstances have now arisen which render it impossible without great injury to himself and to those to whom he owes a natural and legal obligation to continue payments in this sum"; but the only "circumstances" he showed were his second marriage and the birth of two children.

[The court then reviews some of the Maryland decisions.]

The appellant cites a long list of cases in other jurisdictions in which remarriage and the birth of children were factors which were taken into consideration in determining whether or not a modification of the decree should be granted. He admits, however, that in none of these cases did the court hold that remarriage and the birth of children in and of themselves entitled the former husband to any relief from the payment of alimony. . . .

In Newburn v. Newburn, 210 Iowa 639, 231 N.W. 389, 391, the court said: "Perhaps a case might arise in which the facts and circumstances shown in favor of the husband against whom a judgment for alimony exists, would make proper a consideration of his remarriage, in the adjustment of equities on an application to modify the decree." However, the very next sentence of the opinion reads: "There is some diversity in the holding of courts in other jurisdictions upon this question. All, however, agree that the remarriage of the husband, together with the obligations thereby assumed, will not alone present such change in the circumstances of the parties as to justify a modification of the decree."

We conclude . . . that in the absence of changed financial or other conditions affecting one or the other or both of the former spouses or their child, the remarriage of the husband and the birth of a child or children to him and his new wife are not sufficient cause for the reduction of alimony to the first wife or of support for a minor child of the first marriage.

The appellant urges, however, that the trial judge erred in refusing to allow him to introduce evidence "to show from the factual standpoint what this man's financial position is." The court declined to admit such testimony, and counsel then made a proffer of evidence in which he itemized appellant's expenses and compared their total to his "take-home" pay. In view of what we have said above, and in view of the fact that the proffer showed no substantial change in the appellant's financial position, we agree with the learned trial judge that even if all of the facts proffered were proven the appellant would fail to present a sufficient reason for a reduction in alimony. It was therefore proper not to admit such testimony.

The appellant now contends that if he had been allowed to present all his evidence he might have been able to prove to the court's satisfaction that the appellee either had other sources of income or would have been able to earn additional income by working. No such facts were alleged in appellant's petition. His pleadings stated only that payment to appellee and her child could be reduced "without grave injury to them." There are authorities which hold that a party seeking modification of an alimony award must set forth in his pleadings such facts and circumstances as will, if established by proof, entitle him to the relief he desires and that mere claims and conclusions stated in general terms are insufficient. [Citations omitted.] We do not, however, reach that question, since the appellant made no effort or proffer of evidence whatsoever in the trial court to support any such contentions. Therefore this matter is not properly before us for consideration on appeal. Maryland Rule 885.

Order affirmed, with costs.

NOTE

As indicated by the court in Warren, support decrees are normally modifiable where one of the parties shows that there has been a material change of circumstance that was not taken into account in the original award. But see page 953 infra concerning decrees based on an agreement of the parties; see also Kan. Stat. Ann. §60-1610(c) (1964) (alimony may not be increased or accelerated without the obligor's consent). Remarriage of the husband is generally not regarded as a sufficient change of circumstance. See, e.g., Quenstedt & Winkler, What Are Our Domestic Relations Judges Thinking?, Monograph No. 1, A.B.A. Sect. of Fam. L., July 1965, p. 5 (80 per cent of 500 domestic relations officials indicated that husband's remarriage and assumption of new support responsibilities insufficient to warrant modification). But compare Mark v. Mark, 248 Minn. 446, 80 N.W.2d 621 (1957). The rule is otherwise where it is the wife who remarries. In this situation a number of states (sometimes by statute) automatically terminate a support order; in many others, such an event presents a prima facie case for modification. See Annot., 48 A.L.R.2d 270 (1956); Bean v. Bean, 86 R.I. 334, 134 A.2d 146 (1957), 38 B.U.L. Rev. 152 (1958) (modification granted but arrears accrued since W's remarriage unaffected).

Not infrequently the decree itself provides that the support payments will be terminable upon the remarriage of the wife. Suppose the wife goes through another marriage ceremony but the marriage is later annulled. Compare Gaines v. Jacobsen, 308 N.Y. 218, 124 N.E.2d 290 (1954) (although New York originally held that first husband's support obligation would be revived upon annulment of remarriage, subsequent enactment of statute authorizing award of alimony against second husband incident to annulment warrants termination of first husband's support obligation upon remarriage of wife), with Sutton v. Leib, 199 F.2d 163 (7th Cir. 1952) (alimony payable even during period of second marriage since such marriage totally void).[13] See also Robbins v. Robbins, 343 Mass. 247, 178 N.E.2d 281 (1961) (W's remarriage followed by prompt annulment not sufficient change of circumstance to warrant modification of original alimony award); Gloss v. Railroad Retirement Bd., 313 F.2d 568 (D.C. Cir. 1962) (railroad retirement benefits not revived after annulment); Yeager v. Flemming, 282 F.2d 779 (5th Cir. 1960) (contra re social security benefits); N.Y. Times, Jan. 13, 1965, p. 22, col. 1 (Florida Council for Senior Citizens reports that "thousands of elderly couples are living together, out of wedlock, in the Miami area" because marriage would mean reduced social security benefits).

Other contingencies that may warrant a modification of the original award are the death of the wife or husband [14] and material changes in the financial circumstance of either party.[15]

PROBLEM

The following statute has been proposed as a reform measure. How does it change existing law? Would you be in favor of its enactment? What changes would you suggest?

1. *Maintenance Upon Absolute Divorce* — Upon termination of a marriage by absolute divorce, if the property awarded the wife to-

[13] The Gaines cases involved the interpretation of a separation agreement rather than a divorce decree. Some commentators have argued that since a support decree is usually modifiable upon a change of circumstance, the absolute termination rule of the Gaines case should perhaps not be applicable to divorce decrees. See Casenote, 68 Harv. L. Rev. 1076 (1955). Other authorities have urged that the result should depend on whether the second marriage is void or merely voidable.
See also DeWall v. Rhoderick, — Iowa —, 138 N.W.2d 124 (1965) (Iowa court refuses to follow Gaines on ground that Iowa statute authorizing "compensation" to innocent party in annulment action does not warrant award of maintenance).

[14] Compare Stoutland v. Estate of Stoutland, 103 N.W.2d 286 (N.D. 1960), 1 J. Fam. L. 145 (1961) (although alimony normally terminates upon H's death in absence of contrary indication in statute or decree, where decree provides that alimony payable until "W's death or remarriage," it constitutes claim against H's estate), with Harrison v. Union & New Haven Trust Co., 147 Conn. 435, 162 A.2d 182 (1960) (fact that payments out of income implies that they terminate upon H's death). See Annot., 39 A.L.R.2d 1406 (1955).

[15] See, e.g., Arnold v. Arnold, 332 Ill. App. 586, 76 N.E.2d 335 (1947) (H's subsequent great wealth in itself insufficient to justify modification, but coupled with W's increased needs resulting from change in tax law and decrease in purchasing power of dollar warrants increase from $175 to $415 per month); Annot., 18 A.L.R.2d 1 (1951).

gether with any separate property she may own, or income from the same, is insufficient for her reasonable maintenance, the court may award her periodic sums for such maintenance:

a. In the event she is incapable of maintaining herself by her own labor at the time of divorce or at the termination of any award made under paragraph b or c of this section, until such time as she is capable of maintaining herself. When the wife is subsequently able to maintain herself, she may apply for an award under paragraph b of this section.

b. In the event she is capable of maintaining herself by her own labor, and is not eligible for an award under paragraph c of this section, for such period, not to exceed two years, as may be necessary for her to find employment or to undertake training for employment.

c. In the event she has been awarded custody of a child or children, until such time as she ceases to have custody of a child under twelve years of age. When the wife ceases to have custody of a child under twelve years of age, she may apply for a maintenance award under the provisions of paragraph a or b of this section, or for an extension of the original award if special circumstances require her to remain home to care for the child.

2. *Award for Training or Education* — Upon termination of the marriage by absolute divorce, if the property awarded the wife together with any separate property she may own is insufficient to meet such expense, the court may award her a sum, over and above any sum awarded for maintenance, to be used for reasonable training or education for her future employment.

B. CHILD SUPPORT

MAITZEN v. MAITZEN
24 Ill. App. 2d 32, 163 N.E.2d 840 (1959)

SCHWARTZ, J. This is an appeal from an order requiring defendant to pay $150 per month for the education of his daughter for a period of four years. The question presented to us is whether in a divorce case a parent may be ordered to provide a college education for an adult child.

The parties to this action were divorced by decree of the Superior Court on July 28, 1943. Plaintiff was awarded custody of the daughter, the sole issue of the marriage, and defendant was ordered to pay child support of $8 per week. The decree was modified August 19, 1954, increasing payments to $50 per week. On December 18, 1958, when the child was seventeen, the court again modified the decree, requiring defendant to pay $150 per month, as before stated.

The evidence shows that defendant has an interest in a business trust which compensates him at the rate of twenty-two and one-half percent of the earnings of the business during the life of his mother. . . . His gross income in 1957 was $39,000, and his estimated gross income for 1958 was $36,000. His income after taxes was about $28,000. Defendant estimated the worth of the business to be in excess of $400,000, and he has property worth about $56,000. He has remarried, and there are two children of the second marriage, nine and thirteen years old. Linda, the child of the broken marriage, has shown an aptitude for higher education and training. She has maintained an S average (the highest grade) throughout high school, and stood third in a class of 130. . . .

It is true that the general jurisdiction of equity does not encompass divorce and that the court looks to the statute for the measure of its authority to grant a divorce. Jurisdiction over children of broken homes, however, is not dependent upon statutes, as defendant contends, but is an inherent power of equity. . . .

The question, therefore, should be stated thus — does the statute relating to divorce, custody and support in any way diminish the inherent power of equity over children of broken marriages? The pertinent portions of the Divorce Act, Ill. Rev. Stat., ch. 40, sec. 19 (1959) provide that the court upon granting a divorce:

"... may make such order touching . . . care, custody and support of the children . . . as, from the circumstances of the parties and the nature of the cases, shall be fit, reasonable and just, . . . [and] may, on application, from time to time, make such alterations in . . . the care, custody and support of the children, as shall appear reasonable and proper."

Defendant's conclusion that we must interpret the word "children" to mean minor children is not supported by the language of the statute nor attendant circumstances. The term "children" is ambiguous. It may mean a young person or offspring of any age. [Citations omitted.] Its use must be examined and its meaning determined within the context of the particular statute. . . .

The construction of a statute is in modern times moving away from the stubborn determination to extract a meaning when obviously none was intended. In the instant case, the statute was passed more than one hundred years ago. At that time, only a fraction of the population attended high school, and a fraction of that fraction attended college. The legislature had no intention, and expressed none in this Act, with respect to the age at which a parent was exonerated from liability for child support and care. Its attention was focused on the question of jurisdiction, and its purpose was to make clear that jurisdiction included the function of providing for the care, custody and support of children. . . . In the days when this Act was passed, children went to work long before they reached their majority. But even then, education beyond the high school level for children of average or better scholarship was the common aspiration of American parents. Today, it is regarded as a necessity. In a normal household, parents, except as limited by compulsory education laws, direct their children as to when and how they should work or study. That is on the assumption of a normal family relationship, where parental love and moral obligation dictate what is best for the children. Under such circumstances, natural pride in the attainments of a child, such as the one here involved, would demand of parents provision for a college education, even at a sacrifice.

When we turn to divorced parents — a disrupted family — society cannot count on normal protection for the child, and it is here that equity takes control to mitigate the hardship that may befall children of divorced parents. Shall we presume, then, that all obligation ends with minority? The statute does not say so, any more than it requires a parent to care for a child who is self-sustaining at sixteen. It leaves that unspoken. We should rather assume that the legislature of that day, more than one hundred years ago, contemplated that it had better be left unsaid, so that the mores and necessities of the times could determine what a wise discretion should do. Rather than fill in the interstice with a numeral, whether it be fifteen or over, it left that to be decided as the circumstances of a particular case should warrant.

The legislature has shown itself capable of expression when it wishes to limit or expand the area intended to be encompassed by a statute such as the one in question. . . .

— In Strom v. Strom, 13 Ill. App. 2d 354, 142 N.E.2d 172 (1957), we held that a father of ample means must provide a college education for his adult, physically afflicted daughter. In Freestate v. Freestate, 244 Ill. App. 166 (1927), our court similarly required a father to support his physically afflicted adult daughter. On the other hand, the court in Rife v. Rife, 272 Ill. App. 404 (1933) decided not to require a divorced father to support his invalid daughter, where the father was financially unable to do so. In Kreitner v. Kreitner, 285 Ill. App. 602, 2 N.E.2d 569 (1936) (memorandum decision), the court refused to extend support payments to an adult, well educated, healthy daughter. We believe that the facts under consideration in the case at bar fall under the reasoning of the Freestate and Strom cases, supra.

Outside the state, authority in well reasoned cases has held that a court of equity should require divorced parents to contribute toward the support and education of their adult children when circumstances so indicate. . . .

The chancellor did not make an independent decision that this child should go to college. Both parents are in chancery. One, the mother, has had custody of the child since she was two years old. She knows the child's talents and abilities, and she has decided that the child shall attend a university. The father expresses no interest in this proposition. He has had practically no communication with his daughter since her babyhood. Her industry, scholarship and high aspirations do not interest him. With utter indifference to those qualities which would evoke pride in the normal parent, he takes the position that he does not want to contribute toward the cost of sending her to school. The court approved the judgment of the one parent who has a natural relationship with the child. In our opinion this was a proper exercise of a discretionary power. . . .

Judgment affirmed.

NOTE

1. There has been a decided trend since the landmark decision in – Esteb v. Esteb, 138 Wash. 174, 244 Pac. 264 (1926), towards the view that under appropriate circumstances (i.e., a father who is financially capable and a child who is intellectually capable) [16] the child support obligations imposed incident to divorce will include support while the child goes to college, at least until majority. Some jurisdictions have reached this result by treating college expenses as a "necessary" (see page 308 supra); others have come to the same conclusion through interpretation of their general support statutes. See 109 U. Pa. L. Rev. 130, 131 (1960). At least one state has a statute specifically dealing with the subject.[17] Cf. also Allison v. Allison, 188 Kan. 593, 363 P.2d 795 (1961) ("education" specifically mentioned in general support statute). Even in those jurisdictions that have refused to recognize a direct responsibility for educational expenses, the same result is sometimes indirectly achieved through continuation of a pre-existing support order on the ground that the child, while in college, cannot support himself. See Straver v. Straver, 26 N.J. Misc. 218, 59 A.2d 39 (Ch. 1948).

Another out-of-the-ordinary item of support that is now awarded with increasing frequency is medical benefits (usually in the form of compelling the father to take out health insurance for the child). Note also the tendency of some courts (primarily as a security device) to order the father to take out life insurance designating the child as beneficiary; in some situations this may have the effect of giving the child a compulsory inheritance. See Riley v. Riley, 131 So.2d 491 (Fla. Dist. Ct. App. 1961), 36 Tul. L. Rev. 367 (1962), and compare page 311 supra.

2. An additional problem facing the court in Maitzen was the question of support beyond majority (eighteen in Illinois). In the eyes of the law a child is incapable of supporting himself. This presumption is terminated at majority except where the child is physically or psychologically incapable of self-support. Fincham v. Levin, 155 So.2d 883

[16] But see Calogeras v. Calogeras, 163 N.E.2d 713 (Ohio Juv. Ct. 1959) (father ordered to continue to support minor child while child in college despite fact that he had four children by subsequent marriage and despite absence of evidence as to his means).

[17] "The court in decreeing a divorce shall make provision for the guardianship, custody, support, and education of the minor children of such marriage; and the court may require the father to provide all or some specified part of the cost of education of such child or children beyond the twelfth year of education provided by the public schools, taking into consideration the earnings of the father, the station in life of the parents and child or children involved, the aptitude of the child or children as evidenced by school records, the separate property of the child or children, and all other relevant factors . . ." Ind. Stat. Ann. §3-1219 (Supp. 1965).

(Fla. Dist. Ct. App. 1963) (epileptic); Commonwealth ex rel. Groff v. Groff, 173 Pa. Super. 535, 98 A.2d 449 (1953) (psychological divorce from reality). Contra, Kizer v. Kizer, 191 N.E.2d 332 (Ind. Ct. App. 1962) (statute limits liability to minor children). See generally Annot., 1 A.L.R.2d 910 (1948). In Crane v. Crane, 45 Ill. App. 2d 316, 196 N.E.2d 27 (1964), the court was also faced with the relationship between the support statute and pre-existing equitable powers. The majority opinion, without discussing Maitzen, assumed that there was no pre-existing equitable jurisdiction to award support beyond majority and that the statute did not grant such jurisdiction. The Maitzen result was distinguished on the ground that it represented an exercise of continuing jurisdiction over an order entered prior to majority (in Crane the petition to modify the original support order was not filed until after majority).

In contrast to the situation in Illinois, most courts will terminate college support at majority. See Allison v. Allison, 188 Kan. 593, 363 P.2d 795 (1961); Johnson v. Johnson, 346 Mich. 418, 78 N.W.2d 216 (1956). But see Commonwealth ex rel. Decker v. Decker, 204 Pa. Super. 156, 203 A.2d 343 (1964) (monthly support of $150 ordered for three years of college; fact that payments extended beyond majority not discussed). In view of the increasing tendency for children to go to college (usually extending to age twenty-two) and often also an additional three or four years of graduate school, why should the law of support arbitrarily terminate at the age of majority?

Suppose a talented sixteen-year-old child, C, who is resident in Illinois, has been admitted to college. There have been no marital problems in C's family, but C's father, though well off financially, refuses to send him to school on the ground that he wants the boy to come into the family business. C consults you. What will you tell him?

3. In addition to terminating upon the child's emancipation or attainment of majority, child support obligations are usually construed to terminate upon the father's death.[18] See Flagler v. Flagler, page 310 supra. But see Guggenheimer v. Guggenheimer, 99 N.H. 399, 112 A.2d 61, 35 B.U.L. Rev. 596 (1955). In general, see Annot., 18 A.L.R.2d 1126 (1951).

4. Unlike permanent alimony which is sometimes not modifiable without a reservation of jurisdiction in the original decree, child support payments are almost invariably subject to modification upon a material change of circumstance in the needs of the child or the financial capacity of the parent.[19] See, e.g., the broad modification provision in the Illinois statute providing for "alterations" when "reasonable and proper." In Hecht v. Hecht, 189 Pa. Super. 276, 150 A.2d 139 (1959), the wife sought to have a support order for her two children increased following an in-

---

[18] Here, as in the preceding section pertaining to alimony, we are concerned with the scope of court-imposed obligations. See Chapter 11 with respect to agreements entered into by the parties.

[19] The erstwhile exception in Georgia (see Yarborough v. Yarborough, 290 U.S. 202 (1933)) has been modified by statute. Ga. Code Ann. §30-220 (Supp. 1963).

crease in her ex-husband's assets and annual earnings and his refusal to pay $2000 a year to send them to summer camp. The original order was for $325 a month. At that time, the husband was worth $100,000 and earned $12,000 a year. Six years later, owing to a substantial inheritance, his assets had increased to $600,000 and his earnings to $40,000. The court held this increase to be substantial enough to justify a monthly order of $550. The court considered the summer camp a necessity for children of a parent with such wealth. Compare page 917 supra as to the effect of subsequent enrichment on alimony. See also Annots., 89 A.L.R.2d 7 (1963) (effect of change in financial condition of parent or in needs of children), id. at 106 (effect of remarriage of H or W), 58 A.L.R.2d 355 (1958) (effect of marriage of child).

5. As is apparent from the preceding discussion, alimony and child support, although similar in some respects, differ in others. Yet there appears to be a judicial tendency, sometimes spurred by tax considerations (see pages 958-959 infra), to lump the two together in one unallocated award. See, e.g., Commonwealth ex rel. Stanley v. Stanley, 198 Pa. Super. 15, 179 A.2d 667 (1962) (allocation within court's discretion). But see Minn. Stat. Ann. §518.55 (Supp. 1964) (allocation mandatory). What effect should be given in this situation to certain events (such as W's remarriage, or a child's marriage) that affect only one of the two constituent elements? It could be argued that the combined award should be reduced by some amount; on the other hand, it may be that the original award represented the maximum that the defendant could pay even though the needs of the family clearly warranted a greater sum. Another alternative would be to allocate the previously combined award. See Annots., 2 A.L.R.3d 596 (1965), 78 A.L.R.2d 1110 (1961).

A related problem concerns awards that lump together support payments for several children. In Cooper v. Matheny, 220 Ore. 390, 349 P.2d 812 (1960), the court refused to reduce a support order when two of the three children reached majority, on the ground that the original award may have been inadequate for all three children, and that in any event there was no basis for a pro rata reduction since each child's needs are different. Accord, Kuyper v. Kuyper, 244 Iowa 1, 55 N.W.2d 485 (1952). Contra, Ditmar v. Ditmar, 48 Wash. 2d 373, 293 P.2d 759 (1956).

6. The child's right to support may not be bargained away by the parents. See, e.g., N.Y. Family Ct. Act §461(a); Barrow v. State, 87 Ga. App. 572, 74 S.E.2d 467 (1953) (H's refusal to support child in reliance upon W's waiver of child support claims as a result of H's transfer of property to her subjects H to criminal child abandonment charges). However, it is not uncommon for the wife to desire to break all ties with the husband on remarriage. Thus W and H-2 may release H-1 from his duty of support (he often may concurrently waive visitation rights) and agree to assume it themselves. If the child is being adequately cared for, the husband will not be liable for its support. See, e.g., Commonwealth v. Cameron, 197 Pa. Super. 403, 179 A.2d 270 (1962). Alternatively the child may be adopted by W and H-2. See Chapter 5.

7. The authorities are divided as to whether the wife's disregard of

court orders pertaining, e.g., to the husband's visitation rights, justifies a judicial termination of the husband's liability for further child support. The prevailing view is that the wife's contemptuous conduct, though perhaps relevant to her continued ability to enforce her claims for alimony, should not prejudice the rights of the child. Compare Kirkwood v. Kirkwood, 83 Idaho 444, 363 P.2d 1016 (1961), with Snelling v. Snelling, 272 Ala. 254, 130 So.2d 363 (1961). See also Annot., 95 A.L.R.2d 118, 134-142 (1964) (contempt normally unavailable in this situation). This position finds further support in the proposition that two wrongs do not make a right; the wife's violation arguably should be remedied directly by contempt proceedings. This alternative is not available, however, where she has deliberately removed herself from the jurisdiction of the court. See Adams v. Adams, 196 A.2d 915 (D.C. Mun. Ct. App. 1964) (although D.C. normally follows majority rule, where wife took children to Morocco in violation of court order, accumulated support moneys refunded to H and future support terminated). See also page 936 infra.

C. ENFORCEMENT OF SUPPORT

JOHNSON v. JOHNSON
319 P.2d 1107 (Okla. 1957)

JACKSON, J. . . . This appeal is taken by Wilburn Johnson, defendant, in a divorce action pending in the District Court of McCurtain County, from a judgment and order of commitment ordering that he be confined in the County Jail until he shall have purged himself of contempt by paying the sum of $4050 to his wife, Theresa Johnson, the plaintiff.

Action for divorce was commenced on March 19, 1954. On March 20, 1954, the trial court entered an ex parte order by which the defendant, Wilburn Johnson, was ordered to pay $250 per month as temporary alimony and child support, together with an additional $300 as temporary attorney's fee. Defendant made no payments for a period of one year, whereupon plaintiff caused a citation to be issued in March of 1955, and the contempt action was tried to the court on June 27, 1955.

The evidence disclosed the following facts: The defendant is and was at all times involved herein a strong, able-bodied, full-blood Indian but never worked more than one week during the eight years of marriage. For the greater part of the married life of the parties they lived with and were supported by defendant's mother who died approximately six weeks prior to the institution of the divorce action. Thereafter plaintiff and the minor children were supported by plaintiff's father. From the date of the temporary order to the date of plaintiff's last application for citation, defendant received $2000 as advances towards his distributive share of his mother's estate, but paid no part of this to plaintiff. The only excuse offered was that this money was used to pay pre-existing debts. However, it further appeared that the defendant made no effort to secure employment.

In our opinion the trial court was clearly justified and, indeed, compelled to hold defendant in contempt. The burden was upon defendant to prove that he was unable to comply with the order and that he had made an honest effort to do so. Wells v. Wells, 46 Okl. 88, 148 P. 723. So far as reflected by the record the defendant made absolutely no effort to comply with the order.

A more complex question is presented in considering whether the trial court exceeded its authority in imposing continuous confinement in this case. The defendant was ordered to stand "committed to the county jail and kept in close confinement until he shall have paid to the plaintiff" the total sum of $4050.

The evidence established that at the time of the trial the defendant had no funds with which to pay such amount. He did have an interest in his mother's estate but no final distribution had been made and even if such distribution were made he could not obtain any part of it without the approval of the Indian Department. Therefore, in order to obtain the money and gain his release he would first be compelled to make application for a partial distribution to the County Court, and then obtain the approval of the Indian Department which might or might not be granted.

Indefinite conditional commitments of this nature are upheld on the theory that the defendant "carries the keys of his prison in his own pocket." . . .

Can it be said that the defendant in the case at bar "carries the keys of his prison in his own pocket?" We think not because it does not appear that he can do the thing commanded by his own volition, and without the assistance of others.

Whether he can secure the necessary funds with which to gain his release depends upon more than his own will and the sentence imposed could possibly result in life imprisonment, notwithstanding every effort on his part to comply with the court's order.

In some jurisdictions a present inability to pay all of the past due installments is a complete defense even though the past due installments could have been paid as they matured. Snook v. Snook, 110 Wash. 310, 188 P. 502. A closely related question is presented in cases where the defendant is unable to pay the installments as they become due because of the fact that he refuses to work. Here again there are some jurisdictions in which such refusal to work is considered an inalienable right and not punishable by contempt proceedings. Messervy v. Messervy, 85 S.C. 189, 67 S.E. 130. These are extreme views. However, this court in the case of Fowler v. Fowler, 61 Okl. 280, 161 P. 227, adopted an equally extreme view in the opposite direction. In the Fowler case this court properly held that a husband's refusal to work in order to pay alimony and child support is contemptuous and punishable. But the case further holds that refusal to work and absence of an honest effort to comply with the order will justify commitment until all delinquent sums are paid, notwithstanding the fact that the defendant has no apparent means of paying such amount while confined in jail. This latter rule is contrary to the better considered cases and the apparent weight of authority, as will be hereinafter shown, and, in our opinion, constitutes an abandonment of the practical and humanitarian considerations involved in cases of this kind, and we hereby overrule the Fowler case insofar as it conflicts with the views expressed in this opinion. . . .

The only justification for an indefinite conditional commitment is based upon the assumption that the defendant can do the thing commanded. In the case at bar the defendant could apply for a partial distribution but what happens if he is unsuccessful? In the Fowler case it was observed that in such an event the District Court would *probably* release the defendant. An individual's freedom should not be the subject of speculation. Inasmuch as the order of commitment is not expressly so qualified, we cannot assume as a matter of law that the defendant would be released upon proof of his unsuccessful efforts, and it is manifestly more expedient and proper to clarify this point on appeal rather than postponing it to some possible future time upon a writ of habeas corpus hearing before this court. . . .

If the only contemptuous act on the part of the defendant had been his failure to make application for partial distribution, it would have been proper to commit him until he made such application. Such form of commitment is apparently suggested in Wohlfort v. Wohlfort, [116 Kan. 154, 225 Pac. 750 (1924)]. However, in this connection we must state that the suggested language for the form of commitment in that case is entirely too broad in requiring only a good faith expression of "willingness to do what he reasonably can do" as a condition of discharge. But in the instant case, in addition to the defendant's failure to make the application, he also failed to seek employment. This conduct cannot go unnoticed.

In Ramsay v. Ramsay [125 Miss. 185, 87 So. 491 (1921)], a case involving the defendant's failure to seek employment, the court held that it was proper to impose a fine but in this state we have held that the sentence imposed is not to vindicate the dignity of the court but should be remedial and coercive in nature. Hadley v. Hadley [129 Okla. 219, 280 Pac. 1098 (1928)]. In the Hadley case we further held that a fixed imprisonment "not conditioned on a continued failure to pay the sums cannot be made." However, this holding does not prohibit a fixed sentence if it is conditioned in such a manner that the defendant can gain his freedom at any time by paying the amount ordered by the court. A fixed sentence so conditioned would obviously have a coercive effect to the end of forcing the defendant to make the application. If he were unsuccessful in obtaining the funds and forced to serve the entire term so fixed, then upon his release it is equally certain that he would feel more inclined to secure employment in order to comply with future orders of the court.

The only objection to such a commitment is that it is possible the defendant could not obtain the funds and would not carry the "keys in his pocket." This objection is technically sound, but the possibility of being forced to serve a fixed sentence, which is reasonable, does not shock the conscience of a court so long as there is a possibility that defendant will not serve any part of it. On the other hand, the possibility of being confined to prison for life, or at least an indefinite time in a case of this nature, and despite good faith efforts by the defendant to comply with the court's order, impresses us as oppressive and unreasonable.

The judgment of the trial court in holding defendant in contempt is affirmed. The order committing defendant to jail indefinitely is vacated, with instructions to the trial court to reconsider its order of commitment in light of the views herein expressed and, if necessary, impose a fixed commitment reasonably sufficient in duration to provoke an honest effort on the part of the defendant to comply with the court's order.

However, if it now appears to the trial court that defendant has made, or is making, an honest effort to comply with the court's order; or that financial assistance to the plaintiff and the children would be more readily available by entering a new order, the trial court may take evidence and do so under its continuing jurisdiction.

HALLEY and BLACKBIRD, JJ., dissent.

NOTE

1. The opinion by Justice Jackson was the court's second effort in this case. In a prior decision, reported only at 28 Okla. B.A.J. 1010 (1957), the district court's order of indefinite commitment was affirmed, largely on the authority of the Fowler case. Justice Jackson dissented.

2. The Johnson case points up the delicate dividing line between civil and criminal contempt. In theory the distinction is clear. Civil contempt is a coercive sanction designed to compel compliance with a judicial decree; the sentence may be of indefinite duration, but is subject to termination at any time by the defendant's doing that which he was ordered to do (in this case, the payment of support). Criminal contempt, on the other hand, is a punitive sanction that cannot be purged by compliance. See, e.g., N.C. Gen. Stat. §5-4 (1953) (30 days). In practice, however, the distinction often becomes elusive. In the Johnson case, for example, a fixed sentence (characteristic of a criminal contempt) was imposed in a civil situation (the essential objective here was to effectuate compliance, as evidenced by the court's indication that if the defendant satisfied his support obligations, he must be released). See also Smith v. Smith, 248 N.C. 298, 103 S.E.2d 400 (1958) (criminal standard of willfulness applied in civil case).

The general rule is that nonpayment of alimony or support is a civil contempt since the action is brought to coerce the husband into payment. Ibid. However, contempt is also applicable where the husband was once but is no longer capable of paying. In such a case it is more closely akin to punishment for a past act. See Smith v. Smith, 248 N.C. 298, 302-303, 103 S.E.2d 400, 403 (1958) (concurring opinion); cf. Knaus v. Knaus, 387 Pa. 370, 380, 127 A.2d 669, 674 (1956) (dicta). The difficulty is compounded by the fact that the same act may be defined as both a civil and a criminal contempt. Compare N.C. Gen. Stat. §5-1(4) (1953) (criminal contempt) with N.C. Gen. Stat. §5-8(1) (1953) (civil contempt) (disobedience of court order). See also Keller v. Keller, 52 Wash. 2d 84, 323 P.2d

231 (1958). In general, see Goldfarb, The Varieties of the Contempt Power, 13 Syracuse L. Rev. 44 (1961).

3. Another source of complexity derives from the fact that the contempt sanction is only available for support obligations, not for payments in discharge of property rights, since the latter are ordinary debts and cannot be enforced by contempt because of the constitutional immunities against imprisonment for debt. See, e.g., Dickey v. Dickey, 154 Md. 675, 141 Atl. 387 (1928). Such a distinction is not particularly helpful in the common situation where a decree is based on a private agreement that inextricably intertwines support and property obligations (a so-called integrated property settlement). Most state court decisions appear to hold that if any element of the agreement goes beyond the legal obligation of support, the entire agreement becomes contractual and unenforceable by contempt unless the support provisions are clearly severable. Thus if the parties provide that payments of what they designate as "alimony" are to continue after the husband's death until the death or remarriage of the wife or if the award is "in lieu of dower," the payments normally cannot be enforced by contempt. However, in California, following a series of decisions refusing to enforce by contempt divorce decrees embodying integrated property settlements (see, e.g., Plumer v. Superior Court, 50 Cal. 2d 631, 328 P.2d 193 (1958)), the statute was amended so as in effect to render all alimony and support provisions severable and enforceable by contempt. Cal. Civ. Code §139; see 47 Calif. L. Rev. 756 (1959).

4. Aside from bringing contempt proceedings, the wife can seek to garnish the husband's wages,[20] attach his property,[21] or file a criminal nonsupport complaint.[22] The criminal remedy is by far the quickest, cheapest, and most potent in that it results in the immediate police arrest of the defendant. However, some courts will not entertain a criminal complaint so long as the husband makes any support payments, no matter how inadequate. But cf. Ky. Rev. Stat. Ann. §435.240(3)(a) (1963) (violation of support order a separate crime). Also the pendency of contempt enforcement proceedings in the divorce court is sometimes used as a basis for declining jurisdiction, even though the contempt remedy is generally regarded as far less effective because of the difficulties encoun-

[20] N.Y. Pers. Prop. Law §49-b (privity over all other creditors except deductions mandatory by law and union dues); Pa. Stat. Ann. tit. 62, §2043.39(c) (1959) (limited to 50 per cent of amount due employee). See also D.C. Code Ann. §16-312(b) (1961) (prepayment of wages to avoid attachment prohibited); Mich. Acts 1964, No. 175 (employer reprisals prohibited).

[21] Attachment is available even if assets are generally exempt from attachment by statute or agreement. McDonald v. McDonald, 351 Mich. 568, 88 N.W.2d 398 (1958) (pension exempt under city charter); Thiel v. Thiel, 41 N.J. 446, 197 A.2d 354 (1964) (pension exempt under labor contract). See generally Annot., 54 A.L.R.2d 1422 (1957); see also Pa. Stat. Ann. tit. 20, §301.12 (1950) (spendthrift trusts subject to attachment).

[22] See, e.g., Cal. Penal Code §270; Model Penal Code §230.5, reproduced at page 929 infra. One incidental benefit of the criminal action is that the location facilities of the police can thus be utilized.

tered in serving the defendant and because a last-minute part payment normally serves to quash the proceedings, thus necessitating a new citation upon each subsequent default. But see Gilmour v. State, 230 Ind. 454, 104 N.E.2d 127 (1952). In the criminal action the husband is often put on probation if he keeps up the support payments, but once he is imprisoned, payment does not serve to discharge him, as is true of civil contempt. See generally Jones, The Problem of Family Support: Criminal Sanctions for the Enforcement of Support, 38 N.C.L. Rev. 1 (1959); Annot., 73 A.L.R.2d 960 (1960).

5. Perhaps the most troublesome situation is presented where, as in Johnson, the husband is incapable of meeting the support order.[23] Here the criminal remedy may serve to assuage the wife's sense of vengeance but not her financial needs. Compare Model Penal Code §230.5 (Proposed Official Draft 1962) (emphasis supplied): "A person commits a misdemeanor if he persistently fails to provide support *which he can provide* and which he knows he is legally obliged to provide to a spouse, child or other dependent." [24] And although, as indicated in Johnson, the husband can generally be cited for contempt in this situation, this remedy is no more likely to produce the desired funds. However, repeated jail sentences like that imposed in Johnson may impel some husbands to seek employment rather than return to jail. Noteworthy in this connection is the recent New York statute authorizing Family Court judges to specify that violators of its orders in support and certain other proceedings serve their sentence on certain days or parts of days (e.g., on weekends or at night). N.Y. Sess. Laws 1965, c. 522, amending Family Ct. Act §§454, 846.

6. In view of the indicated obstacles, the wife will be well advised to obtain maximum security against nonpayment at the time the original support order is entered. Such security may take the form of a lien against some or all of H's assets,[25] a bond,[26] or a trust.[27] In one recent case a wife who alleged that her husband was in arrears and that he was about to leave the jurisdiction was able to obtain a writ of ne exeat authorizing the arrest of the defendant unless he posted a $1000 security bond. Upon his subsequent default, the wife was able to collect on the bond, but only for sums that had accrued at the time the writ was issued.[28]

[23] Sometimes the husband's inability to pay is self-imposed, as where he transferred all his assets in anticipation of the marital action. See Annot., 49 A.L.R.2d 521, 554-555 (1956) (such transfers normally voidable as fraudulent conveyances).

[24] See also Royal Commission on Marriage and Divorce, Report 1951-1955, Cmd. No. 9678, pars. 1087 et seq. (1956) (recommendation that garnishment of wages be permitted in view of futility of jail sentences in this situation; recommendation adopted in Maintenance Orders Act, 1958, 6 & 7 Eliz. 2, c. 39).

[25] Annot., 59 A.L.R.2d 656 (1958); but see Mo. Stat. Ann. §452.080 (1952) (lien appropriate only if H refuses to post security after being ordered to do so).

[26] See, e.g., N.Y. Dom. Rel. Law §243; Cal. Civ. Code §140.

[27] Annot., 3 A.L.R.3d 1170 (1965).

[28] National Auto. & Cas. Ins. Co. v. Queck, 405 P.2d 905 (Ariz. Ct. App. 1965).

WORTHLEY v. WORTHLEY
44 Cal. 2d 465, 283 P.2d 19 (1955)

TRAYNOR, J. — Plaintiff appeals from a judgment barring further prosecution of this action. The judgment was entered after a trial of defendant's special defense (Code Civ. Proc., §597) to plaintiff's complaint for prospective and retroactive enforcement of defendant's obligations under a separate maintenance decree entered in the New Jersey Court of Chancery on May 19, 1947. Plaintiff and defendant were married in New Jersey in March 1943, and separated in November 1946. In the action for separate maintenance defendant appeared personally and by counsel, and the decree ordered him to pay $9.00 a week for plaintiff's support. About ten months after the decree was entered, defendant left New Jersey for Nevada, and in March 1948 he commenced an action for divorce in that state. Although plaintiff was served in New Jersey with summons and a copy of the complaint in the Nevada action, she did not appear therein. On July 7, 1948, the Nevada Second Judicial District Court granted defendant a divorce.

Defendant had paid all of the sums due under the New Jersey decree at the time the divorce was granted by the Nevada court but made no further payments thereafter. The Nevada decree contained no provision for alimony. On November 16, 1951, plaintiff commenced this action in the Superior Court of Los Angeles County, the county of defendant's present residence. She alleged that the New Jersey decree "has become final and has never been vacated, modified, or set aside" and that defendant is delinquent in his payments thereunder in the amount of $1089. She seeks a judgment for the accrued arrearages and asks that the New Jersey decree be established as a California decree and that defendant be ordered to pay her $9.00 a week until further order of the court. Defendant answered the complaint by a general denial and by alleging, as an affirmative defense, that the Nevada divorce decree had terminated his obligations under the earlier New Jersey separate maintenance decree. On defendant's motion, the affirmative defense was tried first under the procedure established by section 597 of the Code of Civil Procedure. The trial court concluded that the Nevada decree dissolved the marriage and was therefore a bar to the maintenance of an action to enforce defendant's obligations under the New Jersey decree.

Since plaintiff does not question the validity of the divorce granted by the Nevada court, that decree, being regular on its face, must be accorded full faith and credit in this state. [Citations omitted.] The controlling questions on this appeal are, therefore, (1) whether the dissolution of the marriage terminated defendant's obligations under the New Jersey decree and, if not, (2) whether and to what extent those obligations are enforceable in this state.

Since the full faith and credit clause compels recognition of the Nevada decree only as an adjudication of the marital status of plaintiff and defendant and not of any property rights that may be incident to that status (Estin v. Estin, 334 U.S. 541, 548-549), the effect of the dissolution of the marriage on defendant's preexisting obligations under the New Jersey maintenance decree must be determined by the law of New Jersey. [Citations omitted.] The Supreme Court of that state has recently held that a New Jersey "decree for maintenance [is not] superseded by a judgment of the foreign state where jurisdiction has only been obtained by publication entered in an ex parte proceeding in which in personam jurisdiction over the wife to whom the maintenance decree runs was not obtained." (Isserman v. Isserman, 11 N.J. 106 [93 A.2d 571, 575].) We must therefore conclude that defendant's obligations under the New Jersey decree were not terminated by the dissolution of the marriage effected by the Nevada court in a proceeding in which personal jurisdiction over plaintiff was not obtained.

The second question is more difficult. Since the New Jersey decree is both prospectively and retroactively modifiable (N.J.S. §2A:34-23 [1951]), we are not constitutionally bound to enforce defendant's obligations under it. [Citations omitted.] [29] Nor are we bound *not* to enforce them. [Citations omitted.] The United States Supreme Court has held, however, that if such obligations are enforced in this state, at least as to accrued arrearages, due process requires that the defendant be afforded an opportunity to litigate the question of modification. [Citations omitted.] It has also clearly indicated that as to either prospective or retroactive enforcement of such obligations, this state "has at least as much leeway to disregard the judgment, to qualify it, or to depart from it as does the State where it was rendered." (Halvey v. Halvey, . . . 330 U.S. 610, 615.)

[The court then concludes that even though a sister-state decree may be prospectively or retroactively modifiable, the California courts will still enforce it, subject to their determination of the modification claim.]

It is suggested that even if there are no binding California authorities on the question, we should follow certain sister-state decisions holding that alimony and support obligations created by a prospectively and retroactively modifiable decree are enforceable only in the state in which the decree was rendered. The policy implicit in those decisions is that a modifiable duty of support in one state "is of no special interest to other states and . . . is not enforceable elsewhere under principles of Conflict of Laws." (Rest., Conflict of Laws, §458, comment *a*.) This policy was rejected by this court . . . and by the Legislature of this state in enacting

---

[29] In recent cases the United States Supreme Court has expressly reserved judgment on the question of full faith and credit to modifiable judgments and decrees (see Barber v. Barber, 323 U.S. 77, 81; Griffin v. Griffin, 327 U.S. 220, 234; but see Halvey v. Halvey, 330 U.S. 610, 615), and the late Mr. Justice Jackson, a foremost expounder of the law of full faith and credit in recent years, forcefully declared that modifiable alimony and support decrees are within the scope of that clause: "Neither the full faith and credit clause of the constitution nor the Act of Congress implementing it says anything about final judgments or, for that matter, about any judgments. Both require that full faith and credit be given to 'judicial proceedings' without limitation as to finality. Upon recognition of the broad meaning of that term much may someday depend." (Concurring opinion, Barber v. Barber, 323 U.S. 77, 87.)

the Uniform Reciprocal Enforcement of Support Act. (Code Civ. Proc., §§1650-1690.) In proceedings commenced pursuant to the provisions of that act, the California courts must recognize and enforce foreign alimony and support decrees whether modifiable or not (Code Civ. Proc., §1670), and must afford the defendant an opportunity to litigate the issue of modification. (Code Civ. Proc., §1682; Griffin v. Griffin, supra, 327 U.S. 220, 233-234.) If we should now refuse to follow the policy expressed by the Legislature in the Uniform Act, and by this court and the United States Supreme Court . . . , and should hold that even though the courts of this state have personal jurisdiction over the defendant, his obligations under a prospectively and retroactively modifiable sister-state support decree cannot be enforced in this state, the result would be anomalous. There would then be two rules in California, one for proceedings commenced under the Uniform Act, and a contrary one for all other proceedings to enforce foreign-created alimony and support obligations.

Moreover, there is no valid reason, in a case in which both parties are before the court, why the California courts should refuse to hear a plaintiff's prayer for enforcement of a modifiable sister-state decree and the defendant's plea for modification of his obligations thereunder. If the accrued installments are modified retroactively, the judgment for a liquidated sum entered after such modification will be final and thus will be entitled to full faith and credit in all other states. (Magnolia Petroleum Co. v. Hunt, 320 U.S. 430, 438-439, and cases cited.) If the installments are modified prospectively, the issues thus determined will be res judicata so long as the circumstances of the parties remain unchanged. [Citations omitted.] Furthermore, the interests of neither party would be served by requiring the plaintiff to return to the state of rendition and reduce her claim for accrued installments to a money judgment. In the present case, for example, defendant, a domiciliary of this state, would have to travel 3000 miles from his home, family, and job to secure a modification of plaintiff's allegedly stale claim and to protect his interests in any proceeding for the enforcement of his support obligation that she might institute in New Jersey. If defendant is unable to afford the time or money to travel to New Jersey to make an effective appearance in plaintiff's proceedings in that state, his substantive defenses to plaintiff's claims will be foreclosed. By the same token, unless plaintiff elected to proceed under the Uniform Reciprocal Enforcement of Support Act, which has been adopted in New Jersey (N.J.S. §2A:4-30.1-30.22), defendant's failure to pay the installments as they came due would force her constantly to relitigate his obligation to support. Repeated suits for arrearages would have to be brought in New Jersey as installments accrued, to be followed by repeated actions in California to enforce the New Jersey judgments for accrued installments, with the net result that the costs of litigation and the dilatoriness of the recovery would substantially reduce the value of the support to which plaintiff is entitled.

Furthermore, there is no merit to the contention that as a matter of practical convenience the issue of modification should be tried in the courts of the state where the support decree was originally rendered.

Proof of changed circumstances in support cases is no more difficult than in custody cases and, as noted above, a California court that has jurisdiction of the subject matter must undertake to adjudicate a plea for modification of custody rights established by a sister-state decree. (Sampsell v. Superior Court, 32 Cal. 2d 763.) Moreover, in most states the problem of modification is dealt with according to general equitable principles, and the law of the state in which the support obligation originated can be judicially noticed (Code Civ. Proc., §1875) and applied by the California courts.

Accordingly, we hold that foreign-created alimony and support obligations are enforceable in this state. In an action to enforce a modifiable support obligation, either party may tender and litigate any plea for modification that could be presented to the courts of the state where the alimony or support decree was originally rendered.

The judgment is reversed.

[The dissenting opinion of Justice Spence, in which Justices Shenk and Schauer concurred, is omitted.]

NOTE

1. When a marriage breaks up, it is not uncommon for one of the spouses to leave the state of marital domicile and move to another state. As the Worthley case demonstrates, this poses difficult problems in addition to those already alluded to for the wife who seeks to enforce alimony or child support claims.[30] A number of separate issues are involved:

a. *Enforcing an existing support order.* Where there has been a separate maintenance or divorce proceeding in which both parties participated and which culminated in support orders against a husband who subsequently moves to another state, the task, generally speaking, is one of obtaining execution on the outstanding judgment.[31] In the few instances where the husband happens to have property in the state where the wife resides, attachment is the obvious remedy. Usually, however, the husband must be pursued into the state of his new residence. It is here that the problems raised in Worthley come into play. A few cases have followed the lead of Worthley and given comity recognition to modifiable support decrees of sister states;[32] in the remaining jurisdictions

[30] For the sake of simplicity it will be assumed that the wife remains in the state of marital domicile and the husband goes to another state. The student should consider other variations, such as the wife leaving and the husband staying, or the wife going to new State A while the husband goes to new State B.

[31] Where the support orders have not been reduced to judgment, this may be a necessary first step. The absence of the defendant should normally prove no obstacle in view of the fact that by hypothesis he initially submitted himself to the court's jurisdiction.

[32] See, e.g., Hudson v. Hudson, 36 N.J. 549, 178 A.2d 202 (1962); see also McCabe v. McCabe, 210 Md. 308, 123 A.2d 447 (1956) (presumption that past due installments not modifiable; contempt enforcement provided); Light v. Light, 12 Ill. 2d 502, 147 N.E.2d 34 (1958) (plaintiff permitted to register foreign support order encompassing both past due and future installments as local decree, subject, however, to available defenses).

the difficulty of satisfying the requirements of the full faith and credit clause as interpreted by the Supreme Court necessitates invocation of the cumbersome enforcement procedures described by Justice Traynor or resort to the Uniform Reciprocal Enforcement of Support Act. This Act, which is in force in every state, establishes a unique two-step procedure for reaching nonresident support obligors. The process is initiated by the petitioner (usually the wife) filing a complaint in the designated court of her home state. If the court finds that the petition sets forth a plausible claim for support, the petition is forwarded to the appropriate court in the responding state having jurisdiction over the defendant. The district attorney takes over the prosecution of the case. After full notice to the defendant, the matter is set down for hearing. The court may adjudicate defenses asserted by the defendant, although this may create procedural complications in view of the physical absence of the plaintiff. Any judgment rendered is collected by the court in the responding state and forwarded to the plaintiff via the courts of the initiating state. The Act also contains criminal provisions (including extradition remedies), and in those states which have adopted the 1958 amendments, a method for permanently registering a foreign support order in the state where the obligor resides.

Although the URESA does not solve the substantial initial problem of locating the support obligor, it does provide a simple and, on the whole, effective procedure for counteracting the overly rigid interpretation which the full faith and credit clause has received at the hands of the Supreme Court. See Note, 48 Cornell L.Q. 541 (1963). Its provisions, although probably intended primarily for persons of little means, are not so limited and hence appear to be available to any person seeking to assert support claims against a nonresident obligor. See Brockelbank, Interstate Enforcement of Support 36 (1960); Annot., 42 A.L.R.2d 768 (1955). See also Council of State Governments, Reciprocal State Legislation to Enforce the Support of Dependents (published annually).

One possible difference between proceeding under the Uniform Act and suing directly on a foreign support order may be in the applicable law. Justice Traynor suggested in Worthley that the law of the state which rendered the original order should be looked to; the Uniform Act in §7 provides that "the laws of any state where the obligor was present during the period for which support is sought" shall govern, and then adds (in the 1952 amendment version) that the obligor is presumed to have been present in the responding state unless otherwise shown. Suppose, for example, that the suit in Worthley had been brought under the URESA. As Justice Spence pointed out in his dissent, under the then prevailing California law a husband's ex parte Nevada divorce terminated a prior support order obtained by his wife. Thus a California court presumably would have dismissed the wife's claim for support for the period following the entry of the Nevada decree. But as Justice Traynor pointed out, New Jersey did not recognize the ex parte divorce insofar as the support rights of the stay-at-home wife are concerned. If, subsequent to the California dismissal, the wife had been able to serve the husband with process in New Jersey (or had been able to find some of his property there), could he have pleaded the California judgment in bar?

Or suppose a divorce is granted in Pennsylvania, which does not recognize permanent alimony. If H then moves to California, which does, can W, a Pennsylvania resident, assert alimony claims against him under the URESA? Cf. Commonwealth of Pennsylvania ex rel. Dept. of Pub. Assistance v. Mong, 160 Ohio St. 455, 117 N.E.2d 32 (1954), 102 U. Pa. L. Rev. 938 (1954) (suit by Pennsylvania welfare authorities against Ohio citizen to compel support of his indigent Pennsylvania father as required by Pennsylvania law dismissed because Ohio law provides defense to such actions; application of Pennsylvania law would constitute denial of equal protection).

In many situations it may not make much difference what law is applied since the governing consideration will be the discretion of the court. But the reference to the law of the defendant's residence in §7 of the URESA may have the effect, where the total means are severely limited, of giving preference to the defendant's new family.

b. *Absence of outstanding support order.* Where the husband deserts the wife (perhaps in order to institute an ex parte divorce in a foreign state), the question is not one of enforcing an existing decree but rather one of obtaining initial judicial recognition of the husband's support obligation. In this situation the wife can of course bring an original action against him in his state of new residence. Alternatively, she can invoke the procedures of the URESA. See Brockelbank, Interstate Enforcement of Support 35 (1960). Both of these remedies will probably subject her to the law of the husband's domicile. At least one state has extended its long-arm statute to permit actions arising out of

> [l]iving in the marital relationship within the state notwithstanding subsequent departure from the state, as to all obligations arising for alimony, child support, or property settlement . . . , if the other party to the marital relationship continues to reside in the state.[33]

Of course, once a valid judgment in the wife's home state has been obtained, the ensuing problems are similar to those described in subsection a above.

c. *Effect of ex parte foreign divorce.* Suppose the husband leaves the marital domicile and obtains in another state a valid ex parte divorce which makes no provision for alimony. As Justice Traynor pointed out, the Supreme Court has held that, unlike the status of divorce, support is an in personam matter which can only be validly determined if there is jurisdiction over both parties. Thus even if the ex parte Nevada divorce obtained by the husband in Worthley was valid on the ground that he was in fact domiciled there, New Jersey was still free to disregard any alimony (or custody) determinations made by the Nevada court. Vander-

[33] Kan. Stat. Ann. §60-308(b)(6) (1964).

bilt v. Vanderbilt, 354 U.S. 416 (1957).[34] This is the doctrine of divisible divorce. The federal law is merely permissive, however; it is a question of state law whether a support order obtained by the wife survives the husband's ex parte divorce (or whether, if she did not obtain an order before the divorce, she can still do so afterwards).[35] Approximately twenty states (including California) have adopted this doctrine either by statute or judicial decision. See Note, Divisible Divorce, 76 Harv. L. Rev. 1233 (1963).

2. The relationship between child support and visitation rights that was already alluded to (page 923 supra) assumes added importance in the interstate setting. In Kubon v. Kubon, 51 Cal. 2d 229, 331 P.2d 636 (1958), a wife sought to enforce in California a Nevada judgment for child support arrearages. The husband urged the court to refuse enforcement on the ground that the wife was in contempt of a temporary restraining order issued by a California court at his request incident to an attempt by him to gain custody. (She had abducted the child from California in violation of this order.) The California Supreme Court affirmed the lower court's dismissal of the action. Justice Traynor, joined by two other Justices, insisted that the full faith and credit clause compelled California to enforce the Nevada judgment. The wife's contempt of the California court was in his view a matter for the Nevada court to consider, along with all other factors relevant to making a custody disposition that was in the best interests of the child.

THE ADMINISTRATION OF ALIMONY AND CHILD SUPPORT

There is scarcely any branch of family law that illustrates more graphically the characteristic gap between the law on the books and the law in action than the enforcement of support. Troublesome as are some of the legal doctrines, they barely give an inkling of the practical difficulties that lie beneath the surface.

Regrettably little is known about the actual administration of alimony and child support. There have been no major contemporary scientific investigations of the support orders sought from and entered by one or more selected courts during a particular period, with a view to determining such matters as the amount requested, the amount granted, the number of supplementary hearings required, the amount actually collected, the number of husbands imprisoned for contempt, the consequences of such imprisonment, and so on. The only large-scale study of divorce

[34] Of course, if the wife participates in the foreign divorce, she is barred from later support claims which are inconsistent with the determinations of the divorce court. Lynn v. Lynn, 302 N.Y. 193, 97 N.E.2d 748, cert. denied, 342 U.S. 849 (1951).

[35] In Loeb v. Loeb, 4 N.Y.2d 542, 152 N.E.2d 36 (1958), cert. denied, 359 U.S. 913 (1959), the New York Court of Appeals held that a spouse who was not domiciled in New York at the time of the husband's Nevada divorce could not invoke the doctrine of divisible divorce for the purpose of asserting support claims against the husband's New York property.

awards was made by Marshall and May in Maryland and Ohio in the early 1930's. They discovered that alimony (unlike child support) was infrequently sought and even less often obtained.[36] The median amount of alimony and child support awarded in Ohio during the last six months of 1931 was $33 per month. Seventy per cent of these payments were to be made on a weekly basis, and their distribution was as follows:

Weekly payments	*Percentage*
Under $5	10.2
$5-9	49.6
$10	21.1
$11-14	4.9
$15	8.5
$16-19	0.8
$20	2.5
$25	1.0
Over $25	1.5

During the same period the median lump-sum payment to the wife was $386 in the cases in which a figure appeared in the record. The amounts ranged from $10 to $50,000 and were concentrated most heavily between $100 and $200. The wife received money or property in 75 per cent of the 2058 cases in which she was given custody of the children, but this proportion dropped to 19 per cent in the 4528 cases in which she did not receive custody of children.[37]

Recent interviews by Hopson of four Kansas trial court judges cast some light on the relative disfavor with which some courts view requests for alimony. The judges apparently conceived of alimony as something extra to be awarded to the wife after the assets were divided up. They generally disliked to order alimony because the continuing financial relationship might lead to later controversy, and because of the possible long-term burden on the husband. Four main factors seemed to enter into the decision whether to award alimony in a particular case. First, alimony was less important if there were assets that could be distributed. Second, alimony would not be ordered if it appeared that a single fixed settlement would be sufficient to enable the wife to get back on her feet. Third, alimony was seen as something of a reward if the aggrieved wife had remained with her husband for a substantial period

---

[36] Of 3306 actions for divorce, annulment, or alimony filed in Maryland in 1929, alimony was sought in 453 cases and obtained in 218. Of 6485 divorces granted in Ohio in the last six months of 1930, alimony was sought in 1883 cases and obtained in 1131. In these same actions in Ohio, child support was awarded in 1331 cases although it was only sought in the original petition in 889 cases; property settlements were awarded in 848 cases although only sought in 674. 1 Marshall & May, The Divorce Court 18, 311 (1932); 2 id. at 322-323 (1933). See also page 908 note 6 supra.

[37] 2 Marshall & May, note 36 supra, at 330-331, 333-334, 340. For some more recent scattered data of the varying practices of particular judges, see Quenstedt & Winkler, What Are Our Domestic Relations Judges Thinking?, Monograph No. 1, A.B.A. Sect. of Fam. L., July 1965, pp. 2-6.

of time. Fourth, alimony would not be ordered if it appeared that the wife was somehow at fault for the disintegration of the marriage.[38]

A 1955 study of families receiving aid to dependent children, though obviously unrepresentative of the population as a whole,[39] illustrates some of the frustrations inherent in the enforcement of private support obligations among those with insufficient means for self-support. Child support payments averaging $67.63 per month had been ordered or agreed to in 42 per cent of the 162,440 families where the now absent father had once been on the scene, married to the mother of the child.[40] But in only about half of these cases (and only 18.3 per cent of the total cases) was any support actually received from the father.[41] The total contributed annually by these fathers was estimated at $20 million, only about 10 per cent of the total public assistance funds expended on these families.[42] Almost one out of every ten fathers was either currently or had at some time in the past been imprisoned for criminal nonsupport.[43]

One of the principal reasons for the ineffectiveness of the private support remedy for the families covered by the ADC study was the difficulty of locating the absent father. In 54.5 per cent of the cases his whereabouts was unknown.[44] Because the father's payments, if any, generally serve to reduce the public assistance disbursements, the Social Security Act requires that law enforcement officials be notified of deserting fathers whose families are receiving ADC payments.[45] Concomitantly, the federal government has agreed to make available to state or local welfare agencies any information it has acquired as to the deserter's whereabouts.[46] The most obvious source for such information is the records of the Social

[38] Hopson, The Economics of a Divorce: A Pilot Empirical Study at the Trial Court Level, 11 Kan. L. Rev. 107, 126 (1962).

[39] In most middle or upper class divorces the property rights of the parties are determined by agreement. See Chapter 11. In the 3306 actions for divorce, annulment, or alimony filed in Maryland in 1929 and disposed of by 1931, 198 agreements were filed with the court. However, Marshall and May estimated that probably many more agreements existed that were not filed — at least 600. 1 Marshall & May, note 36 supra, at 220-221. See also Hopson, note 38 supra, at 118 (agreements in seventeen out of forty cases).

[40] Kaplan, Support from Absent Fathers of Children Receiving ADC 1955, pp. 7, 15 (U.S. Bureau of Public Assistance Rep. No. 41, 1960).

[41] Id. at 24-25.

[42] Id. at 26, 75 (Table A-50).

[43] Id. at 16.

[44] Id. at 6. Even where his whereabouts was known and the Uniform Reciprocal Enforcement of Support Act was utilizable, in only about 40 per cent of the cases was the Act invoked, and in only one third of these was support actually ordered. Id. at 65 (Table A-27).

[45] Id. at 12.

[46] Until recently, such information could be obtained only with respect to the deserting parent of a child actually receiving ADC. 20 C.F.R. §401.3(g)(3) (1965). However, as a result of a 1965 amendment of the Social Security Act, the information will be supplied in any case where a child under sixteen is "in destitute or necessitous circumstances," and is either a recipient or an applicant for any of a number of specified federal assistance programs, provided that a court has entered a support order for the benefit of such child. Pub. Law 89-97, §340, amending 42 U.S.C.A. §1306 by adding a new subsection (c).

Security Administration indicating contributions made by his current employer. However, the Social Security Administration has so far successfully resisted any attempt to make its files generally available to court officials or private persons seeking assistance in the location of support obligors.[47] Compare page 778 supra.

Undoubtedly the location problems are in part a reflection of the hostility and vindictiveness that frequently characterize the relations between divorced spouses.[48] These feelings are likely to be exacerbated by the continuation of the relationship that is often a corollary of the award of periodic alimony or child support.[49] Just as the husband may do everything in his power to evade his support responsibilities as a means of showing his contempt for the wife, so the wife may often look upon the available legal machinery as a convenient means of harassing the husband.[50] Serious denials of the defendant's legal rights may thus result. In Politano v. Politano, 146 Misc. 792, 262 N.Y. Supp. 802 (1933), the husband was an ignorant immigrant who was ordered to pay alimony to his childless and self-supporting wife. The order was entered while the husband was employed as a bricklayer. Within a few months he was unemployed and penniless. Nevertheless, he was sentenced for contempt and stayed in prison for thirty-one months. In Pennsylvania prior to 1957 a judge could order the posting of a bond to insure payment as a condition to release, even if the defendant had no funds to pay the bond premium. The publicity given to one case in which the husband was sentenced to life imprisonment for failure to post a bond finally resulted in the drafting of legislation to outlaw the practice. See American Civil Liberties Union of Penn., Civil Liberties Record, Feb. 1957, p. 4.

The probationary aspects can also lead to abuse. The probation officer has discretion in his use of sanctions to enforce payment. In the case of Dr. McGill [51] on probation for contempt, the probation officer determined that the defendant's resistance to payment was due to a domineering

---

[47] A number of states have enacted comparable legislation making motor vehicle registration and other files available to specified agencies in their own government and in some instances to agencies of other states. See, e.g., Ark. Stat. Ann. §83-161 (Supp. 1965). Sometimes the authority is limited to public assistance cases. Here, too, private individuals generally have no access to these data. See Council of State Governments, Reciprocal State Legislation to Enforce the Support of Dependents, c. 3 (1964, revised annually) for a state-by-state listing of location services.

[48] See, e.g., N.Y. Times, Nov. 6, 1965, p. 46M, col. 7 (estranged husband shoots wife and four children on day he was to have appeared in contempt proceeding for refusing to make support payments). See also Goode, After Divorce 290 (1956), indicating that 28 per cent of the divorcees in his study admitted that they "frequently" desired to punish their husbands; another 20 per cent stated that they "occasionally" harbored such feelings.

[49] See Peele, Social and Psychological Effects of the Availability and the Granting of Alimony on the Spouses, 6 Law & Contemp. Prob. 283 (1939).

[50] See the report of an undocumented study by a Stanford University psychologist who studied eight hundred women responsible for jailing their former husbands for nonsupport; he concluded that 70 per cent of the women were suffering from "psychoses bordering on sadism." N.Y. Times, Jan. 9, 1960, p. 24, col. 1.

[51] See Keve, Jail Can Be Useful, N.P.P.A. News, Nov. 1956, p. 1.

mother. Although the mother had paid up all the arrearages, and apparently would continue to do so in the future, the officer determined that Dr. McGill was a chronic evader and hence needed "jail therapy" to teach him to shoulder his responsibilities. Accordingly, Dr. McGill was twice jailed briefly.

The general dissatisfaction with the cumbersomeness and inefficacy of the support enforcement machinery has led to a search for new methods. A few jurisdictions have provided for the collection and disbursement of all support obligations through a central office affiliated with the court. Through this device defaults are more likely to be deterred; once they occur, court officials promptly initiate compliance proceedings. See, e.g., the Michigan Friend of Court Act, Mich. Stat. Ann. §§25.171-25.175 (1957). See also Bradway, Why Pay Alimony?, 32 Ill. L. Rev. 295 (1937), reprinted in Selected Essays on Family Law 1040 (insurance fund for alimony proposed). In many situations, however, the problem is simply that there is not enough money to go around, particularly if the husband has taken on responsibility for a new family. It is here that public support programs such as ADC are playing an increasing part. Not unexpectedly, there have been complaints that ADC is encouraging divorce.[52] To the extent these reports have any factual basis, they may be traceable to the fact that under many state plans the wife is required to institute an action for support against the husband before she can qualify for benefits.[53] Presumably such a requirement is based on a desire to collect reimbursements from the father. In light of the data reported above, is this a sound rule? What should be the relationship between private and public support in this situation? Compare pages 66-71 supra.

PROBLEMS

1. The following provision has been proposed as a remedy for the widespread noncompliance with support decrees:

> Section 107. Restrictions on the Issuance of Marriage Licenses — No license to marry shall be issued if either of the applicants for a license has at any time failed to comply with an order to support lawful dependents which is issued by a court of competent jurisdiction, unless a judge of the superior court shall determine that despite such failure said applicant is financially able to discharge his duty to support his existing dependents, and such judge shall have authority to require that the applicant post sufficient security to insure the performance of his support obligation to his existing dependents. Any marriage contracted in violation of this section shall be void, whether entered into this state or elsewhere.[54]

Would you favor the enactment of this provision?

[52] See Quenstedt & Winkler, note 37 supra, at 5. Compare pages 121-122 supra concerning the relationship between ADC and illegitimacy.

[53] See Kaplan, note 40 supra, at 12.

[54] Compare Wis. Stat. Ann. §245.10 (Supp. 1965).

2. The McCarthys were married in Boston, Massachusetts, ten years ago and have lived there since that time. Mr. McCarthy has been very successful in business and is now a man of fairly substantial means; his wife, meanwhile, inherited a considerable estate at the death of her father. There are two children, aged five and eight.

For some time now relations between the McCarthys have been strained, and a year ago Mr. McCarthy finally felt he had evidence of Mrs. McCarthy's adultery. Accordingly, two months thereafter he brought a suit for divorce in the Suffolk County, Massachusetts, Probate Court. But before Mrs. McCarthy could be served, she took the two children and left for Idaho, where her mother lives. Following the elapse of the six-week residence period, she promptly filed for divorce there, alleging extreme cruelty and demanding custody of the children, as well as substantial alimony and child support. These claims were granted following notice by mail to Mr. McCarthy, who, upon the advice of an attorney, filed a special appearance in the Idaho proceedings, calling to the court's attention the pending Massachusetts case and seeking unsuccessfully to challenge the jurisdiction of the Idaho court to enter a valid divorce decree.

Shortly thereafter, Mr. McCarthy's uncontested Massachusetts divorce action came on for hearing, and he was granted a divorce, along with an order relieving him of all future obligations of support towards Mrs. McCarthy in view of her considerable independent assets and her adultery.

Recently Mr. McCarthy has received a number of letters from Mrs. McCarthy's Idaho attorney requesting him to forward the alimony and child support payments ordered by the Idaho court "or face contempt proceedings." Dissatisfied with his prior legal representation, Mr. McCarthy now consults you with respect to his rights and obligations.

CHAPTER 11

Family Dissolution Planning—
The Separation Agreement

A. PUBLIC POLICY LIMITATIONS ON THE PARTIES' FREEDOM TO NEGOTIATE

The separation agreement is the most important tool employed by the lawyer who services middle class divorce clients. It enables him to work out with the attorney for the other spouse the best arrangement for the support of the wife and children, the custody of the latter, and the division of the spouses' accumulated property. By and large, the law leaves great flexibility to the lawyer who negotiates a separation agreement. Hence there is a premium on imagination coupled with a thorough grounding in the requisite skills (both legal and nonlegal). We shall deal with these matters in Section B below. We first turn briefly to a consideration of some doctrines which somewhat limit the lawyer's substantial freedom of choice.

VILES v. VILES
14 N.Y.2d 365, 200 N.E.2d 567 (1964)

BURKE, J. In this action by a former wife to recover arrears due under a separation agreement the defense is illegality. We find the defense well founded under section 51 of the Domestic Relations Law since the affirmed findings of fact conclusively establish that the agreement was made as an inducement to divorce.

The parties agreed that the venue of the divorce action was to be the Virgin Islands and an oral agreement was reached providing for the payment of plaintiff's traveling expenses to that jurisdiction. The check payable to the order of plaintiff's attorney, designed to cover plaintiff's traveling expenses to the Virgin Islands, was delivered to the attorney at the same time the separation agreement was executed. The defendant's attorney stated he was "submitting this agreement for signature to Mr. Viles, predicated upon the understanding arrived at that Mrs. Viles was going to the Virgin Islands for the purpose of obtaining a divorce, and that this was a condition of the execution of this agreement." This testimony, if credited, clearly evidences a collateral oral agreement which had a direct tendency "to alter or dissolve the marriage," and as such invalidated the written separation agreement (Domestic Relations Law,

§51; [further citations omitted]). Though plaintiff at the trial denied knowledge of any agreement relating to a divorce, it was for the trial court to assess the credibility of the witnesses and we are powerless to disturb the finding that there was in fact an agreement relating to a divorce.

Finally there is the circumstance that on December 8, 1951, less than two months after execution of the separation agreement, plaintiff secured a divorce from defendant. Certainly the record, taken as a whole, may be viewed as evidencing the authority of plaintiff's attorney to negotiate a collateral agreement by plaintiff to obtain a divorce. It follows that the trial court committed no error in admitting testimony of defendant's attorney as to conversations with plaintiff's attorney establishing the substance of the agreement.

The order appealed from should be affirmed, without costs.

VAN VOORHIS, J. (dissenting). Plaintiff has been defeated in her suit against her former husband to recover an arrearage under their separation agreement, which was entered into prior to a Virgin Islands divorce. His income averaged $23,200 per year. She was to receive $5500 annually in monthly installments of $458.33, except that the amount which she was to receive was to be reduced to not less than $3600 per annum if the husband's annual income from trust funds were to fall below $10,000. They had been married for about 12 years. The Virgin Islands divorce decree did not incorporate the agreement, but directed the payment of alimony in an equivalent amount which was later reduced.[1]

Both sides concede and assert that the breach between the parties was irrevocable. Their circumstances were such as would be likely to lead to a divorce, which was in contemplation by each of them at the time when the separation agreement was negotiated and signed.

We are at a loss to understand how the public policy of the State will be promoted by relieving defendant from his obligations under this agreement which he signed, and by denying to his former wife recovery thereon. There is no evidence that the value of the rights secured to her by this agreement was out of proportion to what a divorce court would normally direct to be paid for her support, or that it was not a fair equivalent of his legal obligation to support his wife at the time

---

[1] Mr. Viles sought to have the original alimony order reduced because of a drop in his income and because of his subsequent remarriage. The Virgin Islands District Court granted his request, but was reversed on appeal. The appellate court pointed out that the original order required him to pay $5500 per year so long as his income exceeded $17,500, but if his income fell below that figure, he would be required to pay only $3600 per year. Since this formula established a ratio of 11 to 35 between alimony and income, and since even with Mr. Viles's reduced income this ratio justified alimony of at least $3600, the court held that the drop in income was a contingency that was anticipated by the original order and hence did not warrant a modification. As for Mr. Viles's remarriage, the court stated that "[h]e cannot escape his obligation under the original decree by voluntarily assuming new domestic responsibilities which make performance more burdensome [citing Newburn v. Newburn, page 915 supra]." Viles v. Viles, 316 F.2d 31, 35 (3d Cir. 1963). — Ed.

when it was made. Under such circumstances, as [a] matter of law, it cannot correctly be held that this separation agreement constituted a "contract to alter or dissolve the marriage or to relieve the husband from his liability to support his wife", as provided by section 51 of the Domestic Relations Law. On the contrary, it was entered into in order to satisfy his liability to support his wife. Nothing in this agreement purports to require either of the parties to obtain a divorce from the other. It is not even conditioned on divorce, even though we have held, in effect, that such a condition would not invalidate it (Butler v. Marcus, 264 N.Y. 519). A separation agreement may be invalid, to be sure, which is conditioned on the obtaining of a divorce by the wife and which gives her so much more in value than her just deserts, as they would normally be appraised by a matrimonial court, as to constitute an inducement to obtain the divorce (Schley v. Andrews, 225 N.Y. 110; Murthey v. Murthey, 287 N.Y. 740). There is no evidence that this is that sort of situation. Upon the contrary, nobody contends that this agreement caused the dissolution of this marriage, or that it provides excessive benefits for the wife or was entered into for any other reason than to provide suitably for her support. Public policy is not served by compelling estranged marriage partners to contest in court every detail of their marital differences. There is usually bitterness enough as it is. One may think that public policy would be advanced by minimizing the bitterness rather than by increasing it. These people tried to adjust the financial details of an impending divorce which was already inevitable in a peaceful, sensible and civilized manner. He was already paying her $400 a month for support on a temporary basis, and it is difficult to understand how it vitiated the agreement that this was increased as a result of negotiations to $458.33 a month, even if it be true, as the husband's lawyer testified after the wife's lawyer was dead, that her lawyer said that she would not get the divorce unless this slight increase was made in the separation agreement to be signed. There was nothing sinister in the payment of the entirely reasonable amount of $1500 to cover the counsel fee of the wife, nor, as it seems to us, should it make any difference that he likewise paid the sum of $600 to defray her expenses in going to the Virgin Islands and taking up a residence there. Stress has been laid upon the testimony of the husband's lawyer, which has thus far successfully enabled his client to escape his contractual obligation, that her going to the Virgin Islands for the purpose of obtaining the divorce "was a condition of the execution of this agreement." The fact that they itemized these payments in this manner, instead of concealing them under some other heading, does not offend public policy. Indeed, it was commendable that they were straightforward about it. There is no evidence of overreaching on either side. This divorce was not in any sense being bought. The circumstance that there was some jockeying in the negotiations over the amount to be paid and that, in this context, the lawyer for the wife said that she would not go to the Virgin Islands unless he dealt with her on an entirely reasonable basis, implying presumably that the divorce would have to be obtained in some other manner at greater inconvenience to him, has no tendency to indicate that this separation agreement was the procuring cause of the divorce or that it provided more in value for her than would ordinarily be done in court. . . .

[Fuld and Bergan, JJ., concur in this dissent.]

NOTE

1. Compare the following cases:

a. Butler v. Marcus, 264 N.Y. 519, 191 N.E. 544 (1934). A separation agreement provided that if the spouses were still married one year from the date of the agreement, the payments would cease, but if the spouses were then divorced, the payments would continue. The parties did get a Nevada divorce within the year. On the wife's suit to enforce agreement, *held,* the agreement is valid.

b. Matter of Rhinelander, 290 N.Y. 31, 47 N.E.2d 681 (1943). H had obtained an ex parte Nevada divorce. Because of his concern over the questionable validity of the Nevada divorce, and since his wife had subsequently brought an action for separate support against him, the spouses entered a separation agreement whereby the wife would receive certain support payments on condition that she move to reopen the Nevada proceeding and enter her appearance so as to validate the foreign divorce. *Held,* the agreement is valid.

c. Reed v. Robertson, 302 N.Y. 596, 96 N.E.2d 894 (1951). W was eager to get a divorce. H demanded $1,000,000. The parties eventually executed an agreement in New Jersey, obligating the wife to pay $500,000 over a period of years into a trust for the child of the marriage if the husband would enter an appearance in the wife's foreign divorce action and thus assure her of a valid divorce. The wife made the required payments for twelve years. Upon the husband's suit to enforce her continued payments, *held,* the agreement is void. See also Hill v. Hill, 23 Cal. 2d 82, 142 P.2d 417 (1943), indicating that an agreement executed in contemplation of divorce or even one expressly conditioned on the obtaining of a divorce was valid, but that a commitment not to defend or an offer to pay the other party's attorney's fees if a divorce was obtained by him or her did violate public policy. The courts of most states draw similar razor-thin distinctions between valid and invalid agreements. See Lindey, Separation Agreements and Ante-nuptial Contracts 31-11 (1964). And compare Churchward v. Churchward, page 671 supra; Staedler v. Staedler, page 756 supra.

2. An alternative device sometimes resorted to where one of the parties to a separation agreement wants to condition his side of the bargain on the other party's obtaining a valid divorce is to put securities, insurance policies, and other items to be transferred in escrow, pending the rendition of the divorce decree. In the few cases which have passed on the validity of this device, such arrangements have generally been upheld. See, e.g., Dora v. Dora, 392 Pa. 433, 141 A.2d 587 (1958). See also Casenote, 63 Mich. L. Rev. 735, 737-738 (1965), suggesting that the

end result in Viles could have been validly achieved by deferring the formal execution of the separation agreement until the foreign divorce proceeding had been instituted or by incorporating the agreement in the foreign divorce and thus insulating it from attack by bringing it under the protective mantle of the full faith and credit clause.

3. There are a number of other doctrines which may bear on the validity of a separation agreement:

a. In at least one state (New Hampshire), separation agreements independent of a divorce decree appear not to be recognized at all. Some other states (e.g., Vermont) require special formalities — such as the interposition of trustees between the contracting spouses.[2] Occasionally separation agreements are not recognized at law, but are given effect in equity if fair and reasonable. See, e.g., Schlemm v. Schlemm, 31 N.J. 557, 158 A.2d 508 (1960).

b. Where one of the contracting parties is mentally incompetent, the agreement is invalid. See Crosby v. Crosby, 188 Kan. 274, 362 P.2d 3 (1961); see also page 645 supra.

c. Under §5-311 of the New York General Obligations Law (referred to in the principal case by its former title, §51 of the Domestic Relations Law), an agreement between the spouses involving a waiver of support rights is invalid. Similar provisions exist in a number of other states.

d. An agreement which can be shown to be the result of overreaching, or which is otherwise grossly inequitable, may be invalidated by the courts. See Hoch v. Hoch, 187 Kan. 730, 359 P.2d 839 (1961) (dictum); Davis v. Davis, 49 Cal. App. 2d 239, 121 P.2d 523 (1942) (imposition of quasi-fiduciary standards in community property states); Comment, 20 U. Chi. L. Rev. 138, 141 (1952).

e. A separation agreement entered into while the spouses are still living together is regarded as conducive towards their separation, and therefore void. See Day v. Chamberlain, 223 Mich. 278, 193 N.W. 824 (1923). And see page 327 supra. Similarly, an agreement executed by the parties after their separation will normally be invalidated by a subsequent reconciliation. See Annot., 35 A.L.R.2d 707 (1954). Characteristic of the sharp distinctions between support and property rights that prevail in this area, see pages 913 supra and 952 infra, the same requirements do not apply to a property settlement not involving support obligations.

f. As concerns the parties' power to preclude subsequent judicial interference with a fair agreement, compare Kan. Stat. Ann. §60-1610(d) (1964) (no modification except with respect to custody, support, and education of children if court has approved initial agreement and found it "valid, just, and equitable"), with Wilson v. Caswell, 272 Mass. 297, 172 N.E. 251 (1930) (court retains inherent power to determine adequacy of alimony and child support). See also page 953 infra.

---

[2] But see Mass. Gen. Laws Ann. c. 209, §2 (Supp. 1964), repealing a similar requirement.

PROBLEM

Consider the validity of the following separation agreement clauses proposed by H:

1. "The wife shall institute proceedings for an absolute divorce solely on the ground of indignities in the Common Pleas Court of Philadelphia County and shall prosecute the same with diligence to the entry of a final decree granting or refusing the same." [3]

2. "This contract, which has been arrived at after full disclosure of all relevant information and extensive negotiations between the parties, at which both parties were represented by their own attorneys, constitutes the entire agreement between them. Accordingly, in order to enable both parties to plan their future lives with some assurance of financial stability, the wife covenants that she will not seek to obtain any increase in alimony over the amounts here specified; if she does so, in violation of this covenant, she shall be liable to the husband as liquidated damages in an amount equal to the difference between the amount thus awarded and the amount provided in this agreement."

B. NEGOTIATING A SEPARATION AGREEMENT

PROBLEM

Your client is Henry Hopkins, who has asked you to represent him in connection with his pending marital difficulties with his wife Mary. Henry (age forty-five) and Mary (age forty-two) have been married for about twenty years. They have one child, who is fifteen years old. For some time now Mary has been aware that Henry has been having a serious affair with Jane, whom he is anxious to marry. After much tension and quarreling Mary has finally agreed that it would be best if she and Henry lived apart under a separation agreement. Mary is to get custody of the child, providing Henry's interests in the child are properly protected.

Henry's annual income before taxes is approximately $30,000, and he is willing to pay a total of about $12,000 per year for the support of Mary and the child. He has also agreed to let her live in their present residence, which he purchased several years ago for $40,000, taking title with Mary as joint tenants. The house is now worth about $58,000 (including approximately $8000 of personal property located in the house) and is subject to a mortgage of $10,000. Henry has also agreed that he will continue to maintain life insurance (face value $100,000, cash value $40,000) which he now owns and of which Mary is the beneficiary. Aside from these assets, Henry has approximately $75,000 of securities (most of them bequeathed him by his father fifteen years ago), a joint bank account with Mary containing approximately $3000, and

---

[3] For the reason behind this clause, see page 779 supra.

two cars worth about $2000 each. Mary herself owns a small summer house in another state and a few securities.

At Henry's request Mary's lawyer has drafted a proposed agreement (appended hereto) which he says embodies the terms agreed upon and which he would like you to look over. He also tells you that when his client saw this draft, she was shocked at its length and complexity and suggested an alternative under which she would settle for an outright payment to her of $100,000. (By cashing in the insurance, selling the house, and transferring some of his securities, Henry could probably raise this sum.)

SEPARATION AGREEMENT

An agreement made by and between Henry Hopkins of Ames in the State of _____ (hereinafter referred to as the husband) and Mary Hopkins, also of said Ames in said State of _____ (hereinafter referred to as the wife).

Whereas the husband and the wife were married on November 10, 1947, in said Ames and last lived together there, and have one child named Josephine, age fifteen; and

Whereas the parties have experienced marital difficulties which they are desirous of resolving; and

Whereas it is the intention of the husband and the wife to enter into an agreement concerning their respective property rights and liabilities with respect to the support, maintenance, and alimony of the wife as well as all obligations of custody, maintenance, and support of said child; and

Whereas said husband and wife are now and have been living apart for a period of three months;

Now therefore, in consideration of the promises and the mutual covenants herein contained, it is hereby agreed by and between the husband and wife as follows:

1. Beginning _____, the husband shall pay to the wife $500 per month so long as said wife shall live; provided that if said wife shall subsequently remarry, said payments of $500 per month shall cease forthwith.

2. The wife shall be given custody of said child and she shall receive from the husband for the said child's support, payments of $250 per month, beginning on _____. These payments shall continue so long as said child resides with the wife, providing that upon the child's attaining the age of twenty-five years, the payments shall stop forthwith.

3. The husband agrees to give to the wife exclusive possession of the house now owned by him and located at 223 Story Street in said Ames; and the husband further agrees that he will continue to pay the real estate taxes as well as the remaining mortgage payments on said house.

4. By way of interim support of said wife and child, the husband agrees to pay the wife forthwith a lump sum of $3000. The husband also agrees to pay the wife no later than thirty days after the effective date of this agreement the sum of $1500 for her reasonable attorney's fees in connec

tion with the negotiation and signing of this agreement, as well as any subsequent divorce action which may hereafter be commenced by either party.

5. In case the net aggregate medical and dental expenses of said child exceed $600 in any year, the husband agrees to pay any such excess.

6. The husband hereby agrees to continue to maintain the following insurance policies now owned by him and of which the wife is a beneficiary: (listing omitted). In case the husband shall fail to make any of the foregoing payments, the wife shall have the right to compel the husband to surrender said policies for their cash value and to pay such arrearages, along with a 10 per cent penalty payment, to the wife forthwith out of said cash surrender value. However, upon such default, the husband shall have the duty as soon as possible to reinstate the insurance policies to their condition prior to the default.

7. The husband shall have the care and custody of the child each year for a period of 30 days, beginning on the first Saturday in August or such other period or periods aggregating 30 days as may be agreed upon by the parties hereto; in addition, the husband shall have the right to visit the child at least one day each month, providing the husband shall give at least one week's notice of such visitation day to the wife.

8. The wife hereby releases all rights of dower in any real property of which the husband is now seized or possessed and the husband in turn releases all curtesy in real property of which the wife is now or may hereafter be seized or possessed. Each agrees to execute and deliver at the request of the other or their legal representative all such instruments as may be necessary to effectuate this release.

9. The husband and wife shall each be free from all control and interference by the other and neither shall impose any restraint upon or interfere in any manner with the personal liberty of the other or molest or trouble the other in any way.

10. This agreement shall be effective at once, regardless of the entry of a decree of divorce by any court. However, in case a final decree of divorce is subsequently granted to either party to this agreement, this agreement shall be incorporated in said decree.

11. The interpretation and validity of this agreement shall be governed by the law of _____.

(You will need to read the rest of this chapter in order to deal adequately with this problem.)

1. *Introductory Note*

The negotiation and drafting of a separation agreement are a difficult and demanding task. It is no accident that we take up this subject at this point in the book. Since the separation agreement seeks to deal with all the multifold legal relationships (both personal and financial) that have developed between the parties over the years, the lawyer who undertakes this task must at a minimum have a thorough grounding in the legal consequences that would follow if there were no separation agreement. It is within this framework that the divorce lawyer operates.

But the very fact that it is a voluntary agreement of the parties that is involved materially enlarges the parties' range of choice. We cannot here canvass this subject in detail;[4] a few examples must suffice. In Flagler v. Flagler, page 310 supra, the Florida Supreme Court held that the Florida courts had no power to order child support to continue beyond the father's death. But in Simpson v. Simpson, 108 So.2d 632 (Fla. Dist. Ct. App. 1959), the court enforced a clause in a separation agreement that provided that child support was to be binding on the father's estate. Indeed, with the advent of the separation agreement the emphasis shifts from the divorce court's statutory power to the interpretation of the parties' contractual agreement.[5] Thus if a separation agreement provides that alimony is to be paid "so long as the wife is living and remains unmarried," the essential question is not whether a judicial order of alimony terminates upon the husband's death (see page 917 supra) but whether the parties intended the stipulated payments to continue beyond the husband's death. Compare Taylor v. Gowetz, 339 Mass. 294, 158 N.E.2d 677 (1959) (payments held enforcible against H's estate), with Desjardins v. Desjardins, 308 F.2d 111, 117-118 (6th Cir. 1962) (estate not liable because surrounding circumstances, such as H's executory promise to take out life insurance policy, indicated intent not to pay alimony beyond his death). See also Annot., 75 A.L.R.2d 1085 (1961). The implications for the draftsman should be obvious.

The basic skills required of the lawyer who negotiates a separation agreement are therefore similar to those called for in any planning situation — foreseeing and making careful provision for all the reasonably expectable contingencies.[6] Since the agreement often governs major aspects of the lives of the parties for an extended period, and since the parties' relationship frequently is such as to preclude later voluntary adjustments, a rather lengthy and detailed agreement may result. Alternatively, where the relationship is particularly acrimonious and future disputes are almost clearly foreseeable, it may be desirable to explore the possibility of a lump sum settlement. But see page 946 supra with respect to the limitations on the parties' power to arrive at a once-and-for-all settlement. And see page 957 infra concerning the tax disadvantages of such a settlement. A third alternative is the utilization of an arbitration clause for the resolution of future disputes. Compare page 865 supra.

There are, however, a number of aspects in which the divorce lawyer's task calls for special skills and responsibilities. A key question that

[4] For a full-scale examination of all aspects of separation agreements, including a compilation of sample clauses, see Lindey, Separation Agreements and Antenuptial Contracts (1964).

[5] This statement is subject to some qualifications. There may be certain matters to which the parties cannot agree (see page 942 supra). And if the agreement of the parties is later incorporated in a court decree, the statutory powers of the court may still be relevant. See page 954 infra.

[6] See Fisher, Towards Better Separation Agreements, 4 J. Fam. L. 63 (1964), for a suggested method of dealing with some of the most common contingencies affecting the amount of alimony and child support.

assumes particular significance because a separation agreement is usually negotiated in an atmosphere of bitterness and hostility is the role to be played by the lawyer for each of the parties. Consider the following comments by a number of New York lawyers who were questioned on this subject:

> Suppose I get a huge alimony for a wife and I know that it is more than the man can afford in terms of spendable income. Well the wife thinks it's wonderful and I'm a great lawyer in her eyes. But in a few years he won't pay it any more; he can't afford it. He was anxious to get divorced and wasn't too cautious, but now it is impossible. Maybe he wants to re-marry. He's angry. He can't pay. The situation deteriorates. Why? Because the contract was not feasible to begin with. . . . I try for fairness in such situations, a settlement which can serve as a guide for my client for a long time.

* * *

> The lawyer's job is to get the client the results they want. Whatever they want I get for them provided it's not illegal and can be done. . . .

* * *

> In matrimonial cases clients are primarily interested in money. If you represent the wife, then your job is to get as much as possible for her. If you represent the husband, pay out as little as possible.

* * *

> What's fair support? . . . Let's say, on the basis of the man's income . . . the courts have been going along with something between twenty and thirty dollars a week for support. . . . Now the opposing lawyer tells me that the wife wants, or will settle for, twenty-five dollars a week for the children. Now my client can afford twenty-five dollars and probably would go along with it. But he figures that his wife will get part of that for herself, and, besides, he's going to buy clothes, toys, and take the children out. So he hedges a bit. Then he figures, *well, what have I, his lawyer, done for him?* He could have accepted that without a lawyer. So I tell him that legally that is a reasonable solution, but I'll see what I can do. I tell the other lawyer that my client wants to pay twenty dollars. So we dicker back and forth. Finally, we agree on twenty-two-fifty a week. I tell the husband and he agrees, and we end on that. *You have to show the client that you are doing something for him.*[7]

Closely related to this question of the role that the lawyer conceives for himself is his willingness to temper his client's legal rights by certain common sense considerations. The first of the preceding excerpts sug-

[7] O'Gorman, Lawyers and Matrimonial Cases 134-136 (1963). For a description of this study and other excerpts from it, see pages 752, 767, and 835 supra. The omissions in the first and last excerpts are the author's.

gests the importance of fashioning an agreement that the parties can live with. Another example is the not uncommon clause that provides for sharply reduced support upon the wife's remarriage, but does not eliminate it altogether, on the theory that such a clause will act as less of a deterrent to her remarriage where she is receiving substantial alimony, and hence may ultimately redound to the husband's benefit.

Returning now to the purely legal aspects, we have seen that by and large these are derived from the general rules that prevail with respect to the relations between husband and wife and parent and child. There are, however, two areas of special concern here, and it is to these that we now turn.

RELATION OF SEPARATION AGREEMENT
TO DIVORCE DECREE

There is a wide range of possible relationships between the agreement and the decree. At one extreme are the situations where the relationship is a nonexistent one, either because there is an agreement without any subsequent decree or because there is a decree without any prior agreement.[8] At the other end of the scale is the separation agreement which is expressly incorporated in a subsequent divorce decree, and which therefore is generally considered to be "merged" in the decree. Between these two extremes there are a variety of possible situations. For example, the decree may make no mention at all of the agreement, and may impose support and other obligations which are totally at variance with those prescribed in the agreement. Or the decree, with or without express reference to the agreement, may adopt some of its terms but differ from it in other respects. Finally, the decree may impose precisely the same terms as are set forth in the agreement, but without express reference to or incorporation of the separation agreement.

Because a private agreement and a court decree differ in at least two essential respects — modifiability and enforceability — these tend to be the principal issues presented in this area.[9] Thus, if a wife seeks to obtain increased support on account of a subsequent improvement in the husband's financial condition, she will not ordinarily be able to do so if she bases her claim on a mere contractual agreement of the parties. How-

---

[8] The latter is the typical situation in the mass of lower class divorces. See Chapter 10. The former is probably relatively uncommon since separation agreements are usually executed in contemplation of divorce. A recent Kansas amendment apparently requires every separation agreement to be approved by the court and incorporated into any subsequent divorce decree. See Hopson, Divorce and Alimony under the New Code, 12 Kan. L. Rev. 27, 43 (1963). Once this is done, however, the agreement attains a limited immunity against modification. See page 946 supra. Compare a similar recommendation in the Report of the Joint Legislative Committee on Matrimonial and Family Laws 44 (N.Y. Legis. Doc. No. 26, 1958).

[9] An overriding issue is whether the obligations encompassed are on account of support or property rights. If the latter, they are normally not modifiable or enforceable by contempt proceedings even if based on a decree. See Dailey v. Dailey, 171 Ohio St. 133, 167 N.E.2d 906 (1960); Goggans v. Osborn, 237 F.2d 186 (9th Cir. 1956).

ever, if she seeks to modify a divorce decree that incorporated the agreement of the parties, she will have a far better chance of success. Indeed, theoretically a decree based on an agreement is just as modifiable as the bare decree itself would be. See Annot., 166 A.L.R. 675 (1947). In actual fact, however, courts may often be more reluctant to modify a decree where it is based on the agreement of the parties. See, e.g., Viles v. Viles, 316 F.2d 31, 33 (3d Cir. 1963).[10] But see McMains v. McMains, 15 N.Y.2d 283, 206 N.E.2d 185 (1965), which held that a wife could modify the support payments specified in a divorce decree where she was unable to support herself on those payments and the husband's means had substantially increased since the promulgation of the decree. This result was reached even though the decree was based on a prior agreement of the parties that was expressly stipulated to survive the decree.

In the reverse situation, where the husband seeks to reduce his support payments, he will be the one to assert the inherent modifiability of the decree. The wife then will have two strings to her bow — she can resist modification on the merits, and alternatively she can stand on the non-modifiable contractual agreement of the parties (which of course cannot be enforced by the contempt sanction). Whether the agreement retains its independent validity despite the subsequent decree depends upon its precise relation to the decree; if the agreement was expressly incorporated in the decree, it is generally deemed merged in it. But the parties can usually specify that the agreement shall survive the decree (in which case it may or may not be incorporated).[11] See Freeman v. Sieve, 323 Mass. 652, 84 N.E.2d 16 (1949) (survival governed by intent of parties). But see Day v. Day, 80 Nev. 386, 395 P.2d 321 (1964) (no survival unless court decree itself so provides). Compare also McMains v. McMains, supra (two dissenting judges pointed to unfairness of wife looking to decree to obtain increased support but standing on agreement to resist husband's claim for decrease). Here again there are obvious implications for the draftsman. Since all too often he fails to deal explicitly with the issue of merger, the courts have evolved elaborate presumptions as to the par-

[10] For an illuminating illustration of these principles, see Newman v. Newman, 161 Ohio St. 247, 118 N.E.2d 649 (1954), and Hunt v. Hunt, 169 Ohio St. 276, 159 N.E.2d 430 (1959). In Newman, the Ohio Supreme Court held that although a court order for alimony is normally modifiable upon a change of circumstance, where an alimony decree is based on the agreement of the parties, it is not modifiable unless jurisdiction is expressly reserved. Accordingly, a wife who was entitled to a maximum of $4000 under an agreement executed twenty years previously, and whose husband had meanwhile become a millionaire, was not entitled to modification of the decree that incorporated the parties' agreement. But in Hunt the same court held that it would be against public policy not to terminate alimony upon the wife's remarriage to a man capable of supporting her, even though the agreement that formed the basis of the decree said nothing about such termination. See also Miller v. Miller, 317 Ill. App. 447, 46 N.E.2d 102 (1943) (provision of separation agreement that barred modification of alimony on wife's remarriage held not effective to deprive court of inherent power to modify decree in which agreement was incorporated).

[11] There is frequently a tendency to confuse the notions of incorporation and merger. There is no reason why the parties could not have the entire agreement incorporated in specie in the decree and still provide for the survival of the agreement. See Harris v. Commissioner, 340 U.S. 106, 119-120 n.4 (1950).

ties' intent. See, e.g., Metcalf v. Commissioner, 271 F.2d 288, 292 (1st Cir. 1959) (survival presumed because wife would not lightly waive the obvious benefits that this doctrine confers upon her). The result in any particular case may depend not only on the degree of identity between agreement and decree but also on the equities of the case and the precise issue presented.

Apart from the questions of modification and enforcement, there may be certain collateral aspects of the agreement-decree relationship. As pointed out previously, if the agreement itself violates local public policy, a foreign decree incorporating it will usually render the agreement enforcible. See Laufer, Family Law, 34 N.Y.U.L. Rev. 1550, 1556 (1959). Conversely, where, for example, a court has no power to award permanent alimony upon divorce (see page 908 supra), an agreement so providing that is incorporated in the decree will not be effective as a decree (and hence cannot be enforced by contempt). See Note, 31 N.C.L. Rev. 482 (1953). Indeed, in one bizarre case that has now been reversed by statute, it was held that since prior to 1963 the Kansas courts had no power to award alimony in periodic form, a decree that incorporated such an agreement was void; since the agreement was held merged in the decree, the agreement could not be enforced either through a suit on the contract. Conway v. Conway, 133 Kan. 148, 298 Pac. 744 (1931).[12]

In general, see Comment, Divorce Agreements: Independent Contract or Incorporation in Decree, 20 U. Chi. L. Rev. 138 (1952); Note, Control of Post-Divorce Level of Support by Prior Agreement, 63 Harv. L. Rev. 337 (1949).

2. *An Outline of the Tax Considerations*

I.   Income Tax Aspects

Internal Revenue Code of 1954 SEC. 71. Alimony and Separate Maintenance Payments.
(a)   General Rule. —
(1) Decree of divorce or separate maintenance. — If a wife is divorced or legally separated from her husband under a decree of divorce or of separate maintenance, the wife's gross income includes periodic payments (whether or not made at regular intervals) received after such decree in discharge of (or attributable to property transferred, in trust or otherwise, in discharge of) a legal obligation which, because of the marital or family relationship, is imposed on or incurred by the husband under the decree or under a written instrument incident to such divorce or separation.
(2) Written separation agreement. — If a wife is separated from her husband and there is a written separation agreement executed after the date of the enactment of this title, the wife's gross income

---

[12] Other courts have more sensibly concluded that an agreement cannot be merged into a void decree. See, e.g., McBride v. McBride, 256 S.W.2d 250 (Tex. Civ. App. 1953).

includes periodic payments (whether or not made at regular intervals) received after such agreement is executed which are made under such agreement and because of the marital or family relationship (or which are attributable to property transferred, in trust or otherwise, under such agreement and because of such relationship). This paragraph shall not apply if the husband and wife make a single return jointly.

(3) Decree for support. — If a wife is separated from her husband, the wife's gross income includes periodic payments (whether or not made at regular intervals) received by her after the date of the enactment of this title from her husband under a decree entered after March 1, 1954, requiring the husband to make the payments for her support or maintenance. This paragraph shall not apply if the husband and wife make a single return jointly.

(b) Payments to Support Minor Children. — Subsection (a) shall not apply to that part of any payment which the terms of the decree, instrument, or agreement fix, in terms of an amount of money or a part of the payment, as a sum which is payable for the support of minor children of the husband. For purposes of the preceding sentence, if any payment is less than the amount specified in the decree, instrument, or agreement, then so much of such payment as does not exceed the sum payable for support shall be considered a payment for such support.

(c) Principal Sum Paid in Installments. —

(1) General rule. — For purposes of subsection (a), installment payments discharging a part of an obligation the principal sum of which is, either in terms of money or property, specified in the decree, instrument, or agreement shall not be treated as periodic payments.

(2) Where period for payment is more than 10 years. — If, by the terms of the decree, instrument, or agreement, the principal sum referred to in paragraph (1) is to be paid or may be paid over a period ending more than 10 years from the date of such decree, instrument, or agreement, then (notwithstanding paragraph (1)) the installment payments shall be treated as periodic payments for purposes of subsection (a), but (in the case of any one taxable year of the wife) only to the extent of 10 percent of the principal sum. For purposes of the preceding sentence, the part of any principal sum which is allocable to a period after the taxable year of the wife in which it is received shall be treated as an installment payment for the taxable year in which it is received.

(d) Rule for Husband in Case of Transferred Property. — The husband's gross income does not include amounts received which, under subsection (a), are (1) includible in the gross income of the wife, and (2) attributable to transferred property. . . .

SEC. 215. Alimony, Etc., Payments.
(a) General rule. — In the case of a husband described in section

71, there shall be allowed as a deduction amounts includible under section 71 in the gross income of his wife, payment of which is made within the husband's taxable year. No deduction shall be allowed under the preceding sentence with respect to any payment if, by reason of section 71(d) or 682, the amount thereof is not includible in the husband's gross income.

A. *Under the 1954 Code,*[13] *three types of support payments qualify for deduction by the husband and concomitant taxability to the wife, provided certain additional requirements set forth in B infra are complied with:*
  1. Payments pursuant to a decree of divorce or separate maintenance (or a written agreement incident to such decree) (§71(a)(1)).
     a. This provision assumed primary importance before the 1954 Code revision because it was then the only basis for deduction of support payments by the husband. With respect to the deductibility of payments provided for in a separation agreement, there was much controversy over such questions as whether the agreement was "incident" to a decree of divorce.[14] Since the 1954 Code added §71(a)(2), which explicitly covers payments pursuant to a written separation agreement (whether or not incident to a decree), §71(a)(1) is now significant only where there is no written separation agreement or where such was executed prior to August 16, 1954, the effective date of the 1954 Code.
  2. Payments pursuant to a written separation agreement executed after August 16, 1954 (or one executed prior thereto but materially modified subsequent thereto) (§71(a)(2)).
     a. H and W must be "living apart," but there need be no decree of divorce or legal separation. Regs. 1.71-1(b)(2).
     b. If under state law a reconciliation has the effect of invalidating the separation agreement, any subsequent payments would probably be deemed voluntary and not pursuant to the written agreement.
  3. Any judicial order for support entered after March 1, 1954 (or a prior order which is materially altered after this date) (§71(a)(3)).
     a. This subsection, which was also added in 1954, was designed primarily to cover temporary alimony and pendente lite payments. Regs. 1.71-1, Ex. 4.
  4. Purely voluntary payments which do not fall into any of the above categories are not deductible by H or taxable to W. Herrmann, 23 T.C.M. 429 (1964).

[13] For a detailed discussion of the pre-1954 Code law, see Harvard Law School International Program in Taxation. Taxation in the United States 897 (Commerce Clearing House 1963); Powell, Separation and Divorce: Income, Gift and Estate Tax Consequences, 15 N.Y.U. Tax Inst. 763-764 (1957).
[14] See note 13 supra.

B. *Additional Requirements in Order for Above Three Types of Payments to be Deductible by H and Taxable to W*

  1. Payments must be "periodic."

    a. This key term is not defined by the Code. Its apparent purpose is to distinguish between lump sum payments (as to which no special tax treatment is warranted) and periodic payments (which are presumed to come out of the husband's taxable income and hence may create serious financial hardship for him unless they are made deductible).

    b. The statute does state that payments need not be made at regular intervals in order to be periodic. It also specifies that even though a lump sum or principal sum is provided for in the agreement or decree, if it is dischargeable through a series of installments extending over a period of more than ten years from the date of the decree or agreement, then the payments shall nevertheless be treated as periodic. However, the maximum deduction in any one year is 10 per cent of the principal sum. §71(c)(2).

      i. Concerning the manner of computing the ten-year period, a court has held that where a judicial decree substantially modified a separation agreement, the payments must be considered to be pursuant to the decree rather than the agreement, and the ten-year period therefore runs from the date of the decree. Commissioner v. Newman, 248 F.2d 473 (8th Cir. 1957). See also Furrow v. Commissioner, 292 F.2d 604 (10th Cir. 1961).

    c. An alternative basis for treating the payments as periodic was established by judicial decision and is now embodied in the regulations. If the payments are modifiable or terminable upon any of the following contingencies (death or change in economic circumstances of either spouse or remarriage of the wife), then, no matter how long they last, it is not possible readily to compute their lump sum equivalent, and therefore they are treated as periodic. Thus, if a decree provides for alimony payments of $100 per month to last for a period of six years or until the wife dies or remarries, whichever first occurs, then the payments are treated as periodic and hence are deductible by H and taxable to W. Regs. 1.71-1(d)(3)(i).

      i. The contingency may be expressly imposed by the instrument or decree, or it may be supplied by local law. See, e.g., Rev. Rul. 59-190, 1959-1 Cum. Bull. 23, holding that since the statutes of the State of Washington provide for the termination of alimony decrees upon the death of either spouse and also allow for subsequent judicial modification of the amount of a decree upon a change of economic circumstance, payments pursuant to a Washington alimony decree are periodic, whether or not the decree expressly provides for these contingencies. However, if deductibility is desired, it would seem more advisable expressly to set forth the contingency in the agreement or decree since local law may be changed.

ii. In view of the immediately preceding paragraph, where payments are made pursuant to a decree, or an agreement that is merged in a decree, it may be impossible under the law of some states to *prevent* the payments from being treated as periodic payments if such is desired in view of the relative brackets of the spouses. In such cases the best alternative is a lump sum payment.

d. If payments qualify as periodic under both b (ten-year test) and c (contingency test) supra, the latter prevails and the 10 per cent limitation is inapplicable. Regs. 1.71-1(d)(4).

e. Where an agreement or decree contains both lump sum and periodic payments, a question arises whether the two types of payments are clearly severable, or whether, for example, the lump sum payment is really a part of the periodic series. See, e.g., Hilgemeier, 42 T.C. 496 (1964) (where decree specified that H pay W $52,400 in the form of an immediate payment of $2000 plus $350 per month thereafter, all payments are in discharge of a principal sum payable over a period in excess of ten years, and hence W is taxable on them).

f. A lump sum settlement of an arrearage in periodic alimony obligations is itself treated as a periodic payment, Davis, 41 T.C. 815 (1964), but if the lump sum payment is in lieu of all future alimony obligations, it is not treated as periodic, Loverin, 10 T.C. 406 (1948).

2. Payments must be made because of the marital or family relationship (Regs. 1.71-1(b)(4)).

a. Section 71 is not applicable to H's repayment of W's loan, Landa, 11 T.C.M. 420, rev'd on other grounds, 206 F.2d 431 (1953), 211 F.2d 46 (D.C. Cir. 1954), or to H's continuing to pay mortgage payments on their prior residence which is now used by W. Bradley, 30 T.C. 701 (1958).

3. Although the statute is silent on the point, the regulations specify that the payments must be for support rather than dower or other property rights in order to qualify for deduction by H. Regs. 1.71-1(b)(4). This principle has been most significant in the community property states where periodic payments in satisfaction of the wife's community property claims have been repeatedly held nondeductible. See, e.g., Bardwell v. Commissioner, 318 F.2d 786 (10th Cir. 1963).

C. *Support of Children*

1. Amounts "specifically designated" for the support of minor children are not treated as alimony and hence are not deductible by H or taxable to W (§71(b)). However, such amounts count towards child support for exemption purposes. See G infra.

2. Where one amount is designated for the support of both wife and children, the total amount is regarded as alimony and hence is deductible by H and taxable to W if it is in periodic form, even if it is subject to specified diminutions on such contingencies as W's remarriage or the death or majority of the children (and hence indirectly allocates between W and the children). Commissioner v. Lester, 366 U.S. 299 (1961). It makes no difference that W in fact spends the entire sum on the child. Kirby, 35 T.C. 306 (1960). Only sums specifically designated for child support come under §71(b). Where a separation agreement which does not specifically designate a sum for child support is incorporated in a decree which does, the payments are considered child support. Metcalf v. Commissioner, 343 F.2d 66 (1st Cir. 1965).

3. Where the parties make a supplementary side agreement which states that $5000 of $9800 alimony is for child support, but the subsequent divorce decree merely speaks of $9800 alimony, the fact that the side agreement is effective under state law deprives H of a deduction for the $5000 portion of each annual payment. Emmons, 36 T.C. 728 (1961), aff'd, 311 F.2d 223 (6th Cir. 1962).

4. The courts are in disagreement concerning the effect of a nunc pro tunc decree purporting to designate some portion of an initially unallocated sum for child support. See Turkoglu, 36 T.C. 552 (1961).

5. If some amount is specifically designated for the support of children, and the total payment is insufficient to cover both alimony and child support, the payment is presumed to go first for child support. Regs. 1.71-1(e).

6. Federal law governs on the question of who is a "minor child." Thus payments to a nineteen-year-old child are treated as child support, even though under state law the age of majority is eighteen. Borbonus, 42 T.C. 983 (1964).

D. *Property Transfers*

1. General Rule as to Income from Such Property
Where H transfers property of any kind (such as securities, real estate, or insurance, directly or in trust) to W in satisfaction of the agreement or decree, any periodic payments of income therefrom received by W are taxable to her. Such payments are not taxable to H nor deductible by him. Regs. 1.71-1(c), 1.215-1.

2. Realization of Gain by H
H realizes gain when he transfers appreciated property (such as securities or real estate) to W in consideration of her release of marital or support rights. United States v. Davis, 370 U.S. 65 (1962). It is irrelevant whether the transfer is pursuant to a court decree or a voluntary separation agreement. Pulliam v. Commissioner, 329 F.2d 97 (10th Cir. 1964).
Normally such gain is equal to the difference between the fair

market value and the cost of the property transferred; courts assume that the value of the rights surrendered by W is equal to the fair market value of the property received by her. But cf. Hall, 9 T.C. 53 (1947), and Commissioner v. Patino, 186 F.2d 962 (4th Cir. 1950) (value established by agreement of parties permitted to govern).

In order to avoid realization of gain, cash or nonappreciated property should be used where possible.

Gain is usually capital gain if capital assets (see §1221) are transferred. But see §§1239, 1245, and 1250 with respect to transfers of depreciable property.

With respect to community property, the result depends upon whether there is a simple partition of the community (no gain), or whether the two spouses receive disparate distributions (gain). Compare Swanson v. Wiseman, 61-1 U.S.T.C. ¶9264 (W.D. Okla. 1961), with Johnson v. United States, 135 F.2d 125 (9th Cir. 1943). And see Wren, Tax Problems Incident to Divorce and Property Settlement, 49 Calif. L. Rev. 665, 685-692 (1961).

3. Realization of Loss by H

Section 267 prohibits the recognition of losses on sales of property between a husband and wife. Thus H should not transfer depreciated property to W; it is best to sell such property on the open market and transfer the proceeds to W. Where H transfers gain items along with loss items, he may be able to net the two except with respect to a loss on his residence, which can never be recognized in any way. Pulliam, 39 T.C. 883 (1963), aff'd, 329 F.2d 97 (10th Cir. 1964).

4. W's Basis in Property Received

Equal to fair market value of property received. See United States v. Davis, 370 U.S. 65, 73 (1962); cf. Farid-es-Sultaneh v. Commissioner, 160 F.2d 812 (2d Cir. 1947).

5. Transfers in Trust

   a. Essentially the same rules that are described above apply. See, e.g., Rev. Rul. 57-507, 1957-2 Cum. Bull. 511, holding that where H transfers appreciated property in trust, with life income to be paid to W as alimony and the remainder to go to charity, H is taxable only on that portion of the total gain which the value of W's life estate bears to the total value of the transferred property.

   b. Where H assigns to W his interest in a pre-existing trust rather than creating a new alimony trust, §682 (which differs from §71 in certain technical respects, see Regs. 1.682(a)-1(a)(2)) governs the taxability of the income.

   c. In general, see Tax Aspects of Alimony Trusts, 66 Yale L.J. 881 (1957).

E. *Specific Items*
1. Taxes
   If H agrees to reimburse W for any income tax incurred by her as a result of her receipt of alimony payments, this is regarded as additional alimony and is therefore taxable to W and deductible by H. See Rev. Rul. 58-100, 1958-1 Cum. Bull. 31; Mahana v. United States, 88 F. Supp. 285 (Ct. Cl.), cert. denied, 339 U.S. 978 (1950). This may lead to spiraling of taxes, unless the parties make a better arrangement (e.g., by giving W so much that she has the desired amount after tax).
2. Insurance
   a. If H pays premiums on life insurance of which W is the beneficiary, the premiums are not deductible as alimony unless (1) the policies are irrevocably assigned to W, (2) she has all the incidents of ownership, and (3) the premium payments are in periodic form. Hyde v. Commissioner, 301 F.2d 279 (2d Cir. 1962).
   b. An outright transfer of the policy to W will usually give rise to taxable gain. See D supra. It may also limit W's exclusion on H's death. See §101(a)(2).
3. Medical Expenses
   a. Of W
   Deductible if in periodic form. Rev. Rul. 62-106, 1962-2 Cum. Bull. 21.
   b. Of Children
   Not deductible as alimony or child support, but they will count towards meeting the more-than-one-half-support requirement of §152, and hence may help to give H the $600 exemption for a child. See G infra. Once H meets this support requirement, the child becomes his "dependent," and its medical expenses are deductible along with his own, subject to the usual statutory limits (i.e., only expenses in excess of 3 per cent of H's adjusted gross income can be deducted).
4. Real Estate
   a. If H merely allows W to live rent free in his individually owned house, he gets no deduction for the fair rental value. Pappenheimer v. Allen, 164 F.2d 428 (5th Cir. 1947); Bradley, 30 T.C. 701 (1958). Nor can H deduct insurance, taxes, or mortgage payments *as alimony* where he owns the house outright or with W as tenants by the entireties. However, in such cases he can deduct the taxes and mortgage interest as his own itemized deductions. Rev. Rul. 62-38, 1962-1 Cum. Bull. 15.
   Where H and W own the residence in question as tenants in common (and presumably also where they own it as joint tenants), H can deduct one half of all payments for principal, interest, insurance, and taxes as alimony if the payments are

in periodic form, and the wife must similarly include one half of all such payments. W can in turn deduct on her own return that portion of her payments which represents interest and taxes, provided she itemizes her deductions. H can make a similar deduction with respect to the tax and interest payments allocable to his half. Rev. Rul. 62-39, 1962-1 Cum. Bull. 17.

Where H conveys title to the house to W, his subsequent mortgage payments, if in periodic form, are taxable to W as alimony. Mace v. United States, 64-2 U.S.T.C. ¶9732 (S.D. Cal. 1964).

Regardless of the state of the title, H can deduct any periodic utility payments made with respect to a house of which W has exclusive possession. Rev. Rul. 62-39, supra.

  b. If H is directed by the divorce court to pay W's rent, H can deduct it so long as it is in periodic form. See the Commissioner's concession to this effect in Lounsbury, 37 T.C. 163, 168 (1961), aff'd on other grounds, 321 F.2d 925 (9th Cir. 1963).

  c. If H transfers to W his interest in the family residence, he will be taxable on the difference between the current market value and the basis of such interest. Stephen, 38 T.C. 345 (1962). If H purchases another residence, he may be able to defer such gain under §1034.

  d. Where H is ordered by the divorce court to purchase a house for W, the mortgage payments will not be deductible alimony even if they are in periodic form because they represent a discharge of a lump sum obligation. Lounsbury, 37 T.C. 163 (1961), aff'd, 321 F.2d 925 (9th Cir. 1963).

F. *Attorney's Fees*

  1. H cannot deduct his own attorney's fee as a business expense, even where it is incurred in part to protect his income-producing property (such as a controlling stock interest) against W's claims. United States v. Gilmore, 372 U.S. 39 (1963); United States v. Patrick, 372 U.S. 53 (1963). However, H can deduct such portion of his expenses as is allocable to the obtaining of tax advice. Carpenter v. United States, 338 F.2d 366 (Ct. Cl. 1964). This suggests the desirability of the attorney's allocation of his fee into tax-related and nontax-related portions. Any portion of the fee that is nondeductible can be added to the basis of property that the attorney's efforts enable him to retain. Gilmore v. United States, 245 F. Supp. 383 (N.D. Cal. 1965).

  2. W can deduct her attorney's fee to the extent it is related to the collection of amounts includable in gross income (i.e., taxable alimony). Regs. 1.262-1(b)(7); Wild, 42 T.C. 706 (1964). In the alternative, W probably can also deduct that portion of her fee which is related to the obtaining of tax advice and add any

nondeductible portion to the basis of property received.   See 1 supra.

3. If H pays W's attorney's fee, he cannot deduct it.   United States v. Davis, 370 U.S. 65 (1962).   It may therefore be desirable in appropriate cases for H to give W more deductible alimony and let her pay her own attorney's fee and claim deduction therefor under 2 supra.

G. *Exemption for Child*

1. The spouse who contributes more than half of a child's support can take the $600 dependency exemption.   See Regs. 1.152. Thus any spouse claiming an exemption for a child must know the total support costs of that child.   This may involve difficult questions of proof if the other spouse is uncooperative.   See Sijan, 14 T.C.M. 1109 (1955).   It may therefore be desirable to insert a provision in the separation agreement requiring each spouse to supply exemption information to the other.   But an attempt by the spouses to allocate the exemption between themselves is not binding on the Commissioner.

2. H can only count those payments which are specifically designated as child support (and hence are nondeductible). §152(b)(4).

3. If a child has its "principal place of abode" with a spouse who pays at least half the cost of maintaining such abode, then that spouse is entitled to favorable Head of Household treatment, regardless of whether he or she is entitled to an exemption for the child, provided that he or she is "not married," (i.e., there has been a final decree of divorce or separate maintenance). §§1(b)(2), 6013(d)(2).

H. *Interrelation of H's and W's Tax*

1. Normally H gets no deduction unless the payments are taxable to W.   §215; Mandel v. Commissioner, 229 F.2d 382 (7th Cir. 1956).   But after H's death his estate apparently gets no deduction even though the payments are still taxable to W.   Regs. 1.215-1(b); Estate of Jarboe, 39 T.C. 690 (1963).   But see G.C.M. 25999, 1949-1 C.B. 116 (post-death payments from income of estate may be deductible under §§651 and 661).

2. The characterization of the payments in proceedings involving one spouse is not res judicata as far as the other spouse is concerned.   Seligmann v. Commissioner, 207 F.2d 489, 495 (7th Cir. 1953).

3. It is desirable to provide in the separation agreement for (a) the allocation of subsequently asserted deficiencies or refunds on joint returns filed prior to the execution of the separation agreement, and (b) an option to continue filing joint returns after the execution of the separation agreement and prior to a final divorce, including the allocation of the spouses' respective contributions towards such joint returns.

II. Gift Tax Aspects

SEC. 2516. Certain Property Settlements. Where husband and wife enter into a written agreement relative to their marital and property rights and divorce occurs within 2 years thereafter (whether or not such agreement is approved by the divorce decree), any transfers of property or interests in property made pursuant to such agreement —

(1) to either spouse in settlement of his or her marital or property rights, or

(2) to provide a reasonable allowance for the support of issue of the marriage during minority,

shall be deemed to be transfers made for a full and adequate consideration in money or money's worth.

A. *Section 2516 provides the principal basis for exemption from the gift tax. But note that it is not applicable to*

1. Transfers for the support of children beyond their minority, even if state law requires such support (e.g., because the child is disabled).

2. Transfers pursuant to a separation agreement which is not followed by a decree of divorce within two years.

3. Transfers which are in satisfaction of W's support claims as distinguished from her marital or property claims.

4. Judicially ordered transfers, where there is no separation agreement.

However this does not mean that all these excepted types of transfers are subject to the gift tax. Some of them — in particular the last two — are covered by the pre-§2516 law.

B. *Where §2516 is not applicable, the prior law controls.*

1. Basic Support Rights

   Transfers in satisfaction of the support claims of the wife and minor children do not constitute taxable gifts because they are considered to be transfers for consideration. E.T. 19, 1946-2 Cum. Bull. 166.

2. Property Rights

   Transfers in satisfaction of the wife's dower or other property claims are taxable gifts unless they are made pursuant to a court decree. This rule derives from the fact that §2043(b) of the estate tax[15] specifically states that the relinquishment of such claims does not constitute consideration, and this provision has been held applicable to the gift tax also. However, in Harris v. Commissioner, 340 U.S. 106 (1950), the Supreme Court stated

---

[15] "SEC. 2043. . . . (b) Marital Rights Not Treated as Consideration. — For purposes of this chapter, a relinquishment or promised relinquishment of dower or curtesy, or of a statutory estate created in lieu of dower or curtesy, or of other marital rights in the decedent's property or estate, shall not be considered to any extent a consideration 'in money or money's worth.' "

that the purpose of §2043(b) was solely to prevent the evasion of the estate tax through voluntary predeath transfers; accordingly, a judicially decreed transfer was held not subject to this provision and hence not subject to gift tax.

a. When is a transfer pursuant to a court decree, rather than the voluntary agreement of the parties, so as to come within the Harris exemption?

    i. Where a separation agreement requires H to transfer certain property to W, the transfer is not a gift if it does not take place until after the divorce decree, McMurtry v. Commissioner, 203 F.2d 659 (1st Cir. 1953), or if the separation agreement is made expressly contingent upon adoption by the divorce court, Harris v. Commissioner, supra.

    ii. But if the transfer is made prior to and independent of any divorce decree, or if a separation agreement cannot be modified by the divorce court, then the transfer is considered voluntary and taxable unless it comes within one of the other two exemptions (i.e., the support rule, B.1 supra, or §2516). Commissioner v. Barnard's Estate, 176 F.2d 233 (2d Cir. 1949); Estate of Bowers, 23 T.C. 911 (1955).

b. Thus to the extent that a separation agreement is on account of marital and property rights of the wife, it is essential to have a divorce within two years (so as to come within §2516), or else to provide for the approval of the agreement by the divorce court (so as to come within the Harris rule). But see pages 942-947 supra concerning the public policy and other problems that may be presented by clauses that seek to accomplish these objectives.

Another alternative may be to delay the transfer until after a decree of divorce has been obtained, so as to come within the McMurtry case, supra. But this may be unfeasible in some cases; moreover, if some gift tax were nevertheless held to be due, the donor would no longer be able to avail himself of the benefits of the 50 per cent marital deduction (§2523) for gifts from a husband to a wife. Conceivably, in those states which have an interlocutory divorce regime, a transfer during the interlocutory period might satisfy both the McMurtry case and §2523.

3. Support of Children after Minority

a. A number of cases have held that provisions in a separation agreement for the support of children beyond their minority give rise to a gift tax even if the agreement is incorporated into the decree, on the ground that the divorce court normally has no power to award such support and that therefore the Harris rationale is inapplicable. Rosenthal v. Commissioner, 205 F.2d 505 (2d Cir. 1953); Wiedemann, 26 T.C. 565 (1956). Quere whether the same result would follow where state law allows or even requires support beyond the age of twenty-one, as, for example, where a child is disabled. Compare Commissioner v. Greene, 119 F.2d 383 (9th Cir. 1941) (held taxable gift).

III. Estate Tax Aspects

A. Where a separation agreement or decree imposes on the husband the obligation to continue payments beyond his death, the question arises whether such payments are deductible from H's gross estate as claims against the estate. Section 2053(b) provides that where such a claim is based upon "a promise or agreement" it must have been incurred for consideration. (The purpose of this provision is to prevent a decedent from obtaining a deduction for bequests by promising the legatee a specified sum which is then asserted as a claim against the estate.) Thus the principal question that is presented under the estate tax is the same as that which was discussed above under the gift tax, namely, whether a claim is based upon a promise or agreement on the one hand or a court decree on the other. If the latter, it is deductible. Regs. §20.2053-4; Commissioner v. Estate of Watson, 216 F.2d 941 (2d Cir. 1954). If the former, it is not, unless it comes within the support exemption, page 964 supra.[16] Where a claim is based on a separation agreement that is later followed by a decree, see page 965 supra as to whether the claim is based on the agreement or the decree. See also Rev. Rul. 60-160, 1960-1 Cum. Bull. 374, holding that if a divorce court having the power to modify the agreement of the parties in fact approves the separation agreement, any payments stipulated therein are founded on the decree rather then the agreement and hence are deductible from H's gross estate.

Note that there is no counterpart of §2516 under the estate tax. Thus in order for payments to be clearly deductible, they must be based on a court decree.

B. Since the precise amount of the obligation of H's estate often depends on such future facts as the death or remarriage of W, actuarial computations may have to be resorted to. Commissioner v. Maresi, 156 F.2d 929 (2d Cir. 1946). Where state law looks to events occurring after H's death in determining the obligations of the estate, such information must also be utilized for tax purposes. Thus where alimony was payable until the first to occur of W's death or remarriage, and W did remarry soon after H's death, the estate tax deduction is limited to the actual amount paid rather than the actuarially computed liability as of the date of H's death. Commissioner v. Estate of Shively, 276 F.2d 372 (2d Cir. 1960). See also Gowetz v. Commissioner, 320 F.2d 874 (1st Cir. 1963).

[16] Although the Internal Revenue Service has ruled that claims on account of support are deductible whether or not based on a decree, the Tax Court and the Court of Appeals for the Second Circuit have reached a contrary conclusion. Estate of McKeon, 25 T.C. 697 (1956); Meyer's Estate v. Commissioner, 110 F.2d 367 (2d Cir. 1940).

Where the obligation is based on a promise or agreement rather than a decree and the support test is relied upon, it will be necessary to allocate between support rights and marital or property rights. See E.T. 19, 1946-2 Cum. Bull. 166.

C. Another estate tax question that arises is whether alimony trusts that are set up by H are includable in his gross estate. The usual rule is that such a transfer is includable if the grantor has retained too much control over the transferred property or if it has been transferred in contemplation of death. See §§2035-2038. But a transfer is not includable if it is made for consideration. It has been held that sums transferred for the reasonable support of children during their minority are supported by consideration and hence are not includable in H's gross estate. Estate of McKeon, 25 T.C. 697 (1956). Transfers for the support of the wife may be similarly excluded. See Estate of Glen, 45 T.C. No. 30 (1966). Quere whether any transfer based on a divorce decree is ipso facto exempted from the consideration requirement. See Lowndes & Kramer, Federal Estate and Gift Taxes 304-305 (1962), which so asserts. But see United States v. Past, 347 F.2d 7 (9th Cir. 1965).

IV. Selected References

A. Durbin, Tax Considerations in Divorce and Separation Agreements and Proceedings, 38 Taxes 987 (1960).

B. Holland, Piper, Bailey & Sander, Matrimony, Divorce and Separation, 18 N.Y.U. Tax Inst. 901 (1960).

C. Kilbourn, Puzzling Problems in Property Settlements — The Tax Anatomy of Divorce, 27 Mo. L. Rev. 354 (1962).

D. McClennen, Tax Aspects of Divorce Settlement Agreements, 4 Ariz. L. Rev. 26 (1962).

E. Rudick, Tax Consequences of Marriage and Its Termination (A.L.I. A.B.A. 1964).

F. Sander, Planning Tax Aspects of Divorce and Separation Agreements, 9 Prac. Law., Feb. 1963, p. 91.

G. Sander, Divorce and Separation (BNA Tax Management Portfolio No. 95, 1964).

H. Wren, Tax Problems Incident to Divorce and Property Settlement, 49 Calif. L. Rev. 665 (1961).

I. Kurlander, Gift and Estate Tax Consequences of Separation and Divorce, 50 A.B.A.J. 381 (1964).

J. Mills, Tax Checklist for Negotiating Divorce and Separation Agreements, 22 J. Tax. 368 (1965).

TABLE OF CASES

[Italicized page numbers refer to principal cases. Only these cases have been listed under both parties.]

I N D E X

By subject and by name